R

MORE THEATRE

Stage to Screen to Television

Volume I: A–L

by

ALVIN H. MARILL

The Scarecrow Press, Inc.
Metuchen, N.J., & London
1993

British Library Cataloguing-in-Publication data available

Library of Congress Cataloging-in-Publication Data

Marill, Alvin H.
More theatre : stage to screen to television / by Alvin H. Marill.
p. cm.
Originally published under title: Theatre / William Torbert Leonard. 1981.
ISBN 0-8108-2717-4 (acid-free paper)
1. Theater--History--20th century. 2. Drama--Bibliography--Catalogs.
3. Film adaptations--Catalogs. 4. Television adaptations--Catalogs.
I. Leonard, William T. Theatre.
II. Title.
PN2189.M32 1993
792.9'5--dc20 93-4687

Manufactured in the United States of America
Printed on acid-free paper

STAGE TO SCREEN TO TELEVISION

CONTENTS

PREFACE

Chronicling major (and minor) literary works and original stage productions that have been mounted theatrically and also have been done as motion pictures and on TV -- stagings in all three media are the criteria here -- is either a challenge or a nightmare. As a researcher, I have relished both the agony and the ecstasy (to borrow from Irving Stone) of this challenge and of this nightmare.

As in the initial volumes compiled by the late William Torbert Leonard through 1980, a great variety of theatrical presentations performed on stages in America and Great Britain, as well as occasional foreign language productions of major English-language works, have been researched for this update. Nearly 150 titles not chronicled in Bill's earlier compilation -- from *Aladdin* to *Ziegfeld* (yes, even *Nick and Nora* has found a place) -- are included in this one, with cast and credit information on significant stage versions through the years and on motion pictures and television dramas (or comedies) that have been made from them. And that's just the first half of this companion set. The second part updates titles previously chronicled -- productions between 1980 and 1992, along with earlier overlooked or lately uncovered film or TV versions and prominent regional or touring stage presentations or those which have interesting lead or minor players. It also corrects and amends some of the information included in those initial volumes.

Because of the near impossibility of tracking down theatrical productions from 200 to 2000 years ago, this volume, like the initial volumes, does not generally document Greek classics, Shakespeare, Gilbert and Sullivan, and assorted traditional fairy tales. There are exceptions, however: *Antigone* (at least from the modern era -- i.e., Cocteau's version and Anouilh's drama adapted from Sophocles) is here, as is *Henry VIII*. So are *Cinderella*, *Jack and the Beanstalk*, and *Beauty and the Beast*.

Compiling this volume, with research notes left by Bill Leonard and the assistance of friends in London, Paris, Lugano, Brussels, Boston, Los Angeles, Houston and Chicago, has been a challenge -- an exhilarating one. And it couldn't have been done without the cooperation of assorted regional theaters around the United States, the Theater Collection at the Lincoln Center Library for the Performing Arts in New York, the staff of the Bibliotheque de L'Arsenal in Paris, the Ramapo College and Fairleigh Dickinson Libraries in New Jersey, the San Francisco Public Library, the Cape Playhouse (thank you, Margaret Adams), the Williamstown Theatre Festival, the Houston Grand Opera, the Virginia Stage Company, the American Conservatory Theatre, the Long Wharf Theatre, the Paper Mill Playhouse, and the Long Beach Civic Light Opera, plus CBS Program Information, NBC Program Analysis, and BBC Program Archives.

There are also the following individuals (alphabetically listed) who have my very special gratitude:

David Bartholomew, John Behrens (CBS), Giancarlo Bertelli, Hal Biard, John Cocchi, Allen Eyles, Guy Giampapa, Pierre Guinle, Jane Klain, Ed Lelyveld, the late

William Torbert Leonard, Colin Leslie (BBC), Ray and Man-Li Liao, Kruse Ludington, Lee Malone (NBC), Judy Marill, David McGillivray, the late Norman Miller, Vincent Terrace, Jerry Vermilye, Vera Wells (NBC), David and Sylvia Williams.

And of course my wife Sandra, for the hours of microfilm research of *The Times* of London and *The New York Times* as well as other periodicals.

Alvin H. Marill
January 1993

STAGE TO SCREEN TO TELEVISION
Volume I: A-L

ALADDIN

Various adaptations of *The History of Aladdin, or the Wonderful Lamp* from *The Arabian Nights Entertainments*, and a 17th-century translation of the Arabic manuscript *A Thousand and One Nights* by France's Jean Antoine Galland

Synopsis

In China, a magician took young Aladdin to a secret place stored with treasure to find a magic lamp. Impoverished Aladdin filled his robe with treasure but, unable to locate the lamp, was sealed into the cave by the wily magician. Aladdin rubbed the ring given to him by the magician and a genie appeared to guide him home. While cleaning the discovered lamp, Aladdin's mother released another genie who granted the young man's every wish. Aladdin and his genie thwarted the Grand Vizier's plan for his own son's marriage to the Sultan's daughter, Princess Badroulbadour. The genie built a magnificent palace next to the Sultans and Aladdin married the Princess. During Aladdin's absence, though, the magician persuaded the Princess to trade the old, magic lamp for a new one, and with it in his possession, the magician transferred the palace and Princess to Africa. Returning home, Aladdin was threatened with death by the Sultan but rubbed his magic ring summoning its genie who carried him to the disappeared palace and his wife, the Princess. Killing the magician and recovering the magic lamp whose genie transported the Palace back to China, Aladdin then did away with the magician's evil brother who had followed them. With his magic ring and wonderful magic lamp, Aladdin and his Princess lived happily ever after.

Comment and Critique

The History of Aladdin, or the Wonderful Lamp was one of many stories told by Scheherazade to forestall her husband Shahriar's constant threat to kill her in the morning and is one of the tales contained in *The Arabian Nights Entertainments*. Many dramatizations have been made of the tale of *Aladdin and the Wonderful Lamp*; one of the earliest was *Aladdin eller den forunderlige Lampe*, written by Danish playwright Adama Gottlob Oehlenschlager in 1805. Called a "MeloDramatik Romance with Music," *Aladdin; or, the Wonderful Lamp* was produced at London's Covent Garden on November 6, 1813. London's Drury Lane Theatre presented *Aladdin* in April 1926, and the following November, the show was produced at New York's Park Theatre.

The Mirror review of the Park's *Aladdin* in 1826 stated, "We certainly believe that Aladdin eclipses everything of the kind that has heretofore been produced. It is gorgeous with appropriate dresses and decorations, and splendid with beautiful scenery, it is unequalled."

During the next half century, *Aladdin* became a popular attraction in England and America. In 1870, Lydia Thompson appeared in a burlesque in England called *Aladdin the Second*, which crossed the ocean and opened at New York's Olympic Theatre on November 11, 1872. *The New York Times* described the Thompson burlesque as "a spectacular extravaganza, brimful of the needed opportunities for scenic display and for songs and dances." In England, *Aladdin* became one of several virtually annual Christmas pantomimes. *Entr'acte* considered Carry Nelson's performance in *Aladdin* at the Royal Alfred Theatre in 1873 to be "a part exactly suited to her abilities" and described the pantomime as "a thorough amusing entertainment."

Augustus Harris presented *Aladdin and Forty Thieves* at London's Drury Lane Theatre on Boxing Day, 1885. "The Annual -- founded on the legend of *Aladdin* -- is, perhaps, the most gorgeous of all Mr. Harris' productions. Never, perhaps, was seen on a stage at the same time such an agglomeration of magnificent dresses and accessories; the stage at one or two intervals being loaded with the richest combinations of brilliant colour," reported *Entr'acte*. "When the necessary pruning has been performed there is no reason why fun should not play an equal part with spectacle in *Aladdin*."

Alfred Thompson's adaptation of the legend, *The Arabian Nights; or, Aladdin's Wonderful Lamp,* successfully originated in Chicago and, on September 12, 1887, opened at New York's Standard Theatre. *The New York Times* found Thompson's *Arabian Nights* "vastly inferior to the good old versions familiar to playgoers of 20 years ago. But the new arrangement of the story gives ample opportunity for the introduction of spectacular effects, brilliant marches and ballets, gorgeous costumes and scenery...There are a dozen of glistening stage sets in the new production that are as handsome as anything ever seen in spectacle in the city... Altogether, *The Arabian Nights* furnishes a very pleasant entertainment."

While Londoners continued to enjoy *Aladdin* as a Christmas pantomime, New Yorkers saw a Chicago success, *Aladdin, Jr.* which opened April 8, 1895. "One has to send his memory backward a considerable distance into the past to recall a spectacle which, simply as a succession of stage pictures, was superior to *Aladdin, Jr.*," reported *The New York Times*. "An immense amount of well-painted scenery was used...of course, not much of a 'play' is expected in performance of this kind, not many people who can really sing. The lines of *Aladdin, Jr.* served their purpose well enough...the acting and singing presented much the same degree of excellence, and the accompanying music was equally inconspicuous...The types introduced are all old and indefinite, and except for the scenery, there was little to excite applause."

The new century opened at Hammerstein's Victoria Theatre with another Aladdin concoction, *Chris and the Wonderful Lamp,* featuring Jerome Sykes as a contemporary Genie and Edna Wallace Hopper as Chris, a modern Aladdin. One critic noted: "The magic lamp of Aladdin appears once more in buretta and the Genius of Genie of the magical utensil is found to be still a potent personage. This Genie, modernized and brought closely up-to-date, is the very life and soul of the new piece ...The quality of the entertainment ranges from variety farce of the very lowest brand to fairy ballet spectacle of the old pattern. The music, however, is good enough for operetta."

Another variation on *Aladdin and His Wonderful Lamp* was written by F. Anstey in 1909 as *The Brass Bottle*. Following a successful run in London, it opened on Broadway on August 11, 1910 starring Richard Bennett. Anstey's version told of architect Horace Ventimore's purchase of an Oriental brass bottle, and its unleashed Genie gratefully rewards his new owner with untold riches as well as impracticable gifts which make Valentine appear ridiculous. Disgusted with his Genie, Ventimore finally entices it back into the bottle, which he tosses into the Thames River.

"*The Brass Bottle* was staged faultlessly -- the scenery was all that it should be and not more; the transformation scenes were cleverly managed, and the devices for the jinnee's entrances and exits indicated a resourceful director," reported *The New*

York Dramatic Mirror. "The most astonishing exit was the demon's evaporation into the bottle. The orchestra also deserves a word for its especially appropriate music. *The Brass Bottle* is everything that it pretends to be. Mr. Anstey gets a bizarre effect by dropping a fantastic creature, subject to another set of physical laws, into what we regard today as ordinary, respectable surroundings. He treats the whole complication with absurd sobriety. While it is by no means the highest comic art, because it requires fancy instead of imagination, it is undeniably funny and at times quite irresistible."

The most successful adaptation of the *Aladdin* legend on the American stage was the Anne Galdwell and R. H. Burnside musical comedy *Chin-Chin; or, A Modern Aladdin* in 1914 starring David Montgomery and Fred Stone.

"*Chin-Chin* is far and away the biggest show of its kind, which is hardly the way to express it, as it stands in a class by itself, that has ever come to Broadway," raved *The New York Times.* "It is every sort of entertainment rolled into three tremendous, smashing acts, and it provides enough laughter to establish the success of half a dozen Broadway shows...Stone does everything that mortals can do to entertain, from falling out of an airship to riding a horse and playing a piano, and he is closely seconded by Dave Montgomery, who doesn't do quite as much but who is entertaining all the time...While there were no songs which stood out and promised to become popular hits, the music of *Chin-Chin* was all pretty and whistleable. Ivan Caryll was responsible for that end of the entertainment."

Aladdin and his Genie continued their merry way in annual Christmas pantomimes in London, and on December 22, 1926, *Aladdin* was produced at the Palladium. *Bystander*'s "Jingle" wrote, "We who go to pantomimes because they are nothing like real life know that that is just where the fun comes in...I wonder who first gave Aladdin's mother the name of Widow Twankey. She has none at all in the original story, and 'Twankey' does not seem quite to fit in with the flourishing Oriental flavour of the names of the other principals in the story. Here the widowed laundress is represented by Mr. Charles Austin, who obviously does not hold the mirror up to Nature...Yet here he is, and we are expected to believe that he is presenting to us a reliable picture of a typical British washerwoman. Could anything be more artificial? Or more delightfully amusing? Mr. Austin has a genius for provoking laughter. There is a quaver in his voice that enables him to make a commonplace line sound like a funny remark...The Aladdin of the pantomime is Miss Clarice Mayne, who in a part of this kind is, of course, *facile princeps*, and several other complimentary Latin words. Miss Mayne, as we all know, sings and dances with perfect charm, and, being an actress of quality as well, she carries the fine old story of make-believe along with a pleasant swing."

Aladdin continued through the next two decades as an English Christmas attraction, and on December 20, 1945, Emile Littler's pantomime opened in London. *Theatre World* appraised the author's holiday show: "Binnie Hale has everything it takes to be the ideal principal boy, charm, versatility, a pleasing voice and a certain 'fey' quality that belongs in true pantomime...but though this pantomime is built more on traditional lines than many we have seen of recent years, surely some of the magic has been taken out of this annual entertainment. Perhaps modern audiences prefer the new semi-revue technique...Like *Cinderella*, *Aladdin* offers fine scope for elaborate scenic effects, but once again we were disappointed. But perhaps the passing years make us unduly critical, we take our fairy stories more seriously maybe."

On June 24, 1954, Guy Lombardo produced *Arabian Nights*, a musical extravaganza starring Lauritz Melchior at the Jones Beach Marine Theatre on Long

Island, in New York. "Put down Mr. Lombardo's entry as entirely successful. For this new musical extravaganza provides an evening in the out-of-doors set to a pleasant mixture of songs, romance and the exoticism of the East," reported *The New York Times*. "The music and lyrics are credited to Carmen Lombardo and John Jacob Loeb and are pleasant to listen to both as sung by the huge cast and played by a full orchestra...The score is a mixture of Eastern rhythms and sprightly tunes that could adorn any respectable juke box...Having set out to provide color and romance, *Arabian Nights*, under the capable direction of Robert H. Gordon, succeeds nicely."

The second Jones Beach edition of Lombardo's *Arabian Nights* the following year was described by Lewis Funke (*The New York Times*) as "an opulent, sumptuous spectacle, an eye-filling diversion for an evening under the moon and stars. Let no one be misled, fundamentally this is a gigantically colorful enterprise designed more for the eye than for the mind...Getting those elephants on the stage is no mean trick. As another attraction of the evening there is Lottie Mayer's disappearing ballet. In this, an army of young women bedecked in exquisite finery enter the water, disappear again, reappear with some of their raiment left behind and return as swimmers of grace and beauty as they maneuver through an assortment of gyrations...Credit Leon Leonidoff, the Radio City maestro, with a grand job of overall direction."

British music hall star Norman Wisdom delighted London audiences in *The Wonderful Lamp* at the Palladium on December 22, 1956, with his fey Aladdin sparking the Christmas pantomime. Choreographer Robert Helpmann directed Cole Porter's *Aladdin* at London's Coliseum Theatre in December 1959. Porter's *Aladdin* had first been produced on American television in 1958.

Theatre World praised the Coliseum *Aladdin*, especially the decor of production designed by Loudon Sainthill, noting, "Spectacle succeeds spectacle, bizarre and beautiful shapes emerge and fade to be followed by fairy-like pictures equally wonderful, and never is the eye tired because the designer's fund of novelty seems inexhaustible and his colours are so marvelously blended. The lighting by Mr. Michael Northen skilfully enhances the visual magic. Fundamentally, one would say, this is pantomime seen and directed as ballet. It is the ballet of *Aladdin*, choreographed by Mr. Robert Helpmann, with Anne Heaton giving lovely performances as the principal dancer. Without Widow Twankey, it would be pure ballet, almost. Mr. Ronald Shiner, a master in the comic line, holds his own as only a master could, taking in washing and exerting audience appeal with bubbling boiler and dripping tap...*Aladdin* is very likeable presented as a cheerful knave by Mr. Bob Monkhouse...Mr. Cole Porter's music gives artistic homogeneity to the work. The book by Mr. Peter Cook is rather pedestrian."

London's *Sphere* added, "It contains an impressive array of talent, including an American principal girl and songs by the American composer Cole Porter. Doretta Morrow, a singer and actress from the United States, takes the part of the Princess...Robert Helpmann, whose first pantomime attraction this is, is both director and choreographer. The whole presentation has cost about 90,000 pounds."

Aladdin and His Wonderful Lamp, a pantomime by David Croft with music and lyrics by The Shadows, opened in December 1964. "After a lapse of a year, to everybody's delight the Palladium reverted in 1964 to its time-honoured tradition of presenting a pantomime at Christmas. *Aladdin and His Wonderful Lamp*, starring Cliff Richard, The Shadows and Arthur Askey, proved a brilliant success," reported *Plays and Players*.

In December 1970, *Aladdin* returned to the Palladium featuring pop singer Cilla Black in the title role. Nigel Andrews (*Plays and Players*) reported, "The Palladium pantomime has often relied on the instant hilarity of commercial products or the dropping of well-known TV names. This year's *Aladdin* is suitably topical: Terry Scott's Widow Twankey -- a blowsy seducer in place of the usual clumping transvestite -- makes passing reference to the 'permissive dynasty' and tries vainly to 'freak-out' with a somnolent hippie; Leslie Crowther has to deposit his magic carpet at a parking meter. But apart from these vague topicalities, Phil Park's book puts its faith in the power of the story. The only sag comes during a rather tedious balletic interlude illustrating the past history of the lamp -- all too obviously concocted to allow Cilla Black to change for the transformation scene...[she] on the other hand, is hardly off the stage and establishes a terrific rapport with the audience both as a comedienne and romantic lead. Leading the traditional sing-in at the end, she had the audience eating out of her hand. And not just in the matter of freely distributed popcorn."

Hollywood's fascination with the Arabian Night Tales found inspiration in Metro's 1917 *Aladdin's Other Lamp* starring Viola Dana, which combined a magic lamp with a strictly *Cinderella* story. William Fox presented the real fantasy in October 1917 as *Aladdin and the Wonderful Lamp*, directed by C.M. and S.A. Franklin and featuring the Fox Kiddies.

"The Fox production of *Aladdin and the Wonderful Lamp*, an eight-part screen version of the old fairy tale -- again utilizes the remarkable ability of the Fox Kiddies, Francis Carpenter, Virginia Lee Corbin, Violet Radcliffe and Gertrude Messenger...Contrary to the *Jack and the Beanstalk* picture, the rest of the characters are taken by grownups," Edward Weitzel (*The Moving Picture World*) reported. "The production is elaborate, several of the scenes having marked beauty. The magical effects demanded by the story have been supplied by the resources of the screen...Two improvements were possible in making *Aladdin*. The scenes might have been given a more humorous treatment and Messrs. Franklin refrained from teaching all the children the same set of gestures. Some of the scenes could still be shortened to advantage...Elmo Lincoln is an impressive Genie and the other characters are well acted."

England's Stoll Pictures produced the tale of *Aladdin* under the title of *Widow Twan-Kee* which was changed to *One Arabian Night* in the United States in 1923. Britain's celebrated comedian, George Robey, was cast as the Widow Twan-Kee and made an uneasy transition from the vaudeville-music hall stages of London to the screen. The film was noted more for its handsome settings and photography than performance, while remaining faithful to the Aladdin tale.

Universal Pictures, ever intrigued with the tales of Scheherazade, produced *Arabian Nights* in 1942 starring their leading exponents of the mystical East, Jon Hall, Maria Montez and Sabu as the weaver of tales. John Qualen had a minor role as Aladdin. In 1945, Columbia Pictures made its entertaining version of *Aladdin* as *A Thousand and One Nights*.

William R. Weaver (*Motion Picture Herald*) found, "This all-out excursion into the field of fantasy, undertaken primarily for fun and winding up in a gale of laughter, rates with the best of its kind on all points and above the previous best as to humor. It tells again, with all the opulence money and coloration can achieve and with the wit and imagination most undertakings in kind have grievously lacked, the old story of Aladdin, and the lamp, still a hit among hits and all new, bright and shiny...It's a property that can be depended upon to thrive as it plays. Cornel Wilde plays Aladdin, making a neat job of it, and Evelyn Keyes is a feast for the eye and a tonic for tired spirits as the obedient but emotionally rebellious genie...Phil Silvers, as Aladdin's companion, given to thieving and addicted to jive talk a la 1945, carries the comedy burden and collects a thousand laughs without seeming to try...Wilfrid H. Pettitt supplied the original story and collaborated with Richard English and Jack Henley on the script, which roundly kids the Aladdin tale without ever quite doing violence to the basic idea."

Universal-International returned to the popular and profitable sex-and-sand genre in 1950 with its production of *The Desert Hawk* starring Richard Greene as Omar, Yvonne De Carlo as Princess Scheherazade -- and Jackie Gleason as Aladdin! Bosley Crowther (*The New York Times*) dismissed the film with "Somehow we have the feeling we've seen this a hundred times before..." The 1952 *Aladdin and His Lamp* was recommended by William R. Weaver (*Motion Picture Herald)* for "Producer Walter Wanger's special talent for filming a fantasy -- is given full exercise again in this telling in Cinecolor of the tale...Patricia Medina as the princess is an appropriate eyeful...and John Sands as Aladdin has the physique required to run out a script that might have winded the first Fairbanks."

The Wanger epic was followed by Columbia Pictures' minor *Thief of Damascus*, which *The New York Times* described as "another harmless but preposterous entertainment package with an Arabian Nights background... Typical of the tired jauntiness of the whole affair is the labored wisecracking of Jeff Donnell as the snappiest Scheherazade in screen history." Diminutive Robert Clary portrayed a lively Aladdin.

The Italian-produced *The Wonders of Aladdin* (*Le Meraviglie di Aladino*) in 1961 starred Donald O'Connor in the title role. Britain's *Monthly Film Bulletin* wrote: "An *Arabian Nights* parody, this film is probably no more vulgar and unappealing than the current de-teriorated form of London Christmas pantomime. But, with the resources of camera 'magic' and spectacle at its command, it seems a pity that it should lack all charm, wit and fairy tale quality. Donald O'Connor gives a coarse, burlesque performance as Aladdin (a character which calls out for a Danny Kaye). Vittorio De Sica graciously materializes genie-style every so often."

In 1967, Russia's Gorky Studios offered their version of *Aladdin and His Magic Lamp* (*Volshebnaya Lampa Aladdina*). It was followed two years later by *Aladdin and His Magic Lamp* (*Aladin et la Lampe Merveilleuse*), an hour-long animated cartoon by France's Jean Image.

Controversial Italian director Pier Paolo Pasolini reached into the Arabian Nights for a mind-boggling, highly erotic look in his bizarre *Il Fiore delle Mille e una Notte* in 1974, the third part of his "trilogy of life" that also included personalized adaptations of Boccaccio's *Decameron* and Chaucer's *Canterbury Tales*. "In Pasolini's interpretation of Arabian Nights, the creative impulse is aimed at scrupulous realism and down-to-earth erotica in an attempt to pin down a social reality while permeating a big canvas with a liberating libertinism of modern times," *Variety* wrote after the film's introduction at the Cannes Film Festival that year. "It's a tall order and a large part of it is fascinating spectacle, though the sheer weight of his magic carpet excursion into previously untouched landscapes, communes, folklore...finally dulls the senses through sheer excess." Another Italian-made version of the tale of Aladdin, contemporized and set in Miami, was released in 1987 as *SuperFantaGenio*.

The Walt Disney Company's enthiusiastically received feature-length animated musical of *Aladdin* premiered in late 1992 as its follow-up to the previous year's smash *Beauty and the Beast*. In a four-star review, Kathleen Carroll (New York *Daily News*) hailed it as "a wish come true. A fast-paced, hysterically funny cartoon fantasy...*Aladdin* is indeed a magical, wonderfully inventive movie." Richard Corliss (*Time*) found it "exhilarating...a ravishing thrill ride."

F. Anstey's 1909 play, *The Brass Bottle*, utilized the Aladdin tale transferring the basic elements of the story to modern times. Lawrence Grossmith starred in Britain's 1914 screen adaptation of *The Brass Bottle*. First National Pictures released a version of Anstey's *The Brass Bottle* in 1923 and four decades later, Tony Randall and Burl Ives starred in Universal's sound remake. Barbara Eden, the leading lady, later was to find herself materializing from a bottle in TV's *I Dream of Jeannie*.

"Not surprisingly, perhaps, Anstey's novel has here been modernized as well as Americanized," observed Britain's *Monthly Film Bulletin*. "This would matter little if advantage had been taken of the fertile possibilities inherent in the tale as a demonstration of the impracticability of magic in the modern world, told in terms of the camera's own magic...Most of the ingenuous fun provided by the film in fact comes from the casting, with Tony Randall and Burl Ives in their element as a modern Aladdin and his genie."

CBS produced the elaborate *DuPont Show of the Month* production of *Aladdin* on television on February 21, 1958. Despite a score by Cole Porter (his last) and a book by S. J. Perelman, it failed to live up to expectation as one of television's great musicals.

"Cole Porter and S. J. Perelman should send out for the Genie," wrote Jack Gould (*The New York Times)*. "Their attempts last night to make a musical out of *Aladdin*, the imperishable *Arabian Night* story of the boy with the magic lamp, ran headlong into sustained disaster...a pretentious ordeal...It was hard to believe that Mr. Perelman had a hand in the evening's drab affair...Mr. Porter was similarly uninspired. His score seldom was related to the narrative and his individual numbers seemed inserted haphazardly." Critic Gould also felt, "Melodically, the ear was seldom entranced ...Sal Mineo, an idol of the teenagers, played Aladdin, and was hopelessly out of place. His was the awkward performance of a virtual beginner in the acting art... Cyril Ritchard appeared confused by the questionable motivation behind his part of the magician...Dennis King, as the astrologer, had scant opportunity to do much with his part. Geoffrey Holder, as the Genie, was somewhat the most successful of anyone on stage...Basil Rathbone, as the Emperor, also projected some of the true flavor of the tale...Much of the sumptuous production of *Aladdin* went for naught...To paraphrase one of Mr. Porter's less enticing lyrics, '*Aladdin* was saddnin'..."

Shirley Temple Storybook television series presented *The Land of Green Ginger* in Spring 1958. Noel Langley adapted his own fairy-tale to television with Antony Eustrel as Aladdin and Kuldip Singh as Abu Ali, Aladdin's son.

On December 6, 1967, New York's Prince Street Players' delightful television production of *Aladdin* in a one-hour musical adaptation of the Arabian Nights tale was broadcast. More than eighteen years later, another version of the story came to television on *Shelley Duvall's Faerie Tale Theatre* on Showtime. Robert Carradine played Aladdin, Valerie Bertinelli his winsome princess, James Earl Jones the genial genie and Leonard Nimoy the wicked vizier, in *Aladdin and His Wonderful Lamp*.

STAGE

ALADDIN; OR, THE WONDERFUL LAMP, *Theatre Royal, Covent Garden*, London, opened November 6, 1813

A Melo-Dramatick Romance, arranged and produced by Mr. Farley; Music by Mr. Condell; Overture and second-act music by Mr. Ware; Preceded by *The Beggar's Opera* by John Gay

Mrs. H. Johnston (Aladdin); Mr. Farley (Abanazzar); Miss Bristow (The Princess Badroulbadour); Mr. Grimaldi (Kazrac); Mrs. Creswell (Tahi Tongluck); Mr.

Bologna (Karar Hanjou, the Vizier); Mr. Bologna, Jr. (Kalim Azack, the Vizier's Son); Miss Treby (Amrou); Mrs. Parker (Zobyad); Mmes. Carew, Coates, Davies, Findlay, Grimaldi, Herbert (Ladies of the Court of the Princess); Mrs. Davenport (The Widow Ching Mustapha); Miss Worgman (Genie of the Ring); Mr. Jeffries (Orlock, Genie of the Air); Mr. Howell (Genie of the Lamp); Misses Bologna, Cox, Heath, Louis, Ryall, Standen, Herbert (Chinese Dancing Girls)

ALADDIN; OR, THE WONDERFUL LAMP, *Philadelphia Theatre*, Philadelphia, opened January 1, 1817

A Melo-Dramatick Romance; Scenery by H. Warren and T. Reinagle; Costumes, Mr. Harbaugh; Machinery effects, Mr. Cummins

Mr. Burke (Aladdin); Mr. Robertson (Abanazzar); Mrs. Duff (Princess Badroulbadour); Mr. Abercrombie (Kazrac); Mr. Hathwell (Tahi Tongluck); Mr. Willis (Karar Hanjou, the Vizier); Mr. Barrett (Kalim Azack, the Vizier's Son); Mrs. Bloxton (Amrou); Mrs. Jefferson (Zobyad); Mrs. Gilbert, Mrs. Jackson, Miss Prigmore (Ladies of the Court of the Princess); Mrs. Francis (The Widow Ching Mustapha); Master Jefferson (Genie of the Ring); Mr. Steward (Orlock, Genie of the Air); Mr. Jackson (Genie of the Lamp); Messrs. Steward, Francis, McFarland, Entwisle (Citizens of Cham Tartary); Master Joseph Jefferson, Miss Hathwell, Miss Seymour, Miss C. Durrung, Miss H. Durrung (Genie of the Lamp's Attendant Spirits)

ALADDIN, *New Theatre Royal*, London, opened March 2, 1821

A Melo-Dramatic Spectacle

Miss S. Booth (Aladdin); Mrs. McCulloch (The Widow Ching Mustapha); Miss Campbell (Princess Badroulbadour); Mr. Swan (Genie of the Lamp); Mr. Cunningham (Abenazuck); Mr. Clarke (Taghi Tongluck); Mr. Horrebow (Kalim Azack); Mr. Rowswell (Obrock); Miss E. Cunningham (Genie of the Ring); Mr. Good (Wangfungchinglong); Miss Curtis (Amour); Mr. Norman (Kazrac); Mrs. Searle (Zobyad); Miss Wells, H. Lacy, Sullivan, R. Cunningham, Mahon, Mrs. Swan (Dancing Slaves); Mmes. Lyong, Johnson, Broad, Chippendale, Edwards, Norman (Ladies of the Court)

ALADDIN, *Park Theatre*, New York, opened November 25, 1826

An Extravaganza based on the Arabian Nights tale

Mrs. John Barnes (Aladdin); Mr. Lee (Azack); Miss Brundage (Amroy); Mrs. W. A. Conway (Zobyad)

A-LAD-IN THE WONDERFUL LAMP, *Park Theatre*, New York, opened October 7, 1844

A Dramatic Romance based on the Arabian Nights Tale

Mrs. Skerritt (Aladdin); W. Chippindale (Abanazar); Mr. Bridges (Keinong Fong Whang); S. Pearson (Kazini Azack); A. Andrews (Kazrac); Mr. Gourley (Janzi); J. R. Anderson (Orlock); Mr. Fisher (Tonglush, Cham of Tartary); Mrs. Knight (Princess Badroulbadour); Mrs. Flynn (Amroc); Mr. Freeland (Camphine, Genie of the Lamp); Mrs. Boulard (Zobeide); Miss St. Clair (Fatima); Mrs. Dyott (Widow Ching Mustapha)

ALADDIN, *Barnum's American Museum*, New York, opened March 17, 1856

Produced by P. T. Barnum

Mrs. Frank Drew (Aladdin); Milnes Levick (Azack); Mrs. France (The Widow); E.

F. Taylor (Kasrac); Mr. France (Tongluck); Mr. Cunningham (Genie of the Lamp); Mr. Burroughs (Genie of the Ring); Miss Jackson (Princess Badroulbadour)

ALADDIN, Bowery Theatre, New York, opened February 20, 1860
Produced and directed by J. H. Allen; Scenery, Minard Lewis and W. Bowes
Mrs. W. Marden (Aladdin); Mr. W. Petrie (Abenasac); J. C. Reeve (Kasrac); C. Warwick (Tahi Tongluck); W. Marden (Kazim Azack); C. J. Foster (Orlock); J. E. Carden (Genius of the Lamp); Henrietta Lang (Princess Badroulbadour); Miss Frances (Zobeide); Mr. Holland (1st Officer); Mr. Gourlay, Mr. Stevens (Officers); Mr. Moore, Mr. Evans, Mr. Williams (Citizens); Miss Lee (Amroc); Miss Hoyt (Female Slave); Miss Walby (Genie of the Ring); Mrs. Cantor (Widow Ching Mustapha)

ALADDIN; OR, THE WONDERFUL LAMP! Walnut Street Theatre, Philadelphia, opened August 8, 1866
Effie German (Aladdin); S. K. Chester (Abanazar); Owen Fawcett (Kazrac); T. C. Green (Tahi Tongluck); J. Bradford (Ben Mouseff); Mrs. S. K. Chester (Princess Badroulbadour); James Taylor (Kasim Azack); Mark Brooke (Ben Cassim); Mr. Reed (Trewash); Miss M. Price (Zobeide); Miss Stone (Fatima); Miss H. Miller (Amron); J. P. Brelsford (Ching Mustapha); Mr. F. Stull (Orlack); Lysander Thompson (Genie of the Lamp); Rosalie Jack (Genie of the Ring)

ALADDIN; OR, THE WONDERFUL SCAMP, Broadway Theatre, New York, opened February 2, 1867
Produced by the Worrell Sisters; A Burlesque based on the Arabian Nights tale
Jennie Worrell (Aladdin); Irene Worrell (Princess Badroulbadour); T. L. Donnelly (Sultan); Welsh Edwards (Vizier); Mrs. G. H. Gilbert (Aladdin's Mother)

ALADDIN THE SECOND, Olympic Theatre, New York, opened November 11, 1872
Produced by the Lydia Thompson Burlesque Company; Setting, Mr. Hayes
Lydia Thompson (Aladdin, the Second); Willie Edouin (Abanazar); John Bryer (The Sultan); Camille Dubois (Pekoe); Fannie Leslie (Te-To-Tum); Tilly Earle (Slave of the Lamp); Jennie Wheatleigh (Genie of the Ring); Eliza Weatherby (Princess Badroulbadour); Harry Beckett (Widow Twankey)
SONGS: "Genevieve de Brabant," "Cackle, Cackle," and popular songs of the day

ALADDIN, California Theatre, San Francisco, opened December 28, 1872
Maggie Moore (Aladdin); W. A. Mestayer (Abanazar); Minnie Walton (Princess Badroulbadour); Eben Plympton (Genie Orlock); Carrie Wyatt (Amrou); E. N. Thayer (Grand Vizier); Walter Lenon (Taki Tongluck); J. C. Williamson (Kazrac); E. J. Buckley (Azack); Lou Johnson (Genie of the Ring); Mary Chambers (Zobyad); Mrs. Saunders (Mustapha); Charles Henry (Afferu); John Wilson (Genie of the Lamp); Henry Cook, J. S. Torrence (Citizens); Rigi Sisters (Dancers)

ALADDIN; OR, HARLEQUIN SHOEBLACK, THE GOOD FAIRY AND THE EVIL GENII, Royal Alfred Theatre, London, opened January 25, 1873
A Pantomime by Mr. Green
Carry Nelson (Aladdin); Jenny de Burt (Princess Badroulbadour); Mr. Lomax (Widow Mustapha); Mr. Anton (The Marquis); Mr. Bourne (Emperor); Mr.

Rowella (Clown)

ALADDIN, Drury Lane Theatre, London, opened December 26, 1874
Produced by F. B. Chatterton; A Pantomime based on the Arabian Nights tale
Victoria Vokes (Aladdin); Harriet Coveney (Widow Ching); Rosina Vokes (Princess Badroulbadour); Fawdon Vokes (Kazrac); F. Vokes (Abanazar); Fred Evans, W. H. Harvey (Clowns); W. Sampson, Willie Harvey (Harlequins); Paul Herring, P. Morris (Pantaloons); Mlles. L. Grosvenor and S. Harvey (Columbines); A. Rosalind (Harlequina)

Aquarium Theatre, London, opened December 26, 1878
A Pantomime based on the Arabian Nights tale
Kate Phillips (Aladdin); Amy Forrest (Princess Badroulbadour); Charles Collette (Abanazar); Mr. Fawn (Widow Twankey); Mr. Paulo (Emperor of China); Paul Martinetti (Slave); Mlle. Bartoletti (Premiere Danseuse)

ALADDIN, Gaiety Theatre, London, opened December 24, 1881
Produced by John Hollingsworth; A Fantasy by R. Reece; Directors, Robert Soutar and R. Reece; Scenery, H. Hann and E. G. Banks; Music, Herr Meyer Lutz; Costumes, A. Chasemore; Dresses, Miss Thompson; Dances, John D'Auban
E. Farren (Aladdin); Edward Terry (Abanazar); Kathe Vaughan (Princess); Phyllis Broughton (HoFi); Agnes Hewitt (Pooh-Pooh); Connie Gilchrist (Shi-Ning); E. Broughton (Hy-Son); Miss Gilbert (Souchong); Miss Moncrieff (Boo-Lang); Lizzie Nelson (Nu-Moune); J. J. Dallas (Wee Ping); T. Squire (Hang-Yu); E. W. Royce (So-Sli)

ALADDIN, THE LAD WITH THE WONDERFUL LAMP; OR, THE PRETTY PRINCESS AND PRECIOUS GREAT SCAMP, Lyceum Theatre, London, opened October 31, 1884
Produced and written by George Conquest and Henry Spry; An Original Burlesque Grand Comic Pantomime; Scenery, Messrs. J. Soames, Murdoch and Black; Mechanical effects, Fred Gaydon; Limelight by Mordey; Gas effects by F. Dimes; Costumes by Mrs. Dearlove; Vocal music selected and partially composed by Victor Stevens; Instrumental music selected, composed, and the entire music arranged by George Phillips; Properties, Tom Major; Incidental music used by kind permission of Messrs. Metzler & Co., Hopwood & Crew, Francis & Day, Wilcocks, Sheard & Co. Entire production under the superintendence of George Conquest
Maude Stafford (Aladdin); Victor Stevens (The Widow Twankey); Ada Vinnette (Princess Badroulbadour); Willie Edmunds (Poodleoodle); R. Courtneidge (Emperor Rumphiz); Katie Cohen (The Genii of the Lamp); Rosamond Tennyson (The Genii of the Ring); Messrs. Wade & Waller (Caesar and Pompey); George Conquest, Jr. (Slihi/Omihi); H. Edmunds (Magician Abanaza); James Albert (Wazrac); W. P. Dempsey (Unhung); Vinnie Edmunds (La-di-da); Mr. Vickars (The Bat); H. Granville (The Doctor's Lamp); Mr. Spencer (Policeman's Lamp); Peter Pony (The Stable Lamp); Mr. Rightaway (The Railway Lamp); Miss Teesdale (The Electric Light); Carrie Conway (Gem of the Jewels); Master Colza (The Moderator Lamp)

ALADDIN AND FORTY THIEVES, Drury Lane Theatre, London, opened December 26, 1885
Produced and Directed by Augustus Harris; A Pantomime by E. L. Blanchard, revised

by Robert Reece; Scenery W. R. Beverly, William Perkins, J. Johnstone, and Henry Emden

Peggy Pride (Aladdin); Harry Leander (The Widow Wee-Ping, Aladdin's mother); Alfred Lorraine (The Sultan); Frances M. Ryan (Princess Badroulbadour); Mr. Huda (Ali Baba); Alice Rogers (Ganem); E. Vokes (The Vizier); Frank Pierce (Abdallah); Sophia Scott (Selim); Ivy Warner (Ring-Ting); Florence Warner (Sing-Sing); Emelie Holt (Morgiana); Otto Elliott & Berto (Abracadabra and Abracanazar); Claude Randall (Neptune); Florence Warner (Amphritrite); Edith Herbert (Arethusa); Ivy Warner (Britannia); Louie Parker (Father Thames)

ALADDIN AND FORTY THIEVES, *Drury Lane Theatre*, London, opened March 4, 1886
Produced and Directed by Augustus Harris; A Pantomime by E. L. Blanchard; Music, Oscar Barrett; Scenery, W. R. Beverly, William Perkins, J. Johnstone, and Henry Emden; Ballets by Katti Lanner; Costumes by Wilhelm, executed by Madame August et Cie, Miss Fisher, Messrs. Harrison and May; Stage Manager, Charles Harris

Grace Huntley (Aladdin); Victor Stevens (Emperor of China); Harry Nicholls (Widow Twankey); H. M. Edmund (The Prime Minister); Kate Leamar (Princess Badroulbadour); Herbert Campbell (Abanazar); Charles Laurie, Jr. (Kazrac); Nelly Bennett (Genius of the Lamp); Clara Grahame (Saw See); Vinnie Edmunds (Stri Ki); Reuben Inch (Bo-Gee/Ag-i-ta-ti); James Albert, William Albert (Prime Minister's Secretaries); Francesca Zanfretta (Principal Dancer); Nelly Leamar (Chee Kee); The Children of The National Training School for Dancing

ALADDIN, *National Standard Theatre*, London, opened December 24, 1886
A Pantomime Produced, written, and directed by John L. Douglass; Scenery, Richard Douglass; Music by W. Corri

Kate James (Aladdin); Marie Barnum (Princess Badroulbadour); G. W. Cockburn (Grand Vizier); E. J. Allnutt (Widow Twankey); Carrie Laurie (Genii of the Ring); Stella Leigh (Genii of the Lamp); Cyrus Bell (Abanazar)

THE ARABIAN NIGHTS; OR, ALADDIN'S WONDERFUL LAMP, *Standard Theatre*, New York, opened September 12, 1887
Produced by David Henderson; A Spectacular Burlesque; Director, Joseph Brooks; Written and designed by Alfred Thompson; Music, Emil O. Wolff, Anthony Reiff, and others; Scenery, Messrs. Noxon, Albert & Toomey; Costumes by Dazian; Ballet Mistress, Rose Beckett; Musical director, Anthony Reiff; Stage Director, William Gill; Acting Manager, Alfred Joel; Stage Manager, R. O. Percy

Loie Fuller (replaced Emma Chambers) (Aladdin); Helen Harrinton (replaced Lelia Barnett) (The Sultana Scheherazade); Miss Cogan (Genie of the Lamp); Lillie Alliston (The Widow Tootsicum); Sallie Williams (replaced Jennie Ellison) (Fol-Dol); George Clare (The Caliph Haroun Al Raschid); J. H. Ryley (replaced John Gilbert) (The Magician); Lizzie Pierrepont (Spirit of the Ring); Frank W. Holland (Emperor Ski-Hi); Celia Ellis (replaced Clara Ellison) (Princess Badroulbadour); Thomas Martin (Tickily Nokra, Grand Vizier); Lena Merville (Kickapoo); May Yohe (Zal-Am-Bo); Agnes Burke (replaced Zoe Vielli) (Tambo-Rina); Rose Frank (Fal-Lal); Rose Wilson (Ni-See); Linda Bennett (replaced Kate Richards) (Lum-Tum); Linda Linnet (Chid-Dee); Ada Chamberlain (Loot-Lee); Marie Austin (Tip-Top); Richard Golden (replaced Richard E. Carroll) (Klub-Lubba, Inspector of Police); Mlle. Cornalba (Premiere Danseuse)

THE ARABIAN NIGHTS; OR, ALADDIN'S WONDERFUL LAMP, Touring Company, season 1887-88

Produced by David Henderson; A Spectacular Burlesque; Directors, Joseph Brooks, Alfred Thompson; Written and Designed by Alfred Thompson; Musical Director, Emil O. Wolff; Scenery by Messrs. Noxon, Albert & Toomey; Costumes by Dazian; Acting Manager, Alfred Joel; Stage Manager, R. V. Percy

Helen Harrington (Aladdin/Scheherazade); Juliet Martel (Genie of the Lamp); Lillie Alliston (The Widow Tootsicum); Sallie Williams (Fol-Dol), George Clare (Caliph Haroun Al Raschid); Richard Golden (Chow-Chow, the Magician); Lizzie Pierrepont (Spirit of the Ring); Frank M. Holland (Emperor Ski-Hi); May Yohe (Princess Badroulbadour); Tom Martin (Tickily Nokra, Grand Vizier); Lena Merville (Kickapoo), Linda Barnett (Zal-Am-Bo); Agnes Burke (Tambo-Rina); Rose Frank (Fal-Lal); Rose Wilson (Ni-See); Mary Baron (Lum-Tum); Linda Linnet (Chid-Dee); Ada Chamberlain (Loot-Lee); Marie Austin (Tip-Top); William Gill (Klub-Lubba, Inspector of Police); Mlle. Bonfanti (Premiere Danseuse); Mlle. Dorst, Alice Stoddard, Lena Merville, Mons. Oreste (The Doll's Quadrille)

MUSICAL NUMBERS: "Polo"; "I'm the Princess"; "Owl's Dance"; "Listen to My Love, Dolly"; "But He Doesn't Know Everything Yet"; "When the Roses Fade and Die"; "It Is Not Always May"; "The Light of Other Days"; "Cutlass Drill"

ALADDIN, OR THE WONDERFUL LAMP, Touring Company, season 1887-88

Director, John Ellsler

Miss Loduski Young (Aladdin); Miss Ray Briscoe (Princess Badroulbadour); H. B. Kavanaugh (Genii of the Wonderful Lamp); W. H. Pierce (Abenazar); Charles Constantine (Kazrac); Hal Warren (Tahi Tong Luch); P. L. Phillips (Orlock, Genii of the Air); Mlle. Estrella Sylvia (Zee-Zee, Grand Dancer); Albert W. Decker (Kazi Azak); Frank Johnson (Noureddin); Ida Francais (Zobeide); Hattie A. Lewis (Ching Mustapha); Mary Osborne (Fairy Fly-Away); Alexina Lawrence (Fairy-Run-to-Me); Sallie Hatton (Adami-Chow); Alexander Houghton (Ben Mouseff); A. Anderson (Mesrour); W. H. Sanders (Haggi); Oscar Tanner, Jr. (Rom-Chow-Low); A. Messig (Run-Wang-Be); D. A. Sargent (Se-Coo-Lon); Jennie St. Clair (Amrou); Bessie Powers (Alexi-Chang); Ellen Stanley (Alessi-Twang); Alice Stanley (Chow-Rango); Clara Douglass (Bacchini-Wang); Van Stavoren (Croco-Tonga)

Grand Theatre, Islington, London, opened December 26, 1889

A Pantomime by Geoffrey Thorne; Music director, Mr. Brinkworth; Ballets, Paul Valentine

Belle Black (Aladdin); Joe Cheevers (Aladdin's Mother); Sara Beryl (Princess Badroulbadour); Miss Louie Wilmot (Pekoe); Retta Walton (Ah-Rong); Fred Walton (Toy Soldier); Wilfrid Shine (Abanazar); Charles Seel (Wishee-Washee); Wal Curtis (The Emperor of China); Alfred Rivers (Grand Vizier); Mlle. Elsie, Florence Morrison, Grace Elsie, Harry Moore, the Almonti Troupe (Harlequinades)

ALADDIN UP TO DATE, Novelty Theatre, London, opened December 26, 1890 43 performances

Produced by Tolhurst; A Play by Brien McCullough and Frank Green; Acting manager, H. J. Borley; Conductor, Henry T. Parkes

Marie Brian (Aladdin); Ada Douglas (Princess Badroulbadour); H. Buckstone Clair (Abanazar); Charles Lerigo (Emperor Ski-Cri); Owen Wynne (Vizier); Brien

McCullough (succeeded by J. G. Wilton) (Widow Crankey); Annie Shelby (succeeded by T. Clifford) (Slave of the Lamp); Georgie Harris (succeeded by Annie Shelby) (Genii of the Ring); Nellie Nelson (succeeded by Georgie Harris) (Beppo); Wally Brunton (Ching Chow)

ALADDIN, *Alhambra Theatre*, London, opened December 19, 1892
A Dramatic Ballet by John Hollingsworth; Choreography, Signor Carlo Coppi; Costumes, Howell Russell and Mons. and Mme. Alias; Scenery, Bruce Smith; Music, G. Jacobi

Mlle. Marie (Aladdin); Signorina Legnani (Princess Badroulbadour); Fred Storey (The Magician); Signorina Pollini (Spirit of the Lamp)

ALADDIN, JR., *Broadway Theatre*, New York, opened April 8, 1895 48 performances
Produced by David Henderson; A Tale of a Wonderful Lamp; Director, Richard Barker; Libretto by J. Cheever Goodwin; Music, W. H. Batchelor and Jesse Williams; Choreography, Fillberto Marchetti from Ballets composed by Carlo Coppe; Ballet music by M. Georgio Jacobi; Costumes, Howell Russell

Anna Boyd (Aladdin, Jr.); Ada Deaves (Widow Bohea); Henry Norman (Abanazar); Albert Froom (Genie of the Lamp); Frankie M. Raymond (Chee Kee); Allene Crater (Badroulbadour); Irene Verona (Oo-Ong); John E. Cain (Vizier Chow Chow); John J. Burke (Crambo); David Abrahams (Lucifer, the Cat); Bessie Pope (Spirit of the Ring); J. W. Herbert (Ki Yi); Charles Turner (Pansy Mulcahy); John E. Murphy (Lily Mulcahy); L. Easton (Tu Tee Fru Tee); Mary Thorne (Lee Tel Wee Lee); Jose Shalders (Da See Gur Lee); Nellie Lynch (Poo See Wee Lo); Mlles. Catharino Bartho, Martha Irmier (Premieres Danseuses); Nellie Lynch, Flora Evans (Dancers)

MUSICAL NUMBERS: "An Emperor's Lot"; "Laundry Trio"; "The Rackety Boys"; "A Magician of High Degree"; "Women, Wine and Song"; "Message of the Rose"; "I Must Away"; "The Feast of Lanterns"; "Love Among the Freaks"; "Alabama Coon"; "I Don't Suppose You Have"; "The Storm"; "Bow Down!"; "I've Booked the Date"; "The Way He Arranges His Face"; "Beauteous Widow Bohea"; "Didn't I Think He'd Do It!"; "Three Old Sports"; "Infelice"; "Farewell, Fondest and Dear"; "Lazily and Drowsily"; "The Stars Alone Can Tell"; "Fill High! Drink Deep!"

ALADDIN, *Drury Lane Theatre*, London, opened December 26, 1896 138 performances
Produced by Oscar Barrett; A Pantomime by Arthur Sturgess and Horace Lennard; Music by Oscar Barrett; Acting manager, Neil Forsyth; Music director, James Weaver; Scenery, Henry Emden, Joseph Harker, Robert Caney, J. Pritchard Barrett, William Telbin; Costumes designed by Wilhelm; Choreography, Katti Lanner, John d'Auban; Stage manager, Arthur P. Collins

Ada Blanche (Aladdin); Decima Moore (Princess Badroulbadour); Herbert Campbell (Abanazar); Dan Leno (Mrs. Twankey); Paul Cinquevalli (Slave of the Lamp); Walker Marnock (Emperor); Fritz Rimma (Grand Vizier); Geraldine Somerset (Genius of the Ring); Florence Darley (Spirit of Life); Ebb Darcia (Milliner); Joe Griffiths (Washee-Wishee); Fred Griffiths (Chief Constable); Ernest d'Auban (Dancing Master); G. Angelo (Lord Chamberlain); Cleveland (Tax Collector); E. H. Chasemore (Constable); Master Goff (Dog); Leo Mars (Coiffeur); Sawyers (Canvasser); George Aubery (Glover); Clara Jecks (Sau-See); Helene Phillans (Pekoe); Grigolati (Slave of the Ring); C. Gaisford, Lily

Milbank, Levy, Lena Delphine, A. Gordon, Gertrude Claridge, Miro, K. Beardshaw, Dora Rignold, Maud Rignold, G. Briscoe, L. Marsden, Taylor, Ethel Beaumont, Archer, B. Talbot, O. Vaughan, Daisy Sedger, E. Pritchard, Maude Vinton, E. Ward, J. Jones, H. West, J. Goodman, J. Ibberson (Ensemble)

CHRIS AND THE WONDERFUL LAMP, *Hammerstein's Victoria Theatre*, New York, opened January 1, 1900 58 performances
Produced by Klaw and Erlanger and B. D. Stevens; A Musical Extravaganza; Director, Ben Teal; Book by Glen MacDonough; Music by John Philip Sousa; Scenery, Ernest Gros, Homer Emens, Gates & Morange; Costumes, F. Richard Anderson; Dances, Mme. Malvina; Electric Butterfly Dance invented and patented by H. Harndin; Music Director, A. Krause; Stage Managers, Charles H. Drew, Louis Strader

Edna Wallace Hopper (Chris Wagstaff); Jerome Sykes (The Genie, Slave of the Lamp); Emilie Beaupre (Aladdin); Mabella Baker (Miss Prisms); Johnny Page (Scotty Jones); Charles H. Drew (Selwell); Ethel Irene Stewart (Fanny Wiggins); Nellie Lynch (Amine); Randolph Curry (The Grand Vizier/Lovemoney); Herbert Carter (Pettingill/Al Khizar); Frank Todd (Captain of the Guards); Edna Hunter (Stella); Edith Barr (Della); Violet Jewell (Bella); Adele Nott (Ella); Stella Madison (Nella); Delia Sylvester (alternate, May Norton) (Queen of Dreams)

ALADDIN, *Hippodrome Theatre*, London, opened December 26, 1901
Produced by H. E. Moss; A Play by W. H. Risque; Director, Frank Parker; Music, Carl Kiefert; Scenery, Ernest Howard, T. E. Ryan; Dances, Will Bishop; Costumes, Herbert Norris

George Martin (Aladdin); Lily Landon (Princess Badroulbadour); Fitzroy Morgan (Emperor of China); Frank Latona (Abanazar); Beryl Somerset (Slave of the Ring); Fred Williams (Widow Twankey); The Three Missouris (Sli/Peep-Hi/Peep Lo)

THE NEW ALADDIN, *Gaiety Theatre*, London, opened September 29, 1906 203 performances
Produced by George Edwardes; A musical comedy; Acting director, Edward Marshall; Book by James T. Tanner and W. H. Risque; Music by Ivan Caryll and Lionel Monckton; Lyrics by Adrian Ross, W. H. Risque, Percy Greenbank, George Grossmith, Jr.; Additional songs, Frank E. Tours; Scenery, Joseph and Phil Harker, Hawes Craven; Costumes designed by Wilhelm; Music director, Ivan Caryll; Choreography, Harry Grattan; Lighting, G. A. Applebee; Stage manager, Herbert Cathcart

Lily Elsie (succeeded by Gertie Millar) (Lally); George Grossmith, Jr. (Genie of the Lamp); Harry Grattan (succeeded by John A. Warden, W. J. Manning) (Ebenezer); Eustace Burnaby (Billy Pauncefort); Olive May (Laolah); Winifred Dennis (Mrs. Tippin); Edmund Payne (Tippin); S. Hansworth (Tony Cavendish); Robert Nainby (General Ratz); Kitty Mason (Winnie Fairfax); Gladys Desmond (Vi Cortelyou); Violet Walker (Nan Jocelyn); Charles Brown (Ideal Man); J. R. Sinclair (Reggie Tighe); J. W. Birtley (Tax Collector); Doris Beresford (Flo Carteret); Tessie Hackney (Kit Lomax); Florence Lindley (succeeded by Rosa Chesney) (Mary Warrener); Jean Aylwin (Fossette); Enid Leonhardt (Di Tollemache); Gaby Deslys (succeeded by Kitty Lindley) (The Charm of Paris); Connie Ediss (succeeded by Mrs. Watt-Turner, Ruth Argent) (Spirit of the Ring); Alfred Lester (Lost Constable); Arthur Hatherton (Cadi); Adrienne Augarde

(Princess); Edna Loftus (Madge Oliphant); Minnie Baker (Millie Farquhar); Lily Collier, Clara Farren, May Flower, Edith Lee, Kitty Lindley, Gladys Saqui (Dancers)

ALADDIN, Adelphi Theatre, London, opened December 26, 1907 88 performances
Produced by S. Gatti; A Pantomime; Director, Robert Arthur; Book by Frank Dix; Music by Julien H. Wilson; Additional numbers by J. C. Shepherd, Guy Jones, Edward Jackobowski; Scenery, C. M. O'Graph, J. Fowler Hogg, Stafford Hall, W. T. Helmsley, Philip Howden; Costumes, Baruch, Harrison, Miss Hale; Lighting, David Marshall; Choreography, Madge Martin; Music director, Julien H. Wilson; Acting managers, Gifford Stacey, A. C. Belsey; Stage managers, Walter McEwen and Arthur Leigh

Millie Legarde (Aladdin); Malcolm Scott (Widow Twankey); Harry Dent (Abanazar); Sarah Vrubell (Princess So-Shi); Anita Ediss (Pekoe); Harry Cliff (Pi-Krust); M. R. Morand (No-Fang); W. R. Percival (Slave of the Lamp); Percy West (Wizard of the East); J. Stringer (Rickshaw Man); Regan (Li-Chi); Ryan (Chi-Li); Gerrard (Di-a-Bo-Lo); Doris Dean (Cheeki); Happy Fanny Fields (Gretchen); Rene Reel (Genie of the Ring); Martini Troupe, Doris Dean (Dancers)

ALADDIN, Lyceum Theatre, London, opened December 23, 1909 91 performances
Produced by Henry R. Smith; A Pantomime by Mr. and Mrs. Carpenter; Music by H. Sullivan Brooks and Herbert Shelley; Scenery, E. C. Nicholls; Costumes, Mme. Stafford, Elkan Brothers; Costume designer, Robert Crafter; Music director, H. Sullivan Brooke; Lighting, F. B. Fidge; Stage managers, S. Major Jones and Henry Armstrong

Dorothy Craske (Aladdin); Scott Barrie (Widow Twankey); Arthur Poole (Abanazar); Archie Royer (Wishee Washee); Eva Kelland (Princess Badroulbadour); Frank Hemming (Emperor of China); Master Bert Bolder (E-Tuk-is-Ook); Harry Gardner (Polar Bear); Marie Free (Pitti Sing); Marjory Carpenter (Slave of the Lamp); Victoria Slevers (Genie of the Ring); Florence Smithers (Smuttee); Rita Ricardo (Goodwill); Master Alec Oakley (Blubber-Blubber); Kitty Fielder (Saw-See); Belle Hamilton (Ah-Sing); Mabel Crouch (So-Fli); Maud Leonard (Nicee-Nicee); Violet Blyth (Trueheart); Maud Gardner (Gentle Thoughts); Edna Ludlow (Helping Hand); Annie Bevington (Queen of the Fairies); Lizzie Ophir (Fairy Heather Bell)

THE BRASS BOTTLE, Vaudeville Theatre, London, opened September 16, 1909 244 performances
Produced by Gaston Mayer; A Comedy, based on *Aladdin and His Wonderful Lamp*, by F. Anstey; Director, Frederick Kerr; Costumes, Comelli; Music director, Edward Jones; Stage managers, Louis Mercanton and Claud Vernon

Lawrence Grossmith (Horace Ventimore); E. Holman Clark (Fakrash-El-Aamash); Viva Birkett (Sylvia Fut-voye); Alfred Bishop (Professor Anthony Futvoye); Lena Halliday (Mrs. Futvoye); Rudge Harding (Spencer Pringle); Luigi Lablache (Samuel Wacker-bath); Armine Grace (Mrs. Wackerbath); J. H. Brewer (Rap-kin); John Carey (Head Efreet); A. Spencer (Chief of Caravan); Mary Brough (Mrs. Rapkin); Gladys Storey (Jessie); Mabel Duncan (Zobeida); Walter Ringham (Waiter); Phyllis Birkett, Florence A. Pigott, Susie Nainby, Dorothy Beaufey, Nina de Leon, Cynthia Farnham (Dancers)

ALADDIN, Drury Lane Theatre, London, opened December 27, 1909 107 performances

Produced and Directed by Arthur P. Collins; A Pantomime; Book by Sir F. C. Burnaud, J. Hickory Wood and Arthur P. Collins; Music by James M. Glover; Scenery, Henry Emden, R. McCleery, Bruce Smith; Costumes, Alias, Angel & Son, B. J. Simons, Mrs. Hannam, Gloag, Muelle, Harrison Ltd., Baruch, L. Levillion, H. & M. Rayne, Manzo; Music director, James M. Glover; Choreography, Jean Pratesi, John d'Auban; Lighting, H. Mather; Costumes designed by Comelli; Acting manager, Charles F. Taylor; Stage managers, Ernest d'Auban and Edward Spiller

Marie George (Aladdin); Wilkie Bard (Widow Twankey); George Graves (Abanazar); Ida Rene (Princess Badroulbadour); Ernest Langford (Gran Vizier); William Downes (Emperor of China); Salambo (Slave of the Lamp); Nellie Stratton (Pitti Sing); Truly Shattuck (Princess Pekoe); Jimmie James (Imperial Town Crier); George Ali (Bolo, the Dog); Bert Monks (Bam Boo); Fred Penley (Bob Bi); Edward Morgan (Corki Waxi); Harold Belcher (Olrac); Doris Trevelyan (Spirit of the Ring); Mena Brae (San Cee); Bob Pender (Clown); Will Pender (Pantaloon); Joe Pender (Harlequin); Will Comp (Sergeant); T. and G. Pender (Policemen); Arthur Conquest (Kasarac); Maggie Pender (Columbine); Edith Barrington, Marie Lovell, Nan Holmes, L. Hewitson, E. Susini, B. Thorpe, D. Murray Woods, M. Murray Woods, Carrie Murray (Ensemble)

THE BRASS BOTTLE, Lyceum Theatre, New York, opened August 11, 1910 44 performances

Produced by Charles Frohman; A Comedy by F. Anstey; Director, Gustave Von Seyffertitz

Richard Bennett (Horace Ventimore); Edwin Stevens (Fakrash-El-Aamash); Irene Fenwick (Sylvia Futvoye); Fuller Mellish (Professor Anthony Futvoye); Mrs. Thomas Whiffen (Mrs. Futvoye); Ivo Dawson (Spencer Pringle); Louis Massen (Samuel Wackerbath); Cecilia Raddlyffe (Mrs. Wackerbath); Sebastian Smith (Rapkin); Arthur P. Hyman (Head Efreet/Zobeida); Grace Crowley (Jessie); Carrie Perkins (Mrs. Rapkin); Adelaide Orton (A Dancing Girl)

CHIN-CHIN; OR, A MODERN ALADDIN, Globe Theatre, New York, opened October 20, 1914 295 performances

Produced by Charles Dillingham; A Musical Fantasy; Director, R. H. Burnside; Book by Anne Caldwell and R. H. Burnside; Music by Ivan Caryll; Lyrics by Anne Caldwell and James O'Dea; Scenery, Homer Emens, Lee Lash Studios and John H. Young; Costumes designed by Wilhelm of London; Motion picture effect by Lubin Studios; Men's costumes by Dazian; Dresses by Schneider-Anderson Company; Gowns by Jean; Wigs by Hepner; Musical director, W. E. Macquinn; Ballet Master, Luigi Albertieri; Company manager, Arthur Houghton; Stage manager, Charles Mastt

David C. Montgomery (Chin Hop Lo/The Widow/Coolie/ Clown/Gendarme); Fred A. Stone (Chin Hop Hi/ Paderewski/Ventriloquist/Mlle. Falloffski/Gendarme); Douglas Stevenson (Aladdin); Charles T. Aldrich (succeeded by Oscar Ragland) (Abanazar); Zelma Rawlinson (succeeded by Allene Crater) (Widow Twankey); Belle Story (succeeded by Mildred Richardson) (Goddess of the Lamp); R. E. Graham (Cornelius Bond); Helen Falconer (Violet Bond); Eugene Revere (Tzu Yung); Edgar Lee Hay (Li-Dragon Face); Charles Mast (Ring Master); Juliette Day (succeeded by Gladys Zeld) (Sen-Sen); Marjorie Bentley (succeeded by Kitty Lindley) (Silver Ray); Lola Curtis (succeeded by Isabel Falconer) (Moon Blossom); Violet Zeld (Fan-Tan); Evelyn Conway (Lily Petal); Hazel Lewis (succeeded by Lydia Scott) (Lotus Leaf); Lorayne Leslie (succeeded by Tot Qualters) (Cherry Bloom); Agnes McCarthy (Little Wing Wu); George Phelps (Little Lee Toy); Mildred Richardson (Spirit of New Year); Eleanor St. Clair (succeeded by Janet Wallenberg) (Poppy Bud); Tot Qualters (Spring Flower); Margaret St. Clair (Wistaria); Lillian Rice (Honeysuckle); Misses Breen (The Four Bears); Hilda Allison, Claire Bertrand, Cecile Conway, Harriet Leidy, Cassie Qualters, Dorothy Richardson, Grace Beaumont, Bessie Burch, Olive Carr, Marion Davies, Isabel Falconer, Anna Ford, Marjorie Graham, Mazie Leroy, R. C. Bosch, Martin Cox, Roger Davis, Joseph Gormley, Jack Hagner, J. F. Johnson, Arthur Kuesta, Peter Page, H. S. Palmen, E. H. Randall, Harold Russell, Harry Silver (The Company); and The Brown Brothers

MUSICAL NUMBERS: "Quaint Toys"; "Shopping in the Orient"; "Teddy Bear Dance"; "The Chinese Honeymoon"; "Chipper China Chaps"; "Good-Bye, Girls, I'm Through"; "Go Gar Sig Gong Ju"; "In an Oriental Way"; "Violet"; "Temple Bells"; "Will O' the Wisp" "Lightning Changes"; "Wedding Gifts of Silver"; "The Grey Dove"; "The Rag of Rags"; "Love Moon"; "Danse Postique"; "The Clown Band"; "The Ventriloquist"; "Mlle. Falloffski"; "Clown"; "Strollers"; "Chin-Chin"

Dropped from Production: "Jumpety Jumps"; "The Mulberry Tree"; "The Man of a Hundred Faces"; "In January"; "It's A Long, Long Way to Tipperary"

Touring Company, season 1917-18

Produced by Charles Dillingham; A Musical Fantasy; Director R. H. Burnside; Book by Anne Caldwell and R. H. Burnside; Music by Ivan Caryll; Lyrics by Anne Caldwell and James O'Dea; Costumes designed by Wilhelm of London; Motion picture effect by Lubin Studios; Scenery, Homer Emens, Lee Lash Studios and John H. Young; Men's Costumes by Dazian; Dresses by Schneider-Anderson Company; Gowns by Jean; Wigs by Hepner

James Doyle (Chin Hop Lo/The Widow/Coolie/Ventriloquist/Gendarme); Harland Dixon (Chin Hop Hi/ Paderewski/Mlle. Falloffski/Gendarme); Roy Hoyer (Aladdin); Joseph Robinson (Abanazar); Essie Franklyn (Widow Twankey); Ed Reader (Cornelius Bond); Grace Walsh (Violet Bond); Roy Binder (Tzu Yung); Jeanne Mai (Goddess of the Lamp); Edward Donnelly (succeeded by Earl Amos) (Ring Master); Louise Worthington (succeeded Belle Irving) (Sen-Sen); Marie Callahan (Fan-Tan); Gene Merrick (Silver Ray); Marie Cavanaugh (succeeded by Louise Worthington) (Moon Blossom); Leone Wilcox (Lily Petal); Ethel Lawrence (Lotus Leaf); Inez Bauer (Cherry Bloom); George Phelps (Little Lee Toy); Misses Bronson, Mack, McDonald (Teddy Bears); Rose Allen, Mary Barry, Emma Bronson, Patricia Devlin, Helen Gates, Peggy Glendenning, Florence Maxwell, Elsie Miller, Hazel Rix, Marjorie Taylor, Abbie Hadlock, Mary Hadlock, Lottie Mack, May Mack, Helen Russell, Esther Rutland, Truly Elwers, Irene Shaw, Josephine Taylor, Myrtle Turner, Meta Train, Laura Walters, Claire Weston, Dorothy Wright, James Black, Ed McGrath, Keith Pitman, Roy Henderson, Carl Kuebler, Frank Allen, Lew Gould, Dick R. Bosch, Joseph Ackinson (The Company)

ALADDIN, *Drury Lane Theatre*, London, opened December 25, 1917

Director, Arthur Collins: A Play by F. Anstey, Frank Dix, and Arthur Collins; Costumes by Comelli; Magical effects by F. Culpett; Dances, A. H. Majilton; Music by J. M. Glover and Melville Gideon; Additional Lyrics by J. O. Harrington; Ballets, Jean Protesi; Company manager, Charles F. Taylor; Stage managers, Ernest D'Auban and

Clifford Speirr

Dorothy Lane (Aladdin); Robert Hale (Abanazar); Stanley Lupino (Widow Twankey); Galeb Porter (Slave of the Lamp); Will Evans (Slave of the Ring); Harry Claff (Emperor of China); Daisy Bindley (Princess Badroulbadour); Lennie Deane (Toi-Sing); Charles Penley (Chokee); Edward Morgan (Ly-Chee); Marcel Godfrey (The Vizier); K. Lane (Poetry); M. Preston (Prose); Harry Claff (Spirit of the Cave); Alec Johnstone (Executioner); Borneo Gardiner (Solo Whistler); The Tiller Troupe Harlequinade: William Stevens (Pantaloon); George Craig (Harlequin); Jessie Vokes (Columbine); George Cooper (Policeman)

ALADDIN AND THE WONDERFUL LAMP, *London Hippodrome*, London, opened December 21, 1920 185 performances
Produced by Moss Empires Ltd, R. H. Gillespie, Managing Director; A Pantomime; Book by Lauri Wylie and F. Maxwell-Stewart; Music by James W. Tate; Lyrics by Clifford Harris, Donovan Parsons and Valentine; Director, Julian Wylie; Staged by Gus Schilke; Scenery, Marc Henri, Philip Howden, R. McCleery, R. D'Amar, Bruce Smith, Ernest Howard; Costumes designed by Comelli and Dolly Tree; Music director, Julian Jones; Lighting, W. P. Chester; Stage managers, H. E. Bright and W. Armstrong

Elsie Prince (Aladdin); Nellie Wallace (Widow Twankey); Richard Norton (Slave of the Lamp); Stanley Turnbull (Emperor of China); Phyllis Dare (Princess Badroulbadour); Liliane Gilbert (Slave of the Ring); Albert Darnley (Abanazar); Fred Reed (Li Lo); Phil Lester (Clown); Wallace Lupino (Grand Vizier); Fred Regina (Harlequin); Ruth French, Edyth Mayall (Dancers); Lupino Lane (Pekoe)

Palladium Theatre, London, opened December 26, 1921 72 performances
Produced by Capital Syndicate Ltd.; A Pantomime; Director, Ernest C. Rolls; Book and Lyrics by Ernest C. Rolls, Cyril Hemington, and Herbert C. Sargent; Music by Horace Sheldon, Hubert Barth, and Ernest C. Rolls; Additional music by Emmett Adams; Scenery, Hicks, Hemsley, James, Francis H. Bull, Bruce Smith, Howden and Bernard; Costumes, Mary Fisher, Reville Ltd., J. Simmonds & Sons, Reneaux, Maison Getz, Maison Lewis; Choreography, J. W. Jackson

Jennie Benson (Aladdin); Charles Austin (Widow Twankey); Will Evans (Abanazar); Lorna Pounds (Wishee Washee); Bernard Dudley (Emperor); Harold Howard (Town Crier); Toots Pounds (Princess Zobeide); May St. John (Slave of the Lamp); Miss Dimitri Vetter (Geni of the Ring); Victoria Miller (Cheekee); Douglas Byng (Grand Vizier); Lily Bruce (Pekoe); Percival Coyte, Jack Hamilton (Policemen); Roddy Macrae, Joseph La Porte (Firemen); Winton's Water Lions and Diving Nymphs

Palladium Theatre, London, opened December 22, 1926 89 performances
Produced by Harry Day; A Pantomime by Charles Henry, Gilbert Lofthouse; Music by Joseph A. Tunbridge; Lyrics by James Heard; Director, Charles Henry; Costumes by Criscuolo; Scenery, Max Martin; Draperies, Maurice; Illusions, Fred Culpitt; Music director, Horace Sheldon; Choreography, Mlle. Albion; Music arranger, Horace Sheldon; General manager, Gilbert Brown; Stage managers, Robert Smith, Walter Morris

Clarice Mayne (Aladdin); Charles Austin (Widow Twankey); Bransby Williams (Abanazar); Violet Essex (Princess Badroulbadour); Ver Wray (So Shi); Henry Martell (Peke); Edgar Martell (Nese); Bert Randall (Wishee Washee); Picton Roxborough (Sultan/ Emperor); Walter Dunio (Slave of the Lamp); Florence

Helm (Pekoe); Joan Kingdon (Scheherazade/Genie of the Ring); Hymack (Vizier); Edward Stillward (Dog); Pauline Prim (Cat); Mlle. Albion (Scheherazade's Sister/Speciality Dancer); Grosvenor Male Sextette, Terry's Juveniles, Daphne Brayne (Entertainers); Derra de Moroda (Principal Dancer)

Dominion Theatre, London, opened December 24, 1930
A Christmas Pantomime by Lauri Wylie, F. V. Maxwell-Stewart and Julian Wylie; Music by James W. Tate and E. W. Eyre; Lyrics by Clifford Harris, Valentine and Donovan Parsons

Ella Retford (Aladdin); Albert Darnley (Abanazar); S. Griffiths-Moss (The Emperor of China); Wallace Lupino (The Grand Vizier); Lupino Lane (Pekoe); Nellie Wallace (The Widow Twankey); Stella Browne (Princess Badroulbadour); Harry C. Robinson (Slave of the Lamp); George Atterbury (Bonzo); Harry C. Robinson (The Great Roc); Liliane Gilbert (Slave of the Ring); The Three Pirates (Li Hi, Li Ho, Li Lower); Baby Love, Sheila Dexter (Principal Dancers)

Lyric Theatre Hammersmith, London, opened December 22, 1931
Produced by Nigel Playfair; A Pantomime by V. C. Clinton-Baddeley; Directors, Frank Birch and Nigel Play-fair; Music by Walter Leigh

Marie Blanche (Aladdin); V. C. Clinton-Baddeley (Abanazar); Frank Birch (The Widow Twankey); Brian Oulton (Pekoe); Scott Russell (The Emperor of China); Ivy Tresmand (Princess Badroulbadour); Muriel George (Empress); Edward Clarke (The Slave of the Lamp); Nadine March (Fairy Dewdrop); Douglas Allen (The Slave of the Ring); Dorothy Dunkels (Itti Sing); Wilfred Lawson, Leslie Holland (Salmon and Gluckstein); Douglas Allne, Edward Clarke (The Horse); Prudence Hyman (Premiere Danseuse)

Grand Theatre, Croydon, London, opened December 26, 1932
A Pantomime by Joy Beahm, revised by Thomas J. Pigott; Director, Henry Wright

Babs Valerie (Aladdin); Harry Brunning (Widow Twankey); Leslie Sarony (Wishee Washee); Charles Rolfe (The Emperor); Marjorie Browne (Princess Badroulbadour); Eric Le Fre (Abanazar); Hazel Shelley (Pekoe); Anne Bolt (Dar-Ling); Sylvia Binham (Herald); Leon and Kik (Nabbee and Grabbee)

Embassy Theatre, London, opened December 26, 1933
Director, Joan Luxton

Geoffrey Wincott (Aladdin); Ann Casson (Princess Badroulbadour); Basil Radford (Grand Vizier); Brember Wills (Abanazar); Charles Hickman (Widow Twankey); Joan Luxton (Altata)

Golders Green Hippodrome, London, opened December 24, 1934
A Pantomime by C. Denier Warren; Music by Frederick Conquer; Director, Harry Butler

Polly Ward (Aladdin); George Graves (Mrs. Twankee); Cecil Humphreys (Abanazar); Edwin Dodds (Slave of the Lamp); Iza Kilpatrick (Genie of the Ring); Fred Miller (Wishee Washee); Lance Fairfax (Wong Ho); Josie Fearon (Princess Heart's Delight); Murray and Mooney (Pee-Cee and Enn-Gee); Mark Stone (Bung Ho); Hylda Ciro (Pekoe); Barbara Wood (Me-Ne-Mo)

Prince Edward Theatre, London, opened December 26, 1934
A Pantomime and Lyrics by J. Bertini; Music by Fred Freer; Director, George Bishop

Valda Jesmond (Aladdin); Ivan Menzies (Widow Twankey); Dan Rayner (Abanazar); Wilma Vanne (Princess Badroulbadour); Evelyn Gardiner (Slave of the Lamp); Clyde Fields (Genie of the Ring); George Lauri (Hung Hi); Fred Biron (Hung Lo); Lingha Singh (Karsac); Jack Millward (Ho Lung); Chic Williams (No Fang); Rowena Ronald (Pekoe); Joan Lang (Nicee)

Golders Green Hippodrome, London, opened December 26, 1936
Produced and Directed by Emile Littler; A Pantomime by Emile Littler; Music by Ronald Hill; Incidental music by Guy Jones

Polly Ward (Aladdin); Stanley Holloway (Abanazar); Dave Burnsby (Widow Twankey); Anne Holt (Princess Badroulbadour); Tony Sympson (Wishee-Washee); Aimee Fillespie (Prince Pekoe); Laney Weeks (Sing-So); Ellis Carlyle (Kasim); Leo Sheffield (Emperor of China); Joanne Davidson (Moonbeam); Collinson and Dean (Bob-HI and Bend LO)

Adelphi Theatre, London, opened December 24, 1937
Produced by Tom Arnold for Julian Wylie Productions Ltd.; A Pantomime by Dan Leno, Jr., Marriott Edgar, and Tom Arnold; Director, Robert Nesbitt; Scenery, E. Delany; Music by James W. Tate and E. W. Eyre; Dances and Ensembles by Joan Davis; Stage director, H. E. Bright; Stage manager, Maurice Edmonds; Costumes, Gladys Calthrop, L. & N. Nathan Ltd., Alice Shanks, Louis Brooks, Betty S. Roberts

Elsie Randolph (Aladdin); Edwin Styles (Abanazar); Arthur Riscoe (Widow Twankey); Jean Colin (Princess Badroulbadour); Arthur Rigby, Jr. (Emperor); Reginald Newson (Slave of the Lamp); Nan Liddle (So Shi); Ena Moon (Slave of the Ring); J. Delira (The Great Roc); W. S. Percy (The Vizier); Charles Austin (Li-Hi); Willie Lancet (Li-Lo); Jerry Verno (Pekoe); Harry Rignold (Dog); Egbert Brothers (Police); Jack Justin, Charles Leoville (Demons); Reginald Newson (Clown); Daphne Dewar (Harlequin); Doreen Hanson (Columbine); Pickard's Chinese Syncopators; Wilkey & Rae; Sixteen Willoughby Babes; Kirby's Flying Ballet; Adelphi Chorus and Ballet; Kennedy Russell and His Orchestra

Streatham Hall, London, opened December 26, 1939
A Pantomime produced, written, and directed by Prince Littler

Betty Huntley-Wright (Aladdin); Barry Lupino (Widow Twankey); Winifred Scott (Princess So Shi); Jules (Slave of the Lamp); Pratrova (Genie of the Ring); Harry Welchman (Abanazar); Henry Latimer (Emperor of China); Billy Nelson (Wishee Washee); Joan Seton (Pekoe); Sheila Daly (Saucee); Shelagh Cotter (San-Sen); The Three Jokers (Ah-Tish, Ah-Tosh, Ah-Sosh); and Terry's Famous Juveniles: Wilson, Keppel and Betty

Coliseum Theatre, London, opened December 23, 1940
A Pantomime by Francis Laidler; Music composed and arranged by Charles Prentice

Jean Colin (Aladdin); Iris Sadler (Widow Twankey); Sutherland Felce (Abanazar); Alf Alva (Slave of the Lamp); June Holden (Genie of the Ring); Jerry Verno (Wishee Washee); Charles Rolfe (Emperor of China); Jane Corda (Princess So-Shi); Billy Purvis (Blotto); Harry Talbot (Grand Vizier); Fuller Brothers (Ah-Tish, Ah-Tosh); and The Five Lai Founs, The Sixteen John Tiller Girls

Richmond Theatre, London, opened December 26, 1941
A Pantomime produced, written, and directed by Kingsley Lark

Prologue: Charles (Genie of the Lamp); Anita (Slave of the Ring); *The Play*: Olwyn Williams (Aladdin); Leslie French (Widow Twankey); Frank Cochrane (Abanazar); Mary Carr (Princess); Kingsley Lark (Emperor); Nora Kennedy (Pekoe); Jill Hands (Nicee); Crosby and Sands (Koppa, Sloppa); Dave Jackley (Wishee Washee)

Cambridge Theatre, London, opened December 20, 1945
A Pantomime produced, written, and directed by Emile Littler

Binnie Hale (Aladdin); Hal Bryan (Widow Twankey); N'Gai (Abanazar); Mary Meredith (Princess Badroulbadour); Carole Marr (Sing-So); Jasmine Dee (Fairy Moonbeam); Martin Lawrence (Emperor of China); Jack Stanford (Wishee Washee); James Rich (Kazim); April Rose (Pekoe); Agar Young Duo (Penelope, the Horse); Laurie Mellin (Thimble, the Cat); Elstree's Three Stooges (Bend-Hi, Bend-Lo, Bend-To)

Golders Green Hippodrome, London, opened December 22, 1945
Produced and directed by Prince Littler; A Magnificent Pantomime based on *Aladdin and His Wonderful Lamp*, by Sydney Smith; Dances arranged by Janet Cram; Musical director, Van Dam, and his Orchestra; General manager, Frank C. Marshall; Manager and stage director, James Weston; Stage manager, Betty Bellew

Sylvia Welling (Aladdin); Barry Lupino (Widow Twankey); Leslie Barker (The Slave of the Lamp); Johnson Clark (Abanazar); David Basil Gill (The Emperor of China); Brenda Gay (Princess So-Shi); Jackie Hunter (Wishee-Washee); Elizabeth Deane (Pekoe); Sally Tozer (Saucee); Diane Gardiner (The Genii of the Ring); Tiki and Del (Ah-Tish, Ah-Tosh, Policemen); Delly King, The Ben Abderrahman Wazzan Troupe (The Emperor's Entertainers); Barbara Burgess, Eileen Clare, Hazel Clarke, Pat Fisher, Valerie Fowler, Peggy Garland, Sheila Grainger, Daphne Goodacre, Eileen Hennessey, Vicky Jamieson, Hazel Leslie, Sylvia Mathews, Sybil Mathews, Pauline Miller, Pamela Moy, Margo Owen, Delphine Patterson, Dulcie Pyne, Leonie Ray, Olwyn Richards, Rita Rome, Joyce Small Renee Spiller, Pat Wallis, Wendy Warren, Leonie Watkins, Helen Whitam, Alice Williams, Sheila Wynn, Jeanette Yarlette (Attendants, Villagers, Courtiers, Chorus and Ballet)

MUSICAL NUMBERS:"Buy, Buy, Buy"; "Pin-Up Girl"; "Sunshine Over the World"; "I'll Be a Millionaire"; "The Wish I Wish Tonight"; "I'm Wishee Washee"; "A.B.C."; "Policeman's Dance"; "Wedding Waltz"; "I Walk In"; "Coming Home"; "Valse des Fleurs"; "Rub, Rub, Rub"; "The Folks Who Live on the Hill"; "Life Is Nothing Without Music"; "Lovely Lady"; "Down the Mall"

King's Theatre, Hammersmith, London, opened December 24, 1945
A Pantomime by Dan Leno, Jr., and Clarkson Rose; Music by Conrad, Leonard, and Charles Tovey

Rosamund Belmore (Aladdin); Clarkson Rose (Widow Twankey); Claude Chandler (Abanazar); Marjorie Cormack (Princess Badroulbadour); Betty Evans (Chee-Kee); Betty Lynn (Nycee); Rex Korda (The Emperor); Terry Cantor (Wishee Washee); Jack Hurst (Winky-Poo); Sidney Scoon (Spirit of the Lamp); Rupert Gresham (Genie of the Ring); June Phillips (Spirit of Hope); Elsie Miller (Spirit of Justioe); Daphne Willmer (Spirit of Freedom); Anne Martin (Spirit of Peace); Leonie Hodge (Prince Pekoe); Petre Julian (The Vizier); The Java Brothers (Li-HI, Li-LO)

Wimbledon Theatre, London, opened December 23, 1946
A Pantomime; Director, Bert Bright

Beryl Seton (Aladdin); Kathleen West (Widow Twan-key); Ceila Hart (Slave of the Ring); Afrique (Abanazar); Richard Courtney (The Emperor); Kathleen Moody (Princess Badroulbadour); Dicky Hassett (Pekoe); Ricardo Devies (Slave of the Lamp); Lynton Boys (Li-HI, Li-LO); George Arnett (The Vizier); William Yardley (The Great Roc)

Richmond Theatre, London, opened December 26, 1949
A Pantomime written and produced by Russell Thorndike; Director, Maxwell Wray; Music, Noel Gray

Rowena Gregory (Aladdin); Sydney Arnold (Widow Twankey); Russell Thorndike (Abanazar); Olive Walter (Fatima); Patricia Leat (Princess Badroulbadour); Stanley Vilven (Emperor Hang-U-Hi); Jane Fisher (Slave of the Ring); Ian Hardy (Slave of the Lamp); Pamela McHugh (Pekoe); Benny Hill (Wishee-Washee); Kenneth Henry (Grand Vizier of Pekin); Erna Franks (Zobeide); Tiki and Del (Bo-Bi, Bi-Bo); Elizabeth Cooper (Principal Dancer)

Finsbury Park Empire Theatre, London, opened December 21, 1950
A Pantomime with incidental music by George Steele; Director, John Warrington

Charmian Innes (Aladdin); Dennis Lawes (Widow Twankey); Ali Bey (Abanazar); Diana Wong (Princess Badroulbadour); George Thomas (Emperor); Jeanne Grosmont (Slave of the Ring); Robert Dean (Genie of the Lamp); Ann Wakefield (So-Shi); Michael Bird (Grand Vizier); George Doonan (Wishee Washee); Janice Howe (Pekoe); The Three Jokers (Peke, Nese, Pom)

King's Theatre, Hammersmith, London, opened December 23, 1950
A Pantomime by Heath Joyce; Additional comedy scenes and lyrics by Clarkson Rose; Director, Olive Fox

Joan Dowling (Aladdin); Clarkson Rose (Widow Twan-key); Gavin Gordon (Abanazar); Violet Plowman (Princess Badroulbadour); Peter Dare (Wishee Washee); June Leighton (Genie of the Ring); Alan Wren (Slave of the Lamp/Suleiman); Tommy Glen (Emperor of China); Andree Curtis (Nicee); Michael Hall (Grand Vizier); Brenda Rowe (Pekoe); Bel-Louis Brothers (Chinese Policemen)

Grand Theatre, Croydon, London, opened December 26, 1950
A Pantomime by Bertram Montague; Book and Lyrics by Barry Lupino, Arty Ash; Director, Rex London

Marjorie Sandford (Aladdin); Rex London (Widow Twan-key); Philip Godfrey (Abanazar); Clive Drummond (Emperor Wangchow); Paddy Johnson (Pekoe); Ruth Miller (Princess Luvlee); Jack Anton (Wishee Washee); Joyce Down (So-Kay); The Chikolas (Wun Hi, Wun Lung); Arthur Stanley (Grand Vizier)

Casino Theatre, London, opened December 19, 1951
Produced and Directed by Emile Littler; A Pantomime; Music and Lyrics by Guy Jones and Hastings Mann

Jean Carson (Aladdin); Julie Andrews (Princess Badroulbadour); Nat Jackley (Widow Twankey); Walter Crisham (Abanazar); Carole Jeffries (Prince Pekoe); Martin Lawrence (Emperor of China); Gloria George (Sing-So); Jimmy Clitheroe (Wishee Washee); Jacqueline St. Clere (Fairy Moonbeam); David Davenport

(Kazim); Desmond and Marks (Bend Hi and Bend Lo); Ross Harvey (Keeper of the Emperor's Aviary); Fiery Jack (Oriental Road Hog); The Olanders (Royal Tumblers); The Tiller Girls; The Terry Children

Wimbledon Theatre, London, opened December 24, 1951
A Pantomime by Heath Joyce; Additional comedy scenes and lyrics by Clarkson Rose; Director, Frederick Triff

Zena Dell (Aladdin); Ruby Riggs (Princess Badroulbadour); Clarkson Rose (Widow Twankey); Billy West (Emperor of China); Gavin Gordon (Abanazar); Babs Adams (Pekoe); Eddie Reindeer (Wishee Washee); Alen Wren (Slave of the Lamp/Suleiman); June Leighton (Genie of the Ring); Rita Perkins (Nicee)

ARABIAN NIGHTS, *Jones Beach Marine Theatre*, Long Island, New York, opened June 24, 1954
Produced by Guy Lombardo; A Musical Extravaganza based on the *Arabian Nights Tales*; Director, Robert H. Gordon; Book by George Marion, Jr.; Music and Lyrics by Carmen Lombardo and John Jacob Loeb; Settings and Costumes by Richard Rychtarik; Lighting by Paul Morrison; Water Sequences by Lottie Mayer; Ballet Music developed by Alan Moran; Orchestrations, Joe Glover; Musical Direction and Vocal Arrangements by Pembroke Davenport; Choreography, Yurek Lazowski; Production consultant, Lebert Lombardo; Production adviser, Herbert L. Berger; Dances devised by The Ballet Theatre for the Disappearing Water Ballet; Company manager, Roy Jones; Sound, Frank McLaughlin; Costumes for Disappearing Water Ballet, Truman Lord; Underwater Hydraulic Lift, Loomis Engineering and Manufacturing Co.; Production stage manager, Paul Morrison

Lauritz Melchior (Sultan/Chinese Emperor); William Chapman (Aladdin/Sinbad/Prince Ahmed); Helena Scott (Scheherazade/Chinese Princess); Jack Dabdoub (Genie); Hope Holiday (Naeel-ah/Teeny-Weeny Genie); Ralph Herbert (Grand Vizier); Harding Dorn (Ali); The Moroccans (Acrobats); Janik and Arnaut (Snake and Charmer); Herbert Estrow (Major Domo); Gloria Van Dorpe (Kanshee); Mia Slavenska (Premiere Ballerina); Adriano Vitale (Premier Danseur); Ralph Lowe (Trumpeter); Winifred Ainslee (Slave Girl); Margot Campbell, Jean Barrozo, Jeanette Margulis, Sally Mortimer, Moira Paul, Mary Haywood, Ruth Hanna, Nina Popova, Eda Wyatt, Janice Cioffi, Jan Miller, Paula Tennyson, Marilyn Pendell, Naomi Boneck, Nanette Blair, Mariann Bollin, Karolyn Bruder, Pat Diamond, Joan Ann Einwick, June Evans, Janise Gardner, Helen Gorst, Ellen Kampman, Natasha Kelepolska, Victor Duntiere, Hubert Farrington, Albert Fioella, Bruce Hoy, John Kelly, Arthur Mitchel, Tom Reed, George Tomal, Martin Fredricks, Harding Dorn, Angelo Nicelli, Edward Stinnett (Dancing Ensemble); Jane Copeland, Ethel Madsen, Gerrianne Raphael, Ruth Schumacher, Winifred Ainslee, Rosanne Jun, Beth Hawkins, Sybil Lamb, Jane Carlyle, Lucille Lewis, Gloria Van Dorpe, Lois Van Pelt, Astrid Neilson, Betty Zollinger, Toby Dale, Rosalind Phillips, Marie Saucier, Iona Nobel, Doras Smith, Carlos Sherman, Mike Roberts, Larry Anderson, Max Hart, George Geyer, Thomas Rieder, Herbert Estrow, Howard Shaw, James Fox, Steve Roland, Charles Rule, Marvin Zeller, Frank Bouley, Charles Aschmann, Robert Price, Herbert Mazzini, Ralph Lowe, Keith Kaldenberg, Feodore Tedick, Don Phillips, Thomas Edwards, Arthur Ulisse, John Schicklin, Gene Varrone (Singing Ensemble); Inge Bredehorst, Frances Gaar Marvin, Merlyn Gensler, Eileen Grady, Eileen Hiferty, Charlene Hornor, Kesley Ann Knoll, Phoebe Kruge, Kathy McLaughlin, Marjorie Paveglio, Sanita Pelkey, Irene

Roberts, Marlaine Sharak, Pat Sikes, Sandra Smith, Helen Vukotich, Barbara Wallace (Water Ballet Girls)

MUSICAL NUMBERS: "What a Pity"; "It's Great to Be Alive"; "A Thousand and One Nights"; "Grand Vizier's Lament"; "Hail to the Sultan"; "Hero of All My Dreams"; "A Whale of a Story"; "Valley of Jewels"; "Bath Parade"; "How Long Has It Been"; "Teeny-Weeny Genie"; "Genie Ballet"; "A Long Ago Love"; "Marry the One You Love"; "Bridal Fete"

ARABIAN NIGHTS, *Jones Beach Marine Theatre*, Long Island, New York, opened June 25, 1955

Produced by Guy Lombardo; A Musical Extravaganza based on *The Arabian Nights Tales*; Director, Leon Leonidoff; Book by George Marion, Jr.; Music and Lyrics by Carmen Lombardo and John Jacob Loeb; Musical direction and vocal arrangement by Pembroke Davenport; Settings and Costumes by Richard Rychtarik; Orchestrations, Joe Glover; Production consultant, Lebert Lombardo; Water sequences staged by Lottie Mayer; Lighting, Gene Braun, Choreography, Rod Alexander; Production supervisor, Herbert L. Berger; Dances devised by the Ballet Theatre; Underwater Hydraulic Lift, Loomis Engineering and Manufacturing company; Production stage manager, Paul Morrison

Lauritz Melchior (Sultan); William Chapman (Aladdin/ Prince Ahmed/Sinbad); Helena Scott (Scheherazade/ Chinese Princess); Hope Holiday (Na-eel-ah/Tweeny-Weeny Genie); Jack Dabdoub (Genie); Jimmy Fox (Trumpeter); Frank Seabolt (Ali); S. S. Poly (Whale); S. S. Poly, Jr. (Whale, Jr.); James McCracken (Bo'sun/ Chinese Emperor); Buzz Miller (Dancing Aladdin/ Dancing Sinbad); Janick and Arnaut (Snake and Charmer); Shirley Cadle (Swimming Princess); Herbert Estrow (Lord High Executioner); Ralph Herbert (Grand Vizier); Ben Wrigley (Belle of Babylon); Nirska (Nirska); Gloria Van Dorpe (Kanshee)

ALADDIN, *Golders Green Hippodrome*, London, opened December 26, 1955

A Pantomime; Director, Richard Bird

Shani Wallis (Aladdin); Anthea Askey (Princess Tai Hee); Claude Chandler (Abanazar); Dick Emery (Widow Twankey); Margaret Madison (Slave of the Ring); John Scott (Genie of the Lamp); George Betton (Grand Vizier); Molly Munks (Prince Pekoe); Lauri Lupino Lane (Wishee); George Truzzi (Washee); June Grigg (So Shi); Tom Walling (Emperor); The Merry Martins (Tish, Tosh, and Tush); John Whyte, Mark Hashfield, Clive Roslin (Palace Guards)

THE WONDERFUL LAMP, *Palladium Theatre*, London, opened December 22, 1956

A Pantomime by Robert Nesbitt and Phil Park; Songs by Cyril Ornadel, David Croft, and Phil Park; Directors, Robert Nesbitt and Charles Henry; Decor, Edward Delaney; Costumes, R. St. John Roper; Choreography, George Carden

Norman Wisdom (Aladdin); Stephanie Voss (Princess Yasmin); Fisher Morgan (Emperor of China); Sonnie Hale (Widow Twankey); Valentine Dyall (Abanazar); David Keir (Grand Vizier); Ann Cumming (Chi-Lee); Osborne Whittaker (Chamberlain); David Davenport (Genie of the Lamp); Agnes Bernelle (Scheherazade); Tom Gill (Kamar); Hope Jackman (Mrs. Chin Wag); Ken Wilson (Well-Known Character); Dave Jackley, Johnny Volant Trio, Ronnie Brodie (Imperial Police)

Wimbledon Theatre, London, opened December 24, 1956

A Pantomime; Director, William Robertson

Jasmine Dee (Aladdin); Douglas Byng (Widow Twankey); John Law (Abanazar); Elizabeth Wade (Princess); Ruth Porcher (Genie of the Ring); Emma Treckman (Slave of the Lamp/Sulieman); Anne Yorke (Pekoe); Raymond Dyer (Wishee Washee); Gillian Cobbold (Nicee); Douglas Malcolm (Vizier); Peter Haddon (Petah); Hugh Dempster (Emperor); Jimmy Patton, Brian Patton (Policemen)

COLE PORTER'S ALADDIN, *Coliseum Theatre*, London, opened December 17, 1959

Produced by Harold Fielding; A Pantomime; Director and Choreographer, Robert Helpmann; Book by Peter Cook and Robert Helpmann; Music and Lyrics by Cole Porter; Additional Material by Dennis Goodwin; Production Designer, Loudon Sainthill; Lighting, Michael Northen; Musical Director, Bobby Howell; Orchestrations, Ronald Hammer, Len Stevens; Choral Arrangements, Bill Shepherd; Production Manager, Ray Gammon; Costumes, James Parker Ltd, L & H Nathan Ltd., Alec Shanks Ltd., and others; Head Dresses, Hugh Skillen, Connie Olden; Magic Carpet by Eugene's Flying Effects, directed by Arthur Kirby; Ballet Mistress, Shelagh Dey; Costumes Supervisor, Dinah Greet; Company Manager, R. Geoffrey Wood; Stage Manager, Joan Preston

Bob Monkhouse (Aladdin); Doretta Morrow (The Princess); Ronald Shiner (Widow Twankey); David Fallon (Grand Vizier); Ian Wallace (The Emperor); Alan Wheatley (Abanazar); Milton Reid (Genie); Philip Hogan (Wishee); Eddie Sargent (Washee); Reginald Barratt (Fruiterer); Mollie Hare (Florist); Jacqueline Marygold (Jasmine); Anne Heaton (The Diamond Fairy); Jessie Carron (The Slave of the Ring); Kerry Jordan (The Emir of Rammemedam); Golda Casimir (The Margravine of Kastamoni/Doorkeeper of the Hammam Baths); Kerry Jordan (A Petitioner); Reginald Barratt (An Old Man); Geoffrey Webb (A Groom); Sylvia Downing, Carolyn Gray, Angela Langton, Soo-Bee Lee, Maeve Leslie, Alison McGuire, Elizabeth MacKenzie, Barbara Rendall, John Lucas, John Clifford, Kevin Collier, Barry Daniels, Peter Hudson, Griffiths Lewis, Bill Richards, Peter Sugden (The Bill Shepherd Singers); Fred Leopold, Fred Leopold, Jr., Max Riegels, Leslie Davidson, Ted Jones (The Johnny Hutch Five); Bertie Green, Astley Harvey, Elroy Josephz, Kenneth McGregor (Attendants); Geoffrey Webb, Norman McDowell, Bernard Eastoe (Principal Dancers); Dorothy Fraser, Jane Bartlett, Joan Bell, Phyllis Brodie, Wendy Cooper, Virginia Courtney, Patrizia Davey, Pat Goh, Anne Harrison, Valerie Hollman, Jean Mostyn, Joan Palethorpe, Anne Paskevska, Niloufer Pieris, Jacquelyn Sands, Kaye Sargent, Anitra Shore, Gillian Sutcliffe, Caroline Symonds, Angela Vivianne, Carol Yule (Dancers)

MUSICAL NUMBERS: "There Must Be Someone for Me"; "No Wonder Taxes Are High"; "Come to the Marketplace"; "Make Way for the Emperor"; "Aladdin"; "Opportunity Knocks But Once"; "Wouldn't It Be Fun?"; "I Adore You"; "Cherry Pies"; "I Am Loved"; "Ridin' High"; "Trust Your Destiny to Your Star"; "Aladdin" (reprise)

Wimbledon Theatre, London, opened December 23, 1963

A Pantomime; Director, William Robertson

Judy Kenny (Aladdin); Hylda Baker (Widow Twankey); Tommy Cooper (Abanazar); Gavin Hamilton (Genie of the Lamp); Gaynor Rees (Princess Balroulbadour); John Hart Dyke (Suliman); Olivia Breeze (Slave of the Ring); Douglas Malcolm (The Emperor); Bryon O'Leary (The Grand Vizier); Barrie Gosney (Wishee Washee); Ronnie Grainger, Ross Macpherson (The Emperor's

Guards); Lauri Lupino Lane, George Truzzi (Chinese Policemen)

ALADDIN AND HIS WONDERFUL LAMP, *Palladium Theatre*, London, opened December 22, 1964

Produced by Leslie A. MacDonnell & Leslie Grade in association with Bernard Delfont; A Pantomime by David Croft; Music and Lyrics by The Shadows; Producer and Director, Albert J. Knight; Decor, Tod Kingman; Costumes, Cynthia Tingey; Musical supervision, Norrie Paramor; Choreography, Pamela Devis

Cliff Richard (Aladdin); Arthur Askey (Widow Twan-key); Alan Curtis (Abanazar); Una Stubbs (Princess Badroulbadour); Wendy Barry (Genie of the Ring); David Davenport (Spirit of the Lamp); Tom Chatto (Emperor of China); Audrey Bayley (Tai-Ping); Billy Tasker (Town Crier); Michael Henry (Grand Vizier); Charlie Cairoli (Chief Inspector Bathrobe); Joan Palethorpe (So-Shy); Little Jimmy (P. C. Noodles); Henry Lytton (P. C. Boodles); Johnny Volant Five (Patrol Cops); The Shadows: Bruce Welch (Wishee); Hank Marvin (Washee); Brian Bennett (Noshee); John Rostill (Poshee); Paul King (Sergeant Pork); Pamela Devis Boys and Girls; The Shepherd Singers; The Seven Lukacs; The Johnny Volant Five

ARABIAN NIGHTS, *Jones Beach Marine Theatre*, Long Island, New York, opened July 2, 1967 63 performances

Produced by Guy Lombardo; A Musical Fantasy; Direction and Choreography by Yurek Lazowski; Book by George Marion, Jr.; Music and Lyrics by Carmen Lombardo and John Jacob Loeb; Scenery, Peter Dohanos; Lighting, Peggy Clark; Costumes, Winn Morton; Musical director, Oscar Kosarin; Choral director, Robert Monteil; Orchestrations, Joe Glover, John Jacob Loeb; Additional Ballet Arrangements, Vladimir Djury; Company manager, Leonard Soloway; Stage managers, Mortimer Halpern, Norman Shelly, William Krot and Peter Lawrence; Entire production under the supervision of Arnold Spector

James Hurst (Aladdin/Prince Ahmed/Sinbad); Linda Bennett (Scheherazade); Norman Atkins (Sultan/ Chinese Emperor; Norman Riggins (Genie); Edmund Walenta (Captain of the Guard); Lee Cass (Grand Vazir/Lord High Executioner); Judy Knaiz (Na-eel-ah/ Teeny Weeny Genie); Jack Adams (Ali/Court Magician/ Medium Genie); Sherry Lambert (Kan-Shee); Joy Holi-day (Jewel Princess/Court Dancer); Ron Holiday (Royal Dancer); Leslie and Simone (Serpent and Charmer); Sahara Troupe (Court Entertainers); Ron and Joy Holiday, Leslie and Simone, Yurek Lazowski Ballet (Royal Dancers); Katherine Barnes, Doris Galiber, Genevieve George, Barbara Gregory, Sherry Lambert, Leonore Lanzillotti, Carol Marraccini, Joyce Olson, Mary Ann Rydzeski, Dixie Stewart, Marsha Tamaroff, Meggie Worth, Peter Clark, Peter Costanza, Daniel Entriken, Jack Fletcher, Nino Galanti, Leslie Meadow, Robert Monteil, Adam Petroski, Herbert Pordum, Edmund Walenta, David Wilder (Singers); Harriet Ali, Sandra Brown, Joetta Cherry, Peggy Christiansen, Clayde Duvernoy, Jean Ann Einwick, Mimi Funes, Sunny Hannum, Eugenia Hoeflin, Jane Jaffe, Virgina Karczewski, Eileen Lawlor, Melissa Martinez, Ruth Mills, Jannas Perlman, Virginia Putnam, Lucinda Ransom, Ellen Rievman, Francine Storey, Ellen Wollenhaupt, Fred Benjamin, John Giffin, Bijan Kalantari, Alexis Kotimsky, George Lee, Stanley Levy, Robert Lupone, Stephen Reinhardt, Tony Salatino, Don Stromsvik (Dancers); Jean Adams, Barbara Fleming, Patti Lewis, Kathleen Shaughnessy (Mermaids)

MUSICAL NUMBERS: "What a Party"; "It's Great to Be Alive"; "The Grand Vazir's Lament"; "A Thousand and One Nights"; "Hail to the Sultan"; "I Only Live for Today";

"Royal Ritual"; "Bring on the Bride to Be"; "Hero of All My Dreams"; "A Whale of a Story"; "Serpent Dance"; "Ballet of Jewels"; "Marry the One You Love"; "Ladies' Maids in Waiting"; "How Long Has It Been?"; "Teeny Weeny Genie"; "Chinese Wedding"; "Royal Ballet"

ALADDIN, *Wimbledon Theatre*, London, opened December 23, 1967
A Pantomime written and directed by Bill Robertson; Music by Robert Probst
Judy Bowen (Aladdin); Barrie Gosney (Widow Twankey); Tommy Trinder (Abanazar); Laura Symonds (Princess Badroulbadour); Gerry King (Slave of the Ring); Patrick Duggan (Genie of the Lamp); Jimmy Lee (Grand Vizier); Jack Haig (Emperor of China); Bruce Forsyth (Wishee Washee); Eddie Graham (P. C. Wong); Jonny Shack (P. C. Wite)

Players' Theatre, London, opened December 17, 1969
A Pantomine by H. J. Byron, adapted by Dennis Martin; Lyrics by Maurice Browning; Director, Don Gemmell; Decor, Reginald Woolley; Costumes, Reginald Hansom
Julia Sutton (Aladdin Twankey-Jones); Deryk Parkin (Widow Twankey-Jones); Robin Hunter (Abanazar); Tony Bateman (Emperor of China); Rosalyn Dunbar (Princess Badroulbadour); Eleanor McCready (Prince Pekoe); Terence Bayler (Grand Vizier); Richard Dennis (Genie of the Ring); Margaret Ashton (Servant of the Lamp); Susan Jackson (Sokooki); Erich Vietheer (Good Evans); Elwyn Hughes (Dai Hard); Ron Lucas (Attendant); Mark Allington (Policeman)

Palladium Theatre, London, opened December 22, 1970
Produced by Louis Benjamin and Leslie Grade; A Pantomine; Book by Phil Park; Music composed, arranged, and orchestrated by Tony Hatch; Director, Albert J. Knight; Scenery, Tod Kingman Ltd.; Costumes designed by Cynthia Tingey, executed by Bermans; Choreography, Irving Davies; Musical adviser, Eric Tann; Technical adviser, Peter Penrose; Special material by Bryan Blackburn, George Martin and Ronnie Taylor; Music director, Robert Lowe; Flying effects, Kirby's Flying Ballet; Company manager, Sidney Maurice; Stage manager, Tommy Hayes
Cilla Black (Aladdin); Leslie Crowther (Wishee-Washee); Terry Scott (Widow Twankey); Stacey Gregg (Princess Badroulbadour); Tom Chatto (Emperor of China); Milton Reid (The Slave of the Lamp); Libby West (Scheherazade); Bertie Hare (Sultan); Bill Tasker (Town Crier); Sheila Melvin (The Genie of the Ring); Alfred Marks (Abanazar); Lauri Lupino Lane (Chief of Police); Sheila Bernette (So-Shy); Bertie Hare (Grand Vizier); Basil Brush (Himself); Johnny Hutch, Brian Lovering, Max Reigelsky, David Farrar, Rodney Myers, Peter Harrison (The Pekin Police Force); Irving Davies Dancers, Bel Canto Singers (Citizens of Pekin); Lily Corma (Sapphire); Sue Lake (Emerald); Zilpha Beckett (Ruby); Sheila Melvin (Diamond); Michaelle Aslanoff, Wendy Baldock, Alison Basham, Zilpha Beckett, Jilly Coram, Ann Justice Crompton, June Cunningham, Karen Gaeng, Shelagh Gilliard, Lynne Halliday, Debbie Hearnden, Jackie Hearnden, Janet Jones, Sue Lake, Lorrie Layton, Lee Porter, Susan Ritman, Nigel Bars, Gerry Binns, Nigel Grice, Richard Key, Peter Kuczmaida, Michael Lander, Peter Loury, Graham Pattenden, Spencer Shires, Ben Steel, Frank Woodman (Dancers); Russell Leachman (Ballet Master); Richard Ashley, Mark Bodell, Sorralyn Groston, Anabel Danadian, Ray Sauvola, Anne Scott, Pam Scott, Mike Smith, Roslynne Stanley, Nicholas Ward, Libby West, Davie York (Bel Canto Singers)

Old Vic Theatre, Bristol, England, opened December 27, 1976 to February 12, 1977
Produced by the Bristol Old Vic Trust Limited; A Pantomime by John Moffatt; Director, Richard Cottrell; Production Designer, John McMurray; Lighting, Robert A. Shakespeare; Sound, Alastair Goolden; Choreography, Bob Stevenson; Music Director, Neil Rhoden

Ann Hamilton (Aladdin); Henry Moxon (Emperor of China); Georgina Moon (Princess Badroulbadour); Michael Rothwell (Widow Twankey); Trevor Martin (Abanazar); Robert O'Mahoney (Wishee-Washee); Cornelius Garrett (Genie of the Lamp); Lynn Clayton (Genie of the Ring); Peter Birch (Pekoe); Ian Mackenzie (Ho-Kee); Jeffery Kissoon (Po-Kee); Clive Wouters (Grand Vizier); Joan Moon (Chee-Ke); Martin Baker (Spirit of the Cave); Peter Benedict, Adrian Crow-hurst, Paula Dene, Sarah Gaygen, Su Paxton (Citizens of Pekin, Jewels, etc.) Neil Rhoden (Piano); Eric Brown (Bass); Ken Morgan (Percussion)

MUSICAL NUMBERS: "Let's Peek in at Old Pekin"; "The Good Old Times"; "Oh, You Little Darling"; "If Your Face Wants to Laugh"; "The Blasted Oak"; "When the Sun Says Good Morning"; "Lord High Emperor"; "Homely"; "Ha Ha! Hee Hee!"; "I Like Scented Soap"; "Pretty Little Dark Blue Eyes"; "The Tin Gee-Gee"; "Wishee Washee"; "Give Me Thy Hand Oh Fairest"; "One Hour of Love With You"; "Absence Makes My Heart Grow Fonder"; "There's a Friend in Every Milestone"; "Stewdle-Ooodle-Oo"; Finale

Palladium Theatre, London, opened December 20, 1978
A Pantomime

Wayne Sleep (Aladdin); Dilys Watling (Princess Badroulbadour); Danny LaRue (Merry Widow Twanky); Brian Marshall McEvoy (Genie of the Lamp); Alfred Marks (Abanazar)

Lyric Theatre Hammersmith, London, opened December 21, 1979 to February 2, 1980
A Pantomime with book, music, and lyrics by Sandy Wilson; Director, David Giles; Decor, Clive Lavagna and Teresa Seisum; Lighting, Chris Ellis; Musical arrangement, Colin Sell; Choreographer, Geraldine Stephenson; Stage Manager, Barbara Penney

Richard Freeman (Aladdin); Christine McKenna (Princess Badroulbadour); Ernest Clark (Emperor of China); Martin McEvoy (Genie of the Lamp); Audrey Woods (Abanazar); Joe Melia (Tuang Kee Chung); Elisabeth Welch (Fatimah); Belinda Lang (Genie of the Ring); Judy Hopton, Pauline Lewis (Badroulbadour's Maids); Michael Sadler (Herald); Cass Allen (Property Lady); Tony Bancza, Robert Howie (Property Men); Edward Hibbert (Yum Pekoe); Arthur Kohn (Yum Cah'i)

Shaftesbury Theatre, London, opened December 18, 1983
A Pantomime by the Theatre of Comedy Company; Produced and devised by Paul Elliott; Director, Tudor Davies; Settings, Alan Miller Bunford; Lighting, James Baird

Jill Gascoigne (Aladdin); Lyndsey de Paul (Princess Badroulbadour); Derek Griffiths (Abanazar); Tudor Davies (Widow Twankey); Richard O'Sullivan (Wishee Washee); Edmund Hockridge (Emperor of China); Roy Kinnear (Grand Vizier); Doreen Wells (The Genie); Tommy Trinder (Constable); David Janson (Policeman)

Shaw Theatre, London, opened December 5, 1986
A Pantomime by Terry Duggan; Music by Ian Barnett; Director, Ben Benison

Debbie Bishop (Aladdin); Norman Beaton (Widow Twankey); Richard Rees (Wishee Washee); Anna Karen (Empress of China); Jim Dunk (Abanazar)

Empire State Main Theater, Albany, New York, opened May 16, 1987
Empire State Institute for the Performing Arts presentation; A Musical in two acts with book by Elisabeth Ruthman; Music by Dennis Buck; Lyrics by Ruthman and Buck; Director, Peter Webb; Set and costumes, Alexander Okun; Lighting, Victor En Yu Tan; Sound, Abe Jacob; Music director and conductor, Maida Libkin; Orchestrator, Larry Wilcox; Choreographer, Patrice Soriero; Stage manager, Robin Horowitz; Dramaturg, Marilyn Stasio

Ron Bohmer (Aladdin); Alan Weeks (Magician); Anny DeGrange (Princess Badroulbadour); Kim Darwin, Stacey Heinz (Handmaidens); Joel Aroeste (Sultan); Besty Normile (Zubadayah); Gary O. Aldrich (Grand Vizier); John Romero (Zoubir); and Dyann Arduini, Mark Baird, David Bunce, Peter Davis, Christopher Foster, Brent Griffin, John Hamelin, Jeffrey Helm, Christopher Howe, Olof Jansson, Joseph Larabee-Quandt, John Thomas McGuire III, Jacqueline Serebani, Carol Edie Smith, Jeanne Vigilante, Paul Villani, Lea Charisse Woods

SCREEN

ALADDIN AND THE WONDERFUL LAMP, *G.A.S. Films*, Great Britain, released November 1899
Directed by G. A. Smith

ALADDIN UP-TO-DATE, *Edison Films*, released September 1912
Produced by Thomas A. Edison; Story by Henry Kitchell, based on the Arabian Nights tale

Edward O'Connor (Tim); Jessie McAllister (Betsey); William Bechtel (Her Father); Alice Washburn (Her Mother)

ALADDIN IN PEARLIES, *British Anglo-American*, Great Britain, released October 1912
Director, Fred Rains

Fred Rains (Aladdin)

ALADDIN: OR, A LAD OUT, *Hepworth Films*, Great Britain, released November 1914
Director, Hay Plumb; Screenplay, Tom Powers

Tom Powers (The Lad); Alma Taylor (The Girl)

ALADDIN, *Piccadilly*, Great Britain, released November 1915
Directors, Fred Evans and Joe Evans

Fred Evans (Aladdin)

ALADDIN'S OTHER LAMP, *Metro Pictures*, released August 1917
Director, John Collins; Screenplay by June Mathis, adapted from Willard Mack's *The Dream Girl*

Viola Dana (Patricia Smith); Robert Walker (Harry Hardy); Augustus Phillips (Genie Jehawnarara); Henry Hallam (Captain Barnaby); Ricca Allen (Mrs. Duff); Edward Elkas (Luke Stemson); Louis B. Foley (Judge Lawrence); Nellie Grant (Mrs. Helen Smithfield)

ALADDIN AND THE WONDERFUL LAMP, Fox Films, released October 1917
Produced by William Fox; Directors, C. M. and S. A. Franklin; Screenplay by Bernard McConville, based on the Arabian Nights tale

Francis Carpenter (Aladdin); Violet Radcliffe (The Magician); Virginia Lee Corbin (Princess Badr-Al-Budur); Lewis Sargent (Camel Driver, Macist); Elmo Lincoln (The Genie); Gertrude Messenger (Yasmini); Joseph Singleton (The Muessin); Fred Turner (Mustapha/Tailor/Aladdin's Father); Buddy Messenger (The Magician's Evil Spirit or Legal Advisor); Alfred Paget (The Sultan); Raymond Lee, Lloyd Peri (Boys of the Street); Marie Messenger, Carmen DeRue (Dancing girls)

ONE ARABIAN NIGHT (aka *WIDOW TWAN-KEE*), Stoll Pictures, Great Britain, released December 1923
Direction and Screenplay by Sinclair Hill; A Pantomime of *Aladdin* from *The Arabian Nights*

Lionelle Howard (Aladdin); George Robey (Widow Twan-Kee); Julia Kean (Princess); Edward O'Neill (Abanazar); W. G. Saunders (The Emperor); H. Agar Lyons (Li-Pong); Basil Saunders (Slave of the Lamp); Julie Suedo (Fairy of the Ring); Aubrey Fitzgerald (Servant)

ARABIAN NIGHTS, Universal Pictures, released December 1942
Produced by Walter Wanger; Director, John Rawlins; Story and Screenplay by Michael Hogan; Additional dialogue, True Boardman; Photography, Milton Krasner; Production designers, Jack Orterson and Alexander Golitzen; Set decorators, R. A. Gausman and Ira S. Webb; Costumes, Vera West; Music, Frank Skinner, Music director, Charles Previn; Technical Advisor, Jamiel Hasson; Editor, Philip Cahn

Jon Hall (Haroun-Al-Raschid); Maria Montez (Scheherazade); Sabu (Ali Ben Ali); Leif Erickson (Kamar); John Qualen (Aladdin); Billy Gilbert (Ahmad); Edgar Barrier (Nadan); Turhan Bey (Captain); Shemp Howard (Sinbad); Thomas Gomez (Hakim); Richard Lane (Corporal); Elyse Knox (Duenna); William Davis (Valda); Charles Coleman (Eunuch); Harry Cording (Blacksmith); Acquanetta (Ishya); Carmen D'Antonio (Harem Queen); Emory Parnell (Harem Sentry); Robin Raymond (Slave Girl); Robert Greig (Eunuch Storyteller); Adia Kuznetzoff (Slaver); Jeni Le Gon (Dresser); Virginia Engels, Nedra Sanders, Mary Moore, Veronika Pataky, Jean Trent, Frances Gladwin, Rosemarie Dempsey, Patsy Mace, Pat Starling, June Ealey (Harem Girls); and Andre Charlot, Frank Lackteen, Anthony Blair, Robert Barron, Art Miles, Murdock MacQuarrie, Ernest Whitman, Ken Christy, Duke York, Mickey Simpson, Kermit Maynard, Eva Puig, Johnnie Berkes, Alaine Brandes, Cordell Hickman, Paul Clayton, Jamiel Hasson, Crane Whitley, Charles Alvarado, Phyllis Flores, Peggy Satterlee, Helen Pender, Eloise Hardt, Amador Guitierrez, Ben Ayassa Wadrassi, Daniel Barone, Edward Marmolejo, Dave Sharpe

A THOUSAND AND ONE NIGHTS, Columbia Pictures, released July 1945
Produced by Samuel Bischoff; Director, Alfred E. Green; Screenplay by Richard English, Jack Henley and Wilfrid H. Pettitt, based on a story by Pettitt; Photography, Ray Rennahan; Art directors, Stephen Goosson and Rudolph Sternad; Set decorator, Frank Tuttle; Music, Marlin Skiles; Music director, Morris Stoloff; Sound, Lambert Day; Editor, Gene Havlick

Cornel Wilde (Aladdin); Evelyn Keyes (The Genie); Phil Silvers (Abdullah); Adele

Jergens (Princess Armina); Dennis Hoey (Sultan Kamar AlKir/Prince Hadji); Rex Ingram (Giant); Dusty Anderson (Novira); Philip Van Zandt (Grand Vizier Abu-Hassan); Gus Schilling (Jafar); Nestor Paiva (Kahim); Richard Hale (Kafir the Sorcerer); Carole Mathews, Pat Parrish, Shelley Winters (Hand Maidens); Trevor Bardette (Hasson); Dick Botiller (Ramud); Cy Kendall (Auctioneer); Charles LaTorre (Innkeeper); Frank Lackteen (Camel Driver); Vivian Mason (Exotic Girl); Mari Jinishan (Dancer); Frank Scannell, Patric Desmond (Retainers)

THE DESERT HAWK, *Universal-International Pictures*, released August 1950
Produced by Leonard Goldstein; Director, Frederick de Cordova; Screenplay, Aubrey Wisberg, Jack Pollexfen and Gerald Drayson Adams; Photography, Russell Metty; Art directors, Bernard Herzbrun and Emrich Nicholson; Music, Frank Skinner; Editors, Otto Ludwig, Dan Nathan

Yvonne De Carlo (Princess Scheherazade); Richard Greene (Omar); Jackie Gleason (Aladdin); George Macready (Prince Murad); Carl Esmond (Kibar); Marc Lawrence (Samad); Rock Hudson (Captain Ras); Lucille Barkley (Undine); Richard Hale (Iman); Nestor Paiva (Abdul); Lois Andrews (Maznah); Ann Pearce (Yasmin); Joe Besser (Sinbad); Donald Randolph (Caliph); Buddy Roosevelt (Baku); Mahmud Shaikhaly (Akbar); Virginia Hunter (Slave Girl Dancer); Bob Anderson (Judah); Ben Welden (Mokar); Michael Ross (Gorah); Shirley Ballard (Naga); Lane Bradford (Standard Bearer); Frank Lackteen (One-Eyed Arab); Harold Cornsweet (Arab); Jack Raymond (Suif); Ian MacDonald (Yussef); Robert Filmer, Bob Wilke (Camel Drivers); Lester Sharpe, Jan Arvan, Milton Kibbee (Merchants); Dale Van Sickel (Kibar Leader); Eileen Howe, Hazel Shaw, Marian Dennish, Norma De Landa, Barbara Kelly, Vonne Lester (Harem Girls); and Michael Ansara, Fred Libby, Bruce Riley, Louis A. Nicoletti, Wally Walker, Mike Portanova, Wendy Waldron, Shirley Ballard, George Bruggeman, Terry Frost, Lucile Barnes, Chet Brandenberg, Vic Romito, Wilson Millar, Phil Barnes, Frank Malet

ALADDIN AND HIS LAMP, *Monogram Pictures*, released February 1952
Produced by Walter Wanger; Associate producer, Ben Schwalb; Director, Lew Landers; Screenplay, Howard Dimsdale, Millard Kaufman and Sam Roeca; Photography, Gilbert Warrenton; Music, Marlin Skiles; Editor, Jack Ogilvie

John Sands (Aladdin); Patricia Medina (Princess Jasmine); Richard Erdman (Mirza); John Dehner (Bokra); Billy House (Kafan); Charles Horvath (Genie); Noreen Nash (Passion Flower); Ned Young (Hassan); Rick Vallin (Captain of the Guard); Sujata (Dancing Slave Girl); Arabella (Maid-in-waiting)

THIEF OF DAMASCUS, *Columbia Pictures*, released May 1952
Produced by Sam Katzman; Director, Will Jason; Screenplay, Robert E. Kent; Photography, Ellis W. Carter; Art Director, Paul Palmentola; Musical director, Mischa Bakaleinikoff; Editor, William Lyon

Paul Henreid (Abu Andar); Jeff Donnell (Scheherazade); Robert Clary (Aladdin); Lon Chaney (Sinbad); John Sutton (Khalid); Elena Verdugo (Neela); Helen Gilbert (Princess Zafir); Philip Van Zandt (Ali Baba); Edward Colmans (Sultan Raudah)

SABU AND THE MAGIC RING, *Allied Artists*, released November 1957
Produced by Maurice Duke; Director, George Blair; Screenplay by Benedict

Freeman, John Fenton Murray and Sam Roeca, based on the *Arabian Nights Tale of the Magic Ring*; Photography, Harry Neumann; Art director, David Milton; Music, Margaret Skiles; Sound, Del Harris; Editor, William Austin

Sabu (Sabu); William Marshall (The Genie); Daria Massey (Zumeela); John Doucette (Kemal); Peter Mamakos (Muzafar); Vladimir Sokoloff (Fakir); Robert Shafto (Caliph); Bernard Rich (Ali); Robin Morse (Magician); George Khoury (Phransigar)

1001 ARABIAN NIGHTS, *Columbia Pictures*, released December 1959

A UPA Animated feature; Producer, Stephen Bosustow; Director, Jack Kinney; Screenplay, Czenzi Ormonde; Storyboard, Dick Shaw, Dick Kinney, Leo Salkin, Pete Burness, Lew Keller, Ed Nofziger, Ted Allan, Margaret Schneider and Paul Schneider; Production design, Robert Dranko; Music, George Duning; Conducted by Morris Stoloff; Orchestrations, Arthur Morton; Supervising editors, Joe Siracusa, Skip Craig and Earl Bennett

Voices: Jim Backus (Uncle Abdul Azziz Magoo); Kathryn Grant (Princess Yasminda); Dwayne Hickman (Aladdin, Magoo's nephew); Hans Conried (The Wicked Wazir); Herschel Bernardi (The Jinni of the Lamp); Daws Butler (Omar the Rug Maker); Alan Reed (The Sultan); The Clark Sisters (Three Little Maids from Damascus)

Original soundtrack recording: Colpix Records

LE MERAVIGLIE DI ALADINO (WONDERS OF ALADDIN), *Embassy Pictures*, released December 1961

Produced by Embassy-Lux Films; Director, Henry Levin; Screenplay by Luther Davis; Story, Stefano Strucchi, Duccio Tessari; Photography, Tonino Delli Colli; Art director, Flavio Mogherini; Music, Angelo Lavagnino; Assistant directors, Alfredo Cardone and Franco Prosperi; 2nd Unit director, Mario Bava; Choreography, Secondino Cavallo; Costumes, Girgio Desideri; Costumes designed by Rosine Delamare; Editor, Gene Ruggiero

Donald O'Connor (Aladdin); Vittorio De Sica (Genie); Noelle Adam (Djalma); Milton Reid (Omar); Aldo Fabrizi (Sultan); Michele Mercier (Zaina); Mario Girotti (Prince Moluk); Fausto Tozzi (Grand Vizier); Marco Tulli (Fakir); Raymond Bussieres (Magician); Alberto Farness (Bandit Chieftain); Franco Ressel (Vizier's Lieutenant); Vittorio Bonos (Lamp Merchant); Adriana Facchetti (Aladdin's Mother); Giovanna Galletti (Midwife); Luigi Tosi (Man)

VOLSHEBNAYA LAMPA ALADDINA (ALADDIN AND HIS MAGIC LAMP), *Gorky Film Studio*, released August 1968 (USSR in 1967)

Director, Boris Rytsarev; Screenplay by Viktor Vitkovich and Grigoriy Yagdfeld, based on *The Arabian Nights Entertainment*; Photography, V. Dultsev, L. Ragozin; Art directors, A. Anfilov and K. Zagorskiy; Music, Aleksey Muravlev; Sound, S. Gurin; Assistant director, V. Losev; Production manager, I. Morozov

Boris Bystrov (Aladdin); Sarry Karryyev (Genie); Dodo Chogovadze (Princess Boodoor); A. Fayt (Magrabinets); G. Sadykhov (Grand Vizier); Valentin Bryleyev (Mubarak); Ye Verulashvilli (Aladdin's Mother); Otar Koberidze (Sultan); Georgiy Millyar (Wiseman); E. Bilanishvili (Night Watchman); Yu Chekulayev (Mustafa); Boris Andreyev, Ya Belenkiy, I Verdin, E. Geller, N. Gorlov, I. Gordzhiy, V. Maslantsov, Z. Mustafin, P. Mukhin, Ye Pandul, S. Safonov, B. Svetlov, N. Sementsova, Yu Shmagala, M. Shcherbakov, N. Yegin

ALADIN ET LA LAMPE MERVEILLEUSE (ALADDIN AND HIS MAGIC LAMP), Target International, released 1969: An Animated Cartoon
Produced by Les Films Jean Image; Director, Jean Image; Screenplay, Jean and France Image; Photography, Peter Olaf Csongovali; Animation, Denis Boutin and Guy Lehideux; Music, Fred Freed; Songs, Christian Sarrel, Jean-Michel Rival and Frank Thomas

IL FIORE DELLE MILLE E UNA NOTTE (ARABIAN NIGHTS), A United Artists Release, released May 1974
A production of PEA (Rome) and Les Productions Artistes Associes (Paris); Produced by Alberto Grimaldi; Written and Directed by Pier Paolo Pasolini; Based on stories from the Islamic collection; Photography, Giuseppe Ruzzolini; Art director, Dante Ferretti; Costumes, Danilo Donati; Music, Ennio Morricone; Supervising editor, Enzo Ocone

Ninetto Davoli (Aziz); Ines Pellegrina (Zumurrud); Franco Citti (Demon); and Tessa Bouche, Margaret Clementi, Franco Merli, Francelisa Noel, Ali Abdulla, Christian Alegny, Jeanne Gauffin Mathieu, Francesco Paolo Governale, Salvatore Sapienza, Zeudi Biasolo, Barbara Grandi, Elisabetta Vito Genovese, Gioacchino Castellini, Abadit Ghidei, Salvatore Verdetti, Mohamed Ali Zedi, Jocelyne Muchenbach, Luigina Rocchi, Alberto Argentino, Luigi Antonio Guerra, Franca Sciutto, Mohamed Fara Scebani, Hassan Ali Hamed, Ghenet Aielew, Amanuel Mathews, Adila Ibrahim, Rino Hammade

SuperFantaGenio (ALADDIN), An Italian International Film Release, released January 1987
A Cannon Group Presentation; Producer, Ugo Tucci for Compania Generale R. T.; Director, Bruno Corbucci; Screenplay, Mario Amendola, Marcello Fondato; Photography, Silvano Ippoliti; Music, Fabio Frizzi; Editor, Daniele Alabasio

Bud Spencer (The Genie); Luca Venantini (Alan); Janet Agren (Alan's mother); Umberto Raho, Julian Voloshin, Daimy Spencer

LES 1,001 NUITS, A UGC (France) Release, released April 1990
A Cinemax/Telemax/Antenne 2/Films A2/RAI 2/Telepool/ Club Investissement Media coproduction; Executive producer, Maurice Bouz; Producer, Andre Djaoui; Director, Philippe de Broca; Screenplay, Philippe de Broca and Jerome Tonnerre; Photography, Jean Tournier; Art director, Francois de Lamothe; Costumes, Jacques Fonteray; Special effects director, Christian Guillon; Music, Gabriel Yared

Stephane Freiss (Aladdin); Gerard Jugnot (Jimmy Genius); Catherine Zeta-Jones (Scheherazade); Vittorio Gassman (Sinbad); Thierry Lhermitte (Caliph of Bagdad); Roger Carel (Grand Vizier)

ALADDIN, Buena Vista Release, released November 1992
A Walt Disney Pictures production; Produced and directed by John Musker and Ron Clements; Coproducers, Donald W. Ernst and Amy Pell; Screenplay, Ron Clements, John Musker, Ted Elliott and Terry Rossio; Production designer, R. S. Vander Wende; Supervising animators, Glen Keane, Eric Goldberg, Mark Henn, Andreas Deja, Duncan Majorbanks, Randy Cartwright, Will Finn and David Pruiksma; Music, Alan Menken; Songs, Alan Menken, Howard Ashman and Tim Rice; Editor, H. Lee Peterson

Voices: Scott Weinger (Brad Kane, singing) (Aladdin); Robin Williams (Genie); Linda Larkin (Lea Salonga, singing) (Jasmine); Jonathan Freeman (Jafar); Frank

Welker (Abu); Gilbert Gottfried (Iago); Douglas Seale (Sultan); Aaron Blaise (Rajah); and Kathy Zielinski, T. Daniel Hofstedt, Phil Young, Chris Wahl

MUSICAL NUMBERS: "Arabian Nights" (Menken-Ashman); "A Friend Like Me" (Menken-Rice); "A Whole New World" (Menken-Rice) "Prince Ali" (Menken-Ashman); "One Jump Ahead" (Menken-Rice); "Prince Ali Reprise" (Menken-Rice); "A Whole New World (Aladdin's Theme)"

Original soundtrack recording: Walt Disney Records

THE BRASS BOTTLE, *Theatre and General*, Great Britain, released January 1914
Produced by Nicholson Ormsby Scott; Written and directed by Sidney Morgan, based on the play and novel by F. Anstey.

Lawrence Grossmith (Horace Ventmire); Holman Clark (Fakrash-al-Amash); Mary Brough (Mrs. Futvoye); Alfred Bishop (Professor Futvoye); Tom Bowbray (Samuel Wackerbath); J. R. Tozer (King Solomon); Doris Lytton (Sylvia Futvoye); with Vane Feather-stone, Molly Farrell, Rudge Harding

THE BRASS BOTTLE, *Associated First National Pictures*, released January 1923
Presented by M. C. Levee; Produced by Maurice Tourneur Productions; Director, Maurice Tourneur; Screenplay by Fred Kennedy Myton, based on the play by F. Anstey; Photography, Arthur Todd; Art director, Milton Menasco; Production manager, Scott R. Beal; Editor, Frank Lawrence

Harry Myers (Horace Ventimore); Ernest Torrence (Fakresh-el-Aamash); Tully Marshall (Professor Hamilton); Clarissa Selwyn (Mrs. Hamilton); Ford Sterling (Rapkin); Aggie Herring (Mrs. Rapkin); Charlotte Merriam (Sylvia Hamilton); Barbara La Marr (The Queen); Otis Harlan (Captain of the Guard); Edward Jobson (Samuel Wackerbath); Hazel Keener, Julianne Johnston (Ladies)

THE BRASS BOTTLE, *Universal Pictures*, released February 1964
Produced by Robert Arthur; Director, Harry Keller; Screenplay by Oscar Brodney, based on the play by F. Anstey; Photography, Clifford Stine; Art directors, Alexander Golitzen and Henry Bumstead; Set decorator, Oliver Emert; Costumes, Rosemary Odell; Makeup, Bud Westmore; Hair styles, Larry Germain; Music, Bernard Green; Music supervision, Joseph Gershenson; Choreography, Hal Belfer; Special photographic effects, Roswell Hoffman; Sound, Waldon O. Watson, Frank Wilkinson; Editor, Ted J. Kent

Tony Randall (Harold Ventimore); Burl Ives (Fakrash-el-Aamash); Barbara Eden (Sylvia Kenton); Edward Andrews (Anthony Kenton); Ann Doran (Martha Kenton); Kamala Devi (Terza); Philip Ober (William Beevor); Parley Baer (Sam Wackerbath); Richard Erdman (Seymour Jenks); Kathie Browne (Hazel Jenks); Lulu Porter (Dancer)

TELEVISION

ALADDIN, *DuPont Show of the Month*, televised February 21, 1958 CBS 90 minutes
Produced by Richard Lewine; Director, Ralph Nelson; Book by S. J. Perelman, based on *Aladdin and His Wonderful Lamp*; Music and Lyrics by Cole Porter; Settings, Bob Markell; Choreography, Rod Alexander; Music director, Robert Emmett Dolan; Costumes, Irene Sharaff

Sal Mineo (Aladdin); Basil Rathbone (The Emperor); Cyril Ritchard (The Magician); Anna Maria Alberghetti (Princess Ming); Geoffrey Holder (The Genie); Dennis King (The Astrologer); Una Merkel (Aladdin's Mother); Howard Morris (Wu Fang, the Pickpocket); Alexander Clarke (Prime Minister); George Hall (Chamberlain); John McCurry

MUSICAL NUMBERS: "Aladdin"; "I Adore You"; "Trust Your Destiny to Your Stars"; "Make Way for the Emperor"; "No Wonder Taxes Are High"; "Opportunity Knocks But Once"; "Wouldn't It Be Fun?"; "Genie's Theme"; "Come to the Supermarket in Old Peking"

Original soundtrack recording: Columbia Records

THE LAND OF GREEN GINGER, Shirley Temple Storybook, televised April 18, 1958 CBS 1 Hour

Executive Producer, William H. Brown, Jr.; Producer and director, William Asher; Associate producer, Alvin Cooperman; Teleplay by Noel Langley; Story editor, Norman Lessing; Costumes, Don Loper; Songs by Jerry Livingston and Mack David; Hostess, Shirley Temple

Antony Eustrel (Aladdin); Joey Faye (Rubdub Ben Thud); Kuldip Singh (Abu Ali); Sue England (Silverbud); Jack Albertson (Tintac Ping Foo)

ALADDIN, CBS Special, televised December 6, 1967 CBS 1 Hour

A New York Prince Street Players Ltd. Production; Produced by Ethel Burns; Director, Nick Havinga; Teleplay, Jim Eiler; Songs by Jim Eiler and Jeanne Bargy

Fred Grades (Aladdin); Will B. Able (Genie); Vicki Morales (Princess Meiling); Robert Dagny (Magician); David Lile (Abanazar); Avril Gentles (Mother); Don Liberto (Stage Manager)

ALADDIN AND HIS WONDERFUL LAMP, Shelley Duvall's Faerie Tale Theatre, televised July 14, 1986 Showtime 48 minutes

A Platypus Production in association with Gaylord Television Entertainment; Executive producer, Shelley Duvall; Producers, Bridget Terry and Fredric S. Fuchs; Director, Tim Burton; Written by Mark Curtiss and Ron Ash; Production designer, Michael Erler; Art director, Jane Osmann; Costume designer, J. Allen Highfill

Robert Carradine (Aladdin); Valerie Bertinelli (Princess); James Earl Jones (Genie); Ray Sharkey (The Grand Vizier); Leonard Nimoy (Magician); Rae Allen (Gidrah); Joseph Maher (Sultan)

ALI BABA AND THE FORTY THIEVES

Various adaptations of *The History of Ali Baba and the Forty Thieves* from *The Arabian Nights Entertainments*

Synopsis

Persian woodcutter Ali Baba, hiding in a tree, watches a group of strange horsemen approach a huge rock. As bandit leader Abdullah bellows "Open, Sesame!" the rock magically opens exposing an enormous cave. When the horsemen depart, Ali Baba commands the rock once again to open and inside the cave finds a cache of untold riches. Filling his pockets with gold, Ali tells his avaricious brother Cassim of his amazing discovery. Cassim goes to the cave but forgets the password and is killed by the bandits, who then succeed in locating Ali Baba and plan to silence him too. Morgiana, Ali's beautiful slave, discovers the bandits hiding in large oil jars and slays them and their leader, Abdullah. Ali frees Morgiana and permits his own son to marry the former slave, while, keeping the secret of the cave to himself, becoming a rich and very happy man.

Comment and Critique

The History of Ali Baba and the Forty Thieves was one of several stories told, according to legend, by Scheherazade to her husband Shahriar every night to forestall his threat to kill her in the morning, and is included in *The Arabian Nights Entertainments*, or *The Book of the Thousand and One Nights*.

London's statuesque thirty-three-year-old Lydia Thompson and her equally amply proportioned troupe of blondes, clad in tights to display their legs, created a sensation in New York just after the Civil War and began what became known as "Burlesque." The Thompson Troupe made its debut in America on September 28, 1868, in *Ixion; or, The Man at the Wheel* at Wood's Museum. On January 30, 1869, Lydia Thompson Burlesque Troupe's production of *The Forty Thieves* opened at Niblo's Garden for a record engagement of 136 performances.

The New York Times acknowledged the craze for the Thompson Troupe. "The distinguishing symptom of the epidemic is a singular and easily detected appearance of masses of light and golden hair on the stage of the afflicted theatre; after this symptom the spectator is appalled by observing a tendency in the patients to dispossess themselves of their clothing, and it requires the greatest exertion to keep anything on them; then follows a series of piercing screams called comic singing, distorted and incoherent raving called puns, and finally, strong convulsions denominated breakdowns and walk-arounds. Exhaustion supervenes after a fit of two or three hours each night....The music embraces of course all the new airs, all the old ones, and, all the variations which both will bear. Of the *dramatis personae* it is to be said that Miss Lydia Thompson, as Ganem, offers herself from first to last in a succession of every known and unknown dance...and that she gives several new readings of old nursery rhymes, and sings with a nightly increasing consciousness that she has a larger theatre to fill with her voice."

In 1892, David Henderson's successful *Ali Baba; or, Morgiana and the Forty Thieves* was produced at Chicago's Opera House. On April 29, 1899, a revised production of his Chicago hit opened on Broadway at the Herald Square Theatre as *An Arabian Girl and Forty Thieves*, featuring Dorothy Morton in the trouser role of Ali Baba, and a promising new comedian Edwin "Eddie" Foy as Cassim D'Artagnan.

"*An Arabian Girl* is another contribution to the supposed demand for spectacle," recorded *The New York Times*, "Cheever Goodwin, in his least lucid mood, wrote the 'book' which treats the story of *The Forty Thieves* in a characteristically flippant and incoherent way. The obsolete pun is revived in its text with shocking results. So, also, are the collapsing chair and the 'slippery-day' staircase of ancient pantomime...The scenery is all very pretty, especially the picture of the moonlit glen near the robber's cave...The calisthenics of the choristers and ballet girls in the public square of Baghdad, and the march of the forty thieves are graceful. In one scene a Fafner-like dragon with flaming nostrils is suddenly transformed into a whole ballet troupe...Edwin Foy [has] a few droll 'wheezes' [but] most of his 'business,' including his encounters with Ali Baba's donkey, are reminiscent of the era of Grimaldi."

Ali Baba and the Forty Thieves became a popular attraction in England prior to the turn of the century. British actor Oscar Asche wrote, produced and starred in his version of the Arabian Nights tale, which as *Chu Chin Chow* became one of the London stage's greatest hits. Asche has played 222 performances in the leading role of Hajj in Edward Knoblock's *Kismet; or, An Arabian Night* in England and Australia from 1911 to 1914, prior to his monumentally successful production of *Chu Chin Chow.* Asche's spectacular *Chu Chin Chow*, with music by Frederick Norton, opened at London's His Majesty's Theatre on August 31, 1916, to establish a longstanding world record of 2,238 performances.

Asche later wrote about *Chu Chin Chow* as a foreword to the production:

> "For the story of this entertainment I have gone to 'The Arabian Nights,' and have taken as my subject 'The Forty Thieves,' the best beloved, I imagine, of all the tales with which Shahrazad soothed her lord. Providing as it does such opportunities for musical illustration, for decorative dances, for pictorial artistry, for the making of atmosphere -- the theme is irresistible! Mainly, I have used Burton's intimate translation, carefully collating the several variants of the story to be found in other literatures. I would point out that 'The Forty Thieves,' as it is commonly known here, has acquired strange and uncongenial characters and incidents. These I have removed; while the exigencies of a play so spacious as to fill the stages so large as those of His Majesty's Theatre in London and the Manhattan Opera House in New York have needed the introduction of other scenes and personalities. Indeed, I have used the license of the dramatist, with a carefully maintained consciousness of the spirit of the 'Night.' And I hope these magic doors may open on a lifelike and stimulating vision of the romance, the splendour, the inscrutable mystery of the East."

London's *Bystander* wrote, "Mr. Oscar Asche has a bright idea when he decided to take the story of *Ali Baba and the Forty Thieves* and see if it could be treated to some other spirit than that of the Christmas pantomime. Whether his actual treatment of it justified the experiment is another matter. I have nothing to say against the result as a spectacle. From that point of view it is undoubtedly a dazzling affair. Messrs. [Joseph and Phil] Harker and Mr. Percy Anderson were obviously left to do what they pleased, and they have just spread themselves as they have never done before...I also propose to leave to others to discuss the exact relation of the whole gorgeous affair to the question at present agitated in the Press as to the degree of decolletage permissible on the stage....But Mr. Asche's achievements as a playwright are not so satisfying as complete...This bald and not very interesting narrative is eked out with a great quantity of 'thee and thou'ing' -- and all that strange language which is supposed to be spoken in the regions of romance...Mr. Asche and Miss Lily Brayton take it all tremendously in earnest."

The huge London success of *Chu Chin Chow* was unfortunately not repeated on Broadway although the extravaganza did have a respectable run of 208 performances. *Chu Chin Chow*, produced by William Elliott, F. Ray Comstock and Morris Gest, opened on October 22, 1917, at the Manhattan Opera House featuring Tyrone Power, Sr., as Abu Hassan.

"The Manhattan Opera House came into its own last night as the home of gorgeous popular melodrama and spectacle. Saving the reverence of Oscar Hammerstein, *Chu Chin Chow* is also opera," reported *The New York Times*. "Like *Kismet*, *Chu Chin Chow* comes to us after almost two years in London. But there is a difference. Knoblock's play...was a very deft, even imaginative rendering of the spirit of *The Arabian Nights*. It had veracious local color, the true atmosphere of the fabled Orient, and a full measure of Oriental luxury and passion. The present play lacks these finer attributes, but by the same token is sets a newmark as spottable and as entertainment for the million...It cannot be said that, as a whole, the production has novelty or any rare distinction, but it has all the qualities to which the great public instinctively responds...There is no doubt that the great London success will be repeated here -- perhaps surpassed."

The New York Dramatic Mirror felt the producers of *Chu Chin Chow* had "accomplished a theatrical miracle ...Not since the days of *Kismet* has the atmosphere of the East been presented with such sensuality of color, such vitality of characterization, such riotousness of the joy of living. At first, you are dazed by the exquisiteness of the scenes; then you eventually grow accustomed, until you finally become a participant in the exotic pleasures of the offering. Thereby is illusion carried to its greatest height...While not possessing the melodramatic intensity of *Kismet*, *Chu Chin Chow* has more the character of a pageant -- a pageant which now suggests grand opera, now a rich fantasy, now a musical comedy after the manner of *The Mikado*...Tyrone Power gave a sense of sinister authority to the title role...Henry Dixey characterized well the part of Ali Baba, playing it with delightful grace and irresponsibility. Florence Reed was convincing in the role of the chief slave while the part of the singing slave was given the excellent voice of Tessa Kosta."

The story of *Chu Chin Chow* tells of Abu Hassan kidnapping beautiful Zahrat and her bridegroom Omar on their wedding day, and selling Zahrat to Baghdad's usurer, Kasim Baba. Assuming a disguise as a Chinese Prince, Chu Chin Chow, Abu repents and buys back Zahrat, promising her great wealth. United with Omar, Zahrat is taken by Abu to his secret treasure cave, which he discovers has been raided by Ali Baba, whose avaricious brother, Kasim, is then killed by Omar. Ali Baba, with his stolen wealth, gives a great feast in Baghdad, and there, seeking revenge on him, Abu Hassan, disguised as a merchant, delivers forty huge jugs containing his forty thieves instead of oil. Zahrat, freed by Ali Baba, unmasks Abu and the forty thieves are captured. As the populace revolts against Abu, Zahrat stabs him to death and happily returns to Omar.

When Oscar Asche died in London on March 23, 1936, his obituary read, "He was not by any stretch of the imagination a great playwright. Perhaps he was not even a great actor or producer. But thousands who saw his *Chu Chin Chow* and *Kismet* will remember them longer than many a better play. *Chu Chin Chow*, which opened in 1916, became woven into the picture of wartime England. British soldiers on leave made a point of 'taking in' *Chu Chin Chow* [which] closed in July 1921, just short of a five-year run in London. That was a world record at the time and has only been since surpassed by another mediocre production, *Abie's Irish Rose*. Despite its obvious defects, *Chu Chin Chow* had a very definite appeal, not only to the men coming from the mud and squalor of the trenches, but to all who lived through the nervous tension and privations of the war years. The Oriental magnificence of the spectacle was the contrast which the theatergoing world needed at the time, just as the homely sentimentality of *Abie's Irish Rose* was an antidote to the grandiose dreams of wealth and the harsh materialism of the 1920s. Oscar Asche, like Anne Nichols, the author of *Abie's Irish Rose*, had the distinction of giving the public exactly what it wanted -- a job not as easy as it may sound."

A 1940 revival of *Chu Chin Chow* in London, during another war, did not repeat the success of the original World War I production.

In 1936, a comedy by Kennedy Kane called *Bedtime for Ali Baba*, starring elfish Jimmy Savo, opened and closed in Wilmington, Delaware. A Wilmington critic reported, "Beautifully set and costumed and introduced, scene by scene, by musical excerpts on motifs from practically all well-known composers...the short play plimped along...its actors, in colorful costumes, giving their best in their effort to put across something that continued to miss fire...Despite the many laughs, some excellent lines, and the delightfully humorous characterizations, the plays seems thin....But it needs speed, action, lines and more Jimmy Savo."

In England, *Ali Baba and the Forty (Or Thirty-Nine) Thieves* became a favorite Christmas pantomime along with *Cinderella*, *Sleeping Beauty*, *Jack and the Beanstalk*, and other fantasies.

William Fox produced a series of films featuring child actors in adult roles based primarily on fairy tales. On November 24, 1918, Fox released *Ali Baba and the Forty Thieves* with youngster George Stone as Ali Baba and the Messinger Children in other key parts. *The Moving Picture World* described the Fox film as a "dashing melodrama acted by clever children...William Fox has brought the 'Open Sesame' of fiction to swing wide the faculties of photoplay enjoyments; to gladden the observer of this pretty fantasy with every detail of its production and artistic presentation...Only a few of the roles are played by grownups; the children carry off the honors. Because of the juvenile cast, get no idea that this is a play especially for children. It's a treat for both the little ones and their elders; a bit of screen blending of tragedy, seriocomic and dramatic revelations that will make a session before the screen a period of pure delight."

Herbert Wilcox directed a British-produced screen version of *Chu Chin Chow* in 1925, filmed in Berlin, Germany and released in America by Metro-Goldwyn. Wilcox's *Chu Chin Chow* previewed in Washington, D.C. and it was reviewed by C. S. Sewell for *The Motion Picture Herald*. "The story is one of the most colorful and romantic of the *Arabian Nights* tales and the screen version is adapted from the play of the same title which enjoyed a long run as a huge spectacle in the larger cities of this country and England...The only familiar name in the cast if Betty Blythe... Jameson Thomas as the heroine's lover makes a good impression but is given little to do...Herbert Langley has the majority of the action of the picture...*Chu Chin Chow*, despite its colorful theme and the scope of the production, is not outstanding from any angle and we do not feel it will exert appeal on the average audience."

The New York Times deplored the 1925 screen version of *Chu Chin Chow*, feeling "one misses the glorious coloring and the voices of Morris Gest's stage production" and described the Wilcox's production as "a carefully made picture, with imposing settings and pleasing costumes, which often drags in the unfolding of the tale." *Motion Picture* magazine shrugged of *Chu Chin Chow* as "a romance of love and intrigue and offers an 'eye-full' -- tho' very little else."

In 1934, Gainsborough Pictures/Gaumont-British re-filmed *Chu Chin Chow* headlining German actor Fritz Kortner as Abu Hassan, George Robey as Ali Baba and Anna May Wong as Zahrat. The *Motion Picture Herald* praised the production: "All the splendid music is there, plus the opportunity for the wider scope in settings and atmosphere...Retaining all the whimsical flavor of the original, all of the Oriental fantasy... The production is highly entertaining, melodious and amusing."

Chu Chin Chow opened at New York's Roxy Theatre on September 21, 1934, and was provocatively advertised as "Slaves for the Harems of Oriental Potentates! *Spectacle* to spellbind you! *Drama* to thrill you! *Mystery* to intrigue you! *Glamor* to entrance you! *Beauty* to dazzle you! *Oriental* opulence to amaze you! SEE Baghdad's Mammoth Temple of Love! Thousands of Slaves and their Masters in Oriental Revels!" *The New York Times* viewed the $500,000 production as "a tuneful, spectacular and robust adaptation of the Oscar Asche comic operetta -- it is a definite challenge to Hollywood...The photography is not as expert as would be encountered in a Hollywood work of similar scope. The sound is faulty in spots, with whole lines of dialogue lost either through technical flaws or, possibly, a New Yorker's difficulty in understanding British intonation...But there is no fault with the cast, with the music (the original score by Frederic Norton is kept intact), or with the singers. Fritz Kortner, one of Germany's best stage and screen stars, is a brilliant Abu Hassan... George Robey a lovable and laughable Ali Baba, Anna May Wong as the Slave...One can not escape wondering how the same theme might have been treated by DeMille, von Sternberg or even Busby Berkeley...the film is pretty much what it was meant to be -- a comic operetta."

In 1954, America's Lippert Films rereleased Gainsborough's 1934 *Chu Chin Chow* under the title of *Ali Baba Nights*.

In 1937, Eddie Cantor starred in Twentieth Century-Fox's imaginative *Ali Baba Goes to Town*. During the filming, a special effects "magic-carpet" fell killing two workmen, but tragedy aside, the New Deal satire pleased most of the public and the critics. H. N. Swanson (*Redbook* magazine) enthused about *Ali Baba Goes to Town* as having "an abundance of production dazzle; acres of impressive sets, good tunes by [Mack] Gordon and [Harry] Ravel, and gals to your heart's content... Like his *Roman Scandals* of some seasons back, this picture uses a dream sequence to take him, as a modern vagabond, back into the days of old. This enables him to compare current problems with those of that time, and serves as a slick frame for the satire."

Burlesque queen Gypsy Rose Lee was cast as the Sultana in *Ali Baba Goes to Town* but Hollywood's censoring coven known as the Hays Office required her to use her real name, Louise Hovick. *Time* magazine reported, "*Ali Baba Goes to Town*...transports taw-eyed, prancing, little Eddie Cantor to ancient Baghdad, where he physics the ailing realm of Sultan Roland Young with panaceas borrowed from the New Deal. Harounel-Cantor's venture into political satire is tuneful, gay, imaginatively written, generously produced...Cantor is a star-struck autograph hunter on his way to Hollywood and stumbles on the desert location of a cinema company making an episode from the Arabian Nights, becomes an extra and falls asleep in the jar reserved for Ali Baba."

Universal Studios, with its passion for Arabian Nights tales, in 1944 released an opulent *Ali Baba and the 40 Thieves*, reuniting the stars of its 1942 hit, *Arabian Nights*, Jon Hall, Maria Montez and Turhan Bey. The *Motion Picture Herald* labeled the picture, "Technicolored escapism -- the screen is filled with colorful settings in which brilliantly costumed actors disport themselves, struggle, suffer, escape, venture and dare, uttering lines of dialogue which, often as not, overtax both credulity and the skill of the performers. It is in this department that Edmund L. Hartman, who dredged up the plausible and actionful story from the depths of *A Thousand and One Nights*, lets down his players and his customers, occasionally to the embarrassment of all concerned."

France's famous comedian, Fernandel, not long afterward starred in *Ali-Baba et Les 40 Voleurs*, filmed in Morocco. The consensus was the French Moroccan Ali Baba was aimless and disappointing despite the estimable Fernandel and effective color photography. Universal released its *Son of Ali Baba* with Tony Curtis and Piper Laurie in 1952. Of it, *The New York Times*' Howard Thompson wrote: "Talk outweighs the routine skirmishes will hollow-sounding frequency. Straining heroically to project the turbulent protagonists, Mr. Curtis and Miss Laurie [united the year before in *The Prince Who Was a Thief*] suggest instead two nice, uncomplicated American youngsters." A dozen years later, its *The Sword of Ali Baba*, Universal's remake of its *Ali Baba and the 40 Thieves*, appeared. The critic for Britian's *Monthly Film Bulletin* appraised *The Sword of Ali Baba*: "This brand of Oriental hokum is nothing new to Universal Pictures, who produced some corking examples a decade or so ago...the total effect is marred by the inadequacy of the two principal players. Peter Mann's Ali Baba is a colourless figure, and Jocelyn Lane is a staid heroine who will not erase memories of Maria Montez or Yvonne De Carlo."

Ali Baba and the 40 Thieves was produced on television for the *Shirley Temple Storybook* series on November 12, 1958. Richard F. Shepard (*The New York Times*) wrote, "The Arabian Nights story was soundly produced, cast and performed. Nehemiah Persoff carried off the characterization of Ali in his usual excellent style...Although the story was faithful in most essentials, it differed somewhat in detail and spirit from what young readers may find in books."

STAGE

LAST OF THE THOUSAND AND ONE NIGHTS, *Bowery Theatre*, New York, opened June 15, 1846
Produced by A. W. Jackson; A Drama by T. W. Pittman, based on *The Arabian Nights*; Stage manager, James Anderson

Mrs. Phillips (Scheherazade); Frank S. Chanfrau (Kerim); F. L. Davenport (Sultan Schariah); Corson W. Clarke (Malouk); Thomas Hadaway (Badroulbadour); Mrs. Sergeant (Dinazarde); Mr. Sutherland (Ismael); Mr. Milner (Grand Vizier); Mr. Brookes (Mandrille). Mr. Stone (Agib); Mr. Yeoman (Great Baboon); Mrs. Deering (Mrs. Mandrille)

THE FEMALE FORTY THIEVES; OR, THE FAIRY DAUGHTERS OF COCHITUATE WATERS, *Beach Street Museum*, Boston, opened February 21, 1849
Produced and directed by Joseph Proctor; A Burlesque of the tale of Ali Baba

David Whiting (Ali Baba); Mrs. Charles Mestayer (Pondiana/Hassarac); Mrs. W. M. Ward (Fairy Cobweb); John Salmon (Gammon Baba); David Anderson (Chasm); Dan Nourse (Herr Dreesback); La Petite Julie (Glint); Arvilla Phillipe (Spee); Mrs. Reid (Muyphester); W. M. Ward (Horrorbrand); Mr. Mead (John Donkey); G. Warren White (Munchiasa); Miss Provost (Cogie); Miss Ward (First Lieutenant of the Thieves); Mrs. Dan Nourse, Miss Stickney, Miss Williams, Miss Burgess (Officers); Gentlemen in Black (War, Famine, Rapine, Fraud)

THE FORTY THIEVES, *Ford's Theatre*, Washington, D. C. opened June 24, 1864
Produced by John T. Ford; A Musical Extravaganza based on the story of Ali Baba; Stage manager, H. B. Phillips; Scenery, C. S. Getz, J. Lamb

Charles B. Bishop (Ali Baba); Susan Denin (Morgiana); Robert Struthers (Cassim Baba); J. Clinton Hall (Abdallah); George Becks (Gasem); Mr. Murray (Ali Em); James A. Horne (Lieutenant of the Banditti); Mr. Ferguson (Laibout); Mr. O'Brien (Bodee); Mr. Carland (Asip); Frank Murdoch (Satina); J. V. Dailey (Oreerbras); Mrs. Helen Muzzy (Zaida); Mrs. Bishop (Cogie Baba); Owen Fawcett (Mustapha); Mr. Anderson (War); Mr. Morgan (Famine); Mr. Morton (Fraud); Henrietta Osborne (Zeelie); Miss Minnie Monk (Fairy of the Lake); Ada Monk (Gosamer); Miss Dunn (Sylph); Miss Magee (Alladine); Miss Preston (Dinna); Mr. Matthews (Mapise)

MUSICAL NUMBERS: "Fairy of the Gleamy Lake"; "To a Woodsman's Hut"; "Ah! What Is This Bosoom's Commotion?"; "Ah! What Can I Turned for Relief?"; "Pronounce the Charm"; "Last Night I Sat Me Down and Cried"; "Bid the Lively Cymbals Jingle"; "Ah! Cruel Maid"; "Last Week I Look a Wife"; "Happy the Day"

FORTY THIEVES, *New Bowery Theatre*, New York, opened April 23, 1886
Produced By J. W. Lingard; A Comedy by John F. Poole

J. W. Lingard (All-Eye Bah Bah); George Lingard (Gammon Bah Bah); Imogene Tracy (Mortgaged Anna); George Brooks (Has-A-Nack)

THE FORTY THIEVES, *Niblo's Garden*, New York, January 30, 1869 136 performances
The Lydia Thompson Burlesque Troupe's burlesque of *Ali Baba and the Forty Thieves*

W. J. Hill (Ali Baba); Lydia Thompson (Ganem); Lisa Weber (Morgiana); Pauline Markham (succeeded by Edith Challis) (Abdallah); Emma Grattan (Orchobrand); Harry Beckett (Hassarac); George F. Ketchum (Cassim Baba); J. W. Brutone (Cogia); Lizzie Kelsey (succeeded by Clara Thompson) (Amber); Belle Land (The Fairy Queen); Annie Byron, Fraulein Schroetter, Lascelles Sisters, The Clodoche Troupe, La Comete, Normandie (Specialties)

THE FEMALE FORTY THIEVES, *Walnut Street Theatre*, Philadelphia, opened April 21, 1869
Produced by Henry J. Byron; A Burlesque and Grand Oriental Extravaganza featuring the Great London Burlesque Combination (Curtain raiser: *Miriam's Crime*)

W. H. Bailey (Ali Baba); Jenny Willmore (Ganem); Lizzie Willmore (Abdallah); Felix Rogers (Hassarac); W. L. Street (Cassim Baba); Mark Brook (Mirza-"Penny Plain"); D. E. Reilly (Hassan-"Twopence Coloured"); Mrs. S. K. Chester (Orchobrand); Mrs. J. P. Breisford (Cogia Baba); Mrs. W. A. Chapman (Zaide); Mrs. Charles Walcot (Morgiana); 40 Fine Females (The Thieves)

ALI BABA, *Gaiety Theatre*, London, opened September 23, 1872
Produced by John Hollingshead; A Burlesque by R. Reece

Mr. Toole (Ali Baba); Miss E. Farren (Ganem); J. G. Taylor (Cassim Baba); Miss Tremaine (Hassarac); Constance Loseby (Morgiana); H. Collier (Dancer)

ALI BABA AND THE FORTY THIEVES, *Park Theatre*, London, opened December 26, 1873
Produced by John and Richard Douglas; Music director, John Barnard

W. Simpson (Ali Baba); Angie Pelham (Abdallah); Kate Neville (Morgiana); Miss M. Rose (Dancer)

THE FORTY THIEVES, *Gaiety Theatre*, London, opened March 14, 1881
Produced by John Hollingshead; A Burlesque-Drama by R. Reece; Directors, R. Soutar and R. Reece; Music by Herr W. M. Lutz; Scenery, Mr. Banks; Costumes, Miss Thompson; Dances arranged by John D'Auban; Melodies selected by permission of Messrs. Francis and Day, Hopwood and Crew, Howard & Company, Herbert Campbell, Arthur Roberts, A. Sprake, T. W. Barrett, G. Macdermott and Miss E. Victor

Edward Terry (Ali Baba); T. Squire (Cassim Baba); Connie Gilchrist (Abdallah); Miss E. Farren (Ganem); E. W. Royce (Hassarac); Miss Hobson (Mesour); Agnes Hewitt (Hassan); Phyllis Broughton (Ben Zoualle); Miss Gilbert (Bedreddin); J. J. Dallas (Cogia); Kate Vaughan (Morgiana)

Dance: Miss Gilbert and Miss R. Moncrieff (Polka Coquette); Connie Gilchrist (Galop Electric); Phyllis Broughton (Schottische Eccentric); The Two Macs (Eccentric Interlude)

Preceded by *Lischen & Fritzchen* (one-act operetta by Offenbach) and *The Little Mother* (two-act play by John Maddison Morton)

THE FORTY THIEVES, *Drury Lane Theatre*, London, opened December 26, 1886
Produced and directed by Augustus Harris; A Pantomime by E. L. Blanchard; Music by Ferdinand Wallerstein; Scenery by William R. Beverly, Grive and Hart, Henry Emden, T. E. Ryan, William Perkins and William Telbin; Costumes, by Wilhelm, executed by August & Cie, Nelly Fisher, Palmer, Hughman, Felix & Rouy and Alias/Armour and Jewelry, Gutperle of Paris, Kennedy & Phillips; Banners by Kenning; Wigs by Clarkson; Mechanical effects, James Skinner; Dances, John A'Dauban; Ballets by the Children of the National School of Dancing, by Madame Katti Lanner

Harry Nicholls (Ali Baba); Robert Pateman (Cassim); Constance Gilchrist (Morgiana); Herbert Campbell (Cogia Baba); Reuben Inch (Mustapha); John D'Auban (Chief of Police) Charles Luri, Jr. (The Donkey); Paul Martinetti (The Monkey); Victor Stevens (Ally Sloper); Edith Bruce (Ganem); M. A. Victor (Mrs. Cassim); Edith Blande-Brereton (Abdallah); Minnie Maro (Sinbad); Emma D'Auban (Codadad); Minnie Inch (Noureddin Ali); Violet Russell (Young King); Marie Williams (Aladdin); Lizzie Byron, Emeline Simmons, Gertrude Goetze, Bridie Jennings, Gertrude Hilyar, Emily Williams, Marie Stewart, Adelaide Mills, Dora Mannering, Kate Driscoll, Lilly Bradshaw, Minnie Werendel, May Hannam, Mabel Ansell, Ada McKee, Ruth Fraser, Millie Brooking, Maud Lassam, Flo Somerton, Jessie Ross, Adelaide Mathews, Louisa Allen, Beckie Fraser, Lilian Shelbourne, Emily Campbell, Cissy St. George, Maud Constantia, Ethel Stratmore, Mabel St. Claire, Harriet Nicholls, Annie Williams, Florence Heddington, Alice Hargreaves (Thieves); AEnea, the Flying Dancer (Civilisation)

THE FORTY THIEVES, *Surrey Theatre*, London, opened December 24, 1888
Produced by George Conquest; A Pantomime

George Conquest; Henry Spry; Albert and Edmunds Troupe; Constance Moxon; Jennie Lee; H. Vincent, Miss Fedora, H. M. Edmunds, W. Albert, George Conquest, Jr.

THE NAUGHTY FORTY THIEVES, *Grand Theatre*, Islington, London, opened December 26, 1892
A Pantomime by Geoffrey Thorn; Ballets by Mme. Marie

Harry Randall (Ali Baba); Minnie Palmer (Morgiana); J. M. Jones (Clown); with Alice Maydue, Minnie Marlo, Tom Costello, Harry Steele, Harlow Brothers-Willis and Dare, Maitland Marier, Frank Famond

ALI BABA; OR, MORGIANA AND THE FORTY THIEVES, *Chicago Opera House*, opened September 4, 1892
Originated and designed by David Henderson; Director, Richard Barker; Scenery, Frederick Dangerfield; Music composed and selected by W. H. Batchelor; Ballet music by Jesse Williams; Costumes, Howell Russell, Baron DeGrimm, Frderick Dangerfield; Electric effects by Martim Krueger; Mechanical effects by Al Vandenerkwen, George Goodrich; Armor by M. Gutperie, Chatlet Theatre, Paris; Decorations, Henderson Brothers

Frankie M. Raymond (Ali Baba); Ida Mulle (Morgiana); Ada Deaves (Nicotina); Mittie Atherton (Abdallah); Bessie Lynch (Hassan); Miss Le Mar (Zamora); Nellie Lynch (Ganem); Edwin Foy (Cassim Baba); Henry Norman (Arraby Gorrah);

Arthur Dunn (Hackaback); Joseph Done (Alibazan); Jack Guilmetta (Akour); Mak Millan (Alaska); James Thompson (Manitoba); Nellie Brown (Amineh); Alice Stoddard (Seraphina); Helen Dore (Menah); Frances Seymour (Mestour); Kittie Allen (Veramah); Venie Morgan (Backsheesh); Rose Frank (Sequin); Lillie Holt (Salaam); Alice Cassidy (Minaret); Lee Easton (Al Raschid); F. J. McCarthy (Mustapah); William Butters (Bismillah); Edwin Hubbard (Aleikim); W. Moyard (Abuben); Harry Carter (Adhem); George Martin (Haroun); Arthur E. Davidson (Alleka); Misses E. Houston, S. Lavilla, M. Brown, M. Zella, R. Rivers, R. Brown, C. Stevens (The Frunga); Misses M. Lewis, M. Chapin, S. Russell, R. Magnussen, M. Lothian, M. Martini (The Murghian); Misses M. Hart, B. Morris, P. Field, B. Hogan, K. Stevens, S. Morris (The Almazor); Misses G. Tunisi, M. Koepping, S. Meehan, H. Baker, H. Redman, T. Pauline (The Zid-El-Mar); Misses L. Manzoni, A. Stoddard, J. Parry, N. Lynch, E. Avenzini, M. Holden (The Sormutt); Misses H. Rosche,J. Monetti, C. Morando, H. Kuley, N. Pickett, A. Gregory (The Kadiya); Hulda Irmier (Danse Clasique); Signora M. Morando (Danse Fantisque); Herr Paul Marks, Fraulien Martha Irmler (Adagio); Misses H. Rosche, H. Kuley, J. Tusina, S. Meehan, N. Pickett, M. Holden, Kittie Stevens, B. Morris, H. Redmond, E. Manzoni, A. Gregory, H. Baker, Hulda Irmier (Dance Oriental)

MUSICAL NUMBERS: "We're All of Us Detectives, and We Each Have a Clue"; "Dashing Militaire"; "Hail to the Caliph"; "I'm as Honest a Man as You Ever Saw"; "We Are a Troupe of Mountebanks"; "Three Scamps"; "Happy Rhymes"; "Song of the Forty Thieves"; "My Heart Is Thine"; "The Walking Telephone"; "Morgiana's Dream"; "Hurrah, We're on the Track"; "Virginia Skedaddle"; "Your Money or Your Donkey"; "Voices of the Night"; "Forty Gallant Thieves Are We"; "Open Sesame"; "The Birth of the Butterfly"; "The Cobbler's Song"; "A Cobbler in Distress"; "Papa's Pants"; "Hackaback"; "Maiden and the Lamb"; "Jolly Old Tar"; "I Wonder If Dreams Come True?"

THE FORTY THIEVES, *Drury Lane Theatre*, London, Opened December 26, 1898
130 performances

Produced and directed by Arthur P. Collins; A Pantomime by Arthur Sturgess and Arthur P. Collins; Scenery, Bruce Smith, William Perkins, R. C. McCleery, W. B. Spong, Julian Hicks and Robert Caney; Choreography, John d'Auban, Carlo Coppi; Costumes designed by Comelli; Music and Music director, James M. Glover; Stage managers, Frank Damer and Michael Ring

Johnny Danvers (Ali Baba); Dan Leno (Abdallah); Harry Fischer (Cassim Baba); Charles Angelo (Caliban); Herbert Campbell (Fair Zuleika); Nellie Stewart (Ganem); Amelia Stone (succeeded by Rita Presano) (Morgiana); Lillie Belmore (Cogia); Alfred Balfour (Zookeeper); Charles Trevor (Judge); Lillian Lee (Judgess); MMe. Grigolati (Spirit of the Cave); Evelyn Hughes (Prospero); William Morgan (Mustapha); Rita Barrington (Spirit of Malice); Le Brun (Donkey Queen); Ernest d'Auban (Spirit of Malice); Ainslie Burton (Policeman); Whimsical Walker (Clown); Tom Cusden (Harlequin) Ruth Jezard (Columbine); Carl Waller (Pantaloon); Rita Presano (succeeded by Miss Hooten) (Hassan); Maud Fowler (Lurliety); Daisy Stratton (Usher); Augusta Walters, F. Harrison, Phil Sturgess, Charles Danvers, William Morgan, Jr., Bedells, Lloyd, Curry, Howard Russell, C. Chasemore, Daly, DaCosta, Wilson, Belmont, Lily Brooking (Ensemble)

AN ARABIAN GIRL AND FORTY THIEVES, *Herald Square Theatre*, New York, opened April 29, 1899

Produced by David Henderson; An Entertainment based upon the Story of *1001 Nights*; Director, Julian Mitchell; Book by J. Cheever Goodwin; Music by W. H. Batchelor; Scenery and Mechanical effects by Fred Dangerfield; Costumes, Will R. Barnes, Howell Russell; Electrical effects by John Welch; Orchestral Director, John J. Braham; Ballets, Signor Filiberto Marchetti; Wigs by William Hepner; Music composed and selected by W. H. Batchelor, John J. Braham, Jesse Williams and Myer Lutz; Stage manager, William Parry

Dorothy Morton (Ali Baba); Clara Lane (Morgiana); Edwin Foy (Cassim D'Artagnan); Frankie Raymond (Ganem); Blanche Chapman (Nicotina Zaza); Maud Gilbert (Abdallah); Amalia Karle (Hassan); J. K. Murray (Arraby Gorrah); Johnny Page (Hackaback); Harry MacDonough (Alibazan); Agnes Paul (Zamora); Joseph Ratcliff (Akour); Marie Lachere (Amineh); Ruth Ralston (Seraphina); George Ali (Ali Baba's Donkey); Gladys Lester (Menah); Beni (A Lion); Pearl Livingston (Mestour); Grace D'Arvigne (Veramah); June Dale (Backsheesh); Jeanette Ivel (Sequin); Marie Bregazzi (Salaam); Estelle Hoyt (Minaret); William Farreau (Raschid); J. H. Plunkett (Bismillah); Sully Guard (Aleikum); Zach Gilbert (Abuben); H. O. Crane (Adhem); R. Marsh (Haroun); William Scott (Alieka); Julian Walsh (Muza); George Roland (Abreka); W. M. Neil (Al Rashid); F. Ellis, H. Rosche, J. Praezer, L. See, E. Rinquest, N. Weston, Miss Persione, Hottie Rigo, M. Murray, Miss Knorath, Miss Dauble, Miss Omet; Clara Street, Nora Ross, Mattie Martien, Lillian Sterling, Gladys Blake, Fannie Quick, Annie Mulvihill, Emmma Praeger, Daisy Beni, Conchita Ruiz, Kittie Lynch, Jennie Digman, Josie Kirke, May Deyo, Kathie Dameling, Nellie Simons, Julie Devere, Phyllis Lehman, Lizzie Harcrow, Josie Graham; Mlle. Catherina Bartho, Fraulein Jennie Praeger (Corps de Ballet)

MUSICAL NUMBERS: "Detectives Bold"; "Dashing Militaire"; "Hail to the Caliph!"; "An Honest Man"; "Operatic Mountebanks"; "Song of the Forty Thieves"; "Let's Away!"; "I'm a Little Lady"; "To the Cave Away!"; "Virginia Skeddalle"; "Forty Gallant Thieves Are We"; "Open Sesame"; "Danse Diabolique"; "Grand Ballet Orientale"; "Cobblers We"; "The Wedding Bells"; "Pictures"; "Sweet William"; "Orb Divine"; "The Hoo-doo-doo-doo Man"; "Laughing Song"; "The Walking Telephone"; "I'm a Detective"; "I Wonder If Dreams Come True?"

AN ARABIAN GIRL AND FORTY THIEVES, *Touring Company*, season 1899-1900

Produced and directed by David Henderson; A Musical Fantasy based on the Arabian Nights Tale, revised and enlarged by Louis DeLange; Book by Cheever Goodwin; Music by W. H. Batchelor; Music selected from compositions by Meyer Lutz, Jesse Williams and W. H. Batchelor; Manager, David Henderson; Musical director, W. H. Batchelor; Ballet Master, Filiberto Marchetti; Stage managers, Frank Smithson and William Parry

Alexander Clark (Ali Baba); Clara Palmer (Cassim Baba); Charles Danby (The Caliph); George O'Donnell (Mustapha Gottem); Agnes Paul (Patrick Michael O'Donovan Ganem); Snitz Edwards (Otto Turk); Phoebe Coyne (Abdallah); Nancy Sadler (Hassan); Queena Davis (Alaska); Ollie Cooke (Manitoba); O. E. Reufrou (Bismillah); Charles Judels (Haroun); F. E. Stevens (Aleika); Joseph Wurzburger (Abuka); D. R. Gundaker (Akela); A. Mickali (Aleikam); W. L. Mehan (Abuben); James Robinson (Adhem); David Abrahams (Neddy); L. Barrett (The Lion); Gussie Joyce, Josie Clairmont, Hattie Dentz, May Hayes, Edith Marion, Mabel Gliddon (The Frungs); Alice Lyon, Emma Lyon, Adele Mackaye, May Abbey, Dell Grant, Mabel Degan (The Murgian); Mattie Martiene, Emma Praeger, Ollie Young, Vero Belle, Rose Humphries, Nellie Brown (The Almazar);

Inez Marcelle, Marie Coccia, Julie Praeger, Lillie George, Ethel Gibbs, Nora Ross (The Zid-el-mar); Clara Street, Bettie Daubl, Helen Konrath, Josie Kirk, Marie Strauss, Rosie Richards (The Sormutt); Louise See, Ida Omet, Angelina Pessione, Henrietta Rosche, Nellie Weston, Hettie Fedgerley (The Kadiva); Jennie Praeger (Danse Parisienne); Catherina Bartho (Danse Classique)

MUSICAL NUMBERS: "Cobblers We"; "Everybody in Trouble but Ali Baba"; "He Is the Real Thing Now"; "Get a Move On"; "Rose Marie"; "Orb Divine"; "The Hoo-doo-doo Man"

ALI BABA, *Adelphi Theatre*, London, opened May 18, 1903 1 matinee performance
Produced, written and directed by Mrs. Hugh Bell; A Fairy Tale; Conductor, H. Draber; Stage manager, Albert Vernon

Nigel Playfair (Ali Baba); Master George Pearse (Abdallah); Ian Maclaren (Cogia Hassan); Gigia Filippi (Amina); Rosina Filippi (Morgiana); Ashton Pearse (Abou Fisticuffs); Leonard Craske, Harold Lennox, B. Egerton, Walter Pearce, Lingham Power, C. H. Wills, G. H. Winn, S. Yates (Robbers); Compton Coutts (Cassim); Vane Featherston (Mrs. Cassim); Violet Furnival (Slave); Jessie Lennen, Edyth Fenton, Kitty DoyleMiss Alexander (Dancing Slaves)

CHU CHIN CHOW, *His Majesty's Theatre*, London, opened August 31, 1916 2,238 performances
Produced, written and directed by Oscar Asche; A musical Tale of the East; Music by Frederick Norton; Scenery by Phil and Joseph Harker; Colour scheme and Costumes designed by Percy Anderson; Costumes executed by B. J. Simmons, Miss Champion and Miss Leverick; Dances arranged by Espinosa; Musical director and Orchestrations by Percy E. Fletcher; Stage managers, William Holles and Alfred Bellew

Oscar Asche (Abu Hasan); Courtice Pounds (Ali Baba); Lily Brayton (Zahrat-Al-Kulub); Violet Essex (succeeded by Pauline Russell) (Marjanah); Frank Cochrane (succeeded by James Herbert) (Kasim Baba); Julian Cross (succeeded by Charles Wingrove, Spencer Lloyd) (Musab); Aileen d'Orme (succeeded by Mildred Walker) (Alcolm); Sydney Fairbrother (Mahbubah); J. V. Bryant (Nur Al-Huda Ali); Annie Moore (Bostan); W. Davidson (succeeded by Julian Cross, Fred Marten) (Mukbil); William Holles (succeeded by Frederick Pattrick) (Otbah); James Herbert (succeeded by Frank Cochrane) (Baba Mustafa); Norman Williams (succeeded by Bernard Dudley) (Abdullah); Spencer Lloyd (succeeded by W. Davidson, Julian Cross, Stanley Arthur) (Khuzaymah); Bessie Major (Zanim); Lisa Coleman (Fitnah); Dacia (succeeded by Roza Heech) (A Dancer); Ray Doree (Street Dancer)

CHU CHIN CHOW, *Manhattan Opera House*, New York, opened October 22, 1917 208 performances
Produced by William Elliott, F. Ray Comstock and Morris Gest; A Musical Tale of the East by Oscar Asche; Music by Frederick Norton; Director, E. Lyall Swete; Dances arranged by Alexis Kosloff; Musical director, Gustave Ferrari; Orchestrations, Percy E. Fletcher; Scenery, Joseph and Phil Harker; Costumes, Percy Anderson; Electrical effects, Paul Bismarck; Stage manager, Frank McCormack; Assistant stage managers, Julian Winters, George W. Zorn and Lester Sweyd

Tyrone Power (Abu Hasan); Henry Dixey (succeeded by Richie Ling) (Ali Baba); Florence Reed (Zahrat-Al-Kulub); Tessa Kosta (Marjanah); Albert Howson (Kasim Baba); Albert Moore (succeeded by Robert Lee Hill) (Khuzymah); Kate

Condon (Alcolom); Lucy Beaumont (Mabubah); George Rasely (Nur-Al-Huda); Matty Thomas (Bostan); Ida Mulle (Zatel-Demaki); Frank McCormack (Mukbill); Richie Ling (succeeded by Julian Winters) (Otbah); Felice De Gregorio (Baba Mustafa); Francis J. Boyle (Abdullah); Katherine Galanta (A Dancer); Harda Daube (The Woman in Green); Gordon Staples (succeeded by Neal H. Lake) (The Stranger); Olive Prosser (succeeded by Clara Vedera) (The Fortune Teller); George Bell (Son of the Bean Seller); Josephine Emory (The Lady); Robert Lee Hill (The Husband); Lester Sweyd (The Lover); Robert Lee Holl (succeeded by Robert Merriman) (Musab); Gladys Earlcott, Adele Meeker, Olga Merville, Lillian Neilson, Mary Reilly, Rosita Khoury, Beatrice Steiner, Gabrille Pitcher (Javanese Fanners); Helen La Tour, Dolores Brune, Louise Blanid, Joan Remville, Alma Rosine, Margerita Patti, Edith Barr, Ethel Mae Whitely (Javanese Dancers); Inez Borrero, Sallie Roumayne, Eleanor Hargrave, Hazel M. Robertson, Mai Poth, Helen Fox (Nile Girls); Dorothy Lee, Leonore Thompson, Stella Rothacker, Rita Fanning, Bertha Knight, Claire Boyd, Nina Artska, Adele Stollman, Jessie Lorraine, Alma Rosine, Ann Linn, Dorothy Butler (Ballet); Jeanette Kayton, Irene Sparry, Ethel Mae Whitely, Pauline Williams Claire Daste, Louise Rothacker (Extra Dancers); Frances Henricks (Circassian Slave); Claire Burton, Olga Merville (Turkestan Slaves); Clara Vedera, Marion Gray, Mai Poth, Dorothy Butler, Claire Burton, May Copeland (Pot Girls); Suzanne Renard, Beatrice Steiner, Minnie Meyers, Gladys Earlcott (Washer Women); Lillian Neilson, Adele Meeker, Mercedes De Cordoba, Annabelle Hennessey, Clara Vedera, Dolores Brune, Claire Earlcott, Helen La Tour, Rosita Khoury (Fruit Girls); Helen Fox, Mai Poth, Hazel M. Robertson

CHU CHIN CHOW, Touring Company, season 1919-20
Produced by F. Ray Comstock and Morris Gest; A Musical Extravaganza of the Orient; Written and Created by Oscar Asche; Director, E. Lyall Swete; Music by Frederick Norton; Costumes, Percy Anderson; Dances by A. Kosloff; New Dances arranged by Mlle. Guida of His Majesty's Theatre, London; Settings, Harker Brothers

Lionel Braham (Abu Hasan); Don W. Ferrandou (Ali Baba); Marjorie Wood (Zahrat-Al-Kulub); Albert Howson (Kasim Baba); Helen Gunther (Marjanah); Thoral Lake (Khuzymah); Neal Lake (Musab); Eugene Cowles (Abdullah); Stella St. Audrie (Alcom); George Rasely (Nur-Al-Huda); Robert Merriman (Mukbill); Hattie Carmontel (Zatel-Demaki); Gladys Earlcott (Mahbubah); Tina Russell (Bostan); Lorraine Welmer (Fortune Teller); Charles Foster (Son of Bean Seller); Adelaide Mesmer (Lady in Green); Roy Tracy (The Stranger); Martha Lorber (Kasim's Palace Dancer); Felice De Gregorio (Baba Mustafa); Christopher Haues (Otbah); Roy Tracy (Bazaar Peddler); Hattie Carmontel (The Lady); Milton Stiefel (The Lover); Thoral Lake (The Husband); May Copeland, Louise Potter, Claire Blanid, Margaret Weimer, Evelyn Richmond, Violet Kingston, Edna Moore, Virginia Chakarr (Javanese Fanners); Joan Renville, Estelle Granau, Helen Trevor, Bessie Rice, Olive Kingsto, Bertha Knapp, Masie Thomas, Ethel Whiteley (Bermese Dancers); May Irwin, Lorraine Weimer, Julia Fernie, Irene Messmer, Claire Bernard, Anna Colebourne (Nile Girls); Margaret Weimer, Lorraine Weimer, Anna Colebourne, Louise Potter, Clarie Bernard (Slaves); Lillian Kayton, Edith LeRoy, Jeanette Kayton, Hazel Jones, Martha Stewart, Helen McGovern (Carrier Girls); May Copelan, Virginia Chakarr, Margaret Weimer, Violet Kingston, Estelle Granau, Helen Trevor, Bessie Rice, Olive Kingston, Mazie Thomas, Bertha Knapp, Claire Bernard, Julia Fernle, Adelaide Messmer, Louise Potter, Irene Messmer (Fruit Girls); Hazel Jones, Martha

Stewart, Claire Bernard, Mabel Freeman, Irene Messmer, Julia Fernie, Gertrude Royale, Lorraine Weimer, Edith LeRoy, Evelyn Richmond, Suzanne Renaud, Violet Kingston, Helen Lee, Edna Moore, Claire Blanid, Violet Kingston, Olga Barousky, Helen Bowers, Jean Roberts, Helen Trevor, Jeanette Kayton, Carmen Vasylvia, Anna Colebourne, Martha Lorber, Francesco Carmonova (Mannequins) Beatrice Steiner, Eleanor Hargrave, Gabrille Kitcher, Sallie Roumayne, Inez Borrero, Minnie Meyers, Bertha Knight, Louise Blanid, Adele Stollman, Ann Linn, Lenore Thompson, Claire Burton, Joan Remville, Kiyo Okita, Nobu Watuma (Mannequins); Ethel Mae Whitely, Pauline Williams, Alma Rosine, Irene Sparry, Jessie Lorraine, Jeannette Kayton, Claire Daste, Nan Rainsforth (Carrier Girls)

THE FORTY THIEVES, *Lyceum Theatre*, London, opened December 26, 1924 112 performances

Produced and directed by Walter and Frederick Melville; A Pantomime; Book by Leedham Bantock; Music by Guy Jones; Scenery, H. K. Browne and J. Leonard; Costumes, Willie Clarkson; Choreography, Euphan MacLaren; Lighting, John H. Waters; Music director, Guy Jones; Stage managers, Clifford Seyler and Cecil de Lee

Stan Paskin (Ali Baba, a Woodcutter); Albert Letine (Cogi, his wife); Freddy Austin (Donald, his Donkey/ Clown); George Green (Giner, his Dog); Rolf Slater (Cassim, his Rich Brother); Will Richards (succeeded by Dolly Harmer) (Cassim's Wife); Hengler Brothers (Tarry and Ruuno, Bagdad Police); Frank Elsworthy (succeeded by Donald Gulland) (Sesame, Genie of the Cave); Dorita Belmont (Princess Hadgi); Eileen Dagmar (Prince Hakki); Louis Gaye (Hassan); George Jackley (Hassarac); Archie McCaig (Cassarac); Robert Woollard (Caliph of Bagdad); Harry Hartley (Mustapha/Pantaloon); Leon Kelloway (Onyx); George Sparrow (Wizier Dubas); Zellini (Magician Kafur); Doris Clayton (Abdallah); Harry Winpenny, The Masu-Medatsu Troupe (Policemen); Baby Love (Spirit of Youth); Connie Wild (Shahrazad); Connie Browning (Morgiana); Irene Shamrock (Ganem Baba); Helen White (Selim); Betty Cole (Zaidee); Marjorie Kenoyn (Columbine); Irene Bradfield (Harlequin); Mollie Seton, Betty Oliver, Evelyn Montfort, Connie Wilde, Baby Love Lottie Stone Troupe (Dancers)

CHU CHIN CHOW, *Regent Theatre*, London, opened December 26, 1928

Produced by Oscar Asche and Martin Sabine; A Musical Tale of the East by Oscar Asche; Director, Ellis J. Preston; Music by Frederick Norton; Scenery, Joseph and Phil Harker; Costumes, Percy Anderson, Music director, Algernon Holland

Oscar Asche (Abu Hasan); Wensley Russell (Ali Baba); Doris Champion (Zahrat-Al-Kulub); Helen Debroy Somers (Marjanah); William Dewhurst (Kasim Baba/Baba Mustafa); Dorothy Dewhurst (Mahbubah); Ellis J. Preston (Muckhill); Stuart Kern (Nur Al Huda Ali); Savana (Bostan); Betty Williamson (Fortune Teller); Marion Edwards (Alcolom); James Johnson (Bean Seller); Lawrence Shiel (Khuzymah); Hubert Carter (Abdullah); Tom Creegan, John Donegal, William Dawson, Ernest Fenton, W. T. Faber, Donald Hulland, Victor Harvey, Edward Jantze, Paul Jackson, George Maxwell, A. G. Middleton, Hedley Stace, Frank Craig, A. Gray, C. Keene, C. Thomas, Victor Yorke, J. Thomas, G. Williams, C. Wilson, Phyllis Boutell, Dorothy Cooper, Rita Cooper, Hilda Day, Grace Grey, Eily Gerald, Joyce Hinde, Enid Jobson, Joyce Jobson, Vivienne Mai, Jean Onslow, Vera Temple (Ensemble)

THE FORTY THIEVES, *Lyceum Theatre*, London, opened December 26, 1935

A Pantomime produced, written and directed by Walter and Frederick Melville; Music by Charles J. Moore

George Jackley (Ali Baba); Iris Carlisle (Princess Hadgi); Antony Eustrel (Cassim); Albert Letine (Mrs. Cassim); Winifred Wright (Prince Hakki); Charlie Naughton (Cassarac); Maria Sandra (Abdallah); Polly Ward (Morgiana); Florrie Ford (Cogla); Jimmy Gold (Hassarac); Molly Vyvyan (The Caliph of Bagdad); Betty Buckenll (Spirit of Youth); Norman McGlen (Toodles, the Cat); Billy Purvis (Tosser, the Dog); Claude Zola (the Donkey); Duck Tubb, Jr. (Genie of the Magic Cave); Kitty Reidy (Gamiem); Eddie Gray (Mountsewer); Louis Gay (Hassan); Latsha and Laurence (Golden Idol/Spirit of Silver) Syd Clayton (Dubas); Renie Jolliffe (Zaidee); Geoege Belmore (Mastapha)

BEDTIME FOR ALI BABA, *Shubert Theatre*, New Haven, opened November 18, 1936; closed, *Playhouse Theatre*, Wilmington, Del., November 28, 1936

Produced by Philip Dunning; A Comedy by Kennedy Kane; Director, Melville Burke; Settings, Arne Lundborg; Costumes, Russell Patterson; Cooch dance director, Gypsy Rose Lee; Incidental Music, Alexander Haas

Jimmy Savo (Ali Baba); Bramwell Fletcher (Hassan); Margaret Mullen (Scheherazade); John Hammond Dailey (The King); Ruth Gilbert (Morgiana); Edgar Stehli (Cassim); Edwin Phillips (Zeeman); Daisy Atherton (Jullee); Nancy Barnwell (Drunya); William Sanders (Kampoor); Frank Andrews (Weezer); Willie Archie (Dwarf); Day Eliot (Noor-Ed-Deen); Carter Blake (Bekkar); Thomas F. Tracey (General Mustapha); W. J. McCarthy (Dooban); B. L. Carter (El Heddar); Robert Harrison (Chairman); Elmer Brown (Secretary); Richard McMyers, Paul Johnson (King's Guards); Harold Grau, John Raby (Neighbors); William Korn (Soldier); Edward Moore, W. C. McCay (Soldiers)

CHU CHIN CHOW, *Streatham Hill Theatre*, London, opened June 10, 1940; moved to *Palace Theatre*, July 3, 1940

A Spectacular play by Oscar Asche; Director, Robert Atkins and Joseph Fenston; Music by Frederick Norton

Lyn Harding (Abu Hasan); Jerry Verno (Ali Baba); Marjorie Browne (Marjanah); Rosalinde Fuller (Zah-rat-Al-Kulub); Raymond Rollett (Mukbil); Peter Bennett (Kasim Baba); Sydney Fairbrother (Mahbubah); Denis Noble (Nur-Al-Huda Ali); Jill Hands (Bostan); Kay Bourne (Alcolm); Tom Kinniburgh (Abdullah); Katie Kemp (Fortune Teller); Clement Hamelin (Kazaymah); Bruce Dargavel (Baba Mustafa); Lev Bario (Otbah); Carol Hill (Indian Dancer); Unity Grantham (Javanese Dancer); Dorothy Vernon, Clement Hamelin (Slave Buyers); Hugh Thurston (Musab)

ALI BABA, *New England Mutual Hall*, Boston, opened October 17, 1947

A production of the Tributary Children's Theatre; Written and directed by Estelle Ritchie; Lighted and supervised by Eliot Duvey

Richard Kilbride (Ali Baba); Adele Thane (Abrima); Martha Aldrich (Morgiana); Robert Milam (Hasan); Malcolm Rivkin (Abdullah); Richard Dodge (Jafar); Lawrence O'Connor (Baba Mustapha); William Carito (Kasim)

ALI BABA; OR, THE THIRTY-NINE THIEVES, *Players' Theatre*, London, opened December 19, 1950

A Fairy Burlesque Extravaganza by H. J. Byron; Adaptation and additional Lyrics by Hattie Jacques and Joan Sterndale-Bennett; Director, Don Gemmell

Eric Chitty (Ali Baba); Don Gemmell (Cassim Baba); Joan Sterndale-Bennett (Abdallah); Hattie Jacques (Cogia Baba); Miss J. Holman (Ardinelle); D. Wood (Hassarac); J. Hewer (Ganem); J. Heawood (Mirza); T. Sympson (Hassan); Daphne Anderson (Morgiana); Misses P. Ashton, D. Kirner, M. Naison (Fairies, Thieves, Rag Tag and Robertail); *Harlequinade*: J. Heawood (Harlequin); Miss M. Naison (Columbine); Mr. D. Wood (Pantaloon); Mr. V. Russell (Policeman); Mr. T. Sympson (Clown); Miss J. Holman (Fairy Queen); Misses P. Ashton, D. Kirner (Fishergirls); Joan Sterndale-Bennett (The Oyster Cross'd in Love)

ALI BABA, *Barbizon Plaza Theatre*, New York, opened March 26, 1951
Produced by the Children's World Theatre; A Play by Wadeeha Atiyeh, based on the *Arabian Nights* story; Director, Monte Meachum; Settings, Herman Husby; Costumes, Bette Butterworth

Murray Perlman (Ali Baba); Wadeeha Atiyeh (Scheherazade); Charles Avery (Hassan); Lynn Blanchard (Morjana); Don Bouche (Hud-Hud, the Donkey); Betty Serton (Foo-Mee-Ya); Robert Buzzel (Khazzim); Franklin Neil (Bu-Zaid); Suleman (Kuz-Kuz); Kenneth Dobbs (Bou Loos); Elhajaji (Bul-Bul); Nack Becker (Toos)

ARABIAN NIGHTMARE, *New Watergate Theatre*, London, opened December 15, 1954
A "Pantomime for Parents" by Julian More; Director, Allan Davis; Music, Geoffrey Beaumont

Frank Duncan (Ali-Baba-re-Bop); Sonia Graham (Princess Dodo); Gerald Cross (Dame Sitt-Baddeley); Nuna Davey (Slinka Belle); Valerie Frazer (Peter Panning); Roger Cage (Woe); Penny Morrell (Salami); Michael Anthony (Lord Nuffink); Robert Stafford (A Guard); Roger Gage (Wop Cop); Stan Thomason (Edward C. Crusoe/C. Horse)

ALI BABA; OR, THE THIRTY-NINE THIEVES, *Players' Theatre*, London, opened December 18, 1956
A Pantomime by H. J. Byron; Adaptation and Lyrics by Hattie Jacques and Joan Sterndale-Bennett; Director, Don Gemmell; Production designer, Reginald Woolley

Anthony Bateman (Ali Baba); Patricia Rowlands (Morgiana); Michael Hall (Cassim Baba); Brian Tipping Codd (Hassan); Robin Hunter (Ganem); Betty Huntley Wright (Abdallah); Anthony Newlands (Hassarac); Michael Darbyshire (Mirza); Barbara Miller (Cogia Baba); Margaret Ashton (Ardinelle); *Harlequinade*: Denys Palmer (Harlequin); Jeanne Lusby (Columbine); Anthony Bateman (Pantaloon); Michael Darbyshire (Columbine's Mother); Mavis Traill (Ribbon Seller); Patty Berard (Snake); Brian Tipping Codd, Harry Haythorne (Clowns)

ALI BABA; OR, THE THIRTY-NINE THIEVES, *Players' Theatre*, London, opened December 21, 1965
A Pantomime by H. J. Byron; Adaptation and additional Lyrics by Denis Martin and Brian Blades; Director, Don Gemmell; Production designer, Reginald Woolley

John Rutland (Ali Baba); Jenny Wren (Morgiana); Fred Stone (Cassim Baba); Joyce Grant (Cogia Baba); Marion Grimaldi (Ardinelle); Jonathan Dennis (Ganem); Sheila Bernette (Hassan); Roy Desmond (Hassarac); Joan Sterndale-Bennett (Abdallah); David Morton (Mirza); Maria Charles (Fairy Sorayah); Josephine Gordon (Fairy Tittullah); Betty Wheeler (Fairy Ninevah)

ALI BABA AND THE FORTY THIEVES, *Bil Baird Theatre*, New York, opened December 26, 1970 91 performances

Produced by Bil Baird and the American Puppet Arts Council, Arthur Cantor, Executive Director; Director, Gordon Hunt; Book by Alan Stern; Songs by George Kleinsinger, Joe Darion and Bil Baird; Artistic associate, Frank Sullivan; Musical director, Alvy West; Played in conjunction with *Holiday on Strings*

Voices of Marionettes: Frank Sullivan (Ali Baba); Pady Blackwood (Zsa-Zsa); Bil Baird (Cassim); David Canaan (Selim); Olga Felgemacher (Morgiana/Mrs. Ali); Bryon Whiting (Mahmound); Peter Baird (Robber); Carl Harms (Manager)

TALES OF THE ARABIAN NIGHTS, *Alley Theatre*, Houston, season 1984-85

Produced by the Alley Theatre, Pat Brown, artistic director; A Musical by Michael Bigelow; Director, John Vreeke; Original score and musical direction, Jan Cole; Setting, Michael Holt; Lighting, Richard W. Jeter; Costumes, Fontini Dimou; Choreography, Lea Geeslin, Terrence Karn, Abiatha Simpson; Stage manager, Mark Tynan

Scheherazade and the Sultan: Jeff Bennett, Kayce Glasse, Raan Lewis, Bob Rumsby, Scott Fults, Mary Agen Cox, Luisa Amaral-Smith

The Fisherman and His Wife: Gregory Ruhe, Luisa Amaral-Smith

Ali Baba and the 40 Thieves: Raan Lewis, Bob Rumsby, Scott Fults, Luisa Amaral-Smith, Gregory Ruhe

The Snake Charmer and His Wife: Michael Normandy, Kayce Glasse

Shukat and the Princess: Bob Rumsby, Kayce Glasse, Gregory Ruhe, Scott Fults, Michael Normandy, Raan Lewis

SCREEN

ALI BABA AND THE FORTY THIEVES, *Fox Pictures*, released November 1918

Produced by William Fox; Directors, C. M. and S. A. Franklin

George Stone (Ali Baba); Gertrude Messinger (Morgiana); Lewis Sargent (Khaujeh Haussain); Buddie Messinger (Kasim); G. Raymond Nye (Abdoollah); Raymond Lee (Also Talib); Charles Hincus (Aasif Azaar); Marine Messinger (Kasim's Servant); Jack Hull (Janeel)

CHU CHIN CHOW, *Metro-Goldwyn release*, released February 1925

Produced by Graham-Wilson Productions, Ltd.; Director, Herbert Wilcox; Screenplay, Herbert Wilcox, based on Oscar Asche's Musical Tale of the East adapted from *Ali Baba and the Forty Thieves*; Photography, Rene Guissart

Herbert Langley (Abu-Hasan--Chu Chin Chow); Betty Blythe (Zahrat); Jameson Thomas (Omar); Judd Green (Ali Baba); Eva Moore (Alcolom); Randle Ayrton (Kasim Baba); Dora Lewis (Mabubah); Olaf Hytten (Mukbill); Jeff Barlow (The Cobbler); Dacia (The Dancer)

CHU CHIN CHOW, *Gainsborough Pictures/Gaumont-British*, released 1934

Produced by Michael Balcon; Director, Walter Forde; Screenplay, Edward Knoblock, Sidney Gilliat and L. DuGarde Peach, based on Oscar Asche's Musical Tale of the East adapted from *Ali Baba and the Forty Thieves*; Photography, M. Greenbaum; Editor, D. N. Twist

Fritz Kortner (Abu Hassan); Anna May Wong (Zahrat); George Robey (Ali Baba); Laurence Hanray (Kasim Baba); John Garrick (Nur-al-din); Pearl Argyle (Marjanah); Malcolm MacEachern (Abdullah); Denis Hoey (Rakham); Sydney

Fairbrother (Mahbubah); Francis L. Sullivan (Caliph); Thelma Tuson (Alcolom); Frank Cochrane (Mustafa); Kyoshi Takase (Entertainer)

ALI BABA GOES TO TOWN, *20th Century-Fox*, released October 1937
Produced by Darryl F. Zanuck; Associate producer, Lawrence Schwab; Director, David Butler; Screenplay, Harry Tugend and Jack Yellen, based on a story by Gene Towne, Graham Baker and Gene Fowler; Photography, Ernest Palmer; Art director, Bernard Herzbrun; Set decorator, Thomas Little; Costumes, Gwen Wakeley; Musical director, Louis Silvers; Songs by Mack Gordon, Harry Revel and Raymond Scott; Editor, Irene Morra

Eddie Cantor (Ali Baba); June Lang (Princess Miriam); Louise Hovick (Gypsy Rose Lee) (Sultana); Tony Martin (Yusuf); Roland Young (Sultan); John Carradine (Ishak); Alan Dinehart (Boland); Virginia Field (Dinah); Douglass Dumbrille (Omar); Ferdinand Gottschalk (Chief Councilor); Warren Hymer, Stanley Fields (Tramps); Sidney Fields (Assistant director); Jim Pierce (Captain of the Guard); Sam Hayes (Radio Announcer); Charles Lane (Doctor); Eddie Collins (Wife-Beating Arab); Marjorie Weaver (Beaten Wife); Francis McDonald (Peasant Ringleader), Peters Sisters, Jeni Le Gon, The Raymond Scott Quintet, Pearl Twins (Themselves); *Celebrities in Newsreel:* Douglas Fairbanks, Lady Sylvia Ashley, Phyllis Brooks, Eddie Cantor, Dolores Del Rio, Sonja Henie, Victor McLaglen, Tyrone Power, Shirley Temple, Cesar Romero, Michael Whalen, The Ritz Brothers, Ann Sothern

SONGS: "Laugh Your Way Through Life"; "Swing Is Here to Stay"; "I've Got My Heart Set on You"; "Vote for Honest Abe"; "Arabania" (Mack Gordon, Harry Revel); "Twilight in Turkey (Raymond Scott)

ALI BABA AND THE FORTY THIEVES, *Universal Pictures*, released January 1944
Produced by Paul Malvern; Director, Arthur Lubin; Screenplay, Edmund L. Hartmann; Photography, George Robinson and W. Howard Green; Special photography, John P. Fulton; Art directors, John B. Goodman and Richard H. Riedel; Set decorators, R. A. Gausman and Ira S. Webb; Choreography, Paul Oscar; Technical advisor, Jamiel Hassen; Musical director, Edward Ward; Song: "Forty and One For All" by J. Keirn Brennan and Edward Ward; Dialogue director, Stacy Keach; Sound, Bernard B. Brown; Editor, Russell Schoengarth

Jon Hall (Ali Baba); Maria Montez (Amara); Andy Devine (Abdullah); Turhan Bey (Jamiel); Moroni Olsen (Caliph Hassan); Frank Puglia (Cassim); Fortunio Bonanova (Old Baba); Scotty Beckett (Ali Baba, age 12); Yvette Dugay (Amara, age 10); Kurt Katch (Hulagu Khan); Ramsay Ames (Nalu); Harry Cording (Mahmoud); Chris-Pin Martin (Fat Thief); Jimmy Conlin (Little Thief); Noel Cravat, Robert Barron (Mongol Captains); Ethan Laidlaw, Dick Dickinson, John Calvert, Hans Herbert, Joey Ray, David Heywood, Pedro Regas (Thieves); Harry Woods, Dick Alexander, Art Miles (Mongol Guards); James Khan (Persian Prince); Charles Wagenheim (Barber); Alphonse Berge (Barber); Rex Evans (Arab Major Domo); Belle Mitchell (Nursemaid); Wee Willie Davis (Arab Giant); Theodore Patay (Arab Priest); Angelo Rossitto (Arab Dwarf); Norman Willis, Pierce Lyden, Don McGill (Guards); Eric Braunsteiner, Jerome Andrews, Alex Goudovitch, Ed Brown, George Martin, Dick D'Arcy (Dancers)

ALI-BABA ET LES 40 VOLEURS, *Films du Cyclope*, released 1949
Director, Jacques Becker; Screenplay, Jacques Becker, Marc Maurette and Maurice Griffe, based on a story by Cesare Zavattini; Dialogue, Andre Tabet; Photography,

Robert le Febvre; Production designer, Georges Wakhevitch; Music, Paul Misraki; Editor, Marguerite Renoir

Fernandel (Ali Baba); Samia Gamal (Morgiane); Dieter Borsche (Abdul); Henri Vilbert (Cassim); Edouard Delmont, Edmond Ardisson, Jules Maffre, Jose Case, Manuel Gary (Thieves)

THIEF OF DAMASCUS, *Columbia Pictures*, released May 1952
Produced by Sam Katzman; Director, Will Jason; Screenplay, Robert E. Kent; Photography, Ellis W. Carter; Art director, Paul Palmentola; Musical director, Mischa Bakaleinikoff; Editor, William Lyon

Paul Henried (Abu Andar); Jeff Donnell (Scheherazade); John Sutton (Khalid); Lon Chaney (Sinbad); Robert Clary (Aladdin); Philip Van Zandt (Ali Baba); Edward Colmans (Sultan Raudah); Elena Verdugo (Neela); Helen Gilbert (Princess Zafir)

SON OF ALI BABA, *Universal Pictures*, released August 1952
Produced by Leonard Goldstein; Director, Kurt Neumann; Associate Producer, Ross Hunter; Story and Screenplay, Gerald Drayson Adams; Photography, Maury Gertsman; Musical director, Joseph Gershensen; Musical numbers staged by Harold Belfer; Editor, Virgil Vogel

Tony Curtis (Kashma Baba); Piper Laurie (Kiki); Hugh O'Brian (Hussein); Susan Cabot (Tala); Victor Jory (Caliph); Gerald Mohr (Captain Youssef); William Reynolds (Mustafa); Morris Ankrum (Ali Baba); Philip Van Zandt (Kareeb); Leon Belasco (Babu); Barbara Knudson (Theda); Alice Kelley (Calu); Milada Mladova (Zaza); Katherine Warren (Princess Karma); Robert Barrat (Commandant); Palmer Lee (Farouk)

THE SWORD OF ALI BABA, *Universal Pictures*, released April 1964
Produced by Howard Christie; Director, Virgil Vogel; Screenplay, Edmund Hartmann and Oscar Brodney; Photography, William Margulies; Art director, William DeCinces; Set decorator, Julia Heron; Music, Frank Skinner; Sound, Waldon O. Watson and Corson Jowett; Editor, Gene Palmer

Peter Mann (Ali Baba); Jocelyn Lane (Amara); Peter Whitney (Abou); Gavin MacLeod (Hulagu Khan); Frank Puglia (Prince Cassim); Greg Morris (Yusuf); Frank McGrath (Pindar); Frank DeKova (Baba); Morgan Woodward (Captain of the Guard)

ARI-BABATO YONJUPPIKI NO TOZOKU (*Ali Baba and the Forty Thieves*), *Toei Company*, Japan, released 1971
Produced by the Toei Company; An Animated Cartoon; Director, Hiroshi Shidara; Animation, Akira Daikubara; Art director, Saburo Yokoi; Music, Selichiro Uno

TELEVISION

ALI BABA AND THE FORTY THIEVES, *Shirley Temple Storybook*, televised November 12, 1958 NBC 1 hour
Henry Jaffe Enterprises production in association with Screen Gems; Produced by Alvin Cooperman; Associate producers, Norman Lessing and Shelley Hull; Director, James Nielson; Teleplay, F. William Durkee, Jr., and Norman Lessing; Music, David Buttolph; Executive consultant, Mitchell Leisen; Narrated by Shirley Temple

Nehemiah Persoff (Ali Baba); Rafael Campos (Abdullah); Thomas Gomez

(Kasim); Vivian Nathan (Ali's Wife); Miriam Colon (Morgana, the Slave Girl); Bruce Gordon (Leader of the Thieves); Alfred Ryder (Hussein); Robert Carricart (Koali); Joe Duval (Baba Mustapha)

ALICE'S ADVENTURES IN WONDERLAND and
THROUGH THE LOOKING GLASS (AND WHAT ALICE FOUND THERE)
Various adaptations of the stories by Lewis Carroll (1865 and 1871)

Synopsis

ALICE'S ADVENTURES IN WONDERLAND:

While pursuing a White Rabbit, Alice tumbles into a hole, at the bottom of which she sees the Rabbit rushing along complaining he will be too late. Only after drinking from a small bottle, marked "Drink Me," does Alice shrink enough to enter a tiny door and find herself in a garden. Bemoaning Alice's fate, the White Rabbit warns her that the Duchess will be angry if he is late. After falling into a pool created by her own tears, Alice is confronted by an old Dodo bird who persuades her to run a caucus race to dry off. In the Rabbit's home Alice drinks from another bottle which inflates her to great size, but eating a piece of cake reduces her to sufficient height to get back through the door. In a nearby forest, Alice is told by a Caterpillar that eating a piece of the mushroom he's sitting on will stabilize her size. At the house of the Duchess, a grinning Cheshire Cat appears and disappears until nothing but the smile is left, but not before he invites Alice to attend the Mad Hatter's Tea Party. The manic party's guests include a March Hare and a drowsy Dormouse, telling silly riddles and having an insane conversation. Escaping by way of the Queen's garden of talking flowers, Alice saves a gardener from decapitation by hiding him in a large flower pot, and then plays croquet with the Duchess using live flamingos for mallets. The Duchess takes Alice to the seaside to meet a Gryphon and a Mock Turtle and join in the Lobster Quadrille. Alice then is summoned to the trial of a thief accused of stealing tarts, and called as a witness before the King and Queen of Hearts, but claims to know nothing about the theft. The infuriated Queen demands Alice's head be cut off. The entire court rush at Alice who sees they are nothing but a pack of playing cards as she awakens from her dream to find herself well and at home.

THROUGH THE LOOKING GLASS (AND WHAT ALICE FOUND THERE):

Alice imagines the looking glass is made of a gauze and passes through it into a world of chessmen, dominated by the Red King and Queen and the White King and Queen. Reading a poem called *Jabberwocky*, written in reverse for a looking glass, she finds it pretty and pretty incomprehensible. Then, in a garden, Alice talks with loquacious flowers and in her travels meets such strange figures as twins Tweedledum and Tweedledee. Tweedledee recites a poem, *The Walrus and the Carpenter*, and the White Queen explains to Alice the problems of "living backward." On a high wall, Alice encounters Humpty Dumpty, and correctly predicts the great egg's fall. Captured by the Red Knight, Alice is saved by the White Knight who sings her his song, "A-sitting on a Gate," when he isn't falling over on his head. The White Knight tells Alice she is to become a Queen on her next move on the chess board and, sitting between the Red and White Queen, Alice is subjected to tests of manners, mathematics and language. She sings the two Queens to sleep after learning she is to be given a Royal Party, at which she becomes exasperated with the Red Queen. Violently, she shakes the Queen until the latter turns into Alice's kitten Dinah. Alice awakens from her dream.

"Children yet, the tale to hear
Eager eye and willing ear,
Lovingly shall nestle near.
In a Wonderland they lie,
Dreaming as the days go by,
Dreaming as the summers die.
Ever drifting down the stream
Lingering in the golden gleam--
Life, what is it but a dream?"

Comment and Critique

The Reverend Charles Lutwidge Dodgson was born on January 27, 1832, in Daresbury, Cheshire, England. For twenty-six years, Reverend Dodgson was a mathematics lecturer at Christ Church, Oxford, and in 1865, under the pseudonym of Lewis Carroll, published a series of stories he had told to the young daughter of Oxford Dean Liddell. The success of *Alice in Wonderland* convinced Reverend Dodgson to write a sequel, *Through the Looking Glass (And What Alice Found There)* in 1871, based on characters in a chess game, introduced with:

"Child of the pure unclouded brow
And dreaming eyes of wonder!
Though time be fleet, and I and thou
Are half a life asunder,
Thy loving smile will surely hail
The love-gift of a fairy tale."

Lewis Carroll's *Alice* books were expertly illustrated with drawings by John Tenniel. After the author's death on January 14, 1898, seven days before his sixty-sixth birthday, London's Children Hospital perpetually endowed a cot through public subscription as a memorial to the creator of *Alice in Wonderland*. In 1928, Alice Liddell sold Dodgson's original manuscript of *Alice in Wonderland*, written in small, concise handwriting, for 15,400 pounds. Only Sir James Barrie's 1904 fantasy, *Peter Pan*, has had the same enduring appeal to children and adults alike.

Although Lewis Carroll wrote other children's books, including *Phantasmagoria* (1869), *The Hunting of the Snark* (1876), *Rhyme and Reason* (1883), *A Tangled Tale* (1885), and *Sylvia and Bruno* (1889), none of them attained the worldwide success of *Alice in Wonderland*, and its sequel, *Through the Looking Glass*. Under his own name, Dodgson also wrote several academic and scholarly tomes on mathematics. Despite his fame for *Alice in Wonderland* and the other books for children, he constantly denied authorship with a rather pompous statement, "Mr. Dodgson neither claimed nor acknowledged any connection with the books not published under his name."

On December 23, 1886, Henry Saville Clarke adapted Carroll's *Alice in Wonderland* and *Through the Looking Glass* to the stage for a series of matinee performances at London's Prince of Wales's Theatre. Clarke's adaptation with music by Walter Slaughter reappeared at the Royal Globe Theatre two years later, and at

London's Opera Comique ten years after that, to complete 115 performances. In 1905, Nigel Playfair and Rosina Filipi adapted the Carroll classic as *Alice*. H. Saville Clarke's stage version of *Alice in Wonderland* became an annual Christmas pantomime in London.

The Players' Producing Company presented *Alice in Wonderland* at Broadway's Booth Theatre on March 23, 1915, featuring Vivian Tobin as Alice. The production, which originated in Chicago, was reviewed by *The New York Times*: "There have been stage versions of these stories before and doubtless will be again. It must be said that this time, neither play nor production is by any means perfect or entirely satisfying, but it must also be said -- in the same breath -- that there probably never will be and never can be a Wonderland play sure to content those who have happily followed Alice on her dream journeys down the rabbit hole or through the looking glass." The *Times* critic found that: "The *Alice in Wonderland* that is at the Booth is the work of Alice Gerstenberg -- she has performed it with reverence and affection...If the product of her work, for all its considerable charm, remains a trifle slender, it may be ascribed to overscrupulousness...No one could ask for a more perfect embodiment of Carroll's and Tenniel's Alice, than Vivian Tobin... everything she does and says is right and pleasing. It is a delightful performance...One misses Tweedledum and Tweedledee, who are nowhere to be seen, and one misses sadly the optimistic White Knight."

Rachel Barton Butler adapted, produced and directed her stage version *Alice in Wonderland*, which opened at Broadway's Little Theatre on April 12, 1920, with Mabel Taliaferro as Alice. Butler, author of *Mamma's Affair*, named one of the Best Plays of the 1919-20 season, donated the proceeds from the *Alice* production to the New York Kindergarten Association. John J. Martin in *The New York Dramatic Mirror* concluded, "*Alice* has proved herself undramatizable before now. Miss Butler's efforts have been rather truer to the original than most, but her version of the greatest whimsy in the language is just as unactable as any previous version...Tampering with Lewis Carroll or Sir John Tenniel is much the same as tampering with the four gospels ...There is, however, one bright spot in the performance, and that is the Queen of Hearts in the capable hands of Elizabeth Patterson. She alone plays as though she loved Alice and her creator, and she alone is devoid of sophistication. Miss Patterson can always be relied upon for thoroughly satisfactory acting, but in this case she is especially to be praised for her truly delightful work."

Alice continued to delight Yuletide audiences in London, and on December 12, 1932, the adaptation by Eva Le Gallienne and Florida Friebus of *Alice in Wonderland and Through the Looking Glass*, produced and directed by Miss Le Gallienne, opened at her Civic Repertory Theatre to become America's best adaptation of the Carroll-Tenniel classic. Eva Le Gallienne moved her $23,000 production from her 14th Street Civic Repertory Theatre to Broadway's New Amsterdam Theatre. *Alice* continued for 127 performances.

"Since Eva Le Gallienne and Florida Friebus have a wholesome respect for *Alice in Wonderland* they have committed no violence. Their stage transcription... recaptures more of the innocent nonsense of the book than you would think possible...do not blame the collaborators if they have not turned it precisely into a play," Brooks Atkinson (*The New York Times*) wrote. "Rather have they related it in a frankly make-believe pageant of Tenniel scenes and Tenniel costumes to the wood notes wild of Richard Addinsell...Miss Le Gallienne's *Alice in Wonderland* is quite the most interesting variation the theatre has played on its main theme in some years. It is light, colorful and politely fantastic....As Alice, Josephine Hutchinson is innocent without being precocious -- a particularly well-bred Alice altogether...Sayre Crawley is especially biting as the Caterpillar. Joseph Schildkraut's raucous and rowdy Queen of Hearts...and Howard da Silva's White Knight -- all these parts recover the pith of their models in the acting...If the Oxford don had not grown tired of *Alice in Wonderland* long before he died, he would have enjoyed this guileless stage transcription."

Ivor Novello and Tom Arnold produced Clemence Dane's adaptation of *Alice in Wonderland* at London's Scala Theatre on Christmas Eve, 1943. Frances Stephens (*Theatre World*) called Dane's adaptation "a delightful new version [which] made a deep impression....Lewis Carroll's immortal books *Alice in Wonderland* and *Alice Through the Looking Glass* have been transplanted at the Scala with a rare naturalness against backgrounds and costumes which are Tenniel brought to life. Roma Beaumont, scarcely off the stage for a moment, is an ideal Alice and not for a long time shall we forget Dame Sybil Thorndike's sublime inanity as the White Queen."

Eva Le Gallienne revived *Alice* on April 5, 1947, at New York's International Theatre. "The Eva Le Gallienne-Florida Friebus dramatization of the Lewis Carroll fantasy, heeding to the Tenniel illustrations of the classic, is quite as enchanting as it was when it was first shown here some fifteen years ago...Bambi Lynn, who may be gratefully remembered for her performance in *Carousel*, is altogether captivating as the seven-year-old youngster." reported Howard Barnes (New York *Herald-Tribune*). Richard Watts, Jr. (*New York Post*) found the show "gay, humorous and strangely touching, and, as for your children, if they don't find it enchanting, I would advise you to drop them immediately...Bambi Lynn, the reformed ballet dancer, who has the all-important role, is, so far as I am concerned, complete perfection in it."

Brooks Atkinson (*The New York Times*), reflecting on the fifteen years when "*Alice in Wonderland* has been one of the sunniest memories of the Civic Repertory Theatre," added, "This animation of the Lewis Carroll classics by Eva Le Gallienne and Florida Friebus turns out to be a little masterpiece of humorous fantasy, based again on the Tenniel drawings, but freshened by a new production and acted with originality and relish ...Bambi Lynn of the golden hair and dancer's grace is giving an ideal performance...As the excitable White Chess Queen, Miss Le Gallienne is immensely funny...The production is a huge one...The score includes some lovely arias but the undertones of light orchestral music all the way through capture the fairy-story quality of the play."

Robert Garland (*Journal-American*) felt that "Enjoying *Alice* is a drama critic's bounded duty. Fifteen years ago, this Eva Le Gallienne-Florida Friebus 'dramatization' of the Lewis Carroll classic seemed fresh, funny and not too, too whimsical down on 14th Street. Even then, coming uptown to 42nd Street, was none too good for it. Now, having moved further north to Columbus Circle, it has not recovered all its freshness, funniness and charm...Bambi Lynn (by special arrangement with David O. Selznick) is Tenniel-like and graceful as Alice but she seldom manages to get inside the character as did Josephine Hutchinson in 1932."

An Afro-American adaptation of *Alice in Wonderland* and *Through the Looking Glass* was conceived and directed by Vinnette Carroll in 1969 as *But Never Jam Today*. On May 31, 1978, Carroll's concept, with music and lyrics by Micki Grant and retitled *Alice*, opened at Philadelphia's Forrest Theatre, produced by Mike Nichols and Lewis Allen. *Alice*, with Debbie Allen in the lead, was a $1.05 million misadventure (half of the investment made by Universal Pictures) that collapsed in the city of Brotherly Love, closing on June 11.

Thirty-five years after Eva Le Gallienne's last revival of *Alice in Wonderland*, the eighty-three-year-old actress brought her new production of it back to Broadway at the Virginia Theatre just before Christmas 1982. Richard Burton's daughter, Kate, was featured as Alice. Miss Le Gallienne, again played the airborne White Queen, and was observing her sixty-eighth year on the stage, having made her theatrical debut at the age of fifteen in London. Kate Burton, a 1982 graduate of the Yale School of Drama, made her own Broadway debut in July 1982 in Noel Coward's *Present Laughter.*

John Beaufort (*The Christian Science Monitor*) wrote, "Kate Burton heads the numerous cast as the insatiably curious child to whom the Wonderland adventures occur. In her blue frock, white pinafore and socks and shiny black shoes, Miss Burton is a charmingly picture-book Alice with a properly storybook attitude...The adaptors have been laudably faithful to their generous source. Unfortunately, the episodic travelogue seemed not to have hit its stride...With several notable exceptions, the playing tends to be more literal than fanciful."

In his review in *The New York Times*, Frank Rich reported, "In the otherwise flat revival of the Eva Le Gallienne *Alice in Wonderland*...the set designer John Lee Beatty and the costume designer Patricia Zipprodt have done an extraordinary job of bringing to life the celebrated storybook illustrations of Lewis Carroll's collaborator, John Tenniel. Virtually every Tenniel drawing has been rendered to the stage perfectly intact." He then observed: "Something has gone terribly wrong with this sweet mission to restore the pageant that was first performed by the Civic Repertory Company a half-century ago and that was successfully revived in 1947. Even the beautiful physical trappings can't long prevent us from noticing that the current incarnation of *Alice in Wonderland* is lifeless nearly from beginning to end...Kate Burton, who plays the part, is a well-spoken, hard-working young actress...But by no fantastical stretch of the imagination does she have the dazzling personal charm or even the warmth that might draw an audience closely to her...Nor does Miss Burton as yet have the skills that might allow her to vary her performance...She is earnest but boring -- a deadly mix in the starring role of a big Broadway show, especially when that role is the only one to turn up in every single scene."

British producer Cecil Hepworth made a short film based on *Alice in Wonderland* in 1903 with his wife playing both the White Rabbit and the Queen and himself as the Frog. Alice was played by May Clark (not the later American actress who was to take a grapefruit in the face from James Cagney). The first American-made screen Alice was Edison's 1910 one-reeler, *Alice's Adventure in Wonderland*, and Viola Savoy was Alice in the 1915 five-reeler, *Alice in Wonderland*, that was presented by American Motion Picture Corporation. In 1923, Walt Disney first used Carroll's *Alice* in a combined cartoon and live action one-reel series called *Alice's Wonderland* featuring Virginia Davis. Additional *Alice* adventures were developed by Disney into a series: twelve reels in 1924, eighteen in 1925 and twenty-six in 1926.

In 1931, the Unique Foto Film Company released a fifty-five minute feature, *Alice in Wonderland.* Filmed at an old Fort Lee, New Jersey studio, Unique's *Alice* was kindly reviewed by Mordaunt Hall (*The New York Times)*: "Notwithstanding the drawbacks of poor photography and none too efficient vocal recording, the film version of *Alice in Wonderland*...possesses something of the charm Lewis Carroll gave to his memorable work. There is an earnestness about the direction and the acting that elicits sympathy...Ruth Gilbert plays Alice. She wears a blonde wig and give her own sincere impressions, which are acceptable...And although none of the acting is any too good, it will probably meet with favor from youngsters who go to see an articulate Alice on the screen."

The Motion Picture Herald considered the juvenile fantasy to be "a distinct departure from accepted ideas of what constitutes film story material...Sound is erratic in places, although lines are uniformly well enunciated...Ruth Gilbert, as Alice, makes an excellent child heroine in Wonderland."

Paramount Pictures' all-star 1933 version of *Alice in Wonderland* was less than successful. Critics and moviegoers alike carped about their favorite screen stars being all but unrecognizable behind grotesque makeup and masks. *Photoplay*, however, thought, "To lovers of Lewis Carroll's story of *Alice*, this picture will be a source of great amusement with each familiar character coming into being. All the charm, all the whimsical nonsense has been caught by the camera...In this fantasy of the most highly imaginative quality, Charlotte Henry makes a believable and charming *Alice*."

Mordaunt Hall (*The New York Times)* found *Alice in Wonderland* "a marvel of camera magic and staging, but there are times when several of the players appear to be giving more thought to their grotesque appearance than to the inflection of their lines...The film is quite satisfactory, but it does lack the smoothness and high quality of the Eva Le Gallienne stage production ...Charlotte Henry, a 17-year-old girl from New York, fills the part of Alice. It is her idea of Alice and as such is an acceptable portrayal without creating any deep impression, such as Josephine Hutchinson did in the role on the stage...W. C. Fields as the hapless Humpty Dumpty gets everything out of the part, but on the other hand, to mention a disappointing portrayal, Gary Cooper makes a very poor White Knight."

The *New Yorker* called the film "a rather perfunctory and uninspired affair...It hasn't the charm, by a long shot, that the Eva Le Gallienne stage show had, although the screen would seem to offer possibilities for all the wildest fancies of the story... Sometimes you feel a spark of what might have been, such as in the scene with Humpty Dumpty; for as an egg, so to speak, W. C. Fields is superb."

In 1933, Walt Disney had also proposed filming *Alice in Wonderland* with Mary Pickford, then forty years old, combining cartoon animation with live action photography. Again, in 1945, Disney announced that Ginger Rogers would become Alice in a planned film, before finally making an all-cartoon feature of *Alice in Wonderland*, which was released by RKO in summer 1951.

While Disney was making his cartoon feature (over a five year period), Louis Bunin, creator of the unique Bunin's Puppets, was financed by the Union Generale Cinematographic Company in France in producing his live action and puppet version of Carroll's fantasy. A liveaction prologue was filmed at Nice's dilapidated Victorine Studio in both English and French in 1949. Bunin's *Alice* was denied distribution in Great Britain because of what the British censors considered an offensive caricature of Queen Victoria by actress Pamela Brown.

Reviewing Bunin's *Alice* for *Films and Filming* on its release in 1951 (simultaneously with Disney's version), John Pym wrote, "The film's chief interest [is] its whimsically bizarre prologue, with such stalwarts as Felix Aylmer and Ernest Milton in full donnish flight, and Pamela Brown, like some noisy and dangerous bird, memorising the names of the Liddell girls on the carriage ride to Oxford...Stephen Murray, however, is a very callow Dodgson...Bunin's point is to draw a parallel between the Vice-Chancellor and the White Rabbit, Victoria as the Queen of Hearts, etc., rather than to enquire into the nature of Dodgson's love for Alice Liddell." About the 128 articulated puppets Bunin used in the film, Pym added, "The sheer effort of animating them seems to have been so great (and they interact, to complicate matters, with the live Carol Marsh) that no energy remained for the transitions: the film jumps alarmingly. Disney's creations may have had an un-Carrollian Disneyishness, but Bunin's, although he claims they were taken from Tenniel's drawings, often have a lugubriousness all their own."

John Pym also noted Bunin's blast at Disney: "Disney wanted me to hold my picture in storage for three years to let him exploit his film first...so that my one million dollar picture wouldn't benefit from the much larger advertising campaign he'd planned for his three million dollar picture. But I opened my picture first, and when he took me to court over this, the judge threw the case out."

Of Disney's version, Leonard Maltin wrote in his 1973 book, *The Disney Films*: "In all, *Alice in Wonderland* is a very flashy and generally entertaining film, but it lacks that essential thread that made Disney's best features hang together, and moreover, it lacks *warmth*. Of course, *Alice* is not *Snow White* or *Cinderella*, and one shouldn't demand the same things of it."

Josef Shaftel and Derek Horne filmed their *Alice in Wonderland* in England in 1972 featuring Fiona Fullerton as Alice heading an all-star British cast. Despite the stellar roster, it was dismissed by critic Clyde Jeavons in Britain's *Monthly Film Bulletin*: "Like all productions of *Macbeth*, all adaptations of *Alice* seem bound to disappoint; and this stale, flat, if not unprofitable musical version, is certainly no exception ...Visually the film is closer to a Babycham commercial than a Tenniel illustration...Fiona Fullerton makes a pretty enough Alice but she saunters rather woodenly through the film, wearing a fixed expression of mild curiosity as if she were killing time in the Natural History Museum...'Curiouser and curiouser,' sings Alice from time to time, 'Tediouser and tediouser' would be nearer the mark."

Not so unbelievable in the current permissive society, Lewis Carroll's *Alice in Wonderland* was given an erotic filming in 1976 with porno-star Kristine de Bell as Alice. The presumptive billing for this nonsense was "The First X-rated Musical"! The script wisely inquired, "What's a nice girl like you doing on a knight like this?"

On television's *Ford Theatre*, a one hour adaptation of *Alice in Wonderland* was presented in December 1950, featuring Iris Mann. The black and white production had telling performances from Richard Waring, Biff McGuire, Jack Lemmon and others. Its production values were considered exceptional if occasionally raucous.

In May 1954, the Lewis Carroll favorite was again produced for television and violated "the Wonderland spirit," according to Jack Gould (*The New York Times*). "The treasured story of *Alice in Wonderland* was shockingly desecrated...For what was done to the beloved classic there can be neither excuse nor justification...Its whole spirit was wantonly violated and largely changed into a coarse, wisecracking charade that lacked even elementary artistic taste." Gould felt: "In an incredible lapse of judgment, the *Kraft Television Theatre* was not content to let Alice make the trip by herself into Wonderland. On television, she was accompanied by Edgar Bergen, the ventriloquist, and his sidekick, Charlie McCarthy. Given the right setting and the right time, Mr. Bergen and Charlie can be fun. But to let them wander through the delicate narrative of *Alice* with their often earthy gags and vaudeville quips was both outrageous and offensive ...Has the television age so distorted our values that nothing -- not even *Alice in Wonderland* -- can be enjoyed and prized for what it is and be kept free from clumsy hands?...To build up Charlie McCarthy at the expense of Alice is stark madness...The great pity was the tragic waste of talent."

Maurice Evans produced TV's next *Alice in Wonderland* in color for the *Hallmark Hall of Fame* on October 23, 1955. Evans' production was a version of the Eva Le Gallienne-Florida Friebus stage adaptation of Carroll's *Wonderland* tales and featured fourteen-year-old English actress Gillian Barber in the title role. "Somewhere amid all the earnest efforts the gently humorous spirit of Lewis Carroll was inadvertently overlooked," reported Jack Gould (*The New York Times*). "The outcome was a series of episodic glimpses of Wonderland presented with uncommon technical dexterity by George Schaefer, the director...But the production lacked the virtue of simplicity and the unifying influence of a child's imagination, making the unreal both completely plausible and utterly enchanting...Eva Le Gallienne played the White Queen and easily stole the honors...Virtually on a par were Elsa Lanchester as the Red Queen and Hiram Sherman as the King of Hearts."

On March 30, 1966, comedian Bill Dana's animated cartoon spoof of *Alice in Wonderland*, subtitled *What's a Nice Kid Like You Doing in a Place Like This?*, was televised, "In this way-out spoof of Lewis Carroll's children's classic, Alice tumbles through the TV set after her dog Fluff -- and falls into Wonderland," was how the network described it. A delightful version, the Lewis Carroll classic was "voiced" by Janet Waldo as Alice, and other characters by Sammy Davis, Jr., Zsa Zsa Gabor, Howard Morris and Bill Dana. The cartoon characters, Fred Flintstone and Barney Rubble, appeared in special guest roles, and Hedda Hopper was cast as "Hedda Mad Hatter." Original songs were by Lee Adams and Charles Strouse, of *Bye, Bye Birdie* fame.

A sumptuous all-star musical TV production of *Alice Through the Looking Glass* premiered on November 6, 1966. Jack Gould (*The New York Times*) extolled it: "'Twas Brillig on the Home Screen. The advantages of color television were strikingly illustrated last night in NBC's opulent production...In his adaptation, Albert Simmons took assorted liberties with the original, but his touch and attitude were altogether right in weaving a spell of light make-believe...Judi Rolin, playing Alice, was so charmingly fetching...The Moose Charlap-Elsie Simmons score never achieved the lilt and gaiety for which a viewer waited in constant expectation... [*Alice*] was a credit to many: only in song did its spell falter."

Jonathan Miller directed and "recreated" a film made for BBC television in 1966. His reconstructed *Alice in Wonderland* boasted an all-star British cast with superb photography by Richard Bush along with a musical score by Ravi Shankar. The $80,000 production was televised in Great Britain on just after Christmas and was an excellent concept of Carroll's classic with Anne-Marie Malik as Alice, Sir John Gielgud (Mock Turtle), Sir Michael Redgrave (Caterpillar), Peter Sellers (King of Hearts), Leo McKern (The Duchess), Peter Cook (The Mad Hatter), and others. Ten years later, *Alice Through the Looking Glass* was produced in England for television with Sarah Sutton as Alice in combined live action and animated cartoon.

The Eva Le Gallienne-Florida Friebus adaptation of *Alice in Wonderland* was the premiere telecast of PBS' eleventh *Great Performances* season (October 3, 1983). Featured was Kate Burton as Alice, along with, among others, her father Richard, as the White Knight.

"With considerable inventiveness and more than a little trimming, public television's *Great Performances* series has transformed a disastrous stage production *Alice in Wonderland* into one of impressive charm... Putting the entire television enterprise into the skillful directorial hands of Kirk Browning, the producers, Jac Venza and Ann Blumenthal, have also enlisted the aid of Donald Saddler, the choreographer, and have devised a new framework for the play...Kate Burton, who played Alice in the stage revival, retains the title role and is genuinely appealing...Most of the other parts are played by a somewhat odd but fascinating collection of guest stars...And Miss Burton's well-known father, Richard, shows up as the White Knight as done in the style of Don Quixote...This is still not a great *Alice*, a work that has often shown itself resistant to theatrical adaptation, perhaps because its basic punning roots are so literary. This *Alice* is a series of sketches, many marvelously executed, which convey some idea of what can be found in the original Lewis Carroll." So John J. O'Connor's appraised the telecast in *The New York Times*.

Producer Irwin Allen's two-part television adaptation by Pulitzer Prize-winning dramatist Paul Zindel of *Alice in Wonderland* was broadcast during the 1985 Christmas season. It featured a stellar cast of forty "names" headed by ten-year-old newcomer Natalie Gregory, plus nineteen songs written by Steve Allen. "[It] is Irwin Allen's masterpiece. The producer of such blockbuster movies as *The Poseidon Adventure* and *The Towering Inferno* has here risen above the ruck of mere entertainment and delivered a work of art," wrote Lee Winfrey (*The Philadelphia Inquirer*). "In *Alice in Wonderland*, a four-hour mini-series with music, old pro Allen received perfect pint-size help from Natalie Gregory, an adorable little girl who makes the classical role of Alice entirely her own." Winfrey admired the expertise with which Zindel adapted *Alice's Adventures in Wonderland* and *Through the Looking Glass* "into one seamless script...a model of screenplay writing that every aspiring dramatist could benefit from studying."

As the Reverend Charles Lutwidge Dodgson once proclaimed when accused of being Lewis Carroll, the creator of *Alice*, "Mr. Dodgson neither claimed nor acknowledged any connection with the books not published under his name."

Still "Curiouser and Curiouser!"

STAGE

ALICE IN WONDERLAND and THROUGH THE LOOKING GLASS, *Prince of Wales's Theatre*, London, opened December 23, 1886 (matiness only)

Produced by Edward Bruce; A Musical Dream Play, based on the Lewis Carroll stories; Director, Edward Bruce; Book by H. Saville Clarke; Music by Walter Slaughter; Scenery, including dissolving view effects, by John Bateman & Company; Costumes by Mons. and Mme. Alias, based on John Tenniel's illustrations; Incidental dances by Mlle. Rosa; Properties by Labhart; Additional scenery, G. Prodger and E. Banks

Alice's Adventures in Wonderland: Phoebe Carlo (Alice); Master D. Abrahams (White Rabbit); Master S. Solomon (Caterpillar); Florence Levey (Duchess); Charles Adeson (Cheshire Cat); Sydney Harcourt (Mad Hatter); Master Edgar Norton (March Hare); Anna Abrahams (Cook); Dorothy D'Alcourt (Dormouse); Stephen Adeson (King of Hearts); Mlle. Rosa (Queen of Hearts); Kitty Abrahams (Jack of Hearts); H.H.H. Cameron (Executioner); Charles Bowland (Gryphon); William Chessman (Mock Turtle)

Through the Looking Glass: Phoebe Carlo (Alice); Anna Abrahams (White King); Kitty Abrahams (White Queen); H.H.H. Cameron (Carpenter); Stephen Adeson (White Knight); Mabel Love (Rose); Florence Levey (Lily); Master D. Abrahams (Red King); Mlle. Rosa (Red Queen); Master C. Kitts (Red Knight); Sydney Harcourt (Tweedledum); John Ettinson (Tweedledee); William Cheesman (Humpty Dumpty); C. Bowland (The Walrus); Master Charles Adeson (Lion); Master S. Solomon (Unicorn); Master Edgar Norton (Hare); Master Hood (Leg of Mutton); Miss D. D'Alcourt (Plum Pudding)

ALICE IN WONDERLAND and THROUGH THE LOOKING GLASS, *Royal Globe Theatre*, London, opened December 26, 1888

Produced by Richard Mansfield; A Musical Dream Play, based on the Lewis Carroll stories; Directors, H. Saville Clarke and Edgar Bruce; Book by H. Saville Clark; Music by Walter Slaughter; Scenery, E. Banks; Incidental Dances by Mlle. Rosa; Costumes by M. L. Besche, based on the illustrations of John Tenniel, executed by Mons. and Mme. Alias; Musical director, Edward German; Stage managers, Sidney Harcourt and E. B. Norman

Alice's Adventures in Wonderland: Isa Bowman (Alice); Charles Bowman (White Rabbit); Master John Smart (Caterpillar); Miss Norton (Duchess); Edith Vanbrugh (Cook); Charles Adeson (Cheshire Cat); Sidney Harcourt (Mad Hatter); Mr. Godfrey (March Hare); Emmie Bowman (Dormouse); Stephen Adeson (King of Hearts); Miss Dewhurst (Queen of Hearts); Irene Vanbrugh (Knave of Hearts); Mr. Roy (Executioner); Mr. Druce (Gryphon); Mr. T. P. Haynes (Mock Turtle)

Through the Looking Glass: Isa Bowman (Alice); Mr. Godfrey (White King); Irene Vanbrugh (White Queen); Mr. Roy (The Carpenter); Mr. Druce (The Walrus); Stephen Adeson (White Knight); Miss Norton (Lily); Edith Vanbrugh (Rose); Miss Dewhurst (Red Queen); Charles Adeson (Red King); Sidney Harcourt (Tweedledum); T. P. Haynes (Tweedledee); Mr. Druce (Humpty Dumpty); Master Allwood (The Lion); Mr. Godfrey (The Hare); Mr. Smiles (The Cook); Miss D'Alcourt (Plum Pudding)

MUSICAL NUMBERS: "The Song of the Elves"; "How Doth the Little Crocodile"; "You Are Old Father William"; "The Baby and the Cook"; "Twinkle, Twinkle, Little Bat"; "So They Say"; "Can't Be Done"; "He Is the Executioner"; "Beautiful Soup So Rich and Green"; "The Lobster Quadrille"; "Will You Walk a Little Faster?"; "Looking-Glass Land"; "Jabberwocky"; "All the King's Horses and All the King's Men"; "Oh, I've Had Such a Curious Dream"

Opera Comique, London, opened December 22, 1898 115 performances
Produced by Arthur Eliot; Director, Horace Sedger; A Musical Adaptation of *Alice in Wonderland* and *Through the Looking Glass* by Lewis Carroll; Book by Henry Saville Clarke; Music by Walter Slaughter; Production designer and costumes, William Clarkson; Scenery by E. G. Banks; Musical director, Rowland Wood; Choreography, Espinosa; Stage manager, Alec Murray

Rose Hersee (Alice); Master T. Pauncefort (White Rabbit/Red Knight); William Cheesman (Tweedledum/ Mock Turtle); Murray King (Tweedledee/Gryphon); W. R. Staveley (White King/King of Hearts/Walrus); H. Cameron (Humpty Dumpty/Carpenter/Executioner); Bert Sinden (Red King/Knave of Hearts/Dancer); Alice Barth (Red Queen/Duchess); Mrs. Arthur Eliot (White Queen/Queen of Hearts); Master Garnet Vayne (Plum Pudding/Cheshire Cat); Master Harold de Becker (Leg of Mutton/Dormouse); Master Murlis (Caterpillar/ Unicorn); Master Robertson (Lion); Vesta de Becker (Lily/Oyster); Miss Beaden (Rose/Oyster); Miss Doyle (Messenger/Usher); Arthur Eliot (Mad Hatter); Master Leach (White Knight); Alec Murray (Hare); Sisters Marchall (Dancers)

U.S. Touring Company, season 1898-99
Produced by Nixon and Zimmerman; A Play by W. de Wagstaffe, based on *Alice's Adventures in Wonderland* by Lewis Carroll; with reproductions of Sir John Tenniel's illustrations

Little Ruby (Alice); Francis Walsh (King of Hearts); Louise Collins (Queen of Hearts); Leslie Fancourt (Knave of Hearts); Clifford Leigh (White Rabbit); R. Buhler (The Dodo); James Cronin (Mock-Turtle); Dan C. Merrifield (Gryphon); Kate A. Johnson (Dormouse); Mr. Millard (March Hare); Harry J. Koeper (Caterpillar); James Staunton (Frog Footman); Mr. MacKenzie (Fish Footman); Mr. Grimalkin (Cheshire Cat); Harry J. Koeper (The Lobster); Mr. Mallon (Ace of Clubs/ The Executioner); E. Travers (Two of Spades); H. Donalds (Five of Spades); T. Elton (Seven of Spades); Misses Linden, Hawkins, Vaughn, Valletie, Smith, Sanners, Gray, Grenville, Mary Hanson (Court Cards); Paul G.

Taylor (Mad Hatter); Margaret Evans (The Duchess); B. F. Stew (The Cook); Anna Sargent (Alice's Sister); The Browns, The Smiths and the Joneses (The Wise Parrots)

NOTE: This production was presented at *Carnegie Lyceum* in New York for a matinee performance on April 10, 1899 with Little Ruby (Alice); Astrid Ransted (Queen of Hearts); Henry Barfoot (King of Hearts); Jessie Lansing (The Duchess); Louise Collins (Alice's sister); J. B. Cole (The Cook); Ralph Yoerg (replaced Frank Opperman) (Mad Hatter)

Vaudeville Theatre, London, opened December 19, 1900   138 performances
Produced by A. & S. Gatti and Charles Frohman; A Musical Dream based on Lewis Carroll's *Alice in Wonderland* and *Through the Looking Glass*; Director, Seymour Hicks; Book by H. Saville Clarke; Music by Walter Slaughter; Costumes, William Clarkson; Scenery, William Harford; Musical director, Walter Slaughter

Ellaline Terriss (Alice); Florence Lloyd (White Queen); Frank Lincoln (succeeded by Compton Coutts) (White King/Knave of Hearts); H. H. H. Cameron (Humpty Dumpty/Carpenter/Executioner); Emily Miller (Duchess/Red Queen); Seymour Hicks (Mad Hatter); William Cheesman (Tweedledum/Mock Turtle); Murray King (Tweedledee/Gryphon); J. C. Buckstone (King of Hearts/Walrus); Stanley Brett (Red King/Caterpillar); Master George Hersee (Cheshire Cat); Winifred Hall (Dormouse); Kathleen Courtney (March Hare); Clarice Erani (White Rabbit); Master MacDonald (Lion); Master Schmidt (Unicorn); Dorothy Ball (Cook); Hilda Antony (Red Knight); Dorothy King (Plum Pudding); Fred Flexmore (Lobster); Enid Sass (Lobster/Cornflower); Mora Hersee (Lily); Florrie Hersee (Rose); Dorothy Frostick (Oyster); Kitty Grey (Lobster); Lillian Burns (Fairy); Amy Wilde (Leg of Mutton)

ALICE THROUGH THE LOOKING GLASS, *New Theatre*, London, opened December 22, 1903   63 performances
Produced by John Donald and Reginald J. Barker; A Fairy Play by Y. Knott, based on the book by Lewis Carroll; Music by Walter Tilbury; Director, George Grossmith, Jr.; Musical director, Augustus Bingham; Chorus director, Spencer Dickinson; Scenery E. G. Banks; Costumes designed by Robert Crafter; Choreography, W. Ozmond; Stage director, Warwick Nuckland

Maidie Andrews (Alice); Constance Courtenay (White Queen); Rose Temple (Red Queen); Tim Ryley (White King); Dallas Welford (Tweedledum); Lennox Pawle (Tweedledee); Willie Atom (Humpty Dumpty); Algernon Newark (Man in White Paper); Haidie Hemsley (Spirit of Fairy Revels); Daisy Catchcart (Tiger Lily); Hilda Moss (Red Rose); Master H. Ballinger (Beetle); Mabel Martin (Violet); Winnie Crisp (Queen of Fairies); Alexandrina Vercisi (Seaweed); James Lewis (Guard); N. Romaine (Goat Man); Masters Thomas Buffery, Alfred Ward, Sydney Coppin, Alfred Lidman, Frank Chapman, Willie Vokes (Pawns); Masters A. Baines, H. Dobson, C. Knight, H. Wain, J. Thomas, J. Twentyman (Soldiers); Ethel Bowden, Madeline Fuller, Queenie Hills, Beatrice Vokes, Minnie Weppner (Marquerites); Sylvia Hastings, Winnie Howard, Rosie Marks, Ivy Redman, Violet Strong (Blue-Bells); Mina Brunton, Kate Buckland, Annie Heskey, Violet Taylor, Magda Whitfield (Poppies); Sylvia Polini, Mabel Dodd, Violet Shaw, Adeline Roth, Rosie Shaw (Pin Roses); Lillie Dodd, Marie Fuller, Lily Marks, Maude Plumb, Cissie Sewell (Buttercups); Connie Brunton, Ethel Downley, Evelyn Hastings, Cissie Brown, Hattie Burgess (Irises); Nellie Burietta, Violet Bennett, Emily Dawkes, Lily Redman (Butterflies); Florrie Curtis, Maude Stuart

(Dragon-Flies); Dorothy Kemble, Mercedes Suarez (Bees); Daisy Connell, Dora Crisp, Ella Morris, Kay deLang, Hilda Lidman, Florence Metzloff, Esther Sobell, Alexandra Vercisi, E. Whitefield, Nora Wilson (Fairies)

ALICE, *Court Theatre*, London, opened May 5, 1905 1 performance
Produced by J. H. Leigh; A Play adapted from Lewis Carroll's *Alice in Wonderland* and *Alice Through the Looking Glass*; Written and directed by Nigel Playfair and Rosina Filipi; Costumes by William Clarkson; Music director, Theodore Stier

Doris McIntyre (Alice); Marianne Caldwell (White Queen); Ruth Parrott (Queen of Hearts); Nigel Play-fair (Mad Hatter/Tweedledum); George Trollope (Humpty Dumpty/Tweedledee/Executioner); St. Clair Bayfield (March Hare/Caterpillar); Cecil Yapp (King of Hearts); Wescombe Penney (Knave of Hearts); Hilda Gregory (Cheshire Cat); Leyla McGrath (Red Queen); Laura Urquhart (Cook); Beatrix Hillier (Dormouse); Esme Hubbard (Duchess); Maud Buchanan (Mabel); Frank Royde (Fishfootman); Ina Pelly (White Rabbit); Chrissie Stevens (No. 7); Mabel Hillier (No. 5); Winnie Hall (No. 2); Edyth Fenton, Mirabel Hillier, Maud Gill, Violet Furnival, Winnie Hall, Chrissie Stevens, Bewicke, Baylegate, Lee, Taylor (Soldiers)

Prince of Wales's Theatre, London, opened December 20, 1906 27 matinee performances
Produced by Frank Curzon; A Musical Dream by H. Saville Clarke, based on Lewis Carroll's *Alice in Wonderland* and *Through the Looking Glass*; Director, Seymour Hicks; Music by Walter Slaughter; Costumes by William Clarkson; Choreography, Will Bishop; Music director, Percy E. Fletcher

Marie Studholme (Alice); Stanley Brett (Mad Hatter); Florence Lloyd (White Queen/Queen of Hearts); Harold Borrett (White King/Knave of Hearts); Harry Ulph (Red King/Caterpillar); H. H. H. Cameron (Humpty Dumpty/Carpenter/Executioner); Tom Graves (Mock Turtle/Tweedledum); J. C. Buckstone (Tweedledee/ Gryphon); Julian Cross (King of Hearts/Walrus); Florrie Arnold (March Hare); Alice Barth (Red Queen/ Duchess); Marjorie West (Cheshire Cat); Rita Leggerio (White Rabbit); Euphan Maclaren (Cook); Ivy Sawyer (Dormouse); Carmen Sylva (Lilly); Ethel Evans (Plum Pudding); Phyllis Bedells (Cornflower/Oyster); Will Bishop (Lobster/Gollywog); Master Lester Bilbe (Lion); Master John Hobbs (Unicorn); Master Tom Jones (Leg of Mutton); Alice Dubarri (Fairy); Margaret Fraser (Lobster)

Apollo Theatre, London, opened December 23, 1907 19 matinee performances
Produced by Tom B. Davis; A Musical Dream by H. Saville Clarke, based on Lewis Carroll's *Alice in Wonderland* and *Through the Looking Glass*; Director, Seymour Hicks; Music by Walter Slaughter; Costumes, William Clarkson; Choreography, Will Bishop; Music director, Percy E. Fletcher; Acting manager, Herbert J. Sich; Stage managers, Will Bishop and Harry Ulph

Maidie Andrews (Alice); E. H. Kelly (Mad Hatter); Evelyn Hill (White Queen/Queen of Hearts); Julian Cross (King of Hearts/Walrus); Jack Rowlands (White King/Knave of Hearts); Rita Leggerio (White Rabbit); Forrie Arnold (March Hare); Tom Graves (Tweedledum/ Mock Turtle); J. C. Buckstone (Tweedledee/Gryphon); Harry Ulph (Red King/Caterpillar); H. H. H. Cameron (Humpty Dumpty/Carpenter/Executioner); Will Bishop (Gollywog); Master Freeman (Lion); Alice Barth (Duchess/Red Queen); Marjorie West (Cheshire Cat); Ivy Sawyer (Dormouse/Lobster/Cornflower); Alice Dubarri (Rose); Dorrit

MacLaren (Red Knight/Lobster); Winnie Hill (Lily); Ethel Evans (Plum Pudding); Cicely Debenham (Oyster); Master John Hobbs (Unicorn/Leg of Mutton); Euphan McLaren (Lobster); Ivy Sawyer (Dancer)

Court Theatre, London, opened December 27, 1909 40 performances
Produced by J. H. Leigh and R.T.E. Neeves; A Musical play based on Lewis Carroll's *Alice in Wonderland* and *Through the Looking Glass*; Director, Marshall Moore; Book by H. Saville Clarke; Music by Walter Slaughter; Scenery, Cecil and James Hicks; Costumes, H. & H. Rayne; Music director, Archibald H. Benwell; Conductor, Marjorie Slaughter; Choreography, Lilian Leoffeler and Charles E. Sutton; General manager, James Anning; Stage managers, Thomas Bentley and Edmund Goulding

Ivy Sawyer (Alice); Ella Anderson (White Queen/ Queen of Hearts); Franklyn Vernon (Mad Hatter); Roy Jeffries (White King/Knave of Hearts); Amy Frachette (Red Queen/Duchess); Girlie Le Claire (Cheshire Cat); Tom Graves (Tweedledum/Mock Turtle); Edgar K. Favelle (succeeded by Roland Henry) (Tweedledee/ Gryphon); Edmund Goulding (King of Hearts/Walrus); H. H. H. Cameron (Humpty Dumpty/Carpenter/Executioner); Yvonne Schofield (Cook); Archie Gordon (Jabberwock); Dan Leon, Jr. (Red King/Caterpillar); Master Joe Carr (Unicorn); Master Tom Hall (Lion); Bertha Schwartz (White Rabbit/Oyster); Dorothy Edward, Phyllis Munro (Lobsters); Ada Danks (Lily/ Fairy); Crystal Hetherington (Rose); Gladys Barnard (Dormouse/ Oyster); Doris Walker (March Hare/Sailor Boy); Dorothy Edward, Phyllis Munro, Elsie Sawyer, Doris Kent, Ireland, Ibberson, Major, Vivian, Molteno, Munro, Milne, Morgan, Popham, Yates, Trueman, Desmond, Coates, Woodford, Jeason, Sutton, Simpson, Bergin, Naylor (Ensemble)

Savoy Theatre, London, opened December 26, 1910
Produced by Leigh and Neeves; A Dramatization by H. Saville Clark of the book by Lewis Carroll; Music by Walter Slaughter

Ivy Sawyer (Alice); Ella Anderson (Queen of Hearts/ White Queen); Maisie Riversdale (Duchess/Red Queen); Franklyn Vernon (Mad Hatter); Roland Henry (Mock Turtle/Tweedledee); Leedam Stanley (Tweedledum/ Gryphon); Dan Leno (Red King/Caterpillar); Bryan O'Sullivan (King of Hearts/Walrus); Alex M. Lee (Carpenter/ Humpty Dumpty/ Executioner); Christine Jensen (White Rabbit/ Oyster); Doris Walker (March Hare); Yvonne Schofield (Cook); Bertha Schwartz (Cheshire Cat/Oyster); Mattie Block (Dormouse); Hilda Boot (Lobster/Oyster); Viloet Danzel (Fairy); Roy Jefferies (Knave of Hearts/White King); Elaine Lea (Lily); Winifred Linder (Rose); Master Friston (Unicorn); Master Board (Lion)

Lyceum Theatre, New York, opened October 27, 1911
A one-act political skit by Laurence Housman

Eva Moore (Alice); Ernest Thesiger (The Mad Hatter); T. N. Weguelin (The March Hare); Lytton Grey (The Dormouse); W. G. Fay (Bill, the Lizard)

Booth Theatre, New York, opened March 23, 1915 20 performances; moved to *Hudson Theatre*, April 5, 1915 5 matinee performances
Produced by The Players' Producing Company; Director, W. H. Gilmore; A dramatization by Alice Gerstenberg, adapted from Lewis Carroll's *Alice in Wonderland* and *Through the Looking Glass*; Scenery and Costumes by William Penhallow Henderson; Music by Eric Delamater

Vivian Tobin (Alice); Frank Stirling (Reverend Lewis Carroll); Bernice Golden (White Queen); Florence LeClercq (Red Queen); Tommy Tobin (White Rabbit); Alfred Donohoe (Humpty Dumpty); Geoffrey Stein (Mad Hatter/Mock Turtle); Fred W. Permain (March Hare/ Gryphon); Walter Kingsford (Frog Footman/Caterpillar); J. Gunnis Davis (Dormouse); Kenyon Bishop (Duchess); Frederick Annerly (King of Hearts); Winifred Hanley (Queen of Hearts); Foxhall Daingerfield (Knave of Hearts); Alfred Donohue (Cheshire Cat); Joe Barlow (Two of Spades); George Ross (Five of Spades); G. Berliner (Seven of Spades)

Little Theatre, New York, opened April 12, 1920
Produced by Rachel Barton Butler; A Play by Rachel Barton Butler, adapted from the book by Lewis Carroll; Directors, Boyd Agin and Rachel Barton Butler

Mabel Taliaferro (Alice); Boyd Agin (Mad Hatter); William Barton (King of Hearts); Elizabeth Patterson (Queen of Hearts); Carl Reed (The March Hare); Lenard Meeker (The Cheshire Cat); Winona Shannon (Alice's Sister); George Doty (White Rabbit); Morgan Farlay (Caterpillar); Edward Beryl (The Gryphon); Richard Dore (The Mock Turtle); Thomas Knox (The Dormouse); Carlotta Irwin (The Duchess)

Garrick Theatre, London, opened December 23, 1921 24 matinee performances
Produced by Herbert Cottesmore; A Musical Play based on Lewis Carroll's *Alice in Wonderland* and *Through the Looking Glass*; Director, Archibald H. Griffiths; Book and Lyrics by H. Saville Clarke; Music by Walter Slaughter; Scenery, James Hicks; Choreography, Lilian Leoffeler; Musical director, Leonard Hornsey; Company manager, Harold Carson

Phyllis Griffiths (Alice); C. Hayden Coffin (Mad Hatter); Franklyn Vernon (Mock Turtle/Tweedledee); Harry Hearn (Tweedledum/Gryphon); Nan Gray (White Queen/Queen of Hearts); Grahame Herington (King of Hearts/Walrus); Renee Tocher (Cheshire Cat); Amy Fanchette (Red Queen/Duchess); Betty Russan (White Rabbit); Nora Posford (Dormouse); Milly Escekay (Fairy Queen); Roy Corraine (Caterpillar/Red King); Reg Read (White King/Knave of Hearts); Evelyn Colyer (Rose); Clara Dance (Lily); Kitty Vaines (Guardian of the Shell Throne); Gertude Martin (Oyster Queen); Elsie Hutchings, Rowena Hakbly (Oysters); George Benson (Carpenter/Executioner); Madge Wright (March Hare); Linda Lindus (Cook); Gladys Dixon (Lobster); Jean Mudie (Green Man)

Court Theatre, London, opened December 26, 1922 23 matinee performances
Produced by Andre Charlot; A Musical Play based on Lewis Carroll's *Alice in Wonderland* and *Through the Looking Glass*; Book by H. Saville Clarke; Music by Walter Slaughter; Scenery, James Hicks; Costumes, Mrs. Ardley; Music director, Herbert H. Hainton; Choreography, Lilian Loeffeler

Evelyn Joyce (Alice); Nan Gray (White Queen/Queen of Hearts); Edward Sidney (King of Hearts/Carpenter); Franklyn Vernon (Mad Hatter); Nora Posford (White Rabbit); Peggy Ferguson (Red Queen); Clarice Durrant (Dormouse); Thora Swan (March Hare); Harry Hearne (Tweedledee/Gryphon); Bryan O'Sullivan (Tweedledum/ Mock Turtle); George Benson (Walrus/Executioner); Marion Sims (Lily); Eric Sidney (White King); Charles Hersee (Caterpillar); Madge Wright (Cheshire Cat); Kitty Lee (Cook/Guardian of Shell Throne); Haidee Roselle (Lobster/Old Man of the Sea); Gertrude Martin (Oyster Queen); Evelyn Colyer (Rose); Phyllis Griffiths (Fairy Queen)

Golder's Green Theatre, London, opened December 20, 1926
A Musical Dream Play by H. Saville Clark, based on Lewis Carroll's *Alice in Wonderland* and *Through the Looking Glass*; Director, Marshall Moore; Music by Walter Slaughter

Gwen Stella (Alice); C. Hayden Coffin (The Mad Hatter); Muriel Terry (White Queen/Queen of Hearts); Howard Arnell (White King/Knave of Hearts); Leonard Calvert (Mock Turtle/Tweedledum); Cecil G. Calvert (Gryphon/Tweedledee); Theodore Constable (Red King/ Caterpillar); Jean Bruce (Red Queen/The Duchess); Phyllis Jay (March Hare); Ida Millais (The Cook); Phyllis Smiles (White Rabbit); Jean Herbert (Cheshire Cat); Betty Bura (Dormouse); Marie Evans (Fairy Queen); Edward Chester (Carpenter/Executioner); Edward Sydney (Walrus/King of Hearts); Ena Eastland (Duck); Helen Adam (Dodo); Margaret Ralli (The Lily); Alison Ralli (The Rose); C. Edward (Humpty Dumpty); Winnie Esmond, Ruby Cole (Oysters)

Savoy Theatre, London, opened December 23, 1927 25 matinee performances
Produced and Directed by Hugh Marleyn; A Musical Play, based on Lewis Carroll's *Alice in Wonderland* and *Through the Looking Glass*; Book by H. Saville Clarke; Music by Walter Slaughter; Music director, Alexander Humphreys; Choreography, Mme. Varishka; General manager, J. D. Moggridge; Stage manager, Harold Arneil

Myrtle Peter (Alice); Charles Heslop (Mad Hatter); Muriel Terry (White Queen/Queen of Hearts); Ruppet Siddons (King of Hearts/Walrus); Theo Constable (Red King/Knave of Hearts); Ruby Clements (White Rabbit); Joan Hall (Dodo); Reginald Thurgood (Carpenter/ Executioner); Billy Collier (Tweedledum/Gryphon); Billy Fern (Tweedledee/Mock Turtle); Reginald James (Humpty Dumpty); H. Baitchemm (White King); Joan Samman (Duck); Peggy Tindall (Red Queen); Joyce Kirby (Footman/Oyster); Maude Quaife (Rose); Betty Colville (Fairy Queen); Eileen Simmons (Rabbit/ Oyster); Joan Gardner (Mouse/Footman); Doria Carter (Duchess); Phyllis Quaife (Lily); Margaret Bell (Cook); Helen Adam (Cheshire Cat); Cynthia Carlton (March Hare); Wendy Nash (Bunnymum/Narcissue); Flora McLennan (Lizard/Oyster); Peter Michael (Caterpillar); Joyce Vernby (Dormouse)

Savoy Theatre, London, opened December 22. 1930
A Musical Fantasy, adapted from the book by Lewis Carroll; Director, Hugh Marleyn; Music by Hugh Marleyn

Joy Blackwood (Alice); Eileen Rice (The White Rabbit); Ronald Brandon (White Knight/The Mad Hatter); Doria Carte (The Red Queen/Duchess); Dickie Pounds (The March Hare); Swailes Atkinson (The Red King/The Knave of Hearts); Sheila Roy (The White Queen/Queen of Hearts); Yootha Rose (The Cheshire Cat); Iris Terry (The Rose); Lionel Edward (Caterpillar/The Jabberwock); Joyce Grundy (Dodo); Brownie Woolsey (Cook); Fred W. Ring (The King of Hearts/The Walrus); Billy Collier (Tweedledum/The Gryphon); Basil Cooper (Tweedledee/The Mock Turtle); Dagmar Mann (The Violet); Queenie Johnstone (The Tiger Lily); Alexander Franks (The Carpenter/Humpty Dumpty); Joan Kent (Mickey Mouse); Georgina Graham (Lory); Molly Keenan (Fish); Marny Trinder (Bunnymum/The Daisy); Peggy Johnson Smith (Footman); Renee Stirling (Kitchen Maid); Anne Nash (Duchess' Attendant); Pat Wilcocks (Wraith); Lena Martin (Lizard); Sheila Bain (The Dormouse); Maisie Thompson (Red Knight's Esquire); Margaret Sinclair (Red Knight's Attendant); Dot Rickenson (Solo Dancer); Phylliss Bedells (Premiere Danseuse); Hugh Marleyn (The Red Knight)

Jordan Hall, Boston, season 1931-32

Produced under the auspices of the Boston University Women's Council; A Dramatization of the story by Lewis Carroll, written, produced and directed by Clare Tree Major; Settings, Irving Morrow; Costumes, Marion DePew

Dorothy Major (Alice); Ian Martin (White Rabbit); Arthur Kennedy (Fish Footman); Dorothy Slaytor (Queen of Hearts); Phillippa Bevans (Duchess); Frederick Leland (Mad Hatter); John Marshall (King of Hearts); Joseph Hunter (Gryphon); Hayes Moore (Mock Turtle); Sara Dwight (Red Queen); Polly Boynton (White Queen); John M. O'Connor (White King); John Hampshire (Frog Footman/March Hare); Ian Martin (Tweedledee); Frederick Leland (Tweedledum); Richard O'Leary (Dormouse/Knave of Hearts)

ALICE IN WONDERLAND AND THROUGH THE LOOKING GLASS, Civic Repertory Theatre, New York, opened December 12, 1932; moved to *New Amsterdam Theatre*, January 20, 1933 127 performances

Produced and directed by Eva Le Gallienne; Adapted for the stage by Eva Le Gallienne and Florida Friebus; Scenery and Costumes designed by Irene Sharaff, after John Tenniel; Animal heads, masks and marionettes by Remo Bufano; Choreography, Ruth Wilton; Orchestra director, Sig Sanders; Flying effects by Fred Schultz

Josephine Hutchinson (Alice); Eva Le Gallienne (White Chess Queen); Joseph Schildkraut (Queen of Hearts); Florida Friebus (Cheshire Cat/Beetle); Tonio Selwart (Fish Footman); Robert F. Ross (Frog Footman/Gentleman Dressed in White); Walter Beck (Lory/Humpty Dumpty); Leona Roberts (Red Chess Queen); Richard Waring (White Rabbit/Goat); Howard da Silva (White Knight/Cook); Burgess Meredith (Tweedledee/Duck/Dormouse); Landon Herrick (Tweedledum/Mad Hatter); Lester Scharff (Mock Turtle); Joseph Kramm (Dodo); Nelson Welch (Mouse/Gryphon); Harold Moulton (King of Hearts); Robert H. Gordon (Eaglet/Train Guard); Margaret Love (Sheep); Sayre Crawley (Caterpillar); Charles Ellis (Duchess); May Sarton (Gnat); David Marks (Two of Spades); Arthur Swensen (Five of Spades); Donald Cameron (March Hare); Whitner Bissell (Seven of Spades); David Turk (Knave of Hearts); Agnes McCarthy (Gentle Voice); William S. Phillips (Horse-Front Legs); David Nathan (Horse-Back Legs); Ruth Wilton, Adelaide Finch (Singers); Tittoni, Ballantyne, Fox, Cotsworth, Pollock, Scourby, Milne, Marsden, Leonard (Hearts); Jacobson, Lloyd, Green, Dwenger (Clubs); English, Beck, Snaylor, Nurenburg, Hill, Tittoni, Marsden, Bauer, Pollock, (Marionette Workers); A. Spolidoro (Marionette Supervisor); Freddy Rendulic, Doris Sawyer (White Rabbit alternates)

Little Theatre, London, opened December 21, 1932

An Fantasy based on the book by Lewis Carroll, adapted for the stage and directed by Nancy Price

Beryl Laverick (Alice); Frederick Peisley (White Rabbit); Gipsy Raine (Caterpillar); George Hayes (Mad Hatter); Frank Birch (March Hare); Norman Page (Cheshire Cat); Vivienne Chatterton (Duchess); Elizabeth Maude (Queen of Hearts); John Smart (King of Hearts); George Thirlwell (Knave of Hearts/A Dodo); Peter Penrose (The Executioner); Noel Campbell (Mr. Penguin/Frog Footman/Gardener Seven); John Cannon (Fish Footman); Renee Gill (Dormouse/ Bill); Wilfred Babbage (Gryphon/Gardener Four); Kenneth Howell (Mock Turtle/Gardener Two); Joyce Mackie (A Mouse); Jack Skinner (A Snail);

Bunty Bruce (Duck/A Cook); Amy Dalby (Miss Penguin); John Martland (Gardener Five)

ALICE THROUGH THE LOOKING GLASS, *Little Theatre*, London, opened December 21, 1936

A Musical Fantasy based on the book by Lewis Carroll; adapted for the stage and directed by Nancy Price; Music by Jonathan Field

Ursula Hanray (Alice); Elizabeth Maude (White Queen/ Sheep); Fred O'Donovan (White King); Joyce Redman (Tiger Lily/Beetle); Sheila Kay (Tiger Lily/Gnat); May Hallatt (Red Queen); Dennis Allen (Gentleman in White); Andrew Leigh (Tweedledum); Ernest Butcher (Tweedledee); Esme Percy (Humpty Dumpty); Paul Peters (Hatta); Alvina Mullins (Larkspur); Paul Stephenson (Unicorn); Robert Syers (Lion); Ronald Sidney (Red Knight); Wilfred Fletcher (White Knight); Robert Syers (Frog Gardener); Pat Haseltine, Eileen Hicks (Roses); Doreen Lotinga (Violet); Gladys Kent, Betty Thurgood (Daisies); Edward Swinton (Anglo-Saxon Messenger/Guard); Paul Peters, Pin White (White Knight's Horse); David Lewis, Robert Syers (Red Knight's Horse); Vi-Va Young (3rd Tiger Lily)

ALICE THROUGH THE LOOKING GLASS, *Playhouse Theatre*, London, opened December 21, 1938

A Musical Fantasy based on the book by Lewis Carroll, adapted for the stage and directed by Nancy Price; Music by Jonathan Field

Rowena Sanders (Alice); Margaret Halstan (White Queen/Sheep); Margery Bryce (Red Queen); Frank Tickle (Tweedledee/Humpty Dumpty); Andrew Leigh (Tweedledum); Robert Ginns (White King); Valerie Tempess (Larkspur); Esther Morris (Beetle/Horse); Gordon Edwards (Unicorn); Eric Micklewood, Joseph Chelton (White Horse); John Christian, John Wharton (Red Horse); Patricia Fox, Audrey Phelps (Roses); Betty Butler, Pamela Metcalfe (Tiger Lilies); Avril Kentridge (Spider/Tiger Lily); June Lloyd (Violet/ Gnat); Peter Morton (Drummer/ Gentleman in White); Frank Birch (King Messenger-One to Come-March Hare); Peter Gray (King's Messenger-One to Go-Mad Hatter); Nancy Jeffries (Dormouse/Daisy/Guard); Eileen Olliffe (Midge/Daisy); Robert Syen (Lion/Frog Gardener)

ALICE IN WONDERLAND and THROUGH THE LOOKING GLASS, *"Q" Theatre*, London, opened December 23, 1938

A Play based on the books by Lewis Carroll; Adapted for the stage and directed by Ronald Kerr

Joyce Redman (Alice); Margaret Yarde (Queen of Hearts); Leo Gavronsky (King of Hearts); Viola Compton (White Queen); Molly Raynor (Red Queen/ Duchess); W. G. Manning (White Rabbit/Tweedledee); Kenneth Howell (King of Hearts/Caterpillar); Paul Martin (Frog Footman/ Gardener/ Carpenter/ Executioner); J. Hwfa Pryse (Cat/White Knight); S. Greenhalgh (Cook/Tiger Lily); P. Featherstonbaugh (Dormouse/Daisy); S. A. Baily (Lizard/Gardener); John Hewitt, Paul Martin (Horse)

ALICE IN WONDERLAND and THROUGH THE LOOKING GLASS, *Scala Theatre*, London, opened December 24, 1943

Produced by Tom Arnold and Ivor Novello; A Play by Clemence Dane based on the stories by Lewis Carroll; Director, Esme Church; Decor (after Tenniel) by Gladys

Calthrop; Music by Richard Addinsell; Music director, Muir Mathieson; Choreography, Andree Howard; Stage director, Peter Yardley; Orchestra Conductor, Reginald Goodall; Masks by H. Skillan, M. Manasse and Peggy Keeling; Lighting, Stanley Earnshaw; Flying by Kirby; Creature bodies by F. H, Drummond and Peggy Keeling; Stage managers, Ames Fraser and Peter Rich

Alice in Wonderland: Roma Beaumont (Alice); Geoffrey Dunn (Lewis Carroll); Sybil Thorndike (Queen of Hearts); Sidney Young (Mad Hatter); Roy Ellet (March Hare); Franklyn Dyall (King of Hearts/Caterpillar); Eugene Leahy (Gryphon); Kristina Blore (Secunda); Basil Coleman (Cheshire Cat/Mouse); Julian Somers (White Rabbit); Richmond Nairn (Knave of Hearts/Two of Spades); Peter Yardley (Seven of Spades); Peter Diminuantes (Mock Turtle); Elizabeth Aicken (Prima/ Guinea Pig); Philip Desborough (Dodo); Ronald Bruce (Duck); Petrena Lowthian (Dormouse/Baby Crab); Ann Bibby (Crab); Deri Vaughan Roberts (Eagle/Five of Spades); Peter Murray (Executioner); Phyllis Morris (Duchess); Daphne Anderson (Father William); Barry Gasney (Lory); Felicity Andreae (Young Man); Hugh Thurston (Frog Footman); Antony Groser (Fish Footman); Carol Dodgson (Cook)

Alice Through the Looking Glass: Roma Beaumont (Alice); Sybil Thorndike (White Queen); Zena Dare (Red Queen); Julian Somers (Humpty Dumpty); Philip Desborough (White King); Geoffrey Dunn (White Knight); Roy Ellet (Hayha); Sidney Young (Hatta); Eugene Leahy (Lion); Basil Coleman (Unicorn); Elizabeth Aicken (Prima); Kristina Blore (Secunda); Daphne Anderson (Walrus); Felicity Andreae (Carpenter); James Fraser (Red King); Phyllis Morris (Sheep); Peter Dimunantes (Tweedledum); Peter Murray (Tweedledee); Hugh Thurston (Creature); James Fraser, Ronald Bruce, Hugo Squire, Allen Brown, Jonathan Heddings (Soldiers); Geoffrey Dunn (Lewis Carroll)

MUSICAL NUMBERS: "A Boat Beneath a Sunny Sky"; "How Doth the Little Crocodile"; "You Are Old Father William"; "Speak Roughly to Your Little Boy"; "Lobster Quadrille"; "Beautiful Soup"; "White Rabbit's Song"; "Tweedledum and Tweedledee"; "The Walrus and the Carpenter"; "Humpty Dumpty Sat on a Wall"; "The Lion and the Unicorn"; "The White Knight's Song"; "Hush-a-by Lady in Alice's Lap"; "To the Looking Glass World"; "A Boat Beneath a Sunny Sky" (reprise)

ALICE IN WONDERLAND and THROUGH THE LOOKING GLASS, "Q" Theatre, London, opened December 22, 1944

A dramatized version by Herbert M. Prentice of the books by Lewis Carroll; Director, Ronald Kerr

Pamela Carroll (Alice); John Denis (White Rabbit/ Tweedledum); Sidney Bromley (Cheshire Cat/White Knight/Tweedledee); Helen Goss (White Queen/ Duchess); Julian Somers (Mad Hatter/Humpty Dumpty); Tom Ferriman (March Hare/Mock Turtle); Michael Whitaker (Caterpillar/Gryphon); Gordon Phillott (Cook/ Walrus/Gardener); Deidre Doyle (Red Queen/Queen of Hearts); Margaret Cooper (Dormouse/ Violet); Arthur Goullet (King of Hearts); Erica Sartrelli (Tiger Lily); June Carlyle (Rose); Jacqueline Ashman (Daisy); Natasha Sokolova (Dancer); W. Fraser-Brunner (Frog Footman/Carpenter/ Gardener); Oliver Trenner (Fish Footman/Gardener); Pat Rutherford (Knave of Hearts); Robert Hayley (Executioner)

ALICE IN WONDERLAND, Palace Theatre, London, opened December 26, 1944

Produced by Tom Arnold and Ivor Novello; A Play by Clemence Dane based on the stories by Lewis Carroll; Director, Esme Church; Decor (after Tenniel) by Gladys

Calthrop; Music by Richard Addinsell; Music director, Muir Mathieson; Choreography, Andree Howard; Orchestra Conductor, Reginald Goodall

Peggy Cummins (Alice); Graham Payne (Lewis Carroll/ Mock Turtle/ Tweedledum); Sybil Thorndike (Queen of Hearts/ White Queen); Kynaston Reeves (Mad Hatter/ Hatta); Billy Thatcher (March Hare/ Hayha); Arthur Young (King of Hearts); Firth Banbury (White Rabbit/ White Knight); Robert Beaumont (Caterpillar/ Humpty Dumpty/Two of Spades); Peter Doughty (Gryphon/Lion); Maurice Bannister (Tweedledee); Irene Browne (White Queen); Sonia Williams (Secunda/ Cook); Basil Coleman (Cheshire Cat/Mouse/Unicorn); Kenneth Carten (Knave of Hearts/White King); Michael Napper (Seven of Spades/Red King); Arthur Young (King of Hearts); Dennis Carlile (Dormouse); Norman Webb (Dodo); Rupert White (Five of Spades); Ronald Bruce (Father William/Duck/Walrus); John Baker (Eagle); Raymond Farrell (Carpenter/Young Man); Rex Fagen (Lory); Diana Court (Baby Crab); Maidie Andrews (Duchess/Ship); Martin Beckwith (Executioner); Michael Ward (Frog Footman); Stewart Easton (Fish Footman); Jose Waterhouse (Prima); Nena Alvis (Guinea Pig/Oyster); John Cruise, John Spinks (Horse)

ALICE IN THUNDERLAND, *Unity Theatre*, London, opened June 14, 1945
A Political Fantasia by Bill Rowbotham, based on characters created by Lewis Carroll; Director, Bernard Sarron; Music by Ben Norris and Bill Rowbotham

Audrey Hale (Alice); Frank Godwin (Bunny); Una Brandon Jones (Queen); Hazel Wallace (Duchess); Joe Levine (Mad Hatter); Mark Cheney (March Hare); Henry Marshall (Not-So-Simple Simon); John Oliver (King/ Ghost 18B); John Elliot (Dormouse/Second Footman); Bob Gorely (Cheshire Cat/Third Gardener); Elsie Chisnall (Nippy); Charles Warren (Photographer/First Gardener); Alfie Bass (Rooky); Corinthia Lane (Justice); Harry Landis (Too/Second Gardener); Reg Bridger (Worker's Leader); Anne Godwin (Technicolor Tessie); Fred Lazarus (Cook); John North, Leslie Wynyard (Painters); Howard Mann (Clerk of the Court/Announcer/First Footman)

ALICE THROUGH THE LOOKING GLASS, *"Q" Theatre*, London, opened December 24, 1947
A Play for children from the book by Lewis Carroll; Adapted for the stage and directed by Nancy Price

Adrienne Corri (Alice); Elizabeth Maude (White Queen/Sheep); John Edmund (White King); Margery Bryce (Red Queen); Desmond Walter-Ellis (Mad Hatter); Eric Chatty (March Hare); Esme Percy (Humpty Dumpty); Duncan Ross (Unicorn); Andrew Leigh (Tweedledum); Dudley Jones (Tweedledee); Muriel Gleed (Dormouse); Jennifer Fowler (Gant); Jeanne Cryer (Beetle); Jennifer Bush (Spider); John Bass (Horse); Stonor Spiv (Kitten); Anne Somerset, Jean Kutner (Tiger Lilies); Elsie Pinkney, Mary Jenkins (Roses); Mary Labies (Violet); Jane Baylis, Cecile Everard (Daisies); Lita Tovey (Larkspur/Gentleman in White); William Douglas (Lion/Guard); William Douglas, Michael Eversfield (Red Horse); Duncan Ross, Leslie Pitt (White Horse); Leslie Pitt (Frog Gardener)

ALICE IN WONDERLAND and THROUGH THE LOOKING GLASS, *International Theatre*, New York, opened April 5, 1947; moved to *Majestic Theatre*, May 29, 1947
97 performances
Produced by Rita Hassan and The American Repertory Theatre; A play, adapted for the stage by Eva Le Gallienne and Florida Friebus based on Lewis Carroll's books

and the drawings of Tenniel; Production devised and directed by Eva Le Gallienne; Scenery by Robert Rowe Paddock; Costumes by Noel Taylor; Masks and Marionettes, Remo Bufano; Music by Richard Addinsell; Choreography, Ruth Wilton; Conductor, Tibor Kozma; Marionettes operated under the direction of A. Spolidoro

Bambi Linn (Alice); Eva Le Gallienne (White Chess Queen); Julie Harris or William Windom (White Rabbit); Richard Waring (Mad Hatter); Margaret Webster (Red Chess Queen); Philip Bourneuf (White Knight); Robert Rawlings (Tweedledum/ Frog Footman/ Five of Spades); Jack Manning (Tweedledee/ Gryphon); Henry Jones (Humpty Dumpty/ Mouse); John Straub (Dod/ Train Guard/ Seven of Clubs); Angus Cairns (Lory/ Mock Turtle/ Gentle Voices); Eli Wallach (Duck/ Two of Spades/Voice); John Becher (Queen of Hearts); Don Allen (Crab/ Cook/ Dormouse/ Goat); Arthur Keegan (Eaglet/ March Hare); Theodore Tenley (Caterpillar/ Sheep); Ed Woodhead (Fish Footman); Raymond Greenleaf (Duchess); Donald Keyes (Cheshire Cat/ Seven of Spades/ Old Frog); Eugene Stuckmann (King of Hearts); Frederick Hunter (Knave of Hearts); John Behney (Two of Clubs); Bart Henderson (Five of Clubs); Thomas Grace (Nine of Clubs); William Windom (Gentleman in White Paper); Donald Keyes (Beetle Voice); Cavada Humphrey (Gnat Voice); Mary Alice Moore (Other Voice); Charles Townley, Will Davis (Horse); Eloise Roehm, Mara Lunden (Singers); Don Allen, Robert Carlson, Michel Corhan, Will Davis, Robert Leser, Gerald McCormack, Walter Neal, James Rafferty, Dan Scott, Charles Townley (Hearts)

Arena Stage, Washington, opened December 18, 1950
Produced by the Arena Stage Company; A Play by Edward Mangum and Zelda Fichandler, based on Lewis Carroll's *Alice in Wonderland*; Director, Edward Mangum; Technical director, Vera Mowry; Dances by Barbara Cole; Music, Albert Berkowitz; Lighting, Leo Gallenstein; Staff assistants, Fred Chubb, Augusta Convisser, George Grizzard, Hilary Knapp, Pernell Roberts, Sallie Smith; Stage manager, Warner Schreiner

Mary Mangum (Alice); George Grizzard (White Rabbit); Warner Schreiner (Mad Hatter/White Knight/Gryophon); Harry Scully (Queen of Hearts); Dick O'Neill (King of Hearts/Tweedledee); Barbara Cole (Knave of Hearts); Lois Copenhaver (Dormouse); Henry Danilowicz (Caterpillar/March Hare); Lester Rawlins (Duchess/Mock Turtle); Jacqueline Dudley (Red Queen); Henry Oliver (Tweedledum/Humpty Dumpty); Mary Pray Conlin (White Queen); Henry Oliver, Lester Rawlins (Cards)

ALICE IN WONDERLAND--A DREAM WITH MUSIC, Touring company, summer 1951
Produced by Theron Bamberger; A Musical play adapted from Lewis Carroll's *Alice in Wonderland* and *Through the Looking Glass*; Book and Lyrics by Frances Pole; Music by John Charles Sacco; Director, Robert E. Perry; Settings, Richard V. Hare; Costumes, Frances Pole; Choreography, Virginia Johnson; Production supervisor, John Huntington

Florence Forsberg (Alice); Ruth White (White Queen); William Krach (Dodgson/The White Knight); Roy Raymond (Canon Duckworth/The Mock Turtle); Bruce Adams (The Nurse/The Duchess); Gene Blakely (Miss Dodgson/The Red Queen); Ronald Telfer (The White Rabbit); John Henson (The Gryphon); John Dooley (The Mad Hatter); William Ryan (March Hare); Jane Ball (Dormouse); Don Markley (Dodo); Ray Sharp (Frog); Trudy Prager (Pigeon); Joyce Guthrie (Pig); Kitty Cooper (Goat); Russell Oberlin (Fish); Katherine

Harvey (A Bee); Carl White (Humpty Dumpty); Jean Colligan (Mouse); Jane Ball, Jean Colligan, Katherine Harvey, Russell Oberlin, Ray Sharp, Trudy Prager (The Playing Cards); Harry Fuquay and George West (Pianists)

MUSICAL NUMBERS: "Looking Glass World"; "Fill Up Your Glasses"; "Wonderland"; "The Time Has Come"; "Fiddle Faddle Fee"; "If"; "Time's a This and That"; "I Wonder"; "A-Sittin' on the Gate"; "Come Dance With Me"; "Beautiful Soup"; "Speak Roughly"; "The Walrus and the Carpenter"; "Croquet Polka"; "Hippity Hay"; "They Told Me"; "Chop! Chop! Chop!"; "Jabberwocky"; "Lobster Quadrille"; Humpty Dumpty's Requiem"; "Coronation Waltz"

ALICE IN WONDERLAND and THROUGH THE LOOKING GLASS, "Q" Theatre, London, opened December 22, 1953

An adaptation of Lewis Carroll's books; Director, Jonathan Field

Julia Lockwood (Alice); Norman Osborne (White Rabbit/White King); Maidie Andrews (White Queen/ Duchess); Wynne Clark (Red Queen/Queen of Hearts); Gordon Whiting (Cheshire Cat/Gryphon/Humpty Dumpty); Billy Thatcher (Caterpillar/March Hare/Tweedledum); Jonathan Field (King of Hearts/ Tweedledee); Peter Butterworth (Mad Hatter/White Knight); David Scott (Fish Footman/Knave of Hearts); David Howarth (Cook); Rosemary Giles (Dormouse/ Old Gentleman/Pudding/Gardener); Ann Norcombe (Leg of Mutton/Daisy/ Gardener); Rosemary Whitbread (Larkspur/Signpost); Susannah Clay (Guard/ Violet); Frank Atkinson (Frog Footman/Mock Turtle); Anneke Willys (Executioner/ Tiger Lily); Ann Norcombe, Susannah Clay (Passengers); David Howarth, Norman Pepperell (Horse); Diane West (Soldier/Rose)

ALICE THROUGH THE LOOKING GLASS, Prince's Theatre, London, opened February 20, 1954

Produced by Ralph Birch; An Musical adaptation of Lewis Carroll's book; Director, Toby Robertson; Music by David King and Raymond Leppard; Book and Lyrics by Felicity Douglas; Choreographer, John Cranko

Carol Marsh (Alice); Margaret Rutherford (White Queen); Binnie Hale (Red Queen); Michael Dennison (White Knight/Humpty Dumpty/Tweedledee); Griffith Jones (Tweedledum/Red Knight); Walter Crisham (Haigha/Tiger Lily/Horse); Timothy Forbes Adam (Frog Footman); Joyce Graeme (Unicorn/Carpenter); Anne Lascelles (Lion/Walrus); Stringer Davis (White King)

ALICE THROUGH THE LOOKING GLASS, Chelsea Palace Theatre, London, opened December 26, 1955

A Play based on the book by Lewis Carroll; Adapted for the stage and directed by Felicity Douglas; Music by David King

Juliet Mills (Alice); Keslie Henson (White King/ Frog Footman); Binnie Hale (Red Queen); Dulcie Gray (White Queen); Ian Holm (Red King/Guard/Red Castle); Walter Crisham (Tiger Lily/Haigha); Tita Dane (The Rose/Goat); Desmond Walter Ellie (Red Knight/ Tweedledum); Michael Denison (Humpty Dumpty/ Tweedledee); Barry Wade (Hatta/Gentleman in Paper); Isabel Falkner (Beetle/Singer); Lisa Thawnton (Carpenter/First Daisy); Wendy McClure (Unicorn/ Second Daisy); William Lawford (White Bishop/Horse/ Walrus); Gillian Town (Pansy)

Winter Garden Theatre, London, opened December 26, 1959

Produced by Maurice Winnick, in association with the Company of Three Ltd; A

Musical version of Lewis Carroll's story adapted by Philip Beresford; Director, Stanley WillisCroft; Music by Arthur Furby; Choreography and musical staging by Frank Harwood

Delene Scott (Alice); John English (Lewis Carroll); Charlotte Selwyn (Lorina); Richard Goolden (The White Rabbit); Binnie Hale (Queen of Hearts/The Duchess); Frankie Howerd (Mock Turtle/The Caterpillar/The Mad Hatter); Ken Tyllsen (Mouse/ Dormouse); Brian Faubert (Five of Spades/The Skunk); Jack Raynes (Knave of Hearts/Father William/The Owl); Barry Wade (Seven of Spades/Frog Footman/ Gryphon); John English (Cheshire Cat/The Dodo); Desmond WalterEllis (March Hare/Fish Footman/King of Hearts); Heather Astral (The Chick); Patricia Kerry (The Squirrel); Carlotta Barrow (The Hen); Pearson Dodd (The Lizard); Pamela Tagg (The Goose); Elizabeth Wade (The Mother Crab); Dorothy Williams (Baby Crab/Hedgehog); Howard Taylor (The Eagle/ Executioner); Kay Clayton (Cook/Toucan); Sonya Petrie (Parrot); Richard Keenes (Monkey); Dudley Stevens (Cockerel); Charlott Selwyn (The Lory); Diana Field (Duck); Pearson Dodd, Dudley Stevens, Richard Keenes, Ken Tyllsen, Kay Clayton (Soldiers); Heather Astral, Carlotta Barrow, Sonya Petrie (Drummer Boys); Charlotte Selwyn, Elizabeth Wade, Patricia Kerry, Diana Field (Court Ladies); Jack Raynes, Howard Taylor, Dudley Stevens, Richard Keenes, Ken Tyllsen, Pearson Dodd (Lobsters); Diana Field, Charlotte Selwyn, Patricia Kerry, Heather Astral, Carlota Barrow, Sonya Petrie (Fishes)

THROUGH THE LOOKING GLASS, Lyric Theatre Hammersmith, London, opened December 21, 1961

A Play by Felicity Douglas, adapted from the book by Lewis Carroll; Director, Toby Robertson; Music by David King; Production designer, Michael Baldwin

Lucinda Curtis (Alice); Moyra Fraser (The Red Queen); Lally Nowers (The White Queen); Christopher Guinee (The Red Knight/Tweedledee/Old Gentleman in Newspaper/The White King); Mike Hall (Tweedledum/ Frog Footman); Edgar Wreford (Humpty Dumpty/The White Knight); Patricia Cassie (The Walrus/The Unicorn/Daisy); Sylvia Ellis (The Carpenter/Daisy/ The Lion); Gloria Lytton (White Bishop/Daisy); Roland Curram (Tiger Lily/Goat/Haigha); Elizabeth Proud (Rose); Phoebe Coleman (Beetle); Michael Dawson (Horse/The Red King/Red Castle); Michael Wells (Guard/Hatta)

BUT NEVER JAM TODAY, New York City Center, opened April 23, 1969

Produced by the City Center of Music and Drama, Norman Singer, General Administrator; Production of the AfroAmerican Folkloric Troupe and Series of Afro-American Plays; An Afro-American adaptation of Lewis Carroll's *Alice in Wonderland* and *Through the Looking Glass*, conceived and directed by Vinnette Carroll; Settings, Donald Padgett; Lighting, Marshall Williams; Costumes, K. T. Fries; Choreography, Herman Howell; Music, Gershon Kingsley; Gospel arrangements, Alex Bradford; Additional Music and Lyrics by Robert Lorimer; Drums, Danny Barrajanos; Choreography staged by Talley Beatty; Stage manager, Joseph M. Diaz

Marie Thomas (Alice); Tommy Pinnock (White Rabbit); Sherman Hemsley (Mad Hatter); Marvin Camillo (Caterpillar); Lola Hokman (Cheshire Cat/Gryphon/Two of Spades); Alex Alexander (Queen of Hearts/Mock Turtle/Five of Spades); Joseph Perry (Black Queen); Cynthia Towns (Duchess/White Queen); Thelma Drayton (March Hare); Danny Barrajanos (Herald); Wai Ching Ho (Dormouse); Verna Gillis, Winston Savage (Cooks); Sherman Hemsley (Seven of Spades); Sterling Roberts (King of Hearts); Burt Rodriguez (Knave of Hearts); Marvin

Camillo (Humpty Dumpty); Angel Caballero, Johnny Harris, Ernest Holly (Citizens of Wonderland); Charles Augins, Glen Augins, Glen Brooks, Annette Brown, Delores Brown, Matt Cameron, Hope Clarke, Jaquelynne Curry, Trina Frazier, Joan Peters, Gail Reese, Danny Sloan, Andy Torres (Dancers and Members of the Jury)

NOTE: This production was restaged as *Alice* at the *Forrest Theatre*, Philadelphia, opening May 31 through June 11, 1978 (see below)

ALICE IN WONDERLAND, *The Extension Theatre*, New York, opened October 8, 1970 122 performances (weekends only)

An New York USOA Theatre Company Manhattan Project; Produced by Lyn Austin and Olive Smith; Adapted from the writings of Lewis Carroll by the Manhattan Project Company; Director, Andre Gregory; Production designers, Eugene Lee and Franne Newman; Translator, Kenneth Cavander; Stage manager, John P. Holms

Gerry Bamman, Tom Costello, Saskia Noordhock Hegt, Cecil MacKinnon, Jerry Mayer, Angela Pietropinto, Larry Pine

THROUGH THE LOOKING GLASS, *Ashcroft Theatre*, Croydon, England, opened December 26, 1972

Produced by the Cambridge Theatre Company; An adaptation of the story by Lewis Carroll, written and directed by Felicity Douglas; Production designer, Paul Ford; Choreography, Maggy Maxwell; Musical director and orchestrations by Malcolm Rudland

Alison Frazer (Alice); Dulcie Gray (White Queen); Michael Denison (White Knight/Tweedledee); Henry Moxon (White King/Frog Footman); Daphne Anderson (Red Queen); John Vine (Red King/Goat/Red Castle); Kleshna Handel (Lion/Daisy/Carpenter); Michael Graham Cox (Humpty Dumpty/Red Knight/ Tweedledum); Hamish Patrick (White Bishop/Train Guard); John Halstead (Tiger Lily/Haigha/Engine Driver); Stanley Bates (Walrus/Hatta/Gentleman in Newspaper); Jill Streatfield (Daisy/Unicorn); Jill Stanford (Rose); Susan Brown (Beetle)

ALICE IN WONDERLAND, *Bil Baird Theatre*, New York, opened March 1, 1975 51 performances; Reopened November 2, 1975 87 performances

Produced by the American Puppet Arts Council, Arthur Cantor, executive producer; A Musical Play with Bil Baird's Marionettes; Produced and designed after Tenniel's drawings by Bil Baird; Director, Paul Leaf; Book by A. J. Russell; Music by Joe Raposo; Lyrics by Sheldon Harnick; Scenery, Howard Mandel; Lighting, Peggy Clark; Artistic associates, Frank Sullivan and Carl Harms; Associate producer, Susanna Lloyd Baird; Production managers, Arthur Cantor and George Wallace; Performed with *Bil Baird's Variety*

Puppeteers: Rebecca Bondor (Alice/Cheshire Cat/ Turtle/ Dormouse/ Whiting/ Second Creature); Peter Baird (White Rabbit/ Tweedledee/ Frog Footman/ Lobster/ Violet/ First Creature); Steven Hansen (Walrus/ Duchess/ Knave of Hearts/ Humpty Dumpty/ March Hare/ Five of Spades/ Mock Turtle); Wiliam Tost (Fish Footman/ Tweedledum/ Mad Hatter/ King/ Lobster/ Violet); Steven Widerman (Three of Spades/ Executioner/ Cook/ Carpenter/ Violet)

Performers: Mary Case (Alice); Merry Flershem (Person in the Forest)

Singing Voices: George S. Irving (Duchess); Sheldon Harnick (White Rabbit/March Hare/Tweedledee); Rose Mary Jun, Ivy Austin, Margery Gray (Violet Trio); William Tost (Mad Hatter/Tweedledum/Whiting); Margery Gray

(Dormouse); Bil Baird (Mock Turtle/ Walrus/Carpenter)

ALICE THROUGH THE LOOKING GLASS, Theatre London, London, Canada, opened December 30, 1976
Produced by Theatre London, Canada; A Play based on the books by Lewis Carroll, adapted and directed by Keith Turnbull; Setting and costumes, Maurice Strike; Lighting, Richard Smerdon; Music, Walter Buczynski; Additional music, Alan Lasing; Musical director, Berthold Carriere; Stage manager, Brian Longstaff

Nancy Beatty (Alice); Richard Curnock (White Queen); David Dodimead (White Knight); Robert Benson (Humpty Dumpty); Gerald Isaac (Tweedledee); Bernard Hopkins (Tweedledum); Graeme Campbell (Caterpillar); Christopher Britton (Tiger Lily); Jack Medley (Red Queen); Peter Elliott (Man in White/Larkspur); Peter Hutt (Red Knight/Rose); Ken A. Smith (Goat/Beaked Gremlin); Keith McNair (Beetle/Frog); Geordie Johnson (Fawn/Pudding/ Guard/Violet); Keith McNair, Ken A. Smith (Daisies); Christopher Britton, Peter Elliott, Peter Hutt, Geordie Johnson, Keith McNair (Gremlins)

ALICE, Forrest Theatre, Philadelphia, opened May 31 through June 11, 1978
Produced by Mike Nichols and Lewis Allen, in association with Urban Arts Corps and Anita MacShane; Conceived, written and directed by Vinnette Carroll from the works of Lewis Carroll; Music and Lyrics by Micki Grant; Settings, Douglas W. Schmidt; Lighting, Jennifer Tipton; Costumes, Nancy Potts; Choreography, Talley Beatty; Orchestrations and Vocal arrangements, H. B. Barnum; Musical director, Joyce Brown; Sound, Abe Jacobs; General managers, Joseph Harris and Ira Bernstein; Stage managers, Robert L. Borod, Alisa Jill Adler, Robert Charles and Kimako

Debbie Allen (Alice); Alice Ghostley (Lily White/ White Queen); Paula Kelly (Regina/Black Queen); Hamilton Camp (Ted White/White King/White Knight); Ronald Dunham (Ronnie); Charlene Harris (Charlie/ Cook); Clinton Derricks-Carroll (Caterpillar/Tweedledum/Fish/Horse); Cleavant Derricks (Tweedledee/ Carpenter/Cook/Horse/Fish); Alberta Bradford (Bartender/Mushroom/Cook); Thomas Pinnock (Gryph/Cook/ Gryphon); Jane White (Duchess); Marilyn Winbush (Waitress); Douglas Houston (Chauffeur/Cook/ Knight); Roumel Reaux (Prima/Cook); Clif DeRaita (Secunda); Christopher Deane (Tertia); Jeffrey Anderson-Gunter (Eric/Cheshire Cat/Mock Turtle); Brenda Braxton, Roslyn Burrough, Nora M. Cole, Christopher Deane, Clif DeRaita, Ronald Dunham, Ralph Farrington, Maggy Gorrill, Charlene Harris, Linda James, Dwayne Phelps, Roumel Reaux Kiki Shepard, Juanita Grace Tyler, Marilynn Winbush, Charles Wynn, Ramon Colon, Debra Lyman (Ensemble)

MUSICAL NUMBERS: "Disco"; "Hall of Mirrors Ballet"; "Father William"; "Chess"; "Workin' for the Man"; "I Am Real"; "Children Are"; "Everybody's Mad"; "Alice"; "Fun and Games"; "It's Lonely"; "Lobster Rock"; "Consider"

ALICE IN CONCERT, Public Theatre, New York, opened December 29, 1980 32 performances
Produced by the New York Shakespeare Festival Theatre; Joseph Papp, Director; A concert version of *Alice in Wonderland* by Lewis Carroll (Previously titled *Wonderland in Concert*); Director, Joseph Papp (replaced Andrei Serban); Book music and lyrics by Elizabeth Swados; Scenery, Michael H. Yeargan; Costumes, Theoni V. Aldredge; Lighting, Arden Fingerhut; Vocal Arrangements, Carolyn Dutton; Musical director, Elizabeth Swados; Choreography, Graciela Daniele; Production stage manager, Richard Jakiel

Meryl Streep (Alice); Betty Aberlin (Edith); Stuart Baker-Bergen (Tweedledum); Richard Cox (Gryphon/ Jabberwock); Sheila Dabney (Queen of Hearts); Rodney Hudson (Cheshire Cat); Michael Jeter (Tweedledee/ Dormouse/Pig Baby); Charles Lanyer (Mad Hatter/King of Hearts); Mark Linn-Baker (White Rabbit/March Hare/Mock Turtle); Kathryn Morath (White Queen); Amanda Plummer (Walrus); Deborah Rush (Red Queen)

Musicians: David Conrad, Carolyn Dutton, Judity Fleisher, Robert J. Magnuson, David Sawyer, William Uttley, Tony Viscardo

MUSICAL NUMBERS: "What There Is" (based on a poem by Kenneth Patchen); "The Rabbit's Excuse"; "Down, Down, Down"; "Drink Me"; "Goodby Feet"; "The Rabbit's House"; "Bill's Lament"; "Caterpillar's Advice"; "Beautiful Soup"; "Wow, Wow, Wow"; "If You Knew Time"; "No Room, No Room"; "Starting Out Again"; "White Roses Red"; "Alphabet"; "Red Queen"; "Never Play Croquet"; "Mock Turtle Lament"; "Eating Mushrooms"; "Child of Pure Unclouded Brow"; "Jabberwocky"; "The Bird Song"; "Humpty Dumpty"; "Tweedledum & Tweedledee"; "The Walrus and the Carpenter"; "The White Queen"; "The White Knight"; "An Aged, Aged Man"; "The Examination"; "The Lion & the Unicorn"; "Queen Alice"; "What Is a Letter?"; "Pretty Piggy"; "Cheshire Puss"; "The Lobster Quadrille"

Virginia Theatre, New York, opened December 23, 1982 21 performances
Produced by Sabra Jones and Anthony D. Marshall in asociation with WNET Television/Thirteen; A Play by Eva Le Gallienne and Florida Freibus adapted from the book by Lewis Carroll; Entire production conceived and directed by Eva Le Gallienne; Assistant director, John Strasberg; Settings, John Lee Beatty; Lighting, Jennifer Tipton; Costumes, Patricia Zipprodt; Animals, William Berloni Theatrical Animals; Tenniel advisor, Sarah Phelps Smith; Music by Richard Addinsell; Music Conductor, Les Scott; Special effects, Chic Silber; Puppets by the Puppet People; Music adapted and supervised by Jonathan Tunick; Movement by Bambi Linn; Sound, Jack Mann; Makeup, Fred Patton; Stage managers, Alan Hall, Ruth E. Rinklin and Skip Harris

Kate Burton (Alice); Eva Le Gallienne (alternate Joan White) (White Queen); Mary Louise Wilson (Red Queen); Richard Woods (King of Hearts/Voice of Humpty Dumpty); Edward Zang (Duchess); John Heffernan (Caterpillar); Robert Ott Boyle (Tweedledum/Five of Spades); John Remme (Tweedledee/ Mouse/Three of Hearts); James Valentine (Mock Turtle/Dodo); Richard Sterne (Cook/Nine of Hearts); Curt Dawson (White Rabbit/White Knight); MacIntyre Dixon (Mad Hatter); Josh Clark (March Hare/Front of Horse); Cliff Rakerd (Seven of Clubs/Back of Horse); Brian Reddy (Queen of Hearts); Rebecca Armen (Eaglet/Two of Hearts); Geoff Garland (Two of Spades); Edward Hibbert (Gryphon/Old Frog); Nancy Killmer (Eight of Hearts/Singer); Nicholas Martin (Duck/Dormouse/Train Guard); Steve Massa (Seven of Spades/Voice of Leg of Mutton); Mary Stuart Masterton (Small White Rabbit/Four of Hearts); John Miglietta (Lory/Seven of Hearts); Marti Morris (Six of Hearts/Singer); Claude-Albert Saucier (Frog Footman/Five of Hearts/ Goat); John Seidman (Knave of Hearts); Geddeth Smith (Fish Footman/Voice of Cheshire Cat/Ace of Hearts/Man in White Paper); Skip Harris (Three of Clubs)

ALICE, Leeds (Eng.) Playhouse, opened March 22, 1984
Produced by The Leeds Playhouse; A Hi-Tech Rock Musical by Richard Scott and Anthony Phillips, based on Lewis Carroll's *Alice in Wonderland*; Director, Nicholas Hytner; Music arranged by Anthony Phillips, John Owen Edwards and Kevin Fitzsimmons; Choreographer, Heather Seymour; Musical director, John Owen

Edwards; Lighting, Tim Thornalley; Sound, John Del'Nero

Sally Ann Triplett (Alice); Bruce Payne (The Mathmagician); Femi Taylor (Queen of Hearts); Michael Skyers (Security); Peter Alex Newton (The Cat); Andy Hampton (Butterfly Williams); Isabelle Lucas (Duchess); Lisa Kent (Doris); Stanley Fleet (Professor Turtle); David Easter (The Hacker); Michael Skyers (The Cook); Jane Danielle (Clare/ Allocatamates); Lisa Dawn-Hart, Lisa Kent, Alan Forrester, Ray Lewis, Rory McDermott (Rebels and Pupils)

ALICE IN WONDERLAND, *Lyric Theatre Hammersmith*, London, opened December 18, 1986

A Play by John Wells, adapted from the story by Lewis Carroll; Director, Ian Forrest; Production designer, Anthony Ward; Lighting, Richard Caswell; Music by Carl Davis; Musical director, Stuart Hutchinson; Movement, Anthony van Laast

Lesley Manville (Alice); Richard Pescud (White Rabbit); Marilyn Cutts (Cheshire Cat/Guinea Pig/ Jane/ Pigeon/Pig/Cat's Mother); Nuala Willis (Queen/ Mouse/Governess); Teddy Kempner (Duck/Frog Footman/ Gardener); Joan Davis (Duchess/Lory); Charles Lewsen (King/Dodo); David Oakley (Eaglet/Dormouse/ Gardener); Michael Mears (Mad Hatter/Soldier/Magpie); John Hall (Cook/Executioner/Canary); Patrick Clancy (Pat/Mole/Knave); Harold Innocent (Caterpillar/Mock Turtle); Terence Hillyer (Fish Footman/Bill the Lizard/Gardener)

SCREEN

ALICE IN WONDERLAND, *Hepworth Films*, England, released May 1903 One reel

Directed by Cecil Hepworth and Percy Stow; Screenplay, Cecil Hepworth, based on the story by Lewis Carroll

May Clark (Alice); Norman Whitten (Mad Hatter/ Fish); Mrs. Cecil Hepworth (White Rabbit/Queen); Cecil Hepworth (Frog); Stanley Faithfull, Geoffrey Faithfull (Cards)

ALICE'S ADVENTURE IN WONDERLAND, *Edison*, released September 1910 One reel

Director, J. Searle Dawley; Based on the novel by Lewis Carroll

Mary Fuller (Alice); Charles Ogle (The White Rabbit)

ALICE IN WONDERLAND, *Nonpareil Feature Film Corp.*, released January 1915

Presented by American Motion Picture Corporation. Picturized by De Witt C. Wheeler; Director and scenario, W.W. Young, based on Lewis Carroll's novels *Alice's Adventures in Wonderland* and *Through the Looking Glass*

Viola Savoy (Alice); Herbert Rice (The White Rabbit); Louis Merkle (The Dormouse); Harry Marks (Dodo)

ALICE'S WONDERLAND, *1923 Newman Laugh-O-Grams*, mini-cartoons made by Walt Disney; Animated and live action; Producer, Walt Disney; Directors, Ub Iwerks, Rudolf Ising; Cast included Virginia Davis (Alice); voices of Walt Disney, Hugh Harman, Ub Iwerks, Rudolf Ising (One reel and less). General Title *ALICE IN CARTOONLAND*

1924
Alice and the Dog Catcher
Alice and the Three Bears
Alice and the Toreador
Alice and the Wild West Show
Alice Cans the Cannibals
Alice in Dutch at School
Alice Hunting in Africa
Alice Plays the Pipers
Alice the Peacemaker
Alice's Day at Sea
Alice's Fishy Story
Alice's Spooky Adventure

1925
Alice Chops the Suey
Alice Gets Stung
Alice in the Jungle
Alice Is Stage Struck
Alice Lose Out
Alice on the Farm
Alice Picks the Champ
Alice Plays Cupid
Alice Rattled by Rats
Alice Solves the Puzzle
Alice the Jail Bird
Alice Wins the Derby
Alice's Balloon Race
Alice's Egg Plant
Alice's Little Parade
Alice's Mysterious Mystery
Alice's Ornery Orphan
Alice's Tin Pany

1926
Alice at the Carnival
Alice at the Rodeo
Alice Charms the Fish
Alice Cuts the Ice
Alice Foils the Pirate
Alice Helps the Romance
Alice in the Alps
Alice in the Big League
Alice in the Klondike
Alice in the Woolly West
Alice the Beach Nut
Alice the Collegiate
Alice the Fire Fighter
Alice the Golf Bug
Alice the Lumber Jack
Alice the Whaler
Alice's Auto Race
Alice's Brown Derby
Alice's Channel Swim
Alice's Circus Daze
Alice's Knaughty Knight
Alice's Medicine Show
Alice's Monkey Business
Alice's Picnic
Alice's Spanish Guitar
Alice's Three Bad Eggs

ALICE IN WONDERLAND, *Unique Foto Film Company*, released September 1931
Produced by the Unique Foto Film Company; Director and photographer, Bud Pollard; Screenplay by John E. Godson and Ashley Ayre Miller, adapted from Lewis Carroll's *Alice in Wonderland*; Setting by Charles Nasca; Costumes by Tama; Dialogue by Ashley Ayre Miller; Theme song by Irving Berlin; Incidental music arranged by William David

Ruth Gilbert (Alice); Leslie T. King (Mad Hatter); Ralph Hertz (White Rabbit); Vie Quinn (Queen of Hearts); N.R. Cregan (King of Hearts); Pat Glasgow (Knave of Hearts); Mabel Wright (Duchess); Tom Corliss (Cheshire Cat); Meyer Beresen (March Hare); Raymond Schultz (Dormouse); Lillian Ardell (Cook); Gus Alexander (Mock Turtle); Charles Silvern (Gryphon); Jimmy Rosen (Caterpillar)

Paramount Pictures, released December 1933
Produced by Louis D. Lighton; Director, Norman Z. McLeod; Screenplay by Joseph L. Mankiewicz and William Cameron Menzies, based on *Alice's Adventures in Wonderland* and *Alice Through the Looking Glass* by Lewis Carroll; Photography, Henry Sharp and Bert Glennon; Production designed by William Cameron Menzies;

Set decorator, Robert Odell; Costumes and Masks, Wally Westmore and Newt Jones; Choreography and Pageantry, LeRoy Prinz; Music, Dimitri Tiomkin; Music supervisor, Nathaniel Finston; Special Effects, Gordon Jennings and Farciot Edouart; Sound, Eugene Merritt; Editor, Ellsworth Hoagland

Charlotte Henry (Alice); Louise Fazenda (The White Queen); Edna May Oliver (The Red Queen); Gary Cooper (The White Knight); W. C. Fields (Humpty Dumpty); Leon Errol (Uncle Gilbert); Edward Everett Horton (The Mad Hatter); Richard Arlen (The Cheshire Cat); Jack Oakie (Tweedledum); Roscoe Karns (Tweedledee); Skeets Gallagher (The White Rabbit); William Austin (The Gryphon); Alec B. Francis (The King of Hearts); Polly Moran (The Dodo Bird); May Robson (The Queen of Hearts); Charles Ruggles (The March Hare); Ned Sparks (The Caterpillar); Ford Sterling (The White King); Roscoe Ates (The Fish); Sterling Holloway (The Frog); Alison Skipworth (The Duchess); Raymond Hatton (The Mouse); Colin Kenny (The Clock); Baby LeRoy (The Joker); Mae Marsh (The Sheep); Charles McNaughton (Five of Spades); Billy Bevan (Two of Spades); Will Stanton (Seven of Spades); Jackie Searle (Dormouse); Harvey Clark (Father William); Jack Duffy (Leg of Mutton); Billy Barty (The White Pawn/The Baby); Colin Campbell (Garden Frog); Cary Grant (The Mock Turtle); George Ovey (The Plum Pudding); Ethel Griffies (The Governess); Lillian Harmer (The Cook); Lucien Littlefield (Father William's Son); Patsy O'Byrne (The Aunt); Jacqueline Wells [Julie Bishop] (Alice's Sister); Harry Ekezian (First Executioner); Joe Torrillo (Second Executioner); Meyer Grace (Third Executioner)

SONGS: "Alice in Wonderland" (Dimitri Tiomkin, Nathaniel Furston, Leon Robin); "Walk a Little Faster" (Lewis Carroll, Dave Franklin)

ALICE AU PAYS DES MERVEILLES, *Union Generale Cinematographie*, France, released 1949; released in U.S. as *Alice in Wonderland* in August 1951 by *Electric Pictures*

Produced by Lou Bunin (New York)/Union Generale Cinematographie (Paris)/Rank (London); Producers, Lou Bunin, Marc Maurette; Director, Dallas Bower; Screenplay by Henry Myere, Albert E. Lewin and Edward Eliscu, based on *Alice's Adventures in Wonderland* by Lewis Carroll; Photography (live action) Gerald Gibbs (French version, Claude Renoir); Photography (animation), Erwin Broner; Puppet animation, William King, Ben Radin and Oscar Fessler; Animation consultant, Art Babbitt; Production designer, Ben W. Rubin; Layout design, Eugene Fleury; Assistant director, Vincent Permane; Assistant director (French version), Marc Maurette; Puppet designer, Bernyce Polifka; Art director, Irving Block; Special effects, Irving Block, Lloyd Knetchel; Model sculptor, Jacques Lecoz; Models, Russell Bernstein; Model makers, Herrmann Silversheer, Lillian Davis; Music score, Saul Kaplan; Music performed by The London Symphony Orchestra, conducted by Ernest Irving; Choreography, Roland Petit; Costume design and Makeup, Florence Bunin; Music, Steve Dalby; Lyrics, Henry Myers, Edward Eliscu; Supervising Editor, Inman (Ted) Hunter; Editors, Marity Cleris, Jacqueline Thiebot

Carol Marsh (Alice Liddell); Stephen Murray (The Reverend Charles Dodgson); Pamela Brown (Queen Victoria); Felix Aylmer (Dr. Liddell, Dean of Christ Church); Ernest Milton (Vice-Chancellor); David Read (Albert, the Prince Consort); Raymond Bussieres (Tailor); Elizabeth Henson (Lorina Liddell); Joan Dale (Edith Liddell)

Voices: Pamela Brown (Queen of Hearts); Joyce Grenfell (Ugly Duchess); Stephen Murray (Knave of Hearts); Ernest Milton (White Rabbit); Raymond

Bussieres (Mad Hatter); David Read (King of Hearts); Felix Aylmer (Cheshire Cat); and Jack Train, Ivan Staff

ALICE IN WONDERLAND, Walt Disney/RKO Pictures, released July 1951
Produced by Walt Disney; An Animated Cartoon; Production supervisor, Ben Sharpsteen; Directors, Clyde Geronimi, Hamilton Luske and Wilfred Jaxon; Screenplay by Winston Hibler, Bill Peet, Joe Rinaldi, Bill Cottrell, Joe Grant, Del Connell, Ted Sears, Erdman Penner, Milt Banta, Dick Kelsey, Dick Huemer, Tom Oreb, John Walkridge, based on Lewis Carroll's *Alice in Wonderland* and *Through the Looking Glass*; *Directing Animators*, Milt Kahl, Ward Kimball, Frank Thomas, Eric Larson, John Lounsbery, Ollie Johnston, Wolfgang Reitherman, Marc Davis, Les Clark, Norman Ferguson; *Character Animators*, Hal King, Judge Whitaker, Tal Ambro, Bill Justice, Phil Ducan, Bob Carlson, Don Lusk, Cliff Nordberg, Harvey Toombs, Fred Moore, Marvin Woodward, Hugh Fraser, Charles Nichols; *Effects Animators*, Jos Meador, Dan MacManus, George Rowley, Blaine Gibson; Music, Oliver Wallace; Songs, Bob Hilliard, Don Raye, Sammy Fain, Gene DePaul, Mack Davis, Jerry Livingston, Al Hoffman; Special Processes, Ub Iwerks; Editor, Lloyd Richardson; Orchestrations, Joseph Dubin; Vocal arrangements, Jud Conlon

Voices: Kathryn Beaumont (Alice); Ed Wynn (Mad Hatter); Richard Haydn (Caterpillar); Sterling Holloway (Cheshire Cat); Jerry Colonna (March Hare); Verna Felton (Queen of Hearts); Bill Thompson (White Rabbit/Dodo Bird); Pat O'Malley (Tweedledee/Tweedledum/Walrus/Carpenter/Oysters); Heather Angel (Alice's Sister); Queenie Leonard (Bird in Tree); Joseph Kearns (Doorknob); Larry Gray (Bill); Dink Trout (King of Hearts); Doris Lloyd (The Rose); James Macdonald (Dormouse); The MelloMen (Card Painters)

SONGS: "Very Good Alice"; "In a World of My Own"; "All in a Golden Afternoon"; "Alice in Wonderland"; "The Walrus and the Carpenter"; "The Caucus Race"; "I'm Late"; "Painting the Roses Red"; "March of the Cards" (Bob Hilliard and Sammy Fain); "T'was Brilling" (Don Raye and Gene DePaul); "A Very Merry Un-Birthday" (Mack David, Al Hoffman and Jerry Livingston); "We'll Smoke the Blighter Out"; "Old Father William"; "A E I O U" (Oliver Wallace and Ted Sears)

Fox-Rank Pictures, released November 1972
Produced by Josef Shaftel and Derek Horne; Director, William Sterling; Screenplay by William Sterling, based on *Alice Adventures in Wonderland* by Lewis Carroll; Photography, Geoffrey Unsworth; Production designer, Michael Stringer; Special effects, Roy Whybrow; Art directors, Norman Dorme and Bill Brodie; Choreography, Terry Gilbert; Music and music director, John Barry; Lyrics, Don Black; Associate Producer, Rene Dupont; Editor, Peter Weatherley

Fiona Fullerton (Alice); Michael Crawford (White Rabbit); Michael Jayston (Dodgson/Lewis Carroll); Robert Helpmann (Mad Hatter); Ralph Richardson (Caterpillar); Flora Robson (Queen of Hearts); Dennis Price (King of Hearts); Peter Sellers (March Hare); Dudley Moore (Dormouse); Michael Hordern (Mock Turtle); Peter Bull (Duchess); Roy Kinnear (Cheshire Cat); Richard Warwick (Seven of Spades); Frank Cox (Tweedledee); Freddie Cox (Tweedledum); Pasty Rowlands (Cook); Rodney Bowes (Knave of Hearts); Ray Brooks (Five of Spades); Dennis Waterman (Two of Spades); Ian Trigger (Frog Footman); Hywel Bennett (Duckworth); Davy Kaye (Mouse); Spike Milligan (Gryphon); Julian Chagrin (Bill the Lizard); Freddie Earlle (Guinea Pig Pat); Stanley Bates (Monkey); Mike Ellis (Guinea Pig Two); William Ellis (Dodo); Melita Manger (Frog); Angela Morgan (Lory); Peter O'Farrell (Fish Footman); Michael Reardon

(Frog); Victoria Shallard (Lorina); Brian Tipping (Duck); Pippa Vickers (Edith); Mia Nardi, Anita Holden (Owls); Ray Edwards (Eagle); June Kidd (Magpie)

Production Associates Pictures, released 1976
Produced by Cruiser Productions; Executive producer, Roy Cruiser; Producer, William Osco; Director, Bud Townsend; Screenplay by Anthony Fredricks, based on an erotic concept of Lewis Carroll's *Alice's Adventures in Wonderland*; Photography, Joseph Bardo; Art director, Ed Duquette; Music, Jack Stern, Peter Matz and Bucky Searles; Music Directors, Jack Stern and Peter Matz; Choreography, Noah; Choreography (Hawaiian number), Jacques Coote; Editor, Shaun Walsh

Kristine de Bell (Alice); Ron Nelson (William); Bradford Armdexter (Humpty Dumpty); Alan Novak (Mad Hatter); Jerry Spelam (White Rabbit); Sue Tsengoles (Tweedledum); Tony Tsengoles (Tweedledee); Bruce Finklesteen (Black Knight); Juliet Graham (Queen); Astrid Hayase (Tart); John Lawrence (king); Jason Williams (White Knight); J. P. Paradine (Scrugg/ Doctor); Nancy Dore, Terry Hall (Nurses); Angel Barrett, Ed Marshall, Melvina Peoples, Marcia Raven (Jurors); Chris Steen (Oogaloo)

TELEVISION

ALICE THROUGH THE LOOKING GLASS, *Theatre Parade*, televised January 22, 1937 BBC 25 minutes
Presented for television by George More O'Ferrall; Extracts from the play adapted and produced by Nancy Price that opened at the Little Theatre, London, on December 21, 1936, based on the story by Lewis Carroll

Ursula Hanray (Alice); Esme Percy (Humpty Dumpty); Andrew Leight (Tweedledum); Ernest Butcher (Tweedledee); Elizabeth Maude (White Queen); Fred O'Donovan (White King)

ALICE IN WONDERLAND, televised April 29, 1937 BBC 1 hour

(no futher information avaliable)

ALICE IN WONDERLAND, televised December 21, 1937 BBC 30 minutes
Presented for television by George More O'Ferrall

Ursula Hanray (Alice); Walter Tobias (March Hare); Earle Gray (Mad Hatter); Fred O'Donovan (King of Hearts); Alban Blakelock (White Rabbit)

ALICE, televised December 26, 1946 BBC 40 minutes
Presented for television by George More O'Ferrall; Dramatized by Clemence Dane from *Alice in Wonderland* by Lewis Carroll; Designer, James Bould; Music, Richard Addinsell

Vivian Pickles (Alice); Erik Chitty (White Rabbit); Desmond Walter-Ellis (Mad Hatter); John Baker (March Hare); Gwyneth Lewis (Dormouse); Dorothy Stuart (Caterpillar); John Roderick (Dodo); Betty Potter (Mouse); Philip Stainton (Mock Turtle); Hilary Pritchard (Gryphon); Madge Brindley (Ugly Duchess); Miriam Karlin (Cook); Josephine Gundry (First Rose); Nancy Harrison (Second Rose); D. A. Meehan (King of Hearts); Kenneth Buckley (Queen of Hearts); Eric Lindsay (Knave of Hearts); Eric Stocker (Two of Spades); Kevin Sheldon (Five of Spades); Anthony Bridge (Seven of Spades)

ALICE'S ADVENTURES IN WONDERLAND AND THROUGH THE LOOKING

GLASS, televised December 25, 1948 BBC 1 hour 45 minutes
Adapted and directed by John Glyn-Jones from the play by Herbert M. Prentice; Designer, Barry Learoyd; Choreography, Sheila Rawle; Music, Alfred Reynolds

James McKechnie (Lewis Carroll); Margaret Barton (Alice); Roddy Hughes (White Rabbit); Cameron Miller (Caterpillar); Walter Plinge (Frog Footman); Beatrice Rowe (Cook); Olive Walter (Duchess); Morris Sweden (Cheshire Cat); Anthony Oliver (March Hare); Robert Webber (Mad Hatter); Charles Wade (Dormouse); Ray James (Two of Spades); Archie Angus (Five of Spades); Derek Ensor (Seven of Spades); Bruce Belfrage (King of Hearts); Sybil Arundale (Queen of Hearts); Victor Platt (Knave of Hearts); Stewart Vartan (Executioner/Walrus); Dennis Bowen (Gryphon); Gordon Bell (Mock Turtle); Louise Hampton (Red Queen); Ian Wallace (Tweedledum); James Hayter (Tweedledee); Ann Dodrington (White Queen); Charles Rolfe (Carpenter); Jack Howarth (Humpty Dumpty); Harold Scott (White King); Anthony Sharp (White Knight)

ALICE IN WONDERLAND, Ford Theatre, televised December 15, 1950 NBC 1 hour
Produced by Garth Montgomery; Director, Marc Daniels; Settings, Samuel Leve; Costumes, Grace Houston; Music, Cy Feuer; Choreography, Dorothy Jarnac

Iris Mann (Alice); Richard Waring (Mad Hatter); Ralph Riggs (Mock Turtle); Dorothy Jarnac (White Rabbit); Biff McGuire (Tweedledee); Jack Lemmon (Tweedledum); Rex O'Malley (Cheshire Cat); Jack Albertson (March Hare)

Kraft Theatre, televised May 5, 1954 NBC 1 hour
Produced and Directed by Maury Holland; Television adaptation by Jack Roche of the story by Lewis Carroll; Set designer, Duane McKinney; Narrators, Edgar Bergen and Charlie McCarthy

Robin Morgan (Alice); Art Carney (Mad Hatter); James Barton (Mock Turtle); Arthur Treacher (Cheshire Cat); Blanche Yurka (Queen of Hearts); Bobby Clark (King of Hearts); Arnold Moss (Red Knight); Fredd Wayne (March Hare); Ernest Truex (White Knight); Joe E. Marks (Dormouse); Una O'Connor (Cook); Joey Walsh (White Rabbit); Cliff Hall (Duchess); Chandler Cowles (Caterpillar); Iggie Wolfington (Tweedledum); Carl White (Tweedledee); Grant Williams (Knave of Hearts); Jerry Kilty (Fish Footman); Malcolm Beggs (Frog Footman); Yolanta Pike, Carol Lee, Ron Cummings, Mel Turner, Bob McCormack (Turtles); Ed Bryce, Ed Fuller, Mel Turner, Bob McCormack (Guards); Mike Roberts (Executioner); Kay Barton (Court Attendant); Floyd Sherman, Mike Roberts, Grace Dorian, Marilyn Delaney, Bobra Harris (Singers); Bob Stone, Cliff Sundsten, Bill Adler (Barristers); Mortimer Snerd (Baby)

Hallmark Hall of Fame, televised October 23, 1955 NBC 90 minutes
Executive producer, Jack Rayel; Producer, Maurice Evans; Director, George Schaefer; Teleplay by Eva Le Gallienne and Florida Freibus; Music by Richard Addinsell; Musical numbers staged and choreographed by Tony Charmoli; Scenery, Jan Scott; Costumes and Masks, Noel Taylor; Music conductor, Franz Allers; Puppets, Burr Tillstrom; Makeup, Dick Smith

Gillian Barber (Alice); Eva Le Gallienne (White Queen); Elsa Lanchester (Red Queen); Hiram Sherman (King of Hearts); Burr Tillstrom (Cheshire Cat and Mock Turtle); Bobby Clark (Duchess); Martyn Green (White Rabbit); Alice Pearce (Dormouse); Tom Bosley (Knave of Hearts); Reginald Gardiner (White Knight); Noel Leslie (Caterpillar); Mort Marshall (Mad Hatter); Skedge Miller

(Gardener); Karl Swenson (Humpty Dumpty); Ronald Long (Queen of Hearts); J. Pat O'Malley (Gryphon); Ben Tone (Cook); Ian Martin (Tweedledum); Don Hammer (Tweedledee); Robert Casper (March Hare); Don Somers (Red King); Michael Enserro (Fish Footman); Gilbert Mack (Frog Footman)

MUSICAL NUMBERS: "You Are Old, Father William"; "Speak Roughly to Your Little Boy"; "Walrus and Carpenter"; "Beautiful Soup"; "Lobster Quadrille"; "You Told Me You Had Been to Her"; "I Sent a Message to the Fish"; "I'll Tell Thee Everything I Can"; "Hush-a-bye Lady in Alice's Lap"; "Banquet Song"

ALICE THROUGH THE LOOKING GLASS, televised November 6, 1966 NBC 90 minutes

Produced by Alan Handley and Bob Wynn; Director, Alan Handley; Teleplay by Albert Simmons, based on the characters created by Lewis Carroll; Music and lyrics by Moose Charlap and Ebie Simmons; Choreography, Tony Charmoli; Music director, Harper McKay; Arrangements by Don Costa

Judi Rolin (Alice); Jimmy Durante (Humpty Dumpty); Nanette Fabray (White Queen); Ricardo Montalban (White King); Agnes Moorehead (Red Queen); Jack Palance (Jabberwock); Roy Castle (Lester the Jester); Robert Coote (Red King); Richard Denning (Alice's Father); Tom and Dick Smothers (Tweedledum and Tweedledee);

MUSICAL NUMBERS: "Through the Looking Glass"; "There Are Two Sides to Everything"; "I Wasn't Meant to Be a Queen"; "Come Out, Come Out, Wherever You Are"; "The Jabberwock Song"; "Keep on the Grass"; "Some Summer Day"; "The Backwards Alphabet"; "T'Was Brilling"; "Who Are You"; "Alice Is Coming to Tea"

Original soundtrack recording: RCA Records

ALICE IN WONDERLAND; OR, WHAT'S A NICE KID LIKE YOU DOING IN A PLACE LIKE THIS?, televised March 30, 1966 ABC 1 hour

Produced and Directed by Alex Lovy; Animated Cartoon adaptation by Bill Dana of the books by Lewis Carroll; Songs by Lee Adams and Charles Strouse

Voices: Janet Waldo (Alice [talking]); Doris Drew Allen (Alice [singing]); Howard Morris (White Rabbit); Bill Dana (White Knight); Zsa Zsa Gabor (Queen of Hearts); Hedda Hopper (Hedda Hatter); Sammy Davis, Jr. (Cheshire Cat); Daws Butler (King of Hearts/March Hare); Harvey Korman (Mad Hatter); Don Messick (Dormouse); Alan Reed (Talking Caterpillar); Mel Blanc (Barney Rubble); Allan Melvin (Humphrey Dumpty/Father)

MUSICAL NUMBERS: "Life's a Game"; "What's a Nice Kid Like You Doing in a Place Like This?" "They'll Never Split Us Apart"; "Today's a Wonderful Day"; "I'm Home"

ALICE IN WONDERLAND, televised December 28, 1966 BBC 80 minutes

Produced by the British Broadcasting Corporation; Produced, directed and recreated by Jonathan Miller, based on the story by Lewis Carroll; Photography, Richard Bush; Settings, Julia Trevelyan Oman; Editor, Pam Bosworth

Anne-Marie Malik (Alice); Sir John Gielgud (Mock Turtle); Wilfrid Brambell (White Rabbit); Sir Michael Redgrave (Caterpillar); Peter Sellers (King of Hearts); Alison Leggatt (Queen of Hearts); Leo McKern (Duchess); Peter Cook (Mad Hatter); Finlay Currie (Dodo); Michael Gough (March Hare); Malcolm Muggeridge (Gryphon); Mark Allington (Duck); Peter Eyre (Knave of Hearts); David Battley (Executioner); Geoffrey Dunn (Lory); John Bird (Frog Footman); Tony Trent (Fish Footman/Gardener); Alan Bennett (Mouse); Freda Dowie (Nurse/Woman);

Avril Elgar (Peppercock); Nicholas Evans (Eaglet); Gordon Gostelow (Head Gardener); Wilfrid Lawson (Dormouse); Charles Lawson (Foreman of the Jury); Jo Maxwell-Muller (Alice's Sister, Emma); Julian Jebb (Young Crab); with: Leslie Glamer, Eric Idle, Katya Benjamin, Zbyssek Lisak, George Orloff, Alex Jadokimov, Gatina Kollisch, Aloysha Zolutuhin, Erbic Zakariyn, Maria Wolska, J. H. Powell, A. Mideilo, Natasha Ostruskaya, Ludmilla Onackayn, Tamara Koslowska, C. Irinski, M. Balmloff, Dave Prowse, and 79 walkons, 10 Bandsmen and 8 Drummers

MUSICAL NUMBERS:"Will You Walk a Little Faster" (Music, L. Lohman, Lyrics, Lewis Carroll); "Glorious Dawn" (Boulton); "Twinkle, Twinkle, Little Star" (Lyrics, Lewis Carroll; Traditional Air); "Immortal, Invisible, God Only Wise" (Traditional Welsh Hymn); "B Flat Minor Sonata" (Chopin); "Eton Boating Song" (Lyrics, Ionica K. Prowse; Music, A.D.E.W.); "Ala Rakha" (Ravi Shankar); "Praise My Soul the King of Heaven" (Congregational Hymn); "Sussex by the Sea" (Ward, Higgs)

ALICE THROUGH THE LOOKING GLASS, televised December 25, 1973 BBC; in U.S., televised November 25, 1976 PBS 90 minutes

A production of MCA Television and the British Broadcasting Corporation; A Piccadilly Circus Dramatic Special; Produced by Rosemary Hill; Directed and adapted by James Mactaggart, from the classic novel by Lewis Carroll with live action and animation based on the drawings of Sir John Tenniel; Designer, Eileen Diss; Costumes, Mary Woods; Makeup, Toni Chapman; Host, Jeremy Brett

Sarah Sutton (Alice); Brenda Bruce (White Queen); Richard Pearson (White King); Judy Parfitt (Red Queen); John Scott Martin (Red King); Geoffrey Bayldon (White Knight); Freddie Jones (Humpty Dumpty); Anthony Collin (Tweedledum); Raymond Mason (Tweedledee); Bruce Purchase (Walrus); Stanley Lebor (Carpenter); Stephen Moore (Haigha); Jonathan Cecil (Old Father/Hatta); Nicholas Jones (Unicorn); Robin Wentworth (Lion); Ian Trigger (Gnat); Jeffrey Segal (Man in White Paper); June Watson (Tiger Lily); Vivienne Moore (Rose); Douglas Milvain (Aged Aged Man); Samantha Gate (Daisy); Sylvia O'Donnell (Another Daisy); Richard Speight (Beamish Boy)

NEL MONDO DI ALICE (ALICE IN WONDERLAND), televised September 3, 1974 Italy 1 hour

Director, Guido Stagnaro; Teleplay, Guido Davico Bonino and Tinin Mantegazza, based on Lewis Carroll's novel

Milena Vukotic (Alice); Giustino Durano (Caterpillar); Giancarlo Detori (The White King); Edmonda Aldini (The White Queen); Ave Ninchi (The Queen of Hearts); Franca Valeri (The Duchess)

ALICE AT THE PALACE, Project Peacock, televised January 16, 1982 NBC 90 Minutes

A New York Shakespeare Festival production; A Concert version by Elizabeth Swados of Lewis Carroll's *Alice in Wonderland*; Director, Emile Ardolino; Music and lyrics by Elizabeth Swados; Choreographer, Graciela Daniele

Meryl Streep (Alice); Debbie Allen (Red Queen); Betty Aberlin (Edith); Rodney Hudson (Cheshire Cat); Richard Cox (Gryphon/Jabberwock); MarkLinn Baker (White Rabbit/March Hare/Mock Turtle); Michael Jeter (Dormouse/Pig Baby)

ALICE IN WONDERLAND, Great Performances, televised October 3, 1983 PBS 90 minutes

Produced by Jac Venza and Ann Blumenthal; Director, Kirk Browning; Adaptation by Eva Le Gallienne and Florida Friebus of Lewis Carroll's novel; Settings, John Lee Beatty; Costumes, Patricia Zipprodt; Music, Richard Addinsell; Musical director, Jonathan Tunick; Choreography, Donald Saddler

Kate Burton (Alice); Richard Burton (White Knight); Maureen Stapleton (White Queen); Colleen Dewhurst (Red Queen); Eve Arden (Queen of Hearts); James Coco (King of Hearts); Tony Cummings (Knave of Hearts); Donald O'Connor (Mock Turtle); Austin Pendleton (White Rabbit); Fritz Weaver (Caterpillar); Andre Gregory (Mad Hatter); Alan Weeks (Tweedledee); Andre De Shields (Tweedledum); Geoffrey Holder (Cheshire Cat); Sven Swenson (Gryphon); Richard Woods (Humpty Dumpty); Kaye Ballard (The Duchess); Zeljko Ivanek (March Hare); Nathan Lane (Mouse)

ALICE IN WONDERLAND, televised December 9 and 10, 1985 CBS 4 hours
Irwin Allen Productions and Proctor & Gamble Productions in association with Columbia Pictures Television; Produced by Irwin Allen; Director, Harry Harris; Teleplay by Paul Zindel, based on Lewis Carroll's *Alice in Wonderland* and *Through the Looking Glass*; Photography, Fred J. Koenekamp; Art directors, Ross Bellah and Hub Braden; Costumes, Paul Zastupnevich; Special effects, John Dykstra; Music score, Mort Stevens; Songs, Steve Allen; Musical staging, Gillian Lynne; Additional choreography, Miriam Nelson; Makeup supervision, Leo L. Lotito, Jr.; Special effects supervisor: Joseph A. Unsinn; Editors, Richard E. Rabjohn, James W. Miller

Natalie Gregory (Alice); Carol Channing (White Queen); Ann Jillian (Red Queen); Lloyd Bridges (White Knight); Harvey Korman (White King); Steve Lawrence (Tweedledum); Eydie Gorme (Tweedledee); Jayne Meadows (Queen of Hearts); Robert Morley (King of Hearts); Karl Malden (Walrus); Anthony Newley (Mad Hatter); Ringo Starr (Mock Turtle); Red Buttons (White Rabbit); Roddy McDowall (March Hare); Martha Raye (Duchess); Sid Caesar (Gryphon); Imogene Coca (Cook); Donald O'Connor (Lory Bird); Arte Johnson (Dormouse); Sammy Davis, Jr. (Caterpillar); Telly Savalas (Cheshire Cat); Shelley Winters (Dodo Bird); Sherman Hemsley (Mouse); Scott Baio (Pat, the Guinea Pig); Tom McLoughlin (Jabberwocky); Donna Mills (Rose); Sally Struthers (Tiger Lily); Sheila Allen (Alice's Mother); Jonathan Winters (Humpty Dumpty); Ernest Borgnine (Lion); Beau Bridges (Unicorn); Jack Warden (Owl); Steve Allen (The Gentleman); Pat Morita (The Horse); Patrick Duffy (The Goat); George Gobel (The Gnat); Merv Griffin (The Conductor); Louis Nye (The Carpenter); John Stamos (Messenger); with Billy Baver, Scotch Byerley, Robert Axelrod, Laura Carlson, Patrick Culliton, Michael Chieffo, Barbie Allison, Dee Brantlinger, Charles Dougherty, John Walter Davis, Selma Archerd, James Joseph Galante, Kristi Lynes, Don Matheson, Ernie Orsatti, George Savalas, Candace Savalas, Desiree Szabo, Jeffrey Winner, Troy Jordan, Janie Walton

MUSICAL NUMBERS: "I Hate Dogs and Cats"; "Father William"; "There's Something to Say for Hatred"; "There's No Way Home"; "Laugh"; "Off With Their Heads"; "Nonsense"; "I Didn't, You Did"; "Why Do People"; "How Do You Do"; "The Sun Was Shining"; "Jam Tomorrow"; "The Lion and the Unicorn"; "Can You Do Addition?" "Hush-a-Bye Lady"; "Emotions"; "And We Are Dancing"; "To the Looking Glass World"; "Alice"

ALICE THROUGH THE LOOKING GLASS, televised April 8, 1988 Showtime 75 minutes
Burbank Films, Australia/Jambre Productions; A Jameson Brewer Film; Executive

producers, Michael Prevett and Tom Stacey; An animated film written and produced by Jameson Brewer; Director, Angela Brescani; Music, Todd Haven; Songs, Jameson Brewer and Todd Haven

Voices: Janet Waldo (Alice/Red Queen); Mr. T (Jabberwock); Phyllis Diller (White Queen); George Gobel (Humpty Dumpty); Jonathan Winters (Tweedle Dum and Tweedle Dee); Alan Young (C. Biscuit/White Knight); Clive Revill (Old Goat); Townsend Coleman (Tom Fool); Hal Smith (Snipe/Paper Man), Will Ryan (Alligator), Booker Bradshaw (Centaur), Alan Dinehart (Train Conductor)

SONGS: "Here's Looking Glass Land"; "Nothing Is Impossible"; "Nobility"; "Tweedle Dum and Tweedle Dee"; "You Just Gotta Be What You Are"; We're Bad"

ALL MY SONS
A Drama by Arthur Miller (1947)

Synopsis

During World War II, industrialist Joe Keller permitted the shipment to the Air Force of 120 defective airplane cylinder heads resulting in the death of twenty-one pilots. Joe arranged to be exonerated and let his partner, Deever, be sent to prison. Three years after the war, Chris Keller invites Deever's daughter Ann, who had been the fiancee of his pilot brother Larry, killed in the war, to visit the family. Chris and Ann have fallen in love but their proposed marriage is paranoically opposed by Chris' mother Kate who believes her eldest son is only missing in action and will return, supported by neighbor Frank Lubey's horoscope on Larry. Ann's brother George helps to expose Joe's hidden guilt, of which their neighbor Dr. Jim Bayliss is aware, and which Kate has accepted to maintain their lifestyle. Chris is disillusioned and horrified at his father's involvement but revoltingly resolves to accept it as "doing business as usual." To quell Chris' emotional anxiety, Ann forces Kate to read Larry's last letter in which he realized his father's treachery and planned to commit suicide by crashing his airplane. Joe's composure crumbles in the realization he has indirectly killed his own son, and that the other twenty-one men were also all his sons. He goes into the house and kills himself with a pistol.

Comment and Critique

Produced, actress, director Antoinette Perry died at age fifty-eight on June 28, 1946. In her honor, the American Theatre Wing, of which she was executive director, established an annual Tony Award for "distinguished achievement" in the theatre. The first Tony Awards were made at a dinner in the Grand Ballroom of the Waldorf Astoria Hotel on April 6, 1947, consisting of a bill clip for men and vanity cases for women. Designer Herman Rosse's medallion was not awarded until 1949. Elia Kazan received the first Tony Award as the Best Director for *All My Sons* and a special award was given to playwright Arthur Miller.

Miller's Ibsenesque *All My Sons* was also selected by the New York Drama Critics Circle as the Best American Play of 1947. The award read, "Because of the frank and uncompromising presentation of a timely and important theme; because of the honesty of the writing and the accumulative power of the scenes, and because it reveals a genuine instinct for the theatre in an intelligent and thoughtful new playwright."

All My Sons opened on Broadway on January 29, 1947, and ran for 328 performances. *Time* magazine appraised the play as having "a theatrical force that covers a multitude of sins...[Playwright Miller] tends to overload his plot and overheat his atmosphere. His writing is uneven, some of his main characters are sometimes unreal, and most of his minor characters are at all times unnecessary." The *Time* critic added, "This story is written with passion, but without soapbox oratory."

Critic George Jean Nathan wrote, "There is not, for example, any great essential difference between something said by this *All My Sons* and the something said many times more effectively all of seventy years ago by Ibsen in *Pillars of Society*...Yet in both instances the idea is identical: a man who sacrifices the weal of others to his own advantage is a scoundrel, and retribution is one form or another is his due...But though the play is honest, sincere and, as the colleagues would have it, about something, it seems to me to be just another in the line of exhibits which misses out because it says what we already all too well know in a manner we already know as well, and in terms and language that are undistinguished."

Brooks Atkinson (*The New York Times*) felt that "the theatre has acquired a genuine new talent. Arthur Miller, who wrote *The Man Who Had All the Luck* in 1944, brings something fresh and exciting into the drama. He has written and honest, forceful drama...Writing pithy yet unselfconscious dialogue, he has created his characters vividly...He is also a skillful technician. His drama is a piece of expert dramatic construction ...he drives the play along to a startling and terrifying climax." Praise for the acting of the company under Kazan's excellent direction included Ed Begley's Joe Keller, Arthur Kennedy's "superb performance, Beth Merrill as Kate and Karl Malden as the confused George ...they are acting an original play of superior quality by a playwright who knows his craft and has unusual understanding of the tangled loyalties of human beings."

All My Sons opened at the Lyric Theatre Hammersmith in spring 1948 and moved to London's West End Globe Theatre two months later to complete 110 performances. Frances Stephens (*Theatre World*) enthusiastically endorsed it: "Some of the finest acting in London is to be seen in this moving American play by Arthur Miller ...It has it weaknesses, mostly on account of occasional undue sentimentality, although this may not have been felt by American audiences. But at least the author has a message which he gets over with considerable skill without preaching or dull passages ...Joseph Calleia and Margalo Gillmore, as Joe Keller and his wife, give brilliant performances. Neither is afraid to make the appeal to emotion. The supporting actors are inspired by the two stars to give most authentic interpretations."

In the 1970s, Roundabout Theatre's Gene Feist and Michael Fried, acquired a former RKO movie house on 23rd Street in Manhattan and changed the name to Round-about Theatre, Stage One. For their debut production and the beginning of their ninth Off-Broadway season, Feist and Fried presented Miller's *All My Sons*.

Clive Barnes (*The New York Times*), after claiming the New York Critics Circle erred in 1947 in awarding their Best Play Award to Miller's *All My Sons* rather than to Eugene O'Neill's marathon drama, *The Iceman Cometh*, wrote of Roundabout's 1974 revival: "*All My Sons* is a goodbad play, well worth the Broadway traffic of its time, a boulevard melodrama almost stiff with morality and didacticism. It has an air of selfrighteousness about...is a simplistic recruiting poster for black and white morality...The morality is too selfconscious and self-congratulatory...The writing is also heavy...Mr. [Hugh] Marlowe plays Keller with a hollow theatrical voice and a nervous-bullish stance, which at first irritates but later becomes effective ...best of all is the tortured calm of Beatrice Straight as Keller's wife."

Seven years later, *All My Sons* was revived at London's Wyndham's Theatre. Richard Findlater (*Plays and Players*) found, "After watching the American dream being dissolved into cautionary nightmares by crusading moralists and propagandists for 30 years, it's hard to imagine the shock-effect of *All My Sons* on Broadway in 1947...an Ibsenite morality-melodrama written during the last war, in an often clumsily contrived text... Compared with *Death of a Salesman*, staged only two years after the Broadway premiere of *All My Sons*, this play shows its age and the forceps-marks of a play-writing-course Caesarean...Yet, in spite of its flaws, Miller's text combines a driving moral force and grave social concern with a compassionate response to human weakness for which one looks in vain to the didactic political cartoonists of recent British drama...Colin Blakely [brings] to the role a concentrated yet relaxed naturalism...that constitutes one prime reason for seeing *All My Sons*...As I recall the 1947 London production, its Joe Keller (Joseph Calleia) was -- though incontestably American -- inferior to this one; and I preferred Rosemary Harris as Joe's wife...to the mid-Western Lady Macbeth of Margalo Gillmore in 1947. Miss Harris glows beautifully through the role."

London's *Sunday Times* critic, James Fenton, hailed *All My Sons* as "a magnificent new production by Michael Blakemore has come in, as a play, for a certain amount of critical stick....Nevertheless, the piece is written within a convention, one which was 70 years old at the time, although rather newer to the American stage...The father is played by Colin Blakely, a powerful actor with an unrivaled capacity for making himself weak... Rosemary Harris gives a moving portrayal of the mother, an extremely well-drawn character...It has a tremendous, plain, emotional impact."

Robert Cushman (*The Observer*) added, "We still recognize Arthur Miller as one of the few great storytellers in modern theatre...Vocally this performance is superbly fastidious; physically it is full, graceful and economic, creating its own white light, Miss Harris is Britain's great lost actress; there should be legislation to stop her returning to America at the end of the run." Benedict Nightingale (*New Statesman*) proclaimed, "This a play and production that makes the rest of theatrical London seem desiccated, bloodless!"

The film of *All My Sons* in 1948 starring Edward G. Robinson in one of his finest screen characterizations as Joe Keller and Burt Lancaster as his son, Chris. "Under the direction of Universal-International's Irving Reis, the picture loses none of the dramatic dynamite that marked the play," reported *Liberty* magazine. "Edward G. Robinson, an old hand at giving effective performances, gives one of his best."

Time magazine advised, "Playwright Miller uses a good many of Ibsen's devices of gradual disclosure; he has developed a rather mannered, deeply native style of dialogue which is well suited to the stage but does not come happily to life on the screen...*All My Sons* in not so much a moral exploration as a conducted tour." The *New Yorker* considered that there was "a lot of wordiness of the stage version of *All My Sons* [which] has been cut out of the movie, and the result is an effective melodrama, longer on ideas than the usual Hollywood commodity...I can assure you it doesn't make a dull movie." Howard Barnes (*New York Herald-Tribune*) declined approval with "While there are scenes of fine indignation in the motion picture, realized to the full by Edward G. Robinson, Burt Lancaster, Mady Christians and Frank Conroy, they do not offset fabricated situations and blurred characterizations."

In his 1973 autobiography *All My Yesterdays*, Edward G. Robinson wrote about *All My Sons* as "a picture of which I am inordinately proud...It was a part I played with such passion and intensity that the director, Irving Reis, told me constantly to take it easy...And my passion imbued the whole cast. No need to imbue Mady Christians, a superb actress. No need to imbue Burt Lancaster, playing in perhaps his second or third film but showing that animal vitality and suppressed volcano inside that inevitably made him a star."

All My Sons was produced by Granada television of Manchester, England, in 1958 starring Albert Dekker as Joe Keller, Megen Jenkins as his wife Kate, and Patrick McGoohan as his idealistic son Chris. In January 1987, the *American Playhouse* television production of *All My Sons* produced by KCET-TV, Los Angeles, with a cast headed by James Whitmore, was called by Arthur Miller, "Quite simply, the best production of *All My Sons* that has ever been done." And it was!

Television critic David Bianculli reported, "Unlike *Death of a Salesman*, which contains flashback scenes and a few set changes, *All My Sons* is self-contained, taking place in one back yard on one afternoon and evening of a very eventful day. Director Jack O'Brien ...has underlined the claustrophobia by shooting *All My Sons* on videotape, on a stage set. It's an approach that often looks so artificial that it undermines rather than underlines, but Miller's script and the terrific, intense performances take hold midway through the first act -- and never let go....If you have a VCR, use it. *All My Sons* is an *American Playhouse* worth savoring and saving.

James Whitmore gave a forceful performance as Joe Keller and Michael Learned was splendid as Kate, the mother convincing herself her dead son is alive rather than face the truth that her husband is responsible for the deaths of many young men, including his own son. Aidan Quinn was equally as powerful as young Chris. But, as Bianculli noted, "Miller may like this production of the play largely because it's complete, unhampered by interruptions or deletions, but it's most impressive because of the power provided by its cast members."

"This Arthur Miller classic translates magnificently to the small screen -- with strong performances by Whitmore, Learned and Quinn," reported *TV Guide*. *The Hollywood Reporter* added, "A riveting broadcasting experience...Another play superbly transmitted by *American Playhouse* into an uncommon television achievement!" *The New York Times* rated the telecast, "A splendid production," and Los Angeles' *Herald Examiner* underscored the telecast with "Miller's work has never been showcased anymore powerfully."

STAGE

ALL MY SONS, *Coronet Theatre*, New York, opened January 29, 1947 328 performances

Produced by Harold Clurman, Elia Kazan and Walter Fried, in association with Herbert H. Harris; A Drama by Arthur Miller; Director, Elia Kazan; Setting and Lighting, Mordecai Gorelik; Costumes, Paul Morrison; Company manager, Otto Harmon; Stage manager, Robert F. Simon; Assistant stage manager, James Gregory

Ed Begley (succeeded by Thomas Chalmers) (Joe Keller); Arthur Kennedy (succeeded by John Forsythe) (Chris Keller); Beth Merrill (Kate Keller); Karl Malden (succeeded by James Gregory) (George Deever); Lois Wheeler (succeeded by Ann Shepherd) (Ann Deever); John McGovern (Dr. Jim Bayliss); Eugene Steiner [alternate, Donald Harris] (succeeded by Maurice Cavell [alternate, Michael Citro]) (Bert); Hope Cameron (succeeded by Jane Blair) (Lydia Lubey); Peggy Meredith (Sue Bayliss); Dudley Sadler (Frank Lubey)

Lyric Theatre Hammersmith, London, opened May 11, 1948; moved to *Globe Theatre*, June 16, 1948

Produced by H. M. Tennant Productions, Ltd.; A Drama by Arthur Miller; Director,

Warren Jenkins

Joseph Calleia (Joe Keller); Richard Leech (Chris Keller); Margalo Gillmore (Kate Keller); John McLaren (George Deever); Harriette Johns (Ann Deever); Hugh Pryce (Dr. Jim Bayliss); Robin Netscher (Bert); Barbara Todd (Lydia Lubey); Louise Lister (Sue Bayliss); Peter Hutton (Frank Lubey)

U.S. Touring Company, season 1947-48
Produced by Gerald Rado; A Drama by Arthur Miller; Director, Charles Adams; Setting and Lighting, Mordecai Gorelik; Costumes, Paul Morrison

Sidney Blackmer (Joe Keller); Blanche Yurka (Kate Keller); John Forsythe (Chris Keller); Beverly Dennis (Ann Deever); James Gregory (George Deever); John Kessler (Dr. Jim Bayliss); Ellen Mahar (Sue Bayliss); Hope Cameron (Lydia Lubey); J. S. Teague (Frank Lubey); Marc Fallenberg (Bert)

Kungl, Dramatiska Teatern, Stockholm, season 1948
Produced by Sven Barthel; A Drama by Arthur Miller; Director, Rune Carlsten; Setting, Georg Magnusson

Holger Lowenadler (Joe Keller); Elsa Carlsson (Kate Keller); Ulf Palme (Chris Keller); Birgitta Valberg (Ann Deever); Olof Widgren (George Deever); Henrik Schildt (Dr. Jim Bayliss); Barbro Hiort (Sue Bayliss); Kurt-Olof Sundstrom (Frank Lubey); Ellika Mann (Lydia Lubey)

Roundabout Theatre, New York, opened September 27, 1974 60 performances
Produced by the Roundabout Theatre Company -- Stage One, Gene Feist and Michael Fried, producers; A Drama by Arthur Miller; Director, Gene Feist; Setting, Holmes Easley; Lighting, Richard Winkler; Musical score, Philip Campanella; Costumes, Mimi Maxman; Sound, Gary Harris; Stage manager, Ron Antone

Hugh Marlowe (Joe Keller); Drew Snyder (Chris Keller); Beatrice Straight (Kate Keller); Tom Keene (George Deever); Catherine Byers (Ann Deever); Matthew Barry (Bert); Kenneth Kimmins (Dr. Jim Bayliss); Janet Sarno (Sue Bayliss); Jane Dentinger (Lydia Lubey); Rik Pierce (Frank Lubey)

Wyndham's Theatre, London, opened October 27, 1981 308 performances
Produced by the Omega Stage Company; A Drama by Arthur Miller; Director, Michael Blakemore; Production designer, Hayden Griffin; Lighting, Rory Dempster

Colin Blakely (Joe Keller); Rosemary Harris (Kate Keller); Garrick Hagon (Chris Keller); Jill Baker (Ann Deever); Richard Durden (George Deever); David Baron (Dr. Jim Bayliss); Pat Starr (Sue Bayliss); Ken Drury (Frank Lubey); Pamela Merrick (Lydia Lubey); Miles Parsey, or Bryan Rogan, Joseph De Marce, Daniel Holender (Bert)

Zellerbach Theatre, Philadelphia, opened April 21 through May 8, 1983
Produced by the Philadelphia Drama Guild, Gregory Poggi, managing director; A Drama by Arthur Miller; Director, William Woodman; Setting, John Jensen; Lighting, William Armstrong; Costumes, Jess Goldstein

Dan Frazer (Joe Keller); Lenka Peterson (Kate Keller); Court Miller (Chris Keller); Kristin Griffith (Ann Deever); Adrian Sparks (George Deever); Edward Seamon (Dr. Jim Bayliss); Lilene Mansell (Sue Bayliss); Ton Pasqualini (Frank Lubey); Sarah Felder (Lydia Lubey); Morgan Land or Judd Serotta (Bert)

Los Angeles Theatre Center, season 1985-86

Produced by the Los Angeles Theatre Center, Bill Bushnell, artistic producing director; Producers, Diane White and Phillip Esparza; A Drama by Arthur Miller; Director, Bill Bushnell

Philip Baker Hall (Joe Keller); Nan Martin (Kate Keller); Bill Pullman (Chris Keller); Sheila Shaw (Sue Bayliss); Julie Fulton (Ann Deever); Gregory Wagrowski (George Deever); Ruth de Sosa (Lydia Lubey); Jim Jansen (Dr. Jim Bayliss); Jon Menick (Frank Lubey); Eric Ratican (Bert)

Seattle (Wash.) Repertory Theatre, season 1985-86
Produced by the Seattle Repertory Theatre, Benjamin Moore, managing director; Artistic directors, Daniel Sullivan, Douglas Hughes; A Drama by Arthur Miller; Director, Edward Hastings; Setting, Hugh Landwehr; Lighting, Dennis Parichy; Costumes, Robert Wojewodski; Sound, Lindsay Smith

William "Biff" McGuire (Joe Keller); Betty Miller (Kate Keller); Mark Arnott (Chris Keller); Kate Skinner (Ann Deever); Michael Santo (Dr. Jim Bayliss); Patricia Conolly (Sue Bayliss); Jane Bray (Lydia Lubey); Shane Clark (Bert); Paul Redford (Frank Lubey)

Long Wharf Theatre, New Haven, opened October 10 through November 23, 1986
Produced by the Long Wharf Theatre Company, M. Edgar Rosenblum, executive director; A Drama by Arthur Miller; Director, Arvin Brown; Setting, Hugh Landwehr; Lighting, Ronald Wallace; Costumes, Bill Walker; Stage manager, Anne Keefe

Ralph Waite (Joe Keller); Joyce Ebert (Kate Keller); Jamey Sheridan (Chris Keller); Frances McDormand (Ann Deever); Christopher Curry (George Deever); Dan Desmond (Dr. Jim Bayliss); Carol Androsky (Sue Bayliss); Stephen Root (Frank Lubey); Dawn Didawick (Lydia Lubey); Nicholas Tamarkin (Bert)

John Golden Theatre, New York, opened April 22, 1987 29 performances
Produced by Jay H. Fuchs and Steven Warnick, in association with Charles Patsos presentation of a Long Wharf Theatre production; A Drama by Arthur Miller; Director, Arvin Brown; Setting, Hugh Landwehr; Lighting, Ronald Wallace; Costumes, Bill Walker; Stage manager, Zoya Wyeth

Richard Kiley (Joe Keller); Joyce Ebert (Kate Keller); Jamey Sheridan (Chris Keller); Jayne Atkinson (Ann Deever); Dan Desmond (Dr. Jim Bayliss); Stephen Root (Frank Lubey); Christopher Curry (George Deever); Dawn Didawick (Lydia Lubey); Michael Maronna (Bert); Kit Flanagan (Sue Bayliss)

NOTE: This production, slightly recast from the Long Wharf Theatre staging of 1986, also played at the *Ford's Theater*, Washington, February 9 through March 15, 1987

Westport (Conn.) Country Playhouse, opened July 6 through 18, 1987; *Cape Playhouse*, Dennis, Mass., opened July 25 through August 1, 1987
Connecticut Theatre Foundation Inc., James B. McKenzie, executive producer; Produced in association with Jay H. Fuchs; A Drama by Arthur Miller; Director, Jose Ferrer; Scenery adaptation and costume design, Steven Perry; Lighting design, John McClain; Stage manager, Camille Calman

Lee Richardson (Joe Keller); Frances Sternhagen (Kate Keller); Tracy Griswold (Chris Keller); Felicity La Fortune (Ann Deever); Guy Paul (Dr. Jim Bayliss); Stephen Root (Frank Lubey); Dan Butler (George Deever); Dawn Didawick (Lydia Lubey); Liann Pattison (Sue Bayliss); Alex Ruchelman (Bert)

SCREEN

Universal Pictures, released May 1948
Produced by Universal-International; Producer, Chester Erskine; Director, Irving Reis; Screenplay by Chester Erskine, based on Arthur Miller's play; Photography, Russell Metty; Art directors, Bernard Herzbrun, Hilyard Brown; Set decorators, Russell A. Gausman, Al Fields; Music, Leith Stevens; Orchestrations, David Tamkin; Costumes, Grace Houston; Editor, Ralph Dawson

Edward G. Robinson (Joe Keller); Burt Lancaster (Chris Keller); Mady Christians (Kate Keller); Louisa Horton (Ann Deever); Howard Duff (George Deever); Frank Conroy (Herbert Deever); Lloyd Gough (Jim Bayliss); Arlene Francis (Sue Bayliss); Henry "Harry" Morgan (Frank Lubey); Elisabeth Fraser (Lydia Lubey); Walter Soderling (Charlie); Harry Harvey (Judge); Therese Lyon (Minnie); Helen Brown (Mrs. Hamilton); William Johnstone (Attorney); Charles Meredith (Ellsworth); Herbert Vigran (Wertheimer); Pat Flaherty (Bartender); George Sorel (Headwaiter); Joseph Kerr (Norton); Walter Bonn (Jorgenson); Victor Zimmerman, George Slocum (Attendants); Herbert Haywood (McGraw); Jerry Hausner (Halliday); Frank Kreig (Foreman); William Ruhl (Ed); Al Murphy (Tom); Richard Lamarr (Bill); Jack Gargan (Workman)

TELEVISION

American Playhouse, televised January 19, 1987 PBS 2 hours
Produced by Michael Brandman Productions; A Drama by Arthur Miller; Executive producer Michael Brandman; Producer, Irene Merlis; Director, Jack O'Brien; Production designer, David Jenkins; Lighting, John Bothilo; Costume designer, Juul Haalmeyer; Music, Conrad Susa

James Whitmore (Joe Keller); Michael Learned (Kate Keller); Aidan Quinn (Chris Keller); Joan Allen (Ann Deever); Alan Scarfe (Dr. Jim Bayliss); Joanna Miles (Sue Bayliss); Zeljko Ivanek (George Deever); Layne Coleman (Frank Lubey); Mary Long (Lydia Lubey); Marlowe Vella (Bert)

ALL THE KING'S MEN
Various adaptations of the Pulitzer Prize novel by Robert Penn Warren (1946)

Synopsis

Educated by his schoolteacher wife, Southern redneck farmer Willie Stark decides to use his gift of oratory to enter politics. Opposition to political boss Tiny Duffy has Willie arrested, his wife fired, and his son Tom beaten up. A quick learner, Stark becomes a lawyer and runs for Governor with the help of newspaper reporter Jack Burden and devoted, astute political campaigner Sadie Burke, who becomes his mistress. Stark embraces acceptable political corruption while accomplishing his idealistic goals under the banner of "Truth, Honesty and Integrity." He quickly discovers honesty impedes his progress and shuffles right from wrong by finding the profitable and justifies the means. Stark's accomplishments, sudden fame and power completely corrupt him. To Sadie's disgust and dismay, Stark takes Burden's girlfriend Anne, the daughter of Judge Stanton, as his mistress, and cleverly clears himself of justifiable charges of political corruption, bribery and impeachment proceedings. Blackmailed by Stark for votes he controls, Judge Stanton commits suicide. Stark abandons Anne Stanton and returns to his wife Lucy. Jack Burden, having witnessed enough of Stark's amorality, deserts him, and Stark is assassinated by Anne's brother, Dr. Adam Stanton.

Comment and Critique

Huey Pierce Long, the controversial, dictatorial Governor of Louisiana and United States Senator was born in Winnfield, Louisiana on August 30, 1893. Huey "The Kingfish" Long made constant national headlines and was given intense media coverage throughout his career. Amos (Freeman F. Gosden) and Andy (Charles J. Correll) provided America with a great deal of laughter for many years with their radio show, and one of the greatest sources of that laughter came from their creation of an indolent, unscrupulous con artist, wheeler-dealer, George "Kingfish" Stevens, potentate of Harlem's "Mystic Knights of the Sea" lodge. "The King-fish" became a synonym for the life and political demagoguery of Huey Pierce Long.

Robert Penn Warren's novel *All the King's Men* was published by Harcourt in 1946 and won the year's Pulitzer Prize for fiction. America's first Poet Laureate (Consultant), Warren was the first American author to win the Pulitzer Prize for fiction and two Pulitzers for poetry. Although he insisted his novel was not based on Huey Long, the parallels were obvious. "If the late Huey Long is Mr. Warren's prototype, as seems likely, complaint may be made that the author has been too kind to his subject. What he has aimed at is apparently explanation rather than accusation or defense. At any rate, the story of the depths to which ambition and power can bring a man is sufficiently appalling," reported *The Christian Science Monitor*.

George Mayberry (*New Republic*) described Warren's novel as "primarily a superbly written narrative in which the surface of the writing is brilliantly integrated with the character of the narrator and the nature of his experience...All together it is the finest American novel in more years than one would like to have to remember."

On September 9, 1935, Long was shot by twenty-nine-year-old Dr. Carl A. Weiss, the son-in-law of anti-Long advocate Judge B. H. Pavy whom "The Kingfish" was trying to force out of office. Three State Highway policemen, George McQueston, E. D. Cole and Murphy Rosen, simultaneously fired at Dr. Weiss and killed him. Long died the next day in Baton Rouge's Our Lady of the Lake Sanitarium.

Joe Marcy (Nathan Sherman) and Jacob A. Weiser first dramatized the Huey Long saga in their play *First American Dictator*, which opened for nine performances at the Nora Bayes Theatre on March 14, 1939. Using actual names for the characters, the short-lived play related Long's victory over impeachment as Governor of Louisiana and included his thirteen-hour filibuster and virulent harangue supporting his share-the-wealth proposal in the United States Senate. The play concluded with news of his assassination.

The non-Equity cast of *First American Dictator* played some eighty parts, and a program note read, "The authors have proof that all the incidents in this play are true in essence. But dramatic license was taken quite freely with innumerable details." Commenting on the "innumerable details," Brooks Atkinson (*The New York Times*) wrote, "Since the Kingfish was a noisy demagogue who made fantastic headway in American in the depths of the Depression, no one can be exactly indifferent to the story of his cheap and shifty career...Although most of *First American Dictator* appears to be reasonably factual, it is hard now to believe that so much screaming made so deep an impression on the nation." About the freely taken dramatic license, Atkinson added, "That probably accounts for their staging the assassination in Washington after his sensational filibuster....As a drama, *First American Dictator* is practically a filibuster in itself."

Two years after winning the Pulitzer Prize for his novel, Robert Penn Warren adapted *All the King's Men* to the stage, and it was directed for The Experimental Theatre in New York by Erwin Piscator at the President Theatre in mid January 1948. (Warren had originally written his story as a verse play, prior to rewriting it as a novel.) "As a work for the theatre, [it] runs an uneasy but almost invariably interesting course between its virtues and shortcomings. Mr. Warren can write pungent dialogue, meaty situations and characters that seem real," wrote the critic for *The New York Times*. "What defeats him is a curious mixture of over-wrought melodrama and underdone philosophizing...More fundamentally, the play suffers from a morally muddy attitude toward its protagonist, Willie Stark... It is a perspective that attempts a sympathetic understanding of Stark's character, but it smacks too much of justification for means that no democratic political morality can condone." The *Times* also noted, "One performances, Robert Osterloh as Willie Stark, is a solid portrayal that stands above the rest."

A second production of it by Piscator was staged at the President Theatre in the summer of 1950 with Steve Gravers as Willie Stark (The Kingfish). Reviewing the recasting of *All the King's Men* from the 1948 Experimental Theatre of Erwin Piscator, *Billboard* felt "as a student exercise in dramaturgy, *Men* had its definite points. As a professional competitor in the Broadway scene at $3.60 top, its chances seem something less than limited...So, like it or lump it, the substances of Warren's saga of a political Humpty-Dumpty, who could be no other than the late Huey Long, must be familiar to many. In the current play structure, Warren makes use of explanatory narration in the form of dialog between some sort of professor of social science and a reporter and exhenchman of the politico... Production-wise, the group has done right well by *Men*. Erwin Piscator, who staged the Workshop edition, has been called in for a repeat chore on this one. Willis Knighton's turntable settings, and background projections, are again in use and are the biggest kind of asset in the telling of a multiple scene story."

Nine years later, *All the King's Men* was revived at the 74th Street Theatre. Robert Penn Warren's revised script was viewed by Brooks Atkinson (*The New York Times*): "The skeletonized form seems old-fashioned now; it is never willing to let one more detail alone. By the time of the third act, the intellectualized view of politics looks self-conscious and sounds a little pious...Does Mr. Warren need all the arguments that he weaves in and out of the portrait? He seems to making the same points repeatedly..But, why argue with Mr. Warren since, after all, he has written an engrossing play that raises some profound moral questions? The production and performance are generally admirable Clifton James' portrait of Willie is excellent..."

In 1974, Vinnette Carroll directed an all-black cast in the Urban Art Corps Theatre's revival of Warren's play, and in 1986, Adrian Hall directed his Dallas Theatre Center production of his adaptation of the Warren novel, with music by Randy Newman. In its review of the staging *Variety* felt: "Hall has succeeded in fashioning a stage work with so much power, with such emotional impact and epic force, and containing so many electrifying performances, that the rough edges serve as only minor distractions...*All the King's Men* has largescale dramatic scale and sweep. Hall's frequent collaborator, designer Eugene Lee, has used the vast open area of the DTC's Art District Theatre for an Olympic-sized set." *Variety* called Peter MacNichol's Jack Burden (through whose eyes the action takes place) "spellbinding," Jack Willis' Willie Stark "forcefully played," and Candy Buckley's Sadie Burke "mesmerizing." It also noted that at the first preview of this version, the play ran three hours and forty-five minutes, but by opening night, five performances later, it was cut down (or "fine tuned") by a full hour.

All the King's Men was turned into an opera called *Willie Stark* in 1981 by Carlisle Floyd, and was staged by Harold Prince at the Houston Grand Opera and then at the John F. Kennedy Center for the Performing Arts. A taped version of this production later was shown on PBS' *Great Performances*.

Robert Rossen produced, wrote and directed the screenplay for Columbia Pictures' acclaimed 1949 screen version of *All the King's Men* which won the year's Academy Award as Best Picture of the Year. Broderick Crawford received the Oscar as Best Actor for his compelling portrayal of Willie Stark and Mercedes McCambridge was named Best Supporting Actress for her Sadie Burke. John Ireland's Oscar nomination for Best Supporting Actor for his playing of Jack Burden lost out to Dean Jagger's performance in *12 O'Clock High*.

The New York Times' Bosley Crowther described the Rossen film as bouncing "from raw-boned melodrama into dark psychological depths and thrashes around in those regions until it claws back to violence again... Consistency of dramatic structure or of character revelation is not in it. But it has a superb pictorialism which perpetually crackles and explodes...it gathers a frightening comprehension of demagoguery in this land." Crowther concluded: "In short, Mr. Rossen has assembled in this starkly unprettified film a piece of pictorial journalism that is remarkable for its brilliant parts ...and you may count as pictorial detail the performance which Broderick Crawford gives...[He] concentrates tremendous energy into every delineation he plays."

In Great Britain, the movie was appraised by one critic: "This long, ambitious and scrupulously authentic film arrives in the wake of its own Oscars [although he erroneously included one for Best Screen-play, which went to Joseph Mankiewicz that year for *A Letter to Three Wives*]. It is not untypical in quality of American award winners, being more conspicuous for scope and worthiness of intention than for inspiration."

Between the acclaim director Robert Rossen achieved for *All the King's Men* and that he was given for *The Hustler* more than a dozen years later, he fell victim to McCarthy Era paranoia and ended up before the House Un-American Activities Committee where he admitted having been a former member of the Communist Party and named fifty-seven industry colleagues and acquaintances he had known as party members. (After *The Hustler*, Rossen directed one other film, *Lillith*, in 1964. He died two years later at age fifty-seven.)

In 1945, James Cagney and his producer brother William purchased the screen rights to Adria Locke Langley's *A Lion Is in the Streets*, which fictionalized the career of Huey Long. In the meantime, Robert Penn Warren's novel, play and motion picture came along. Ultimately, in 1953, William Cagney made a film of Langley's novel with brother James as Huey Long demagogic prototype, Hank Martin. *The New York Times*' Bosley Crowther found the Raoul Walsh-directed *A Lion Is in the Streets*, "a headlong and dynamic drama...and the portrait which Mr. Cagney draws of this loud and lively man could be an intended imitation of the bumptious and pugnosed 'Kingfish' Long...There never was any secret that Miss Langley's popular tale was based on the concrete example of the grotesque career of Huey Long."

The real Huey Long came to the screen in 1985 through Ken Burns and Richard Kilberg's acclaimed documentary of his life, later to have its television premiere on PBS. *All the King's Men* came to television in a two-part May 1958 production on *Kraft Theatre*. Sidney Lumet directed Don Mankiewicz's adaptation of Robert Penn Warren's novel and screenplay. John Shanley (*The New York Times*) found it "a powerfully-charged version of the saga of Willie Stark ...Neville Brand gives a dynamic performance." Although he felt the ending was "anti-climactic, Shanley praised the production for its "great emotional force" and for the "fine portrayals of Maureen Stapleton as a rejected woman...Fred J. Scollay as a disillusioned investigator and Frank Conroy as a judge." Nearly two decade later, another version of the Huey Long story came to TV in writer/director Robert Collins' *The Life and Assassination of the Kingfish*. Originally titled *Every Inch a King*, it starred Edward Asner as Long and was filmed in and around Baton Rouge. John J. O'Connor viewed it as "retrieving Huey Long's reputation and image from the black and white demagoguery thinly disguised as fiction in All the King's Men." In his review in *The New York Times*, he also felt that the teleplay got "snared in its own dramatic machinery...The result is less illuminating that curiously waffling, simultaneously implying evaluations but withdrawing direct statements...The script's multi-faceted conception of Long is overprotected."

STAGE

FIRST AMERICAN DICTATOR, *Nora Bayes Theatre*, New York, opened March 14, 1939 9 performances
Produced by George Lewis; A Drama by Jor Marcy (Nathan Sherman) and Jacob A. Weiser; Director, Humphrey Davis

Conrad Noles (Governor Huey Long); Gilbert Green (Frank Darcy); Oscar Jacobson (Representative Saunders); Humphrey Davis (Representative Buckley); John Culbertson (Representative Madden); Lewis Fisher (Senator Wheatley); Edmond LeCompte (Gus); Thomas Daly (Oscar)

ALL THE KING'S MEN, *President Theatre*, New York, opened January 14, 1948 21 performances
Produced by The Experimental Theatre, under the sponsorship of the American National Theatre and Academy; A Drama by Robert Penn Warren, based on his Pulitzer Prize novel; Directed and designed by Erwin Piscator; Setting and projections by Willis Knighton; Lighting, Hans Sondheimer; General manager, Leo Mittler; Stage manager, Martin Spohn

Robert Osterloh (Willie Stark); Helen Bernstein or Margret Wyler (Sadie Kovak); Dan Matthews (Jack Burden); Michael Michelas or Paul Curtis (Tom Stark); Andrea Johnson (Anne Stanton); Paul Ransom or Loren Denny (Adam Stanton); Thom Carney (Tiny Duffy); S. Woodrow Parfrey (Judge Erwin); S. Joseph Fantl or Scott Landers (Larson); Rosa Kudish or Helen Clarke (Lucy Stark); Claude Traverse (Professor); Louis Pasternack (Slade); Paul Brown (Mr. Sandeen); Elaine Eldridge (Mrs. Burden); Bill Beckham or Bob Lindsay (Sugar Boy); Jack Sorian (Frey); Theresa Lotito (Nurse); Janet Shannon or Babette Towbis (Doris); Harry Berhman or Louis Pasternack (Policeman); Roger Johnson or Richard Kraft (Politician); Egbert Swackhamer or Howard Jessor (Man)

President Theatre, New York, opened July 18, 1950
Produced by the President Players; A Drama by Robert Penn Warren; Director, Erwin Piscator; Setting and projections by Willis Knighton; Lighting, Hans Sondheimer; Stage manager, Norman Howard

Steve Gravers (Willie Stark); Doe Avedon (Sadie Burke); Dan Matthews (Jack Burden); Lori March (Anne Stanton); Scott Hale (Adam Stanton); Al Henderson (Tiny Duffy); Arthur Jarrett (Judge Erwin); Murray Druck (Larson); Madeleine Sherwood (Lucy Stark); Claude Traverse (Professor); Jack Bittner (Slade/ Frey); Robert Gibbons (Mr. Sandeen); Alice Edwards (Mrs. Burden/Doris); Gerald Ito

(Sugar Boy); Norman Howard (Policeman/Man); Terry Henderson, James Carti, Doris Schwartz, Seymore Geldin, Charles Jonas, Marylyn Dove, Fred Jaroslowsky (Townspeople, etc.)

74th Street Theatre, New York, opened October 15, 1959 40 performances
Produced by Michel Bouche, Arnold M. Brockman and Iris Michaels; A New Dramatization of the novel and play by Robert Penn Warren; Director, Mark Schoenberg; Scenery, Gary Smith; Lighting, Jules Fisher; Costumes, Sue Spector; Technical director, Ivor Balding; Stage manager, Louis Napoleon

Clifton James (Willie Stark); Marian Reardon (Sadie Burke); John Ragin (Jack Burden); Donald Quine (Tom Stark); Joan Harvey (Anne Stanton); Richard Kneeland (Dr. Adam Stanton); Roger C. Carmel (Tiny Duffy); Alex Reed (Judge Irwin); Mary Van Fleet (Lucy Stark); Stan Watt (Director of Tom Clark Memorial Hospital); Jay Kobler (Slade); Stephen J. Hall (Mr. Frey/Man in the Capitol/Man in the crowd); Will Corry (Sugar Boy); Elizabeth Farley, Alfred de Graff, Edna Jean Lundy, Ralph Maurer, Patricia Doyle, Jay Kobler (Crowd)

Forum Theater, Brandeis University, Waltham, Mass., opened July 10, 1963
Presented by the Brandeis University Forum Theater; A Revival of the play by Robert Penn Warren; Director, Robert Blackburn; Production designer, Ariel Ballif; Stage manager, Ray Duffy

Thomas Hill (Willie Stark); Eve Roberts (Sadie Burke); Roy R. Scheider (Jack Burden); Ron Huntewr (Tom Stark); Beverlee McKinsey (Anne Stanton); Robert Rees Evans (Adam Stanton); Whitney Haley (Tiny Duffy); Ned Cary (Judge Irwin); Johanna Madden (Lucy Stark); Anne Gerety (Jack's mother); William Swetland (The Professor); Harry Cooper (Larson); Ray Duffy (Slade); John Peters (Mr. Frey); Tucker Ashworth (Sugar Boy); Robert Blackburn (Heckler); Paul Lawrence (Goon)

Urban Arts Corps Theatre, New York, opened May 8, 1974 16 performances
Produced by The Urban Arts Corps; A Play by Robert Penn Warren; Director, Vinnette Carroll; Setting, Marty Kappell; Lighting, Ken Billington; Costumes, Edna Watson; Choreography, Edmond Kresley; Musical direction, Danny Holgate; Choral direction, Chapman Roberts; Songs, Gerry Richelson and Malcolm Dodds

Palmer Deane (Willie Stark); Maryce Carter (Sadie Burke); Nick Smith (Jack Burden); Marie Thomas (Anne Stanton); Brel Barbara Clarke (Lucy Stark); Damien Lake (Tom Stark); Everett Ensley (Tiny Duffy); Samuel Barton (Sugar Boy); Freeman Parks (Judge Irwin); Russell Gustafson (Larson); John Danelle (Adam Stanton); Samuel Barton (Mr. Frey); Brel Barbara Clarke (Mother)

WILLIE STARK, *Jones Hall for the Performing Arts*, Dallas, opened April 24, 26, 28, May 1, 1981; moved to *Opera House*, *John F. Kennedy Center*, Washington, D.C. opened May 9, 1981 12 performances
A Production of the Houston Grand Opera and the John F. Kennedy Center for the Performing Arts; A Musical Play based on Robert Penn Warren's *All the King's Men*; Director, Harold Prince; Music and libretto by Carlisle Floyd; Scenery, Eugene Lee; Lighting, Ken Billington; Costumes, Judith Dolan; Choreography, Francis Patrelle; Musical direction, John DeMain, Hal France; Chorus preparation, Norman Scribner; Sound, Jack Mann; Stage managers, David F. King, Steven Kelley, Darlene Durant

Timothy Nolen (Willie Stark); Jan Curtis (Sadie Burke); Alan Kays (Jack Burden); Dana Matles (Lucy Stark); Julia Conwell (Anne Stanton); Don Gerrard

(Judge Irwin); Lynn Griebling (Mrs. Stark); David Vosburgh (Tiny Duffy); Roger Moulson (Sugar Boy); Joseph Pearson (George Williams); Harry Torno (Reporter); Donald Bass (Mayor); Robert W. Ousley, Robert Williamson (Hugh and Jeff)

NOTE: This production was taped for PBS' *Great Performances*

Becton Theater, Fairleigh Dickinson University, Teaneck, N.J., opened April 18 through May 11, 1986 (Premier attraction)

Produced by The American Stage Company, Paul Sorvino, artistic director; A Play by Robert Penn Warren; Director, Victor D'Altorio; Sets and Lighting, Robert Klingelhoefer; Costumes, Deborah Jackson; Sound, Jim Rabkin; Stage manager, Sandra M. Bloom

Paul Sorvino (Willie Stark); Jo Twiss (Sadie Burke); Reed Jones (Jack Burden); Valerie Leonard (Anne Stanton); Penny Templeton (Lucy Stark); Clement Fowler (Judge Irwin); Paul Goodman (Adam Stanton); Ken Jennings (Sugar Boy); Susan Keenan (Jack's mother); Joe Rose (The Professor); Jim Hillgartner (Tiny Duffy); G. Denny French (William Larson); Mark Leonard Daniels (Tom Stark); Larry Attile (Frey); Robert Richman (Slade)

Dallas (Texas) Theater Center Arts District Theater, opened November 25, 1986

Produced by the Dallas Theater Center; A Play written and directed by Adrian Hall, based on Robert Penn Warren's novel; Settings, Eugene Lee; Lighting, Natasha Katz; Costumes, Donna M. Kress; Music, Randy Newman; Musical director, Richard Cumming

Jack Willis (Willie Stark); Candy Buckley (Sadie Burke); Peter MacNichol (Jack Burden); Linda Gehringer (Anne Stanton); Christina Ward (Lucy Stark); Neil Vipond (Judge Irwin); Sean Hennigen (Adam Stanton); Rudy Young (Sugar Boy); Ann Gerety (Jack's mother); Kelly Wright (Phoebe); and Bill Bolender, Ann Hamilton, William Larsen, Randy Moore, Kurt Rhoads

Trinity Repertory Company, Providence, R.I., opened April 13, 1987

Presented by the Trinity Repertory Company; A Play by Robert Penn Warren, based on his novel; Director, Adrian Hall; Scenery, Eugene Lee; Lighting, Natasha Katz; Costumes, William Lane; Dramaturg, Marsue Cumming MacNichol; Music, Randy Newman; Musical direction, Richard Cumming

Peter Gerety (Willie Stark); Candy Buckley (Sadie Burke); Peter MacNichol (Jack Burden); Anne Scurria (Anne Stanton/Ensemble); Richard Kneeland (Judge Irwin/Old Timer/Hugh Miller); Cynthia Strickland (Lucy Stark/Ensemble); Derek Meader (Adam Stanton/ Ensemble); James Carruthers (Tiny Duffy/Old Timer/ Ensemble); Brian McEleney (Theodore Murrell/Slade/ Mr. Pettus); Janice Duclos (Mrs. Patton/Lily Littlepaugh/Ensemble); Timothy Crowe (Editor/ Mr. Patton/ Ensemble); Becca Lish (Miss Dumonde/Nurse/Ensemble); Frederick Sullivan, Jr. (Tom Stark/Ensemble); Daniel von Bargen (Dolph Pillsbury/Byram B. White/George); Barry Blier (Sugar Boy/Ensemble); Barbara Orson (Mother/Ensemble); Akin Babatunde (Servant/ Sanitarium Attendant/Ensemble); David C. Jones (Ellis Burden/Old Timer/Hugh Miller); Stella Reed (Servant/ Ensemble)

THE KINGFISH, *John Houseman Theatre*, New York, opened March 24, 1991 52 performances

Claudet and Christen Productions Inc.; Produced by Michel Claudet and Darryl K. Christen; A oneman show by Larry L. King and Ben Z. Grant; Director, Perry Martin; Production design, R.S.E. Limited; Lighting, F. Mitchell Dana; Sound, Tom Gould

John McConnell (The Kingfish)

SCREEN

Columbia Pictures, released November 1949

Produced, directed and written by Robert Rossen; Based on the novel by Robert Penn Warren; Photography, Burnett Guffey; Art director, Sturges Carne; Set decorator, Louis Diage; Music by Louis Gruenberg; Assistant director, Sam Nelson; Montages, Donald W. Starling; Music director, Morris Stoloff; Costumes and gowns by Jean Louis; Sound recording, Frank Goodwin; Technical adviser, Robert Parrish; Editor, Al Clark

Broderick Crawford (Willie Stark); John Ireland (Jack Burden); John Derek (Tom Stark); Mercedes McCambridge (Sadie Burke); Joanne Dru (Anne Stanton); Sheppard Strudwick (Adam Stanton); Ralph Dumke (Tiny Duffy); Anne Seymour (Lucy Stark); Katharine Warren (Mrs. Burden); Raymond Greenleaf (Judge Stanton); Walter Burke (Sugar Boy); Will Wright (Dolph Pillsbury); Grandon Rhodes (Floyd McEvoy); H. C. Miller (Pa Stark); William Bruce (Commissioner); A. C. Tillman (Sheriff); Richard Hale (Hale); Helene Stanley (Mrs. Hale); Phil Tully (Football Coach); Truett Myers (Minister); Houseley Stevenson (Madison); Judd Holdren, Pat O'Malley (Politicians); Paul Maxey (Local Chairman); Reba Watterson (Receptionist); Ted French (Dance Caller); Louis Mason (Second Minister); John Skins Miller (Drunk); King Donovan (Reporter); Edwin Chandler (Radio Announcer); Paul Ford, Frank Wilcox (Men); Frank McLure (Doctor); Irving Smith (Butler)

A LION IS IN THE STREETS, *Warner Bros.*, released September 1953

A William Cagney Production; Producer, William Cagney; Director, Raoul Walsh; Screenplay, Luther Davis, based on the novel by Adria Locke Langley; Photography, Harry Stradling; Production designer, Wiard Ihnen; Music, Franz Waxman; Set decorator, Fred M. MacLean; Special effects, Roscoe Cline; Sound, John Kean; Editor, George Amy

James Cagney (Hank Martin); Anne Francis (Flamingo); Barbara Hale (Verity Wade); John McIntyre (Jeb Brown); Jeanne Cagney (Jeannie Brown); Warner Anderson (Jules Bolduc); Frank McHugh (Rector); Larry Keating (Robert); Lon Chaney, Jr. (Spurge); Onslow Stevens (Guy Polli); Sara Haden (Lula May); Roland Winters (Prosecutor); James Millcan (Mr. Beach); Mickey Simpson (Tim Beck); Burt Mustin (Smith); Irene Tedrow (Sophy); Ellen Corby (Singing Woman); Sarah Selby (Townswoman)

HUEY LONG, *RKB-Florentine Films*, released September 1985

Produced by Ken Burns and Richard Kilberg; A Documentary Film of the life of Huey Long; Director, Ken Burns; Screenplay, Geoffrey C. Ward; Photography, Buddy Squires and Ken Burns; Consultants, William Leuchtenburg, Alan Brinkley, Arthur M. Schlesinger, Jr., William Snyder and Jerome Liebling; Music, John Colby; Additional music, Randy Newman; Sound, Greg Moring

David McCullough (Narrator)

TELEVISION

ALL THE KING'S MEN, Kraft Theatre, televised May 14 and 21, 1958 NBC two 60 minute segments
Produced by Robert Herridge; Director, Sidney Lumet; Adaptation by Don Mankiewicz of Robert Penn Warren's novel

Neville Brand (Willie Stark); Maureen Stapleton (Sadie Burke); Fred J. Scollay (Jack Burden); Anne Meacham (Anne Stanton); William Prince (Adam Stanton); Robert Emhardt (Tiny Duffy); Frank Conroy (Judge Irwin); John Fiedler (Sugar Boy)

THE LIFE AND ASSASSINATION OF THE KINGFISH, televised March 21, 1977 NBC 2 hours
Tomorrow Entertainment; Executive Producer, Thomas W. Moore; Producer, Paul Leaf; Writer/Director, Robert Collins; Photography, Ric Waite; Music by Fred Karlin; Song "Kingfish" performed by Randy Newman; Costume designer, Ruth Morley; Set decorator, Joanne MacDougall; Associate producer, Robert Grand; Editor, Patrick Kennedy

Edward Asner (Huey Long); Diane Kagan (Rose Long); Nicholas Pryor (Manners); Frederic Cook (Earl Long); Steven Ramay (Russell Long); Dorrie Kavanaugh (Alice Grosjean); Gary Allen (J. R.); Stanley Reyes (Seymour Weiss); Jake Staples (O. K. Allen); Wilbur Swartz (Gerald L.K. Smith); Tom Alden (Dr. Vidrine); Edward Hoerner (Dr. Rives); Jean Mayre (Sister Michael); Jerry Leggio (Jack Williamson); Brooks Read (Rep. Fruge); Donegan Smith (Harley Bozeman); Rod Masterson (Murphy Roden); Don Draper (Desobre); Walter Krousel (House Speaker); and Robert Adams, Eliott Keener, J. Frank Lucas, Don Lutenbacher, Pat McNamara

WILLIE STARK, Great Performances, televised September 28, 1981 PBS 2 hours 30 minutes

(see Houston Grand Opera production above under stage)

HUEY LONG, Documentary Film shown on PBS Television, 1987 (see screen)

THE AMAZING DR. CLITTERHOUSE
A Play by Barre Lyndon (1936)

Synopsis

Dr. Clitterhouse, a professor writing a detailed volume on criminal mentality who has become an amateur cracksman himself, decides to study his subject from the inside. He ventures into a life of crime -- for research purposes, of course, and becomes involved with a gang of thieves under one Benny Keller, helping to mastermind a huge fur robbery. The doctor finds that he enjoys the camaraderie, finding it a lot warmer than in other professions, and the adventure exhilarating. Ultimately, his research into the criminal mind comes to an end, but he discovers that retiring from the profession and returning to medicine is not quite as easy as he thought. He is pressured into helping fleece his rich friends. At this point, he decides that perhaps he needs a chapter on the rationale and act of homicide and does in the now-blackmailing Keller, recording Keller's reactions as he dies.

Eventually, Dr. Clitterhouse is arrested, but he manages to convince a jury, after pleading insanity as his defense, that he actually was sane during the crimes he committed -- and he is acquitted. The jury, it seems, felt that any man who insists he is insane at one point and sane at another must in fact be insane.

Comment and Critique

London-born playwright Barre Lyndon (1896-1972) had been a onetime journalist and short-story writer before turning to the stage. His first play was a minor one called *Speed* (1931). Next came *The Amazing Dr. Clitterhouse* in 1936, a somewhat lighthearted play about psychology and gangsterism. He later went on the write *They Came by Night* and then *The Man in Half Moon Street*, which, like *Clitterhouse*, was adapted to the screen. Lyndon himself went to Hollywood in 1941 to write such memorable fare as *The Lodger*, *Hangover Square*, *The House on 92nd Street*, *Night Has a Thousand Eyes*, *The Greatest Show on Earth*, and *War of the Worlds*, among others.

The Amazing Dr. Clitterhouse had its premiere in London in the summer of 1936, with Ralph Richardson in the lead, Charles Mortimer as his "subject" and subsequently his nemesis, and Meriel Forbes as the gangster's moll. Its popularity prompted Jack Warner to purchase the screen rights and to stage it in America with producer Gilbert Miller. It came to Broadway the following March, this time with Cedric Hardwicke in the lead, together with Clarence Derwent and Muriel Hutchison. Hardwicke, *The New York Times*' Brooks Atkinson found, "acts his part with the greatest of ease, relishing the excitement and sweetening the irony by the modesty of his style of playing. Like a good many minor pieces from the English stage, *The Amazing Dr. Clitterhouse* is not overburdened with story or ingenuity. It is a crime play in the genre of frank make-believe. But Mr. Lyndon has set his story down with so much quiet dexterity, and Sir Cedric is playing the chief part with so much grace and good humor that no one will be satisfied with a lawful life as long as this criminal calendar remains on the boards."

The Amazing Dr. Clitterhouse ran for just eighty performances, toured briefly, then seemed to have vanished from the stage repertoire. It had a much longer life as a film starring Edward G. Robinson, adapted by John Wexley and up-and-coming John Huston. Supporting Robinson, who of course had the title part, were Claire Trevor and Humphrey Bogart, plus the venerable Warner Bros. stock company of players. Of the 1938 film, critic Howard Barnes wrote in the *New York Herald Tribune*: "A deft and amusing job of screen transcription has been done with *The Amazing Dr. Clitterhouse*...Edward G. Robinson would not have been my choice for the Clitterhouse role, but he performs the assignment capably. Perhaps it is because he has been so clearly identified with gangster roles that he has trouble in underlining the Jekyll and Hyde quality which Cedric Hardwicke accomplished so suavely in the drama. In any case, he never fails to give the picture dramatic punch when it requires it, whether he is calmly stealing or murdering, or testing the reflexes of his henchmen in the very act of lawbreaking."

The play came to television in 1957 in a staging by the BBC, with Hugh Sinclair starring. "The flattering assumption that law-abiding citizens, if they chose, could show hardened criminals a thing or two about their profession has animated many a plot," the critic for *The London Times* wrote, "but in Barre Lyndon's *The Amazing Dr. Clitterhouse*, produced on BBC, it comes in an unpleasingly pretentious guise. For Dr. Clitterhouse is no genial raffles undertaking amateur burglary merely for amusement; his object, it is often stated, is research. Friendly, but never too familiar, he moves among his shady associates, who are shown regarding him with puzzles reverence as a master mind and a superior counsellor...Mr. Hugh Sinclair, playing Clitterhouse with dignity and restraint, kept the character firmly at arm's length."

STAGE

THE AMAZING DR. CLITTERHOUSE, Theatre Royal Haymarket, London, opened August 6, 1936

Produced by Frederick Harrison Trust Ltd.; A Melodrama by Barre Lyndon; Director, Claud Gurney; Decor, Aubrey Hammond; Meriel Forbes' dresses, Janet Jackson Ltd.; Stage manager, Charles La Trobe

Ralph Richardson (Dr. Clitterhouse, M.D.); Meriel Forbes (Daisy); Charles Mortimer (Benny Kellerman); Charles Farrell ("Pal" Green); Frederick Worlock (Sir William Grant); Joan Marion (Nurse Ann); Eric Stanley (Chief Inspector Charles); Vincent Holman (Sergeant Bates); Ralph Michael (A Constable); S. Victor Stanley (Oakie); Norman Pierce ("Tug" Wilson); Hugh E. Wright ("Badger" Lee)

Hudson Theatre, New York, opened March 2, 1937 80 performances

Produced by Gilbert Miller in association with Warner Brothers; A Melodrama by Barre Lyndon; Director, Lewis Allen; Settings, Raymond Sovey

Cedric Hardwicke (Dr. Clitterhouse, M.D.); Muriel Hutchison (Daisy); Clarence Derwent (Benny Keller); Ernest Jay ("Pal" Green); Frederick Worlock (Sir William Grant); Helen Trenholme (Nurse Ann); Edward Fielding (Chief Inspector Charles); Stephen Fox (Sergeant Bates); Ralph Sumpter (A Constable); Alexander Field (Oakie); Ross Chetwynd ("Tug" Wilson); Victor Beercroft ("Badger" Lee)

SCREEN

Warner Bros.-First National, released 1938

Associate producer, Robert Lord; Director, Anatole Litvak; Screenplay, John Wexley and John Huston, based on the play by Barre Lyndon; Photography, Tony Gaudio; Art director, Carl Jules Weyl; Wardrobe, Milo Anderson; Music, Max Steiner; Music conductor, Leo F. Forbstein; Sound, C. A. Riggs; Editor, Warren Low

Edward G. Robinson (Dr. Clitterhouse); Claire Trevor (Jo Keller); Humphrey Bogart ("Rocks" Valentine); Gale Page (Nurse Randolph); Donald Crisp (Inspector Lane); Allen Lane ("Okay"); Thurston Hall (Grant); John Litel (Prosecuting Attorney); Henry O'Neill (Judge); Maxie Rosenbloom (Butch); Curt Bois (Rabbit); Bert Hanlan (Pat); Ward Bond (Tug); Vladimir Sokoloff (Popus); Billy Wayne (Candy); Robert Homans (Lieutenant Johnson); William Haade (Watchman); Thomas Jackson (Connors); Edward Gargan (Sergeant); Winifred Harris (Mrs. Ganswoort); Eric Stanley (Dr. Ames); Loia Cheaney (Nurse Donor); Wade Boteler (Captain MacLevy); Libby Taylor (Mrs. Jefferson); Edgar Dearing (Patrolman); Sidney Bracy (Chemist); Irving Bacon (Jury Foreman); Vera Lewis (Woman Juror); Bruce Mitchell (Bailiff)

TELEVISION

THE AMAZING DR. CLITTERHOUSE, televised July 7, 1957 BBC 80 minutes

Produced by the British Broadcasting Corporation; A Play by Barre Lyndon; Director,

Alan Bromly; Designer, Frederick Knapman

Hugh Sinclair (Dr. Clitterhouse, M.D.); Vera Day (Daisy); David Lander (Benny Kellerman); Jerold Wells ("Pal" Green); Andrew Cruickshank (Sir William Grant); Joy Parker (Nurse Ann); Ronald Leight-Hunt (Chief Inspector Charles); Frank Sieman (Sergeant Bates); Reginald Jessup (A Constable); Bill Owen (Oakie); Michael Bird ("Tug" Wilson); Wilfrid Brambell ("Badger" Lee)

THE AMAZING DR. CLITTERHOUSE, televised April 23, 1962 BBC 80 minutes
Produced by the British Broadcasting Corporation; A Play by Barre Lyndon; Director, George Foa; Designer, Roy Oxley

Leo McKern (Dr. Clitterhouse, M.D.); Patsy Rowlands (Daisy); John Bennet (Benny Kellerman); William Marlowe ("Pal" Green); Ian Colin (Sir William Grant); Jill Dixon (Nurse Ann); Robert Cawdron (Chief Inspector Charles); Ian Paterson (Sergeant Bates); Barry Wilsher (Oakie); Charles Kay ("Badger" Lee)

ANATOL

A Comedy cycle of one-act plays by Arthur Schnitzler (1893); translated into English as *The Affairs of Anatol* by Harley Granville-Barker (1911)

Synopsis

Vienna: Turn of the Century

Questioning Fate: Bachelor Anatol hypnotizes Hilda to discover her love and faithfulness to him but finds he can not go through with the hypnotic inquisition.
Christmas Shopping: Anatol's conquest of Gabrielle collapses when she gives him her Christmas bouquet for his mistress with the message: "From a woman, who, perhaps, might know how to love as well as you -- but who hasn't the courage."
Episode: Anatol decides to bury his past by burning a large collection of love letters in his friend Max's fireplace, but saves one letter from Bibi, a woman who will never forget nor cease loving him. Max's friend Bianca arrives, kisses Max, and politely nods to Anatol, asking if they have not met before in the dim, dark past. Anatol leaves abruptly and Max asks "Bibi" to stay.
Milestones: Anatol's jealously of Emily erupts when she refuses to part with two treasured rings: a ruby and a black diamond given to her by former lovers. A furious Anatol cancels their forthcoming marriage and calls her a "harlot."
The Farewell Supper: Determined to end his affair with ballerina Mimi, Anatol and Max await her arrival at the Hotel Sacher Restaurant. Between huge quantities of wine and food, Mimi tells Anatol she is in love with Carl of the ballet's orchestra and that this is their farewell supper.
Dissolution: Anatol, convinced "there is nothing more disagreeable than to be the lover of a married woman," unhappily ends his affair with Elsa.
Anatol's Wedding Morning: Max is appalled to discover Anatol has spent the night before his wedding with actress Lona. Lona decides they should all stay at Anatol's for a quiet day, but he regrets he has other plans -- like getting married. Explosive Lona threatens to disrupt the ceremony and vows never to let him go, but Max quiets the enraged actress by assuring her the wedding is a mere formality and Anatol will soon return to her.

Comment and Critique

Arthur Schnitzler, M. D. (1862-1931) was born in Vienna where he practiced medicine, wrote novels and plays, the best of which was his delightful 1893 comedy *Anatol*, later translated into English by Harley Granville-Barker as *The Affairs of Anatol*. With John Barrymore as the passionate, philandering bachelor, *The Affairs of Anatol* opened on Broadway in late 1912.

"The piece is not strictly a play. It is a succession of five short episodes in which Anatol and Max are recurring characters," reported *The New York Dramatic Mirror*. "With each scene we have a new heroine...John Barrymore makes Anatol one of the best characters he has ever played -- one, moreover, that gives him opportunity to show that he is one of the best light comedians we have...He makes Anatol his own...If humor and a rich fancy in the form of a wholly unconventional comedy with a thousand facets, and delightfully played, can exercise an appeal in New York, *The Affairs of Anatol* ought to fill Mr. Ames's little playhouse for a long time."

The Affairs of Anatol lasted seventy-two performances, during which time Marguerite Clark replaced Doris Keane, and Barrymore's first wife, Katherine Corri Harris, whom he married on September 1, 1910, succeeded Miss Clark.

The New York Times headed its review, "Very Smart Are Anatol's Affairs," and praised the overall acting of the company adding, "good taste marks the presentation of *Anatol* from start to finish, and the setting are charmingly appropriate and beautiful...Mr. Barry-more plays here with charming variety and plenty of the right sort of humor."

Nearly two decades later, *Anatol* reappeared on Broadway on in early 1931. The production was praised but the acting was not. "Bela Blau has mounted it handsomely, not forgetting the Viennese Waltzes," reported Brooks Atkinson (*The New York Times*). "And Joe [sic] Mielziner has lavished upon Schnitzler's anatomy of love some of the most alluring settings in years... As Anatol, Joseph Schildkraut is mechanical and constricted in a part that should be romantically exhilarating. He has little of the free improvisation that is the charm of Schnitzler's bundle of episodes. But Walter Connolly is quietly merry as Anatol's knavish comrade...As the operatic hussy Miriam Hopkins is vastly amusing...*Anatol* without a dynamic Anatol is makeshift entertainment."

John Mason Brown (*The Evening Post*) wrote a long appraisal of the 1931 production, considering it "as heavy in its touch as the text is light. What is more fatal still is the sad fact that all of its six scenes are played so monotonously that they emerge with the deadening similarity of some many peas in a pod...Mr. Schildkraut's Anatol is far from ideal...for the most part [it] is insensitive to the illusions he seeks to preserve in each new appearance...On the whole, however, the production at the Lyceum manages to make *Anatol* about as sophisticated as those vaudeville skits used to be that dealt with love, marriage and divorce ...I can only advise you to reread your *Anatol* at home, and forswear this current performance."

Robert Benchley in *The New Yorker* admired the "six of the loveliest stage sets I have ever seen, designed by Jo Mielziner," but acknowledged, "*Anatol* is very nice to read and might possibly have acted well with Mr. John Barrymore in the title role, but with Mr. Schildkraut taking his own good time (and ours) to get his laughs, the scenes which occur in the first hour seemed interminable...Mr. Walter Connolly, who, as Max, carries on throughout the whole thing with a comforting ease and grace." Richard Lockridge (*The Evening Sun*) also admired the magnificent designs for each scene by Mielziner but found "few things are less convincing than such a ghostly play as Arthur Schnitzler's *Anatol*."

Fay and Michael Kanin adapted *Anatol* to the musical stage as *The Gay Life*, which opened on Broadway in November 1961 to generally good reviews. Walter Kerr (*Herald Tribune*), however, found the Kanin's libretto had "mistaken the elegance of a chase among the chaise longes for the energy and industry of an ice hockey rink." Robert Coleman (*New York Mirror*) felt *The Gay Life* "isn't gay enough...It's a beautiful, tuneful and driving show, but it lacks humor, and takes a long time to work up speed...in this old-fashioned musical," and found the Kanin's libretto, "a lacklustre adaptation."

Howard Taubman *(The New York Times)* described *The Gay Life* as "colorful, cheerful and leisurely in an Old World Way," with "Anatol, played with a pleasant, good-looking diffidence by Walter Chiari, Italian stage and film performer...Howard Dietz and Arthur Schwartz, too long absent from Broadway, have written some agreeable songs, mingling memories of Old Vienna and modern Broadway...But the nicest of all the gemutlich things in *The Gay Life* is Barbara Cook."

Richard Watts, Jr. (*New York Post*) reported, "The happiest feature of *The Gay Life* is its lovely pictorial evocation in setting and costume of the romantic spirit of Vienna at the turn of the century...as well as some striking dance numbers and the lively performances of Barbara Cook and Elizabeth Allen. But heaviness sets in when it gets around to its libretto ...And I'm afraid it isn't easily helped by the performance of the Italian actor, Walter Chiari in the important central role."

John Chapman (*Daily News*) called *The Gay Life* a "Stunningly handsome, engaging musical of Old Vienna... There are 15 scenes telling this jam-packed story, all for them elegant. Highlights are a spectacular ball and an exciting Gypsy dance staged by Herbert Ross, a lovely picture of a Viennese street on Christmas Eve and a breathtakingly beautiful wedding finale." John McClain (*Journal-American*) conceded that, after a slow start, *The Gay Life* was "colorful and melodic...an Evening of Good Fun."

Fifteen years after *The Gay Life* disappeared from Broadway after an unsatisfactory 113 performances for which lyricist Howard Dietz blamed its leading man, Walter Chiari, who "couldn't act, dance, sing, or speak English, which was a handicap," *Anatol* was revived at London's Open Space Theatre. Ned Chaillet (*Plays and Players*) reported: "I have my doubts that an homage to Schnitzler constitutes experimental theatre. Certainly it is not experimental to present Schnitzler's insights of the 1890s as though they were relevant to the 1970s...Derek Godfrey plays Anatol as the smooth but cowardly mesmerist...It is Prunella Scale's energetic portrayal of the six women in the play that keeps the performance lively."

In 1985, Ellis Rabb and Nicholas Martin reworked Schnitzler's *Anatol* and retitled it *The Loves of Anatol*. The "revamped Schnitzler," featuring Stephen Collins as Anatol, was viewed by Frank Rich (*The New York Times*) as "not, as such calamities usually are, merely an inept production. Nor is it a radical reinterpretation of the text, about which reasonable people might disagree. What the director Ellis Rabb has done to Schnitzler's work is to mutilate it willfully, with a thoroughness that could brings fans of the original text to tears even as the rest of the audience is put to sleep." Rich went on: "In *The Loves of Anatol*, every aspect of *Anatol* has been inverted. A delicate, melancholy comedy has been transformed into a vulgar and unfunny boulevard farce...Due to Mr. Rabb's insistence on caricaturing most of Anatol's lovers as shrieking burlesque tarts, the playwright instead emerges as a misogynist -- and his exploration of the unbridled erotic impulse is rendered completely sexless."

Douglas Watt (*Daily News*) described the Rabb-Martin corruption of Schnitzler "clumsily adapted and unbecomingly acted...Stephen Collins, though dashing enough in appearance, is about as romantic as a yard-stick...Michael Learned pumps some life into the second half...Ellis Rabb, who is responsible, along with Nicholas Martin, for the awkward and, in at least one instance, ungrammatical adaptation, has tried to stage the play with some style, but what could he hope to do with such a cast? The scenery, striking costumes, and lighting achieve more."

London's Gate Theatre Club produced *Anatol* in March 1987. John Walsh (*London Evening Standard*) reported, "Arthur Schnitzler -- best known to us through the filming of his 10-part play, *La Ronde*, and the televising of his stories as *Vienna 1900* -- was both the poet and the great debunker of late nineteenth century romanticism...A hundred years on, the sophisticated dialogue of these ironic encounters remains fresh and witty -- the Coward of *Private Lives* would have felt quite at home among the dressing gowns and bitten back emotions. Director Michael Robinson provides a new translation, plays it lightly but misses no nuance of regret or retribution. Simon Shepherd and Malcolm Sinclair play Max and Anatol as cocksure public-school roues with precisely the right combination of hypocrisy and charm. And, playing all seven women, Jane Bertish -- imperious, calculating or enraged as the occasion demands -- is a marvel of hot-blooded Viennese chic."

Francis King (*Sunday Telegraph*) added, "Through emigre Central European film directors and script-writers of the Thirties, clearly influenced by him, the tone of Arthur Schnitzler's voice-witty, worldly-wise, sophisticated, detached [is] better known to most Anglo-Saxons than all but one of his works, *Reigen* (*La Ronde*)...His 1895 *Anatol* [is] an unsparing little masterpiece, far ahead of its time. It has now been brilliantly revived under Michael Robinson's direction at the little Gate Theatre...There are first-rate performances from Malcolm Sinclair as Anatol...from Simon Shepherd as the cynical friend...and from Jane Bertish as all seven of the women."

Giles Gordon (*London Daily News*) noted that "Schnitzler was a near contemporary and friend of Freud, and also studied medicine. As a writer, he was drawn to the psychological depiction of his neurotic characters. Stylistically, he never repeated himself. *Anatol* consists of seven episodes, each self-contained ...Michael Robinson, who provides the new, reasonably colloquial translation, also directs on the pocket handkerchief-sized stage."

In 1921, Cecil B. DeMille filmed *Anatol*, altering the title to *Five Kisses*, based on a scenario by Jeanie Macpherson which included a few of Schnitzler's characters but virtually nothing of his play. The film was released as *The Affairs of Anatol*, starring matinee idol Wallace Reid with Gloria Swanson, Bebe Daniels, Agnes Ayres and Wanda Hawley as the women in his life.

Fritz Tidden (*Moving Picture World*) wrote, "Should that famous Austrian, the good Dr. Arthur Schnitzler, view the Cecil B. DeMille-Jeanie Macpherson-Paramount version of his celebrated play, *The Affairs of Anatol*, he would probably turn pale and then surely recognize as the last remaining shred of his work that title of the picture. That is absolutely all there is left of the brilliant, cynical, ultra-sophisticated continental comedy." Adele Whitely Fletcher (*Motion Picture Magazine*) noted, "If a huge sum was given to the screen right to Schnitzler's *The Affairs of Anatol* in order that the new Cecil B. DeMille production might be, it is a glaring example of extravagance...Certainly this *deluxe* review of ladies fair, boudoirs and cabarets is a far-fetched version of the sophisticated Viennese tale."

Cecil B. DeMille in his *Autobiography* (Prentice-Hall, 1959) admitted that his motion picture version was "Based on, or it would be more accurate to say, suggested by, the play by Arthur Schnitzler." W. Somerset Maugham accused DeMille and Macpherson of plagiarism until DeMille convinced the author "there was only the remotest superficial resemblance between his story and ours." Maugham had suggested the filming of Schnitzler's *The Affairs of Anatol* to both DeMille and Jesse L. Lasky. The hand-tinted DeMille opus was judged by Robert E. Sherwood, then a motion picture reviewer for *Life* magazine: "Should be enormously popular, especially with those who think Schnitzler is a cheese."

Prior to the opening of *Anatol* as *The Gay Life* on Broadway, *The Affairs of Anatol* was produced on television's *Hollywood Playhouse* in March 1961. John Van Dreelen was *Anatol* but the teleplay by Robert Boon was condensed for TV's time-frame and lost much of the Viennese zest and content in the transition. Far more appealing with the 1965 BBC production with Robert Hardy, John Wood, and Moira Redmond, that came to the U.S. four years later.

STAGE

CONVERSATIONS OF ANATOL, *Little Theatre*, London, opened March 11, 1911
Anatol dialogues by Arthur Schnitzler, paraphrased by Granville Barker
Ask No Questions and You'll Hear No Stories:
Granville Barker (Anatol); Nigel Playfair (Max); Gertrude Robins (Hilda)
A Christmas Present:
Granville Barker (Anatol); Katharine Pole (Gabrielle)
A Farewell Supper:
Granville Barker (Anatol); Nigel Playfair (Max); Lillah McCarthy (Mimi); A. B. Tapping (Waiter)
An Episode:
Granville Barker (Anatol); Nigel Playfair (Max); Dorothy Minto (Bianca)
The Wedding Morning:
Granville Barker (Anatol); Nigel Playfair (Max); Alice Crawford (Lona); Harry Dodd (Franz)

THE AFFAIRS OF ANATOL, *Little Theatre*, New York, opened October 14, 1912 72 performances
Produced by Winthrop Ames; A sequence of seven episodes, a comedy by Arthur Schnitzler; English adaptation by Harley Granville-Barker; Director, George Foster Platt; Miss Keane's dresses by Mme. Allouise; Miss Kane's and Miss Emmett's dresses by Lucille, Ltd.; Miss Lee's dresses by Henri Bendel; General manager, E. E. Lyons
John Barrymore (Anatol); Doris Keane (succeeded by Marguerite Clark) (Mimi); Marguerite Clark (succeeded by Katherine Harris) (Hilda); Gail Kane (Bianca); Oswald Yorke (succeeded by Frank Reicher) (Max); Isabelle Lee (Lona); Alfred de Bell (Waiter); Albert Easdale (Franz); Katherine Emmett (Gabrielle)

Elitch's Gardens, Denver, opened July 18, 1915
A Comedy by Arthur Schnitzler; Director, Daniel Fager
Forrest Winant (Anatol); Charles Dow Clark (Max); Leona Powers (Mimi); Marion Dentler (Hilda); Jessie Mueller (Gabrielle); Louise Valentine (Lona); Wilfred Lytell (Waiter); Robert Homans (Butler); Gabrielle Gelinas (Bianca)

Greenwich Theatre, New York, opened November 4, 1929
Produced by Chamberlain Brown; A Comedy by Arthur Schnitzler; Director, Samuel T. Godfrey
Rollo Peters (Anatol); Margaret Namara (Gabrielle); Sylvia Breamer (Elsa); Douglas Wood (Max); Georgette Cohan (Minna); Frances Dale (Bianca); Mary Law (Lona); Don Ameche (Waiter); Cyril Wild (Franz)

ANATOL, *Lyceum Theatre*, opened January 16, 1931 45 performances
Produced by Bela Blau, Inc.; A Comedy by Arthur Schnitzler, adapted by Harley Granville-Barker; Director, Gabriel Beer-Hoffmann; Settings, Jo Mielziner; Costumes and Uniforms, Helene Pons; Music arranged by Macklin Morrow; Music director, Alexander Hass; Company manager, L. S. Leavitt; Stage managers, Royal C. Stout and Roger Ramsell

Joseph Schildkraut (Anatol); Miriam Hopkins (Mimi); Dennie Moore (Hilda); Walter Connolly (Max); Ruthelma Stevens (Lona); Elena Miramova (Bianca); Patricia Collinge (Gabrielle); Anne Forrest (Emily); Roger Ramsdell (Franz); Oswald Yorke (Waiter);

SONGS: "Wien, du Stadt meiner Traume"; "Im Prater bluh'n wieder die Baume"

ANATOL, *Gate Theatre*, London, opened October 9, 1935
Dialogues by Arthur Schnitzler; Paraphrased in English by Harley Granville-Barker

Basil Bartlett (Anatol); Vincent Price (Max); Joan Collier (Hilda); Sylvia Coleridge (Elsa); Pamela Stanley (Mimi); Betty Hardy (Lona); Lindisferne Hamilton (Emily); Phillada Sewell (Bianca); Frederic Madell (Franz Waiter)

Bucks County Playhouse, New Hope, Pa., summer, 1940
Produced by Kenyon Nicholson and Theron Bamberger; A Comedy by Arthur Schnitzler; Director, Heinrich Schnitzler; Settings, John Koenig

Louis Calhern (Anatol); Hunter Gardner (Max); Barbara Parker (Hilda); Natalie Schafer (Gabrielle); Mary Mason (Bianca); Haila Stoddard (Mimi); Florence McGee (Lona); Thomas Coley (Waiter)

Touring Company, season 1960-61
Produced by The Repertory Company of the Association of Producing Artists; A Musical adaptation of Schnitzler's dialogues; Adapted from the German translation by Lilly Lessing; Music by Tom Jones, based on themes from Offenbach; Director, Ellis Rabb; Settings, William D. Roberts; Lighting, Richard Bolfson; Costumes, Oliver Olsen; Musical director, Conrad Susa; Musical supervisor, Edward Muller; Choreographers, Rhoda Levine and Tao Strong; Assistant directors, Richard Easton and Keene Curtis; Company manager, Robert Alan Gold

Richard Easton (Anatol); David Hooks (Max); Rosemary Harris (Gabrielle); Eve Roberts (Cora); Olive Dunbar (Annie); Dorothy Victor (Ilona); Betty Hellman (Annette); Keene Curtis (Franz); Earl Montgomery (Baron Dieble); Edward Grover (Fleider); Paul Sparer, Jack McQuiggan, Robert Gold, Janell MacArthur (Viennese); Conrad Susa (Pianist)

THE GAY LIFE, *Shubert Theatre*, New York, opened November 18, 1961 113 performances
Produced by Kermit Bloomgarden; A musical comedy based on Arthur Schnitzler's play *Anatol*; Book by Fay and Michael Kanin; Director, Gerald Freedman; Music by Arthur Schwartz; Lyrics by Howard Dietz; Settings, Oliver Smith; Lighting, Jean Rosenthal; Costumes, Lucinda Ballard; Musical numbers staged by Herbert Ross; Musical director and vocal arrangement, Herbert Greene; Orchestrations, Don Walker; Dance music arrangements, Robert Starer; Magical illusions created and designed by Jack Adams; Stage managers, Kermit Kegley, Cliff Cothren, Charles McDaniel, Rico Froehlich

Walter Chiari (Anatol); Barbara Cook (Liesl Brandel); Jules Munshin (Max); Jeanne Bal (Helene); Elizabeth Allen (Magda); Loring Smith (Herr Brandel); Lu Leonard (Frau Brandel); Leonard Elliott (Franz); Jack Adams (The Great Gaston); Yvonne Constant (Mimi); Joanne Spiller (Anna); Sterling Clark (Usher); Michael Quinn (Proprietor); Rico Froehlich (Otto/Doorman); Ted Lambrinos, Russell Goodwin (Waiters); Aura Vainio (Grandmother); Gerald Teijelo (Photographer); Carl Nicholas (Headwaiter); Hal Norman (Waiter); Ken Ayers, Russell Goodwin, Tony LaRusso, Ted Lambrinos, Carl Nicholas, Hal Norman, Michael Quinn, Loyce Baker, Joan Bishop, June Card, Luce Ennis, Jeanne Grant, Carole O'Hara, Nancy Radcliffe, Joanne Spiller (Singers); Kip Andrews, Karoly Barta, Sterling Clerk, Thatcher Clark, Ray Kirchner, Louis Kosman, Michel Stuart, Gerald Teijelo, Patrick King, Bonnie Brandon, Carolyn Clark, Marion Fels, Carol Flemming, Leslie Franzos, Bettye Jenkins, Doris Ortiz, Eleonore Treiber, Aura Vainio, Jenny Workman (Dancers)

MUSICAL NUMBERS: "What a Charming Couple"; "Why Go Anywhere at All?"; "Bring Your Darling Daughter"; "Magic Moment"; "Now I'm Ready for a Frau"; "Who Can?, You Can"; "Oh, Mein Liebchen"; "The Label on the Bottle"; "This Kind of Girl"; "The Bloom Is Off the Rose"; "I'm Glad I'm Single"; "Something You Never Had Before"; "You Will Never Be Longly"; "You're Not the Type"; "Come A-Wandering With Me"; "I Never Had a Chance"; "I Wouldn't Marry You"; "For the First Time"

Original cast recording: Capitol Records

ANATOL, Open Space Theatre, London, opened February 11, 1976

Produced by the Open Space Company with the assistance of the Goethe Institute; Produced and Directed by Charles Marowitz; A Comedy by Arthur Schnitzler, English translation by Frank Marcus; Settings, Robin Don; Costumes, Susan Thompson

Derek Godfrey (Anatol); Nicholas Selby (Max); Prunella Scales (Mimi, Hilda, Bianca, Gabrielle, Lona, Emily)

ANATOL, *Hartford (Conn.) Church Street Theatre*, opened October 27, 1984

Produced by the Hartford Stage Company, William Stuart, managing director; A Comedy by Arthur Schnitzler; English translation by Frank Marcus; Director, Mark Lamos; Setting and Costumes by John Conklin; Lighting, Pat Collins; Wigs, Paul Huntley; Sound, David Budries

Mark Lamos (Anatol); David Schramm (Max); Carol Calkins (Cora); Mary Layne (Gabrielle); Leslie Geraci (Bianca); Giulia Pagano (Emily); Michele Farr (Annie); Susan Pellegrino (Elsa); Patricia Mauceri (Ilona); Howie Muir (Franz); Mark Wayne Nelson (Waiter); Elise Stone, Ken Mayer, Charles Johnson (Others)

THE LOVES OF ANATOL, *Circle in the Square Theatre*, New York, opened March 6, 1985 46 performances

Produced by the Circle in the Square Theatre, Theodore Mann, artistic director; A play by Ellis Rabb and Nicholas Martin, adapted from *Anatol* by Arthur Schnitzler; Director, Ellis Rabb; Scenery, Lawrence Miller; Lighting, Richard Winkler and James Tilton; Costumes, Robert Morgan; Musical staging, Donald Saddler; Music design, Catherine MacDonald; Improvision on solo piano, John Bavless; Hair Stylist, Paul Huntley

Stephen Collins (Anatol); Philip Bosco (Max); Mary Joan Negro (Cora and Emille); Michael Learned (Gabrielle and Ilona); Valerie Mahaffey (Annie and Annette); Louis Turenne (Johann); Pamela Sousa (Bianca and the Lady in

Black); Daniel Southern (Fileder); Mark Fotopoulos (Baron Diebl); Reed Jones (Franz and The Young Gentleman); Louis Turenne, Mark Fotopoulos, Daniel Southern (Gentlemen)

THE GAME OF LOVE, *Ohio Theatre*, Cleveland, opened October 5, 1985
Produced by the Great Lakes Theater Festival; A Musical Comedy based on *Anatol* by Arthur Schnitzler; Director, Gerald Freedman; Book and Lyrics by Tom Jones, as translated by Lily Lessing; Music by Jacques Offenbach; Settings, John Ezell; Lighting, Spencer Mosse; Costumes, Lewis D. Rampino; Musical director, Stuart W. Raleigh; Arrangements and additional music by Nancy Ford

John Reeger (Anatol); Robert Black (Max); Mark Alan Gordon (Fritz); Donna English (Cora); Mimi Wyche (Annie); Alison Bevan (Gabrielle); Angelina Fiordellisi (Ilona); Jossie De Guzman (Annette); Doug Montgomery (Franz); John Abarjian (Flieder); David Manis (Baron Diebel)

ANATOL, *Gate Theatre*, London, opened March 3, 1987 31 performances
A Play by Arthur Schnitzler, translated by Michael Robinson; Director, Michael Robinson; Production designer, Anthony Waterman; Lighting, Herl Wallace; Music, Colin Guthrie

Malcolm Sinclair (Anatol); Simon Shepherd (Max); Jane Bertish (The Women); Roy Niles (Waiter/Franz)

SCREEN

THE AFFAIRS OF ANATOL, *Paramount Pictures*, released September 1921
Produced by Paramount Pictures-Famous Players-Lasky; Director, Cecil B. DeMille; Screenplay, Jeanie Macpherson, Beulah Marie Dix, Lorna Moon and Elmer Harris, based on Arthur Schnitzler's comedy *Anatol*; Photography, Alvin Wyckoff and Karl Struss; Art director, Paul Iribe; Editor, Anne Bauchens

Wallace Reid (Anatol De Witt Spencer); Gloria Swanson (Vivian Spencer); Elliott Dexter (Max Runyan); Bebe Daniels (Satan Synne); Wanda Hawley (Emilie Dixon); Monte Blue (Abner Elliott); Agnes Ayres (Annie Elliott); Theodore Roberts (Gordon Bronson); Theodore Kosloff (Nazzer Singh); Charles Ogle (Dr. Bowles); Winter Hall (Dr. Johnson); Julia Faye (Tibra); Polly Moran (Orchestra Leader); Raymond Hatton (Hoffmeier); Guy Oliver (Spencer's Butler); Zelma Maja (Nurse); Shannon Day, Alma Bennett (Chorus Girls); Ruth Miller (Spencer's Maid); Lucien Littlefield (Spencer's valet); Elinor Glyn, Lady Parker (Bridge Players); William Boyd, Maud Wayne (Guests); Fred Huntley (Stage manager)

TELEVISION

Hollywood Playhouse, televised March 30, 1961 PBS 90 minutes
Produced by Alexander Ramati; Director, Ezra Stone; Teleplay by Robert Boon, based on the play by Arthur Schnitzler

John van Dreelen (Anatol); Oscar Beregi (Max Runyan); Kathleen Crowley (Ilona); Susan Silo (Lita); Didi Ramati (Cora); Jack Tesler, Ralph Smiley (Anatol's Servants)

ANATOL, televised March 11, 1965 BBC 90 minutes; in U.S. on *NET Playhouse*, televised March 14, 1969

Produced by the British Broadcasting Corporation; Producer, Bernard Hepton; Director, Christopher Morahan; Adapted by Rosemary Hill from the play by Arthur Schnitzler; Designer, Frederick Knapman; Music, Harry Rabinowitz

Robert Hardy (Anatol); John Wood (Max); Moira Redmond (Mimi); Priscilla Morgan (Bianca); Elvi Hale (Lona); Margaret Read (Lady); Tony Sympson (Waiter); Beatrice Greeke (Flower Seller)

ANNE OF GREEN GABLES

Various adaptations of the novel by Lucy Maud Montgomery (1908)

Synopsis

Fiery, redheaded young Anne Shirley is mistreated by a blacksmith's family and returned to the orphanage, but comes to the attention of spinster Marilla Cuthbert and her bachelor brother Matthew, owners of a farm in the small village of Avonlea on Canada's Prince Edward Island. They had hoped to adopt a boy from the orphanage to help work the farm. The orphanage mistakenly has sent Anne to the rustic, elderly couple who are perplexed at the strong-willed, intelligent, young girl with a thriving and vivid imagination. Anne soon captures the heart of shy, retiring Matthew, and taciturn Marilla grudgingly accepts the lively girl. Anne's romantic dreams and penchant for dramatics constantly create problems. But Anne excels at school, sharing top scholastic honors with Gilbert Blythe, who finds her entrancing. Anne brilliantly recites "The Highwayman" and becomes a candidate for college. Matthew's sudden death, however, alters her decision to accept a scholarship and she chooses to remain with her foster mother Marilla, who finally realizes her love and devotion to her adopted daughter. Anne remains on Prince Edward Island to teach school and support herself and Marilla. There is also the incentive of being close to Gilbert, who also stays on the island.

Comment and Critique

Canadian writer Lucy Maud Montgomery wrote *Anne of Green Gables* in 1908. Its immediate success spawned several "Anne" sequels: *Anne of Windy Polars*, *Anne of Avonlea*, *Anne of Ingleside*, *Anne of the Island*, and *Anne's House of Dreams*. The Montgomery tales of Anne gained international popularity over the years, and in 1965, Canadian actor Donald Harron and Canadian director Norman Campbell adapted *Anne of Green Gables* to the stage as a musical play. It opened in late June at Canada's Charlottetown Festival Theatre and became a successful summer attraction for several seasons.

In spring 1969, *Anne of Green Gables* opened at London's New Theatre to excellent reviews and public support. Harold Hobson (*Sunday Times*) found the Canadian musical offering "an evening when it was good to be alive and in a theatre!" And Eric Shorter (*Daily Telegraph*) described it as "a bouncing show of engaging charm." Felix Barker (*Evening News*) proclaimed, "If London's heart doesn't embrace this show, the town is in urgent need of a transplant." While Irving Wardle (*London Times*) added, "A family musical at its best...London has seen more ambitious musicals than the New Theatre version of *Anne of Green Gables*, but few that applied show business skills more single-mindedly to adapting a children's classic with sincerity and affection."

Clive Barnes (*The New York Times*) reported from London, "This musical has been the biggest sleeper since *Rip Van Winkle*...It had been around in Canada for some three or four years before this season...Here is the mini-hit of the town...The music is naive and charming, the jokes are so clean they appear not only washed but starched, and there is an amiability and sweetness about the show that is hard to resist...Polly James as Anne is a bundle of pure urchin vitality...Barbara Hamilton, with a face of sweet vinegar, and Hiram Sherman, with his sheep-dog charms, are most beguiling. *Anne of Green Gables* may not be very stimulating theatre, but it really does provide at least a partial answer to those people who have been asking about, yet, innocence and its flight."

Anne of Green Gables opened a limited engagement of sixteen performances at New York's City Center Theatre just before Christmas 1971. Julius Novick (*The Village Voice*) reported, "The musical version was first presented in 1965 at the Charlottetown Festival on the island; they loved it in Charlottetown, and they have loved it all over again every year since then. They also loved it on tour in Canada; they loved it in London. I understand that they even loved in Osaka when it was presented there as part of Canada's contribution of Expo '70. I can see why; if you love this sort of thing, this is the sort of thing you'll love. It is what it is -- sweet and simple -- very intensely and full; it makes *The Music Man* look like 'The Dirtiest Show in Town.'...I think that people whose self-image forbids them to enjoy things like *Anne of Green Gables* are missing something -- not much, but something. Simplicity has its place as a part of multiplicity...The worst thing about the show is Grace Finley's performance in the title role: arch, knowing, fake, overstated, and surpassingly obnoxious...if you can stand it, *Anne of Green Gables* is a nice little show."

Walter Kerr (*The New York Times*) was less impressed with the Canadian import, which he labeled as "Canadian Cornbred," adding he "didn't much care for. As staged, the show's deliberate simplicity seemed to me synthetic and bit pushy, its pigtailed heroine seemed constantly on the verge of turning herself into Donald Duck...The whole thing was manufactured, and you could see the plotpistons turning routinely. Nonetheless, the thing done, the generous deed, the warm impulse, was plausible...as an outline of something actual. It was more than plausible. It was necessary. Some human gestures carry their rightness about with them."

Paramount Pictures filmed *Anne of Green Gables* in 1919 starring blonde and buoyant Mary Miles Minter, its threat to Mary Pickford, as Anne Shirley, with young Paul Kelly as Gilbert Blythe. *The Moving Picture World* reported, "It is claimed that the Realart picture, *Anne of Green Gables* [is] founded on four of the "Anne" books, written by L. M. Montgomery and made into a scenario by Frances Marion. This may well be believed. There is a profusion of incident, but it all unfolds the career of the little freckle-faced orphan who comes to live at Green Gables and keeps the neighbors busy talking about her pranks and her powers of imagination ...The whole story is sweet and wholesome...William D. Taylor, the director, chose a wonderful old place for the home -- many of his locations are rare examples of rural landscape effects...Mary Miles Minter has the youth and personal charm required for the part of Anne, and responds quickly and convincingly to the character's varying moods. Paul Kelly makes a likeable boyish lover, and the cast is uniformly satisfactory."

Photoplay magazine called *Anne of Green Gables*, "A faithful and sympathetic screen adaptation of the novel -- suitable for the whole family...Romance, humor and pathos, well balanced." *The New York Times* found that "Humor, pathos, melodrama and romance are the reliable ingredients of the story, to which William Desmond Taylor, the director, has added a number of pleasing pictures. He has also brought much of the story's rural atmosphere naturally to the screen."

Mary Miles Minter had made her Broadway stage debut at the age of six with Nat Goodwin in *Cameo Kirby* and first appeared in motion pictures in 1912 as Juliet Shelby. Her film career flourished until the early 1920s and ended abruptly with the murder on February 2, 1922 of her director and mentor, William Desmond Taylor. Mary has implicated in the Taylor murder and her motion picture career ended, with her films generally withdrawn from circulation.

The still "unsolved" murder of handsome, six-foot tall Irish director and actor, William Desmond Taylor, became a puzzling, quixotic affair in which obvious clues and pertinent facts were totally ignored while lurid details of Taylor's sexual aberrations and homosexuality were exposed. Evidence recently unearthed alleges director Taylor was shot and killed by Mary's irate mother.

In 1934, RKO remade *Anne of Green Gables* featuring a young actress known on the screen as Dawn O'Day (nee Dawn Evelyeen Paris). She adopted Lucy Maud Montgomery's beloved Anne Shirley as her future screen name. *The Motion Picture Herald* found "Potential showmanship values of this production are embodied in the popularity of the L. M. Montgomery novel, on which the film is based, and the general excellence of production. This one whistles right up the alley of Pollyanna customers, faithfully depicting the adventures of a little orphan girl adopted into a country family...first class program entertainment...Well etched characters make the rural atmosphere felt rather than seen...This is essentially family fodder." About Anne Shirley's performance as Anne Shirley, *The New York Times* said, "Her performance is as warm, as honest and as beguiling a piece of acting as Hollywood has offered us all year."

Telefilm Canada produced an acclaimed television version of *Anne of Green Gables* shown on in the United States on PBS in two parts in December 1985. The expertly produced and directed telefilm by Kevin Sullivan featured Megan Follows as Anne with the remarkable Colleen Dewhurst as Marilla and Richard Farnsworth as Matthew. The four-hour production, filmed on Prince Edward Island, glowed with beautiful photography by Rene Ohashi, and Megan Follows as Anne was a total delight. Character roles by Dewhurst and Farnsworth were played with imposing professionalism and director Sullivan brought out all the warmth, humor and pathos of the story without oozing sentimentality.

Of the $3.5 million film, Dennis Foon, Vancouver's playwright and drama critic, felt "Lovers of *Anne of Green Gables* can relax: Canada's favorite orphan, Anne Shirley, has been lusciously, lovingly resurrected." Mark Twain had called the novel "The sweetest creation of childlife yet written" and twenty-nine-year-old Toronto filmmaker, Kevin Sullivan ably described his television film as "A Valentine from another era."

The television production was given ten Gemini Awards by the Academy of Canadian Cinema and Television in December 1986. Presented at Toronto's Metro Convention Center, the awards went to PBS for Best Drama Mini-Series; Best Actress (Megan Follows); Best Supporting Actor and Actress (Richard Farnsworth and Colleen Dewhurst); Best Drama Series (writers Kevin Sullivan and Joe Wisenfeld); Best Photography (Rene Ohashi); Best Costumes (Carol Spier); Best Art Design (Martha Mann), and to Hagood Hardy for his original music. *Anne of Green Gables* was also selected by the readers of *TV Guide* as the year's most popular program. The Sullivan Film Company, producers of the series, also received Canada's first television Gemini Award.

The 1987 television sequel to *Anne of Green Gables*, with much of the same cast and crew reunited, garnered the same type of critical and popular acclaim as its predecessor.

STAGE

ANNE OF GREEN GABLES, *Charlottetown Festival Theatre*, Prince Edwards Island, Canada, opened June 29, 1965
Produced by the Charlottetown Festival Theatre; A Musical play, based on the novel by Lucy Maud Montgomery; Directed and Choreographed by Alan Lund; Book and lyrics by Donald Harron and Norman Campbell; Music by Norman Campbell; Additional lyrics by Mavor Moore and Elaine Campbell; Musical director, Fen Watkin; Settings, Murray Laufer; Lighting, Ron Montgomery; Costumes, Marie Day; Production stage manager, Ron Francis; Stage manager, Pat Thomas

Malorie-Ann Spiller (Anne Shirley); Elizabeth Mawson (Marilla Cuthbert); George Merner (Matthew Cuthbert); Barrie Wood (Gilbert Blythe); Maud Whitmore (Mrs. Rachel Lynde); Glenda Landry (Diana Barry); Wanda Cannon (Miss Stacy); Doug Chamberlain (Mr. Phillips); Amanda Hancox (Josie Pye); Joyce Landry (Prissy Andrews); Cleone Duncan (Mrs. Barry); Connie Martin (Mrs. Pye); Sharon Dyer (Mrs. MacPherson); Glen Kotyk (Tommy Sloane); Brian Harris (Charlie Sloane); Jim White (Moody MacPherson); Sharon Dyer (Mrs. Spencer); Wanda Cannon (Mrs. Sloane); Scott Walker (The Minister); Sharry Flett (Lucilla); Susi Cuthbert (Ruby Gillis); Valerie Smith (Tillie Boulter); Bonnie Monaghan (Gertie Pye); Scot Denton (Earl/The Stationmaster); George Murray (Cecil); Sharry Flett (Mrs. Blewett); Scott Smith (Malcolm Andrews)

MUSICAL NUMBERS: "Where Is Matthew Going?"; "Gee I'm Glad I'm No One Else But Me"; "We Clearly Requested"; "The Facts"; "Humble Pie"; "Oh, Mrs. Lynde"; "Back to School Ballet"; "Avonlea We Love Thee"; "Wondrin'"; "Did You Hear?"; "Ice Cream"; "Where Did the Summer Go To?"; "Learn Everything"; "Kindred Spirits"; "When I Say My Say"; "I'll Show Him"; "Nature Study Ballet"; "General Store"; "If It Hadn't Been for Me"; "Anne of Green Gables"; "The Words"

Charlottetown Festival Theatre, Prince Edwards Island, Canada, opened July 5, 1966
Produced by the Charlottetown Festival Theatre; A Musical Play, based on the novel by Lucy Maud Montgomery; Directed and Choreographed by Alan Lund; Book and lyrics by Donald Harron and Norman Campbell; Music by Norman Campbell; Additional Lyrics by Mavor Moore and Elaine Letterman; Scenery, Murray Laufer; Lighting and Aristides Gazetas; Costumes, Marie Day; Musical direction and arrangements, John Fenwick; Production stage manager, Ron Francis

Jamie Ray (Anne Shirley); Barbara Hamilton (Marilla Cuthbert); Peter Mews (Matthew Cuthbert); Dean Reagan (Gilbert Blythe); Maud Whitmore (Mrs. Rachel Lynde); Marylyn Stuart (Diana Barry); Judy Armstrong (Miss Stacey); Diane Nyland (Josie Pye); Jane Casson (Mrs. Pye); Anne Linden (Prissy Andrews); Darlene Hirst (Mrs. Barry); Flora MacKenzie (Mrs. MacPherson); Brian Lund (Tommy Sloane); Roy Urbach (Charlie Sloane); Robert Ainslie (Moody MacPherson); Esther Pietch (Mrs. Spencer); Judy Armstrong (Mrs. Blewett); Donald Saunders (Mailman); Marci Thomas (Tillie Boulter); Maurice Lemay (Gerry Boute); Jack Duffy (Schoolmaster); Lloyd Malenfant (Minister); Flora MacKenzie (Store Clerk); Richard Braun (Stationmaster); Douglas Chamberlain (Storekeeper); Jules Boswell, Larry Brazel; Michael Brazel, Janet Farrar, Amanda Hancox, Robin Willis (Children)

New Theatre, London, opened April 15, 1969
Produced by Bill Freedman, by arrangement with Donald Albery; A Musical play

based on the novel *Anne of Green Gables* by Lucy Maud Montgomery; Director and Choreographer, Alan Lund; Book and lyrics by Donald Harron and Norman Campbell; Music by Norman Campbell; additional lyrics by Mavor Moore and Elaine Campbell; Settings, Henry Bardon; Lighting, Francis Reid; Costumes, Michael Stennett; Musical supervision and Orchestrations, John Fenwick; Musical director, Martin Goldstein; Assistant choreographer, Robert Ainslie

Polly James (Anne Shirley); Hiram Sherman (Matthew Cuthbert); Barbara Hamilton (Marilla Cuthbert); Bettina Dickson (Rachel Lynde); Susan Anderson (Diana Barry); Robert Ainslie (Gilbert Blythe); Pat Starr (Miss Stacy); Ian Burford (Mr. Phillips); Liz Edmiston (Josie Pye); Janis Dunning (Prissy Andrews); Joan Ryan (Mrs. Barry); Marion Wilson (Mrs. Pye); Betty Benfield (Mrs. MacPherson); John Chester (Tommy Sloane); Gerard Hunt (Charlie Sloane); Roy Urbach (Moody MacPherson); Barbara Miller (Mrs. Spencer); Kathy Dunkerley (Mrs. Sloane); Ian Burford (Reverend Smythe-Hankinson); Colette Gleeson (Lucille); Kenneth Waller (Minister); Laurie Webb (Mailman); Jonathan Poole (Farmer); Philip Summerscales (Townsman); Pat Starr (Mrs. Blewett); Josie Ashcroft (Ruby Gillis); Judith Cox (Tillie Boulter); Rita Henerson (Gertie Pye); Laurie Webb (Station Master)

MUSICAL NUMBERS: "Where Is Matthew Going?"; "Gee I'm Glad I'm No One Else But Me"; "We Clearly Requested"; "The Facts"; "Humble Pie"; "Oh Mrs. Lynde"; "Back to School Ballet"; "Avonlea We Love Thee"; "Wondrin'"; "Did You Hear?"; "Ice Cream"; "Where Did the Summer Go To?"; "Learn Everything"; "Kindred Spirits"; "When I Say My Say"; "Nature Study Ballet"; "I'll Show Him"; "General Store"; "If It Hadn't Been for Me"; "Anne of Green Gables"; "The Words"

Original cast recording: CBS Records

City Center Theatre, New York, opened December 21, 1971 16 performances (Limited engagement)

Produced by the City Center of Music and Drama, Norman Singer, executive director, in association with the Charlottetown Festival (Prince Edward Island, Canada); The Canadian National Theatre Production; Director and Choreographer, Alan Lund; A Musical play based on the novel by Lucy Maud Montgomery, adapted by Donald Harron; Music by Norman Campbell; Lyrics by Donald Harron and Norman Campbell; Additional Lyrics by Mavor Moore and Elaine Campbell; Production designer, Murray Laufer; Lighting, Ronald Montgomery; Music Director and Orchestrations, John Fenwick; Costumes, Marie Day; Stage managers, David Loynd, J.P. Regan and Ernie Abugov

Grace Finley (Anne Shirley); Elizabeth Mawson (Marilla Cuthbert); Peter Mews (Matthew Cuthbert); Jeff Hyslop (Gilbert Blythe); Glenda Landry (Diana Barry); Sharlene McLean (Prissy Andrews); Barbara Barsky (Josie Pye); Deborah Millar (Gertie Pye); George Juriga (Charlie Sloane); Dan Costain (Moody MacPherson); Andre Denis (Gerry Buote); Maud Whitmore (Mrs. Rachel Lynde); Cleone Duncan (Mrs. MacPherson); Nancy Kerr (Mrs. Barry); Flora MacKenzie (Mrs. Sloane); Kathryn Watt (Mrs. Pye); Jack Northmore (Reverend Smythe Hankinson); Bill Hosie (Earl); George Merner (Cecil); Roma Hearn (Mrs. Blewett); Lynn Marsh (Tillie Boulter); Calvin McRae (Malcolm Andrews); Cleone Duncan (Lucilla); Roma Hearn (Miss Stacy); Flora MacKenzie (Mrs. Spencer); Bill Hosie (Stationmaster); John Powell (Tommy Sloane); Jack Nortmore (Mr. Phillips); Lloyd Malen-fant (Minister); Patti Toms (Ruby Gillis)

MUSICAL NUMBERS: "Great Workers for the Cause"; "Where Is Matthew Going?";

"Gee I'm Glad I'm No One Else But Me"; "We Clearly Requested"; "The Facts"; "Where'd Marilla Come From?"; "Humble Pie"; "Oh, Mrs. Lynde!"; "Back to School Ballet"; "Avonlea We Love Thee"; "Wondrin'"; "Did You Hear?"; "Ice Cream"; "The Picnic"; "Where Did the Summer Go?"; "Kindred Spirits"; "Open the Window"; "The Words"; "Nature Hunt Ballet"; "I'll Show Him"; "General Store"; "Pageant Song"; "If It Hadn't Been for Me"; "Anne of Green Gables"

SCREEN

Paramount-Realart Pictures, released December 1919

Director, William Desmond Taylor; Screenplay by Frances Marion, based on the novel by Lucy Maud Montgomery

Mary Miles Minter (Anne Shirley); Paul Kelly (Gilbert Blythe); Mildred Harris (Marilla Cuthbert); Frederick Burton (Matthew Cuthbert); Laurie Lovelle (Diana Barry); Leila Romer (Mrs. Pie); Caroline Lee (Mrs. Barry); Jack B. Hollis (Reverend Figtree); Lincoln Stedman, J. T. Chailee, Russell Hewitt, Beatrice Allen, Mary Hall, George Stewart, Albert Hackett

RKO Radio Pictures, released November 1934

Produced by Kenneth Macgowan; Director, George Nicholls, Jr.; Screenplay by Sam Mintz, based on the novel by Lucy Maud Montgomery; Photography, Lucien Andriot; Music, Max Steiner; Editor, Arthur Schmidt

Anne Shirley (Anne Shirley); Tom Brown (Gilbert Blythe); O. P. Heggie (Matthew Cuthbert); Helen Westley (Marilla Cuthbert); Gertrude Messinger (Diana Barry); Murray Kinnell (Mr. Phillips); Sara Haden (Mrs. Barry); Charley Grapewin (Dr. Tatum); Hilda Vaughn (Mrs. Blewett); June Preston (Her Daughter)

ANNE OF WINDY POPLARS, RKO Radio Pictures, released June 1940

Executive Producer, Lee Marcus; Producer, Cliff Reid; Director, Jack Hively; Screenplay by Michael Kanin and Jerry Cady, based on the novel by Lucy Maud Montgomery; Photography, Fred Redman; Costumes, Edward Stephenson; Sound, John L. Cass; Editor, George Hively

Anne Shirley (Anne Shirley); James Ellison (Tony Pringle); Patric Knowles (Gilbert Blythe); Henry Travers (Matey); Elizabeth Patterson (Rebecca); Slim Summerville (Jabez Monkman); Katharine Alexander (Ernestine Pringle); Minnie Dupree (Kate); Louise Campbell (Catherine Pringle); Joan Carroll (Betty Grayson); Alma Kruger (Mrs. Stephen Pringle); Marcia Mae Jones (Jen Pringle); Ethel Griffies (Hester Pringle); Clara Blandick (Mrs. Morton Pringle); Gilbert Emery (Stephen Pringle); Wright Kramer (Morton Pringle); Jackie Moran (Boy)

TELEVISION

ANNE OF GREEN GABLES, Telefilm Canada, televised December 2 and 3, 1985 PBS 4 hours

Produced by Sullivan Films, Inc., CBC, PBS WonderWorks; Executive Producer and Director, Kevin Sullivan; Co-Producer, Ian McDougall; Teleplay by Joe Wisenfeld and Kevin Sullivan, based on the novel by Lucy Maud Montgomery; Photography, Rene Ohashi; Costumes, Carol Spier; Art design, Martha Mann; Set decorator, Elmor Galbraith; Original musical score, Hagood Hardy; Editors, Maureen Wilkinson and James Lahti

Megan Follows (Anne Shirley); Colleen Dewhurst (Marilla Cuthbert); Richard

Farnsworth (Matthew Cuthbert); Jonathan Crombie (Gilbert Blythe); Patricia Hamilton (Rachel Lynde); Schuyler Grant (Diana Barry); Marilyn Lightstone (Miss Stacy); Jayne Eastwood (Mrs. Hammond); Samantha Langevin (Matilda Bluewit); Rosemary Radcliffe (Mrs. Barry); Robert Collins (John Barry); Joachim Hanson (John Sadler); Christine Krueger (Elspeth Allen); Cedric Smith (Reverend Allen); Paul Brown (Mr. Phillips); Miranda DePoncier (Josie Pye); Trish Nettleton (Jane Andrews); Jennifer Inch (Ruby Gillis); Wendy Lyon (Prissy Andrews); Jackie Burroughs (Amelia Evans); Dawn Greenhalgh (Mrs. Cadbury); Jack Mather (Stationmaster); Vivien Reins (Mrs. Spencer); Nancy Beattie (Essie); David Roberts (Tom); Morgan Chapman (Minnie May); Charmion King (Aunt Josephine Barry); Sean McCann (Dr. O'Reilly); David Hughes (Thomas Lynde); and Robert Haley, Michael Tait, Fiona McGillivray, Zack Ward, Sharon Dyer, Rex Southgate, Juliana Saxton, Molly Thom, Jennifer Irwin, Peter Sturgess, Ray Ireland, Daw Taylor, Patrick Allard, Adrian Dorbal, Martha Cornyn, Martha Maloney, John Conway

ANNE OF AVONLEA: THE CONTINUING STORY OF ANNE OF GREEN GABLES, Telefilm Canada, televised May 19, 26, June 2, 9, 1987 The Disney Channel 4 hours (later shown on PBS)
Produced by Sullivan Films, Inc., CBC, The Disney Channel, PBS WonderWorks; Executive Producer/Director/ Writer, Kevin Sullivan, based on the books *Anne of Avonlea*, *Anne of the Island* and *Anne of Windy Poplars* by Lucy Maud Montgomery; Photography, Marc Champion; Costumes, Martha Mann; Art Director, Susan Longmire; Music, Hagood Hardy; Editors, Maureen Wilkinson and James Lahti

Megan Follows (Anne Shirley); Colleen Dewhurst (Marilla Cuthbert); Jonathan Crombie (Gilbert Blythe); Schyler Grant (Diana Barry); Patricia Hamilton (Rachel Lynde); Frank Converse (Morgan Harris); Dame Wendy Hiller (Mrs. Harris); Marilyn Lightstone (Miss Stacy); Rosemary Dunsmore (Miss Brooke); Suzanna Hoffman (Jen Pringle); Genevieve Appleton (Emmeline Harris); Les Carlson (Mr. Lawson); Mag Ruffman (Alice Lawson); Kay Hawtrey (Mabel Sloanne); David Fox (John Blythe); David Hughes (Thomas Lynde); Charmion King (Aunt Josephine); Rosemary Radcliffe (Mrs. Barry); Robert Collins (Mrs. Barry); Kate Lynch (Pauline); Charles Joliffe (Alec McGuiness); Nuala Fitzgerald (Mrs. Tom Pringle); Miranda DePoncier (Josie Pye); Trish Nettleton (Jane Andrews); Jennifer Inch (Ruby Gillis); Morgan Chapman (Minnie May); Kathryn Trainor (Essie); and Bruce McCollogh, Anna Ferguson, Patty Carroll Brown, Chick Roberts, Ian Heath, Larry Aubrey, Zack Ward, Sheila Harcourt, Janice Bryan, Dora Dainton, Amerlea Weston, Brigit Wilson, Martin Donlevy, Molly McNeil, Juno Mills-Cockell, Dave Foley, Marilyn Boyle, Araby Lockhart, Lynne Gorman, Maxine Miller, Meg Hogarth, Carolyn Hetherington, Robert Galbraith, Michael Fletcher, Gladys O'Connor, Glori Gage, Fred Booker, Ingrid Bauer, Louise Nicol

AVONLEA, televised begining March 5, 1990 The Disney Channel 13 episodes (1 hour each) (second series began January 1991; third series began January 1992)
Produced by Rose Cottage Productions, Inc.; Sullivan Films, Inc., CBC, The Disney Channel, Telefilm Canada; Executive Producer, Kevin Sullivan; Produced by Trudy Grant; Director (premiere), Paul Shapiro; Teleplay (premiere), Heather Conkie, based on the books *The Story Girl*, *The Golden Road*, *Chronicles of Avonlea* and *Futher Chronicles of Avonlea* by Lucy Maud Montgomery; Photography, Manfred Guthrie; Art Director, Perri Gorrara; Costumes, Martha Mann; Music, John Weisman; Editors, Maureen Wilkinson, James Lahti and Gordon McClellan

Sarah Polley (Sara Stanley); Jackie Burroughs (Aunt Hetty King); Mag Ruffman (Aunt Olivia Dale); Frances Hyland (The Governess); Cedric Smith (Alec King); Lally Cadeau (Janet King); Gema Zamprogna (Felicity King); Harmony Camp (Cecily King); Zachary Bennett (Felix King); Patricia Hamilton (Rachel Lynde); R. H. Thomson (Jasper Dale); Colleen Dewhurst (Marilla Cuthbert); Peter Coyote (Romney Penhallow); Madeline Kahn (Miss Pigeon Plumtree); Michael York (Ezekial); and Lloyd Bochner, Zoe Caldwell, Malcolm Stoddard, Fiona Reid, Kate Nelligan, Christopher Lloyd, Christopher Reeve, Ned Beatty

ANTIGONE

A Drama by Jean Anouilh, based on Sophocles' tragedy, *Antigone*, English translation by Lewis Galantiere (1943)

Synopsis

King Oedipus' sons, Eteocles and Polynices, kill each other battling for the throne of Thebes. Their Uncle Creon takes the throne and has Eteocles buried with royal honors but decrees Polynices' body be left outside the city's walls for the vultures, with death to anyone who buries him. Oedipus' daughter, Antigone, engaged to Creon's son Haemon, is determined to give Polynices a decent burial despite pleading from her sister, Ismene, to forget their rebellious brother. Antigone is caught attempting to cover her brother's body with earth and taken before Creon whom defies: "Nay, be what thou wilt; but I will bury him; well for me to die in doing that. I shall rest, a loved one with him I have loved, sinless in my crime; for I owe a longer allegiance to the dead than to the living; in that world I shall abide forever." Creon sentences Antigone to death by being sealed alive into a mountain cave. A messenger relates to Chorus that Haemon has entered the tomb where Antigone has hanged herself. Haemon refuses Creon's plea to leave the tomb and stabs himself, falling into a pool of blood beside Antigone's body. Creon returns to the palace to find his wife, Eurydice, having learned of Haemon's suicide, has cut her own throat. Creon is left to bury his own dead.

Comment and Critique

Sophocles' tragedy *Antigone* was first presented in Greece in 441 B.C. In 1943, during the Nazi occupation of Paris, Jean Anouilh adapted the ancient tragedy as *Antigone and the Tyrant*. Anouilh's play struck responsive chords in patriotic Frenchmen while completely eluding the Nazi occupiers in the audience. The play ran to packed houses for several years at the Theatre de l'Atelier in Paris. Anouilh's wife, Monelle Valentin, portrayed Antigone in the Paris production, with Jean Davy as Creon.

Lewis Galantiere, who adapted Anouilh's play to the English-speaking stage, wrote, "It was impossible for a Greek of the Periclean Age (and Sophocles was a con-temporary of Pericles) to forget altogether the relations of Man and the State, Ruler and People, even when his subject was religion. Creon was what the Greeks call a tyrant and we call a dictator. We, in our age, do not call injustice a sin; the Greeks did; and this explains how it happens that Antigone plays a political role despite herself. All of this has been brilliantly perceived by M. Anouilh and brilliantly incrusted in his eloquent and powerful play...the triumph of Antigone, that with no other weapons than her purity, her instinctive sense of what is just in the eyes of God and of man, she literally breaks and humbles the most persuasive, the most ruthless, the most 'reasonable' of tyrants."

During the winter of 1945, Katharine Cornell and her brave company of troupers arrived in Paris on their tour of Europe with her great stage success, *The Barretts of Wimpole Street*. While there, Miss Cornell saw a performance of *Antigone and the Tyrant* and, after returning to America, asked producer Gilbert Miller to secure the American stage rights to Anouilh's play. Impressed with the "superhuman courage and ingenuity to accomplish this play under the German occupation... For Frenchmen, *Antigone* symbolized France herself, France heroically rejecting the 'New Order,'" Katharine Cornell produced *Antigone and the Tyrant* on Broadway.

"It was an experience in the theatre I shall not soon forget," wrote Burton Rascoe (*New York World-Telegram*). "I am grateful to Miss Cornell and Gilbert Miller for undertaking it, to all those connected with the presentation, to Jean Anouilh for the French adoption of the 2500-year-old drama, and to Lewis Galantiere, the sensitive bilingual translator, who has recreated Mr. Anouilh's adaptation. On the part of all of them, this an act of faith in the finer things of the theatre and more than a cultural gesture in recognition of our link, through the centuries, with the life of Greece during its great age of art and enlightenment."

Lewis Nichols (*The New York Times*) felt, "*Antigone* is not a fullbodied evening at the theatre. Where it should be moving and strong it too often seems empty. Too much of its length drifts away in unrationalized talk by characters who are not quite living human beings...With her beauty and low, distinct voice, Miss Cornell never fails to get something out of a part, but even she cannot make Antigone as moving or as real as she should be." Howard Barnes (*Herald Tribune*) found *Antigone* "telescoped into an hour and a half's playing time without intermission and garbed in tails and tea gowns, the new offering is more interesting than satisfying...*Antigone* is an acting exercise for Miss Cornell and Cedric Hardwicke, with the latter taking the major honors."

The *New Yorker* recognized that "it is easy to see how the Germans might have regarded Creon as a perfect symbol of benevolent authority, since he is clearly a reasonable, efficient man, seriously devoted to the interests of the State and marvelously patient with Antigone's morbid behavior." John Chapman (*Daily News*) reported, "This modern-dress version of Sophocles was Hardwicke's play. I felt that the tyrant and not Antigone had won...The work of Jean Anouilh, it was a devilishly clever flaunting of Nazi authority -- for playing with Nazi consent, it exposed the foibles and fallacies of personal dictatorship and proclaimed the rights of the human spirit...But somehow Creon isn't quite bowled over...Hardwicke has made Creon just too damned sure of himself."

Robert Garland (*Journal-American*) believed, "It is easy to understand why, when boldly displayed in Paris during the German occupation, the Jean Anouilh condensed version of this ancient hocus-pocus assumed a pertinence infrequently evident here in New York... Katharine Cornell, actress to her own manager, giving a sultry, unreasonable impersonation of sultry, unreasonable Antigone. America's only actress-manager, in the 15th play of her 15 years of acting-manager, gives more to the Greek who has words for it than the Greek who has words for it gives back to her. She is also strangely beautiful."

In his 1946 book *Seeing Things*, John Mason Brown presented a reasonable solution in accepting and enjoying *Antigone*, writing, "Forget that the strange man in the seat next to you is an American. Substitute a brown shirt for his business suit. Imagine him to be a Stormtrooper or a Gestapo agent; pretend the playhouse is enemyfilled. That New York is Nazi-held...It is not hard to guess how Parisians felt when they saw the tyrant defied. Or how their hearts must have been lifted when in Anouilh's text they heard that the citizens of Thebes were with Antigone, and there was an ominous rumbling in the city...As I say, it is, or ought to be, easy to read into *Antigone* the meanings which it must have held for the French."

Time magazine expressed the opinion that *Antigone* reached Broadway but "its symbolic side had lost its urgency...The Antigone of Anouilh, unswayed by religion, unfond of her brother, and in love with life, can only be accounted a fanatical idealist -- a character into whom Katharine Cornell finds it almost impossible to breathe life. On the other hand, Anouilh's Creon is at once the least Sophocles and the most successful person in the play."

On February 10, 1949, Anouilh's *Antigone* opened in London starring Vivien Leigh and Laurence Olivier, as Chorus, with George Relph as Creon. "*Antigone* (in modern dress) has proved a most interesting experience of gripping topicality," reported Frances Stephens (*Theatre World*), "As the Chorus, Laurence Olivier, in immaculate evening dress, is superb, and memorable performances come from George Relph, a tower of strength and a sympathetic figure as Creon, and from Vivien Leigh in the title role...Olivier's production of Jean Anouilh's provocative play proved the season's most stimulating experience...Very wisely, *Antigone* is produced to run without an interval, and to add lightness to the evening's entertainment Sir Laurence has added a delightful curtain raiser in Chekov's *The Proposal*."

On October 28, 1841, Felix Mendelssohn's incidental music written for Sophocles' *Antigone* was first performed, and in 1961, Sophocles' play was adapted to the screen and directed in Greece by George Tzavellas starring Irene Papas as Antigone. One British critic observed, "This film gives a good impression of the march of Sophoclean tragedy, with sorrow heaped on sorrow. George Tzavellas has filmed the play with only a few cuts in the text, and on natural locations... Irene Papas conveys the essential nobility and utter devotion of Antigone, but it is Manos Katrakis who carries away the acting honors as Creon."

Gordon Gow (*Films and Filming*) wrote, "This is a Greek film of a classic Greek tragedy and the director, George Tzavellas, adheres to the Sophocles dramatisation of the legend but compromises discreetly, now and then, between the most venerable form of theatre and the flexibility of cinema...Tzavellas has set himself the formidable task of reconciling Sophocles with cinema, and has succeeded sometimes...The acting is no more excessive than need be in the circumstances. As Antigone, Irene Papas compromises expertly between theatrical tradition and the cinema closeup; her strong, expressive face, closely observed, is especially eloquent in moments of silent suffering. Manos Katrakis is a persuasive, gaunt-cheeked Creon... Ideally, a more fluent technique was needed to make this *Antigone* consistent cinema as well as faithful Sophocles, but it remains a brave try, intermittently awkward to be sure, but often enough aglow with enterprise."

Dancer-turned-filmmaker Amy Greenfield wrote, produced, directed, choreographed, edited, and starred in a 1990 silent film version of *Antigone* interlaced with another Sophocles play, *Oedipus at Colonus*, told exclusively through dance and movement. An imaginative vanity production which most critics found disappointing premiered at the Museum of Modern Art in New York. Greenfield chose the Empire State Plaza in Albany to suggest the Greek City of Thebes. *The New York Times* dance critic Jennifer Dunning reviewed the film: "Ms. Greenfield's strong-faced Antigone is obdurate and high-minded from the start. She has no chance to grow or change, as Janet Eilber's Ismene does so persuasively...Bertram Ross, the former Martha Graham star who is now a gifted actor, lends the project a good deal of authority with his strong presence and classical delivery in the roles of Oedipus and Creon."

The world premiere of John Cranko's ballet, *Antigone*, was given at London's Covent Garden on October 19, 1959. The critic for London's *Sphere* noted, "Performed in one continuous act, the tragic work compresses the incidents of the Greek legend of *Antigone*; the story of the ballet has been freely adapted not form Sophocles but from Racine's version, *Les Freres Ennemis*...Although the ballet with music by Greek composer Mikis Theodorakis and scenery by the Mexican artist, Rufino Tamaya, met with a mixed reception, there was unanimous praise for the young ballerina, Svetlana Beriosova as Antigone."

Sidney Lumet directed Anouilh's *Antigone* for the November 21, 1954 *Omnibus* telecast with Beatrice Straight giving an outstanding performance in the title role opposite Philip Bourneuf's Creon. This *Antigone* received critical praise and was found exciting television, beautifully acted by an exceptionally talented cast, and rightly described as "one of the highlights of the TV season."

In September 1956, Lewis Galantiere's translation of Anouilh's modern-dress *Antigone* was restaged for television's *Kaiser Aluminum Hour*. Jack Gould (*The New York Times*) found it to be "a potentially provocative experiment in drama [which] floundered most disappointingly...Claude Rains in the part of Creon strove earnestly and sometimes very tellingly to impart meaning and emotion to the tragedy...But *Antigone* needs an Antigone...For the part of the regal figure who puts human dignity above materialistic happiness, the producer selected Marisa Pavan. The beautiful child was simply out of her depth...she was capable only of a recitation...The aimlessness of [Franklin Shaffner's] direction did not help the tragedy toward its climax ...Experimentation in TV drama is certainly to be encouraged; however, it is wise not to forget that a title role generally needs acting before glamour. Inexperience at the top handicaps everyone all the way down the line."

Harry Harris (*The Philadelphia Inquirer*) described 1956's *Antigone* as a "watered-down Greek tragedy, in modern dress, loaded with slang and other concessions to the limited attention span of TV audiences...The only trouble is, that as written, sharply abbreviated and played by Claude Rains as Creon and Marisa Pavan as Antigone, all the sympathy last night went to the supposedly 'cruel role'... Nonetheless, the play was provocative and always interesting, many cuts above the usual level of TV drama. Rains is always a delight to watch as an actor, and Miss Pavan was a delight to watch as a woman, especially in last night's muted TV colors."

PBS televised *Playhouse New York's Classics for Today* production of *Antigone* in October 1972 starring young French-Canadian actress Genevieve Bujold in the title role. "Genevieve Bujold wasn't merely superior as Antigone; she was superb," wrote Harry Harris (*The Philadelphia Inquirer*). Noting Bujold's success as *Saint Joan* on television and her splendid performance as Anne Boleyn opposite Richard Burton in the screen version of *Anne of the Thousand Days*, Harris added, "Her performance as Oedipus' daughter was yet another acting gem...Fritz Weaver strove valiantly to be worthy adversary as Creon. And Stacy Keach, as an urbane, cigar-puffing commentator, kept chiding the characters and instructing the audience."

An unusual telecast from the ancient theatre of Dionysus in Athens, retracing the development of Greek drama on September 11, 1963, featured a scene from Sophocles' *Antigone* in which Lynn Fontanne appeared as Chorus and Rosemary Harris and Alfred Drake as Antigone and Creon. This telecast, the premiere production of a CBS series of periodic specials under the umbrella title *Roots of Freedom*, was produced by Perry Wolff, directed by Tom Donovan and hosted by Alfred Lunt and Lynn Fontanne.

STAGE

ANTIGONE, American Laboratory Theatre, New York, opened April 24, 1930
Produced by the American Laboratory Theatre; A tragedy by Jean Cocteau, from the play by Sophocles, translated and directed by Francis Fergusson; performed in repertory with Cocteau's *Le Boeuf Sur le Toit*

Marjorie Bretnall (Antigone); T. Renick Hayes (Creon); William Anderson (Haemon); Emily Floyd (Ismene); Karl Swenson (Chorus); Richard Gaines (Tiresias); Satu Sen (Boy Who Leads Him); Frances Williams (Eurydice); J. Mac Dixon (Messenger); Charles Kradoska (Guard); W. Robert Spruill, Christian A. Hagen (Palace Guards)

ANTIGONE, Theatre de L'Atelier, Paris, opened February 14, 1944
A Drama by Jean Anouilh; Costumes, Andre Barsacq; Music, Henri Sauguet

Monelle Valentin (Antigone); Jean Davy (Creon); Andre Le Gall (Hemon); Odette Talazac (Nurse); Edmond Beauchamp (Jonas, a guard); Auguste Boverio (Choir)

ANTIGONE AND THE TYRANT, Cort Theatre, New York, opened February 18, 1946
64 performances
Produced by Katharine Cornell in association with Gilbert Miller; A Drama by Jean Anouilh; English adaptation by Lewis Galantiere; Director, Guthrie McClintic; Setting, Raymond Sovey; Costumes by Valentina; Music arranged by Alexander Haas; General Manager, Gertrude Macy; Company manager, William Tisdale; Stage manager, James Neilson

Katharine Cornell (Antigone); Cedric Hardwicke (Creon); Wesley Addy (replaced James Monks) (Haemon); Horace Braham (Chorus); Bertha Belmore (Nurse); Ruth Matterson (Ismene); Merle Maddern (succeeded by Eveline Vaughan) (Eurydice); Oliver Cliff (Messenger); Albert Biondo (Page); George Matthews, David J. Stewart, Michael Higgins (Guards)

New Theatre, London, opened February 10, 1949
Produced and directed by Laurence Olivier; A Drama by Jean Anouilh; English translation by Lewis Galantiere; Setting by Roger Ramsdell; Costumes by Sophie Harris

Vivien Leigh (Antigone); George Relph (Creon); Laurence Olivier (Chorus); Dan Cunningham (Haemon); Meg Maxwell (Ismene); Eileen Beldon (Nurse); Helen Beck (Eurydice); Terence Morgan (Messenger); Michael Reddington (Page); Thomas Heathcote, Hugh Stewart, George Cooper (Guards)

Preceded by Anton Chekhov's *The Proposal*, English translation by Constance Barnett

Carnegie Hall Playhouse, New York, opened April 2, 1956
Produced by Mazda Productions, Sanford Friedman and Henry Boettcher; A Drama by Jean Anouilh; English translation by Lewis Galantiere; Director, Henry T. Weinstein; Setting by Richard Mason; Lighting by George Corrin; Costumes, Alfred Lehman

Nancy Marchand (Antigone); Stiano Braggiotti (Creon); Tani Seitz (Ismene); Paul Stevens (Haemon); William Myers (Chorus); Jean Rose (Nurse); Jane Hughes (Eurydice); Michael Conrad (Jonas)

East 74th Street Theatre, New York, opened September 15, 1959
Produced and Directed by Harry Joe Brown,Jr.; A Drama by Jean Anouilh; Scenery and Lighting by Joe Weishar; Technical director, Ivor Balding; Costumes, Hal George; Stage manager, Joe Cunningham

Marcia Stillman (Antigone); David Hooks (Creon); Edith Lebok (Ismene); Owen Cunliffe (Haemon); Roscoe Lee Browne (Chorus); Pearl Sheffy (Nurse); Jo McManus (Eurydice); Michael Troy (Page); Jock Livingston (Private Jones); Tom Pedi (Private Dousse); Ian Cadenhead (Messenger); John Kennedy (Guard)

Royal Court Theatre, London, opened November 23, 1960
Two one-act Plays by Christopher Logue under the title of *TRIALS BY LOGUE* (*ANTIGONE* and *COB AND LEACH*); Director, Lindsay Anderson; Decor, Jocelyn Herbert; Music by Bill Le Sage

ANTIGONE: Mary Ure (Antigone); George Rose (Creon); Zoe Caldwell (Ismene); Peter Holmes (Haemon); Morris Perry (Head Steward); Dickie Owen (Head Guard); Peter Duguid (Sentry); Trevor Martin, Murray Evans (Stewards); Peter Fraser, Tony Selby, Laurence Harrington (Guards)

Midway Theatre, New York, opened December 28, 1962
Produced by the Mermaid Repertory Company; A Tragedy by Jean Cocteau from Sophocles, translated by Carl Wildman; Director, Matt Cimber; Prologue and choreography staged by Virginia Mason; Scenery and Lighting, Gary Meir; Costumes, Nancy Azara; Stage manager, Saylor Creswell; Performed in repertory with Cocteau's *Orthee*

Rosemary Tory (Antigone); Leigh Wharton (Creon); Neil Vipond (Haemon); Nikki Stiller (Ismene); Don Dawson (Chorus); Lenora Robinson (Mime); Ira Lewis (Guards); E. M. Margolese (Tiresias); Shirley Cox (Eurydice); Robert Dorn (Messenger)

Sheridan Square Playhouse, New York, opened January 13, 1967 5 performances
Produced by the Young People's Repertory Theatre, Terese Hayden, artistic director; A Drama by Sophocles, adapted by Dudley Fitts and Robert Fitzgerald; Director, Terese Hayden; Designed by Michael Harwood; Lighting, Joe Pacitti; Artistic supervisors, William and Jean Eckart; Chorus direction, Irma Jurist; Movement, Barrie Landauer; Music, Harvey Sollberger; Production manager, Allen Davis III; Stage manager, Penelope H. Parkhurst

Sima Gelbart (Antigone); Gregory Reese (Creon); Robert Fielding (Haemon); Eva Alexandria (Ismene); Annett Oliver (Eurydice); Joseph Ross (Sentry); William Beckwith (Tiresias); Steven Mencher (Boy); Kenneth Aaron (Messenger); Marc Mantell (Second Messenger); Sonya Abbye, Anthony Abeson, Sheryl Blevins, Harvey Brown, Lile Fiszman, Ira Kozinsky, Christina Lawrence, Tina Mann, Linda Rein, Beaty Schulman, Carlos Skeete, Peter Thomas (Chorus)

American Shakespeare Festival Theatre, Stratford, Conn., opened June 18, 1967
Produced by Joseph Verner Reed, Sr. and Joseph Verner Reed, Jr.; A Drama by Jean Anouilh; English translation by Lewis Galantiere; Director, Jerome Kilty; Scenery, Donald Oenslager; Lighting, Tharon Musser; Costumes, Gordon Micunis; Music and musical director, John Duffy; Lyrics, John Devlin; Stage managers, David

Clive, Lo Hardin, Robert Herrman; Performed in repertory with Shakespeare's *A Midsummer Night's Dream*, *The Merchant of Venice*, and *Macbeth*.

Maria Tucci (Antigone); Morris Carnovsky (Creon); Anthony Mainionis (Haemon); Tom Aldredge (Chorus); Marian Hailey (Ismene); Jane Farnol (Eurydice); Doris Rich (Nurse); John Devlin (Messenger); Billy Partello (Page); Peter Norden, Elliot Paul (Secret Service); Richard Castellano, Garry Mitchell, Edward Rudney (Guards); Bill MacAdama, Peff Modelski, Michael Scotlin, Ian Tucker (Singers)

THE ANTIGONE OF SOPHOKLES, *Brooklyn Academy of Music*, opened October 9, 1968

Produced by the Living Theatre Company under the direction of Julian Beck and Judith Malina; Adaptation by Bertolt Brecht, based on the German translation by Frederich Holderlin of the Drama by Sophocles; English translation by Judith Malina; Scenery, Julian Beck; Costumes, Birgit Knabe

Judith Malina (Antigone); Julian Beck (Kreon); Steve Thompson (Hamon); Henry Howard (Megareus); Cal Barber (Warhorse); Jenny Hecht (Ismene); Rufus Collins (Tiresias); Steven Ben Israel (Guard); Carl Einhorn (Eteokles); Echnaton (Polyneikes); Micharl Shari (Child); Jim Anderson, Pamela Badyk, Cal Barber, Rod Beere, Gene Gordon, Roy Harris, Frank Hoogeboom, Birgit Knabe, Sandy Linden, Gunter Pannewitz, William Shari, Luke Theodore, Jim Tiroff, Petra Vogt, Diana Van Tosh (People of Thebes)

Vivian Beaumont Theatre, New York, opened May 13, 1971 46 performances

Produced by The Repertory Theatre of Lincoln Center; A Drama by Sophocles; English version by Dudley Fitts and Robert Fitzgerald; Director, John Hirsch; Setting, Douglas W. Schmdit; Lighting, John Gleason; Costumes, Jane Greenwood; Music, Lukas Foss; Stage managers, Barbara-Mae Phillips and Jean-Daniel Noland

Martha Henry (Antigone); Philip Bosco (Creon); David Birney (Haemon); Tandy Cronyn (Ismene); Charles Cioffi (Choragos); Sydney Walker (Teiresias); Dimitra Arliss (Eurydice); John Harkins (Messenger); Pauline Flanagan (Chorus Leader); Robert Legionaire, Frank T. Wells (Guards); Timmy Ousey (Boy); James Blendick (succeeded by Ray Fray) (Sentry); Diana Kirkwood, David Little, Myra Rubin, George Van Den Houten (Chorus)

Greenwich Theatre, England, opened October 14, 1971

A Drama by Sophocles, translated by Leo Aylen; Director, Leo Aylen; Production designer, Digby Howard

Freda Dowie (Antigone/Teiresias/Messenger); Freddie Jones (Creon); Eric Flynn (Haemon); Susan Glanville (Ismene); Ann Horn (Eurydice); Alan Vicars (Guards); Annette Battam, Eric Flynn, Susan Glanville, Annie Graham, Trevor Griffiths, Ann Horn, Robert Lister, Alan Vicars (Chorus)

Touring Company, season 1972-73

Produced by the National Shakespeare Company, Philip Meister, Artistic Director; A Drama by Sophocles; Director, Louis Criss; Setting, Philip Meister; Scenery, Karl Eigsti; Lighting, Richard Ronald Beebe; Costumes, James Berton Harris; Music, Arnold Black; Managing director, Elaine Sulka; Stage managers, Cynthia Darlow, Grade Woodard and Richard Romald Beebe

Megan McTavish (Antigone); Richard Boddy (Creon); James Lavin (Haemon); Cynthia Darlow (Ismene); Grace Woodard (Eurydice); John Hostetter

(Teiresias); Richard LeVene (Chorus Leader); Antonio Pandolfo (Sentry); Mary Noel (Girl); Aidn Jaro (Messenger); Charles Davis, Jeffrey DeMunn, Jere O'Donnell (Chorus)

Abbey Theatre, New York, opened December 9, 1975 40 performances
Produced by the Classic Stage Company, Christopher Martin, director; A Drama by Sophocles, translated by Alex Szogyi; Director and production designer Christopher Martin; Assistant director, Rene Buch; Stage manager, John Shannon

Karen Sunde (Antigone); Christopher Martin (Creon); Jose Rodriguez (Haemon); Lisa Carling (Ismene); Deborah Dennison (Eurydice); Carol Flemming (Nurse); Wayne Wofford (Boudousse); Peter Van Norden (Durand); Alberto Tore (Jonas); Noble Shropshire (Messenger); Earl Trussell (Chorus)

Public Theatre/Martinson Hall, New York, opened April 27, 1982 62 performances
Produced by the New York Shakespeare Festival, Joseph Papp, producer; A Drama by Sophocles; New translation by John Chioles; Director, Joseph Chaikin; Scenery and Costumes, Sally Jacobs; Lighting, Beverly Emmons; Music, Richard Peaslee; Production supervisor, Jason Steven Cohen; Stage managers, Ruth Kreshka and Jane Hubbard

Lisa Banes (Antigone); F. Murray Abraham (Creon); Rosemary Quinn (Ismene); Peter Francis-James (Haemon); George Lloyd (Chorus); Raymond Barry (Messenger); Shami Chaikin (Eurydice); Roger Babb (Guard); Priscilla Smith (Teiresias); Jeffrey Bravin (Boy); B. Constance Barry, Hunt Cole, Ann Dunigan, Richard Frisch, Ronnie Gilbert, Clark Morgan (Chorus)

Shakespeare Festival Theatre, Stratford, Canada, opened June 18, 1985
Produced by the Stratford Festival Theatre; Director, David William; A Play by Sophocles, translated by Paul Roche; Production designer, Lesley Macauley; Lighting, Louise Guinand; Musical director, Laura Burton; Choreography, Paula Thomson; Stage manager, Michael Benoit

Caro Coltman (or Gwynyth Walsh) (Antigone); Kevin McNulty (Creon); Janet MacDonald (Ismene); Donald Adams (Haemon); Caro Coltman (or Gwynyth Walsh) (Eurydice); Lucy Peacock (Lady-in-Waiting); Keith Thomas (A Guard); William Needles (Tiresias); Ron Rees (A Boy); Ted Dykstra (An Officer); Maurice Godin (Chorus Leader); Kim Coates, Ted Dykstra, Richard Gilbert-Hill, Robert McClure, John Moffat, Laurence Russo, Keith Thomas (Chorus, Citizens of Thebes)

Duke of Cambridge Theatre, London, opened October 29, 1986 33 performances
Produced by the Duke of Cambridge Company; A Play by Jean Anouilh, translated by Lewis Galantiere; Director, Malcolm Sherman

Anne Harris (Antigone); Adam Kimmel (Creon); Kya Dyson (Ismene); Adrian Beaumont (Haemon); Tony Marshall (Chorus); Margaret Hotine (Nurse); David Finch (Guards); Deborah Lester-George (Singer)

BALLET

Covent Garden, London, opened October 15, 1959
Produced by the Royal Ballet of London; A Ballet by John Cranko based on the play *Antigone*; Music by Mikis Theodorakis; Scenery, Rufino Tamayo; Adaptation from Racine's *Les Freres Ennemis*; Musical Conductor, Hugo Rignold

Svetlana Beriosova (Antigone); Michael Somes (Creon); David Blair (Polynices); Leslie Edwards (Oedipus); Julia Farron (Jocasta); Gary Burne (Etiocles); Donald McLeary (Haemon)

SCREEN

ANTIGONE, Norma Pictures, released 1961

Executive Producer, Sperie Perakos; Producer, Demetrios Paris; Written and Directed by George Tzavellas; Based on the tragedy by Sophocles; Photography, Dinos Katsouridis; Art director, G. Anemoyannis; Music, Arghyris Kounadis; Sound, N. Despotides

Irene Papas (Antigone); Manos Katrakis (Creon); Nikos Kazis (Haemon); Maro Kontou (Ismene); Ilia Livikou (Eurydice); T. Karousos (Teiresias); John Arghyris (Sentry); Byron Pallis (Messenger); T. Moridis (Leader of the Chorus)

ANTIGONE/RITES FOR THE DEAD, ASA Communications, released October 1990

An Eclipse Production; Associate producer, Robert Haller; Produced, adapted, directed and choreographed by Amy Greenfield from Sophocles' *Antigone* and *Oedipus at Colonus*; Photography, Hilary Harris and Judy Irola; Costume design, Betty Howard; Music, Glenn Branca, Diamanda Galas, Paul Lemos, Elliott Sharp and David van Tieghem; Editors, Amy Greenfield and Bernard Hajenberg

Amy Greenfield (Antigone); Bertram Ross (Oedipus/ Creon); Janet Eilber (Ismene); Sean McElroy (Haemon); Henry Montes (Polynices); Silvio Facchin (Eteocles)

NOTE: This production premiered at the Museum of Modern Art, New York

TELEVISION

Omnibus, televised November 21, 1954 CBS 90 minutes

Produced by Robert Saudek for the CBS Television and Radio Workshop; Director, Sidney Lumet; The play by Sophocles

Beatrice Straight (Antigone); Barry Jones (Creon); Marian Seldes (Ismene); Kevin McCarthy (Haemon); Philip Bourneuf (Chorus); Sheppard Strudwick (Teiresias); Virginia Kaye (Nurse); Martin Brooks (Messenger); Bruce Gordon (Guard)

Kaiser Aluminum Hour, televised September 11, 1956 NBC 1 hour

Produced and directed by Franklin Shaffner; Lewis Galantiere's adaptation of the play by Jean Anouilh of the Sophocles classic; Sets, Rouben Ter Arutunian

Claude Rains (Creon); Marisa Pavan (Antigone); Felicia Montealegre (Ismene); Mildred Natwick (Nurse); Alexander Scourby (Chorus); Paul Stevens (Haemon); Clint Young (Guard); Chris Snell (Page); Theseus George (Second Guard); Mel Arrighi (Third Guard); Marc May (Polynice's Body)

Play of the Week, televised October 27, 1959 BBC 1 hour

Produced by thge British Broadcasting Corportation; Director, Michael Elliott; Lewis Galantiere's adaptation of the play by Jean Anouilh of the Sophocles classic; Decor, Frederick Knapman

Dorothy Tutin (Antigone); Basil Sidney (Creon); Jennifer Wilson (Ismene); David

McCallum (Haemon); Rosalind Atkinson (Nurse); Noel Willman (Chorus); Enid Porimer (Eurydice); Peter Hempson (Page); James Maxwell (Messenger); Sam Kydd (First Guard); Richard Klee (Second Guard); Edwin Brown (Third Guard)

Roots of Freedom, televised September 11, 1963 CBS 1 hour
Produced by Perry Wolff; Director, Tom Donovan; Hosts, Alfred Lunt and Lynn Fontanne (A section from *Antigone*, taped at Theatre of Dionysus in Athens, was part of the premiere program of this series of periodic specials, this one entitled *Athens, Where the Theatre Began*)

Rosemary Harris (Antigone); Alfred Drake (Creon); Lynn Fontanne (Chorus)

Playhouse New York's Classic for Today, televised October 7, 1972 PBS 90 minutes
Executive producer, Jac Venza; Director, Gerald Freedman; Lewis Galantiere's adaptation of the play by Jean Anouilh of the classic by Sophocles. (Rebroadcast on PBS' *Theatre in America*, February 13, 1974)

Genevieve Bujold (Antigone); Fritz Weaver (Creon); Stacy Keach (Chorus); James Naughton (Haemon); Aline MacMahon (Nurse); Leah Chandler (Ismene); Louis Zorich (Jonas)

The Theban Plays, televised October 2, 1988 PBS 2 hours
Films for the Humanities, Inc. and Bioscope, in association with BBC-TV; Produced by Louis Marks; Adapted and directed by Don Taylor from the classic by Sophocles; Costumes, June Hudson; Music, Derek Bourgeosis; Commentary, Michael York

Juliet Stevenson (Antigone); John Shrapnel (Creon); Mike Gwilym (Haemon); John Gielgud (Teiresias); Rosalie Crutchley (Euridice); Gwen Taylor (Ismene); and Tony Selby, Paul Russell, Bernard Hill

(Juliet Stevenson, John Shrapnel and Gwen Taylor played the same roles in *Oedipus at Colonus*, the previous entry in the BBC trilogy of Theban Plays, televised one week before)

AROUND THE WORLD IN 80 DAYS

Based on the novel by Jules Verne (1872)

Summary

Punctilious English gentleman Phileas Fogg, during a card game with several of his wealthy friends at London's Reform Club, wagers 20,000 pounds that he can circle the globe in eighty days, and accompanied by his new valet, Passepartout, begins his journey in high spirits. Everything conspires against him. An avalanche blocks the railroad...winds blow his balloon off course ...a bullfight in Spain changes his intinerary...a Scotland Yard detective, hot on his trail thinking he's the man who, coincidentally, robbed the Bank of England the day Fogg departed, creates fresh obstacles at every port...an angry mob in India delays his passage in India, where he and Passepartout save a newly widowed princess from being tossed on the funeral pyre with her late husband...Fogg his separated from his tickets in Hong Kong when the detective tricks Passepartout, but hires a junk that gets him to Yokohama...a political rally holds up the party in San Francisco, and they are attacked by Indians while crossing the plains... arriving in New York too late to catch the steamer to Liverpool, he bribes the captain of a trading schooner headed for South America to change course, and then has to burn the boat to the waterline as the fuel runs out almost within sight of England. The question of whether Phileas Fogg wins his wager as time runs out is well known to all as, after first thinking he'd lost, but then realizing he'd gained a full day having crossed the International Dateline from East to West, he strolls into the Club at the last moment.

Comment and Critique

Jules Verne was born in Nantes, France, on February 8, 1828, and eventually made his way to Paris to study law. He drifted into the theatre where, at twenty, he wrote the librettos for a pair of operettas with Michel Carre, and then did the verse comedy *Les Pailles rompues* with Alexandre Dumas fils. Ultimately he turned his vision toward achievements of marvelous scientific and mechanical invention and began writing what today would be called science-fiction. His first success in this area was his tale of adventure, *Cinq semaines en balloon* (*Five Weeks in a Balloon*), written for Hertzel's *Magazin d'Education* in 1862. This was followed by *Voyage au centre de la terre* (1864), *De la terre a la lune* (1865), *Vingt mille lieuses sous les mers* (1869), *Les Anglais au pole nord* (1870), and finally *Voyage autour de monde en quartrevingts jours*, which appeared in the magazine *Le Temps*. It was adapted to the stage two years later by Adolphe R. d'Ennery, who premiered the play as *Le Tour du monde en 80 jours*, at Paris' Porte St. Martin Theatre on November 7, 1874. A five act play (plus prologue), it was a huge success and played for more than two years. Six years later, he and d'Ennery had another stage hit with *Michael Strogoff*. Verne died in Amiens on March 24, 1905.

Through the years, assorted versions of the Jules Verne adventure came to the stage, including a 1939 Belgian production and a Czech one in the early 1960s that's played for years in East Bloc countries and other places in the world.

Around the World in 80 Days came to Broadway four decades after Verne's death. It was Orson Welles who chose to turn the adventure into a musical extravaganza. Welles not only adapted the Verne book but also produced and directed the show through his Mercury Productions but also played the part of crafty Detective Dick Fix (Phileas Fogg was played by Arthur Margetson) and no less than Cole Porter provided the score. (It was not vintage Porter and remains one of his least known -- probably he was more interested in his next musical, *Kiss Me Kate*.) "Although he is an old acquaintance of interplanetary space, Orson Welles has cut himself down to a single world in [the musical]," Lewis Nichols wrote in *The New York Times*. "*Around the World* is only fitfully amusing. Based roughly on Jules Verne, the story gives Mr. Welles the chance to pour a little of everything upon the stage, but, as in politics, the one world lacks a cohesion and basic plan. It can be said to Mr. Welles' credit, however, that he goes down as a showman should, with pistols blazing, feathers showering on the audience and cymbals clashing. Part of the time -- the better part, by the way -- *Around the World* is a blood brother to *Hellzapoppin'*...In other words, *Around the World* has the makings for an hilarious evening. It does not come off because it lacks unity."

"*Around the World* is one of those ideas that must have seemed hilarious on paper. The trouble is that it is just not very funny. The basic story must have appeared a perfect foundation for humorous situations and nonsensical wit. Instead, for the most part the story is left to produce its own laughs, or is needled by entirely extraneous vaudeville," said the *New York World-Telegram*'s William Hawkins. "One gets the feeling that Mr. Welles, the author, got his character to a certain spot, then said to himself in desperation, 'What must I do now?' Then he answered, 'Let's have a circus,' or 'Let's run another reel of a movie,' or more frequently, 'Let's shoot some more guns off.'"

Howard Barnes thought in the *Herald Tribune*: "Orson Welles has quite a field day for himself in *Around the World*. He has adapted the Jules Verne novel to the musical comedy stage with brash enthusiasm, combining silent movies, Hoboken melodramatic satire, a magic show and Olsen and Johnson japes in a popular potpourri...All in all, it is a very uneven musical which the producer-author-actor must answer for. In this instance, he is more often exhibitionistic than entertaining...The Porter song are not in the finest Porter tradition, but they serve the plot adequately when it deserves it." *Around the World* lasted seventy-five performances. Welles then went to Hollywood to make *The Lady from Shanghai*; Porter went to Hollywood to score *The Pirate*.

On the screen, an early German production in 1918 entitled *Die Reise um die Welt* (*The Trip Around the World*) was one of the first filmings of the Verne tale. Difficulties with Verne's estate forced a change in the title from *Around the World in 80 Days*. It fell to another audacious showman, Mike Todd, to out-Orson Welles Orson Welles and make the definitive *Around the World in 80 Days* in 1956. The flamboyant Todd was heretofore known primarily for his lavish, often gaudy stage productions like *The Hot Mikado* (1939), *Star and Garter* (1942), *Something for the Boys* (1943), *Mexican Hayride* (1944), *Up in Central Park* (1945), *Peep Show* (1950), and *A Night in Venice* (1952). He also produced a *Hamlet* on Broadway in the mid-1940s.

Todd's maiden effort on film was to be the most spectacular thing movies had yet seen. To this end, he began coaxing all of his show business contacts into joining him on his grand project. At first, reportedly, he was less than successful, until Frank Sinatra agreed to make a token appearance gratis. Then by the dozens, name actors hopped aboard the Todd bandwagon in "cameo" appearances (as the producer chose to describe the participation of each in a term that since has gone into the show business lexicon). In all, aside from the four leading roles played by David Niven, Cantinflas (the beloved Mexican actor/clown in his first American role), Shirley MacLaine and Robert Newton, forty-four international stars became part of the festivities in nothing more than walk-on appearances. Interestingly, the legendary picture, in the expansive wide-screen process known as Todd-AO, became Michael Todd's *Around the World in 80 Days*--not Jules Verne's (his name was all but buried in the lavish advertising and on the screen).

"The most fantastic entertainment event in the entire history of the motion picture industry!" is how *Newsweek* described Todd's oeuvre -- as if Todd himself had written the review. Bosley Crowther wrote in *The New York Times*: "This mammoth and mad pictorial rendering of the famous old novel of Jules Verne...is a sprawling conglomeration of refined English comedy, gigantic screen travel and slam-bang Keystone burlesque. It makes like a wild adventure picture...It is, undeniably, quite a show." Crowther also observed that Todd "with an onslaught of highly heterogeneous and untraditional musical shows, is apparently out to shatter the fundamental formation of the screen."

One spectacular opening followed another around the country as the film premiered on reserved seats. It went on to do remarkable business and win the Academy Award as Best Picture of the Year, with Oscars also going for Best Screenplay (James Poe, John Farrow and S.J. Perelman), Best Color

Cinematography (Lionel Lindon), Best Film Editing (Gene Ruggiero and Paul Weatherwax), and Best Scoring of a Dramatic or Comedy Picture (Victor Young, who died three months before Oscar night). Nomination also went to director Michael Anderson (who lost to George Stevens for *Giant*) and to art directors James W. Sullivan and Ken Adam, set decorator Ross J. Dowd, and costume designer Miles White (the awards went to their counterparts for *The King and I*). It also won honors worldwide.

Todd's grand, bigger-than-life scheme, with the encouragement of his wife Elizabeth Taylor, whom he married in February 1957, was then to turn *Around the World in 80 Days* into a ballet. At first, he envisioned a television spectacular, then broadened his dream into an event at the Metropolitan Opera House in New York (October 17, 1957, was his target date--the first anniversary of the film's premiere in New York). Composer Harold Adamson was commissioned to write lyrics to Victor Young's existing score, and Gower and Marge Champion were to play (and dance) Phileas Fogg and Princess Aouda, backed by an enormous chorus. *The Around the World Ballet* was put aside briefly as Todd and Taylor came up with an even more extravagant idea: *A Little Party for a Few Friends* (18,000 to be exact) at Madison Square Garden. Mike Todd's ballet was to remain an unfulfilled dream. He was killed in a plane crash near Grants, New Mexico, on March 22, 1858, at age forty-nine. He was en route to New York to be toasted as "Showman of the Year" by the National Association of Theater Owners. Rather than having *Around the World in 80 Days* staged as a musical ballet, a recording of the score was produced by Michael Todd, Jr., and released later in 1958.

For three decades, Michael Todd's vision of the Jules Verne adventure was to stand as the definitive one, until NBC decided to attempt to top it with a star-laden six-hour, three part mini-series. With Pierce Brosnan as Fogg, the spectacular new version went into production in the summer of 1988 on location in five countries. It took twelve weeks to film and like its predecessor was packed with "cameo" appearances. Eric Idle, a member of the Monty Python troupe, was Passepartout, and Peter Ustinov hammed it up as Detective Fix (ironically, he was to have played Fix in Todd's movie but another film commitment at the time forced he to relinquish the part to Robert Newton). Two others in the TV cast, Robert Morley and John Mills, were also in the theatrical version thirty-odd years earlier.

In his review in *The New York Times*, TV critic John J. O'Connor observed: "This television version has one fairly consistent virtue. It assumes that the Verne story is something more than a glitzy vehicle for guest-star actors...Pierce Brosnan plays Phileas Fogg in a slyly attractive manner that makes it easy to see why this Irish actor was once a top candidate to become James Bond...[He] takes the clever approach of ignoring his looks and, with a bow in the direction of Cary Grant, showing with considerable charm that he isn't afraid to look silly. The aristocratic Phileas is, after all, very much the cold fish, the finicky perfectionist who will no doubt do tomorrow what he's done today."

STAGE

LE TOUR DU MONDE EN 80 JOURS, *Le Theatre de La-Porte-St-Martin*, Paris, opened November 7, 1874 (played for more than two years)
A Play in Five Acts by M. Adolphe d'Ennery and Jules Verne

M. Lacressionniere (Phileas Fogg); M. Dumaine (Archibald Corsican); M. Vannoy (Detective Fix); M. Alexandre (Passepartout); M. Rene Didier (Stuart);

M. Fraizier (Sullivan); M. Rolle (Ralph); M. Renot (Flanagan); M. Mangin (Captain Comarty); Mme. Angele Moreau (Princess Aouda); Mme. Pauline Patry (Nemea); Mme. Berthe Marietti (Nakahira); Mme. Marie-Laure (Margaret); and Messieurs Danjou, Bouyer, Machanette, Murray, Perrier, Emrol, Bellet, Neraut, Besson, Lansoy, Leroy, Abel, Leon, Adolphe; and Mme. Pauline Moreau

LE TOUR DU MONDE EN 80 JOURS, *L'Alhambra*, Brussels, opened October 14, 1939

Roger Beaulieu (Phileas Fogg); M. Mussiere (Passepartout); M. Stredon (Archibald Corsican); Nelly Corbusier (Princess Aouda); M. Davray (Detective Fix); Mony Doll (Nemea)

AROUND THE WORLD, *Adelphi Theater*, New York, opened May 31, 1946 75 performances

A Mercury Production, presented by Orson Welles; A Musical Comedy with music and lyrics by Cole Porter and a book adapted by Orson Welles from the novel by Jules Verne; Directed by Orson Welles; Settings, Robert Davison; Costumes, Alvin Colt; Circus arranged by Barbette; Musical director, Harry Levant

Arthur Margetson (Mr. Phileas Fogg); Larry Laurance (Passepartout, a Yankee); Orson Welles (Dick Fix); Mary Healy (Mrs. Aouda); Brainerd Duffield (A Bank Robber); Guy Spaull (A Police Inspector); Nathan Baker, Jack Pitchon, Myron Speth, Gordon West (London Bobbies); Genevieve Sauris (A Lady); Stefan Schnabel (Avery Jevity); Julie Warren (Molly Muggins); Brainerd Duffield (Mr. Benjamin Cruett-Spew); Guy Spaull (Mr. Ralph Runcible); Bernard Savage (Sir Charles Mandiboy); Billy Howell (Lord Upditch); Bruce Cartwright (A Servingman); Gregory McDougall (Another Servingman); Billy Howell (A Station Attendant); Dorothy Bird (Meerahlah); Lucas Aco, Myron Speth (Two Dancing Fellas); Bernard Savage (British Consul in Suez); Stefan Schnabel (An Arab Spy); Brainerd Duffield (A Second Arab Spy); Eddy Di Genova, Victor Savidge, Stanley Turner (Snake Charmers); Lucas Aco (A Fakir); Guy Spaull (Maurice Goodpile); Spencer James (A Sikh); Arthur Cohen (A High Priest); Phil King, Billy Howell, Lucas Aco, Nathan Baker (Various sinister Chinese); Jackie Cezane (Lee Toy); Lee Morrison, Nancy Newton (Two Daughters of Joy); Brainerd Duffield (Mr. Oka Saka); The Three Kanasawa (Foot Jugglers); Adelaide Corsi (Rolling Globe Lady); Miss Lu (Contortionist); Ishikawa (Hand Balancer); Mary Broussard, Lee Vincent, Patricia Leith, Virginia Morris (Aerialists); Billy Howell, Lucas Aco, Gregory McDougall (Circus Assistants); Ray Goody (The Slide for Life); Jack Pitchon, Tony Monteli (Roustabouts); Stefan Schnabel (Mother); Nathan Baker (Father); Bernie Pisarski (Child); Cliff Chapman (Bride); Larry Laurance (Groom); Arthur Cohen (Minister); Jack Cassidy (Policeman); Eddy Di Genova (Monkey Man); Allan Lowell (Kimona Man); Bruce Cartwright, Gordon West (Firemen); Daniel DePaolo (Dragon); Stanley Turner (An Attendant); Eddy Di Genova (A Bartender); Dorothy Bird, Bruce Cartwright (Mexican Dancers); Victoria Cordova (Lola); Brainerd Duffield (Sol); Billy Howell (Sam); James Aco (Jim); Spencer James (Jake); Stefan Schnabel (A Medicine Man); Bernard Savage, Billy Howell (Other Medicine Men); Allan Lowell (Jail Guard)

MUSICAL NUMBERS: "Look What I Found"; "There He Goes, Mr. Phileas Fogg"; "Meerahlah"; "Suttee Procession"; "Suez Dance"; "Sea Chantey"; "Should I Tell You I Love You"; "Pipe Dreaming"; "Oka Saka Circus"; "California Scene Dance"; "If You Smile At Me"; "Wherever They Fly the Flag of Old England"

Dropped during tryout in Boston, New Haven and Philadelphia: "Missus Aouda"; "Slave Auction"; "Snagtoota Gertie"

NOTE: Larry Lawrence later became singer Enzo Stuarti

LE TOUR DU MONDE EN 80 JOURS, S. K. Neumann Theatre, Prague, opened January 27, 1962

A Comedy in Five Acts by Pavel Kohout, adapted from the play by Jules Verne and Adolphe D'Ennery; Director, Vaclav Lohnisky; Decor, Vladimir Synek; Costumes, Jan Skalicky

(Following is the Belgian cast of this production which opened at *Le Theatre National de Belgique* during the 1964-65 season:)

Andre Debaar (Phileas Fogg); Jo Rensonnet (Passepartout); Georges Bossair (Detective Fix); Liliane Vincent (Princess Aouda); and in multiple roles: Paul Clairy, Michel Fasbender, Billy Fasbender, Yves Larec, Marcel Roels, Jacques Dorval, Jean Pascal, Fernand Leane, Andre Clarence, Boris Stoikoff, Nicole Karis, Veronique Balaes, Yves Dailly

LE TOUR DU MONDE EN 80 JOURS, Comedie des Champs Elysees, Paris, opened March 1, 1979

Produced by Les Acteurs Francais Associes; A Comedy by Pavel Kohout, adapted from the play by Jules Verne and Adolphe D'Ennery; French translation by Jacques Ziller; Director, Guy Descaux; Decor, Philippe Bruneau

Daniel Ceccaldi (Phileas Fogg); Maurice Sarfati (Passepartout); Jean-Pierre Darras (Detective Fix); Ariele Semenoff (Princess Aouda); and in multiple roles: Jacques Dynam, Jean-Pierre Delage, Bruno Balp, Jacques Marchand, Bernard Lanneau, Luis Amiel

LE TOUR DU MONDE EN 80 JOURS, Belgian Tour, 1980-81

Andre Brevers (Phileas Fogg); Alex Trasset (Passe-partout); Jean Brouwers (Detective Fix); Claire Servais (Princess Aouda); plus Marcel Liben and Jose Brouwers playing 54 other characters

80 DAYS, La Jolla Playhouse, Mandell Weiss Theater, San Diego, Calif., opened August 28, 1988

La Jolla Playhouse presentation. A Musical in two acts, based on the novel by Jules Verne; Director, Des McAnuff; Book by Snoo Wilson; Music and Lyrics by Ray Davies; Sets, Douglas W. Schmidt; Costumes, Susan Hilferty; Lighting, David F. Segal; Sound, John Kilgore; Musical supervision, Danny Troob; Musical director, Jonny Bowden; Orchestrations, Robby Merkin; Vocal arrangements, Danny Troob and Jonny Bowden; Incidental music, Ada Janik; Choreographer, Dianne McIntyre

Stephen Borgadus (Jules Verne); Timothy Landfield (Phileas Fogg); Yamil Borges (Indian Princess); and Brooks Almy, Don Amendolia, Matthew Eaton Benett, Jay Garner, Randy Graff, Ernest Harada, Scott Harlan, Paul Kandel, Scotch Ellis Loring, Deborah Nishimura, Lannyl Stephens, Cynthia Vance, Matthew Wright, Rise Benson, Kevin Connell, Karen Gedissman, Mindy Hull, Sylvia MacCalla, Jim Morlino, Andrew Weems, Christopher Zelno

LE TOUR DU MONDE EN 80 JOURS, Theatre Dejazet, Paris, season 1988-89

A Musical Comedy adapted from the play by Jules Verne and Adolphe D'Ennery; Book and direction by Jean-Marie Lecoq; Music and musical direction by Louis

Dunoyer de Segonzac; Decor, Claude Acquart; Costumes, Barbara Ryschlowska; Choreography, Eveline Drach

Claude Legendre (Phileas Fogg); Jean-Marie Lecoq (Passepartout); Maxime Casa (Detective Fix); Jocelyne Sand (Princess Aouda); and in multiple roles: Lise Durand, Agnes Host, Nelly-Anne Rabas, Gilles Butin, Bonnafet Tarbouriech, Bernard Valdeneige

SCREEN

DIE REISE UM DIE WELT (*The Trip Around the World*), *Oswald Film GmBH*, Germany, released July 1921

Written and directed by Richard Oswald, based on Jules Verne's *Around the World in 80 Days*

Conrad Veidt (Phileas Fogg); Reinhold Schunzel (Passepartout); Eugen Rex (Detective Fix); Anita Berber (Prince Aouda); and Kate Oswald, Max Gulstorff

AROUND THE WORLD IN 80 DAYS, *United Artists*, released October 1958

A Michael Todd Production for The Michael Todd Co.; Associate producer, William Cameron Menzies; Director, Michael Anderson; Screenplay, James Poe, John Farrow and S. J. Perelman, based on the novel by Jules Verne; Photography, Lionel Linden; Costumes, Miles White; Art directors, James Sullivan and Ken Adams; Music, Victor Young; Choreography, Paul Godkin; Foreign location director, Kevin McClory; Editors, Gene Ruggiero and Paul Weatherwax

David Niven (Phileas Fogg); Cantinflas (Passepartout); Robert Newton (Mr. Fix); Shirley MacLaine (Princess Aouda); Charles Boyer (Monsieur Gasse); Joe E. Brown (Stationmaster at Fort Kearney); Martine Carol (Pretty Tourist in Paris); John Carradine (Col. Stamp Proctor, San Francisco Politician); Charles Coburn (Clerk in Hong Kong Steamship Office); Ronald Colman (Official on Railroad in India); Melville Cooper (Chief Steward on "SS Mongolia"); Noel Coward (Roland Hesketh-Baggott); Finlay Currie (Reform Club Member); Reginald Denny (Chief of Police, Bombay); Andy Devine ("SS Henrietta" First Mate); Marlene Dietrich (Barbary Coast Saloon Proprietress); Luis Miguel Dominguin (Bullfighter in Chincon, Spain); Fernandel (Paris Coachman); Sir John Gielgud (Foster, Fogg's exemployee); Hermione Gingold (London Club "Sporting Lady"); Jose Greco (Spanish Dance in Cave of the Seven Winds); Sir Cedric Hardwicke (Brigadier-General Sir Francis Cromarty); Trevor Howard (Reform Club Member); Glynis Johns (Drinker in London Pub); Buster Keaton (Central Pacific Railroad Conductor); Evelyn Keyes (Pretty Flirt in Paris); Beatrice Lillie (Revivalist Captain in London); Peter Lorre (Japanese Steward on "SS Carnatic"); Edmund Lowe ("SS Henrietta" Engineer); Victor McLaglen ("SS Henrietta" Helmsman); Colonel Tim McCoy (U.S. Cavalry Commander at Fort Kearney); A. E. Matthews (Reform Club Member); Mike Mazurki (Character in Hong Kong Waterfront Dive); John Mills (Hiccupping London Cabbie); Alan Mowbray (British Consul at Suez); Robert Morley (Bank of England Governor); Edward R. Murrow (Narrator of Prologue); Jack Oakie ("SS Henrietta" Captain); George Raft (Bouncer at Barbary Coast Saloon); Gilbert Roland (Achmed Abdullah); Cesar Romero (Abdullah's henchman); Frank Sinatra (Barbary Coast Piano Player); Red Skelton (Barbary Coast Saloon Drunk); Ronald Squires (Reform Club Member); Basil Sydney (Reform Club Member); Richard Wattis (Scotland Yard Inspector at Lloyds); Harcourt Williams (Hinshaw, Reform Club Servant)

Music from the soundtrack: Decca Records (a version of the score with lyrics by Harold Adamson added to Victor Young's music, and featuring the Jack Saunders Orchestra and Chorus under Franz Allers' direction, was released in 1958 on Everest Records)

TELEVISION

AROUND THE WORLD IN 80 DAYS, animated cartoon, televised December 29, 1988 HBO 65 minutes
An API Television Production/Active Home Video. Producer, Walter J. Hocker; Director, Leif Gram; Script, Chet Stover; Animators, Tom Baron, Ray Bartle, Gairden Cooke, John Ewing, Don Exard, Mick Faulkner, Susan Gilbert, Sam Harvey, Ed De Matteia, Ralph Peverill, Barnev Posner, William Toh; Animation Supervisor, Jean Tych; Storyboard, Chris Coddington; Layouts, Robert Smit, Alex Nicholas, Bruce Davis; Backgrounds, Peter Connell, Jann Sender, Cherie Hayes, Ros Kyle, Azmi Mounir; Camera, Jenny Ochse, Kim Humphreys, Carl Keller, Robert Bates; Music, John Sangster; Editor, Eddy Graham

Voices: Alistair Duncan, Ross Higgins, Max Osbiston, Owen Wingott

AROUND THE WORLD IN 80 DAYS, televised April 16-18, 1989 NBC 2 hours (each part)
A Harmony Gold & ReteEurope Production in association with Valente/Baerwald Productions; Executive producers, Paul Baerwald and Renee Valente; Coproducers, Frank Agrama and Daniele Lorenzano; Line producer, Allesandro Tasca; Director, Buzz Kulik; Teleplay by John Gay, based on the novel by Jules Verne; Photography, Nic Knowland; Production designer, Michael Porter; Art directors, Ian Watson, Jonathan Cheung and Vladislav Lasic; Costume designer, Emma Porteous; Music, Billy Goldenberg; Makeup supervisor, Giancarlo del Brocco; 2nd unit director, Burr Smidt; 2nd unit photographer, Jacques Renoir; Editors, Les Green, David Beatty and Peter Parasheles

Pierce Brosnan (Phileas Fogg); Eric Idle (Passepartout); Julia Nickson (Princess Aouda); Peter Ustinov (Detective Fix); Ariel Dombasle (Lucette); Gabrielle Ferzetti (Rimani); Henry Gibson (Train Conductor); John Hillerman (Sir Francis Commarty); Rick Jason (Cornelius Vanderbilt); Jack Klugman (Captain Bunsby); Christopher Lee (Thomas Flanagan); Patrick Macnee (Gautier Ralph); Anna Massey (Queen Victoria); Roddy McDowall (Gerald McBaines); Darren McGavin (Mr. Mudge); Sir John Mills (Faversham); Robert Morley (Sir Forbes-Keith Wentworth); Stephen Nichols (Jesse James); Lee Remick (Sarah Bernhardt); Pernell Roberts (Captain Speedy); James B. Sikking (Engineer Jenks); Jill St. John (Mrs. Bennett); Robert Wagner (Alfred Bennett); Simon Ward (Andrew Stuart); Jean-Pierre Castaldi (Lenoir); Hugo de Vernier (Louis Pasteur); and John Abineri, Yves Aubert, Bill Bailey, Peter Birrell, John Carlin, Lane Cooper, Julian Curry, Ellis Dale, Bruce Troy Davis, Edward Dentith, Geraldo DiMiglio, Roy Evans, Don Ferguson, Henry Fong, Mike Gable, Maurice Gar-dette, Arne Gordon, Olivier Hemon, Colin Higgins, Mark Holmes, George Ip, Subash Ioshi, Abraham Lee, Michael Lee, Lily Leung, Joseph Long, Victor Maddern, Ian McNeice, Ajay Mehta, Christopher Munche, Pierre Olaf, Stuart Ong, Arvin Pathela, John Rapley, Terence Scammell, Peter Sharman, Eve Shickle, Cassie Stuart, Tommy Tam, Ted Thomas, Violette, Ed Wiley, Tariq Yanus

AROUND THE WORLD IN 80 DAYS, televised January 7 through February 18, 1990
Arts and Entertainment 7 episodes (1 hour each)
A British Broadcasting Corporation Production; Produced by Clem Vallence; Director, Roger Mills; Written by Michael Palin, based on the concept by Jules Verne; Photography, Nigel Meakin; Graphic design, Liz Friedman; Sound, Ron Brown; Editor, David Thomas

Michael Palin (retracing Phileas Fogg's journey starting on September 25, 1988)

BABE RUTH
Various dramatizations of the life of George Herman Ruth

Synopsis, Comment and Critique

George Herman Ruth, Jr., was born in Baltimore on February 6, 1895, and grew up to become the most celebrated baseball player of all time. His youth though was quite troubled and his parents, George, a saloon-keeper, and Katherine, found themselves frustrated by hid incorrigible behavior and shipped him off at age seven to St. Mary's Industrial School for Boys where he came under the tutelege of Brother Mathias. There he learned sports and a trade, and in 1914, his prowess as a left-handed pitcher caught the eye the Baltimore Orioles. Owner Jack Dunn adopted the teenager and signed him with the team where he earned the nickname "Babe." He was sold shortly thereafter to the Boston Red Sox and helped them win the 1915 and 1916 world championships. He played six seasons for the Red Sox, and his slugging prowess convinced the manager, Ed Barrow, to take him off the mound and put him in the outfield where he could play regularly and set a major league record with 29 home runs.

In 1920 the Sox electrified baseball by selling Ruth to the New York Yankees where he was to become a national hero, breaking record after record until his release in 1934. His sixty home runs in 1927 marks a record that still stands (for a 154-game season) and his 714 career home runs were unsurpassed until 1974. Babe Ruth became probably the most famous player ever and was baseball's leading celebrity with a mystique that made him the stuff of legends. Off the diamond, he led a rather undisciplined life however, a reputation that kept him from being selected a manager after retiring as an active player following a season with the Boston Braves in 1935. In 1936 he was voted a charter member of the newly established National Baseball Hall of Fame. Ruth died of cancer in New York City on August 16, 1948, not long after attending the movie premiere of a rather uninspired "popcorn biography" (as one critic dubbed it) based on his life with William Bendix as The Babe.

Bosley Crowther (*The New York Times*) felt that "it is hard to concieve that anyone -- Mr. Ruth's fans least of all -- will be entirely happy about *The Babe Ruth Story* on the screen. For the sober fact is that this movie...is a good bit too much of a muchness in the line of heroics and tears." He also found that "it is hard to accept the presenation of a great, mawkish, noblespiritred buffoon which William Bendix gives in this picture as a reasonable facsimile of the Babe... When all is said and done, [it] has much more tha tone of low-grade fiction than it has of biography." *Variety*'s critic was somewhat kinder, feeling that "*The Babe Ruth Story* tells a fanciful, romanticized version of the life and deeds of the King of Swat, mixing screen licencse with fact to dish out a load of chuckles, tears and sentiment that should pay off... William Bendix does an excellent job of the title role. While he's still Bendix, he gives the performance the color, of Ruth and a reasonable facsimile of the Bambino's mannerism, batting stance and walk."

For the next four decades, Ruth would remain the figure of legend until Max Gail (who had gained fame as the shambling Wojo of television's *Barney Miller*) chose to play the famed Sultan of Swat on stage. Of Gail's venture, Douglas Watt wrote in the *Daily News*: "*The Babe*, last night's error at the Princess, is a dull, plodding account of the career of the most celebrated of all ball players...this one-man show belongs in a sandlot, preferably six feet under." In *The New York Times*, Mel Gussow found that "the play superficially considers the athlete's life, somewhat in the manner of a television documentary...As directed by Noam Pitlik, the evening is so intent on being inclusive in a relatively short span of time -- about the man, and, on film, about his era -- that it succeeds in short-changing his amazing baseball accomplishments as well as his prodigious personal life...As a dramatic portrait of the Sultan of Swat, *The Babe* is as deep as a bunt." *The Babe* played on Broadway only briefly, but it was captured on tape for later presentation on television.

In the early nineties, Babe Ruth's colorful life was dragged before the cameras twice in a span of six months -- once on television, once on the big screen. Of the former, premiering at World Series time in 1991, *Variety* wrote: "[It] is about as deep as a pop fly to first base. When all the pitches are thrown, *Babe Ruth* strikes out." The paper's critic thought that its star, Broadway actor Stephen Lang, "does a good job in the title role, and aside from the silly-looking gobs of rubber added to make his appearance similar to Ruth's, he does his job convincingly. However it is the lack of substance in the writing that fails to provide Lang with the meat needed to carry his performance over the fence." John Goodman starred in the big-budget theatrical 1992 film, called simply *The Babe*. It was received with only slightly more enthusiasm. "With an engaging and convincing performance by John Goodman," *Variety* found, "*The Babe* is better than one might expecty, but producer John Fusco's uninspired script never gives this film a reason for being...the thinly dramatized, overly episodic *Babe* resembles a telepic that has lost its way onto the big screen."

STAGE

THE BABE, Princess Theater*, New York, opened May 17, 1984 8 performances (and 5 previews)
Presented by Corniche Productions and Peter F. Buffa; A One-man Play by Bob and Ann Costa; Director, Noam Pitlik; Scenery, Ray Recht; Lighting, F. Mitchell Dana; Costumes, Judy Dearing; Makeup, Steve Laporte; Production stage manager, Doug Laidlaw

Max Gail (George Herman Ruth)

*This production was later taped for television presentation in 1985

SCREEN

THE BABE RUTH STORY, Allied Artists, released July 1948
Produced and directed by Roy Del Ruth; Associate producer, Joe Kaufman; Screenplay, Bob Considine and George Callahan, based on the book by Considine; Photography, Philip Tannura and James Van Trees; Art director, Paul Sylos; Music, Edward Ward; Editor, Richard Heermance

William Bendix (Babe Ruth); Claire Trevor (Claire Hodgson); Charles Bickford

(Brother Mathias); Sam Levene (Phil Conrad); William Frawley (Jack Dunn); Gertrude Niesen (Nightclub Singer); Fred Lightner (Miller Huggins); Stanley Clements (Western Union Boy); Bobby Ellis (Babe Ruth as a Boy); Lloyd Gough (Baston); Matt Briggs (Col. Jacob Ruppert); Paul Cavanaugh (Dr. Menzies); Pat Flaherty (Bill Corrigan); Tony Taylor (The Kid); Richard Lane (Coach); Mark Koenig (Himself); Harry Wismer, Mel Allen (Sports Announcers); H. V. Kaltenborn (News Announcer); Knox Manning (Narrator)

THE BABE, *Universal Pictures*, released April 1992
Executive producers, Bill Finnigan and Walter Coblenz; Written and produced by John Fusco; Coproducer, Jim Van Wyck; Director, Arthur Hiller; Photography, Haskell Wexler; Production designer, James D. Vance; Costume designer, April Ferry; John Goodman's makeup, Kevin Haney; Music, Elmer Bernstein; Editor, Robert C. Jones

John Goodman (George Herman Ruth); Kelly McGillis (Claire Hodgson Ruth); Trini Alvarado (Helen Woodford Ruth); Bruce Boxleitner (Jumpin' Joe Dugan); Peter Donat (Harry Frazee); James Cromwell (Brother Mathias); J. C. Quinn (Jack Dunn); Joe Ragno (Miller Huggins); Bernard Kates (Col. Jacob Ruppert); Michael McGrady (Lou Gehrig); Andy Voils (Young George Herman Ruth); Dylan Day (Johnny Sylvester, age 10); Stephen Caffrey (Johnny Sylvester, age 30)

TELEVISION

THE BABE, televised October 15, 1985 ESPN (Sports Network) 90 minutes
Produced by Coreniche Productions; Executive producers, Terry M. Giles and Robert C. Acosta; Producer, Peter F. Buffa; Director, Noam Pitlik; Written by Robert and Ann Acosta

Max Gail (George Herman Ruth)

BABE RUTH, televised October 6, 1991 NBC 2 hours
A Lyttle Production Company and Elliott Friedgen Production in association with Warner Bros. Television; Executive producer, Lawrence A. Lyttle; Producer, Frank Pace; Director, Mark Tinker; Teleplay, Michael de Guzman, based on the books *Babe Ruth, His Life and Legend* by Kal Wagenheim and *Babe; The Legend Comes to Life* by Robert W. Creamer; Photography, Donald M. Morgan; Production designer, Donald Light Harris; Special makeup designed by Michael Westmore; Music, Steve Dorf; Editor, Stanford C. Allen

Stephen Lang (Babe Ruth); Brian Doyle-Murray (Bill Slocum); Donald Moffat (Col. Jacob Ruppert); Yvonne Suhor (Helen Woodford Ruth); Lisa Zane (Claire Hodgson Ruth); Bruce Weitz (Miller Huggins); William Lucking (Brother Mathias); Neal McDonough (Lou Gehrig); Pete Rose (Ty Cobb); John Anderson (Judge Landis); Cy Bunyak (Eddie Bennett); William Flatley (Emil Fuchs); Stephen Prutting (Jimmy Walker); Jeff Blanchard (Jimmy Barton); Brandi Chrisman (Dorothy Ruth); Matthew Glave (Joe Dugan); Deborah Anne Gorman (Julia Hodgson; Clint Nageotte (Young Babe); Annabelle Weenick (Mrs. Woodford); Philip J. Stone (Graham McNamee); and Frankie Thorne, Thomas Wagner, Gregory Adams, Dana Craig, Charles J. Flick, Adam Goldberg, Thomas B. Hall, John Kolibab, Andrew May, Nathan Lisle, Mickey Manners, Troy Startoni, Gary Wilbanks, Jerry O'Donnell, Fred Ornstein, Joe Schratz, Rohn Thomas, Tom Tully

THE BAD SEED
A Drama by Maxwell Anderson, adapted from William March's novel *The Bad Seed* (1954)

Synopsis

Angelic appearing eight-year-old Rhoda Penmark covets a penmanship medal won by her classmate Claude Diagle, and during a school outing, beats him over the head with her shoes reinforced with iron heel cleats until he falls from a pier. Rhoda placidly watches him drown, then persistently denies any knowledge of Claude's death to her own mother Christine, to the victim's distraught, alcoholic mother, Hortense, and the school's headmistress, Miss Claudia Fern. Christine later discovers Claude's medal in Rhoda's room. From her father, noted criminologist-author Richard Bravo, Christine learns she was adopted and is the daughter of a notorious murderess, Bessie Denker, known as "The Destroying Angel," whose lurid criminal career began as a child. When dimwitted janitor LeRoy taunts Rhoda about her classmate's death and claims he has found her half-burned shoes in the incinerator, she sets fire to LeRoy's quarters with him in it. Aware that Rhoda set the fire, Christine forces her to admit to the killing of Claude and the earlier death of elderly Mrs. Post whom Rhoda pushed down a stairway. Convinced she has produced a hereditary "bad seed," Christine gives Rhoda an overdose of sleeping pills, and when her daughter is asleep, Christine kills herself with a pistol. Learning of the tragedy, Richard Bravo has a fatal heart attack. As neighbors Monica and her brother Emory console Christine's grief-stricken husband Colonel Penmark, Rhoda emerges from her room to enchant and charm her unsuspecting father.

Comment and Critique

Maxwell Anderson's adaptation of William March's novel to the stage was, justifiably, considered one of the "Best Plays of 1954-1955." Brooks Atkinson (*The New York Times*) reported that the play was "written with reserve and skill. *The Bad Seed* is an extraordinarily literate horror story and a superior bit of theatre... It is a shattering story, largely because it involves such decent people." Walter Kerr (*New York Herald-Tribune*) found *The Bad Seed* "A genuine fourteen-carat, fifteen-below chiller...thrilling entertainment....As a work of purely theatrical excitement, it is beautifully carpentered, suspensefully acted, craftily sustained... *The Bad Seed* is an ingenious piece of straight showmanship."

Time magazine reported "*The Bad Seed*...will not be easily dislodged as the season's most harrowing drama ...In its recital, its crescendo of horrors...it has gripping scenes and many chilling moments...For all its force, *The Bad Seed* betokens neither art nor life; for all its grimness, it can only be classified as entertainment." *The New Yorker* critic believed the psychological premise of the plot might tax the audiences' credulity but still found "*The Bad Seed* a highly competent piece of work, shocking enough, in its fabricated and deliberately implausible fashion, to suit all but the most exacting taste."

Burns Mantle, in his *Best Plays of 1954-1955*, named it one of the best of the season, calling it "the season's overwhelmingly most harrowing play...The horror grows, moreover, through the play's quasi-realistic tone, its reassuringly middle-class atmosphere. As a literate shocker, *The Bad Seed* is successful....The misfortune of the play is that it succeeds on unattractive terms; that something so hard-hitting should betoken neither art nor life, that something so grim can only be classified as entertainment."

Kenneth Tynan viewed the London production of *The Bad Seed* as containing "some leaden prose and a highly tendentious theory about hereditary evil; yet, judged as sheer dramatic vivisection, it works. The audience is jabbed with acid, and the sting is real. What we need from cast and director is the strictest Hitchcock realism; what we got from the London production was amateur operatic." Frances Stephens (*Theatre World*) found, "The constant discussion along psychological lines has a tendency to overlay the real human interest of the plot," but noted, "Diana Wynyard as Christine Penmark, the mother, gives a most sensitive performance."

Veteran film actress Nancy Kelly first made her mark on Broadway as the daughter of Gertrude Lawrence in Rachel Crothers' 1937 play *Susan and God*. For her splendid portrayal of Christine Penmark in *The Bad Seed*, Nancy Kelly received Broadway's 1955 Tony Award as Best Dramatic Actress and was nominated for an Oscar as Best Actress for her performance in the film version, but lost to Ingrid Bergman's *Anastasia*. Young Patty McCormack also received an Oscar nomination for her deceptively diabolical Rhoda in *The Bad Seed* but lost in the Best Supporting Actress category to Dorothy Malone in *Written on the Wind*.

Maxwell Anderson, who died at the age of seventy on February 28, 1959 at Stamford, Connecticut, had thirty-two plays produced on Broadway. His first success in the theatre was in 1924 with *What Price Glory?* coauthored with Laurence Stallings. In 1933, Anderson was awarded the Pulitzer prize for his play *Both Your Houses* and received the New York Critics Circle Award in 1935 for *Winterset* and in 1936 for *High Tor*. His Broadway-produced play was his most successful: his adaptation of William March's novel *The Bad Seed*.

Alistair Cooke in his review of *The Bad Seed* for *The Manchester Guardian* in 1954 wrote, "I dare to go on believing that William March is still the unrecognized genius of our time." Born William Edward March Campbell in Mobile, Alabama, on September 18, 1893 (the second of eleven children), he was the author of several novels including *Company K*, *Come in at the Door*, *The Tallons*, *The Looking Glass*, *Trial Balance*, and *October Island*. Posthumous fame arrived for March, who died at the age of sixty on May 15, 1954 in New Orleans.

Judith Crist, reviewing the 1985 television adaptation of *The Bad Seed*, found the story "as fascinating and chilling as ever. Blair Brown and Carrie Wells come close to the unsurpassable performances of Nancy Kelly and Patty McCormack as mother and child, and one finds a fine thriller endures." *Variety* found that "William March's tight little horror novel, with all its cunningly placed signposts, has been cleverly and frighteningly adapted by exec producer George Eckstein into a satisfyingly chilling telefilm that's sure to raise hackles. *The Bad Seed* springs forth like a Halloween bloom...It has lots of excitement and conviction no matter how unlikely the premise -- lack of morality can be in the genes -- might be. [It] is, quite simply, good fun."

STAGE

THE BAD SEED, *46th Street Theatre*, New York, opened December 8, 1954 334 performances

Produced by The Playwrights' Company; A Drama by Maxwell Anderson adapted from the novel by William March; Director, Reginald Denham; Setting and lighting by George Jenkins; Costumes by Sal Anthony; Company manager, Ben Rosenberg; Stage managers, Porter Van Zandt and Malcolm Wells

Nancy Kelly (Christine Penmark); Patty McCormack (Rhoda Penmark); Henry

Jones (LeRoy); Evelyn Varden (Monica Breedlove); Lloyd Gough (Reginald Tasker); Thomas Chalmers (Richard Bravo); John O'Hare (Col. Kenneth Penmark); Joseph Holland (Emory Wages); Eileen Heckart (succeeded by Pert Kelton) (Mrs. Daigle); Wells Richardson (Mr. Daigle); Joan Croydon (Miss Fern); George Gino (succeeded by Ted Mann, Philip Pruneau) (Messenger)

NOTE: Alice Frost played the role of Christine during Nancy Kelly's vacation

Aldwych Theatre, London, opened April 14, 1955

Produced by H. M. Tennent Ltd.; A Drama by Maxwell Anderson, adapted from the novel by William March; Director, Frith Hanbury; Setting, Stewart Chaney; Costumes, Berman Ltd.

Diana Wynyard (Christine Penmark); Carol Wolveridge (Rhoda Penmark); Malcolm Keen (Richard Bravo); Margalo Gillmore (Monica Breedlove); Bernard Breslaw (LeRoy); Jon Farrell (Emory Wages); Andrew Crawford (Reginald Tasker); Miriam Karlin (Mrs. Daigle); Mark Baker (Mr. Daigle); Robert Ayres (Col. Kenneth Penmark); Joan Sanderson (Miss Fern); David Geary (Messenger)

Touring Company, opened *Playhouse Theatre*, Wilmington, Del., December 1, 1955; closed *Harris Theatre*, Chicago, June 30, 1956

Produced by The Playwrights' Company; A Drama by Maxwell Anderson, adapted from the novel by William March; Director, Reginald Denham; Setting and lighting by George Jenkins; Costumes by Sal Anthony; Company manager, George Oshrin; Stage managers, Peter Van Zandt, Tom Tyrrell

Nancy Kelly (Christine Penmark); Kimetha Laurie (Rhoda Penmark); Roy Poole (LeRoy); Ann Shoemaker (Monica Breedlove); Lloyd Gough (Reginald Tasker); Arthur Jarrett (Richard Bravo); James Field (Col. Kenneth Penmark); Gordon B. Clarke (Emory Wages); Virginia Maddocks (Mrs. Daigle); Donald Keyes (Mr. Daigle); Elizabeth Council (Miss Fern); Tom Tyrrell (Messenger)

MALA SEMILLA (*BAD SEED*), *Neuvo Teatro Fabrigas*, Mexico City, opened September 14, 1955

A Comedias Internacionales Production; A Drama by Maxwell Anderson, adapted from the novel by William March and translated by Julia Guzman; Director, Jesus Valero; Setting, Julia Prieto; Costumes, Armando Valdez-Peza; Background music by Hector Gonsalez de La Barrera

Rita Macedo (Christine Penmark); Angelica Maris (Rhoda Penmark); Alfonso Torres (Richard Bravo); Consuelo Guerrero de Luna (Monica Breedlove); Yerye Beirute (LeRoy); Armando Gutierrez (Emory Wages); Luis Manuel Pelayo (Reginald Tasker); Angelines Fernandez (Mrs. Dayly); Arturo Soto Urena (Mr. Dayly); Lola Tinoco (Miss Fern); Hector Godoy (Kenneth Penmark); Eduardo Lugo (Messenger)

Touring Company, summer 1956

Director, Robert Caldwell; A Drama by Maxwell Anderson, adapted from the novel by William March; Setting, Hal Shafer; Lighting, Elliott Krancer

Mary Sinclair (Christine Penmark); Claudia Crawford (Rhoda Penmark); Jack Harley (Richard Bravo); Dorothy Patten (Monica Breedlove); Arthur Malet (LeRoy); Hal Burdick (Emory Wages); George Cotton (Reginald Tasker); Pert Kelton (Mrs. Daigle); Martin Cohen (Mr. Daigle); Charles Mundy (Col. Kenneth Penmark); Gloria Shipley (Miss Fern); W. Broderick Hackett (Messenger)

Touring Company, summer 1988
Director, Porter Van Zandt; A Drama by Maxwell Anderson, adapted from the novel by William March; Setting, Herbert Senn; Lighting, Joanne Zaharis; Costumes, Susan O'Donnell

Sandy Dennis (Christine Penmark); Sky Cash (Rhoda Penmark); Carl Low (Richard Bravo); Bella Jarrett (Monica Breedlove); Edward Seamon (LeRoy); John Scanlan (Emory Wages); Jack Davidson (Reginald Tasker); Susan Kellerman (Mrs. Daigle); Douglas Fisher (Mr. Daigle); Ron Harper (Col. Kenneth Penmark); Mary-Alan Hokanson (Miss Fern)

SCREEN

THE BAD SEED, *Warner Bros. Pictures*, released September 1956
Produced and Directed by Mervyn LeRoy; Screenplay by John Lee Mahin, based on the play by Maxwell Anderson and novel by William March; Photography, Hal Rosson; Art director, John Beckman; Music, Alex North; Sound, Stanley Jones; Editor, Warren Low

Nancy Kelly (Christine); Patty McCormack (Rhoda); Henry Jones (LeRoy); Evelyn Varden (Monica); Paul Fix (Bravo); Jesse White (Emory); Eileen Heckart (Mrs. Daigle); Frank Cady (Mr. Daigle); William Hopper (Kenneth); Gage Clarke (Tasker); Joan Croyden (Miss Fern)

TELEVISION

THE BAD SEED, televised February 7, 1985 ABC 2 hours
Hajeno Production for Warner Bros. Television; Producer, George Eckstein; Director, Paul Wendkos; Teleplay by George Eckstein, based on the play by Maxwell Anderson and the novel by William March; Photography, Ted Voigtlander; Art director, Fredric P. Hope; Music, Paul Chihara; Associate producer, Maria Padilla; Editor, Steve Cohen

Blair Brown (Christine Penmark); Carrie Wells (Rachel Penmark); David Carradine (LeRoy); Lynn Redgrave (Monica Breedlove); David Ogden Stiers (Emory Breedlove); Richard Kiley (Richard Bravo); Anne Haney (Alice Fern); Weldon Bleiler (Fred Daigler); Carol Locatell (Rita Daigler); Chad Allen (Mark Daigler); Eve Smith (Mrs. Post)

BARNUM
Various adaptations of the life of Phineas Taylor Barnum (1810-91)

Synopsis

Phineas Taylor Barnum was born on July 5, 1810, at Bethel, Connecticut, the first of five children of Philo and Irena Barnum. He was named for his maternal grandfather, Phineas Taylor. P.T. Barnum's early occupation as the owner of grocery store -- augmented by a profitable lottery -- soon gave way to a new career as the editor of *The Herald of Freedom* in nearby Danbury. In 1829, the selfnamed "Prince of Humbug" married twenty-one-year-old Charity Hallett. Erroneously credited with the immortal statement, "There's a sucker born every minute," Barnum had his first success as a showman with the purchase in Philadelphia of an elderly black slave, Joice Heth, for $1,000. He was given an "authentic" yellowed bill of sale dated February 5, 1727. The originator of "advertising promotion," "ballyhoo" and "hype" first exhibited the "slave woman who was 161 years old and formerly the nurse of George Washington" at Niblo's Garden. Barnum described the ancient, pipe-smoking centenarian in his *Autobiography* as looking "as if she might have been far older than her advertised age. She was apparently in good health and spirits, but from age or disease was unable to change her position; she could move one arm at will, but her lower limbs could not be straightened; her left arm lay across her bosom and she could not remove it; the nails on her left hand were almost four inches long. She was toothless and totally blind and her head was covered with a thick bush of grey hair.... Everything seemed so straightforward. She was quite garrulous about her protege, 'dear little George,' at whose birth she declared she was present." Joice's recitation of being Washington's nurse, ending with the singing of old hymns, was hugely profitable to Barnum and Niblo.

On December 27, 1841, Barnum acquired John Scudder's Chambers Street, New York American Museum, and in 1843, he engaged a young, twenty-five-inch-tall midget, Charles Sherwood Stratton, dubbing him "General Tom Thumb." Barnum's success in exhibiting "The General" led to lavish praise and profits at home and abroad, where a Royal Command Performance was given before Queen Victoria at Buckingham Palace. In 1850, Barnum remodeled the Museum's lecture room into a three-thousand-seat theatre. His opening play was *The Drunkard*, which ran more than one hundred performances, establishing a long-run record for the era. Although fire twice destroyed Barnum's Museum, he rebuilt his showplace. The greatest coup of his fabulous career was the importation of Jenny Lind, dubbed "The Swedish Nightingale," whose 1850-52 American tours became the sensation of the continent and firmly established P. T. Barnum as "The World's Greatest Showman." In 1866, Barnum lost in the Connecticut congressional election after serving four terms in the state legislature. From England's Royal Zoological Garden, Barnum purchased their prized elephant, Jumbo, for $10,000. It became a beloved attraction and as profitable as General Tom Thumb, Giant Girl, Jane Campbell, and midget Lavinia Warren, who married "The General" in 1863.

In 1871, Barnum merged his circus, aptly named "The Greatest Show on Earth," with one owned by James A. Bailey. Barnum and Bailey's three-ring circus toured the American continent in tents, touted by the high-flown Barnum ballyhoo. His fascinating and amusing *Autobiography* was published in 1854, followed by *The Humbugs of the World* (1865), *Struggles and Triumphs* (1869), and *Money-Getting* (1883). Six-foot-two-inch Phineas Taylor Barnum, with a bulbous nose on a large head covered with an unruly mop of curly hair, died at his home on April 7, 1891. The "Mighty Barnum" left an estate estimated at $5 million.

Comment and Critique

"A Musical Romance based on the life of Jenny Lind," called *The Nightingale*, opened on the road starring Peggy Wood and Lee Beggs and featuring Alexander Gray. During the road tour, the stars were replaced by Eleanor Painter and Tom Wise, with Glen Dale as the romantic lead. Eleanor Painter, described by Gerald Bordman (*The American Musical Theatre*) as "one of the many multitalented actresses who grace the lyric stage of her generation," had last appeared on Broadway for three months in 1924 in *The Chiffon Girl* and was coaxed out of "retirement" by the Shuberts to replace the talented and popular Peggy Wood as

Jenny Lind in *The Nightingale*.

The Nightingale was written by Guy Bolton and P. G. Wodehouse with music by Armand Vecsey, orchestra leader of New York's Hotel Ritz, who had supplied the musical score for the 1924 Bolton and Wodehouse musical *The Rose of China*. Shubert's Jolson Theatre was where *The Nightingale* opened on January 3, 1927.

"The heroine of *The Nightingale* is Jenny Lind, but those who are a bit fearful of historical backgrounds need not stay away on the account," reported *The New York Times*. "Rightful enough, *The Nightingale* subordinates history to the exigencies of the musical comedy stage...The book is sufficient for the occasion: Mr. Wodehouse's lyrics, as you would expect, are workmanlike, and there is a first-rate comedian in the person of Stanley Lupino. Nevertheless, the evening belongs primarily to music. Mr. Vecsey's score is a mixture of the operatic and the popular requiring good voices and getting them. The best of them belonged to Eleanor Painter, who seems to retire periodically and then emerge again as good as ever, if not a little better." *The Times* critic noted: "Mr. Barnum figures in the person of Tom Wise and there is a line now and then that recalls the period...It is in all respects a perfect evening for operetta lovers..."

Fifty-three years later, *Barnum* musically burst upon Broadway. "*Barnum* humdinger story of a humbug," headlined the New York *Daily News* critic Douglas Watt. "*Barnum* may not be the greatest show on earth, but last night's circusy new musical at the St. James is colorful, eye-catching and abundantly high-spirited. Set to a buoyant, tuneful score by Cy Coleman, and with the agile Jim Dale in the title role, it radiates good cheer. Joyously staged by Joe Layton...*Barnum* has a sketchy but reasonably serviceable book by Mark Bramble. It skims the career and private life of the flamboyant 19th century American impresario and master of flimflam...It is a lively, fun-filled evening of theatre, and one with style. If nothing else, it's likely to make your kids, or even you, run away from home to 'join the circus' as the finale stimulatingly beckons."

Frank Rich (*The New York Times*) asked, "Is there anything that Jim Dale can't do?...This man can create magic -- the magic of infectious charm -- even on those rare occasions when he's standing still...*Barnum* has plenty of other virtues besides its star...but, it doesn't have a book. Mark Bramble, the writer, tries to create a sympathetic portrait of P. T. Barnum, the 19th century circus man and self-styled 'Prince of Humbug' and he tries to use show business as an all-purpose metaphor for the vagaries of life...Perhaps Michael Stewart's lyrics are a bit prosaic...One of the unspoken advantages of writing the score for a bookless musical is that almost every song can be plucked from the show's context and sung in a saloon." Rich also observed that "For Joe Layton, the director-choreographer, the principal mission of the evening is to keep the numbers whizzing by as fast as possible... His staging is a veritable riot of sleight-of-hand effects. He not only keeps his company changing in and out of a seemingly endless supply of vivid Theoni V. Aldredge costumes, but he also has them swing on ropes, fall through midair and charge through the audience streaming balloons, handbills and confetti....But it is not the greatest show on earth...*Barnum* and its crack ringleader nonetheless deliver an evening of pure, exhilarating fun."

Clive Barnes (*New York Post*) extolled the musical: "Jim Dale is a one-man, three-ring, four-star circus in *Barnum*...It is boisterous, brash and bright and has a catchy, clever and occasionally very beautiful score by Cy Coleman and some tongue-twisting adroit lyrics by Michael Stewart...Mark Bramble has struggled hard to inject life into Barnum's life, but Bramble rambles, and his book emerges as a library of good intentions." Barnes said of the show's star: "What makes Dale a great performer is his nerveless, yet still nervy skills...As Barnum he is a knockout. He sings, he juggles, he jumps, he tells jokes, he makes discreet love to the audience, not to mention the cast, he does a little trapeze work, and walks across the stage on a high-wire singing a happy song...To Joe Layton has fallen the task of evolving a concept musical from a book show and his staging has the virtuosity of class ...The cast is lovely; Glenn Close, as the wife, has the ungrateful task of playing to Dale's vermilion and succeeds. Marianne Tatum is gorgeous as Jenny Lind."

Time added, "It is lucky that Dale is so irresistible, since the book makes him a horseless rider. Writer Mark Bramble has sketched in the details of Barnum's career like a superficially canned guided tour ...As for Joe Layton's staging, the blinding speed of his now-you-see-now-you-don't direction makes playgoers forget that they can see right through *Barnum*."

John Beaufort (*The Christian Science Monitor*) wrote, "In paying tribute to America's definitive showman and self-proclaimed Prince of Humbug, *Barnum* goes for the spectacular. The entertainment begins with calliope music in the foyer, clowns in the auditorium, and a curtainless stage festooned with ladders and bunting, and littered with the paraphernalia of the big top...A big bonanza of a show. And, in the words of the sideshow barker, a feast for the eye and ear. As for Jim Dale, he's simply amazing."

In May 1981, Tony Orlando, who gained fame on records and his television show with his two lady associates as Tony Orlando and Dawn, made his Broadway debut as a replacement from the vacationing Jim Dale. On October 13, 1981, American-born Israeli actor Mike Burstyn was signed to replace Jim Dale in the title role of *Barnum*. A number of actors had been approached to replace Dale, including Lee Majors, Robert Morse, Treat Williams and Malcolm MacDowell, but several rejected the offer, reluctant to be compare with the inestimable Jim Dale. Burstyn, having relocated to Israel in 1962 and having fought with the Israeli Army during the 1967 war, was a Yiddish Theatre actor. He continued playing *Barnum* until the Broadway show closed on May 16, 1982.

In June 1981, *Barnum* opened in London at the Palladium starring Michael Crawford. Most of the reviews were unabashed raves. "Michael Crawford is pure genius," felt the *Daily Express*. "Michael Crawford thrills the audience with a performance so brilliant it's impossible to top," was the judgement of the *Daily Mirror*. The *Observer* noted, "Mr. Crawford won the standingest ovation I have ever seen." The *New Standard* proclaimed, "Crawford walks to tightrope triumph. *Barnum* could run for years. Even the orchestra applauded!" The *Daily Telegraph* called *Barnum* "A triumph of the showman's art."

Paul Bailey (*Plays and Players*) was less impressed: "Michael Crawford, forever panting and forever young, plays Phineas T. Barnum, the great showman whose life story the musical purports to tell. The Puckish Crawford is here a lightweight actor possessed of ex-traordinary energy, he even brings an electric charge to the raising of his eyebrows. His very grin is effortful. He leaps and prances and wriggles and walks with, as they say, a vengeance...Crawford shares with Jim Dale, who is playing the role on Broadway, a rare ability to make acting look like hard work. Both performers solicit admiration by dint of the amount of honest sweat they exude -- each drip signals Energy, and therefore Effort." Critic Bailey concluded that "This is a show that lacks depth, though it does allow itself an occasional portentousness...The trouble is that one can't accept the Crawford Barnum as a flaming and burning individual: he's a scatterbrained comedian, that's all, with a demoniacal urge to be energetic at every turn."

Harold Fielding reproduced *Barnum* in 1985, opening the show at London's

Victoria Palace on March 14. The reviews were, again, ecstatic. "Four years later -- and the man has done it again. Michael Crawford is back in town in *Barnum* -- the show in which he first triumphed in 1981. Then 39, he is now 43...Time may catch up with him some day, but I wouldn't bet on it," wrote Kenneth Hurren (*Mail on Sunday*).

*Daily Mail*s Jack Tinker found, "Were I ever asked to pick eight performances from a lifetime's theatre-going to keep me company for the rest of my life on a desert island...then undoubtedly Michael Crawford's *Barnum* would be among the first ashore...I know of no artist alive on the British stage today who could return to a role of these extraordinary physical and artistic demands four years after unveiling it and make it shine out fresher, more vital and invigorating than when it was first seen. Yet here he is back in the West End with the first night audience once again on its feet screaming for more...A tireless and talented cast aid him in this small miracle. Eileen Battye gives Mrs. Barnum a mettle that is a match for a husband's waywardness while Christina Collier adds a teasing wit to Jenny Lind's obvious allures."

Sheridan Morley (*Plays and Players*) suggested, "Every now and then in the commercial theatre, if you are lucky, you get to see a star invade and inhabit and overtake an entire musical...In London now, you can see Michael Crawford doing it with *Barnum*...This is a performance and a production which ought to be shown to anyone who has ever wondered about the nature of star quality; it is a victory parade of a single stage talent, and the curious thing is how much better it is now as a performance than as a show. Ever since it first opened on Broadway in 1980 with Jim Dale, *Barnum* has suffered from a deep uncertainty about whether it is supposed to be a musical circus or a musical about a circus...*Barnum* is a great sawdust singalong, and Mr. Crawford is giving in the title role the greatest star-turn performance in the whole of the West End..."

Michael Billington (*The Guardian*) noted, "*Barnum* is a triumph of styles over content, of spectacle over substance...I still wish Mark Bramble had written a meatier book...But even if the show is weak on biography, it is an utterly beguiling spectacle blending the riotous colour of a Dufy painting with a lot of genuine acrobatic skill...The evening, however, unquestionably belongs to Michael Crawford...It is the most energetic performance I have ever seen in a musical."

This second version of Michael Crawford's *Barnum* turn was taped by the BBC during one (or more) of the performances and it premiered on TV in late 1986. It would take more than three years for it to arrive in the United States, premiering on PBS in mid-March 1990.

Earl Derr Biggers' *Saturday Evening Post* story, *Broadway Broke*, was adapted to the screen in 1923. Maclyn Arbuckle was cast as P. T. Barnum, a minor role in what the *Exhibitors Herald* classified as "a story of the stage, of New York theatrical people and the motion picture industry." Seven years later, Metro-Goldwyn-Mayer introduced opera star Grace Moore to the screen as Jenny Lind in *A Lady's Morals*, in which Wallace Beery gave his first Phineas Taylor Barnum portrayal.

Originally called *The Soul Kiss*, MGM considered *A Lady's Morals* a more provocative title, although neither suggested the career of Jenny Lind. "Grace Moore, soprano of the Metropolitan Opera Company, makes her audible screen debut at the Capitol in a fictional story of Jenny Lind, 'the Swedish Nightingale,' which bears the meaningless and unsuitable title of *A Lady's Morals*," wrote Mordaunt Hall (*The New York Times*). "Sidney Franklin, who directed the picture, has for the most part performed his task with intelligence and care. He has not, however, taken full advantage of sound perspective and a few of the flashes of comedy hardly belong in such a production...In certain instances, Miss Moore's charming voice is admirably recorded...Miss Moore is a genuine asset to vocalized films, for not only is her singing agreeable, but she is an actress of some distinction and is endowed with a most pleasing personality. This story, one of half-truths and fiction, was subscribed to Dorothy Farnum and the dialogue came from the combined pens of Hans Kraly and Claudine West...Reginald Denny gives an ingratiating performance...Wallace Beery appears briefly as P. T. Barnum."

Photoplay enthused, "Introducing Grace Moore, young and beautiful prima donna of the Metropolitan Opera, to pictures. And what a voice! The story is based on incidents in the life of Jenny Lind, and Miss Moore sings several lovely numbers, notably one written especially for the picture by Carrie Jacobs Bond. Reginald Denny is fine opposite the star. This will surely please you."

Four years later, Wallace Beery was signed by 20th Century-United Artists to star as P. T. Barnum in Darryl F. Zanuck's production of *The Mighty Barnum*. The 1934 film was hailed by *Photoplay*: "Step right up, folks, and see just about the grandest show you ever paid your money for...Wallace Beery as *Phineas T. Barnum* gives his best performance since *The Champ*, and the rest of the cast is right up with him. Virginia Bruce, as Jenny Lind, is the big surprise, looking more beautiful than anyone can think of, and singing like an angel...The opulent production, the movement, color, fantastic characters, the smoothness and direction, all combine into a brilliant background for some grand acting...This picture of the greatest showman on earth, who was the originator of present-day exploitation, is salty and vigorous and one of the best evening's entertainment you will ever enjoy."

England's *Bystander* stated, "*The Mighty Barnum*...it is definitely a picture to see. Wallace Beery has said that Zanuck told him he 'wanted Barnum, not Beery.' If so, he asked the impossible. The stove-pipe hats and frock-coats of the 'eighties and 'nineties cannot obliterate a personality such as this. But in his own gloriously recognizable way, Beery gives a vastly entertaining interpretation of the great showman, vulgarian, humbug optimist and opportunist, but with a great heart and a 'flair' for freaks which founded 'the greatest show on earth.' The freaks, themselves, provide a large part of the interest of the film. General Tom Thumb and his lovely little 'wife' are charming incidentals, and the episodes between Barnum and the Bearded Lady are genuinely, although grossly, funny...This is another picture in which good teamwork contributes to success."

Time added, "When the script for this picture was published in book form, reporters asked author Gene Fowler if he had tried to follow history. Said he, 'We tried to throw it out the window.' Except that it truthfully portrays Phineas Taylor Barnum as a loud and ingenuous oddity, *The Mighty Barnum* succeeds admirably in its intention. A spirited mixture of legend, libel and exhilarating fiction, it is a first-rate cinema extravaganza which Barnum would have loudly applauded."

In November 1986, a colorfully fictionalized biography of the showman, called *Barnum*, was televised on CBS. Starring Burt Lancaster as Phineas Taylor Barnum and German actress Hanna Schygulla as Jenny Lind, *Barnum* was filmed on location in Montreal.

Richard F. Shepard (*The New York Times*) found television's *Barnum* to be "good family entertainment... This is a simple and sympathetic (probably too much so of each) portrait with Burt Lancaster in the title role -- or mostly in the title role, because John Roney, who plays P. T. Barnum as a young man and a child, represents his tender years. Barnum is a figure absolutely made for a piece of acting, as we have seen on stage and in film. Mr. Lancaster gives us a rather laid-back Barnum, one who is seen recalling his life in flashbacks that put his magnificent deceptions in the best of lights...Hanna Schygulla, who appeared in many of Rainer Werner Fassbinder's films, plays the singer (Jenny Lind) with charm and astuteness -- the sort of show that has its attractions here and there for an audience of any age -- as Barnum might have put it."

STAGE

THE NIGHTINGALE, Jolson Theatre, New York, opened January 3, 1927 96 performances

Produced by the Messrs. Shubert; A Musical Romance based on the life of Jenny Lind; Director, Lewis Morton; Book and Lyrics by Guy Bolton and P. G. Wodehouse; Music by Armand Vecsey; Settings, Watson Barratt; Dances, Carl Hemmer; Musical director, Thomas L. Jones; Costumes, Barbiere, executed by Max Weldy

Eleanor Painter (replaced Peggy Wood) (Jenny Lind); Tom Wise (replaced Lee Beggs) (Phineas Taylor Barnum); Stanley Lupino (Mr. Carp); Glen Dale (replaced Alexander Gray) (Capt. Rex Gurnee); Nicholas Joy (Stephen Rutherford); Robert Hobbs (Capt. Joe Archer); Lucius Henderson (Major-General Gurnee); Sophie Everett (Mrs. Gurnee); John Gaines (Colonel Wainwright); Eileen Van Biene (Alice Wainwright); Clara Palmer (Mrs. Vischer Van Loo); William Tucker (Otto Goldschmidt); Ivan Dneproff (Signor Belletti); Victor Bozardt (Col. Robert E. Lee/Cornelius Vanderbilt); Violet Carlson (Josephine); Harold Woodward (Whistler); Eileen Carmody (Piper); John Gaines (Butler); Robert Harper (Usher); Neal Frank (Footman); Vira Galli, Ruth Johnston, Florence O'Brien, Ruth Ramsey, Viola Paulson, Marian Lynn, Ileen May, Madeline Biltmore, Mimi Hayes, Mabel Zoeckler, Dorothy Johnson, Dorothy Maurice, Ray Ramsey, Marie Chase, Catherine Janeway, Marie Muselle, Theo Loper (Ladies of the Ensemble); Harry Quinn, Gerald Goff, Neal Frank, Tom Denton, John Russell, Herbert Stanley, George Glasgow, Henry Riebeselle, Robert Harper, Walter Lunt, Jack Edmunds, Sonintu Syrjala, Edward Hoffman, George Brent, Albert Valnor, Jack Connett, Donald Black, Richard Bartlett, Sydnie Smith, Fred Barth, Bruce King, Lee Borough, John Muccio, John Gutscher, Luther Talbert, William Dillon, James McKay, Raymond Cullen, Byron Way, Leon Abrahamson, Robert W. Davis (Gentlemen of the Ensemble)

MUSICAL NUMBERS: "Breakfast in Bed"; "March Song"; "Waltz Song"; "Homeland"; "May Moon"; "Two Little Ships"; "He Doesn't Know"; "Fairyland"; "Trio"; "Santa Claus"; "Josephine"; "Once in September"; "The Last Rose of Summer"

Dropped during tryout tour: "Days of Long Ago"; "My Nightingale"; "Rabbits Make Wonderful Fathers"; "Look Sharp, Send for Carp"; "Little Old New York"

BARNUM, St. James Theatre, New York, opened April 30, 1980 854 performances

Produced by Judy Gordon, Cy Coleman, Maurice Rosenfield, Lois F. Rosenfield, in association with Irvin Feld and Kenneth Feld; A Musical Comedy; Directed and choreographed by Joe Layton; Music by Cy Coleman; Lyrics by Michael Stewart; Book by Mark Bramble; Scenery, David Mitchell; Lighting, Craig Miller; Costumes, Theoni V. Aldredge; Orchestrations, Hershy Kay; Vocal arrangements, Jeremy Stone, Cy Coleman; Music director, Peter Howard; Production supervisor, Mary Porter Hall; Technical supervisor, Peter Feller; Sound, Otts Munderloh; General manager, James Walsh; Company manager, Susan Bell; Stage managers, Mary Porter Hall, John Beven, Michael Mann and Fred Feldt.

Jim Dale (succeeded by Tony Orlando [during vacation], Mike Burstyn) (Phineas T. Barnum); Glenn Close (succeeded by Catherine Cox, Deborah Reagan) (Chairy Barnum); Marianne Tatum (succeeded by Suellen Estey [during vacation], Catherine Gaines) (Jenny Lind); William C. Witter (succeeded by

Terrence V. Mann, Kelly Walters) (Ringmaster/Julius Goldschmidt/James A. Bailey); Terrence V. Mann (succeeded by R. J. Lewis, R. Robert Melvin) (Chester Lyman/Humbert Morissey); Terri White (succeeded by Lillias White) (Joice Heth); Kelly Walters (succeeded by Richard Gervais) (Amos Scudder/Edgar Templeton); Leonard John Crofoot (Tom Thumb); Karen Trott (Susan B. Anthony) Steven Michael Harris (One-Man Band); Catherine Carr (succeeded by Missy Whitchurch) (Lady Plate Balancer); Barbara Nadel (succeeded by Mary Testa, Andrea Wright) (Lady Juggler); Edward T. Jacobs (succeeded by Fred Garbo Garver, Navarre Matlovsky) (Chief Bricklayer); Andy Teirstein (succeeded by Marshall Coid) (White-Face Clown); Dirk Lumbard (succeeded by R. J. Lewis) (Sherwood Stratton); Sophie Schwab (succeeded by Andrea Wright (Mrs. Stratton); Bruce Robertson (succeeded by R. J. Lewis) (Wilton); Robbi Morgan (succeeded by Colleen Flynn) (Lady Aerialist)

MUSICAL NUMBERS: "There's A Sucker Born Every Minute"; "Thank God I'm Old"; "The Colors of My Life"; "One Brick at a Time"; "Museum Song"; "I Like Your Style"; "Bigger Isn't Better"; "Love Makes Such Fools of Us All"; "Out There"; "Come Follow the Band"; "Black and White"; "Prince of Humbug"; "Join the Circus"

Original cast recording: CBS Records

Touring Company, opened *Saenger Performing Arts Center*, New Orleans, May 12, 1981; closed *Fisher Theatre*, Detroit, August 22, 1981

Produced by Judy Gordon, Cy Coleman, Maurice and Lois Rosenfield, Irvin and Kenneth Feld; A Musical Play; Director, Joe Layton; Music by Cy Coleman; Lyrics by Michael Stewart; Book by Mark Bramble; Scenery, David Mitchell; Lighting, Craig Miller; Costumes, Theoni V. Aldredge; Sound, Otts Munderloh; Orchestrations, Hershy Kay; Music director, Robert Billing; Circus Training by The Big Apple Circus/The New York School for Circus Acts; Production supervisor, Mary Porter Hall; Technical supervisor, Peter Feller; General management, James Walsh; Company manager, John Corkill; Stage managers, Warren Crane, Kate Pollock and Steve Wappel

Stacy Keach (Phineas Taylor Barnum); Dee Hoty (Chairy Barnum); Catherine Gaines (Jenny Lind); Gabriel Barre (Ringmaster/James A. Bailey); Melvin Roberts (Chester Lyman); Terri White (Joice Heth); Andrew Hill Newman (Amos Scudder); Bobby Lee (Tom Thumb); Malcolm Perry (Acrobat Extraordinaire); Stephanie Nash (Lady Plate Balancer/Mrs. Stratton); Richard Gervais (Sherwood Stratton/Wilton); K. Leslie (Lady Bricklayer); Darlene Cory (Baton Twirler); Michael Oster (White-Face Clown); Andrea Wright (High-Wire Lady); Steve Hall (Julius Gold-schmidt/Humbert Morrissey); Paul Browne (One-Man Band/Edgar Templeton); Diane Abrams (Lady Aerialist)

London Palladium, opened June 11, 1981 655 performances

Produced by Harold Fielding and Louis Benjamin; A Musical Play; Director, Peter Coe; Music by Cy Coleman; Lyrics by Michael Stewart; Book by Mark Bramble; Scenery, David Mitchell; Lighting, Eric Delzenne; Costumes, Theoni V. Aldredge; Choral director, John McCarthy; Orchestrations, Hershy Kay; Vocal and dance arrangement by Cy Coleman; Musical director, Michael Reed; Sound, Edward Fardell; Circus training by The Big Apple Circus/The New York School for Circus Arts; Original choreography recreated by Buddy Schwab; Produced by arrangement with Judy Gordon, Cy Coleman, Maurice and Lois F. Rosenfield, in association with Irvin and Kenneth Feld; Production stage manager, David Freeman

Michael Crawford (Phineas Taylor Barnum); Deborah Grant (Charity "Chairy" Barnum); Jennie McGustie (Joice Heth); Christopher Beck (Tom Thumb); Sarah Payne (Jenny Lind); William C. Witter (Julius Goldschmidt/James A. Bailey/Ringmaster); Tony Kemp (Chester Lyman/Sherwood Stratton); Grant Smith (Amos Schudder/Humbert Morrissey); Jane Watts (Lady Clown); Sean Kay (Wire Walker); John Alexander (Juggler); Daniel John-Jules (Flying Trapeze); Jennie McGustie (Blues Singer); Perry Davey (Balancer); Lindsey Betts (Lady Contortionist); Terry Williams (Acrobat); Christopher Beck (Edgar Templeton); Christine Cartwright (Mrs. Sherwood Stratton); Peter Barbour, Sue Barbour (Beefeaters); Lorenza Johnson (Circus Lady); Jane Ash (Baton Twirler); Sally Brelsford (Waitress); Ken Smith (White-Face Clown)

Original cast recording: Chrysalis Records

Touring Company, opened *Golden Gate Theatre*, San Francisco, December 16, 1981; closed *Pantages Theatre*, Los Angeles, April 4, 1982
Produced by Judy Gordon, Cy Coleman, Maurice and Lois F. Rosenfield, Irvin and Kenneth Feld; A Musical Play; Directed asnd choreographed by Joe Layton; Music by Cy Coleman; Lyrics by Michael Stewart; Book by Mark Bramble; Scenery, David Mitchell; Lighting, Craig Miller; Costumes, Theoni V. Aldredge; Sound, Otts Munderloh; Orchestrations, Hershy Kay; Music director, Ross Allen; Production supervisor, Mary Porter Hall; Stage managers, Marc Schlackman, Bethe Ward, Steve Wappel and Leslie Wing

Jim Dale (Phineas Taylor Barnum); Glenn Close (Chairy Barnum); Catherine Gaines (Jenny Lind); Ray Roderick (Tom Thumb); Terri White (Joice Heth); Terrence V. Mann (Ringmaster/Julius Goldschmidt/ James A. Bailey); Bruce Robertson (Chester Lyman/ Wilton); Gordon Weiss (Amos Scudder/Edgar Templeton); Malcolm Perry (Acrobat Extraordinaire); Catherine Carr (Lady Tightrope Walker); Darlene Cory (Baton Twirler); Skip Lackey (Chief Bricklayer); Derek Meader (White-Face Clown); Charles Edward Hall (Sherwood Stratton/One-Man Band); Barbara Nadel (Mrs. Stratton); Robbi Morgan (Mrs. Wilson); Betty LaRusso (Susan B. Anthony); Bo Gerard (Humbert Morrissey); Dennis Buck, Jack Mezzano (Pianists)

Touring Company, season 1982-83
Produced by Tom Alloe and the Municipal Opera Company of St. Louis, in association with James Janek; A Musical Play; Director, Joe Layton; Music by Cy Coleman; Lyrics by Michael Stewart; Book by Mark Bramble; Scenery, David Mitchell; Lighting, Craig Miller; Costumes, Theoni V. Aldredge; Sound, Otts Munderloh; Orchestrations, Michael Gibson; Vocal and Dance Arrangements, Cy Coleman; Musical director, Ross Allen; Production stage manager, Harold Goldfaden; Directorial assistant, Michael Mann; Pianists, Kristen Blodgette and David Rhodes

Harvey Evans (Phineas Taylor Barnum); Jan Pessano (Chairy Barnum); Robin Kersey (Joice Heth); Gordon Weiss (Amos Scudder); R. Robert Melvin (Chester Lyman/Wilton); Charles Edward Hall (Sherwood Stratton/Humbert Morrissey); Leonard John Crofoot (Tom Thumb); Susan Dawn Carson (Susan B. Anthony); Kelly Waters (Julius Goldschmidt/James A. Bailey); Kathy Lynn (Lady Aerialist); Fred Feldt (Juggler Extraordinaire); Diane Abrams (Mrs. Sherwood Stratton); Robert D. Newell (White-Face Clown); Kathleen Marsh (Jenny Lind); Charles Edward Hall (One-Man Band); Gordon Weiss (Edgar Templeton); Skip Lackey (Chief Bricklayer); Darlene Cory (Baton Twirler); Susan Dawn Carson (Lady

Jeggler); Mary Ellen Richardson (Lady Plate Balancer); Malcolm Perry (Acrobat Extraordinaire)

Victoria Palace Theatre, London, opened March 14, 1985 383 performances
Produced by Harold Fielding; A Musical Play; Director, Peter Coe; Music by Cy Coleman; Lyrics by Michael Stewart; Book by Mark Bramble; Production designer, David Mitchell; Lighting, Eric Delzenne; Costumes, Theoni V. Aldredge; Musical Director, Michael Reed; Orchestrations, Hershy Kay; Sound, Edward Fardell; Circus Training, Terry and Danuta Parsons; Presented by arrangement with the American Producers, Judy Gordon, Cy Coleman, Maurice and Lois F. Rosenfield, in association with Irvin and Kenneth Feld; Associate producer, Wendy Toye; Original choreography recreated by Buddy Schwab

Michael Crawford (Phineas Taylor Barnum); Eileen Battye (Charity Barnum); Sally Lavelle (succeeded by Sharon Benson) (Joice Heth); Paul Leonard (Amos Scudder/Edgar Templeton); Michael Heath (Ring-master/James A. Bailey/Julius Goldschmidt); Stephen Beagley (succeeded by Paul Miller) (Tom Thumb); Alan Heap (Sherwood Stratton); Nadine Shenton (Mrs. Sherwood Stratton); Christina Collier (Jenny Lind); Graham Fawcett (Humbert Morrissey); Michael Herview (Juggler); Debbie Steel (Acrobat); Perry Davey (Balancer); Paul Miller (Flying Trapeze); Jane Watts (Lady Clown); Joanne Robley-Dixon (Circus Lady); Paul Goddard (Professor Crusp); Richard Gauntlett (White-Face Clown); Peter Barbour, Sue Barbour (Beefeaters); James Francis-Johnson (Chester Lyman); Amanda Newman (Waitress); Sally Lavelle (Blues Singer)

NOTE: This production was taped by BBC and shown in 1986. It premiered in the U.S. on PBS in March 1990 (see Television).

Shepherd's Bush Garden (tent), West London, opened December 27, 1989 through January 4, 1990
An LMC Production; A Musical Play; Director, John Redgrave; Music by Cy Coleman; Lyrics by Michael Stewart; Book by Mark Bramble; Production designer, Inigo Monk; Lighting, John Redgrave; Costumes, Richard Callaghan; Choreography, Kenn Oldfield; Musical Director, David Beer

Peter Duncan (Phineas Taylor Barnum); Roni Page (Charity Barnum); Sally Lavelle (Joice Heth/Blues Singer); Alan Mosley (Amos Scudder/Humbert Morrissey); Chris Talman (Ringmaster/James A. Bailey); John Melvin (Chester Lyman/Edgar Templeton); Vincent Shiels (Tom Thumb); Robert Hopkins (Sherwood Stratton/Wally/Julius Goldschmidt); Ann Woodfield (Mrs. Sherwood Stratton); Maria Kesselman (Jenny Lind); Vanessa Skaer (Juggler); Dougie Mann (Acrobat); Zoey Rayner (Baton Twirler/1st Waitress); Nicky Forsyth (2nd Waitress); Juliana and Michelle Inaros (Flying Trapeze); Phillipa Rae (Lady Contortionist); Ruby-Marie Hutchinson (Circus Lady); Jackie Sysum (White-Face Clown/Wire Walker); Elizabeth Haywood, Deborah Woolley (Beefeaters); Tony Rossouw (Cloud Swing)

SCREEN

BROADWAY BROKE, Selznick Distributing Corporation, released October 1923
Produced by Murray W. Garsson Productions; Director, J. Searle Dawley; Screenplay by John Lynch, based on the *Saturday Evening Post* story by Earl Derr Biggers; Photography, Bert Dawley

Mary Carr (Nellie Wayne); Maclyn Arbuckle (P. T. Barnum); Percy Marmont

(Tom Kerrigan); Gladys Leslie (Mary Karger); Edward Earle (Charles Farrin); Dore Davidson (Lou Gorman); Macey Harlam (Claude Benson); Pierre Grendon (Jack Graham); Henrietta Crosman (Madge Foster); Frederick Burton (Augustin Daly); Billy Quirk (Joe Karger); Sally Crute (Augusta Karger); Leslie King (Mark Twain); Albert Phillips (General Grant); Lassie Bronte ("Chum"--a dog)

A LADY'S MORALS, *Metro-Goldwyn-Mayer*, released November 1930
A Cosmopolitan Production; Director, Sidney Franklin; Screenplay, Hans Kraly, Claudine West; Dialogue, John Meehan, Arthur Richman; Based on a story by Dorothy Farnum; Photography, George Barnes; Art director, Cedric Gibbons; Dance, Sammy Lee; Gowns, Adrian; Sound, J. K. Brock, Douglas Shearer; Editor, Margaret Booth; Original title: *The Soul Kiss*

Grace Moore (Jenny Lind); Wallace Beery (Phineas Taylor Barnum); Reginald Denny (Paul Brandt); Gus Shy (Olaf); Jobyna Howland (Josephine); Gilbert Emery (Brougham); George F. Marion (Innkeeper); Paul Porcasi (Maretti); Giovanni Martino (Zerga); Bodil Rosing (Innkeeper's Wife); Joan Standing (Louise); Mavis Villiers (Selma); Judith Vosselli (Rosatti)

MUSICAL NUMBERS: "Is It Destiny?"; "Student's Song"; "I Hear Your Voice" (Clifford Grey, Oskar Straus); "Oh, Why?" (Arthur Freed, Herbert Stothart, Harry M. Woods); "Lovely Hour" (Carrie Jacobs Bond); "Swedish Pastorale" (Howard Johnson, Herbert Stothart); "Casta Diva" (from *Norma* by Bellini); "Rataplan" (from *The Daughter of the Regiment* by Donizetti)

THE MIGHTY BARNUM, *20th Century-United Artists*, released November 1934
A Joseph M. Schenck presentation; Produced by Darryl F. Zanuck; Director, Walter Lang; Screenplay, Gene Fowler and Bess Meredyth; Photography, Peverell Marley; Music, Alfred Newman; Editors, Allen McNeil and Bobbie McLean

Wallace Beery (Phineas Taylor Barnum); Virginia Bruce (singing voice dubbed by Diana Gaylen) (Jenny Lind); Adolphe Menjou (Mr. Walsh); Rochelle Hudson (Ellen); Janet Beecher (Nancy Barnum); Tammany Young (Todd); Lucille La Verne (Joice Heth); George Brasno (General Tom Thumb); Olive Brasno (Lavinia Thumb); May Boley (Bearded Lady); Herman Bing (Man with Three-headed Frog); Richard Branso (Gilbert); John Hyams (Skiff); Tex Madsen (Cardiff Giant); Ian Wolfe (Swedish Consul); Davison Clark (Horace Greeley); George MacQuarrie (Daniel Webster); Charles Judels (Maitre d'Hotel); Christian Rub (Ole); Franklyn Ardell (Sam); Ethel Wales (Mrs. Wendell-Wendell); Theresa A. Conover (Mrs. Waldo Astor); Brenda Fowler (Mrs. Rhinelander-Fish)

TELEVISION

THE LEGEND OF JENNY LIND, *Matinee Theatre*, televised May 2, 1956 NBC 1 hour
Producer, Albert McCleery; Director, Walter Grauman; Teleplay, Irve Tunick

Dorothy Kirsten (Jenny Lind); James Flavin (P. T. Barnum)

BARNUM, televised November 30, 1986 CBS 2 hours
Robert Halmi Productions; Executive producer, Robert Halmi; Supervising producer, Ira Halberstadt; Produced by David Patterson; Director, Lee Phillips; Teleplay, Michael Norell; Photography, Reginald Morris; Production design, William Beeton; Art director, Claude Pare; Costumes, Ann Marie Newson; Music, Charles Gross; Editor, George Jay Nicholson.

Burt Lancaster (Phineas Taylor Barnum); John Roney (Young Barnum); Hanna Schygulla (Jenny Lind); Sandor Raski (Young Tom Thumb--Charles Stratton); Laura Press (Charity Barnum); Kirsten Bishop (Nancy); Patty Maloney (Older Tom Thumb); Joan Heney (Mrs. Stratton); Lorena Gale (Joice Heth); Michael Higgins (Phineas Taylor); Bronwen Mantel (Queen Victoria); and Joe Cazalet, Rummy Bishop, Andrew Bednarski, Richard Dumont, Deborah Hancock, Sean Hewitt, Harry Hill, Sam Lemarquand, John McCorkell, Shawn Lawrence, Tony Rabinow, Rob Roy, Michael Sinelnikoff, John Stanzil, Philip Spensely, Thick Wilson, Chris Wiggins, The Royal Hanneford Circus.

BARNUM, televised December 26, 1986 BBC; in U.S., televised March 14, I990 PBS 110 minutes
A BBC-TV Production in association with Harold Fielding; Producer, Harold Fielding; Associate producer, Wendy Toye; A Musical by Mark Bramble; Director for London stage, Peter Coe; Television director, Terry Hughes; Music by Cy Coleman; Lyrics by Michael Stewart; Scenic designer, David Mitchell; Lighting designer, Eric Delzene; Costume designer, Theoni V. Aldredge; Vocal and dance arrangements, Cy Coleman; Orchestrations, Hershy Kay; Musical director, Michael Reed; Makeup, Lesley Rawstone; Sound design, Edward Fardell; Production manager, David Freeman

Michael Crawford (Phineas Taylor Barnum); Eileen Battye (Charity "Chairy" Barnum); Michael Heath (The Ringmaster); Christina Collier (Jenny Lind); Sharon Benson (Joice Heth/Blues Singer); Paul Miller (Tom Thumb); Peter Barbour and Sue Barbour (Beefeaters); Michael Cantwell (Amos Scudder); Perry Davey (Balancer); James Francis-Johnston (Chester Lyman); Graham Fawcett (Humbert Morrissey); Richard Gauntlett (White-Face Clown); Paul Goddard (Professor Cusp); Alan Heap (Sherwood Stratton); Michael Herview (Juggler); Amanda Newman (Waitress); Joanne Robley-Dixon (Circus Lady); Nadine Shenton (Mrs. Sherwood Stratton); Debbie Steel (Acrobat); Christopher Talman (Edgar Templeton); Jane Watts (Lady Clown); Paul Bateman, Bunny Thompson (Pianists)

BEAUTY AND THE BEAST

Various adaptations of the fairy tale by Mme. Leprince de Beaumont and/or Gabrielle Suzanne (Mme. de Villeneuve), and by the Brothers Grimm (1757)

Synopsis

Losing his fortune, a once-wealthy merchant relocates his family to labor on a country farm. His two pretentious, arrogant daughters ridicule their younger sister Beauty for her placid acceptance of their misfortune. When their father prepares to leave to recover merchandise in town, he goes with requests from the older daughters for luxuries, but Beauty asks him to bring back only a rose. During a snowstorm, the merchant is lost and finds shelter in a large, quite remote castle where he is wined and dined and sheltered by an unseen host. In leaving the following morning, he picks for Beauty a spray of roses, miraculously growing through the drifts. He is soon confronted by a beast in human form who accuses him of stealing his prize roses after receiving the hospitality of the manor. The beast demands the merchant forfeit his life but then permits him to return home in exchange for the life of one of his daughters. To save her father, Beauty offers to return to the Beast.

At the castle, the Beast falls in love with Beauty who treats him with kindness while refusing his offer of marriage. Learning ultimately that her sisters have married and that her father is now alone, Beauty requests permission to return home for eight days. There she discovers that the Beast has magically provided her with a stunning wardrobe woven of gold and diamonds. Her jealous sisters, aware of Beauty's promise to return to the Beast, spitefully persuade her to remain home for another eight days. Beauty reproaches herself for being untruthful to the Beast and goes back to the castle, and there she discovers the Beast unconscious. Beauty, remorseful, vows to marry the Beast, which is suddenly transformed into a handsome Prince. She has broken the spell, it appears, that was placed upon the Prince years earlier until a beautiful woman consented to marry him despite his grotesque, beastly form. A fairy appears to Beauty praising her choice of a husband of kindness and merit over physical appearance. After Beauty's marriage to the Prince, the fairy changes her despicable sisters into statues to stand at the castle door forever and silently observe the happiness of Beauty and her Prince, transformed from a Beast.

Comment and Critique

There is disagreement over who actually wrote *Beauty and the Beast*, but most literary historians attribute the modern version to Mme. Leprince de Beaumont (1711-80), who apparently adapted it from the fairy tale by the Brothers Grimm, although the British Museum found an original by Mme. de Villeneuve predating it by nearly two decades. The Leprince version dates back to 1757, but one of the earliest stagings was Madame Vestris' in 1841 at London's Covent Garden with her husband Charles James Mathews as The Beast. In America, actress Mary Taylor captured audiences with her interpretation of Beauty in one of three productions that opened in New York in 1843.

In 1890, John d'Auban starred with Belle Bilton in Augustus Harris' London production of *Beauty and the Beast*. In this century, the tale was adapted to a Christmas pantomime that paid annual Yuletide visits to London, and as recently as 1985, when the Old Vic produced a version, it has retained its popularity. Jack Linder (*Daily Mail*) wrote of the Old Vic adaptation which starred Vanessa Redgrave's daughter Joely, "Louise Page [who adapted the story] has spared nothing in the retelling of *Beauty and the Beast*...it is a potent play."

Jeremy Kingston determined in *The London Times*: "Playwrights tinker with fairy tales at their peril, since they express, so psychologists tell us, conflicts that lie too deep to be resolved except by fairy aid. Louise Page's retelling of this tale reserves the story we all know...Joely Richardson moderates the inevitably rather trying 'goodiness' of the heroine with an occasional jab of wit...Best of all is Jack Klaff's fine-speaking Beast, whose snarls of despair, bursting out of his gentle speech, have the true tragic passion of the imprisoned hero."

As early as 1899, the French had made a film version of *Beauty and the Beast*. A onereeler was made that year and another in color in 1908. In between, there was a British film of the story. The earliest American version was H. C. Matthews' for Universal-Rex Pictures in 1913, with Elsie Albert as Beauty. "...a splendid adaptation of the old fairy story...While the photography of the interiors is not at all times what it might be, this cannot be said of the exteriors," wrote George Blaisdell (*The Moving Picture World*). "In the latter, it is uniformly excellent -- sharp and clear. The settings were chosen with great care and discrimination; the artificial are noteworthy for attention to details so essential to a costume or period picture; the natural, the outdoor, are selected with an eye for artistic effect...Elsie Albert, who portrays Beauty, seems particularly adapted to these pretentious fairy productions. She does excellent work in this picture." Blaisdell concluded: "That *Beauty and the Beast* is an expensive production is apparent. Likewise it is apparent that the money has been expended."

The most famous of all the screen versions (aside from the *King Kong* variations) of *Beauty and the Beast* remains Jean Cocteau's 1946 masterpiece with Josette Day and Jean Marais in the leads. In his published diary about its making, Cocteau wrote on the eve of the start of production in August 1945, "My method is simple: not to aim at poetry. That must come of its own accord. The mere whispered mention of its name frightens it away. I shall try to build a table. It will be up to you then to eat at it, to examine it or to chop it up for firewood." What he accomplished, it turns out, generally has been accepted as poetry and remains one of the great achievements of the screen. *Life* magazine called it "sensuously fascinating." *The New York Times* described it as "priceless, gorgeous, exquisite."

Beauty and the Beast had its American premiere in New York on Christmas Eve, 1947. "The oft-tried but seldom-known accomplishment of telling a familiar fairy-tale with pure imagery and enchantment through the sensuous devices of the screen has been almost perfectly realized by the French poet-playwright, Jean Cocteau," Bosley Crowther wrote in *The Times*. "An eminent model of cinema achievement in the realm of poetic fantasy. It is a fabric of gorgeous visual metaphors, of undulating movement and rhythmic pace, of hypnotic sounds and music, of casually congealing lines."

Other lesser screen versions followed over the years. There was a minor American one in 1962 with Mark Damon and Joyce Taylor, an animated version from the USSR in the early 1970s, and an ambitious Czech one in 1978. The *Hallmark Hall of Fame* TV production of it in 1976 with George C. Scott and Trish Van Devere was released theatrically in Great Britain. Filmed in the disused church of St. Mary's, Lambeth, the version, written by Sherman Yellin and directed by Fielder Cook, had Scott spending ten hours in a boar's head which required two and a half hours to put on every morning.

Tom Milne wrote of the production in *Monthly Film Bulletin*: "Limping lamely in the wake of Cocteau's marvelously magic *La Belle et La Bete*, this resetting of Perrault's fairy tale is embarrassingly flat-footed and hopelessly cloy in its use of language. Introduced with hideous inappropriateness through a distorted lens, sorely lacking the enchantment of Bernard's designs and Cocteau's living statuary...Small wonder in the circumstances that the film remains obstinately earthbound and more than a little tedious..."

In 1987, producers Menachem Golan and Yoram Globus made a number of screen fairy tales in Israel to be released under their Cannon Movie Tales banner. Several of them premiered at the Cannes Film Festival that year. One was *Beauty and the Beast*. It was not well received by the critics. *Variety*, for one, noted: "Rebecca DeMornay is Beauty and John Savage is her beast-prince. She has cameo-brooch looks and his beast makeup closely resembles every 'Wolf Man' pic...Acting overall, including DeMornay and Savage, is so flat and direction so weak that pic might be presumed to be an intended spoof. It's passed off seriously, however, with overstaged and overlong scenes, hardly any action, a harsh mix of accents and a castle that looks snapped together far too quickly...Film buffs with a taste for dumb pics might find some fun. Kiddies, for whom the pic is intended, won't." *Beauty and the Beast* seems never to have been released theatrically in the

United States, but premiered on The Disney Channel on television.

The Disney Company made its own feature-length animated version of the classic fairy tale over a seven year period during the 1980s, and on its release in late 1991, it was greeted enthusiastically, with a number of critics placing it among the best of Disney of the past. It boasted a score by Alan Menken and Howard Ashman, who had written Disney's previous *The Little Mermaid* as well as the cult musical *Little Shop of Horrors*. Disney's *Beauty and the Beast* went on to become the first animated movie ever to be nominated for the Academy Award as Best Picture of the year.

Earlier television productions of *Beauty and the Beast* were presented on *Shirley Temple Storybook* (the show's premiere) in January 1958 with Claire Bloom and Charlton Heston, and as an ABC special in a staging by the San Francisco Ballet Company in 1969. In 1984, Shelley Duvall's *Faerie Tale Theatre* offered an engaging production of it with Klaus Kinski as The Beast and Susan Sarandon as Beauty. It marked French director Roger Vadim's American TV debut.

In September 1987, CBS premiered a *Beauty and the Beast* series, contemporizing the story, setting it in Manhattan -- above and below ground, with a pretty lady prosecutor being saved from a savage beating by muggers by a beastly figure living in a tunnel world. The show, which starred Linda Hamilton and Ron Perlman (made up as a lion-like man-beast and emerging as a rather offbeat romantic idol), became a cult favorite. Over the course of the series, the two fall in love and ultimately have a child -- just as the show comes to an abrupt end with the withdrawal of the leading lady. (The departure was a personal choice; her murder was written into the script.) Without a beauty a *Beauty and the Beast* is virtually impossible to sustain, and the show limped along into more or less oblivion, much to the distress of its devoted fans. A closing episode ultimately was filmed so that the Beast could avenge Beauty's death, and the series was gone in the spring of 1990.

STAGE

BEAUTY AND THE BEAST, Covent Garden, London, opened March 4, 1841
A Play by James Robinson Planche; Performed as an afterpiece to Dion Boucicault's *London Assurance*

Madame Vestris (Beauty); Charles James Mathews (The Beast)

Olympic Theatre, New York, opened January 23, 1843 14 performances
Produced and directed by William Mitchell; Music and lyrics by H. C. Timm and W. Alpers

Mrs. H. C. Timm (Beauty); Charles M. Walcot (The Beast/Prince Axor); Mary Taylor (Dressylinda); Mrs. Mossop (Marygolda); John Nickinson (Croton Pump, Esq.); William Mitchell (John Quill); Miss Clark (Queen of the Roses); Miss Singleton (Zephyr); Master Wood (Black Cupid)

Bowery Theatre, New York, opened January 28, 1843
Produced and directed by James Wallack

Mrs. Ellen Herbert (Beauty); James Wallack (The Beast); C. Hill (Sir Aldgate Pump); W. F. Gates (John Quill); Mrs. C. Hill (Queen of the Roses)

Olympic Theatre, New York, opened September 15, 1843
Produced and directed by William Miitchell; Music and lyrics by H. C. Timm and W. Alpers

Mary Taylor (Beauty); James C. Dunn (The Beast); William Mitchell (John Quill)

Broadway Theatre, New York, opened December 10, 1855
Produced and directed by George Washington Marsh

Mary Guerineau Marsh (Beauty); Louise Marsh (The Beast); Carrie Marsh (Aldgate Pump); George Washington Marsh (John Quill); Georgina Marsh (Marygolda); Helen Brooks (Dressylinda); Miss Salome (Queen of the Roses); Cora Ames (Zephyr)

Pavilion Theatre, London, opened December 26, 1877
Produced by Morris Abrahams; A Pantomime by Frank Green; Director, Isaac Cohen

Marion Webster (Beauty); Mr. Holdsworth (The Beast); J. F. Alexander (Harlequin); Rose Alexander (Columbine); Arthur Alexander (Pip); Johnny Alexander (Clown); Mr. Gibbs (Pantaloon); Gus Connolly (John Quill); H. Lynn, J. Wilton, G. English. J. Cifion, A. Wolff, Katie Cohen, Polly and Constance Alexander (Dancers)

Prince of Wales Theatre, London, opened December 26, 1890 140 performances
Produced and directed by Augustus Harris; A Pantomime by William Yardley and Augustus Harris; Scenery, Robert Caney, T. E. Ryan, Kautsky, William Perkins; Costumes, Edel & Russell, Auguste, Harrison, M. Landolf, Miss Palmer; Chorus master, Stedman; Choreography, John d'Auban; Musical director, P. Bucalossi; Stage manager, Arthur P. Collins

Belle Bilton (Beauty); John d'Auban (The Beast); Harry Nicholls (Mary Anne); Jane Herbert Campbell (Sarah); Charles Wallace (Monmorency); George Temple (Old Bogie); Tom Pleon (McSkipper); Dan Leno (Lombarde Streete); Fred Walton (Private Block); J. Griffiths (Maxwelton); F. Griffiths (Sheepshead); Master Coleman (Lt. Gen. Shrimp); Terriss (Postman); Vesta Tilley (King Courage); Florence Paltzer (Fairy Rosebud); Retta Walton (Vivandiere); Emma d'Auban (Fairy Chamberlain); Ethel Salisbury (King's Chamberlain); Baton Nicholls (Field Marshal); C. Mabel Coates (Major Key); Daisy Baldry (Lieutenant Wright); Cissy St. George (Field Marshalless Baton); Leopold Troupe (Envy/Hatred/Malice/Slander/Lying); Sybil Grey (King of Diamonds); Violet Ellicott (Maj. Gen. Plume); Violet Granville (Captain Jinks); C. Benton (Lt. Col. Filbert); A. Moore (Ensign Flagg); Whimsical Walker, Harry Leopold, Fred Leopold, Joseph Leopold, Georgina Cook (Harlequinade)

Lyceum Theatre, London, opened December 26, 1928
A Pantomime written and directed by Walter and Frederick Melville; Music, Charles J. Moore

Jean Colin (Beauty); Dorothy Seacombe (The Beast/ Prince Hal); Ernie Mayne (Pickles); Fred Yule (Leander); Frank Attree (Hook o'Crook, a Witch); Gladys Hall (Florizel); Molly Vyvyan (Lord Ferdinand); Hermione Darnborough (Spirit of the Rose); Albert Letine (Mignonette); Dick Tubb (Marigold); Archie McCraig (Sergeant Brown); J. Edwards-Martin (Sebastian); Lionel Scott (Captain of the Guard); Louis Gaye (Bundle); Olive Layton (Robbie); Eileen Dagmar (Silverstone); Joe Bogannay (Dr. Addlepate); Errol Addison (Sunray); Gertrude Mitrenga (The Butterfly); Marjorie Lancaster (Goodheart); Peggy Walton (Wormwood); Leslie Dale (Jack); Ivy Wensley (Jill); Austin and Scott (Felstead); Margie Noel (Jasmine); Lois Fuller (The Flame); Bogannay Troupe (The Collegiates); Zellini (The Witch's Butler)

Lyceum Theatre, London, opened December 27, 1937
A Pantomime written and directed by Frederick Melville; Music, Conrad Leonard
Anne Leslie (Beauty); Jill Esmond (The Beast/Prince Hal); Albert Murdon (Pickles); Norman Greene (Leander); Noel Carey (Hook o'Crook, a Witch); Olive Green (Florizel); Molly Vyvyan (Lord Ferdinand); Hermione Darnborough (Spirit of the Rose); Johnny Cavanaugh (Mignonette); Clarkson Rose (Marigold); Sydney Claydon (Mother Shipton); Betty Bucknell (Snowflake); Billy Purvis (Caesar); Newman and Wheeler with Yvonne (Saturn, Mars and Venus); Wally Mark (Tiddles); Dick Edwards (Herr von Pumpernickle); Vivian Ashdown (Scout Trumpeter); William Norman (Lord Chief Constable); June Melville (Sunray); Dave and Joe O'Gorman (Eustace and Percy); Roberta Petley (Spirit of Joy); Billy Raw (Fido); D'Amzel (Consomme); The Two Jays (Hoppem and Coppem)

Mercury Theatre, London, opened December 21, 1949
A Play by Nicholas Stuart Gray; Director, Mary Morris
Carol Marsh (Beauty); John Byron (The Beast/ Prince); Hugh Pryce (Mr. Hodge); Barry MacGregor (Mikey); Jill Raymond (Jessamine); June Rodney (Jonquiline); Donald Finlay (Mr. Clement)

Westminster Theatre, London, opened December 19, 1950
A Play by Nicholas Stuart Gray; Director, Charles Hickman
Patricia Dainton (Beauty); Alan Badel (The Beast/ Prince); John Byron (Mr. Hodge); Alaric Cotter (Mikey); Jill Raymond (Jessamine); Ann Summers (Jonquiline); Donald Finlay (Mr. Clement)

Mercury Theatre, London, opened December 22, 1952
A Play written and directed by Nicholas Stuart Gray
Jane Griffiths (Beauty); Shaun O'Riordan (The Beast/ Prince); Hugh Pryse (Mr. Hodge); Christine Finn (Mikey); Rosemary Wallace (Jessamine); Elizabeth Regan (Jonquiline); Donald Finlay (Mr. Clement)

Embassy Theatre, London, opened December 22, 1953
A Play by Nicholas Stuart Gray; Director, Chloe Gibson
Helena Hughes (Beauty); Kenneth Haigh (The Beast/ Prince); Richard Goolden (Mr. Hodge); Leon Garcia (Mikey); Margaret Dale (Jessamine); Cora Bennett (Jonquiline); Nigel Arkwright (Mr. Clement)

Players' Theatre, London, opened December 20, 1955
A Fairy Extravaganza by J. R. Planche; Director Don Gemmell
Sonia Graham (Beauty); Anthony Newlands (The Beast); Margaret Ashton (Queen of the Roses); Ormerod Greenwood (Sir Aldgate Pump); John Harmer (Zephyr); Patricia Rowlands (Marygolda); Sally Miles (Dressalinda); Michael Darbyshire (John Quill); Beverley Richards, Yvonne Olena, Hazel Wiscombe, Barbara Viner (Rose Fairies); *Harlequinade*: John Harmer (Harlequin); Barbara Viner (Columbine); Brian Tipping Gold (Clown); Ormerod Greenwood (Pantaloon); Michael Darbyshire (Toff); Beverely Richards (Page); Hazel Whitcombe (Dog); Yvonne Olena (Fairy)

Arts Theatre Club, London, opened December 23, 1959
Produced by the Arts Theatre Club; A Play by Nicholas Stuart Gray; Directors, Ruth

Atkinson and Nicholas Stuart Gray; Settings, Joan Jefferson Farjeon

Lesley Nunnerley (Beauty); Michael Atkinson (The Beast/Prince); Jonathan Meddings (Mr. Hodge); Dudy Nimmo (Mikey); Julia Puccini (Jessamine); Gillian Muir (Jonquiline); Stanley Beard (Mr. Clement)

Hampstead Theatre Club, London, opened December 20, 1965
Produced by the Hampstead Theatre Club; A Play by Nicholas Stuart Gray; Director, Hywel Jones; Setting, Dawn Pavitt

Maureen O'Brien (Beauty); David Andrews (The Beast/ Prince); Robert Eddison (Mr. Hodge); Richard Howard (Mikey); Jane Bond (Jessamine); Lucinda Curtis (Jonquiline); John Frawley (Mr. Clement)

Sydney (Australia) Opera House, opened December 26, 1980
Produced by the Festival of Sydney and Sydney Theatre Company, in association with the Sydney Opera House; A Play adapted and directed by Louis Nowra and Rex Cramphorn, based on the story by Mme. Leprince de Beaumont; Production designer, Silvia Jansons; Lighting, Alan Crossey; Choreographer, Michael O'Reilly; Musical director, Sarah de Jong

Michele Fawdon (Beauty); Brandon Burke (The Beast); Vic Rooney (Father); Andrew Tighe (George); Kerry Walker (Felicity); Janice Finn (Adelaide); Tony Mack (Eric); Kim Deacon (Statue)

Old Vic Theatre, London, opened December 19, 1985 47 performances
Produced by The Women's Playhouse Trust and Liverpool Playhouse, by arrangement with Brendon Street Investments and Allside Asset Management Company; A Play by Louise Page, based on Mme. de Villeneuve's 1740 story; Director, Jules Wright; Settings, Annie Smart; Lighting, Dave Horn; Costumes, Shay Cunliffe; Choreography, Jacky Lansley; Fights staged by Malcolm Ranson; Sound, Ilona Sekacz

Joely Richardson (Beauty); Jack Klaff (Hew the Beast); Natasha Parry (Finagle); Cathryn Harrison (Mielle); Veronica Quilligan (Zephyr); Mark Tandy (Bear/ Nossail); Terence Harvey (Bearkeeper/Duke/ Argent); Souad Faress (Lady/ Jen/ Fairy/ Sophy/ Monkey/ Pomfret); Philip Bretherton (Courtier/ Boye/ Simon); Jack Ellis (Soldier/Earl/Kit/Monkey); Tricia Kelly (Lady/ Ann/ Mother of the Fairies/ Governess/ Clarice/ Monkey); Marty Cruickshank (Hortense/ Monkey)

SCREEN

LA BELLE ET LA BETE, *Pathe Films*, France, released 1899 1 reel
Based on the tale by Gabrielle Suzanne

BEAUTY AND THE BEAST, *Clarendon/Gaumont Pictures*, released November 1905 1 reel
Director, Percy Snow

LA BELLE ET LA BETE, *Pathe Films*, France, released 1908 1 reel colored
Based on the tale by Gabrielle Suzanne

BEAUTY AND THE BEAST, *Universal-Rex Pictures*, released 1913 1 reel
Produced and directed by H. C. Matthews; Based on the tale by Gabrielle Suzanne

and the Brothers Grimm
Elsie Albert (Beauty)

BEAUTY AND THE BEAST, International Film Service, Inc., released 1916
Written and directed by H. E. Hancock
Mineta Timayo (Beauty)

BEAUTY AND THE BEAST, Stoll Pictures, released January 1922
Produced by George Clark; Written and directed by Guy Newell
Ivy Duke (Beauty); Guy Newell (The Beast); Douglas Munro (Father); Winifred Sadler (Mother)

LA BELLE ET LA BETE, Discina Films, France, released 1946
Produced by Andre Paulve; Adapted and directed by Jean Cocteau, based on the story by Mme. Leprince de Beaumont, attributed to Perrault; Photography, Henri Alekan; Decor and costumes, Christian Berard; Settings, Moulaert; Lighting, Raymond Meresse; Techical adviser, Rene Clement; Makeup, Hagop Arakelian; Music, George Auric; Editor, Claude Iberia
Josette Day (Beauty); Jean Marais (The Beast/ Avenant/Ardent--Prince Charming); Marcel Andre (The Merchant); Mila Parely (Adelaide); Nane Germon (Felicia); Doudou (Diana); Carrier (Bit Player); Diot (Jean Marais's Standin); Michel Auclair (Beauty's Brother)

BEAUTY AND THE BEAST, United Artists, released May 1962
Produced by the Harvard Company; Producer, Robert E. Kent; Director, Edward L. Cahn; Screenplay, George Bruce and Orville H. Hampton; Photography, Gilbert Warrenton; Art director, Franz Bachelin; Editor, Richard Carlisle
Mark Damon (The Beast/Duke Eduardo); Joyce Taylor (Beauty/Lady Althea of Sardi); Eduard Franz (Baron Orsini); Michael Pate (Prince Bruno); Merry Anders (Princess Subil); Dayton Lummis (Count Roderick); Walter Burke (Garfield)

BEAUTY AND THE BEAST, Studio Bartranov, Prague, released 1978
A Czechoslovakian Film Production; Director, Juraj Herz; Screenplay, Ota Hofmann
Zdena Studenkova (Beauty); Vlastimil Harapes (The Beast); Vaclav Vosko (Beauty's Father); Jana Brejchova (Gabina, Beauty's Sister); Zuzana Kocurikova (Malinka, Beauty's Sister)

BEAUTY AND THE BEAST, Cannon Films, released May 1987
A Golam-Globus Production; Executive producer, Itzik Kol; Producers, Menahem Golan and Yoram Globus; Associate producer, Patricia Ruben; Director, Eugene Marner; Screenplay, Carole Lucia Satrina, based on the story by Mme. de Villeneuve; Photography, Avi Karpick; Production designer, Marek Dobrowolski; Costumes, Buki Shiff; Music, Lori McKelvey; Editor, Tova Ascher
Rebecca DeMornay (Beauty); John Savage (The Beast); Yossi Graber (Father); Michael Schneider (Kuppel); Carmela Marner (Bettina); Ruth Harlap (Isabella); Joseph Bee (Oliver)

BEAUTY AND THE BEAST, Buena Vista, released November 1991
A Walt Disney Production in association with Silver Screen Partners IV; Executive producer, Howard Ashman; Producer, Don Hahn; Directors, Gary Trousdale and Kirk Wise; Animation screenplay, Linda Woolverton; Based on the classic French fairy

tale; Art direction, Brian McEntee; Visual effects supervisor, Randy Fullmer; Music, Alan Menken; Songs, Howard Ashman and Alan Menken; Editor, John Carnochan

Voices: Paige O'Hara (Belle); Robby Benson (Beast); Jerry Orbach (Lumiere); Angela Lansbury (Mrs. Potts); Richard White (Gaston); David Ogden Stiers (Cogsworth/Narrator); Jesse Corti (LeFou); Rex Everhart (Maurice); Bradley Michael Pierce (Chip); Jo Anne Worley (Wardrobe); Kimmy Robertson (Featherduster)

MUSICAL NUMBERS: "Belle"; "Gaston"; "Be Our Guest"; "Something There"; "Beauty and the Beast"; "The Mob Song"; "Beauty and the Beast" (reprise)

Original soundtrack recording: Walt Disney Records

KING KONG, *RKO Radio Pictures*, released March 1933
Executive producer, David O. Selznick; Directors, Merian C. Cooper and Ernest B. Schoedsack; Screenplay, James Creelman and Ruth Ross, based on a story by Edgar Wallace and Merian C. Cooper; Photography, Edward Linden, Verne Walker and J. O. Taylor; Art directors, Carroll Clark and Al Herman; Costumes, Walter Plunkett; Chief Technician, Willis O'Brien; Production Assistants, Archie Marshek and Walter Daniels; Music, Max Steiner; Sound, E. A. Wolcott; Sound Effects, Murray Spivak; Editor, Ted Cheeseman

Robert Armstrong (Carl Denham); Fay Wray (Ann Darrow); Bruce Cabot (John Driscoll); Frank Reicher (Captain Englehorn); Sam Hardy (Weston); Noble Johnson (Native Chief); James Flavin (Briggs); Steve Clemento (Witch Doctor); Victor Long (Lumpy); Ethan Laidlaw (Mate); Dick Curtis, Charlie Sullivan (Sailors); Vera Lewis, LeRoy Mason (Theater Patrons); Paul Porcasi (Apple Vendor); Lynton Brent, Frank Mills (Reporters)

KING KONG NO GYAKUSHU (KING KONG ESCAPES), *Toho Films*, Japan, released 1967
Produced by Toho Film Company; American version by Rankin/Bass productions; Producer, Tomoyuki Tanaka (American version: Arthur Rankin, Jr.); Director, Inoshiro Honda; Screenplay, Kaoru Mabuchi (American version: William J. Keenan); Photography, Hajime Koizumi; Art director, Takeo Kita; Special effects, Eiji Tsuburaya; Music, Akira Ifukube

Rhodes Reason (Commander Nelson); Mie Hama (Madame Piranha); Linda Miller (Susan); Akira Takarada (Lt. Jiro Nomura); Eisei Amamoto (Dr. Who)

KING KONG, *Paramount Pictures*, released December 1976
A Dino De Laurentiis production; Executive producers, Frederick de Laurentiis, Christian Ferry; Director, John Guillermin; Screenplay, Lorenzo Semple, Jr., based on a script by James Creelman and Ruth Rose from a concept by Edgar Wallace and Merian C. Cooper; Photography, Richard H. Kline; Visual consultant, Dale Hennessy; Special photographic effects, Frank Van Der Veer; Art directors, Archie J. Bacon, David Constable, Robert Gundlach; Set decorator, John Franco, Jr.; Costumes, Moss Mabry, Anthea Sylbert; Music, John Thompson; Editor, Ralph E. Winters

Jeff Bridges (Jack Prescott); Jessica Lange (Dwan); Charles Grodin (Fred Wilson); John Randolph (Captain Rose); Rene Auberjonois (Bagley); Julius Harris (Boan); Dennis Fimple (Sunfish); Jack O'Halloran (Joe Perko); Ed Lauter (Carnahan); Jorge Moreno (Garcia); Mario Gallo (Timmons); John Lone (Chinese Cook); Garry Walberg (Army General); John Agar (City Official); Keny Long (Ape Masked Man); Sid Conrad (Petrox Chairman); George Whiteman

(Army Helicopter Pilot); Wayne Heffley (Air Force Colonel); and Kong, The Eighth Wonder of the World

KING KONG LIVES, De Laurentiis Entertainment Group, released December 1986
Executive producer, Ronald Shusett; Producer, Martha Schumacher; Director, John Guillermin; Screenplay, Steve Pressfield, based on characters created by Edgar Wallace and Merian C. Cooper; Photography, Alec Mills; Production designer, Peter Murton; Art directors, Fred Carter, Tony Reading, John Wood; Creature creation and construction, Carlo Rambaldi; Costume designer, Clifford Capone; Music, John Scott; Editor, Malcolm Cooke

Linda Hamilton (Amy Franklin); Brian Kerwin (Hank Mitchell); John Ashton (Colonel Nevitt); Peter Michael Goetz (Dr. Ingersoll); Frank Maraden (Dr. Benson Hughes); Peter Elliot (King Kong); George Yrasomi (Lady Kong)

TELEVISION

BEAUTY AND THE BEAST, Shirley Temple Storybook, televised January 12, 1958 NBC 1 hour
Executive producer, William H. Brown, Jr.; Producer, William Asher; Teleplay, Joseph Schrank; Hostess, Shirley Temple

Claire Bloom (Beauty); Charlton Heston (The Beast); E. G. Marshall (The Merchant); June Lockhart, Barbara Baxley (Beauty's Sisters)

BEAUTY AND THE BEAST, televised December 31, 1969 ABC 1 hour
Produced by the San Francisco Ballet Company; Executive producer, David Sacks; Producer, Gordon Waldear; Director, Seymour Robbie; Settings, Dik Rose; Costumes, Tony Duquette; Choreography, Lew Christiansen

Hayley Mills (Narrator); Lynda Meyer (Beauty); Robert Gladstein (The Beast); David Anderson (Prince Charming); Members of the San Francisco Ballet Company

Hallmark Hall of Fame, televised December 3, 1976 NBC 90 minutes
Produced by Thomas M. C. Johnston and Hank Moonjean; Director, Fielder Cook; Teleplay, Sherman Yellin, based on Perrault's fairy tale; Photography, Jack Hildyard and Paul Beeson; Art director, Elliott Scott; Costume designer, Albert Wolsky; Beast makeup, Del Acevedo; Music, Ron Goodwin; Editor, Freddie Wilson

George C. Scott (The Beast); Trish Van Devere (Belle); Virginia McKenna (Lucy); Bernard Lee (Beaumont); Michael Harbour (Anthony); William Relton (Nicholas); Patricia Quinn (Susan)

CBS Family Classics, televised November 25, 1983 CBS 1 hour
Produced by Ruby-Spears Entertainment in association with Triple Seven Concepts; Executive producers, Joseph Ruby amd Ken Spears; Producer, Larry Huber; Director, Rudy Larriva; Animated special written by Steve Gerber and Martin Pasko, adapted from Mme. Leprince de Beaumont's story; Animation supervisor, Michael Longden; Art director, Ric Gonzalez; Music, Dean Elliott and Paul DeKorte; Narrator, Paul Kirby

Voices: Janet Waldo (Beauty/Jacqueline/Queen/Old Crone); Robert Ridgley (The Beast/The Prince); Linda Gary (Erwina/Stately Lady/Messenger Boy); Alan Young (Rene/Cockatoo); Stacy Keach, Sr. (Merchant/Sailor/ Male Voice); Paul Kirby (Gerard)

Shelley Duvall's Faerie Tale Theatre, televised August 13, 1984 Showtime I hour
Produced by Think Productions, Inc.; Executive producer, Shelley Duvall; Producers, Bridget Terry and Frederic S. Fuchs; Teleplay, Robert C. Jones, based on Perrault's fairy tale; Director, Roger Vadim; Production designer, Michael Erler; Art director, Jane Osmann; Costume designer, J. Allen Highfill

Klaus Kinski (The Beast); Susan Sarandon (Beauty); Stephen Elliott (The Father); Angelica Huston, Nancy Lenehan (Beauty's Sisters); Stanley Wilson (Nicholas)

BEAUTY AND THE BEAST (series), televised September 25, 1987 through June 2, 1989 and December 12, 1989 through January 24, 1990 CBS 1 hour each (56 episodes in regular series plus three extra ones on July 21, 28 and August 4, 1990)
Produced by Ron Koslow Films and Witt/Thomas Productions in association with Republic Pictures Corporation; Executive producers, Paul Junger Witt and Tony Thomas; Producer, Ron Koslow; Coproducer, Lynn H. Guthrie; Director, Richard Franklin (premiere) and others; Teleplay, Ron Koslow (premiere) and others; Photography, Roy H. Wagner; Production designer, John Mansbridge; Beast designed and created by Rick Baker; Music, Lee Holdridge; Editor, Andrew London

Linda Hamilton (Catherine Chandler); Ron Perlman (Vincent the Beast); Roy Dotrice (Father); Ren Woods (Edie); Jay Acovone (Joe Maxwell); Edward Albert (Elliot Burch); Stephen McHattie (Gabriel); Jo Anderson (Diana Bennett); David Greenlee (Mouse)

THE BEGGAR'S OPERA
A Comic Opera by John Gay (1727)

Synopsis

Crooked lawyer Peachum and his wife are appalled when their daughter Polly marries handsome highwayman Captain Macheath. Although he has acted as a fence for Macheath's stolen goods, Peachum plots to have the highwayman arrested and pocket the reward money. Warned by Polly, Macheath escapes and meets his gang at a Newgate tavern, advising them to lay low. Assisted by two female pickpockets holding Macheath captive with his own pistols, Peachum has him arrested and jailed in Newgate prison overseen by Peachum's greedy partner, Turnkey Lockit. Lockit's daughter Lucy, once Macheath's mistress, hopes to marry the highwayman. While Peachum is learning from Mrs. Coaxer that his dishonest partner Lockit has been pocketing their illegally obtained funds, Macheath is attempting to convince Lucy of his faithfulness when his wife Polly arrives at the prison. Lucy, however, relents and steals her father's keys and Macheath returns to his gang. Peachum and Lockit again recapture Macheath, who has been betrayed by Jenny Diver, in Mrs. Trape's bordello and he is returned to prison. Distraught, Polly and Lucy join forces to beg their father for Macheath's life. Before his transfer to Old Bailey to be hanged, Macheath is visited by four more "wives" -- each with a child -- who create such a furor proclaiming rich men and their vices escape the gallows but poor men are hanged for theirs, that Macheath is reprieved and charges against him dropped. Vowing to shun vice but still endeavor to live like the rich, Macheath decides that Polly will remain his one and only wife since:

"My Heart was so free,
It rov'd like the bee.
'Til Polly my passion requited;
I sipt each flower,
I chang'd ev'ry hour,
But here ev'ry flower is united."

Comment and Critique

Irish satirist and author of *Gulliver's Travels* Jonathan Swift suggested to English poet and librettist John Gay that he should write a satirical, bawdy comedy, "A Newgate pastoral among the whores and thieves there might make an odd pretty sort of thing." Gay, who was born at Barnstaple, Devonshire, on June 30, 1685, and died in London on December 4, 1732, depicted the thieving politicians of their day, especially the blatant bribery perfected by Prime Minister Sir Robert Walpole and the corrupt government of King George II. Using traditional airs and old songs, Gay created *The Beggar's Opera.* Sixty-nine airs were familiar to the audience; many mainly from parodies of those in Tom D'Urfey's *Pills to Purge Melancholy.*

After actor James Quin declined to play the role of Macheath, Drury Lane Theatre's Colley Gibber refused to produce the play. John Rich produced *The Beggar's Opera* at London's Lincoln's Inn Field on January 29, 1728, with Thomas Walker as Macheath and, as Polly, Lavinia Fenton. (She was for twenty-three years the mistress of Charles Powlett, Duke of Bolton, who married her in 1751 after the death of the Duchess.)

A year after the soaring success of *The Beggar's Opera*, which was said to have "made Gay rich and Rich gay," John Gay's sequel to his comic opera, *Polly*, was banned from the stage by the Lord Chamberlain on the insistence of Sir Robert Walpole. In 1729, Sir Archibald Grant commissioned satirical artist William Hogarth to paint a scene from *The Beggar's Opera.* The Hogarth painting, now in London's Tate Gallery, depicts Polly and Lucy pleading with Turnkey Lockit and Peachum for Macheath's release.

The Very Reverend Dr. Herring, Archbishop of Canterbury, denounced *The Beggar's Opera* from the pulpit for glorifying Macheath and permitting him to go unpunished. Chief Magistrate Sir John Fielding requested the inflammatory comic opera to be suppressed due to "the dangerous effect it is supposed to have on the morals of the people." As was and ever will be, such righteous damnation only increased attendance.

Lucia Elizabetta Vestris, celebrated actress Madame Vestris, appeared as Macheath in London's Haymarket Theatre revival of Gay's *The Beggar's Opera* on July 22, 1820. In his biography, *Madame Vestris and Her Times*, Charles Pearce noted that Vestris was not the first actress to portray Macheath, explaining, "In 1820, the opera had not been performed for seven years. With Vestris as Macheath it came as a refreshing surprise -- a surprise all the greater as the costume revealed the exquisite form of one of the most beautifully proportioned women who had ever appeared upon the English stage. It is not a little singular that, coarse and vulgar as was the taste of the day, some people professed to see impropriety in an actress in a 'breeches' part. However, the *Theatrical Inquisitor*...was fain to admit that 'though our sentiment of this lady's appearance in Macheath are not precisely such as will blazon her merit or confirm her success ...we are half inclined to instance this momentous effort as the most amusing personation in which we have hereto beheld her. The muses, according to Gay's *Beggar*, pay no attention to dress....but Madame Vestris in her scarlet frock and blue cravat...her dapper appearance, high spirits and unflagging activity, were apparent in every branch of her impersonation and rendered her Captain Macheath...one of the prettiest rattles for overgrown children with which the stage can at present supply them.' The opera ran for ten consecutive nights."

Earlier, Captain Macheath was played by Anne Catley in Henry Mossop's production in 1764 at Dublin's Smock Alley Theatre. Spranger Barry produced Gay's comic-opera in competition with Mossop's acclaimed presentation with himself as Macheath, Mrs. Dancer as Polly Peachum and Mrs. Abington as Lucy Lockit. In 1779, Mrs. Kennedy played Macheath at London's Covent Garden, and the following year, Mrs. Cargill appeared in the "breeches" role. Anne Catley again abandoned her role as Polly to oppose Mrs. Cargill's travesty of Macheath.

Gay's comic opera first appeared in America at New York's Nassau Street Theatre on January 7, 1850, produced by England's Murray and Kean Company. ("The Theatre on Nassau Street," as it was called, was a two-story wooden building owned by the estate of Rip Van Dam, where six candles served as footlights for the stage.) Gay's expose of the political shenanigans of his day found great favor in the emerging theatre of the American colonies. *The Beggar's Opera* has been successfully produced around the world for nearly three hundred years.

On the bicentenary of *The Beggar's Opera*, using Gay's original text and the original music by Frederic Austin, the opera was staged on February 14, 1928, at the Lyric Theatre Hammersmith, London, where, in 1920, Gay's 18th-century romp completed 1,468 performances. The 1920 London Company toured several cities in the United States and Canada. After playing several engagements on the West Coast, the Company terminated its tour in Chicago on April 1, 1922.

Eugen Bertolt Friedrich Brecht's secretary, Elisabeth Hauptmann, suggested that he should adapt Gay's comic opera to the German stage. Brecht's adaptation *Die Dreigroschenoper* (*The Threepenny Opera*) completed 600 consecutive performances with Kurt Weill's musical comedy wife, Lotte Lenya, as Spelunken-Jenny. Novelist-playwright, Leon Feuchtwanger, suggested the title *Die Dreigroschenoper*.

Lotte Lenya later recalled in *Theatre Arts* (1956), "From that day Berlin was swept by a *Dreigroschenoper* fever. In the streets, no other tunes were whistled. A *Dreigroschenoper* bar opened, where no other music was played. Immediately, the 'Brecht style' and the 'Weill style' were slavishly imitated by other dramatists and composers."

The Threepenny Opera was first produced on Broadway on April 1, 1933 at the Empire Theatre but closed after twelve performances. Brecht's German text had been adapted into English by Gifford Cochran and Jerrold Krimsky who also produced the musical.

Lewis Nichols (*The New York Times*) compared 1728's *The Beggar's Opera* to 1931's *Of Thee I Sing* and viewed *The Threepenny Opera* as "a three-dimensional satire, or humor, or whatever such an aggregation of things would be. It does form, however, a gently made evening in the theatre... *The 3-Penny Opera* has a splendid score, one that is interesting, pleasant and quite in the air of the early day sinners of London...Bert Brecht has been responsible for the book. He has chosen from *The Beggar's Opera* all the necessary material, and has built thereon...The cast for the opera has been chosen excellently and Francesco Von Mendelssohn has directed them gayly...Rex Weber has the part of the greatest scoundrel of them all, Jonathan Peachum...Steffi Duna is excellent as Polly Peachum." But Mr. Nichols considered Robert Chisholm "perhaps, just a shade too well-bred for *The Beggar's Opera* as Macheath."

John Gielgud directed a revival of Gay's *The Beggar's Opera* at London's Haymarket Theatre in 1940. *Theatre World*, reflecting on the hugely successful Lyric Theatre Hammersmith productions of the opera throughout the 1920s, reported, "It is doubtful whether the Hammersmith brigade with their rigid insistence on ritual, would approve of Mr. Gielgud's treatment. In place of formality and what might be termed stylised bawdiness, he has post-dated Gay's play by a hundred years and, to quote a programme note, 'sought inspiration, with the aid of Motley, in the early drawings of George Cruikshank'...If there are certain elements of the Playfair-Lovat-Fraser production that one misses, and some performances which, to my mind, don't come within a mile of the originals, there is much to admire, a pervading sense of freshness and gaiety, and some gay and deft invention...Michael Redgrave cuts a gallant figure as Macheath, using a pleasant voice with grace and style, and extracting full humour from every situation. Audrey Mildmay sings beautifully as Polly, but her acting is artificial in the operatic tradition ...The most striking performance comes from Linda Gray, who sings and acts with fine dramatic force as the dark termagant, Lucy." Frederic Austin created a new musical score for the revival.

John Latouche adapted Gay's opera to the stage to Duke Ellington's music as *Twilight Alley* which arrived at the Broadway Theatre just after Chrismas 1946 as *Beggar's Holiday*. Howard Barnes (*Herald-Tribune)* reported, "From the standpoint of size or general activity, *Beggar's Holiday* is quite an entertainment. This very free musical adaptation of the John Gay classic has a company which literally crowds the stage....But the satisfactions of the show are, at best, fragmentary...Neither John Houseman, who originally staged the show, nor George Abbott, who worked on it more recently, have succeeded in achieving a sustained mood or an engrossing line of action. [Zero] Mostel appears to be improvising in most of his scenes and the individual encounters are as dreary as the sagging libretto deserved them to be."

Brooks Atkinson (*The New York Times*), however, noted, "Let appropriate salutes be fired in honor of Duke Ellington and John Latouche. Using John Gay's *Beggar's Opera* as a ground plan, they have composed a flaring musical play in modern style...Mr. Ellington and Mr. Latouche have translated the footpad Macheath into a modern gangster who lives off the rackets of the town -- a garish and bitter dance of extraordinary quality. Mr. Ellington and Mr. Latouche have given Broadway a score and lyrics we can be proud of."

Richard Watts, Jr. (*New York Post*) found *Beggar's Holiday*, "A colorful but confused show," and allowed for last minute cast changes, a parade of directors and other symptoms which made it appear that "it never quite makes up its mind whether to be social satire, melodramatic burlesque or just plain musical extravaganza...But the show just doesn't work out." Robert Garland (*Journal-American*) felt, "it must have seemed like a good idea at the time...*Beggar's Holiday* is, for the time being, having the courage of its unorthodox convictions...Zero Mostel is an impressive example of undercasting. His Mr. Peachum does not belong in *The Beggar's Opera* as conceived by the dead Mr. Gay or reconceived by the quick Mr. Latouche. On the other hand, the Macheath of Alfred Drake belongs whole-heartedly. I have never seen a better singing-dancing-acting bad man than his...But with valor gone and vaudeville substituting, even Max Meth's masterful orchestral direction of Duke Ellington's fine, fresh music fails to keep the early promise of this latest revamping of John Gay's ballad opera."

In 1948, England's Benjamin Britten composed a new musical score based on original English folk-airs for the Sadler's Wells Theatre production of *The Beggar's Opera*. The production featured Peter Pears as Macheath and Nancy Evans as Polly.

It was not until 1954 that Brecht and Weill's reconstruction of Gay's masterpiece finally became successful in America, when Carmen Capalbo, Stanley Chase, and Louise Lortel managed to raise $10,000 to produce the German *Die Dreigroschenoper*, translated for the English-speaking stage by Marc Blitzstein as *The Threepenny Opera*. The highly praised 1954 revival at Off-Broadway's Theatre De Lys eventually completed 2,611 performances. Aside from Kurt Weill's brilliant score, from which the song "Moritat" (also known as "Mack the Knife") gained international fame, Brecht's text, translated by Blitzstein, was described by Virgil Thompson as "the finest thing of its kind in existence."

In *The World of Musical Comedy*, author Stanley Green explained the durability of Brecht-Weill-Blitzstein *Threepenny Opera* this way: "In the twilight years of the Weimar Republic in Germany, audiences could see in the raffish, sardonic story all the venality and bitterness then so much a part of daily life in Central Europe. An empathy was created between the play and audience that no other work of that period could approach. The social illness within the United States thirty years later may not be so pronounced, but they have caused many sociologists to express concern at the decline of moral values within an apparently healthy society. Thus, *The Threepenny Opera* still has something pertinent to say, while, at the same time, delivering its message with broad humor, a certain romantic charm, and an unflagging musical appeal."

Lotte Lenya, the widow of Kurt Weill (he died at the age of fifty on April 3, 1950), sang the role of Jenny in the Theatre De Lys production during the first year of its record run. Lenya, the original Jenny in Berlin's 1928 production of *Die Dreigroschenoper*, was born Karoline Blamauer in Vienna, Austria, on October 18, 1900, and died in New York City on November 27, 1981. Bertolt Brecht died at age fifty-eight on August 14, 1956, in East Germany.

Richard Baldridge's version of Gay's comic opera with music adapted and arranged by Daniel Pinkham was produced at New York's City Center Theatre on March 13, 1957, and in Chicago, Paul Sills' adaptation of *The Beggar's Opera* featuring Alan Arkin as Macheath, with music by William Mathieu, was called *Big Deal*. The Theatre De Lys' *Threepenny Opera* featuring Scott Merrill, their original Macheath, and Gypsy Rose Lee as Jenny, opened a national tour in Toronto, Canada, on September 19, 1961 but folded there on September 30.

Tony Richardson directed the new British production of *The Threepenny Opera* which opened in February 1972 at London's Prince of Wales Theatre, featuring Joe Melia as Macheath and Vanessa Redgrave as Polly Peachum. Hugh Leonard reviewed Richardson's production for *Plays and Players*, noting, "The point of *The Threepenny Opera* is rammed home at the end of the first act. The characters are scum; thieves, cutthroats, prostitutes, corrupt policemen; and they advance to the edge of the stage and ask if we are any better than they, since we have permitted them to exist. Brecht does not deign to argue or even demonstrate; instead he *tells* us, and there is no more to be said...*The Threepenny Opera* was written in 1928 and set in Soho of the 1890s...But there seemed little reason for Tony Richardson in directing the play 44 years after it was written, to update the action -- setting it in the 1920s. In this context, it hardly works. Macheath and his gang are shown as cheap hoods, so raffish that they must steal the appurtenances of a wedding night, and the brothel patronized by Macheath is the most scabrous establishment west of Calcutta ...stylistically, Mr. Richardson's production is at odds with Brecht's head-on methods. As well as being a poet -- although one would hardly think so from Hugh McDiarmid's uncertain adaptation -- Brecht was also a theoretician who knew exactly how he wanted his work to be presented."

In early May 1972, England's Chichester Festival Theatre also produced

Gay's *The Beggar's Opera*, starring John Neville and Millicent Martin. "It's a sound measure of the indestructibility of John Gay's *The Beggar's Opera* that its sweet and sour soul, the strong beat of its stout heart and the tang of its lemon wit have survived attempts at prettification, of gimmicks to make it more socially 'relevant.' Lousy singing, indifferent acting, it absorbs with good will," wrote *Plays and Players*. "At Chichester, in Robin Phillips' production, it even manages to override, at moments of menace, a noise resembling the baying of the Hound of the Baskervilles in heat. It is a work of unsentimental conscience, persistent life and magic undimmed by 244 years of toil and treachery... The best things about this latest version are the musical arrangements by Martin Best...Millicent Martin's Polly substitutes a pleasingly pert romanticism and her true yet roomy voice is perfectly pitched to ballad form. As Macheath, John Neville occasionally looks a bit like Richard II fallen among thieves and, initially, a shaky nasal Cockney twang sounded as though it was going to bung up his delivery. But, with a little less stiffness along the vertebrae, he'll make an attractively relaxed roue of a hero. Already, his 'if the heart of a man,' without playing for sentimentality, brings a catch to the throat and a tear to the eye..."

Gay's *The Beggar's Opera* emerged season after season in various adaptations, and in 1973, the City Center Acting Company included the opera in its repertory. The zesty revival was reviewed by Clive Barnes (*The New York Times*): "Any production of *The Beggar's Opera* has to run the gauntlet of strange comparisons. Gay's original text has served for many springboards. Obviously, Brecht's *The Threepenny Opera*, with its Kurt Weill score, is one competitor, and then, rather closer to the original is Benjamin Britten's version, which is almost operatic in scope....Kevin Kline sings well but is less than totally commanding as Macheath...Far better is Patti Lupone as Lucy Lockit ...this *Beggar's Opera* will give you a fun evening in the theater."

Richard Watts (*New York Post*) wrote, "Actually, Brecht and Weill improved *The Beggar's Opera* when they changed it into *The Threepenny Opera*, largely because Kurt Weill composed such wonderful songs for it. Gay's songs were bright and pleasant, but they lack something of Weill's rich tunefulness. Yet seeing it in the original version, although less satisfying theatrically, is rewarding because it offers us such a vivid and persuasive picture of the seamy side of low life in the colorful 18th century."

Ralph Manheim and John Willett made an English adaptation of Brecht's *Threepenny Opera* which was produced by Joseph Papp in 1976 with Raul Julia as Mack the Knife (Julia earlier had played the part at Williamstown). Clive Barnes (*The New York Times*) found the translation "shocking...the Brecht script still has the tremorious undertone of an earthquake to it. But this production is shocking for another reason -- the familiar Blitzstein version sanitized and popularized, defanged and, at times, even traduced the Brecht original. It had been made far more socially acceptable, the scatological references had been removed, for example, and also it was politically far tamer. Brecht's socialistic philosophy remained in large part, but the corrosiveness had been removed or at least softened." Barnes observed: "Mr. Papp has gone to another source for his version with a new translation by Ralph Manheim and John Willett that, if memory serves, because I have not compared the text, is even tougher than Mr. Feingold's. It works very well indeed and what is particularly significant about Mr. Papp's production is that he has gone to the two people in American who are best fitted to stage the piece."

Tony Award nominations for this *Threepenny Opera* went to Joseph Papp (Most Innovation Production of a Revival), Raul Julia for his Macheath a.k.a. Mack the Knife, Ellen Greene for her Jenny Towler, costume designer Theoni V. Aldredge and scenic designer Santo Loquasto.

Robert David MacDonald's English translation of Brecht's *Die Dreigroschenoper*, directed by Peter Wood at London's Olivier Theatre in 1986, was deplored by Rodney Milnes (*Plays and Players*): "There are many curious things about this truly dreadful performance, or rather the first half of it. What on earth was it doing [in] the Olivier?... Most curious of all was a production that flew in the face of everything that Brecht stood for -- indeed he could well have coined the work 'culinary' simply to describe it. The mordant satire on middle-class mores was turned by Peter Wood into a quaint little musical comedy....I fled the theatre at the interval...unable to take any more of Mr. Wood's all-too-successful hatchet job on one of the masterpieces of 20th-century musical theatre."

Newsweek's comment on the Peter Wood's *Threepenny* fiasco: "Adrift in the vast space of the National's Olivier Theatre, [it] was similarly forced to puff itself out with fancy and incongruous effects, along with the epicene prancing of Tim Curry's Mack the Knife. But, at least, the National Theatre's music director, Dominic Muldowney, wisely insisted on going back to Weill's vivid, original jazz-band orchestration of *Threepenny*."

The Guardian's critic, Michael Billington, wrote, "I was fascinated to read in the National's programme for *The Threepenny Opera* that the *Red Flag* condemned the 1928 Berlin production as 'Culinary theatre, totally lacking in concrete social awareness.' Whatever claim to revolutionary status the work has stems from its ironic, low-life, inversion of the operatic form; and that point goes crucially missing from Peter Wood's bland, smooth, pretty new production at the Olivier ...Irony is the key. Brecht himself in a conversation with Giorgio Strehler in 1955 (recorded in the Methusen edition) explained the show's underlying idea. "Beggars are poor people. They want to make a grand opera but lack money and have to make do as best they can.' What Brecht underlined was that the actors' effort to achieve something grandiose ended each time as a fiasco...Mr. Wood's production has no such savagery and no such framing device; it is basically a pleasant bourgeois spectacle with some indestructible Kurt Weill tunes."

Warner Bros.-First National Pictures released G. W. Pabst's screen production of the BrechtWeill *Die Dreigroschenoper* in 1931. "Herr Pabst's direction reveals occasional brilliant moments," reported Mordaunt Hall (*The New York Times*), "but his characters in their attire look more German than English...It is a production filled with anachronism...What purports to be Newgate Prison looks to be almost an up-to-date jail... Rudolf Forster, who plays Messer, gives quite a clever performance, considering the circumstances. Carola Neher also does well in this conception of Polly Peachum. Reinhold Schunzel's portrayal of Tiger Brown likewise has a certain merit. The melodies are quite agreeable and one would not complain if there were more of the singing and less of some of the action. It is, however, a fantastic affair which has none of the charm, vitality and bitter satire of Gay's *Beggar's Opera*."

In 1974, Tony Rayns wrote a retrospective of the Pabst production, noting, "Brecht hated Pabst's version of *Die Dreigroschenoper*. In October, 1930 -- while the film was still in production -- he and Kurt Weill sought a court order forcing Nebenzal's Nero-Film to bring the project into line with its author's wishes; Weill won control of the score, but Brecht's case was dismissed, the court ruling that he had shown insufficient readiness to work on the film in its pre-production stage. When released, the film enjoyed considerable success (until banned by the Nazis in 1933), but remained under attack (from Marxists: Bela Balasz, in particular, was criticized for having lent his name to a flagrantly capitalist venture -- his response being that he had remained on the film precisely in order to preserve as much as possible of its left-wing position). Ironically, this furor was coincident with the period of Pabst's own greatest social commitment: he had just been elected leader of Dacho, the German film technicians' union, and was about to go on to make his urgent call for socialist pacifism in *Kameradschaft*...Weill's ballads are incorporated without the slightest deviation from the tone of the rest of the action, strengthening the dream-like style further (although Ernst Busch's delivery of the 'Moritat' and Lotte Lenya's song would be showstoppers in other circumstances)."

Georg-Wilhelm Pabst simultaneously directed a French version of *Die Dreigroschenoper*, adapted by Andre Mauprey, Solange Bussi and Ninon Steinhoff. Called *L'Opera de quat'sous*, it featured Albert Prejean as Mackie, Odette Florelle as Polly and Margo Lion as Jenny.

Laurence Olivier and Herbert Wilcox produced Gay's *The Beggar's Opera* for the screen in 1953. The handsome British film was directed by Peter Brook and starred Olivier as Macheath, Dorothy Tutin as Polly, George Devine and Mary Clare as the Peachums, and Stanley Holloway as Lockit. The *New York Post* critic enthused about the Olivier film, "A feast of color brought to furious movement! The performances are a fine and lusty set. A unique romp...place it high on the list of screen classics!"

Arthur Knight (*Saturday Review*) reported, "Olivier himself plays the dashing Macheath with keen appreciation of the satire implicit in the role. He also sings his own part, revealing a light tenor that is always agreeable if not always true...Opera on film requires a bold hand as well. Sir Laurence has played it to perfection."

Britain's *Monthly Film Bulletin* wrote, "Much, perhaps too much, was to be expected of *The Beggar's Opera*, the first film of Peter Brook, the most gifted stage director of his generation...Unfortunately the failure is equalled only by the ambition. One has the feeling that much went wrong with this film almost from the start. The ragged construction, the scrappy, often unfinished-looking succession of episodes, the variable colour, the discordant mixture of styles, the whole potted 90 minutes of a work more than twice that length -- all this suggests an initial lack of grasp. The basic flaw lies in the handling itself, which shows surprisingly little aptitude for the cinema...Sir Arthur Bliss' incidental music adopts an incongruous modern idiom, and much of it sounds merely bombastic...But behind all these surface faults one is aware of the inner vacuum -- the failure to convey any feeling of Hogarthian London, or any acceptable formalization of it; the lack of robustness, of breadth, in the whole thing; and its faltering, confused development as a piece of narrative."

C. A. Lejeune in London's *The Observer* proclaimed, "Olivier's Macheath, to my mind, is the most comfortable piece of work he has given us yet in pictures. He romps through the part, whether acting, singing, dancing or riding, without any touch of self-consciousness, and as though all these exercises were a joy, and the player's impression of ease, of relaxation, is irresistibly communicated to the audience."

"This Technicolor screen version of John Gay's 225-year-old work is a kaleidoscopic view of truly colorful facets of the London dear to Hogarth and is as unrestrained as its author's name," appraised *The New York Times* critic A. H. Weiler. "While it deviates from the original intent and now lampoons neither opera nor political personalities, it is still a spirited musical ...While this *Beggar's Opera* is closer to horse opera than Covent Garden, its principals and its basic story lines are recognizable...Although the plot and motivations are sometimes vague and pointless without the satirical thrusts that made it the biting jest of its day, *The Beggar's Opera* is unusual and not static fare. It has movement and authentic color, attributes missing from most filmed operas."

In 1963, Germany remade the Brecht-Weill *Die Dreigroschenoper* in three languages: German, French and English. *Films and Filming* noted "This second film adaptation of the Brecht-Weill opera (it was filmed by G. W. Pabst in 1931) is directed by Wolfgang Staudte. A few years ago, he started directing a film of *Mutter Courage*, but quit because of disagreements with Brecht. Staudte has aimed at an authentic period style. The tendency of *Die Dreigroschenoper* was basically already outmoded at the time of the first performance in 1928. Yet Brecht's work is such that a relation to any specific era seems unimportant."

Die Dreigroschenoper was released in English in Great Britain and America as *The Threepenny Opera* and featured Curt Jurgens (Mack, the Knife), June Ritchie (Polly), Hildegard Knef (Pirate Jenny) and Sammy Davis, Jr. as the Ballad Singer. Attempting to expound the often advertised Brecht-Weill adaptation of "Seven different shows for one admission price: a period crime thriller, a political satire, a folklore ballad, a social-message play, a sex show, a tuneful opera, and a hilarious parody of opera," the film fell short of its goal despite its lavish production. The 1989 German remake of *The Threepenny Opera*, set in Victorian England, has Raul Julia once again playing the role of Macheath, as he had in Joseph Papp's 1976 Shakespeare Festival version, together with Richard Harris, opera star Julia Migenes, Julie Walters, Clive Revill and Roger Daltrey (Macheath in Jonathan Miller's 1983 BBC-TV production). By the time it made its way to the U.S. in late January 1990, this Menachem Golan production was retitled *Mack the Knife*. (It opened in New York less than a month after the Broadway production with Sting closed.)

"Broadway Dickens, which is the real inspiration for this aggressively ragtag adaptation by the Israeli mogul Menachem Golan, is a far cry from the scathing tone of *The Three Penny Opera*. But Golan has determinedly turned the material into the basis for an extended variety show," Janet Maslin wrote of *Mack the Knife* in *The New York Times*. "The qualified best than can be said for Mr. Golan is that he made all this even more unpleasant than might be thought...The actors, who have been savaged by a costume designer intent on repellent blowsiness for one and all, are sometimes much better than their surroundings. Mr. Julia makes a fine, cynical Macheath, with all the wiliness and power that the role demands. And Ms. Migenes, the opera singer, has a regal presence even under the most sordid circumstances. Richard Harris makes a broad but amusing Peachum, though he seems too often to be playing Fagin; Clive Revill, who *has* played Fagin on the stage, makes an entertaining Money Matthew here."

John Gay's *The Beggar's Opera* became an experiment for the CBS Television Workshop on March 2, 1952. The telecast was found to be rather heavy-handed despite excellent performances from Stephen Douglass as Macheath and Doretta Morrow as Polly.

Kirk Browning produced and directed another version of *The Beggar's Opera* for television on February 5, 1967. Jack Gould (*The New York Times*) considered the telecast "a poor *Beggar's Opera*...ill advised revival of the original play with music was a spiritless marathon, wordy beyond tolerance, and, melodically, two hours that went determinedly unsung... Browning might have mitigated the tedium by having high fun with the old vehicle and doing it as a stylish lark. But the fantasy of the highwayman and his sundry loves in Newgate Prison was unfolded at a snail's pace and the portrayals of the cast were rarely endowed with touches of point of view of personality as that might have compensated for the musical notes beyond reach."

Philadelphia television critic Harry Harris, however, considered: "*The Beggar's Opera* was a television treat. Some of the vocalizing was hardly of even mock-operatic quality but since this classical musical satire is supposed to be performed by 18th century inmates of London's Newgate Prison, it didn't much matter...there were deliciously disreputable performances as the Peachums by Howard Da Silva and, of all unexpected people! -- Shirl Conway."

In 1983, Jonathan Miller staged his BBC production of *The Beggar's Opera* with a cast that included Roger Daltrey as Macheath, Bob Hoskins, Patricia Routledge and Carol Hall. *The London Times* critic found it "a production which startled more for its precise faithfulness to the period and mood of the original than for any revelatory redating. I am surprised Miller was not tempted by the glamorously vicious London crime scene of the 1960s. But here the music came first: gone was the folksy prissiness of the familiar Dent and Britten versions of the score. I did not count, but most of the 69 original songs seemed to be included...Roger Daltrey's much-heralded Macheath turned out to be mainly swagger and girl-groping; he hit his songs with a blunt instrument...The best match of voice and acting came from Macheath's two rival loves: Carol Hall's Polly, pure of voice but passionate in temper, and Rosemary Asche's Lucy, small and fierce, who suddenly blossomed in one of Purcell's three superb melodies." This BBC production premiered in the U.S. on the Arts and Entertainment Channel four years later.

STAGE

THE BEGGAR'S OPERA, *Lincoln's Inn Fields Theatre*, London, opened January 29, 1728 63 performances
Produced by John Rich; A Comic Opera by John Gay

Thomas Walker (Macheath); Lavinia Fenton (Polly Peachum); John Hippisley (Peachum); Mr. Hall (Lockit); Mrs. Egleton (Lucy Lockit); H. Bullock (Jemmy Twitcher); Mr. Clark (Filch); Mrs. Martin (Mrs. Peachum); Mrs. Clarke (Jenny Diver); Mrs. Pit (Nimming Ned); Mr. Houghton (Crook'd-Finger Jack); Mrs. Holiday (Mrs. Coaxer); Mrs. Martin (Diana Trapes); Mr. Eaton (Harry Paddington); Mr. Lacy (Robin of Bagshot); Mr. Spiller (Matt of the Mint); Mr. Morgan (Ben Budge); Mrs. Sallee (Molly Brazen); Mrs. Rice (Mrs. Vixen); Mrs. Rogers (Betty Doxy); Mrs. Lacy (Dolly Trull); Mrs. Smith (Wat Dreary); Mrs. Chapman (Beggar); Mr. Milward (Player); Mrs. Morgran (Mrs. Slammekin); Mrs. Palin (Sukey Tawdry)

John Street Theatre, New York, opened November 19, 1753
A Comic Opera by John Gay

Louis Hallam (Mr. Peachum); Mr. Adcock (Captain Macheath); Mrs. Becceley (Polly); Mrs. Adcock (Mrs. Peachum); Mr. Malone (Lockit); Mrs. Clarkson (Lucy Lockit); Mr. Miller (Filch); Mr. Bell (Matt o' the Mint); Mr. Singleton (Wat Dreary); Mr. James Hulett (Nimming Ned); Miss Hallam (Mrs. Coaxer); Mrs. Rigby (Mrs. Vixen); Mrs. Adcock (Diana Trapes); Mr. Clarkson (Moll Brazen); Mrs. Love (Jenny Diver)

Theatre on Society Hill, Philadelphia, opened August 24, 1759
A Satirical Opera by John Gay

Mr. Harman (Captain M'Heath); Mr. Tomlinson (Peachum); Mrs. Love (Polly); Mrs. Harman (Mrs. Peachum); Mrs. Scott (Lockit); Mrs. Harman (Lucy Lockit); Owen Morris (Beggar); David Douglas (Player); Adam Allyn (Jemmy Twitcher); Mr. Reed (Matt o' the Mint); Mr. Horne (Harry Paddington); Adam Hallam (Filch); Mrs. David Douglas (Mrs. Coaxer); Mrs. Tomlinson (Mrs. Slammekin)

John Street Theatre, New York, opened May 21, 1773
A Comic Opera by John Gay

Louis Hallam (Captain Macheath); David Douglas (Mr. Peachum); Miss Mallam (Polly); Mrs. Morris (Mrs. Peachum); Owen Morris (Lockit); Ann Storer (Lucy Lockit); Mr. Wall (Matt o' the Mint); Miss Richardson (Jenny Diver); Mr. Parker (Ben Budge); Mr. Dermot (Nimming Ned); Mr. Byerley (Jemmy Twitcher); Mrs. Maria Henry (Mrs. Coaxer); Mrs. Wall (Mrs. Slammekin)

Southwark Theatre, Philadelphia, opened November 28, 1776
A Comic Opera by John Gay; Dances by Mr. Matthews

Stephen Woolls (Captain Macheath); Adam Allyn (Peachum); Miss Wainwright (Polly); Catherine Maria Harman (Mrs. Peachum); Owen Morris (Beggar); Mrs. Tomlinson (Lockit); Mrs. Owen Morris (Lucy Lockit); Mrs. Matthews (Jemmy Twitcher); Mr. Wall (Filch); Miss Dowthwait (Mrs. Slammekin); Mrs. David Douglas (Molly Brazen)

New Theatre, Montego Bay, Jamaica, opened March 29, 1777
Produced by The American Company of Comedians; A Comic Opera by John Gay

John Henry (Cap'n M'Heath); E. Allen (Mr. Peachum); Mrs. Owen Morris (Mrs. Peachum); Miss Wainwright (Polly); Thomas Wignell (Filch); Maria Storer (Lucy Lockit); Owen Morris (Lockit); Mr. Dermot (Matt o' the Mint); Mr. Johnson (Crook'd-Finger Jack); William Wignell (Wat Dreary); George Hughes (Ben Budge); Mrs. E. Allen (Mrs. Coaxer); David Benjamin Roberts (Molly Brazen)

Covent Garden, London, opened April 6, 1785
A Comic Opera by John Gay

John Henry Johnstone (Captain Macheath); Eliza Wheeler (Polly); John Cochran Booth (Peachum); Mrs. Harriett Davenport (Mrs. Peachum); Mary Morton (Jenny Diver); Elizabeth Wilson (Filch); Joshua Painter (Jemmy Twitcher); Mrs. Thomas Kennedy (Lucy Lockit); William Darley (Matt o' the Mint); Robert Bates (Crook'd-Finger Jack); Mrs. Richard Webb (Lockit); John Ledger (Ben Budge); Miss Platt (Mrs. Slammekin); William Stevens (Jailor); Mrs. Helme (Drawer)

SONGS: "The Sorrows of Charlotte at the Tomb of Werter"; "The Soldier Tir'd of War's Alarms" (sung by Eliza Wheeler)

New Theatre, Philadelphia, season 1793-94
A Satirical Opera by John Gay; Music director, James Hewitt

John Hodgkinson (Macheath); Mr. Prigmore (Peachum); Mrs. Miller (Mrs. Peachum); Mrs. John Hodgkinson (Polly Peachum); John Martin (Filch); William King (Matt o' the Mint); Mrs. Pownall (Lucy Lockit); Mr. Ashton (Lockit); Mrs. Hamilton (Mrs. Coaxer); Mrs. Wilson (Mrs. Slammekin)

Drury Lane Theatre, London, opened December 17, 1799
A Comic Opera by John Gay

Michael Kelly (Captain Macheath); Miss Stephens (Polly Peachum); William Dowton (Peachum); Mrs. Walcot (Mrs. Peachum); Thomas Hollingsworth (Lockit); Maria De Camp (Lucy Lockit); Mrs. Hugh Sparks (Diana Trapes); Mr. Suett (Filch)

Theatre Royal, Covent Garden, London, opened March 6, 1802
A Comic Opera by John Gay

Mr. Hill (Captain Macheath); Mr. Davenport (Peachum); Mrs. Davenport (Mrs. Peachum); Mrs. Billington (Polly Peachum); Mr. Thompson (Lockit); Mrs. Martyr (Lucy Lockit); Mr. Simmons (Filch); Mr. Klanert (Ben Budge); Mr. Curties (Crook'd-Finger Jack); Mr. Harley (Jemmy Twitcher); Mr. Street (Wat Dreary); Mr. Atkins (Nimming Ned); Mr. Wilkinson (Harry Paddington); Mr. Wilde (Robin of Bagshot); Mr. Abbot (Drawer); Mrs. Cstelle (Jenny Diveri; Mrs. Edwards (Mrs. Coaxer); Mr. Blurton (Jailor); Mrs. Iliff (Dolly Trull); Mrs. Norton (Mrs. Vixen); Miss Cox; (Betty Doxy); Miss Leferve (Mrs. Slammekin); Mrs. Watts (Sukey Tawdry); Mrs. Lloyd (Molly Brazen); Mr. Cory (Matt o' the Mint)

Theatre Royal, Covent Garden, London, opened October 8, 1806
A Comic Opera by John Gay

Charles Incledon (Captain Macheath); Mr. Munden (Peachum); Mrs. Davenport (Mrs. Peachum); A Young Lady who has never yet appeared on any stage (Polly); Mr. Emery (Lockit); Mr. Taylor (Matt o' the Mint); Mr. Simmons (Filch); Mrs. Charles Kemble (Lucy Lockit); Miss Cox (Jenny Diver); Mr. Klanert (Ben Budge); Mr. Jeffries (Crook'd-Finger Jack); Mr. Treby (Jemmy Twitcher); Mr. Street (Wat Dreary); Mr. Atkins (Nimming Ned); Mr. King (Harry Paddington); Miss Cranfield (Mrs. Vixen); Mrs. Bologna (Mrs. Coaxer); Mrs. Iliff (Betty Doxy); Mr. Wilde (Robin of Bagshot); Mr. W. Murray (Drawer); Miss Leferve (Mrs. Slammekin); Mrs. I. Bologna (Molly Brazen); Mrs. Grimaldi (Dolly Trull); Mrs. Watts (Sukey Tawdry)

New Theatre Royal, Covent Garden, London, opened September 19, 1809
A Comic Opera by John Gay

Charles Incledon (Captain Macheath); Mr. Munden (Peachum); Mrs. Davenport (Mrs. Peachum); Mrs. Dickons (Polly); Mr. Emery (Lockit); Mrs. Charles Kemble (Lucy Lockit); Mr. Field (Ben Budge); Mr. Simmons (Filch); Mr. Jefferies (Crook'd-Finger Jack); Mr. Taylor (Matt o' the Mint); Mr. Wilde (Robin of Bagshot); Mr. W. Murray (Drawer); Mrs. Bologna (Mrs. Coaxer); Mrs. Coates (Dolly Trull); Miss Cranfield (Mrs. Vixen); Miss Cox (Jenny Diver); Mrs. Iliff (Betty Doxy); Mr. King (Harry Paddington); Mrs. I. Bolgna (Molly Brazen); Mrs. Watts (Sukey Tawdry); Mr. Treby (Jemmy Twitcher); Mr. Atkins (Nimming Ned); Mr. Street (Wat Dreary); Miss Leferve (Mrs. Slammekin)

Theatre Royal, Covent Garden, London, opened September 15, 1812
A Comic Opera by John Gay

Charles Incledon (Captain Macheath); Mr. Blanchard (Peachum); Mrs. Davenport (Mrs. Peachum); Mrs. Sterling (Polly); Mr. Emery (Lockit); Mrs. Charles Kemble (Lucy Lockit); Mr. Taylor (Matt o' the Mint); Mr. Hickman (Ben Budge); Mr. Simmons (Filch); Mr. Jeffries (Crook'd-Finger Jack); Mr. Treby (Jemmy Twitcher); Mrs. Bologna (Mrs. Coaxer); Mrs. Grimaldi (Dolly Trull); Mrs. Coates (Mrs. Vixen); Miss Cox (Jenny Diver); Mr. Tinney (Robin of Bagshot); Mr. Menage (Drawer); Miss Leferve (Mrs. Slammekin); Mrs. Simes (Betty Doxy); Mrs. Watts (Sukey Tawdry) Mrs. Davies (Molly Brazen); Mr. Norris (Wat Dreary); Mr. Atkins (Nimming Ned); Mr. King (Harry

Paddington)

Theatre Royal, Covent Garden, London, opened November 6, 1813
A Comic Opera by John Gay

Charles Incledon (Captain Macheath); Mr. Blanchard (Peachum); Mrs. Davenport (Mrs. Peachum); Miss Stephens (Polly); Mr. Emery (Lockit); Mrs. Liston (Lucy Lockit); Mr. Higman (Ben Budge); Mr. Taylor (Matt o' the Mint); Mr. Norris (Wat Dreary); Mr. Atkins (Nimming Ned); Mr. King (Harry Paddington); Mr. Menage (Drawer); Miss Cox (Jenny Diver); Mrs. Bologna (Mrs. Coaxer); Mr. Simmons (Filch); Mrs. Heath (Dolly Trull); Mrs. Coates (Mrs. Vixen); Miss Adamo (Betty Doxy); Mr. Treby (Jemmy Twitcher); Mr. Jeffries (Crook'd-Finger Jack); Mr. Tinney (Robin of Bagshot); Miss Leferve (Mrs. Slammekin); Mrs. Davies (Molly Brazen); Mrs. Watts (Sukey Tawdry)

New Theatre Royal, Drury Lane, London, opened February 13, 1821
A Comic Opera by John Gay

Mr. Pearman (Captain Macheath); Miss Byrne (Polly Peachum); Mr. Williams (Peachum); Mrs. McCulloch (Mrs. Peachum); Mt. Fullam (Lockit); Mrs. Humby (Lucy Lockit); Mr. Johnson (Filch); Mr. A. Lee (Matt o' the Mint); Mr. Grey (Ben Budge); Miss Mahon (Jenny Diver); Mr. Turner (Crook'd-Finger Jack); Mr. O'Rourke (Harry Paddington); Mr. Digges (Nimming Ned); Mr. Sutcliffe (Wat Dreary); Mr. Tobin (Robin of Bagshot); Mr. Hart (Turnkey); Mrs. Chippendale (Mrs. Coaxer); Mrs. Grey (Mrs. Slammekin); Miss Cunningham (Molly Brazen); Miss E. Mahon (Dolly Trull); Miss Sullivan (Sukey Tawdry); Mr. Good (Waiter)

New Theatre Royal, Drury Lane, London, opened March 8, 1823
A Comic Opera by John Gay

Mr. Horn (Captain Macheath); Mr. Terry (Peachum); Mrs. Harlowe (Mrs. Peachum); Miss Stephens (Polly); Mr. Gattie (Lockit); Miss Cubitt (Lucy Lockit); Mr. Fitzwilliam (Matt o' the Mint); Mr. Knight (Filch); Mr. G. Smith (Jemmy Twitcher); Mr. Hughes (Crook'd-Finger Jack); Miss Smith (Jenny Diver); Mrs. Coveney (Mrs. Coaxer); Mr. W. H. Williams (Wat Dreary); Mr. D. Smith (Robin of Bagshot); Mr. Turnorr (Nimming Ned); Mr. Read (Ben Budge); Mr. Coveney (Harry Paddington); Mr. Randall (Waiter); Mr. Gibbon (Jailor); Double Hornpipe in Fetters by Mr. Ridgway and Mr. Southby

Theatre Royal Haymarket, London, opened July 12, 1826
A Comic Opera by John Gay

A. Lee (Captain Macheath); W. Farren (Peachum); Mrs. C. Jones (Mrs. Peachum); Miss Forde (Polly); Mr. Williams (Lockit); Mrs. Humby (Lucy Lockit); W. West (Filch); Mr. Ebsworth (Ben Budge); Mr. Hickel (Matt o' the Mint); Mr. Coates (Jemmy Twitcher); Mr. Bishop (Wat Dreary); Mrs. W. Johnson (Jenny Diver); Miss Wood (Sukey Tawdry) Mr. Moore (Harry Paddington); Mr. C. Jones (Drawer)

The Theatre, New York, opened October 14, 1828
A Comic Opera by John Gay

Charles E. Horn (Macheath); John Barnes (Peachum); Mrs. Austin (Polly); Mrs. Hackett (Lucy Lockit); Thomas Placide (Filch); Peter Richings (Matt o' the Mint)

Park Theatre, New York, opened November 27, 1840
A Comic Opera by John Gay

Joseph Wood (Macheath); John Fisher (Peachum); Mrs. F. Wheatley (Mrs. Peachum); Mrs. Wood (Polly); William Chippindale (Lockit); Clara Fisher Maeder (Lucy Lockit); William A. Chapman (Filch); W. F. Brough (Matt o' the Mint)

Bowery Theatre, New York, opened June 4, 1849
A Cominc Opera by John Gay

James C. Dunn (Macheath); Mary Taylor (Polly); John Gilbert (Peachum); Charles Bass (Lockit); Mrs. Herbert (Lucy Lockit); Mrs. John Gilbert (Mrs. Peachum); John Winans (Filch); Mrs. James C. Dunn (Mrs. Vixen)

Adelphi Theatre, London, opened March 17, 1873
A Comic Opera by John Gay; Musical director, E. Ellis

William Terrott (Captain Macheath); Miss Furtado (Polly Peachum); B. Egan (Peachum); J. B. Jonstone (Lockit); Cicely Nott (Lucy Lockit); Augustus Glover (Matt o' the Mint); John Clarke (Filch); Mrs. Addie (Mrs. Peachum)

Performed with *The Double Marriage*; *Up a Tree* and *The Yule Long*

Greenwich Village Theatre, New York, opened December 27, 1920, followed by tour, seasons 1920-22
Nigel Playfair's London production of John Gay's comic opera; Produced by Arthur Hopkins; New Settings of the Airs and Additional Music by Frederic Austin; Scenery and Costumes by C. Lovat Fraser; Wigs by Clarkson; Dances arranged by Marian Wilson; Curtailment and selection by Arnold Bennett under the direction of J. C. Duff; Musical conductors, John Mindy (New York), Sebastian Unglada (Tour); Dances for Tour arranged by Gladys Johnson; Stage manager, Phyllis Hiller

Percy Heming (succeeded by Joseph Farrington) (Macheath); Sylvia Nelis (succeeded by Darianne Bawn) (Polly Peachum); Arthur Wynn (Peachum); Charles MacGrath (Lockit); Fedora Roselli (succeeded by Celia Turrill) (Lucy Lockit); Lena Maitland (Mrs. Peachum); Alfred Heather (Filch); Nonny Lock (Jenny Diver); C. C. Lewis (succeeded by Halley Mostyn) (Drawer); Edith Bartlett (succeeded by Julia Meo) (Diana Trapes); William Eville (succeeded by George Tawade, Charles MacGrath) (The Beggar); Charles Tobin, Edward Ciannelli, James Wolff, Walton Macafee, Mario Carboni, S. Rossmussen (succeeded by Messrs. Ahern, St. John, Millman, Ward, Cummings) (Members of Macheath's Gang); Meg Mellors, Clytie Hine, Gladies Johnson, Julie Meo, Vera Hurst, Enid Lindsay (succeeded by Marjorie Chard, Elsie Williams, Christie Murray, Gertrude West, Marguerite Perdifa) (Women of the Town)

Lyric Theatre Hammersmith, London, opened June 5, 1920 1,469 performances
Produced and Directed by Nigel Playfair; A Comic Opera by John Gay; Music by Frederic Austin; Scenery and Costumes designed by C. Lovat Fraser; Scenery, Victor Hembrow; Costumes, Charles Wilson & Company; Choreography, Marian Wilson; Conductors, Eugene Goossens and Herbert Withers; Stage manager, Stephen Thomas

Frederick Ranalow (succeeded by Clive Carey, Pitt Chatham, Arthur Hosking) (Macheath); Frederic Austin (succeeded by Scott Russell, Arthur

Wynn) (Peachum); Sylvia Nelis (succeeded by Vivian Roberts, Katharine Arkandy, Rose Hignell, Kathlyn Hilliard, Alice Mason, Lillian Stanford, Sydney Leon, Pamela Baselow) (Polly Peachum); Arnold Pilbeam (succeeded by Stephen Thomas, Fergus Leslie) (The Beggar); Violet Marquesita (succeeded by Ella Milne, Dorothy Smithard) (Lucy Lockit); Elsie French (Mrs. Peachum); Alfred Heather (succeeded by Frederick Davies, Malcolm Rignold, Scott Russell (Filch); Nonny Lock (succeeded by Angela Baddeley, Sydney Leon, Mildred Watson) (Jenny Diver); Scott Russell (Matt o' the Mint); Jack Girling (Turnkey); David Hodder (succeeded by Charles Straite) (Drawer); Alan Trotter, Malcolm Rignold, John Clifford, Edward Barrs, Charles Straite (Members of Macheath's Gang); Beryl Freeman (succeeded by Edith Bartlett, Iris Fraser Foss) (Diana Trapes); Vera Hurst, Enid Lindsey, Ella Milne, Winifred Christie, Lillian Stanford, Edith Bartlett, Mildred Watson, A. Dennison (Women of the Town)

Lyric Theatre Hammersmith, London, opened June 23, 1925 63 performances
Produced and Directed by Nigel Playfair; A Comic Opera by John Gay; Music by Frederic Austin; Production designer Claude Lovat Fraser; Scenery, Victor Hembrow; Costumes, Charles Wilson & Company, Mrs. C. Lovat Fraser; Choreography, Marian Wilson; Conductor, Alfred Reynolds; Stage manager, Stephen Thomas

Frederick Ranalow (Macheath); Scott Russell (Peachum); Kathlyn Hilliard (Polly Peachum); Arnold Pilbeam (The Beggar); Arthur Wynn (Lockit); Fedora Bernard (Lucy Lockit); Sara Allgood (Mrs. Peachum); Miles Malleson (Filch); Nonny Lock (Jenny Diver); Jack Girling (Turnkey); Pilton Wilson (Drawer); Beryl Freeman (Diana Trapes); John Dean, Arnold Beauvais, Ralph Humble, James Topping, Lawrence Hepworth, Cavan O'Connor (Macheath's Gang); Vera Hurst, Jules Godby, Marjorie Dixon, Ruth Williamson, Valerie Russell, Ita Hope, Jean Duncan (Women of the Town)

Lyric Theatre Hammersmith, London, opened May 22, 1926 25 performances
Produced and Directed by Nigel Playfair; A Comic Opera by John Gay; Music by Frederic Austin; Production designer, Claude Lovat Fraser; Scenery, Victor Hembrow; Costumes, Charles Wilson & Company, Mrs. C. Lovat Fraser; Choreography, Marian Wilson; Conductor, Richard Austin; Stage manager, Phyllis Hiller

Frederick Ranalow (Macheath); Scott Russell (Peachum); Sylvia Nelis (Polly Peachum); Arnold Pilbeam (The Beggar); Elsie French (Mrs. Peachum); Frederick Davies (Filch); Jack Girling (Turnkey); Ita Cope (Jenny Diver); Arthur Wynn (Lockit); Beryl Freeman (Diana Trapes); Dunstan Hart (Drawer); Violet Marquesita (Lucy Lockit); Owen Bryngwyn, Arnold Beauvais, John Dean, Malcolm Rignold, Frank Enright, Sydney Wilson (Members of Macheath's Gang); Gwyneth Edwards, Marjorie Dixon, Nelly Meyrat, Dorothy Saunders, Maisie Evans, Jean Duncan, Clarice Coles (Women of the Town)

Lyric Theatre Hammersmith, London, opened February 14, 1928 69 performances
Produced and Directed by Nigel Playfair; A Comic Opera by John Gay; Music by Frederic Austin; Production designer, Claude Lovat Fraser; Scenery, Victor Hembrow; Costumes, Charles Wilson & Company, Mrs. Claude Lovat Fraser; Choreography, Marian Wilson; Conductor, Richard Austin; Stage manager, Stephen Thomas

Frederick Ranalow (Macheath); Scott Russell (Peachum); Rose Hignell (Polly

Peachum); Elsie French (Mrs. Peachum); Arnold Pilbeam (The Beggar); Sydney Granville (Lockit); Violet Marquesita (Lucy Lockit); Betty Warner (succeeded by Vera Robson) (Jenny Diver); Mark Raphael (succeeded by James Topping) (Filch); Dewey Gibson (Matt o' the Mint); David Hodder (Drawer); Harry Hilliard (Turnkey); Patrick Ward, Harold Ching, Frank Goulding, John Mottershead, Cavan O'Connor (Members of Macheath's Gang); Cicely Nicks (Diana Trapes); Phyllis Dawn, Guelda Waller, Dorris Halley-Stewart, Nelly Meyrat, Marjorie Dixon, Mona Benson, Vera Maconochie (Women of the Town)

Original cast recording (1920 Production): Victor Records, with Frederick Ranalow, Scott Russell, Dorothy Smithard, Violet Marquesita, Tristan Rawson, Kathlyn Hilliard, Frederick Davies, Colin Ashdown, etc.

Touring Company, season 1927-28 and *48th Street Theatre*, New York, opened March 28, 1928 36 performances
Produced by J. C. Duff; The 200th Anniversary Tour of the comic opera by John Gay; New Settings of the Airs and Additional music by Frederic Austin; Musical director, Sebastian Unglada; Company manager, H. M. McFadden; Stage manager, Phyllis Hiller

George Baker (Macheath); Sylvia Nelis (Polly Peachum); Charles MacGrath (Peachum); Norman Williams (Lockit); Celia Turell (Lucy Lockit); Lena Maitland (Mrs. Peachum); Alfred Heather (Filch); Julia Meo (Diana Trapes); Allison Ramsay (Jenny Diver); Marjorie Chard (Mrs. Coaxer); Beatrice Morson (Dolly Trull); Vera Hurst (Mrs. Vixen); Audrey Mildmay (Mrs. Slammekin); Zaidee White (Molly Brazen); Julia Cornelius (Sukey Tawdry); George Gregson (Drawer/The Beggar); Julie Meo (Betty Doxy); Boris Milman, Leon Mandas, Raimonda Aubray, Harry Taylor, Norman Stengel (Macheath's Gang); Orchestra: Hazel Grouppe (Harpsichord); Jean Stockwell (First Violin); F. May Taylor (Violin); Sadie Tilkin (Violincello); Irene Scott (Double Bass); Joseph Marino (Oboe); Rose Fishbein (Flute)

Program Note: "This entire organization and production, consisting mainly of the original cast who appeared at the Lyric Theatre Hammersmith, London, when this opera was revived by Mr. Nigel Playfair on May 12, 1920, have been brought to this country by Mr. Duff direct from England for this tour."
(Sylvia Nelis was the only "original cast member")

> "In this version of Mr. Gay's famous English Ballad Opera every possible effort has been made to recapture the spirit of the original work, much of which was 'improved away' in the representations of the early nineteenth century. Unfortunately in an age which lacks the leisure of the eighteenth century the opera cannot be given in its entirety; in the work of curtailment and selection, the producer has been much helped by Mr. Arnold Bennett."

Touring Company, season 1928-29
The London Company production of John Gay's comic opera; New settings of the Airs and Additional Music by Frederic Austin; By arrangement with the Lyric Theatre

Hammersmith, London, on the Bicentennial Tour of America; Produced by J. C. Duff; Costumes, C. Lovat Fraser; Production director, Alfred Heather; General manager, H. M. McFadden

Clive Carey (Macheath); Sylvia Nelis (Polly Peachum); Charles MacGrath (Peachum); Norman Williams (Lockit); Beatrice Morson (Lucy Lockit); Alfred Heather (Filch); Lena Maitland (Mrs. Peachum); Audrey Mildmay (Jenny Diver); Helen Arden (Diana Trapes/Mrs. Coaxer); Kathleen Ogilvie (Dolly Trull); Mae Marvis (Mrs. Vixen); Ruth Whisman (Betty Doxy); George Gregson (Drawer/The Beggar); Eugenia Andrus (Mrs. Slammekin); Zaidee White (Molly Brazen); Jean Sands (Sukey Tawdry); Ernest Cole (Ben Budge); Charles Ross (Crook'd-Finger Jack); Robert Sterling (Jemmy Twitcher); Thomas Mengert (Robin of Bagshot); Maurice Genest (Nimming Ned); James Dale (Matt o' the Mint); Orchestra; Carl Bengston (Harpsichord); Betty Gould (First Violin); Esther Steinberg (First Violin); F. May Taylor (Viola); Sadie Tilkin (Violincello); Irene Scott (Double Bass); Joseph Moreno (Oboe); Rose Fishbein (Flute)

Lyric Theatre Hammersmith, London, opened March 11, 1929 38 performances
Produced and Directed by Nigel Playfair; A Comic Opera by John Gay; Music by Frederic Austin; Production designer Claude Lovat Fraser; Scenery, Victor Hembrow; Costumes, Charles Wilson & Company, Mrs. C. L. Fraser; Choreography, Marian Wilson; Conductor, Alfred Reynolds; General manager, A. P. Horne; Stage managers, A. E. Filmer and Eric Bloom

Frederick Ranalow (Macheath); Scott Russell (Peachum); Rose Hignell (Polly Peachum); Arnold Pilbeam (The Beggar); Leslie Howard (Filch); Colin Cooper (Lockit); Violet Marquesita (Lucy Lockit); Vera Robson (Jenny Diver); Elsie French (Mrs. Peachum); Dewey Gibson (Matt o' the Mint); Harry Hilliard (Turnkey); Mary Ogden (Diana Trapes); Ella Milne (Mrs. Coaxer); Cavan O'Connor, Geoffrey Dunn, Haigh Jackson, John Anthony (Macheath's Gang); Molly Iverson, Betty Baxendale, Margaret Elwes, Yootha Rose, Jane Connard, Arabella Tulloch (Women of the Town)

DIE DREIGROSCHENOPER, *Schiffbaurdamm Theatre*, Berlin, opened August 28, 1928 600 performances
Produced by Ernst-Josef Aufricht; A Musical Play; Director, Erich Engel; Music by Kurt Weill; Libretto by Bertolt Brecht; Settings, Caspar Neher; Production manager, Henrich Fischer

Harald Paulsen (Mackie); Roma Bahn (replaced Carola Neher) (Polly); Erich Ponto (Peachum); Rosa Valletti (Mrs. Peachum); Kurt Gerron (Tiger Brown/ Street Singer); Lotte Lenya (Jenny)

THE THREEPENNY OPERA, *Empire Theatre*, New York, opened April 1, 1933 12 performances
Produced by Jerrold Krimsky and Gifford Cochran; A Musical Play, adapted into English by Gifford Cochran and Jerrold Krimsky from *Die Dreigroschenoper* by Bertolt Brecht, based on John Gay's *The Beggar's Opera*; Music by Kurt Weill; Director, Francesco von Mendelssohn; Settings by Cleon Throckmorton after designs by Caspar Neher; Musical director, Macklin Morrow; Costumes, Brooks Costume Company; Stage manager, J. Edward Shugrue

Robert Chisholm (Captain Macheath); Steffi Duna (Polly Peachum); Rex Weber (Jonathan Peachum); Evelyn Beresford (Mrs. Peachum); Marjorie

Dille (Jenny Diver); George Heller (Legend Singer); Burgess Meredith (Crook'd-Finger Jack); Herbert Rudley (Filch); Rex Evans (Sheriff Brown); Josephine Huston (Lucy Brown); Anthony Blair (Matthew); Harry Bellaver (Walter); George Heller (Robert); Francis Kennelly (Jimmy); H. L. Donsu (Wing); John Connolly (Reverend Kimball); Mary Heberden (Vixen); Eugenie Reed (Trull); Lotta Burnell (Madame); Hilda Kosta (Tawd); Ruth Thomas (Dolly); Lilian Okun (Betty); Jean De Koven (Molly Brazen); Harry Hornick (Beggar); Gerald Hamer (Police Inspector Smith); Arthur Brady, Clyde Turner, Larry Larkin, James Harvey (Constables); Tom Morgan, Harold Imber, Gus Alexander, Thomas Murphy, Richard Bengali, Morton Ullman, Louis Halprin, Jack Carstairs, Geraldine Lusby, Lillian Ardell, Barbara Winchester, Ellen Love, Corinne Anderson (Beggars)

MUSICAL NUMBERS: "The Legend of Mackie Messer"; "Wedding Song"; "The Pirate Jenny"; "The Soldier's Song"; "Love Duet"; "First Finale"; "Farewell Song"; "Tango Ballad"; "Lucy Song"; "Ballad of the Easy Life"; "Jealousy Duet"; "Second Finale"; "Song of the Aimlessness of Life"; "Cry From the Dungeon"; "Third Finale-Testament"

Haymarket Theatre, London, opened March 5, 1940

A Musical version of John Gay's Comic Opera by Frederic Austin; Director, John Gielgud

Michael Redgrave (Macheath); Roy Henderson (Peachum); Audrey Mildmay (succeeded by Irene Eisinger) (Polly Peachum); Constance Willis (Mrs. Peachum); Joseph Farrington (Lockit); Linda Gray (Lucy Lockit); Frank Napier (The Beggar); Noel Willman (The Player); Bruce Flegg (Filch); Ruby Gilchrist (Jenny Diver); Maldwyn Thomas (Matt o' the Mint); Alys Brough (Diana Trapes)

Bucks County Playhouse, New Hope, Penn., Opened August 11, 1941

Produced by Kenyon Nicholson and Theron Bamberger; Lehman Engel's production of John Gay's comic opera; Music by Frederic Austin; Staging, choreography and musical direction by Lehman Engel; Settings, Howard Bay

Walter Cassel (Macheath); Jane Pickens (Polly Peachum); Richard Hale (Mr. Peachum); Edith King (Mrs. Peachum); Robert Challener (Filch); Wallace Acton (Lockit); Shirley Brown (Lucy Lockit); Otto Hulett (Matt o' the Mint); Carmen Gagliardi (Crook'd-Finger Jack); Samuel Liff (Ben Budge); Zonia Porter (Jenny Diver); Emily Buckeley (Mrs. Coaxer); Inez Harris (Dolly Trull); Vivian Bloch (Betty Doxey); David Weiss (Harry Paddington); Mitchell Agruss (Nimming Ned); Steve Brody (Wat Dreary); John Harrold (Drawer); Curt Conway (Beggar); James Gregory (Player); Garry Davis (Jemmy Twitcher); Bernice Sherman (Mrs. Vixen); Eleanor Knapp (Molly Brazen); Dorothy Johnson (Mrs. Diana Trapes); John Harrold (Jailor); Ruth Fremont (Sukey Tawdry); Robert Shaw (Robin of Bagshot); Josephine Silver (Mrs. Slammekin); Mitchell Agruss (Harper); Garry Davis, Samuel Liff (Constables); Carmen Gagliardi (Turnkey); Julia Huffman, Margaret Wallace, Vivian Bloch, Eleanor Knapp (Women); Everett Roudebush (Accompanist)

NOTE: Plans to open this production on Broadway in the fall of 1941 never materialized.

BEGGAR'S HOLIDAY, *Broadway Theatre*, New York, opened December 26, 1946

111 performances

Produced by Perry Watkins and John R. Sheppard, Jr; A musical comedy based on

The Beggar's Opera by John Gay; Director, Nicholas Ray (succeeded John Houseman and George Abbott); Book and Lyrics by John Latouche; Music by Duke Ellington; Settings, Oliver Smith; Supervision and lighting, Peggy Clark; Choreography, Valerie Bettis; Costumes, Walter Florell; Musical director, Max Meth; Orchestrations supvervised by Billy Strayhorn; General manager, Leo Rose; Stage manager, Frank Coletti; Original title *Twilight Alley*

Alfred Drake (The Beggar); Bernice Parks (replaced Libby Holman) (Jenny); Zero Mostel (Hamilton Peachum); Avon Long (Careless Love); Jet MacDonald (Polly Peachum); Dorothy Johnson (Mrs. Peachum); Lewis Charles (The Knife); Alfred Drake (Macheath); Lavina Nielson (Dolly Trull); Leone Hall (succeeded by Margaret Wilson) (Betty Doxy); Herbert Ross (Bartender); Rollin Smith (Chief Lockit); Mildred Smith (Lucy Lockit); Pan Theodore (Blenkinsop); Tommy Gomez (The Pursued/The Other Eye); Nini Korda (Minute Lou); Marjorie Bell (The Lookout/The Girl); Paul Godkin (The Boy/Wire Boy); Bill Dillard (The Horn); Enid Williams (Flora, The Harpy); Elmire Jones-Bey (Bessie Buns); Malka Farber (Trixy Turner); Marie Bryant (The Cocoa Girl); Tommie Moore (Tawdry Audrey); Jack Bittner (Highbinder); Stanley Carlson (Fingersmith); Gordon Nelson (O'Heister/Customer/Black Marketeer); Archie Savage (Cop/Gunsel); Albert Popwell (Plainclothesman/Slam); Herbert Ross, Lucas Hoving (Policemen); Doris Goodwin (Mrs. Trapes); Royce Wallace (Annie Coaxer); Claire Hale (Baby Mildred); Perry Bruskin (The Drunk); Lucas Hoving (Strip); Perry Bruskin (Mooch); Pan Theodore (The Eye); Douglas Henderson (The Caser); Hy Anzel (Customer)

MUSICAL NUMBERS: "The Chase"; "When You Go Down by Miss Jenny's"; "I've Got Me"; "TNT"; "Take Love Easy"; "I Wanna Be Bad"; "When I Walk With You"; "Wedding Ballet"; "The Scrimmage of Life"; "Ore From a Gold Mine"; "Tooth and Claw"; "Maybe I Should Change My Ways"; "The Wrong Side of the Railroad Tracks"; "Tomorrow Mountain"; "Chorus of Citizens"; "Girls Want a Hero"; "Lullaby for Junior"; "Quarrel for Three"; "Folde-rol-rol"; "Women, Women, Women"; "The Hunted"; "Brown Penny" (Lyrics based on a poem by W. B. Yeats)

BEGGAR'S HOLIDAY, *Shubert Theatre*, Chicago, opened April 5, 1947
Produced by Perry Watkins and John R. Sheppard, Jr.; A Musical Comedy based on *The Beggar's Opera* by John Gay; Director, Nicholas Ray; Book and Lyrics by John Latouche; Music by Duke Ellington; Settings, Oliver Smith; Technical supervision and Lighting, Peggy Clark; Choreography, Valerie Bettis; Orchestrations, Billy Strayhorn; Costumes, Walter Florell

Alfred Drake (Macheath/The Beggar); Jet MacDonald (Polly Peachum); Claudia (Miss Jenny); Zero Mostel (Hamilton Peachum); Dorothy Johnson (Mrs. Peachum); Rollin Smith (Police Chief Lockit); Mildred Smith (Lucy Lockit); Bill Dillard (The Horn); Russell Ford (Highbinder); Gordon Nelson (O'Heister); Paul Godkin (Wire Boy/Dancer); Dorothy Etheridge (The Lookout/Dancer); Archie Savage (Gunsel/Cop); Stanley Carlson (Fingersmith/Miss Jenny's Bartender); Raymond Dorian (Strip/ Policeman); Perry Bruskin (Mooch/Drunk); Tommy Gomez (The Other Eye/The Pursued); Albert Popwell (Slam/ Plainclothesman); Douglas Henderson (The Caser); Lewis Charles (The Knife); Edmund J. Howland (Policeman); Marie Bryant (The Cocoa Girl); Nina Franklin (Dolly Trull); Margaret Wilson (Betty Doxey); Jean Dwyer (Mrs. Trapes); Claire Hale (Annie Coaxer); Roxy Foster (Baby Mildred); Rita Morrow (Minute Lou); Malka Forbes (Trixy Turner); Royce

Wallace (Bessie Buns); Enid Williams (Flora, the Harpy)

THE BEGGAR'S OPERA, Sadler's Wells Theatre, London, opened September 6, 1948
A Comic Opera by John Gay; Director, Tyrone Guthrie; Music by Benjamin Britten from original airs

Peter Pears (Captain Macheath); George James (Mr. Peachum); Nancy Evans (Polly Peachum); Flora Nielsen (Mrs. Peachum); Otakar Kraus (Lockit); Rose Hill (Lucy Lockit); Norman Platt (Filch/Jemmy Twitcher); Jennifer Vyvyan (Jenny Diver); Norman Lumsden (Matt of the Mint); Catherine Lawson (Mrs. Coaxer); Mildred Watson (Betty Doxy); Lesley Duff (Mrs. Vixen); Elisabeth Parry (Mrs. Slammekin); Anne Sharp (Molly Brazen); Lily Kettlewell (Suky Tawdry) Roy Ashton (Harry Paddington); Denis Dowling (Ben Budge); Gladys Parr (Beggar/Mrs. Diana Trapes/Dolly Trull); John Highcock (Wat Dreary/Drawer); Max Worthley (Jailer/Nimming Ned)

Lyric Theatre Hammersmith, London, opened July 17, 1950
A Comic Opera by John Gay; Directors, Tyrone Guthrie and Basil Coleman; Music by Benjamin Britten

Bruce Boyce (Captain Macheath); David Franklin (Peachum); Esther Salaman (Mrs. Peachum); Nancy Evans (Polly Peachum); Otakar Kraus (Lockit); Rose Hill (Lucy Lockit); Max Worthley (Filch/Numming Ned); John Highcock (Jemmy Twitcher); Mary Grimmett (Jenny Diver); Norman Lumsden (Matt o' the Mint); Esther Darlington (Mrs. Coaxer); Mildred Watson (Betty Doxy); Lilly Kettlewell (Dolly Trull); Lesley Duff (Mrs. Vixen); Anne Sharp (Molly Brazen); Cecilia Cardoza (Suky Tawdry); Andrew Gold (Harry Paddington/Jailer); Geoffrey Connor (Ben Budge); Gladys Parr (Beggar/ Mrs. Trapes); George Prangnell (Wat Dreary/The Drawer)

THE THREEPENNY OPERA, Theatre De Lys, New York, opened March 10 through May 30, 1954 95 performances
Produced by Carmen Capalbo and Stanley Chase; Director, Carmen Capalbo; English adaptation of John Gay's *The Beggar's Opera*, and lyrics by Marc Blitzstein; Music by Kurt Weill; Original text by Bertolt Brecht; Settings, William Pitkin; Lighting, Peggy Clark; Costumes by Bolasni; Musical director, Samuel Matlowsky; Original orchestrations by Kurt Weill; General manager, Zelda Dorfman; Stage managers, Gene Perlowin, Charles Bellin

Scott Merrill (Macheath--Mack the Knife); Jo Sullivan (succeeded by Gerrianne Raphael) (Polly Peachum); Lotte Lenya (Jenny); Charlotte Rae (succeeded by Mildred Cook) (Mrs. Peachum); Leon Lishner (succeeded by Martin Wolfson) (Mr. J. J. Peachum); Gerald Price (Street Singer); Joseph Berud (Crook'd-Finger Jake); George Tyne (Tiger Brown); Beatrice Arthur (Lucy Brown); John Astin (Readymoney Matt); Bernard Bogin (Bob the Saw); William Duell (Filch); Paul Dooley (Walt Dreary); Donald Elson (Reverend Kimball); Marcella Markham (Betty); Marion Selee (Molly); Gerrianne Raphael (Dolly); Gloria Sokol (Coaxer); Chuck Smith (Smith); William Duell (Messenger); Stan Schneider, Miles Dickson (Constables)

Theatre De Lys, New York, reopened September 20, 1955 2,611 performances
Produced by Carmen Capalbo and Stanley Chase in association with Lucille Lortel; Director, Carmen Capalbo; English adaptation of John Gay's *The Beggar's Opera*,

and lyrics by Marc Blitzstein; Music by Kurt Weill; Original text by Bertolt Brecht; Settings, William Pitkin; Lighting, Peggy Clark; Costumes supervised by William Pitkin; Original orchestrations by Kurt Weill; Musical director, Kelly Wyatt; General manager, Zelda Dorfman; Stage managers, Herbert DuFine and Rome Smith

(During the extensive engagement of *The Threepenny Opera*, there were many cast changes. Performers of the various roles are listed below:

Macheath--Mack the Knife: Scott Merrill; James Mitchell; Gerald Price; Jerry Orbach; Charles Rydell

Polly Peachum: Jo Sullivan; Jo Wilder; Judith Paige; Paula Stewart; Cynthia Price; Gail Johnston; Elizabeth Hubbard; Cherry Davis

Jenny: Lotte Lenya; Grete Mosheim; Katharine Sergave; Christine Felsmann; Marion Brash

Mrs. Peachum: Jane Connell; Nina Dova; Jenny Lou Law; Madeline Lee; Rosemary O'Reilly; Annette Warren; Lu Leonard; Jo Hurt

Mr. J. J. Peachum: Frederic Downs; Edward Asner; Leon Janney; Emile Renan; Mitchell Jason

Street Singer: Tige Andrews; Jerry Orbach; Mordechai Sheinkman; Len Ross; Chuck Smith

Crook'd-Finger Jake: Eddie Lawrence; Sidney Kay; Maurice Shrog

Tiger Brown: Richard Verney; Angus Cairns; Ronald Weyand; Noam Pitlik; Alfred Spindelman

Lucy Brown: Beatrice Arthur; Jean Arnold; Ann Mitchell; Mary Louise Wilson; Nadyne Turney

Readymoney Matt: John Astin; Mitchell Lear; Stan Schneider; Mal Throne

Bob the Saw: Bernie Fein; Mitchell Lear; Gerald Austin; Bob Darnell; Joseph Masolo; Brendan Fay

Filch: William Duell

Wat Dreary: Joseph Elic; Gordon Matthews; Pierre Epstein; Tony Ballen; Noam Pitlik; Stephen Pearlman

Reverend Kimball: Carroll Saint; Alfred Russell; Mitchell Jason; Alan Haller; Arnold Kelly; Charles Gilbert

Betty: Joan Coburn; Barbara Sohmers; Joanne Spiller; Barbara Louis; Mary Harmon

Molly: Marion Selee

Dolly: Irene Kane; Elizabeth Perry; Judith Paige; Cynthia Price; Nona Chandler; Gail Lucas; Sherry Lambert

Coaxer: Bea Barrett; Betinna Barret; Gianna Rossilli; Estelle Parsons; Wesley Marie Tackitt

Smith: Rome Smith; Stefan Gierasch; Pierre Epstein; Hank Andrews; Noam Pitlik; William Crossett; Robert Fass

Messenger: William Duell

Constables: Albert Valentine; Steve Palmer; Len Ross; Louis Lippa; Jerry Orbach; Pierre Epstein; Noam Pitlik; Ken Chapin; Pete Martine; Rome Smith; Sim Landres; Arnold Kelley

MUSICAL NUMBERS: "Ballad of Mack the Knife"; "Morning Anthem"; "Instead-Of-Song"; "The Bide-a-Wee in Soho"; "Wedding Song"; "Army Song"; "Love Song"; "Ballad of Dependency"; "The World Is Mean"; "Polly's Song"; "Pirate Jenny"; "Tango-Ballad"; "Ballad of The Easy Life"; "BarbaraSong"; "Jealousy Duet"; "How to

Survive"; "Useless Song"; "Solomon Song"; Call From the Grave"; "Death Message"; "The Mounted Messenger"

Original cast recording: MGM Records

Scenes from the Theatre de Lys production were televised on NBC's *Wide Wide World* program on March 16, 1958.

THE BEGGAR'S OPERA, *Sadler's Wells Theatre*, London, opened October 4, 1954
Produced by the Sadler's Wells Company; A Comic Opera by John Gay; Director, Michael Langham

James Johnston (Macheath); Norman Lumsden (Mr. Peachum); Valetta Iacopi (Mrs. Peachum); Marjorie Thomas (Polly); John Ford (Filch); Otakar Kraus (Lockit); Rose Hill (Lucy Lockit); Norma Morgan (Jenny Diver); Frank Tickle (The Beggar); Trevor Anthony (Matt o' the Mint); Frederick Westcott (Harry Paddington); Roger Stalman (Wat Dreary); Lloyd Strauss-Smith (Nimming Ned); Maurice Wearmouth (Crook'd-Finger Jack); David Oddie (Jemmy Twitcher); Gladys Parr (Mrs. Trapes); Mildred Watson (Mrs. Vixen); Betty Sagon (Sukey Tawdry); Catherine Lawson (Mrs. Coaxer); Johanna Paterson (Mrs. Slammekin); Ann Dowdall (Molly Brazen); Vivetta Hendriks (Betty Doxy); Claire Duchesneau (Mrs. Flimzy); Ronald Maconaghie (Ben Budge); Walter Hudd (Theatre Manager); Nora Ogonovsky (Dolly Trull)

THE THREEPENNY OPERA, *Royal Court Theatre*, London, opened February 9, 1956 140 performances
A Musical Play; Director, Sam Wanamaker; Based on John Gay's comic opera, *The Beggar's Opera*; Book by Bertolt Brecht; Music by Kurt Weill; English adaptation by Marc Blitzstein; Production designer, Casper Neher

Bill Owen (Macheath); Daphne Anderson (Polly Peachum); Eric Pohlmann (Mr. J. L. Peachum); Lisa Lee (Mrs. Peachum); Victor Baring (Filch); Warren Mitchell (Crook'd-Finger Jake); Charles Hill (Wat Dreary); Geroge A. Cooper (Tiger Brown); Maria Remusat (Jenny Diver); Georgia Brown (Lucy Lockit); Renee Goddard (Mrs. Coaxer); Aliki Hansen (Betty Doxy); Patricia Black (Molly); Sylva Langova (Dolly Trull); George Murcell (Readymoney Matt); George Tovey (Bob the Slasher); Charles Stanley (Smith); Ewan MacColl (Street Singer); Una Victor (Street Urchin); Roland Randel (Reverend Kimball); Michael Murray, John Crobett (Constables)

THE BEGGAR'S OPERA, *City Center Theatre*, New York, opened March 13, 1957 15 performances
Produced by The New York City Center Light Opera Company, Jean Dalrymple, director; A musical comedy based on John Gay's play. Adaptation and direction by Richard Baldridge; Music adapted and arranged by Daniel Pinkham; Setting, Watson Barratt; Costumes, Robert Fletcher; Lighting, Jean Rosenthal; Musical staging by John Heawood; Musical director, Miles Morgan; Entire production supervised by Burt Shevelove as originally produced at the Cambridge (Mass.) Drama Festival; General manager, Buford Armitage; Stage managers, Bernard Pollock, John Maxtone-Graham and Jack Emrek

Jack Cassidy (Macheath); Shirley Jones (Polly Peachum); Constance Brigham (Jenny Diver); George S. Irving (Mr. Peachum); Zamah Cunningham (Mrs. Peachum); Peter Turgeon (Beggar Poet); Charles

Bolender (Filch); George Gaynes (Mr. Lockit); Jeanne Beauvais (Lucy Lockit); Paula Laurence (Mrs. Coaxer); William Inglis (Tom Tizzle); Jack De Lon (Slippery Sam); David Nillo (Bob Booty); J. C. McCord (Nimming Ned); Maurice Edwards (Crook'd-Finger Jack); Francis Barnard (Wat Dreary); Hal England (Jemmy Twitcher); Robert Burr (Matt o' the Mint); Maria Karnilova (Dolly Trull); Charlotte Rae (Molly Brazen); Shirley Chester (Sukey Tawdry); Jenny Lou Law (Betty Doxy); Anita Cooper (Mrs. Vixen); Adnia Rice (Mrs. Slammekin); William Ashley, Hal Barnet, George Broadhurst, Willie Cooper, Joan DuBrow, Jack Emrek, James Karr, Sara Meade, Louis Saporito, Lee Warren, Hurd Wiese (Prisoners, Guards and other Ladies of the Town); Louis Algarra, Jennie Andrea, Evelyn Aring, Robert Atherton, Nicola Barbusci, Don Becker, June Bucknor, Julia Gerace, Peter Held, Maurice Kostroff, Mary Lesawyer, Maria Martell, John Person, Thomas Powell, Robert Ruddy, Mary Thompson, Mara Yavne (Chorus of Prisoners)

MUSICAL NUMBERS: "Let Us Take the Road"; "My Heart Was Free"; "Were I Laid on Greenland Coast"; "Virgins Are Like the Fair Flowers"; "Our Polly Is a Sad Slut"; "The Turtle Thus With Plaintive Crying"; "'Tis Woman That Seduces All Mankind"; "Through All the Employments of Life"; "Hanging Is My Only Sport"; "O, What a Pain It Is to Part"; "No Power on Earth Can Ever Divide"; "Man May Escape From Rope and Gun"; "Why How Now Madam Flirt"; "Is Then His Fate Decreed, Sir?"; "Fill Every Glass"; "The Ways of the World"; "If the Heart of a Man"; "Youth's a Season Made for Joys"; "When Young at the Bar"; "In the Days of My Youth"; "At the Tree I Shall Suffer With Pleasure"; "I'm Like a Skiff on the Ocean Toss'd"; "Come, Sweet Lass"; "The Charge Was Prepar'd"; "Would I Might Be Hanged"; "Since Laws Were Made for Every Degree"; "See the Conquering Hero"

NOTE: Shirley Jones and Jack Cassidy had performed *The Beggar's Opera* on July 25, 1956, at Boston's Cambridge Drama Festival.

THE BEGGAR'S OPERA, *Festival Theatre*, Stratford, Ontario, season 1958-59
Produced by the Stratford Festival of Canada; A Comic Opera by John Gay, arranged by Frederic Austin; Director, Tom Brown; Production Designer, Brian Jackson; Orchestra Conductor, Louis Applebaum

Robert Goulet (Macheath); Chester Watson (Mr. Peachum); Maxine Miller (Polly Peachum); Ann Casson (Mrs. Peachum/Mrs. Vixen); William Cole (Filch); Ernest Adams (Nimming Ned/Constable); Robert Christie (Mr. Lockit); Marie Gauley (Lucy Lockit); Alan Crofoot (Matt o' the Mint/Constable); Brendon Dillon (Beggar/Robin of Bagshot/ Turnkey); Igors Gavon (Ben Budge); Mary Savidge (Mrs. Coaxer); Jacqueline Smith (Dolly Trull); Sylvia Grant (Jenny Diver); Helen Burns (Diana Trapes/Molly Brazen); Norman Welsh (Player/Jemmy Twitcher/Turnkey)

THE THREEPENNY OPERA, *Marines Theatre*, San Francisco, opened September 13, 1960
Produced by the Actor's Workshop, by arrangement with Carmen Capalbo and Stanley Chase; A Comic Opera by Bertolt Brecht based on John Gay's *The Beggar's Opera*; English adaptation by Marc Blitzstein; Director, Carmen Capalbo; Music by Kurt Weill; Scenery, Costumes and Lighting by William Pitkin; Musical director, Samuel Matlovsky

Scott Merrill (Macheath); Anna Sten (Jenny Diver); Frederick Downs (Peachum); Jo Wilder (Polly Peachum); Estelle Parsons (Mrs. Peachum);

Robert Bell (Filch); Tige Andrews (Streetsinger); Grace Lee Whitney (Lucy Brown); Richard Verney (Tiger Brown); Len Lesser (Readymoney Matt); Phil Arnold (Crook'd-Finger Jack); Gail Lucas (Dolly Trull); Chris Paoti (Bob the Saw); Josip Elic (Wat Dreary); Donald Elsen (Reverend Kimball); Hal Jon Norman (Warden Smith); Helen Goodman (Molly); Gloria Victor (Mrs. Coaxer); Curt Matson, Mike Foran (Constables); Wesley Marie Tackitt (Betty Doxy)

BIG DEAL, *Playwrights' Theatre*, Chicago, opened August 16, 1961
Produced by Bernard Sahlins, Paul Sills and David Shepherd; A Musical Comedy-Drama, based on John Gay's *The Beggar's Opera*; Written and directed by Paul Sills; Music by William Mathieu; Lyrics by David Shepherd; Settings, Stanley Kadailis; Lighting, Sheldon Patinkin and Del Close

Alan Arkin (William Macheath); Dolores Alton (Polly Peachum); Win Stracks (Jonathan Jeremiah Peachum); Mary Brady (Mrs. Peachum); Ann Raim (Jenny Diver); Caty Cook (Lucy Brown); Stephen Pearlman (Jacob Maro); Bob Coughlan (George Filch); Del Close (Avery Welch); Richard Schaal (Benjamin Frank); Mona Burr (Clea Mae Hilton); Avery Schreiber (Max Gruber); Floyd Mutrux (Exio); George Poulas (Bartender); Jeri Jensen (Stevie Garret); Tom Erhart (Lieutenant Thomas Brown); Charles Lewsen (Sergeant John Marjoriebanks); Jerry Cunliffe (Sergeant Silinski); Anthony Gronner (Reporter)

THE THREEPENNY OPERA, *Royal Alexandra Theatre*, Toronto, opened September 19 through 30, 1961
Produced by Carmen Capalbo, Stanley Chase and Lucille Lortel; English adaptation by Marc Blitzstein of John Gay's *The Beggar's Opera*; Director, Carmen Capalbo; Music by Kurt Weill; Original text by Bertolt Brecht; Settings, William Pitkin; Lighting, Peggy Clark; Musical director, Samuel Matlovsky; Original orchestrations by Kurt Weill; Associate producers, Herbert R. Steinmann and George M. Peters; General manager, Harold Kusell; Stage managers, Hugh Lester and Don Sheffey

Scott Merrill (Macheath); Gypsy Rose Lee (Jenny); Didi Van Eyck (Polly Peachum); Jane Connell (Mrs. Peachum); Mitchell Jason (Mr. Peachum); Martyn Greene (Crook'd-Finger Jack); Henry Howard (Ready-money Matt); Richard Verney (Tiger Brown); Buzz Halliday (Lucy Brown); Jack Whalen (Bob the Saw); Leonard Rogel (Filch); Herbert Edelman (Wat Dreary); Everett Fisch (Reverend Kimball); Marcia Gilford (Betty Doxy); Jane Dougher (Molly Brazen); Betty Stanton (Dolly Trull); Daryl Thornton (Coaxer); G. Kennedy Osborn (Smith, Warden); Chris Ponti, Everett Fisch (Constables); Leonard Rogel (Messenger)

Billy Rose Theatre, New York, opened October 27, 1966 15 performances
Produced by Jay K. Hoffman; The Stockholm Marionette Theatre of Fantasy's production of *The Threepenny Opera*; Michael Meschke, founder and artistic director; Director, Michael Meschke; Text and lyrics by Bertolt Brecht; Music by Kurt Weill; English adaptation by Marc Blitzstein; Puppets, Masques and Settings by Franciszka Themerson; Lighting, Jules Fisher; Choreography, Holger Rosenquist; Production assistant, Agneta Pauli; Company manager, Artie Solomon

Puppet Players	*Spoken Voices*	*Role*
Per Nielsen	Goran Graffman	Macheath
Zanza Lidums	Helena Brodin	Polly Peachum
Ulf Hakan Jansson	Ingvar Kjellson	Mr. J. J. Peachum
Zanza Lidums	Ulla Sjoblom	Mrs. Peachum
Arne Hogsander	Hakan Serner	Streetsinger/Filch
Ellika Linden	Ulla Sjoblom	Jenny
Arne Hogsander	Hakan Serner	Tiger Brown
Lydia de Lind van Wijngaarden	Meta Velander	Lucy Brown

and: Jan Blomberg (Matt); Heinz Spira (Jake); Folke Trgardh (Bob); Michael Meschke (Wat)

THE BEGGAR'S OPERA, *Aldwych Theatre*, London, opened July 16, 1963
Produced by the Royal Shakespeare Company; A Comedy by John Gay; Director, Peter Wood; Decor, Sean Kenny; Costumes, Leslie Hurry; Choreography, Pauline Grant; Music by Raymond Leppard

Derek Godfrey (Macheath); Dorothy Tutin (Polly Peachum); Ronald Radd (Peachum); Doris Hare (Mrs. Peachum); Patience Collier (Diana Trapes); Malcolm Rivers (Crook'd-Finger Jack); Richard Rippon (Jemmy Twitcher); Patricia Kilgarriff (Jenny Diver); Denise Coffey (Mrs. Coaxer); Elizabeth Spriggs (Mrs. Vixen); Tony Church (Lockit); Virginia McKenna (Lucy Lockit); Ann Cooper (Betty Doxy); Gareth Morgan (Matt o' the Mint); John Harwood (Wat Dreary); John Cobner (Robin of Bagshot); Peter Bramble (Tom Tipple); Tim Bamber (Slippery Sam); Darien Angadi (Drawer); Joan Alcorn (Molly Brazen); Patricia Conolly (Dolly Trull); Mary Webster (Sukey Tawdry); Valerie Griffiths (Mrs. Slammekin); John Cobner (Jailer); Donald Bisset (Marine Officer); Donald Layne- Smith (Ben Budge); Darien Angadi (Nimming Ned); Gordon Honeycombe (Harry Paddington); Gareth Morgan (Poet); Barry Ashton, Richard Arthure, Kenneth Gardiner, Dane Howell, April Walker (Beggars and Guards)

THE THREEPENNY OPERA, *Old Vic Theatre*, London, opened August 11, 1965
Production of The Berliner Ensemble Theatre; A Musical Play based on John Gay's *The Beggar's Opera*; Director, Erich Engel; Book by Bertolt Brecht; Music by Kurt Weill; Production designer, Karl von Appen

Wolf Kaiser (Macheath); Peter Kalisch (Jonathan Peachum); Carola Braunboch (Celia Peachum); Christine Gloger (Polly Peachum); Siegfried Kilian (Tiger Brown); Annemone Haase (Lucy Brown); Felicitas Ritsch (Ginny Jenny); Peter Beske (Filch); Martin Florchinger (Money-Matthew); Erhard Koster (Hookfinger-Jacob); Hermann Hiesgen (Saw-Robert); Stefan Lisewski (Lightfinger Ede); Hans-Georg Voigt (Weeping Willow Walter); Erich Haubmann (Beggar); Gunter Naumann (Ballad Singer); Werner Dissel (Jimmy; Dieter Knaup (Executioner); Agnes Kraus (Vixen); Angelica Domrose (Betty); Gisela May (Dolly); Ruth Berghaus (Molly); Renate Richter (Kitty); Herbert Manz (Smith); Wolfgang Lohse (The Reverend Kimball); Manfred Wagner (Policeman); Siegfried Weib (Aristocrat); Manfred Karge, Mattias Langhoff, Klaus Tilsner, Gunter Voigt (Policemen); Bruno Carstens (General)

THE BEGGAR'S OPERA, *Apollo Theatre*, London, opened September 12, 1968
Produced by Richard Pilbrow and Harold Prince, in association with Prospect

productions; A Comic Opera by John Gay, edited by David Turner; Director, Toby Robertson; Music orchestrated by Pearce Higgins; Production designer, Voytels; Lighting, Toby Corbett; Costumes, Nadine Baylis; Musical Director, Neil Rhoden

Peter Gilmore (Captain Macheath); James Cossins (Mr. Peachum); Hy Hazell (Mrs. Peachum); Jan Waters (Polly Peachum); John Cater (Mr. Lockit); Frances Cuka (Lucy Lockit); Angela Richards (Jenny Diver); Peter Kenton (Filch); Richard Durden (Beggar); David Calder (Matt o' the Mint); Tony Robinson (Nimming Ned); Gordon Reid (Ben Budge); Peter Forest (Crook'd-Finger Jack); Kenneth Shanley (Wat Dreary); Carol Gillies (Mrs. Coaxer); Patricia Fuller (Dolly Trull); Jessie Barcley (Mrs. Vixen); Pamela Miles (Mrs. Slammekin); Suzanne Heath (Sukey Tawdry); Vivian Brooks (Molly Brazen); Margaret Blay (Betty Doxy); Hy Hazell (Mrs. Trapes); Peter Forest (Turnkey); Colin Prockter, Allan Tennock (Constables); Adama Deane (Jemmy Twitcher)

THE THREEPENNY OPERA, *Prince of Wales Theatre*, London, opened February 10, 1972

Produced by Michael White; A Musical Play; Director, Tony Richardson; Based on John Gay's *The Beggar's Opera* and Bertolt Brecht's *Die Dreigroschenoper*, English translation by Hugh McDiarmid; Book by Bertolt Brecht; Music by Kurt Weill; Production designer, Patrick Robertson; Lighting, Richard Pilbrow; Costumes, Rosemary Vercoe; Choreography, Eleanor Fazan

Joe Melia (Macheath); Vanessa Redgrave (Polly Peachum); Ronald Radd (Mr. Peachum); Hermione Baddeley (Mrs. Peachum); Henry Woolf (Filch); Lon Satton (Narrator); Dan Meaden (Tiger Brown); Barbara Windsor (Lucy Brown); Victor Maddern (Matt); John Hartley (Bob); Declan Mulholland (Wat Dreary); Derry Power (Father Kimble); Annie Ross (Jenny Diver); Patricia Quinn (Dolly Trull); Diana Quick (Betty Doxy); Stella Courtney (Mrs. Coaxer); Miriam Margolyes (Nelly); Kevin Flood (Smith); Arthur Mullard (Jake); John Cording, David WeldonWilliams (Constables); Bill Bailey, Tom Bentley-Fisher, Timothy Davies, Christopher Taynton (Beggars)

THE BEGGAR'S OPERA, *Chichester (Eng.) Festival Theatre*, opened May 3, 1972

Produced by the Chichester Festival Theatre; An Opera by John Gay with music arranged by Martin Best; Director, Robin Phillips; Decor, Daphne Dare; Choreography, Sheila O'Neill; Stage managers, Christine Roberts, Bill Capel, Jenny Courtenay-Dunn and Anthony Morris

John Neville (Macheath); Millicent Martin (Polly Peachum); Harold Innocent (Mr. Peachum); Maggie Fitzgibbon (Mrs. Peachum); Angela Richards (Lucy Lockit); Jonathan Elson (Filch); Sarah Atkinson (Jenny Diver); June Jago (Sukey Straddle); Michael Aldridge (Mr. Lockit); Brian Poyser (Matt o' the Mint); Richard Cornish (Ben Budge); David Grayson (Jemmy Twitcher); Richard Dennis (Crook'd Finger Jake); Charles Dance (Wat Dreary); Christopher Molly (Robin of Bagshot); David Robb (Nimming Ned); John Rogan (Harry Paddington); Kenneth McClellan (Tom Tipple); Laurie Webb (Slippery Sam); Ian Milton (Drawer); Josephine Gordon (Mrs. Coaxer); Myvanwy Jenn (Dolly Trull); Nelda Quilliam (Betty Doxy); Pamela Manson (Mrs. Vixen); Maggie Fitzgibbon (Mrs. Slammekin); Olwen Hughes (Sukey Tawdry); Valerie Minifie (Mollie Brazen); John Rogan (Jailer); Charles Dance (Hangman); David Robb (Servant); Robert Selbie (Constables); Laurie Webb (Beggar)

THE THREEPENNY OPERA, *Avon Stage*, Stratford, Ontario, opened June 30, 1972
Produced by the Stratford Festival, Ontario, Canada; A Musical Play, adapted from John Gay's *The Beggar's Opera*; Director, Jean Gascon; Book by Bertolt Brecht; Music by Kurt Weill; English adaptation by Marc Blitzstein; Decor, Robert Prevost; Lighting, Gil Wechsler; Musical director, Alan Laing

Anton Rodgers (Macheath); Monique Leyrac (Polly); Jack Creley (Mr. Peachum); Lila Kedrova (Mrs. Peachum); Robin Marshall (Filch); Denise Ferguson (Jenny); Jeff Jones (Crook'd-Finger Jake); J. Kenneth Campbell (Street Singer/Money Matthew); Kenneth Wickes (Wat Dreary); Lewis Gordon (Bob the Saw); Bernard Engel (Reverend Kimball/Smith); Henry Ramer (Tiger Brown); Anni Lee Taylor (Betty); Anne Linden (Dolly); Elsie Sawchuk (Molly); Iris MacGregor (Coaxer); Marilyn Gardner (Lucy); Michael Fletcher, Errol Slue (Constables); Leo Burns, Vincent Cole, Eric Hutt, Stephen Nesrallah, Tim Whelan (Beggars)

THE BEGGAR'S OPERA, Brooklyn Academy of Music, New York, opened March 21, 1972 28 performances; reopened *McAlpin Rooftop Theatre*, May 30, 1972
Produced by the Chelsea Theatre Center of Brooklyn; Michael David, artistic director; John Gay's classic, musical score newly realized by Ryan Edwards; Director, Gene Lesser; Settings, Robert U. Taylor; Lighting, William Mintzer; Costumes, Carrie F. Robbins; Dances, Elizabeth Keen; Musical director, Roland Gagnon; Production manager, Burl Hash; Technical director, Neil Bleifeld; Stage managers, James Doolan and David Elyah

Stephen D. Newman (succeeded by Peter Lombard, Timothy Jerome) (Macheath); Kathleen Widdoes (succeeded by Leila Martin) (Polly Peachum); Gordon Connell (succeeded by Rex Robbins) (Mr. Peachum); Tanny McDonald (succeeded by Irene Frances Kling) (Jenny); Jeanne Arnold (succeeded by Charlotte Jones, Mary Louise Wilson) (Mrs. Peachum); John Long (Filch); William Newman (succeeded by Steven Gelfer) (Matt o' the Mint); Neil Hunt (Crook'd-Finger Jack); Joseph Palmieri (succeeded by Roy Brocksmith) (The Beggar/Jimmy Twitcher); Connie Van Ess (Diana Trapes); Lynn Ann Leveridge (succeeded by Carol Hanzel) (Mrs. Coaxer); Reid Shelton (succeeded by Howard Ross, Ralston Hill) (Lockit); Marilyn Sokol (succeeded by June Helmers) (Lucy Lockit); Joan Nelson (succeeded by Jill Eikenberry) (Dolly Trull); Irene Frances Kling (succeeded by Deborah Deeble) (Suky Tawdry); Roy Brocksmith (Ben Budge)

Billy Rose Theatre, New York, opened December 22, 1973 limited 8 performance engagement
Produced by the City Center Acting Company, John Houseman, Artistic Director; John Gay's classic; Director, Gene Lesser; Settings, Robert Yodice; Lighting, Martin Aronstein; Costumes, Carrie F. Robbins; Dances arranged by Elizabeth Keen; Musical direction and arrangements by Roland Gagnon; Stage managers, Peter B. Mumford, Robert Buckler and John Michalski

Kevin Kline (Macheath); Cynthia Herman (Polly Peachum); Mary-Joan Negro (Jenny Diver); David Ogden Stiers (Peachum); Mary Lou Rosato (Mrs. Peachum); Norman Snow (Filch); Sam Tsoutsouvas (Lockit); Patti Lupone (Lucy Lockit); Jared Sakren (Crook'd Finger Jack); Richard Ooms (Matt o' the Mint); Benjamin Hendrickson (Beggar); Joel Colodner (Harry Paddington); Gerald Shaw (Nimming Ned); Nita Angeletti (Mrs. Trapes);

David Schramm (Wat Dreary); Leah Chandler (Dolly Trull); Gisela Caldwell (Sukey Tawdry); Mary Lou Rosato (Betty Doxy); Peter Dvorsky (Jimmy Twitcher)

THE THREEPENNY OPERA, *Williamstown (Mass.) Theatre Festival*, opened July 30 through August 3, 1974
Produced by the Williamstown Theatre Festival, Nikos Psacharopoulos, artistic director; English translation of Bertolt Brecht's *Die Dreigroschenoper* by Marc Blitzstein; Music by Kurt Weill; Director, Peter Hunt; Scenery and costumes, John Conklin; Lighting, Richard Devin; Musical director, Herbert Kaplan; Stage manager, Franklin Keysar

Raul Julia (Mack the Knife); JoBeth Williams (Polly Peachum); Virginia Vestoff (Jenny Diver); Louis Beachner (Jonathan Peachum); Peggy Pope (Mrs. Peachum); David Ford (Tiger Brown); Donna McKechnie (Lucy Brown); Stuart Ross (Crook'd-Finger Jake); Purcell McKamey (Bob-the-Saw); David Ackroyd (Ready-Money Matt); John Basil (Walt Dreary); Austin Pendleton (Ballad Singer); Emerry Battis (Reverend Mr. Kimball); Peggy O'Neill (Betty); Deborah Boily (Dolly); Barbette Tweed (Molly); Carolyn Descoteaux (Coaxer); Gary Lahti, David Pilot (Cops)

THE THREEPENNY OPERA, *Vivian Beaumont Theatre*, opened May 1, 1976
Produced by the New York Shakespeare Festival, Joseph Papp, Producer; Associate producer, Bernard Gersten; English translation of Bertolt Brecht's *Die Dreigroschenoper* by Ralph Manheim and John Willett; Music by Kurt Weill; Director, Richard Foreman; Setting, Douglas W. Schmidt; Lighting, Pat Collins; Scenery, Santo Loquasto; Costumes, Theoni V. Aldredge; Musical director, Stanley Silverman; Stage managers, D. W. Koehler, Michael Chamers and Frank DiFilia

Raul Julia (Mack the Knife); Caroline Kava (Polly Peachum); Ellen Greene (Jenny Towler); C. K. Alexander (Jonathan Peachum); Elizabeth Wilson (Mrs. Peachum); David Sabin (Tiger Brown); Blair Brown (Lucy Brown); William Duell (Crook'd-Finger Jake); K. C. Wilson (Bob-the-Saw); Max Gulack (Wat Dreary); Ralph Drischell (Ready-Money Matt); Rik Colitti (Ned); Robert Schlee (Jimmy); Roy Brock-smith (Ballad Singer); John Ridge (Reverend Mr. Kimball); Glenn Kezer (Smith); Alison Mills (Whore/Ballad Singer); Tony Azito (Samuel); Ed Zang (Charles Filch); Penelope Brown, Nancy Campbell, Gretel Cummings, Brenda Currin, Mimi Turque (Whores); Pendleton Brown, M. Patrick Hughes, George McGrath, Rick Petrucelli, John Ridge, Craig Rupp, Armin Shimerman, Jack Eric Williams, Ray Xito (Beggars and Policemen)

Original cast recording: Columbia Records

Delacorte Theatre, New York, opened July 6 to July 24, 1977 27 performances
Produced by the New York Shakespeare Festival, Joseph Papp, producer; Associate producer, Bernard Gersten; English translation of Bertolt Brecht's *Die Dreigroschenoper* by Ralph Manheim and John Willett; Music by Kurt Weill; Director, Richard Foreman; Setting, Douglas W. Schmidt; Lighting, Pat Collins; Scenery, Santo Loquasato; Costumes, Theoni V. Aldredge; Musical director, Stanley Silverman; General manager, Robert Kamlot; Technical director, Darrell Ziegler; Production supervisor, Jason Steven Cohen

Philip Bosco (Mack the Knife); Caroline Kava (Polly Peachum); Ellen Green (Jenny Towler); Jerome Dempsey (Jonathan Peachum); Gretel Cummings

(Mrs. Peachum); William Duell (Jake); Ed Zang (Charles Filch); David Sabin (Tiger Brown); Penelope Bodry (Lucy Brown); Roy Brocksmith (Ballad Singer); Ralph Drischell (Matt); K. C. Wilson (Bob); Paul Ukens, Jr. (Ned); Tony Azito (Samuel); Robert Schlee (Jimmy); John Ridge (Wat Dreary); Marc Jordan (Smith); Jack Eric Williams (Messenger); Barbara Andres, Nancy Campbell, Alexandra Ivanoff, Lisa Kirchner, Mimi Turque (Whores); Pendleton Brown, Peter Iacangelo, George McGrath, Art Ostrin, Rick Petrucelli, Craig Rupp, Armin Shimerman, Jack Eric Williams, Ray Xito (Beggars and Policemen)

THE THREEPENNY OPERA, *Globe Theatre*, Regina, Saskatchewan, Canada, opened April 15, 1977
A Musical Play by Bertolt Brecht based on John Gay's *The Beggar's Opera*; Director, Kenneth Kramer; Translation by John Willet and Ralph Manheim; Music by Kurt Weill; Costumes, Marian Buller; Stage manager, Charles Harper

Stanley Coles (Macheath); Stephen Walsh (Mr. Peachum); Rita Deverll (Mrs. Peachum); Anne Wright (Polly Peachum); Kim McCaw (Filch); Jacqueline McLeod (Jenny Diver); Robert Clinton (Street Singer); David Miller (Tiger Brown); Trudy Cameron (Lucy Brown); James Brewer (Matthew); Bill Hugli (Jake); Jonathan Harrison (Wat Dreary); Gabriel Prendergast (Robert); Kyra Harper, Linda Huffman, Frances Kotowich, Carl Ann Reid, Janet Blancher (Whores); Charles Harper, Thomas McCarthy, Stan McGaffin (Beggars); Kim McCaw (Reverend Kimball); Jonathan Harrison (Smith); Sheila Ottenbreit (Pianist); Jonathan Harrison (Musical Saw, Harmonica)

THE THREEPENNY OPERA, *Citizen's Theatre*, Glasgow, Scotland, opened September 29, 1978
A Musical Play by Bertolt Brecht based on John Gay's *The Beggar's Opera*; Director, and Production Designer, Philip Prowse; Lighting, Gerry Jenkinson; Musical director, David Cann

Patrick Hannaway (Macheath); Ciaran Hinds (J. J. Peachum); Judy Lloyd (Polly Peachum); Fidelis Morgan (Mrs. Peachum); Peter Jonfield (Tiger Brown); Angela Chadfield (Lucy Lockit); Sian Thomas (Jenny Diver); Robert Gwilym (Walt Dreary); John Breck (Matt); Daniel Webb (Crook'd-Finger Jake); Christopher Jagger (Mouth); David Gann (Moss Fingers)

Stanford (Conn.) Repertory Theatre, opened January 28, 1978
Produced by the Stanford Repertory Theatre; A Comic Opera by John Gay; Director, John Wright; Setting, Dwight Richard Odle; Lighting, Paul Landry; Costumes, Carolyn Parker; Technical direction, Larry Davidson; Makeup consultant, Barbara Hiken; Music research by Wye Jamison; Music arrangements by Isiah Jackson; Stage managers, Albert L. Gibson and Katherine Robertson

Paul E. Richards (Macheath); Paul E. Winfield (Peachum); Jane Hoffman (Mrs. Peachum); Carol Androsky (Polly Peachum); Ruth Hunt (Lucy Lockit); Jerome Raphel (Lockit); Glenn Cannon (Filch); Jennifer Haefele (Jenny Diver); Ann Heller (Mrs. Coaxer); Barbara Richards (Diana Trapes); Stephen D. Newman (Matt o' the Mint); Joseph G. Medalis (Ben Budge); Carrillo Gantner (Jemmy Twitcher); Sergei Tschernisch (Crook'd-Finger Jack); Steven Polinsky (Wat Dreary); Randolph McKee (Robin of Bagshot); Norbert Davidson (Nimming Ned); Joel Lawrence (Henry Paddington); Charles Edelman (Drawer); Sheldon Feldner (Beggar); Ruth Henderson (Betty Doxy);

Pat Berthrong (Mrs. Vixen); Ruth Silviera (Sukey Tawdry); Ellen Perry (Molly Brazen); Sally Kemp (Dolly Trull); Lucille Medalis (Mrs. Slammekin); Holly Worthen (Holly Trollop); Chuck Hogan (Turnkey); Joel Lawrence, Jon Hardy, Dustin, W. Holmquist (Constables); Susan Baker, Dale Hopkins, Deborah Pauly, Cecile Raphel (Wives)

THE BEGGAR'S SOAP OPERA, *Duo Theatre*, New York, opened July 5, 1979
Produced by the Duo Theatre Spanish-English Ensemble Theatre; A Musical satire based on John Gay's *The Beggar's Opera*; Director, Manuel Martin Jr.; Book and Lyrics by Rolores Prida; Music by Paul Radelate; Music director, Tania Leon; Choreography, Rosemary Rios, Daria Atandian; Settings, Diego Vallejo; Lighting, Jenny Ball; Costumes, Bud Santora; Stage manager, Robert Morgen

Dionis Enrique (Maki Navaja); Brenda Feliciano (Jenny Dive); Juan Manuel Aquero (Juan Ramon Pichon); Cynthia Lopez (Maria Josefa Pichon); Sandra Nieves (Poll Pichon); Henry Ravelo (Papo); Miquel Sierra (Pipo); Richard Adan (Pepe); Armando Rivas (Tiger Bravo); Jeannie Kauffman (Fifi); Paula Denise Martinez (Chichi); Miquel Sierra (Prison Guard); Brunilda Colon (Receptionist); Armando Rives (Felipe Filcho); Henry Ravelo (Mr. Bemba); Miquel Sierra (Mr. Pluma); Richard Adan (Mr. Buche); Brunilda Colon (Mimi); Juan Manuel Aguero (Reverend Euallo Perez); Brunilda Colon, Paula Denise Martinez (Western Union Messengers)

Cottesloe Theatre, London, opened July 1, 1982
A National Theatre Production; A Satirical Musical by John Gay; Director, Richard Eyre; Production designer, John Gunter; Lighting, Peter Radmore; Music adapted by Dominic Muldowney; Dances by David Toguri

Paul Jones (Macheath); Belinda Sinclair (Polly Peachum); Harry Towb (Peachum); June Watson (Mrs. Peachum); Kevin Williams (Filch); David Ryall (Lockit); Imelda Staunton (Lucy Lockit); Fiona Hendley (Jenny Diver); Richard Walsh (Matt o' the Mint); Norman Warwick (Crook'd-Finger Jack); Irlin Hall (Mrs. Trapes); Sally Cooper (Sukey Tawdry); Gail Rolfe (Mrs. Coaxer); Kevin Quarmby (Nimming Ned); June Watson (Mrs. Slammekin); William Armstrong (Beggar); Kevin Williams (Pickpocket/Wat Dreary); Paul Jones (Pimp); Larrington Walker (Ben Budge); Imelda Staunton (Molly Brazen); Vincent Pickering (Harry Paddington/Drawer); Norman Warwick, Kevin Quarmby (Gentlemen); David Ryall (Fence); Harry Towb (Irish Cockney Sneak Thief); Rachel Izen (Mrs. Vixen); Belinda Sinclair (Dolly Trull); Kevin Quarmby (Gaoler); William Armstrong (Jemmy Twitcher); Musicians: Rory Allam (clarinet); Robn Jeffrey (guitar/mandolin); Tim Laycock (concertina); Roderick Skeaping (violin)

THE LITTLE THREEPENNY CAFE, *Olio Theatre*, Los Angeles, opened October 17, 1984
Produced by the Los Angeles Arts Repertory Theatre; A Musical Play, conceived and directed by Louis Fantasia; Music and Lyrics by Bertolt Brecht, Kurt Weill, Hans Eisler, Paul Dessaru; Production designer, Philip J. Cizewski; Costumes, Doug Spessert; Choreography, Louise Kawabata; Musical director, Norman Bergen

Joe Spano (The Streetsinger/Bertolt Brecht); Louis R. Plante (The Owner); Marilyn Child (The Owner's Wife); Donald Craig (Man at Table); Melissa Converse (Woman at Table); Rick Lieberman (The Waiter); Susie G. Dixon (The Waitress)

MUSICAL NUMBERS: "Ballad of Mack the Knife"; "Tango Ballade"; "Pirate Jenny"; "Ballad of the Easy Life"; "Threepenny Finale"; "The Bilbao Song"; "Surabaya Johnny"; "Nanna's Song"; "The Alabama Song"; "The Barbara Song"; "Song of Supply and Demand"; "Ballad of Marie Sanders"; "Song of the German Mother"; "Song of Moldau"; "Change the World"; "To Those Not Yet Born"; "Easter Sunday 1938"; "Sprinkling the Garden"; "Mask of Evil"; "Friedenlieder"; "I Came to the Cities"; "The Benares Song"; "Mother Courage Song"; "Remembering Marie A"; "Praise Ye the Night"

THE THREEPENNY OPERA, *Olivier Theatre*, London, opened March 13, 1986
Produced by The National Theatre; English translation of Bertolt Brecht's *Die Dreigroschenoper* by Robert David MacDonald; Music by Kurt Weill; Director, Peter Wood; Production designer, Timothy O'Brien; Lighting by Robert Bryan; Choreography, David Toguri; Musical direction, Dominic Muldowney

Basil Henson (Narrator); Tim Curry (Macheath, a.k.a. Mack the Knife); Sally Dexter (Polly Peachum); Stephen Moore (Jonathan Jeremiah Peachum); Sara Kestelman (Celia Peachum); Neil Daglish (Filch); Barry James (The Ballad Singer/ Matt o' the Mint); Michael Bryant (Crook'd Finger Jake); Paul Stewart (Bob the Saw); Eve Adam (Jenny); Barry James (Ballad Singer); Steven Law (Ned the Finger); Martin Howells (Jimmy the Second); Basil Henson (Weeping Willow Water); Alan Haywood (Reverend Kimball/Constable); Saul Reichlin (Angry Beggar); Niall Buggy (Tiger Brown); Roz Clifton (Dolly); Judith Coke (Vixen); Joanna Foster (Lucy); Paul Stewart (Smith); Peter Gordon (Execution Constable); Edna Dore (Betty)

THE BEGGAR'S OPERA; OR, PEACHUM'S POORHOUSE, *Royal Lyceum Theatre*, Edinburgh, Scotland, opened April 18, 1986
Produced by the Royal Lyceum/Wildcat Stage; A Satirical Musical by David MacLennan, based on John Gay's comic opera; Director, Ian Wooldridge; Music and Lyrics by David McNiven; Production designer, Colin McNeil; Lighting, Martin Palmer; Musical director, David McNiven; Sound, John A. Harper

Martin Black (Macheath); Gerry Mulgrew (Peachum); Andrea Miller (Mrs. Peachum); Maggie Ryder (Polly Peachum); Greig Alexander (Filch); Steven Wren (Lockit); Lesley Robertson (Jenny Diver); Rab Handleigh (Lieutenant Mat); Mike Travis (Sergeant Budge); Catherine Ann Jack (Betty Doxy); Andy Munroj (Robin of Bagshot); Stewart Hanratty (Wat Dreary); Neil Hay (Jemmy Twitcher); Steve Kettley (Harry Paddington); Blythe Duff (Lucy Lockit); Gordon Dougall (Corporal Ned)

L'OPERA DE QUAT'SOUS (THE THREEPENNY OPERA), *Chatelet Theatre*, Paris, opened November 10, 1986
Produced and Directed by Giorgio Strehler; An Opera by Bertolt Brecht based on *The Beggar's Opera* by John Gay; Music by Kurt Weill; Settings, Ezio Frigerio and Franca Squarciapino; Musical director, Peter Fischer; Assistant conductor, Nicolas Kemmer

Michael Heltau (replaced Michel Piccoli) (Mackie); Barbara Sukowa (replaced Nastassja Kinski) (Polly Peachum); Annick Cisaruk (Lucy Lockit); Milva (Jenny)

THE THREEPENNY OPERA, *Lunt-Fontanne Theatre*, New York opened November 5, 1989 (World premiere: *National Theater*, Washington, September 14, 1989) 65 performances

Produced by Jerome Hellman in association with Haryki Kadokawa and James M. Nederlander; A Musical in three acts; Director, John Dexter; Book and lyrics by Bertolt Brecht, translated by Michael Feingold; Music by Kurt Weill; Musical staging, Peter Gennaro; Scenery and costumes, Jocelyn Herbert; Lighting, Andy Phillips and Brian Nason; Musical director, Julius Rudel; Associate producers, Margo Lion, Hiroshi Sugawara and Lloyd Phillips, Kiki Miyake; Production stage manager, Bob Borod

Sting (Macheath); Maureen McGovern (Polly Peachum)*; Georgia Brown (Mrs. Peachum); Alvin Epstein (Jonathan Peachum); Suzzanne Douglas (Jenny Diver); Kim Criswell (Lucy); Ethyl Eichelberger (Ballad Singer); Jeff Blumenkrantz (Filch); Josh Mostel (Matt of the Mint); Mitchell Greenberg (Crook'd-Finger Jack); David Schechter (Sawtooth Bob); Philip Carroll (Ed); Tom Robbins (Wat Dreary); Alex Santoriello (Jimmy); Steven Major West (Beggar); Larry Marshall (Police Chief); Anne Kerry Ford (Dolly); Jan Horvath (Betty); Teresa De Zarn (Vixen); Nancy Ringham (Molly); K. T. Sullivan (Suky Tawdry); Fiddle Viracola (Old Whore); David Pursley (Police Constable Smith); Macintyre Dixon, Michael Pointek (Policemen); Kim Criswell (Lucy Brown); Philip Carroll, MacIntyre Dixon, Michael Pointek, David Schechter, Steven Major West (Beggars and Bystanders)

MUSICAL NUMBERS: "Overture"; "Ballad of Mack the Knife"; "Peachum's Morning Hymn"; "Why-They-Can't Song"; "Wedding Song"; "Pirate Jenny"; "Soldier's Song"; "Love Song"; "Barbara's Song"; First 3 Penny Finale; "Melodrama and Polly's Song"; "Ballad of the Prisoner of Sex"; "Pimp's Ballad (Tango)"; "Ballad of Living in Style"; "Jealousy Duet"; Second 3 Penny Finale; "Ballad of the Prisoner of Sex" (Reprise); "Song of Futility"; "Lucy's Aria"; "Solomon Song"; "Call From the Grave"; "Epitaph"; "March to the Gallows"; Third 3 Penny Finale

* Due to illness following the Washington premiere, Maureen McGovern left the show for several weeks and Nancy Ringham played Polly Peachum on Broadway on opening night, and Lesley Castay played Molly.

THE THREEPENNY OPERA, *Williamstown (Mass.) Theatre* Festival, opened June 2 through July 5, 1992

Produced by the Williamstown Theatre Festival, Peter Hunt, artistic director; A Musical in three acts; Director, Peter Hunt; Book and lyrics by Bertolt Brecht, English adaptation by Marc Blitzstein; Music by Kurt Weill; Choreography, Ann Reinking; Sets, John Conklin; Lighting, Peter Hunt; Costumes, Merrily Murray-Walsh; Musical director, Christopher Drobny; Musical supervision, Arthur B. Rubinstein; Stage manager, Roy Backes

Clifford David (Macheath); Stephanie Zimbalist (Polly Peachum); Molly Regan (Mrs. Peachum); Rex Robbins (Mr. J.J. Peachum); Betty Buckley (Jenny Diver); Linda Purl (Lucy Brown); Laurent Giroux (Ballad Singer); Ralph Williams (Filch); Tom Tammi (Ready-Money Matt); Danny Parker (Crook-Finger Jake); Lee Clew (Bob the Saw); Jeffrey Shore (Wat Dreary); Graham Leach-Krouse (The Kid); Don Perkins (Reverend Kimball); Conrad L. Osborne (Tiger Brown); Bob Mirrsey (Smith); Allegra di Carpegna (Dolly); Isabel Rose (Betty); Patricia Jones (Molly); Arija Bareikis (Coaxer); James Ryan, Jason Dittmer (Constables); Grayson McCouch (Beggar); Diana Gardner, Liz Mamana, Cynthia Newman, Emile Schreiner, Darlene Bel Grayson, Sarah Anderson, Barbara Collins, Jennifer Fox, Merry Grisson, Kate Guillory, Karen Lee, Tertia Lynch, Angelina Orlandi, Emily Weiner,

David Ari, Gene Barry, Anthony Beasley, Jason Bohner, Tom Caruso, Blake Ferger, Larry Filas, Joe Lucas, David Simonds, David Strauss, Scott Thomson (Beggars and Bystanders)

SCREEN

DIE DREIGROSCHENOPER (*THE THREEPENNY OPERA*), *Tobis-Klangfilm/ Nero Film (Berlin) Warner Bros.-First National Pictures release*, released May 1931
Produced by Seymour Nebenzal; Director, G. W. Pabst; Screenplay by Bela Balasz, Leo Lania, Ladislaus Vajda, based on the musical play by Bertolt Brecht, inspired by John Gay's *The Beggar's Opera*; Photography, Fritz Arno Wagner; Art director, Andrei Andreiev; Music by Kurt Weill; Orchestrations, Theo Mackeben; Sound recording, Adolf Jensen; Editor, Hans Oser

Rudolf Forster (Mackie Messer); Carola Neher (Polly Peachum); Reinhold Schunzel (Tiger Brown); Fritz Rasp (Peachum); Valeska Gert (Mrs. Peachum); Vladimir Sokoloff (Prison Warder Smith); Ernst Busch (Street Singer); Lotte Lenya (Jenny); Hermann Thimig (Priest); Paul Kemp, Gustav Puttjer, Oska Hocker, Kraft Raschig (Mackie's Gang); Herbert Grunbaum (Filch)

NOTE: Reissued in 1960 in a reedited version assembled by Thomas Brandon (Brandon Films). Edited by James Townsend with revised musical score by Henry Schuman

French Version: *L'OPERA DE QUAT'SOUS* (*THE THREEPENNY OPERA*), *Societe des Films Sonores Tobis (Paris)*, released 1930
Screenplay, Solange Bussi, Andre Mauprey and Ninon Steinhoff; Editor, Henri Rust

Albert Prejean (Mackie Messer); Odette Florelle (Polly Peachum); Jacques Henley (Tiger Brown); Gaston Modot (Peachum); Jane Marken (Mrs. Peachum); Vladimir Sokoloff (Prison Warder Smith); Bill Bocketts (Street Singer); Margo Lion (Jenny); Antonin Artaud (Apprentice Beggar); Hermann Thimig (Priest); Arthur Duarte, Marcel Merminod, Pierre Leaud, Albert Broquin (Mackie's Gang); Marie-Antoine Buzet, Prejeane (Women)

THE BEGGAR'S OPERA, *British Lion Films*, released June 1953
Imperadio Pictures Ltd.; Produced by Laurence Olivier and Herbert Wilcox; Director, Peter Brook; Screenplay by Denis Cannan adapted from the comic opera by John Gay; Additional dialogue and Lyrics by Christopher Fry; Photography, Guy Green; Technicolor consultant, John Bridge; Art director, William C. Andrews; Opera sets and Costumes, George Wakhevitch; Wardrobe supervison, Maude Churchill; Special effects, Wally Veevers and George Samuels; Set decorator, Leonard Townsend; Music arranged and conducted by Sir Arthur Bliss; Score conducted by Muir Mathieson; Sound recording, Peter Handford, Red Law; Dance arrangements, Frank Staff; Editor, Reginald Beck

Laurence Olivier (Captain Macheath); Stanley Holloway (Lockit); Mary Clare (Mrs. Peachum); George Devine (Peachum); Dorothy Tutin (Polly Peachum); Yvonne Furneaux (Jenny Diver); Athene Seyler (Mrs. Trapes); Daphne Anderson (Lucy Lockit); Margot Grahame (The Actress); Laurence Naismith (Matt of the Mint); Hugh Griffith (The Beggar); Edward Pryor (Filch); Edith Coates (Mrs. Coaxer); Sandra Dorne (Suky Tawdry); Mercy Haystead (Dolly

Trull); Patricia Raine (Mrs. Slammekin); Isabel George (Mrs. Vixen); Helen Christie (Betty Doxy); Felix Fenton (The Governor); Max Brent (A Drunkard); Eric Pohlmann (Innkeeper); Kenneth Williams (Jack, the Pot Boy); Madge Brindley (Gin Seller); George Rose (Turnkey); Stuart Burge, Cyril Conway, Gerald Lawson (Prisoners); Eileen Harvey (Young Female Traveler); Oliver Hunter, John Baker (Chairmen); Tamba Alleney (Negro Page); Terence Greenidge (Chaplain); Billy Wells (Hangman); John Kidd, H. C. Walton, Eugene Leahy, Edgar Norfolk (Turnkeys); Jocelyn Jones (Molly Brazen); Dennis Cannan (Footman)

DIE DREIGROSCHENOPER (*THE THREEPENNY OPERA*), released in Germany, February 1963 by *Gloria Films*; released in U.S. in October 1964 by *Embassy Pictures* (filmed in German, French and English)
Produced by Kurt Ulrich Film in collaboration with C.E.C., Paris; Director, Wolfgang Staudte; Screenplay, Wolfgang Staudte and Guenther Weisenborn, based on Bertolt Brecht's adaptation of John Gay's *The Beggar's Opera*; Music by Kurt Weill; English text by Marc Blitzstein; Photography, Roger Fellous; Settings and Costumes, Hein Heckroth; Music adaptation, Peter Sandloff; Music scoring, Karl Helmer, Erwin Drager; Choreography, Dick Price; Sound, Fritz Schwarz; Editor, Wolfgang Wehrun

Curt Jurgens (Mack, The Knife); June Ritchie (Polly Peachum); Hildegard Knef (Pirate Jenny); Sammy Davis, Jr. (Ballad Singer); Marlene Warrlich (Lucy Brown); Lino Ventura (Tiger Brown); Hilde Hildebrand (Mrs. Peachum); Gert Froebe (J. J. Peachum); Walter Giller (Filch); Hans W. Hanacher (Constable Smith); Adelaine Wagner (Suky Tawdry); Henning Schluter (Pastor Kimball); Hans Reiser (Tourist Guide); Siegfried Wieschnewski (Counterfeit Matthew); Walter Feuchtenberg (Hook-finger'd Jack); Stanislav Ledinek (Robert the Saw); Martin Berliner (Weeping Willow Walter); Max Strassberg (Ede); Steven Wigger (Jimmy); Robert Manuel (Executioner); Jurkin Feindt (Executioner); Erna Heffner, Clessia Wade, Jacqueline Pierreux (Whores)

Original soundtrack recording in German: London Records (Maria Korber singing the role of Polly; Konrad Wagner the role of Tiger Brown)

Original English language soundtrack recording: RCA Records (George S. Irving singing the role of Mack the Knife; Martha Schlamme the role of Jenny; Jo Wilder the role of Polly)

THE THREEPENNY OPERA,* *21st Century Films*, released October 1989
A Golan-Globus Production; Executive producers, Menachem Golan and Yoran Globus; Produced by Stanley Chase; Written and directed by Menachem Golan; Based on the play by Bertolt Brecht; Music by Kurt Weill; Photography, Elemer Ragalyi; Production design, Tivadar Bertalan; Costumes, John Bloomfeld; Music director, Dov Seltzer; Choreography, David Toguri; Sound, Cyril Collick; Editor, Alan Jakubowicz

Raul Julia (Macheath); Richard Harris (Peachum); Julia Migenes (Pirate Jenny); Roger Daltrey (Street Singer), Julie Walters (Mrs. Peachum); Rachel Robertson (Polly Peachum); Clive Revill (Money Mathew); Bill Nighy (Tiger Brown); Erin Donovan (Lucy Lockit); Julie T. Wallace (Coaxer)

* Also released as *Mack the Knife*

TELEVISION

THE BEGGAR'S OPERA, *CBS Television Workshop*, televised March 2, 1952 CBS 1 hour
Produced by Norris Houghton; Director, Richard Linkroum; A Comic Opera by John Gay
Stephen Douglass (Macheath); Doretta Morrow (Polly Peachum); with Odette Myrtil, Joseph Silver, Richard Kates, Jack Diamond, Karen Lindgren, Wyatt Cooper

THE BEGGAR'S OPERA, *NET Playhouse*, televised February 5, 1967 PBS 2 hours
Produced and Directed by Kirk Browning; A Comic Opera by John Gay; Settings, Eugene Gurlitz; Costumes, John Boxer
Kenneth Haigh (Macheath); Nancy Dussault (Polly Peachum); Howard Da Silva (Peachum); Shirl Conway (Mrs. Peachum); Barry Morse (Lockit); Linda Lavin (Lucy Lockit)

THE BEGGAR'S OPERA, televised October 10, 1983 BBC 3 hours (in the U.S. on Arts & Entertainment Channel, 1987)
A BBC/RM Arts Coproduction; Produced and directed by Jonathan Miller; A Comic Opera by John Gay; Designer, David Myerscough-Jones; Costumes, Alun Hughes; Lighting, Dennis Channon; Musical director, John Eliot Gardiner; Musical arrangements, Jeremy Barlow and John Eliot Gardiner; Choreography, Sally Gilpin; Makeup, Eileen Mair
Roger Daltrey (Macheath); Carol Hall (Polly Peachum); Stratford Johns (Peachum); Patricia Routledge (Mrs. Peachum); Peter Bayliss (Lockit); Rosemary Ashe (Lucy Lockit); Isla Blair (Jenny Diver); Paddy Navin (Suky Tawdry); Gary Tibbs (Filch); Bob Hoskins (Beggar); Gawn Grainger (Ben Budge); Anthony Pedley (Matt of the Mint); Don Estelle (Crook-finger'd Jack); Richard Stuart (Wat Dreary); Tim Brown (Robin of Bagshot); Leslie Sarony (Nimming Ned); Peter Spraggon (Harry Paddington); Derek Deadman (Drawer); Jeannie Crowther (Mrs. Coaxer); Elaine Sharling (Dolly Trull); Kay Stonham (Mrs. Vixen); Iris Saunders (Betty Doxy); Lucie Skeaping (Mrs. Slammekin); Jacqueline Davis (Molly Brazen); Gaye Brown (Mrs. Trapes); John Benfield (Gaoler); Graham Crowden (Player); The English Baroque Soloists, Elizabeth Wilcock, leader

BELLE STARR

Various interpretations of the life of Belle Starr (1848-89)

Synopsis

Belle Starr was born Myra Belle Shirley on February 5, 1848 in Carthage, Missouri. At eighteen, she gave birth to Cole Younger's illegitimate daughter, Pearl. Myra Belle later married outlaw Jim Reed of Rich Hill, Missouri, and their son Edward was born in Los Angeles. Reed and Belle, dressed in men's clothing, tortured a California prospector Watt Grayson and stole over $30,000 in gold coins. Reed was later shot and killed by Deputy Sheriff John T. Morris near Paris, Texas, and Belle became the lover of an Indian outlaw named Blue Duck, leaving him for Cherokee

Indian Tom Starr's son, Sam, whom she married in 1876 and named their home "Younger's Bend." Belle and Sam Starr became the most notorious leaders of a band of horse and cattle thieves in the country. In 1882, Belle and Sam received a sentence of six months in jail for horse stealing from Fort Smith, Arkansas, Judge Isaac Parker. Sam Starr was killed in December 1886 by an Indian policeman, Frank West, and Belle took Jim Reed's cousin, John Middleton, for her lover. He too was soon killed. Belle's daughter, Pearl, became a noted prostitute, especially for the outlaw Dalton brothers, and son Ed Reed was sent to prison in Columbus, Ohio, for bootlegging. Belle, supposedly, married a Creek Indian, Jim July, who was wanted by the authorities. She was shot by E. A. Watson, rumored to be a former lover (or some sources say her eighteen-year-old son), in Eufalla, Oklahoma, on February 3, 1889, and died in the arms of her daughter, Pearl. Rumors also were rife that Jim July paid $200 for Belle's murder; he was shot to death in 1891 by Deputy J. R. Hutchins. Over her mother's grave, daughter Pearl erected a monument inscribed with a poem, the last lines reading: "Tis but the casket that lies here. The gem that fills it sparkles yet."

Comment and Critique

"The gem that fills it sparks yet" was accurately described by Jay Robert Nash in his definitive encyclopedia of American criminals, *Bloodletters and Badmen*: "Belle was a cheap, free-living horse-thief with the morals of an alley cat." Like Jesse James, Billy the Kid and other infamous outlaws, dime novels, the press and, especially, Hollywood have glamorized their lives in crazily romanticized fiction that rivals the tales of the Brothers Grimm. In keeping with the public concept of Belle, several beautiful actresses have portrayed her on stage, screen and television: Betty Grable, Gene Tierney, Ruth Roman (daughter Pearl), Jane Russell and Elizabeth Montgomery. Actually, 5'1" Belle Starr was anything but beautiful. Her sharp, masculine features were accentuated by thin lips, black beady eyes, large ears and, below her rounded, men's hat, a shock of black hair slicked down over the forehead above the right eye.

On April 1, 1969, a musical comedy called *The Piecefull Palace* opened at Glasgow, Scotland's Alhambra Theatre for a testrun of three weeks. Produced by actor Rory Calhoun, Jerry Schaefer and Clarke Reynolds, its book was written by Warren Douglas with music by Steve Allen. The preposterous musical starred Betty Grable as Belle Starr, the madam of the PieceFull Palace Saloon of Fort Baker (Las Vegas) where Sheriff J. J. Sarno invited the most infamous American outlaws under a grant of amnesty to celebrate the first anniversary of the settlement's founding in 1869. Belle finds love with Jesse James before her bawdy housesaloon is burned to the ground, which in the judgement of all should have happened to the book.

Undeterred by this Hollywoodesque nonsense, the show opened on April 30, 1969, as *Belle Starr* at London's Palace Theatre. It folded in two weeks.

John Russell Taylor (*Plays and Players*) headed his review: "A Star Without a Show...the average musical's book is something one can quite well do without anyway, but if the whole weight of the evening is to be thrown on the musical numbers, I think they have to be just a mite stronger than those devised by composer Steve Allen and choreographer Jack Card. The tunes are absolutely unmemorable...The dances involve a certain amount of careful acrobatics from the male dancers and a lot of squealing and legwaving from the girls...and then there is Betty Grable, who seems to me the only reason anybody would go and see *Belle Starr*....The lady is evidently a star, but this time there is hardly any way she can show it..." The *Daily Express* pictured Betty Grable as "a performer whose talents are best described as modest," while the *Evening Standard* deplored "her weak voice that not even the microphones could aggrandize; a timid wiggle masquerading as voluptuousness and the wholesome appeal of Miss Vanilla Ice Cream of 1936." R. A. Young (*The Financial Times*) added, "A pathetically inadequate story, unmemorable songs and dialogue so unbelievably awful that the miserable performance it gets are only what it deserves." The *Daily Mail* dismissed the fiasco as "Excruciating rubbish."

On November 2, 1975, *Jesse and the Bandit Queen*, David Freeman's two-character drama, was produced by the New York Shakespeare Festival. Freeman's fictionalized mating of Belle Starr and Jesse James recounted their exploits compiled by the *Police Gazette*. The play was set in the early 1880s in Missouri, Kansas and the Indian Territory, by which time in Western history Jesse James had been killed (April 3, 1882) and Belle was serving time in an Arkansas prison. Freeman's dramatic license was applauded by Clive Barnes (*The New York Times*): "This is unquestionably a play I would recommend -- it is most sweetly performed and it has a technical daring to it that is in itself fascinating." About playwright Freeman's text, Barnes wrote, "He has devised a quite unusual dramatic form. It is basically a dialogue between Jesse and his Belle, his sometime mistress....I really urge you to see *Jesse and the Bandit Queen* -- largely to see the most ingratiating, technical and natural acting of Pamela PaytonWright as Belle and Kevin O'Connor as Jesse..."

If the stage version of *Belle Starr* was less than believable, Hollywood had won the laurels of legend in *Belle Starr*, its glamorized screen version of the famed bandit queen's life in a highly imaginative, if entertaining, motion picture produced by 20th Century-Fox in 1941. Myra Belle Shirley, here materialized in glorious Technicolor, is a heroine of the Confederacy attended by her Mammy. Refusing to end the Civil War and uniting with former Confederacy Captain Sam Starr, li'l old innocent Belle discovers that Starr's men are not dedicated to the restoration of the South but are desperadoes! Belle joins the gang and, after arranging the captain's escape from prison, decides to surrender to federal authorities, but is killed by some poor white trash on her journey to respectability.

Lovely Gene Tierney starred in the title role with Randolph Scott as Captain Starr. "There are good, solid entertainment values in this story of a young woman who carries on the Confederate cause in Missouri following the official conclusion of the Civil War," reported the *Motion Picture Herald*. "Gene Tierney, playing the heroine, gives a performance that should do much towards raising her up among the most popular stars. Randolph Scott, as Captain Sam Starr, the leader of the guerrilla band, is convincing...The color in *Belle Starr* ranks with the best produced thus far. Many scenes have great naturalness and beauty..." *The New York Times* critic Theodore Strauss wrote: "To the panel of neurotic unreconstructed rebels spawned in the aftermath of the Civil War, Twentieth Century-Fox has added the portrait of a guntoting lady in *Belle Starr* ...And a strange melange of Technicolored fuss-and-feathers they have made of it. As has become almost habitual by now in films of post-war desperadoes, Hollywood has turned the tables on history. Instead of a female thug she turns out to be a sort of border Joan of Arc fighting bravely for the lost cause of the Confederacy...This Belle Starr was never a scourge and legend in the West. She is a cantankerous school child fighting over jacks and marbles, not life and death. When you're playing with hokum it's best not to fudge. You get caught too easily."

Henry Fonda, originally cast as Sam Starr, wisely convinced producer Darryl Zanuck to release him from *Belle Starr* and the part fell to Randolph Scott. Gene Tierney inherited the title role when Barbara Stanwyck was unavailable.

During filming, Gene Tierney suffered from a serious eye infection called angioneurotic edema which precluded her appearing before the cameras for several days. In her memoir *Self-Portrait*, written with Mickey Herskowitz in 1979, she noted, "I was not, needless to say, at the top of my form for *Belle Starr*, and the reviews reflected it. In addition to the anxiety I felt over my allergy, the role of a female outlaw was not exactly custom-made for someone recently out of a finishing school. I loved to ride, but I was no stunt lady. Still, my director, Irving Cummings, was determined that I do as much riding as possible." Her agent, Leland Hayward later dubbed her *Belle* Tierney.

Seven years later, 20th Century-Fox produced a sequel of sorts to *Belle Starr*, called, not unnaturally, *Belle Starr's Daughter*, in which Belle's daughter, known here as "Rose of Cimarron" (Ruth Roman), is converted to law and order and leaves her lover Bob Yauntis (Rod Cameron) for stalwart Marshal Tom Jackson (George Montgomery). *Motion Picture Herald* classified *Belle Starr's Daughter* as "a standard routine story...Thanks to the direction of Lesley Selander, the picture moves at a brisk clip with action stressed all the way." In between the two Fox films, Belle Starr was portrayed by Isabel Jewell in RKO's 1946 Western, *Badman's Territory*, and she repeated the role in *Belle Starr's Daughter*.

Jane Russell, who had burst upon the screen as Billy the Kid's seductive gal Rio in Howard Hughes' notorious 1943 film *The Outlaw* and had appeared as Calamity Jane in 1948 in Paramount's *The Paleface*, was cast as Belle Starr in RKO Pictures' *Montana Belle* (1952) actually filmed by Fidelity Pictures at Republic Studios in 1948. Howard Hughes, then owner of RKO, paid $600,000 for the Trucolor print of *Montana Belle* and let it sit on the shelf for four years.

Montana Belle in some quarters was called a good western "with its full share of tough excitement, to which Scott Brady and Forrest Tucker contribute handsomely...In the part of *Belle Starr*, Jane Russell gives another highly skilled performance."

The New York Times' appraisal of *Montana Belle* was that "it is the understatement of the overstated Western of the year," and about Jane Russell's Belle, "...pine for the unvarnished vehicles of William S. Hart. Miss Russell shares his jaw line but precious little else...The actress is exhausting, her singular histrionics gamut once more as the outlaw bandit, Belle Starr. Miss Russell does a nice job of warbling [but] she's beginning to look saddle sore."

Merry Anders portrayed Belle Starr in *Young Jesse James* (1960), while in *The Long Riders* (1980), which more accurately illuminated the steaming affair between Belle (Pamela Reed) and Cole Younger (David Carradine), good ol' Belle was finally exhibited for what she was: a tough prostitute.

Marie Windsor had played the part of Belle Star on the syndicated series *Stories of the Century* in 1954 and Jeanne Cooper was Belle on *The Tales of Wells Fargo* episode televised September 9, 1957, while on April 2, 1980, a CBS made-for-television movie with a decidedly feminist attitude, *Belle Starr*, starred Elizabeth Montgomery. The two-hour television movie was advertised as "The legend of outlaw Belle Starr. How she became the West's most wanted -- and most desired -- woman."

John J. O'Connor (*The New York Times)* reported: "This Belle Starr's talent for holdups in the Old West takes second place to her sexual appetites" and described Elizabeth Montgomery's portrayal of Belle as "occasionally, a touch too elegant, suggesting a Ralph Lauren mannequin in chic western duds, but Miss Montgomery makes the most of the few dramatic pressure points. And the supporting cast, most notably Cliff Potts as Cole Younger, keep the western cliches bubbling along nicely."

A more concise epitaph for Myra Belle Shirley Starr was *Photoplay*'s comment on 20th Century-Fox's 1941 *Belle Starr*: "When Hollywood is through white-washing historical characters of unsavory fame, their own mothers wouldn't know them -- or even like them."

STAGE

BELLE STARR, *Palace Theatre*, London, opened April 30, 1969 16 performances
Produced by Jerry Schafer, Rory Calhoun and Clarke Reynolds; A Musical play; Director, Jerry Schafer; Book by Warren Douglas; Music by Steve Allen; Lyrics by Steve Allen, Jerry Schafer and Warren Douglas; Musical numbers and Choreography staged by Jack Cord; Production designer, Peter Proud; Lighting, Michael Northen; Costumes by David Crowther; Musical director and Chorus master, Maurice Arnold; Musical adviser, R. V. Brand; Action coordinator, Dick Shane

> Betty Grable (Belle Starr); Ray Chiarella (Jesse James); Blayne Barrington (Billy the Kid); Valerie Walsh (Calamity Jane); Michael Hawkins (Killer Malone); Sally Mates (Lady Jane); Mostyn Evans (Sheriff J. J. Sarno); Mike Rowlett (L. D. Sloane); Thick Wilson (Ned Buntline); Terry Williams (Boliver Shagnasty); Keith Galloway (P. U. Lule); Frank Blanch (Joker); Angela Ryder (Big Buttes); Ron Eagleton (Luscious); Maggie Vickers (Flea); Tina Scott (Charity); Georgia Jee (Dumb Nora); Peter Honri (Professor); Delia Sainsbury (Rotary Rosie); Ross Petty (Skeeter); Walter Cartier (Bat); Richard Manuel (Turkey Lucas); Marc Urquhart (San Francisco Sam); John Alexander (Rowdy Joe); Malcolm Chessman (Odie Thudpucker); Debbie Roberts (replaced Yolanda Callaghan) (Lulu); Judy Clare (Juddy); Tammy Filbert (Cowboy Maggie)

MUSICAL NUMBERS: "Story Song"; "Belle"; "Happy Birthday to Vegas"; "We're Gonna Make History"; "The Gun-fighter's Ballad"; "A Lady Don't Do"; "Ladylike Lady Like Me"; "It Takes One to Know One"; "Dirty, Rotten, Vicious, Nasty Guys"; "Dance Polka"; "Gee You're Pretty"; "I'm a Lady"; "The Biggest Pair of 38's in Town"; "Never Had This Feeling Before"

NOTE: This production premiered at Alhambra Theatre, Glasgow, Scotland, on April 1, 1969, as *The Piecefull Palace*

JESSE AND THE BANDIT QUEEN, *Other Stage, Public Theatre*, New York, opened November 2, 1975 155 performances
Produced by the New York Shakespeare Festival, Joseph Papp, producer, Bernard Gersten, associate producer; A Duo-Drama by David Freeman; Director, Gordon Stewart; Setting, Richard J. Grazlano; Lighting, Arden Finger-hut; Costumes, Hilary M. Rosenfeld; Stage managers, Penny Gebhard and Miklos Horvath

> Pamela Payton-Wright (succeeded by Dixie Carter) (Belle Starr); Kevin O'Connor (succeeded by Barry Primus) (Jesse James)

Belle Starr was also included as a character in the London world premiere of Arthur Kopit's 1968 play, *INDIANS*. Belle, however, was excised from the 1969 Broadway production. Cast and credits for *INDIANS* are included here under *JESSE JAMES*.

JESSE AND THE BANDIT QUEEN, *Kingston Playhouse*, San Diego, Cal., opened June 4 through 30, 1990
Produced by the Bowery Theater; A Play by David Freeman; Director, Ollie Nash; Set, John Blunt and Ralph Elias; Lighting, Kris Sabel; Sound Lawrence Czoka

Mickey Mullany (Belle Starr); Tim Reilly (Jesse James)

SCREEN

BELLE STARR, 20th Century-Fox, released September 1941
Produced by Darryl F. Zanuck; Associate producer, Kenneth Macgowan; Director, Irving Cummings; Screenplay by Lamar Trotti, based on a story by Cameron Rogers and Niven Busch; Photography, Ernest Palmer and Ray Rennahan; Art directors, Richard Day and Nathan Juran; Set decorator, Thomas Little; Technicolor director, Natalie Kalmus; Costumes, Travis Banton and Roger Heman; Music, Alfred Newman; Sound, E. Clayton Ward; Editor, Robert Simpson

Gene Tierney (Belle Starr); Randolph Scott (Sam Starr); Dana Andrews (Maj. Thomas Crail); Sheppard Strudwick (Ed Shirley); Elizabeth Patterson (Sarah); Chill Wills (Blue Duck); Olin Howland (Jasper Tench); Louise Beavers (Mammy Lou); Joseph Sawyer (John Cole); Joseph Downing (Jim Cole); Charles Trowbridge (Colonel Bright); Paul Burns (Sergeant); Howard Hickman (Colonel Thornton); James Flavin (Sergeant); Charles Middleton (Carpetbagger); Mae Marsh (Preacher's Wife); Kermit Maynard (Union Officer); Stymie Beard (Young Jakes); Franklyn Farnum (Barfly); Cecil Weston (Mother)

BADMAN'S TERRITORY, RKO Radio Pictures, released April 1946
Produced by Nat Holt; Director, Tim Whelan; Screenplay, Jack Nettleford and Luci Ward; Additional sequences, Clarence Upton Young and Bess Taffel; Photography, Robert de Grasse; Art directors, Albert S. Agostino and Walter E. Keller; Set decorators, Darrell Silvera and James Altwies; Music, Roy Webb; Music director, C. Bakaleinikoff; Montage, Harold Palmer; Sound, Jean L. Speak, Terry Kellum; Editor, Philip Martin

Randolph Scott (Mark Rowley); Ann Richards (Henryette Alcott); George "Gabby" Hayes (Coyote Kid); Lawrence Tierney (Jesse James); Tom Tyler (Frank James); Isabel Jewell (Belle Starr); Steve Brodie (Bob Dalton); Phil Warren (Grat Dalton); William Moss (Bill Dalton); Nestor Paiva (Sam Bass); Ray Collins (Colonel Farewell); Virginia Sale (Meg); James Warren (John Rowley); Morgan Conway (Bill Hampton); John Halloran (Hank McGee); Andrew Tombes (Doc Grant); Chief Thundercloud (Chief Tahlequah); Richard Hale (Ben Wade); Harry Holman (Hodge)

BELLE STARR'S DAUGHTER, 20th Century-Fox, released November 1948
Produced by Edward L. Alperson; Associate producer, Jack Jungmeyer; Director, Lesley Selander; Screenplay by W. R. Burnett; Photography, William Sickner; Art director, Lucius Croxton; Music, Dr. Edward Kilenyi; Editor, Joseph Bernie

Ruth Roman (Rose of Cimarron); George Montgomery (Marshal Tom Jackson); Rod Cameron (Bob Yauntis); Wallace Ford (Lafe Bailey); Charles Kemper (Gaffer); Edith King (Mrs. Allen); Isabel Jewell (Belle Starr); J. Farrell MacDonald (Doc Benson); Lane Chandler (Marshal Evans); Jack Lambert (Bronc); William Phipps (Yuma); Fred Libby (Slim); Chris-Pin Martin (Spanish George); Kenneth MacDonald (Jim Davis); William Perrott (Loftus); William Ruhl (Chris); Frank Darrien (Old Man); Larry Johns (Jed Purdy); Charles Stevens (Cherokee Joe); Paul E. Burns (Clearwater Doctor); Mary Foran (Bonnie); Henry Hull (Old Marshal); Bill Kennedy (Kiowa Marshal); Harry Harvey (Drunk Citizen); John Cason (Kiowa Posseman)

MONTANA BELLE, RKO Radio Pictures, released December 1952*
A Fidelity Picture; Produced by Howard Welch; Associate producer, Robert Peters; Director, Allan Dwan; Screen-play by Horace McCoy and Norman S. Hall; Photography, Jack Marta; Art director, Frank Arrigo; Costumes, Adele Palmer; Music, Nathan Scott; Song: "The Gilded Lily" by Portia Nelson and Margaret Martinez; Editor, Arthur Roberts; Special effects, Howard and Theodore Lydecker

Jane Russell (Belle Starr); George Brent (Tom Bradfield); Scott Brady (Bob Dalton); Forrest Tucker (Mac); Andy Devine (Peter Bivins); Jack Lambert (Ringo); John Litel (Matt Towner); Roy Mallinson (Grat Dalton); Roy Barcroft (Jim Clark); Ray Teal (Emmett Dalton); Holly Bane (Ben Dalton); Eugene Roth (Marshal Ripple); Gregg Barton (Deputy Stewart); Stanley Andrews (Marshal Combs); Kenneth MacDonald (Sheriff Irving); Glenn Strange, Pierce Lyden, George Chesebro (Deputies); Ned Davenport (Bank Clerk); Rodney Bell (Hotel Clerk); Dick Elliott (Banker Jeptha Rideout); Iron Eyes Cody (Cherokee); Charles Soldani (Indian); Hank Bell (Bartender); Rex Lease (Barfly); Dennis Moore (Messenger); Franklyn Farnum (Man in Audience); Frank Ellis (Kibitzer); Paul Stader (Double for Scott Brady); Terry Wilson (Double for Forrest Tucker); Dave Sharpe (Rider for Iron Eyes Cody); Tom Steele (Rider for Stanley Andrews); Joe Yrigoyen (Double for Jack Lambert)

* Filmed in 1948 before Jane Russell starred as Calamity Jane in *The Paleface.*

TELEVISION

BELLE STARR, episode of *Stories of the Century*, syndicated 1954
Producer, Rudy Ralston

Jim Davis (Matt Clark); Mary Castle (Frankie Adams); Marie Windsor (Belle Starr)

YOU ARE THERE: THE TRIAL OF BELLE STARR, televised November 21, 1954 CBS 30 minutes
Executive producer, William Dozier; Associate producer, Leo Davis; Director, Byron Paul

BELLE STARR, episode of *The Tales Of Wells Fargo*, televised September 9, 1957 NBC 30 minutes

Jeanne Cooper (Belle Starr); George Keymas (Blue Duck); Edmund Hashim (Jim July); Harry Ivans (Conductor); Kit Carson (Haskell); Dale Robertson (Jim Hardie, Narrator)

*BELLE STARR (*aka *WAY OF THE WEST), Schlitz Playhouse of the Stars*, televised June 6, 1958 CBS Pilot 30 minutes
Producer, Frank Rosenberg; Director, David Butler; Teleplay, Edna Anhalt, William Fay

Abby Dalton (Belle Starr); John Forsythe (Dr. John Carter); Staats Cotsworth (Colonel Taylor); K. L. Smith (Slim Enfield); Sheridan Comerate (Ed Coats); Claude Akins (Gus Garner); Mona Carrole (Elaine); Ciney Gray (Doreen); Michael Landon (Don Burns); Jack Bartell (Sentry); Robert Darin (Joe); John Bryant (Harry Ryan); Malcolm Atterbury (Johnson); Maudie Prickett (Miss Piper)

BELLE STARR, televised April 2, 1980 CBS 2 hours
Produced by Hanna-Barbera Productions/Entheos Unlimited Productions; Executive

producers, Barry Krost and Joseph Barbera; Producer, Doug Chapin; Directed and photographed by John A. Alonzo; Teleplay, James Lee Barrett; Art director, Robert Kinoshita; Music, Dana Kaproff; Editor, David Garfield

Elizabeth Montgomery (Belle Starr); Cliff Potts (Cole Younger); Michael Cavanaugh (Jesse James); Jesse Vint (Bob Dalton); Alan Vint (Grat Dalton); Gary Combs (Frank James); Fred Ward (Ned Christie); Geoffrey Lewis (Reverend Weeks); Michelle Stacy (Pearl Younger); Peter Hobbs (Jenkins); Sandy McPeak (Pratt); David Knell (Ed Reed); Geno Silva (Blue Duck); Morgan Paull (Latham); Sarah Cunningham (Mrs. Chandler); Burt Edwards (Bank Manager); Stony Bower (Summerville); James Burke (Fuller); Dee Cooper (Morris); Gilbert Combs (Baggage Clerk); Kate Williams (Woman); John Edwards (Stockyard Clerk)

THE BIG KNIFE
A Drama by Clifford Odets (1948)

Synopsis

Charlie Castle, a successful movie star, is in the process of turning down a $4-million, fourteen-year contract offered by studio tycoon Marcus Hoff. Charlie not only believes he has lost his integrity by acting in run-of-the-mill movies but also wishes to return to the New York stage. In addition, his estranged wife Marion threatens to divorce him if he does sign with Hoff, who now is holding a long hushed-up secret over Charlie's head: a hit-and-run accident that the actor had had in which a child was killed and for which a friend had taken the rap and gone to prison. Out of fear, Charlie reluctantly signs the contract, then realizes he has sold his self-respect. Learning of a studio plot to murder the starlet who was in the car with him the night of the accident--to prevent her from talking, Charlie comes to a full awareness of what his "success" really means and takes drastic steps.

Comment and Critique

Clifford Odets has been hailed as "the greatest American playwright since Eugene O'Neill." When he wrote *The Big Knife* in 1948, he had just spent several years in Hollywood writing screenplays (Cary Grant's *None But the Lonely Heart*, Susan Hayward's *Deadline at Dawn*, and the Joan Crawford-John Garfield *Humoresque*) and was endeavoring to clear his name from charges made in 1947 by the House Un-American Activities Committee that he was "active in Communist work in the film colony."

His controversial, hard-hitting drama about greed and avarice in the film industry during its studio system heyday, *The Big Knife* opened on Broadway in late February 1949. Lee Strasberg directed a cast that included John Garfield, Nancy Kelly, J. Edward Bromberg and Joan McCracken--"an enthralling group of players," noted *The New York Times*' Brooks Atkinson following its premiere, "and Mr. Odets revealed some of Hollywood's most monstrous abominations...But the characters in *The Big Knife* are not worth so much of Mr. Odets' indignation on so cosmic a plane. As in a soundly motivated melodrama, they get what they deserve in the last act...[The play] seems to be a study of the immorality of success measured solely in terms of money ...For Lee Strasberg, working in a minor key, has designed a beautiful performance that has a spontaneity and tension at the same time. Although he does not force it, it is never colorless or tepid."

Howard Barnes' disappointing critique in the *New York Herald-Tribune* pointed out that "Were it not for the fact that John Garfield plays the starring role with tremendous intensity and conviction, it would be a sorry dramatic hodgepodge. The actor has never been finer...His sensitive performing does not save [the play] from tedium and confusion. The author has employed a specious premise to spring his savage indictment of filmmaking...Garfield has expended genuine artistry to little avail in *The Big Knife*." In a similar vein, Robert Garland (*Journal American*) wrote that "Everything about *The Big Knife* is superior to what *The Big Knife* is about. Neither Clifford Odets' playwriting, John Garfield's play acting nor Dwight Deere Wiman's play producing succeeds in making [it] more than showy, superficial and Holly-wooden stage stuff. I am sure that, as a reformed scenarist who has frankly acknowledged the error of his ways, Mr. Odets has given *The Big Knife* the best that remains in him...yet [his] first off-screen scripting in the eight years since *Clash By Night* lived up to its title remains an over-written, over-acted, over-produced play about nobody in particular."

Of London's initial production of *The Big Knife* (it premiered in Wimbledon at the end of November 1953 and opened on the West End on New Year's Day 1954), produced, directed by and starring American expatriate Sam Wanamaker, the London *Times* wrote, "By treating it with tragic seriousness, Mr. Odets makes the film community appear as remote and alien as though it belonged to another planet." *The Observer* felt, "All this anti-Hollywood left-wing stuff is suspect because it pours all its censure on the capitalist who provides colorful trash and none of the proletarian who revels in such wares." In the *Manchester Guardian*, there was this: "Mr. Odets is good at moral indignation. We shall be lucky if many days of the New Year produce any play half as effective."

The Big Knife never became a major stage piece after its initial (108 performance) Broadway run, and except for its 1954 West End production in 1954, it effectively vanished from the repertoire save for a brief Off Broadway revival by Peter Bogdanovich in late 1959 and another one nearly three decades after that by the Capital Repertory Company in Albany, New York. (There also was a 1987 London revival.)

Brooks Atkinson wrote of young, later-to-have-screen-fame Bogdanovich's version with John Lasell, Eve Roberts and Carroll O'Connor in the leads: "If Peter Bogdanovich had staged a tauter, brisker performance, it is possible that *The Big Knife* would not seem so overwritten...it is the sort of gaudy melodrama that needs to be hurried along before the audience starts asking questions...In this theatregoer's opinion, all the acting would improve if the pace were swifter and the tone more metallic." The *Times* critic concluded that "As a melodramatic contrivance, *The Big Knife* is generally effective in the theatre. But as an indictment of Hollywood it is shrill and excessive. Where is Mr. Odets today? In Hollywood, earning a living."

Writer James Poe's 1955 film version of *The Big Knife*, produced and directed by Robert Aldrich, starred Jack Palance, Ida Lupino, Shelley Winters and Rod Steiger at the head of a strong cast. "The legiter was something of a bore," *Variety* felt. "This is one of the more interesting new entries which, despite its phony story angles and other shortcomings, is a possible sleeper of wideawake boxoffice proportion...It's sometimes so brittle and brutal as to prove disturbing... It mirrors the ruthlessness of talent-studio relations and overall 'company town' operations...It's an anomaly, of course, that when Hollywood spoofs or exposes another industry, it is circumspect to have a titular explanation that this is not 'typical' nor is the expose or exposition as frank and forthright as is the job director-producer Robert Aldrich did on a certain phase of Hollywood."

The New York Times' Bosley Crowther less enthusiastically found that "without intending any reflection upon the people who wrote and made this film, we suggest that they are asking the audience to have sympathy for a dunce...Actually, it looks as though *The Big Knife* originally was written and aimed at an angry, vituperative incident of the personal and professional morals of Hollywood. This is the clear implication of what is presented on the screen...[Odets and Poe] were more disposed at extreme emotionalism than to actuality and good sense. They picture a group of sordid people jawing at one another violently. But their drama arrives at a defeatist climax."

Forty years after its Broadway premiere, *The Big Knife* came to television -- as a British production debuting on PBS' *American Playhouse* -- starring Peter Gallagher in the lead, Nehemiah Persoff as the studio head, expatriate American actor Stubby (*Guys and Dolls*) Kaye and an all-English cast. "Gallagher fails to make film star Charlie Castle any more a protagonist than did his predecessors, who at least gave him tension. *The Big Knife*, dated, expository and lesser Odets, plays here like community theater," felt *Daily Variety*'s "Tone." "The play's structure is old-fashioned, with its artificiality putting off any true dramatic persuasion. Awkward explanations, clumsy entrances and exits continue to plague Odets' unhappy opus."

STAGE

THE BIG KNIFE, *National Theatre*, New York, opened February 24, 1949 108 performances

Produced by Dwight Deere Wiman; A Drama by Clifford Odets; Director, Lee Strasberg; Setting, Howard Bay; Costumes, Lucille Little

John Garfield (Charlie Castle); Nancy Kelly (Marion Castle); J. Edward Bromberg (Marcus Hoff); Joan McCracken (Dixie Evans); Leona Powers (Patty Benedict); Reinhold Schnuzel (Nat Danziger); Paul McGrath (Smiley Coy); Frank Wilson (Russell); William Terry (Buddy Bliss); Mary Patton (Connie Bliss); Theodore Newton (Hank Teagle); John McKee (Dr. Frary)

Duke of York's Theatre, London, opened January 1, 1954, moved to *Westminster Theatre*, March 28 through May 1, 1954

Produced and directed by Sam Wanamaker; A Drama by Clifford Odets

Sam Wanamaker (Charlie Castle); Renee Asherson (Marion Castle); Frederick Valk (Marcus Hoff); Diane Cilento (Dixie Evans); Natalie Lynn (Patty Benedict); Meier Tzelniker (Nat Danziger); George Coulouris (Smiley Coy); John Harrison (Russell); Philip Vickers (Buddy Bliss); Heather Stannard (Connie Bliss); Joseph O'Connor (Hank Teagle); Mayne Linton (Dr. Frary)

NOTE: This production was originally staged at *Wimble-don Theatre* beginning November 30, 1953, with Stuart Nichol as Hank Teagle, Jacqueline Knott as Connie Bliss and Arthur Owen as Dr. Frary

Seven Arts Playhouse, New York, opened November 12, 1959

Produced by Peter Bogdanovich, Alfred Tataciore and Carlos Salgado, in association with Walt Framer; A Drama by Clifford Odets; Director, Peter Bogdanovich; Sets and lighting, Peter Wexler

John Lasell (Charlie Castle); Eve Roberts (Marion Castle); Carroll O'Connor (Marcus Hoff); Nancy McCarthy (Dixie Evans); Clare Justice (Patty Benedict);

Robert Davis (Nat Danziger); Ryan MacDonald (Smiley Coy); Ral Tasco (Russell); Steve Pluta (Buddy Bliss); Norma Cates (Connie Bliss); Sidney Kay (Hank Teagle); Walton Butterfield (Dr. Frary)

Walnut Street Playhouse, Philadelphia, opened January 10 through 31, 1987
Produced by the Walnut Street Theatre Company, Bernard Havard, Executive director; A Drama by Clifford Odets; Director, Malcolm Black; Sets and lighting, Paul Wonsek; Costumes, Kathleen Blake, Production manager, Ryszard Lukaszewicz; Stage manager, Frank Anzalone

Tony Musante (Charlie Castle); Deborah Strang (Marion Castle); Donald Buka (Marcus Hoff); Zita Godfrey (Dixie Evans); Tresa Hughes (Patty Benedict); Lionel Croll (Nat Danziger); Douglas Wing (Smiley Coy); Ronal Stepney (Russell); Allen Fitzpatrick (Buddy Bliss); Lisa Emery (Connie Bliss); Geddeth Smith (Hank Teagle); Carl Harms (Dr. Frary)

Albery Theatre, London, opened September 21 through October 24, 1987
Produced by Bill Kenwright; Director, Robin Lefevre; A Drama by Clifford Odets; Sets, Grant Hicks; Costumes, Tim Shortell; Lighting, Dave Horn

Martin Shaw (Charlie Castle); Gayle Hunnicutt (Marion Castle); James B. Sikking (Marcus Hoff); Georgia Allen (Dixie Evans); Delia Lindsay (Patty Benedict); David de Keyser (Nat Danziger); Brian Greene (Smiley Coy); Mark Heath (Russell); Jon Yule (Buddy Bliss); Marella Oppenheim (Connie Bliss); Ray Jewers (Hank Teagle); Donald Pelmear (Dr. Frary)

Capital Repertory Company, Market Theatre, Albany, New York, opened March 27 through May 1, 1988
Produced by Capital Repertory Company; A Drama by Clifford Odets; Director, Bruce Bouchard; Scenic design, Rick Dennis; Costumes, Lynda L. Salsbury; Lighting, Jackie Manassee; Sound, Andy Luft

Frank Muller (Charlie Castle); Nicole Orth-Pallavicini (Marion Castle); Frank Biancamano (Marcus Hoff); Carol Wade (Dixie Evans); Barbara Perry (Patty Benedict); William Newman (Nat Danziger); Burke Pearson (Smiley Coy); Hugh L. Hurd (Russell); William Leone (Buddy Bliss); Heather Rattray (Connie Bliss); James DeMarse (Hank Teagle)

SCREEN

United Artists Release, released September 1955
An Associates and Aldrich Production; Produced and directed by Robert Aldrich; Screenplay, James Poe, from the play by Clifford Odets; Photography, Ernest Laszlo; Music, Frank DeVol; Editor, Michael Luciano

Jack Palance (Charlie Castle); Ida Lupino (Marion Castle); Rod Steiger (Stanley Hoff); Miss Shelley Winters (Dixie Evans); Wendell Corey (Smiley Coy); Jean Hagen (Connie Bliss); Ilka Chase Patty Benedict); Everett Sloane (Nat Danziger); Wesley Addy (Hank Teagle); Paul Langton (Buddy Bliss); Nick Dennis (Nick); Bill Walker (Russell); Mike Winkelman (Billy Castle); Mel Wells (Bearded Man); Robert Sherman (Bongo Player); Strother Martin (Stillman); Ralph Volke (Referee); Michael Fox (Fight Announcer)

TELEVISION

American Playhouse, televised July 20, 1988 PBS 2 hours
A Coproduction of HTV Ltd. (London) and American Playhouse; Executive producer, Johnny Goodman; Produced and directed by John Jacobs; Teleplay, Kenneth Jupp, adapted from the Clifford Odets play; Designer, Douglas Thorpe; Lighting director, Wally Hazelhurst; Production manager, Douglas Thorpe; Makeup supervisor, Cherry West; Wardrobe supervisor, Gilly Brock

Peter Gallagher (Charlie Castle); Betsy Brantley (Marion Castle); Nehemiah Persoff (Marcus Hoff); Melinda McGraw (Dixie Evans); Stubby Kaye (Nat Danziger); Irene Worth (Patty Benedict); William Hootkins (Buddy Bliss); Debora Weston (Connie Bliss); Harry Ditson (Smiley Coy); Errol John (Russell); Colin Bruce (Hank Teagle)

BILLY THE KID
Various adaptations of the legend, saga and life of Billy the Kid

Synopsis

William H. Bonney was born Henry McCarty in New York City on November 23, 1859. Migrating west in 1873 with his tubercular mother, Catherine McCarty, he and his elder brother Joseph attended her wedding to William H. Antrim in Santa Fe, New Mexico. Before his twenty-first birthday, Billy had *supposedly* shot and killed twenty-one men. Documentations of the men gunned down by Billy the Kid (also known as Kid Antrim and Billy Bonney) amounted to four: Frank P. Cahill (1877), Joe Grant (1880) and, in 1881, Bob Olinger and J. W. Bell. Before Billy's twenty-second birthday, he himself was shot dead.

The Lincoln County (New Mexico) range war pitting L.G. Murphy and J.J. Dolan against neighboring ranchers Alexander McSween and Englishman John Tunstall, who were supported by cattle baron and trailblazer, John Chisum, led to the Kid's eventual downfall. Billy accepted employment on the Rio Feliz ranch of friendly John Tunstall who was killed by Jesse Evans and Billy Morton of the Murphy-Dolan posse on February 18, 1878. Billy (reportedly) killed eighteen members of the gang responsible for Tunstall's murder, including Sheriff Brady and deputy George Hindman, heads of the posse.

The raging Lincoln County War prompted President Rutherford B. Hayes to appoint General Lew Wallace (author of *Ben-Hur*) as Governor of New Mexico. Wallace promised Billy amnesty if he testified against J.J. Dolan and his men, but Billy later reneged on the arrangement and returned to his life of crime. In 1880, Patrick Floyd Garrett, a small-time cattle thief, was elected Lincoln County Sheriff. After a three month pursuit, Garrett killed Billy at the Maxwell ranch on Thursday, July 13, 1881, and through a special act passed by the New Mexico legislature, later collected a $500 reward for the life of Billy the Kid.

Pat Garrett in 1882 had his highly fictionalized version of Billy's life, *The Authentic Life of Billy the Kid* (written by Ash Upton), published. It attempted to justify Garrett's killing of Billy by crediting the Kid with multiple murders and a marathon of crime. Garrett's legend had been preceded in 1881 by Edmund Noble's dime novel, *Billy the Kid, the New Mexico Outlaw; or, The Bold Bandit of the West*, and by Don Jernado's *The True Life of Billy the Kid*.

[Other fictionalized tales included J. C. Cowdrick's *Silver-Mask, The Man of Mystery; or, The Cross of the Golden Keys* (1884) and Francis W. Doughty's *Old King Brady and "Billy the Kid"; or, The Great Detective's Chase* (1890).]

Billy the Kid was buried on the Maxwell ranch beneath a cross made by Deluvina Maxwell, bearing the words "Duerme bien, Querido" ("Sleep well, beloved"), but the outlaw's body was later moved to Fort Sumner. In 1961, the Lincoln County Commissioners protested the Fort's advertisement of "The Home of Billy the Kid" and officially requested that Billy's body be disinterred and reburied in Lincoln County, "the rightful resting place of the Southwest's foremost personality." But there may be no body to be relocated.

The late Leslie Traylor, an agent of the U.S. Immigration and Naturalization Service, formerly of San Antonio, Texas, claimed in 1964 at age eighty-five that Billy, or Henry McCarty, was not killed by Pat Garrett, his onetime friend, but maintained his promise to alter his lifestyle for freedom and persuaded Garrett to release him. According to Traylor, Billy changed his name to Henry Street Smith and lived until the age of ninety-seven when he died at the Arizona Pioneer's Home in Prescott, Arizona, on October 17, 1955. Traylor supported his claim by producing pictures taken of Billy in 1880 and of 5'7", unhandsome, buck-toothed Henry Street Smith in 1907, an exact description of William H. Bonney of the 1870s.

Patrick Floyd "Pat" Garrett, Billy's 6'4" nemesis, was killed by a disgruntled employee on February 29, 1908. Garrett's murderer, Wayne Brazel, was acquitted.

Comment and Critique

The legendary life of William H. Bonney, known as Billy the Kid, has been staged, screened and televised in much the same variation on the theme of folk-hero as have the lives of Jesse James, Belle Starr and other infamous Old West outlaws. The truth about these criminals and desperadoes has been lost in a maze of glamorized fiction in which they emerge as romanticized, oppressed heroes. The Billy the Kid legend was dramatized in a play written by Walter Woods, gaining great popularity after the turn of the century through performances by various stock companies and touring companies.

Walter Woods and Joseph Santley's melodrama, *Billy the Kid*, opened New Star Theatre in New York on August 13, 1906. "This is a dramatization of some *Boys' Own Weekly*, full of heroics and superpuerile bravado, and embellished with clever dialogue and character drawing," reported *The New York Dramatic Mirror*. "The plot is weak, though consistent, and the lines that tell the story are the stock phrases of melodrama...One noticeable fault is the length of some of the scenes; they are not played fast enough to keep the audience in the state of excitement demanded by patrons of this type of drama...Joseph Santley makes good use of his boyishness in the role of Billy, and while his acting might be criticized, his voice carries conviction and he is active in the scenes calling for quick movements...Marion Leonard as Nellie Bradley does as much as possible with an insipid role."

Joseph Santley, at the age of nine, starred in *Boy of the Streets* and toured in title role of *Billy the Kid* for several seasons in repertory with *From Rags to Riches*. *Billy the Kid* became a popular touring melodrama and played twice daily (admission 25 cents) with Santley in the title role and his horse "Silverheels" prominently featured. Several members of the cast, Sidney Olcott, Marion Leonard, and Robert G. Vignola later had careers in Hollywood films. Santley subsequently became a motion picture actor and director and died on August 8, 1971, at age eighty-one.

By 1913, when Joseph Santley was becoming a leading musical comedy juvenile on Broadway in such fare as *When Dreams Come True*, his former successful melodrama, *Billy the Kid*, was still extensively touring the provinces with Billy still telling Nellie in his curtain speech, "Come Nellie, we'll wander down life's pathway together, where the sun shines always."

Elizabeth McCormick revived *Billy the Kid* on August 20, 1951, at New York's Carnegie Recital Hall, with Michael Higgins as Billy. Brooks Atkinson (*The New York Times*) noted, "To come face to face with a melodrama enjoyed by our betters in 1906 is a chastening experience...*Billy the Kid* is still good entertainment...But the old Walter Woods melodrama goes on to gaudier doings that are hard to have much confidence in... Michael Higgins is a winning Billy the Kid...If the good burghers in New York believed this in 1906, they must have been more amiable than we are today, or the acting and the direction must have been more cunning."

Four decades after Santley's *Billy the Kid*, the fabled character emerged on stage as the antihero of a musical called *Shootin' Star* featuring David Brooks as Billy. After a three-week tryout, *Shootin' Star*, despite rather good reviews for the principals if not for the story, died a less violent death in Boston on April 27, 1946, than did William Bonney. The American Lyric Theatre had plunged Billy into ballet in 1939 with Eugene Loring's choreographed *Billy the Kid* to the nowclassic music by Aaron Copland. In 1973 and 1977, Michael Ondaatje's play *The Collected Works of Billy the Kid* was produced in Canada.

Based on Walter Noble Burns' 1926 novel, *The Saga of Billy the Kid*, with a screenplay by Charles MacArthur and Laurence Stallings, King Vidor directed Metro-Goldwyn-Mayer's *Billy the Kid* (1930). Filmed mainly in New Mexico's Lincoln County where Billy had participated in the Lincoln County Wars, the picture was shot in a 70mm process called *Realife*, which in its enlarged screen projection covered the entire proscenium of Broadway's Capitol Theatre. Mordaunt Hall (*The New York Times*) called the *Realife* process "tremendously effective," feeling that "the scenes in the open are impressive and often they have a stereogenic illusion ...the views on the wide screen are so compelling."

John Mack Brown, who had appeared in several MGM silent films, was featured as Billy with Wallace Beery in an admirably restrained performance as Pat Garrett, who permits the Kid to escape. After the release of *Billy the Kid*, Beery was starred over Brown. "The story is merely a moderately entertaining and often unconvincing Western melodrama," reported Mordaunt Hall. "Twentyeight or thirty persons are killed and more reports of firearms are heard here than in any other film." Hall classified *Billy the Kid* as "a muddled piece of work...Mr. Brown gives an ingratiating performance [and] Mr. Beery also does his bit to make things interesting...the rest of cast do creditable work considering the nature of the tale."

In 1941, while producer Howard Hughes was deeply involved in filming his screen version of *Billy the Kid* called *The Outlaw*, MGM remade Burns' *The Saga of Billy the Kid*, combined with a story by Bradbury Foote and Howard Emmett Rogers, developed into a scenario by Gene Fowler and directed by David Miller. Despite William Bonney's short stature and far from handsome features, Louis B. Mayer assigned the role of Billy to his resident romantic leading man, Robert Taylor.

Redbook magazine selected *Billy the Kid* as their "Picture of the Month" and noted the legend of the Kid "has assumed the nature of a Robin Hood of the frontier...It perhaps is well for Metro-Goldwyn-Mayer that the folklore of New Mexico dominates the history of Billy the Kid. Anything that is told about this colossus of bad men is believable. Metro has not injured his reputation; they have merely taken advantage of the tales that have been told about him, and fashioned an exciting and interestcompelling drama with Robert Taylor as the star. Taylor is excellent in the title role of *Billy the Kid*." The *Redbook* critic found that "Surrounding Taylor are a competent lot of saints and sinners. All are fictitious characters as far as history is concerned, and yet every one is a counterpart of some figure who crossed the path of the outlaw....As with all good Westerns, the film is brightened by exceptional scenery, this time photographed in color. Much of it was made in the fantastic Monument Valley of Arizona. In the clear desert air the photography has a stereoscopic quality. Even if *Billy the Kid* had no story, it would be worth seeing just for a view of the scenery."

Roy Rogers starred as Billy the Kid in Republic's *Billy the Kid Returns* (1938). In the prologue to the film, Rogers was seen as Billy the Kid being shot by Pat Garrett and as himself during the final reels, being mistaken for The Kid. Two years later, Sigmund Neufeld began PRC's series of *Billy the Kid* "B" Westerns featuring, initially, Bob Steele. In 1941, Buster Crabbe took over the role in the Neufeld series with the character alternating between The Kid and Billy Carson.

Almost as notorious as the life of Billy the Kid was Howard Hughes' highly publicized screen version called *The Outlaw* which started production in 1941. For the role of Billy, Hughes signed a twenty-three-year-old Texas-born actor, Jack Buetel, and, after consideration was given to Leatrice Joy Gilbert (the daughter of Leatrice Joy and John Gilbert) for the role of Rio, a nineteen-year-old dentist's receptionist, Ernestine Jane Geraldine Russell, was contracted for the femme fatale.

After two weeks on location in the Arizona desert at Moencopi, director Howard Hawks resigned from the $440,000 budgeted production and persistent Howard Hughes moved into the director's chair. Ben Hecht's original screenplay was reworked by Jules Furthman, again romanticizing Billy's life, ending with Pat Garrett handcuffed to a pillar while Billy and Rio ride off into the sunset and happiness ever after. The Hays Office demands for cuts in the script (i.e., the voluptuous Rio "keeping Billy warm" in bed during his illness, and the winner of a poker game given a choice of Rio or a horse) were reluctantly met by Hughes who continued to direct the picture after business hours at his aircraft empire, to the growing impatience (and bank accounts) of veteran actors Thomas Mitchell and Walter Huston.

Hughes lavished most of his directorial efforts on the curvaceous Jane Russell, whose attributes were described by Hughes as "the most beautiful pair of knockers I've ever seen in my life!" Hughes signed Jane Russell (dimensions 38-24-35) to a seven-year contract beginning at $50 a week. To promote his latest sex symbol, and overshadow publicity earlier given to Jean Harlow (vital statistics 34-25-35) in his 1930 screen epic, *Hell's Angels*, Hughes engaged expert publicist Russell Birdwell who announced Jane Russell to be "the new Jean Harlow." Hughes' new starlet was extensively photographed in explicit sensuous poses emphasizing her physical assets.

Captioned with "Sex has not been rationed," a huge billboard featuring Jane in a seductive pose was installed outside San Francisco's Geary Theatre proclaiming "the picture that couldn't be stopped." The world premiere of *The Outlaw* was at the Geary on February 5, 1943, over fourteen months after the film's completion. For the premiere, a stage sketch was presented in which Jane Russell appeared as Rio, Jack Buetel as Billy with Rosalyn Vojola as "the other girl" and Robert Baron as Buck.

A twenty-minute epilogue was deleted from the 117-minute film which was nationally denounced by the Legion of Decency. A ban on the film by the San Francisco police was overruled by a court order and *The Outlaw* had a profitable run of three weeks at the Geary Theatre and another four weeks at the Tivoli Theatre -- and then withdrawn. Four years later, *The Outlaw* was scheduled to open in Manhattan at three theatres, underscored with Birdwell's continuing publicity campaign and alluring pictures of Jane, captioned with "What are the TWO great reasons for Russell's success?"

Although Hughes' film had been passed by the New York Board of Censors, the

Commissioner of Licenses and the City Police Commissioner publicly denounced *The Outlaw* as obscene. Hughes' appeal to the Appellate Division Court and the New York Court of Appeals to force the contracted theatres to screen *The Outlaw* was denied by Superior Court Justice Shientag as "unthinkable that a court should order defendants to do an act which almost certainly will subject them to be convicted of a crime." In Philadelphia, Roman Catholic Cardinal Dougherty threatened a one-year ban on all theaters unless *The Outlaw* was withdrawn from the Erlanger Theatre. In Baltimore, the film was banned and the judge upheld the state's verdict by acknowledging that Miss Russell's breasts "hung over the picture like a thunderstorm spread out over a landscape" which, of course, was what Hughes intended.

Added to Hughes' craftily orchestrated efforts to get his *Outlaw* screened if not pardoned, was a breachof-contract suit filed against the Hughes Tool Company on April 4, 1947, by descendants of Sheriff Pat Garrett protesting the characterization of Garrett by Thomas Mitchell in *The Outlaw*.

Time magazine on February 22, 1943, had dismissed *The Outlaw* as "a strong candidate for the flopperoo of all time." *The New Yorker*'s 1943 response was "In this inflated saga of Billy the Kid, Mr. Hughes has managed to create the definitive burlesque of all cow-town dramas....Both Miss Russell and Mr. Buetel perform with a desperate earnestness that sets off neatly the activities of Walter Huston and Thomas Mitchell, who invest two supporting roles with a marvelous frivolity."

The Outlaw finally opened at New York's Broadway Theatre on Thursday, September 11, 1947, on a twenty-four-hour-a-day screening schedule. Ads heralded the contested epic as "At Last You Can See Howard Hughes' Production, *The Outlaw*." *The New York Times* classification of the leading lady's acting debut: "Miss Russell is hopelessly inept as an actress." The *New York Herald-Tribune* found "her sultry advances to the young desperado are more amusing than licentious." *The Outlaw* opened at London's Pavillion Theatre in February 1947 to less than ecstatic reviews although admiration was given to Tchaikovsky's background music. Two years later, the picture was shown in Italy under the title of *Il Mio Corpo Ti Scaldera (My Body Will Warm You)* which should have delighted Mr. Hughes. The national U.S. release of *The Outlaw* did not come about until 1950, with Jane Russell accompanying the movie on stage in major cities.

In 1962, William K. Everson and George N. Fanin, in their book *The Western*, described *The Outlaw* as "one of the better film biographies of Billy the Kid (no more accurate than the others, but less sentimentalized), it would in fact have been a good Western but for the obtrusive eroticism." Bosley Crowther (*The New York Times*) had pondered, "One wonders what all the excitement was about. This is a strictly second-rate Western, long and tedious and crudely acted for the most part."

Jane Russell later disclosed that Howard Hughes filmed two versions of *The Outlaw*. one released to commercial theatres and the second for his private viewing with close friends. The second stressed Hughes' mammary mania featuring Miss Russell nude from the waist up with the camera recording her welldeveloped frame.

In 1950, Universal-International released *The Kid from Texas* starring Audie Murphy. "The verdict on this newest addition to the film annals of an untamed West ...is that Billy picked mighty nice country in which to operate even if those operations were not especially exciting," reported *The New York Times*. "Lincoln County in New Mexico is the area involved and it is a locale which seems to have been created for the Technicolor cameras...Audie Murphy is handsome, sits a horse well and wears a solitary expression through the proceedings...*The Kid from Texas* doesn't give special stature to a noted saga."

Gore Vidal's 1955 television script, *The Death of Billy the Kid*, was filmed in 1958 by Warner Bros. as *The Left-Handed Gun*. Paul Newman, who had appeared in the 1955 television version, starred as Billy Bonney in Hollywood's *The Left-Handed Gun* -- although the legendary Billy Bonney was *righthanded*. "The life and times of Billy Bonney, or Billy the Kid, may have been as dull as they were yesterday in *The Left-Handed Gun*, but let's hope not," wrote Howard Thompson in *The New York Times*. "The sad thing about this Warners release, starring Paul Newman, is that some television people have obviously tried to make a Western that's different. And, by golly, it is...a Gore Vidal script shaped a moody psychological vignette, long on reactions and short on motivations, that had the hero fatally traipsing around a prairie town....The picture moves self-consciously, at a snail's pace."

Charles Neider's *The Authentic Death of Hendry Jones*, published in 1956, became the source for *One-Eyed Jacks*, Marlon Brando's monumental failure as a director requiring nearly four years of production and an initial cut of nearly five hours. (It was released in 1960 in a 141-minute version.) *One-Eyed Jacks* was presumably a highly fictionalized account of Billy the Kid, in which the characters' names were altered and the locale shifted to California. In 1970, John Wayne's *Chisum* came as close as any of the myths, legends, and fictions about "The Kid."

Michael Pollard played Billy Bonney in Columbia Pictures' 1972 *Dirty Little Billy*, described as being "what must be the ultimate in Old West authenticity." Vincent Canby (*The New York Times*) wrote of *Dirty Little Billy*: "The physical production is stunningly squalid and Michael Pollard is spectacularly runty in the title role, that of a very androgynous Billy the Kid who literally wanders into legend through mud up to his knees." Columbia's press release for the film was as strange as the subject, reading "*Dirty Little Billy* is a different kind of movie. It's not about the Billy the Kid you've known and loved. It's about the real William H. Bonney. And the real William H. Bonney was a loser. *Dirty Little Billy* is the end of his legend."

Sam Peckinpah's 1973 *Pat Garrett and Billy the Kid* was influenced by Charles Neider's fictionalized account. Kris Kristofferson portrayed Billy and James Coburn was seen as Pat Garrett. Critic Richard Coombes noted, "Production difficulties with the studio; a team of six editors credited on a film that seems to be missing several connections, and the director subsequently protesting over the way his work has been assembled: *Pat Garrett and Billy the Kid* is likely to be pigeonholed as Peckinpah's *Major Dundee* of the '70s...*Pat Garrett* seems in its very conception a paralyzed epic, an impenetrable mood piece. Its title characters are static figures on a landscape of closed possibilities; and the studio's ditching of the framework depicting Garrett's death at the hands of his own employers has not so much undermined the film as simply abbreviating its catalogue of the circles of Hell...Sporadic outbursts of action...attest Peckin-pah's brilliant sharpening of the Western; but for the main part, the story disappears and the fiction is disrupted in order to make the heroes' dilemma crystal clear; the director himself putting in a brief appearance towards the end to goad Garrett on to his final, self-destructive act."

A revisionist version of the Billy the Kid tale was found in both *Young Guns* (1988) and its sequel *Young Guns II* (1990), in which Emilio Estevez portrayed William H. Bonney.

In addition to the portrayal on television by Paul Newman on *Philco Playhouse*'s telecast of July 24, 1955, there have been Billy the Kid interpretations by Robert Vaughn on *Tales of Wells Fargo* in 1957 and by Robert Walker, Jr., on *The Time Tunnel* series in 1967. Billy's longest television fictionalized tale was seen from September 10, 1960, to May 26, 1962, on NBC's series, *The Tall Man*, in which Barry Sullivan portrayed Pat Garrett and Clu Gulager was the legendary Billy.

Jack Gould (*The New York Times*) described *The Tall Man* as "a characteristic item of uninventive tripe... the Sheriff's playmate for this series is Billy the Kid, who is made to resemble a Kookie of the Sagebrush, an assignment well within the acting resources of Clu Gulager."

The American Ballet Theatre's televised *Billy the Kid* on December 15, 1976, narrated by Paul Newman, was less-than-favorably reviewed by John J. O'Connor (*The New York Times*): "The artistic powers that be decided to impose a pointless and thoroughly annoying narration over the performance of *Billy the Kid*...the decision to give him a voice-over narration does a disservice to the ballet and to Mr. Newman."

In May 1989, Gore Vidal again tackled the familiar legend of the Old West in *Gore Vidal's Billy the Kid* with British actor Val Kilmer as Billy and Canadian actor Duncan Regehr as Pat Garrett. It premiered on Ted Turner's Turner Network Television (TNT). Of *Gore Vidal's Billy the Kid*, Walter Goodman (*The New York Times*) said "it is more like Billy the Kid's Gore Vidal. The essayist and novelist, known for construing American history in his fashion, has accepted many of the conventions of the Western form in his script of the most written-up good-bad boys of the Old West. The result is an O.K. low-key show that brings the smiles and yawns of familiarity...Val Kilmer, who at moments resembles and sounds a little like the young Marlon Brando, turns in an easygoing, nicely contained performance as Billy. What he lacks in force, he makes up in amiablity. Duncan Regehr looks determined as Pat Garrett. And Wilford Brimley, everybody's favorite codger, makes an undemanding appearance as Gen. Lew Wallace."

Kay Gardella, in the New York *Daily News*, viewed Vidal's latest vision of Billy the Kid as "a good, gritty Western...As perceived by Vidal, Billy wasn't a thief, or an outlaw in the true sense of the word. Played with a kind of youthful trust and openness by Val Kilmer, he's portrayed as a guy who was liked by neighbors and friends...[and] seems very much a nice enough kid who never intentionally meant to wind up on the wrong side of the law."

STAGE

BILLY THE KID, *New Star Theatre*, New York, opened August 13, 1906
A Melodrama by Walter Woods and Joseph Santley

Joseph Santley (Billy the Kid); Marion Leonard (Nellie Bradley); John C. Fenton (Col. Wayne Bradley); Sidney Olcott (Con Hanley); Robert G. Vignola ("Peanut" Giovanni); Lorena Ferguson (Mary Wright); Paul Barnett (Boyd Denver); Thomas J. MacMahon (Stephen Wright/Bud Monroe); George M. De Vere (Mose Moore); T. Jerome Morley (Hank Burke); James Early (Arizona Jake); Jennie Lansing (Molly); Adele Lyndon (Jennie); Frank Gordon (Jim Storm); James Liet (Bill White)

Touring Company, season 1912-13
Director, Edward Riley; A Drama by Walter Woods and Joseph Santley; Company manager, Herbert Farrar; Stage managers, H. C. Horne, Edward Riley

Berkeley Haswell (Billy the Kid); Alice Mortlock (Nellie Bradley); Rex Turner (Col. Wayne Bradley); Edward Riley (Con Hanley); George C. Hall (Stephen Wright); Lydia Willmore (Mary Wright); H. T. Adams (Boyd Denver); Paul Hamlin (Mose Moore); H. C. Horne ("Peanut" Giovanni); Will White (Hank Burke); James Spear (Arizona Jake); Marion Morton (Jennie); G. C. Hall (Bud Monroe)

Touring Company, season 1914-15

Director, Edward Riley; A Drama by Walter Woods and Joseph Santley

Berkeley Haswell (Billy the Kid); Gladys Royal (Nellie Bradley); Frederick Hoadley (Col. Wayne Bradley); Joseph H. Lee (Con Hanley); Edward J. DeVelde (Stephen Wright); Edna Holloway (Mary Wright); H. T. Adams (Boyd Denver); Edward Baker (Mose Moore); Ben Stoddard (Hank Burke); Edgar Hoadley (Arizona Jake); Edna Holloway (Jennie); Ed J. DeVelde (Bud Monroe)

BILLY THE KID, *Carnegie Recital Hall*, opened August 20, 1951 16 performances
Produced by the Phoenix Theatre, Elizabeth McCormick and Stanley Cobleigh, producers; A Play by Walter Woods; Director, Elizabeth McCormick; Setting, Maurice Gordon

Michael Higgins (Bill Wright/Billy the Kid); Carol Teitel (Nellie); Edwin Christie (Stephen Wright); Tom Rutherford (Boyd Denver); John Regan (Mose Moore); Guy Arbury (Con Hanley); Walter F. Appler (Col. Wayne Bradley); Nolia Trammel (Mary Wright); Mario Alcaldo (Bud Monroe); James Harwood ("Peanut" Giovanni); Marion Moore (Molly); Adeline Hiatt (Jennie); Harry Bergman (Hank)

SHOOTIN' STAR, opened in New Haven, April 4, 1946; closed in Boston, April 27, 1946
Produced by Max Liebman and Joseph Kipness; A Musical Story of *Billy the Kid* by Walter Hart, Louis Jacobs and Halsted Welles; Director, Halsted Welles; Music by Sol Kaplan; Lyrics by Bob Russell; Settings, Frederick Fox; Costumes, Kenn Barr; Musical director, Pembroke Davenport; Orchestrations, Hershy Kay; Choreography, Lester Horton; General manager, Jack Small; Stage managers, Eddie Dimond, Rex King and Peter Gray

David Brooks (Billy); Doretta Morrow (Amy); Howard Da Silva (Ross Dixon); Edward Andrews (Fancy); Bernice Parks (Lorraine); Clay Clement (Francis T. Corey); Art Smith (Cash Claghorne); Margaret Irving (Sarilla); Larry Stewart (Hank); Lee Fairfax (Beaver); James Moore (Sheriff Brody); Aldo Cadena (Willy); Susan Reed (Folk Singer); Marco Rosales (Curley); Richard Gibbs (Windy); Everett Gammon (Mr. Barry); Elliott Sullivan (Buckshot); Walter Stane (Soldier); Rex King (Chuck Wagner); Peter Gray (Spike); Emily Earle (Lola); Sandra Grubel (Teaser); Ruth K. Hill (Paradise); Elline Walther (Velvet); Jean Olds (Saddle Jane); Nelle Fisher (Sally); Ray Harrison (Jerry); Thom Conroy (Mr. Eliot); Jock McGraw (Mr. MacDonald); Edward Cullen (Mr. Adams); Larry Anderson (Olie); Larry Gray (Luke); Jerry Bercier (succeeded by Rex King) (Bartender); James Moore (Raphael Ventura); Emily Earle ((Maria Ventura); Sonia Shaw (Conchita); Nathan Kirkpatrick (Pedro); Bram Nossen (General Wallace); Sandra Crubel, Eileen Avers, Christine Scoville, Mollie Cousely, Ethel Madsen, Jean Olds, Helen Whitney, Elline Walther, Ruth K. Hill, Everett Gammon, Richard Anderson, Lawrence Gray, Larry Anderson, Jerry Bercier, Alan Leonard (Singers); Barbara Steele, Nancy Lang, Doris Ebener, Patricia Schaeffer, Nona Schurman, Billie Kirpich, Lavina Nielsen, Edythe Uden, Jimmy Kirby, Aldo Cadena, Forrest Bonshire, Francisco Moncion, Herbert Ross, Walter Stane, David Ahdar (Dancers)

MUSICAL NUMBERS: "Saga of Billy the Kid"; "Footloose"; "Kid Stuff"; "Friendly Country"; "Payday"; "What Do I Have to Do"; "Mighty Big Dream"; "He'll Make Some Girl a Wonderful Husband"; "Sometime Tomorrow"; "It's a Cold Cruel World"; "No Ross Dixon, Lincoln Plaza Saloon"; "Music to a Dancing Bird"; "Chin-Che"; "Free"; "Nothin"; "I'm Paying' You"; "Hip-di-di-Otee"

WANTED, Cherry Lane Theatre, opened January 19, 1972 79 performances
Produced by Arthur D. Zinberg; A Musical Play; Director, Lawrence Kornfeld; Music and Lyrics by Al Carmines; Book by David Epstein; Scenery, Paul Zalon; Lighting, Roger Morgan; Costumes, Linda Giese; Musical direction, Susan Romann; Stage manager, Jimmy Cuomo

Reathel Bean (Billy the Kid); Peter Lombard (Jesse James); Frank Coppola (John Dillinger); Andra Akers (Starr Faithful Brown); Lee Guilliatt (Ma Barker); Stuart Silver (Doc Barker); John Kuhner (Jelly Barker); Jerry Clark (Babycakes); Cecelia Cooper (Opal); June Gable (Shorty); Merwin Goldsmith (Jacob Hooper); Gretchen Van Aken (Miss Susanah Figgit/ Sister Powhatan Lace); John Kuhner (Deafy); Stuart Silver (Sheriff Sweet)

MUSICAL NUMBERS: "I Am the Man"; "Where Have You Been Up to Now?"; "Outlaw Man"; "Who's on Our Side"; "Parasol Lady"; "Jailhouse Blues"; "I Want to Ride With You"; "You Do This"; "Guns are Fun"; "I Do the Best I Can"; "Whispering to You"; "I Want to Blow Up the World"; "The Indian Benefit Ball"; "The Lord Is My Light"; "It's Love"; "As I'm Growing Older"

Billy the Kid was also one of the characters included in Arthur Kopit's 1968 play, *INDIANS*. Cast and credits for *INDIANS* are included here under *JESSE JAMES*.

THE COLLECTED WORKS OF BILLY THE KID, Third Stage, Stratford, Canada, opened July 10, 1973 23 performances
Produced by the Stratford, Ontario, Canada Festival; A Play by Michael Ondaatje; Director John Hayes; Music by Alan Laing; Production designer, Jean Gascon; Lighting, Gil Wechaler

Neil Munro (Billy the Kid); Ted Follows (Pat Garrett); Michael Donaghue (John Chisum); Nancy Beatty (Sallie Chisum); Cherry Davis (Angela Dickinson); Art Hindle (Charlie Bowdre); Marilyn Lightstone (Manuela Bowdre); P. M. Howard (Tom O'Folliard)

THE COLLECTED WORKS OF BILLY THE KID, Brooklyn Academy of Music, opened October 13, 1975 10 performances
Produced by the Canadian Council Touring Office in association with the Brooklyn Academy of Music; The Neptune Theatre Company of Nova Scotia Production of a play by Michael Ondaatje; Director, John Wood; Production designer, John Ferguson; Lighting, Robert A. Elliott; Stage manager, Catherine McKeehan

Neil Munro (Billy the Kid); Ivar Brogger (Pat Garrett); David Renton (John Chisum); Carole Galloway (Sallie Chisum); Patricia Collins (Angela Dickinson); John Sweeney (Charlie Bowdre); Suzanne Ristic (Manuela Bowdre); P. M. Howard (Tom O'Folliard)

THE COLLECTED WORKS OF BILLY THE KID, Folger Theatre, Washington, D.C., opened October 10, 1975
Produced by the Folger Theatre Group and Louis W. Scheeder; A Play by Michael Ondaatje; Director, Louis W. Scheeder; Setting, David Chapman; Lighting, Hugh Lester; Costumes, Randy Barcelo; Music Director, Pete Jabekay; Incidental Music by Desmond McAnuff

Allan Carlsen (William Bonney); Anne Stone (Sallie Chisum); Brad Sullivan (Pat Garrett); Richard Greene (John Chisum); Guy Boyd (Tom O'Folliard); Mark Robinson (Charlie Bowdre); Sandy Faison (Angela Dickinson); Albert Malafronte (Dave Rudabaugh)

THE COLLECTED WORKS OF BILLY THE KID, Theatre 3, Edmonton, Alberta, Canada, opened July 9, 1977
Produced by Theatre 3; A Play by Michael Ondaatje; Director, Randy Maertz; Production designer, Doug Welch; Music by Des McAnuff; Additional music by Gordon Christie and Gregory Tuck; Stage manager, Larry Farley

Gregory Tuck (Billy the Kid/Charlie/Maxwell/Emory/ Wilson); Michael Ray Cunningham (Pat Garrett/Toro); Susan Andre (La Princess/Sally); Richard Gishler (Wilde/Reporter/Narrator); Gordon Christie (Musician/Poe); Jim Love (Billy--the Reality); Marie Hawkins (Angie/Celsa); Bob Collins (Chisum/Clinger); Sam Gilbert (Tom/Bell/McKinnon)

BALLET

BILLY THE KID, Martin Beck Theatre, opened May 24, 1939 2 performances
Produced by the American Lyric Theatre, in association with The League of Composers, Robert Edmond Jones, managing director; A Character ballet based on the legend of *Billy the Kid*, choreographed by Eugene Loring; Director, Lincoln Kirstein; Costumes by Jared French; Music composed by Aaron Copland; Music conductor, Fritz Kitzinger; Performed in conjunction with *Air and Variations* (a classic ballet by Nicolas Nabokoff) and *Pocahontas* (a ballet-legend by Lew Christensen under general heading of *The Ballet Caravan*)

Eugene Loring (Billy the Kid); Todd Bolender; Marie-Jeanne; Lew Christensen; Misses Campbell, Tompkins, Dekova, Friedlich, Shea, Tucker, Heater, London, Asquith, Colbath, Quarequio; Valon, Wagner; Messrs: Kidd, Godwin, Hawkins, Lahee, Weamer

City Center Theater, New York, opened November 1, 1989
Produced by the Joffrey Ballet, Gerald Arpino, artistic director; A Character Ballet based on the legend of *Billy the Kid*, choreographed by Eugene Loring; Director, Gerald Arpino; Music conductor, John Miner

Douglas Martin (Billy the Kid); Beatriz Rodriguez (Young Billy's Mother/Older Billy's Sweetheart); Tyler Walters (Pat Garrett)

SCREEN

BILLY THE KID, Metro-Goldwyn-Mayer, released October 1930
Director, King Vidor; Screenplay by Laurence Stalling and Charles MacArthur, based on *The Saga of Billy the Kid* by Walter Noble Burns; Continuity, Wanda Tuchock; Photography, Gordon Avil; Art director, Cedric Gibbons; Recording Engineer, Douglas Shearer; Wardrobe, David Cox; Editor, Hugh Wynn; Technical adviser, William S. Hart

John Mack Brown (Billy the Kid); Wallace Beery (Pat Garrett); Kay Johnson (Claire); Wyndham Standing (Tunston); Karl Dane (Swenson); Russel Simpson (McSween); Blanche Frederici (Mrs. McSween); Roscoe Ates (Old Stuff); Nelson McDowell (Hatfield); Warner P. Richmond (Ballinger); James Marcus (Donovan); Jack Carlyle (Brewer); Aggie Herring (Mrs. Hatfield); Marguerita Padula (Nicky Whoosiz); John Beck (Butterworth); Christopher Martin (Santiago)

BILLY THE KID, Metro-Goldwyn-Mayer, released May 1941
Producer, Irving Asher; Director, David Miller; Screenplay by Gene Fowler, based on

The Saga of Billy the Kid by Walter Noble Burns, and a story by Howard Emmett Rogers and Bradbury Foote; Photography, Leonard Smith, William V. Skall; Music, Ormond B. Ruthven and Albert Mannheimer; Song, "Viva La Vida" by Ruthven and Mannheimer;-Editor, Robert J. Kern

Robert Taylor (Billy Bonney); Brian Donlevy (Jim Sherwood); Ian Hunter (Eric Keating); Mary Howard (Edith Keating); Gene Lockhart (Dan Hickey); Lon Chaney, Jr. ("Spike" Hudson); Henry O'Neill (Tim Ward); Guinn "Big Boy" Williams (Ed Bronson); Cy Kendall (Sheriff); Ted Adams ("Buzz" Cobb); Frank Conlan (Judge Blake); Frank Puglia (Pedro Gonzalez); Mitchell Lewis (Bart Hodges); Dick Curtis (Kirby Claxton); Grant Withers (Ed Shanahan); Joe Yule (Milton); Earl Gunn (Jesse Martin); Eddie Dunn (Pat Shanahan); Carl Pitti ("Bat" Smithers); Kermit Maynard (Thad Decker); Chill Wills (Tom Patterson); Aline Blakeney (Mrs. Patterson); Ethel Griffies (Mrs. Hanky)

BILLY THE KID RETURNS, *Republic Pictures*, released September 1938

Produced by Charles E. Ford; Director, Joe Kane; Original screenplay by Jack Natteford; Photography, Ernest Miller; Music, Cy Fever; Songs, Eddie Cherkose and Smiley Burnette

Roy Rogers (Billy the Kid); Smiley Burnett (Frog); Lynn Roberts (Ellen); Morgan Waller (Morganson); Fred Kohler, Sr. (Matson); Wade Boteler (Pat Garrett); Edwin Stanley (Moore); Horace Murphy (Miller); Joseph Crehan (Conway); Robert Emmett Keane (Page)

SONGS: "Born to the Saddle (Eddie Cherkose); "Sing a Little Song About Anything" (Eddie Cherkose, Smiley Burnette); "When the Sun Is Setting on the Prairie (Eddie Cherkose, Alberto Columbo); "When I Camped Under the Stars" (Vera and Tim Spencer)

BILLY THE KID IN TEXAS, *Producers Releasing Corporation*, released November 1940

Produced by Sigmund Neufeld; Director, Peter Stewart (Sigmund Neufeld); Original screenplay by Joseph O'Donnell; Photography, Jack Greenhalgh; Musical director, Lew Porter; Editor, Holbrook N. Todd

Bob Steele (Billy the Kid); Al St. John (Fuzzy); Terry Walker (Mary); Carlton Young (Gil); Charles Wittaker (Windy); Frank La Rue (Jim); Charles King (Dave); John Merton (Flash)

BILLY THE KID'S FIGHTING PALS, *Producers Releasing Corporation*, released June 1941

Produced by Sigmund Neufeld; Director, Sherman Scott (Sam Newfield); Screenplay, George Plympton; Photography, Jack Greenhalgh; Music director, David Chudnow; Editor, Holbrook N. Todd

Bob Steele (Billy the Kid); Al St. John (Fuzzy); Phyllis Adair (Ann); Edward Peil, Sr. (Hardy); Forrest Taylor (Hanson); Carleton Young (Jeff); Charles King (Badger); Curley Dresden (Burke); Hal Price (Burroughs); George Chesebro (Sheriff); Bud Buster (Mason); Julian Ravero (Lopez)

BILLY THE KID IN SANTE FE, *Producers Releasing Corporation,* released July 1941

Produced by Sigmund Neufeld; Director, Sherman Scott (Sam Newfield); Screenplay, Joseph O'Donnell; Photography, Jack Greenhalgh; Music director, Lew Porter; Editor, Holbrook N. Todd

Bob Steele (Billy the Kid); Al St. John (Fuzzy); Rex Lease (Jeff); Marin Sais

(Pat); Dennis Moore (Bank Clerk); with Karl Hackett, Steve Clark, Hal Price, Charles King, Frank Ellis, Dave O'Brien, Ken Duncan

BILLY THE KID WANTED, Producers Releasing Corporation, released November 1941
Produced by Sigmund Neufeld; Director, Sherman Scott (Sam Newfield); Screenplay, Fred Myton; Photography, Jack Greenhalgh; Editor, Holbrook N. Todd
Buster Crabbe (Billy the Kid); Al St. John (Fuzzy); Dave O'Brien (Jeff); Glenn Strange (Matt); Charles King (Saunders)

BILLY THE KID'S ROUND UP, Producers Releasing Corporation, released December 1941
Produced by Sigmund Neufeld; Director, Sherman Scott (Sam Newfield); Screenplay, Fred Myton; Photography, Jack Greenhalgh; Editor, Holbrook N. Todd
Buster Crabbe (Billy the Kid); Al St. John (Fuzzy); Carleton Young (Jeff); Glenn Strange (Landreau)

LAW AND ORDER, Producers Releasing Corporation, released October 1942
Produced by Sigmund Neufeld; Director, Sherman Scott (Sam Newfield); Screenplay, Sam Robins; Photography, Jack Greenhalgh; Editor, Holbrook N. Todd
Buster Crabbe (Billy the Kid); Al St. John (Fuzzy Jones); Sarah Padden (Aunt Mary); Wanda McKay (Linda); Charles King (Crawford); Tex O'Brien (Jeff); Hal Price (Simms); Ted Adams (Sheriff); Ken Duncan (Dugan); John Merton (Turtle)

THE KID RIDES AGAIN, Producers Releasing Corporation, released March 1943
Produced by Bert Sternbach; Director, Sherman Scott (Sam Newfield); Screenplay, Fred Myton; Photography, Jack Greenhalgh; Editor, Holbrook N. Todd
Buster Crabbe (Billy the Kid); Al St. John (Fuzzy Jones); Iris Meredith (Joan); Glenn Strange (Tom); Slim Whitaker (Texas Sheriff); Charles King (Vic); I. Stanford Jolley (Mort); Edward Peil, Sr. (Ainsley); Ted Adams (Sheriff)

WESTERN CYCLONE, Producers Releasing Corporation, released June 1943
Produced by Sigmund Neufeld; Director, Sam Newfield; Screenplay, Patricia Harper; Photography, Robert Cline; Editor, Holbrook N. Todd
Buster Crabbe (Billy the Kid); Al St. John (Fuzzy Jones); Marjorie Manners (Mary Arnold); Karl Hackett (Governor Arnold); Kermit Maynard (Hank); Milton Kibbee (Senator Peabody); Glenn Strange (Dirk Randall); Charles King (Ace Harmon); Hal Price (Sheriff)

BLAZING FRONTIER, Producers Releasing Corporation, released September 1943
Produced by Sigmund Neufeld; Director, Sam Newfield; Screenplay, Patricia Harper; Photography, Robert Cline; Editor, Holbrook N. Todd
Buster Crabbe (Billy the Kid); Al St. John (Fuzzy Jones); Marjorie Manners (Helen); Milton Kibbee (Barstow); I. Stanford Jolley (Sharp); Kermit Maynard (Pete)

CATTLE STAMPEDE, Producers Releasing Corporation, released December 1943
Produced by Sigmund Neufeld; Director, Sam Newfield; Screenplay, Joe O'Donnell; Photography, Robert Cline; Editor, Holbrook N. Todd
Buster Crabbe (Billy the Kid); Al St. John (Fuzzy Jones); Frances Gladwin (Mary); Charles King (Coulter); Ed Cassidy (Sam Dawson); Hansel Werner (Ed

Dawson); Frank Ellis (Elkins); Bud Buster (Jensen); Steve Clark (Turner); Ray Bennett (Stone); Roy Brent (Slater); John Elliott (Doctor)

DEVIL RIDERS, Producers Releasing Corporation, released January 1944
Produced by Sigmund Neufeld; Director, Sam Newfield; Screenplay, Joe O'Donnell; Photography, Robert Cline; Editor, Robert Crandall

Buster Crabbe (Billy "The Kid" Carson); Al St. John (Fuzzy Jones); Patti McCarthy (Sally Farrell); Ed Cassidy (Doc); Charles King (Del Stone); Kermit Maynard (Red); John Merton (Jim Higgins); Frank LaRue (Tom Farrell); Jack Ingram (Turner); George Chesebro (Curley)

THUNDERING GUNSLINGERS, Producers Releasing Corporation, released March 1944
Produced by Sigmund Neufeld; Director, Sam Newfield; Screenplay, Fred Myton; Photography, Robert Cline; Editor, Holbrook N. Todd

Buster Crabbe (Billy Carson); Al St. John (Fuzzy Jones); Karl Hackett (Jeff Halliday); Frances Gladwin (Bab Halliday); Charles King (Steve Kirby); Jack Ingram (Vic)

THE DRIFTER, Producers Releasing Corporation, released June 1944
Producer, Sigmund Neufeld; Director, Sam Newfield; Screenplay, Patricia Harper; Photography, Robert Cline; Editor, Holbrook N. Todd

Buster Crabbe (Billy Carson/Drifter Davis); Al St. John (Fuzzy Jones); Carol Parker (Sally Dawson); Kermit Maynard (Jack); Jack Ingram (Trent); Roy Brent (Sam)

FRONTIER OUTLAWS, Producers Releasing Corporation, released July 1944
Produced by Sigmund Neufeld; Director, Sam Newfield; Screenplay, Joe O'Donnell; Photography, Robert Cline; Editor, Holbrook N. Todd

Buster Crabbe (Billy Carson); Al St. John (Fuzzy Jones); Marin Sais (Ma Clark); Frances Gladwin (Pat); Kermit Maynard (Wallace); Charles King (Harlow); Jack Ingram (Taylor); Edward Cassidy (Sheriff); Emmett Lynn (Judge); Bud Buster (Clerk)

VALLEY OF VENGEANCE, Producers Releasing Corporation, released August 1944
Produced by Sigmund Neufeld; Director, Sam Newfield; Screenplay, Joe O'Donnell; Photography, Jack Greenhalgh; Editor, Holbrook N. Todd

Buster Crabbe (Billy Carson); Al St. John (Fuzzy Jones); Evelyn Finley (Helen); Donald Mayo (Young Billy); David Polonsky (Young Fuzzy); Glenn Strange (Marshal Baker); Charles King (Burke); Steve Clark (Happy); John Merton (Kurt); Jack Ingram (Brett); Bud Osborne (Dad Carson); Nora Bush (Ma Carson); Lynton Brent (Carr)

WILD HORSE PHANTOM, Producers Releasing Corporation, released October 1944
Produced by Sigmund Neufeld; Director, Sam Newfield; Screenplay, George Milton, Photography, Jack Greenhalgh; Editor, Holbrook N. Todd

Buster Crabbe (Billy Carson); Al St. John (Fuzzy Jones); Elaine Morey (Marian); Kermit Maynard (Daggett); Bud Buster (Ed Garnet); Hal Price (Walters); Bob Cason (Lucas); John Elliott (Warden); Frank McCarroll (Moffett)

RUSTLER'S HIDEOUT, *Producers Releasing Corporation*, released October 1944
Produced by Sigmund Neufeld; Director, Sam Newfield; Screenplay, Joe O'Donnell; Photography, Jack Greenhalgh; Editor, Holbrook N. Todd

Buster Crabbe (Billy Carson); Al St. John (Fuzzy Jones); Charles King (Buck Shane); Patti McCarty (Barbara); John Merton (Harry); Hal Price (Dave Crockett); Terry Frost (Jack Crockett); Ed Cassidy (Sheriff); Frank McCarroll (Squint); Lane Chandler (Hammond); Al Ferguson (Steve)

STAGECOACH OUTLAWS, *Producers Releasing Corporation*, released September 1945
Produced by Sigmund Neufeld; Director, Sam Newfield; Screenplay, Fred Myton; Photography, Jack Greenhalgh; Editor, Holbrook N. Todd

Buster Crabbe (Billy Carson); Al St. John (Fuzzy Jones); Frances Gladwin (Linda); I. Stanford Jolley (Steve); Kermit Maynard (Vic); Ed Cassidy (Jed); Robert Kortman (Matt); Steve Clark (Sheriff); Bob Casson (Joe)

BORDER BADMEN, *Producers Releasing Corporation*, released October 1945
Produced by Sigmund Neufeld; Director, Sam Newfield; Screenplay, George Milton; Photography, Jack Greenhalgh; Musical director, Frank Sanucci; Editor, Holbrook N. Todd

Buster Crabbe (Billy Carson); Al St. John (Fuzzy Jones); Lorraine Miller (Helen); Marlyn Gladstone (Roxie); Raphael Bennett (Deputy Sheriff); Marin Sais (Mrs. Bentley)

LIGHTING RAIDERS, *Producers Releasing Corporation*, released December 1945
Produced by Sigmund Neufeld; Director, Sam Newfield; Screenplay, Fred Myton; Photography, Jack Greenhalgh; Editor, Holbrook N. Todd

Buster Crabbe (Billy Carson); Al St. John (Fuzzy Jones); Mady Lawrence (Jane); Henry Hall (Wright); Steve Darrell (Hayden); I. Stanford Jolley (Kane); Karl Hackett (Murray); Roy Brent (Phillips); Marin Sais (Mrs. Murray); Al Ferguson (Lorren)

PRAIRIE RUSTLERS, *Producers Releasing Corporation*, released January 1946
Produced by Sigmund Neufeld; Director, Sam Newfield; Screenplay, Fred Myton; Photography, Jack Greenhalgh; Editor, Holbrook N. Todd

Buster Crabbe (Billy Carson); Al. St. John (Fuzzy Jones); Evelyn Finley (Helen); Karl Hackett (Dan Foster); I. Stanford Jolley (Matt); Kermit Maynard (Vic); Bud Osborne (Bert)

TERRORS ON HORSEBACK, *Producers Releasing Corporation*, released April 1946
Produced by Sigmund Neufeld; Director, Sam Newfield; Screenplay, George Milton; Photography, Jack Greenhalgh; Editor, Holbrook N. Todd

Buster Crabbe (Billy Carson); Al St. John (Fuzzy Jones); Patti McCarty (Roxie); I. Stanford Jolley (Grant Barlow); Henry Hall (Doc Jones); Kermit Maynard (Wagner); Bud Buster (Sheriff Bartlett); Marin Sais (Mrs. Bartlett); Karl Hackett (Ed Sperling); Steve Clark (Cliff Adams); Steve Darrell (Jim Austin)

GENTLEMEN WITH GUNS, *Producers Releasing Corporation*, released May 1946
Produced by Sigmund Neufeld; Director, Sam Newfield; Screenplay, Fred Myton;

Photography, Jack Greenhalgh; Editor, Holbrook N. Todd

Buster Crabbe (Billy Carson); Al St. John (Fuzzy Jones); Patricia Knox (Matilda); Steve Daskell (McAllister); George Chesebro (Slade); Karl Hackett (Justice of Peace); Bud Buster (Sheriff); Frank Ellis (Cassidy)

PRAIRIE BADMEN, *Producers Releasing Corporation*, released July 1946
Produced by Sigmund Neufeld; Director, Sam Newfield; Screenplay, Fred Myton; Photography, Robert Cline; Music director, Lee Zahler; Editor, Holbrook N. Todd

Buster Crabbe (Billy Carson); Al St. John (Fuzzy Jones); Patricia Knox (Linda); Charles King (Cal); Ed Cassidy (Doc Lattimer); Kermit Maynard (Lon)

THE OUTLAW, *RKO Radio Pictures*, released 1943*; rereleased September 1947; national release, 1949
Produced by Howard Hughes; Supervising director, Otto Lovering; Directors, Howard Hawks, Howard Hughes; Screenplay by Jules Furthman; Photography, Gregg Toland; Art director, Perry Ferguson; Special effects, Roy Davidson; Music director, Victor Young; 2nd Unit Camera, Lucien Ballard; Editor, Walter Grissell

Jack Buetel (Billy the Kid); Jane Russell (Rio); Walter Huston (Doc Holliday); Thomas Mitchell (Pat Garrett); Pat West (Bartender); Mimi Aguglia (Guadalupe); Joe Sawyer (Charley); Carl Stockdale (Minister); Nina Quartaro (Chita); Edward Peil, Sr. (Swanson); Emory Parnell (Dolan); Julian Rivero (Pablo); Frank Darien (Shorty); Carl Stockdale (Minister); Ethan Laidlow, Ed Brady, William Steele (Deputies); Lee "Lasses" White (Coach Driver); Ted Mapes (Guard); William Newell (Dunken Cowboy); Martin Garralaga (Waiter); Arthur Loft, Dick Elliott, John Sheehan (Salesmen); Lee Shumway (Dealer); Cecil Kellogg (Officer); Wally Reid, Jr. (Bystander); Dickie Jones, Frank Ward, Bobby Callahan (Boys); Gene Rizzi (Stranger); Rosalyn Vajda (Girl); Robert Baron (Buck)

* World premiere: Geary Theatre, San Francisco, February 5, 1943

RETURN OF THE BAD MEN, *RKO Radio Pictures*, released May 13, 1948
Executive producer, Jack J. Gross; Producer, Nat Holt; Director, Ray Enright; Screenplay by Charles O'Neal, Jack Natteford and Luci Ward, based on a story by Natteford and Ward; Photography, J. Roy Hunt; Art directors, Albert S. D'Agostino, Ralph Berger; Set decorators, Darrell Silvera, James Altwies; Music, Paul Sawtell; Music director, C. Bakaleinikoff; Special effects, Russell A. Cully; Editor, Samuel F. Beetley

Randolph Scott (Vance); Robert Ryan (Sundance Kid); Anne Jeffreys (Cheyenne); Dean White (Billy the Kid); Steve Brodie (Cole Younger); Tom Keene (Jim Younger); Robert Bray (John Younger); George "Gabby" Hayes (John Pettit); Jacqueline White (Madge Allen); Lex Barker (Emmett Dalton); Walter Reed (Bob Dalton); Michael Harvey (Grat Dalton); Robert Armstrong (Wild Bill Doolin); Tom Tyler (Wild Bill Yeager); Lew Harvey (Arkansas Kid); Gray Gray (Johnny); Walter Baldwin (Muley Wilson); Minna Gombell (Emily); Jason Robards (Judge Harper); Warren Jackson (George Mason); Robert Clarke (Dave); Harry Shannon (Wade Templeton); Charles McAvoy (Elmer); Larry McGrath (Scout); Ernie Adams (Townsman Leslie); Billy Vincent, Howard McCrorey (Deputies); George Nokes (Donald Webster); Ronnie Ralph (Tim Webster); Polly Bailey (Mrs. Webster); Forrest Taylor (Farmer); Lane Chandler (Posse Leader Ed); Bud Osborne (Stagecoach Driver); Brandon Beach (Conductor); Charles Stevens (Grey Eagle); Kenneth McDonald (Colonel Markham); Ida Moore (Mrs. Moore); Dan Foster (Outlaw); Richard Thorne

(Soldier); John Hamilton (Doc Peters); Cy Ring (Bank Clerk); Earle Hodgins (Auctioneer)

SON OF BILLY THE KID, Screen Guild Production, released August 1949
Produced by Ron Ormond; Associate producer, Ira Webb, Director, Ray Taylor; Screenplay, Ron Ormond, Ira Webb; Photography, Ernest Miller; Art director, Fred Preble; Music, Walter Greene; Editor, Hugh Winn

Al "Lash" La Rue (Jack Gardner); June Carr (Norma); Al St. John (Fuzzy); with Marion Coby; George Baxter; Terry Frost, Johnny Jones; House Peters, Jr; Clark Stevens

THE KID FROM TEXAS, Universal Pictures, released February 1950
Produced by Paul Short; Director, Kurt Neumann; Screenplay by Robert Hardy Andrews and Karl Lamb; Photography, Charles Van Enger; Art director, Bernard Herzbrun; Emrich Nicholson; Music director, Milton Schwartzwald; Editor, Frank Gross

Audie Murphy (Billy the Kid); Frank Wilcox (Sheriff Pat Garrett); Gale Storm (Irene Kain); Albert Dekker (Alexander Kain); Shepperd Strudwick (Jameson); Will Geer (O'Fallon); William Talman (Minniger); Robert H. Barrat (General Lew Wallace); Dennis Hoey (Major Harper); Ray Teal (Sheriff Rand); Paul Ford (Copeland); Martin Garralaga (Morales); Walter Sande (Crowe); Don Haggerty (Morgan); Rosa Turich (Marita); Dorita Pallais (Lupita); Pilar Del Rey (Margarita); Tom Trout (Denby); Zon Murray (Lacas); Harold Goodwin (Matt Curtis); John Phillips (Sid Curtis)

I SHOT BILLY THE KID, Lippert Pictures, released August 1950
A Don Barry Production; Produced and directed by William Berke; Screenplay by Orville Hampton; Photography, Ernest Miller; Music, Albert Glasser; Editor, Carl Pierson

Don Barry (Billy the Kid); Robert Lowery (Pat Garrett); Tom Neal (Bowdre); John Morton (Ollinger); Wendy Lee (Francesca); Wally Vernon (Vicenti); Richard Farmer (McSween); Claude Stroud (Wallace); Henry Marce (Juan); Felice Richmond (Mrs. McSween); Tommy Monroe (Maxwell); Billy Kennedy (Poe); Archie Twitchell (Grant); Jack Geddes (Sheriff); Jack Perrin (Man)

THE BOY FROM OKLAHOMA, Warner Bros., released January 1954
Produced by David Weisbart; Director, Michael Curtiz; Screenplay by Frank Davis and Winston Miller, based on a *Saturday Evening Post* story, *The Sheriff Was Scared*, by Michael Fessier; Photography, Robert Burks; Music, Max Steiner; Editor, James Moore

Will Rogers, Jr. (Tom Brewster); Nancy Olsen (Katie Brannigan); Tyler MacDuff (Billy the Kid); Lon Chaney (Crazy Charlie); Anthony Caruso (Barney Turlock); Merv Griffin (Steve); Slim Pickens (Shorty); Wallace Ford (Wally Higgins); Clem Bevans (Pop Pruty); Louis Jean Heydt (Paul Evans); Sheb Wooley (Peter Martin); Skippy Torgerson (Johnny Neil); James Griffith (Joe Downey); Charles Watts (Harry)

THE LAW VERSUS BILLY THE KID, Columbia Pictures, released July 1954
Produced by Sam Katzman; Director, William Castle; Screenplay, John T. Williams; Photography, Henry Freulich; Art director, Paul Palmentola; Music supervisor, Mischa Bakaleinikoff; Editor, Aaron Stell

Scott Brady (Billy the Kid); James Griffith (Pat Garrett); Betta St. John (Nita Maxwell); Alan Hale, Jr. (Bob Ollinger); Paul Cavanaugh (John H. Tunstall); Benny Rubin (Arnold Dodge); William "Bill" Phillips (Charlie Bowdro)

STRANGE LADY IN TOWN, Warner Bros. released April 1955
Produced and directed by Mervyn LeRoy; Story and screenplay by Frank Butler; Photography, Harold Rosson; Art director, Gabriel Scognamillo; Costumes, Emile Santiago; Music composed and conducted by Dimitri Tiomkin; Title song by Dimitri Tiomkin and Ned Washington, sung by Frankie Laine; Choreography, Peggy Carroll; Editor, Folmar Blangsted

Greer Garson (Julia Garth); Dana Andrews (Dr. Rork O'Brien); Cameron Mitchell (Lt. David Garth); Nick Adams (Billy the Kid); Lois Smith (Spurs); Walter Hampden (Father Gabriel Mendoza); Adele Jergens (Bella Brown); Bob Foulk (Joe); Ralph Moody (General Lew Wallace); Louise Lorimer (Mrs. Wallace); Pedro Gonzalez-Gonzalez (Martinez Martinez); Joan Camden (Norah Muldoon); Jose Torvay (Bartolo Diaz); Anthony Numkena [Earl Holliman] (Tomasito Diaz); Russell Johnson (Shadduck); Gregory Walcott (Shannon); Douglas Kennedy (Slade Wickstrom); Jack Williams (Rebstock); Joey Costarello (Alfredo); Jose Lopez (Pueblo Indian); Bob Wilke (Karg); Frank de Kova (Anse Hatlo); Marshall Bradford (Sheriff); George Wallace (Curley); Joe Hamilton (Mr. Harker); Helen Spring (Mrs. Harker); Jose Gonzalez-Gonzalez (Jose); The Trianas (Dancers)

LAST OF THE DESPERADOS, Associated Film Releasing Corporation, released December 1955
Produced and directed by Sigmund Neufeld; Screenplay, Orville Hampton; Photography, Eddie Linden; Music, Paul Dunlap; Editor, Holbrook N. Todd

James Craig (Pat Garrett); Jim Davis (John W. Poe); Barton MacLane (Mosby); Dona Martel (Paulita); Margia Dean (Sarita); Myrna Dell (Bowdre); Stanley Clements (Bert)

THE PARSON AND THE OUTLAW, Columbia Pictures, released 1957
Executive producer, Robert Gilbert; Produced by Charles "Buddy" Rogers; Director, Oliver Drake; Screenplay, Oliver Drake and John Mantley; Photography, Clark Ramsey; Music, Joe Sodja; Sound, Harry Smith

Anthony Dexter (Billy the Kid); Marie Windsor (Tonya); Sonny Tufts (Jack Slade); Jean Parker (Mrs. Jones); Robert Lowery (Colonel Morgan); Buddy Rogers (Reverend Jericho Jones); Madalyn Trahey (Elly McCloud); Bob Steele (Jardine)

THE LEFT-HANDED GUN, Warner Bros., released April 1958
Produced by Fred Coe; Director, Arthur Penn; Screenplay by Leslie Stevens, based on Gore Vidal's teleplay *The Death of Billy the Kid*; Photography, J. Peverell Marley; Art director, Art Loel; Set decorator, William Kuehl; Costumes, Marjorie Best; Music, Alexander Courage; Ballad by William Goyen and Alexander Courage; Makeup, Gordon Bau; Assistant director, Russ Saunders; Sound, Earl Crain, Jr.; Editor; Folmar Blangsted

Paul Newman (Billy Bonney); John Dehner (Pat Garrett); Lita Milan (Celsa); Hurd Hatfield (Moultrie); James Congdon (Charlie Boudre); James Best (Tom Folliard); Colin Keith-Johnston (Tunstall); Bob Anderson (Hill); Wally Brown (Moon); Martin Garralaga (Saval); Denver Pyle (Ollinger); Ainslie Pryor (Joe Grant); Paul Smith (Bell); Anne Barton (Mrs. Hill); Robert Foulk (Brady); Nestor

Paiva (Maxwell); Jo Summers (Mrs. Garrett); John Dierkes (McSween)

ONE-EYED JACKS, Paramount Pictures release, released March 1961
Produced by Pennebaker Company; Executive producers, George Glass, Walter Seltzer; Producer, Frank P. Rosenberg; Director, Marlon Brando; Screenplay by Guy Trosper and Calder Willingham, based on the novel *The Authentic Death of Hendry Jones* by Charles Neider; Photography, Charles Lang, Jr.; Art directors, Hal Pereira, J. McMillan Johnson; Set decorators, Sam Comer, Robert Benton; Costumes, Yvonne Wood; Music, Hugo Friedhofer; Choreography, Josephine Earl; 2nd unit photography, Wallace Kelley; Editor, Archie Marshek

Marlon Brando (Rio); Karl Malden (Dad Longworth); Katy Jurado (Maria); Pina Pellicer (Louisa); Ben Johnson (Bob Amory); Slim Pickens (Lon); Larry Duran (Modest); Sam Gilman (Harvey); Timothy Carey (Howard Tetley); Miriam Colon (Redhead); Elisha Cook (Bank Teller); Rudolph Acosta (Rurales' Leader); Ray Teal (Bartender); John Dierkes (Bearded Townsman); Margarita Cordova (Flamenco Dancer); Hank Worden (Doc); Nina Martinez (Margarita); Snub Pollard (Townsman)

BILLY THE KID VS. DRACULA, Embassy Pictures, released April 1966
Produced by Carroll Case; Director, William Beaudine; Story and Screenplay by Carl K. Hittleman; Photography, Lothrop Worth; Music, Raoul Kraushaar

Chuck Courtney (Billy the Kid); John Carradine (Dracula); Melinda Plowman (Betty Bentley); Harry Carey, Jr. (Ben); Virginia Christine (Eva Oster); Walter Janovitz (Franz Oster); Bing Russell (Red Thorpe); Lennie Geer (Yancy); Roy Barcroft (Marshal Griffin); Olive Carey (Dr. Henrietta Hull); Hannie Landman (Lila Oster); Marjorie Bennett (Mrs. Ann Bentley); William Forrest (James Underhill); George Cisar (Joe Flake); Charlita (Nana); Richard Reeves, Max Kleven, Jack Williams, William Challee

EL HOMBRE QUE MATAO BILLY EL NINO (THE MAN WHO KILLED BILLY THE KID), Richard Schulman release (Spain/ Italy) 1967
Produced by Aitor Films (Madrid) and Kinesis Film (Rome); Producer, Silvio Battistini; Director, Julia Buchs; Screenplay by Frederico de Urrutia and Julio Buchs, based on the legend of *Billy the Kid* and a story by Jose Mallorqui, Frederico de Urrutia and Julio Buchs; Photography, Miguel Mila; Art director, Franco Calabrese; Music director, Gianni Ferrio; Editor, Cecilia Gomez

Peter Lee Lawrence (Karl Hirenbach) (William Bonney, aka Billy the Kid); Fausto Tozzi (Pat Garrett); Dianik Zurakowska (Helen); Gloria Milland (Mrs. Bonney); with Luis Prendes, Barta Barry, Carlos Casaravilla, Antonio Pica, Enrique Avila, Orlando Baralla, Paco Sanz, Luis Rivera, Tomas Blanco, Luis Induni, Milo Quesada, Miguel de la Riva, Margot Cottens

CHISUM, Warner Bros., released July 1970
A Batjac Production; Executive producer, Michael A. Wayne; Producer, Andrew J. Fenady; Director, Andrew W. McLaglen; Screenplay, Andrew J. Fenady; Photography, William H. Clothier; Art director, Carl Anderson; Set decorator, Ray Moyer; Music, Dominic Frontiere; Music supervisor, Sonny Burke; Special effects, Howard Jensen; Editor, Robert Simpson

John Wayne (John Chisum); Geoffrey Deuel (Billy The Kid); Forrest Tucker (Lawrence Murphy); Bruce Cabot (Sheriff Brady); Christopher George (Dan Nodeen); Ben Johnson (James Pepper); Glenn Corbett (Pat Garrett); Andrew

Prine (Alex McSween); Patric Knowles (John H. Tunstall); Richard Jaeckel (Jess Evans); Pamela McMyler (Sally Chisum); Lynda Day (Sue McSween); John Agar (Patton); Lloyd Battista (Neemo); Robert Donner (Morton); Ray Teal (Justice Wilson); Edward Faulkner (Dolan); Ron Soble (Bowdre); Alan Baxter (Governor Axtell); Alberto Morin (Delgado); Glenn Langan (Dudley); William Bryant (Jeff); Pedro Armemdariz, Jr. (Ben); Christopher Mitchum (O'Folliard); Abraham Sofaer (White Buffalo); Gregg Palmer (Riker)

SONGS:"Turn Me Around" (Dominic Frontiere, Norman Gimbel); "Ballad of John Chisum" (Dominic Frontiere, Andrew J. Fenady), sung by Merle Haggard

UNE AVENTURE DE BILLY LE KID, *Moullet Productions*, France, released March 1971

Produced by Moullet Productions; Written and directed by Luc Moullet; Photography, Jean Gonnet, Jean-Jacques Flori; Music, Patrice Moullet; Lyrics, Luc Moullet; Title song sung by Mlle. Hesterber; Editor, Jean Sustanche

Jean-Pierre Leaud (Billy the Kid); Rachel Hesterber (Ann); Michel Minaud (Sheriff); Jean Valmont (Hunter); Bernard Pinon (Soldier); Bruno Kresoja (Indian); Kathy Maloney (Squaw)

DIRTY LITTLE BILLY, *Columbia Pictures*, released May 1972

Produced by Jack L. Warner and WRG/Dragoti Productions; Director, Stan Dragoti; Screenplay, Charles Moss and Stan Dragoti; Photography, Ralph Woolsey; Art director, Malcolm Bert; Set decorator, George Hopkins; Music composed and conducted by Sascha Burland; Editor, Dave Wages

Michael J. Pollard (Billy Bonney); Lee Purcell (Berle); Richard Evans (Goldie Evans); Charles Aidman (Ben Antrim); Dran Hamilton (Catherine McCarty); Willard Sage (Henry McCarty); Josip Elic (Jawbone); Mills Watson (Ed); Alex Wilson (Len); Ronnie Graham (Charlie Niles); Richard Stahl (Earl Lovitt); Gary Busey (Basil Crabtree); Cherrie Franklin (Gerta Schmidt); Dick Van Patten (Harry); Rosary Nix (Louisiana); Frank Welker (Young Punk); Scott Walker (Stormy); Craig Bovia (Buffalo Hunter); Severn Darden (Big Jim); Henry Proach (Lloyd); Len Lesser (Slits); Ed Lauter (Tyler); Doug Dirksen (Swille)

PAT GARRETT AND BILLY THE KID, *Metro-Goldwyn-Mayer*, released May 1973

Produced by Gordon Carroll; Director, Sam Peckinpah; Screenplay, Rudolph Wurlitzer; Photography, John Coquillon; Art director, Ted Haworth; Set decorator, Ray Moyer; Special photographic effects, A. J. Lodman; Music, Bob Dylan; 2nd unit director, Gordon Dawson; 2nd unit photography, Gabriel Torres; Editors, Garth Craven, David Berlatsky, Richard Halsey, Roger Spottiswoode, Robert L. Woolfe, Tony de Zarraga

Kris Kristofferson (Billy the Kid); James Coburn (Pat Garrett); Bob Dylan (Alias); Richard Jaeckel (Sheriff Kip McKinney); Katy Juardo (Mrs. Baker); Chill Wills (Lemuel); Slim Pickens (Sheriff Baker); R. G. Armstrong (Deputy Ollinger); Jason Robards (Governor Lew Wallace); Luke Askew (Eno); Rita Coolidge (Maria); John Beck (Poe); Richard Bright (Holly); Matt Clark (J. W. Bell); Jack Dodson (Howland); Jack Elam (Alamosa Bill); Emilio Fernandez (Paco); Paul Fix (Maxwell); L. Q. Jones (Black Harris); Jorge Russel (Silva); Charlie Martin Smith (Bowdre); Harry Dean Stanton (Luke); Claudia Bryar (Mrs. Horrell); John Chandler (Norris); Mike Mikler (Denver); Aurora Clavel (Ida); Rutanya Alda (Ruthie); Walter Kelley (Rupert); Rudy Wurlitzer (O'Folliard); Elisha Cook, Jr. (Cody); Gene Evans (Horrell); Donnie Fritts (Beaver); Dub Taylor (Josh); Don

Levy (Sackett); Sam Peckinpah (Will)

YOUNG GUNS, *20th Century-Fox*, released August 1988

A James G. Robinson and Joe Roth presentation of a Morgan Creek production; Executive producers, John Fusco and James G. Robinson; Producers, Joe Roth and Christopher Cain; Coproducers, Irby Smith and Paul Schiff; Director, Christopher Cain; Screenplay, John Fusco; Photography, Dean Semler; Production designer, Jane Musky; Art director, Harold Thrasher; Set decorator, Robert Kraick; Costume design, Richard Hornung; Music, Anthony Marinelli and Brian Banks; Editor, Jack Hofstra

Emilio Estevez (William H. Bonney); Kiefer Sutherland (Doc Scurlock); Lou Diamond Phillips (Chavez y Chavez); Charlie Sheen (Dick Brewer); Dermot Mulroney (Dirty Stephens); Casey Siemaszko (Charley Bowdre); Terence Stamp (John Tunstall); Jack Palance (L. G. Murphy); Terry O'Quinn (Alex McSween); Sharon Thomas (Susan McSween); Geoffrey Blake (J. McCloskey); Alice Carter (Yen Sun); Brian Keith (Buckshot Roberts); Tom Callaway (Texas Joe Grant); Patrick Wayne (Pat Garrett); Lisa Banes (Mallory); Sam Gauny (Morton); Cody Palance (Baker); Gadeek (Henry Hill); Victor Izay (Justice Wilson); Allen Robert Keller (John Kinney); Craig M. Erickson (Poppin); Jeremy M. Lepard (Dolan); Daniel Kanin (Sheriff Brady); Richela Renkun (Bar Girl); Pat Lee (Jenny); Gary Kanin (Colonel Dooley); Forrest Broadley (Rynerson); Alan Tobin (Bartender); Joey Hanks (Hindman); Loyd Lee Brown (Soldier); Elena Farres (Manuela's Mother)

YOUNG GUNS II, *20th Century-Fox*, released August 1990

A James G. Robinson presentation of a Morgan Creek production; Executive producers, John Fusco, Joe Roth and James G. Robinson; Producers, Irby Smith and Paul Schiff; Director, Geoff Murphy; Screenplay, John Fusco; Photography, Dean Semler; Production designer, Gene Rudolph; Art director, Christa Munro; Set decorator, Andy Bernard; Costume design, Judy Ruskin; Music, Alan Silvestri; Songs, Jon Bon Jovi; Editor, Bruce Green

Emilio Estevez (William H. Bonney); Kiefer Sutherland (Doc Scurlock); Lou Diamond Phillips (Chavez y Chavez); Christian Slater (Arkansas Dave Rudabaugh); William Peterson (Pat Garrett); Alan Ruck (Hendry French); R. D. Call (D. A. Rynerson); James Coburn (John Chisum); Balthazar Getty (Tom O'Folliard); Jack Kehoe (Ashmun Upson)

TELEVISION

THE DEATH OF BILLY THE KID, *Philco Playhouse*, televised July 24, 1955 NBC 1 hour

Produced by Fred Coe; Director, Robert Mulligan; Teleplay, Gore Vidal

Paul Newman (Billy the Kid); Frank Overton (Pat Garrett); Jason Robards, Jr. (Joe Grant); George Mitchell (Pete Maxwell); Frank Conrad (Charles Bowdrie); Muriel Berkson (Celsa Gutierrez); Harold Stone (Saval Gutierrez); Michael Strong (John Poe); Matt Crowley (Governor Lew Wallace); Frank Marth (Guard); Joseph Anthony (Drunk)

BILLY THE KID, episode of *Tales of Wells Fargo*, televised October 21, 1957 NBC 30 minutes

Produced by Overland Productions/Juggernaut, Inc., Producer, Earle Lyon; Director,

R. G. Springsteen; Created by Frank Gruber; Photography, Bud Thackery; Art director, Alexander A. Mayer; Costume supervisor, Vincent Dee; Theme music, Harry Warren; Musical scoring, Morton Stevens, Executive story consultant, Milton S. Gelman; Sound, Earl Crain, Jr.; Editor, Richard G. Wray

Dale Robertson (Jim Hardie); Robert Vaughn (Billy the Kid); Aline Towne (Nell Forrester); Addison Richards (General Lew Wallace)

THE TALL MAN, televised September 10, 1960 to May 26, 1962 NBC 30 minutes each (75 episodes)

Executive Producers, Nat Holt, Edward J. Montagne; Producers, Samuel A. Peeples, Frank Price; Directors, Herschel Daugherty, Lesley Selander and others; Teleplays, Samuel A. Peeples, David Lang and others; Photography, Lionel Lindon; Art director, John J. Lloyd; Makeup, Jack Barron; Costume supervision, Vincent Dee; Music, Juan Esquivel; Editors, Richard G. Wray, David J. O'Connell

Clu Gulager (William H. Bonney/"Billy the Kid"); Barry Sullivan (Pat Garrett); Robert Middleton (Paul Masson); Denver Pyle (Dave Leggett); King Donovan (Spieler); Ron Soble (Evers); Ken Lynch (Gorman); and guests including Jim Davis (Bob Orringer); Ford Rainey (Sheriff Brady); Leonard Nimoy (Johnny Swift); Harold J. Stone (Ben Myers); Marianne Hill (Rita); Claude Akins (Dan Rees); Robert McQueeney (Bragg); Andy Clyde (Pa McBean); George Macready (Roy A. Barlow); Harry Carey, Jr. (Dusty); Jack Mather (Sheriff); Olive Sturgess (May); R. G. Armstrong (Bailey); Jan Merlin (Hendry Grant); Richard Jaeckel (Denver); James Coburn (John Miller); John Archer (Ben Webster); Jeanne Cooper (Elmira); Martin Landau (Francisco); Ellen Corby (Hannah Blossom); Russell Collins (Sam Masters); Robert J. Wilke (Marshal Ben Hartley); Faith Domergue (Kate Elder); Robert Lansing (Doc Holliday); Lyle Bettger (Vince Ober); Michael Pate (Young); James Griffith (Clint); Kathleen Hughes (Nita Jardine); Raymond Hatton (Stage Driver); Frank de Kova (Mike Gray Eagle); Michael Forest (Ledall); Monica Lewis (Sal); Wesley Lau (Jason Cleary); Alan Baxter (Fallon); Joe De Santis (Waco); Connie Gilchrist (Big Mamacita); Frank Ferguson (Lew Wallace); Miriam Colon (Angelita Sanchez); Nan Leslie (Beth); Joan Evans (Lou Belle Martin); Nancy Davis (Sarah Wiley); Charles Aidman (Bill Wiley); Edgar Buchanan (Archie Keogh); Colleen Gray (Edna); George Kennedy (Jake Newton); Mona Freeman (Amy Dodds); Vic Morrow (Skip Farrell); Judi Meredith (Mattie Arnold); Robert Foulk (Gimp); Berry Kroeger (Dean Almond); Howard McNear (Cyrus Skinner); Rafael Lopez (Fosforito); Sherry Jackson (White Moon); J. Pat O'Malley (Sam Barlett); Jan Clayton (Janet); Harry Von Zell (Murphy); Joan O'Brien (Marilee); Robert Emhardt (Judge Oliver Cromwell); Barbara Lawrence (Sadie Wren); Harry Townes (Henry Stewart); Lori March (Isabel Stewart); Roberta Shore (Sally); Gregory Morton (Don Diego); Adele Mara (Rosa); Ed Nelson (Dr. Wade Parsons); Mabel Albertson (Kate Baines); June Kenney (Mary Curtis); Paul Hartman (Marlowe); Richard Reeves (Santee); George Macready (Cyrus Caufield); Patricia Barry (Sylvia); Ken Lynch (Gorman); Richard Ney (Edward Van Doren); Madge Kennedy (Elizabeth Van Doren); Wally Brown (Ethan); Alan Carney (Wino)

BILLY THE KID, episode of *The Time Tunnel*, televised February 10, 1967 ABC 60 minutes

Producer, Irwin Allen; Director, J. Juran; Written by William Welch; Photography, Winston Hoch; Special effects, L. B. Abbott; Music, Johnny Williams

Robert Walker, Jr. (Billy the Kid); Allen Case (Sheriff Pat Garrett); Pitt Herbert (McKinney); Harry Lauter (Wilson); John Crawford (Deputy John Poe); Phil Chambers (Marshal); with regular characters: James Darren (Tony Newman); Whit Bissell (Gen. Heywood Kirk); Lee Meriweather (Ann); Robert Colbert (Doug Phillips); John Zaremba (Dr. Raymond Swain); Wesley Lau (Sergeant Jiggs)

BILLY THE KID, American Ballet Theatre, Great Performances, televised December 15, 1976 PBS 60 minutes
Produced by WNET/13 New York; Executive producer, Jac Venza; Producer, Emile Ardolino; Director, Merrill Brockway; Production designer, Jac Venza; Music by Aaron Copland; Choreographer, Eugene Loring; (Televised with *Les Patineurs [The Skaters]*; Choreographer, Frederick Ashton)

Paul Newman (Narrator); Terry Orr (Billy the Kid); Frank Smith (Pat Garrett); Clark Tippet (Alias); Marianna Tcherkassky (Sweetheart/Mother); Victor Barbee (Prospector); Michael Owen (Mailman); Kirk Peterson (Cowboy in Red); Francia Kovak, Christine Spizzo (Mexican Girls); Marie Johanson, Ruth Mayer, Patricia Wesche (Dance Hall Girls)

GORE VIDAL'S BILLY THE KID, televised May 10, 1989 TNT 2 hours
A von Zerneck/Sertner Films Production for Turner Network Television; Executive producers, Frank von Zerneck and Robert M. Sertner; Producers, Gregory Prange and Phillips Wylly, Sr.; Director, William A. Graham; Teleplay, Gore Vidal; Photography, Denis Lewiston; Production designer, Donald LightHarris; Set decorator, Nigel Clinker; Costume designer, Molly Maginnis; Music, Laurence Rosenthal; Sound, Glenn Berkovitz; Editor, William B. Stich

Val Kilmer (Billy the Kid); Duncan Regehr (Pat Garrett); Julie Carmen (Celsa); Rene Auberjonois (Drunk); Wilford Brimley (Gov. Lew Wallace); Tom Everett (Joe Poe); Michael Parks (Rynerson); Albert Salmi (Pete Maxwell); Red West (Joe Grant); Gore Vidal (Minister); Patrick Massett (Tom); Ned Vaughn (Charlie); Nate Esformes (Valdez); Andrew Bicknell (John Tunstall); John O'Hurley (J. J. Dolan); Burr Steers (Billy's Gang Member); Mike Casper (Ollinger); Jack Dunlap (Brady); Billy Joe Patton (Peppin); Bing Blenman (Deputy Sheriff); Roberto Guajardo (Photographer); Richard Glover (Beaver Smith); Richard Blake (Bartender); Sam Smiley (Hotel Clerk); Ed Adams (Posse Member); Kirk Nelson (Lieutenant); Clark Roy (Mulligan); Henry Max Kendrick (Dolan's Man); Ric Sannicholas (Bell); Rich Wheeler (Carpenter); Tiny Wells (Cowman); Will Hannah (Duff)

BREAKFAST AT TIFFANY'S

Various productions based on the novel by Truman Capote (1958)

Synopsis

Holly Golightly is a capricious New York partygirl, given to "chasing the mean reds, worse than the blues," by standing outside of Tiffany's at dawn, nibbling a bun, sipping coffee and gazing at the gems in the window. She has had her marriage at fifteen to Doc Go-lightly, a good-hearted Texan, annulled and now supports herself and her cat in a partially furnished apartment on Manhattan's East Side on $100 a week earned from visiting mobster Sally Tomato at Sing Sing and an occasional $50 from gentleman escorts. The Tiffany visits she finds keep her from becoming depressed. At one of her freewheeling parties, she meets writer Jeff Claypool, who learns that her wild bashes are the constant annoyance of her upstairs neighbor, Yunioshi, a myopic Japanese photographer. It isn't long before Jeff falls in love with Holly, only to find that she's determined to marry South American millionaire Jose Ybarra. It also isn't long before Holly is exposed as the innocent carrier of information from Sally Tomato to his former underworld, drugdealing cronies. When Ybarra learns of this, he dumps her. Deeply distressed, Holly tosses her cat into the street and, after one more visit to Tiffany's window, she decides to leave town -- until Jeff persuades her to stay.

Comment and Critique

Producer David Merrick's plan to bring Truman Capote's *Breakfast at Tiffany's* to the stage as a musical holds a special place in the modern history of the Broadway theater -- becoming one of the alltime famous bombs. He apparently was perspicacious enough to sense disaster and closed it during previews after a disastrous tryout engagement first in Philadelphia and then in Boston.

The Capote novel, which had been turned successfully into a movie in 1961, first had been adapted to the musical stage by Nunnally Johnson, but it never got produced. Writer/director Abe Burrows next tried his hand at it under Merrick's aegis and, with Mary Tyler Moore and Richard Chamberlain in the leads, it got its first staging in Philadelphia in October 1966. It had a score by Bob Merrill and choreography by Michael Kidd. It was not well received -- but it was sold out. *The Philadelphia Inquirer*'s Barbara L. Wilson wrote that "the show that lurched about the Forrest stage comes close to being a totally unsatisfactory adaptation of Capote's *Breakfast at Tiffany's*...The Holly Golightly remembered here was a charming dreamer, a tramp, perhaps, but a delightful one...As played by Mary Tyler Moore, within the tasteless and humorless confines of Abe Burrows' adaptation, the current Holly is a gold digger with a heart of ice..."

Ernest Schier (*The Evening Bulletin*) described Burrows' adaptation as "tedious and purely irrelevant." He also found the Mary Tyler Moore performance "quite tiresome." Schier had kinder words for composer Bob Merrill "who has written the music and lyrics, not only read *Breakfast at Tiffany's*, he also understands it. He has transferred the original into musical terms that are tough, appealing, amusing and, except in one obvious number, always appropriate...While Merrill is entitled to sue for non-support, his bright score raises hope that *Holly Golightly* can be salvaged, once the mass of underbrush has been cleared away and Miss Moore gets to like the girl she is impersonating."

The Boston critics, Merrick found, were no kinder, and he brought in Pulitzer Prize-winner Edward Albee to doctor Burrows' script. Burrows apparently did not appreciate the move and asked out of the production. He was replaced as director by Joseph Anthony. With Albee, out went the title *Holly Golightly* and in came Capote's original *Breakfast at Tiffany's*.

The bumpy road that finally led to Broadway's Majestic Theatre caused Merrick to throw in the towel after four preview performances prior to the scheduled day-after-Christmas 1966 opening, and take a $400,000 loss. For years afterward, Merrick referred to *Breakfast at Tiffany's* as "my Bay of Pigs."

Totally different, of course, was the outcome of George Axelrod's screen adaptation of the Capote story, which, under Blake Edwards' direction and with Audrey Hepburn in the lead, became one of the most delightful movies of its time (1961). Complementing the fine performances was Mancini and Mercer's memorable

Oscar-win-ning song, "Moon River," which became one of the musical evergreens of the last half of the 20th century. Mancini also got an Oscar for his music score. Academy Award nominations, in addition, went to Hepburn, Axelrod, and for art and set decoration.

Ironically, a 1969 television adaptation, designed as a pilot to a prospective series revolving around Holly Golightly, as played by Stefanie Powers, was produced but never shown -- duplicating the dubious fate of Merrick's stage musical that never opened officially on Broadway.

STAGE

*HOLLY GOLIGHTLY (*aka *BREAKFAST AT TIFFANY'S), Forrest Theatre*, Philadelphia, opened October 15, 1966; closed during previews at *Majestic Theater*, New York, December 14, 1966

Produced by David Merrick; A Musical by Abe Burrows (replaced by Edward Albee), based on the novel by Truman Capote; Director, Abe Burrows (replaced by Joseph Anthony); Music and lyrics, Bob Merrill; Scenery, Oliver Smith; Lighting, Tharon Musser; Costumes, Freddy Wittop; Musical staging, Michael Kidd; Vocal arrangements and musical direction, Stanley Lebowsky; Orchestrations, Ralph Burns; Assistant choreographer, Tony Mordente; Associate producer, Samuel Liff; Stage manager, Harry Clark

Mary Tyler Moore (Holly Golightly); Richard Chamberlain (Jeff Claypool); Sally Kellerman (Mag Wildwood); Art Lund (Doc Golightly); Mitchell Gregg (Jose Ybarra); Paul Mitchell (succeeded by Murvyn Vye) (Sally Tomato); Martin Wolfson (O. J. Berman); Brooks Martin (succeeded by Thayer David) (Rusty Trawler); Stephen Cheng (Yunioshi); Charles Welch (Joe Bell); Sid Raymond (Sid Arbuck); J. Frank Lucas (Oliver O'Shaughnessy); Maryann Kerrick (Madam Spanella); Sally Hart (Mrs. Zimmermann); John Anania (Warden); John Sharpe (Banker); Bob Gorman (Gent); Bill Stanton (Ukelele Player); Stan Mazin (Westerner); Richard Terry (Colonel); Mitch Thomas (Jose's Cousin/Disguised Man); Justin McDonough (TV Announcer); Larry Devon (Toupee Man); John Sharpe (Messenger); Bud Fleming (Off-Duty Cop); Robert Donahue (Detective); Teak Lewis, Justin McDonough (Men with Gift Boxes); Larry Devon, Justin McDonough, Bob Gorman, Robert Donahue (Prison Guards); John Anania, Richard Terry, Bob Gorman (Brazilian Trio); Carolyn Kirsch, Bob Gorman, Robert Donahue, John Sharpe, Richard Terry (Customers); Sally Hart, Lee Hooper, Maryann Kerrick, Marybeth Lahr, John Anania, Henry LeClair, Robert Donahue, Bob Gorman, Justin McDonough, Richard Terry (Singers); Barbara Beck, Trudy Carson, Judy Dunford, Carolyn Kirsch, Priscilla Lopez, Debe Macomber, Sally Ramsome, Pat Trott, Bud Fleming, Teak Lewis, Stan Mazin, Dom Salinaro, John Sharpe, Paul Solen, Bill Stanton, Kent Thomas, Mitch Thomas (Dancers)

NOTE: In addition to Moore, Chamberlain, Kellerman, Lund and Wolfson, the cast after Edward Albee's rewrite included James Olsen (Mr. Buckley); Larry Kert (Carlos); Paul Michael (Giovanni); William Stanton (Mr. Moss); Charles Welch (Joe Howard); Robert Donahue (Patrick O'Connor); Paul Bauersmith (Sheila Fezzonetti); John Sharpe (Messenger); Richard Terry (O. J. Assistant); Paul Solen (Hospital Attendant); Justin McDonough (Announcer); John Anania (Voice); Sally Hart, Maryann Kerrick, Marybeth Lahr (Giovanni's Girls); Bill Stanton, John Sharpe, Mitchell Thomas (Bar Patrons); John Anania, Scott Schultz, Feodore Tedick, Robert Donahue (Guests)

MUSICAL NUMBERS (in Philadelphia): "I've Got a Penny"*; "Holly Golightly"; "So Here We Are Again"; "Traveling"*; "Freddy Chant"; "Holly Gollucci"; "Scum-De-Dum"*; "Lament for Ten Men"; "Bessie's Blues"*; "Who Needs Her"; "Nothing Is New in New York"*; "Stay in the Sun"; "The Bachelor"*; "The Rose"*; "Breakfast at Tiffany's"
* dropped during revisions
MUSICAL NUMBERS (added in Boston): "Wittiest Fellow in Pittsburgh"; "The Party People"; "Ciao Compare"; "The Girl Who Used to Be"
ADDITIONAL NUMBERS (in New York previews): "When Daddy Comes Home"; "Ulamae"; "I'm Not the Girl"; "Grade 'A' Treatment"; "Better Together"; "Same Mistakes"

SCREEN

BREAKFAST AT TIFFANY'S, *Paramount Pictures*, released October 1961
A Jurow-Shepherd Production; Producers, Martin Jurow and Richard Shepherd; Director, Blake Edwards; Screenplay, George Axelrod, based on the novel by Truman Capote; Photography, Franz F. Planer; Art directors, Hal Pereira and Roland Anderson; Set decoration, Sam Comer and Ray Moyer; Costume supervisor, Edith Head; Audrey Hepburn's wardrobe, Hubert Givinchy; Patricia Neal's wardrobe, Pauline Trigere; Music, Henry Mancini; Song "Moon River" by Henry Mancini and Johnny Mercer; Editor, Howard Smith

Audrey Hepburn (Holly Golightly); George Peppard (Paul Varjak); Patricia Neal ("2E"); Buddy Ebsen (Doc Golightly); Martin Balsam (O. J. Berman); Mickey Rooney (Mr. Yunioshi); Villalonga (Jose de Silva Perreira); Alan Reed (Sally Tomato); Dorothy Whitney (Mag Wildwood); Stanley Adams (Rusty Trawler); John McGiver (Tiffany's Salesman); Miss Beverly Hills (Nightclub Dancer); Claude Stroud (Sid Arbuck)

TELEVISION

HOLLY GOLIGHTLY, unaired pilot 1969-70 season ABC 30 minutes
Produced by 20th Century-Fox Television; Produced and directed by James Frawley; Teleplay, James Henerson, based on characters created by Truman Capote

Stefanie Powers (Holly Golightly); and George Furth, Jack Kruschen, Jean-Pierre Aumont

CALAMITY JANE
Various interpretations of the life of Calamity Jane

Synopsis

Martha Jane Cannary, better known as "Calamity Jane," reportedly was born in Princeton, Missouri, in 1852. Frontier-woman Martha Jane dressed in men's clothing earning her living as a mule skinner in Wyoming and as a laborer on the Union Pacific Railroad. Jane also was called a prostitute during her brief stay near Fort Laramie and considered a "sporting woman" by the customers of E. Coffey and Cuney's Trading Post. On September 1, 1870, at Deadwood, Dakota Territory, Jane claimed that the Reverend W. F. Warren married her to James Butler "Wild Bill" Hickok, and in 1873, her daughter was born, sired by Hickok. Three years later, at age fortyeight, 6'2" Wild Bill Hickok was killed while playing cards by a drunken, crosseyed varmint, Jack McCall, in Carl Mann's Deadwood Saloon. Although admitting he killed Hickok to avenge his brother's shooting, McCall was found not guilty.

McCall later was retried by a Federal Court at Yankton, Dakota Territory, and his sentence to be hanged was carried out on March 1, 1877. In 1885, Jane married Clinton Burke in California, but the marriage failed. She returned to Wyoming where her wild behavior and hard drinking increased her already tarnished reputation. Eight years later, Calamity Jane joined Buffalo Bill Cody's Wild West Show which toured the United States and England. After an appearance as a star of Western characters exhibit at Buffalo, New York's Pan-American Exposition, Jane was constantly discharged for drunkenness, assaulting police and general hellraising. In 1895, Jane was arrested for drunken, disorderly conduct but jumped bail and returned to the West. Using her name of Martha Cannary Burke, Jane wrote her autobiography, *Life and Adventures of Calamity Jane*. "Calamity Jane" died of pneumonia and acute alcoholism at the Callaway Hotel in Terry, South Dakota, on August 1, 1903. She was buried, as she had requested, next to Wild Bill Hickok in Deadwood.

Comment and Critique

Like Belle Starr, Hollywood more or less glamorized Martha Jane Cannary. In 1923, William S. (Surrey) Hart appeared on the screen in the title role of *Wild Bill Hickok* with blonde Ethel Grey Terry as Calamity Jane. Hart, whose first feature film was *The Bargain* (1914), had been successful on the stage in *Ben-Hur* and other epics before entering motion pictures. He prided himself in producing "authentic" Western films which were favorably compared with the realistic, exciting paintings of Western artists Frederic Remington and Charles M. Russell.

Photoplay considered Hart's *Wild Bill Hickok* "an old fashioned Western," adding, "The return to the screen of William S. Hart is marked with much gunfighting, most of which is successful." *The New York Times* found the 1923 Hickok and Calamity more of a calamity than Jane, claiming, "Nobody connected with this picture seems to have the vaguest notion of the chief character...[Mr. Hart] is just about the same as he was, except that his acting, compared with modern screen celebrities, appears to belong to an old, old school. His efforts are puerile."

Cecil B. DeMille brought Calamity Jane and Wild Bill Hickok to the screen in 1936 in an exciting, if not historically pure, motion picture called *The Plainsman*. Gary Cooper gave a splendid performance as Hickok and Jean Arthur was vigorous and compelling as Calamity Jane. The *New York World-Telegram* reported, "The performances are excellent. Gary Cooper acts Wild Bill Hickok with considerable force, humor and salty flavor, and Jean Arthur makes the high-spirited Calamity Jane a genuine character by the authenticity of her play."

London's *Bystander* praised *The Plainsman*, finding, "The characterizations of Wild Bill, Calamity Jane, Buffalo Bill Cody and the rest is established deftly and firmly...Jean Arthur has the mixture of toughness and charm required for Calamity Jane, Texas Guinan's predecessor in one phase of her activities, was also given to driving mule teams, scouting and Indian fighting; when she tired of the charms of booze and saloon hurdy-gurdies...despite the epitaph on her grace, 'She Was a Holy Terror,' she must have had charm to get away with half of the misdemeanors she is charged with."

The volatile and beautiful Frances Farmer was Calamity Jane in Universal's 1941

Western, *Badlands of Dakota*. Despite her sincere and rugged performance, *Photoplay* found the film "over-fictionalized," noting, "Everybody and everything that belong to our historical and even hysterical old West have been incorporated in this shoot'em-up movie!" For Paramount's comedy Western, *The Paleface* (1948), Jane Russell was an amusing Calamity Jane packing pistols in her petticoat and marrying bumbling dentist Bob Hope to cover her true identity. Howard Barnes (*New York Herald-Tribune*) wrote, "Miss Russell does not exactly act in the part of Calamity Jane, but she is extremely effective in underlying the ludicrous quality of the show." In 1967, Universal remade *The Paleface* as *The Shakiest Gun in the West* with Don Knotts as the nervous dentist and Barbara Rhoades as the Calamity Jane character, here called Penelope Cushings.

Adding to Hollywood's corruption of history was Universal-International's *Calamity Jane and Sam Bass* (1949). Small-statured Sam Bass was an inept train robber who was killed at Round Rock, Texas, on July 19, 1878, at which time Martha Jane Cannary was mourning the death of Wild Bill Hickok in Deadwood, Dakota Territory. Yvonne De Carlo, a beauteous sight in skintight buckskin, was Calamity in this overly fictitious Western. *The New York Times* opined that De Carlo was "playing Jane in the style of Mae West," while Howard Barnes (*New York Herald-Tribune*) found "Miss De Carlo is properly swaggering as Calamity Jane, but she always looks as though she had just come from a beauty parlor, even when she is shooting it out with the law on a craggy hillside."

The least likely, but most effective, Calamity Jane was brought to the screen by, of all people, Doris Day in Warner Bros.' very popular 1953 Technicolor musical, *Calamity Jane*. Bosley Crowther (*The New York Times*) described the film as "a shrill and preposterous musical Western," adding, "James O'Hanlon has written a script that is utterly cheerful and abandoned in tangling a quite unlikely tale...As for Miss Day's performance, it is tempestuous to the point of becoming just a bit frightening -- a bit terrifying at times... David Butler, who directed, has wound her up tight and let her go. She does everything but hit the ceiling in lashing all over the screen."

Photoplay found Doris Day's *Calamity Jane* "broad as a barn door, a lively sketch of a guntoting tomboy whose feminine heart languishes for a handsome Army lieutenant...The story is shamelessly reminiscent of *Annie Get Your Gun*, but the picture is lighter and fresher than *Annie*, though the score -- ballads and novelty numbers -- doesn't measure up." Sammy Fain and Paul Francis Webster's "Secret Love," performed by Doris Day, won the Academy Award as Best Song.

The *New York Herald-Tribune*'s comment was "*Calamity Jane* can pride itself on one good tune and an energetic performance in the title role by Doris Day... Miss Day stomps and hollers her way around the town of Deadwood like Betty Hutton in a holiday mood." The *Hollywood Reporter* called *Calamity Jane*, "A rollicking musical filled with humor, vitality and sure-fire song hits... With Doris Day in the title role delivering what easily may be her most sparking performance to date...Miss Day obviously had a lot of fun playing Calamity...In top singing form, she is an appealing hoydenish, rowdy Jane, a fast-shooting, dead-eyed markswoman with a flair for adding bellowing exaggerations to her fantastic exploits."

Several second-generation actors James Mitchum (Robert's son), Alana Ladd (Alan's daughter) and Jody McCrea (Joel's son) starred in a minor 1962 Western called *Young Guns of Texas*, in which Calamity Jane was played by an unknown actress named Barbara Mansell (who remains unknown). In 1963's *The Raiders*, Robert Culp and Judi Meredith were Hickok and Calamity Jane, and in the 1966 remake of DeMille's *The Plainsman*, Don Murray and Abby Dalton played Wild Bill and Calamity, with Guy Stockwell turning up as Buffalo Bill Cody.

In 1961, James O'Hanlon's *Calamity Jane* screenplay was adapted to the stage by Charles K. Freeman using the Sammy Fain/Paul Francis Webster musical score from the 1953 film. Betty O'Neil opened in the title role of *Calamity Jane* at Fort Worth's Casa Manana Theatre on May 28, 1961. Fain and Webster added a few more songs to their score for the stage production. *Calamity Jane* was popular as a summer theatre attraction at St. Louis' Municipal Opera Theatre (MUNY) in June 1961 with Edie Adams as star, and in Kansas City, Missouri, the following month with Carol Burnett as the rough and tumble Jane.

Two years later, Carol Burnett brought her Calamity Jane to television. The much traveled Fain-Webster-O'Hanlon musical was broadcast as a ninety-minute CBS Special in November 1963. Jack Gould (*The New York Times*) found Burnett's television version "hardly worthy of her talents. It was the awkward musical called *Calamity Jane* which wasn't too good a film and did not benefit by further compression for TV."

Twenty-one years after the musical, Jane Alexander produced and starred in a rather loose adaptation of the Calamity-Hickok legend on television. "She rode hard, she drank hard, she loved hard!" was how CBS promoted its movie-made-for television that premiered in March 1984. Jane Alexander was splendid in the title role in a wellpaced script written by Suzanne Clauser, based on Martha Jane Cannary's diary. Richard F. Shepard (*The New York Times*) praised the colorful story, adding, "the best thing here is the performance in the title role by Jane Alexander, who makes Calamity Jane most credible and turns what might have been a quite sentimental bit of unbelievable business into a very human experience...Under James Goldstone's direction, *Calamity Jane* moves along scenically when it does not do so dramatically, with a capable cast that includes Frederic Forrest as a hirsute Hickok."

STAGE

CALAMITY JANE, Casa Manana Theatre, Fort Worth, Texas, opened May 28, 1961
Produced by Casa Manana Musicals Company; A Musical Comedy; Director, Michael Pollock; Book by Charles K. Freeman adapted from the screenplay by James O'Hanlon; Music by Sammy Fain; Lyrics by Paul Francis Webster; Settings, Hal Shafer; Lighting, Jules Fisher; Costumes, Evelyn Norton Anderson; Choreography, Harding Dorn; Musical direction, Boris Kogan; Orchestrations and choral arrangements, Philip J. Lang

Betty O'Neil (Calamity Jane); Danny Scholl (Wild Bill Hickok); Freshy Marker (Katie Brown); William Pickett (Henry Miller); Johnny Sullivan (Rattle-snake); Linda Johnson (Susan); Carl Hoyt (Colorado Charlie); Vern Taylor (Doc Pierce); Bud Cruse (Joe); Jim Hampton (Francis Fryer); Charley James (Hank); Dick Hitt (Pete); Robert Simpson (Lieutenant Gilmartin); Ronald Knight (Hugh Kingsley); Janan Hart (Adelaide Adams); Carl Hoyt (Stage Doorman); Jim Gurley, Bill Olfekehn, Eric Scott, Michael Waco (Stagedoor Johnnies); Carol deOnis, Barbara Ellers, Kay Sutton, Rosemary Webb (Chorus Girls); Ellen Ray (Solo Dancer); Bill Cook, Jody Cross, Georgia Ebly, Jim Frazier, Jack Hairston, Jack Stuteville, Tia Lou Taylor, David Worsley (Deadwood City Residents)

MUSICAL NUMBERS: "Secret Love"; "The Deadwood Stage"; "Higher Than a Hawk"; "'Tis Harry I'm Plannin' to Marry"; "I Can Do Without You"; "Just Blew in From the Windy City"; "Keep It Under Your Hat"; "I've Got a Hive Full of Honey"; "A Woman's Touch"; "The Black Hills of Dakota"

St. Louis (Mo.) Municipal Opera Theatre, opened June 12, 1961

Produced by the Municipal Theatre Association of St. Louis; The World Outdoor Premiere of *Calamity Jane*; Produced by John Kennedy; Director, James Vincent Russo; Adapted for the stage by Charles K. Freeman, based on the screenplay by James O'Hanlon; Music by Sammy Fain; Lyrics by Paul Francis Webster; Orchestrations and Vocal arrangements by Philip J. Lang; Music director, Edwin McArthur; Settings, Paul C. McGuire; Choreography and Ensembles by Frank Westbrook; Costumes, Bill Hargate, Eaves Costume Company, Andrew Geoly; Modern dances and ensembles, Dan M. Eckley

Edith Adams (Calamity Jane); George Gaynes (Wild Bill Hickok); Nolan Van Way (Lt. Danny Gilmartin); Allyn Ann McLerie (Katie Brown); Edmund Lyndeck (Henry Miller); April Shawhan (Susan); Lou Wills, Jr. (Francis Fryer); Lila Gage (Adelaid Adams); Joseph Cusanelli (Rattlesnake); F. J. O'Neil (Doc Pierce); Pablo Flores (Joe); Graham Green (Pete); Robert Kelly (Hank); Carroll Wayham (Kingsley); Charles Sherwood (Prospector); Eb McIntire (Doorman); Bill Wood (Preacher); Bill Bradley (Lead Dancer)

MUSICAL NUMBERS: "The Deadwood Stage"; "Adelaid"; "Everyone Complains About the Weather"; "Weather Dance"; "Men"; "Careless With the Truth"; "Hive Full of Honey"; "Weather Dance Lesson"; "I Can Do Without You"; "'Tis Harry I'm Planning to Marry"; "Windy City"; "Keep It Under Your Hat"; "Barroom Dance"; "Higher Than a Hawk"; "A Woman's Touch"; "Love You Dearly"; "Black Hills of Dakota"; "Secret Love"

Starlight Theatre, Kansas City, Mo., opened July 17, 1961

Produced by the Starlight Theatre Association of Kansas City; A Musical Play; Production supervisor, Richard H. Berger; Director, Bertram Yarborough; Adapted for the stage by Charles K. Freeman from screenplay by James O'Hanlon; Music by Sammy Fain; Lyrics by Paul Francis Webster; Scenery and Lighting by G. Philippe de Rosier; Costumes designed by Audre; Musical director, Roland Fiore; Musical ensembles staged by Ted Forlow; Orchestrations and vocal arrangements by Philip J. Lang; Choreography, Harding Dorn; Associate musical director and choral master, Dean Ryan; Dance music arranged by Jack Lee; Stage managers, Anthony Ferrara and Jerold D. Funk

Carol Burnett (Calamity Jane); Norwood Smith (Wild Bill Hickok); Joseph Macaulay (Henry Miller); Beryl Towbin (Katie Brown); Judy St. John (Susan); Walter Hook (Francis Fryer); Stephen Elmore (Rattlesnake); Paul Elsom (Doc Pierce); Don Larson (Bartender); William Ledbetter (Hank); Keith Lee Thomas (Pete); Art Matthews (Lieutenant Gilmartin); Patti Karr (Adelaid Adams); Raymond Highley (Doorman); Steve Bray, Linda Eikel, Frank McConnell, Melissa Stoneburn, Gretchen White (Children's Ballet); Dorothy Ansmith, Jim Dybas, Dolores Lipinski, Wayne Boyd, Elaine Loughead, David Milnes, Evelyne Maubert, Wayne Foster (Corps de Ballet)

CALAMITY JANE TO HER DAUGHTER, *Dance Theater Workshop*, New York, opened October 22, 1990 2 performances

Produced by the Dance Theater Workshop; Director/ lighting designer, Charles Otte; Book and music, Ben Johnston; Costumes, Claudia Brown; Presented on a program of seven music-theater pieces titled *Urban Diva*

Dora Ohrenstein (Calamity Jane)

SCREEN

WILD BILL HICKOK, *Paramount Pictures*, released November 1923
Presented by Adolph Zukor; Producer, William S. Hart; Director, Clifford S. Smith; Screenplay by J. H. Hawkes based on a story by W. S. Hart; Photography, Dwight Warren and Arthur Reeves

William S. Hart (Wild Bill Hickok); Ethel Grey Terry (Calamity Jane); James Farley (Jack McQueen); Kathleen O'Connor (Elaine Hamilton); Carl Gerard (Clayton Hamilton); Jack Gardner (Bat Masterson); William Dyer (Colonel Horatio Higginbotham); Bert Sprotte (Bob Wright); Leo Willis (Joe McCord); Naida Carle (Fanny Kate); Herschel Mayall (Gambler)

CAUGHT, *Paramount Pictures*, released August 1931
Director, Edward Sloman; Screenplay, Agnes Brand Leahy and Keene Thompson; Additional dialogue, Bella and Sam Spewack; Photography, Charles Lang

Louise Dresser (Calamity Jane); Richard Arlen (Lt. Tom Colton); Frances Dee (Kate Winslow); Tom Kennedy (Jard Harmon); Martin Burdon (Curly Braydon); Marcia Manners (Goldie); Sid Saylor (Sergeant Weems); Guy Oliver (McNeill); E. J. LeSaint (Haverstraw); Charles K. French (Bradford); Lon Poff (Clem); James Mason (Scully); Jack Clifford (Drunk); Hal Price (Pal)

THE PLAINSMAN, *Paramount Pictures*, released November 1936
Produced and directed by Cecil B. DeMille; Screenplay by Waldemar Young, Harold Lamb and Lynn Riggs, based on the stories *Wild Bill Hickok* by Frank J. Wilstach and *The Prince of Pistoleers* by Courtney Riley Cooper and Grover Jones; Adaptation by Jeanie MacPherson; Photography, Victor Milner, George Robinson; Special camera effects, Gordon Jennings, Farciot Edouart; Art directors, Hans Dreier and Roland Anderson; Set decorator, A. E. Freudeman; Costumes, Natalie Visart, Dwight Franklin and Joe De Young; Music director, Boris Morros; Music, George Antheil; Sound, Harry M. Lindgren; Editor, Anne Bauchens

Jean Arthur (Calamity Jane); Gary Cooper (Wild Bill Hickok); James Ellison (Buffalo Bill Cody); Charles Bickford (John Latimer); Porter Hall (Jack McCall); John Miljan (General George Armstrong Custer); Victor Varconi (Painted Horse); Helen Burgess (Louisa Cody); Frank McGlynn, Sr. (Abraham Lincoln); Paul Harvey (Chief Yellow Hand); Granville Bates (Van Ellyn); Purnell Pratt (Captain Wood); Pat Moriarty (Sergeant McGinnis); Charles Judels (Tony); Fuzzy Knight (Dave); Edwin Maxwell (Stanton); John Hyams (Schuyler Colfax); Fred Kohler (Jack); George "Gabby" Hayes (Breezy); George MacQuarrie (General Merritt); Charlie Stevens (Injun Charlie); Leila McIntyre (Mary Todd Lincoln); Harry Stubbs (John F. Usher); Davison Clark (James Speed); William Humphries (Hugh McCulloch); Sidney Jarvis (Gideon Welles); Wadsworth Harris (William Dennison); C. W. Herzinger (William H. Seward); Lona Andre (Southern Belle); Frank Albertson (Young Soldier); Anthony Quinn (Cheyenne Warrior); Bruce Warren (Captain of the Lizzie Gill); Mark Strong (Wells Fargo Agent); George Ernest (Urchin); Irving Bacon (Soldier); Francis MacDonald (Boat Gambler); Edgar Dearing (Custer's Messenger); Arthur Aylesworth, Douglas Wood, George Cleveland (Van Ellyn's Assistants); Harry Woods (Quartermaster Sergeant); Francis Ford (Veteran); Bud Flanagan [Dennis O'Keefe], Gail Sheridan, Lane Chandler, Hank Bell, Jane Keckley, Cora Shumway, Tex Driscoll, Wilbur Mack, Francis Sayles, Louise Stuart, James Mason, Franklyn Farnum, Stanhope Wheatcroft, Noble Johnson, Ted Oliver, Bud Osborne, Blackjack Ward (Extras)

YOUNG BILL HICKOK, *Republic Pictures*, released September 1940
Produced and directed by Joseph Kane; Screenplay, Norton S. Parker and Olive Cooper; Photography, William Nobles; Musical director, Cy Feuer; Editor, Lester Orlebeck

Roy Rogers (Bill Hickok); Sally Payne (Calamity Jane); George "Gabby" Hayes ("Gabby"); Jacqueline Wells (Louise Mason); Monte Blue (Marshal Evans); Hal Taliaferro (Morrell); Ethel Wales (Mrs. Stout); Archie Twitchell (Phillip); John Miljan (Nicholas Tower); Jack Ingram (Red); Monte Montague (Majors)

BADLANDS OF DAKOTA, *Universal Pictures*, released September 1941
Associate producer, George Waggner; Directer, Alfred E. Green; Screenplay, Gerald Geraghty; Story by Harold Shumate; Photography, Stanley Cortez; Art director, Jack Otterson; Musical director, H. K. Salter; Songs, Carson Robinson; Editor, Frank Gross

Richard Dix (Wild Bill Hickok); Frances Farmer (Calamity Jane); Robert Stack (Jim Holliday); Ann Rutherford (Anne Grayson); Broderick Crawford (Bob Holliday); Hugh Herbert (Rocky); Andy Devine (Spearfish); Lon Chaney, Jr. (Jack McCall); Fuzzy Knight (Hurricane Harry); Addison Richards (General Custer); Bradley Page (Chapman); Samuel S. Hinds (Uncle Wilbur); Carleton Young (Mercer); Glenn Strange (Russell); Don Barclay (Joe); Emmett Vogan (Benson); Willie Fung (Chinaman); Edward Fielding (Judge); Dwight Latham, Walter Carlson, Guy Bonham (The Jesters)

SONGS: "No One to Love" and "Goin' to Have a Big Time Tonight" (Carson Robinson); "McNamara's Band" (Shamus O'Connor and J. J. Stamford)

THE PALEFACE, *Paramount Pictures*, released December 1948
Produced by Robert L. Welch; Director, Norman Z. McLeod; Screenplay by Edmund Hartman, Frank Tashlin; Additional dialogue, Jack Rose; Photography, Ray Rennahan; Art directors, Hans Drier, Earl Hedrick; Set decorators, Sam Comer, Bertram Granger; Costumes, Mary Kay Dodson; Choreography, Billy Daniels; Music, Victor Young; Special effects, Gordon Jennings; Sound, Gene Merritt, John Cope; Assistant director, Alvin Ganzer; Editor, Ellsworth Hoagland

Bob Hope ("Painless" Peter Porter); Jane Russell (Calamity Jane); Robert Armstrong (Terris); Iris Adrian (Pepper); Jack Searl (Jasper Martin); Joseph Vitale (Indian Scout); Robert Watson (Toby Preston); Charles Trowbridge (Governor Johnson); Clem Bevans (Hank Billings); Stanley Andrews (Commissioner Emerson); Wade Crosby (Webb); Jeff York (Joe); Chief Yowlachie (Chief Yellow Feather); Iron Eyes Cody (Chief Iron Eyes); Francis McDonald (Lance); Frank Hagney (Greg); Skelton Knaggs (Pete); Olin Howlin (Undertaker); John Maxwell (Village Gossip); Tom Kennedy (Bartender); Henry Brandon (Medicine Man Wapato); Earl Hodgins (Clem); Arthur Space (Zach); Charles Cooley (Mr. "X"); Eric Alden (Bob); Edgar Dearing (Sheriff); George Chandler, Nestor Paiva (Patients); Dorothy Grainger (Bath House Attendant); Duke York, Ethan Laidlow (Henchmen); John Miller (Bellhop); Wally Boyle (Hotel Clerk); Babe London (Wagon Train Woman); Billy Engle, Houseley Stevenson, Al M. Hill (Pioneers); Laura Corbay, Margaret Field (Guests); Lane Chandler (Tough Guy); Oliver Blake (Westerner); Dick Elliott (Mayor); Carl Andre, Ted Maples, Kermit Maynard (Horsemen); Harry Harvey, Paul Burns (Justices of the Peace); Loyal Underwood (Man with Beard); June Glory, Marilyn Gladstone, Charmienne Karker, Betty Hannon, Dee La Nore, Marie J. Tavares (B-Girls); Stanley Blystone, Bob Kortman (Bystanders)

SONGS: "Buttons and Bows" (Jay Livingston and Ray Evans) -- Academy Award-winning song for 1948

NOTE: The 1968 remake of this film, *The Shakiest Gun in the West*, starring Don Knotts and Barbara Rhoades, used different character names with no Calamity Jane included.

CALAMITY JANE AND SAM BASS, *Universal-International Pictures*, released July 1949

Produced by Leonard Goldstein; Associate producer, Aaron Rosenberg; Director, George Sherman; Screenplay by Maurice Geraghty, based on an original story by George Sherman, adapted by Maurice Geraghty and Melvin Levy; Photography, Irving Glassberg; Art directors, Bernard Herzbrun and Richard Riedel; Set decorators, Russell A. Gausman and Al Fields; Costumes, Yvonne Wood; Music director and orchestrator, Milton Schwarzwald; Sound, Leslie I. Carey, Glenn E. Anderson; Editor, Edward Curtiss

Yvonne De Carlo (Calamity Jane); Howard Duff (Sam Bass); Willard Parker (Sheriff Will Egan); Dorothy Hart (Katherine Egan); Norman Lloyd (Jim Murphy); Lloyd Bridges (Joel Collins); Marc Lawrence (Dean); Houseley Stevenson (Dakota); Milburn Stone (Abe Jones); John Rodney (Morgan); Roy Roberts (Marshal Peak); Ann Doran (Mrs. Egan); Charles Cane (J. Wells); Walter Baldwin (Doc Purdy); Clifton Young (Link); Paul Maxey (Underwood); George Carleton (Mr. Sherman); Harry Harvey (Station Agent); Jack Ingram (Mayes); Francis McDonald (Starter); Douglas Walton (Bookmaker); Russ Conway (Baggage Man); Nedrick Young (Parsons); Jimmy Ames (Blacksmith); Stanley Blystone (Cowboy); I. Stanford Jolley (Wilson); Anthony Backus, Pierce Lyden (Deputies); Ezelle Poule (Woman Customer); Roy Butler, Frank McCaroll, Charles Sullivan, Bob Perry, James Linn, Bill Sundholm (Bits)

THE TEXAN MEETS CALAMITY JANE, *Columbia Pictures*, released October 1950

Produced, directed and written by Andre Lamb; Photography, Karl Stuss; Music, Rudy de Saxe; Editor, George McGuire

Evelyn Ankers (Calamity Jane); James Ellison (Cordon Hastings); Lee "Lasses" White (Colorado Charley); Frank Pharr (Sheriff Atwood); Ruth Whitney (Cecelia Mullen); Jack Ingram (Matt Baker); Sally Weidman (Emmy Stokes); Hugh Hooker (Sam); Walter Strand (Carlos); Rudy de Saxe (Herbert); Ferrell Lester (Rollo); Ronald Marriott (Nick); Paul Barney (Dave); Bill Orisman (Shotgun Messenger); Lou W. Pierce (Elmer and the Horse); Elmer Herzberg (Henry the Whistler)

CALAMITY JANE, *Warner Bros. Pictures*, released November 1953

Produced by William Jacobs; Director, Daivd Butler; Screenplay by James O'Hanlon; Photography, Wilfred M. Cline; Art director, John Beckman; Set decorator, G. W. Bertsen; Costumes, Howard Shoup; Songs by Sammy Fain and Paul Francis Webster; Musical direction, Ray Heindorf; Musical numbers, staged and directed by Jack Donohue; Editor, Irene Morra

Doris Day (Calamity Jane); Howard Keel (Wild Bill Hickok); Allyn McLerie (Katie Brown); Philip Carey (Lieutenant Gilmartin); Dick Wesson (Francis Fryer); Paul Harvey (Henry Miller); Chubby Johnson (Rattlesnake); Lee Shumway (Bartender); Gale Robbins (Adelaide Adams); Rex Lease (Buck); Forrest Taylor (MacPherson); Monte Montague (Pete); Francis McDonald (Hank); Emmett

Lynn (Artist); Lane Chandler, Glenn Strange, Zon Murray, Budd Buster, Terry Frost, Ton Landon, Billy Bletcher (Prospectors); Buddy Roosevelt, Reed Howes, Stanley Blystone, Lee Morgan, Kenne Duncan, Bill Hale Tom Monroe (Cowboys, Citizens, etc.)

MUSICAL NUMBERS: "Secret Love"; "Higher Than a Hawk"; "'Tis Harry I'm Plannin' to Marry"; "The Deadwood Stage"; "I Can Do Without You"; "Keep It Under Your Hat"; "Just Blew in from the Windy City"; "I've Got a Hive Full of Honey"; "A Woman's Touch"; "The Black Hills of Dakota"

Original soundtrack recording: Columbia Records

YOUNG GUNS OF TEXAS, *20th Century-Fox*, released 1962

Producer and director, Maury Dexter; Screenplay, Henry Cross; Photography, John Nickolaus, Jr.; Production Supervisor, Harold E. Knox; Art Director, Harry Reif; Music, Paul Sawtell; Title Song written by Paul Sawtell and John Herring, sung by Kenny Miller, Sound, William Bernds and Harry M. Leonard; Editors, Jodie Copelan and Richard Einfield

James Mitchum (Morgan Coe); Alana Ladd (Lily Glendenning); Jody McCrea (Jeff Shelby) Barbara Mansell (Martha "Calamity" Jane Cannary); Robert Lowery (Jesse Glendenning); Fred Krone (Pike); Alex Sharpe (Red); Chill Wills (Sam Shelby); Gary Conway (Tyler Duane); Troy Melton (Luke); Robert Hinkle (Sheriff); Will Wills (Cowhand)

THE RAIDERS, *Universal-International Pictures*, released 1963

Producer, Howard Christie; Director, Herschel Daugherty; Screenplay, Gene L. Coon; Photography, Bud Thackery; Art director, Alexander A. Mayer; Set decorators, John McCarthy and Robert C. Bradfield; Music, Morton Stevens; Sound, David H. Moriarty; Assistant director, Edward K. Dodds; Editor, Gene Palmer

Robert Culp (James Butler "Wild Bill" Hickok); Judi Meredith (Martha Jane "Calamity Jane" Cannary); Alfred Ryder (Captain Benton); James McMullan (William F. "Buffalo Bill" Cody); Brian Keith (John G. McElroy); Simon Oakland (Sergeant Austin Tremaine); Ben Cooper (Tom King); Trevor Bardette (Uncle Otto Strassner); Harry Carey, Jr. (Jellico); Dick Cutting (Jack Goodnight); Addison Richards (Huntington Lawford); Cliff Osmond (Duchamps); Paul Birch (Paul King); Richard Deacon (Commissioner Mailer); Michael Burns (Jimmy McElroy)

THE PLAINSMAN, *Universal Pictures*, released 1966

Produced by Richard E. Lyons; Associate producer, Jack Leewood; Director, David Lowell Rich; Screenplay, Michael Blankfort; Photography, Bud Thackery; Costumes, Helen Colvig; Art Directors, Alexander Golitzen and William DeCinces; Set decorators, John McCarthy and Ralph Sylos; Music, Johnny Williams; Music supervisor, Stanley Wilson; Makeup, Bud Westmore; Assistant director, Edward K. Dodds; Sound, Waldon O. Watson and David H. Moriarty; Editor, Danny B. Landres

Don Murray (Wild Bill Hickok); Abby Dalton (Calamity Jane); Guy Stockwell (Buffalo Bill Cody); Bradford Dillman (Lt. Stiles); Henry Silva (Crazy Knife); Edward Binns (Lattimer); Simon Oakland (Black Kettle); Leslie Nielsen (Colonel George A. Custer); Michael Evans (Estrick); Percy Rodrigues (Brother John); Terry Wilson (Sergeant Womack); Walter Burke (Abe Ireland); Emily Banks (Louisa Cody)

TELEVISION

CALAMITY JANE, televised November 12, 1963 CBS 90 minutes
Executive producer, Bob Banner; Produced by Joe Hamilton; Directors, Dick Altman and Ernest Flatt; Teleplay by Phil Shuken, based on the screenplay by James O'Hanlon; Music by Sammy Fain; Lyrics by Paul Francis Webster; Music director, Harry Zimmerman; Choreography, Ernest Flatt

Carol Burnett (Calamity Jane); Art Lund (Wild Bill Hickok); Beryl Towbin (Katie Brown); Bernie West (Henry Miller); Don Chastain (Lt. Danny Gilmartin); Cathryn Damon (Adelaide Adams); Mark Harris (Francis Fryer)

CALAMITY JANE, televised March 6, 1984 CBS 2 hours
Executive producer, Bernard Sofronski; Produced by Herbert Hirschman and Jane Alexander; Director, James Goldstone; Teleplay by Suzanne Clauser; Photography, Terry K. Meade; Production designer, Albert Heschong; Music, Fred Karlin; Costume designer, Brienne; Editor, Edward A. Biery

Jane Alexander (Calamity Jane); Frederic Forrest (Wild Bill Hickok); Ken Kercheval (Buffalo Bill Cody); David Hemmings (Captain James O'Neill); Gilliam Eaton (Mrs. O'Neill); Walter Olkewicz (Will Lull); Talia Balsam (Jean); Walter Scott (Charlie Burke); Jack Murdock (Reverend Warren); Larry Cedar (Reverend Sipes); Isabell Monk (Nell); Doug Toby (Jackie); Laurie O'Brien (Mamie); Sara Abeles (Jean, age 7); Don Hepner (Barker); Jessica Nelson (Patty); Henry M. Kenrick (Station Boss); Gloria Henry, Mavis Neal Palmer (Ladies); Theresa DePaolo (Young Woman)

CAMELOT

A Musical Play by Alan Jay Lerner and Frederick Loewe (1960)

Synopsis

After the death of his ancient tutor, King Arthur, shy and nervous over his forthcoming marriage, anxiously awaits his bride Guenevere. Without at first revealing his identity, Arthur tells Guenevere, who deplores the prospect of marriage robbing her of the simple joys of maidenhood, that he has heard wicked tales about the King but that Camelot is a place of wonder where it only rains at night and "there's not a more congenial spot for happy everaftering." After their marriage, Arthur establishes a Round Table of Knights dedicated to peace and righting wrongs. Lancelot du Lac, a dashing, egotistical Frenchman, arrives in Camelot to join the Round Table. Guenevere encourages Sir Dinadan, Sir Sagramore and Sir Lionel to challenge Lancelot to a joust. Lancelot defeats Dinadan and Sagramore but fatally spears Sir Lionel. Before the awestricken court, Lancelot, through his great faith and purity, brings Sir Lionel back to life, winning the respect of the court and knighthood from Arthur.

Lancelot and Guenevere fall in love. They maintain their love in silence from afar, however, out of respect and love for Arthur, who is aware of their devotion. Villainous Mordred, Arthur's illegitimate son, arranges Arthur's absence and traps the innocent lovers. Lancelot escapes but Guenevere is condemned to be burned at the stake. The Queen is rescued from her fate by Lancelot and taken to France. Arthur pursues the lovers but forgives them on learning that Guenevere has entered a convent and maintains Lancelot as his still-devoted friend. Before a battle with the

French, Arthur encounters a stowaway English boy Tom begging to join his renowned Round Table. The boy's request instills renewed hope in Arthur that Camelot's "fleeting wisp of glory" and "one, brief shining moment" will be remembered and recaptured.

Comment and Critique

Camelot was the last Broadway collaboration by composer Frederick Loewe and lyricist Alan Jay Lerner. They had first worked together in 1942 for a musical version of Barry Conner's 1925 play *The Patsy*, retitled *Life of the Party*, which opened and closed in Detroit. Lerner and Loewe's Broadway contributions included *What's Up* (1943); *The Day Before Spring* (1945); *Briga-doon* (1947); *Paint Your Wagon* (1951); and *My Fair Lady* (1956). Between *My Fair Lady* and *Camelot*, they wrote *Gigi* for the screen.

Camelot was based on T. H. White's (1906-64) classic five novels written over a period of twenty years: (*The Sword in the Stone* (1939); *The Witch in the Wood (The Queen of Air and Darkness*) (1940); *The Ill-Made Knight* (1941); *The Candle in the Wind* (1958); *The Once and Future King* (1958), published under the general title of *The Once and Future King.*

The opening of *Camelot* on Broadway was postponed from November 19 to December 3, 1960, with advance ticket sales amounting close to $2 million. Director Moss Hart had died during the show's Boston tryout and Lerner himself had taken over the direction. "Alan Jay Lerner, Frederick Loewe and Moss Hart spent so much to mount *Camelot* that the wisecrackers have been calling it *Costallot*," reported Robert Coleman (*New York Mirror*). "...It's no *Fair Lady*. The words and music are just fair. We suspect that Lerner set out to pen a serious satire on knighthood in flower, and missed the boat. His philosophy lacks true depth, and there's too little wit about the premises...*Camelot* is an expensive disappointment."

John Chapman (*Daily News*) wrote, "*Camelot* is magnificent. Its songs are lovely and unfailingly right. Its cast is superb. The sets and costumes of its twenty scenes have far more than splendor; together they make a single, thrilling work of art." Frank Aston (*New York World-Telegram and The Sun*) added, "This...version of the Arthurian legend, with its crowds, vistas, colors and costumes is about as reportable as the Grand Canyon...*Camelot* has gayety and grandeur. Its beauty is almost unbelievable."

"Although its people are handsome and its vistas beautiful, *Camelot* is a partly enchanted city," claimed Howard Taubman (*The New York Times*), "Visually, *Camelot* is never less than a thing of beauty. Graceful and sumptuous though it is, *Camelot* leans dangerously in the direction of old-hat operetta. It has intervals of enchantment, as it must with talented men like Lerner, Loewe and Hart in charge. It would be unjust to tax them with not attaining the heights of *My Fair Lady*, but it cannot be denied that they badly miss their late collaborator, Bernard Shaw."

John McClain (*Journal-American*) appraised *Camelot* as "Beautiful to behold, but lacks distinction...the Frederick Loewe music lacks great distinction and Alan Jay Lerner's story buckles at the knees...The result, of course, is that the splendor of the surroundings overpowers everything else, and if it weren't for the great masculine authority of Richard Burton, and Julie Andrews, winsome voice and fragile beauty, there might be times when the action of the play would become an unwelcome interruption of a poetic reverie...The fine hand of Moss Hart never falters in the direction; it is a pity the book offered him so little subtlety in situation."

Moss Hart, whose long career in the theatre included several of his plays and others written with George S. Kaufman, had directed the Lerner and Loewe 1956 smash, *My Fair Lady*. Hart had a heart attack while directing *Camelot* and the musical legend would be his last contribution to the American theatre. On Wednesday, December 20, 1961, he died in Palm Springs, California at fifty-seven.

Camelot was a huge success on Broadway and on national tours for the next four years. On August 19, 1964, *Camelot* opened at the Drury Lane Theatre in London, with Laurence Harvey in the lead. Hugh Leonard (*Plays and Players*) recalled a New York friend describing *Camelot* as "the only musical play from which he ever came away whistling the scenery," adding, "There are many things wrong with *Camelot* but nothing -- not even the wild veering from legend to reality to fairy tale and back again, with side trips to Disneyland *en route* -- equals the havoc wreaked by the character of Pellinore. It was once axiomatic that every musical play must have its low comedian, but even Rodgers and Hammerstein in their worst excesses -- Ali Hakim in *Oklahoma!*, for example -- never sunk to the depths plumbed by Alan Jay Lerner in recreating Pellinore...Frederick Loewe's tunes were not merely undistinguished but almost undistinguishable...Laurence Harvey, who must surely be the world's most unpopular popular star, was a skittish and sympathetic Arthur."

Producer Jack Hylton lavished some $300,000 on the London production of *Camelot*, but Herbert Kretzmer (*Daily Express*) felt the opulence of the show was "all dressed up and nowhere to go...If spectacle were all, *Camelot* would run for five years, but otherwise it is too often insecure, unsure of its own directions. It lacks spine." In the *Daily Mail*, Bernard Levin found both the book and music "totally forgettable" in the "least interesting, least witty, least colorful, least bearable series of works ever spoken by a substandard cast." Arthur Thirkell (*Daily Mirror*) added, "It may draw the crowds on the strength of its magical sets and costumes, but I wish the magic could have spread to the story and the dialogue."

Twenty years after *Camelot* first burst upon Broadway with Richard Burton in his first musical, and Arthur's final acknowledgement that Camelot's "fleeting wisp of glory" and its "one, brief shining moment" became a tribute to the brief presidency of John Fitzgerald Kennedy, fifty-four-year-old Richard Burton returned to the stage to once again reign over *Camelot*.

The 1980 revival of *Camelot* opened at Toronto's O'Keefe Center Theatre (where the 1960 production had first tried out) prior to a national tour and reappearance at New York's State Theatre. Patrick Pacheco (*After Dark*) reviewed the Toronto engagement, feeling "In our present gray times, *Camelot* reaches for the stars with unapologetic romanticism, bound in myth and legend to what now seems a golden era. The hero-hungry crowd grabs for a fleeting wisp of glory like children too long deprived of fantasy." Burton told Pacheco, "It's inevitable, I suppose, that this show should conjure up memories of the good ol' days -- but people forget that in those good ol' days, people were hungering for the good ol' days. You never catch up. As for me, I've had a pretty wonderful life, despite all the selfinduced physical punishment." Burton conceded, "I always felt that I was too young to do the role justice when I first did it. Now I sometimes wonder if it isn't the other way around."

The revived Burton and revival of *Camelot* opened again on Broadway in July 1980, to play fifty-six per-formances. Annalyn Swan (*Newsweek*) felt Richard Burton was "more memorably moving as good King Arthur than he was in the original Broadway production twenty years ago," and noted that Alan Jay Lerner had revised *Camelot* to open with and end with the battle scene with the story told in flashbacks. "Unfortunately, in Frank Dunlap's ponderous staging, idyllic *Camelot* emerges as a realm you wouldn't much care to visit, let alone live in...By the end Burton seems more like a hamlet than a music man as he proclaims the final ringing benediction of the 'one brief, shining moment that was known as Camelot.' A kingdom may be lost in *Camelot*, but the crown rests secure on Burton's head."

Douglas Watt (*Daily News*) found that "twenty years later, *Camelot* is still in trouble -- not just the place, but the whole gorgeous whooping crane of a show -- half lovely, half dopey and ultimately a bore. *Camelot* is too long and too often silly and pretentious. Eventually, Burton is the whole show." Frank Rich (*The New York Times*) was pleased with the revisions Lerner had made in the script, considering them "generally for the better, "but they don't remake *Camelot* into a seamless, light-footed entertainment. Without Burton, it might well be a chore to sit through."

Burton had remarked about his scheduled year-long national tour in *Camelot* (for which he was reputedly paid $50,000 a week), "I considered this my tryout for a six-month run of *King Lear*. After a year of this, I'll be ready for 'Blow, winds, and crack your cheeks! Rage! Blow!'" On March 11, 1981, *Camelot* opened at Los Angeles' Pantages Theatre, and on March 23, 1981, Burton found himself confined in Santa Monica's St. Johns Hospital with a virus and an impinged nerve in the cervical area of his right arm.

Burton gave his last performance as King Arthur on March 17 and was replaced by his understudy William Parry, who completed the run of *Camelot* on June 7 (it had opened with an advance sale of over $3 million). Burton had missed only one performance during the tour of *Camelot* on July 17 in New York. Richard Burton died of cerebral hemorrhage at fifty-eight on August 5, 1984.

Richard Harris, who had played Arthur in the 1967 screen version of *Camelot*, took over the role for an extensive road tour and appeared on November 15, 1981, at Broadway's Winter Garden Theatre. "Maybe there can be *Camelot* without Richard Burton," reported Frank Rich (*The New York Times*), "but it didn't happen in the revival that opened at the Winter Garden...Mr. Harris' Arthur, while by no means bad, is far more dour. This performance is, heaven knows, a regal piece of showmanship -- full of grand, arrogant gestures, royal pauses and vocal extravagances of the old school... What's fatally missing from his King, however, are sexual passion and a sense of humor...Richard Muenz, the major cast holdover, remains a vibrant and amusing Lancelot...*Camelot* now lives best on the original cast album - and in our fond memories of round tables past." (The Harris production of *Camelot* was taped at the Winter Garden for subsequent showing on Home Box Office the following September.)

In 1982, when *Camelot* reappeared in London, Frank Marcus (*Plays and Players*) wrote, "Alan Jay Lerner (Book and Lyrics) and Frederick Loewe (Music) cannot match ability to ambition...they attempt to extract contemporary significance from the Arthurian legend. There is nothing dishonourable in wanting to do so, although their manifest fear of overtaxing the mental powers of their audience is somewhat patronising.... Musically the show suffers from anoerexia nervosa -- I have never seen or heard a musical success of yester-year that was so lacking in inspiration...Richard Harris' King Arthur, weighed down by the burden of his suffering and nobility (not to mention the script), hurtles downhill into the vale of tears, fairly choking with selfpity."

Harris returned to the American stage, both directing and starring as King Arthur in a final six-month tour of *Camelot* in 1986, beginning at Wolf Trap outside of Washington, D.C., and in 1990, Robert Goulet, having grown into the role of King Arthur, toured the country in a version of *Camelot*.

Several film versions of the Arthurian legend were made, based mainly on Sir Thomas Malory's *Morte d'Arthur*, Alfred Lord Tennyson's *The Idylls of the King*, Hennius' *Historia Brittenum*, or myriad historical legends out of folklore. Mark Twain set his humorous novel *A Connecticut Yankee in King Arthur's Court* in legendary Camelot, but it remained for T. H. White to complete the Arthurian legend in four novels under the general title of *The Once and Future King*. In 1975, a fifth novel by T. H. White, *Merlyn's Folly*, was found and published. English archaeologists in 1969 uncovered many artifacts in South Cadbury, near Glaston-bury, England, which could have been the site of Camelot. Walt Disney produced an animated film of White's first novel *The Sword in the Stone* in 1963, and it was inevitable that Lerner and Loewe's *Camelot* would be transferred to the screen.

In 1964, Warner Bros. produced an excellent screen version of Lerner and Loewe's superb *My Fair Lady*, and in 1967, the studio issued a press release titled *Camelot Rises Anew From Mists of a Myth* extoling the magnificence of *Camelot*. "Conceived by Jack L. Warner as monumental entertainment, Warners have spared nothing to create a worthy successor to *My Fair Lady*...The sets alone cost more than $2.5 million, while the costumes were executed for an estimated $2,250,000... *Camelot* began a year of production with two months filming in Spain, where the exteriors of eight genuine castles were used to illuminate Sir Lancelot's Quest to enlist Arthur's Knights of the Round Table. The castles were in Sergovia, Bilbao, Avila, Penafiel, Manzanares, Medina del Campo, and Coca (representing *Camelot*), besides Castle Bellver near Palma, Majorca. At the Warner studios, other *Camelot* settings were constructed. Among 45 different sets, the castle measured 400 by 300 feet, rising almost 100 feet from ground to turret tops. Another setting, the King's study, held Arthur's celebrated Round Table; weighing 2,750 pounds with a 38-foot diameter and 119-foot circumference, it accommodated 150 seated knights in armor." (The huge studio castle used in *Camelot* was refurbished for the 1973 musical remake of *Lost Horizon*.)

"Now it is our turn to stand alone at the end of this film version and yearn for the grandeur of a fully consummated *Camelot* that might have been, that never was and probably never will be," eulogized *Newsweek* magazine. "The proportions are all wrong, the pieces still refuse to fit and the vision is clouded by an immense accumulation of conventional claptrap. The most notable improvement is in Vanessa Redgrave's delicious portrayal of Guenevere...Richard Harris's King Arthur is a commanding figure...Much of Franco Nero's performance as the insufferably invincible Lancelot is wonderful...Three creditable performances cannot save a disjointed epic that lumbers along for more than three hours...A few sparkling exteriors of Arthur's castle come too late to efface an initial impression that the residents of Camelot inhabit an old Walt Disney set."

Bosley Crowther (*The New York Times*) wrote, "It is still the same sort of clutter of supernaturalism ornately displayed with conventional romantic realism, all set to music, as it was on the stage -- only more so because of the extravagance of Warner Brothers and the massiveness of the Panavision screen....The music is played and sung with great charm, but the settings are vastly overdone -- much too massive and vulgar for the delicacy and grace that should prevail."

David Austen (*Plays and Players*) found that "*Camelot* is by no means entirely successful but there are certainly enough good things in it to provide an entertaining evening...Richard Harris, a player that I've never had much liking for, is quite excellent... Vanessa Redgrave's voice is somewhat inadequate but, since this is not an all-singing musical, it hardly matters...Lancelot does suffer from the playing of Franco Nero [who] cannot cope with the complexities of the French champion."

"Unfortunately, there is nothing royal about *Camelot*'s curious screen version. It has been brought crunchingly down to earth by the churlish touch of director Joshua Logan," reported *Time* magazine, "Even on Broadway, *Camelot* never quite succeeded in capturing the wonderful, free imagination of White's original... The movie, which should have opened up the drama, shuts it down instead...Even the makeup seems to have been applied by an amateur: Harris' eye shadow is heavier than Redgrave's...But it is Vanessa Redgrave who emerges as the film's most telling virtue...Without her, *Camelot* would be disastrous."

The Academy of Motion Picture Arts and Sciences members were more impressed with Jack L. Warner's "monumental entertainment" and in 1967 awarded Oscars to John Truscott for costume design and art direction, Alfred Newman and Ken Darby for their musical scoring of the film, and Edward Carrers and John W. Brown for set decoration.

Cable television's Home Box Office televised the Winter Garden Theatre production of *Camelot* in September 1982, starring Richard Harris. The telecast staged by Marty Calliner expertly captured the stage production including well directed closeups.

STAGE

CAMELOT, Majestic Theatre, opened December 3, 1960 873 performances
Produced by Alan Jay Lerner, Frederick Loewe and Moss Hart; A Musical play; Director, Moss Hart; Book and Lyrics by Alan Jay Lerner, based on *The Once and Future King* by T. H. White; Music by Frederick Loewe; Settings, Oliver Smith; Lighting, Feder; Costumes, Adrian, Tony Duquette; Choreography and Musical numbers by Hanya Holm; Musical director, Franz Allers; Orchestrations, Robert Russell Bennett and Philip J. Lang; Dance and Choral Arrangements by Trude Rittman; Hairstylist, Ernest Adler; Company manager, Charles Gnys; Stage managers, Robert Downing, Edward Preston and Bernard Hart

Richard Burton (succeeded by William Squire) (Arthur); Julie Andrews (succeeded by Patricia Bredin, Janet Pavek, Kathryn Grayson) (Guenevere); Robert Goulet (succeeded by Robert Peterson) (Lancelot); Robert Coote (succeeded by Arthur Treacher) (Pellinore); Roddy McDowall (succeeded by Christopher Cary) (Mordred); John Cullum (succeeded by Robert Peterson) (Sir Dinadan); Jack Dabdoub (Sir Lionel); M'el Dowd (succeeded by Madeleine Sherwood) (Morgan Le Fey); David Hurst (succeeded by Louis Turenne) (Merlin); Peter Deign (Sir Sagramore); Virginia Allen (Lady Catherine); Marjorie Smith (Nimue); Michael ClarkeLawrence (succeeded by Byron Webster) (Dap); Gene GeBauer (succeeded by Son Strong) (Clarius); Michael Kermoyan (Sir Ozanna); Robert Peterson (succeeded by John Starkweather) (Sir Gwilliam); Don Stewart (Sir Colgrevance); Frank Bouley (Sir Castor); Judith Hastings (Lady Jane); Steve Curry (succeeded by Royston Thomas) (Tom); Leland Mayforth (A Page); Christina Gillespie (suc-ceeded by Adriana Keathley) (Lady Anne); Leesa Troy (A Lady); Tommy Long (succeeded by Richard Mills) (A Page); John Starkweather (succeeded by Jerry Bowers) (Herald); Joan August, Mary Sue Berry, Elizabeth Lamkin, Judith Hastings, Janet Hayes, Shelia Swenson, Leesa Troy, Dorothy White, Frank Bouley, Jack Dabdoub, Daniel P. Hannafin, Jack Irwin, Jack McMinn, Robert Neukum, Philip Rash, George Ritner, Don Stewart, Jack Eddleman, Robert Mackie (Singers); Virginia Allen, Carlene Carroll, Joan Coddington, Kathie Dalton, Katia Geleznova, Adriana Keathley, Phillis Lear, Dawn Mitchell, Joan Volkman, Toodie Wittmer, Jerry Bowers, Peter Deign, Richard Lyle, Frank Piper, Loren Hightower, James Kirby, Paul Olson, Lowell Purvis, John Starkweather, Don Strong, Jimmy Tarbutton (Dancers)

MUSICAL NUMBERS: "I Wonder What the King Is Doing Tonight?"; "The Simple

Joys of Maidenhood"; "Camelot"; "Follow Me"; "C'Est Moi"; "The Lusty Month of May"; "How to Handle a Woman"; "The Jousts"; "Before I Gaze at You Again"; "If Ever I Would Leave You"; "The Seven Deadly Virtues"; "Fie on Goodness"; "What Do Simple Folk Do?"; "The Persuasion"; "I Loved You Once in Silence"; "Guenevere"

Original cast recording: Columbia Records

Touring Company, opened *Fisher Theatre*, Detroit, January 8, 1963; closed *National Theatre*, Washington, D.C., August 1, 1964

Produced by Alan Jay Lerner, Frederick Loewe and Moss Hart; Book and Lyrics by Alan Jay Lerner, based on *The Once and Future King* by T. H. White; Music by Frederick Loewe; Director, Moss Hart; Settings by Oliver Smith; Lighting by Feder; Costumes, by Adrian and Tony Duquette; Choreography and Musical Numbers by Hanya Holm; Musical Director, Dobbs Frank; Orchestrations by Robert Russell Bennett and Philip J. Lang; Dance and Choral arrangements by Trude Rittman; Hairstylist, Ernest Adler; Company manager, James S. Miller; Stage managers, Edmund Baylies, Tom A. Larson, Edward Becker

William Squire (succeeded by Louis Hayward, George Wallace) (Arthur); Kathryn Grayson (succeeded by Anne Jeffreys) (Guenevere); Robert Paterson (Lancelot); Arthur Treacher (Pellinore); Christopher Cary (Mordred); Bob Rue (succeeded by Peter Costanza) (Sir Dinadan); Jan Moody (Morgan Le Fey); Byron Webster (Merlin); Charles Vick (succeeded by William James, Jack Villari) (Sir Sagramore); Frederick Griesinger (succeeded by Charles Vick) (Sir Lionel); Maureen Bailey (Lady Anne); Marie Grasso (succeeded by Kathryn Humphreys) (Nimue); Jane Coleman (Lady Sybil); Ginny Gagnon (Lady Catherine); Thomas Barry (Dap); Don Strong (Clarius/Herald); Arthur Sussis (succeeded by Royston Thomas) (Tom); Jimmy Stiles (succeeded by Marc Castle) (Page); Ricky Cameron (Page); George Tregre, Don Strong (Horses); Maureen Bailey, Jame Coleman, Paula Coonen, Marie Grasso, Anne Doughty, Ginny Gagnon, Kathryn Humphreys, Julie Stomme, Abbie Todd, Thomas Barry, Ed Becker, Peter Costanza, Frederic Griesinger, Bill James, Dugan Miller, Laired Montgomery, Byrne Piven, Rob Rue, Charles Vick (Singers); Pat Drylie, Audrey Hayes, Marion Hunter, Joan Kall, Elaine King, Marcia Paterson, Carol Perea, Zoya Terzetta, Eileen Woliner, Joan Volkman, Myron Curtis, Paul Gleason, George Gregre, Jerry Kent, Ed Kerrigan, Gerard Leavitt, George Mozer, Haydon Smith, Don Strong, Jerry Trent

Touring Company, opened *Masonic Temple*, Scranton, Pa., November 10, 1963; closed December 19, 1964

Produced by Henry Guettell and Arthur Cantor (by arrangement with Jenny Productions); Book and Lyrics by Alan Jay Lerner, based on *The Once and Future King* by T. H. White; Music by Frederick Loewe; Director, Lawrence Kasha; Settings by Oliver Smith; Lighting by Feder; Costumes by Stanley Simmons; Choreography and Musical Numbers by Hanya Holm; Musical directors, John Anderson, Edward Simons; Orchestrations, Robert Russell Bennett and Philip J. Lang; Company manager, Charles Mooney; Stage managers, Eddie Dimond, Ruth Newton and Jay Gregory

Biff McGuire (succeeded by George Wallace) (Arthur); Jeannie Carson (succeeded by Jan Moody) (Guenevere); Sean Garrison (succeeded by Igors Gavon) (Lancelot); Melville Cooper (Pellinore); George Hearn (Sir Dinadan); Brendan Burke (Mordred); Gwyllum Evans (Merlin); Ewel Cornett (Sir Lionel);

Jane Bergerman (Nimue); Charles May (Dap); Dennis Wayne (Clarius); Edgar Mastin (Sir Sagramore); Daryl Alford (Tom/A Page); Yvonne Lynn (Lady Anne); Sur Babel, Jane Bergerman, Sandra Brewer, Laura Graham, Barbara Gregory, Gracia Littauer, Peff Modelski, Eva Marie Sage, Susanne Whitcomb, Marjorie Wood, Daryl Alford, Paul Glover, Jay Gregory, Don Lawrence, Arnott Mader, Andre St. Jean (Ladies and Knights)

Touring Company, summer 1964
Produced by Musicarnival, Inc.; A Musical Play; Director, Otto W. Pirchner; Book and Lyrics by Alan Jay Lerner; Music by Frederick Loewe; Original production staged by Moss Hart; Scenery, Edward Graczyk II; Lighting, Florine Pulley; Costumes, Evelyn Norton Anderson; Choreography, Sandra Devlin; Musical direction, Dickson Hughes; Ballet Costumes, Charles Autry

Harry Theyard (Arthur); Monte Amundsen (Guenevere); Don Stewart (Lancelot); Leonard Elliott (Pellinore); David Hladik (Sir Sagramore); Tom Rolla (Mordred); Sondra Wolf (Morgan Le Fey); Steve Rydell (Sir Dinadan); Justin Morley, Jr. (Sir Lionel); William Boehm (Merlin); Suzanne Pritchard (Nimue); Robert Miragliotta (Squire Dap); Rosanna Huffman (Lady Anne); Patrick Swann (Tom); Robert Mintz, Mark Macho (Pages); Karen Bair, David Hladik, Rosanna Huffman, Virginia Kerr, Leeanne Mitchell, Robert Miragliotta, Justin Morley, Jr., Susanne Pritchard, Steve Rydell, Richard Resseger (Singers); Frank Brooks, Gregory Drotar, Anna Maria Fanizzi, Kevin Kamis, Sybil Lukoff, Ann McKinley, Alexia Allen Rydell (Dancers)

Drury Lane Theatre, London, opened August 19, 1964   518 performances
Produced by Jack Hylton; A Musical Play based on T. H. White's novel *The Once and Future King*; Director, Robert Helpmann; Book and lyrics by Alan Jay Lerner; Music by Frederick Loewe; Settings and Costumes by John Truscott; Choreography, Robert Helpmann, assisted by Shelagh Dey; Lighting, Richard Pilbrow; Musical director, Kenneth Alwyn; Orchestrations, Robert Russell Bennett, Philip J. Lang; Production assembled by Alec Shanks

Laurence Harvey (succeeded by Paul Daneman) (Arthur); Elizabeth Larner (Guenevere); Barry Kent (Sir Lancelot); Cardew Robinson (Pellinore); Nicky Henson (Mordred); Victor Flattery (Sir Dinadan); Raymond Edwards (Sir Lionel); Paul Ferris (Sir Clarius); Brian Hewitt Jones (Sir Sagramore); Miles Malleson (Merlin); Maryetta Midgeley (Lady Anne); Elaine Hewitt (Lady Sybil); Josephine Gordon (Nimue); Morya Fraser (Morgan Le Fey); John Scarborough (Archbishop/Squire Dap); Kit Williams (Tom); Kevin Crowhurst, Frank Knight (Pages); John Bannon, Disus Bradney, James Christensen, Gilliam Elvins, Robert Ivan Foster, Richard Hazell, Peter Johnston, Lynn Leishman, Margaret McQueen, Bryan Payne, Robin Sherringham, Wallace Stephenson, Tom Walling, Jennie Walton, Diana Beall, Yvonne Chaplin, John Clifford, Joyce Endcan, Norman Furber, Lewis Henry, Michael Jones, Jill Longstaffe, George Nichol, Jeanette Roach, Anthea Slattern, Gordon Traynor, John Walsh, Annabella Weston, Theresia Bester, Ann Chivers, Joyanna Delancey, Penny Everton, Caroline Haig, Robert Howe, Tony Kemp, Jean Mostyn, Alan Pace, Bernard Sharpe, Lorraine Smith, Heather Walford, Jane Walters, Ralph Wood, Felicity Wright, Gordon Yeats (Singers and Dancers)

St. Louis (Mo.) Municipal Opera Theatre, opened June 23 through July 9, 1969
Produced by the St. Louis Municipal Opera Association; Producer, Glenn Jordan; A

Musical Play; Director, Jack Beaker; Book and Lyrics by Alan Jay Lerner; Music by Frederick Loewe; Settings, C. Murawski; Costumes, Don Foote; Musical director, Anton Coppola; Choreography, Raymond George; Stage managers, John Wessel and Stephen Jarrett

John Cullum (King Arthur); Sally Ann Howes (Guene-vere); Richard Fredericks (Sir Lancelot); John Lynch (Sir Dinadan); Michael Reinhart (Sir Lionel); Frank Andre (Mordred); Erik Rhodes (Merlin); Laurie Mann (Pellinore); Julie Lee Conwell (Nimue); David Alt (Sir Sagramore); Charles Collins (Guilliam); Bonnie Hinson (Lady Anne); Paul Renaud (Squire Dap); Craig Pomranz (Tom of Warwick); Spencer Henderson (Dinadan's Squire); Mark Diamond (Lionel's Squire); Mark Bugler (Sagramore's Squire); Jon Adams, Ronald Gibbs, Keith Dyvig, Joe Ziegenfuss, Jay Holthouser, Lawrence Rieders, Kelly Donnell, Jim Pailer (Pages and Heralds)

Touring Company, season 1977-78

Produced by William Ross; A Musical play; Director, Stockton Briggle; Book and Lyrics by Alan Jay Lerner based on *The Once and Future King* by T. H. White; Music by Frederick Loewe; Scenery and Lighting Design, Michael J. Hotopp and Paul DePass (for theatres-in-the-round); Settings for proscenium theatres by Peter Wolf Associates; Musical staging and Dances by George Bunt; Musical director, Jonathan Anderson; Assistant musical director, Richard Riskin; Costumes, Brooks Van Horn; Mr. Hudson's Costumes designed by Arthur Boccia; Stage manager, Pat Tolson

Rock Hudson (Arthur); Sherry Mathis (Guenevere); Jerry Lanning (Lancelot); Iggie Wolfington (Pellinore); Robert Ousley (Sir Dinadan); Courtney Burr (Mordred); Mark Mensch (Merlin); William James (Sir Sagramore); Bettye Malone (Nimue); Austin Colyer (Dap); Peter Schroeder (Sir Gwilliam); John Leslie Wolfe (Sir Castor of Cornwall); J. Martin Byrne (Tom); Anna McNeely (Lady Anne); Michael Licata, Michael Radigan, Rodney Reiner (Pages) Kenneth Bell (Herald); Kenneth Bell, Lee Bellaver, J. Martin Byrne, Austin Colyer, Kenneth Frett, Rebecca Hoodwin, William James, Kelley Kristen, Michael Licata, Bettye Malone, Anna McNeeley, Robert Ousley, Frances Roth, Peter Schroeder, John Leslie Wolfe (Singers); Karen Krossley, Larry Kingery, Nancy Lynch, Nancy Miller, Michael Radigan, Rodney Reiner (Dancers)

New York State Theatre, opened July 8, 1980 56 performances

Produced by Mike Merrick and Don Gregory in association with James M. Nederlander; A Dome/Cutler-Herman Production; A Musical play; Director, Frank Dunlop; Book and Lyrics by Alan Jay Lerner, based on *The Once and Future King* by T. H. White; Music by Frederick Loewe; Settings and Costumes by Desmond Heeley; Lighting, Thomas Skelton; Choreography, Buddy Schwab; Musical director, Franz Allers; Conductor, James Martin; Orchestrations, Robert Russell Bennett and Philip J. Lang; Musical coordinator, Robert Kreis; Production supervisor, Jerry Adler; Sound, John McClure; Artistic Consultant, Stone Widney; Technical supervisor, Arthur Siccardi; Hairstylist, Vincenzo Prestia; Incidental music, Robert Kreis; Company manager, James Awe; Stage managers, Jonathan Weiss and Cathy Rice

Richard Burton (Arthur); Christine Ebersole (Guenevere); Richard Muenz (Lancelot Du Lac); Paxton Whitehead (Pellinore); Robert Fox (Mordred); Andy McAvin (Sir Sagramore); James Valentine (Merlin); Robert Molnar (Dap); William Parry (Sir Dinadan); Jeanne Caryl (Nimue); Nora Brennan (Lady Anne); Deborah Magid (Lady Sybil); Thor Fields (Tom); James Valentine (Friar); William James (Sir Lionel); Davis Grimes (His Squire); Steve Soborn (Sir Sagramore's

Squire); Herndon Lackey (Sir Dinadan's Squire); Ken Henley, Gary Jaketic, Jack Starkey, Ronald Bennett Stratton (Knights of the Investiture) Bob (Horrid); Nora Brennan, Jeanne Caryl, Melanie Clements, Stephanie Conlow, Van Craig, John Deyle, Debra Dickinson, Richard Dodd, Cecil Fulfer, David Grimes, Lisa Ann Grant, Ken Henley, John Herrera, Gary Jaketic, William James, Kelby Kirk, Herndon Lackey, Deborah Magid, Andy McAvin, Laura McCarthy, Robert Molnar, Steve Osborn, Patrice Pickering, Janelle Price, Nancy Rieth, Patrick Rogers, Deborah Roshe, D. Paul Shannon, Jack Starkey, Ronald Bennett Stratton, Sally Ann Swarm, Sally Williams, Lynn Keeton, Richard Maxon (Knights, Ladies, Lords)

Touring Company, opened *Arie Crown Theatre*, Chicago, August 26, 1980; reopened *Winter Garden Theatre*, New York, November 15, 1981 for 37 performances
Produced by Mike Merrick and Don Gregory; A Musical Play; Director, Frank Dunlop; Book and Lyrics by Alan Jay Lerner, based on *The Once and Future King* by T. H. White; Music by Frederick Loewe; Settings and Costumes by Desmond Heeley; Lighting by Thomas Skelton; Orchestrations, Robert Russell Bennett and Philip J. Lang; Artistic consultant, Stone Widney; Musical director, Franz Allers; Musical coordinator, Robert Kreis; Associate producers, Steve Herman and Jon Cutler; General manager, Arthur Anagnostou; Assistant company manager, Kathleen Turner; Stage managers, Jonathan Weiss and Cathy Rice

Richard Burton (succeeded by William Parry, Richard Harris) (Arthur); Christine Ebersole (succeeded by Meg Bussert) (Guenevere); Richard Muenz (Lancelot Du Lac); Paxton Whitehead (succeeded by Barry Ingham) (Pellinore); Robert Fox (Mordred); Andy McAvin (Sir Sagramore); William Parry (Sir Dinadan); James Valentine (Merlin/Friar); Jeanne Caryl (Nimue); Robert Molnar (Dap); Nora Brennan (Lady Anne); Deborah Magid (succeeded by Patrice Pickering) (Lady Sybil); William James (Sir Lionel); Davis Gaines (succeeded by Steve Osborn) (His Squire); Steve Soborn (succeeded by Randy Morgan) (Sir Sagramore's Squire); Herndon Lackey (succeeded by Craig Mason) (Sir Dinadan's Squire); Thor Fields (Tom); Ken Henley, Gary Jaketic, Jack Starkey, Ronald Bennett Stratton (Knights of the Investiture); Michael James Fisher (Friar); Bob (succeeded by Daisy) (Horrid); Nora Brennan, Bjarne Buchtrup, Jeanne Caryl, Melanie Clements, Stephanie Conlow, John Deyle, Debra Dickinson, Cecil Fulfer, Lisa Ann Grant, Ken Henley, Gary Jaketic, William James, Peter Kapetan, Kelly Kirk, Dale Kristien, Lorraine Lazarus, Kevin Marcum, Craig Mason, Andy McAvin, Laura McCarthy, Robert Molnar, Randy Morgan, Steve Osborn, Patrice Pickering, Nancy Rieth, Patrick Rogers, Deborah Roshe, D. Paul Shannon, Jack Starkey, Ronald Bennett Stratton, Sally Ann Swarm, Sally Williams, Ellyn Arons, Richard Maxon (Knights, Lords and Ladies)

Winter Garden Theatre, opened November 15, 1981 57 performances
Produced by Mike Merrick and Don Gregory; A Dome/Cutler-Herman Production; A Musical Play; Director, Frank Dunlop; Book and Lyrics by Alan Jay Lerner, based on *The Once and Future King* by T. H. White; Music by Frederick Loewe; Settings and Costumes by Desmond Heeley; Lighting by Thomas Skelton; Music director, Franz Allers; Orchestrations, Robert Russell Bennett and Philip J. Lang; Artistic consultant, Stone Widney; Musical coordinator, Robert Kreis; Associate producers, Steve Herman, Jon Cutler; Special Effects by Robert Joyce; Conductor, Terry James; Sound, John McClure; Choreography, Buddy Schwab; Hairstylist, Vincenzo Prestia; Assistant choreographer, Dee Erickson; General manager, Arthur Anagostou;

Company managers, Carl Sawyer and Kathleen Turner; Stage managers, Alan Hall, Steven Adler and Sally Ann Swarm

Richard Harris (Arthur); Meg Bussert (Guenevere); Richard Muenz (Lancelot Du Lac); Barrie Ingham (Pellinore); Richard Backus (Mordred); Andy McAvin (Sir Sagramore); William Parry (Sir Dinadan); James Valentine (Merlin); Jeanne Caryl (Nimue); Robert Molnar (Dap); Vincenzo Prestia (Friar); Sally Williams (Lady Anne); Patrice Pickering (Lady Sybil); William James (Sir Lionel); Steve Osborn (His Squire); Randy Morgan (Sir Sagramore's Squire); Richard Maxon (Sir Dinadan's Squire); Thor Fields (Tom); Bruce Sherman, Jack Starkey, Ken Henley, Richard Bennett Stratton (Knights of the Investiture); Daisy (Horrid); Elaine Barnes, Marie Berry, Bjarne Buchtrup, Jeanne Caryl, Melanie Clements, John Deyle, Norb Joerder, Kelby Kirk, Debra Dickinson, Kathy Flynn-McGrath, Ken Henley, William James, Dale Kristien, Lorraine Lazarus, Lauren Lipson, Craig Mason, Richard Maxon, Andy McAvin, Robert Molnar, Randy Morgan, Ann Neville, Steve Osborn, Patrice Pickering, Joel Sager, Mauriellen Sereduke, D. Paul Shannon, Bruce Sherman, Jack Starkey, Ronald Bennett Stratton, Nicki Wood, Ellyn Arons, Gary Wales (Knights, Lords and Ladies)

Apollo Victoria Theatre, London, opened November 23, 1982 83 performances

Produced by Paul Gregg and Lionel Becker for Apollo Theatre Productions; A Musical Play; Director, Michael Rudman (from the New York Production as directed by Frank Dunlop); Book and Lyrics by Alan Jay Lerner, based on *The Once and Future King* by T. H. White; Music by Frederick Loewe; Settings and Costumes by Desmond Heeley; Choreography by Ronald Hynd; Orchestrations by Robert Russell Bennett and Philip J. Lang; Musical director, Gerry Allison; Produced in association with Mike Merrick and Paul Gregory

Richard Harris (King Arthur); Fiona Fullerton (Guenevere); Robert Meadmore (Lancelot Du Lac); Robin Bailey (Pellinore); Michael Howe (Mordred); William Squire (Merlin); David Bexon (Sir Lionel); Roger Nott (Sir Dinadan); Claire Moore (Nimue); Trever Griffiths (Dap); Sandra Carrier (Lady Anne); Care Gurney (Lady Sybil); Neil Michael (Sir Sagramore); Darren Rheault or Paull Denny (Tom); Sue Aldred, Peter Barry, Neil Boyle, Neil Braithwaite, Sue Burton, Sandra Carrier, David Donegan, Bruce Graham, Caro Gurney, Gail Ivey, Morag Mackay, Marcus Mackenzie, Kim Mendez, Lyndon Miles, Stephen Miles, Claire Moore, Sue Nye, Donal O'Sullivan, Jenny Sawyer, Tony Stansfield, Mandy Stone, Caroline Tatlow, Geoff Thomas, Philip Tsaras, Nevil Whiting (Knights and Ladies of the Court)

Touring Company, opened *Wolf Trap*, Vienna, Va., August 26, 1986; closed Hershey, Pa., December 7, 1986

King Arthur Productions, Ltd., Miles C. Wilkin, executive producer; A Musical play; Staged and directed by Richard Harris; Book and lyrics by Alan Jay Lerner; Music by Frederick Loewe; Based on *The Once and Future King* by T. H. White; Set design, Tom Barnes; Lighting design, Norman Coates; Sound design, Christopher "Kit" Bond; Choreography, Norb Joerder; Music director, Terry James; Additional costumes, Michael Bottari and Ronald Case

Richard Harris (King Arthur); Martha Traverse (Guenevere); Patrick Godfrey (Lancelot du Lac); James Valentine (Pellinore/Merlin); S. Chris Pender (Mordred/Sprite/Court Dancer); William Thomas Bookmyer (Tom of Warwick/Young Arthur); Mark Vitale (Sir Lionel); Dennis Skerik (Sir Dinadan); Marcia Brushingham (Nimue); Robert Ousley (Squire Dap/Turquine of Glenfield);

Tracey Moore (Lady Anne); Gloria Ptak (Lady Margaret); William Solo (Sir Sagramore); Dennis Collado (Fool); Wallace K. Sheretz (Sir Bliant of Westchester); Martin Van Treuren (Lord Chancellor/Forest Merlin); Marcia Brushingham, Tarry Caruso, Dennis Collado, Bob Cucciole, Diane DiLascio, Joan Henry, Mark Hoebee, William James, Norb Joerder, Tracey Moore, Andre Noujaim, Robert Ousley, Gloria Ptak, Barbara Scanlon, J. C. Sheets, Wallace K. Sheretz, Dennis Skerik, William Solo, Martin Van Treuren, Kathy Vestulo, Mark Vitale (Knights, Lords and Ladies)

Sacramento (Cal.) Music Circus, opened February 13 through 18, 1990; then on tour
Produced by Sacramento Light Opera Association, Leland Ball, producing director; Producers, Russell Lewis and Howard Young; Associate producer, Richard Lewis; A Musical play; Directed and choreographed by Norb Joerder; Book and lyrics by Alan Jay Lerner; Music by Frederick Loewe; Based on *The Once and Future King* by T. H. White; Set design, Tom Barnes; Lighting design, Clarke W. Thornton; Costume designer, Ray Delle Robbins (Gail Hecht on tour); Sound design, Robert Sereno; Music director, John Vissier; Production stage manager, Robert Raby

Robert G Goulet (King Arthur); Patricia Kies (Guenevere)*; Chuck Wagner (succeeded by Richard White) (Lancelot du Lac); James Valentine (succeeded by Steve Pudenz) (Pellinore); Kenneth Boys (Mordred); Kenny Lund (succeeded by Danny Bergold) (Tom of Warwick/Young Arthur); Neil Badders (succeeded by Viri Andrick) (Sir Lionel); Paul Hope (succeeded by Chip Huddleston) (Sir Dinadan); Charles Krohn (succeeded by Newton Gilchrist) (Merlin); Mary Kay Buehler (succeeded by Cynthia Marty) (Nimue); Steve Minow (succeeded by Newton Gilchrist) (Squire Dap); Laura Burton (succeeded by Julie Ann Fogt) (Lady Anne); Paul Grant (succeeded by Brian Jeffrey Hurst) (Sir Sagramore); Ollie Bear (Horrid); Susan Danielle Mills (Lady Catherine); Jennie Welch (Lady Sybil); Chris Alexander, Mikhael Plain (Pages); John Almanza, Marie Bain, Karla Cave, Marybelle Chaney, Jonathan Charles, Debi Davis, Rebecca George, Peggy Hickey, Ken Johnson, Timothy Killops, Brady McKay, Paul Plain, Jason Schafer, Kevin Schwarz, Rodney Stenborg, Nancy Wulff (Knights, Lords and Ladies)

* Patricia Kies also starred in the 1986 Sacramento Light Opera production opposite Noel Harrison

Touring Company, opened *Fisher Theatre*, Detroit, September 9, 1992
A Music Fair presentation; A Musical play; Directed and choreographed by Norbert Joerder; Book and lyrics by Alan Jay Lerner; Music by Frederick Loewe; Based on *The Once and Future King* by T. H. White; Set supervision and lighting, Neil Peter Jamopolis; Costumes, Franne Lee; Sound design, Tom Morse; Music director, John Monaco; Production stage manager, Martin Gold

Robert Goulet (King Arthur); Patricia Kies (Guenevere); Steve Blanchard (Lancelot du Lac); James Valentine (Pellinore/Merlin); Kenneth Boys (Mordred); Justin March (Tom of Warwick/Young Arthur); Viri Andrick (Sir Lionel); Richard Smith (Sir Dinadan); Vanessa Shaw (Nimue); Newton R. Gilchrist (Squire Dap); Jean Mahlmann (Lady Anne); Cedric D. Cannon (Sir Sagramore); Steve Asciolla, Greg Brown, Ben Starr Coates, William Thomas Evans, Lisa Guignard, Theresa Hudson, Brian Jeffrey Hurst, Donald Ives, Ted Keegan, Stephanie Park, Raymond Sage, Barbara Scanlon, Verda Lee Tudor, Kimberley Wells (Knights, Lords and Ladies)

PRODUCTIONS PERTAINING TO KING ARTHUR AND CAMELOT

MERLIN, *Metropolitan Opera House*, opened January 3, 1887
Produced by the Metropolitan Opera Company; An Opera by Karl Goldmark; Conductor, Walter Damrosch

Adolf Robinson (King Arthur); Max Alvary (Merlin); Frau Kemlitz (Mordred); Wilhelm Basch (Lancelot); Marianne Brandt (Morgana); Max Heinrich (Gawein); Lilli Lehmann (Viviane); Rudolph von Milde (Bedwye); George Sieglitz (Gelndower); Emil Fischer (Demon); Leonore Better, Ida Klein, Silvia Franconi, Wilhelmenia Mayer (Viviane's Maids)

ELAINE, *Madison Square Theatre*, opened April 28, 1887
A Dramatization by Geroge Parsons Lathrop and Harry Edwards of the poem by Alfred Lord Tennyson

H. M. Pitt (King Arthur); Annie Russell (Elaine); Alexandro Salvini (Sir Lancelot); Robert Hilliard (Sir Gawain); L. F. Massen (Sir Torre); Walden Ramsey (Lavaine); Harry Edwards (Lord of Astolat); Marie Burroughs (Queen); May Robson (Llaynd); Marie Greenwald (Roselle); Harry Millward (Hermit Friar); C. P. Flockton (The Dumb Servitor); H. Holliday (The Harper)

LANCELOT THE LOVELY; OR, THE IDOL OF THE KING, Avenue Theatre, London, opened February 27, 1889
Produced by Henry Watkin; A Burlesque based on the Arthurian Legend by Richard Henry; Scenery, Julian Hicks; Costumes, J. W. Houghton; Dances, W. Warde; Music, John Crook; Stage manager, R. Soutar

Arthur Roberts (Lancelot the Lovely); Annie Halford (Guenevere); Alec Marsh (Arthur Pendragon); E. D. Ward (Merlin); Sallie Turner (Morgan le Fay); Joseph Tapley (Tristram); A. Collini (Leodograunce); H. Grattan (Gareth); G. Capel (Kaye); Carrie Coote (Lynette); Nelly Woodford (Iseult); Madle Vanoni (Vivien); Hettie Bennet (Gawaine); Mildred Mildren (Bedivere); F. Woolf (Geraint); Miss Lloyd (Enid); Miss Garthorne (Elaine); Lillie Marsden, J. Woolf, Paddy Sinclair, A. Sinclair, T. Thompson, Gladys Garthorne, Avelina Bartlett, Maria Mitchell, Mary Medas, Emily Ellis, Violet Vizard, Carrie Carlyle, Dorothy Douglas, Beatrice Bertram, Millie Warren, Baby Waltham, Clara Carini, Rosy Reynolds, Eva Evans, Edith Edevaien, Nelly Norval, Flora Franklyn, Beila Buckland, Mary Maryon, Wilhelmina Wood, Elfreda Esmond, Selina Shergold, Wynnie Wynter; Messrs. Betzmann, Bridgeman, Carpenter, Foude, Handel, Hartt, Baldwin, Winterbottom (Knights of the Round Table, Squires, Men-at-Arms, Populace of Camelot, Dames of Honour, Pages, etc.)

KING ARTHUR, *Lyceum Theatre*, London, opened January 12, 1895 105 performances
Produced and Directed by Henry Irving; A Play by J. Comyns Carr; Settings and Costumes by Edward Burne-Jones; Music director, J. Meredith Ball; Acting manager, Bram Stoker; Music by Arthur Sullivan; Stage manager, H. J. Loveday

Henry Irving (succeeded by Frank Tyars) (King Arthur); Ellen Terry (succeeded by Maud Milton) (Guenevere); Johnston Forbes-Robertson (succeeded by Ben Webster) (Sir Lancelot); Sydney Valentine (Merlin); Genevieve Ward (Morgan Le Fay); Frank Cooper (succeeded by William Haviland) (Sir Mordred); Frank Tyars (succeeded by Clarence Hague) (Sir Kay); Clarence Hague (succeeded by W. Lionel Belmore) (Sir Gawaine); Fuller Melish (Sir Bedevere); Mr. Lacy (Sir

Agravaine); Mr. Buckley (Sir Perivale); Julius Knight (Sir Lavaine); Lena Ashwell (Elaine); Annie Hughes (Clarissant); John Martin Harvey (Sir Dagonet); R. P. Tabb (Gaoler); W. Lionel Belmore (Messenger); Maud Milton (succeeded by Alisa Craig) (Spirit of the Lake)

NOTE: This production was staged at New York's *Abbey's Theatre* beginning November 4, 1895 with the above cast except changes: Mary Rork (Morgan Le Fay); Julia Arthur (Elaine); Alisa Craig (Clarissant) and Lionel Belmore (Sir Percivale)

THE QUEST OF THE HOLY GRAIL, *Court Theatre*, London, opened July 3, 1908 1 performance

Produced by Edith Rhys, William Poel; A Play by Ernest Rhys; Music by Vincent Thomas; General manager, Patrick E. Doherty; Choreography, Maude Douie; Music director, Harrison Frewin; Stage manager, A. S. Aspland

Wingfield Heals (King Arthur); Miss Douie (Guenevere); C. F. Barrett (Sir Lancelot); Miss Gwendollen Lally (Sir Galahad); Launcelot Crane (Sir Percival); C. Court Treatt (Sir Gawain); Allan Gomme (Sir Kay); Edith Rhys (Nimue/Tradition) Esther Tilley (Tradition's Child); Joseph Payne (Timor Mortis/Arch Druid); Mr. Dixon (Court Minstrel); Miss O'Auvergne Upcher (Arch Druidess); W. H. Nicholson (Sailor)

ARTHUR, *Royal Victoria Hall*, London, opened March 12, 1923

A Poetic Drama by Laurence Binyon, in collaboration with Sir John Martin Harvey; Incidental music by Sir Edward Elgar

Wilfrid Walter (King Arthur); Florence Buckton (Guenevere); Douglas Burbidge (Sir Lancelot); Rupert Harvey (Sir Mordred); Reyner Barton (Sir Gawaine); Kingsley Baker (Sir Bedivere); Jane Bacon (Elaine); John Laurie (Sir Torre); Guy Martineau (Lavaine); John Garside (Sir Bernard of Astolat); Hugh McNeill (Sir Gareth); Hilton Edwards (Sir Agravino); Maxwell Wray (Sir Bors); Sidney Scott (Sir Kay); Ernest Meads (Sir Colegravance); Ronald Nicholson (Sir Lucan); Robert Glennie (Sir Patrice); Rolfe Davies (Sir Mador); Henry Cohen (Dumb Simon); Nancy Harker (Lady-in-Waiting); Eileen Butler (The Damsel of Peace); Rolfe Davies (A Bishop); Henry Cohen (Man-at-Arms); Ether Harper (Lynned); W. Douglas Mattinson (Guard); M. M. Francis (Sir Gaheris)

GUINEVERE, BE GOOD, *Royal Artillery Theatre*, Woolwich, England, opened October 6, 1953

A Play by Charles Nielson Gattey and Zelma Bramley-Moore, based on the Arthurian legends; Director, Vere Lorrimer

Rory MacDermott (King Arthur); Anne Ridley (Queen Guinevere); James Sharkey (Sir Launcelot du Lac); Reginald Selleck (Merlin); Caroline Swinton (Annie); Margaret Boyd (Nurse); Pamela Jackson (Lady Vivien); Glyn Davys (Master Bores)

KING ARTHUR, *Atlanta (Ga.) Municipal Theatre*, opened October 29, 1968

Produced by the Atlanta Ballet, Opera and Repertory Theatre, Christopher B. Manos, General Director; A Musical Drama; Director, Michael Howard; Book by John Dryden; Music and Lyrics by Arthur Purcell (Lyrics adapted by Blanche Theborn); Prologue by John Lewin; Scenery, Richard Gullicksen; Lighting, Nananna Porcher; Costumes, Kurt Wilhelm; Choreography, Joyce Trisler; Dance director, Robert Barnett; Musical director, Jonathan Sternberg

Edward Lally (Arthur); Claudette Nevins (Emmeline); Lee Wallace (Merlin);

Clayton Corbin (Oswald); David Gold (Grimbald); Francis McDonald (Gulilmar); Christian Grant (Narrator); John Ferrante (His Grace); Elaine Kerr (His Lady); Bernard Cates (Osmund); Ed Avery (Aurelius); Robert McKenzie (Canon); George Loros (Albanact); Joelle Jons, Enzo Cirillo, Maryce Carter (Lackeys); Betty Lord, Lana Paulk, Kay Bates, Linda Cook (Guests); Harry Ellerbe, Richard Russ, Steven Bush (Soldiers); Sandra Seacat (Matilda); Janette Moody (Philidel); Edward White (Genius of Winter); Patricia Buchanan, Joanne Greene, Bonnie Hargrove, Karen Kimble, Janetta Moody, Nancy Myers, Jan Saxon, Elinore Bucholtz, Susan Claflin, Eleanor Davidson, Barbara Dean, Jill Ericson, Judith Flint, John Ferrante, Henry Grossman, Samuel Hagan, Walter Richards, Douglas Robinson, Alvin Rogel, David Schwartz, Bruce Cheney, William Nethercut, Patrick Shelby, Russell Thompson, Wayne Turnage, Edward White (Singers); Colette Albert, Dwight Arno, Rose Barrie, Barbara Barrington, Russell Chambers, Kathleen Essex, Mary Fellman, Barbara Fisher, Margaret Florin, Jo Lind Hulse, Lynne Hitelin, Wendy Johnston, Charles Kennedy, Richard Lee, Sharon Long, Claire Mesnard, Mannie Rowe, Cathy Sharp, Claudia Simmons, Gretchen Stock, Ann Vorus, John Walker, Deborah Wisehart (Dancers)

MUSICAL NUMBERS: "Hither This Way"; "You Say 'Tis Love"; "How Blest Are Shepherds"; "Shepherd, Shepherd"; "Oh Shepherds, Lead Up a Lively Measure"; "We've Cheated the Parson"; "What Ho, the Genius of the Clime"; "'Tis I, 'Tis I"; "Two Daughters of This Aged Stream"; "How Happy the Lover"; "Ye Blustering Brethren"; "Fairest Isle"

A KING FOR ALL AGES, *Grace Rainey Rogers Auditorium*, Metropolitan Museum of Art, New York, opened October 9, 1971 3 performances only.

Produced by the Metropolitan Museum of Art; A Play written and directed by Carella Alden; Technical director, Douglas Wallace; Projectionist, Louis J. Cardamone; Lighting, Sy Wong; Costumes, Brooks-Van Horn; Art consultant, Roberta Paine; Tapes, George Mittag; Stage managers, Chester Chorney, Vito Luonogo, Lori Shepard and Nancy Cole

Marshall Borden (King Arthur); Christine Lienard (Queen Guenevere); Claude Marks (Merlin); John H. Fields (Sir Lancelot); Joseph Frances (Sir Mordred); Tom McDermott (Sir Hector); George Gitto (Sir Kay); Richard Kuss (Sir Agravaine); Igors Gavon (Sir Gawain); Raymond Lynch (Sir Gaheris); David Kerman (Sir Bedivere); Dean Crane, Jr. (Arthur, as a Boy); Anne Countryman (Lady of the Lake); Michael Arle (Sir Gareth); Michelle Bayard (Lynette); April Gilmore (Lady Lyonors); Lori Shepard (Unicorn); Jo Ann Williams (Sir Tristan); Jack Adams, (Wizard); Gregory Long (Sir Galahad); David Kerman, William Kiehl (Warriors); Stanley Bakis (Archbishop); Susan Tabor, Betty George, Dorothy Leeds, Jean Baur (Ladies of the Court); Elsa Raven, William Kiehl (Narrators); Raymond Lynch, Joseph Francis (Jousters); Stanley Bakis (An Ancient); Lori Shepard (Chaperone); Michael Colleary, David Bloch (Pages); William Kiehl (Sir Lucan)

THE ISLAND OF THE MIGHTY, *Aldwych Theatre*, London, opened December 5, 1972

Produced by the Royal Shakespeare Company; A Drama by John Arden, with Margaretta D'Arcy; Director, David Jones; Scenery Timothy O'Brien and Tezeena Firthl; Lighting, Stewart Leviton; Music, Carl Davis; Choreography, David Toguri

Patrick Allen (Arthur); Emrys Jones (Merlin); Richard Pesco (Medraut); Morgan Sheppard (Bedwyr); Roger Rees (Balin); Lisa Harrow (Pictish Princess); David

Calder (Belen); Anthony Pedley (Prince of Strathclyde); Richard Mayes (Tallesin); Tony Church (Pictish Poet); Michael Shannon (Pictish WarLeader); Peter Geddis (Chief Porter); Susan Fleetwood (Bondwoman); Lloyd McGuire (Sacred King); Mike Pratt (Gerion); Lila Kaye (Queen of Picts); Heather Canning (Pictish Ambassador); Forbes Collins, Lloyd McGuire (Pictish Fishermen); Lynn Dearth (Fisherman's Wife); Denis Holmes (King Pellam); Bernard Lloyd (Aneurin); Gordon Gostslow (Prince of Gododdin); Estelle Kohler (Gwenhwyvar); Heather Canning (Gwenddydd); Matthew Roberton (Monk); Ted Valentine (Caradoc); Peter Machin (Dylan); John Hug (English Captive); Beatrix Lehmann (Morgan); Michael Shannon (Cowman); Julie Bislock (Cowman's Wife); Valerie Colgan, Marion Line (Pictish Messengers); Matthew Roberton, Michael Walker, Ted Valentine (Companions); Forbes Collins, Denis Holmes (Chief Poets)

SIR GAWAIN AND THE GREEN KNIGHT, Lyttelton Theatre, London, opened December 8, 1977
Produced by the National Theatre; A Play devised by Michael Bogdanov and adapted by Peter Stevens from Brian Stone's translation of a 14th-century poem; Director, Michael Bogdanov; Decor, Paul Bannister; Lighting, Chris Ellis; Music by Iwan Williams; Sound, David Foister; Fights staged by William Hobbs; Movement, Frederick Warder

Frederick Warder (Gawain); James Keith (Arthur); Julia Pascal (Guenevere); Liz Bagley (Morgan the Fay); John Labanowski (Bertilak); Warren Clarke (Merlin/Storyteller); Caroline Harrington (Gay Lady); Chris Hunter, Robert Ralph, Philip Wilde, Drew Wood (Courtiers); The Albion Band

LANCELOT AND GUINEVERE, Old Vic Theatre, London, opened September 10, 1980
Produced by the Old Vic Theatre Company; A Play by Gordon Honeycombe based on Thomas Malory's *Le Morte d'Arthur*, Director, Martin Jenkins; Setting, Anthony Dean; Lighting, Brian Harris; Music, David Cain

Timothy West (Thomas Malory); David Summer (King Arthur Pendragon); Maureen O'Brien (Queen Guinevere); Bryan Marshall (Sir Lancelot du Lac); Philip Sully (Sir Mordred/Sir Galahad); Bernard Archard (King Pelles/The Hermit/Bishop); Ron Meadows (Sir Ector de Maris); Stephen Jenn (Sir Bors de Gants); Kevin Quarmly (Sir Lucan); Lois Butlin (Elaine); Jane Cussons (Dame Brusen); Peter Marinker (Sir Gawain); John Hug (Sir Agravain); Peter Roberts (Sir Gareth); Bernard Bresslaw (Sir Melliangance); Christopher Fulford (Sir Bevedere the Bold/Carrier); John Hug (Sick Knight)

MERLIN, Mark Hellinger Theatre, New York, opened February 13, 1983 199 performances
Produced by Ivan Reitman, Columbia Pictures Stage Productions, Marvin A. Krauss, James M. Nederlander; A Musical; Director, Ivan Reitman; Book by Richard Levinson and William Link; Songs and Incidental Music by Elmer Bernstein; Lyrics by Don Black; Magic Illusions, Doug Henning; Scenery, Robin Wagner; Lighting, Tharon Musser; Costumes, Theoni V. Aldredge; Choreography, Christopher Chadman; Musical Direction and vocal arrangements, David Spear; Dance arrangements, Mark Hummel; Magic consultant, Charles Reynolds; Production supervisor, Jeff Hamlin; Sound, Jesse Heimlich and Abe Jacobs; Orchestrations, Larry Wilcox; Technical coordinator, Arthur Siccardi; Stage managers, Jeff Lee, Bonnie Panson and B. J. Allen

Doug Henning (Merlin); Christian Slater (succeeded by Knowl Johnson) (Arthur/Young Merlin); George Lee Andrews (Old Merlin/Old Soldier); Edmund Lyndeck (The Wizard); Chita Rivera (The Queen); Nathan Lane (Prince Fergus); Rebecca Wright (Philomena); Gregory Mitchell (The Queen's Companion); Debby Henning (Merlin's Vision/Water); Michelle Nicastro (Ariadne); Peggy Parten (Earth); Robyn Lee (succeeded by Andrea Handler) (Air); Spence Ford (Fire); Alan Brasington (Acolyte/Manservant); Robin Clever, Spence Ford, Pat Gorman, Andrea Handler, Debby Henning, Leslie Hicks, Sandy Laufer, Robyn Lee, Peggy Parten, Iris Revson, Claudia Shell, David Asher, Ramon Galindo, Todd Lester, Joe Locarro, Fred C. Mann, III, Gregory Mitchell, Andrew Hill Newman, Eric Roach, Robert Tanna, Robert Warners (Ensemble)

MUSICAL NUMBERS: "It's About Magic"; "I Can Make It Happen"; "Beyond My Wildest Dreams"; "Something More"; "The Elements"; "Fergus' Dilemma"; "Nobody Will Remember Him"; "Put a Little Magic in Your Life"; "He Who Knows the Way"; "We Haven't Fought a Battle in Years"; "Satan Rules"

Original cast recording: Arista Records

KING ARTHUR IN THE REALM OF THE DRAGON, TUCC Stage 3, Philadelphia, opened November 26, 1990

Presented by Novel Stages; A Play by Brian Joyce; Director, David Bassuk; Setting, Franco Colavecchia; Lighting, Russell Wadbrook; Costumes, Barbra Kravitz; Fight director, Ian Rose; Stage manager, Kristin H. Waskowicz

David Urrutia (King Arthur); Alyssa Weiss (Guenevere); Christopher Stewart (Lancelot); George T. Spillane (Merlin); Clista Townsend (Morgana); Hazel Weinberg Bowers (Vivian); Arturo Castillo (Sir Gawain); Charles McMahon (Uther/Gareth); Larry Barcus (Sir Kay); Leigh Smiley (Lady Tenet); Donna Browne (Nimiane); Adam Horn (Percival)

SCREEN

CAMELOT, Warner Bros.-Seven Arts Productions, released October 1967

Produced by Jack L. Warner; Director, Joshua Logan; Screenplay by Alan Jay Lerner, based on the musical play by Lerner and T. H. White's book *The Once and Future King*; Book and Lyrics by Alan Jay Lerner; Music by Frederick Loewe; Photography, Richard H. Kline; Production and Costume designer, John Truscott; Art director, Edward Carrere; Set decorator, John W. Brown; Music director, Alfred Newman; Orchestrations, Leo Shuken, Jack Haynes; Sound recording, M. A. Merrick, Dan Wallin; Assistant director, Arthur Jacobson; Action-sequence directors, Tap and Joe Canutt; Editor, Folmar Blangsted

Richard Harris (King Arthur); Vanessa Redgrave (Guenevere); Franco Nero (Lancelot du Lac); David Hemmings (Mordred); Lionel Jeffries (King Pellinore); Laurence Naismith (Merlin); Pierre Olaf (Dap); Estelle Winwood (Lady Clarinda); Peter Bromilow (Sir Sagramore); Gary Marshall (Sir Lionel); Anthony Rogers (Sir Dinadan); Sue Casey (Lady Sybil); Nicholas Beauvy (King Arthur as a Boy); Gary Marsh (Tom of Warwick)

KING ARTHUR WAS A GENTLEMAN, Gainsborough Pictures, released December 1942

Produced by Edward Black; Director, Marcel Varnel; Screenplay by Val Guest, Marriott Edgar; Photography, Arthur Crabtree; Art director, John Bryan; Music,

Manning Sherwin; Lyrics, Val Guest; Musical director, Louis Levy; Orchestrations, Bob Busby; Dances, Buddy Bradley; Editor, R. E. Dearing

Arthur Askey (Arthur King); Evelyn Dall (Susan Ashley); Anne Shelton (Gwen Duncarron); Max Bacon (Maxie); Jack Train (Jack); Peter Graves (Lance); Vera Frances (Vera); Al Burnett (Slim); Brefni O'Rorke (Colonel Duncarron); Ronald Shiner (Sergeant); Freddie Crump (Feldman)

ADVENTURES OF SIR GALAHAD, *Columbia Serial*, released 1949 15 episodes
Produced by Sam Katzman; Director, Spencer Bennet; Screenplay by George H. Plympton, Lewis Clay and David Mathews, based on the Arthurian legends; Photography, Ira H. Morgan; Art director, Paul Palmentola; Music, Mischa Bakaleinikoff; Editors, Earl Turner and Dwight Caldwell

George Reeves (Sir Galahad); Nelson Keigh (King Arthur); Marjorie Stapp (Queen Guenevere); William Fawcett (Merlin); Pat Barton (Morgan Le Fay); Hugh Prosser (Sir Lancelot); Jim Diehl (Sir Kay); Don Harvey (Bartog); John Merton (Ulric); Pierce Lyden (Cawker); Charles King (Bors); Lois Hall (Lady of the Lake)

EPISODES: The Stolen Sword; Galahad's Daring; Prisoners of Ulric; Attack on Camelot; Galahad to the Rescue; Passage of Peril; Unknown Betrayers; Perilous Adventure; Treacherous Magic; The Sorcerer's Spell; Valley of No Return; Castle Perilous; The Wizard's Vengeance; Quest for the Queen; Galahad's Triumph

KNIGHTS OF THE ROUND TABLE, *Metro-Goldwyn-Mayer*, released December 1953
Produced by Pandro S. Berman; Director, Richard Thorpe; Screenplay by Noel Langley, Talbot Jennings and Jan Lustig, based on Sir Thomas Malory's *Le Morte d'Arthur*, Photography, F. A. Young and Stephan Dade; Art directors, Alfred Junge, Hans Peters; Costume design, Roger Furse; Music, Miklos Rozsa; Editor, Frank Clarke

Robert Taylor (Lancelot); Ava Gardner (Guenevere); Mel Ferrer (King Arthur); Stanley Baker (Mordred); Anne Crawford (Morgan Le Fay); Felix Aylmer (Merlin); Robert Urquhart (Gawain); Gabriel Woolf (Percival); Anthony Forwood (Gareth); Maureen Swanson (Elaine); Niall MacGinnis (The Green Knight); Barry McKay, Derek Tansley (Green Knight's Squires); Stephen Vercoe (Agravaine); Ann Hanslip (Nan); Jill Clifford (Bronwyn); Howard Marion Crawford (Simon); Alan Tilvern (Steward); Gwendoline Evans (Enid); Roy Russell (Leogrance); Dagmar Wuhter (Vivien); John Brooking (Bedivere); Peter Gawthorne (Bishop); John Sherman (Lambert); Martin Wyldeck (John); Michel De Lutry (Dancer); Mary Germaine (Brigid)

THE BLACK KNIGHT, *Columbia Pictures*, released August 1954
Produced by Warwick Productions, England; Producers, Irving Allen, Albert R. Broccoli; Director, Tay Garnett; Screenplay, Alec Coppel; Photography, John Wilcox; Art director, Vetchinsky; Music, John Addison; Choreography, David Poltenghi; Editor, Gordon Pilkington

Alan Ladd (John); Patricia Medina (Linet); Anthony Bushell (King Arthur); Peter Cushing (Sir Palamides); Jean Lodge (Queen Guenevere); Basil Appleby (Sir Hal); Laurence Naismith (Major Domo); Harry Andrews (Earl of Yeonil); Andre Morell (Sir Ontzlake); Patrick Troughton (King Mark); Olwen Brookes (Lady Ontzlake); Pauline Jameson (Countess Yeonil); Ronald Adam (Abbot); John

Laurie (James); Bill Brandon (Bernard); Tommy Moore (Apprentice); John Kelly (Wood Cutter); Elton Hayes (Troubadour)

THE SWORD IN THE STONE, *Buena Vista Pictures*, released December 1963
Produced by Walt Disney; Director, Wolfgang Reitherman; Screenplay by Bill Peet, based on the novel by T. H. White; Art director, Ken Anderson; Character design, Milt Kahl, Bill Peet; Layout: Don Griffith, Basil Davidovitch, Vance Gerry, Sylvia Cobb, Dale Barnhart, Homer Jonas; Backgrounds, Walter Peregoy, Bill Layne, Al Dempster, Anthony Rizzo, Ralph Hulett, Fil Mottola; Character animation, Eric Cleworth, Hal King, Eric Larson, Hon Sibley, Cliff Nordberg, Hal Ambro, Dick Lucas; Animation, Frank Thomas, Milt Kahl; Effects Animation, Dan MacManus, Jack Boyd, Jack Buckley; Music, George Bruns; Songs, Richard M. Sherman, Robert B. Sherman; Title Song sung by Fred Darian; Sound, Robert O. Cook; Editor, Donald Halliday

Voices: Rickie Sorenson (Wort); Karl Swenson (Merlin); Sebastian Cabot (Sir Ector); Junius Matthews (Archimedes); Alan Napier (Sir Pelimore); Norman Alden (Sir Kay); Martha Wentworth (Madam Min/Granny Squirrel); Barbara Joe Allen (Scullery Maid); Ginny Tyler (Little Girl Squirrel); The Mellowmen [Richard Reitherman and Robert Reitherman]

LANCELOT AND GUINEVERE, *Emblem Productions*, Great Britain, released 1962; released in U.S. as *SWORD OF LANCELOT* by *Universal-International*, April 1963
Executive producer, Cornel Wilde; Producer, Bernard Luber; Director, Cornel Wilde; Screenplay by Richard Schayer and Jefferson Pascal; Photography, Harry Waxman; Additional photography, Robert Thomson; Art director, Maurice Carter; Costumes, Terence Morgan; Music, Ron Goodwin; Sound, Don Sharpe; Editor, Frederick Wilson

Cornel Wilde (Lancelot); Jean Wallace (Guinevere); Brian Aherne (King Arthur); Michael Meacham (Sir Mordred); George Baker (Sir Gawaine); Adrienne Corri (Lady Vivian); Mark Dignam (Merlin); John Barrie (Sir Bedivere); Archie Duncan (Sir Lamorak); Iain Gregory (Sir Tors); Richard Thorp (Sir Gareth); Reginald Beckwith (Sir Dagonet); Joseph Tomelty (Sir Kaye); Walter Gotell (Sir Cedric); John Longden (King Leodogran); Bob Bryan (Sir Dorjak); Geoffrey Dunn (Edric); Graham Stark (Rian); Christopher Rhodes (Ulfus); Peter Prowse (Brandagorus); Violetta Farjeon (French Serving Maid)

SIEGE OF THE SAXONS, *BLC/Columbia Pictures*, released 1963
Produced by Ameran Company; Producer, Jud Kinberg; Director, Nathan Juran; Screenplay, John Kohn and Jud Kinberg; Photography, Wilkie Cooper and Jack Mills; Art director, Constable; Production manager, Ted Wallis; Editor, Maurice Rootes

Ronald Lewis (Robert Marshall); Mark Dignam (King Arthur); Jerome Willis (Limping Man); Janette Scott (Katherine); Ronald Howard (Edmund); John Laurie (Merlin); Richard Clarke (Saxon Prince); Francis De Wolff (Blacksmith); Charles Lloyd Pack (Doctor); John Gabriel (Earl of Chatham); Peter Mason (Young Monk); Michael Mellinger (Thief); Gordon Boyd (Captain); Robert Gillespie (Solider); Kenneth Cowan (Soldier)

GAWAIN AND THE GREEN KNIGHT, *United Artists*, released 1974
A Sancrest Production; Produced by Philip Breen; Associate producer, Charles Athey; Director, Stephen Weeks; Screenplay, Philip Breen and Stephen Weeks, based on the medieval poem; Additional dialogue, Rosemary Sutcliff; Photography, Ian Wilson; Art director, Anthony Woollard; Set decorator, Peter Young; Costume designer, Shura Cohen; Music, Ron Goodwin; Special effects, Les Hillman; Editor,

John Shirley

Murray Head (Sir Gawain); Ciaran Madden (Linet); Nigel Green (The Green Knight); Anthony Sharp (The King); Robert Hardy (Sir Bertilak); David Leland (Humphrey); Murray Melvin (Seneschal); Tony Steedman (Fortinbras); Ronald Lacey (Oswald); Willoughby Goddard (Knight); George Merritt (Old Knight); Peter Forbes-Robertson (Young Knight); Pauline Letts (Lady of Lyonesse); Richard Hurndall (Bearded Man); Peter Copley (Vosper); Geoffrey Bayldon (Wise Man); Jerold Wells (Sergeant); Michael Crane (Giant); Jack Woolgar (Porter); Sue Ellis Jones (Ermyntrude)

LANCELOT DU LAC, *Mara Films*, France, released May 1974

Produced by Mara Films-Laser Productions-ORTF Paris; Producers, Jean-Pierre Rassam, Jean Yanne, Alfredo Bini and Francois Rochas; Directed and written by Robert Bresson; Photography, Pasqualino De Santis; Art director, Pierre Charbonnier; Special effects, Alain Bryce; Costumes, Gres; Music, Philippe Sarde; Editor, Germaine Lamy

Luc Simon (Lancelot); Laura Duke Condominas (Guinevere); Arthur De Montalembert (Lionel); Patrick Bernard (Mordred); Humbert Balsan (Sir Gawain); Vladimir Antolek-Oresek (Artus); and Joseph Patrick Le Quidre, Charles Balsan, Christian Schlumberger, Jean-Paul Leperlier, Guy de Bernis, Philippe Chleq, Jean-Marie Becar, Antoine Rabaud, Marie-Louise Buffet, Marie-Gabrielle Cartron

SWORD OF THE VALIANT--THE LEGEND OF GAWAIN AND THE GREEN KNIGHT, *Cannon Group release*, released November 1984

Produced by Golan-Globus Productions; A London-Cannon Films Ltd. Production; Executive Producers, Michael Kagan, Phillip M. Breen; Producers, Menachem Golan and Yoram Globus; Associate Producers, Sture Rydman and Basil Keys; Director, Stephen Weeks; Screenplay by Stephen Weeks, Phillip M. Breen and Howard C. Pen; Additional dialogue, Rosemary Sutcliff and Therese Burdon; Photography, Freddie A. Young and Peter Hurst; Production designers, Maurice Fowler and Derek Nice; Set decorator, Val Wolstenholme; Costumes, Shuna Harwood; Makeup, Richard Mills; Special effects supervisor, Nobby Clarke; Special effects prosthetics, Daniel Parker; Green Knight head effects, Aaron Sherman; Music, Rob Geesin; Sound, George Stephenson, Malcolm Davies; Action sequences director, Anthony Squire; Second Unit director, Sture Rydman; Editors, Richard Marden and Barry Peters

Miles O'Keeffe (Sir Gawain); Sean Connery (The Green Knight); Trevor Howard (King Arthur); Emma Sutton (Morgan Le Fay); Cyrielle Claire (Linet); Leigh Lawson (Humphrey); Peter Cushing (Seneschal); Lila Kedrova (Lady of Lyonesse); Ronald Lacey (Oswald); John Rhys-Davies (Baron Fortinbras); Douglas Wilmer (The Black Knight); Brian Coburn (Friar Vosper); Bruce Lidington (Sir Bertilak); John Serret (Priest); Thomas Heathcoate (Armourer); Mike Edmonds (Tiny Man); David Rappaport (Sage); John Pierce-Jones (Sergeant); James Windsor (First Recruit); Ric Morgan (Second Recruit); Peter MacKriel (Third Recruit); Jerold Wells (First Torturer); Harry Jones (Second Torturer); John C. Carney (Messenger); Wilfred Brambell (Porter)

TELEVISION

THE ADVENTURES OF SIR LANCELOT, televised September 24, 1956 through

September 16, 1957 (NBC) and October 1, 1957 through September 26, 1958 (ABC) 30 minutes each episode
A Whitehall Production; Produced by Hamneh Weinstein, Dallas Bower; Directors, Ralph Smart, Bernard Knowles, Arthur Crabtree and Anthony Squire; Theme Song, Bruce Campbell, Alan Lonex

William Russell (Sir Lancelot de Lac); Bruce Seton (King Arthur); Jane Hylton (Queen Guenevere); Cyril Smith (Merlin); Robert Scroggins (Squire Brian); Howard Pays (Sir Richard of Taunton); Derry Nesbitt (Sir Tristram); Alison Leggett (Morgana); Mary Manson (Helga); Bailard Berkeley (Urgan); Jack Bowie (Norrin); Norah Gersen (Igrane); Douglas Argent (Prince Boudwin); Patricia Kneale (Ellen); Brown Derby (John); Duncan Lewis (King Meliot); Peter Assinder (Happy Thief); Pauline Olsen (Enid); George Woodbridge (Sir Melius); Sidney Head (Wooden Leg); Derek Waring (Balin); Robert Hardy (Rupert); Carol Marsh (Sybil); Michael Benson (Hassin); Chin Yu (Vuleika); Lynne Furlong (Princess Kathleen); Jerome Willis (Prince); Tony Quinn (King Anguish); Mary Steele (Princess Ann); Linda Gray (Marta); John Horsley (Athelred); Reginald Herne (Evanston); Derry Nesbitt (Andred); Derek Aylward (King Marhaus); Jack May (Caradoc); Eric Corrie (Priest)

MERLIN, THE MAGICIAN, episode of *The Time Tunnel* series, televised March 17, 1967 ABC 60 minutes
Produced by Irwin Allen; Director, Harry Harris; Written by William Welch; Photography and Special Effects, L. B. Abbott; Music, Johnny Williams

James McMullan (King Arthur); Lisa Jak (Guenevere); Christopher Carey (Merlin); Vincent Beck (Wogan); and regulars: James Darren (Tony Newman); Robert Colbert (Doug Phillips); Whit Bissell (General Heywood Kirk); Lee Meriweather (Ann); John Zaremba (Dr. Raymond Swain); Wesley Lau (Sergeant Jiggs)

CAMELOT, HBO Theatre, televised September 26, 1982 HBO 2 1/2 hours
A Mike Merrick and Don Gregory production; A Musical play, based on *The Once and Future King by T. H. White*; Television director, Marty Callner; Stage director, Frank Dunlop; Book and lyrics by Alan Jay Lerner; Musical by Frederick Loewe; Sets and costumes, Desmond Heeley; Art director, Bill Groom; Lighting, Greg Burton; Musical director, Terry James; Orchestrations, Robert Russell Bennett and Philip J. Lang; Choreography, Buddy Schwab; Taped at New York's Winter Garden Theatre

(See Stage: Winter Garden Theatre, November 15, 1981)

ARTHUR THE KING, televised April 25, 1985 CBS 3 hours
Produced by Martin Poll; Director, Clive Donner; Teleplay by J. David Wyles; Photography, Denis C. Lewiston; Production design, Francisco Chianese; Music, Charles Gross; Costumes, Phyllis Dalton; Makeup, Barbara Daly; Editor, Peter Tanner; Sound, David Hilyard

Malcolm McDowell (King Arthur); Rosalyn Landor (Queen Guenevere); Rupert Everett (Sir Lancelot); Candice Bergen (Morgan Le Fay); Edward Woodward (Merlin); Dyan Cannon (Katherine); Lucy Gutteridge (Niniane); Patrick Ryecart (Sir Gawain); Ann Thornton (Lady Ragnell); Joseph Blatchley (Mordred); Liam Neeson (Grak); Philip Sayer (Agravain); Dennis Lil (King Pelinore); John Quarmley (Sir Kai); Michael Gough (Archbishop); Milance Avramovic (Gorgo); Terry Torday (Enchanted Queen); and Mary Starin, Carole Ashby, Alison Worth, Peter Blythe, Pat Starr, Marie Elise, Maryam D'Abo, Tina Robinson, Pia

Constance-Churcher, Linda Fontana, Christine Hunt, Cia Ford, Miro Pfeiffer, Vlado Spindler, Mise Martinovic, Tom Vukusic

NOTE: Filmed in 1982.

THE LEGEND OF KING ARTHUR, televised 1985 BBC 4 parts (1 hour each); in U.S., televised December 31, 1989 through January 21, 1990 Arts and Entertainment Network
Produced by the British Broadcasting Corporation, Time-Life Television and the Australian Broadcasting Commission, in association with Lionheart Television; Producer, Ken Riddington; Director, Rodney Bennett; Dramatized by Andrew Davies; Designer, Kenneth Sharp; Lighting, Sam Barclay; Costume designer, Amy Roberts; Makeup, Joan Stribling; Music, Dudley Simpson; Fights arranged by B. H. Berry

Andrew Burt (King Arthur); Felicity Dean (Guinevere); David Robb (Lancelot); Robert Edison (Merlin); Maureen O'Brien (Morgan Le Fay); Godfrey James (Bors); Brian Coburn (Uther Pendragon); Morgan Sheppard (Duke Gorlois); Anne Kidd (Igrayne); Richard Austin (Young Arthur); Patsy Kensit (Young Morgan Le Fay); Ivor Roberts (Leodograunce); Peter Burroughs (Branic); Richard Beale (Sir Ector); Martin Chamberlain (Sir Kay); Anthony Dutton (Accolon); Jon Croft (Lot); Hilary Mason (Midwife); Terence Soall (Bard)

CANDIDE
A Comic Operetta by Lillian Hellman; Music by Leonard Bernstein (1956), adapted from the novel by Voltaire (1759)

Synopsis

In the Westphalia castle of Baron Thunder-Ten-Tronck live four young people: the impoverished Candide, the Baron's beautiful daughter Cunegonde, her handsome brother Maximillian, and the luscious serving maid Paquette. Philosopher and metaphysician Dr. Pangloss is giving marital counseling to Candide, who is about to marry Cunegonde, and advising him that this is the best of all possible worlds. As the wedding is about to begin, though, war breaks out between Westphalia and Hesse. Westphalia is destroyed and Cunegonde is seemingly killed, and Candide takes comfort in the Panglossian doctrine, deciding to see the world. In Lisbon, he stumbles across a ragged beggar in the person of Pangloss, but then gets caught up in the Inquisition, escaping only in the aftermath of an earthquake. In Paris, he discovers Cunegonde again, having turned up alive and, through the machinations of the Old Lady, having become a courtesan bedecked in jewels and finery.

The three flee France with a band of devout Pilgrims and make their way to the New World. Arriving in Buenos Aires, the group finds itself the Governor's prisoners, but Cunegonde catches his eye and is put up at the palace with the Old Lady as her duenna. Fired by reports of Eldorado, Candide escapes once more to seek his fortune and then rescue Cunegonde whom the Governor has tied into a sack and shipped back to Venice. Candide is overjoyed to find his old teacher, Dr. Pangloss, who accompanies him back to Europe, where, having just found Cunegonde again, working as a scrubwoman in a palazzo, Candide is swindled out of his fortune by an avaricious crowd. Disillusioned, he returns to the ruined Westphalia, refuting Pangloss' philosophy about a beautiful, pure world. Cunegonde, Pangloss and the

Old Lady then appear, and within them the spark of optimism flickers, and Candide decides that the only way to live is to try to make some sense of life.

Comment and Critique

French critic, acerbic satirist, iconoclastic philosopher and playwright Voltaire was born Francois Marie Arouet in Paris on November 21, 1694, and died at age eighty-eight on May 30, 1778. Among his works: *Oedipe* (1718), *Artemire* (1720), *Marianne* (1724), *Brutus* (1730), *La Morte de Cesar* (1731), *Zaire* (based on Shakespeare's jealousy motif in *Othello*) (1732), *Alzire* (1736), *Zulime* (1740), *Mahomet* (1741), *Merope* (1743), *L'Orphelin de la Chine* (1755), *Tancrede* (1760), and *Irene* and *Nanine* (1778). Voltaire's satirical "philosophical tale" *Candide* was published as a short novel in 1759.

Michael Myerberg presented Charles Weidman's ballet based upon *Candide* at New York's Booth Theatre on May 15, 1933 for eight performances. Danced in two acts and four cantos, Weidman's *Candide* was seen by Richard Lockridge (*The Evening Sun*) as "a three-way compromise between the dance, the drama and Voltaire...It is an interesting experiment, has moments of visible wit and is to be recommended with only moderate reservations to those who like to see Mr. Weidman dance and do not mind having Voltaire reduced to words of one syllable...The result seems to me to have been the reduction of the whole matter to a primer status...It also lacks incisiveness, in the manner of dance narratives and -- the narration aside -- does rub it in a bit with pantomime... The whole affair, incidentally, mellows alarmingly at the end..."

Candide, adapted to the stage by Lillian Hellman with a memorable score by Leonard Bernstein, became a notable *succes d'estime* in the theatre. "As a man of the theatre, Voltaire would doubtless be overwhelmed by the splendor and variety of the musical *Candide*... Lillian Hellman and Leonard Bernstein have recognized in *Candide* an intellectual attitude that is apposite to the 20th century. By using all the arts of the theatre with taste and skill, they have produced the first musical of the season that has distinction," reported Brooks Atkinson (*The New York Times*). "In departing from standard formulas, *Candide* has put the musical stage on a superior intellectual and artistic level. It is civilized. It has lost some of Voltaire's harshness and ferocity. But it has lost none of his scorn for humbug, and it has found grace and beauty in the modern theatre."

Other critics, and a large portion of audiences, found *Candide* bewildering, as reflected in John McClain's review in the *Journal-American*, finding the musical "a tough one to call. Here they have taken a satire by Voltaire, a most tenuous idea in itself dealing with the general perversity of life, and transposed it into an operetta. *Candide* is ambitious and brilliant, and it is loaded with talent. Sorry it didn't quite score." Walter Kerr (*Herald-Tribune*) called *Candide*, "a really spectacular disaster... pessimism is the order of the evening."

Richard Watts, Jr. (*New York Post)* felt that Lillian Hellman had failed to translate Voltaire's biting satire in "effective dramatic terms...the final effects of this adventurous new theatrical work is one of disappointment. There is so much that is brilliant about it, so much in the way of musical excellence, visual beauty, grace of style and boldness of design, that it deserves attention and respect from playgoers who are interested in artistic enterprise...But, in general, the libretto, while it sticks to the Voltaire outline, is not satirically powerful or dramatically striking...But there should be no denying the musical and visual eminence of a brave adventure in operetta."

Tom Donnelly (*New York World Telegram and The Sun*) appraised *Candide* as the "Best Musical News of Year... this comic operetta derived from Voltaire doesn't hang together very well, but the bits and pieces of it are invariably fascinating... Leonard Bernstein's music is lush, lovely and electric...It is easily the best score Mr. Bernstein has written for the theatre...It is scarcely surprising that Miss Hellman hasn't really succeeded in whipping these unyielding materials into a readily comprehensive shape...*Candide* may be an example of reach exceeding grasp, but what a reach is there!"

Brooks Atkinson (*The New York Times*) added, "Let's admit that the 18th century philosophical tale is not ideal material for a theatre show for it is plotless and repetitious. And let's further concede that the *Candide* that Miss Hellman, Mr. Bernstein and [Robert] Rounseville have created is not the blithering idiot whom Voltaire invented. He is more like a disillusioned hero."

Caryl Brahms reviewed London's *Candide*, which opened at the Saville Theatre in April 1959, and noted that "the world of the wideeyed Candide cannot be said to be the best of all possible worlds, because it, too, is mainly twodimensional. But at least one can take pleasure in its neat, bright ironies...There is more goodish music than there is dialogue to carry it...And the music and its singing is the best thing in this second best of all possible kinds of musicals." Brahms continued his *Plays and Players* review by describing Lillian Hellman's adaptation as "unreal and quite without dramatic form and meaning" but praised the cast, especially Mary Costa as Cunegonde, Denis Quilley's Candide, Ron Moody and James Cairncross, adding, "And Mr. Laurence Naismith is superb as the genial, hopeful, clown, Pangloss."

Candide finally found success on Broadway eighteen years after its initial production when the Chelsea Theatre Center of Brooklyn's production, directed by Hal Prince, arrived on Broadway to complete 740 performances. Not the least of *Candide*'s success was a new libretto written by playwright Hugh Wheeler, who had won acclaim for his 1973 adaptation of Ingmar Bergman's *Smiles of a Summer Night* into Stephen Sondheim's charming theatre piece, *A Little Night Music*.

"*Candide* may at least have stumbled into the best of all possible productions," enthused Walter Kerr (*The New York Times*). "I take back 'stumbled,' instantly. For there is nothing at all inadvertent about the magician's pass director Harold Prince has made at the song-and-dance celebration of Voltaire's calculated insult to 'the best of all possible worlds'...a new and freefloating libretto by Hugh Wheeler and then simply rebuilt a theater to suit Leonard Bernstein's sweetly irreverent score... no one -- until now -- had thought of making the entire evening spin just as Voltaire's novel spins... The original is short, breathless, cantankerous and cavalier. Mr. Prince has thrown words, notes and players at us with the same windswept effrontery."

Clive Barnes (*The New York Times*), acknowledging that *Candide* in its initial staging "had been an unhappy, unlucky failure," found that "this is now a new musical, a fun musical...Mr. Wheeler's new book exults in Voltaire and his sardonic world picture of Panglossian philosophy that we all live in the best of all possible worlds...I always knew that the Bernstein music was a great score but somehow had been lost on the way to the theater. Here it has at last been found. Mr. Bernstein, Mr. Wheeler, Mr. Prince and, of course, Mr. Voltaire, have given us a new and effervescent musical...This is a doll of a show. I love it and loved it. I think Voltaire would have loved it, too. If he didn't -- to hell with him."

Candide possibly found its proper milieu when the New York City Opera Company included it in its repertoire in October 1982. Donal Henahan (*The New York Times*) reported, "The new 'opera house version' of *Candide* was performed so brilliantly that one would have thought it had been running for months rather than being mounted as part of the opera company's hectic schedule...Harold Prince's staging was not without its cliches -- it brought singers down into the audience at times for no pressing reason, for instance...Everything clicked so neatly that one could ignore the fact that most of the effects were fairly standard Broadway musical stuff, guessed up for a night at the opera. The principals could hardly have been better...This is, in effect, a new *Candide* in all but its music, and even that has been touched up a great deal. Mr. Bernstein and his musical elves have gone back to his original score to restore some deleted pages and reorchestrate others...The failure of the original *Candide* has always seemed puzzling to those who have cherished the original cast album for a quarter of a century...If this were the best of all possible operatic worlds, the new *Candide* would become a repertory staple of all companies all over the world."

The London revival in 1988 of *Candide* brought this observation from *Variety*: "[It] has probably found its proper comic opera stride with this revised yet again Old VicScottish Opera edition...A spare, visually witty style (with prop models of famous landmarks) and a strong cast both vocally and dramatically make for a broadly pleasing production...it's still a sweetly sardonic and often highly risible show in a smoothpaced production that, among other things, niftily mocks the conventions of opera. The lush and melodic Bernstein score remains a joy, and the lyrics by Richard Wilbur et al. are delights of clever pastiche and paradox..."

British critic Peter J. Dyer said of Norbert Car-bonnaux's 1960 film version, *Candide, ou L'Optimisme au XXeme Siecle*, "Just as Voltaire's eighteenth-century satire was inspired by the Lisbon earthquake which killed thirty thousand, so the film finds its inspiration in the Atom Bomb which dealt destruction to ten times that number...The script, a disjointed series of revuetype sketches, never builds...This ugliness -- too facile to earn comparison with Voltaire's original -- extends to the sheer look of the thing, with its crude closeups and eye-straining camera pans; and to the performance of such generally reliable actors as [Pierre] Brasseur, who plays the dogged Pangloss on a note of monotonous, graveltoned oratory..."

Raymond Durgnat (*Films and Filming*) later wrote, "Voltaire's *Candide* in a satire on Liebniz, caricatured (and distorted) as Professor Pangloss, who taught his pupil Candide that all is for the best in the best of all possible worlds and that only man's lack of logic keeps him from the consolations of this knowledge... Carbonnaux' film is most stinging when he forgets Voltaire and hares after moral hypocrisies...The better ideas would have had more punch in a less tongue-in-cheek story and for my taste, Carbonnaux lumbers and lurches clumsily between the facetious and the seriously satirical. The mixture of an absurd story, wartime atrocity newsreels and sketches like those decorating British farces, is an uneasy one, and the attempt to squeeze humour out of mincing 18th-century behaviour in 20th-century dress is feeble because irrelevant...Taken at too quick a clip to be positively tedious, the film struck me as rather inert at heart. It's for those who like their satire broad, but the random whimsy-whamsy kills the real mordant of Voltaire's humour."

Newsweek wrote of *Candide* on its American premiere on 1962: "The film lampoons virtually every country and every pretension to sanity. A screamingly funny picture." And Wanda Hale (New York *Daily News*) labeled it: "Farcically funny French satire lampooning the morals, culture and politics of the 20th century."

Voltaire's *Candide* was produced for television by the BBC and televised in the United States on October 30, 1975. The fantasy, starring Frank Finlay as Voltaire with Ian Ogilvy in the title role, was advertised as "A satire that pokes fun at witless optimism." Adapted for television and directed by James Mactaggart, *Candide* was a spirited and amusing video presentation.

The New York City Opera Company's brilliant production of *Candide* found its proper home on the operatic stage. The 1986 telecast, directed by Kirk Browning, based on Harold Prince's highly theatrical presentation, was an inspired piece of nonsense, blessed with Leonard Bernstein's excellent score. During the interval, Harold Prince explained to New York City Opera's director, Beverly Sills, how Hugh Wheeler had altered the original book, opening it up to a side-show aspect and that "Hellman's book was too serious, too angry."

STAGE

CANDIDE, *Booth Theatre*, New York, opened May 15, 1933 8 performances
Produced by Michael Myerberg; An adaptation of Voltaire's novel arranged by Charles Weidman; Music arranged and composed by Genevieve Pitot and John Coleman; Narrated by Ian Wolfe; Choreography in two acts and four cantos by Charles Weidman

Charles Weidman (Candide); Eleanor King (Cunegonde); John Glenn (Dr. Pangloss); Katharine Manning (Baroness/Materialistic Hag); Jose Limon (Master of Ceremonies/Don Fernando/Priest); William Matons (Martin/Jew); Cleo Athenos (Paquette/Demi-Mondaine); Gene Martel (Baron Thunder); Richard Abbott (Voice)

Martin Beck Theatre, New York, opened December 1, 1956 73 performances
Produced by Ethel Linder Reiner in association with Lester Osterman, Jr.; A Comic Operetta, based on Voltaire's satire; Director, Tyrone Guthrie, assisted by Tom Brown; Book by Lillian Hellman; Music by Leonard Bernstein; Lyrics by Richard Wilbur; Additional Lyrics by John Latouche and Dorothy Parker; Production designed by Oliver Smith; Lighting by Paul Morrison; Costumes by Irene Sharaff; Musical director, Samuel Krachmalnick; Orchestrations by Leonard Bernstein and Hershy Kay; Hairstylist, Ronald de Mann; Dance supervisors, Wallace Seibert and Anna Sokolow; Company manager, Joseph Moss; Stage managers, Peter Zeisler, Jack Merigold and Joseph Bernard

Westphalia:

Robert Rounseville (Candide); Max Adrian (Dr. Pang loss); Barbara Cook (Cunegonde); Conrad Bain (King of Hesse); Robert Mesrobian (Baron); Louis Edmonds (Maximilian); Norman Roland (Hesse's General)

Candide Travels to London:

Robert Rounseville (Candide); Boris Aplon (Man); Doris Okerson (Woman); Margaret Roy (Dutch Lady); Tony Drake (Dutch Man); Robert Rue (Athiest)

Lisbon:

Robert Rounseville (Candide); Max Adrian (Dr. Pangloss); Maria Novotna (Infant Casmira); Robert Barry (Arab Conjuror); William Chapman (Lawyer); Robert Cosden (Junkman); Stanley Grover (Wine Seller); Robert Rue (Bear Man); Charles Morrell (Bear); Conrad Bain (Very, Very Old Inquisitor); Charles Aschmann (Very Old Inquisitor/Alchemist); Margaret Roy (Grocery Lady)

Candide Travels to Paris:

Robert Rounseville (Candide); Maud Scheerer (French Lady); Margaret Roy, Robert Cosden, Thomas Pyle (Beggars)

Paris:

Irra Petina (Old Lady); Barbara Cook (Cunegonde); Boris Aplon (Marquis Milton); Joseph Bernard (Sultan Milton); Robert Rue (Pilgrim Father); Robert Rounseville (Candide)

They Travel to Buenos Aires:

Robert Rounseville (Candide); Barbara Cook (Cunegonde); Irra Petina (Old Lady); Conrad Bain (Captain); Robert Rue (Pilgrim Father); Dorothy Krebill (Pilgrim Mother)

Buenos Aires:

Robert Rounseville (Candide); Barbara Cook (Cunegonde); Max Adrian (Martin); Conrad Bain (Captain); Robert Rue (Pilgrim Father); Irra Petina (Old Lady); Louis Edmunds (Maximilian); William Olvis (Governor of Buenos Aires); George Blackwell, Tony Drake, Thomas Pyle (Officers)

Candide Travels to Venice:

Robert Rounseville (Candide); Max Adrian (Dr. Pangloss/Martin)

Venice:

Robert Rounseville (Candide); Irra Petina (Madame Sofronia); Barbara Cook (Scrub-Lady); William Chapman (Ferone); Maud Scheerer (Duchess); Norman Roland (Prefect of Police); Robert Mesrobian (Prince Ivan); Max Adrian (Dr. Pangloss); Joseph Bernard (Sultan Milton); Dori Davis (Lady Cutely); George Blackwell (Lady Toothly); Fred Jones (Lady Soothly); Thomas Pyle (Lady Richmond); Robert Barry (Croupier); Charles Aschmann (Duke of Naples); Boris Aplon (Marquis Milton)

Westphalia:

Robert Rounseville (Candide); Barbara Cook (Cunegonde); Louis Edmunds (Maximilian); Irra Petina (Old Lady); Max Adrian (Dr. Pangloss)

Singers:

Peggyann Alderman, Charles Aschmann, Robert Barry, George Blackwell, Dori Davis, Jack Delon, Tony Drake, Naomi Farr, Stanley Grover, Fred Jones, Mollie Knight, Dorothy Krehill, Vivian Laurence, Henry Lawrence, Robert Mesrobian, Lois Monroe, Doris Okerson, Thomas Pyle, Margaret Roy, Robert Rue, Mara Shorr, Dorothy White

Dancers:

Alvin Beam, Charles Czarny, Marvin Gordon, Carmen Gutierrez, Charles Morrell, Frances Noble, Liane Plane, Gloria Stevens

MUSICAL NUMBERS: "The Best of All Possible Worlds"; "Oh, Happy We"; "It Must be So"; "Lisbon Sequence"; "It Must Be Me"; "Mazurka"; "Glitter and Be Gay"; "You Were Dead, You Know"; "Pilgrim's Procession"; "My Love"; "I Am Easily Assimilated"; "Quartet"; "Quiet"; "Eldorado"; "Bon Voyage"; "What's the Use"; "Gavotte"; "Make Our Garden Grow"

Original cast recording: Columbia Records

THE OPTIMIST, Avenue Theatre, Toronto, opened September 20, 1956
Produced by the New Play Society; A Musical Satire, based on Voltaire's *Candide*; Director, Richard Knowles; Book, Lyrics and Music by Mavor Moore; Musical arrangements, Howard Cable; Lighting, Alan Benson; Costumes, Suzanne; Choreography, Gladys Forrester

Robert Goulet (Candide); Drew Thompson (Dr. Voltaire); Margo MacKinnon (Lady Cunegonde); Paul Kligman (Pangloss); Barbara Hamilton (Cacambo); Alan Crofoot (King of the Gregarianna); Ernest Adams (King of El Dorado); Peter Mews (King of Corsica); Sydney Melville (King of Poland); Alexander Gray (King of England); Andrew Macmillan (Grand Inquisitor/Emperor of Russia); Enrest Adams (King of the Abares); Alan Crofoot (Sultan of Morocco); Peter Mews (Governor of Buenos Aires)

MUSICAL NUMBERS: "Times Flies"; "Don't Kiss Me Now"; "Have You Ever Been in Love Before"

Bucks County Playhouse, Pennsylvania, opened September 22, 1958
Produced by Lester Osterman and Hillard Elkins; A Concert Version of a Musical based on Voltaire; Director, David Alexander; Book by Lillian Hellman; Music by Leonard Bernstein; Lyrics by Richard Wilbur; Other Lyrics by John LaTouche and Dorothy Parker; Concert adaptation by Michael Stewart; Musical director, Samuel Krachmalnick; Production designed and lighted by W. Broderick Hackett and David Hale Hand; Pianists, Urey Krasnopolsky and Moreland Kortkamp; General manager, John J. Crowley; Stage manager, Harvey Medlinsky

Robert Rounseville (Candide); Martyn Green (Dr. Pangloss/Martin); Mary Costa (Cunegonde); Irra Petina (Old Lady); Lee Bergere (Ferrone/ Governor/ Sultan/First Inquisitor); Jack Matthew (Maximilian); Charles May (Marquis/ Extortionist/First Man With Bread); Ralston Hill (Baron Thunderton Tronch/Second Man With Bread/Pilgrim); Wayne McIntyre (Second Inquisitor/Third Man With Bread/ Prefect/Man in Eldorado); Jeanne Beauvais (Madame); Claire Alexander (Woman in Buenos Aires); Veronica Kusmin (Gretchen); Luba Tcheresky (First Woman in Lisbon); Shirley Delp (Second Woman in Lisbon); Charlotte Pierson (Woman in Buenos Aires); Paul Veglia (Soldier)

Saville Theatre, London, opened April 30, 1959
Produced by Linnit and Dunfee; A Musical based on the satire by Voltaire; Director, Robert Lewis; Book by Lillian Hellman, assisted by Michael Stewart; Music by Leonard Bernstein; Lyrics by Richard Wilbur; Other Lyrics by John LaTouche and Dorothy Parker; Production designer, Osbert Lancaster; Choreography, Jack Cole; Sets and Costumes by Obsert Lancaster

Denis Quilley (Candide); Laurence Naismith (Dr. Pangloss/Martin); Mary Costa (Cunegonde); Dennis Stephenson (Maximilian/Second Inquisitor); Edith Coates (Old Lady); Vernon Rees (Baron Thunder-Ten-Tronch/Dutch Man); Vincent Charles (King of Hesse/ Atheist); Lauverne Gray (Flower Girl); Alan Thoms (Pastry Cook/First Senor); Lorna Lee (Pastry Cook's Wife/Duchess); Patricia Moore (Cunegonde's Maid); Silvia Beamish (Swiss Woman); Roy Pattison (Spanish Gentleman/Guard/Chief of Police); Victor Spinetti (Marquis Milton/First Inquisitor); Ron Moody (Governor of Buenos Aires); James Cairncross (Sultan Milton/Third Inquisitor); Shirley Lee (Woman Prisoner); Rudi Szigeti (Executioner); Margot Barry (A Guest); Patricia Kilgarriff (Another Guest);

Lawrence Richardson (Croupier); Leighton Camden (A Desperate Gentleman); Tom Fletcher (First Lady Mary); Byron O'Leary (Second Lady Mary/Second Senor/ Policeman); Bernard Jamieson (Third Lady Mary); Brian Scott (Fourth Lady Mary); Vernon Lee (Extortionist); Dorothy Buttery, Helen Fox, Maretta Grace, Patricia Hawkes, Vivienne Hetzel, Derina House, Ross Howard, Bernard Jamieson, Brian Scott, Tommy Shaw, Rudi Seigeti, Gordon Wales (Dancers)

Touring Company, opened *Curran Theatre*, San Francisco, July 6, 1971; closed *Kennedy Center*, Washington, D.C., November 13, 1971
Produced by The San Francisco Civic Light Opera Association, Allen L. Chickering, President; Edwin Lester, General Director, in association with the Kennedy Center, Washington, D. C.; A New Musical version of the satire by Voltaire, based on the play by Lillian Hellman; Conceived and Directed by Sheldon Patinkin; Music by Leonard Bernstein; Lyrics by Richard Wilbur; Other Lyrics by John LaTouche and Dorothy Parker; Scenery by Oliver Smith; Lighting, Peggy Clark; Costumes, Freddy Wittop; Choreography, Michael Smuin; Music director, Maurice Peress; Orchestrations, Leonard Bernstein and Hershy Kay; Additional orchestrations, Maurice Peress; Technical director, Warren Merkle; Production stage manager, Phil Friedman

Frank Porretta (Candide); Douglas Campbell (Voltaire/Dr. Pangloss/Martin); Mary Costa or Barbara Meister (Cunegonde); Rae Allen (The Old Lady); William Lewis (Baron of Westphalia/Marquis Milton/ Ship Captain/Governor of Buenos Aires/First Inquisitor); Annette Cardona (Baroness of Westphalia/ Princess Casmira/Lady of Paris/Pilgrim Mother/ Governor's New Mistress/Lady Frilly); Robert Ito (Baron's Body Guard/Inquisitor's Herald/Milton's Major Domo/First Mate/Governor's Page/Keeper of the Masks); Joshua Hecht (King of Hesse/Second Inquisitor/Sultan Milton/Pilgrim Father/Maximilian/ Chief of Police); Harold Brown (First Hessian General/Arab Conjurer/Gentleman of Paris/Pilgrim/ Senores I/Croupier); Eugene Green (Herman, Second Hessian General/Third Inquisitor/Party Guest/ Pilgrim/Senores II/Gambler); Juleste Salve, Garold Gardner (Soldiers of Lisbon); Danny Villa (Assistant to Second Inquisitor); Lucy Andonian, Marvin Samuels, James L. Cutlip (Beggars); Cecile Wilson (Lady Silly); Tina Blandy (Lady Willy Nilly); Maris O'Neill (Lady Lightly); Damita Freeman (Lady Brightly); Marie Patrice (Lady Fly-by-Nightly); Dana Alexis, Lucy Andonian, Lonna Arklin, Tin Blandy, Catherine Drew, Susan Gayle, Damita Freeman, De Maris Gordon, Anne Kaye, Brenda Lynn, Daphne Payne, Maris O'Neill, Marie Patrice, Kelley Maxwell, Anne Turner, Cecile Wilson, Karen Yarmat, Robert Bakanic, David Bender, Howard Chitjian, James L. Cutlip, Clifford Fearl, Garold Gardner, Gerogeton McClain, Autris Paige, Casper Roos, Marvin Samuels, Juleste Salve, Ben Vargas, Paul Veglia, Danny Villa (Ensemble)

The Chelsea Theatre Center, Brooklyn Academy of Music, opened December 18, 1973 for 48 performances; moved to *Broadway Theatre*, New York, opened March 5, 1974 740 performances
Produced by the Chelsea Theatre Center of Brooklyn; Robert Kalfin, artistic director; Michael David, executive director; Burl Hash, production director; A Musical play; Director, Harold Prince; Book by Hugh Wheeler adapted from Voltaire; Music by Leonard Bernstein; Lyrics by Richard Wilbur; Additional lyrics, Stephen Sondheim and John LaTouche; Settings, Eugene Lee; Lighting, Tharon Musser; Costumes, Franne Lee; Choreography, Patricia Birch; Musical director, John Mauceri, Paul Gemignani; Orchestrations, Hershy Kay; Assistant conductor, Joseph D. Lewis;

Hairstylist, Sondra Muir; General manager, Howard Haines; Stage managers, George Martin, Errol Selsby and Carlos Gorbes; Produced in association with Harold Prince and Ruth Mitchell

Mark Barker (Candide); Maureen Brennan (Cunegonde); Lewis J. Stadlen (succeeded by Charles Kimbrough) (Voltaire/ Dr. Pangloss/ Governor Host/ Sage); Sam Freed (Maximillian); Deborah St. Darr (Paquette); June Gable (succeeded by Niki Flacks) (Old Lady); David Horwitz (Huntsman/Recruiting Officer/ Agent/ Spanish Don/ Eunuch/ Cartagenian/ Sailor); Joe Palmieri (Baron/ Grand Inquisitor/ Slave Driver/ Captain/ Guest); Jim Corti (Coolie/ Soldier/ Priest/ Spanish Don/ Sailor/ Lion/ Guest); Mary-Pat Green (Baroness/ Harpsichordist/ Penitente/ Houri/ Steel Drummer); Robert Henderson (Servant/ Agent of Inquisition/ Spanish Don/ Cartagenian Sailor); Peter Vogt (Recruiting Officer/ Aristocrat/ Cartagenian); Gail Boggs (succeeded by Lisa Wilkinson) (Penitente/ Whore/ Houri); Carolann Page (Aristocrat/ Cartagenian/Second Sheep); Carlos Gorbea (Bulgarian Soldier/ Aristocrat/ Vendor/ Sailor/ Pygmy/ Cow); Kelly Walters (Bulgarian Soldier/ Penitente/ Cartagenian/ Sailor/ Cow); Chip Garnett (Westphalian Soldier/ Agent/ Governor's Aide Pirate/ Guest); Jeff Keller (Rich Jew/ Man in Black/ Cartagenian/ Pirate/ German/ Botanist/ Guest); Becky McSpadden (Aristocrat/ Cartagenian/ Houri); Kathryn Ritter (Aristocrat/ Whore/ Houri/ Cunegonde alternate for matiness); Renee Semes (Lady with knitting/ Cartagenian/ First Sheep); Rhoda Butler (succeeded by Lisa Wilkinson) (Swing Girl)

MUSICAL NUMBERS: "Life Is Happpiness Indeed"; "The Best of All Possible Worlds"; "Oh Happy We"; "It Must Be So"; "O Miserere"; "Glitter and Be Gay"; "Auto da Fe (What a Day)"; "This World"; "You Were Dead, You Know"; "I Am Easily Assimilated"; "My Love"; "Alleluia"; "Sheep's Song"; "Bon Voyage"; "Make Our Garden Grow"

New original cast recording: Columbia Records

Avon Stage, Stratford, Ontario, opened June 8, 1978

Produced by the Stratford Festival; A Musical Play; Director, Lotfi Mansouri; Book by Hugh Wheeler; Music by Leonard Bernstein; Lyrics by Richard Wilbur; Additional lyrics, Stephen Sondheim and John Latouche; Production designer, Mary Kerr; Lighting, Michael J. Whitfield; Choreography, Brian MacDonald; Music director, Berthold Carriere

Edward Evando (Candide); Caralyn Tomlin (Cunegonde); Michael Fletcher (Dr. Voltaire/Pangloss); Andrea Martin (Old Lady); Gerald Isaac (Maximillian); Cathy Wallace (Paquette); Richard Whelan (Baron/Grand Inquisitor); Susan Gudgeon (Baroness); Richard McMillan (Judge/Jew); Elias Zarou (Inquisition Agent); Robert Vigod (Penitent/Sailor); Anne Linden, Maida Rogerson (Prostitutes); Stephen Beamish, Donald Hunkin (Penitents/Westphalian Soldiers); Theodore Baerg (Executioner/Governor); David Dunbar, Barrie Enders (Spanish Dons/Executioners); Ricardo Keens-Douglas (Spanish Don/Sailor); Iris Fraser, Edda Gaborek, Pamela MacDonald, Marylu Moyer, Peggy Watson (Dancers/Townspeople/Slaves)

New York State Theatre, New York, opened October 13, 1982

Produced by the New York City Opera Company; A Musical Play; Director, Harold Prince; Book adapted from Voltaire by Hugh Wheeler; Music by Leonard Bernstein; Lyrics by Richard Wilbur; Additional Lyrics, Stephen Sondheim and John Latouche;

Scenery, Clarke Dunham; Lighting, Ken Billington; Conductor, John Mauceri; Choreography, Patricia Birch; Chorusmaster, David Leighton; Orchestrations, Leonard Bernstein and Hershy Kay; Costumes, Judith Dolan

John Lankston (Voltaire/Dr. Pangloss/Businessman/ Governor); David Eisler (Candide); Erie Mills (Cunegonde); Scott Reeve (Maximillian); Bonnie Kirk (Baroness); Muriel Costa-Greenspon (Old Lady); James Billings (Don Issacher/Maximillian's Servant); Deborah Darr (Paquette); Don Yule (Huntsman); Jack Harrold (Baron/Grand Inquisitor/Slave Driver/Pasha/ Prefect)

Old Vic Theater, London, opened December 6, 1988 34 performances

Old Vic-Scottish Opera presentation; A Musical in two acts, adapted from Voltaire; Directed by Jonathan Miller and John Wells; Book by Hugh Wheeler; Music by Leonard Bernstein; Lyrics by Richard Wilbur; Additional lyrics by Stephen Sondheim and John Latouche, Lillian Hellman and Dorothy Parker; Choreography, Anthony Van Laast; Settings, Richard Hudson; Lighting, Davy Cunningham; Sound, Julian Beech; Orchestrations, Leonard Bernstein and Hershy Kay; Additional orchestrations, John Mauceri; Music direction, Peter Stanger

Nickolas Grace (Voltaire/Dr. Pangloss); Mark Beudert (Candide); Rosemary Ashe (Cunegonde); Patricia Routledge (Old Lady); with Alexander Oliver, Gaynor Miles, Mark Tinkler, Leon Greene, Howard Goorney, Besty Marrion, Harriet Neave, Helen Garton, John Brackenridge, Jonathan Coad, Bill Snape

MUSICAL NUMBERS: "Life Is Happiness, Indeed"; "The Best of All Possible Worlds"; "Oh Happy We"; "It Must Be So"; "Battle Chorale"; "Candide's Lament"; "Dear Boy"; "Auto-da-fe"; "It Must Be Me"; "Paris Waltz"; "Glitter and Be Gay"; "You Were Dead, You Know"; "Easily Assimilated"; "To the New World"; "My Love"; "We Are Women"; "Alleluia"; "Ballad of El Dorado"; "Laughing Song"; "Bon Voyage"; "Money Money"; "Pass It Along"; "Venice Gavotte"; "Nothing More Than This"; "Universal Good"; "Make Our Garden Grow"

New York State Theatre, New York, opened July 20, 1989

Produced by the New York City Opera Company; Director, Albert Sherman; Book adapted from Voltaire by Hugh Wheeler; Music by Leonard Bernstein; Lyrics by Richard Wilbur; Additional Lyrics, Stephen Sondheim and John Latouche; Scenery, Clarke Dunham; Lighting, Ken Billington; Conductor, Scott Bergeson; Choreography, Patricia Birch; Orchestrations, Leonard Bernstein and Hershy Kay; Costumes, Judith Dolan

John Lankston (Voltaire/Dr. Pangloss/Businessman/ Governor); Mark Beudert (Candide); Cyndia Sieden (Cunegonde); James Javore (Maximillian); Bonnie Kirk (Baroness); Muriel Costa-Greenspon (Old Lady); James Billings (Don Issacher/Maximillian's Servant); Maris Clement (Paquette); Don Yule (Huntsman); Jack Harrold (Baron/Grand Inquisitor/ Slave Driver/Pasha/ Prefect)

CSC Theatre, New York, opened April 22, 1992

Produced by CSC Repertory, Casey Perloff, artistic director; A Play in two acts by Len Jenkin, adapted from the book by Francois Marie Arouet de Voltaire; Directors, David Esbjornson and Casey Perloff; Sets, Hugh Landwehr; Lighting, Brian MacDevitt; Costumes, Teresa Snider-Stein; Music, David Lang; Sound, John Kilgore III; Production stage manager, Crystal Huntington

Victor Mack (Candide); Julia Gibson (Cunegonde/ King of Eldorado); Edward Hibbert (Pangloss/Pococurante); Rebecca Schull (Baroness/Old Woman); Kimberley Pistone (Pacquette/Clarion); Dennis Reid (Baron Sr./Cacambo);

Michael Gaston (Baron Jr./Vanderdendur); and William Keeler, Kent Gash, Ani Apardian, D'Metrius Fitzgerald Conley, Roberta Kastelic, Elena McGhee, Katherine Puma, Denis Sweeney, Julina Tatlock, Heather Traber, Rebecca West, Michael R. Wilson

SCREEN

CANDIDE, OU L'OPTIMISME AU XXEME SIECLE, *Connaisseur Film*, France, released 1960; in U.S. as *Candide*, released 1962
Produced by C.L.M.S.N. PatheCinema; Producer, Clement Duhour; Director, Norbert Carbonnaux; Screenplay by Norbert Carbonnaux and Albert Simonin, based on Voltaire's novel; Photography, Robert Le Febvre; Art director, Jean Douarinou; Sound, Jean Bertrand; Music, Hubert Rostaing; Production manager, Andre Deroual; Editor, Paulette Robert

Jean-Pierre Cassel (Candide); Dahlia Lavi (Cunegonde); Michel Simon (Colonel Nanar); Jean Tissier (Dr. Jacques); Louis de Funes (French Gestapo Officer); Jean Richard (BlackMarketeer); Pierre Brasseur (Dr. Pangloss); Nadia Gray (The Confidante); Jean Constantin (Fourak); Albert Simonin (Major Simpson); Jean Poiret and Michel Serrault (Policemen); Dario Moreno (Don Fernando d'Ybarrara y Figueroa; Luis Mariano (Don Mascarena); Jean Tissier (Dr. Jacques); Jacqueline Maillan (The Puritan Mother); John William (Native Chieftain); Don Ziegler (The Gangster Father); Robert Manuel (Various German Officers); and Mathilde Casadesus, Don Ziegler, John William, Harold Kay, Michel Garland, Alice Sapritch, Jacques Balutin, Jean Droze, Michel Dacquin, Maurice Biraud, Michel Thomass, Jean Franval, Pierre Repp

TELEVISION

CANDIDE, *Play of the Month*, televised February 16, 1973 BBC; in U.S. on PBS' *Classic Theatre*, televised October 30, 1975 90 minutes
Produced by the British Broadcasting Corporation in association with WGBH-TV, Boston; Producer, Cedric Messina; A Comedy by Voltaire, adapted and directed by James MacTaggart; Designer, Eileen Diss; Lighting, Dennis Channon; Costumes, Elizabeth Waller

Frank Finlay (Voltaire); Ian Ogilvy (Candide); Angela Richards (Cunegonde); Emrys James (Dr. Pangloss); Clifton Jones (Cocambo); Kathleen Helme (Old Woman); Leonard Maguire (Martin); Nicholas Jones (Young Baron); and Douglas Milvain, Robin Hunter, John Woodnutt, Jerome Willis, Anthony Collin, Geoffrey Matthews, Elspeth Macnaughton, Johnny Wade, Rita Davies

CANDIDE, *Live From Lincoln Center*, televised November 12, 1986 PBS 2 1/2 hours
Produced by the New York City Opera; A Musical Play; Director, Harold Prince; Television director, Kirk Browning; Book by Hugh Wheeler adapted from Voltaire; Music by Leonard Bernstein; Lyrics by Richard Wilbur; Additional lyrics by Stephen Sondheim and John Latouche; Orchestrations, Leonard Bernstein and Hershy Kay; Set designer, Clarke Dunham; Lighting, Ken Billington; Costumes, Judith Dolan; Conductor, Scott Bergeson; Chorus Master, Joseph Colaneri; Choreographer, Patricia Birch

John Lankston (Voltaire/Dr. Pangloss/Businessman/ Governor/Gambler/Police Chief/Sage); David Eisler (Candide); Erie Mills (Cunegonde); Muriel Costa-Greenspon (Old Lady); Deborah Darr (Paquette); Ruth Golden (Baroness/Calliope Player); Jack Harrold (Baron/ Grand Inquisitor/ Slave Driver/ Pasha/ Prefect); Don Yule (Huntsman); Scott Reeve (Maximilian); James Billings (Servant/Judge/Father Bernard/Don Issachar/Gambler); Ralph Bassett (Heresy Agent); Robert Brubaker (Lion); Ivy Austin, Rhoda Butler (Pink Sheep)

CAPTAINS COURAGEOUS
A Novel by Rudyard Kipling (1897)

Synopsis

Harvey Chayne, the pampered son of a millionaire under the impression that his father's wealth will get him anything, buys his way into a school club and tries to bribe a teacher. Too preoccupied with business to this time to be a real father, Mr. Chayne decides to take his son on an ocean cruise to Europe so that perhaps they can better understand one another. Shortly after sailing, young Harvey topples overboard and is plucked from the sea by Manuel, a Portuguese fisherman from nearby Gloucester fishing boat *We're Here*, skippered by crusty Captain Disko Troop. The boy makes himself obnoxious to the crew and unsuccessfully orders the captain to return him to his father at once. Harvey sulks around the vessel but eventually Manuel is able to bring him around and they soon become fast friends. Manuel teaches him to fish and takes him out in his dory, instructing him in the principles of good sportsmanship and fair play, lessons hard to come by for the boy because of the way he was raised.

At last considered one of the crew, Harvey is thrilled to be part of the great race back to Gloucester after the boat is filled with fish. An old rival of the captain's is ahead of him but by daring and skillful sailing, Disko overhauls him, but will need to break out more canvas in order to keep the lead. Manuel offers to go aloft and tend the topsails, but the mast breaks and he his thrown into the water, entangled in rope and canvas. Harvey rows out to him with one of the ship's mates, but Manuel cannot be saved and there is a tearful farewell. When *We're Here* finally makes port in Gloucester, Harvey is reunited with his father, and having learned some lessons in life from the goodhearted Manuel, lights a candle in his friend's memory, then tosses a wreath into the water as is tradition for those who have died at sea.

Comment and Critique

Rudyard Kipling's famous sea story and the transformation of a spoiled brat into a man became a movie first as one of the screen's great adventures films, then a television drama, and latterly a stage musical (!), adapted not from the novel but from the 1937 movie.

English short-story writer, poet and novelist Kipling was born in 1865 in India of British parents and at age six was taken to England and left to board with paid foster parents. He entered an inferior boarding school for the sons of fathers in the Indian Services, and at age seventeen, he returned to India where his father had secured for him a position at the *Civil and Military Gazette* of Lahore, where he began his first stories about life in Britishruled India. From these came *The Man Who Would Be King*. He went back to England in 1889 by way of Japan and America and soon enjoyed spectacular success as a writer. He briefly was collaborated with Woolcott

Balestier, whose sister Caroline he married in 1892, and moved to her family's estate in Brattleboro, Vermont. There he wrote, among others, *The Jungle Book* and *Captains Courageous*. Dissatisfied with life in America, he moved back to England after five years and settled in Sussex, returning to America only once in 1899 when he daughter died of pneumonia in New York.

Despite his enormous popularity in America, he spoke of it in bitterness in the ensuing years while turning out a prolific body of work. In 1907, he became the first English writer to be awarded the Nobel Prize. His autobiography *Something of Myself* was left unfinished at his death in 1937, not living to see *Captains Courageous* brought to the screen.

The film version, which began as a screen vehicle of young Freddie Bartholomew, not only made Spencer Tracy a star of the first rank but also brought him the first of his two consecutive Academy Awards as Best Actor. Lionel Barrymore as the captain, Melvyn Douglas as the father, and Mickey Rooney as the captain's son and Freddie's cabin boy pal headed the memorable cast. The film proved over the years to be a true screen classic, and *Time* magazine noted on its premiere: "So magnificent are its sweep and excitement, so harmonious its design, that *Captains Courageous* ranks above more current cinematic efforts [and] offers its credentials for admission to the thin company of cinema immortals." *Variety* thought it to be "one of the best pictures of the sea ever made." In the *New York Herald-Tribune*, Howard Barnes felt that "with such eloquence, authority and beauty...[it] is certain to become a classic in its new medium. *Captains Courageous* belongs with the screen's few masterpieces." Interestingly, not only was the film unfaithful to Kipling, but the relationship between Manuel and young Harvey was not even in the book.

Forty years later, *Captains Courageous* came to television as a Bell System special with Karl Malden as the captain, Jonathan Kahn as brattish Harvey Cheyne, and Ricardo Montalban as Manuel. "This time around, *Captains Courageous* has been adapted by John Gay, who freely concedes that he has added his own 'third act' to a story that lacks a 'structured dramatic climax,'" TV critic John J. O'Connor noted in *The New York Times*. "Mr. Gay's tinkering, his putting story ideas into the head of a dead author, is certainly questionable, but the rest of his screenplay remains remarkably faithful to the book." O'Connor concluded that "this *Captains Courageous* adds up to respectably pleasant television." In *TV Guide*, Judith Crist wrote: "Most movie buffs' off-the-cuff reaction to a remake of Kipling's *Captains Courageous* is bound to be 'Who needs it?' Deep in our hearts lies MGM's 1937 salt-water classic...On the cuff, however, and forty years later, one has to credit John Gay's new TV adaptation for its shift of emphasis from sentiment to storyline and its concentration on character rather than spectacular seascapes."

In late summer 1992, a musical stage adaptation of the Kipling tale had its world premiere at Ford's Theatre in Washington, D.C., with a score by Frederick Freyner and Patrick Cook. Reviews were decidedly split. On one hand, the *Washington Post* found this *Captains Courageous* "not worth its salt" and "a pretty humdrum show" that was "adapted from the film with Spencer Tracy, not the book by Rudyard Kipling." On the other, the *Baltimore Sun*'s critic found it "a stunning debut that deserves nothing less than a berth on Broadway."

STAGE

CAPTAINS COURAGEOUS, *Ford's Theatre*, Washington, opened September 23 through November 22, 1992

Presented by the Ford's Theatre Society, Frankie Hewitt, producting director; A Musical based on the 1937 MGM film adapted by John Lee Mahin, Marc Connelly amd Dale Van Every from the novel by Rudyard Kipling; Directed and choreographed by Graciela Daniele; Book and lyrics by Patrick Cook; Music by Frederick Freyer; Sets, Christopher Barreca; Lights, Jules Fisher and Peggy Eisenhauer; Costumes, Ann Hould-Ward; Musical direction, James Kowal; Orchestrations, Doug Besterman; Sound, Peter Fitzgerald; Flying by Foy; Production stage manager, Leslie Loeb

John Dossett (Manuel); Kel O'Neill (Harvey Elles-worth Cheyne); Don Chastain (The Captain); Walter Hudson (Long Jack); Mark Aldrich (Nate); Larry Alexander (Tom); Frank DiPasquale (Simon); Michael Greenwood (Murphy); George Kmeck (Walters); Joseph Kolinski (Stevens); Michael Mandell (Doc); John Mineo (Hermans); Ric Ryder (Evans); Michael Shelle (Harris); Richard Thomsen (Ollie); John Leslie Wolfe (Peters)

MUSICAL NUMBERS: "Little Fish"; "Nothin' to Do"; "I'm Harvey Ellesworth Cheyne" "Ten Seconds/Not So Bad"; "Anybody Else"; "I Make Up This Song"; "Right Here"; "Lord, Could She Go"; "That's Where I'm Bound"; "Jonah"; "You Never Saw"; "Song of the Sea"; "The Grand Banks"; "One More Year"; "Regular Fellas"; "I'm Home"; "I Make Up This Song" (reprise); "Song of the Sea" (reprise)

SCREEN

Metro-Goldwyn-Mayer, released June 1937

Producer, Louis D. Lighton; Director, Victor Fleming; Screenplay, John Lee Mahin, Marc Connell and Dale Van Every, based on the novel by Rudyard Kipling; Photography, Harold Rosson; Art director, Cedric Gibbons; Sound, Douglas Shearer; Music, Franz Waxman; Songs, Franz Waxman and Gus Kahn; Editor, Elmo Vernon

Freddie Bartholomew (Harvey Cheyne); Spencer Tracy (Manuel); Lionel Barrymore (Captain Disko Troop); Melvyn Douglas (Mr. Cheyne); Charley Grapewin (Uncle Salters); Mickey Rooney (Dan Troop); John Carradine ("Long Jack"); Oscar O'Shea (Cushman); Jack LaRue (Priest); Walter Kingsford (Dr. Finley); Donald Briggs (Tyler); Samuel McDaniels ("Doc"); Billy Burrud (Charles); Christian Rub (Old Clement); Leo G. Carroll (Burns); William Stack (Elliott); Charles Trowbridge (Dr. Walsh); Richard Powell (Steward); Jay Ward (Pogey); Katherine Kenworthy (Mrs. Disko); and Dave Thursby, Roger Gray, Gladden James, Philo McCullough, James Kilgannon, Bill Fisher, Dick Howard, Larry Fisher, Gil Perkins, Jack Sterling, Stubby Kreuger, Murray Kinnell, Dave Wengren. Goldie Sloan, Myra McKinney, Lee Van Atta, Gene Reynolds, Billy Gilbert, Jimmy Conlin, Frank Sully, Lester Dorr, Lloyd Ingraham, Jack Kennedy, Wade Boteler, Norman Ainsley

TELEVISION

Bell System Special, televised December 4, 1977 ABC 2 hours

A Norman Rosemont production; Producer, Norman Rosemont; Director, Harvey Hart; Teleplay, John Gay, based on the novel by Rudyard Kipling; Photography, Philip Lathrop; Production designer, Hilyard Brown; Music, Allyn Ferguson; Editor, Jack McSweeney

Karl Malden (Captain Disko Troop); Jonathan Kahn (Harvey Chayne); Ricardo Montalban (Manuel); Fritz Weaver (Mr. Cheyne); Neville Brand (Little Penn); Fred Gwynne (Long Jack); Jeff Corey (Salters); Charles Dierkop (Tom Platt); Johnny Doran (Dan Troop); Stan Haze (Cook); Redmond Gleeson (Phillips);

Shay Duffin (Chief Steward); Milton Frome (Mr. Atkins); Stanja Lowe (Mrs. Cheyne); Len Wayland (McLean); Don Plumley (Captain Olley); Orville Young (Captain Bush); Randy Faustino (Boy)

CASABLANCA

Adaptations of the play *Everybody Comes to Rick's* by Murray Burnett and Joan Alison (1939)

Synopsis

Richard Blaine, an American expatriate, is the tough, cynical owner of a Casablanca watering hole that's popular with international travelers of the late Thirties and early Forties. He calls his gin joint Rick's Cafe Americain, and he oversees the place with his piano player Sam, his bartender Ahmed, and his head waiter Carl. (Rick, according to the play but unmentioned in the movie, had been a disillusioned criminal attorney back in the States and left behind a wife and two kids.) Rick's Place has come increasingly a haven for war refugees and has fallen under the eye of Nazi officials, on the lookout for certain targets in transit out of Europe, and caught in the middle is Luis Renault, the expedient local police prefect who has an uneasy alliance with Rick while picking up "the usual suspects" whenever Major Strasser, the Gestapo head, snaps his fingers.

Into Rick's Place comes a Polish underground leader, Victor Laszlo, with a Yank, Lois Meredith, on his arm. (In the film, she was turned into Ilsa Laszlo, Victor's wife.) Lois, it turns out, is an old flame from Rick's Paris days, and she and Rick quickly become romantically involved once again. Victor, meanwhile, is seeking a visa to go to America, and it falls to Rick to get him -- and Lois -- letters of transit. Rick is left to wrestle with his conscience: should he risk his life to get the proper documents for Victor and Lois, or might Lois stay behind if Victor gets out, or would it be doing the right thing to get Lois to walk out on him again?

Comment and Critique

The genesis of what was to become one of the most enduring movies of all time was a play written in 1939 by a couple of New Yorkers, Murray Burnett, who subsequently became a prolific writer, producer and director on radio and then television, and Joan Alison, who later went to Hollywood to write screenplays.

Shortly after they wrote a play called *Everybody Comes to Rick's* (their only one together), about an American adventurer who ended up running a fancy watering hole in Morocco at the outbreak of World War II, Jack L. Warner optioned it for the movies, and it was to go unproduced on the stage for fifty years. Originally, as by now everybody knows, George Raft turned down the part of Rick, and contract players Ann Sheridan and Ronald Reagan were assigned the roles that ultimately went to Ingrid Bergman and Humphrey Bogart, not quite yet a star. (Bogart was reported to have commented to Hal Wallis, the film's producer, when assigned to the project: "He drinks, he smokes, he makes love. They say goodbye. So what's the pitch?") The film, now called *Casablanca*, didn't even have an ending until the last moment, in the script concocted from the play by twins Julius J. and Philip F. Epstein, and Howard Koch, Orson Welles' Mercury Theatre associate, was brought in to doctor. According to trade stories at the time, Wallis found himself stuck with a clinker and director Michael Curtiz and his cast, in effect, "winged it" as the script came in piecemeal. In one of her final television interviews, Ingrid Bergman told of how everyone in the cast was totally confused as to what was happening and not knowing what their character's motivation was. Miraculously, as time has proven, *Casablanca* all came together.

Although given a limited release in November 1942 (making it officially a 1942 film), *Casablanca* was not seen widely until the following January, causing confusion in Academy Award listings, with the film winning the Oscar as Best Picture of 1943 (!), and Curtiz being named Best Director, and the Epstein brothers and Koch getting Academy Awards for Best Screenplay. Humphrey Bogart was nominated as Best Actor (losing to Paul Lukas for *Watch on the Rhine*), while Ingrid Bergman got her nomination as Best Actress not for this but for *For Whom the Bell Tolls*, and Claude Rains was nominated as Best Supporting Actor. Also nominated were cinematographer Arthur Edeson, editor Owen Marks, and Max Steiner for his score.

Casablanca came to television twice as a series -- both times (in the 1950s and the 1980s) unsuccessfully. Charles McGraw played Rick (his last name then was Jason) in the first series, one of the elements in the *Warner Bros. Presents* anthology, and David Soul had the role when producer David L. Wolper resurrected the *Casablanca* concept three decades later.

In between the two television versions, David Kelsey, a British film buff, learned that the source play was never produced and began a seventeen-year search for the rights. He discovered one of the coauthors, Murray Burnett alive and well in New York with a virgin script (unproduced) in his bottom drawer. The next step was to find an enterprising producer. "I think the turning point which set the project in motion was the recent [1989-90] political eruption in Europe, the confusions of national barriers, refugees fleeing for freedom; precisely the same background as *Casablanca*, which has the added gem of a potent love story," Kelsey has written. "So we have a warring conflict which is directly reflected by the two main protagonists -- a 'fight for love and glory' between a tormented man and a woman who redeems him from soulless isolation." Kelsey persuaded London impresario Paul Elliott to secure the performing rights, and the play, now called *Rick's Bar Casablanca*, received its premiere staging in late February 1991 at the Churchill, an Off-Broadway-like repertory theatre in London's South End before transferring to the West End some weeks later, fifty two years after being written.

With the long shadow of one of the alltime popular movies hovering over the project, *Rick's Bar Casa-blanca* was greeted with a decidedly mixed reception. *Variety* reported that "the play is simply spooked by an enduring movie masterpiece," finding it to be "an archaeological novelty that ironically might survive for a while in the West End by the grace of curious." The paper's critic continued: "A bummer it isn't. It's just that the play's undercut at every turn by the film. Lines indelibly etched by the movie, with its mix of intrigue, suspense, romance and cynical humor, lack the same snap, sparkle or schmaltzy resonance on stage. The acting is constantly bedeviled by one's mental images of those inimitable screen performances, a handicap David Gilmore's lackluster staging doesn't begin to ease."

The *Sunday Times* found that the play "has all the makings of as great Hollywood success" and said of popular British television star Leslie Grantham, in the role of Rick: "It's not often that someone so famous makes such an impeccable West End debut." The *London Evening Standard*s critic felt, however, that "stripped of those compelling performances, [the play] is only a precis of the picture," and called it "a misconceived venture." *Rick's Bar Casablanca* made it through just six weeks.

STAGE

RICK'S BAR CASABLANCA, *Whitehall Theatre*, London, opened April 3, 1991 53 performances

A presentation of George Wieser, Hugh J. Alexander, Paul Elliott, International Artistes and Greg Smith; A Churchill Theatre, Bromley Production; Associate producers, David Kelsey, Brian Hewitt-Jones and Chris Moreno; The original play [*Everybody Comes to Rick's*] by Murray Burnett and Joan Alison; Director, David Gilmore; Designer, Saul Radomsky; Lighting, Michael Calf; Musical associate, Trevor Michael Georges

Leslie Grantham (Richard Blaine [Rick]); Shelley Thompson (Lois Meredith); Richard Durden (Victor Laszlo); Edward De Souza (Louis Renault); Trevor Michael Georges (Sam); Ken Bones (Major Heinrich Strasser); Robert Schofield (Guillermo Ugarte); David Weston (ForresterSmith); Lisa Bowerman (Annina Viereck); Paul Aves (Jan Viereck); Geoffrey Drew (Carl, the Head Waiter); Guy Gregory (Ahmed, the Barman); Louise Bangay (Yvonne); Malcolm Terris (Senor Martinez); Maria Darling (Rosa); Jonathan Byard, Daniel Davies, Jo Edkins, Maria Galante, John Walters (Guests); Philip Childs, Graham Padden, Peter Hurle, John Walters (French Officers, German Officers, Gendarmes)

SCREEN

CASABLANCA, *Warner Bros.-First National*, released November 1942

Producer, Hal B. Wallis; Director, Michael Curtiz; Screenplay, Julius J. & Philip G. Epstein and Howard Koch; Based on the play *Everybody Comes to Rick's* by Murray Burnett and Joan Alison; Photography, Arthur Edeson; Art director, Carl Jules Weyl; Sets, George James Hopkins; Gowns, Orry-Kelly; Music, Max Steiner; Orchestrations, Hugo J. Friedhofer; Songs: "As Time Goes By," Herman Hupfeld; "Knock on Wood," M. K. Jerome and Jack Scholl; Montages, Don Siegel and James Leicester; Editor, Owen Marks

Humphrey Bogart (Rick Blaine); Ingrid Bergman (Ilsa Laszlo); Paul Henreid (Victor Laszlo); Claude Rains (Capt. Louis Renault); Conrad Veidt (Colonel Strasser); Sydney Greenstreet (Senor Farrari); Peter Lorre (Ugarte); S. Z. Sakall (Carl); Dooley Wilson (Sam); Madeleine LeBeau (Yvonne); Joy Page (Annina Brandel); John Qualen (Berger); Leonid Kinsky (Sascha); Helmut Dantine (Jan Brandel); Curt Bois (Pickpocket); Marcel Dalio (Croupier); Corinna Mura (Singer); Ludwig Stossel (Mr. Leuchtag); Ilka Gruning (Mrs. Leuchtag); Charles La Torre (Italian Officer Tonelli); Frank Puglia (Arab Vendor); Dan Seymour (Abdul)

TELEVISION

CASABLANCA, televised September 27, 1955 through April 24, 1956* ABC Series 10 episodes (1 hour each)

Producer, Joel Robinson; Directors, Don Weis, John Peyser, Alvin Ganzer and Richard Bare; Writers, various; Adapted from the 1942 film; Music, David Buttolph; Host, Gig Young

Charles McGraw (Rick Jason); Clarence Muse (Sam); Marcel Dalio (Captain Renault); Dan Seymour (Senor Ferrari); Michael Fox (Sascha); Ludwig Stossel (Ludwig); Peter Van Eyck (Victor Laszlo); Anita Ekberg (Ilsa Lund Laszlo); and guests including Nicole Maurey, William Hopper, Maureen O'Sullivan, Karin

Booth, Rosanna Rory, Mari Blanchard, Patty McCormack
* Presented along with "Kings Row" and "Cheyenne" as revolving anthology elements of *Warner Bros. Presents*

CASABLANCA, televised April 10 through 24, 1983, and August 27 through September 3, 1983 NBC Series 5 episodes (1 hour each)
Executive Producer, David L. Wolper; Directors, Ralph Senensky, Robert Michael Lewis and Mel Stuart; Writers, James M. Miller, Bob Foster, Nelson Gidding, Chester Krumholtz, Harold Gast; Adapted from the 1942 film; Music, Peter Matz

David Soul (Rick Blaine); Scatman Crothers (Sam); Hector Elizondo (Capt. Louis Renault); Patrick Horgan (Major Strasser); Reuben BarYotam (Ferrari); Ray Liotta (Sascha); Kai Wulff (Lieutenant Heinz); Arthur Mallet (Carl); and guests including Trisha Noble, Madolyn Smith, Shanna Reed, Daniel Pilon, Michael Horton, Melinda O. Fee, Andrea Millian, Persis Khambatta

CASANOVA
A Drama by Lorenzo de Azertis, translated by Sidney Howard (1923), and other adaptations of *The Memoirs of Giacomo Casanova*

Synopsis

Sidney Howard's translation from the Italian play by Lorenzo de Azertis had eighteenth-century Giacomo Casanova, self-styled Chevalier de Seingalt, admitting to a mere three hundred mistresses from his self-proclaimed 1,001. The drama centered on Casanova's one true love, Henriette. Having won a considerable amount of gold at the gambling table in Cesena, Casanova persuades Henriette, who has left her despicable husband, to live with him in luxurious, glorious sin for ninety days on Lake Geneva. Casanova's reckless gambling once again reduces him to poverty and, although madly in love with Henriette, permits his lover to leave with rescuing friends sent by her contrite husband. Depressed by Henriette's absence and haunted by her note, "You'll also forget Henriette," scratched with her diamond ring on the window pane, Casanova returns to the gambling casino where he wins a small fortune. Learning that Henriette is pregnant with his child, Casanova unsuccessfully engages several postillions to find her. The couriers do return with three other Henriettes, a governess, a dancer from Milan and a courtesan, with whom Casanova exercises his libidinous hunger. Twenty years later, Casanova meets his and Henriette's daughter in Geneva. Old, impoverished, but still in hot pursuit of l'amour with kitchen maids, Casanova is unable to identify himself to his beautiful illegitimate daughter. After she leaves, the old roue kisses the carpet where she walked, and then dies.

Comment and Critique

Giacomo Casanova, born in 1725 in Venice, was the son of Gaetana Casanova and a vivacious actress, Zanetta Farusi. His father died early on and Zanetta became a lifetime member of the Dresden State Theatre. Unhampered by family, Casanova entered, of all things, the priesthood and became Abbe Casanova, but confused sacramentals with seduction and was dismissed. Arrested in 1775 for "sedition and irreligion," he was imprisoned in the impenetrable Leeds Prison of the Palazzo

Ducale. After nearly two years in Leeds, Casanova made what is recorded by William Bolitho in his fascinating book *Twelve Against the Gods*, "the most extraordinary, if not the most extraordinary, escape in history."

Reaching Paris, Casanova found fortunes improved by his appointment to the State Lottery fund which he carefully but generously looted to become a wealthy man. Gradually, Casanova precipitated his own downfall through arrogance and greed. He records persistent failures in London, Prussia and Russia and becomes persona non grata in most of the capitals of Europe. At age fifty-two, he returned to Venice becoming, amazingly, a "vicereporter" for the government under the name of Antonio Pratolini.

Finally, Casanova in his old age was engaged as a librarian in Court Waldstein's Dux Castle in Bohemia. There he wrote his *Memoirs* (later published in the 1920s by The Venetian Society in eight volumes). Casanova died at the age of seventy at Dux Castle. His name became part of most languages designating "lover," "libertine" and overshadowed the likes of Don Juan and Romeo as the "Great Lover" with his exotic and highly erotic adventures.

Havelock Ellis, an appropriate commentator on the life of Casanova, wrote as preface to the *Memoirs*, "This supreme book of adventures is a real man's record of his own real life. It remains a personal document of a value which will increase rather than diminish as time goes by. It is one of the great autobiographical revelations which the ages have left us, with Augustine's, Cellini's, Rousseau's...of its own kind supreme."

The Sidney HowardAzertis play *Casanova* opened on Broadway at the Empire Theatre in September 1923, starring Lowell Sherman. *Time* magazine advised, "The only real amour that dramatic exigencies permit him is one with Henriette. The 300 others are sufficiently indicated in the delightful ballet-prologue...The costumes are glittering and colorful; Katharine Cornell, superb; Lowell Sherman, sedulously rakish."

Theatre magazine reported, "What a character to tempt the imagination of a dramatist or test the ability of an actor!...The dramatist has taken for the purpose of the present play Casanova's affair with Henriette -- a brief *liaison* that is but a passing incident in the eight formidable volumes which form the remarkable autobiography...The play departs only slightly from the facts...Casanova must have possessed unusual powers of fascination, charms of person and charm of manner. We know that he was handsome, witty, eloquent. Lowell Sherman only partly fulfills these requirements. He lacks the grace, the elegance, the grand air of the period. His love making is conventional. In his wooing he appears sinister rather than tender. His performance is labored, mechanical. He saws the air too much with his arms. He was at his best in the death scene, but at no time did he ever let us think it was anything but acting. Not so with Katharine Cornell, who plays Henriette. Piquant, vivacious, arch, she was the life of the play. It was a beautiful performance, the memory of which will linger...As drama, *Casanova* is somewhat wanting, but as a romantic spectacle, it is picturesque and interesting."

Erik Charell produced a version of *Casanova* in London in 1932 with music by Johann Strauss; it ran for more than a year. Trinculo (*The Bystander*) wrote, "*Casanova*, at the Coliseum, is a chronic case of elephantiasis of the scenic organs. There are eight revolving stages and two sets of principals...The book, adapted by one German from two others and anglicised by Harry Graham, is hardly a riot of humour...The Strauss music certainly requires well singing, but otherwise the parts are not particularly onerous. Dorothy Dickson [has] little to do and Oriel Ross still less as the Empress Catherine...Little need be added concerning the story. As a romantic record of Casanova's wandering sex-appeal, it is as dull and decorous as a mothers' meeting. Casanova himself, in the personage of Fernando Autori, emerges from it as an operasinger with chivalrous instincts on his best behaviour. The romance is lost in the scenery which so dominates actors and authors...The scenery, dresses, crows, dwarfs, acrobats, dancers, ballet girls, Gipsies, singers, animals -- all that colossal pageant of bedazzlement is beyond my powers of description...The final scene is a revolving panorama of Venice in which carnival crowds of revelers advance at the double over the bridges of the Grand Canal to the Rialto. Nothing more supremely spectacular or mechanically perfect has been done on the stage...wither Casanova returns without a stain on his character or anything to suggest the wholesale slaughter of feminine virtue."

A 1985 *Casanova* opera by Dominick Argento, staged by Arthur Masella for the New York City Opera, premiered at the New York State Theater in Lincoln Center at the beginning of November (after first having earlier in the year in Minneapolis). The three-act work was hailed by Donal Henahan of *The New York Times* as an "inspired account of one of the great lover's autumnal escapades...a thorough-going delight...handsomely sung and acted by Timothy Nolen. Critic Henahan also noted: "As far as I have been able to discover, this was a historic event [as] the first opera in English with English captions, and probably not the last." The same production was again staged at Lincoln Center in September 1987.

Casanova was brought to the screen in 1927 by France's Albatross Films, founded by expatriate Russian stage and screen professionals after the Russian Revolution and led by actor Ivan Mosjoukine. *The New York Times* reviewed the showing of the French production in New York on June 23, 1927, describing it thusly: "The colorful adventures of Casanova have been woven into a remarkable film...In presenting the episodes of Casanova's adventurous career, Mosjoukine brought to the screen probably for the first time a gripping picturization of Venice in the 18th century ...The picture is a triumph of artistic photography and the interpretation of the leading roles is competent throughout... Into the life of Casanova, Mosjoukine and his assistants have introduced situations, which make for dramatic cohesion and unity."

In 1986, the French film was unearthed, and Jon Pareles (*The New York Times*) wrote, "After decades of obscurity, *Casanova* was rediscovered in the archives of the Cinematheque Francaise...The film's restoration -- tracking down usable versions of every sequence and editing them together -- took three years for Renee Lichtig at the Cinematheque...Like many silent films, it is tinted, but its climactic sequences -- the Carnival of Venice -- were hand-tinted, frame by frame, in not one but four colors."

Shown for one performance at New York's Alice Tully Hall on July 11, the film was accompanied by "a new score composed and conducted, in person, by Georges Delerue," according to Walter Goodman (*The New York Times*). "This ambitious and accomplished film seems to have been the inspiration of Ivan Mosjoukine...The director was another Russian emigre, Alexander Volkoff. The cast was international...The writers did not exert themselves to be faithful to the *Memoirs*...Given the nostalgia for Mother Russia of the emigres who made the movie, the emphasis on a brief trip that Casanova paid to St. Petersburg and his meeting with Catherine the Great is not surprising, but this, too, is mostly make-believe...Mosjoukine plays the role as a combination of Rudolph Valentino, Errol Flynn and George Arliss... *Casanova* is not in the highreaching class of Abel Gance's epic *Napoleon*, also made in France in 1927 and recently released in restored form, but its two hours and 15 minutes abound in invention and heady spirits. It is said to be the first film shot on location -- in Venice and the Austrian Alps -- and much is made of those picturesque places...The spectacle is enhanced by tints of color...*Casanova* is a brilliant pastiche, and Mr. Delerue's score, with its hints of the 18th century and its spirited airs of battle and ballroom, has been carefully synchronized to the action...Mosjoukine captures the essence and plays it for all its worth... *Casanova* is a rich find."

Considered a bit lascivious even for American's "Roaring Twenties," *Casanova* was shown in New York on April 29, 1929 as *The Loves of Casanova.* Mordaunt Hall (*The New York Times*) found the French import to be "an expurgated edition -- a French production with competent acting and pretentious scenes....Only seven of the original 15 or more reels are offered over here, but, except for a few passages that have been sheared too short to convey their full meaning, this picture still affords a good entertainment. In Paris, due to its extraordinary length, it was exhibited in two installments on different days." Critic Hall also felt: "Edwin Justus Mayer, who was responsible for the play *The Firebrand,* has done excellent work for the captions...Several of the episodes in this film are hand-painted, and while this is not particularly effective in certain stretches, it is quite impressive in the sequence when Catherine makes her entry into court. Her regal robe has a train that is about 40 feet long... Ivan Mosjoukine is in his element in the role of *Casanova.*"

Casanova was remade in France in 1933. The sound version, directed by Rene Barberis, also starred the ubiquitous Ivan Mosjoukine but was less effective than the silent version. France's admiration for Casanova emerged yet again in 1948 in *Les Amours de Casanova* with musical comedy star Georges Guetary. Bosley Crowther (*The New York Times*) described the 1948 edition as a "flouncy French costume picture" which was "about as spirited and daring as an old copy of Godey's Lady's Book. And M. Guetary's performance as the lover of great renown suggests nothing quite so strongly as the posturing of a back-row chorus boy. How this anemic romance ever came to be produced or got all the way to this country is a mystery in international trade."

A burlesque of Casanova's lascivious life was produced in 1954 as a vehicle for Bob Hope. "The role of the tinhorn Lothario is so familiar and hackneyed for Bob Hope that he starts off with two strikes on him in *Casanova's Big Night,*" reported *The New York Times'* Bosley Crowther, "a frank burlesque of the great-love-hero...The third strike is pitched by Hal Kanter and Edmund Hartmann who wrote the script...Paul Jones has given the picture a handsome color-film production for Paramount. It's just too bad that some exalted genius can't imagine another characterization for Mr. Hope."

Italy's *Casanova* came along in 1957 starring Gabriele Ferzetti. "For nearly two hours we are treated to the dreary spectacle of Casanova's triumphs over the fair sex...The colour is not unpleasing, the costumes attractive and the ladies are all splendid; but there is no real plot and not the faintest trace of satire, and we are expected to be as guiltily fascinated by the *contes drolatiques* that make up the action as a schoolboy pouring over the *Decameron,*" was Leo Harris' summation in *Films and Filming.*

Carlo Ponti's 1965 production, *Casanova '70,* was an updated farce in which Marcello Mastroianni portrayed an Italian officer, a latter-day Casanova, assigned to NATO who becomes obsessed by the prospect of impotency. Britian's *Monthly Film Bulletin* found that "its single joke is endlessly repeated, the only variation being the succession of pretty girls with whom it is played -- so many of them that they become indistinguishable before the end....Even the everreliable Mastroianni seems bored. But who can wonder?"

Casanova returned to the screen in Italy's 1969 *Infanzia, Vocazione e Prime Esperienze di Giacomo Casanova, veneziano* (*Giacomo Casanova: Childhood and*

Adolescence). The $2 million production starred British actor Leonard Whiting as young Casanova. Directed by Luigi Comencini, the performances were excellent, the dialogue crisp and witty and the production was beautifully designed by the two-time Oscar winner, Piero Gherardi.

In 1976, *Casanova di Federico Fellini* garnered a more scathing press than Casanova would have imagined. Starring Donald Sutherland, in grotesque makeup, the film was judged "spectacular, but singularly joyless" by Vincent Canby (*The New York Times*). "*Fellini's Casanova* is much less about the self-proclaimed 18th-century philanderer, his life and his times, than it is the surreal, guilt-ridden confessions of a nice, middle-class Italian husband of the 20th-century. This fellow, on reaching middle age shortly before the sexual revolution, is still tormented by fantasies that seem to him to be wicked and to the rest of us merely exhausting...The production is gigantic, but the ideas and feelings are small."

Stanley Kauffmann (*The New Republic*) reported, "The original book promised boredom. I've read the one-volume condensation of Casanova's lengthy memoirs, hardly a literary gauge -- and if that volume is the highs, there must be wilderness of lows. The next bad news was the casting of Donald Sutherland as Casanova ...the choice of this actor for Casanova suggested that Fellini was planning a series of fabrications, beginning with makeup...*Casanova* is a disjointed set of dreary episodes, which could have been expanded or contracted, which have only occasional glimmers of visual richness, and which move to a heavily predicted conclusion that takes two and three-quarter hours to arrive."

Andrew Sarris (*Village Voice*) found *Fellini's Casanova*, "A joyless, sexless, often pointless caricature of Casanova...Ignoring Sutherland's conscientious study of Casanova's memoirs and the role they implied, Fellini set out to transform this idealistic, intellectual actor into a grotesque puppet devoid of all seductive charm. Yet, if anything redeems *Fellini's Casanova* from convulsive futility it is Sutherland's indestructible dignity and integrity as an actor...The continuity is so ragged and so gratuitous that the present film seems to have been hacked out of a much bigger version with all the vital thematic connections severed. Except for Sutherland's performance, there is no acting worthy of the name, only primping and posing in the most selfconsciously Satanic tradition. There is no particular insight into -- nor even much information about -- either Casanova or the 18th century. There is no eroticism or sensuality, and no good conversation."

Tony Curtis starred as Casanova in a bawdy 1977 romp that was a coproduction of Austria, Italy, France and West Germany. It got little or no play in the U.S. despite its having been filmed in English with an international cast that included Britt Ekland, Sylva Koscina, Marisa Berenson, Hugh Griffith, Marisa Mell and others. Of *Casanova & Company*, Britain's *Monthly Film Bulletin* said: "Marginally more lavish than the average sexploitation romp (if trailing far behind the Fellini opus which it was presumably intended to exploit), this effort is otherwise indistinguishable from the competition...effectively smothered by flat direction and dialogue which alternates between puerile salaciousness and lumbering anachronisms." *Variety* tended to agree, finding that "The film might be able to please an unassuming audience which would be content with a senseless jumble of a twin Curtis, mild smut, and an overdose of (admittedly) beautiful bare bosoms of every imaginable size." (It's been shown on cable TV in the U.S. under the title *Some Like It Cool*.)

The BBC's six-part *Casanova*, shown on American TV in mid-1981 in syndication (rather than on PBS), got most of its (few) good notices because of the script by Dennis Potter, who had gotten raves for his earlier *Pennies from Heaven*. Reviewing the first episode, *Variety* found that it "fails to show how [Casanova] managed to interest so many women, but maybe that comes later. What it does show is plenty of bare skin, lots of Venetian pomp and scenery, and Casanova himself suffering in prison; It's pretty slow stuff...[Frank] Finlay insinuates himself into the role, edging his study with a suggestion of emotional instability... Casanova as a literate, freedom worshipping gentleman of the old Italian school doesn't make it in this chapter."

A lush, lighthearted TV movie of *Casanova* was filmed in Venice, Madrid and other locations in Spain starring Richard Chamberlain as the legendary lover. The three-hour telecast of *Casanova*, stylishly directed by Simon Langton and beautifully filmed in color by Jose Luis Alcaine, was promoted thusly by ABC: "Casanova proceeds to make a career of pleasure -- which lands him in a formidable Venice prison as 'a notorious profligate and corrupter of public morals.' Casanova's daring -- and fact-based -- escape attempt from this fortress is one of the highlights of the film, which also dramatizes more fanciful escapades." Richard Chamberlain gave a wellpolished portrayal of Casanova with Frank Finlay (who had the title role in the earlier BBC series) garnering acting honors as his nemesis, Razetta.

STAGE

CASANOVA, *Empire Theatre*, New York, opened September 26, 1923
Produced by A. H. Woods and Gilbert Miller; A Drama by Lorenzo de Azertis, translated by Sidney Howard; Director, Gilbert Miller; Settings, Herman Rosse; Costumes designed by Georges Barbier, executed by Max Weldy of Paris; Ballet pantomime by Michel Fokine; Incidental music by Deems Taylor; Stage manager, Edward Broadley

Prologue: *The Return from the Carnival*:

Beatrice Belreva (Columbine); George Royale (Pul-cinella); Horace Healy (A Gentleman in Black); Herbert James (Battista); Harry Fielding (A Fat Man); George Blackmore (A Roman Soldier); Doris and Dursha (Guitar Players); Lora Vinci, Alice Wynne, Desha, Renee Wilde (Harlequins); Marguerite Denys, Valentina Sanina, Janet Justice, Dinarzade, Nellie Savage, Helen Raskin (Masked Women)

The Play:

Lowell Sherman (Giacomo Casanova, Chevalier de Seingalt); Katharine Cornell (Henriette); Ernest Cossart (Leduc); Judith Vosselli (The Courtesan); Nellie Burt (Manon); A. G. Andrews (The Innkeeper); Horace Braham (The Abbe Bernis); Philip Wood (Alfani-Celli); Mario Majeroni (Captain Michael Echedy); Victor Benoit (Monsieur Dubois); David Glassford (Monsieur Antoine); Gypsy O'Brien (The Beautiful Governess); Sheila Hayes (Rose); Mary Ellis (The Dancer from Milan); B. N. Lewin (Manzoni); Walter Soderling (A Waiter); William Marr (A Gambler); Ralph Belmont (A Lieutenant); Edward Le Hay (An Inn-keeper); J. C. Wallace, Edward F. Snow (Archers); Harold Hartsell (A Banker in Cesena); Harry Redding (A Gambler); James Powers, Jacob Kingsberry, Frank Newcomb, Charles Vincent (Postillions); Dinarzade (Giulietta)

London Coliseum, opened May 24, 1932 429 performances
A Musical Play of Love and Adventure; Produced and Directed by Erik Charell; Book by Hans Muller, adapted from a play by Schanzer and Welisch; English book and lyrics by Harry Graham; Music by Johann Strauss, arranged by Ralph Benatsky

Fernando Autori (Casanova, May 24); Arthur Fear (Casanova, May 25); Grete

Natzler (Barbarina, May 24); Margaret Carlisle (Barbarina, May 25); Soffi Schonning (Laura); Walter Outhwaite (Menuzzi); Ben Williams (Lieutenant Franz Von Hohenfels); Douglas Wakefield (Costa); Mary Lawson (Annuschka); John Deverell (Prince Potomski); Dorothy Dickson (Princess Potomska); Robert Cheesman (Gipsy Boy); Tamara Desni (Dolores); Leonard Hayes (Perez); Veronica Brady (Ignacia); Eleanor Darville (Abbess); Marie Lohr (Empress Marie Therese of Austria); A. D. Robertson (Chamberlain); Oriel Ross (Empress Catherine of Russia); Charles Cautley (Chamberlain); John Kevan (Alexei); Fred Louin (Gipsy Leader); Richard Neller (Street Singer); Jack Barty (Count Waldstein); Billy Nelson (Stage Manager); The Bourbonnel Trio (Acrobats); R. Stringer (Waiter); Marienne Winkelstern (Prima Ballerina); Alexander von Swaine (Soloist); The Waldo Trio (Court Jesters); Nick Walla (Kitchen Boy); Chuck O'Neill (Old Man); Alexander von Swaine (Harlequin); Billy Nelson (Housemaid); Robert Hine (Waldestein's Servant); Richard Harris (Cook)

CASANOVA, *The New Dramatists, Inc.*, New York, opened October 28, 1977
Produced by The New Dramatists, Inc.; A Work-in-Progress production; Officers, L. Arnold Weissberger, Zilla Lippmann; Administration director, Stephen Harty; Workshop coordinator, Peter Kozik; Director Eric R. Cowley; Book and Lyrics by John Wolfson; Music by Ralph Affoumado

A Concert reading with Irwin Pearl, Faith Catlin, Ruth Jaroslow, Michael Enserro, Ken Shuey, Edmund Lyndeck, Spring Condoyan, Richard Dahlia, Dottie Dee, Alan Brooks, William Starrett

CASANOVA, New York State Theater, *Lincoln Center*, New York, opened November 2, 1985
Produced by the New York City Opera; An Opera by Dominick Argento; Director, Arthur Masella; Libretto by Dominick Argento; Scenery, Franco Colavecchia; Costumes, Lewis Brown; Lighting, Duane Schuler; Choreography, Jessica Redel; Conductor, Scott Bergeson

Timothy Nolen (Casanova); John Lankston (Marquis de Lisle); Joyce Castle (Mme. d'Urfe); Carol Gutknecht (Giulietta); Susanne Marsee (Bellino); Michele McBride (Barbara); Mark Thomsen (Gabrielle); Melissa Fogarty (Marcantonio); Jerold Siena (First Inquisitor/Pulcinello); David Hamilton (Lorenzo da Ponte); Ralph Bassett (Businello)

CASANOVA, *New York State Theater*, *Lincoln Center*, New York, opened September 20, 1987
Produced by the New York City Opera; An Opera by Dominick Argento; Director, Arthur Masella; Libretto by Dominick Argento; Scenery, Franco Colavecchia; Costumes, Lewis Brown; Lighting, Duane Schuler; Choreography, Jessica Redel; Conductor, Scott Bergeson

Timothy Nolen (Casanova); John Lankston (Marquis de Lisle); Joyce Castle (Mme. d'Urfe); Leigh Munro (Giulietta); Susanne Marsee (Bellino); Diana Walker (Barbara); Dale Smith (Gabrielle); and Michael Wilson, Jonathan Green, Clark Utterback; Robert Brubaker, William Ledbetter, Joseph McKee

SCREEN

CASANOVA, *Albatross Films*, released June 1927; released in U.S. as *The Loves of Casanova* by *Cineromans Films* in April 1929

Director, Alexander Volkoff; Screenplay by Norbert Falk, Alexander Volkoff, Ivan Mosjoukine, based on the *Autobiography of Casanova*; Art director, Noel Bloch; Costumes, Paul Leni; Settings, Lockhakoff

Ivan Mosjoukine (Giovanni Giacomo Casanova); Suzanne Bianchetti (Catherine the Great); Rina de Liguoro (Mme. Corticelli); Diana Karenne (Countess Maria Mari); Rudolph Klein-Rogge (Peter II); Carlo Tedeschi (Le Duc); Michel Simon (Servant); Jenny Jugo, Olga Day, Paul Guide

CASANOVA (aka *LES AMOURS DE CASANOVA*), France, released 1933

Production of M. J. Films; Director, Rene Barberis; Photography, Fedote Bourgassoff, Raoul Auboudier and Pierre Velle; Production designer, Marcel Magniez; Costumes, Boris Bilinsky; Music, Pierre Vellones, Walter Winnig

Ivan Mosjoukine (Giacomo Casanova); Madeleine Ozeray (Angelica); Jeanne Boitel (Ann Roman); Marcelle Denys (Madame de Pompadour); Leda Ginelly (Mme. Binetti); Pierre Larquey (Pogomas); Henry Laverne (Le Duc); Colette Darfeuil (Mme. Corticelli); Marguerite Moreno (Mme. Morin); Saturin Fabre (Binetti); Pierre Moreno (Castelbougnac); Nicole de Rouves, Marthe Mussine (Servants); Wanda Warel, Suzy Delair, Jacqueline Hopstein, Vera Markels, Loulou Rex (Women); Emile Drain (de Bernis); Jean Guilton, Allain Dhurtal, Raymond Faure, Jean Delannoy, George Jamin, Victor Vina, Jacques Norman, Leon Larive, Marcel La Montagne, J. P. de Baer (Men)

ADVENTURES OF CASANOVA, *Eagle-Lion*, released February l948

A Bryan Foy production; Producer, Leonard S. Picker; Director, Roberto Gavaldon; Screenplay, Crane Wilbur, Walter Bullock and Karen DeWolf, from a story by Wilbur; Photography, John Greenhalgh; Art directors, Alfred Ybarra and Jorge Fernandez; Music, Hugo Friedhofer; Music director, Irving Friedman; Editor, Louis H. Sackin

Arturo de Cordova (Casanova); Lucille Bremer (Lady Bianca); Turhan Bey (Lorenzo); John Sutton (Count de Brissac); George Tobias (Jacopo); Noreen Nash (Zanetta); Lloyd Corrigan (D'Albernasi); Fritz Lieber (D'Anneci); and Nestor Paiva, Jorge Trevino, Cliff Carr, Jacqueline Dalya, Miroslava, Rafael Alcaide, Jacqueline Evans

LES AVENTURES DE CASANOVA (*THE LOVES OF CASANOVA*), *Vog Film*, released as two films in February and March 1947; released in U.S. as a single film September 1948

Produced by Sirius; Director, Jean Boyer; Adaptation and Screenplay by Marc Gilbert Sauvajon; Photography, Charles Suin; Art director, Jacques Krauss; Montage, Fanchette Mazin; Music, Rene Sylviano; Lyrics, Vandair and Rouzaud; English Titles, George Slocombe

Le Chevalier de l'aventure: Jacqueline Gauthier (Coraline); Gisele Preville (Mme. Van Hope); Noelle Norman (Clotilde du Manoir); Luce Feyrer (La Borelli); Barbara Shaw (Lady Ancliff); Helene Dassonville (Henriette); Claude Falco (Le Fille du Juge); Micheline Gary (Consuela); Gisele Casadesus (Genevieve de Cerlin); Marguerite Ducouret (Concepcion); and Monique Ravot, Marylou, Gaby Blanche, Gisele Frappa, Paola Manelli, Annie Avril, Gaby Bruyere

Les mirages de l'enfer: Georges Guetary (Jacque Casanova de Seingalt); Aime Clariond (Don Luis); Albert Dinan (Jasmin); Jean Tissier (Van Hope); Pierre Labry (Le Moine); Lucien Pascal (Francois); Georges Tourreil (Piquebise); Raymond Loyer (Maxime de Carlin); Raymond Faure (Seigneur Tortoli); Marcel Peres (Sergeant); Georges Jasmin (Police Officer); Nicolas Amato (Theatre

Director); Andre Bervil (Croce); and Gaston Mauger, Julien Maffre, Pierre Juvenet, Guy Saint-Clair, Marcel Charvey, Jean Duvaleix, Pierre Dargout

IL CAVALIERE MISTERIOSO, Lux Films, Italy, released 1948
Produced by Dino De Laurentiis; Director, Riccardo Freda; Screenplay, Riccardo Freda, Steno and Mario Monicelli; Photography, Rodolfo and Guglielmo Lombardi; Art director, Piero Filippone; Costumes, Vittorio Nino Novarese; Music, Alessandro Cicognini; Editor, Otello Colangeli

Vittorio Gassman (Giacomo Casanova); Maria Mercader (Elisabeth); Yvonne Sanson (Caterina II); Gianna Maria Canale (Contessa Lehmann); Elli Parvo (Il Dogaressa); and Antonio Centa, Alessandra Mamis, Hans Heinrich, Dante Maggio, Aldo Nicodemi, Guido Notari, Vittorio Duce, Tino Buazzelli, Renato Valente

CASANOVA'S BIG NIGHT, Paramount Pictures, released March 1954
Produced by Paul Jones; Director, Norman Z. McLeod; Screenplay by Hal Kanter, Edmund Hartmann, based on a story by Aubrey Wisberg, Photography, Lionel Lindon; Art directors, Hal Pereira and Albert Nozaki; Choreography, Josephine Earl; Music, Lyn Murray; Songs by Jay Livingston and Ray Evans; Editor, Ellsworth Hoagland

Bob Hope (Pippo); Joan Fontaine (Francesca); Vincent Price (Casanova); Basil Rathbone (Lucio); Audrey Dalton (Elena); Hugh Marlowe (Stefano Di Gambetta); Arnold Moss (The Doge); John Carradine (Minister Foressi); John Hoyt (Maggiorin); Hope Emerson (Duchess of Castelbello); Robert Hutton (Raphael, Duke of Castelbello); Lon Chaney (Emo); Raymond Burr (Bragadin); Frieds Inescort (Signora Di Gambetta); Primo Carnera (Corfa); Frank Puglia (Carabaccio); Paul Cavanagh (Signor Alberto Di Gambetta); Romo Vincent (Giovanni); Natalie Schafer (Signora Foressi); Henry Brandon (Captain Rugello); Joan Shawlee (Beatrice D'Brizzi); Oliver Blake (Amadeo); Nestor Paiva (Gnocchi); Barbara Freking (Maria); Paul Newlan (Regniatti); Bess Flowers (Marquesa); and Keith Richards, Skelton Knaggs, John Doucette, Torben Meyer, Kathryn Grant, Marla English, Douglas Fowley, Lucien Littlefield, Joseph Vitale, John Alderson, Richard Karlan, Fritz Feld, Walter Kingsford, Eric Alden, Charley Cooley, Rexene Stevens, Arline Hunter, Dick Sands, Charles Hicks

LE AVVENTURE DI GIACOMO CASANOVA (SINS OF CASANOVA), Gala Pictures, Italy-France, released 1954; released in Great Britain as *Casanova*, May 1957
Produced by Orsolris (Rome), C.F.P.C. (Paris); Producer, Emo Bistolfi; Director, Steno (Stefano Vanzina); Screenplay, Steno, Emo Bistolfi, Sandro Continenza, Luigi Fulci, Mario Guerra and Carlo Romano; Photography, Mario Bava; Art director, Mario Chiari; Music, Angelo Francesco Lavagnino; Sound, Bruno Brunacci; Costumes, Maria de Matteis; Editor, Giuliana Attenni

Gabriele Ferzetti (Giacomo Casanova); Corinne Calvet (Contessa Luisa di Charpillon); Nadia Gray (Margrave Maria Theresa); Mara Lane (Barbara); Irene Galter (Dolores); Marina Vlady (Fulvia); Carlo Campanini (Le Duc); Aroldo Tieri (Lt. Jose Ramirez); Anna Amendola (Gertrude); Florence Arnaud (Angelica); Fulvia Franco (Bettina); Lia De Leo (Lucrezia); and Nuri Neva, Nico Pepe, Arturo Bragaglia, Nero Bernardi, Ursula Andress

CASANOVA '70, Paramount Pictures, released 1965
Produced by C. C. Champion (Rome), Films Concordia (Paris); Executive producer,

Joseph E. Levine; Producer, Carlo Ponti; Director, Mario Monicelli; Screenplay, Furio Scarpelli, Agenore Incrocci, Mario Monicelli and Suso Cecchi D'Amico, based on a story by Antonio Guerra and Giorgio Salvioni; Photography, Aldo Tonti; Art director, Mario Garbuglia; Music, Franco Bassi, Armando Trovajoli; Sound, Ennio Sensi; Assistant director, Renzo Marignano; Editor, Ruggiero Mastroianni

Marcello Mastroianni (Major Andrea Rossi-Colombetti); Virna Lisi (Gigliola); Michele Mercier (Noelle); Enrico Maria Salerno (Doctor); Marisa Mell (Thelma); Guido Alberti (The Monsignor); Margaret Lee (Dolly Greenwater); Rosemarie Dexter (Chambermaid); Yolanda Modio (Addolarata); Seyna Seyn (Indonesian Airline Hostess); Moira Orfei (Santina); Liana Orfei (Lion Tamer); Beba Loncar (Girl in Museum); Bernard Blier (Commissioner)

INFANZIA, VOCAZIONE E PRIME ESPERIENZE DI GIACOMO CASANOVA VENEZIANO (*GIACOMO CASANOVA: CHILDHOOD AND ADOLESCENCE*), *Mega Films*, released November 1969

Produced by Panta-Cinemetografica/Ugo Santalucia Productions; Director, Luigi Comencini; Screenplay by Suso Cecchi D'Amico and Luigi Comencini, based on the *Memoirs of Casanova*; Photography, Ajace Parolin; Production designer and costumes, Piero Gherardi; Music, Fiorenzo Carpi; Editor, Nino Baragli

Leonard Whiting (Giacomo Casanova); Senta Berger (Millescudi); Lionel Stander (Don Tosello); Maria Grazia Buccella (Zanetta); Wilfred Brambell (Malipiere); Tina Aumont (Marcella); Cristina Comencini (Angela); Raul Grassilli (Don Gozzi); Claudio De Kunert (Giacomo Casanova, as a boy); Mario Peron (Casanova's Father); Silvia Dionisio (Mariolina); Elisabetta Fanti (Princess Contarini); Sara Franchetti (Suor Lucia); Isabella Savone (Teresa); Mario Scaccia (Dr. Zambelli)

IL CASANOVA DI FEDERICO FELLINI (FELLINI'S CASANOVA), 20th Century-Fox, released December 1976

Produced by PEA Cinematografica; Producer, Alberto Grimaldi; Director, Federico Fellini; Screenplay by Federico Fellini and Bernardino Zapponi, based on the book *Histoire de Ma Vie* by Giacomo Casanova de Seingalt; Photography, Giuseppe Rotunno; Production designers, Danilo Donati and Federico Fellini; Set designers, Giantito Burchiellaro and Giorgio Giovannini; Costumes, Danilo Donati; Paintings, Rinaldo Geleng, Giuliano Geleng; Sculptures, Giovanni Gianese; Frescoes, Mario Fallani; Magic Lantern designs, Roland Topor; Choreography, Gino Landi; Makeup, Rino Carboni (Donald Sutherland), Giannetto De Rossi, Fabrizio Sforza; Production supervisor, Giorgio Morra; Special effects, Adriano Pischiutta; Music, Nino Rota; Glass Harp, Bruno Hoffman; Music director, Carlo Savina; English dialogue, Anthony Burgess; English dialogue director, Frank Dunlop, Christoper Cruise; Dialogue editor, David Hawkins; Editor, Ruggero Mastroianni

Donald Sutherland (Giacomo Casanova); Tina Aumont (Henriette); Cicely Browne (Mme. D'Urfe); Carmen Scarpitta (Mme. Charpillon); Clara Algranti (Marcolina); Daniela Gatti (Giselda); Margareth Clementi (Sister Maddalena); Olimpia Carlisi (Isabella); Silvana Fusacchia (Silvana); Adela Angela Lojodice (Mechanical Doll); Sandra Elaine Allen (Giantess); Clarissa Mary Roll (Anna-Maria); Daniel Emilfork-Berenstein (Dubois); Luigi Zerbinati (Pope); Hans Van Den Hoek (Prince Del Brando); Dudley Sutton (Duke of Wurtemberg); John Karlsen (Lord Talou); Reggie Nalder (Faulkircher); Vim Hiblom (Edgard); Harold Innocent (Count of Saint-Germain); Micha Bayard (Owner of Workshop); Nicolas Smith (Casanova's Brother); Chesty Morgan (Barberina); Donald Hodson

(Hungarian Captain); Alessandra Belloni (Princess); Marica Rivera (Astrodi); Angelica Hansen (Hunchbacked Actress); Mario Cencelli (Dr. Mobius); Dan Van Husen (Viderol); Gabriele Carrara (Count of Waldenstein); Marjorie Bell (Countess of Waldenstein); Marie Marquet (Casanova's Mother); Marcello Di Folco (Captain)

CASANOVA & COMPANY (aka *THE RISE AND RISE OF CASANOVA*), A Trident Barber release (World Premiere: Vienna, February 1977); released in U.S. as *Some Like It Cool* in 1978
A Coproduction of Neue Delta Film (Austria), Panther Film (Italy), COFCI (France) and TV13 (Germany); Producers, Franz Antel, Carl Szokoll; Coproducer, Peer Oppenheimer; Associate producers, Claude Giroux, George Glass; Director, Francois Legrand (Franz Antel); Screenplay, Joshua Sinclair, Tom Priman; Additional dialogue, Jose Villeverde; Photography, Hanns Matula; Art director, Nino Borghi; Costumes, Helga Bandini; Makeup, Otello Sisi, Giancarlo De Leonardis; Music, Riz Ortolani; Editor, Michel Lewin

Tony Curtis (Giacomo Casanova/Giacomino); Marisa Berenson (Calipha of Shiraz); Hugh Griffith (Caliph of Shiraz); Marisa Mell Duchess Francesca); Britt Ekland (Countess Trivulzi); Sylva Koscina (Gelsomina); Jean Lefevre (Sergeant); Andrea Ferreol (Beatrice); Victor Spinetti (Prefect); Umberto Orsini (Count Tiretta); Jacques Herlin (Senator Dell'-Acqua); Jenny Arrasse (Cecilia); Werner Pochath (Fulgenzio); Jeanne Bell (Fatme); Liliane Mueller (Beata); Olivia Pascal (Angela); Roswitha Kobald (Senator Dell'Acqua's Secretary); Umberto Raho (Doge); Katja Christine (Fiorabella); Mauro Vestri (Father Anselmo); Gerard Jugnot (Valente); Giacomo Rossi Stuart (Coppafratta)

TELEVISION

CASANOVA, televised November 11 through December 19, 1971 BBC 6 episodes 1 hour each; in U.S. in 1981 in syndication
Produced by BBC/Time-Life Television; Producer, Mark Shivas; Associate producer, Fraser Lowden; Directors, John Glenister and Mark Cullingham; Teleplay, Dennis Potter; Photography, John Wyatt; Art director, Peter Seddon; Choreographer, Geraldine Stephson; Music, John Burrows; Music conductor, Oliver Butterworth; Editor, Graham Dunn

Frank Finlay (Giacomo Casanova); Zienia Merton (Christina); Norman Rossington (Lorenzo); Christine Noonan (Barbarina); George Benson (Christina's Uncle); Geoffrey Wincott (Senator Bragadin); Ronald Adam (Senior Inquisitor); Igor Silic (Carlo); Patrick Newell (Schalon); Julie Cornelius (Rose); Bridget Bates (Nanan); Carolyn Bowbesvio (Anna); Ania Larson (Ann Coupier); Arthur Pentelow (Caretaker); Rowan Wylie (Columbia); Gillian Hills (Caroline); Roger Hammond (Father Balbi); Jean Holness (Madame Morin); Richard Dennis (Tiretta); Simon Barclay (Damiens); Claire Davenport (Madame Lenoir); Norman Glynn (Violinist); Enid Burton, Julia Desmond, Sue Bond (Prostitutes); Victor Baring (Messr. Grand); Alfred Hoffman, Ray Martoni (Constables); Lynn Yladman (Genovessa); Valerie Gearon (Pauline); Basil Clarke (Dr. Belotti); Gillian Brown (Nun); Elaine Donnelly (Helena); Lynn Turner (Street Crier)

CASANOVA, televised March 1, 1987 ABC 3 hours
The Konigsberg/Sanitsky Company in association with Reteitalia; Executive producers, Frank Konigsberg and Larry Sanitsky; Produced by Sam Manners;

Director, Simon Langton; Teleplay by George MacDonald Fraser, based on the *Memoirs* of Giacomo Casanova; Photography, Jose Luis Alcaine; Production designer, Gil Parrondo; Art director, Jose Maria Alacron; Set decorator, Julian Mateos; Costumes, Yvonne Blake; Makeup Supervisor, Cristobal Criado; Music, Michel Legrand; Associate producer, Luciana Paluzzi Solomon; Editor, Bud S. Isaacs

Richard Chamberlain (Giovanni Casanova); Faye Dunaway (Madame Durfay); Frank Finlay (Count Razetta); Sylvia Kristel (Maddalena); Ornella Muti (Henriette); Toby Rolt (Young Casanova); Sophie Ward (Jacqueline); Hanna Schygulla (Zanetta, Casanova's Mother); Kenneth Colley (Le Duc); Roy Kinnear (Balbi); Richard Griffiths (Cardinal Acquaviva); Jean-Pierre Cassel (Louis XV); Janis Lee Burns (Louison O'Murphy); Patrick Ryecart (De Bernis); Bruce Purchase (Major Grandi); Traci Lin (Heide); and Christopher Benjamin, John Wells, Michael Balfour, John Boswall, Marina Baker, Eros De Simone, Chris Edmonds, Anibal Blas Franco, Ignacio Munoz Gallo, Paul Geoffrey, Gilda Germano, Ivana Gianferdi, Aitana Sanchez Gijon, David Hart, William Job, Fernando Hilbeck, Alvaro Labra, Paul Lacoux, Savino Maneri, Elizabeth Mason, Elmer Modling, Rose McVeigh, Gary Piquer, Dennis Rafter, Dennis Vaughan, Christine Walker

CASEY JONES

A Drama by Robert Ardrey (1938)

Synopsis

Dedicated railroad engineer, fifty year old Casey Jones, had spent his life enslaved to his Engine #4 and gained the reputation as the finest locomotive engineer in the country. Physically deteriorating Casey set a new record driving his #4 from Chicago to St. Louis. Having missed two signals en route due to his failing eyesight, Casey is demoted to a whistle-stop stationmaster. Despairing of his physical breakdown and gradual loss of eyesight, he rebels against his isolation, flags down his beloved #4, regains his engineer's seat in the locomotive cab and pushes it westward, perhaps to start a new, if not better, life.

Comment and Critique

Chicago-born (1908) Robert Ardrey lectured for two years on anthropology at Chicago's Century of Progress Exposition which expertise resulted in his fascinating 1961 book, *African Genesis*. Bolstered by a Guggenheim Fellowship, Ardrey's first play, *Star-Spangled*, was produced on Broadway in 1936 for a brief run. His second play, *How to Get Tough About It*, opened at Broadway's Martin Beck Theatre on February 8, 1938, for a dis-appointing twenty three performances. Twelve days later, Ardrey's subsequent drama, *Casey Jones*, premiered at the Fulton Theatre.

Produced by The Group Theatre, *Casey Jones* was the first Broadway directorial assignment for Elia Kazan, who had appeared as an actor in The Group Theatre productions of *Men in White* (1933), *Waiting for Lefty* (1935), *Johnny Johnson* (1936) and *Golden Boy* (1937). Charles Bickford, recalled to Broadway from a depressed Hollywood screen career, expertly acted the title role. But the real star of *Casey Jones* was Mordecai Gorelik's ingenious design of locomotive #4.

Life magazine announced that "neither Charles Bickford's acting nor Robert

Ardrey's play is the real hero of *Casey Jones*. The real hero is a locomotive that in two scenes looms black and monstrous across the stage...It shakes and rocks and trembles and roars and pants. By some magic of designing it seems, though it never moves forward, to be tearing through the night at 90 miles an hour...It is made of lath, covered with black velours. Its fire is a red spotlight. Its steam is real steam blown by a fan...its bell is a sound record taken on the New York Central line...its cost was $1,500...*Casey Jones*, its locomotive aside, is not a good play but it has the makings of a superb movie."

George Jean Nathan (*Newsweek*) felt *Casey Jones* "shows no promise at all. It is poorer than [Ardrey's] second play, which was poorer than his first...but this play about a locomotive engineer who at the dimsighted 50 finds his profession taken away from him persuades me to believe that I may be unpleasantly right." Mr. Ardrey's play did not impress Mr. Nathan.

Brooks Atkinson (*The New York Times*) felt, "Robert Ardrey's second play of the month is a railroad saga with a swaying, rattling locomotive pounding the rails through three scenes...Never much of a hand to write a play, Mr. Ardrey offers this one as the character sketch of a fabulous engineer, named in honor of the ballad hero...*Casey Jones* is a free hand sketch...All Mr. Ardrey's plays are long on character and short on sustained drama. *Casey Jones* is no exception. It is written with humorous insight into the character of odd and muscular men; the dialogue is spontaneously original; the scenes are comic and sympathetic. Mr. Ardrey has extraordinary flair. But he has not yet written a fully developed drama with a story that pledges all the characters to a significant meaning... has difficulty in making his ideas stand on their two feet in a theatre, and this one fizzles out before it is finished." Atkinson also obvserved: "[Charles] Bickford plays it appreciatively but he has not yet caught the inner toughness of a superman...Elia Kazan might help him some by tightening the performance in direction...Van Heflin gives a gloriously agile, humorous and roaming performance...For the third time in his career, Mr. Ardrey has chosen a fresh subject and populated it with pungent characters...But with all his gifts he does not write plays that exhaust their subject in terms of the theatre."

Jonathan Luther Jones was born on March 14, 1864 in Cayce, Kentucky, and became the best and most publicized engineer on the Illinois-Central Railroad. Nicknamed "Casey" (after the place of his birth, Cayce), Jones was killed in the wreck of his old #382 Cannonball Express on April 30, 1900. "Casey" Jones became a legend. Joe Hill, T. Lawrence Seibert and Carl Sandburg glorified "Casey" in poems and ballads and folk songs materialized written by black troubadour Wallis Sanders, H. M. Harris, and others.

The folklore, ballads and poems varied in interpretation of Casey's death on his Cannonball Express running from Memphis to Canton and the famous wreck fourteen miles north of Canton in Vaughn, Mississippi.

Casey's engine #382 was a tenwheel McQueen mounted with six driving wheels six-feet high and equipped with a six-lute calliope whistle, donated by an admirer, which played a "whip-poor-will" tune. Casey's fireman was a young black man, Sim T. Webb, who idolized the famous engineer. After finishing his run at 9:00 PM on April 29, 1900, Casey volunteered to replace an ill engineer, Sam Tate, on his scheduled run with the Cannonball Express #1, providing he could use his beloved #382. Six-feet-four-inches tall, the handsome, thirty-six-year-old Casey was married and the father of three. Reportedly, he had become so well-known for his on-time schedule that people along his railroad route set their watches by his "whip-poor-will" whistle.

At 12:50 AM on April 30, 1900, Casey moved the ninety-five minute overdue

Cannonball Express out of Memphis determined to make up the lost time. Telling Sim to shovel on more coal, Casey gained speed of more than one hundred miles per hour and over the level 102-mile track to Grenada, Mississippi, made up an hour of lost time. From Grenada to Winona, Casey knocked off another fifteen minutes over the twenty-three-mile stretch as Sim furiously shoveled coal. By the time Casey pulled into Durant, he had forced #382 to almost maintaining the scheduled time and yelled to Sim, "The old lady's got her high-heel slippers on tonight!" Leaving Durant, Casey clocked seventy-five miles an hour over a supposedly clear single-track. But as he neared Vaughn, Mississippi, four-teen miles from his final destination, and having made up ninety-one minutes over the 174 miles from Memphis, Casey steered #382 around an "S" curve and saw the red lights of a freight train caboose through the fog.

Casey shouted to Sim to jump, shut off the throttle, pulled the reverse lever, applied the air-brakes and sounded a long blast on the whistle. He slowed the train to thirty-five miles an hour as Sim jumped from the cab. The crash was heard for miles and #382 demolished the caboose, rammed into cars loaded with hay and corn and jumped the track, grinding into the earth on its side. Casey Jones was found crushed under bales of hay with an iron bolt piercing his neck. Casey was the only fatality of the wreck. Sim Webb was found unconscious and recovered.

The Mississippi Department of Archives and History erected a memorial at the Vaughn wreck site which reads, "Casey Jones: A famous ballad, the folklore of American railroading and a postage stamp commemorate the colorful and courageous engineer who was killed in a wreck here in 1900." On the fiftieth anniversary of Casey Jones' famous wreck, the United States issued a commemorative stamp in his honor. In Jackson, Tennessee, the famed engineer's home was purchased by the city and opened in 1956 as the Casey Jones Museum with a locomotive similar to #382, a duplicate of the well-known "whip-poor-will" whistle and many of Casey's personal belongings.

Wallace Saunders, an Illinois Central engine-wiper, shortly after Casey's death composed a ballad about his friend which began, "Casey Jones, Casey Jones, he was all right. Stuck to his duty both day and night..." An Illinois Central engineer, William Leighton, sent Saunders' ballad to his vaudevillian brothers, Bert and Frank Leighton, who popularized the song across the country. Later, from the many variations of the ballad, T. Lawrence Seibert and Eddie Newton, a professional songwriting team, published and copyrighted their version in 1909. Seibert and Newton called their version "Casey Jones (The Brave Engineer)." The sheet music, which sold thousands of copies, was headed "The Original Comedy Railroad song: this world famous railroad song relates the tragic story of the wreck of the CANNONBALL EXPRESS on April 29, 1900 in which the brave engineer, John Luther was killed."

Seibert and Newton's version, although the best known, was also highly inaccurate. They had Casey driving a locomotive on a Western railroad heading for San Francisco and colliding with another one and had Mrs. Jones with "another papa" on the Salt Lake River Line! Several ballads cropped up after Casey's death of unknown origin, the lyrics set to old folk tunes. "Mama Have You Heard the News! (Daddy got killed on the C-B-and Q's)" was one of many, and other ballads sung by railroad men were published in the periodical, *The Railroad Man's Magazine*. Some of the songs were recorded from cotton field versions, such as "The Wreck of the Six-Wheel Driver" and "Nachul-Born Easman":

"Casey Jones was a li'l behin',
He thought prob'ly he could make de time,
Got up in his engine, an' he walked about,
Gave three loud whistles an'-a he pulled out."

In 1927, W. Ray Johnston and Dwight C. Leeper produced a motion picture based on the nationally famous ballad, *Casey Jones*. "Announced as based on the perennially popular railroad song, *Casey Jones* shows an engineer of that name and forgets the 'other father on the Salt Lake line.' The title merely advertises the fact that this is a railroad play," reported *Motion Picture Herald*. "The story has not been built along high art lines...It follows railroading closely and, with the exception of one miniature, this atmosphere is convincing...Ralph Lewis is capital as the engineer and Kate Price, as the buxom wife, makes a good second. Anne Sheridan as the girl plays intelligently." *Photoplay* claimed, "Most people are familiar with the old song *Casey Jones* and will be expecting the story." Arthur Hoerl's screenplay was run-of-the-mill melodrama in which Casey, Jr. saves a train carrying bullion from a planned wreck, rescues his father, Casey, and wins the gal.

Screen Gems produced a television series, *Casey Jones*, syndicated in 1957 in thirty-minute episodes, starring Alan Hale, Jr. as the famed Casey featuring his legendary engine #382 and the Illinois Central's Cannonball Express.

STAGE

CASEY JONES, Fulton Theatre, New York, opened February 19, 1938 25 performances
Produced by The Group Theatre; A Drama by Robert Ardrey; Director, Elia Kazan; Settings, Mordecai Gorelik

Charles Bickford (Casey Jones); Van Heflin (Jed Sherman); Frances Williams (Mrs. Jones); Peggy Conklin (Portsmouth Jones); Robert Strauss (Jones); Joseph Sawyer (Mac); Curt Conway (Elgy); Charles Thompson (Brakeman); Howard Da Silva (Old Man); Clancy Cooper (Gassiman); Charles J. Dingle (John Collins); Eunice Stoddard (Mrs. McGuiness)

SCREEN

CASEY JONES, Rayart Pictures, released December 20, 1927
Produced by Trem Carr Production, W. Ray Johnston, producer; Director, Charles J. Hunt; Screenplay by Arthur Hoerl, based on the 1909 song by T. Lawrence Seibert and Eddie Newton; Titles, Richard Weil; Photography, Hap Depew; Editor, J. S. Harrington

Ralph Lewis (Casey Jones); Kate Price (Mrs. Casey Jones); Jason Robards (Casey Jones, Jr.); Anne Sheridan (Peggy Reynolds); Al St. John (Jock MacTavish); Brooks Benedict (Roland Ayres); Violet Kane (Baby Kathleen Jones); Jimmy Kane, Charlie Kane (Bandits)

TELEVISION

Syndicated Series, 1957 32 episodes 30 minutes each
Produced by Harold Green

Alan Hale, Jr. (Casey Jones); Mary Lawrence (Alice Jones); Bobby Clark (Casey

Jones, Jr.); Dub Taylor (Willie Sims, the Cannonball Fireman); Eddy Waller (Red Rock, the Cannonball Conductor); Pat Hogan (Indian Sam Peachpit); Paul Keast (Mr. Carter)

CHARLIE AND ALGERNON

Adaptations of the short story and 1966 novel *Flowers for Algernon* by Daniel Keyes

Synopsis

Charlie Gordon is a retarded thirty-year-old with the mind of a child. By day he works as a sweeper in a bakery; by night, in a fruitless attempt to better himself, he diligently attends evening classes taught by Alice Kinian, who is touched and impressed by his desire to learn. Before long, she arranges to have him examined by a pair of neurosurgeons who have successfully cured mentally defective mice by surgery and are now looking for a human guinea pig. In his initial tests, Charlie is unable to keep pace with Algernon, a mouse. It isn't long however before Charlie miraculously improves and his mind improves to genius proportions, although he is slower to develop emotionally. Suddenly, with his whole life before him, Charlie envisions a terrible return to his moronic state when his tiny pal Algernon goes into decline and dies. Realizing he too might be doomed, Charlie, speaking before a gathering of distinguished scientists, startles the assembly with a bitter attack on modern civilization. The neurosurgeons who performed the initial experiments on him make a desperate attempt to prevent his retardation, but it soon becomes apparent that they are fighting a losing battle. Charlie reluctantly faces his future and returns to his room to await his impending mental retardation alone, despite Alice's plea to stay with him.

Comment and Critique

In one of the infrequent reversals of the production process, Thomas Jefferson High School (Brooklyn) teacher Daniel Keyes' prize-winning science fiction story (it won the Hugo Award in 1960) began its life on television in 1961, later became an Oscar-winning movie in 1968, and subsequently became a short-lived stage musical in 1980. Cliff Robertson starred in the first two productions, winning an Academy Award as Best Actor in the film version. Fielder Cook directed The Theatre Guild's one-hour *U.S. Steel Hour* TV adaptation of the story, adapted by James Yaffee and called *The Two Worlds of Charlie Gordon*. Robertson, who costarred with Mona Freeman, playing his sympathetic teacher, had enough faith in the story that he purchased screen rights, but it was years before he could get backing to film it.

Ultimately he joined forces with one-time TV director Ralph Nelson and brought it to the screen as *Charly*, with Claire Bloom as a clinical psychologist (rewritten from the original teacher role). His starring performance turned out to be one of the only elements the critics applauded. "*Charly* is a self conscious contemporary drama, the first ever to exploit mental retardation for -- if not the fun -- the bitter-sweet romance of it," Vincent Canby wrote in *The New York Times*. "The movie didn't work for me. I'm not sure that somebody couldn't pull this off effectively, although it might be only slightly less difficult than making a comedy about cancer. *Charly* is not so much an offbeat movie as one that is out of synchronization with its apparent sentimental aim...Because *Charly* -- even though Cliff Robertson gives an earnest performance --

remains on a level either below or above the rest of us, it's really impossible to identify with him."

Arthur Knight *(Saturday Review)* said: "On the surface, *Charly*, a new film lovingly directed by Ralph Nelson and knowingly written by Stirling Silliphant, would seem to have almost as many strikes against it as Charly, its ill-fated hero...Although the kind of operation that Charly undergoes is still in the realm of science-fiction, the filmmakers made no attempt to gadget it up, realizing that the focus had to remain upon the man, not the machinery. Perhaps the most fascinating part of the picture is to watch Cliff Robertson's subtle alterations of posture and expression as this change takes place. Similarly, the love story, such as it is, is kept properly muted."

Daniel Keyes' story, novelized in 1966, was converted into a fairly unlikely one-act musical in 1979 and was premiered in Edmonton, Alberta (Canada), as *Flowers for Algernon*, with staging by Peter Coe. Coe then took the production to London where it opened at the Queen's Theatre in mid-June with Michael Crawford in the lead. According to *Variety*, "[It] provides Crawford, a gifted and versatile performer with ample scope for his talents as singer and hoofer, and the musical's interest owes a lot to his personal appeal and authority...no smash but a worthy and involving effort." It lasted on the West End for twenty-nine performances.

Now called *Charlie and Algernon*, the show had a twenty-one-song score by David Rogers (book and lyrics) and Charles Strouse (music), and was next staged in summer 1980 at the Kennedy Center in Washington at the relatively tiny Terrace Theatre before moving into the roomier Eisenhower Theatre. It boasted an acclaimed performance by P. J. Benjamin and a showstopping one by a performing mouse! *Variety's* critic called the show "enchanting" but felt that "Strouse's music is the weak link in this otherwise exemplary Folger Theatre production" while admitting that "much of the credit goes to director Louis Scheeder, who obviously counsels restraint for the major characters so the story can work its own magic ...*Charlie and Algernon* offers plenty of charm with its endearing story and loveable characters, and should be particularly successful with the younger set." *Charlie and Algernon* came to Broadway briefly in September, but closed after seventeen performances.

On its opening, Douglas Watt wrote in the *Daily News*: "Despite a resourceful performance in the leading role -- make that roles, for one mustn't underestimate the appearance of a performing mouse -- [it] is a hapless affair...To one unfamiliar with either the book or subsequent movie, the story, especially as set to music, both trivializes and sentimentalizes the subject of mental retardation. It is, oddly, a work that while taking unfair advantage of our emotions, fails to move us." Of the performers, Watt said: "P. J. Benjamin is winning on the whole, most at ease as the smartly attired genius-lover who sings and dances skillfully and acts acceptably, as well. He is less successful as the hunched-over, grinning moron...Sandy Faison gives an attractive performance in the limited and somewhat contradictory, as well as unconvincing, part of the teacher who accepts her former pupil as her lover and slips unhappily away, at his will."

The New York Times' Frank Rich felt: "If *Charlie and Algernon* had the grace or pizzazz of a firstrate musical, perhaps it would be easier to ignore its simplistic content. Unfortunately the distractions are few...Many of the crucial plot transitions are accompanied not by the score or the book but by voice-over readings from the hero's journal. Rich called P. J. Benjamin "gifted" and concluded, "Of course, I'm not forgetting about Algernon. He's a cute little mouse -- perhaps too little to be seen from the back of the Helen Hayes [Theatre] -- and he does a mean little softshoe."

STAGE

FLOWERS FOR ALGERNON, Queen's Theatre, London, opened June 19, 1979 29 performances
Produced by Michael White in association with Isobel Robins Kopecky; A Musical based on the novel by Daniel Keyes; Director, Peter Coe; Book and lyrics by David Rogers; Music by Charles Strouse; Scenery, Lawrence Schaefer; Lighting, Spike Gaden; Choreography, Rhoda Levine; Musical director, Alexander Faris; Orchestrations, Philip J. Lang; Associate producer, Robert Fox

Michael Crawford (Charlie); Cheryl Kennedy (Alice Kinian); Aubrey Woods (Dr. Strauss); Ralph Nossek (Dr. Nemur); Betty Benfield (Mrs. Donner); Sharon Lee Hill (Gina); George Harris (Frank); Jeanne L'Esty (Mother); Jason Ash (Little Charlie); Richard Owens (Father); Amanda Holmes, Brian Honeyball, Betty Turner, Barry Wade (Nurses)

CHARLIE AND ALGERNON, Eisenhower Theatre, Washington, D.C., opened August 4 through 31, 1980; moved to *Helen Hayes Theatre*, New York, opened September 14 through September 28, 1980
Produced by the Kennedy Center, Isabel Robins Konecky, Fisher Theatre Foundation and Folger Theatre Group; A Musical based on the novel *Flowers for Algernon* by Daniel Keyes; Director, Louis W. Scheeder; Book and lyrics by David Rogers; Music by Charles Strouse; Scenery, Kate Edmonds; Lighting, Hugh Lester; Costumes, Jess Goldstein; Choreography, Virginia Freeman; Musical director, Liza Redfield; Orchestrations, Philip J. Lang; Sound, William H. Clements

P. J. Benjamin (Charlie); Sandy Faison (Alice Kinian); Edward Earle (Dr. Strauss); Robert Sevra (Dr. Nemur); Nancy Franklin (Mrs. Donner); Loida Santos (Lita); Patrick Jude (Frank); Julienne Marie (Mother); Matthew Duda (Little Charlie); Michael Vita (Father)

MUSICAL NUMBERS: "Have I the Right?"; "I Got a Friend"; "One Step at a Time"; "Jelly Donuts and Chocolate Cake"; "Hey Look at Me"; "Reading"; "No Surprises"; "Midnight Riding"; "Dream Sale With Me"; "Midnight Riding" (reprise); "Not Another Day Like This"; "I Can't Tell You"; "Now"; "Charlie & Algernon"; "The Maze"; "Whatever Time There Is"; "Everything Was Perfect"; "Charlie"; "I Really Loved You"; "Whatever Time There Is" (reprise)

SCREEN

CHARLY, Cinerama Releasing Corporation, released September 1968
A Selmur Picture in association with Robertson Associates; Executive producer, Selig J. Seligman; Produced and directed by Ralph Nelson; Screenplay, Stirling Silliphant; Based on the short story and novel *Flowers for Algernon* by Daniel Keyes; Photography, Arthur J. Ornitz; Art director, Charles Rosen; Set decorator, Clint Marshall; Music, Ravi Shankar; Editor, Frederick Steinkamp

Cliff Robertson (Charly Gordon); Claire Bloom (Alice Kinian); Leon Janney (Dr. Richard Nemur); Lilia Skala (Dr. Anna Straus); Dick Van Patten (Bert); William Dwyer (Joey); Ed McNally (Gimpy); Dan Morgan (Paddy); Barney Martin (Hank); Ruth White (Mrs. Apple); Freak Nolan (Eddie); Ralph Nelson (Convention Speaker)

TELEVISION

THE TWO WORLDS OF CHARLIE GORDON, U. S. Steel Hour, televised February

22, 1961 CBS 1 hour
Produced by George Kondolf for The Theatre Guild; Director, Fielder Cook; Teleplay, James Yaffee, based on the story *Flowers for Algernon* by Daniel Keyes

Cliff Robertson (Charlie Gordon); Mona Freeman (Alice Kinian); Gerald S. O'Loughlin (Dr. Richard Nemur); Joanna Roos (Dr. Anna Straus); Maxwell Shaw (Bert)

CHARLIE CHAN
Various adaptations of the character created by Earl Derr Biggers

Synopsis

KEEPER OF THE KEYS: A Mystery Drama by Valentine Davies (1933)

Convinced that his former wife, noted opera singer Ellen Landini, gave birth to a son after their divorce and has concealed the boy from him, Dudley Ward invites the prima donna, two of her former husbands and her current spouse to his Nevada mountain hunting lodge. He also invites wily Honolulu detective Charlie Chan to help resolve his claim. Ellen is found shot to death on the balcony, and the following day one of her former husbands meets a similar death. The crafty Charlie Chan carefully examines the various and conflicting motives of each guest and those of his host, and finally succeeds in unmasking the murderer: Dudley Ward himself.

Comment and Critique

George M. Cohan successfully adapted Earl Derr Biggers' novel *Seven Keys to Baldpate* to the stage in 1913. Biggers' *Keeper of the Keys*, originally titled *Inspector Charlie Chan* by adaptor Valentine Davies, was the only Charlie Chan novel to reach the stage. *Keeper of the Keys* was unsuccessful, and Richard Lockridge (*The Evening Sun*) considered it "the last and the best of Earl Derr Biggers' detective novels" but, "though the play follows the novel closely enough, is not really very interesting. William Harrigan is an excellent Charlie...It has been so nicely cast and conscientiously done that it is quite a pity it does not turn out to be much of a play." *The New York Times* critic agreed with Lockridge's appraisal, noting, "Charlie Chan is not at his best on the stage...and, further, William Harrigan does not catch the spirit with which the novelist graced the figure of the detective."

Earl Derr Biggers, born at Warren, Ohio, on August 26, 1884, did not see his creation of Charlie Chan materialize on Broadway. Biggers died at age forty-eight on April 5, 1933. He conceived the plot of his first Charlie Chan novel while vacationing in Honolulu in 1919. Four years later, he researched the careers and exploits of two Honolulu Chinese detectives, Chang Apana and Lee Fook and his Chan, a composite of the two, first emerged in *The House Without a Key*, serialized in *The Saturday Evening Post* in 1925.

Biggers later qualified his Chan creation in *The House Without a Key*: "So Charlie appeared in the Hono-lulu mystery, starting as a minor and unimportant character. As the story progressed, however, he modestly pushed his way forward, and toward the end he had the lion's share of the spotlight. Scarcely had the story stopped running in the *Post* when I began to hear from people all over the country who wanted another Charlie Chan story. The idea had never occurred to me to write a series, but the possibilities looked good. So I wrote *The Chinese Parrot*."

The House Without a Key was adapted to the screen by Frank Leon Smith as a ten-chapter Pathe serial in 1926. *The Motion Picture Herald* synopsized its plot on December 26. The tale relates the animosity between two brothers, Amos and Dan Witherslip, who erected a spite fence between their Honolulu properties for twenty years. "Their sister comes from Boston to patch up their quarrel. John Witherslip, a nephew, is entrusted by his Uncle Dan with the doing away of a strong box which holds the Witherslip secret. On his boat is Cary, daughter of Amos Witherslip's partner. The mystery is finally unraveled and Cary and John, many times thwarted, are reunited at the end and marry."

Biggers followed his initial Chan adventure with five more novels featuring the Chinese detective: *The Chinese Parrot* (1926); *Behind That Curtain* (1928); *The Black Camel* (1929); *Charlie Chan Carries On* (1930) and the last Chan adventure, *Keeper of the Keys* (1932), the only Chan novel not filmed.

The casting of Charlie Chan reflected Charlie Chaplin's later riposte to Jack Oakie when Oakie initially rejected caricaturing Benito Mussolini in Chaplin's *The Great Dictator*. Oakie observed that they were many Italian actors in Hollywood who could play the part. Chaplin replied, "What's so unusual about an Italian playing an Italian?" No Chinese actor ever portrayed Charlie Chan. That observation holds true a half century later.

The screen's first Charlie Chan was Japanese actor George Kuwa and the second Chan was Kamiyama Sojin, also Japanese. The finest of the screen's Chans was Warner Oland. Born October 3, 1880, at Ulmea, Sweden, he portrayed Charlie in sixteen films. After Oland's death on August 6, 1938, several actors were tested for the part of Charlie Chan including Leo Carrillo and Noah Beery, but Twentieth Century-Fox assigned the role to actorplaywright Sidney Toler, born of Scottish parents at Warrensburg, Missouri, on April 28, 1874. Toler made twenty-two Charlie Chan adventures, first at Fox and then at Monogram Studios. After Toler's death at age seventy-two on February 12, 1947, Boston-born (November 22, 1904) character actor Roland Winters portrayed Charlie Chan in the last six films in the Monogram series.

Warner Oland had played Oriental villains early on in his film career: in the 1917 serial *Patria* as Japanese Baron Hurokio, and he was Charlie Yong in First National's 1922 picture *East Is West*. Paramount featured Oland as Fu Manchu in its *The Mysterious Dr. Fu Manchu* (1929) and *The Return of Fu Manchu* (1930). Between his assignments as Charlie Chan, Oland played Henry Chang opposite Marlene Dietrich in Paramount's *Shanghai Express* (1932) and he was General Yu in Garbo's 1934 MGM film *The Painted Veil*.

On radio over the years, Charlie Chan was played by Walter Connolly (1932), Ed Begley (1944-47), Santos Ortega (1947-48) and William Rees (1950)

Television's Charlie Chan was portrayed by J. (Joseph) Carrol Naish, born in New York City on January 27, 1897, who died in La Jolla, California, on January 24, 1973. Naish was an expert dialectician and adept at unusual makeup. *The New Adventures of Charlie Chan*, a British-made series syndicated on television in 1957, featured the very versatile Naish as the Chinese sleuth. An animated cartoon series called *The Amazing Chan and the Chan Clan* was televised for two years over CBS beginning in 1972. Keye Luke, who had played Charlie's Number One son in the Warner Oland theatrical Chan series, supplied the master detective's voice..

Universal Television made a pilot film in 1973 titled *Happiness Is a Warm Clue* featuring Ross Martin as Charlie Chan, which was eventually televised in the United States on July 17, 1979, as *The Return of Charlie Chan*. (Martin's casting was vociferously opposed by the increasingly active Asian-American faction of the Screen Actors Guild.) Another non-Oriental, British actor Peter Ustinov, was the screen's next Charlie Chan (although he is more renowned as a sleuth for his seven movie and television appearances as Agatha Christie's imperious Belgian sleuth, Hercule Poirot). Ustinov played the ever-popular Oriental detective in *Charlie Chan and the Curse of the Dragon Queen* (1980), heading a stellar cast but enthralling few reviewers or Charlie Chan purists.

STAGE

KEEPER OF THE KEYS, Fulton Theatre, New York, opened October 18, 1933 23 performances

Produced and directed by Sigourney Thayer; A Play by Valentine Davies, from the novel by Earl Derr Biggers; Setting and Lighting by Donald Oenslager; Technical director, Felix Jacoves; Costumes, Edith Hiatt; General manager, John Yorke

William Harrigan (Inspector Charlie Chan); Romaine Callender (Dr. Swan); Roy Roberts (Don Holt); Dwight Frye (Ah Sing); Ruth Easton (Kathleen Ireland); Robert Lynn (Michael Ireland); Roberta Beatty (Ellen Landini); Fleming Ward (Dudley Ward); Howard St. John (John Ryder); Warren Parker (Cash Shannon); Elwood K. Thomas (Seth Leahy); Aristides de Leoni (Luis Romano)

SCREEN

THE HOUSE WITHOUT A KEY, Pathe Serial (10 episodes), released November 1926

Director, Spencer Bennet; Screenplay, Frank Leon Smith, based on Earl Derr Biggers' first Charlie Chan novel; Photography, Edward J. Snyder

George Kuwa (Charlie Chan); Walter Miller (John Quincy Winterslip); Allene Ray (Cary Egan); William Norton Bailey (Harry Jennison); John Webb Dillon (Amos Winterslip); Betty Caldwell (Barbara Winterslip); Frank Lackteen (Kachla); E. H. Calvert (Uncle Dan Winterslip); Jack Pratt (James Egan); Natalie Warfield (Minerva Winterslip); Charles West, Harry Semels, John Cossar, Scott Seaton, Clifford Saum

EPISODES: The Spite Fence; The Mystery Box; The Missing Numeral; Suspicion; The Death Buoy; Sinister Shadows; The Mystery Man; The Spotted Menace; The Wrist Watch; The Culprit

THE CHINESE PARROT, Universal Pictures, released October 1927

Produced by Carl Laemmle; Director, Paul Leni; Screenplay and adaptation by J. Grubb Alexander, based on Earl Derr Biggers' 1926 novel; Photography, Ben Kline; Titles, Walter Anthony

Kamiyama Sojin (Charlie Chan); Marion Nixon (Sally Phillimore); Hobart Bosworth (Philip Madden/Jerry Delaney); Florence Turner (Sally Phillimore); Edward Burns (Robert Eden); Albert Conti (Martin Thorne); Fred Esmelton (Alexander Eden); Ed Kennedy (Maydorf); George Kuwa (Louie Wong); Anna May Wong (Nautch Dancer); Jack Trent (Jordan); Slim Summerville, Dan Mason (Prospectors); Etta Lee (Gambling Den Habitue)

BEHIND THAT CURTAIN, Fox Films, released June 1929

Produced by William Fox; Director, Irving Cummings; Screenplay by Sonya Levien and Clarke Silvernail, based on Earl Derr Biggers' novel (*Saturday Evening Post*

March 31 to May 5, 1928); Photography, Conrad Wells, Dave Ragin, Vincent Farrar; Titles, Wilbur Morse; Assistant director, Charles Woolstenhulme; Editor, Al DeGaetano

E. L. Park (Charlie Chan); Warner Baxter (John Beetham); Lois Moran (Eve Mannering); Gilbert Emery (Sir Frederic Bruce); Claude King (Sir George Mannering); Philip Strange (Eric Durand); Boris Karloff (Karlov); Finch Smiles (Dobbins); Jamiel Hassen (Habib Hanna); Montague Shaw (Hilary Galt); Peter Gawthorne (Inspector Thomas); John Rogers (Alf Pornick); Mercedes De Valaco (Nunah)

CHARLIE CHAN CARRIES ON, *Fox Films*, released April 1931
Produced by William Fox; Director, Hamilton MacFadden; Screenplay by Philip Klein and Barry Connors, based on a story by Earl Derr Biggers, Photography, George Schneiderman; Editor, Al DeGaetano

Warner Oland (Charlie Chan); John Garrick (Mark Kenaway); Marguerite Churchill (Palema Potter); Warren Hymer (Max Minchin); Marjorie White (Sadie); C. Henry Gordon (John Ross); George Brent (Captain Ronald Keane); William Holden (Patrick Tait); John Swor (Elmer Benbow); John T. Murray (Dr. Lofton); Peter Gawthorne (Inspector Duff); Goode Montgomery (Mrs. Benbow); Jason Robards (Walter Honeywood); Lumsden Hare (Inspector Hanley); Zeffie Tillbury (Mrs. Luce); Betty Francisco (Sybil Conway); Harry Beresford (Kent); John Rogers (Martin); J. C. Davis (Eben); James Farley (Liner Captain)

ERAN TRECE, *Fox Films*, released 1932
Director, David Howard; Screenplay by Philip Klein and Barry Connors, based on *Charlie Chan Carries On* by Earl Derr Biggers; Photography, George Schneiderman; Editor, Al DeGaetano; Spanish Film Version

Manuel Arbo (Charlie Chan); with Ana Maria Custodio; Raul Roulien; Juan Torena; Blanca de Castejon; Martin Garralaga; Antonio Vidal; Jose Nieto; Rafael Calvo; Miguel Ligero; Carmen Rodriguez; Amelia Sante, Luana Alcaniz

THE BLACK CAMEL, *Fox Films*, released June 1931
Produced by William Fox; Director, Hamilton MacFadden; Screenplay by Hugh Stange, Barry Connors, Philip Klein, based on the novel by Earl Derr Biggers; Photography, George Schneidermann; Editor, Al DeGaetano

Warner Oland (Charlie Chan); Sally Eilers (Julie); Robert Young (Jimmy Bradshaw); Bela Lugosi (Tarneverro); Dorothy Revier (Shelah Fane); Victor Varconi (Robert Fyfe); J. M. Kerrigan (Thomas MacMasters); Mary Gordon (Mrs. MacMasters); William Post, Jr. (Alan Jaynes); C. Henry Gordon (Von Hart); Murray Kinnell (Smith); Richard Tucker (Wilkie Ballou); Marjorie White (Rita Ballou); Dwight Frye (Jessop); Violet Dunn (Anna); Otto Yamaoka (Kashimo); Robert Homans (Chief of Police); Louise Mackintosh (Housekeeper); Rita Roselle (Native Girl, Luana)

CHARLIE CHAN'S CHANCE, *Fox Films*, released January 1932
Produced by William Fox; Director, John Blystone; Screenplay by Philip Klein and Barry Connors, based on a novel by Earl Derr Biggers; Photography, Joseph August; Editor, Alex Troffey; Remake of *Behind That Curtain*

Warner Oland (Charlie Chan); Alexander Kirkland (John Douglas); Marion Nixon (Shirley Marlowe); Linda Watkins (Gloria Garland); James Kirkwood (Inspector Flannery); Ralph Morgan (Barry Kirk); H. B. Warner (Inspector Fyfe); James

Todd (Kenneth Dunwood); Herbert Bunston (Garrick Enderly); Charles McNaughton (Paradise); Edward Peil, Jr. (Li Gung); Jimmy Wang (Kee Lin); Joe Brown (Doctor)

CHARLIE CHAN'S GREATEST CASE, Fox Films, released October 1933
Director, Hamilton MacFadden; Screenplay by Lester Cole and Marion Orth, based on Earl Derr Biggers' novel *The House Without a Key*; Photography, Ernest Palmer; Music director, Samuel Kaylin; Editor, Alex Troffey

Warner Oland (Charlie Chan); Heather Angel (Carlotta Egan); John Warburton (John Quincy Winterslip); Robert Warwick (Dan Winterslip); Frank McGlynn (Amos Winterslip); Virginia Cherrill (Barbara Winterslip); Francis Ford (Captain Hallett); Walter Byron (Harry Jennison); Clara Blandick (Minerva Winterslip); Claude King (Captain Authur Cope); Cornelius Keefe (Steve Letherbee); Gloria Roy (Arlene Compton); Roger Imhof (The Beachcomber); William Stack (James Eagen); Ivan Simpson (Brade)

CHARLIE CHAN'S COURAGE, Fox Films, released August 1934
Directors, George Hadden and Eugene Forde; Screenplay by Seton I. Miller, based on Earl Derr Biggers' novel *The Chinese Parrot*; Photography, Hal Mohr; Music director, Samuel Kaylin; Editor, Alex Troffey

Warner Oland (Charlie Chan); Donald Woods (Bob Crawford); Paul Harvey (J. P. Madden/Jerry Delaney); DeWitt C. Jennings (Constable Bracken); Jerry Jerome (Maydorf); Harvey Clark (Professor Gamble); Drue Leyton (Paula Graham); Murray Kinnell (Martin Thorne); Si Jenks (Will Holley); Jack Carter (Victor Jordan); Reginald Mason (Mr. Crawford); James Wang (Wong); Virginia Hammond (Mrs. Jordan); Francis Ford (Hewitt)

CHARLIE CHAN IN LONDON, Fox Films, released September 1934
Produced by John Stone; Director, Eugene Forde; Screenplay by Philip MacDonald, based on a story by Earl Derr Biggers; Photography, L. W. O'Connell; Music director, Samuel Kaylin; Editor, Alex Troffey

Warner Oland (Charlie Chan); Raymond Milland (Neil Howard); Drue Leyton (Pamela Gray); Douglas Walton (Paul Gray); Alan Mowbray (Geoffrey Richmond); Mona Barrie (Lady Mary Bristol); Madge Bellamy (Becky Fothergill); David Torrence (Home Secretary, Sir Lionel Bashford); George Barraud (Major Jardine); E. E. Clive (Detective Sergeant Thacker); Paul England (Bunny Fothergill); Walter Johnson (Jerry Garton); Murray Kinnell (Phillip); Reginald Sheffield (Flight Commander King); Claude King (R.A.F. Commandant); Perry Ivins (Kemp); John Rogers (Lake); Margaret Mann (Housemaid); Helena Grant (Miss Johnson); Montague Shaw (Doctor); Phyllis Cochlan (Nurse); Arthur Clayton (Warden); Elsa Buchanan (Alice Perkins); Carli Taylor, Doris Stone (Guests); Ann Doran (Woman)

CHARLIE CHAN IN PARIS, Fox Films, released January 1935
Produced by John Stone; Director, Lewis Seiler; Screenplay by Edward T. Lowe and Stuart Anthony from a story by Philip MacDonald, based on the Charlie Chan character created by Earl Derr Biggers; Photography, Ernest Palmer; Music director, Samuel Kaylin; Editor, Al DeGaetano

Warner Oland (Charlie Chan); Mary Brian (Yvette Lamartine); Keye Luke (Lee Chan); Thomas Beck (Victor Descartes); Erik Rhodes (Max Corday); John Miljan (Albert Dufresne); Murray Kinnell (Henri Latouche); Dorothy Appleby (Nardi);

Minor Watson (Renard); John Qualen (Concierge); Henry Kolker (M. Lamartine); Ruth Peterson (Renee Jacquard); Perry Ivins (Bedell); Harry Cording (Gendarme)

CHARLIE CHAN IN EGYPT, Fox Films, released June 1935
Produced by Edward T. Lowe; Director, Louis King; Screenplay by Robert Ellis and Helen Logan, based on the Charlie Chan character created by Earl Derr Biggers; Photography, Daniel B. Clark; Art director, William Darling; Music director, Samuel Kaylin; Editor, Al DeGaetano

Warner Oland (Charlie Chan); Pat Paterson (Carol Arnold); Thomas Beck (Tom Evans); Rita Cansino [Rita Hayworth] (Nayda); Frank Conroy (Professor Thurston); Nigel de Brulier (Edfu Ahmad); Jameson Thomas (Dr. Anton Racine); James Eagles (Barry Arnold); Paul Porcasi (Fouad Soucida); Arthur Stone (Drageman); Stepin Fetchit (Snowshoes); Anita Brown (Snowshoes' Friend); John Davidson (Daoud Atrash); Frank Reicher (Dr. Jaipur); George Irving (Professor Arnold); John George (Dwarf Egyptian Helper); Gloria Roy (Woman)

CHARLIE CHAN IN SHANGHAI, Fox Films, released October 1935
Produced by John Stone; Director, James Tinling, Screenplay by Edward T. Lowe and Gerald Fairlie, based on the Charlie Chan character created by Earl Derr Biggers; Photography, Rudolph Mate; Music, Samuel Kaylin; Editor, Nick De Maggio

Warner Oland (Charlie Chan); Irene Hervey (Diana Woodland); Charles Locher [Jon Hall] (Philip Nash); Russell Hicks (James Andrews); Keye Luke (Lee Chan); Neil Fitzgerald (Dakin); Halliwell Hobbes (Chief of Police); Frederik Vogeding (Burke); Harry Strang (Chauffeur); Max Wagner (Taxi Driver); Pat O'Malley (Belden)

CHARLIE CHAN'S SECRET, 20th Century-Fox, released December 1935
Produced by John Stone; Director, Gordon Wiles; Screenplay by Robert Ellis, Helen Logan and Joseph Hoffman, based on the Charlie Chan character created by Earl Derr Biggers; Photography, Rudolph Mate; Music director, Samuel Kaylin; Editor, Nick De Maggio

Warner Oland (Charlie Chan); Henrietta Crosman (Henrietta Lowell); Rosina Lawrence (Alice Lowell); Charles Quigley (Dick Williams); Astrid Allwyn (Janice Gaige); Edward Trevor (Fred Gaige); Jerry Miley (Allen Coleby); Herbert Mundin (Baxter); Arthur Edmund Carew (Professor Bowan); Jonathan Hale (Warren T. Phelps); Egon Brecher (Ulrich); Ivan Miller (Morton); James T. Mack (Fingerprint Man); Landers Stevens (Coroner); Francis Ford (Boat Captain)

CHARLIE CHAN AT THE CIRCUS, 20th Century-Fox, released March 1936
Produced by John Stone; Director, Harry Lachman; Screenplay by Robert Ellis and Helen Logan, based on the Charlie Chan character created by Earl Derr Biggers; Photography, Daniel B. Clark; Music director, Samuel Kaylin; Editor, Alex Troffey

Warner Oland (Charlie Chan); J. Carrol Naish (Tom Holt); Keye Luke (Lee Chan); George Brasno (Tim); Olive Brasno (Tiny); Francis Ford (John Gaines); Shirley Deane (Louise Norman); John McGuire (Hal Blake); Paul Stanton (Joe Kinney); Wade Boteler (Lieutenant Macy); Maxine Reiner (Marie Norman); Boothe Howard (Dan Farrell); Drue Leyton (Nellie Farrell); Shia Jung (Su Toy); Franklyn Farnum (Mike)

CHARLIE CHAN AT THE RACE TRACK, 20th Century-Fox, released July 1936

Produced by John Stone; Director, H. Bruce Humberstone; Screenplay by Robert Ellis, Helen Logan and Edward T. Lowe, based on the Charlie Chan character created by Earl Derr Biggers and a story by Lou Breslow and Saul Elkins; Photography, Harry Jackson; Music director, Samuel Kaylin; Editor, Nick De Maggio

Warner Oland (Charlie Chan); Helen Wood (Alice Fenton); Alan Dinehart (George Chester); Keye Luke (Lee Chan); Thomas Beck (Bruce Rogers); Gavin Muir (Bagley); Gloria Roy (Catherine Chester); Jonathan Hale (Warren Fenton); G. P. Huntley, Jr. (Denny Barton); Robert Warwick (Chief of Police); Frankie Darro ("Tip" Collins); Junior Coghlan (Eddie Brill); John Rogers (Mooney); Harry Jans (Al Meers); Jack Mulhall (Second Purser); George Irving (Major Kent); John H. Allen ("Streamline" Jones); Paul Fix (Gangster)

CHARLIE CHAN AT THE OPERA, 20th Century-Fox, released November 1936

Produced by John Stone; Director, H. Bruce Humberstone; Screenplay by W. Scott Darling and Charles Belden, based on the Charlie Chan character created by Earl Derr Biggers and a story by Bess Meredyth; Photography, Lucien Androit; Opera *Carnival* Composed by Oscar Levant and William Kernell; Music director, Samuel Kaylin; Art directors, Duncan Cramer and Lewis Creber; Editor, Alex Troffey

Warner Oland (Charlie Chan); Boris Karloff (Cravelle); Charlotte Henry (Kitty); Keye Luke (Lee Chan); Margaret Irving (Lilli Rochelle); Gregory Gaye (Enrico Barelli); Thomas Beck (Phil Childers); Nedda Harrigan (Anita Barelli); Frank Conroy (Whitley); William Demarest (Sergeant Kelly); Guy Usher (Inspector Regan); Maurice Cass (Arnold); Tom McGuire (Morris); Fred Kelsey, Stanley Blystone, Bud Geary, Lee Shumway, Larry Fisher, Richard Powell, Harry Strang, Ed Parker (Policemen); Harland Tucker (Private Detective); Gladden James (Secretary); Hilda Vaughan, Jane Keckley (Wardrobe Women); Dedo Newton (Bar Maid); Anthony Hughes (Ambulance Driver); Tony Merlo, Pat Cunning, Milton Gowman, Leonard Mellon, Myrte Donnilias, Marjorie May Timm, Herschel Graham, Mary Louise Smith, Tony Roux (Villagers); Billy Wayne (Electrician); Eddie Tamblyn (Call Boy)

CHARLIE CHAN AT THE OLYMPICS, 20th Century-Fox, released May 1937

Produced by John Stone; Director, H. Bruce Humberstone; Screenplay by Paul Burger, Robert Ellis and Helen Logan, based on the Charlie Chan character created by Earl Derr Biggers; Photography, Dan Clark; Music director, Samuel Kaylin; Editor, Fred Allen

Warner Oland (Charlie Chan); Katherine De Mille (Yvonne Roland); Allan Lane (Richard Masters); Pauline Moore (Betty Adams); Keye Luke (Lee Chan); John Eldredge (Cartwright); C. Henry Gordon (Arthur Hughes); Morgan Wallace (Zaraka); Jonathan Hale (Hopkins); Layne Tom, Jr. (Charlie Chan, Jr.); Frederik Vogeding (Inspector Strasser); Howard Hickman (Dr. Burton); Edward Keane (Colonel); Selmer Jackson (Navy Commander); Don Brodie (Radio Announcer); George Chandler (Ship's Radio Announcer); Andrew Tombes (Chief Scott); Minerva Urecal (Woman); Paul W. Panzer, Philip Morris, Lee Shumway, Stanley Blystone (Men)

CHARLIE CHAN ON BROADWAY, 20th Century-Fox, released October 1937

Produced by John Stone; Director, Eugene Forde; Screenplay by Art Arthur, Robert Ellis, Helen Logan, Charles B. Belden and Jerry Cady, based on the Charlie Chan character created by Earl Derr Biggers; Photography, Harry Jackson; Music director, Samuel Kaylin; Editor, Al De Gaetano

Warner Oland (Charlie Chan); Joan Marsh (Joan Wendall); Keye Luke (Lee Chan); J. Edward Bromberg (Murdock); Louise Henry (Billie Bronson); Leon Ames (Buzz Moran); Joan Woodbury (Marie Collins); Donald Woods (Speed Patton); Douglas Frawley (Johnny Burke); Harold Huber (Inspector Nelson); Marc Lawrence (Thomas Mitchell); Creighton Hale (Reporter); Lon Chaney, Jr. (Desk Man); Charles Williams (Meeker); Willian Jeffrey (Coroner); Toshie Mori (Ling Tse); Eugene Borden (Louis); Sidney Fields (Porter); Norman Ainsley (Stewart); Philip Morris (Customs Officer); George Regas (Hindu); Sherry Hill, Billy Wayne, Don Brodie, Franklin Parker, Allen Fox, (Reporters); George Guhl (Smitty); Charles Haefli (Pickpocket); Sam Ash (Waiter); Harry Depp (Snapper); Beulah Hutton (Telephone Operator); Victor Adams (Gangster); Art Miles (Porter); Paddy O'Flynn, Lester Dorr (Photographers)

CHARLIE CHAN AT MONTE CARLO, 20th Century-Fox, released November 1937
Produced by John Stone; Director, Eugene Forde; Screenplay by Charles S. Belden, Jerry Cady, Robert Ellis and Helen Logan, based on the Charlie Chan character created by Earl Derr Biggers; Photography, Dan Clark; Music director, Samuel Kaylin, Editor, Nick De Maggio

Warner Oland (Charlie Chan); Virginia Field (Evelyn Gray); Sidney Blackmer (Karnoff); Keye Luke (Lee Chan); Harold Huber (Inspector); Kay Linaker (Joan Karnoff); Robert Kent (Gordon Chase); Edward Raquelo (Paul Savarin); George Lynn (Al Rogers); Louis Mercer (Cab Driver); George Renavant (Renault); John Bleifer (Ludwin); George Sorrel (Gendarme); George David (Pepito)

CHARLIE CHAN IN HONOLULU, 20th Century-Fox, released December 1938
Produced by John Stone; Director, H. Bruce Humberstone; Screenplay by Charles S. Belden; Art directors, Richard Day and Haldane Douglas, based on the Charlie Chan character created by Earl Derr Biggers; Photography, Charles Clarke; Music, Samuel Kaylin; Editor, Nick De Maggio

Sidney Toler (Charlie Chan); Phyllis Brooks (Judy Hayes); Sen Yung (Jimmy Chan); Claire Dodd (Carol Wayne); John King (Randolph); Eddie Collins (Al Hogan); George Zucco (Dr. Cardigan); Robert Barrat (Captain Johnson); Marc Lawrence (Johnnie McCoy); Richard Lane (Detective Arnold); Layne Tom, Jr. (Tommy Chan); Philip Ahn (Wing Foo); Paul Harvey (Detective); Richard Alexander (Sailor)

CHARLIE CHAN IN RENO, 20th Century-Fox, released June 1939
Produced by John Stone; Director, Norman Foster; Screenplay by Philip Wylie, Frances Hyland, Albert Ray and Robert E. Kent, based on the Charlie Chan character created by Earl Derr Biggers; Photography, Virgil Miller; Editor, Fred Allen

Sidney Toler (Charlie Chan); Ricardo Cortez (Dr. Ainsley); Phyllis Brooks (Vivian Wells); Slim Summerville (Sheriff Tombstone Fletcher); Sen Yung (Jimmy Chan); Pauline Moore (Mary Whitman); Kane Richmond (Curtis Whitman); Kay Linaker (Mrs. Russell); Louis Henry (Jeanne Bently); Robert Lowery (Wally Burke); Iris Wong (Choy Wong); Morgan Conway (George Bently); Eddie Collins (Cab Driver); Hamilton MacFadden (Night Clerk); Charles D. Brown (Police Chief)

CHARLIE CHAN AT TREASURE ISLAND, 20th Century-Fox, released September 1939
Produced by Edward Kaufman; Director, Norman Foster; Screenplay by John Larkin,

based on the Charlie Chan character created by Earl Derr Biggers; Photography, Virgil Miller; Editor, Norman Colbert

Sidney Toler (Charlie Chan); Cesar Romero (Fred Rhadini); Pauline Moore (Eve Cairo); Douglas Fowley (Peter Lewis); Sen Yung (Lee Chan); June Gale (Myra Rhadini); Douglass Dumbrille (Thomas Gregory); Sally Blane (Stella Essex); Billie Seward (Bessie Sibley); Charles Halton (Redley); Trevor Bardette (Abdul); Donald McBride (Chief Kilvaine); Wally Vernon (Elmer Keiner); Gerald Mohr (Dr. Zodiac); Louis Jean Heydt (Paul Essex); John Elliott (Doctor)

CHARLIE CHAN IN THE CITY OF DARKNESS, 20th Century-Fox, released December 1939

Produced by John Stone; Director, Herbert I. Leeds; Screenplay by Robert Ellis, Helen Logan, Gina Kaus and Ladislaus Fodor, based on the Charlie Chan character created by Earl Derr Biggers; Photography, Virgil Miller; Editor, Harry Reynolds

Sidney Toler (Charlie Chan); Lynn Bari (Marie Dubon); Harold Huber (Marcel); Pedro de Cordoba (Antoine); Richard Clarke (Tony Madero); Dorothy Tree (Charlotte Rondell); C. Henry Gordon (Romaine); Leo G. Carroll (Louis Sentinelli); Lon Chaney, Jr. (Pierre); Noel Madison (Belescu); Douglass Dumbrille (Petroff); Louis Mercier (Max); George Davis (Alex); Adrienne d'Ambricourt (Landlady); Barbara Leonard (Lola); Frederik Vogeding (Captain); Tommy Seidel (Hilip); Paul Irving (Doctor); and Albert Conti, Alphonse Martell, Eugene Borden, Albert Pollet, Jean De Val, Merek Windheim, George Sorel, Anota Pike, Michael Mark, Gino Corrado, Vyola Vonn, Harry Fleischmann, Fred Farrell, Frank Puglia

CHARLIE CHAN IN PANAMA, 20th Century-Fox, released March 1940

Produced by Sol M. Wurtzel; Director, Norman Foster; Screenplay by John Larkin, Lester Ziffren, based on the Charlie Chan character created by Earl Derr Biggers; Photography, Virgil Miller; Editor, Fred Allen

Sidney Toler (Charlie Chan); Jean Rogers (Kathi Lenesch); Lionel Atwill (Cliveden Compton); Mary Nash (Jennie Finch); Sen Yung (Jimmy Chan); Kane Richmond (Richard Cabot); Chris-Pin Martin (Lieutenant Montero); Jack La Rue (Manolo); Helen Ericson (Stewardess); Edwin Stanley (Governor Webster); Frank Puglia (Achmed Halide); Addison Richards (Godley); Edward Keane (Dr. Fredericks); Lane Chandler (Officer); Eddie Acuff (Sailor); Ed Gargan (Plant Worker); Jimmy Aubrey (Drunken Sailor); Wally Vernon (Man); Lionel Royce (Dr. Grosser); Don Douglas (Captain Lewis)

CHARLIE CHAN'S MURDER CRUISE, 20th Century-Fox, released June 1940

Produced by John Stone; Director, Eugene Ford; Screenplay by Robertson White and Lester Ziffren, based on the Charlie Chan character created by Earl Derr Biggers; Photography, Virgil Miller; Editor, Harry Reynolds

Sidney Toler (Charlie Chan); Marjorie Weaver (Paula Drake); Lionel Atwill (Doctor Suderman); Robert Lowery (Dick Kenyon); Leo G. Carroll (Professor Gordon); Cora Witherspoon (Susie Watson); Sen Yung (Jimmy Chan); Kay Linaker (Mrs. Pendleton); Harlan Briggs (Coroner); Charles Middleton (Mr. Walters); Claire DuBrey (Mrs. Walters); Leonard Mudie (Walter Pendleton); Don Beddoe (James Ross); James Burke (Wilkie); Richard Keene (Buttons); Layne Tom, Jr. (Willie Chan); Montague Shaw (Inspector Duff); Cliff Clark (Policeman); Harry Strang (Guard); Walter Miller (Officer)

CHARLIE CHAN AT THE WAX MUSEUM, *20th Century-Fox*, released September 1940
Produced by Walter Morosco and Ralph Dietrich; Director, Lynn Shores; Screenplay by John Larkin, based on the Charlie Chan character created by Earl Derr Biggers; Photography, Virgil Miller; Art directors, Richard Day and Lewis Greber; Music, Emil Newman; Editor, Harry Reynolds

Sidney Toler (Charlie Chan); C. Henry Gordon (Dr. Cream); Marguerite Chapman (Mary Bolton); Sen Yung (Jimmy Chan); Marc Lawrence (Steve McBirney); Ted Osborn (Tom Agnew); Michael Visaroff (Dr. Otto Von Brom); Hilda Vaughn (Mrs. Rocke); Joe King (Inspector O'Matthews); Charles Wagenheim (Willie Fern); Harold Goodwin (Edwards); Archie Twitchell (Carter Lane); Edward Marr (Grenock); Joan Valerie (Lily Latimer)

MURDER OVER NEW YORK, *20th Century-Fox*, released December 1940
Produced by Sol M. Wurtzel; Director, Harry Lachman; Screenplay by Lester Ziffren, based on the Charlie Chan character created by Earl Derr Biggers; Photography, Virgil Miller; Editor, Louis Loeffler

Sidney Toler (Charlie Chan); Marjorie Weaver (Patricia Shaw); Robert Lowery (David Elliott); Ricardo Cortez (George Kirby); Sen Yung (Jimmy Chan); Donald McBride (Inspector Vance); Melville Cooper (Herbert Fenton); Kane Richmond (Ralph Percy); Joan Valerie (June Preston); John Sutton (Richard Jeffrey); Leyland Hodgson (Boggs); Frederick Worlock (Hugh Drake); Frank Coghlan, Jr. (Gilroy); Clarence Muse (Butler); Shemp Howard (Shorty McCoy); Trevor Bardette (Suspect); Lal Chand Mehra (Ramullah)

DEAD MEN TELL, *20th Century-Fox*, released March 1941
Produced by Walter Morosco and Ralph Dietrich; Director, Harry Lachman; Screenplay by John Larkin, based on the Charlie Chan character created by Earl Derr Biggers; Photography, Charles Clarke; Editor, Harry Reynolds

Sidney Toler (Charlie Chan); Sheila Ryan (Kate Ransome); Ethel Griffies (Patience Nodbury); Sen Yung (Jimmy Chan); Robert Weldon (Steve Daniels); Don Douglas (Ked Thomasson); Paul McGrath (Charles Thursday); Kay Aldridge (Laura Thursday); George Reeves (Bill Lydig); Truman Bradley (Captain Kane); Lenita Lane (Dr. Anne Bonnery); Milton Parsons (Gene La Farge); Stanley Andrews (Inspector)

CHARLIE CHAN IN RIO, *20th Century-Fox*, released September 1941
Produced by Sol M. Wurtzel; Director, Harry Lachman; Screenplay by Samuel G. Engel and Lester Ziffren, based on the Charlie Chan character created by Earl Derr Biggers; Photography, Joseph P. MacDonald; Art director, Richard Day; Music director, Emil Newman; Music and Lyrics, Mack Gordon and Harry Warren; Editor, Alex Troffey

Sidney Toler (Charlie Chan); Mary Beth Hughes (Joan Reynolds); Cobina Wright, Jr. (Grace Ellis); Victor Jory (Alfredo Marana); Harold Huber (Chief Souto); Ted North (Clark Denton); Sen Yung (Jimmy Chan); Richard Derr (Ken Reynolds); Kay Linaker (Helen Asby); Jacqueline Dalya (Lola Dean); Ann Codee (Margo); Eugene Borden (Armando); Truman Bradley (Paul Wagner); Hamilton MacFadden (Bill Kellogg); Leslie Denison (Rose); Iris Wong (Lili)

CASTLE IN THE DESERT, *20th Century-Fox*, released February 1942
Produced by Ralph Dietrich; Director, Harry Lachman; Screenplay by John Larkin,

based on the Charlie Chan character created by Earl Derr Biggers; Photography, Virgil Miller; Editor, John Brady

Sidney Toler (Charlie Chan); Arleen Whelan (Brenda Hartford); Richard Derr (Carl Detheridge); Douglass Dumbrille (Manderley); Sen Yung (Jimmy Chan); Henry Daniell (Watson King); Edmund MacDonald (Walter Hartford); Lenita Lane (Lucretia Manderley); Ethel Griffies (Madame Saturnie); Lucien Littlefield (Professor Gleason); Milton Parsons (Fletcher); Steve Geray (Dr. Retling); Paul Kruger (Bodyguard); George Chandler (Bus Driver); Oliver (Blake); Prickett (Wigley)

CHARLIE CHAN IN THE SECRET SERVICE, *Monogram Pictures*, released February 1944

Produced by Philip N. Krasne and James S. Burkett; Director, Phil Rosen; Screenplay by George Callahan, based on the Charlie Chan character created by Earl Derr Biggers; Photography, Ira Morgan; Art director, Dave Milton; Music director, Karl Hajos; Editor, Martin G. Cohn

Sidney Toler (Charlie Chan); Mantan Moreland (Birmingham); Benson Fong (Tommie Chan); Gwen Kenyon (Inez); Arthur Loft (Jones); Lela Tyler (Mrs. Winters); Marianne Quon (Iris Chan); Eddie Stutueroth (Von Vogan); Eddie Chandler (Lewis) George Lessey (Slade); George Lewis (Paul); Muni Seroff (Peter)

THE CHINESE CAT, *Monogram Pictures*, released May 1944

Produced by Philip N. Krasne and James S. Burkett; Director, Phil Rosen; Screenplay by George Callahan, based on the Charlie Chan character created by Earl Derr Biggers; Photography, Ira Morgan; Art director, Dave Milton; Editor, Fred Allen

Sidney Toler (Charlie Chan); Mantan Moreland (Birmingham); Benson Fong (Tommie Chan); Ian Keith (Racknick); Weldon Heyburn (Harvey Dennis); Joan Woodbury (Leah Manning); Cy Kendall (Deacon); Sam Flint (Tom Manning); Anthony Warde (Catlen); Dewey Robinson (Salos); John Davison (Carl/Kurt); Betty Blythe (Mrs. Manning); Jack Norton (Hotel Clerk); I. Stanford Jolley (Henchman)

CHARLIE CHAN IN BLACK MAGIC, *Monogram Pictures*, released August 1944

Produced by Philip N. Krasne and James S. Burkett; Director, Phil Rosen; Screenplay by George Callahan, based on the Charlie Chan character created by Earl Derr Biggers; Photography, Arthur Martinelli; Art director, Dave Milton; Music director, Alexander Laszlo; Editor, John Link; Reissued as *Meeting at Midnight*

Sidney Toler (Charlie Chan); Mantan Moreland (Birmingham); Jacqueline DeWit (Justine Bonner); Claudia Dell (Vera Starkey); Charles Jordan (Tom Starkey); Frances Chan (Frances); Joseph Crehan (Matthews); Ralph Peters (Rafferty); Frank Jaquet (Paul Hamlin); Helen Beverley (Norma Duncan); Dick Gordon (Bonner); Geraldine Wall (Harriet Green); Harry Depp (Charles Edwards); Edward Earle (Dawson)

THE JADE MASK, *Monogram Pictures*, released January 1945

Produced by James S. Burkett; Director, Phil Rosen; Screenplay by George Callahan, based on the Charlie Chan character created by Earl Derr Biggers; Photography, Harry Neumann; Art director, Dave Milton; Music, Edward J. Kay; Assistant director, Eddie Davis; Editor, Richard Currier

Sidney Toler (Charlie Chan); Mantan Moreland (Birmingham); Hardie Albright (Meeker); Edith Evanson (Louise); Janet Warren (Jean); Edwin Luke (Tommy); Frank Reicher (Harper); Alan Bridge (Mack); Cyril Delevanti (Roth); Dorothy Granger (Stella); Jeo Whitehead (Peabody); and Ralph Lewis, Jack Ingram, Lester Dorr, Henry Hall

THE SCARLET CLUE, *Monogram Pictures*, released June 1945
Produced by James S. Burkett; Director, Phil Rosen; Screenplay by George Callahan, based on the Charlie Chan character created by Earl Derr Biggers; Photography, William Sickner; Art director, Dave Milton; Music, Edward J. Kay; Assistant director, Eddie Davis; Editor, Richard Currier

Sidney Toler (Charlie Chan); Mantan Moreland (Birmingham); Benson Fong (Tommy Chan); Helen Devereaux (Diane Hall); Robert Homans (Captain Flynn); Virginia Brissac (Mrs. Marsh); Reid Kilpatrick (Wilbur Chester); I. Stanford Jolley (Ralph Brett); Jack Norton (Willie Rand); Charles Sherlock (Sergeant McGraw); Janet Shaw (Gloria Bayne); Milt Kibbee (Herbert Sinclair); Ben Carter (Ben); Victoria Faust (Hulda Swenson); Charles Jordan (Nelson); Leonard Mudie (Horace Carlos); Kernan Cripps (Detective)

THE SHANGHAI COBRA, *Monogram Pictures*, released September 1945
Produced by James S. Burkett; Director, Phil Karlson; Screenplay by George Callahan and George Wallace Sayre, based on the Charlie Chan character created by Earl Derr Biggers; Photography, Vince Farrar; Music, Edward J. Kay; Assistant director, Eddie Davis; Editor, Ace Herman

Sidney Toler (Charlie Chan); Mantan Moreland (Birmingham); Benson Fong (Tommy Chan); Walter Fenner (Inspector Harry David); James Cardwell (Ned Stewart); Janet Warren (Lorraine); Addison Richards (John Adams/Jan Van Horn); Joan Barclay (Paula Webb); James Flavin (Jarvis); Arthur Loft (Bradford HarrisHume); Joe Devlin (Taylor); Roy Gordon (Walter Fletcher); Gene Stutenroth (Morgan)

THE RED DRAGON, *Monogram Pictures*, released December 1945
Produced by James S. Burkett; Director, Phil Rosen; Screenplay by George Callahan, based on the Charlie Chan character created by Earl Derr Biggers; Photography, Vincent Farrar; Art director, Dave Milton; Music, Edward J. Kay; Assistant director, Eddie Davis; Editor, Ace Herman

Sidney Toler (Charlie Chan); Fortunio Bonanova (Inspector Luis Carvero); Benson Fong (Tommy Chan); Willie Best (Chattanooga Brown); Robert E. Keane (Alfred Wyans); Carol Hughes (Marguerite Fontan); Marjorie Hoshelle (Countess Irena); George Meeker (Edmond Slade); Charles Trowbridge (Prentiss); Barton Yarborough (Joseph Bradish); Mildred Boyd (Josephine); Jean Wong (Iris Chan); Donald Dexter Taylor (Dorn); Don Costello (Charles Masack)

DARK ALIBI, *Monogram Pictures*, released May 1946
Produced by James S. Burkett; Director, Phil Karlson; Screenplay by George Callahan, based on the Charlie Chan character created by Earl Derr Biggers; Photography, William A. Sickner; Art director, Dave Milton; Music, Edward J. Kay; Editors, Richard Currier and Ace Herman

Sidney Toler (Charlie Chan); Mantan Moreland (Birmingham); Benson Fong (Tommy Chan); Teala Loring (June Harley); Edward Earle (Thomas Harley); Ben

Carter (Carter); George Holmes (Hugh Kenzie); Joyce Compton (Emily Evans); Janet Shaw (Miss Petrie); John Eldredge (Morgan); Edna Holland (Mrs. Foss); Ray Walker (Danvers); Russell Hicks (Warden Cameron); William Ruhl (Thompson); Milton Parsons (Johnson); Anthony Warde (Slade); Tim Ryan (Foggy); Frank Marlowe (Barker); George Eldredge (Brand)

SHADOWS OVER CHINATOWN, *Monogram Pictures*, released 1946
Produced by James S. Burkett; Director, Terry Morse; Screenplay by Raymond Schrock, based on the Charlie Chan character created by Earl Derr Biggers; Photography, William Sickner; Music, Edward J. Kay; Editor, Ralph Dixon

Sidney Toler (Charlie Chan); Mantan Moreland (Birmingham); Victor Sen Yung (Jimmy Chan); Tanis Chandler (Mary Conover); John Galaudet (Jeff Hay); Paul Bryar (Mike Rogan); Bruce Kellogg (Jack Tilford); Alan Bridge (Captain Allen); Mary Gordon (Mrs. Conover); Dorothy Granger (Joan Mercer); Jack Norton (Cosgrove); Charlie Jordan (Jenkins); John Hamilton (Bus Passenger); and George Eldredge, Lyle Latell, Myra McKinnon

DANGEROUS MONEY, *Monogram Pictures*, released 1946
Produced by James S. Burkett; Director, Terry Morse; Screenplay by Miriam Kissinger, based on the Charlie Chan character created by Earl Derr Biggers; Photography, William Sickner; Music, Edward J. Kay; Editor, William Austin

Sidney Toler (Charlie Chan); Victor Sen Yung (Jimmy Chan); Joseph Crehan (Captain Black); Willie Best (Chattanooga); Elaine Lange (Cynthia Martin); Dick Elliott (P. T. Burke); Amira Moustafa (Laura Erickson); Gloria Warren (Rona Simmonds); Joe Allen, Jr. (George Brace); Bruce Edwards (Harold Mayfair); Emmett Vogan (Professor Martin); John Harmon (Freddie Kirk); Alan Douglas (Whipple); Leslie Denison (Reverend Whipple); Dudley Dickerson (Big Ben); Tristram Coffin (Scott Pearson); Rito Punay (Pete); Selmer Jackson (Ship's Doctor); Rick Vallin (Tao Erickson)

THE TRAP, *Monogram Pictures*, released 1947
Produced by James S. Burkett; Director, Howard Bretherton; Screenplay by Miriam Kissinger, based on the Charlie Chan character created by Earl Derr Biggers; Photography, James Brown, Art director, Dave Milton; Music director, Edward J. Kay; Editors, Ace Herman and Richard Currier

Sidney Toler (Charlie Chan); Mantan Moreland (Birmingham); Victor Sen Yung (Tommy Chan); Tanis Chandler (Adelaide); Rita Quigley (Clementine); Helen Gerald (Ruby); Larry Blake (Rick Daniels); Kirk Alyn (Sergeant Reynolds); Lois Austin (Mrs. Thorn); Barbara Jean Wong (San Toy); Minerva Urecal (Mrs. Weebles); Margaret Brayton (Madge Mudge); Anne Nagel (Marcia); Bettie Best (Winifred); Jan Bryant (Lois); Walden Boyle (Doc Brandt); Howard Negley (Cole King)

THE CHINESE RING, *Monogram Pictures*, released December 1947
Produced by James S. Burkett; Director, William Beaudine; Screenplay by Scott Darling, based on the Charlie Chan character created by Earl Derr Biggers; Photography, William Sickner; Music, Edward J. Kay; Editors, Ace Herman and Richard Heermance

Roland Winters (Charlie Chan); Mantan Moreland (Birmingham); Victor Sen Yung (Tommy Chan); Warren Douglas (Sergeant Davidson); Byron Foulger (Armstrong); Louise Currie (Peggy Cartwright); Philip Ahn (Captain King);

Thayer Roberts (Captain Kelso); Paul Bryar (Sergeant); Charmienne Harker (Stenographer); Jean Wong (Princess Mei Ling); Chabing (Lilly Mae); and George L. Spaulding, Thornton Edwards, Lee Tung Foo; Richard Wang, Spencer Chan, Kenneth Church

THE DOCKS OF NEW ORLEANS, Monogram Pictures, April 1948
Produced by James S. Burkett; Director, Derwin Abrahams; Screenplay by W. Scott Darling, based on the Charlie Chan character created by Earl Derr Biggers; Photography, William Sickner; Music, Edward J. Kay; Editors, Ace Herman and Otho Lovering

Roland Winters (Charlie Chan); Mantan Moreland (Birmingham); Victor Sen Yung (Tommy Chan); Virginia Dale (Rene); John Gallaudet (Captain McNally); Carol Forman (Nita Aguirre); Douglas Fowley (Grock); Harry Hayden (Swendstrom); Howard Negley (Pereaux); Stanley Andrews (Von Scherbe); Emmett Vogan (Henri Castanaro); Boyd Irwin (La Fontaine); Rory Mallinson (Thompson); George J. Lewis (Dansiger); and, Diane Fauntelle, Ferris Taylor, Haywood Jones, Eric Wilson, Paul Conrad, Wally Walker, Frank Stephens, Fred Miller

THE SHANGHAI CHEST, Monogram Pictures, released July 1948
Produced by James S. Burkett; Director, William Beaudine; Screenplay by W. Scott Darling and Sam Newman, based on the Charlie Chan character created by Earl Derr Biggers; Photography, William Sickner; Music, Edward J. Kay; Editor, Ace Herman

Roland Winters (Charlie Chan); Mantan Moreland (Birmingham); Victor Sen Yung (Tommy Chan); Tim Ryan (Lieutenant Ruark); Deannie Best (Phyllis); Tristram Coffin (Ed Seward); John Alvin (Vic Armstrong); Russell Hicks (District Attorney Bronson); Pierre Watkin (Judge Armstrong); Philip Van Zandt (Tony Pindello); Milton Parsons (Mr. Grail); Erville Alderson (Walter Somerville); Olaf Hytten (Bates); George Eldredge (Finley); Louis Mason (Custodian); Willie Best (Willie); David Hoffman (Graves); Bill Woolf (Juror); and Edward Coke, Charlie Sullivan, Paul Scardon, William Ruhl, Lois Austin, John Shay

THE MYSTERY OF THE GOLDEN EYE, Monogram Pictures, released August 1948
Produced by James S. Burkett; Director, William Beaudine; Screenplay by W. Scott Darling, based on the Charlie Chan character created by Earl Derr Biggers; Photography, William Sickner; Music, Edward J. Kay; Editors, Ace Herman and Otho Lovering

Roland Winters (Charlie Chan); Mantan Moreland (Birmingham); Victor Sen Yung (Tommy Chan); Wanda McKay (Evelyn); Evelyn Brent (Teresa); Bruce Kellogg (Bartlett); Lois Austin (Mrs. Driscoll); Tim Ryan (Lieutenant Ruark); Ralph Dunn (Driscoll); Forrest Taylor (Manning); Lee "Lasses" White (Pete); Edmund Cobb (Miner); and Tom Tyler, John Merton, George L. Spaulding, Barbara Jean Wong, Richard Loo, Lee Tung Foo, Bill Walker, Herman Cantor

THE FEATHERED SERPENT, Monogram Pictures, released December 1948
Produced by James S. Burkett; Director, William Beaudine; Screenplay by Oliver Drake, based on the Charlie Chan character created by Earl Derr Biggers; Photography, William Sickner; Music, Edward J. Kay; Editor, Otho Lovering

Roland Winters (Charlie Chan); Mantan Moreland (Birmingham); Keye Luke (Lee Chan); Victor Sen Yung (Tommy Chan); Robert Livingston (John Stanley); Nils Asther (Professor Paul Evans); Jay Silverheels (Diego); Martin Garralaga

(Pedro); Carol Forman (Sonia Cabot); George J. Lewis (Captain Juan); Leslie Dennison (Professor Farnsworth); Beverly Jons (Joan Farnsworth)

SKY DRAGON, *Monogram Pictures*, released May 1949
Produced by James S. Burkett; Director, Lesley Selander; Screenplay by Clint Johnstone and Oliver Drake, based on the Charlie Chan character created by Earl Derr Biggers; Photography, William Sickner; Music, Edward J. Kay; Editors, Otho Lovering and Roy Livingston (Working title: *Murder in the Air*)

Roland Winters (Charlie Chan); Mantan Moreland (Birmingham); Keye Luke (Lee Chan); Noel Neill (Jane Marshall); Tim Ryan (Lieutenant Ruark); Iris Adrian (Wanda LaFern); Elena Verdugo (Marie Burke); Lyle Talbot (Andy Barrett); Milburn Stone (Tim Norton); Paul Maxey (John Anderson); John Eldredge (William French); Joel Marston (Don Blake); Eddie Parks (Mr. Tibbets); Louise Franklin (Lena); Lyle Latell (Ed Davidson); Bob Curtis (Watkins); and Gaylord Pendleton, Emmett Vogan, Edna Holland, Lee Phelps, Frank Cady, Charles Jordan, Suzette Harbin, Joe Whitehead

CHARLIE CHAN AND THE CURSE OF THE DRAGON QUEEN, *United Artists* released February 1980
Produced by American Cinema Productions and Jerry Sherlock Productions; Executive producers, Michael Leone and Alan Belkin; Producer, Jerry Sherlock; Director, Clive Donner; Screenplay by Stan Burns and David Axelrod, based on the character created by Earl Derr Biggers, and a story by Jerry Sherlock; Photography, Paul Lohmann; 2nd unit photography, Ed Koons; Production designer, Joel Schiller; Special effects, Gene Crigg, Mike Wood and Sam Price; Music, Patrick Williams; Orchestrations, Herbert Spencer and Arthur Morton; Dance Coordinator, Jill Okura; Costumes, Jocelyn Rickards (Men); David McGough (Women); Makeup, Charles Schram, Fred Williams and Gene Bartlett; Stunt coordinator, Richard Washington; Editors, Walt Hannemann and Phil Tucker

Peter Ustinov (Charlie Chan); Lee Grant (Mrs. Lupowitz); Angie Dickinson (Dragon Queen); Richard Hatch (Lee Chan, Jr.); Brian Keith (Police Chief); Roddy McDowall (Gillespie); Rachel Roberts (Mrs. Dangers); Michelle Pfeiffer (Cordelia); Paul Ryan (Masten); Johnny Sekka (Stefan); Bennett Ohta (Hawaiian Chief of Police); David Hirokane (Lee Chan, Sr.); Karlene Crockett (Brenda Lupowitz); Michael Fairman (Bernard Lupowitz); James Ray (Haynes); Momo Yashima (Dr. Yu Sing); Alison Hong (Maysie Ling); Duane Tucker (Cocktail Waiter); Pavla Ustinov (Cherie); Trevor Hook (Colonel Blass); Paul Sanderson (Mr. Finnegan); Molly Roden (Lady Rodeworthy); Kael Blackwood, Jerry Loo (Medical Assistants); Laurence Cohen, Robin Hoff, Kathie Kei, James Bacon (Reporters at Clinic); Frank Michael Liu (Homicide Detective); John Hugh, George Chiang, David Chow (Shopkeepers); Dewi Yee (TV Interviewer); Joe Bellan, Garrick Huey (Reporters at Pier); Don Parker (Hotel Manager); Kai Wong (Murdered Messenger); John Fox, Kenneth Snell, Nicholas Gunn, Din Murray (Pimps); Gerald Okamura (Bouncer); Lonny Carbajal (Spacedout Dancer); Miya (Club Shanghai Hostess); Peter Michas (Dragon Queen's Chauffeur); Vic Hunsberger (Traffic Cop); Larry Duran (Man Getting Traffic Ticket); Kay Kimler (Riding Instructor); Jim Winburn (Beach Cop); Tony Brubaker, Chuck Hayward, Bear Hudkins, Rock Walker (Hansom Drivers); Beth Beardsley, Sheryl Brown, Jeannie Epper, Stephanie Epper, Carrie Salazar, Sammy Thurman, Sunny Woods (Saddled Riders); Jade David, Angelo Lamonea, Bob Minor, Bob Orrison, Joe Stone (Bareback Riders); Robert Black, Bob Baiver, Vince

Cadiente, Allison Klokman, Tom Orga, Tom Rosales (Reporters at Pier); Greg Elam, Nancie Kawata, Henry Kingi, Faith Minton, Sharon Schaeffer, Peter Stader, Mike Vendrell (Tourists); Ken Denoso, Bill Ryasaki, Bill Saito, Leland Dun (Shopkeepers); Davi Caliente, Rosemary Johnston, Reg Parton, Mary Peters, George Sawaya (Elevator Sequence)

MURDER BY DEATH, *Columbia Pictures*, released June 1976
A Rastar Production; Produced by Ray Stark; Director, Robert Moore; Associate producer, Roger M. Rothstein; Screenplay, Neil Simon; Photography, David M. Walsh; Production designer, Stephen Grimes; Music, Dave Grusin; Costumes, Ann Roth; Editor, Margaret Booth

Peter Sellers (Sidney Wang); David Niven (Dick Charleston); Maggie Smith (Dora Charleston); Eileen Brennan (Tess Skeffington); Truman Capote (Lionel Twain); James Coco (Milo Perier); Peter Falk (Sam Diamond); Elsa Lanchester (Jessica Marbles); Nancy Walker (Yetta); Estelle Winwood (Miss Withers); Richard Narita (Willie Wang); James Cromwell (Marcel); Alec Guinness (Bensonmum)

Neil Simon's original movie spoof of various famous fictional detectives in *Murder by Death* included Peter Sellers' impersonation of Charlie Chan under the character name of Sidney Wang

TELEVISION

THE NEW ADVENTURES OF CHARLIE CHAN, televised 1957-58 Syndicated 39 episodes 30 minutes each
A Lew Grade Production; Executive producer, Leon Fromkess; Producers, Rudolph Flathow, Sidney Marshall; Directors, Alvin Rakoff, Leslie Goodman, Don Chaffey; Based on the characters created by Earl Derr Biggers

J. Carrol Naish (Charlie Chan); James Hong (Barry Chan, Number One Son); Hugh Williams (Inspector Carl Marlowe); Rupert Davies (Inspector Duff)

THE AMAZING CHAN AND THE CHAN CLAN, televised September 9, 1972 to September 22, 1974 CBS 30 minutes each Animated cartoon
Executive producers, William Hanna and Joseph Barbera; Producer, Alex Lovy; Directors, Hanna and Barbera; Animation director, Charles Nichols; Music, Hoyt Curtis

Voices: Keye Luke (Charlie Chan); Robert Ito (Henry Chan); Stephen Wong, Lennie Weinrib (Stanley Chan); Virginia Ann Lee, Cherylene Lee (Suzie Chan); Brian Tochi (Alan Chan); Leslie Kumamoto, Jodie Foster (Anne Chan); Michael Takamoto, John Gunn (Tom Chan); Jay Jay Jue, Gene Andrusco (Flip Chan); Debbie Je, Beverly Kushida (Nancy Chan); Leslie Kawai, Cherylene Lee (Mimi Chan); Robin Toma, Michael Morgan (Scooter Chan); Don Messick (Chu Chu, the Clan Dog); Additional voices: Lisa Gerritsen, Hazel Shermit, Janet Waldo, Len Wood

HAPPINESS IS A WARM CLUE, televised BBC, England, July 1973; televised in U.S. as *THE RETURN OF CHARLIE CHAN*, July 17, 1979 ABC 2 hours
Produced by Universal Television; Executive Producer, John J. Cole; Producer, Jack Laird; Director, Daryl Duke; Teleplay by Gene Kearney from a story by Simon Last and Gene Kearney, based on the Charlie Chan character created by Earl Derr

Biggers; Photography, Richard C. Glouner; Art director, Frank Arrigo; Music, Robert Prince; Editor, Frank Morriss

Ross Martin (Charlie Chan); Richard Haydn (Andrew Kidder); Louise Sorel (Ariane Hadrachi); Kathleen Widdoes (Irene Hadrachi); Joseph Hindy (Paul Hadrachi); Peter Donat (Noel Adamson); Don Gordon (Lambert); Leslie Nielsen (Alexander Hadrachi); Rocky Gunn (Peter Chan); Virginia Lee (Doreen Chan); Soon Teck-Oh (Stephen Chan); Ernest Harada (Oliver Chan); Pearl Hong (Jan Chan); Adele Yoshioda (Mai-Ling Chan); William Nunn (Fielding); Pat Gage (Sylvia Grombach); Ted Greenhalgh (Dr. Howard Jamison); Graham Campbell (Inspector McKenzie); Neil Dainard (Richard Lovell); John Guiliani (Giancarlo Tui); Otto Lowy (Anton Grombach)

CHRISTOPHER COLUMBUS

Various dramatizations of the life of Christopher Columbus (1451-1506)

Synopsis

Christopher Columbus (or Colombo, or Colon, or Coullon depending on Christopher's varying self-proclaimed ancestry) of Genoa, Italy, was a soft-goods salesman who dreamed of a Western route to the West Indies despite a lack of expertise in navigation, exploration or seamanship. In 1482, Columbus sought financial support from King John II of Portugal who rejected the Genoan's plan but secretly sent a Portuguese ship to sail the proposed route. The Portuguese sailors lost heart and courage, ridiculed Columbus' project and returned to Lisbon. In 1485, a year after the death of his wife, Filepa Moniz Perestrello, Columbus was befriended by the Franciscan monks of the Spanish Palos monastery, La Rabida. The abbe of the monastery, Juan Perez de Marchena, with the aid of the Duke of Medina Celi, persuaded King Ferdinand and Queen Isabella to support Columbus' expedition. Leaving his young son, Diego, with the Franciscan monks and his mistress Beatriz Enriquez de Arana with their illegitimate son, Ferdinand, Columbus sailed for the West Indies on August 4, 1492, from Palos with three small ships, the Nina, the Pinta and the Santa Maria, supplied by experienced seamen, the Pinzon brothers, and manned by 121 hands.

Overcoming the fear and anxiety of his crew, self-appointed Admiral Columbus, believing he had reached China, arrived on October 12 on an island he named San Salvador. Later, he discovered the islands of Cuba and San Domingo where be began a colony called Hispaniola. Columbus returned to Spain on March 15, 1493, to great acclaim. With financing by the Duke of Medina and Queen Isabella's profit from the confiscated property of 1,700,000 Jews she had banished from Spain, a second Columbus expedition included seventeen ships and 1500 men and sailed from Cadiz in September. The Caribee Islands and Jamaica were discovered for Spain. In 1498, Columbus sailed for a third time, discovering Trinidad and the tip of South America. Returning to Hispaniola, Columbus found that miserly King Ferdinand had sent Francesco de Bobadilla to supersede him. A victim of political intrigue, Columbus was brought back to Spain in chains. Despite his disgrace, Columbus sailed on his fourth and last voyage, leaving Cadiz on May 11, 1502, with four ships and 150 men, seeking a passage he believed existed between the Atlantic and Pacific Oceans. His crews mutinied and he reluctantly returned to Spain. Queen Isabella died soon after his return and Ferdinand refused to further sponsor his explorations. Columbus died in poverty on May 20, 1506, at Valladolid, Spain.

Comment and Critique

Early dramatizations based on the life and adventures of Christopher Columbus included John Marston's 1599 drama, *Columbus*; Thomas Morton's *Columbus; or, A World Discovered*, written in 1792, and *Columbus; or, The Original Pitch in a Merry Key* by Elfred Thompson, which was performed at London's Gaiety Theatre on May 17, 1869. In France, Gilbert de Pixerecourt's play, *Christophe Colomb*, was produced.

Columbus became a favorite hero for many operas. Among the first were Cardinal Ottoboni's *Colombo*, written about 1650, and *Il Colombo* by Fabrizzi in 1765. Other operas based on the life of Columbus are listed later in this text.

Dublin-born comedian-playwright, John Brougham, made his American stage debut in 1842 and, according to Joseph Jefferson, "always acted a part as though it were a joke." Years later, twentieth-century author Richard Moody described Brougham as "a mid-nineteenth century combination of W. C. Fields and George S. Kaufman." On December 30, 1857, Brougham's burlesque, *Columbus Filibuster*, opened at Burton's Theatre with the author portraying Christopher Columbus. The Brougham farce, ambiguously subtitled, "The legendary romance of the French Captain and the Maid of Mobile" was, according to historian George Odell, "put on with excellent scenery...[and] had a soul-satisfying run."

On July 28, 1858, Otto Hoym produced and starred in Linkgemann's German-language play, *Columbus*, at his New York theatre. John Brougham revised his 1857 burlesque as *Columbus Reconstructed* and again played the leading role at the Winter Garden Theatre beginning July 9, 1886.

Tullio Carminati, later to find Broadway success as composer Bruno Mahler in Jerome Kern and Oscar Hammerstein II's 1932 musical, *Music in the Air*, starred in a seven performance Hawthorne Hurst comedy, *Christopher Comes Across*, at the Royale Theatre beginning in late May 1932. Brock Pemberton, who had presented Preston Sturges' 1929 Broadway hit, *Strictly Dishonorable* (in which Carminati had starred), produced the Hurst comedy which he codirected with Antoinette Perry.

"It is Hawthorne Hurst's whim to conceive of Columbus as a professional palace philanderer in *Christo-pher Comes Across*," reported J. Brooks Atkinson (*The New York Times*). "Brock Pemberton has given his author the encouragement of a mettlesome troupe of actors, brilliant costumes and medieval settings of solid charm by Dale Stetson. But Mr. Hurst's piquant whim and Mr. Pemberton's craftsmanlike encouragement are prodigally wasted. For *Christopher Comes Across* is only an obvious prank that mistakes a commonplace leer for skimming humor...Writing a costume play in the modern vernacular, Mr. Hurst represents the court of Ferdinand in terms of modern graft and vices...But this sort of costume travesty requires more inventive humor and fleeting wit than Mr. Hurst has at this command, and a keener relish of the historical characters he is winking at...As Columbus, the insinuating Tullio Carminati plays exclusively in the key of Gallic wiles; he is singularly lacking in humor in a farce that attempts nothing else."

Robert Garland (New York *WorldTelegram*) added, "With small attempt at subtlety and in the spirit of good unclean fun, the new arrival at the Royale performs a Lou Holtz on that old so-and-so Columbus... The piece is *Christopher Comes Across* and Hawthorne Hurst, the author, refers to it as farce-comedy. Farce it certainly is, with the Court Scandaler predicting blessed events with the assistance of a keyhold, King Ferdinand getting his Queen a new pair of shoes with the assistance of yet galloping dominoes, and the great explorer himself acquiring his ships and sailors with a little bit of 'it' and a good deal of Isabella." Garland felt that "Anyway, the fault wasn't entirely Mr. Hurst's. Miscasting had something to do with it. Miscasting that misused such excellent actors as Ernest Lawford and Charles Brown and asked Tullio Carminati to stop singing and look sexy. In *Christopher Comes Across* and the tights provided by the Brooks Costume Company, [Carminati] is scarcely the combination of Clark Gable, Casanova and Commander Byrd the text demands...Brock Pemberton has given it a tasteful production...As you've gathered, Mr. Carminati is not altogether in his element as God's and Italy's gift to Queen Isabella."

Paul Claudel's French play *Christophe Colomb* was presented in England and America by Sol Hurok under the auspices of the Government of the French Republic and produced by the Compagnie Madeleine Renaud/Jean-Louis Barrault in 1956 and 1957. The Renaud-Barrault Repertory Company included *Christophe Colomb* in its repertoire of eight plays presented at Broadway's Winter Garden Theatre on January 30, 1957. (An American production of *Christophe Colomb* would not happen for another thirty-five years, at the Brooklyn College Opera Theater, on the eve of the Columbus quincentenary.)

Herbert L. Matthews *(The New York Times)* called *Christophe Colomb* "a piece of theatrical magic by the late Paul Claudel...It is not a play to like or dislike; in fact, it is not a play at all. It is a poem, a pageant, a series of tableaus, accompanied by music written by the French composer Darius Milhaud -- and it is very beautiful music. There is a ballet. There is even a movie screen in the back, always distorted by the sail of Columbus' ship, which is the one prop on the stage." The *Times* critic decided that "The plot is nothing but a series of episodes in the great and tragic life of the man who was the most colossal failure and the greatest discovery in the history of the world...The part of Columbus is not one to bring out M. Barrault's best gifts as an actor, but the play does show his genius as a director...Everything is unusual about *Christophe Colomb* and, most certainly, it is a remarkable theatrical experience."

American playwright Richard Nelson's imaginative *Columbus and the Discovery of Japan* had its initial staging in the Royal Shakespeare Company's production at the Barbican Theatre in London in the summer of 1992. "His Columbus is recognizably by the man who created *Two Shakespearean Actors* and *Some Americans Abroad*, other plays given their first outings by the Royal Shakespeare Company," critic Benedict Nightingale wrote in *The London Times*. "A wry, watchful intelligence is always evident, but energy and momentum are mostly missing...[Jonathan Hyde's] is a Columbus who talks seldom about 'ambition and need' and shows those qualities even less frequently. Hyde fidgets about, gesticulating, scratching himself, and exuding insecurity; but he lacks drive and charisma."

In 1923, the Yale University Press produced a chronicle of *Columbus* for the silent screen featuring Fred Eric as the explorer. In 1949, England's Gainsborough Pictures produced a lavish but slowmoving screen version, *Christopher Columbus*, starring Fredric March. *The Motion Picture Herald* found that "the film, in beautiful Technicolor, is most elaborately mounted -- granted that a film biography of such a famous man is difficult to make, the story of Christopher Columbus as a motion picture should have turned out better. Hardly anyone would expect to see almost two-third's of the film devoted to court scenes. An hour of running time passes before a ship is seen..."

Universal-International released *Christopher Columbus* in the United States and Bosley Crowther (*The New York Times*) noted in his review, "This film embraces the legend of Columbus with more solemn respect than passionate zeal. Full of elaborate tableaux of the fifteenth century Spanish court, of costumes gentlemen and ladies, of swarthy sailors and ships, this Technicolored chronicle of Columbus' discovery of the New World gives large pictorial illustration to everything but the man himself...is largely an uninspired succession of legendary but lifeless episodes, of tableaux consecrated by history with a few fictional fancies thrown in. And the only positive characteristic with which Columbus himself is endowed is a rugged determination to prove that the world is round. As Fredric March performs him, this urge is made eminently plain in his piercing eye and firm demeanor. But that's about all he reveals. Likewise, Queen Isabella, as played by Florence Eldridge (Mrs. March), is a rigid representation of the legendary queen...The costumes, however, are authentic, the palace scenes are lush and the sailing ships of Columbus are colorfully reproduced."

Time saw the picture as turning "an exciting bit of history into a series of dull tableaux in antiqued color. Even 10-year-olds, at whom this British-made movie is plainly aimed, will find it about as thrilling as an afternoon spent looking at Christmas cards." *The New Yorker*'s appraisal was: "The scriptwriters have managed to transform some fine historical material into a film about as stimulating as a trip through the Hudson tubes...As Columbus, Fredric March is about the most dour mariner I've ever laid eyes on, and as Queen Isabella, Florence Eldridge seems a bit less lively than Her Majesty was reported to have been. Francis L. Sullivan is the expansive villain, but even his impressive talents are pretty well lost in this over-stuffed picture."

No other Columbus came to the screen (except for a cameo by Anthony Dexter in the 1957 *The Story of Mankind*) until the quincentenary celebration in 1992 of his voyage to the New World. Three films then were forthcoming -- one British spoof and two very expensive international productions that were found quite wanting. First there was the campy *Carry On Columbus*, the thirtieth entry in the "Carry On" series dating back to 1958 (and the first in fourteen years), with Jim Dale as a freewheeling Christopher Columbus. This was followed by a pair of competing multimilliondollar spectaculars.

From Alexander and Ilya Salkind (the men behind the *Superman* movies) came *Christopher Columbus: The Discovery*, a box-office disaster that billed cameo players Marlon Brando as Torquemada and Tom Selleck as King Ferdinand above the title and buried "unknown" French actor George Corraface, starring as Columbus, below. Brando, in fact, commanded $10 million for his eight-minute-or-so part and wanted his name taken off the credits in protest against the script's treatment of Indians. "Surprisingly little is known about Columbus and his life," Vincent Canby wrote in *The New York Times*. "Yet the filmmakers' imaginations seem to have fallen over the edge." Canby found this Columbus movie "expensive, sloppy and, at its most ambitious, a frail reminder of the Warner Brothers swashbucklers that Michael Curtiz used to turn out with Errol Flynn...The film preserves, but never enlivens, all those gestures so dear to old-time Hollywood costumes dramas: people sweeping into and out of throne rooms, kissing royal rings and unrolling parchments that are of more interest to them than to us" Britain's *Sight and Sound* concluded: "Regularly punctuated with bursts of over-orchestrated music, *Christopher Columbus: The Discovery* is bereft of historical curiosity, and is of no more interest as a genre film."

The "other" Columbus movie of 1992, titled *1492: Conquest of Paradise*, starred French matinee idol Gerard Depardieu and received a slightly better reception at the box office, although the critics weren't that much kinder. *Variety* felt that "All of [director] Ridley Scott's vaunted visuals can't transform [it] from a lumbering, one-dimensional historical fresco in-to a complex, ambiguous character study that it strives to be...As for Depardieu's Columbus, the great French actor does his best to get his mouth around the long speeches and harangues, and is comprehensible most of the time." Critic Roger Ebert, one of the few generally favorably inclined toward this version, found that "*1492* is a satisfactory film. Depardieu lends it gravity, the supporting performances are convincing, the locations are realistic, and we are inspired to reflect that it did indeed take nerve to sail off into nowhere just because an orange was round."

A six-hour TV miniseries, *Christopher Columbus*, was produced by Italy's RAI-Televisione in association with America's Lorimar Productions in 1985. The $15 million production of *Christopher Columbus* was filmed in twenty-six weeks with another six months of post- production in London and Rome, where the musical score was added.

"*Christopher Columbus*," reported Richard F. Shepard (*The New York Times*), "was made in Malta, Spain and the Dominican Republic, and it is a splashy production both in the literal sense of its storms at sea and in the flamboyant context of colorful scenes such as the triumphant return of Columbus from his discovery, a reception in Granada that in the mini-series required a thousand extras a day for five days in the making. The casting is in the think-big Cecil B. DeMille tradition: 46 major roles, 82 minor ones, more than 200 speaking parts by actors from 10 different countries, some of them ignorant of English except for the ability to make the sounds of it as written in the script...Gabriel Byrne portrays Columbus. His star support, whose roles are important and certainly not cameos, includes Nicol Williamson and Faye Dunaway (the Spanish King and Queen), Virna Lisa, Eli Wallach, Rossano Brazzi, Oliver Reed, Raf Valone and Max Von Sydow. The director is Alberto Lattuada...Although even historians disagree on much about Columbus, the mini-series tried for historical accuracy."

A documentary on Christopher Columbus was produced for television in 1956 by John Haldi and directed by Carl Papai. Chet Long and Don Riggs did the commentary including an interview with Admiral Samuel Eliot More-son, author of the Pulitzer Prize-winning biography *Admiral of the Ocean Sea*. A widely-heralded seven-part Columbus documentary, filmed in twenty-seven countries, was telecast on PBS in October 1991. "A rich, rambling $5 million documentary," is how *Variety* described it, "a coffee-table look at the Admiral of the Ocean Sea without plumbing much depth. Handsome, timely [and] expansive, the program sails on and on -- and on." Walter Goodman (*The New York Times*) found that "it is at times more like a ceremonial journey than a voyage of discovery. It puts in at all the obligatory ports but often the winds of imagination fail and the program finds itself becalmed in colorful settings."

STAGE

COLUMBUS FILIBUSTERO, *Burton's Theatre*, New York, opened December 30, 1857

Produced and directed by William Burton; A play, based on the adventures of Christopher Columbus

John Brougham (Christopher Columbus); Mark Smith (King Ferdinand); Mrs. George Holman (Queen Isabella); Lawrence Barrett (Talavera); George Holman (de Fonesca); Mr. Gledhill (Alonzo de Quintenella); Josephine Orton (Diego); Mrs. L. W. Davenport (Columbia); Miss Taylor (Little Kansas); Arthur Alleyn (Luis St. Angel)

COLUMBUS, *Hoym's Theatre*, New York, opened July 28, 1858
A Play for Herr Linkgemann

Edward Furst (Christopher Columbus); Elise Hoym (Queen Isabella); Herr Scherer (Bovadella); D. E. Bandmann (Diego); Otto Hoym (Matnei)

COLUMBUS; OR, THE DISCOVERY OF AMERICA, *Touring Company*, season 1862-63
A Play by Barton Hill, adapted from the French play by M. Mestepes and E. Barre; Director, E. L. Davenport; Original Music by Mr. Cunnington

Edward L. Davenport (Christopher Columbus); Mrs. E. L. Davenport (Queen Isabella); J. S. Wright (Diego Columbus); B. Young (Don Luis de Fonseca); H. Bascomb (Bartholomew Columbus); E. N. Thayer (Don Escobar); Miss Perry (Pellegrino); E. I. Tilton (Roldan); G. Johnson (Maschera); S. Barth (Francisco); S. H. Verney (Caiman); J. E. Whiting (Antonio); J. Porter (Captain); J. Reed (Citizen); S. Brown (Pedro); Mr. Matthews (Herald); Miss Crowell (Donna Maria de Guzman); Miss Johnson (Onea, Queen of Hayti); Miss West (Una); Miss Peters (Nun)

COLUMBUS RECONSTRUCTED, *Winter Garden Theatre*, New York, opened July 9, 1866
A Burlesque, produced, directed and written by John Brougham

John Brougham (Christopher Columbus); James Dunn (King Ferdinand); E. Andrews (Queen Isabella); Miss Johnson (Diego Columbus); Emilie Melville (Colmbiz, Goddess of America)

CHRISTOPHER COMES ACROSS, *Royale Theatre*, New York, opened May 31, 1932 7 performances
Produced by Brock Pemberton; A Comedy by Hawthorne Hurst; Directors, Antoinette Perry and Brock Pemberton; Settings, Dale Stetson

Tullio Carminati (Captain Christopher Columbus); Patricia Calvert (Queen Isabella of Spain); Walter Kingsford (King Ferdinand of Spain); Fania Marinoff (Beatriz, Marchioness of Moya); Ernest Lawford (Don Alfonso); Gregory Gaye (Prince Otar of Homamb); Kirby Hawkes (Duke of Medinia Sedonia); Patrick Glasgow (Isadoro); Gilda Oakleaf (Zita); Charles Brown (The Marquis of Moya); Irene Homer (Lady in Waiting); Hamilton Brooks (Don Sebastian de Corazilla); Betty Lawrence (Dolores De Arana); Gilbert Douglas (Hernando De Arana); Clarence Redd (A Porter); John Gilchrist (A Sentry)

CHRISTOPHE COLOMB, *Palace Theatre*, London, opened November 19, 1956
Presented by Sol Hurok under the auspices of the Government of the French Republic; Produced by the Compagnie Madeleine Renaud/Jean-Louis Barrault; A Play by Paul Claudel; Director, Jean-Louis Barrault; Decor and Costumes by Max Ingrand and Marie-Helene Daste; Photography, Michael Boyer; Music by Darius Milhaud; Orchestra and Chorus under the direction of Pierre Boulez

Jean-Louis Barrault (Christopher Columbus of the Drama); Regis Outin (Christopher Columbus of the Legend); Madeleine Renaud (Isabelle the Catholic); Natalie Nerval (Wife of Christopher Columbus); Marie-Helene Daste (Mother of Christopher Columbus); Francoise Golea (Sister of Christopher Columbus); Jean Juillard (King of Spain/Cook/Wise Man/Major-domo/Officer); Francoise Ledoux (A Woman of the People); Pierre Bertin (The Exponent); Jean Desailly (The Defender); Jean-Pierre Granval (The Opponent); Beauchamp (The

Inn-Keeper/ Old Sailor/ Creditor/ Delegate/Wise Man); Georges Cusin (Court Dignitary); Gabriel Cattand (Friend/ Guitarist); Dominique Rozan (Commander/ Guitarist); Gerard Dournel (Quadrille/ Tialoc/ Sailor); Jacques Galland (Sailor/ Creditor/ Father of Christopher Columbus/ Dignitary); Andre John (Wise Man/ Sailor); Rene Lanier (A Bourgeois); Andre Batisse, Jean Lancelot, Emile Noel, Serge Merlin (Servants and Dancers)

NOTE: This production opened at New York's *Winter Garden Theatre*, January 30, 1957 6 performances

COLUMBUS AND THE DISCOVERY OF JAPAN, *Barbican Theatre*, London, opened July 22, 1992

Presented by the Royal Shakespeare Company; A Play in three ascts by Richard Nelson; Director, John Caird; Sets, Timothy O'Brien; Lighting, David Hersey; Costumes, Jenny Jones; Music, Shaun Davey

Jonathan Hyde (Christopher Columbus); Jane Gurnett (Beatrice); Simon Magnus or Luke Nugent (Diego); Christopher Benjamin (Martin Pinzon); Philip Voss (Rodrigo Pulgar); Bernard Gallagher (Miguel Garcia); Michael Poole (Pero de Soria); Michael Higgs (Juan de la Enzina); Christopher Luscombe (Pedro de Terreros); Don Gallagher (Vincente); Tim Hudson (Francisco); Helen Batch (Felipa); Terence Wilton (Fr. Juan Perez); Christopher Saul (Christobal Quinteros); Howard Crossley (Juan Ninos); David Hirrell (Luis de Torres); Albie Woodington (Juan Sanchez); Robert Demeger (Diego de Harana); Daniel Robson or Robbie Gill (Cabin Boy); and Constance Byrne, Oliver Darley, Ian Hartley, Andrew McDonald, Stephen Moyer, Nick Simons, Biddy Wells

THE VOYAGE, *Metropolitan Opera House*, New York, opened October 12, 1992 6 performances (in repertory through October 31)

An Opera in three acts, a prelude and an epilogue by Philip Glass; Libretoo by David Henry Hwang; Story by Glass; Production, David Puntney; Conductor, Bruce Ferden; Set design, Robert Israel; Costumes, Dunya Ramicova; Lighting, Gil Wechsler; Choreography, Quinny Sacks

Timothy Noble (Columbus); Tatiana Troyanos (Isabella); Patricia Schumann (Commander); Douglas Perry (Scientist/First Mate); Kaaren Erickson (Ship's Doctor/Space Twin 1); Julien Robbins (Second Mate/Space Twin 2); Jane Shaulis, Jan Opalach (Earth Twins)

SCREEN

COLUMBUS, *Pathe Exchange*, released October 1923

A Chronicle of America Series Production; Produced by Yale University Press; Director, Edwin L. Hollywood; Screenplay and adaptation by Arthur E. Krows based on *The Spanish Conquerors: A Chronicle of Empire Overseas* by Irving Berdine Richman

Fred Eric (Christopher Columbus); Dolores Cassinelli (Queen Isabella); Robert Gaillard (King Ferdinand); Paul McAllister (King John II of Portugal); Howard Truesdell (The Bishop of Ceuta); Leslie Stowe (Juan Perez, Prior of La Rabida)

CHRISTOPHER COLUMBUS, *Universal-International Pictures*, released June 1949 (England) and October 1949 (U.S.)

A Sydney Box Production/A Gainsborough Picture; Presented by J. Arthur Rank; Producer, A. Frank Bundy; Director, David Macdonald; Screenplay, Cyril Roberts,

Muriel and Sydney Box; Photography, Stephen Dade, David Harcourt; Music, Arthur Bliss; Editor, V. Sagovsky

Fredric March (Christopher Columbus); Florence Eldridge (Queen Isabella); Francis Lister (King Ferdinand); Francis L. Sullivan (Francisco de Bobadilla); Derek Bond (Diego de Aranas); Kathleen Ryan (Beatriz); Nora Swinburne (Joanna de Torres); Abraham Sofaer (Luis de Santangel); James Robertson Justice (Martin Pinzon); Linden Travers (Beatriz de Peraza); Dennis Price (Francesco Pinzon); Richard Aherne (Vincente Pinzon); Felix Aylmer (Father Perez); Edward Rigby (Pedro); Niall MacGinnis (Juan de la Cosa); Ralph Truman (Captain); David Cole (Columbus' Son)

CARRY ON COLUMBUS, *Island World*, released July 1992

An Island World production and Comedy House production in association with Peter Rogers Productions; Executive producers, Peter Rogers and Audrey Skinner; Producer, John Goldstone; Director, Gerald Thomas; Screenplay, Dave Freeman; Photography, Alan Hume; Production designer, Harry Pottle; Costume design, Phoebe de Gaye; Music, John Du Prez; Title song, Malcolm McLaren and Lee Gorman, performed by Jayne Collins and Debbie Holmes; Editor, Chris Blunden

Jim Dale (Christopher Columbus); Peter Richardson (Bart); Sara Crowe (Fatima); Bernard Cribbins (Mordecai Mendoza); Julian Clary (Diego); Richard Wilson (Don Felipe); Leslie Phillips (King Ferdinand); June Whitfield (Queen Isabella); Keith Allen (Pepi); Nigel Planer (Wazir); Rik Mayall (Sultan); Andrew Bailey (Genghis); Burt Kwouk (Wang); Jon Pertwee (Duke of Costa Brava); James Faulkner (Torquemada); and Tony Slattery, Martin Clunes, Sara Stockbridge, Maureen Lipman, Holly Aird, Su Douglas, Rebecca Lacey, Don Henderson, Charles Fleischer, Reed Martin

CHRISTOPHER COLUMBUS: THE DISCOVERY, *Warner Bros.*, released August 1992

An Alexander and Ilya Salkind production; Executive producer, Jane Chaplin; Producer, Ilya Salkind; Coproducer, Bob Simmonds; Director, John Glen; Screenplay, John Briley, Cary Bates and Mario Puzo from a story by Puzo; Photography, Alec Mills; Production designer, Gil Parrondo; Costume design, John Bloomfield; Music, Cliff Eidelman; Editor, Matthew Glen

Marlon Brando (Torquemada); Tom Selleck (King Ferdinand); George Corraface (Christopher Columbus); Rachel Ward (Queen Isabella); Robert Davi (Martin Pinzon; Catherine Zeta Jones (Beatriz); Oliver Cotton (Harana); Benicio Del Torro (Alvaro); Mathieu Carriere (King John); Manuel de Blas (Vicente Pinzon); Glyn Grain (De La Cosa); Peter Guinness (Fra Perez); Nigel Terry (Roldan); and Nitzan Sharron, Steven Hartley, Nigel Black, Nigel Harrison, Chris Hunter, Simon Dormandy, Christopher Chaplin, Michael Gothard, Clive Arindell, Richard Cubison, Mark Long, Nicholas Selby, John Grillo, Serge Malik, Joseph Long, Branscombe Richmond, Anthony Sarda, Tailinh Forest Flower, Gerard Langlais, Michael Halphie, Genevieve Allenbury, Michael Gunn, Vincent Pickering, Trevor Sellers, Caleb Lloyd, Andrew Dicks, Georgi Fisher, Steven Fletcher, Ivan De Sono

1492: CONQUEST OF PARADISE, *Paramount Pictures*, released October 1992

A Percy Main/Legende/Cyrk production; Executive producers, Mimi Polk Sotela and Iain Smith; Producers, Ridley Scott and Alain Goldman; Coproducers, Marc Boyman, Roselyne Bosch and Pere Fages; Director, Ridley Scott; Screenplay, Roselyne

Bosch; Photography, Adrian Riddle; Production designer, Norman Spencer; Supervising art directors, Benjamin Fernandez and Leslie Tomkins; Costume designers, Charles Knode and Barbara Rutter; Music, Vangelis; Editors, William Anderson and Francoise Bonnot

Gerard Depardieu (Christopher Columbus); Armand Assante (Sanchez); Sigourney Weaver (Queen Isabella); Loren Dean (Older Fernando); Angela Molina (Beatriz); Fernando Rey (Marchena); Michael Wincott (Moxica); Tcheky Karyo (Pinzon); Kevin Dunn (Captain Mendez); Frank Langella (Santangel); Mark Margolis (Bobadilla); Kario Salem (Arojaz); Billy Sullivan (Fernando at 10); John Hefernan (Brother Buyl); and Arnold Vosloo, Steven Waddington, Fernando G. Cuervo, Jose Luis Ferrer, Bercelio Moya, Juan Diego Botto, Achero Manas, Fernando Garcia Rimada, Albert Vidal, Isabel Prinz, Angel Rosal, Jack Taylor

TELEVISION

CHRISTOPHER COLUMBUS, televised May 19 and 20, 1985 CBS 6 hours

An RAI-Television Italiana/Cliesi Cinematografica/Antenne 2/Bavaria Atelier coproduction in association with Lorimar Productions; Executive producers, Malcolm A. Stuart and Ervin Zavada; Producers, Silvio and Anna Maria Clementelli; Supervising producer, Fabrizio Castellani; Director, Alberto Lattuada; Teleplay by Laurence Heath, based on the screenplay by Adriano Bolzano, Tullio Pinelli and Albert Lattuada; Photography, Franco DiGiacomo; Production designer, Mario Chiari; Music, Riz Ortolani; Costume designers, Maria De Mattheis and Enrico Luzzi; Editor, Russell Lloyd; Research by Professor Paolo Emilio Taviani

Gabriel Byrne (Christopher Columbus); Faye Dunaway (Queen Isabella); Max Von Sydow (King John of Portugal); Nicol Williamson (King Ferdinand); Oliver Reed (Martin Pinzon); Audrey Matson (Dona Felipe); Anne Canovas (Beatriz Enriguez); Eli Wallach (Hernando de Talavera); Raf Vallone (Jose Vizinho); Rossano Brazzi (Diego Ortiz de Vilhegas); Virna Lisa (Dona Moniz Perestrello); Mark Buffery (Bartholomew Columbus); Larry Lamb (Don Castillo); Murray Melvin (Father Linares); Michel Auclair (Luis de Santangel); Keith Buckley (Luis de Torres); Elpidia Carrillo (Coana); Massimo Girotti (Duke Medina Celi); Stefano Madia (Federico); Jack Watson (Father Marchena); Hal Yamanouchi (Guacanabo); and Claudio Aliotti, Patrick Bauchau, Kasimir Berger, Salvatore Borgese, Charles Borromel, Tony Camilleri, Scott Coffey, Cyrus Elias, Francesco Lattuada, Patrick Longhi, Alexander Lopez, Antonio Marsina, David Mills, Lino Mintoff, Brizio Montinaro, Joseph Murphy, Luca Orlandini, Iris de Peynado, Jean Francois Poron, Gregory Snegoff, Erik Schumann, John Suda, Fabiola Toledo, Sergio Testori, Josefina Vetencourt, Heinz Weiss

COLUMBUS AND THE AGE OF DISCOVERY, televised October 6-9, 1991 PBS 7 parts (1 hour each)

Executive producer, Zvi Dor-Ner; Senior producer, Thomas Friedman; Directors, Zvi Dor-Ner, Stephen Segaller and Graham Chedd; Written by Thomas Freedman, Zvi Dor-Ner and Graham Chedd; Photography, Peter Hoving, D'Arcy Marsh, Chris Openshaw and Jean de Segonzac; Music, Sheldon Mirowitz; Advisers, Juan Gil, Franklin Knight, William McNeill, Mauricio Obregon and Consuelo Varela; Editors, Sarah Holt, Simon McCabe and David Berenson; Narrator, Will Lyman

Episodes: Columbus' World; An Idea Takes Shape; Worlds Lost and Found (2 parts); God, Gold...and Disease; The Columbian Exhange

THE TRUE ADVENTURES OF CHRISTOPHER COLUMBUS, televised July 27-30, 1992 BBC 1 hour each
Produced by the British Broadcasting Corporation; Directors, Patrick Barlow and Philip Bonham-Carter; Teleplay, Patrick Barlow

Patrick Barlow (Christopher Columbus); Tim Piggott-Smith (Ferdinand of Aragon); Miranda Richardson (Isabella of Castile); Victor Banerjee (Indian chief); Tanveer Ghani (Chief's son); and Graham Stark, Freddie Jones, Carmela Romero, Hugh Quarshie

OPERA

Composer	*Title*
Barbieri, C.E.	Christopher Columbus
Bignami, E.	Christopher Columbus
Blaze, A. J. M.	Colombe
Bottesini, G.	Cristoforo Colombo
Bristow, George Frederick	Columbus
Carnicier, R.	Cristoforo Colombo
Casella, Felicita	Cristoforo Colombo
Coppola, R.	Cristoforo Colombo
Corradi, D.	Cristoforo Colombe
Fabrizi, V.	Colombo, Il
Fava, A.	Colombo
Fioravanti, Vincent	Colombo,all Scoperta delle Indie
Franchetti, Alberto	Cristoforo Colombo
Giambini	Colombo, Il
Gianetti, R.	Colomba di Barcellona, La
Gomez, Antonio Carlos	Cristoforo Colombo
Grandjean, A. K. W.	Colombo
Hanson, Daryl	Christopher Columbus
Liepe, E.	Colombo

Llamos Berete, A.	Colombo
Mackenzie, A. C.	Colombo
Marcora, C.	Cristoforo Colombo
Mela, V.	Cristoforo Colombo
Milhaud, Darius	Christophe Colomb
Morales, M. G.	Cristoforo Colombo a San Domingo
Morlacchi, F.	Colombo in America, Il
Ottoboni, Cardinal	Colombo
Ricci, L.	Colombo
Sangiorgio-Rabitti,A.G.B.	Colombo, Il
Van Fossen, David	Christopher Columbus
Zador, E.	Christopher Columbus

CINDERELLA
Various adaptations of the fairy tale by Charles Perrault (1697)

Synopsis

After her widowed father marries a domineering woman with two unattractive daughters, Cinderella is forced to become a house slavey consigned to a garret room. One day an invitation arrives from the king's son for all persons of high degree to attend his ball. Cinderella's wicked stepmother and her wretched step-sisters feel qualified and prepare for the event after giving Cinderella her working orders. Arrayed in their finest finery, the three leave for the ball and Cinderella, alone, succumbs to tears. Into her life suddenly comes her Fairy Godmother who arranges for her to attend the ball, too. Miraculously Cinderella's ragged clothes are changed into a jewel-bedecked gown of gold and silver with a pair of glass slippers, and then a woeful-looking pumpkin transforms into a magnificent gilded coach, six mice into dappled grey horses, a large rat into a coachman, and a half dozen mice into wellattired lackeys. As she sees Cinderella off, the Fairy Godmother reminds her that she must return before midnight, otherwise all will revert to their original state at the stroke of twelve.

Making her grand entrance at the ball, Cinderella accepts the admiring stares of the Prince, her step-mother and her sisters, all of whom are entranced by the unknown girl they take to be a Princess. The Prince saves as many dances as he can for her and she regales in the glory. As the clock strikes quarter to twelve, Cinderella finds she must make a hasty departure, and in her rush, leaves a glass slipper behind on the palace stairs. Finding it, the Prince issues a proclamation that he would wed the girl whose foot the slipper fit. All eligible ladies in the realm are visited, and ultimately the Prince comes across the cindercovered slavey whose foot easily slides into the slipper. The Prince has found his Princess of the ball and a marriage is arranged, with all -- except the evil stepmother and the stuckup stepsisters -- living happily ever after.

Comment and Critique

Charles Perrault, the first author to write a book exclusively for children, in 1687 had his *Histories ou Contes du Temps, passe aven des Moralites* published (it was subtitled *Contes de ma Mere l'Oye (Tales of Mother Goose)*. Madame d'Aulnoy's *Les Contes des Fees* and *Contes Nouveaux au les Fees a la Mode* soon followed, and in France, Jean Antoine Galland's adaptation of the fifteenth century Arabic manuscript *A Thousand and One Nights* gained great popularity. In the theater, Perrault's *Cinderella* became a standard work over the next three centuries, and the myriad productions of it and its rags-to-riches offspring would require a separate volume. The theater, knowingly or not, utilized the Cinderella *leitmotif* from gaslights to television, and beyond drama and comedy, the musical stage for many years found the rags-to-riches formula successful. The Cinderella theme is evident in many of the stage's greatest musical successes and plays from the very beginning, and Hollywood has done variations on it from the earliest days of sound up into the nineties.

Perhaps the greatest "Cinderella Era" on Broadway was the period of the 1920s which gave rise to many variations under assorted names. Among theme were *Irene* (1919); *Cinderella on Broadway*, *Poor Little Ritz Girl* and *Sally* (1920); *The O'Brien Girl*, *Good Morning, Dearie* and *Suzette* (1921); *Sue, Dear*, *Little Nelly Kelly* and *Glory* (1922); *The Dancing Girl*, *Cinders*, *Poppy*, *The Magic Ring* and *The Rise of Rosie O'Reilly* (1923); *Lollipop*, *Sitting Pretty*, *Plane Jane* and *Princess April* (1924); *Mayflowers* and *Tip-Toes* (1925), and *The Five O'Clock Girl* (1927). Even George Bernard Shaw's *Pygmalion* of 1913 is an extension of *Cinderella*.

Gioacchino Antonio Rossini composed a twoact opera set to a libretto by Jacopo Ferretti, based on Perrault's 1697 *Cendrillon, ou la Petite Pantoufle*, and Charles-Guillaume Etienne's libretto for Niccolo Isourard's 1810 failed opera *Cendrillon*. Rossini's *La Cenerentola* premiered at the Teatro Valle in Rome on January 25, 1817, with Geltrude Righetti-Giorgi singing the title role. The opera was first performed in London at the Haymarket Theatre in 1820, sung in Italian. On April 13, 1830, it was sung at London's Covent Garden, with an English libretto by Michael Rophino Lacy.

New York first heard Rossini's *Cinderella* sung in Italian at the Park Theatre on June 27, 1826. *La Cenerentola*, with Maria Felicita Garcia singing the title role, was performed by the Garcia Company headed by Spanish tenor Manuel del Popola Vincente Garcia, who established the first Italian opera company in New York the previous year.

A new production was mounted at the Park Theatre in January 1831. Theater historian George Odell wrote: "The season of 1830-31 was notable for three features -- the first appearance of Charles Kean, the first of Master Joseph Burke, and the bringing out of *Cinderella*. The last came on January 24th, and was the event of the year, so far as production goes. It at once ranged itself with the bigoperatic spectacular successes of recent years...It was offered about fifty times during its first season...One Cinderella after another sang her way into the hearts of playgoers, though none quite equalled the original representative -- the lovely Mrs. Austin.

Rossini's *Cenerentola* had been sung in New York by the divine Signorina; it was to figure within a few years in the repertoire of Italian opera companies in the city. But it was not quite Rossini's opera that now enthralled New York. It was an English adaptation by Rophino Lacy and the advertisements of the first day announced that the music by Rossini was selected from *Cenerentola*, *Armida*, *Maometto* and *Guillaume Tell*."

The *Mirror* reflected the general enthusiasm with "This charming opera has completely surmounted all obstacles. The most incredible transformation takes place with a beautiful and dreamlike facility... It is acknowledged that *Cenerentola* offers an attraction superior to anything of the kind every produced in the United States." During the mid-1800s, Mary Taylor was to be a popular *Cenerentola*.

Cinderella; or, the Little Glass Slipper opened at New York's Booth Theatre in October 1880 with Rossini's music arranged by Max Maretzek. The *Mirror* called it "a musical entertainment. *Cinderella* has considerable merit, from the first merry note to the wedding chorus at the altar. As a spectacle, it possesses many features of interest. The costumes are new and bright, and the stage setting magnificent...[Director Henry] Jarrett's *Cinderella* is not the old burlesque but a newly written piece, with touches of beauty, melody, color, sparkle and dash..."

In England, *Cinderella* became a favorite Christmas pantomime from the 1880s onward. On December 26, 1882, Frank Green's pantomime of the fairy tale opened at London's Pavilion Theatre. "*Cinderella* lends itself excellently to pantomime," recorded *Entr'Acte*. "It gives plenty of scope to the scenic artist, to the musicians, to the costumier, and to the performers. It is a legend, too, with which everybody is familiar, and it appeals to popular sentiment..."

A competing version opened on the same date as the Drury Lane Theatre's Christmas attraction, and *Entr'Acte* reported: "[It] is perhaps the best of all the popular pantomime subjects, and this is the story which the most poetic of all writers of this staple has this season utilized for the Drury Lane annual. Mr. Augustus Harris has done every justice to the excellent material which has been furnished by Mr. [E. L.] Blanchard, and has produced the spectacular comicality with much sumptuousness...The scenery is in every sense complete and beautiful; the dresses are, on the whole, most rich and rare, and the music by Mr. Oscar Barrett has been most tastefully selected and composed..."

David Henderson, impresario of the Chicago Opera House, moved his successful "spectacular extravaganza" *The Crystal Slipper* to Broadway's Star Theatre in late November 1888. Alfred Thompson, librettist and costume designer for London's Gaiety Theatre Christmas pantomimes, was imported to write the book (with Harry B. Smith) and execute the costumes for Henderson's production which had a six-month run in Chicago, but ran only four weeks in New York. It featured Marguerite Fish, who played Cinderella with her native Viennese accent, and an up-and-coming performer named Eddie Foy.

On December 2, 1891, a pantomime *Cinderella* opened at Philadelphia's Academy of Music. The *Mirror* found: "The entire stage of the Academy was made, several times, a dazzling and lively picture of dancing women, with a background of exceptional richness...*Cinderella* is a return to the gold old days of *The Black Crook*, *The White Dawn* and *Aladdin's Lamp*. It is just such a pantomime as the patrons of the Drury Lane and Covent Garden expect annually...Fannie Ward, in the title part, was dainty and engaging..."

In September 1904, *The Catch of the Season*, Seymour Hicks and Cosmo Hamilton's updating of *Cinderella*, became one of London's greatest stage hits of the day lasting 616 performances. Years later, writer Harry Stone (*Plays and Players*) recalled, "Perhaps the most blatant version of *Cinderella* was a musical version called *The Catch of the Season* which Seymour Hicks put on at the Vaudeville in 1904." The following August it came to Broadway with Edna May as Cinderella and had a respectable run of 104 performances.

The musical *A Stubborn Cinderella* opened on Broadway in 1909 with Sallie Fisher in the title role along with John Barrymore, in his only musical comedy. "The Cinderella of the title is Lady Leslie...This play has the spirit of youth as its main recommendation. It has snap and brightness," wrote the critic for *The New York Times*. "The book possesses humor and the music is tuneful and light. Also there is a real plot with dramatic moments, actors capable of performing their parts, and scenery and costumes designed with an evidence of taste...John Barrymore and Sallie Fisher must be credited with helping the piece well on toward success. Mr. Barrymore as Mac plays the part vigorously and humorously, and makes one attempt at singing with some success. He is really funny..."

Charles Dillingham's production of the Victor Herbert musical, *The Lady of the Slipper*, opened on Broadway at the Globe Theatre in late October 1912 for 232 performances. *The New York Times* found that it wasn't necessary "to use more than a fragment of the old fairy tale for the purposes they had in hand in the making of a typical musical comedy play...Victor Herbert [has] done better in the past...However, he has provided a pleasant and useful score, the kind that enables Miss Elsie Janis to come into the limelight and sing, or dance, or give imitations, as the case may be, and which also provides plenty of opportunities for Fred Stone to tie himself into all sorts of dancing knots and twists, and, with the assistance of his agile partner, Dave Montgomery, gives an effect of singing that is always very funny."

Throughout the 1920s, *Cinderella* continued to be revived as a Christmas pantomime in England. In America, the Shuberts' pastiche, *Cinderella on Broadway*, had little to do with the fairy tale, although in 1925, The Theatre Guild brought the Cinderella story to Broadway via Ferenc Molnar's comedy, *The Glass Slipper*, in which Cinderella becomes a serving girl in Budapest mistreated by a grayhaired Prince. Rudolph Friml's musical comedy, *Cinders*, was a modernized version of the tale, and in 1929, a gender switch provided London with a smash hit in *Mr. Cinders*, which ran for 528 performances. Thirty years later, Harry Stone (*Plays and Players*) reflected on that show's success: "Changing Sex: In *Mr. Cinders*, produced in 1929, Cinderella was changed into a male role, played by Bobby Howes, and Prince Charming became a neighbouring heiress in the attractive person of Binnie Hale...Here again there was a tuneful score, this time by Vivian Ellis and included the songs 'One Man Girl' and 'Spread a Little Happiness.' From all this, it is clear there is nothing unusual in authors and composers purloining from the classic fairy story..."

Of the annual *Cinderella* Christmas pantomimes in London, the Drury Lane Theatre's 1934 version brought this report from *The Bystander* critic: "...let me say that the 1934-35 brand of Drury Lane pantomime, with its gorgeous spectacle and amusing scenes, will assuredly delight young and old, who will also find in [British musical comedy actor of the day] June an ideal Cinderella...The part of Prince Charming is played by Phyllis Neilson-Terry."

Herbert and Eleanor Farjeon's adaptation of *Cinderella*, called *The Glass Slipper*, received a glowing press in 1944, and the following year, Robert Donat revived the play with music by Clifton Parker. "Donat's production of the charming Herbert and Eleanor Farjeon's fairy tale, telling the story of Cinderella without the usual trappings of pantomime and knockabout comedy, is a revival of crystal prettiness, wrote *Theatre World*. Sara Gregory is a new recruit as Cinderella and she plays the part and sings the songs with spontaneous sweetness..." Not so enthusiastic was the publication about Jack Hylton's pantomime of *Cinderella* at the Adelphi the same year. Theatre world found it to have "a poor book...To allow Gavin Gordon to play the thankless role of the Baron is a dog-in-the-manger piece of casting...the choice of songs was uninspired...Clever music-hall acts were inserted without any introduction and still less justification."

Leonard Sillman's *If the Shoe Fits* in 1946 on Broadway managed twenty performances despite lackluster reviews. Wolcott Gibbs (*The New Yorker*) called the musical comedy based on *Cinderella* "one of the most godforsaken entertainments that have been inflicted on us in many a black night...*If the Shoe Fits* was bad in almost every conceivable way -- the book was some tangled, hopeless variant of the Cinderella story; the music was derivative and tinny; the comedy, based largely on homosexuality, was tasteless; the costumes were unattractive; the dancing was negligible; and the acting, with a few exceptions, was precisely in keeping with its surroundings." This was hardly a "money" review.

The 1953 Christmas pantomime of *Cinderella* at the London Palladium starred Julie Andrews in one of her early roles. She was to star in the role again on American television in 1957 in the classic version written by Richard Rodgers and Oscar Hammerstein. The Rodgers and Hammerstein musical premiered on the London stage in December 1958 at the Coliseum with Yana as Cinderella and then rock 'n' roll idol Tommy Steele as Buttons, and another production of it followed two years later at the Victoria Palace. On the American stage, meanwhile, there was not to be another major *Cinderella* until the St. Louis Municipal Theatre's 1961 staging of Rodgers and Hammerstein's TV production.

One of the more unusual variations on the tale was the British musical, *I Gotta Shoe*, which was a first commissioned by the BBC in 1957 and broadcast for Christmas as *Cindy-Ella* and later became a novel, illustrated by Tony Walton, the noted set designer then married to Julie Andrews. It premiered at the Garrick Theatre in London in December 1962 with Cleo Laine starring.

In 1964, an Off-Broadway musical called *Cindy* began what would be a successful run and make it a cult favorite. Transforming Cinderella into a mid-Sixties American teenager, Jacqueline Mayro starred in the show which opened at the Gate Theatre and moved first to the Orpheum and later to the Cricket Theatre. "Cindy is magical and great," wrote the *New York Herald Tribune*. And *Cue* magazine found that "A talented exuberant cast made this fairy tale sparkle all over again." It amassed a run of just over 400 performances and in May 1968, found its way to London.

Twiggy made what apparently was her stage debut as Cinderella in the 1974 *Cinderella* Christmas pantomime in London, while Fiona Fullerton starred in the 1976 pantomime. In spring 1983, *Mr. Cinders* had its first major revival in London, and it is that production which was captured on record. *Mr. Cinders* had its belated (not very well received) American premiere at the Forum Theatre in Metuchen, New Jersey, in spring 1986. In October 1988, the Goodspeed Opera House in Connecticut, however, gave it a grand revival. "A 1929 West End hit that didn't make it to the U. S. initially, *Mr. Cinders* may be too sweetly gentle for the rigors of Broadway, *Variety*'s critic wrote, "but it has the ideal home in the intimate Goodspeed in a cherishable production that, if carefully handled and placed, could do well elsewhere...The musical is a clever twist on the Cinderella story with a male poor-relation stepson at its heart."

Joseph Papp produced Janusz Glowacki's drama, *Cinders*, adapted from the Cinderella story, in February 1984 as part of The New York Shakespeare Festival. Lucinda Jenney played Cinderella. Contemporary audiences know the stage

Cinderella from the Stephen Sondheim musical *Into the Woods*, which premiered at San Diego's Old Globe Theatre in December 1986 and came to Broadway the following November, with a touring company crisscrossing America during 1988 and 1989. It opened in London in September 1990.

Countless ballet and opera productions of *Cinderella* have been performed around the world as standard works through the years. Among the many stagings of the ballet with Prokofiev's score: the 1945 premiere with the great Galina Ulanova at the Bolshoi Theatre in Moscow, where a pantomime *Cinderella* ballet had inaugurated the venue in 1825; the Royal Ballet of Great Britain (the former Sadler's Wells Ballet Company) 1956 *Cinderella* choreographed by Frederick Ashton and danced by Margot Fonteyn; the Berlin Opera Ballet's *Cinderella* with former Kirov Ballet stars Valery Panov and Galina Panova, dazzling critics and audiences at the New York State Theatre in summer 1978; Rudolf Nureyev's production of the fairy tale for the Paris Opera Ballet that won wide acclaim in London in 1986 and toured the United States in 1988. In 1990, the Fort Worth Ballet did *Cinderella* at the City Center in New York, choreographed by Paul Mejia who did the first version for his wife Suzanne Farrell in 1981 for the Chicago City Ballet.

The Rossini opera of *Cinderella* was staged by the New York City Opera in English in November 1980 and telecast live on PBS. The 1981 La Scala production with Frederica von Stade was televised on PBS' *Great Performances* in February 1984.

Charles Perrault's tale of *Cinderella* was a natural for the screen, which over the years has utilized the story in a number of guises. One of the earliest filmings was by George Albert Smith as *Cinderella and the Fairy Godmother* in England in 1898. Smith's seventy-five-foot film featured Laura Bayley as Cinderella and was advertised as "The First Double Exposure and Stop Action Film." Britain's Hepworth Pictures released a short film version of *Cinderella* in 1907 and America's Thanhauser Pictures produced the fairy tale with Florence La Badie in the title role in 1911. The following year, Britain's Empire Films produced a one-reel *Cinderella*, animated by toys. Hepworth experimented with *Cinderella* and sound by synchronizing a short film to a Columbia record in 1913.

William N. Selig produced a three-reel feature film of *Cinderella* in 1912 featuring Mabel Taliaferro in the title role. A studio press release claimed that 300 people participated in the five week filming of some 99 scenes. *The Moving Picture World* called *Cinderella* "a great filmed subject...There is such a wealth of settings, both out-door and indoor; such a great variety of properties and costumes, selected with the utmost care, so much of action and heart interest throughout these 3,000 feet of film that one cannot possibly take in at one sitting more than a small fraction of the actual values. Always prominent throughout, and holding one with heart grips, is the Cinderella of Mabel Taliaferro...T. J. Corrigan is an excellent Prince Charming..."

Mary Pickford starred in *Cinderella* in 1914. *The Motion Picture World* reported: "It is a delightful interpretation the Famous Players have given us of this old friend of childhood. In the title role of *Cinderella*, which is shown in four parts, Miss Pickford brings to bear all her native charm...*Cinderella* is well done."

Ludwig Berger's Germanmade 1924 screen version of *Cinderella* came to the United States two years later, and *The New York Times* described it as an "enchanting photoplay...*Cinderella* was pleasing...although some sterling portions of this picture could not be shown because they had unfortunately been destroyed. The portion that was haplessly destroyed chances to deal with the transforming of the mice into footmen and rats into horses, for the entrancing glass carriage...Helga Thomas fills the part of Cinderella. She is beautiful, a type that never seems quite real, and in some scenes she reminds one of a graceful figure on a piece of Sevres china."

Variations of the *Cinderella* story or motif filled the screen during the 1920s and 1930s. In 1925, Paramount filmed James Barrie's *A Kiss for Cinderella* with Betty Bronson, and the next year, Colleen Moore starred in *Ella Cinders*, an update of the tale. Other Hollywood features, while having no reference to Cinderella, also told the now time-honored poor working girl-handsome man with money rags-to-riches story.

The best remembered screen version of *Cinderella* fell to Walt Disney to create in 1950 -- one of his most enduring animated features. "Though no chef d'oeuvre, [the film] is well worth the love and labor spent. As the Fairy Godmother puts it, 'Even miracles take a little time,'" wrote Bosley Crowther in *The New York Times*. "For Mr. Disney and his craftsmen have brilliantly splashed upon the screen a full-blown and flowery animation of the perennially popular fairy tale ...in extravagant story-book terms, matching the romance of the fable with lushly romantic images...The beautiful Cinderella has a voluptuous face and form -- no to mention an eager disposition -- to compare with Al Capp's Daisy Mae. Prince Charming resembles Li'l Abner in a Student Prince soldier suit, and the Evil Stepmother is completely the stock comicstrip villainess...To the fellows who dreamed up these fancies we are heartily grateful, indeed. They have sprinkled in *Cinderella* -- along with sugar and wit -- some vagrant art." The musical score to this Disney treat was highlighted by such songs as Oscar-nominated "Bibbidi Bobbidi Boo" and "A Dream Is a Wish Your Heart Makes."

In 1954, MGM brought Herbert and Eleanor Farjeon's London hit of a decade earlier, *The Glass Slipper*, to the screen with Leslie Caron and Michael Wilding, somewhat of an age-wise mismatch. Comparing the screen version with the London musical, British critic David Robinson found: "It has, however, cast aside most of the action, all the ballets and musical decorations and a good deal of the charm of the original, in favor of a semi-psychological rationalization of the story...This rationalization is characterized by a heavy-voiced pseudo-psychoanalytical narration [by Walter Pidgeon] ...The drama and the magic gone, some of the characters remain. Leslie Caron defies a script which would make her a neurotic orphan from *East of Eden*...Elsa Lanchester appears briefly, but with her usual superior sense of comedy...The only other character who is really faithful to the spirit of the Farjeon original is, unexpectedly, a creation of the film: Mrs. Toquet, the fairy godmother, is an engaging and whimsical creature perfectly played by Estelle Winwood..."

Following its spring 1955 opening at Radio City Music Hall, Bosley Crowther (*The New York Times*) said of *The Glass Slipper*: "*Cinderella* has turned up in the movies under a variety of circumstances and names that it is thoroughly disarming and refreshing to see her played frankly by the girl of *Lili*, little Leslie Caron...No complicated sophistication -- save a richly designed ballet, a slightly psycho-conscious narration and a fairy godmother who talks like a character out of Lewis Carroll -- confuses the pretty presentation of the details of the fairy tale." Crowther felt that "Miss Caron clearly mirrors an unlovely and muchdisquieted girl...Charles Walters' direction of the acting is gracious and leisurely, but this is a fanciful story and dancing should be its medium..."

The 1960 Bolshoi Ballet film version of *Cinderella* from the USSR was found by *Films and Filming*'s David Hunt to be "skillfully condensed and adapted for the screen by Alexander Row, who has specialized in filming fairy stories...This wide-screen record of the Bolshoi's production of *Cinderella* -- first given in 1945 with Lepshinskaya in the title role -- provides ballet-lovers with an interesting opportunity to make comparisons with Ashton's 1948 version for the Royal Ballet. Rather strangely, considering its fairy tale subject, it reflects perhaps more strongly than any other Soviet ballet film, the Russians' deeply humanist approach to ballet and the arts generally...The photography retains the magic while transcending the limitations of a stage performance...The soft pastels and burnished opulence of Piotr Williams' well-designed sets and costumes are attractively reproduced."

Jerry Lewis' *CinderFella* of 1960 was a change-of-sex version of the tale, with Anna Maria Alberghetti as the Princess, Judith Anderson as the wicked stepmother and Ed Wynn as the Fairy Godfather. It was not well-received by the critics, but audiences -- especially Lewis' -- loved it. A sample of the reviews it got on its week-before Christmas release: "We'll bet good money that even the kids will be bored stiff, said Howard Thompson in *The New York Times*. "The gags are stale, the pacing is pure molasses and the camera glues to Mr. Lewis' feeble prancing with royal fascination."

In 1967, Sophia Loren and Omar Sharif costarred in the Italian film *C'era Una Volta* (*Happily Ever After*), another variation on the Cinderella story, set in Naples circa 1600. In Great Britain, it was released as *Cinderella, Italian Style*; in the United States, it became *More Than a Miracle*. "With Omar Sharif at his romantic best, and Sophia Loren as everyone's idea of what a desirable woman should be, director Francesco Rosi has woven his pepped-up Cinderella story into a fantasy of enormous charm," Peter Buckley wrote in *Films and Filming*. "It is lovingly photographed...and the wide screen is filled with some of the most attractive people in the cinema today...One should never become too old to believe in fairy tales, so sit back and let this physically beautiful film waft over your senses and remember the days when studios were not afraid to make films that appealed directly to everyone's sense of innocence."

Less enthusiastic was Vincent Canby (*The New York Times*), who felt that "It seems that one of Miss Loren's most important functions in her private life is to upgrade those motion pictures produced by her husband, Carlo Ponti, that turn into poverty (not disaster) areas ...If anyone could save the film of course, it would be Sophia, but even she fails, though she does spend most of the picture in one of those breakaway peasant mini-dresses in which she first burst upon the public consciousness."

In the ensuing years, there were other Cinderella movie, ranging from animated ones for the youngsters to X-rated ones (like *Sinderella and the Golden Bra* in 1964 and *Grimm's Fairy Tales for Adults* in 1971).

Rivaling the 1950 Disney feature-length cartoon classic, however, was the exquisitely made 1976 British musical fairy tale, *The Slipper and the Rose*, written Bryan Forbes (who also directed) and Robert B. and Richard M. Sherman (who were responsible for *Mary Poppins*). Gemma Craven and Richard Chamberlain were ideally cast as Cinderella and her Prince, heading a stellar lineup of British notables: Edith Evans (in her last role), Kenneth More, Margaret Lockwood, Michael Hordern, and others. "The quality of fairy tales is sustained with charm, taste and the *soupcon* of sophistication that the British customarily provide for such entertainments in *The Slipper and the Rose: The Story of Cinderella*," reported Arthur Knight in *Saturday Review*. He called the film "a wonderfully lush, lilting and lavish musical -- with some neat twists of plot and personality to refresh the legend, and some imaginative and divertingly witty variations added. Freed from Disney strictures, the brothers Sherman have let loose with jolly and sweet tunes and some Gilbert & Sullivanish lyrics...Richard Chamberlain emerges as the ultimate singing charming prince, with Gemma Craven a lovely Cinderella...It's a treat for the eye and the ear -- and the young in heart."

London's *Daily Mirror* called the film, "A work of rare distinction, full of wonder and enchantment...A film it would be madness to miss." David Robinson (*The London Times*) found it to be "a bold innovation in contemporary cinema, as a film which sets out only to please, charm, seduce and entertain..." *The New York Times*' Vincent Canby was notably less enchanted. After the film's Radio City Music Hall premiere, he felt that "one begins to long for a bit of Julie Andrews' chic and sophistication...As the young lovers, Mr. Chamberlain and Miss Craven have impossible roles that are less like characters in a fairy tale than pictures on a jar of peanut butter." Canby also found that the Shermans have written "a whole bunch of forgettable songs [and] sound as if they're parodying the worst of the Broadway musical theater of the '50s." One of those songs, though, "The Slipper and the Rose Waltz," was Oscar nominated, as was the Sherman Brothers' score.

In 1987, *Maid to Order* turned the Cinderella story upside down in a good-hearted comedy that had a spoiled rich girl turned by her fairy godmother into a maid for a gauche Malibu Beach couple to learn humility.

Richard Rodgers and Oscar Hammerstein II brought *Cinderella* to television in March 1957. It was to be their only TV musical and it became an enduring classic. (A black and white kinescope of that ninety-minute production is in the collection of the Museum of Television and Radio in New York, and the recording of that show has become a collector's item.) Julie Andrews, who had played Cinderella on the London stage several years before, starred in the title role, heading a cast that included stage veterans Dorothy Stickney, Howard Lindsay and Ilka Chase, plus Kaye Ballard, Alice Ghostley, Jon Cypher (as the Prince) and Edie Adams (then known as Edith). There were nearly two dozen songs in the score, the best known of which were "In My Own Little Corner" and "Do I Love You Because You're Beautiful?" (Only ten of these appear on the original cast recording.)

Of the show, Jack Gould wrote in *The New York Times*: "It had the heaven-sent blessing of Miss Andrews, who, particularly in lovely color video, was a beguiling vision. When she and Jon Cypher, making his debut in a major role, raised their voices in songs that had not already been played to death on the air, it was most pleasant theatre. The home screen has so few moments of genuine charm that the attractive interludes in *Cinderella* were something to be savored." *Variety*'s critic felt: "For fashioning their musicalization of the ageless fairy tale for television, Rodgers and Hammerstein delivered a whale of a show in their first time up with an original contribution for the medium. And if it wasn't a perfect show, there was always Miss Andrews to lend it special enchantment and to make most of the 90 minutes a delight...It was a class show." (In 1958, Mary Martin recorded several of the *Cinderella* songs for one side of an album for RCA.)

Nine years later, Rodgers and Hammerstein's *Cinderella* was restaged for television with a new cast headed by Lesley Ann Warren and Stuart Damon, plus Ginger Rogers, Walter Pidgeon and Celeste Holm. This time it was in color (the first version also apparently was in color but there were so few color sets available at the time that most saw it only in black and white) and one new song was added: "Loneliness of Evening," written originally for *South Pacific* and then cut before the show opened. This version was first shown in February 1966 and then repeated in February 1968. (The Rodgers and Hammerstein show has occasionally been staged theatrically, most notably by the St. Louis Municipal Theater in 1961, 1965, 1980 and 1990.)

A month after CBS broadcast the Rodgers and Hammerstein musical originally, NBC's *Producers Showcase* presented a version of *Cinderella* by the Royal Ballet of London using the music of Prokofiev. Margot Fonteyn danced the title role, with choreography by Frederick Ashton (who played one of the two ugly stepsisters). In November 1977, *Cinderella* emerged on television again in one of eight segments of a CBS Children's Special entitled *Once Upon a Brothers Grimm*. The following March, ABC telecast an original TV movie musical called *Cindy*, which updated the story to World War II Harlem. It was produced and written by the team behind *The Mary Tyler Moore Show* and remains one of a handful of enchantingly unique television movies (though rarely seen).

Shelley Duvall offered her engaging vision of *Cinderella* on *Faerie Tale Theatre* in the summer of 1985, with Jennifer Beals and Matthew Broderick as Cinderella and her Prince, Jean Stapleton as the Fairy Godmother, and Eve Arden as the Wicked Stepmother. PBS' *Great Performances* offered several versions of *Cinderella* in the 1980s: the San Francisco Ballet's production of Prokofiev's ballet and the 1981 La Scala and 1988 Vienna State Opera productions of Rossini's *La Cenerentola*. And in June 1990, PBS televised the Lyon Opera Ballet's production of Prokofiev's *Cinderella* on *Alive From Off Center*. Dance critic Jennifer Dunning (*The New York Times*) called it "not for purists. Choreographed by Maguy Marin, the chic maverick of French ballet, the production is a child's-eye vision of the fairy tale, with fat-faced, stiff-moving doll figures with padded bodies enacting all the roles."

STAGE

CINDERELLA, *Park Theatre*, New York, opened March 30, 1808
Director, William Twaits; Scenery, Mr. Holland; Dresses, Mrs. Gibbons; Original music, Mr. Kelly

Mrs. Darley (Cinderella); John Darley (Prince); William Twaits (Pedro); Miss Dillinger, Mrs. Ald-mixon, Miss White (Nymphs)

Vauxhall Theatre, New York, opened August 17, 1808

Mrs. Wilmot (Cinderella); Mr. Mills (Prince); Master Harris (Hyman); Mrs. Mills, Mrs. William Francis (Cinderella's Sisters); Miss Delamater (Cupid); Miss Seymour (Venus)

LA CENERENTOLA, *Teatro Valle*, Rome, opened January 25, 1817
An Opera by Gioacchino Antonio Rossini; Libretto by Jacopo Ferretti entitled *Angiolina, ossia La Bonta in trionfo*, based on Charles Perrault's *Cendrillon, ou La Petite Pantoufle*

Geltrude Righetti-Giorgi (Angiolina--Cenerentola); Andrea Verni (Don Magnifico); Guiseppe Debegnis (Dandini); Giacomo Guglielmi (Don Ramiro); Caterina Rossi (Clorinda); Teresa Mariani (Thisbe); Zenobio Vitarelli (Alidoro)

CINDERELLA; OR, THE LITTLE GLASS SLIPPER, *Philadelphia Theatre*, opened February 26, 1824
A Pantomime; Director, Charles Durang; Scenery, H. Warren, Joseph Jefferson and I. Darley; Costumes, Mr. Harbaugh; Music, Mr. Kelly

Mrs. James W. Wallach (Cinderella); Charles Durang (The Prince); Mrs. Greene, Mrs. Mestayer (The Step-sisters); Mrs. H. Hathwell (Cupid); Charles Burke (Pedro); George Mestayer (Hyman); Mrs. Charles Burke (Venus); Miss Hathwell, Mrs. Charles Durang, Mrs. Mestayer, Miss Parker (Graces); Mrs. Murray, Mrs. Darlay (Nymphs)

LA CENERENTOLA, *Park Theatre*, New York, opened June 27, 1826

Produced and directed by Manuel del Popola Vincente Garcia; An Opera by Rossini; Libretto by Ferretti

Maria Felicita Garcia (Angiolina--Cenerentola); Signor Rosich (Don Magnifico); Manuel Garcia, Jr. (Dan-dini); Signor Milon (succeeded by Signor Crivelli) (Don Ramiro); Madame Barbiere (Clorinda); Mme. Manuel Garcia (Thisbe); Signor Angrisani (Alidoro)

CINDERELLA; OR, THE FAIRY AND THE LITTLE GLASS SLIPPER, Covent Garden, London, opened April 13, 1830

A Comic Opera by Rossini adapted by Michael Rophino Lacy from Jacopo Ferretti's libretto for *La Cenerentola*, with music from pieces from Rossini's *Armida*, *Guillaume Tell*, *La Cenerentola* and *Maometto II*

Mary Ann Paton (Cinderella); Joseph Wood (Felix, Prince of Salerno); G. Penson (Baron Pompolino); Miss H. Cawse (Clorinda); Miss Hughes (Thisbe)

MUSICAL NUMBERS: "While Sunbeams Are Glancing"; "Morning Its Sweets Is Flinging"; "Music Floats in the Air"; "Bless Now Attend Thee"; "Hark!-Around-Above"; "What Wild Sounds the Hunters Attending"; "Our Noble Prince If Found"; "No, No, With Steps So Light"; "Grant Me Charity"; "Ye Tormentors, Wherefore Came Ye?"; "All Around Is Silent"; "This Mansion a Desert Seems"; "Whence This Soft and Pleasing Flame?"; "Of the Baron's Lovely Daughters"; "My Lord Deign But to Hear Me"; "Dare But to Breathe Again"; "Softly, Softly, in a Whisper"; "Sir, a Secret Most Important"; "Cease Cinderella!"; "Delightful Hour of Rapture"; "In Light Tripping Measure"; "Whilst to Joy We Sing Inviting"; "Let Thine Eyes on Mine Mildly Beaming"; "What Demon's Opposing Malice"; "Now With Grief No Longer Lending"

CINDERELLA; OR, THE FAIRY AND THE LITTLE GLASS SLIPPER, Park Theatre, New York, opened January 24, 1831

A Comic Opera by Rossini adapted by Michael Rophino Lacy from Jacopo Ferretti's libretto for *La Cenerentola*, with music from pieces from Rossini's *Armida*, *Guillaume Tell*, *La Cenerentola* and *Maometto II*; Scenery, Evers; Costumes by Mead; Musical director, De Luce; Choral director, Mr. Meta; Stage manager, Mr. Chambers

Mrs. Austin (Cinderella); John Jones (Felix, Prince of Salerno); Henry Placide (Baron Pompolino); Mrs. W. R. Blake (Clorinda); Jane Vernon (Thisbe); Thomas Placide (Pedro); Mrs. Henry Wallack (Fairy Queen); James Thorne (Dandini); Peter Richings (Alidoro); Mr. Poney (Hunter); Mrs. Durie, Juliet Godey, B. Benjamin, C. Jessop, Julia Turnbull, Julia Wheatley, Emma Wheatley, Miss Simms, Miss Turnbull (Fairies)

CINDERELLA; OR, THE FAIRY AND THE LITTLE GLASS SLIPPER, Chestnut Street Theatre, Philadelphia, opened April 13, 1832

A Comic Opera by Rossini adapted by Michael Rophino Lacy from Jacopo Ferretti's libretto for *La Cenerentola*, with music from pieces from Rossini's *Armida*, *Guillaume Tell*, *La Cenerentola* and *Maometto II*; Scenery, Smith and Carr; Costumes by Mead; Musical director, Mr. Cross, Jr.

Mrs. Austin (Cinderella); John Jones (Felix, Prince of Salerno); Mr. Rowbottom (Baron Pompolino); Mrs. Rowbottom (Clorinda); Miss A. Fisher (Thisbe); Mr. Watson (Pedro); Mrs. Smith (Fairy Queen); Mr. Mercer (Dandini); Mr. Whiting (Alidoro); Messrs. Still, Derr, Whitney, D. Eberle, Broad, Sprague, Johnson, Dickson, Thompson, Read, Ryan, Elliot, Weaver, Young (Hunters); Mmes. Green, Roberts, Misses Armstrong, J. Turner, E. Turner, Durang, Fox, Fairfield,

Resad, Nichols, More, Clements, Tailor, Smith (Fairies)

CINDERELLA; OR, THE FAIRY AND THE LITTLE GLASS SLIPPER, Niblo's Garden, New York, opened August 14, 1837
A Comic Opera by Rossini adapted by Michael Rophino Lacy from Jacopo Ferretti's libretto for *La Cenerentola*, with music from pieces from Rossini's *Armida*, *Guillaume Tell*, *La Cenerentola* and *Maometto II*

Mrs. Knight (Cinderella); John Jones (Felix, Prince of Salerno); William Chippindale (Baron Pompolino); Mrs. Archer (Clorinda); Mrs. Vernon (Thisbe); John Sefton (Pedro); Mrs. Durie (Fairy Queen); Peter Richings (Dandini); John Povey (Alidoro)

CINDERELLA; OR, THE FAIRY AND THE LITTLE GLASS SLIPPER, Touring company, season 1837-38
A Comic Opera by Rossini adapted by Michael Rophino Lacy from Jacopo Ferretti's libretto for *La Ceneren-tola*, with music from pieces from Rossini's *Armida*, *Guillaume Tell*, *La Cenerentola* and *Maometto II*

Eliza Petrie (Cinderella); J. M. Field (Felix, Prince of Salerno); Vincent DeCamp (Baron Pompolino); Miss Vogt (Clorinda); Mrs. Hubbard (Thisbe); Thomas Placide (Pedro); Miss Henning (Fairy Queen); Sol Smith (Dandini); Matt Field (Alidoro)

CINDERELLA; OR, THE FAIRY AND THE LITTLE GLASS SLIPPER, Olympic Theatre, New York opened February 19, 1844 16 performances
Produced and directed by William Mitchell; A Comic Opera by Rossini adapted by Michael Rophino Lacy from Jacopo Ferretti's libretto for *La Cenerentola*, with music from pieces from Rossini's *Armida*, *Guillaume Tell*, *La Cenerentola* and *Maometto II*; Costumes, Mrs. Skaats

Mary Taylor (Cinderella); Mrs. H. C. Timm (Felix, Prince of Salerno); John Nickinson (Baron Pompolino); Mrs. J. B. Booth, Jr. (Clorinda); Mrs. Watts (Thisbe); George Holland (Pedro); Constantia Clark (Fairy Queen); Charles M. Walcot (Dandini); George Graham (Alidoro)

CINDERELLA, Olympic Theatre, New York, opened March 20, 1844 20 performances
Produced and directed by William Mitchell; A Burlesque by Horncastle

Mrs. H. C. Timm (Cinderella); Mary Taylor (Prince Perseverance); Charles M. Walcot (Nedamid); John Nickinson (Alderman Sollipop); George Graham (Peter); Mrs. J. B. Booth, Jr. (Bessy Boxer-Ears); Mrs. Watts (Sissy Slycuff); Constantia Clarke (Biddy); Miss Roberts (Judy)

CINDERELLA; OR, THE FAIRY AND THE LITTLE GLASS SLIPPER, Bowery Theatre, New York, opened February 5, 1847
Produced and directed by William Mitchell; A Comic Opera by Rossini adapted by Michael Rophino Lacy from Jacopo Ferretti's libretto for *La Cenerentola*, with music from pieces from Rossini's *Armida*, *Guillaume Tell*, *La Cenerentola* and *Maometto II*

Mary Taylor (Cinderella); Henry Hunt (Felix, Prince of Salerno); Mr. Vache (Baron Pompolino); Mrs. J. B. Booth, Jr. (Clorinda); Mrs. Sergeant (Thisbe); Thomas Hadaways (Pedro); Miss Lockyer [Mrs. Joseph Jefferson] (Fairy Queen); H. Chapman (Dandini); John Winans (Alidoro)

CINDERELLA; OR, THE FAIRY AND THE LITTLE GLASS SLIPPER, Olympic Theatre, New York, opened October 1, 1849
Produced and directed by William Mitchell; A Comic Opera by Rossini adapted by Michael Rophino Lacy from Jacopo Ferretti's libretto for *La Cenerentola*, with music from pieces from Rossini's *Armida*, *Guillaume Tell*, *La Cenerentola* and *Maometto II*
Mary Taylor (Cinderella); T. Bishop (Felix, Prince of Salerno); John Nickinson (Baron Pompolino); Miss Sinclair (Clorinda); Julia Miles (Thisbe); Thomas Hadaways (Pedro); Mrs. W. Conover (Fairy Queen); Charles M. Walcot (Dandini); Mr. Stafford (Alidoro)

CINDERELLA, Wallack's Theatre, New York, opened June 15, 1851
A Fair Tale Extravaganza by William Brough
Adelaide Gougenheim (Cinderella); Josephine Gougen-heim (Prince Rodolphe); J. G. Burnett (Baron Sold-off); Mrs. Junius Booth, Jr. (Baroness Soldoff); Ida Vernon (Rondoletia); Miss C. Howard (Patchoulia); Charles Peters (Capillaire); Mr. Zavistowski (Red Man of Agar)

CINDERELLA; OR, THE FAIRY AND THE LITTLE GLASS SLIPPER, Park Theatre, New York, opened January 19, 1852 12 performances
Produced and directed by William Mitchell; A Comic Opera by Rossini adapted by Michael Rophino Lacy from Jacopo Ferretti's libretto for *La Cenerentola*, with music from pieces from Rossini's *Armida*, *Guillaume Tell*, *La Cenerentola* and *Maometto II*
Mary Taylor (Cinderella); George Holman (Felix, Prince of Salerno); Henry Placide (Baron Pompolino); Mrs. Blake (Clorinda); Mrs. Holman (Thisbe); William H. Burton (Pedro); Jane Hill (Fairy Queen); F. Meyer (Dandini); Mr. Rea (Alidoro)

LA CENERENTOLA, Astor Place Theatre, New York, opened December 27, 1852 4 performances
An Opera by Rossini; Libretto by Ferretti
Madame Marietta Alboni (AngiolinaCenerentola); Agostino Rovere (Don Magnifico); Signor Colletti (Dandini); Signor Sangrovanni (Don Ramiro); Signora Avogadro (Clorinda); Signor Albertazii (Thisbe); Signor Barili (Alidoro)

CINDERELLA, Bowery Theatre, New York, opened June 15, 1858
A Fair Tale Extravaganza by William Brough
Adelaide Gougenheim (Cinderella); Josephine Gougenheim (Prince Rodolphe); J. G. Burnett (Baron Soldoff); Mrs. Junius Booth, Jr. (Baroness Soldoff); Ida Vernon (Rondoletia); Miss C. Howard (Patchoulia); Charles Peters (Capillaire); Mr. Zavistowski (Red Man of Agar)

CENDRILLON, New York Theatre, opened December 13, 1866
Produced and directed by Augustin Daly; A Play translated and adapted by L. R. Beneux from Charles Perrault's *Cinderella*
Mrs. W. Gomersal (Cendrillon); Eliza Newton (Prince Charming); Mark Smith (King Hurlyburly XIX); Marie Wilkins (Urania de la Houspignolle); Lewis Baker (M. de la Pinchonnaire); Mrs. H. Bland (President of Cupid's Court); Blanche Chapman (Javotte); Alicia Mandeville (Madelon); Sallie Hinckley (Luciola); Annie Yeamons (Oculi); Rosa St. Clair Leland (Aurora); Frank Champman (Maclon); H. Bland (Farhulas); W. Gomersal (Jolicoco); Fred Percy (Riquiqui)

CINDERELLA, *Theatre Comique*, New York, opened March 23, 1872
Produced and directed by Josh Hart; A Burlesque by the Worrell Sisters

Irene Worrell (Cinderella); Sophie Worrell (Prince Petty Pet); Jeannie Worrell (Dandini); E. D. Gooding (Baron); Jennie Hughes (Thisbe); Larry Tooley (Clorinda); Ada Wray (Fairy Queen); John Wild (Buttons); Harry Owen (Alidoro); Jennie Benson (Dancer)

CINDERELLA; OR, HARLEQUIN AND THE LITTLE GLASS SLIPPER, *Standard Theatre*, London, opened December 26, 1872
A Pantomime written and directed by John L. Douglas

Marian Inch (Cinderella); Mlle. Tonnelier (Prince Poppet); Mr. W. Brunton (Clorinde); Mrs. Aynsley Cooke (Thisbe); Miss Osborne Armstrong (King Cocoa); J. Wallace (Baron Pompolini); John Barnum (Dandini)

CINDERELLA, *Drury Lane Theatre*, London, opened December 26, 1873
Produced by F. B. Chatterton; A Pantomime by E. L. Blanchard

Victoria Vokes (Cinderella); Jessie Vokes (The Prince); Fred Vokes (Baron Pumpernickel); Miss Hudspeth (Vixena); Miss Warden (Pavonia); Fred Evans (Clown); Fowdon Vokes (Buttons)

CINDERELLA IN BLACK, *Bryant's Minstrel Theatre*, New York, opened December 22, 1873
A Minstrel version of Cinderella, written, produced and directed by the Bryant Brothers

Eugene (Cinderella); W. Raymond (The Prince); J. Unsworth (Pedro); Dan Bryant, Nelse Seymoure (The Wicked Sisters); Bob Hart (Baron Pomp); Dave Reed (The Witch)

OUR CINDERELLA, *Touring company*, season 1878-79
Produced by the Colville Company; A Burlesque by William Gill; Director, Samuel Colville; Music, H. Sayter (selections mainly from the Chimes of Normandy)

Marian Elmore (Cinderella); Mlle. Emma Roseau (Elfina, Fairy Queen); Marie Williams (Prince Hildebrando Poppetti); Lina Merville (Hightoni); William Gill (Clorinda); Eleanor Deering (Thisbe); W. H. Cahill (Baron de Boulevard); A. W. Maflin (Dryasdust); C. H. Drew (Seraph); Kate Everleigh (Peontype); Susie Winner (Hon. Miss Barebell/Sweetsugar); LePetite (The Coachman); Ada Lee (Hon. Miss Honeydew); Elsie Dean (Ducksydaisy); Annie Deacon (Orfulnice); Mary Winner (Prettysapicture; Annie Winner (Numbetta); Messrs. Harper, Amburg, DeSmith, Francis (Four Watchmen)

THE MAGIC SLIPPER, *Haverley's Theatre*, New York, opened August 25, 1879
Produced by Samuel Colville's Opera Burlesque Company; Director, Samuel Colville; Musical director, Jesse Williams

Emma Roseau (Cinderella); Alice Hastings (The Prince); Ella Chapman (Hightoni); R. E. Graham (Clorinda); Fannie Wright (Thisbe); Edward Chapman (Baron de Boulevard); Carrie McHenry (Swagger); Roland Reed (Seraph); Ada Lee (Peontype); Annie Deacon (Hon. Miss Barebell/Sweetsugar); A. W. Malfin (Petitoe); Alice Wright (Hon. Miss Honeydew); Rose Leighton (Her Imperial Highness); Susie Winner (Daffydowndilla); Bessie Temple (Primrose); Elsie Dean (Violetta); Louise Loring (Daisyana); Mary Winner (Cloverina); Annie Winner (Heartsena); Nita Gerald (Wheatina); Theresa Lamborn (Roseleafa);

Messrs. Amsberg, Horace, Fell (Huntsmen)

CINDERELLA; OR, THE FAIRY AND THE LITTLE GLASS SLIPPER, Booth's Theatre, New York, opened October 12, 1880 30 performances
Produced by John D. Mishler; A Play adapted and directed by Henry C. Jarrett from the Comic Opera by Rossini; Scenery, Catherine Lewis and Henry E. Hoyt; Music arranged by Max Maretzek; Conducted by Anthony Reiff

Annie Shaffer (Cinderella); Catherine Lewis (Prince Paragon); William H. Seymour (Baron Pompolino); Elma Delaro (Clorinda); Jennie Hughes (Thisbe); James Vincent (Pedro); Little Katie Seymour (Fairy Queen); Mark Smith (Dandini); Edward Connell (Alidoro); Ethel Delmont (Colin); William Lloyd (Count Primrose); Charles Bright (Lord Daisy); Leonard Saville (Sir William Rocket); Arthur German (Viscount Dash); George Topack (Humpty); William Moore (Dumpty); Rose Courtland (Dazzle); Lizzie Sims, Lillian Lancaster (Principal Dancers); Folly Gymnasts (Specialty)

CINDERELLA, *Pavilion Theatre*, London, opened December 26, 1882
Produced by Morris Abraham; A Pantomime by Frank Green; Director, John Alexander; Designer, Isaac Cohen

Constance Alexander (Cinderella); Bessie Bonehill (Prince Paragon); Nellie Leamar (Dandini); Sam Holdsworth (Baron Pumperino); George English (Scratchface); John Alexander (Spitfire/Clown); Julia Kent (Fairy Kindheart); Katie Leamar (Petronella); Arthur Alexander (Dozy); C. Reeves (The Demon King); Children of the Matthews Family (Midgets); Mme. Bioletta Amadi (Musician)

CINDERELLA, *Drury Lane Theatre*, London, opened December 26, 1882
Produced and directed by Augustus Harris; A Pantomime by E. L. Blanchard; Music, Oscar Barrett

Kate Vaughan (Cinderella); Minnie Mario (The Prince); Dot Mario (His Attendant); J. W. Hanson (Baron Filletoville); Harry Nicholls (Blondina); Herbert Campbell (Brunetta); M. A. Victor (Baroness Filletoville); Kate Sullivan (Fairy Godmother); Master Abrahams (Tortoiseshell Tom); Fred Storey (General Sharpwitz); Reuben Inch (King Gallopade); George Lupino (Spirit of Mischief); Mlle. Emma Palladino, The Rosa Troupe (Dancers)

CINDERELLA, *Drury Lane Theatre*, London, opened December 26, 1883
Produced and directed by Augustus Harris; A Pantomime by E. L. Blanchard; Music, Oscar Barrett

Kate Vaughan (Cinderella); Minnie Mario (The Prince); Dot Mario (Pousette); Harry Parker (Baron Filletoville); Harry Nicholls (Blondina); Herbert Campbell (Brunetta); M. A. Victor (Baroness Filletoville); Kate Sullivan (Fairy Godmother); Master Abrahams (Tortoiseshell Tom); Fred Storey (General Sharpwitz); Reuben Inch (King Gallopade); George Lupino (Spirit of Mischief); J. W. Hanson (Hobbedyhoy); Alma Stanley (Captain Piccadilly); Mlle. Aenea (Electra); Emily Duncan (Lt. Pall Mall); Emily Clare (Lord Tomnoddy); Challie Clayton (Hon. Charley Wot); Cissie St. George (Viscount Dash); Annie Akers (Lord Broke); Lilly May (Captain Hardup); Rosie Roy (Lieutenant Tique); May Johnstone (Marquis of Must); Minnie Inch (Jeames); Elsie Ward (Baron Johnnie); Selina Delphine (Thomas); May Mellow (Adolphus); Millie Gerard (John); Bridie Jennings (Alphonse); Kate Talbot (Otto); Emma Palladino (Premiere Danseuse);

The Rosa Troupe (Dancers); George Lupino (Harlequin); Tully Louis (Pantaloon); Florence Valeria (Columbine); Will Harley (Policeman XO); Harry Payne (Clown); and Children of the National Training School of Dancing

CINDERELLA, *Sanger's Theatre*, London, opened December 24, 1886
Produced and directed by George Sanger; A Pantomime by William Muskery

Eunice Irving (Cinderella); Stella de Vere (Prince Charming); Mr. Ouseley (Baron Pompolino); Jessie Phillips (Dandini); Tom Wallace (Quisbe); Alfred Bourne (Clawrinda)

CINDERELLA, *Pavilion Theatre*, London, opened December 24, 1886
Produced by Morris Abraham; A Pantomime by Oswald Allen; Director, John Alexander; Designer, Isaac Cohen

Helena Lisle (Cinderella); Miss Louie Gilbert (Prince Brilliant); Arthur Alexander (Dandini); George English (Baron Pomposo); James Stephenson (Clorinda); George Lewis (Thisbe); Mrs. Brunton (Baroness Pomposo); Little Tich (King Mischief); The Albert and Edmund's Troupe (Harlequinade)

THE CRYSTAL SLIPPER; OR, PRINCE PRETTIWITZ AND LITTLE CINDERELLA, *Star Theatre*, New York, opened November 26, 1888 32 performances
Produced by David Henderson; A Spectacular Extravaganza by Harry B. Smith and Alfred Thompson; Director, Richard Barker; Music by Frank David and others; Lyrics by William Jerome; Ballets by Signor Novissimo; Miseenscene, ballet costumes and effects by Alfred Thompson; Scenery, William Voegtlin; Costumes, Dazian

Marguerite Fish (Cinderella); Edwin Foy (Yosemite); R. E. Graham (Baron Anthracite); Mamie Cerbi (Prince Pollydore von Prettiwitz); Daisy Ramsden (Mardi Gras); Tom Martin (Count Twobetter); James E. Sullivan (Tweedledum); Harry Kelly (Tweedledee); Homie Weldon (Fairy Graciosa); Charles Warren (Angostura); Topsy Vann (Flordefuma); Ada Chamberlaine (Captain Riffraff); Babette Rodney (TipTop); Ida Haggard ("She"); George Ali (succeeded by Eddie Rategan) (Thomas Cat); Jessie Rogers (Flick); Lulu Hesse (Flock); Rose Franck (Tric); Olive Lynne (Trac); Lillian Le Mont (Piff); Beatrice Mooney (Paff); Alice Morgan (Hostess of the "Golden Pretzel"); Mabel Morris (Lischen); Addie Inness (Gretchen); Belle Bowles (Rosa); Minnie Murray (Theresa); Mary James (Indian Queen); Mlles. Qualitz, Clara Neumann, Madeline Morando (Dancers); Fanny Quick (Jack); Lena Mazone (Jill); Laurie Brooks (Little Boy Blue); Mlle. Morando (Little Bo Peep); Louis Ronaldo (Frog); Mlle. Qualitz (Duck)

MUSICAL NUMBERS: "A Fool Is My Brother"; "We Are a Daisy Family"; "A Cent for This and a Cent for That"; "Zing Boom"; "I Am a Prince"; "Maypole Dance"; "When the Wheels Go Round"; "The Baron's Song"; "You Shall Be Present at the Prince's Ball"; "The Irish Reel"; "Cinderella"; "Merrily We Trip the Dainty Measure"; "How to Receive an Invited Guest"; "Nothing Like Us"; "Whispered Love"; "Court Gavotte"; "I'm Not Old Enough to Know"

SWEET CINDERELLA, *Grand Theatre*, London, opened Decem-ber 26, 1888
Produced by Charles Wilmot; A Pantomime

Dot Mario (Cinderella); Julia Warden (The Prince); E. C. Dunbar (Dandidi); Fred Williams, Mark Kinghorne (The Ugly Sisters); Joe Burgess (The King); Will Crackles (Chamberlain); Miss Maxwell (The Good Fairy); Miss Douglas (The Bad Fairy); The Paragon Quartette (Singers)

CINDERELLA; OR, LADYBIRD, LADYBIRD, FLY AWAY HOME, Her Majesty's Theatre, London, opened December 26, 1889

Produced and directed by Charles Harris; A Pantomime by Richard Henry; Music by Alfred Cellier, Edward Solomon, Ivan Caryll, Robert Martin and Henry J. Leslie; Lyrics by Clement Scott; Scenery, Messrs. W. Telbin, Henry Emden, W. Hann, E. J. Banks and W. Perkins, T. E. Ryan; Costumes, Mme. Auguste, Miss Fisher, J. A. Harrison, Morris Angle, Potter & Dolman, M. and Mme. Alias; Ballets arranged by M. Gredlue of the Grand Opera, Paris; Children of Her Majesty's Training School and Incidental Dances by John D'Auben

Minnie Palmer (Cinderella); Fanny Robins (The Prince); Eily Coghlan (Ladybird); Alice Young (Beeswing); Laura Linden (Spirit of the Age); Harry Parker (Baron Brokestone); Charles Wallace (Cloddini); Julian Girard (Father Christmas); Robert Dezano (Sinuoso); Irena Verona (Quicksilver); Ella Chapman (Chappini); Annie Volkes (Queen); Mrs. Henry Leigh (The Baroness); Florence Melville (Mayfairio); Violet Elliott (Milendio); Johnny Hanson (The King); F. E. McNish (The King's Herald); Fred Esmond (The Spider King); D. Abrahams (The Cat); S. H. Albert (The Coachman); J. W. Lawrence (John); Tom Lovell (The Cook); The Two Armstrongs (James I and James II); Fawdon Vokes (The Kangaroo); John Le Hay (Tottina Ann); Sheila Barry (Scroogins); Charles Coborn (Glorvina Jane); The Sisters Milton (Maids of Honor); Edith Lester (Page); Marie Knight (Mustard Seed); Jeanette Desborough (Moth); Marie Branhardt (Cobweb); Alice Douglas (Peasblossom); Ellis Jeffrey (Butterfly); Maude Richards, Florence Beresford, Ethel Carlington, Maude Mayron (Black Dominos); The Sisters Hepworth, Jessie Consuela, Kitty Montague, C. Sommerville, A. Jolly, Amy Pedro, Ida Ferrers (Huntsmen); Lucia Cormani (Premiere Danseuse Assoluta); Mlle. Prioria (Premiere Danseuse)

THE CRYSTAL SLIPPER, OR, PRINCE PRETTIWITZ AND LITTLE CINDERELLA, Touring Company, season 1889-90

Produced by David Henderson; A Spectacular Extravaganza by Harry B. Smith and Alfred Thompson; Director, Richard Barker; Music by Frank David and others; Lyrics by William Jerome; Ballets by Signor Novissimo; Miseenscene, ballet costumes and effects by Alfred Thompson; Scenery, William Voegtlin; Costumes, Dazian

Ida Mulle (Cinderella); Edwin Foy (Yosemite); Henry Norman (Baron Anthracite); Louise Montagu (Prince Pollydore von Prettiwitz); Daisy Ramsden (Mardi Gras); Tom Martin (Count Twobetter); Joseph M. Donner (Tweedledum); E. H. Carroll (Tweedledee); Babette Rodney (Fairy Graciosa); Fanny Daboll (Ango-stura); Topsy Vann (Flordefuma); Frankie M. Raymond (Captain Riffraff); Lizzie Winner (Tip-Top); Ida Haggard ("She"); Master Pohey (Thomas Cat); Kitty Allen (Flick); May Wheeler (Flock); Edith Shaw (Tric); Rose Franck (Trac); Lillian Le Mont (Piff); Beatrice Mooney (Paff); Alice Morgan (Hostess of the "Golden Pretzel"); Mabel Morris (Lischen); Addie Inness (Gretchen); Edith Seymour (Rosa); Suzie Winner (Theresa); Rose Franck (Indian Queen)

Academy of Music, Philadelphia, opened December 5, 1891 29 performances

A Spectacular Pantomime Extravaganza by Henry John Leslie

Fannie Ward (Cinderella); Bertha Ricci (The Prince); Nina Farrington (Duke of Chappies); Jennie Reeves (Fairy Queen); Edwin H. Carroll (Tattina Ann); Fred Merdoza (Gloriana Jage); Katherine Pyke (Prunella Gaiters); Norma Cole (Earl of Dudies); Charles Burke (Chauncey); Lillie Alliston (Belva); Lillian De Wolf (Quicksilver); Marie Levton (Spirit of the Age); George D. Melville (Clown);

William Burke (Pantaloon); Augustus Lahlke (Harlequin); W. Lowe (Sprite); J. J. Geary (Policeman); Edith Craske (Columbine); Mlle. Paris (Premiere Assoluta); Mlle. Chitten (Premiere Danseuse)

CINDER-ELLEN UP TOO LATE, *Gaiety Theatre*, London, opened December 24, 1891 181 performances
Produced by George Edwardes; A Musical Comedy by A. C. Torre (Fred Leslie) and W. T. Vincent, based on the fairy tale *Cinderella*; Director, Walter Raynham; Music* and musical direction by W. Meyer Lutz; Costumes designed by Wilhelm, Hugh Patterson; Choreography, Katti Lanner and Willie Warde; Stage manager, Frank Parker

Nellie Farren (succeeded by Kate James, Letty Lind) (Cinder-Ellen); Arthur Williams (Sir Ludgate Hall); Fred Leslie (Servant); Sylvia Grey (Linconzina); Florence Levey (Fettalana); E. J. Lonnen (Prince Belgravia); Maude Hobson (Lord Taplow); Blanche Massey (Lord Eastbourne); Hetty Hamer (Lord Soho); Janet Norton (Sir Waterloo Bridge); Lillian Price (Catherine); Maude Wilmot (Grazina); Violet Monckton (Furnivalzina); Eva Greville (Griffina); Adelaide Astor (Templina); C. Walker (Gnorwood); Mr. Harris (Peckham); Mr. Hill (Footman); Maud Boyd (Sir Peterborough Court); Lily MacIntyre (Victorina); Emily Milly (Mrs. Kensington Gore); Dunville (Lord Whitefriars)

* Music selected from compositions by Osmond Carr, Scott Gatti, Lionel Monckton, Jacobi, Robertsoin, Walter Slaughter, Leopold Wenzel and Sidney Jones

Novelty Theatre, London, opened December 26, 1891 58 performances
Produced and directed by Mrs. J. F. Brian; A Pantomime by H. Buckstone Clair; Scenery, G. Swell, Edgerton and A. Terraine

Florrie Turner (Cinderella); Bella Brian (Prince Peerless); Patti Florence (Fairy Queen); H. Buckstone Clair (Baron Oofless); Rose Crawford (Dandini); Eleanor Lloyd (Baroness Oofless); Francis Rossiter (Sir Algernon Fitznooks); Harriett Ware (Rosebud); Owen Wynne (Dr. Syntax); Frederick Ellis (Pauline); Alice Butler (Rosetta); Beatrice Hurst (Sir Augustus Smyth); Martini (Columbine); Val Seymour (Gertrude); A. St. Lawrence (Grab 'Em); George Arnold (Seize 'Em/A Masher); Mr. Holdun (Pantomime); Mr. Reeves (Lord Chamberlain); Master Buck Williams (Father Time); A. Whittaker (Harlequin); W. Garrett (Jeames/Clown); Carlotta Parks (Harebell)

Lyceum Theatre, London, opened December 26, 1893 126 performances; reopened *Abbey's Theatre*, April 23, 1894 64 performances
Produced by Henry Irving; A Pantomime by Horace Lennard; Director, Oscar Barrett; Music by Oscar Barrett; Choreography, Katti Lanner; Ballet director, J. R. Crawford; Scenery, Henry Enden, J. Pritchard Barrett and Hawes Craven; Musical director, James Weaver; Stage manager, Arthur Bruston

Ellaline Terriss or Bessie Rignold (Cinderella); Kate Chard (Prince Felix); Susie Vaughan (Fairy Godmother); Alice Brookes (succeeded by Katie Barry) (Dandini); Victor Stevens (succeeded by Seymour Hicks) (Thisbe); Harry Parker (Baron Pumpolino); Clara Jecks (succeeded by Minnie Inch) (Baroness); Fred Emney (succeeded by Fred Eastman) (Clorinda); Richard Blunt (succeeded by S. B. Steele) (Alidoro); Charles Wallace (succeeded by Reuben Inch) (Pedro); Florrie Harmon (Fernando); Deane Brand (Grand Chamberlain); William Lugg (succeeded by W. Bestic) (Minister of War); Thomas Terriss (succeeded by W. Jacobson) (Minister of Marine); Willie Temple (succeeded by C. Jacobson)

(Minister of Finance); Guy Waller (succeeded by Mr. Carzley) (Minister of Agriculture); Harry Kitchen (Harlequin); Minnie Tight (Columbine); Louise Loveday (Pigeon); Francesca Zanfretta (succeeded by Lottie Dickens) (Fox); Violet Darrell (succeeded by Nina Gillette (Fairy of the Slipper); Emily Earle (succeeded by E. Clark) (Fairy Potter); Dora Barton (succeeded by Cissie Chamberlain (Fairy Weaver); Dorothy Harwood (succeeded by Edwina Brooke (Fairy Electrician); George Aubrey (Ticket Inspector); Charles Lauri (succeeded by D. Abrahams) (Clown/Black Cat); Enrico Zanfretta (Pantaloon); Fred Kitchen (Policeman); Minnie Terry (succeeded by Victoria Inch) (Sylph Coquette); H. Evans (Boot); Cassie Bruce (succeeded by N. Clark) (Fairy Brassfounder); Grace Leslie (Beauty); Dora Rignold (Virtue); Hilda Thorpe (Industry); Mary Barton (Patience)

Drury Lane Theatre, London, opened December 26, 1895 179 performances
A Pantomime written and produced by Augustus Harris; Director, Arthur Sturgess; Music by James M. Glover; Lyrics by Mary and Joseph Watson, Constance Bache; Choreography, Carlo Coppi and John D'Auban; Scenery, Joseph Harker, Bruce Smith and Robert Caney; Costumes, Comelli; Musical director, James M. Glover; Stage manager, Arthur P. Collins

Isa Bowman (Cinderella); Ada Blanche (Prince Felix); Lily Harold (Fairy Godmother); Alexander Dagmar (Dandini); Herbert Campbell (The Baron); Emily Miller (Clorinda); Sophie Larkin (Angelina); Lionel Rignold (Tutor); Dan Leno (The Baroness); Maggie Ripley (Lord Chamberlain); Buffy Hoby (Harlequin); E. Walker (Columbine); Carl Waller (Pantaloon); V. Knight (Prime Minister); Marguerite Cornille (French Ambassador); H. Hastings (Italian Ambassador); A. Fricker (German Ambassador); L. Feverll (Austrian Ambassador); Tom Lovell (Clown); Lillie Comyns (Demon); Kate Jocelyn (King Toy); Griffiths Brothers (Two Bailiff's Officers) M. Ring (Policeman); Helen Lee (Spirit of Pantomime); Lena Delphine (Lord-in-Waiting); Harrison (Captain of the Guard-at-Arms); M. Bryer (Prince's Aide-de-Camp); M. Shields (Master of the Horse)

Garrick Theatre, London, opened December 27, 1897 86 performances
Produced and directed by Oscar Barrett; A Pantomime by Geoffrey Thorne; Music by Oscar Barrett; Choreography, Katti Lanner; Ballet director, J. R. Crawford; Scenery, Henry Enden, J. Pritchard Barrett and Hawes Craven; Costumes, Wilhelm; Musical director, James Weaver; Stage manager, Arthur Bruston

Grace Dudley (Cinderella); Helen Bertram (Prince Felix); Cicely Richards (Fairy Godmother); Florrie Harmon (Dandini); Harry Nicholls (Thisbe); William Lugg (Baron Pumpolino); Kate Phillips (Baroness); John Le Hay (Clorinda); Guy Barrett (Alidoro); Fred Kaye (Pedro); Lillie Thurlow (Fernando); C. Thornburn (Grand Chamberlain); William Regina (Weary); Lilian Pollard (Susan Soft); Gertrude Claridge (Mrs. Green); Jessie Danvers (Martha Blobbs); George Belmore (Clown); John Wheaton (Pantaloon); E. Hoby (Columbine/Fox); H. Thomas (Harlequin); W. Ritter Ryley (Stallkeeper); Guy Barrett (Fitzalladash); Charles Ross (Policeman); O. E. Lennon (Black Cat); Charles Lilford-Delph (Marmaduke); Edward Morehen (Green); Violet Darrell (Modiste); Georgina Leno (Fancy); Elsa Moxter, Ethel Vivian, Ethel Kern, Kate Dudley, Lilian Pollard, Maggie Byron, Maude Vinton, Ethel Wallis, Lily Twyman, Daisy Sedger, M. Maude, A. Selwyn, M. Romney, M. Graham, Gertrude Claridge, Lily Millbank, Minnie Grist (Ensemble)

THE CATCH OF THE SEASON, *Vaudeville Theatre*, London, opened September 9, 1904 616 performances

Produced by A. & S. Gotti and Charles Frohman; A Musical Comedy by Seymour Hicks and Cosmo Hamilton; based on the fairy tale *Cinderella*; Director, Seymour Hicks; Music by Herbert E. Haines and Evelyn Baker; Lyrics by Charles H. Taylor; Scenery, William Harford; Choreography, Edward Royce; Musical director, Howard Carr; Stage manager, George Fielder

Zena Dare (succeeded by Maie Ash, Ellaline Terriss, Phyllis Dare, Madge Crichton) (Angela); Seymour Hicks (succeeded by Stanley Brett) (Duke of St. Jermyns); Hilda Jacobson (succeeded by Hilda Jeffreys, Florence Lloyd, Gladys Ward) (Higham Montague); Compton Coutts (William Gibson); Charles Daly (Sir John Crystal); Mollie Lovell (succeeded by Ethel Matthews) (Lady Crystal); Rosina Filippi (Lady Caterham); Philip Desborough (succeeded by Ralph Westcombe-Penney) (Almeric Montpelier); Sam Sothern (succeeded by Vera Smith) (Lord Dundreary); Mervyn Dene (Captain Rushpool); Cecil Kennard (succeeded by Philip Desborough) (Lord Yatton); Barbara Dane (Miss Caw); Ethel Matthews (succeeded by Olive Morrell, Louie Pounds) (Hon. Sophia Bedford); Ruby Day (Duchess of St. Jermyns); Kate Vesey (succeeded by Elsie Kay) (Enid Gibson); Lily Maynier (Princess Schowenhohe-Hohenschowen); Helene Blanche (succeeded by Andres Corday, Irena Langlois) (Clotilde); Master A. Valchera (Bucket); William Jefferson (succeeded by Cecil Tresilian (First Footman); C. J. Evans (succeeded by H. N. Mason) (Second Footman); William Jefferson, R. Williams, J. Henry, Ralph Westcombe-Penney, R. Drewitt, C. J. Evans (Guests); Hilda Jeffreys, Lily Mills, G. Karri, Elsie Kay, Kathleen Dawn, Marie Ashton, Marion Cecil, Irene Allen, Barbara Roberts, Alexandra Carlisle (Gibson Girls); Winnie Hall, Winnie Geoghegan, Alice Dubarry, Crissy Bell (Bridesmaids); Lily Eyton, Edith Lee, Munro Ross, Ida Mann, Stella de Marney, Maie Ash, Clara Webber, Lily Maynier, Eve Carrington, Jennie Bateman, Elsie Melville, Genee Hayward (Guests)

MUSICAL NUMBERS: "All Done by Kindness"; "Little Bit of Dinner"; "Back to Harrow"; "Cinderella"; "Auf Wiedersehen" (W. T. Francis); "Seaweed" (Fred Earle); "Raining"; "Won't You Kiss Me Once Before You Do?" (Kern and Harris); "Cupid Is the Captain of the Army" (Dave Reed, Jr.); "Around the World" (Cass Freeborn and Grant Stewart); "Edna May's Irish Song" ["Molly O'Halleron"]

THE CATCH OF THE SEASON, *Daly's Theatre*, New York, opened August 28, 1905 104 performances

Produced by Charles Frohman; A Musical Comedy by Seymour Hicks and Cosmo Hamilton; based on the fairy tale *Cinderella*; Director, Ben Teal; Music by Herbert E. Haines and Evelyn Baker; Lyrics by Charles H. Taylor; Scenery, Ernest Gros; Choreography, Edward Royce

Edna May (Angela); Farren Soutar (Duke of St. Jermyns); Fred Kaye (succeeded by George Frothingham (Lord Bagdad Monteagle); Fred Wright, Jr. (William Gibson); W. L. Branscombe (Sir John Crystal); Annie Esmond (Lady Crystal); Maud Milton (Lady Caterham); Jack H. Millar (Almeric Montpelier); Frank Norman (Captain Rushpool); Bert Sindon (succeeded by Harry Hudson) (Lord Yatton); June May (Hon. Sophia Bedford); Margaret Fraser (Hon. Honoria Bedford); Mrs. J. P. West (Duchess of St. Jermyns); Margaret Greet (Princess SchowenhoheHohenschowen); Dora Sevening (Clotilde); James F. O'Sullivan (Hon. William Dorking); Vivian Vowles (Ermytrude Dorking); Master Louis Victor (Bucket); Vivian Graham (Badminton); Lillian Burns (Lady Louise D'Orsay);

William Jefferson (First Footman); C. J. Evans (Second Footman); Leroy Berry, Talleur Andrews (Guests); Dorothy Zimmermann, Gladys Lockwood, Ethel Kelly, Dorothy Reynolds, Ethel Fillmore, Muriel St. Quinten, Enid Gibson, Violet Conrad, Evelyn Powys, Adele McNeil, Sylvia Egan (Gibson Girls)

Drury Lane Theatre, London, opened December 26, 1905 131 performances
Produced and directed by Arthur P. Collins; A Pantomime by Sir F. C. Burnand, J. Hickory Wood and Arthur P. Collins; Scenery, Robert Caney, Henry Emden, Bruce Smith and Julian Hicks; Costumes, Comelli; Choreography, Ernest d'Auban; Music and musical director, James M. Glover

May de Sousa (Cinderella); Queenie Leighton (Prince Jasper); Walter Passmore (Baroness de Bluff); Arthur Williams (Baron de Bluff); Harry Fragson (Dandigny); Johnny Danvers (Samuel Snap); Arthur Conquest (Spirit of Midnight/Cat); Tom Wootwell (Growler); Daisy Cordell (Fairy Godmother); Emilie Spiller (Aemone); Pollie Emery (Hippolyta); Minnie Abbey (Ferdinand); Alec Davidson (Father Time); Tom Cusden (Harlequin); Whimsical Walker (Clown); Charles Ross (Pantaloon); Sid Cotterell (Policeman); M. Pennell (Columbine); Le Brun (Trim/Trott); Harry Randall (Alphonse); Arthur Nelstone (Sentry); Edward Morgan (Beadle); Bob Ronina, Florence Hooton, Edith Russell, Mabel Mitchell, Mabel Robbins, Renee Roma, Mary Gray, Eva Fairleigh, Edward Morgan, Sid Cotterell, Harold Chapin, D. Mills, W. Green, The Tiller Troupe (Ensemble)

Adelphi Theatre, London, opened December 24, 1908 91 performances
Produced by George Edwardes and Robert Courtneidge; A Pantomime by A. M. Thompson and Robert Courtneidge; Scenery, Conrad Tritschler, W. R. Coleman and R. McCleery; Costumes, Mrs. E. Walcott and Wilhelm; Choreography, Elsie Clerc; Music, Alfred Haines; Musical director, Arthur Wood; Stage manager, Reginald Highley

Phyllis Dare (Cinderella); Gertrude Sinclair (Fairy Godmother); Fred Leslie (Dandini); Louie Lochner (Malvolentio); Dan Rolyat (Archibald, Baron Lacklands); Stephen Adeson (Choodles); Mabel Russel (Mopsa); Marie Ringold (Arethusa); Carrie Moore (Rudolph); Maudie Thornton (Gaston); Marjorie Manners (Marquis Oakdeans); Dorothy Laine (Princess Roxana); Violet Graham (Duchess of Foxbrush); Muriel Vana (Lord Beechwood); Lily Banlon (Lady Sweetbriar); Rhoda Clighton (Earl of Hawthorn); Maisie Sinclair (Earl of Marshmallow); Margaret Keane (Icicle); Charles James, Charles Charmier (Woodcutters); George Parte, G. Smith (Prince's Footmen); John Humphries (Daisy); Belle Ross (Lord Chestnut); Norah Dwyer (Gretchen)

A STUBBORN CINDERELLA, *Broadway Theatre*, New York, opened January 25, 1909 88 performances
Produced by Mort H. Singer; A Musical Play by Frank B. Adams and Will H. Hough; Director, George Marion; Music by Joseph E. Howard; Scenery, Gates and Morange; Costumes, Will R. Barnes; Musical director, William Loraine

Sallie Fisher (Lady Leslie); John Barrymore ("Mac"); Charles Prince (Fat); Alice Dovey (Lois); Helen Salinger (Lady Evelyn); Dorothy Brenner (Sallie); Alan Brooks (A Tutor); Robert Harrington (succeeded by Bobby Barry) (Skeeter); Charles Rankin (Thaddeus Leonardo); James C. Marlowe (Colonel Hunt); Don Merrifield (The President/An Indian); Ben Turbett (Police Sergeant/An Engineer); Charles Wedlake (Officer/A Porter); John Wheeler (A Cab Driver); Clarence Lutz (Grid); Frank Magin (Hotel Manager); Misses Adams, Baker, Boswell, Cecil,

Carleton, Cummings, Deskaw, Downing, Edwards, Everette, Feltes, Francis, Gilbert, Harrington, Horlock, Harris, Hubbard, Le Clare, Lockwood, Merrill, Miller, Moon, A. Notter, H. Notter, Oty, O'Day, Porterfield, Rodriguez, Stephenson, Stone, Stoy, Vose, Webb, White, Younge (Show Girls); Messrs. Damarel, Diamond, Gates, Hamilton, Headley, Hutchins, Lansky, Lasher, Lutz, Merrill, McDermott, McKittridge, Murray, Sampson, Wood, Yorkshire (Boys)

MUSICAL NUMBERS: "Love Me Just Because"; "Don't Be Cross With Me"; "I'm in Love With All the Girls I Know"; "None But the Brave Deserve the Fair"; "The Land of the Sky"; "Adios, Senorita"; "Don't Be Anybody's Moon But Mine"; "Cinderella"; "Dream Minuet"; "Don't Teach Me to Swim Alone"; "If They'd Only Let Poor Adam's Rib Alone"; "The Orange Fete"; "When You First Kiss the Last Girl You Love"

Strand Theatre, London, opened December 12, 1909 15 performances
A Play written and directed by Austin Fryers; Music, Moritz Lutzen

Mary Glynne (Cinderella); Rosie Fitzgerald (Prince); Clara Cooper (Dandini); Harry Dean (Baron); Mabel Wall (Orynthia); Minnie Dean (Ermyntrude); Agnes Glynne (Fairy Godmother); Cynthia Eckert (Chamberlain)

OUR LITTLE CINDERELLA, *Playhouse Theatre*, London, opened December 20, 1910
A Musical Play by Leo Trevor; Music, Herman Lohr; Lyrics, Arthur Wimperis

Margery Maude (Cinderella); Herbert Bromilow (The Prince); Dorothy Dayne (Witch Hazel); Cyril Maude (Lord Punterfield); H. Robert Averell (Hurlingham); Neville Knox (Roehampton); Rix Curtis (Ranelagh); John Harwood (Lord Chamberlain); Maidie Hope (Mrs. Bloomer); Ethel Morrison (Marathon); Emma Chambers (Crecy); Renee Mayer (Fairy Teenie Wee); Nora Roylace (Fairy Icklesing); Marcella Kreutz (Fairy Squibb); Beatrice Griffiths (Fairy Tinymite); Dorothy Turner (Fairy Wiggley Wog); Dolly Summers (Coachman); Lillian Drew, Kathleen Hayes, Muriel Hall, Nora Laming, Eva Rowland, Gertrude Hanne, Hilda Harita, Dorothy Lane, Doris Champneys, Violet Lingard, Lillian Bell, Clarissa Batchelor, Elsie Spencer, Patrick Murray, Percival Thorne, Wilfred Essex, Kingsford Shortland, Albert Derrick, Charles Stedman, George Gregson, Otto Alexander (Fairies, Guests, Huntsmen, Trumpeters); Henry J. Ford (Messenger)

THE GOLDEN LAND OF FAIRY TALES, *Aldwych Theatre*, London, opened December 14, 1911
A Fairy Play translated and adapted by A. H. Quaritch and Maurice Raye; Music by Heinrich Berte

Mary Glynne (Cinderella); Bobbie Andrews (Prince Richard); Lena Flowerdew (Stepmother); Rhode Beresford, Honoria Elliot (Stepsisters); Maud Cressall (Fairy Queen); Shakespeare Stewart (King); Blanka Stewart (Queen); Basil Seymour (Minister of State); Ada Glynne (Page); Alfred Latell (Bull Dog); Charles A. White (Court Marshal); Arthur Cleave (Master of Churchill)

THE LADY OF THE SLIPPER; OR, A MODERN CINDERELLA, *Globe Theatre*, New York, opened October 28, 1912 232 performances
Produced by Charles Dillingham; A Musical Fantasy; Director, R. H. Burnside; Book by Anne Caldwell and Lawrence McCarty; Music by Victor Herbert; Lyrics by James O'Dea

Elsie Janis (Cinderella); David C. Montgomery (Spooks); Fred A. Stone (Punks); Douglas Stevenson (Crown Prince Maximilian); Vivian Rushmore (Fairy

Godmother); Charles Mason (Baron von Nix); Edgar Lee Ray (replaced Vernon Castle) (Atzel); Allene Carter (Romneya); Samuel Burbank (Albrecht); Florence Williams (Sophia); Lillian Lee (Dollbabia); Queenie Vassar (Freakette); Peggy Wood (Valerie); Edna Bates (Irma); James Reaney (Captain Ladislaw); Eugene Revere (Prince Ulrich); David Abrahams (Mouser); Harold Russell (Louis); Lillian Rice (Maida); Angie Wiemers (Gretchen); Edgar L. May (Joseph); Don Abrahams (Don the Dog); Lydia Lopoukowa (Premier Danseuse); Marie Gordon, Marion Henry, Estelle Richmond, Marguerite St. Clair, Carol Lynn, Claire Bertrand, Gladys Feldman, Selma Mantell, Esther Lee, Kathryn Daly, Isabel Falconer, Olive Carr, Edna Dana, Evelyn Conway, Alice Keene, Anna Stone, Mazie LeRoy, Lola Curtis, Dolly Filly (Ladies-in-Waiting, Oriental Women of the Harem); R. C. Bosch, R. C. Bell, Harry Silvey, John Roberts, J. F. Johnson, Joseph Donnelly (Soldiers, Courtiers); Ethel Rose-bud, Lottie Crossland, Maud Crossland, Phyllis Erroll, Violet Horlock, Mattie Cronin, Marjory Graham, Annie Ray (Dancing Girls); Marie Walsh, Helen Shea, Irene Kearney, Alice Moriarty, Marion O'Neill, Myrtle Zeigler, Adelaide Zeigler, Josephine Taylor, Sadie Howard, Margie Moriarty, Ida Goldstein, Emily Callen, Helen Ward, Helen Elsworth, Mazie Goss, Jeanette Wollenberg (Corps de Ballet); Agnes McCarthy, Evelyn Whalan, Juliet Strahl, Marie Carroll, Joe Quinn, George Phelps, Charles Jackson, Herbert Zeigler (Halloween Kiddies); *Harlequinade*: David C. Montgomery, Fred A. Stone (Harlequins); Lillian Rice (replaced Vernon Castle) (Columbine); David Abrahams (Cat); Ed Randall, George Phelps (Policemen)

MUSICAL NUMBERS: "Once Upon a Time"; "Fond of the Ladies"; "Meow! Meow! Meow!"; "Love Me Like a Real, Real Man"; "All Halloween"; "Witch Ballet"; "Princess of Far Away"; "At the Bal Masque"; "Them Was the Childhood Days"; "Youth"; "Bagdad"; "Little Girl at Home: "Punch Bowl Glide"; "The Drums of the Nations"; "The Lady of the Slipper"; "Cinderella's Dream"; "Put Your Best Foot Forward, Little Girl"; "And They Lived Happily Ever Afterwards"

Dropped from production: "The Garden Party"; "The Voice of the Waltz"; "My Russian Girlski"; "Reuben Glue"

CINDERELLA ON BROADWAY, *Winter Garden Theatre*, New York, opened June 24, 1920 126 performances

Produced by Lee and J. J. Shubert; A Fantasy of the Great White Way; Director, J. C. Huffman; Dialogue and lyrics by Harold Atteridge; Music by Bert Grant; Incidental music, Al Goodman; Art director, Watson Barratt; Costumes, Cora MacGeachy, Homer Conant, S. Zalud and Madame Haverstick; Dance numbers staged by Allan K. Foster; The Top of the World and the Circus designed by Homer Conant; Musical director, Oscar Radin

Prologue: Al Sexton (Broadway); Norma Gallo (Peter Pan); Burtress Dietch (Boy); Delores Mendez (Girl)

A Toy Shop and Book Store: Norma Gallo (Peter Pan); James Daly (Old King Cole); John Kearns Santa Claus); Arthur Cardinal (Jack Horner); Roger Little (Jack in the Box); Joe Neimeyer (A Toy); Byron Halsted (Whistle); Georgie Price (Tad); Eileen Van Biene (Cindy); Steward Baird (Prince Charming); Jessica Brown (Joy); John T. Murray (Gloom); Renee Dentling (Beauty); The Glorias (Themselves); Marie Stafford (Marie); Charlotte Sprague (Charlotte); Mildred Soper (Mildred); Lyola White (Lyola); Florence Elmore (Mrs. Content); Jane Green (Jane)

Cafe de Paris: Bert Savoy (Mlle. Pretty); Jay Brennan (Baron Rock)

Humpty Dumpty Lane: El Brendel (Yonson); Flo Burt (Miss Moffet); Georgie Price (Simon); Eileen Van Biene (Cindy); Joe Neimeyer (Jack); Al Sexton (Jill); Florence Elmore (Mrs. Content)

The Husband and the Friend: Al Sexton (Broadway); Albert Howson (The Husband); Renee Dentling (The Wife); George Baldwin (The Friend); Walter Brower (The Other Man)

Anywhere: Walter Brower (Artie)

Sweetie Land: Olga Cook (Sweetie)

The Devil Examines His Accounts: John T. Murray (Gloom); Stewart Baird (Prince); Renee Dentling (Princess)

The Top of the World: Dorothy Bruce (A Vampire); Flo Summerville (The Joker); Isabelle Holland (Dice); Grace Keeshon (Queen of Hearts); Mae Deveraux (Jack of Hearts); Lyola White (Ace of Diamonds); Ann Delmore (Queen of Spades); Mae Daley (Misfortune); Louise Wayne (Poverty); De Anguilliar (Hope Abandoned); Mar McCreary (Vice); Madge McCarthy (Shame); Mildred Soper (Hope Gone Wrong); Marie Farrell (Degradation); Llora Hoffman (Voice); Maryon Vadie (Laughter); Constantin Kobeleff (Dance); Violet Gleason (Another)

Honeymoon Cottage: El Brendel (Yonson); Flo Burt (Miss Moffet)

The Silver Slipper Ball: Roger Little (Butler); Georgie Price (Tad); Jessica Brown (Joy); George Baldwin (Hal); Walter Brower (Artie); Renee Dentling (Beauty); Stewart Baird (Prince); Billy Wagner (Maid); Eileen Van Biene (Cindy); John T. Murray (Gloom); Llora Hoffman (Miss Walz); Flo Burt (Miss Moffet); Al Sexton (Broadway); Joe Neimeyer (Jack); Purcella Brothers (Themselves); The Glorias (Themselves)

The Old Music Masters: Steward Baird (Prince); Albert Howson (Mendelssohn); Maryon Vadie ("Spring Song"); Roger Little (Paderewski); The Glorias ("Minuet"); James Daly (Liszt); Mlle. Vadie-Kubeleff ("Hungarian Rhapsodies")

Caproni Station: Eileen Van Biene (Cindy); John T. Murray (Inventor); Al Sexton (Broadway); George Baldwin (Hal); Olga Cook (Mary); Georgie Price (Tad); El Brendel (Yonson); Flo Burt (First Mate)

At the Circus: Eileen Van Biene (Cindy); John T. Murray (The Ring Master); Tarzan (Himself); Felix Patty (The Keeper); Mijares and Brother (Themselves)

Lies: Norma Gallo (Peter Pan); Al Sexton (Broadway); Eileen Van Biene (Edith); George Baldwin (Ralph); Stewart Baird (Tommy); Flo Burt (Amy)

The Primrose Path: Rene Dentling (Beauty); Stewart Baird (Prince)

Out Front: John T. Murray (Gloom); Al Shayne (An Opera Singer); William Kinley (A Musician)

Watteau Land: Olga Cook (Susie); Jessica Brown (Joy); Joe Neimeyer (Folly); Al Sexton (Broadway); El Brendel (Yonson); Flo Burt (Miss Moffet); Albert Howson (Minister); John Y. Murray (Gloom)

On Broadway: Al Sexon (Broadway); Georgie Price (Tad)

MUSICAL NUMBERS: "Chair Ballet"; "Old King Cole"; "Beyond the Candle Light"; "All the Little Glooms Start Dancing"; "My Phantom Loves"; "Romantic Blues"; "Whistle"; "Cindy"; "Why Don't You Get a Sweetie?"; "Wheel of Fate"; "Roulette Dance"; "Minuet"; "The Last Waltz I Had With You"; "Cinderella on Broadway"; "Joy Dance"; "Any Little Melody"; "Old Music Masters"; "Lady of Mars"; "Primrose Path"; "Naughty Eyes"; "Girl Belongs to You"; "Precious Jewels"

Covent Garden, London, opened December 27, 1920 65 performances
Produced by Arthur P. Collins and Alfred Butt; A Pantomime by Frank Dix and Arthur P. Collins; Director, Arthur P. Collins; Scenery, Alfred Terraine, Bruce Smith, R. C.

McCleery, E. J. Humphries, Marc Henri and John Bull; Costumes, Comelli; Choreography, Jean Pratesi; Music and musical director, James M. Glover; Stage managers, Ernest d'Auban and Arthur Conquest

Kathlyn Hilliard (Cinderella); Marie Blanche (Prince of Floravia); Winifred Davis (Fairy Godmother); Mabel Green (Dandini); G. Clark (Lord Chamberlain); George Craig (Harlequin); F. Schuster (Columbine); Arthur Conquest (Dr. Crowley); E. Morgan (Oliver); Seth Egbert (Baroness de Beauxchamps); Harry Claff (Baron de Beauxchamps); Lily Long (Maxie); Louise Maisie (Butterfly); Whimsical Walker (Clown); B. Bennett (Archbishop); William Stevens (Pantaloon); Bell (Wagstaff); Brennan (Flunkey); Robb Gilmore (Minnie); Albert Egbert (Walter); and The Penders, Fred Cinnett & Co., Wyko, M. Crawley, Avis, Simpson, J. Clarke, Bennett, Bowden, J. Crawley, The Drury Lane Girls

Lyceum Theatre, London, opened December 26, 1921 96 performances
Produced and directed by Walter and Frederick Melville; A Musical Pantomime by Leedham Bantock and Bert E. Hammond; Music by H. Sullivan Brooks; Scenery, H. K. Browne, A. E. Payne and I. Morgan; Lighting, John H. Waters; Costumes, Willie Clarkson; Choreography, Euphran MacLaren; Stage managers, S. Major Jones, Cecil de Lee and Jack Vincent

Dainty Doris (Cinderella); Louie Beckman (Prince Charming); Doris Lennox (Fairy Godmother); Ruby Kimberley (Dandini); Dorothy Mudge (Spirit of the Slipper); George Jackley (Baron Pas de Largent); Jack Vincent (Father Time); Norman Astridge (Demon Malvino); Jimmy Commerford (Pantaloon/Toodles the Cat); Walter Commerford (Clown/Poodles the Dog); Connie Wilde (Sunbeam); Minnie Pine (Clorinda); Poppy H. Asquin (Dorothy Bag); Violet Beatrice (Rosy Bloom); Eva Wilton (Gold Stick); M. S. Carr (Copper Stick); Vera Mills (Silver Stick); Fred Sylvester and His Company (Sir Ajax/Tiny Tim/Much/Little); Fred Dixon (Moon Man); Augustus Bowerman (Father Christmas); Billy Danvers (Buttons); Freddy Regent (Araminta); Joe Mott (Put); Len Kilroy (Take); Babe Livesey (Dancer)

Hippodrome Theatre, London, opened December 21, 1922 176 performances
Produced by Moss Empires Ltd., R. H. Gillespie, managing director; A Musical Pantomime; Director, Julian Wylie; Book and lyrics by Clifford Harris and Valentine; Music by James W. Tate; Scenery, Marc Henri, Laverdet, Philip Howden and John Bull; Lighting, W. P. Chester; Costumes, Dolly Tree; Musical director, Julian Jones; Stage managers, Colin Bryce and W. Armstrong

Daisy Burrell (Cinderella); Clarice Mayne (Prince Charming); Daisy Wood (Dandini); Stanley Lupino (Buttons); Bert Errol (Minnie Mumm); Victor Crawford (Baron Mumm); Dolly Harmer (Maxie Mumm); C. Leoville (Harlequin); Ted Reed (Pantaloon); Bob Reed (Clown); Evelyn Lynn (Columbine); Winifred Roma (Silverlight); Harry C. Robinson (Demon Nightshade); Fred Whittaker (Chummie); Nervo and Knox (Broker's Men)

Palladium Theatre, London, opened December 23, 1925 101 performances
Produced by Harry Day; A Musical Pantomime by Charles Henry and Gilbert Lofthouse; Director, Charles Henry; Music by Vivian Ellis; Lyrics by James Heard; Scenery, Max Martin and H. Good; Costumes, Jefferson Arthur and Criscuolo; Musical director, Horace Sheldon; Stage managers, Robert Smith and Gregory Croke

Lennie Deane (Cinderella); Clarice Mayne (Prince Charming); Charles Austin (Buttons); Susie Belmore (Dandini); Gordon Terry (Story Book Man); George

Mozart (Baron Bardupp); Cherry Hardy (Good Fairy); Isabelle Dillon (Caroline); Lily Lansdown (Prudence); Jeanie Gregson (Gertrude); Picton Roxborough (Squire/Footman); Charles Naughton, Jimmy Gold (Debt Collectors); Guy and Billy Shanks (Horse); Daphne Brayne (Specialty Dancer); Derra de Moroda (Principal Ballet Dancer)

CINDERS, *Dresden Theatre*, New York, opened April 3, 1923
Produced and directed by Edward Royce; A Music Comedy; Book and lyrics by Edward Clark; Music by Rudolf Friml; Scenery, P. Dodd Ackerman; Gowns, Paul Poiret; Fashion parade gowns, Evelyn McHorter; Musical director, Victor Baravelli; Stage managers, Frank Rainger and Denny Murray

Nancy Welford (Cinders); Queenie Smith (Tillie Olsen); W. Douglas Stevenson (John Winthrop); Margaret Dale (Mrs. Horatio Winthrop); Fred Hillebrand (Slim Kelly); John H. Brewer (Major Drummond); Roberta Beatty (Mrs. Delancey Hoyt); George Bancroft (Great Scott); Mary Lucas (Geraldine Hoyt); Thomas Fitzpatrick (Winthrop's Butler); Lillian Lee (Miss Breckenridge); Edith CampbellWalker (Mme. Duval); Kitty Kelly (Tottie); Estelle Levelle (Lottie); Alta King (Hortense); Diana Stegman (Annabelle); Dagmar Oakland (Mathilde); Evelyn Darville (Julie); Elaine Gholson (Yvette); Eden Grey (Ninette); Vera Da Wolfe (Cecelia); Louise Bateman (Simone); Jack Whiting (Bruce); Nathaniel Gennes (Nat); Frank Curran (Frank); Harry Howell (Harry); Denny Murray (Denny); Abner Barnhart (Cliff); Dewitt Oakley (Dewitt); Thomas Green (Thomas); Eugene Jenkins (Gene); Gertrude McDonald, Elva Pomfretm Mildred Lunnay, Sydney Reynolds (Dancers); Ralph Riggs and Katharine Witchie (Specialty Dancers)

MUSICAL NUMBERS: "One Good Time"; "Get Together"; "You Got What Gets 'Em"; "I'm Simply Mad About the Boys"; "You and I"; "The Argentine Arango"; "Finaletto"; "Hawaiian Shores"; "You Remind Me of Someone"; "Fashion Parade"; "Cinders"; "The Belles of the Bronx"; "Rags Is Royal Rainments"

THE GLASS SLIPPER, *Guild Theatre*, New York, opened October 19, 1925 65 performances
Produced by The Theatre Guild; A Comedy by Ferenc Molnar; Acting version and direction by Philip Moeller; Settings and costumes, Lee Simonson; Stage managers, Ralph MacBan and Rowland Hoot

June Walker (Irma Szabo); George Baxter (Paul Csaszar); Helen Westley (Adele Romajzer); Armina Marshall (Kati); Lee Baker (Lajos Sipos); Martin Wolfson (Stetner/Police Clerk); Erskine Sanford (Captain Gal/Police Sergeant); Veni Atherton (Adele's Mother); Maud Brooks (Viola); Ethel Westley (Julcsa); Louis Cruger (Bandi Sasz/Sergeant at Arms); Day Tuttle (Parish Priest); Elizabeth Pendleton (Cook); Stanley G. Wood (Janitor); Amelia Summerville (Mrs. Rotics); Jeanne La Gue (Mrs. Rotics' Companion); Ralph MacBane (Dr. Theodore Sagody); John McGovern (Photographer); Roland Hoot (Assistant Photographer); Ethel Valentine (Ilona Keczeli); Milton S. Salisbury (Policeman); Edward Fielding (Police Magistrate); Eddie Wragge (Lilly)

CINDERELLA, *Metropolitan Opera House*, Philadelphia, opened February 22, 1927
Produced by the Peerless Juvenile Extravaganza Company; A Musical version of the fairy tale; Dances and Play directed and staged by Ethel QuirkPhilips, Edward Quirk-Philips, Karlene Franz and Leslie Kelley, under the direction of Ethel Quirk-Philips and Al White; Costumes, Mrs. M. S. Barry-Louise Muir

Artennis Faque (Cinderella); Leslie Kelley (The Prince); Myrtle Quirk-Philips (Dandini); Phyllis Battles (Alidoro); Ethel Quirk-Philips (Fairy God-mother); Audrey Shestack (Clorinda); Katherine Dougherty (Thisbe); Dennis Welch (Baron Pompolino); Thomas Cannan (Pedro); Anna Hagen (Page); Lucile Bremer, Paul Treadway, Margery Jane Moss, Thelma Pooler, Leone Nolle, Mildred Davis, Sylvia Folstein, Anna Hagen, Margery Tams, Vera Rosenthal, Dolores Able, Dot Denneker, Dorothy Leatherman, Marcelle McKenna, Maria Magazu, Minerva Wiley, Franklin Tettener, Dorothy Lipschultz, Lorraine and Faust, Margaret Mitchell, Pearl Leaf, Mary Moss, Mabel Smith, Regina Pinto, Mae Whitlock and the Stanley Brothers, Ruth Warner, Amanda Clayes, Helen Hill, Phyllis Battles, Katherine Dougherty, Thomas Cannan, Uncle Whip (Specialties)

Palladium Theatre, London, opened December 24, 1927 85 performances
Produced by Charles Gulliver and Harry Day; A Musical Pantomime; Director, Charles Henry; Book by Gilbert Lofthouse and Charles Henry; Music by Vivian Ellis; Lyrics by James Heard; Scenery, Max Martin; Costumes, Criscuolo; Choreography, Mlle. Albion; Musical director, Horace Shelton; Stage managers, Robert Smith and Gregory Croke

Lena Chisholm (Cinderella); Clarice Mayne (Prince Charming); George Jackley (Buttons); Peggy Surtees (Good Fairy); Susie Belmore (Dandini); Alec Dane (Story Book Man); Harry Ford (Baron Hardup); Ronnie Howard (Gertrude); Daphne Payne (Prudence); Isabelle Dillon (Caroline); Picton Roxborough (Squire/ Footman); Jack Frost, Hengler Brothers, Terry's Juveniles (Footmen); Queen and Le Brun (Animals); Nervo and Knox (Debt Collectors); Mlle. Albion (Premiere Danseuse)

THE TALE OF CINDERELLA, *Scala Theatre*, London, opened December 26, 1928 50 performances
Produced and directed by Frederick G. Lloyd; A Pantomime by Peter Davey, Arthur Stanley and H. N. Gibson; Music by Brer White; Additional music by Kathleen Simpson; Scenery, Leonard Mortimer; Costumes, Bevan Lorimer; Choreography, Gracie Cone; Musical director, Brer White; Stage manager, A. E. Macey

Iris Adair (Cinderella); Ouida MacDermott (Prince Glorio); Chester Fields (Buttons); Maudie Olmar (Dandini); Edwin Dodds Baron Shotocash); Cedric Percival (Mr. Wellworth); Audrey King (Crooked Sixpence); Marjorie Geach (Fairy Queen); Dot Rikenson (Mme. Vanite); Harold Stanley Barker (Clown); Jill Evans (Priscilla); Egbert Brothers (Bill/Walter); Charles James (Jeames); Jimmie Jones, Hilary Fryer, Frank Quinton, Charles Bright, Charles Knight (Footmen); Mary Milburn, Iris Moore, Joan Bourne, G. Waddington, Beryl Reeves, Freda Tree, Sylvia Pope (Huntsmen)

MR. CINDERS, *Adelphi Theatre*, London, opened February 11, 1929; moved to *Hippodrome Theatre*, July 16, 1929 528 performances
Produced by Moss Enterprises Ltd. and J. C. Williams Ltd.; Producer, Julian Wylie; A Musical Comedy; Director, George D. Parker; Book and lyrics by Clifford Grey and Greatrex Newman; Music by Vivian Ellis and Richard Myers; Additional lyrics, Leo Robin; Dances, Max Rivers; Costumes, Revielle and Mme. Blanche; Stage manager, H. E. Bright

Bobby Howes (Jim); Binnie Hale (succeeded by Rene Mallory) (Jill Kemp); Charles Cautley (Henry Kemp); Sebastian Smith (Sir George Lancaster); Lorna

Hubbard (Phyllis Patterson); Reita Nugent (Minerva Kemp); Jack Melford (Lumley); Ruth Maitland (Lady Lancaster); Rene Mallory (succeeded by Vera Wilson) (Lucy Smith); Basil Howes (Guy); Paddy Duprez (P. C. Marks); Edith Saville (Donna Lucia d'Esmeralda); Thorp Devereaux (Smith); Phil Lester (Hodgins/ Butler); Daphne Day, Sheila Armstrong, Doris Collins, Rita Elsie, Doris Greene, Ella Fairbanks, Gracie May, Vera Wilson, Billy Reynolds, Harry Webster, Norman Lonsdale, Freddie Nye (Principal Guests)

MUSICAL NUMBERS: "Blue Blood"; "True to Two"; "I Want the World to Know"; "One-Man Girl"; "On With the Dance"; "Spread a Little Happiness"; "Le Cygne"; "At the Ball"; "Seventeenth Century Drag"; "Jill"; "On the Amazon"; "Every Little Moment"; "I've Got You, You've Got Me"; "Honeymoon for Four"

Lyceum Theatre, London, opened December 26, 1931

A Pantomime written, produced and directed by Walter and Frederick Melville; Music by Charles J. Moore

Constance Carpenter (Cinderella); Kitty Reidy (Prince Charming); John E. Coyle (Buttons); Iris Rowe (Fairy Godmother); Helen Binnie (Dandini); Irene Vere (Arabella); Dorothy Vernon (Clorinda); George Jackley (The Baron); Edward Law (Father Time); Betty Bucknell (Fairy of the Slipper); Molly Vyvyan (Lord Goldstick); Mary Penney (Lord Silverstick); Jessica Noble (Lord Copperstick); Ethel Beatrice (Lord Leadstick); John Lloyd (Mr. Whey [Milkman]); Freddy Austin (Neddy the Donkey); Dan Swanson (Mr. Bones [Butcher]); Charles Naughton (Joe Muggitt); Jimmy Gold (Bill Riff Raff); Neigh and Neigh (Horse the Horse); Wally Mack (Thomas the Cat); Errol Addison (Spirit of the Mirror); George Belmore (Sloth); Iris Kirkwhite (Vanity)

Drury Lane Theatre, London, opened December 26, 1934

Produced and directed by Prince Littler; A Pantomime by Marriott Edgar; Music by Tom Lewis; Special compositions by Tom Lewis and Eric Coates

June (Cinderella); Phyllis Neilson-Terry (Prince Charming); Clarice Hardwicke (Dandini); Bill Danvers (Buttons); Ethel Revnell (Maxie Mumm); Gracie West (Minnie Mumm); Dan Leno, Jr. (Baron Mumm); The Three Sailors

Coliseum Theatre, London, opened December 24, 1936

Produced and directed by Prince Littler; A Pantomime by Marriott Edgar; Music by Tom Lewis

Edna Best (Cinderella); Madge Elliott (Prince Charming); Lupino Lane (Buttons); Anona Winn (Dandini); Reginald Matthews (Father Time); Rita Stirling (Fairy); Jack Butler (Jake); Chuck O'Neill (Sydney); Wallace Lupino (Baron Stoneybroke); Douglas Wakefield, Billy Nelson (The Ugly Sisters, Julie and Myrtle); Bert Evremonde (Bromo)

Princes' Theatre, London, opened December 24, 1937

Produced and directed by Prince Littler; A Pantomime by Marriott Edgar, with additional scenes by Stanley Lupino; Music by Tom Lewis; Special compositions by Tom Lewis and Eric Coates

Greta Payne (Cinderella); Madge Elliott (Prince Charming); Stanley Lupino (Buttons); Pat Kirkwood (Dandini); Jack Leonard (Father Time); Helen Crerer (Fairy Godmother); Leslie Barker (Jake); Will Russell (Sydney); Arty Ash (Baron Stoneybroke); Ken Douglas, Freddie Foss (The Ugly Sisters, Julie and Myrtle); George Hayes (Bromo)

Coliseum Theatre, London, opened December 26, 1939
A Pantomime written, produced and directed by Francis Laidler

Joan Cole (Cinderella); Patricia Burke (Prince Charming); Leslie Sarony (Buttons); Jane Corda (Dandini); Leslie Holmes (Baron de Broke); Joan FredEmney (Julie); Doris Fred-Emney (Trixie); Monti Ryan (Fairy Godmother); Charlie Jass (Neddy the Donkey); Ferguson Brothers (Dobbins the Horse); Marjorie Verne (James); The Three Loose Screws (Dottem, Skinnem, Rookem); The Turner Twins (Specialty Dancers)

AFTER THE BALL, *Clinton* (Conn.) *Playhouse*, opened August 6, 1940
Produced by Alexander Kirkland and Dorothy Willard; A Musical Fantasy conceived and directed by Alexander Kirkland; Book and lyrics by Edward Eager; Music from Verdi, Audran, Cellier, Millocker, Offenbach, Strauss, Wagner, von Suppen, Lecocq, Debussy and Planquette; Settings, David Sarvuse; Lighting, Willard Simonds; Costumes and choreography, Jacques Cartier; Musical director, Robert Bates; Musical arrangements, Howard Lindberg

Patricia Bowman (Cinderella); Natalie Hall (Prince Fortunato); Howard Freeman (Baroness Gertrude); Marian Warring-Manley (Fairy Queen); Virginia Coyle (Snow White); Carol Deis (Tarantella); Elizabeth Ashley (Citronella); Sol George (Clorinda); John Call (King Parvo I); Helen Sobol (Sleeping Beauty); Jean Reynolds (Rapunzel); Mary Hopple (Dandini); Eleanor Searle (Tantivi); Alfred Drake (Adolfino, Lord High Chancelor); Jack George (Thisbe); Donald Gustafson (Seventh Dwarf); Martha Eberle (Alice Before); Janet Anderson (Alice After); Charles Hart (Herald); Donald Murphy (Slipper Bearer); Steven Howard (Dragon); Jacques Cartier (Marble Faun); Doris Bernard (Veil Bearer); Osbert Chevers (Malkin, Cinderella's Cat); Bronson Dudley (Allspice, an Elf); Jill Edward, Carole Freeman (Dryads); Rose Moran (Signorina Columbina); Richard Sheridan, Frank Hall (Attendants); Richard Sheridan, Steven Howard (Spies); Carolyn West (Page Boy); Carol Dies (Echo); Alan Currier, Frank Pujol (Forest)

Golder's Green Hippodrome, London, opened December 26, 1941
Produced and directed by Prince Littler; A Pantomime by Marriott Edgar; Music by Tom Lewis; Special compositions by Tom Lewis and Eric Coates

Nancy Burne (Cinderella); Norah Chapman (Prince Charming); Duggie Wakefield (Buttons); Lillian Keyes (Dandini); Tom Squire (Father Time); Winifred Evayne (Fairy Godmother); Jack Butler (Jake); Leslie Barker (Sydney); Johnny Kavanaugh (Baron Stoneybroke); Billy Nelson, Chuck O'Neil (The Ugly Sisters, Julie and Myrtle); Tony Swain (Bromo); Gerald Fitzgerald, Couth Griffiths (Footmen)

Stoll Theatre, London, opened December 24, 1942
A Pantomime written and directed by Emile Littler

Linda Carroll (Cinderella); Fay Compton (Prince Charming); Ted Ray (Buttons); Sylvia Clive (Fairy Godmother); Phyllis Hunter (Dandini); Kenneth Blain (Baron Hardup of Stoneybroke); Naughton & Gold (Flip and Flop); Nervo & Knox (Cecilia and Anastasia); Frank Holloway, Edward Law (Flunkeys)

Streatham Hill, London, opened December 26, 1942
Produced and directed by Prince Littler; A Pantomime by Marriott Edgar; Music by Tom Lewis; Special compositions by Tom Lewis and Eric Coates

Nancy Burne (Cinderella); Sylvia Welling (Prince Charming); Freddie Foss (Buttons); Lillian Keyes (Dandini); Tom Squire (Father Time); Winifred Evayne (Fairy Godmother); Leslie Barker (Jake); Harold Scott (Sydney); Johnny Kavanaugh (Baron Stoney-broke); Victor Thomas, Charles Jones (The Ugly Sisters, Julie and Myrtle); Tony Swain (Bromo); Arthur Owen, Sonny Bentley (Footmen)

His Majesty's Theatre, London, opened December 27, 1943
A Pantomime by Arty Ash and Barry Lupino; Music arranged by Freddie Bretherton and Bernard Grun

Carole Lynne (Cinderella); Evelyn Laye (Prince Charming); Natasha Sokolova (Fairy Godmother); George Moon (Buttons); Nancy Hunks (Dandini); Kenneth Blain (Baron Hardup); Reginald Mann (His Dog); Tessie O'Shea (Trixie); Gordon Whelan (Major Domo/Father Time); Gaston Palmer (Jake); Sid Plummer (Julie); Burton Brown (Myrtle); Sirdani (Sydney); Jack Coult, William Hinton Jones, Dewey Gibson, Reginald Hayes (Singers)

THE GLASS SLIPPER, *St. James's Theatre*, London, opened December 22, 1944
A Fairy Tale with Music by Herbert and Eleanor Farjeon; Director, William Armstrong; Music by Clifton Parker; Ballet, Andree Howard

Audrey Hesketh (Cinderella); Eric Micklewood (The Prince); Elliot Mason (The Stepmother); Doris Gilmore (Araminta); Megs Jenkins (Arethusa); John Ruddock (The Father); Gerald Kent (The King); Betty Baskcomb (The Queen); Gabrielle Daye (The Fairy Godmother); Geoffrey Dunn (The Herald); Rex Rodgers (The Trumpeter); Robin Christie (The Footman); John Oliver (The Coachman/Toastmaster); Stanley Newby (Rat Coachman); Tony Blake, Philip Kay (Lizard Footmen/Pages); Tita Dane (Marquise of Cinnamon); Inez Torode (Countess of Caraway); Jean Lammond (Baroness of Allspice); Irene Lister (Archduchess of Cochineal); Iris Tully (Viscountess of Cloves); Meg Maxwell-Lyle (Margravine of Mace); Nina Shelley, Helen Lawrence (Ladyin-Waiting); Martita Kern (Blackamoors); Voices of Things: Roy Elliott (Clock); Joan Dunn (Tap); Gerald Kent (Broom); Betty Baskcomb (Fire); Benita Lydal (Rocking Chair); Four Spriits: Margaret Scott (Earth); Brenda Hamlyn (Air); Marguerite Stewart (Fire); Nina Shelley (Water); *Harlequinade*: Walter Gore (Harlequin); Sally Gilmour (Columbine); Geoffrey Dunn (Street Singer); John Oliver (Bass Singer); Michael Holmes (Doctor); Michael Bayston (Merchant); Rex Reid (Captain); The Three Graces: Jean Stokes (Truth); Joyce Graeme (Love); Brenda Hamlyn (Beauty)

Winter Garden Theatre, London, opened December 24, 1944
Produced by Julian Wylie Productions Ltd., in association with Bernard Delfont and Mala de la Marr; Producer, Tom Arnold; A Pantomime; Director, Frank P. Adey; Dances and ensembles arranged by Alison McLaren; Scenery, E. Delany; Musical director, Van Phillips

Kathleen Moody (Cinderella); Binnie Hale (Prince Charming); Bobby Howes (Buttons); Marianne Lincoln (Dandini); Prudence Hyman (Fairy Godmother); Jack Morrison (Baron Mumm); Hermione Baddeley (Minnie); Muriel White (Maxie); Syd Harrison, Max Harrison (Spottem and Grabbem)

THE GLASS SLIPPER, *St. James's Theatre*, London, opened December 20, 1945
Produced by Robert Donat; A Fairy Tale with Music by Herbert and Eleanor Farjeon;

Directors, Stephen Thomas and Robert Donat; Music by Clifton Parker; Ballet, Andree Howard

Sara Gregory (Cinderella); Michael Anthony (The Prince); Elsie French (The Stepmother); Sterndale Bennett (Araminta); Olga May (Arethusa); Lawrence Hanray (The Father); Harry Brindle (The King); Glae Carrodus (The Queen); Helen Cherry (The Fairy Godmother); Lulu Dukes (Zany); Geoffrey Dunn (The Herald); George Lowndes (The Trumpeter); Roy Elliott (The Footman); Michael Holmes (Rat Footman); Charles Heinemann (Lizard Footmen/Page); Ian Wallace (Toastmaster); Mary Leahy (Marquise of Cinnamon); Elsie Ford (Countess of Caraway); Mary Reed (Baroness of Allspice); Rosemary Morgan (Archduchess of Coch-ineal); Joan Maffett (Viscountess of Cloves); Jean Lammond (Margravine of Mace); Helen Lawrence (Lady-in-Waiting); Arthur Ayton (Archduke); Robert King (Duke); Arthur Bell (Marquis); William Lambourne (Earl); Renee Nichols, Isla Gill (Blackamoors); Voices of Things: Harry Brindle (Clock); Mary Leahy (Tap); Glae Carrodus (Broom); Roy Elliott (Fire); Jean Lammond (Rocking Chair); Four Spriits: June Konopasek (Earth); Isla Gill (Air); Renee Nichols (Fire); Patricia Dainton (Water); The Masque: Frank Staff (The Husband); Elizabeth Schooling (The Wife); Ann Lascalles (The Maid); Sara Luzita (The Strange Lady); Rex Reid (The Gay Cavalier); Michael Holmes (The Lackey); Harlequinade: Frank Staff (Harlequin); Annette Chappell (Columbine); Geoffrey Dunn (Street Singer); Ian Wallace (Bass Singer); Michael Holmes (Doctor); Anthony Deaden (Merchant); Rex Reid (Captain); The Three Graces: Ann Lascelles (Truth); Elizabeth Schooling (Love); Sara Luzita (Beauty)

Adelphi Theatre, London, opened December 24, 1945

Produced by Jack Hylton; A Pantomime by Bud Flanagan and Jack Hylton; Director, Bud Flanagan; Additional songs and lyrics by Bud Flanagan; Settings, Alock Johnstone; Costumes, Alec Shanks; Dances, Dorothy McAusland; Music arranged by Freddie Bretherton; Musical director, Sydney Jerome; Stage manager, Harry Gould

Lois Green (Cinderella); Jean Adrienne (Prince Charming); Bebe de Roland (Fairy); Peggy Tawlings (Dandini); Angela Glynne (Tinki); Gavin Gordon (Baron); Desmond Campbell (Demon King); Baker, Dove and Allen (Broker's Men); Dudley's Midgets; Beams' Children

Golder's Green Hippodrome, London, opened December 21, 1946

Produced by Prince Littler; A Pantomime by Marriott Edgar; Additional scenes by Arty Ash and Barry Lupino; Director, Albert Locke; Scenery, Bert Reynolds; Costumes, Max Weldy, J. H. Simmons and Mac Rogers; Dances arranged by Betty Oliphant; Stage managers, Anthony Gordon and Betty Bellew

Nancy Burne (Cinderella); Gwyneth Lascelles (Prince Charming); George Moon (Buttons); Wyn Henry (Fairy Godmother); Rene Powell (Dandini); Johnny Kavanaugh (Baron Stoneybroke); Anthony Gordon (Father Time); Harry Nicol (Sidney); Bert Nicol (Jake); Billy de Haven (Myrtle); Dandy Page (Julie); William Best (Bromo); George Simmons, Tom Clarke (Footman); Dorothy Britain, Sally Brock, Greta Brennan, Audrey Cooper, Edna Gee, Gilian Grey, Dulcie Hone, Daphne Johnson, Maureen Love, Buntz Lyne, Sylvia Matthews, Billie Metcalf, Sylvia Myers, Lorna McAllister, Moya McCormack, Sheila O'Connor, Billie O'Day, Antonio Palmer, June Price, Patricia Rapley, Ann Richmond, June Rose, Kay Taylor, Joy Shaw, Dora Thomas, Jill Thomas, Joan Walker, Peggy Wilding (Chorus)

MUSICAL NUMBERS: "Hunters Horn"; "Shake Hands With a New Tomorrow";

"When the Sun Says Good Morning to You"; "A Love Song"; "This Heart of Mine"; "Post Horn Galop"; "I Have Cinderella"; "The Stars Will Remember"; "Pretending"; "Music in the Air"; "Cinderella Ballet"; "Going to the Ball"; "Little Sleepy Head"; "Minuet"; "My Love Is Only for You"; "Lovely Lady" "We Push the Damper In"; "Ali Baba"; "Down the Mall"

IF THE SHOE FITS, *Century Theatre*, New York, opened December 5, 1946 20 performances

Produced by Leonard Sillman; A Musical Comedy by June Carroll and Robert Duke, based on the Cinderella fairy tale; Director, Eugene Bryden; Music by David Raksin; Lyrics by June Carroll; Settings, Edward Gilbert; Costumes, Kathryn Kuhn; Choreography, Charles Weidman; Tap routines, Don Liberto; Musical director, Will Irwin; Orchestrations, Russell Bennett; Vocal director, Joe Moon; Production supervisor, Leonard Sillman; Stage manager, T. C. Jones

Leila Ernst (Cinderella); Edward Dew (Prince Charming); Florence Desmond (Lady Eve); Jody Gilbert (Mistress Spratt); Marilyn Day (Delilah); Sherle North (Thais); Joe Besser (Herman); Edward Lambert (King Kindly); Jack Williams (Broderick); Jean Olds (Dame Crinkle); Joyce White (Dame Crumple); Chloe Owen (Dame Crackle); Ray Cook (The Baker); Adrienne (Widow Willow); Frank Milton (His Magnificence, the Wizard); Richard Wentworth (The Butcher Boy); Gail Adams (Lorelei); Eileen Ayers (Lilith); Youka Troubetzkoy (Major Domo); Eleanor Jonesa (Lady Guinevere); Dorothy Karroll (Lady Persevere); Barbara Perry (Kate); Vincent Carbone (Court Dancer); Robert Penn (Town Crier); Don Mayo, Walter Kattwinkel (Undertakers); Harvey Braun, Stanley Simmonds (Lawyers); William Rains, Ray Morrissey, Richard Wentworth (Three Troubadours); Fin Olsen (Their Arranger); Richard D'Arcy (Sailor); Billy Vaux (Dancing Attendant); Eugene Martin (Singing Attendant); Jane Vinson, Paula Dee (Acrobatic Attendants); Vincent Carbone, Harry Rogers, Allen Knowles, Ferd Bernaski (Four Sprites); Marcia Maier, Marybly Harwood (Sailor's Sweethearts)

MUSICAL NUMBERS: "Start the Ball Rollin'"; "I Wish"; "In the Morning"; "Come and Bring Your Instruments"; "Night After Night"; "Every Eve"; "With a Wave of My Wand"; "Am I a Man or a Mouse?"; "I'm Not Myself Tonight"; "Three Questions"; "If the Shoe Fits"; "What's the Younger Generation Coming To?"; "Have You Seen the Countess Cindy?"; "This Is the End of the Story"; "I Took Another Look"; "I Want to Go Back to the Bottom of the Garden"; "My Business Man"

CINDERELLA; OR, THE LOVER, THE LACKEY, AND THE LITTLE GLASS SLIPPER, *Players' Theatre*, London, opened December 21, 1946

A Fairy Burlesque Extravaganza by Henry J. Byron, adapted by Archie Harradine; Director, Don Gemmell

Joyce Cummings (Cinderella); Elma Soiron (Prince Poppetti); Owen Holder (Buttoni); Joan Stendale-Bennett (Dandini); Bill Shine (Baron Balderdash); Don Gemmell (Clorinda); May Hallett (Thisbe); Phillada Sewell (Fairy Queen); Therese Langfield (Honeydew); Marguerite Stewart (Harebell); Peggy Attfield (Prince's Page); *Harlequinade*: John Hewer (Pantaloon); Therese Langfield (Columbine); Marguerite Stewart (Harlequin); Bill Shine (Policeman); Owen Holder (Dandy); Peggy Attfield (The Butcher's Boy); David Kier (Clown); Joan Sterndale-Bennett (The Oyster Cross'd in Love)

Casino Theatre, London, opened December 20, 1947

A Pantomime produced, written and directed by Emile Littler

Carole Lynne (Cinderella); Eve Lister (Prince Charming); Arthur Askey (Buttons); Anna Claire (Fairy Godmother); April Rose (Dandini); Dick Thorpe (Baron Hardup); Chevalier Brothers (Flip and Flop); Ben Wrigley (Buttercup); Henry Lytton (Daisy); Jeffrey Piddock, Gerald Seymoure (Flunkeys)

Palladium Theatre, London, opened December 24, 1948

A Pantomime by Michael Bishop; Director, Charles Henry

Roma Beaumont (Cinderella); Evelyn Laye (Prince Charming); Tommy Trinder (Buttons); Jane Hilary (Fairy Godmother); Zoe Gail (Dandini); Franklin Bennett (Baroness); Coral Woods (Prudence); Syd Hamilton (Justice of the Peace); George and Bert Bernard (Buttercup and Dandelion); Leopold Brothers (The Horse); Casavecchi Troupe (Broker's Men); Patricia Sinnott (Premiere Danseuse)

CINDERELLA; OR, NO ROOM IN THE SHOE, *Embassy Theatre*, London, opened December 27, 1948

A Pantomime by Patrick Cargill; Directors, Anthony Hawtrey and Patrick Cargill

Maureen McGregor (Cinderella); Diana King (Prince Charming); Patrick Cargill (Buttons); Phyllis Owen (Fairy Godmother); Lesley Lindsay (Dardini); Reginald Selleck (Baron Hampstead); Peggy Banks (Maid Marion); Seymour Green (Figarol); Joan Sanderson (Pneumonia); Freda Jackson (Claustrophobia); Mary MacKenzie (Marge Irene); Gerald Welch (Usher)

CINDERELLA COMES OF AGE, *Torch Theatre*, London, opened December 22, 1949

A Comic Fantasy by J. A. Saunders; Director, Leon Lehmann

Eileen Cleveland (Cinderella); Bertie Watts (Prince Charming); Lucienne Hill (Fairy Godmother); Frederick Peisley (Prime Minister Gulasch); Jean Peterson, Maureen Oliver (Ugly Sisters); Geoffrey Best (Wedlock); Herbert Haycock (General Pomposities)

People's Palace Theatre, London, opened December 26, 1949

A Pantomime by Emile Littler; Director, Hastings Mann

Jasmine Dee (Cinderella); Gladys Stanley (Prince Charming); Derek Roy (Buttons); Pauline Johnson (Fairy Godmother); Madeleine Hearne (Dandini); Charles Stephen (Baron Hardup); The Three Stooges (Flip, Flop and Flap); Charles Jones (Buttercup); Fred Beck (Daisy); Ronald Barnes (Flunkey)

Richmond Theatre, London, opened December 23, 1950

A Pantomime written and directed by Fred Noon; Lyrics, Brenda Rockett

Pamela Galloway (Cinderella); Hilary Allen (Prince Charming); Jackie Norman (Buttons); Jean Ireland (Fairy Godmother); Fred Noon (Dandelion); Stanley Vilven (Baron Nodo); Dudley Hale (Crocus); Keith Leggett (Lamplighter); Kim Grant (Major Domo/Shopkeeper); John Beresford Cooksey (Hurdy Gurdy Man); The Playboys (Tic and Tac); Vida Goodall (Principal Dancer)

Streatham Hill Theatre, London, opened December 26, 1950

Produced by Prince Littler; A Pantomime by Marriott Edgar; Additional scenes by Arty Ash and Barry Lupino; Director, Sydney Smith; Scenery, Bert Reynolds; Costumes, Max Weldy, J. H. Simmons and Mac Rogers; Dances arranged by Betty Oliphant

Nancy Burne (Cinderella); Gwyneth Lascelles (Prince Charming); Eddie Leslie (Buttons); Betty Sagon (Fairy Godmother); Stella Moravy (Dandini); Johnny Kavanaugh (Baron Stoneybroke); Anthony Gordon (Father Time); Tim Dormonde (Sidney); Clive Dunn (Jake); Freddie Foss (Myrtle); Fred Kitchen (Julie); William Best (Bromo); The Alva Brothers (Donkey); Pauline Innes (Principal Dancer)

Prince's Theatre, London, opened December 21, 1951
Produced by Maxwell Wray; A Pantomime by Marriott Edgar; Additional scenes by Arty Ash and Barry Lupino; Director, Bertram Montague; Scenery, Joseph Carl; Costumes, Max Weldy, J. H. Simmons and Mac Rogers; Dances and ballets arranged by Iris Kirkwhite and Mme. Darmora

Cherry Lind (Cinderella); Christine Norden (Prince Charming); Derek Roy (Buttons); Shelagh Day (Fairy Godmother); Janet Brown (Dandini); Charles Stephen (Baron Hardup); Vic Ford (Hedy); Chris Sheen (Veronica); Barbour Brothers (The Artful Brokers); Peggy O'Farrell's Tiny Tappas, Loyal Max and Lole; Barbour Brothers; Mabel and Foure Chesters, Peter Brothers' Comedy Horse "Thunder"; The Vocalion Quartette, The Iris Kirkwhite Singers, Owen Walters and His Orchestra (Specialties)

King's Theatre, London, opened December 24, 1952
A Pantomime by Arty Ash and Barry Lupino; Director, Heath Joyce

Barbara Leigh (Cinderella); Paula Grey (Prince Charming); Lupino Lane (Buttons); Virginia Tate (Fairy Godmother); Elsie Percival (Dandini); Leslie Spuring (Baron Bentonbroke); George Atterbury (Bonzo); Bunny Baron (Bud); Harry Arnold (Blossom); Barbour Brothers (The Artful Brokers)

Golder's Green Hippodrome, London, opened December 24, 1952
Produced by Maxwell Wray; A Pantomime by Marriott Edgar; Additional scenes by Arty Ash and Barry Lupino; Director, Leonard Dainton

Lisabeth Webb (Cinderella); Gwyneth Lascelles (Prince Charming); Eddie Leslie (Buttons); Betty Sagon (Fairy Godmother); Ray Johnson (Dandini); Johnny Kavanaugh (Baron Stoneybroke); Anthony Gordon (Father Time); Hal Collins (Sidney); Harold Childs (Jake); Freddie Foss (Myrtle); Richard Gilbert (Julie); William Best (Bromo); The Alva Brothers (Donkey); Pauline Innes (Principal Dancer)

Players' Theatre, London, opened December 22, 1953
A Victorian Pantomime adapted by Hattie Jacques; Director, Don Gemmell

Carole Keith (Cinderella); Juno Stevas (Prince Poppetti); John Hewer (Buttons); Hattie Jacques (Fairy Fragrant); Annie Leake (Fairy Aida); Barbara Burke (Dandini); Michael Mellinger (Baron Cuthbert); Brenda Stanley (Baroness); Ian Wallace (Scarlatina); Geoffrey Dunn (Brunetta); Denys Palmer (Discord); Norman McDowell (Datcord); Michael Derbyshire (Demon King); Josephine Gordon, Jeanne Lusby, Shirley Rees (Fairies); Robin Hunter (Flunkey/Cabby); *Harlequinade*: Robin Hunter (Harlequin/Policeman); Norman McDowell (Pantaloon); Jeanne Lusby (Columbine); John Hewer (Clown); Shirley Rees (Dance of Delight); David Thomson, John Terry (Dobbin); Josephine Gordon (Poodle Pooh); Michael Derbyshire (Toff)

Palladium Theatre, London, opened December 24, 1953

A Pantomime by Michael Bishop, Eric Sykes and Spike Milligan; Director, Val Parnell

Julie Andrews (Cinderella); Adele Dixon (Prince Charming); Max Bygraves (Buttons); Elaine Garreau (Fairy Godmother); Joan Mann (Dandini); Richard Hearne (Baron Pastry); Cyril Wells (Baroness Pastry); Jon Pertwee (Dandelion); Tony Sympson (Buttercup); William Barrett (Harlequin); Edna Busse (Columbine); David Dale (Squire of Tumbleweed); Silvia Ashmole (Fairy); Ted and George Durante (Herbert and Patrick Fitzherbert); Casavecchia Troupe (Clown, Pantaloon, Policemen)

Palace Theatre, London, opened December 21, 1955

A Pantomime by produced, written and directed by Emile Littler; Music and lyrics by Hastings Mann and Jack Strachey

Erica Yorke (Cinderella); Jean Telfer (Prince Charming); David Nixon (Buttons); Sylvia Norman (Fairy Godmother); Paula Marshall (Dandini); Peter Evans (Father Time); San Woodcock (Baron Hardup); Billy Nelson (Flip); Billy Morris (Flop); Chuck O'Neil (Flap); Desmond and Marks (Lizzie and Dizzie); Linda McMullin (Principal Dancer)

Wimbledon Theatre, London, opened December 24, 1957

A Pantomime written and directed by William Robertson

Jasmine Dee (Cinderella); Pamela Charles (Prince Charming); Danny O'Dea (Buttons); Ruth Porcher (Fairy Godmother); Anne Yorke (Dandini); Peter Haddon (Baron Hardup); Margaret St. Barbe West (The Baroness); John Hart-Dyke (Humphrey); Elsie Waters (Gert); Doris Waters (Daisy); Mike Hope (Charlie Staircase, Jr.); Albie Keene (Charlie Staircase, Sr.); Gillian Cobbold (Principal Dancer)

Coliseum Theatre, London, opened December 18, 1958 101 performances

Produced by Harold Fielding; A Pantomime adapted for the stage by Don Driver; Director, Freddie Carpenter; Music by Richard Rodgers; Lyrics by Oscar Hammerstein II; Settings and costumes, Loudon Sainthill; Lighting, Michael Northen; Choreography, Tommy Lindsen; Musical director, Bobby Howell; Orchestrations, Robert Russell Bennett and Ronnie Hammer; Choral arrangements, Bill Shepherd; Additional material, Ronnie Wolfe

Yana (Cinderella); Bruce Trent (The Prince); Tommy Steele (Buttons); Betty Marsden (Fairy Godmother); Kenneth Williams (Portia); Jimmy Edwards (The King); Enid Howe (The Queen); Godfrey James (Dandini); Ted Durante (Joy); Prudence Rodney (The Crystal Fairy); Robin Palmer (Lord Chamberlain); Maryon Leslie (Baby Bear); Frank Raymond (Flunkey); Tom Merrifield (Principal Male Dancer); The Bill Shepherd Singers; Dianna Atherton, Linda Blackledge, Sheila Browning, Sylvia Cardew, Elaine Carr, Jean Cragg, Sidonie Darrell, Jane Don, Irene Dunn, Ann Edgar, Sylvia Ellis, Susanne Foster, Ann Gotelee, Annette Hylton, Merle Lee, Maryon Leslie, Jill Love, Virginia Minoprio, Vicki Mitchell, Margot Pritchard, Christine Reynolds, Maureen Rudd, Kaye Sargent, Christine Skilton, Marilyn Stevenson, Michael Ashlin, Larry Haider, George Lucas, Ron Lucas, Perry McCann, Larry Oaks (Dancers)

MUSICAL NUMBERS: (Same as in 1957 television production), plus "A Very Special Day"; "Marriage Type Love"; "No Other Love" (from Me and Juliet); and "You and Me" (written by Tommy Steele)

LA CENERENTOLA, Glyndebourne, England, opened July 16, 1959

Produced by the Glyndebourne Festival Opera Company; An Opera by Rossini; Libretto by Jacopo Ferretti; English translation based on the original production by Carl Ebert; Production designer, Oliver Messel; The Royal Philharmonic Orchestra conducted by Vittorio Giu

Teresa Berganza (Angelina); Juan Oncina (Don Ramiro); Sesto Bruscantini (Dandini); Ian Wallace (Don Magnifico); Silvana Zanolli (Clorinda); Miti Traccato Pace (Thisbe); Hervey Alan (Alidoro)

Sadler's Wells Theatre, London, opened October 25, 1959
Produced by the Sadler's Wells Company; An Opera by Rossini; English libretto by Arthur Jacobs; Director, Douglas Craig; Scenery and costumes, Carl Toms; Musical conductor, Bryan Balkwill

Patricia Kern (Angelina); Alexander Young (Don Ramiro); Denis Dowling (Dandini); Howell Glynne (Don Magnifico); Nancy Creighton (Clorinda); Anna Pollck (Thisbe); Stanley Clarkson (Alidoro)

Victoria Palace, London, opened December 23, 1960 101 performances
Produced by Harold Fielding; A Pantomime adapted for the stage by Don Driver; Director, Freddie Carpenter; Music by Richard Rodgers; Lyrics by Oscar Hammerstein II; Settings and costumes, Loudon Sainthill; Lighting, Michael Northen; Choreography, Tommy Lindsen; Musical director, Bobby Howell; Orchestrations, Robert Russell Bennett and Ronnie Hammer; Choral arrangements, Bill Shepherd; Additional material, Ronnie Wolfe

Janet Waters (Cinderella); Bill Newman (The Prince); Ted Rogers (Buttons); Joan Heal (Fairy Godmother); Richard Wakeley (Portia); Jimmy Edwards (The King); Betty Bowdon (The Queen); Graham Squire (Dandini); Ted Durante (Joy); Gillian Lynne (The Crystal Fairy); Arthur Howard (Lord Chamberlain); Maryon Leslie (Baby Bear); Frank Raymond (Flunkey); Tom Merrifield (Principal Male Dancer); The Bill Shepherd Singers

St. Louis (Mo.) Municipal Theatre, opened August 14 through 20, 1961
Produced by the St. Louis Municipal Theatre Association; A Musical Comedy adapted for the stage by Don Driver; Director, John Kennedy; Music by Richard Rodgers; Lyrics by Oscar Hammerstein II; Settings, Paul C. McGuire; Costumes, Andrew Geoly; Choreography and ensembles staged by Frank Westbrook; Modern dances and ensembles staged by Dan. M. Eckley; Musical director, Edwin McArthur; Orchestrations, Robert Russell Bennett

Marie Santell (Cinderella); Harry Snow (The Prince); Hal LeRoy (Portia); Jack Gilford (The King); Mary M. Cook (The Queen); Will B. Able (Joy); F. J. O'Neil (Lord Chamberlain); Edmund Lyndeck (The Herald); Lila Gage (The Plume Lady); Pablo Flores (The Chef); Walter Richardson (The Steward); Lupe Serrano (Premier Ballerina)

NOTE: Rodgers and Hammerstein's *Cinderella* also was staged at *Musicarnival*, Cleveland, June 5 through 8, 1961, with Monte Amundsen as Cinderella, Tommy Rall as The Prince, and Hal LeRoy as Portia, and at *Swope Park Auditorium*, Kansas City, Mo., July 10 through 16, 1961, with Carla Alberghetti as Cinderella along with Tommy Rall and Hal LeRoy, plus Murray Matheson as The King and Mimi Randolph as The Queen

MUSICAL NUMBERS: "The Prince Is Giving a Ball"; "The Entrance of the Prince"; "A Very Special Day" (from *Me and Juliet*); "Ladies in Waiting" [written by Don Driver];

"In My Own Little Corner"; "Keep It Gay" (from *Me and Juliet*); "When You're Driving Through the Moonlight"; "A Lovely Night"; "Boys and Girls Like You and Me" (dropped from *Oklahoma!*); "Impossible"; "The Transformation Ballet"; "It's Possible"; "A List of Bare Necessities"; "The Grand March"; "Gavotte"; "The Grand Ballet"; "Ten Minutes Ago"; "Stepsisters' Lament"; "Do I Love You Because You're Beautiful?"; Finale

Players' Theatre, London, December 19, 1961
A Pantomime by Henry J. Byron, adapted by Archie Harrington with additional dialogue and lyrics by John Heawood; Director, Don Gemmell; Production designer, Reginald Wooley

Sydonie Platt (Cinderella); Katy Sadler (Prince Poppetti); John Rutland (Buttoni/Clown); Stella Moray (Dandini); Tony Sympson (Baron Balderdash/Pantaloon); Margaret Ashton (Fairy Queen); John Heawood (Clorinda); Brian Blades (Thisbe); Wendy Barper (Harebell); Mary Coulson (Honeydew); Anne Asprey (Foxglove); Wendy McClure, Delia Corrie (Pages); Barrie Wilkinson (Harlequin); Robin Haig (Columbine/ Eglantine); Anne Asprey, Wendy Barker, Mary Coulson (Her Confidantes); Bill Duthie (Toff)

Golder's Green Hippodrome, London, opened December 26, 1961
A Pantomime by Emile Littler; Director, Marjorie Ristori; Music and lyrics, Hastings Mann; Production designer, Doria Zinkiesen

Erica Yorke (Cinderella); Elizabeth Larner (Prince Charming); Arthur Askey (Buttons); Jean Ramsay (Fairy Godmother); Christine Taylor (Dandini); Charles Stephen (Baron Hardup); Terry Wall (Father Time); Billy Nelson (Flip); Billy Morris (Flop); Chuck O'Neil (Flap); Dawkes & Webb (Dizzie & Lizzie)

Wimbledon Theatre, London, opened December 22, 1962
A Pantomime with incidental music by Robert E. Probst and Ken Phillips; Director, William Robertson; Choreography, Rita King

Tricia Money (Cinderella); Terry Donovan (Prince Charming); Hughie Green (Buttons); Jasmine Dee (Dandini); Arthur Lane (Baron Hardup); Fred Desmond (Copem); Jack Marks (Snatchem); Barri Chat (Orbit); Terri Gardner (Satellite); Nancy Roberts (Nancy); Ronald Wayne (Major Domo); Julie de Marco (Julie); Vic Hallums (Willie the Ghille); Keith Ashley (Demon King)

CINDY-ELLA; OR, I GOTTA SHOE, *Garrick Theatre*, London, opened December 17, 1962; reopened *New Arts Theatre*, London, December 23, 1963
Produced by Michael Codron; A Musical Entertainment by Caryl Brahms and Ned Sherrin; with additional music by Peter Knight and Ron Grainer; Director, Colin Graham; Designer, Tony Walton; Lighting, Richard Pilbrow

Cleo Laine (Cindy-Ella/Mammy/Mr. Abedingo/Pigmee/ Lord Chamberlain); Elisabeth Welch (Mr. Smith/ Esmee/Lovable/Fairy Godmammy/Major Domo); Cy Grant (Prince Charming Jones/Peanuts/Mr. Meshak/Herald); George Browne (Mr. Shadrak/Pappy/Uncle/ Uncle Lazy-Do-Nothing/Coachman/Regent/Chucker-Out)

MUSICAL NUMBERS: "I Gotta Shoe"; "Troubles of the World"; "Motherless Child"; "Shine Shine Shoe"; "Li'l Ella Play On Yo' Harp"; "Round Like a Melon, Sweet Like a Peach"; "You Ain't-a Gonna Sit and Take Yo' Ease"; "Go 'Way F'om Mah Window"; "Man No Good for Nothin'; "Nobody Knows the Trouble I've Seen"; "You're Worried Now"; "You Gotta Look Disdainful"; "Stranger"; "Git Along Home, Cindy, Cindy";

"High Summer Day"; "Look on Me With a Loving Eye"; "There's a Man Goin' Roun' Givin' Cards"; "Raise a Ruckus"; "Plenty Good Room"; "Bring a Little Pumpkin, Cindy"; "Cindy-Ella"; "Swing Low, Sweet Chariot"; "Nobody's Business"; "Oh the First Time"; "Look on Me With a Loving Eye"; "De Midnight Special"; "Let Me Hold Your Hand"; "Hush-a-Bye"; "I Gotta Shoe"; "Stranger" (reprise); "Hush-a-Bye" (reprise)

Original cast recording: Decca (London)

CINDY, *Gate Theatre*, New York, opened March 19, 1964 86 performances; reopened *Orpheum Theatre*, September 24, 1964, and moved to *Cricket Theatre*, January 19, 1965 318 performances

Produced by Chandler Warren and Philip Temple by arrangement with Stuart Wiener and Jerry Grace; A Musical Comedy by Joe Sauter and Mike Sawyer; Director and choreographer, Marvin Gordon; Music and lyrics by Johnny Brandon; Scenery, Robert T. Williams; Lighting, Martin Aronstein; Costumes, Patricia Quinn Stewart; Musical conductor, Sammy Benskin; Orchestrations and musical direction, Clark McClellan; Restaged for the Cricket Theatre by Tommy Karaty; Director for the Cricket Theatre, Ruth Nastasi; Production stage manager, Nathan Caldwell, Jr.

Jacqueline Mayro (succeeded by Kelly Wood, Isabelle Farrell) (Cindy Kreller); Mike Sawyer (David Rosenfeld); Sylvia Mann (succeeded by Nancy Carroll, Milly Weitz) (Mama Kreller); Frank Nastasi (succeeded by David Howard) (Papa Kreller); Johnny Harmon (succeeded by Tommy Karaty, Jerry Wilkins, Rick Landon) (Lucky); Dena Dietrich (succeeded by Mary Betten, Alyce Beardsley) (Della Kreller); Amelia Varney (Golda Kreller); Lizabeth Pritchett (succeeded by Elizabeth Parrish, Evelyn Bell) (Ruth Rosenfeld); Joe Maisell (succeeded by Joe Bellomo) (Chuck Rosenfeld); Thelma Oliver, Tommy Karaty (succeeded by Rick Landon), Mark Stone (succeeded by Michael Loman), Robert Becker (succeeded by Charles Abbate) (Storytellers)

MUSICAL NUMBERS: "Once Upon a Time"; "Let's Pretend"; "Is There Something to What He Said"; "Papa, Let's Do It Again"; "A Genuine Feminine Girl"; "Cindy"; "Think Mink"; "Tonight's the Night"; "Who Am I?"; "Ballroom Sequence"; "If You've Got It, You've Got It"; "The Life That I've Planned for Him"; "If It's Love"; "Got the World in the Palm of My Hand"; "Call Me Lucky"; "Laugh It Up"; "What a Wedding"

Original cast recording: ABC Records

St. Louis (Mo.) Municipal Theatre, opened July 19 through 25, 1965

Produced by the St. Louis Municipal Theatre Association; A Musical Comedy adapted for the stage by Don Driver; Director, John Kennedy; Music by Richard Rodgers; Lyrics by Oscar Hammerstein II; Settings, Paul C. McGuire; Costumes, Andrew Geoly; Choreography and ensembles staged by Frank Westbrook; Musical director, Edwin McArthur; Orchestrations, Robert Russell Bennett

Judith McCauley (Cinderella); William Lewis (The Prince); Hal LeRoy (Portia); Jack Harrold (The King); Mary M. Cook (The Queen); Will B. Able (Joy)

Golder's Green Hippodrome, London, opened December 24, 1965

A Pantomime by with book, music and lyrics by Harry Bright; Director, Jeffrey Choyce

Veronica Page (Cinderella); Erica Yorke (Prince Charming); Dickie Henderson (Buttons); Camilla Powell (Fairy Godmother); Patricia Kilgariff (Dandini); Lionel Murtin (Baron Hardup); Danny La Rue (Fabrina); Alan Haynes (Marlene); Alan Barnes (The Bailiff/Major Domo); Wendy Cameron (Premiere Danseuse)

Palladium Theatre, London, opened December 20, 1966
Produced by Leslie A. Macdonnell and Lesie Grade in association with Bernard Delfont; A Pantomime by David Croft; Director, Albert J. Knight; Music and lyrics by The Shadows; Settings, Tod Kingman; Costumes, Cynthia Tingley; Choreography, Pamela Davis; Musical supervisor, Norrie Paramor

Pippa Steel (Cinderella); Peter Gilmore (The Prince); Cliff Richard (Buttons); Tudor Davies (Dandini); Patricia Merrin (Fairy); Jack Douglas (Baron Hardup); Terry Scott (Teresa); Hugh Lloyd (Eunice); Avril Yarrow (Mistress Maybelle); Bruce Welch, Hank Marvin, John Rostill, Brian Bennett (Broker's Men); Bill Tasker (Town Crier/Vicar of Stoneybroke); Jack Francois (Innkeeper/Major Domo); Bel Canto Singers (Footmen); Aida Foster Children (Pages); Pamela Davis Dancers

MUSICAL NUMBERS: "Welcome to Stoneybroke"; "Why Wasn't I Born Rich?"; "Where Can My Man Be?"; "Poverty"; "Peace and Quiet"; "The Flyder and the Spy"; "In the Country"; "The Hunt"; "Come Sunday"; "Dare I Love Him?"; "Wouldn't It Be Nice?"; "Ballet Themes"; "Waltz Theme"; "At the King's Place"; "Cossack Number"; "Gavotte"; "She Needs Him More Than Me"; "Hey Doctor Man"; Finale

CINDY, *Fortune Theatre*, London, opened May 30, 1968
Produced by Haymarket Stage Productions Ltd.; A Musical Comedy by Joe Sauter and Mike Sawyer; Director, Alexander Bridge; Music and lyrics by Johnny Brandon; Scenery, Kenneth Sharpe; Choreography, Bob Howe

Geraldine Morrow (Cindy Kreller); Alan Selwyn (David Rosenfeld); Hy Hazell (Zelda Kreller); Kalman Glass (Irving Kreller); Johnny Tudor (Lucky); Ann Stillman (Della Kreller); Angela Darren (Golda Kreller); Rose Hill (Ruth Rosenfeld); Dudley Stevens (Chuck Rosenfeld); Tina Scott, Hal Davis, BrianJay Smith (Storytellers)

LA CENERENTOLA, *Festival Theatre*, Stratford, Ontario, opened June 10, 1968
Produced by the Stratford Festival of Canada, Jean Fascon and John Hirsch, artistic directors; An Opera by Rossini; Libretto by Jacopo Ferretti; English translation by Arthur Jacobs; Director, Douglas Campbell; Production designer, Leslie Hurry; Lighting, Robert Reinholt; Musical director, Lawrence Smith

Patricia Kern (Angelina); JeanLouis Pellerin (Don Ramiro); Robert Savoie (Dandini); Howell Glynne (Don Magnifico); Gwenlynn Little (Clorinda); Muriel Greenspon (Thisbe); Peter Van Ginkel (Alidoro); Anne Maire Clark, Nancy Gottschalk, Muriel James, Peter Milne, David Norris, Danielle Pilon, Oskar Raulfs, Herman Rombouts, Rene Rosen, Donald Rutherford, Daniel Tait, Leslie Westman (Chorus)

Players' Theatre, London, opened December 20, 1968
Produced by the Players' Theatre; A Burlesque Pantomime by H. J. Byron, adapted with additional lyrics by Maurice Browning; Director, Don Gemmell; Music selected by Denis Martin; Scenery, Reginald Hanson; Dances and musical numbers staged by Doreen Hermitage; Musical arrangements, Geoffrey Brawn; Stage managers, David Jonathan Gatrell and Philip Mayer

Frances Barlow (Corella); Keith Jones (Prince Edward Burgundi); Kim Grant (Mick Buttons); Alec Bregonzi (Edmundo Dandini); Brian Blades (Baron O'Leary); Josephine Gordon (Goner O'Leary); Barbara Miller (Regan O'Leary); James Bree (Paddy); Dudley Stevens (Shamus); Joan Sterndale Bennett (Fairy

O'Lympia); Eleanor McCready (Fairy Randida); Jenny Wren (Fairy Lilyborda); Diane Grayson (Fairy Chatterina); Clifton Todd (Lord Curandi); Dinny Jones, Lorraine Todd, Larry Drew (Courtiers/Footmen)

Wimbledon Theatre, London, opened December 24, 1970
Produced by Bernard Delfont and Tom Arnold; A Fairy Tale Extravaganza; Choreography, Michael Tye-Walker; Decor, Robert Weaver; Costumes, Anthony Holland and R. St. John Roper; Musical conductor, Robert Probst

Andree Silver (Cinderella); Elizabeth Larner (Prince Charming); Roy Castle (Buttons); Jenny Wren (Dandini); Annette Holt (Fairy Godmother); Clive Bennett (Baron Hardup); John Inman (Lucinda); Barry Howard (Lavinia); Josephine Palmer (Dandini's Friend); Stuart Anderson (Major Domo/Demon); Michael Tye-Walker, Corinne Duvernay (Principal Dancers); Franklyn and His Doves (Specialty); The Derek Taverner Singers; Douglas Cavill Ponies; Betty Algar Babes; Corps de Ballet

Palladium Theatre, London, opened December 21, 1971
Produced by Louis Benjamin and Leslie Grade; A Pantomime devised and directed by Alfred J. Knight; Book by Phil Park, with additional scenes by Brian Blackburn, Barry Cryer, Dave Freeman and Spike Millins; Decor, Tod Kingman; Costumes, Cynthia Tingey; Choreography, Tommy Shaw

Clodagh Rogers (Cinderella); Malcolm Roberts (The Prince); Ronnie Corbett (Buttons); Brian Hills (Dandini); Dorothy Dampier (Fairy Godmother); David Kosoff (Baron Hardup); Georgia Jee (Mistress Maybelle); Terry Scott (Teresa Hardup); Julian Orchard (Julia Hardup); Bill Trasker (Town Cryer/ Old Man); Bertie Hare (Major Domo); The Patton Brothers (The Broker's Men); Tommy Merrifield, Jilly Coram (Principal Dancers)

Wimbledon Theatre, London, opened December 22, 1973
Produced by Bernard Delfont and Richard M. Mills (for Tom Arnold and Bernard Delfont Enterprises Ltd.); A Fairy Tale Extravaganza; Director, Jeffrey Choyce; Assisted and choreographed by Roy Pennell; Decor, Tod Kingman; Special material for David Nixon and Basil Brush written by George Martin; Musical conductor, Robert Probst

Rita Phillips (Cinderella); Terry Mitchell (Prince Charming); Peter Kaye (Buttons); Earl Adair (Dandini); Sula Cartier (Fairy Godmother); David Nixon (Baron Hardup); Basil Brush (Himself); Barrie Gosney (Lucinda); David Morton (Lavinia); Alistair (Baron's Servant); George Giles (Lord Chamberlain); Peter Salmon, Wendy Barrie (Principal Dancers); The Royal Dancers; Derek Taverner Singers; Douglas Cavill Ponies; Corps de Ballet

Casino Theatre, London, opened December 18, 1974
Produced by Bernard Delfont and Richard M. Mills (for Tom Arnold and Bernard Delfont Enterprises Ltd.); A Pantomime by Frank Hauser; Directors, Dick Hurran and Frank Hauser; Decor, Tod Kingman; Costumes, R. St. John Roper and Cynthia Tingey; Choreography, Irving Davies; Musical conductor, Ray Cook

Twiggy (Cinderella); Marc Urquhart (Prince Charming); Nicky Henson (Buttons); Bob Horney (Dandini); Joyce Grant (Fairy Godmother); John Rutland (Baron Hardup); Harry H. Corbett (Ben); Wilfrid Brambell (Badger); Roy Kinnear (Valeria); Hugh Paddick (Cornucopia); John J. Moore (Gumble); Betty Benfield (The Queen); Lenny the Lion with Terry Hall; Perry O'Farrell Children; The Irving

Davies Dancers
NOTE: This marked Twiggy's stage debut

I GOTTA SHOE, Criterion Theatre, London, opened December 15, 1976
An AD & J. Arlon Production, presented by H. M. Tennent Ltd.; A Musical Entertainment by Caryl Brahms and Ned Sherrin, with additional music by Peter Knight and Ron Grainer; Directors, Ned Sherrin and David Toguri; Designer, Berkeley Sutcliffe; Lighting, John Wood

Linda Lewis (CindyElla/ Mammy/ Mr. Abedingo/ Pigmee/ Lord Chamberlain); Elisabeth Welch (Mr. Smith/ Esmee/ Lovable/ Fairy Godmammy/ Major Domo); Felix Rice (Prince Charming Jones/ Peanuts/ Mr. Meshak/ Herald); Clarke Peters (Mr. Shadrak/ Pappy/ Uncle/ Uncle Lazy-Do-Nothing); Eric Roberts (Coachman/ Regent/ Chucker-Out)

Palladium Theatre, London, opened December 21, 1976
Produced by Louis Benjamin and Leslie Grade; A Pantomime devised and directed by Alfred J. Knight; Book by Brian Blackburn; Decor, Tod Kingman; Costumes, Cynthia Tingey; Choreography, Pamela Davis

Fiona Fullerton (Cinderella); Robert Young (The Prince); Richard O'Sullivan (Buttons); Roger de Courcey (Dandini); Mary Laine (Fairy Godmother); Richard [Mr. Pastry] Hearne (Baron Hardup); Erica Yorke (Mistress Maybelle); Yootha Joyce (Mildred Hardup); Brian Murphy (Georgina Hardup); Bill Boazman (Town Cryer/Major Domo); Gordon and Bunny Jay (The Broker's Men); Robin Sherringham, Jilly Coram (Principal Dancers); Nookie the Bear; The Palladium Singers and Dancers; Perry O'Farrell Children

THE AMUSING SPECTACLE OF CINDERELLA AND HER NAUGHTY-NAUGHTY SISTERS, Theatre Royal, Stratford-upon-Avon, England, opened December 15, 1977
Produced by the Theatre Royal; A Christmas Show with words and music by Martin Duncan; Directors, Martin Duncan and John Ashford; Decor, David Fisher, assisted by Jenny Teramani; Lighting, Stephen T. Mead

Pauline Siddle (Cinderella); Darlene Johnson (Goody Biddy Bean, a Fairy); Geoffrey Freshwater (Baron Poorasachurchmouse); Brian Protheroe (Little Johnny Buttons); Peter Benson (Pearl, the Naughty Sister); Rhys McConnochie (Deidre, the Other Naughty Sister); Margot Leicester (The Widow Peahen); Susan Jameson (Prince Fritz Fitz-Pince); Felicity Harrison (Dandy-Knee); Robert Pugh (Fred); Vincent Brimble (Needle); Sebastian Born, Stephen Ormrod (Proscenium Servants); The Italian Band: Martin Duncan (Tifacio, the Maestro); Stephen Warbeck (Sapristi); Deborah Findlay (Donna Rita); Bob Critchley (Giuseppe)

MR. CINDERS, Fortune Theatre, London, opened April 27, 1983
Produced by Charles Ross and Dan Crawford, by arrangement with Joel Spector; A Musical Comedy; Director, Tony Craven; Book and lyrics by Clifford Grey and Greatrex Newman; Music by Vivian Ellis and Richard Myers; Additional lyrics by Leo Robin; Settings, Norman Coates; Lighting, Mark Henderson; Costumes, Peter Rice; Choreography, Kenn Oldfield; Musical director, Michael Reed; Stage managers, Iain McAvoy, Michael Lightfoot and Isabel Arnett

Denis Lawson (Jim Lancaster); Christina Matthews (Jill Kemp); Donald Douglas (Henry Kemp); Steven Percy (Guy Lancaster); Graham Hoadley (Lumley Lancaster); Derek Smee (Sir George Lancaster); Angela Vale (Lady Lancaster);

Helen Blizard (Penelope Parks/Lucy Jones); Tony Stansfield (Bunny Hayes); Stephanie Lunn (Becky Bartlett); Diana Martin (Minerva Kemp); John Atterbury (Smith the Butler); Julie Anne Blythen (Enid Brinkly); Janthea Williams (Cynthia Boyce); Mark Hutchinson (Charles Wylde); Geoff Steer (Billy Whymper); Andrea Kealy (Phyllis Patterson); Andrew Livingston (Policeman); Jeanna L'Esty (succeeded by Joanna Douglas) (Donna Lucia d'Esmeralda); Andrew Livingston (P. C. Merks)

NOTE: This revival originated at *The Kings Head Theatre Club*, London, in January 1983

Original cast recording: "That's Entertainment" Records

Lyttelton Theatre, London, opened December 15, 1983 through February 24, 1984
Produced by the National Theatre; A Pantomime by Trevor Ray; Director, Bill Bryden; Decor, William Dudley; Costumes, Deirdre Clancy; Music, John Tams

Janet Dibley (Cinderella); Marsha Hunt (Dandini); Tony Haygarth (Buttons); Stephen Petcher, Anthony Trent (The Horse); Susan Fleetwood (Fairy Godmother); Trevor Ray (Indian); James Grant (Demon)

CINDERS, *Public/LuEsther Theatre*, New York, opened February 20, 1984 56 performances
Produced by the New York Shakespeare Festival; Producer, Joseph Papp; A Drama by Janusz Glowacki, translated by Christina Paul; Director, John Madden; Scenery, Andrew Jackness; Lighting, Paul Gallo; Costumes, Jane Greenwood; Incidental music, Richard Peaslee; Musical director,, Deena Kaye; Fights staged by B. H. Barry; Stàge managers, James Harker and Tracy B. Cohen

Lucinda Jenney (Cinderella); Christopher Walker (Director); Dori Hartley (Prince); Greta Turken (Fairy Godmother); Melissa Leo (Stepmother); Anna Levin, Johann Carlo (Ugly Sisters); Eli Marder (Mouse); Peter McRobbie (Inspector/Soundman); George Guidall (Principal); Robin Gammell (Deputy); Martha Gehman (Father); Kevin McClarnon (Electrician); Jonathan Walker (Cameraman)

MR. CINDERS, *Forum Theatre*, Metuchen, N. J., opened April 30, 1986
Produced by the Forum Theatre Group in association with Dan Crawford and Kings Head Productions; A Musical Comedy; Director, Peter Loewy; Book and lyrics by Clifford Grey and Greatrex Newman; Music by Vivian Ellis and Richard Myers; Additional lyrics by Leo Robin; Settings, Diane Mandel and Lisa Meyers; Lighting, Edward R. F. Matthews; Costumes, Debbie Stasik; Choreography, June Tartaglia; Musical director, Richard Christman; Stage manager, Michael Price

Michael Lengel (Jim Lancaster); Lynne Wilson (Jill Kemp); Andrew Scopellite (Henry Kemp); Robert Jensen (Guy Lancaster); Jonathan Smedley (Linden Lancaster); Donald J. Baumgardner (Sir George Lancaster); Sue Winik (Lady Lancaster); Joanne King (Penelope Crawford); Mary Lynn Susek (Becky Bartlett); Rose Pedone (Minerva Kemp); Dan Chiel (Smith the Butler); Sally Weller (Enid Brinkly); Kim White (Cynthia Boyce); Paul Panella (Charles Wylde); Rob Reynolds (Billy Whymper); Margaret Bakes (Phyllis Patterson); John DeMeglio (Benny); Carl Fitzgerald (P. C. Merks)

MR. CINDERS, *Goodspeed Opera House*, East Haddam, Conn., opened October 22 through December 18, 1988

Produced by the Goodspeed Opera House, Michael P. Price, executive director; A Musical Comedy; Director, Martin Connor; Book and lyrics by Clifford Grey and Greatrex Newman; Music by Vivian Ellis and Richard Myers; Additional lyrics by Leo Robin; Settings, James Leonard Joy; Lighting, Curt Osterman; Costumes, David Toser; Choreography, Dan Siretta; Musical director, Lynn Crigler; Orchestrations, Russell Warner and Lynn Crigler; Stage manager, Michael Brunner

Charles Repole (Jim Lancaster); Beth Austin (Jill Kemp); Tom Batten (Henry Kemp); Bill Ullman (Guy Beardsley-Lancaster); Drew Tayler (Lumley Beardsley-Lancaster); Iggie Wolfington (Sir George Lancaster); Patricia Kilgarriff (Lady Lancaster); Angela Nicholas (Penelope Spencer); Reness Laverdiere (Becky Bartlett); Pamela Clifford (Minerva Kemp); Ian Thomson (Smith the Butler); Holly Evers (Enid Brinkly); Mikki Whittles (Cynthia Boyce); David Monzione (Charles Wylde); Ken Skrzesz (Freddie Whymper); Katy Cavanaugh (Phyllis Patterson); Tim Foster (Harry Fortesque); Gary Kirsch (Bunny Hayes); Teresa Parent (Lucy Larkin); Farnham Scott (P. C. Merks)

CINDERELLA, Terrace Theatre, Long Beach, Cal., opened August 3 through 20, 1989

Produced by the Long Beach Civic Light Opera; Producers, Martin Viviott and Keith Stava; A Musical Comedy adapted for the stage by Don Driver; Director, Fran Soeder; Music by Richard Rodgers; Lyrics by Oscar Hammerstein II; Set design, Eduardo Sicangco; Lighting, Jeff Calderon; Costumes, Delmar L. Rinehart, Jr.; Choreography, Gene Castle; Musical director, Steve Smith; Orchestrations, Robert Russell Bennett; Special effects, Adam Bezark

Julie Lambert (Cinderella); Greg Louganis (The Prince); Pat Carroll (Fairy Godmother); Alan Young (The King); Marilyn Child (The Queen); Elmarie Wendel (The Stepmother); Pamela Myers (Portia); Kathryn Skatula (Joy); Raymond Saar (Herald/ Steward); Bill Bateman (Chef)

CINDERELLA ON ICE, St. Louis (Mo.) Municipal Theatre, opened July 23 through 29, 1990

Produced by the St. Louis Municipal Theatre, Paul Blake, executive producer; A Musical on Ice; Director, Paul Blake; Music by Richard Rodgers; Lyrics by Oscar Hammerstein II; Production designer, Paul Wonsek; Choreography, Robin Cousins; Musical director, Bruce Pomahac; Production stage manager, Robin Rumpf

Rachelle Ottley (Cinderella); Robin Cousins (The Prince); Gretchen Wyler (The Stepmother); Nancy Dussault (Fairy Godmother); Adolph Green (The King); Phyllis Newman (The Queen); Barbara Sharma (Joy); Lois Foraker (Portia); Cliff Bemis (The Herald); Michael Jokerst (The Chef); Neal Frederiksen (The Steward); Shirley Carron, Maria Causey, Kevin Kurth, Karen Moehsmer, Sherry Ollar, Terry Pagano, Tony Paul, Bob Pellaton, Gina Randazzo, Dennis Sveum, John Taylor, Ken Webb (Skating Chorus); Elizabeth Breckenride, Kelsey Lents, Kelsey Woddail (Children's Skaters); Cliff Bemis, Jane Boschert, Michele Burdette-Elmore, Neal Fredriksen, Michael Jokerst, Debby Lennon, Rebecca Ann Lillie, Kevin McMahon (Singing Chorus)

Pantages Theatre, Los Angeles, opened December 12 through 30, 1990

Produced by the Los Angeles Civic Light Opera; Producers, Martin Viviott and Keith Stava; A Musical Comedy adapted for the stage by Don Driver; Director, Charles Repole; Music by Richard Rodgers; Lyrics by Oscar Hammerstein II; Set design, Eduardo Sicangco; Costumes, Garland Riddle; Choreography, Timothy Smith;

Musical director, Carol Weiss; Orchestrations, Robert Russell Bennett; Special effects, Adam Bezark

Bobbie Eakes (Cinderella); Jeff Trachta (The Prince); Rose Marie (Fairy Godmother); Steve Allen (The King); Jayne Meadows (The Queen); Carol Swarbrick (The Stepmother); Pamela Hamill (Portia); Sandy Rosenberg (Joy)

Playhouse 91, New York, opened December 19, 1991 through March 8, 1992
Presented by the Riverside Shakespeare Company, Gus Kaikkonen, artistic director; A Musical by Norman Robbins; Director, Laura Fine; Music composed and arranged by Dan Levy; Lyrics by Amy Powers and Dan Levy; Set design, Harry Feiner; Lighting, Stephen Petrilli; Costumes, Gail Baldoni; Stage manager, Paula Gray

Melanie Wingert (Cinders); Anthony Stanton (Prince Charming); Mark Honan (Buttons); Fredi Walker (Dandini); Lora Lee Cliff (Fairy Godmother); Diana Ciesla (Baroness Medusa Hardupp); Robert Mooney (Asphyxia); John Keene Bolton (Euthanasia); Jim Fitzpatrick (Ammer); Jay Brian Winnick (Tongs)

INTO THE WOODS, *Old Globe Theatre*, San Diego, Cal., opened December 4, 1986 through January 11, 1987
(see *Jack and the Beanstalk* entry for complete cast and credits)

Kim Crosby (Cinderella); Kenneth Marshall (Cinderella's Prince); George Coe (Cinderella's Father); Merle Louise (Cinderella's Mother); Joy Franz (Cinderella's Stepmother); Kay McClelland (Florinda); Lauren Mitchell (Lucinda)

INTO THE WOODS, *Martin Beck Theatre*, New York, opened November 5, 1987 750 performances
(see *Jack and the Beanstalk* entry for complete cast and credits)

Kim Crosby (Cinderella); Robert Westenberg (Cinderella's Prince); Edmund Lyndeck (Cinderella's Father); Merle Louise (Cinderella's Mother); Joy Franz (Cinderella's Stepmother); Kay McClelland (Florinda); Lauren Mitchell (Lucinda)

INTO THE WOODS, National tour opened *Parker Playhouse*, Fort Lauderdale, November 22, 1988; closed *Naples/Marco Philharmonic*, Naples, Fla., December 17, 1989
(see *Jack and the Beanstalk* entry for complete cast and credits)

Kathleen Rowe McAllen (succeeded by Jill Geddes) (Cinderella); Chuck Wagner (Cinderella's Prince); Don Crosby (Cinderella's Father); Anne Rickenbacker (Cinderella's Mother); Jo Ann Cunningham (Cinderella's Stepmother); Susan Gordon-Clark (Florinda); Danette Cuming (Lucinda)

INTO THE WOODS, *Phoenix Theatre*, London, opened September 25, 1990 186 performances
(see *Jack and the Beanstalk* entry for complete cast and credits)

Jacqueline Dankworth (Cinderella); Clive Carter (Cinderella's Prince); John Rogan (Cinderella's Father); Eunice Grayson (Cinderella's Mother); Ann Howard (Cinderella's Stepmother); Elizabeth Price (Florinda); Liza Sadovy (Lucinda)

SCREEN

CINDERELLA, *G.A.S. Films*, England, released August 1898 1 reel
Director, George A. Smith

Laura Bayley (Cinderella)

Hepworth Pictures, England, release December 1907 1 reel
Director, Lewis Fitzhamon
Dolly Lupone (Cinderella); Frank Wilson (Prince Charming); Gertie Potter (Fairy Godmother); Thurston Harris (Baron)

Thanhauser Pictures, released December 1911 1 reel
Written and directed by Theodore Marston
Florence La Badie (Cinderella); Frank Crane (Prince); Miss Rosamonde (Fairy Godmother); Alphonse Ethier (Baron)

Selig Pictures, released January 1912
Producer, William N. Selig; Director, Colin Campbell; Adapted by Henry Mitchell Webster from the Grimm Brothers fairy tale
Mabel Taliaferro (Cinderella); Thomas J. Corrigan (Prince Charming); Frank Weed (Cinderella's Father); Lillian Leighton (Cinderella's Stepmother); Josephine Miller, Olive Cox (Stepsisters); Baby Griffin (Fairy Godmother); and Charles Clary, Adrienne Kroell, Jessie Stevens, George Cox, William Stowell, Winifred Greenwood and a cast of 300

Empire Films, England, released November 1912
Written and directed by Arthur Collins
(Animated one-reel film enacted by toys)

LORD BROWNING AND CINDERELLA, *Vitagraph Films*, released November 1912
Director, Van Dyke Brooke; Screenplay, Josephine N. Crawford
Clara Kimball Young (Cinderella Gibson); Maurice Costello (Lord Browning); Julia S. Gordon (Mrs. Gibson); Flora Finch (Sylvia); Leah Baird (Adrienne); Van Dyke Brooke (Old Morgan)

Hepworth Pictures, released December 1913
Director, Harry Buss
(Sketch of Cinderella synchronized with a "Vivaphone" to a Columbia recording)

CINDERELLA'S GLOVES, *Essanay Pictures*, releaed June 1913
Ruth Hennessey (Millie, a Waif); Billy Mason (Ned Forrester, Prince Charming); Eleanor Blanchard (Millie's Aunt); Dolores Cassenelli (Mille's Cousin); Charles Hitchcock (Millie's Uncle); Frances Mason (Mrs. Depuyster)

CINDERELLA, *Paramount Pictures*, released December 1914
Produced by Famous Players/Lasky; Director, James Kirkwood
Mary Pickford (Cinderella); Owen Moore (Prince Charming); Isabel Vernon (Stepmother); Georgia Wilson, Lucille Carney (Stepsisters); W. N. Cone (The King)

CINDER-ELFRED, *Hepworth Pictures*, England, released 1914
Director, Hay Plumb
Tom Powers (Elfred)

DER VERLORENE SCHUH, *UFA Films*, Berlin, released January 1924
A Decla-Bishop production; Director, Ludwig Berger; Titles, Robert A. Sanborn;

Photography, Gunther Krampf; Art director, Rudolph Bamberger; Editor, Joseph R. Freisler

Helga Thomas (Cinderella); Paul Hartmann (Prince); Frida Richard (Fairy Godmother); Hermann Thiemig (Baron); Lucie Hofflich (Stepmother); Mady Christians, Olga Tschechowa (Stepsisters); Max Gulstoroff (Cinderella's Father)

A KISS FOR CINDERELLA, *Paramount Pictures*, released December 1925

Produced by Famous Players/Lasky; Director, Herbert Brenon; Adapted by Willis Goldbeck from the play by Sir James Barrie and Townsend Martin; Photography J. Roy Hunt; Art director, Julian Boone Fleming

Betty Bronson (Cinderella); Tom Moore (Policeman/ Prince Charming); Esther Ralston (Fairy Godmother); Ivan Simpson (Mr. Cutaway); Dorothy Walters (Mrs. Maloney); Henry Vibart (Richard Bodie); Edna Hagen (Gretchen); Mary Christian (Sally); Marilyn McLain (Gladys); Flora Finch, Juliet Brenon (Customers); Dorothy Cumming (The Queen); Pattie Coakley (Marie-Therese)

ELLA CINDERS, *First National Pictures*, released June 1926

Producer, John McCormick; Director, Alfred E. Green; Screenplay, Frank Griffin and Mervyn LeRoy, based on the play *Cinderella in the Movies* by William Conselman and Charles Plumb; Titles, George Marion, Jr.; Photography, Arthur Martinelli; Art director, E. J. Shulter; Editor, Robert J. Kern

Colleen Moore (Ella Cinders); Lloyd Hughes (Waite Lifter); Vera Lewis ("Ma" Cinders); Doris Baker (Lotta Pill); Emily Gerdes (Prissy Pill); Jed Prouty (The Mayor); Jack Duffy (The Fire Chief); Mike Donlin (Film Studio Gateman); Barry Allen (The Photographer); Alfred E. Green (The Director); D'Arcy Corrigan (The Editor); Harry Langdon, E. H. Calvert, Russell Hopton, Chief Yowlache (Movie People)

CINDERELLA, *Jean Levy-Strauss Productions*, France, released 1937

Producer, Jean Rossi; Director, Pierre Caron; Screenplay, Jean Montazel; Photography, Boris Kaufman; Production designer, Jean Douarinou; Music by Vincent Scotto; Lyrics by George Koge

Joan Warner (Cinderella); Christiane Delyne (Dany Rosy); Suzanne Dehelly (Virginia); Maurice Escande (Gilbert); Marcel Vallee (The Director); Paul Faivre (Mataplan); Felix Paquet (Electrician); Philippe Janvie (A Student); Jeanne Fusier-Gir, Jane Stick, Eva Barcinska, O'Dett, Jacques Josselin, Guy Berry, Charles Lemontier, Titys, Raphael Medina, Georges Grey (The Boys and Girls of the Folies-Bergere); Jo Bouillon and His Orchestra; Willie Lewis and His Entertainers

CINDERELLA, *Lenfilm*, Russia, released 1947

Produced and directed by Nadezhda Kosheverova and Mikhail Shapiro; Screenplay, E. Schwartz; Photography, E. Shapiro

Yanina Zheimo (Cinderella); A. Konovsky (Prince Charming); F. Ranevskaya (Stepmother); F. Garin (King)

LA CENERENTOLA, *Artisti Associati*, Italy, released 1948; in U.S. May 1953

An Opera film produced by Marie and Ugo Trombetti; Director, Fernando Cerchio; Screenplay, Piero Ballerini, Angelo Besozzi, Fernando Cerchio, Fulvio Palmieri and Aldo Rossi, based on the libretto by Jacobo Feretti; Music by Gioachhino Rossini; Photography, Mario Albertelli; Scenery, Gastone Simonetti; Costumes, Flavio

Mogherini; Music conductor, Oliviero De Farbritiis; Editor, Renzo Lucidi

Lori Randi (Cenerentola/Cinderella); Fedora Barbieri (Voice of Cinderella); Gino Del Signore (Prince Don Ramiro); Vito De Taranto (Don Magnifico); Afro Poli (Dandini); Fiorelli Carmen Forti (Clorinda); Enrico Formichi (Alidoro the Magician); Franca Tamantini (Tisbe); Fernanda Cadoni (Voice of Tisbe); Orchestra and Chorus of the Rome Opera Company

CINDERELLA, *Walt Disney/RKO Radio Pictures*, released 1950

A Walt Disney Animated Cartoon Feature Film; Production supervisor, Ben Sharpsteen; Directors, Wilfred Jackson, Hamilton Luske and Clyde Geronimi; Directing animators, Eric Larson, Ward Kimball, Norman Ferguson, Marc Davis, John Lounsberg, Milt Kahl, Wolfgang Reitherman, Les Clark, Oliver Johnston, Jr., and Franklin Thomas; Screenplay based on the original story by Charles Perrault; Story, Kenneth Anderson, Ted Sears, Homer Brightman, Joe Rinaldi, William Peet, Harry Reeves, Winston Hibler and Erdman Penner; Musical directors, Oliver Wallace and Paul J. Smith; Orchestrations, Joseph Dubin; Songs, Mack David, Jerry Livingston and Al Hoffman; Special processes, Ub Iwerks; Editor, Donald Halliday

Voices: Ilene Woods (Cinderella); William Phipps (Prince Charming); Eleanor Audley (Stepmother); Rhoda Williams, Lucille Bliss (Stepsisters); Verna Felton (Fairy Godmother); Luis Van Rooten (King/ Grand Duke); James MacDonald (Jacques/Gus)

MUSICAL NUMBERS: "Bibbidi Bobbidi Boo"; "So This Is Love"; "A Dream Is a Wish Your Heart Makes"; "Cinderella"; "The Work Song"; "Sing, Sweet Nightingale"

THE GLASS SLIPPER, *Metro-Goldwyn-Mayer*, released March 1955

Producer, Edwin H. Knopf; Director, Charles Walters; Screenplay, Helen Deutsch, based on *Cinderella* by Charles Perrault and the 1944 musical play by Herbert and Eleanor Farjeon; Photography, Arthur E. Arling; Art directors, Cedric Gibbons and Daniel B. Cathcart; Costumes, Helen Rose and Walter Plunkett; Choreography, Roland Petit; Music, Bronislau Kaper; Song "Take My Love" by Bronislau Kaper and Helen Deutsch; Editor, Ferris Webster; Narrator, Walter Pidgeon

Leslie Caron (Ella); Michael Wilding (Prince Charles); Estelle Winwood (Mrs. Toquet, the Fairy Godmother); Elsa Lanchester (Widow Sonder); Keenan Wynn (Kovin); Barry Jones (Duke); Amanda Blake (Birena); Lisa Daniels (Serafina); Lurene Tuttle (Cousin Loulou); Liliane Montevecchi (Tehara); Reginald Simpson (Valet); Tyler McDuff (Willie); Bud Osborne (Coachman); Lucille Curtis (Mistress); Mary Ellen Clemons, Dawn Bender, Sue George (Girls); Gail Bonney, Doris Kemper, Elizabeth Slifer (Women); Robert Dix, Richard Emory, Ronald Green (Young Men); and The Ballet de Paris

ASCHENPUTTEL, *Fritz Genshow-Film*, West Germany, released 1955; in U.S. released by *Childhood Productions*, 1966

Written, produced and directed by Fritz Genschow; Adapted from the Grimm Brothers fairy tale; Photography, Gerhard Huttula; Art director and costumes, Waldemar Volkmer; Music, Richard Stauch (German version), Milton DeLugg (American version); Songs, Milton and Anne DeLugg; Dances, Carola Krauskopf; Editor, Albert Baumeister; Narrator, Paul Tripp (American version)

Rita-Maria Nowotny (Cinderella); Rudiger Lichti (Prince); Renee Strobawa (Fairy Godmother); Fritz Genschow (Father); Aenne Bruck (Stepmother); and Werner Stock, Herbert Weissbach, Joachim Rodel, Gisela Schauroth

GRUSTAINI BASHMACHOK (CINDERELLA), Gorky Films, Russia, released February 1960; in U.S. December 1961

A Ballet film written and directed by Alexander Row and Rostislav Zakharov; Photography, Alexander Ginzburg; Art direction and costumes, Piotr Williams; Choreography, Rostislav Zakharov; Music, Sergei Prokofiev; Performed by The Bolshoi Orchestra conducted by Yuri Faier; Sound, Anatoli Dikan; Editor, Ye. Abdirkina

Raisa Struchkova (Cinderella); Gennadi Lediakh (The Prince); Elena Vanke (The Stepmother); Lesma Chadarin (Haughty); Natalya Rizhenko (Spiteful); Alexander Pavlinov (Cinderella's Father); Yekaterina Maximova (Spring); Elena Riabinkina (Summer); Marina Kolpakchi (Autumn); Natalya Taborko (Winter); L. Shvachkin (Midnight Gnome); Y. Vyrenkov (Jester); Y. Skott (Snake Dancer); V. Ferbakh, N. Papko (Mazurka Soloists); Nina Simonova, V. Kudryashov (Andalusian Dancers); G. Tarasov (Steward); Aleksandr Lapauri, V. Zakharov, Y. Ignatov (Foreign Guests); Aleksandr Radunskiy (Master of Ceremonies)

CINDERFELLA, Paramount Pictures, released December 1960

A Jerry Lewis Production; Associate producer, Ernest D. Glucksman; Written and directed by Frank Tashlin; Photography, Haskell Boggs; Art directors, Hal Pereira and Henry Bumstead; Costumes, Edith Head; Musical numbers staged by Nick Castle; Music, Walter Scharf; Songs, Harry Warren and Jack Brooks; Sound, Gene Merritt; Editor, Archie Schmdit

Jerry Lewis (Fella); Anna Maria Alberghetti (Princess Charmein); Ed Wynn (Fairy Godfather); Judith Anderson (Wicked Stepmother); Henry Silva (Maximilian); Robert Hutton (Rupert); Alan Reed (Father); Count Basie and His Orchestra with Joe Williams

SINDERELLA AND THE GOLDEN BRA, Manson Distributing, released 1964

Producer, Paul Mart; Associate producers, Ed Ludlom and Sy De Bardas; Director, Loel Minardi; Screenplay, Frank Squires, freely adapted from the Cinderella fairy tale; Photography, Mario Tosi; Art director, Tod Jonson; Music and lyrics, Les Szarvas; Musical director, Jacques Montreaux; Editor, Karl Von

Suzanne Sybele (Sinderella); Bill Gaskin (Prince David); David Duffield (King); Sid Lassick (Godfather); Patricia Mayfield (Stepmother); Joan Lemmo (Fanny); June Faith (Flossy); Gerald Strickland (Adviser); Kay Hall (Matron); John Bradley (Page); Althea Currier, Jackie DeWitt, Justine Scott, Lisa Carole, Donna Anderson, Beverly Frankell (Village Maidens)

C'ERA UNA VOLTA (HAPPILY EVER AFTER), Champion Cinematographica (Rome)/*Les Films Concordia* (Paris), released 1967; in Great Britain, released by MGM as *CINDERELLA--ITALIAN STYLE*; in U.S., released by MGM as *MORE THAN A MIRACLE*

A Carlo Ponti production; Producer, Carlo Ponti; Director, Francesco Rosi; Screenplay, Tonino Guerra, Raffaele La Capria, Giuseppe Patroni Griffi and Francesco Rosi; Photography, Pasquale De Santis; Art director, Piero Poletto; Costumes, Giulio Coltellacci; Music, Piero Piccioni; Editor, Jolanda Benvenuti

Sophia Loren (Isabella); Omar Sharif (Prince Ramon); Dolores Del Rio (Queen Mother); Georges Wilson (Monzu); Leslie French (Brother Joseph de Copertino); Marina Malfatti (Devout Princess); Anna Nogara (Impatient Princess); Rita Forzano (Greedy Princess); Rosemary Martin (Vain Princess); Carlotta Barilli

(Superstitious Princess); Fleur Mombelli (Haughty Princess); Anne Liotti (Infant Princess); Carla Pisacane, Gladys Dawson, Kathleen St. John, Beatrice Greack (Witches)

GRIMM'S FAIRY TALES FOR ADULTS, West Germany, released 1969; released in U.S. by *Cinemation*, 1971
Produced by Jerry Gross; Director (German version), Rolf Thiel; Supervisor (English version), Perry Oxenhorn; Screenplay, Tom Bau; Art director, Helen Gary; Music, Joe Beck and Regis Mull

Eva V. Rueber Stairer (Cinderella); Marie Liljedahl (Snow White); Ingrid Van Bergen (Wicked Queen); Gaby Fuchs (Sleeping Beauty); Kitty Gschopf, Evelin Dufree (The Stepsisters); Walter Giller (Hans); Peter Hohberger (Heinz); Hugo Lipdinger (Farmer); Isolde Stiegler (The Old One)

THE SLIPPER AND THE ROSE: THE STORY OF CINDERELLA, *Universal Pictures*, release October 1976
A Paradine CoProductions Film; Executive producer, David Frost; Producer, Stuart Lyons; Director, Bryan Forbes; Screenplay, Bryan Forbes, Robert B. Sherman and Richard M. Sherman; Photography, Tony Imi; Production designer, Raymond Simm; Costumes, Julie Harris; Music and lyrics, Robert B. Sherman and Richard M. Sherman; Choreography, Marc Breaux; Musical arranger and conductor, Angela Morley; Editor, Timothy Gee

Gemma Craven (Cinderella); Richard Chamberlain (Prince Edward); Annette Crosbie (Fairy Godmother); Edith Evans (Dowager Queen); Christopher Gable (John); Michael Hordern (King); Margaret Lockwood (Stepmother); Kenneth More (Lord Chamberlain); Julian Orchard (Montague); Lally Bowers (Queen); Sherrie Hewson (Palatine); Rosalind Ayres (Isobella); John Turner (Major Domo); Keith Skinner (Willoughby); Polly Williams (Lady Caroline); Norman Bird (Dress Shop Proprietor); Roy Barraclough (Tailor); Elizabeth Mansfield, Ludmilla Nova (Queen's Ladiesin-Waiting); Peter Graves (General); Gerald Sim (Lord of the Navy); Geoffrey Bayldon (Archbishop); Valentine Dyall (Second Major Domo); Tim Barrett (Minister); Vivienne McKee (Bride); Andre Morell (Bride's Father); Myrtle Reed (Bride's Mother); Peter Leeming (Singing Guard); Marianne Broome, Tessa Dahl, Lea Dreghorn, Eva Reuber-Staier, Ann Rutherford, Suzette St. Clair (Princesses); Jenny Lee Wright (Milk Maid); Patrick Jordan, Rocky Taylor (Prince's Guards); Bryan Forbes (Herald)

MUSICAL NUMBERS: "Why Can't I Be Two People"; "What Does Love Have to Do With Getting Married?"; "Once I Was Loved"; "What a Comforting Thing to Know"; "Protocoligorically Correct"; "A Bride Finding Ball"; "Suddenly It Happens"; "Secret Kingdom"; "The Slipper and the Rose Waltz" ("He Danced With Me"/"She Danced With Me"); "Position and Positioning"; "Tell Me Anything (But Not That I Love Him)"; "I Can't Forget the Melody"

Original soundtrack recording: MCA Records

CINDERELLA, *Group One Productions*, released June 1977
Executive producers, Lenny Shabes and Ronald Dormont; Producer, Charles Band; Director, Michael Pataki; An erotic version by Frank Ray Perilli of the Charles Perrault fairy tale; Photography, Joseph Mangine; Art director, Sherman Loudermilk; Costumes, Christine Boyer; Choreography, Russell Clark; Music, Andrew Belling; Lyrics, Lee Arries; Editor, Laurence Jacobs

Cheryl Smith (Cinderella); Yana Nirvana (Drucella); Marilyn Corwin (Marbella); Jennifer Doyle (Stepmother); Sy Richardson (Fairy Godmother); Bret Smiley (Prince); Kirk Scott (Lord Chamberlain); Buckley Norris (King); Pamela Stonebrook (Queen); Jean-Claude Smith (Swedish Ambassador); Shannon Korbel (Swedish Ambassador's Wife); Elizabeth Halsey, Linda Gildersleeve (Farm Girls); Robert Stone (Farm Girls' Father); Mariwin Roberts, Roberta Tapley (Trapper's Daughters); Gene Wernikoff (Trapper); Bobby Herbeck (Court Jester); Frank Ray Perilli (Italian Ambassador); and Joe X. Cantu, Larry Eisenberg, Bob Leslie, Dewi Silver, Susan Hill, Lois Owens, Jamie Lynn, Jenny Charles, Dwight Krizman, Bill X. Mason

CENERENTOLA '80, Compania Distribuzione Europea (CDE) release, released March 1984
An RAI-TV Channel 2/TVC-Television Center/Strand Art coproduction; Produced and directed by Roberto Malenotti; Screenplay, Ugo Liberatore, Ottavio Alessi and Roberto Malenotti; Photography, Dante Spinotti; Art director, Paolo Biagetti; Music, Guido and Maurizio de Angelis; Editor, Angelo Curi

Bonnie Bianco (Cindy); Pierre Cosso (Mizio); Sandra Milo (Marianne); Adolfo Celi (Prince Gherardeschi); Sylva Koscina (His Wife); Vittorio Caprioli (Harry)

MAID TO ORDER, New Century/Vista Film Co., release July 1987
A Vista Organization production; Producers, Herb Jaffe and Mort Engelberg; Director, Amy Jones; Screenplay, Amy Jones, Perry Howze and Randy Howze; Photography, Shelly Johnson; Production designer, Jeffrey Townsend; Costume designer, Lisa Jensen; Music, Georges Delerue; Editor, Sidney Wolsinsky

Ally Sheedy (Jessie Montgomery); Michael Ontkean (Nick McGuire); Beverly D'Angelo (Sheila); Valerie Perrine (Georgette Starkey); Dick Shawn (Stan Starkey); Tom Skerritt (Charles Montgomery); Merry Clayton (Audrey James); Begona Plaza (Maria)

TELEVISION

CINDERELLA, televised March 31, 1957 CBS 90 minutes
Produced by Richard Lewine; Director, Ralph Nelson; A Musical Fable; Book and lyrics by Oscar Hammerstein II; Music by Richard Rodgers; Settings and costumes, William and Jean Eckart; Set decorator, Gene Callahan; Lighting, Robert Barry; Choreography, Jonathan Lucas; Orchestrations, Robert Russell Bennett; Musical director, Alfred Antonini; Stage manager, Joseph Papp

Julie Andrews (Cinderella); Jon Cypher (Prince Charming); Howard Lindsay (King); Dorothy Stickney (Queen); Ilka Chase (Stepmother); Kaye Ballard (Portia); Alice Ghostley (Joy); Edith Adams (Fairy Godmother); Robert Penn (Town Crier); Alec Clarke (Captain of the Guard); Iggie Wolfington (Chef); George Hall (Steward); David F. Perkins (Court Tailor); Eleanor Phelps, Martha Greenhouse, Jerome Collamore, Julius J. Bloom, Jacquelyn Paige, Jon Call (Townspeople); Kathy Kelly, Karen Lock, Leland Mayforth, Johnny Towsen, Karen Waters (Children); Charles Aschmann, Herb Banke, Donald Barton, Hank Brunjes, Robert Burland, Jean Caples, Jean Coates, Sally Crane, Richard Crowley, William Damian, Grace Dorian, Debbie Douglas, Jose Falcion, Pat Finch, Marvin Doodis, Gloria Hamilton, Dorothy Hill, Stuart Hodes, Diana Hunter, Joseph Layton, Margot Moser, Giselle Orkin, Hazel Patterson, Alex Polermo, Earl Rogers, John Smolko, Tao Strong, Jayne Turner (Ensemble)

MUSICAL NUMBERS: "The Prince Is Giving a Ball"; "Cinderella March"; "In My Own Little Corner"; "Impossible"; "It's Possible"; "Folderol"; "Gavotte"; "Ten Minutes Ago"; "Stepsisters' Lament"; "Waltz for a Ball"; "Do I Love You Because You're Beautiful?"; "When You're Driving Through the Moonlight"; "A Lovely Night"; "The Search"; Finale

Dropped before rehearsals: "If I Weren't King"

Original soundtrack recording: Columbia Records
Additional recording of songs performed by Mary Martin: RCA Records

Producers Showcase, televised April 29, 1957 NBC 90 minutes
The Royal Ballet of London presentation; Music, Sergei Prokofiev; Choreography, Frederick Ashton; Musical director, Robert Irving

Margot Fonteyn (Cinderella); Michael Somes (The Prince); Frederick Ashton, Kenneth MacMillan (The Ugly Sisters); Julia Farron (Fairy Godmother); Alexander Grant (Jester); Merle Park (Spring); Elaine Fifield (Summer); Annette Page (Autumn); Svetlana Bertosova (Winter)

NOTE: Originally presented in London in 1956 with Fonteyn, Somes and Ashton when the Royal Ballet was still the Sadler's Wells Ballet

CINDERELLA, televised February 22, 1965 CBS 90 minutes
Executive producer, Richard Rodgers; Produced and directed by Charles S. Dubin; Associate producer, James S. Stanley; A Musical Fable; Teleplay, Joseph Schrank; Book and lyrics by Oscar Hammerstein II; Music by Richard Rodgers; Set decorator, Antony Mondello; Lighting, Edwin S. Hill; Costumes, George Whittaker; Choreography, Eugene Loring; Orchestrations, Robert Russell Bennett and John Green; Musical director, John Green

Lesley Ann Warren (Cinderella); Stuart Damon (Prince Charming); Walter Pidgeon (King); Ginger Rogers (Queen); Jo Van Fleet (Stepmother); Celeste Holm (Fairy Godmother); Pat Carroll (Prunella); Barbara Ruick (Esmerelda); Joe E. Marks (Prince's Aide); Don Heitgerd (The Herald); Butch Sherwood (Small Boy); Bill Lee (Father); Betty Noyes (Mother); Trudie Adams (Daughter); Alice Mock (Grandmother); Jack Tygett, Paul Gleason (Magic Grooms); Myra Stephens, Linda Howe, Francesca Bellini, Alicia Adams, Rosemarie Rand, Jackie Ward, Debbie Megowan, Robin Eccles

MUSICAL NUMBERS: Same as original production with addition of "Loneliness of Evening"

Original soundtrack recording: Columbia Records

Dance Special, televised December 25, 1976 PBS 1 hour
Produced by the South Carolina Educational Television Network; The Ballet by Sergei Prokofiev; Performed by the Columbia (S.C.) City Ballet; Director, Sidney Palmer; Production designer, Ann Brodie; Music recorded by the Moscow Symphony Orchestra

Mimi Wortham (Cinderella); Henry Everett (Prince Charming); Lou Martin (Fairy Godmother)

ONCE UPON A BROTHERS GRIMM, CBS Children's Special, televised November 23, 1977 CBS 2 hours
Produced by Bernard Rothman and Jack Wohl; Director, Norman Campbell;

Teleplay, Jean Holloway; Art director, Ken Johnson; Set decorator, Robert Checci; Costumes, Bill Hargate; Choreographer, Ron Field; Music by Mitch Leigh; Lyrics by Sammy Cahn

Dean Jones (Jacob Grimm); Paul Sand (Wilhelm Grimm);

Cinderella segment: Stephanie Steele (Cinderella); John McCook (Prince Charming); Corinne Conley (Fairy Godmother); Gordon Connell (Carriage Driver)

CINDY, televised March 24, 1978 ABC 2 hours

John Charles Walters Company in association with Paramount Television; Producers, David Davis, Ed. Weinberger, James L. Brooks and Stan Daniels; Director, William A. Graham; Teleplay, David Davis, Ed. Weinberger and Stan Daniels, based on the Cinderella fairy tale; Photography, Larry Boelens; Production designer, James D. Vance; Costume designer, Sandy Stewart; Choreography, Donald McKayle; Music and lyrics, Stan Daniels; Arranged and orchestrated by Howard Roberts; Editors, Kenneth R. Koch and Vince Humphrey

Charlaine Woodard (Cindy); Alaina Reed (Venus); Nell-Ruth Carter (Olive); Clifton Davis (Capt. Joe Prince); Mae Mercer (Sara Hayes [Stepmother]); Scooey Mitchlll (Father); Cleavant Derricks (Michael Simpson); W. Benson Terry (Miles Archer); John Hancock (Wilcox); Richard Stahl (Recruiter); Burke Byrnes (Swearing-in Officer); Don Dandridge (Military Policeman); Graham Brown (Minister); Noble Willingham (Sergeant); Helen Martin (Flower Lady); Bill P. Murry (Emcee); Boyd Bodwell (Recruit); Joseph George (Doctor); Spo-de-ooee (Wino)

CINDERELLA, *Live From Lincoln Center*, televised November 6, 1980 PBS 3 hours

Produced by Lincoln Center for the Performing Arts in association with WNET/13; Producer, John Goberman; The Opera by Rossini with a libretto by Jacopo Ferretti, English translation by Gimi Beni; Director, Lou Galterio; Scenery and costumes, Rouben TerArutunian; Lighting, Gilbert V. Hemsley, Jr.; The New York City Opera Orchestra conducted by Brian Salesky; Televised live from the New York State Theater

Susanne Marsee (Cinderella); Rockwell Blake (Don Ramiro); James Billings (Don Magnifico); Alan Titus (Dandini); Gianna Rolandi (Clorinda); RoseMarie Freni (Tisbe); Ralph Bassett (Alidoro)

LA CENERENTOLA, *Great Performances*, televised February 6, 1984 PBS 2 hours

A production of Unitel, Munich; The 1981 La Scala staging of the Opera by Rossini with a libretto by Jacopo Ferretti; Executive director, Horant H. Hohlfeld; Staged by Jean-Pierre Ponnelle; Photography, David Watkin; Set design and costumes, Jean-Pierre Ponnelle; The Orchestra and Chorus of La Scala conducted by Claudio Abbado; Chorusmaster, Romano Gandolfi

Frederica von Stade (Angelina [Cenerentola]); Francisco Araiza (Don Ramiro); Paolo Montarsolo (Don Magnifico); Claudio Desderi (Dandini); Margherita Guglielmi (Clorinda); Laura Zannini (Tisbe); Paul Plishka (Alidoro)

CINDERELLA, *Shelley Duvall's Faerie Tale Theatre*, televised August 14, 1985 Showtime 50 minutes

Platypus Productions Inc. and Gaylord Television Entertainment in association with Lion's Gate Films; Executive producer, Shelley Duvall; Producers, Bridget Terry and

Fredric S. Fuchs; Teleplay, Mark Curtiss and Rod Ash; Production designer, Michael Erler; Lighting, George Riesenberger; Music, Jimmy Webb; Editor, Marco Zappia

Jennifer Beals (Cinderella); Matthew Broderick (Prince Henry); Jean Stapleton (Fairy Godmother); Eve Arden (Wicked Stepmother); Edie McClurg, Jane Alden (Stepsisters)

CINDERELLA, *Great Performances/Dance in America*, televised December 3, 1985 PBS 90 minutes

Produced by the San Francisco Ballet; The Ballet by Prokofiev; Choreographed by Lew Christensen and Michael Smuin; Coproducers, Judy Kinberg and Michael Smuin; Director, Emile Ardolino; Sets and costumes, Robert Fletcher; Hosts, Kermit the Frog and Miss Piggy

Evelyn Cisneros (Cinderella); Alexander Topicy (Prince); Catherine Batcheller (Fairy Godmother); Tomm Ruud (Lucretia); Vane Vest (Anastasia); Julian Montane (Jester); Kirk Peterson (Dance Master); Van Caniparoli (Father); Anita Paciotti (Stepmother); Nancy Dickson (Spring); Jamie Zimmerman (Summer); Christina Fagundes (Fall); Eda Holmes (Winter); Ricardo Bustamante, Andre Reyes (Companions to the Prince)

ROSSINI'S CINDERELLA, *Great Performances*, televised June 2, 1989 PBS 3 hours

A production of ORF, Vienna, in association with WNET/13; The 1988 Vienna State Opera staging of the Opera by Rossini with a libretto by Jacopo Ferretti; English translation and subtitles, Sonya Haddad; Executive producer for ORF, Ernst Neuspiel; Staged by Michael Hampe; Television director, Claus Viller; Set design and costumes, Mauro Pagano; The Vienna Philharmonic and Vienna State Opera Chorus conducted by Riccardo Chailly

Ann Murray (Angelina [Cenerentola]); Francisco Araiza (Don Ramiro); Walter Berry (Don Magnifico); Gino Quilico (Dandini); Angela Denning (Clorinda); Daphne Evandelatos (Tisbe); Wolfgang Schoene (Alidoro)

CINDERELLA, *Alive From Off Center*, televised June 1, 1990 PBS 90 minutes

Produced by SVTI Drama and RM Arts in association with La Sept, Channel 4 and ZDF; Executive producer, John Schott; Producer, John Ligon; Director, Maas Reutersward; The Lyon Opera Ballet's production of the Prokofiev ballet; Choreographed by Maguy Marin; Lyon Opera Orchestra conducted by Yakov Kreisberg

Francoise Joullie (Cinderella); Bernard Cauchard (The Prince); Nathalie Delassis (Fairy Godmother); Patrick Azzopardi (Father); Dominique Laine (Stepmother); Jayne Plaisted, Daniele Pater (Stepsisters); Miriam Yous (Little Girl)

INTO THE WOODS, *American Playhouse*, televised March 20, 1991 PBS 3 hours

(see Broadway production)

COME BLOW YOUR HORN

A Comedy by Neil Simon (1961)

Synopsis

Alan Baker is a thirty-three-year-old playboy who owns a bachelor apartment on Manhattan's upper East Side, into which flows a constant stream of single girls. To him comes his brother Buddy, a diffident twenty-one-year-old hoping to escape from his mother's babying and his father's insistence that he settle into the family business, manufacturing waxed fruit. Alan passes Buddy off as an up-and-coming movie producer to help him impress the ladies but soon becomes righteously indignant seeing his brother a reflection of himself in his wild oats sowing sibling.

Comment and Critique

TV comedy writer-turned-playwright Neil Simon (see *The Odd Couple*) had contributed to a couple of flop Broadway revues (*Catch a Star* in 1955 and *New Faces of 1956*) before turning to plays, and had a smash with his very first one, *Come Blow Your Horn*, in 1961. His succeeding twenty-eight shows (through 1992) would make him the most successful Broadway playwright of the century, with performances in excess of 15,100, unmatched, according to *Variety*, by any other dramatic author. When *Come Blow Your Horn* (with TV game show host Hal March in the lead) opened at the Brooks Atkinson Theatre in late February 1961, it was greeted with modified cheers from the critics while theater-goers loved it.

In *The New York Times*, Howard Taubman called it "a slick, lovely, funny comedy...[it] will not go down in the dramatic annals as a masterpiece [but] it is smoothly plotted and deftly written." Taubman felt, "[Simon] has provided some explosively hilarious moments rooted in character. His choicest and funniest creation is Harry Baker, owner of the biggest artificial fruit business in the East...played by Lou Jacobi with a wonderful mixture of brawling brusqueness and injured sensibility." John McClain, critic for the *Journal American*, wrote: "The audience at the opening ...whistled, screamed and all but tore up the seats in approval of this new comedy by Neil Simon...And, indeed, it is funny -- but it ISN'T THAT funny. This is Mr. Simon's first Broadway venture, after a successful hitch in television writing, and it struck me that he is still under the whammy of the small red eye...but he has an abundance of solid yoks, some very adept character delineation, and the whole production moves with pace and professional slickness."

McClain found that Hal March "comes off as an assured and very likeable comedic actor" and that "Stanley Prager, in his Broadway debut as a director, shows a clear appreciation of the pace required and the proper timing of the frequent boffos." Walter Kerr's report in the *Herald Tribune* skewered the comedy, although nice words were heaped upon the individual actors. Kerr's conclusion was: "It is imperative that I report a blockbuster response on the part of the customers, no matter whether the jokes were satisfying, soso, or seedy. This duty done, and the major performances acknowledged, we can only years for the years of Anne Nichols' maturity."

Come Blow Your Horn, despite its popularity, never became a touring or stock staple through the years, and it would be two decades before another major staging of it would be mounted. In between, there was the film version, refashioned as a vehicle for Frank Sinatra in 1963 (his "ring-a-ding-ding" days). This was the movie he made on the heels of *The Manchurian Candidate*. As a Sinatra film, it was quite popular, but most critics felt that it threw the Simon play off balance. "The main thing they have done is to throw the play out the window -- all but the bones and central situation. (After all you have to start somewhere)," Arthur Knight observed in *Saturday Review*. "By shifting the focus from the younger to the older brother, they have strengthened what remains a feeble and familiar story line. But they have also opened it out with gay and inventive business, and paced it with breakneck speed."

Less forgiving was *The New York Times*' Bosley Crowther: "Even if you have never seen the play on the stage, you would be likely to get that feeling of vapid boredom when you see it on the screen. For the dismal fact is that the producers and Frank Sinatra have really butchered the play in their garish screen version which came to Radio City Music Hall.. It is not only that they have dressed it out of all proportion to the style and logic of the situation and the characters involved...The worst thing about this picture is the dullness with which it is played -- the lack of pace in [Bud] Yorkin's direction complements the clumsy performances."

Newcomer Tony Bill played the younger brother in this one. He went on to have a fitful acting career but became better known as a producer (*The Sting*) and a director (*My Bodyguard*). Veteran Yiddish theater actress Molly Picon made her Hollywood film debut here as the boys' doting other and went on to play in only two other English-language movies (*Fiddler on the Roof* and Barbra Streisand's *For Pete's Sake*). Phyllis McGuire, of the singing McGuire Sisters, also made her film acting debut here. Outlasting the film itself, which is not seen too often, is the title song written for Sinatra by Sammy Cahn and James Van Heusen. The composers did not get Oscarnominated for their tune (although they did win that year for *Call Me Irresponsible*), but art directors Hal Pereira and Roland Anderson and set decorators Sam Comer and James Payne did get nominated for *Come Blow Your Horn*. They lost however to their artisan counterparts on *Cleopatra*.

Just as Tony Bill (the screen Buddy Baker) moved into directing subsequently, so did Warren Berlinger (the stage Buddy Baker). It was Berlinger who directed the 1981 revival of the play, first at the Burt Reynolds Dinner Theatre in Jupiter, Florida, and then at the Huntington Hartford Theatre in Los Angeles. Elliott Gould had the role of the older brother, and Lou Jacobi reprised his hilarious original performance as the befuddled father. Alice Ghostley and Alfie Wise played the mother and the younger brother. "Neil Simon's *Come Blow Your Horn* has not matured as gracefully as have some of his other comedies. Many laughs are still to be found in this 1961 show, but the premise of a generation gap...is dated from the perspective of the 1980s...Gould's character is the centerpiece, and he plays it like one: an inanimate object. As unemotional as wax fruit. Gould's performance stays at one level, whether he's mad, making love or conversing...If the play seems remote for the 1980s, it might be at least more interesting with a lead whose performance has some spark," *Daily Variety* felt. "Production's best moments come when Lou Jacobi as the domineering papa and Alice Ghostley as the archetypical Jewish mama are on stage. Both play these plum roles to the hilt, provoking the strongest and most frequent laughter with the sheer ease and skill of their deliveries."

This production of the Simon play subsequently was taped for television and broadcast in November 1981 on cable's *Broadway on Showtime* series.

STAGE

COME BLOW YOUR HORN, *Brooks Atkinson Theatre*, New York, opened February 22, 1961 677 performances

Produced by William Hammerstein; A Comedy in three acts by Neil Simon; Director, Stanley Prager; Setting and lighting, Ralph Alswang; Costumes, Stanley Simmons; Stage managers, Harvey Medlinsky and E. M. Margolese

Hal March (succeeded by Tom Poston) (Alan Baker); Lou Jacobi (Mr. Baker); Pert Kelton (Mrs. Baker); Arlene Golonka (Peggy Evans); Sarah Marshall (succeeded by Natalie Ross) (Connie Dayton); Warren Berlinger (succeeded by

Joel Grey) (Buddy Baker); Carolyn Brenner (A Visitor)

Touring Company, opened *Moore Theatre*, Seattle, October 8, 1962; closed *Civic Theatre*, Chicago, February 2, 1963
Produced by William Hammerstein and Michael Ellis; A Comedy in three acts by Neil Simon; Director, Stanley Prager; Setting and lighting, Ralph Alswang; Costumes, Stanley Simmons; Stage managers, Harvey Medlinsky and Julius Adler

Hal March (Alan Baker); Morris Carnovsky (Mr. Baker); Henrietta Jacobson (Mrs. Baker); Patty Joy Harmon (Peggy Evans); Karen Thorsell (Connie Dayton); Warren Berlinger (Buddy Baker); Helen Verbit (A Visitor)

Cape Playhouse, Dennis, Mass., opened July 29 through August 3, 1963
Produced by Charles Mooney; A Comedy by Neil Simon; Director, Porter Van Zandt; Seting, Helen Pond

Julius La Rosa (Alan Baker); Jerome Cowan (Mr. Baker); Paula Trueman (Mrs. Baker); Jane Culley (Peggy Evans); Lyla Van (Connie Dayton); Will Mackenzie (Buddy Baker); Eleanor Cody Gould (A Visitor)

Touring Company, summer 1977
Produced by Charles Forsythe; A Comedy by Neil Simon; Director, John Going

Doug McClure (Alan Baker); Lou Jacobi (Mr. Baker); Audrey Christie (Mrs. Baker); Sydney Blake (Peggy Evans); Monica Merryman Connie Dayton); Georgeanna Spelvin (A Visitor)

Burt Reynolds Dinner Theatre, Jupiter, Fla., opened August 5 through September 19, 1981; then *Huntington Hartford Theatre*, Los Angeles, opened October 9 through November 8, 1981
Produced by Karen Poindexter (Burt Reynolds Theatre), Fred Amsel, Ted Witzer, Michael Mann and Warren Berlinger; A Comedy in three acts by Neil Simon; Director, Warren Berlinger; Set, Steven J. Normandale; Lighting, Pamela Mara (Burt Reynold Theatre), Paulie Jenkins; Costumes, Sarah Bradford

Elliott Gould (Alan Baker); Lou Jacobi (Mr. Baker); Alice Ghostley (Mrs. Baker); Alfie Wise (Buddy Baker); Lynne Marta (Connie Dayton); Jennifer Richards (Peggy Evans); Miriam Dady (A Visitor)

NOTE: This version was taped for television presentation on cable, and premiered the day after the Los Angeles stage production closed

Jewish Repertory Theater, opened December 30, 1987
Presented by the Jewish Repertory Theater, Ran Avni, artistic director; A Comedy by Neil Simon; Director, Charles Maryan; Sets, Atkin Pace; Lighting, Brian Nason; Costumes, Barbara Bush; Sound, Aaron Winslow; Stage manager, Catherine Heusel

Mark Sawyer (Alan Baker); Stephen Perlman (Mr. Baker); Chevi Colton (Mrs. Baker); Lonny Price (Buddy Baker); Julia Mueller (Connie Dayton); Susan Batten (Peggy Evans); Arlene Mantek (A Visitor)

SCREEN

COME BLOW YOUR HORN, Paramount Pictures, released June 1963
An Essex-Tandem Production; Executive producer, Howard W. Koch; Producers, Norman Lear and Bud Yorkin; Director, Bud Yorkin; Screenplay, Norman Lear, based on the play by Neil Simon; Photography, William H. Daniels; Art directors, Hal Pereira

and Roland Anderson; Costumes, Edith Head; Set decorators, Sam Comer and James Payne; Makeup, Wally Westmore; Music, Nelson Riddle; Orchestrations, Gil Grau; Title Song, Sammy Cahn and James Van Heusen; Editor, Frank P. Keller

Frank Sinatra (Alan Baker); Lee J. Cobb (Papa Baker); Molly Picon (Mama Baker); Barbara Rush (Connie); Jill St. John (Peggy); Tony Bill (Buddy Baker); Dan Blocker (Mr. Eckman); Phyllis McGuire (Mrs. Eckman); Herbie Faye (Waiter); Romo Vincent (Barber); Charlotte Fletcher (Manicurist); Greta Randall (Tall Girl); Vinnie De Carlo (Max); Jack Nestle (Desk Clerk); Eddie Quillan (Elevator Operator); Grady Sutton (Manager); Joyce Nizzari (Snow Eskanazi); Carole Welles (Eunice); John Indrisano (Cab driver); Dean Martin (Wino)

TELEVISION

COME BLOW YOUR HORN, *Broadway on Showtime*, televised November 9, 1981
Showtime 2 hours
Paramount Television Distribution in association with Burt Reynolds Dinner Theater; Executive producer, David Gershenson; Directed for the Stage by Warren Berlinger; Directed for television by Bill Caruthers; The play by Neil Simon

Elliott Gould (Alan Baker); Lou Jacobi (Mr. Baker); Alice Ghostley (Mrs. Baker); Alfie Wise (Buddy Baker); Lynne Marta (Connie); Jennifer Richards (Peggy); Miriam Dady (A Visitor)

THE CORSICAN BROTHERS

A Play by Dion Boucicault, based on *Les Freres Corses* by Alexandre Dumas (1852)

Synopsis

Born Siamese twins but miraculously separated after their birth, Louis and Fabien dei Franchi remain bound in soul, heart and mind. In 1840, the brothers falls in love with, Emilie, daughter of a general, and Louis is persuaded to leave Corsica for Paris and tell the beautiful girl of his love for her. There he discovers that Emilie has married Admiral de l'Esparre, and in her husband's absence at sea, is being amorously pursued by Monsieur de Chateau Renaud, a notorious rake. Chateau Renaud agrees to return Emilie's compromising letters if she attends Baron de Montgiron's dinner party. Emilie finds herself the center of attention among the Baron's allmale guests and pleads for Louis' protection. Louis challenges Chateau Renaud to a duel and is killed by the blackmailing rogue. At the dei Franchi castle in Corsica, the vision of Louis appears before his twin, Fabien, describing his death. Fabien, declaring revenge, finds Chateau Renaud in Paris and challenges him to a duel on the very ground in the Forest of Fontainebleau where his twin brother was slain. Fabien pierces Chateau Renaud in the heart and cries out his vendetta victory to his twin.

Comment and Critique

In 1852, the year the novel was published, Charles Fechter appeared as the twins in the first dramatization of *The Corsican Brothers*, adapted by Eugene Grange and Xavier de Montepin, at the Theatre Historique in Paris. Dumas based his story on the widely publicized telepathic attunement of the twin Tremayne brothers, born in

1660 at Tavistock, Devon, England. Dumas relocated his adventure of love and vendetta to Corsica and France.

Dion Boucicault adapted the novel to the stage for Edmund Kean's son, Charles, who included it as one of the most successful plays in his repertoire. Charles Fechter later portrayed *The Corsican Brothers* on the London stage, but audiences preferred Charles Kean's interpretation. *The Corsican Brothers* was first produced in America in April 1852, at New York's Bowery Theatre with Edward Eddy as the dei Franchi twins.

In his *Annals of the New York Stage*, historian George Odell noted, "The really notable success at the Bowery was the much discussed foreign novelty, *The Corsican Brothers*, with its trick ghost and special effects, its magnificent scenery, its exciting episodes." Competitive twins found equal success at the Astor Place Theatre in May 1852 with Gustavus Vaughan Brooke in the leading roles. In March 1856, New York's German-language Stadt Theatre produced *The Corsican Brothers* featuring Otto Hoym as the twin brothers.

Henry Irving produced *The Corsican Brothers* in London on September 18, 1880, and submitted the following advertisement in the London press:

> NOTICE/LYCEUM THEATRE, MR. IRVING wishes to announce to the Public that the written applications for booked places for the First Representation of THE CORSICAN BROTHERS so far exceeds the holding capacity of the Theatre that he has been obliged to allot all seats available according to priority of application...

The performance began with the one-act *Bygones* by Arthur Wing Pinero, who also played the leading role as well as the part of Monsieur Alfred Meynard in *The Corsican Brothers*.

Henry Irving selected Dion Boucicault's adaptation as had been played by Charles Kean. Laurence Irving, Sir Henry's grandson, wrote in his biography, *Henry Irving, The Actor and His World*, "No doubt he chose *The Corsican Brothers* (a play which Henry James dismissed as hackneyed and preposterous) because it offered him considerable scope as a producer and because its lack of any part of female interest made it a good stopgap until Ellen Terry returned to the Lyceum at the end of the year. The play was an old favorite with the public; indeed for a quarter of a century, it had been acted to death. Their eagerness to see him in it was a measure of his hold over them...The notices of his own performance were perfunctory; on the whole he was judged to be too solemn and inert -- in fact, too middle-aged to be convincing as a hardy Corsican mountaineer. One critic went so far as to say that as Louis he was better in the spirit than in the flesh. The public, however, were not deterred by these qualifications. *The Corsican Brothers* ran until the end of the year..." At one performance, Irving persuaded William Ewart Gladstone, then Chancellor of the Exchequer, to be a super in Scene I of Act II in the Paris Opera House Bal de l'Opera.

Actress Violet Vanbrugh later described to writers H. A. Saintsbury and Cecil Palmer for their biography, *We Saw Him Act: A Symposium on the Art of Sir Henry Irving*, "He held you literally spellbound. Then came the haunting music as, by the device of a sliding trap, the ghost of Louis dei Franchi stole across the stage to his brother, his hand upon the wound on his chest. Irving's lighting effects were wonderful. No one ever realized more clearly than he did the power that lighting has upon the imagination of the audience. He only used gas and limelights, but with what perfection he blended colours, diffused light and created shadows ...In the second act, his portrayal of Louis dei Franchi showed us a polished, courtly man, weaker in fibre than Fabien, like yet unlike his brother. He made you realize the similarity of their upbringing, and just what had been the effect on each nature of their experiences after they had separated."

Saintsbury and Palmer added, "*The Corsican Brothers*, a crude melodrama with its dual *role* of twins, miraculously alike, its stilted language, its vendettas, its ghosts, its duel in the snow, would seem strange fare now to set before a London audience. And indeed in 1880, when it was revived at the Lyceum, it would have appeared almost equally old-fashioned had not Henry Irving been there to play Fabien and Louis dei Franchi."

Ten years after Irving's successful experiment with the dei Franchi, New York saw Robert Mantell's interpretation of *The Corsican Brothers* at the 14th Street Theatre. *The New York Times* called it "A very good performance of a very old play...As the twins, Mr. Mantell has grown somewhat heavier in method as well as physique...He retains the athletic grace, the suggested force and the rich, melodious voice...The revival is, on the whole, very captivating."

The New York Dramatic Mirror reviewed *The Corsican Brothers* as being presented "with a claim of being a grand spectacular production. The mechanical effects were the well-known vision scenes, but they were badly managed in the lighting and the illusion was accordingly dispelled by the gauzes being visible...The double role of Louis and Fabien de [sic] Franchi was undertaken by Robert Mantell in a satisfactory and artistic manner, but with less vigor than the accomplished actor has shown in other pieces..."

Henry Irving continued reviving *The Corsican Brothers* until the turn of the century when Martin Harvey appeared as the brothers in 1907 and 1908. Seven decades later, John Bowen adapted his television script of *The Corsican Brothers* to the stage as a musical.

"The result is not unenjoyable but it shows, I fear, the difficulties of trying to rework a melodrama without accepting the clear-cut moral attitudes it originally embodied," Michael Billington (*Plays and Players*) found. "Mr. Bowen's solution is clearly to try and provide something for everyone: the problem is he doesn't really supply quite enough for anyone. One the most basic level, he seeks to combine the narrative drive and theatrical flair of authentic melodrama...On to this simplest tale of revenge and retribution, Mr. Bowen has grafted several agreeable songs with music by Offenbach, Gounod, Auber and Donizetti and lyrics by himself and John Holmstrom."

Irving Wardle reported from London to *The New York Times* that "In Boucicault's 1850s, the piece was famous for doubling the parts of the rough Corsican squire and his smooth emigre sibling. Mr. Bowen's version also uses one actor for both roles and speeds up their overlapping into a virtuoso routine, including trick scenes presenting the brothers simultaneously...and equips the piece with excellently pointed lyrics to old favorites from Offenbach and Gounod...sophisticated hindsight robs the story telling of its energy..."

The Corsican Brothers provided the screen with an opportunity for experimentation. In 1898, George Albert Smith produced a seventy-five-foot film of the scene in which the ghost of Louis appears before his brother Fabien. It was heralded as "the first double exposure" produced for the screen in England. Britain's Dicky Winslow produced a three-hundred-foot film in 1902 of *The Corsican Brothers* with A. W. Fitzgerald as Fabien and Louis dei Franchi depicting the death of Fabien after Louis' death in the duel with Chateau Renaud. Edison's 1912 short film featured

George A. Lessey and Benjamin F. Wilson.

On May 14, 1915, Universal-Imp Pictures of America released their three-reel version of *The Corsican Brothers*. "Following up a presentday practice among film producers, namely, the modernizing of stories which were originally set by their authors in a period more or less remote from our own, the Universal version of the Dumas novel, adapted and produced by George Lessey, brings to our vision the Paris of today, with a Corsica that might have belonged in part to the period referred to by the novelist," Margaret I. MacDonald (*The Moving Picture World*) wrote. "The production has, however, lost little if any by the transposition of its story to the modern atmosphere. King Baggot, playing a dual role, does remarkably well with the characters of the twin brothers...There is, of course, as always in such cases, a noticeable lack of freedom in action on the double exposure scenes...The production cannot fail to please, regardless of the fact that the modernizing of the story may not please all of us."

Andre Antoine directed a French version of *Les Freres Corses* in 1915 with Henry Krauss as the brothers and Rose Dione as Emilie. On December 28, 1919, United Pictures released Louis J. Gasnier's production of *The Corsican Brothers* with Dustin Farnum in the dual role.

"The story of *The Corsican Brothers* by Alexandre Dumas, containing a wealth of material for spectacular and dramatic presentation, has not yet been converted to the screen with the best accouterments of art. Stories of lesser dramatic values and more ordinary problems have been filmed with a larger degree of artistry and monied magnificence," reported Margaret I. MacDonald in *The Moving Picture World*. "While the production contains many point of merit, including excellent double exposure work -- it has not the earmarks of a finished production. The construction is choppy and lacks breadth of vision...The old-fashioned charm of Emilie de Lesparre as portrayed by Winifred Kingston is exquisite...Dustin Farnum, while he is a bit stagey in his 'double role,' presents an attractive figure..."

Les Freres Corses was filmed again in France in 1938 with Pierre Brasseur and Jacques Erwin as the twin brothers. Edward Small's American production of *The Corsican Brothers* starring Douglas Fairbanks, Jr. as the dei Franchi brothers was released in 1941. "This is the kind of movie that made movies popular," advised *Photoplay*. "It has romance, thrills, rescues, sword play and all the unbelievable things that went into the dream world of movies -- the romance and thrills that abound in a well-knit story are many and will keep you entranced throughout..."

Time magazine, on the other hand, noted "*The Corsican Brothers* are (both of them) Douglas Fairbanks, Jr., who has yet to make up his mind who he is: his father, or Ronald Colman...is accomplished with heavy-handed, uninspired direction and all the corny hokum that accompanies the routine Hollywood romantic picture. In the realms of farce or horror, *The Brothers'* situation might have amounted to something."

Liberty magazine observed, "Swashbuckling costume melodrama is generally sure-fire on the screen...One of the best of these is *The Corsican Brothers*...With Douglas Fairbanks, Jr., playing a dual role with florid dash, the picture is colorful and engrossing...Call it a wild and wooly fable, if you want, but it makes superior entertainment for those who like costume romantic melodrama. Fairbanks plays the brother roles with vigor and considerable versatility. Ruth Warrick is a pleasant heroine and Akim Tamiroff makes a sinister villain. *The Corsican Brothers* is strictly hokum, but it is beguiling hokum."

United Artists released Edward Small's new screen version of the Dumas classic in 1953 as *Bandits of Corsica* starring Richard Greene as the two Franchis plus one.

The film was released in England as *The Return of the Corsican Brothers* where one British critic carped that "Confusion necessarily arises by Richard Greene having to play *three* characters; for the rest, the film is quite efficient in its unexacting way."

The Corsican Brothers was brought to television in Great Britain in 1965 with Alan Dobie in the lead(s) and Anne Lawson as the love interest. It received a lavish new production two decades later on the *Hallmark Hall of Fame* featuring Trevor Eve as the brothers and Olivia Hussey as the romantic interest.

"A good adventure yarn, no matter how familiar or farfetched, carries a kind of visceral charge that makes it perennially irresistible as popular entertainment. And *The Corsican Brothers*...is just such a yarn," reported Stephen Holden (*The New York Times*). "The twohour, made-for-television movie version of the story...may be giddy escapist hokum. But the film, produced by David A. Rosemont and directed by Ian Sharp, nevertheless skillfully recaptures the flavor and rhythm of old-time Technicolor swords-and-daggers romps, with a seasoning of contemporary elements such as a *Godfather*-like score... Written for television by Robin Miller, [it] revels in vintage movie cliches, and almost every sentence is an oracular costume-drama pronouncement." Critic Holden also felt that "Trevor Eve's Louis/Lucien does not exude the sheer physical delight that Douglas Fairbanks (senior and junior) and Errol Flynn brought to the swashbuckling genre. His tense, glowering presence is closer to the mood of modern gangster movies. Uncharming as he is, however, Mr. Eve gives the movie a psychological edge that helps hold together the mounds of fluffy cliche."

STAGE

(Variation in the spelling of character names are given as listed on programmes)

THE CORSICAN BROTHERS, *Bowery Theatre*, New York, opened April 21, 1852
40 performances
A Play based on the novel by Alexandre Dumas

Edward Eddy (Fabian dei Franchi/Louis dei Franchi); W. R. Goodall (Chateau Renaud); Mrs. Yeamans (Emilie); Mr. Hamilton (Montgiron); Mr. Stevens (Martelli); Caroline Hiffert (Maria); M. W. Leffing-well (Orlando); G. H. Griffiths (Colonna); S. W. Glenn (Alfred Meynard); Mr. Browne (Verner); Mr. Reed (Beauchamp); Mr. Bowes (Antonio Sanoli); Mr. Moore (Boissac); Mr. Daly (Surgeon); Mrs. Jordan (Madame dei Franchi)

Theatre d'Astor Place, New York, opened May 19, 1852
A Play based on the novel by Alexandre Dumas

Gustavus Vaughan Brooks (Fabian dei Franchi/Louis dei Franchi); George Jordan (Chateau Renaud); Mrs. Hale (Emilie); G. J. Arnold (Montgiron); Mr. Harris (Martelli); Mrs. Vickery (Madame dei Franchi)

Princess Theatre, London, opened December 29, 1852
A Play by Dion Boucicault, based on the novel by Alexandre Dumas; Scenery, W. Gordon, F. Lloyds, Adams and Cuthbert; Costumes, Sefton and Hoggins; Dances, Oscar Byrn; Stage manager, Mr. Gelks

Charles Kean (Fabian dei Franchi/Louis dei Franchi); Walter Lucy (Chateau Renaud); James Vining (Montgiron); Miss Murry (Emilie); Charles Wheatleigh (Martelli); G. Everett (Meynard); Miss Phillips (Madame dei Franchi); Mr. Chester (Boissec); Mr. Ryder (Orlando); Mr. Meadows (Colonna); F. Cooke (Sanoli); Mr. Paulo (Griffo); Mr. Daly (Surgeon); Mr. Stoakes (Tomaso); Mrs.

Daly (Celestine); J. Marston (Maria); Miss Vivashe (Estelle); Mr. Stacey (Beauchamp); Mr. Rolleston (Mons. Verner); C. Leclercq (Carolie); Mr. Haines, Mr. Wilson (Servants)

New Theatre, Greenwich, England, opened October 16, 1854
A Play by Dion Boucicault, based on the novel by Alexandre Dumas

James Fernandez (Fabian and Louis Dei Franchi); G. Robinson (Chateau Renaud); Bessie Foote (Emilie); W. Howard (Meynard); Mr. Ricketts (Martelli); W. Arthur (Montgiron); W. Foote (Orlando); J. Francis (Colonna); Mrs. C. Wharton ((Madame dei Franchi); Miss Lynn (Griffo); Mr. Watson (Tomaso); Mr. Smith (Surgeon); S. Turner (Estelle); Miss Sylvester (Maria); Miss Powell (Coralie); Miss M. Foote (Celestine); W. J. Hurlstone (Boissec)

Varieties Theatre, London, opened February 26, 1855
A Play by Dion Boucicault, based on the novel by Alexandre Dumas; Director, W. R. Floyd

Mary Gladstone (Fabian and Louis dei Franchi); W. E. Sheridan (Chateau Renaud); W. J. Cogswell (Meynard); Josie Orton (Emilie); O. H. Barr (Martelli); H. W. Mitchell (Montgiron); F. P. Pierce (Orlando); Vining Bowers (Colonna); Willie Seymour (Griffo); Mrs. Preston (Madame dei Franchi); J. K. Power (Antonio Sanoli); W. J. Stanton (Boissec); Annie Vaughan (Maria); Bella Wallace (Estelle); Mrs. Seymour (Celestine); Kate Wood (Coralie)

DIE CORSIKANISCHEN BRUDER, *Stadt Theatre*, New York, opened March 4, 1855
A Play derived from the novel by Alexandre Dumas

Otto Hoym (Fabian and Louis dei Franchi); C. Worret (Chateau Renaud); Frau Hoym (Emilie); Herr Buchheister (Orlando); Herr Czmock (Colonna); Herr Fortner (Montgiron); Herr Wolf (Martelli); Johann Wetzler (Canolo); Herr Jakobi (Griffo); Frau Schmidt (Mme. dei Franchi); Frau Kress-Jakobi (Maria); Herr Klein (Vernett)

Niblo's Garden Theatre, New York, opened April 26, 1865
A Play based on the novel by Alexandre Dumas; Scenery, Hillyard; Costumes, Mons. Phillippe; Music, S. Wallis

William Wheatley (Fabian and Louis dei Franchi); Charles Pope (Chateau Renaud); George Becks (Alfred Meynard); J. W. Blaisdell (Giordano Martelli); J. Numan (Orlando); J. G. Burnett (Colonna); Maria Maeder (Emilie); Mrs. Farren (Madame dei Franchi); Mr. Elliot (Beauchamp); H. Danvers (Griffo); E. Barry (Sanoli); E. B. Holmes (Boissec); Mr. Rendle (Tomaso); Mr. Neil (Surgeon); Mrs. Skerett (Estelle); Miss Burke (Celestine); Mrs. Reeves (Maria); Miss Burnard (Coralie); Miss Richardson (Domino); Mr. Burke (Servant)

Howard Anthaneum, New York, opened November 18, 1865
A Play based on the novel by Alexandre Dumas

Helen Western (Fabian and Louis dei Franchi); James Herne (Chateau Renaud); G. Clair (Alfred Meynard); D. Oakley (Baron Montgiron); Mr. Norris (Giordano Martelli); W. P. Sheldon (Gaetano Orlando); E. A. Locke (Mario Colonna); Mr. Webster (Griffo); Mr. Burgess (Sanoli); Miss Athena (Emilie); Miss L. Morse (Madame dei Franchi); Miss Smith (Estelle); Miss Prescott (Marie); Miss L. Ellem (Celestine); Miss A Benedict (Coralie); Mr. Sever (Tomaso); W. R. Crolius (Surgeon)

Royal Lyceum Theatre, London, opened June 11, 1866
Produced and directed by Charles Fechter; A Play based on the novel by Alexandre Dumas; Scenery, T. Grieve; Costumes, Mme. May and Miss Dickenson; Music W. H. Montgomery; Dances, McCormack

Charles Fechter (Fabian and Louis dei Franchi); G. Jordan (Chateau Renaud); Mrs. Henrade (Emilie); Hermann Vezin (Montgiron); C. Horsman (Meynard); M. Fitzpatrick (Martelli); S. Emery (Orlando); H. Widdecomb (Colonna); Mrs. Ternan (Madame dei Franchi); Mr. Moreland (Sanoli); Mr. Westland (Beauchamp); Mr. Stanley (Favrolle); Mr. Morton (Griffo); Mrs. C. Horsman (Maria); Miss Hatch (Doree); E. Lavenu (Rosette); Mr. Regan (Servant); Miss Duverney (Minie)

Princess Theatre, London, opened July 15, 1871
Produced by Benjamin Webster; A Play based on the novel by Alexandre Dumas; Stage manager, Mr. Billington

Charles Fetcher (Fabian and Louis dei Franchi); J. C. Cowper (Chateau Renaud); C. H. Fenton (Meynard); Mr. Billington (Montgiron); Mr. Clifford (Martelli); Rose Leclercq (Madame dei Franchi); Lizzie Price (Emilie); Howard Russell (Orlando); J. Clarke (Colonna); Mr. Tapping (Favrolle); Mr. Travers (Beauchamp); Mr. Northcote (Tomaso); W. R. Bruton (Griffo); Miss Hudspeth (Rosette); Miss Montague (Doree); Miss D'Arcy (Marie); Miss Lee (Domino); C. Seyton (Woodcutter); Mr. Naylor (Servant); Edith Stuart (Minie)

Boston Museum, Boston, opened March 1, 1873
A Play based on the novel by Alexandre Dumas

Charles Barron (Fabian and Louis dei Franchi); F. Hardenbergh (Chateau Renaud); Hart Conway (Meynard); J. A. Smith (Montgiron); H. N. Wilson (Martelli); N. Saisbury (Orlando); J. Nolan (Colonna); F. Carlos (Griffo); J. H. Ring (Boissec); S. W. Standish (Tomaso); Laura Phillips (Emilie); Miss M. Parker (Madame dei Franchi); Mr. Johnston (Judge); C. H. Lucas (Francois); Fannie Skerritt (Estelle); Amy Ames (Celestine); Josie Browne (Coralie); Belle Bailey (Marie)

Grand Opera House, New York, opened June 2, 1873
Produced by J. Augustin Daly; A Play by Dion Boucicault, based on the novel by Alexandre Dumas

Charles Albert Fechter (Louis and Fabian dei Franchi); Charles Wheatleigh (Chateau Renaud); Lizzie Price (Emilie); George F. DeVere (Montgiron); B. T. Ringgold (Giordano); Cyril Searle (Beauchamp); Mrs. J. W. Chapman (Mme. dei Franchi); J. W. Jennings (Colonna); J. G. Peaker (Meynard); Josephine Henry (Rosette); J. H. Golden (Judge); Charles Leclercq (Orlando)

Princess Theatre, London, opened June 17, 1876
A Play based on the novel by Alexandre Dumas; Director, Horace Wigan; Scenery, Maugham; Costumes, S. May; Dances, Clara Morgan Fay

John Clayton (Fabian and Louis dei Franchi); J. H. Barnes (Chateau Renaud); J. R. Crauford (Meynard); A. Elwood (Montgiron); P. C. Beverley (Martelli); G. Yarnold (Orlando); F. W. Irish (Colonna); Mr. Dormar (Beauchamp); Caroline Hill (Emilie); Miss St. Henry (Madame dei Franchi); M. Johnstone (Mons. Verner); J. W. Lawrence (Griffo); Mr. Tyndale (Sanoli); Mr. Swann (Boissac); Mr. Harrison (Tomaso); C. Brabant (Maria); Miss Wade (Coralie); Miss H. Herrick (Celestine);

Daisy St. Henry (Louise); Miss Fern (Marguerite); Miss Eilly (Berthe); Mr. Newbold, Mr. Wright (Servants)

Theatre Royal, Edinburgh, Scotland, opened October 4, 1878
A Play based on the novel by Alexandre Dumas

G. W. Harris (Fabian and Louis dei Franchi); Hector Mackenzie (Chateau Renaud); W. Vincent (Meynard); G. H. Leonard (Montgiron); W. Moodee (Martelli); John Birchenough (Orlando); G. K. Maskell (Colonna); Amy Biornette (Emilie); Lizzie Doyne (Marie); Mrs. T. B. Bannister (Madame dei Franchi); F. Rogers (Boissac); Mr. Shaw (Tomaso); W. J. Lancaster (Beauchamp); G. B. Prior (Griffo)

Niblo's Garden Theatre, New York, opened October 7, 1878
A Play by Dion Boucicault, based on the novel by Alexandre Dumas

Charles Pope (Fabian and Louis dei Franchi); Frank Roche (replaced by Frank Tannehill) (Chateau Renaud); Annie Ward Tiffany (Emilie); Ogden Stevens (Montgiron); Mrs. Berrell (Madame dei Franchi); T. G. Riggs (Colonna); Lottie Murray (Marie); H. Montgomery (Meynard); Simcoe Lu (Orlando); J. F. Herne; John E. Ince; T. G. Rogers

Boston Theatre, Boston, opened November 22, 1880
A Play by Dion Boucicault, based on the novel by Alexandre Dumas

Charles Barron (Fabian and Louis dei Franchi); B. R. Graham (Chateau Renaud); William Seymour (Meynard); J. B. Mason (Montgiron); Maurice Strafford (Martelli); May Davenport (Emilie); J. Burrows (Orlando); J. Nolan (Colonna); Mary Shaw (Madame dei Franchi); Frank Carlos (Boissec); J. S. Maffitt, Jr. (Griffo); Frederick P. Ham (Sanola); Rose Temple (Estelle); Charles E. Hoyle (Tomaso); W. T. Clark (Beauchamp); Lizzie Jeremy (Celestine); Carrie Hopgood (Coralie); Kate Ryan (Marie)

Booth's Theatre, New York, opened March 26, 1883; moved to the *Globe Theatre*, April 30, 1883
Produced by John Stetson; A Play by Dion Boucicault, based on the novel by Alexandre Dumas; Director, Frederick De Belleville; Scenery, William Voegtlin and Joseph Clare; Mechanical effects, Benson Sherwood; Gas effects, J. Thompson; Music, Charles Puerner; Ballet, Charles Constantine; Stage manager, L. H. Everett

F. C. Bangs (Fabian and Louis dei Franchi); Theodore Hamilton (succeeded by Frederick De Belleville, Barton Hill) (Chateau Renaud); George Parkes (succeeded by A. H. Forrest, Henry Sanit Maur) (Montgiron); Clinton Stuart (Meynard); Henry Saint Maur (succeeded by Fred Ross) (Martelli); Lizzie Goode (Estelle); E. Lamb (succeeded by Luke Martin) (Colonna); J. W. Shannon (succeeded by Fred Lotto) (Orlando); H. A. Weaver (succeeded by J. A. McCabe) (Salona); William Richardson (Griffo); W. T. Harris (succeeded by William Mack) (Jose); Emily Rigl (Emilie); Kate Meek (succeeded by Clara Baker) (Madame dei Franchi); Katie A. Stokes (succeeded by Alice Hector) (Celestine); J. A. Wilks (succeeded by H. Edwards) (Boissac); J. Swinburne (succeeded by G. W. Ellison) (Tomaso); Margaret Cone (succeeded by Elly Pferdner) (Marie); Anna Boudinot (succeeded by Emily Herbert) (Grain D'Or); Lillian Lewis (succeeded by Pauline Barrett) (Coralie); Frank Lawlor (succeeded by James Fagan) (Surgeon); J. E. Hynes (Francois)

THE CORSICAN BROTHERS & COMPANY; OR, WHAT LONDON LAUGHS AT, Park Theatre, New York, opened September 8, 1884
Produced by Moore and Holmes's Royal British Burlesque and Specialty Company; A Satire on *The Corsican Brothers* by Alexandre Dumas
Edward J. Henley (Louis and Fabien dei Franchi); Grace Pedley (Mlle. de Lesparre); Marie Loftus (Renaud); Patrick Feeney (Madame dei Franchi)

THE CORSICAN BROTHERS, 14th Street Theatre, New York, opened January 13, 1890
Produced by Augustus Pitou; A Play by Dion Boucicault, based on the novel by Alexandre Dumas; Scenery, Homer E. Emens; Stage managers, Fred Lotto, J. Fedris
Robert Mantell (Fabian and Louis dei Franchi); Mark Price (Chateau Renaud); Charlotte Behrens (Emilie de l'Esparre); B. T. Ringgold (Baron Montgiron); Kendall Weston (Alfred Maynard); Frederick Lotto (Orlando); Guy Lindsley (Martelli); G. F. James (Sanoli); E. A. Barrow (Boissac); George Hammond (Tomaso); Minnie Monk (Madame dei Franchi); George Darrell (La Fond); Murry Woods (succeeded by Adolph Bernard) (Colonna); Charles Hawley (La Croix); Clara Flagg (Estelle); Marie Sheldon (Celestine); Louisa Evans (Marie); Ferris Stetson (Surgeon); Annie Weaver (Coralie); Fanny Barton (Pomponette); William Ashton (Genee); Archie Lindsay (Griffo); James Hartley (Jose); Harry Peabody (Verner); Martin Clark (Beauchamp)

Grand Opera House, Boston, opened May 23, 1890
Produced by Augustus Pitou; A Play by Dion Boucicault, based on the novel by Alexandre Dumas
Robert Mantell (Fabian and Louis dei Franchi); Albert Bruning (Chateau Renaud); Charlotte Behrens (Emilie de l'Esparre); Nathaniel Hartwing (Meynard); B. T. Ringgold (Baron Montgiron); George F. Bird (Orlando); W. Morton Baker (Martelli); Charles E. Odlin (Sanoli); Sid Pryor (Colonna); Harry Stanhope (Boissac); Minnie Monk (Madame dei Franchi); Henry Peabody (Verner); James Hyner (Jose); Charles Hawley (La Croix); Willian Jansen (Genee); George Darrell (La Fond); Charlotte Malcolm (Celestine); Jessie D. Busley (Estelle); Violet Evans (Marie); Harry Stanhope (Woodcutter); Verna Clarges (Griffo); Walter Ashton (Genee); John F. Leney (Servant)

Novelty Theatre, London, opened August 4, 1890
Produced and directed by Joseph A. Cave; A Play by Dion Boucicault, based on the novel by Alexandre Dumas; Scenery, W. H. Drury; Lighting, J. Wells; Mechanical effects, Walter Lee; Acting manager, Thomas Crawford; Musical director, Henri G. French
Charles Sennett (Fabian and Louis dei Franchi); George Bryne (Chateau Renaud); Jessie Robertson (Emilie de l'Esparre); Henry Crane (Alfred Meynard); H. Moss (Tomaso); Norman Clarke (Le Baron Giodano Martelli); Mr. Druce (Le Baron Montgiron); Ada Pitte (Gran D'Or); Kate Long (Pomponnetti); R. Robertson (Gaetano Orlando); Mr. Russell (Marco Colonna); T. Brownlow (Antonio Sanoli); Charles Steyen (Blaze); W. Blake (Surgeon); Marie Brian (Marie); Mrs. J. F. Brian (Madame dei Franchi); S. Charles (Griffo)

People's Theatre, St. Louis, Mo., opened September 10, 1890
A Play based on the novel by Alexandre Dumas
McKee Rankin (Fabian and Louis dei Franchi); Percy Rede (Chateau Renaud);

Isabel Evesson (Emilie); B. F. Haning (Meynard); Lilford Arthur (Martelli); George S. Paxton (Baron Montgiron); Fred Lotto (Orlando); Henry Wilson (Griffo); Jacques Martin (Colonna); Mrs. Sol Smith (Madame dei Franchi); F. E. Allen (Tomaso); J. H. Hoxie (Sanola); Charles Roberts (Surgeon); Eme Walters (Estelle); May Smith (Grain d'Or); Fanny Lewis (Pomponette); Alice Brown (Marie); John Ward (Marcolo)

Lyceum Theatre, London, opened May 12, 1891 57 performances
Produced and Directed by Henry Irving; A Play by Dion Boucicault, based on the novel by Alexandre Dumas; Scenery, Hawes Craven and Joseph Harker; Costumes, Auguste, Mrs. Nettleship and Mrs. Reid; Choreography, Espinosa; Music director, J. Meredith Ball; Acting manager, Bram Stoker; Stage manager, H. J. Loveday

Henry Irving (Louis and Fabien dei Franchi); William Terriss (Monsieur de Chateau); Annie Irish (Emilie de l'Esparre); Thomas E. Wenman (Orlando); Frank Tyars (Martelli); William Haviland (Alfred Meynard); F. H. Macklin (Baron de Montgiron); John Martin Harvey (Antonio Sanola); John Archer (Griffo); Kate Phillips (Coralie); Mrs. Paucefort (Madame dei Franchi); Amy Coleridge (Estelle); T. Reynolds (Boissec); Samuel Johnson (Colonna); Gordon Craig (Beauchamp); Mr. Gurney (Surgeon); Mr. Lacy (Verner); Miss Foster (Celestine); E. Oldcaste (Eugenie); Miss Clive (Rose); N. de Silva (Marie); R. P. Tabb (Tomaso); Frederick Evans, Zietz Brothers, A. Giavanelli, Carl Waller, Mr. Eugene, Mr. Romaine, Mr. Morgan, Leon Espinosa (Pierrots); Misses Braithwaite, Holt, Hemmonda, Giles, Sismondi, Symonds, French Evans (Chicardes); Misses Hamilton, Brandon, Phillips, Gibbs, Whitefoot, Powell, Richards (Debardeurs)

Preceeded by *Nance Oldfield*, a one-act comedy by Charles Reade with Ellen Terry

Lyceum Theatre, London, opened July 15, 1895 6 performances
Produced and directed by Henry Irving; A Play by Dion Boucicault, based on the novel by Alexandre Dumas; Scenery, Hawes Craven and Joseph Harker; Costumes, Auguste, Mrs. Nettleship and Mrs. Reid; Costume designer, Faustin; Choreography, Espinosa; Music director, J. Meredith Ball; Acting manager, Bram Stoker; Stage manager, H. H. Loveday

Henry Irving (Fabian dei Franchi/Louis dei Franchi); Julia Arthur (succeeded by May Whitty) (Emilie de l'Esparre); Frank Kemble Cooper (Chateau Renaud); Ben Webster (Montgiron); Mary Rorke (Madame dei Franchi); Sam Johnson (Colonna); William Haviland (Alfred Meynard); John Archer (Griffo); T. Reynolds (Boissec); W. Lionel Belmore (Beauchamp); Maud Milton (Coralie); Sydney Valentine (Orlando); John Martin Harvey (Antonio Sanola); Brenda Gibson (Estelle); K. Rivington (Surgeon); R. P. Tabb (Tomaso); Mr. Lacy (Verner); N. de Silva (Marie); Miss Foster (Celestine); Frank Tyars (Giordano Martelli); Miss Davis (Eugenie)

Academy Theatre, Milwaukee, opened January 28, 1901
Produced by the Academy Thanhauser Company, Edwin Thanhauser, manager; A Play based on the novel by Alexandre Dumas; Director, Frederick Pauling; Assistant director, Colin Campbell; Scenery, P. J. Donigan

Eugene Moore (Fabian and Louis dei Franchi); Lee Baker (Chateau Renaud); Edith Evelyn (Emilie); Harry Mestayer (Montgiron); Edgar Baume (Martelli); Walter Goodrich (Meynard); William Yearance (Orlando); R. C. Chamberlain (Colonna); Duane Dotie (Beauchamp); Daisy Lovering (Estelle); Kate Woods

Fiske (Mme. dei Franchi); Robert O'Connor (Favrollers); Colin Campbell (Sanola); Dexter Johnson (Paulo); Frederick Loomis (Boissec); Sarah Turnbull (Coralie); Lulu Hastings (Celestine); Elsie Kaufer (Marie); Miss McDonald (Domino); H. Knoeckel (Francois)

NOTE: Edwin Thanhauser later abandoned the stage for a career in motion pictures, forming the Thanhauser Film Company with several of the above players as its nucleus.

Murray Hill Theatre, New York, opened February 3, 1902
Produced by the Henry Donnelly Stock Company; A Play by M. M. E. Grange and X. DeMontepin, based on the novel by Alexandre Dumas

William Bramwell (Fabian and Louis dei Franchi); Sheldon Lewis (Chateau Renaud); John S. Robertson (Martelli); Charles Mason (Montgiron); George T. Raab (Meynard); Isabel O'Madigan (Madame dei Franchi); Alice Johnson (Emilie); Robert McWade, Jr. (Orlando/Brissac); George Henry Trader (Colonna); William Short (Sanola); Frederic Gibbs (Griffo); Laura Hope Crews (Estelle); Frances Starr (Celestine); Henry Hawtry (Beauchamp); Eva Grau (Marie); Agnes Mack (Coralie); Frank Jaeger (Servant); The Althea Sisters (Dancers)

Castle Square Theatre, Boston, opened June 30, 1902
Produced by the Castle Square Dramatic Stock Company, J. H. Emery, Manager; A Dramatic Romance by M. M. E. Grange and X. DeMontepin, adapted from the novel by Alexandre Dumas; Director, James R. Pitman

Hallett Thompson (Fabian dei Franchi/Louis dei Franchi); Edmund Breese (M. De Chateau Renaud); Fanny Addison Pitt (Madame Savilia dei Franchi); Katherine Clinton (Emilie De Lespare); James L. Seeley (Alfred Meynard); Lindsay Morison (Orlando); James A. Keane (Le Baron de Montgiron); Edward Wade (Le Baron Giordano Martelli); John T. Craven (Colonna); George R. Simpson (M. Beauchamp); Cordelia MacDonald (Celestine); W. Paul Linton (M. Faverollers); William H. Hasson (Griffo); Warren Cook (Antonio Sanola); Louis Thiel (Boissec); B. F. Duffy (Tomaso); Nelson Lewis (A Surgeon); Sarah Kingsley (Coralie); Alexia Durant (Marie); W. C. Mason, H. C. Wetherbee (Servants); Izetta Jewel (Estelle)

Adelphi Theatre, London, opened June 17, 1907 8 performances
Produced by Tom B. Davis; A Play based on Alexandre Dumas' novel, *Les Freres Corses*, revised from the play by Dion Boucicault; Director, H. J. Loveday; Scenery, George J. Dodson; Music director, Clemens Franckenstein; Fight director, Felix Bertrand; Stage managers, Alfred Rivers, Frank J. Arlton

Martin Harevy (Fabian dei Franchi/Louis dei Franchi); Vincent Sternroyd (Chateau Renaud); Amy Coleridge (Emilie De Lespare); Alfred Mansfield (Alfred Meynard); Albert E. Raynor (Le Baron de Montgiron); Paul Barry (M. Beauchamp); J. Barber (Antonio Sanolo); Maud Milton (Madame Savilla del Franchi); Fred Wright (Colonna); George Cooke (Baron Martelli); Charles J. Cameron (Monsieur Favrollers); Maud Rivers (Coralie); Ethel Patrick (Celestine); Leslie Palmer (Griffo); Philip Hewland (Orlando); H. Earle (Surgeon); Bessie Elder (Frisette); Marjorie Field (Estelle); Madge Fabian (Maria); R. Allen, D. Holm (Servants); Denham Muir (Tomaso); P. Alexander (Boissec)

Adelphi Theatre, London, opened September 9, 1908 26 performances; Reopened November 23, 1908 14 performances
Produced by George Edwardes; A Play based on Alexandre Dumas' novel, *Les Freres Corses*, revised from the play by Dion Boucicault; Director, H. J. Loveday; Scenery, George J. Dodson; Music director, W. H. Hudson; Fight director, Felix Bertrand; Acting manager, Eugene Bertram; Stage managers, Alfred Rivers and Henry Watson

Martin Harvey (Fabian dei Franchi/Louis dei Franchi); Vincent Sternroyd (succeeded by William Haviland) (M. de Chateau Renaud); Amy Coleridge (succeeded by Maud Hoffman) (Emilie De Lesparre); George Cooke (Baron Martelli); Albert E. Raynor (Baron de Montgiron); Philip Hewland (Orlando); Bernard Sloane (succeeded by Charles J. Cameron) (Favrollers); J. Barber (Antonio Sanola); Percy Foster (Boissec); Alfred Mansfield (Alfred Meynard); C. Charles (succeeded by Bernard Sloane) (Beauchamp); Maud Rivers (Coralie); Marjorie Field (Estelle); Mary Rorke (Madame Savilla dei Franchi); Fred Wright, Sr. (Colonna); Leslie Palmer (Griffo); Ethel Patrick (Celestine); Madge Fabian (Maria); Denholm Muir (Tomaso); Henry Watson (Surgeon); Bessie Elder (Frisette); R. Allen, D. Holm (Servants)

Birmingham (Eng.) Repertory Theatre, opened November 24, 1917
Produced by the Birmingham Theatre Repertory Company; A Play based on the novel by Alexandre Dumas; Director, Frank D. Clewlow

William J. Rea (Fabian and Louis dei Franchi); William Dexter (Chateau Renaud); Dorothy Massingham (Emilie); Margaret Chatwin (Madame dei Franchi); Frank Moore (Meynard); Noel Shannon (Martelli/ Griffo); Alfred J. Brooks ((Montgiron/Orlando); Joseph A. Dodd (Colonna); Frank D. Clewlow (Senola); Richard Wayne (Tomaso); William Bache (Surgeon); Cathleen Orford (Estelle); Hilda Vane (Marie); Maud Gill (Coralie); Dorothy Taylor (Celestine); Sydney Leon, Nancy Staples, Minnie Suckling, Hud Vane, William Bache, Sydney Smith (Peasants)

Greenwich Theatre, London, opened March 17, 1970
Director John Cox; A Musical, adapted from Alexandre Dumas' novel, with Book and Music by John Bowen; Lyrics, John Holmstrom and John Bowen; Music by Gounod, Offenbach, Auber and Donizetti; Production designer, Sue Plummer; Musical director, Richard Gill; Fights arranged by William Hobbs; Richard Gill (Pianist)

David Cook (Fabian dei Franchi/Lucien Dei Franchi); Fiona Walker (Melanie Saint Bernard); George Howe (General Saint Bernard/A Priest); Romy Baskerville (Dominique); Hope Jackman (Aunt Lucille); Gerald Harper (Chateau Renaud); Roger Ostime (Montgiron); Paul Chapman (Captaine Gerard Leparc); Marika Rivera (Madame Orsini); Diana Bishop (Madame Colonna); Peter Porteous (Orsini); Godfrey Jackman (Colonna); Robert Lister (Fabrice/Joseph); Leonie Collins (Minette); Liz Moscrop (Minou); Robert Bennett (Carlo/A Surgeon); Bronson Shaw (Alfred); Bill Stewart (An Inspector of Police); Alexander Green (A Drunken Guest); Jackie Cox, Rosemary Croft, George Howe, Romy Baskerville, Hope Jackman, Paul Chapman, Roger Ostime, Marika Rivera, Diana Bishop, Peter Porteous, Godfrey Jackman, Robert Lister, Robert Bennett, Bronson Shaw, Leonie Collins, Liz Moscrop, Alexander Green, Bill Stewart (Servants, Dancers, Fencers, Ball Guests, etc.)

SCREEN

THE CORSICAN BROTHERS, G.A.S. Films, England, released 1898
Director, George A. Smith
A seventy-foot film, said to be first using double exposure, dealing with one scene from the Dumas novel

Harrison Films, England, released 1902 1 reel
Adapted and directed by Dicky Winslow from Alexandre Dumas' novel
A. W. Fitzgerald (Fabian and Louis di Franchi)

The Edison Company, released 1912
Director, J. Searle Dawley. Adapted from Alexandre Dumas' novel
George A. Lessey (Fabian di Franchi); Benjamin A. Wilson (Louis)

Universal-Imp Pictures, released May 1915 3 reels
Adapted and directed by George A. Lessey from the novel by Alexandre Dumas
King Baggot (Louis and Fabien de Franchi); Jane Gale (Emilie De Esparrde); Ned Reardon (Meynard): Hal Clarendon (Renard); Frank W. Smith (Montgiron); Mathilde Brundage (Madame dei Franchi)

LES FRERES CORSES, Pathe Films, France, released 1915
Director, Andre Antoine; Screenplay, based on Alexandre Dumas' novel
Henry Krauss (Fabian dei Franchi/Louis dei Franchi); Rose Dione (Emilie de l'Esparre); Jacques Gretillat (M. Chateau Renaud); Romuald Joube (Montgiron)

United Pictures, released December 1919
Producer by Louis J. Gasnier; Director, Colin Campbell; Screenplay, Katherine Carr, based on the novel by Alexandre Dumas
Dustin Farnum (Fabian dei Franchi/Louis dei Franchi); Winifred Kingston (Emilie de l'Esparre); Andrew Robson (General de l'Esparre); Fanny Midgley (Madame Savilla del Franchi); Wedgewood Nowell (M. Chateau Renard); Will Machin (Le Baron Montegiron); Ogden Crane (Gaeno Orlando)

LES FRERES CORSES, Distribution Europeene Films, France, released 1938
Produced by Lucien Mavro; Director, Geo Kelber; Assistant director, Georges Brunot; Screenplay, Gilles Dartevelle, based on *The Corsican Brothers* by Alexandre Dumas; Adaptation by Leo Lania; Photography, Georges Stilly and Marcel Grignon; Music, Henri Tomasi; Dialogue, Alexandre Arnoux
Pierre Brasseur (Tonio); Jacques Erwin (Angelo); Jean Aquistapace (Bruno Ferraz); Lucienne Le Marchand (Gina); Jacqueline Daix (Laeticia); Lucien Galas (Jerome); Paul Azais (Andre); Raymond Rognoni (Priest); Jean Brochard (Policeman); Zoia Jollson, Sylvia Bataille, Ruth Pally (Women); Jacques Vitry, Bruno Clair (Men)

United Artists, released December 1941
Produced by Edward Small; Director, Gregory Ratoff; Screenplay, George Bruce and Howard Estabrook, based on the novel by Alexandre Dumas; Photography, Harry Stradling; Art director, Nicholai Reimisoff; Musical Score, Dimitri Tiomkin; Dances, Adolf Blum; Editor, Williams Claxton
Douglas Fairbanks, Jr. (Mario Franchi/Lucien Franchi); Ruth Warrick (Isabelle);

Akim Tamiroff (Colonna); J. Carrol Naish (Lorenzo); John Emery (Tomasso); H. B. Warner (Dr. Paoli); Henry Wilcoxon (Comte Franchi); Gloria Holden (Countess Franchi); Walter Kingsford (Monsieur Dupre); Nan Bryant (Madame Dupre); Pedro de Cordoba (Gravini); Veda Ann Borg (Maria); William Farnum (Priest); Manart Keppen (Martelli); Sarah Padden (Nurse); Ruth Robinson (Angela)

EL CAMINO DE SACRAMENTO, Mexico, released 1945
Director Chano Ureta; Screenplay, based on *The Corsican Brothers* by Alexandre Dumas

Jorge Negrete; Rosario Granadas; Julia Villareal; Peper Martinez

BANDITS OF CROSICA (a.k.a. *THE RETURN OF THE CORSICAN BROTHERS*), United Artists, released February 1953
A Global Production. Produced by Edward Small; Director, Ray Nazarro; Screenplay, Richard Schayer, based on *The Corsican Brothers* by Alexandre Dumas, adapted by Frank Burt; Photography, George E. Diskant; Art Director, Edward L. Ilou; Music, Irving Gertz; Production supervisors, Ben Hirsch and Michel Kraike; Editor, Grant Whylock

Richard Greene (Lucien/Carlos/Mario Franchi); Paula Raymond (Christina); Raymond Burr (Jonatto); Dona Drake (Zelda); Raymond Greenleaf (Paoli); Lee Van Cleef (Nerva); Frank Puglia (Riggio); Paul Cavanaugh (Dianza); Nestor Paiva (Lorenzo); Peter Mamakos (Diegas); Clayton Moore (Ricardo); Francis J. McDonald (Grisha); Peter Brocco (Angelo); George Lewis (Arturo); Virginia Brissac (Maria); Michael Ansara (Blacksmith); William Forrest (Marquis); John Pickard (Coachman)

LOS HERMANOS CORSOS, Argentina, Sono Film release, released 1955
Director, Leo Flieder; Screenplay, Ariel Cortazzo; Photography, Anibal Gonzalez Paz; Production design, Dimas Garrido; Music, Teddy Giorgio; Editor, Jorge Garate

Antonio Vilar (Los Hermanos Corsos); Amalia Gade; Tomas Blanco, Nestor Deval, Pedro Hurtado, Adolfo Linvell, Alberto Barcel, Josefa Goldar, Francisco Lopez Silva, Felix Rivero, Oscar Llomart, Maruja Montes

I FRATELLI CORSI, *Italia-France Production*, released 1961
Director, Anton Giulio Majano; Screenplay, Antonio Civlic Majans, Diego Fabbri and Gian Uti; Photography, Adalberto Albertini; Music, Angelo Lavagnino

Geoffrey Horne (dei Franchi Twins); Valerie Lagrange (Edith); Gerald Barray (Giovanni); Jean Servais (Sagona); Amedeo Nazzari (Orlandi); Emma Danieli (Madame dei Franchi)

TELEVISION

THE CORSICAN BROTHERS, *Play of the Week*, televised November 11, 1965 ATV (London) 80 minutes
Producer, Cecil Clarke; Director, John Llewellyn Moxey; Adapted by John Bowen from the novel by Alexandre Dumas; Designer, Tom Lingwood

Alan Dobie (Fabian de Franchi/Louis de Franchi); Anne Lawson (Emilie); Clement McCallin (General Saint-Hays); Anita Sharp Bolster (Aunt Lucy); Jeremy Longhurst (Capt. Gerald Leparc); Harry R. Fripp (Major domo); Michael Balfour (Old Orlando); Nancy Nevinson (Mme. Orlando); Gary Hope (Alfred

Resnard); Tony Beckley (Montgiron); Gerald Harper (Chateau Renaud); Michael Lynch (Old Colonna); Ann Tirard (Mme. Colonna); Barry Halliday (Carlo Orlando); Sandor Eles (Josef Colonna); Ann Sharp (Minette); Peter Madden (Police Inspector); Brown Derby [sic] (Priest); Stanley Jacob (Surgeon); Peter Torquil (Drunken Guest)

Hallmark Hall of Fame, televised February 5, 1985 CBS 2 Hours
Produced by Norman Rosemont Productions; Executive producer, Norman Rosemont; Producer, David A. Rosemont, Director, Ian Sharp; Teleplay, Robin Miller, based on the novel by Alexandre Dumas; Photography, Frank Watts; Production design, John Stoll; Costume design, Rosine Delamare; Music, Allyn Ferguson; Editors, Alan Pattillo, David Spiers

Trevor Eve (Louis de Franchi/Lucien de Franchi); Olivia Hussey (Annemaria de Guidice); Simon Ward (Duc Chateau-Renaud): Jean Marsh (Mazzere); Donald Pleasence (Chancellor); Geraldine Chaplin (Madame de Franchi); Patsy Kensit (Emilie du Cailland); Nicholas Clay (Giordano Martelli); James Hazelsine (Vincente da Franchi); Benedict Taylor (Georges du Gaillaud); Mark Ryan (Bernardo de Guidice); Jennie Linden (Countess Wolski); Margaret Tyzack (Madame de Guidice); Kevork Malikyan (Orlandi); and Peter Howell, Bernard Fontaine, Anthony Pedley, Francoise Trumpette, Peter Cellier, Marc Estrada de Tourmiel, Toby Salaman, Liselote Palm, Daniel Auguste, Marina Bonin, Raynald Bandry, Anne Bruner, Flora Alberti, Abbe Fantozzi, Lise Roy, Nancy Mooy, Mirelle Chaulet, Louis LaLanne, Mark Brooks, David Brooks, Rosette Jaubert, Mike Bainsborough, Joe Maalouf, Pietro Jianni

DAVID COPPERFIELD

Various adaptations of the novel by Charles Dickens (1849-50)

Synopsis

Born six months after his father's death, David Copperfield is sent to London by his sadistic stepfather, Mr. Murdstone, after his meek and gentle mother Clara dies in childbirth. David is lodged with the expansive and impecunious Micawber family, but after Mr. Micawber is sent to debtor's prison, David runs away to Dover to his Aunt Betsey Trotwood, who adopts him. Attempts by Murdstone and his cruel sister to reclaim the boy are vigorously opposed by Aunt Betsey, and David is sent to school at Canterbury where he lives with Aunt Betsey's lawyer, Mr. Wickfield, and Wickfield's daughter Agnes. After graduation, David marries sickly, childlike Dora Spenlow who soon dies. He is later asked by Wickfield to investigate the mismanagement of his business by his unscrupulous clerk, Uriah Heep. With the help of the crafty Mr. Micawber, David exposes Heep's duplicity and thievery, and Heep is sent to prison. The Micawbers leave for Australia, and David, realizing Agnes Wickfield has always loved him, asks her to become his wife.

Comment and Critique

David Copperfield, perhaps the most famous of the Dickens novels, was the author's favorite work and was published initially in twenty monthly installments during 1849 and 1850. English actor William Evans Burton had converted and refurbished New York's dilapidated Palmo's Opera House into his Chambers Street

Theatre in 1848, and his first production of a Dickens work was *Dombey and Son*. On November 30, 1850, Burton produced Dr. Northall's dramatization of *David Copperfield* and portrayed Micawber during the play's healthy run (for that era) of eighty-two performances.

Burton's late 1850 success with *David Copperfield*, naturally, spawned other productions. The Bowery Theatre opened its version just over a month later, on January 6, and on the same night, John Brougham presented yet another adaptation at his Lyceum Theatre. Burton's production, according to historian George Odell, "was the thing, distinctly, of the season." *The Albion* reported, "All the hero's early adventures at the Blunderstone Rookery, his sufferings under the tyranny of the Murdstones, and in London, are lost in the play; also his love for and marriage with Dora; indeed, the 'child-wife' is never once alluded to. Barkis, the carrier [and] Peggotty, the faithful nurse, are also lost...Micawber, the 'fallen tower' [found] a capital representative in Manager [producer/director William Evans] Burton, who never does anything badly and most things excellently well...the Uriah Heep of [T. B.] Johnston was perhaps the most characteristic and best played part in the whole play."

The Albion found that in Brougham's competitive version, "[He] has judiciously retained the nurse Peggotty, for the sake of introducing his clever and lively wife, and has reduced Copperfield, Steerforth and Mrs. Micawber to very subordinate positions...Mr. Brougham shows less of the brandy-and-water side of Micawber's character than Burton, but is very telling and effective in his attitudinizing and rhodomontade."

Micawber, George Fawcett Rowe's dramatization of Dickens' novel, opened at the Union Square Theatre in April 1873. *The New York Times* recorded, "The flimsiness of the sketch [upon] incidents in *David Copperfield* is to be regretted...Mr. Rowe's picture of Dickens' impecunious hero is, however, an exceedingly amusing one." During the next decade, Rowe's dramatization of *David Copperfield* as *Little Em'ly* found great success on Broadway and on extensive road tours, and his interpretation of Micawber was, according to historian George Odell, "long esteemed a triumph of Dickensian."

Louis N. Parker's 1914 *David Copperfield* dramatization, as *The Highway of Life*, opened at the Wallack's Theatre in late October. *The New York Dramatic Mirror* found that "Mr. Parker's latest contribution to the stage of Wallack's, where he has been so successful in two previous offerings. *Pomander Walk* and *Disraeli*, is a unique and most interesting entertainment. It may be set down as an impracticable task to reduce a story of Dickens' *David Copperfield* to a consistently developed play of concentric interest, as the dramatic cohesion is absent in a tale of such complex incidents. But the author has contrived, cleverly enough, to develop the relations of David and Agnes into a fairly consistent dramatic theme, and to compensate for some sacrifice in this direction, has given us the Dickens characters in their serious outlines as well as their purely humorous elements, in an aspect extremely apt manner." The *Mirror* concluded, "The production is handsomely staged, and every detail of the performance is closely and carefully looked after."

The Evening Post, noting that playwright Parker had written *The Highway of Life* for Sir Herbert Beerbohm-Tree and His Majesty's Theatre Company (where Tree produced his *David Copperfield* on Christmas Eve 1914), stressed that "no playwright, of course, has ever succeeded, or ever can succeed, in a task which, on the face of it, is impossible. In the path of Mr. Parker lay peculiar obstacles. He not only had to employ as many persons as possible for the sake of a spectacular setting, and to prepare an intelligible synopsis, but he had to contrive to give special prominence to the two characters, Daniel Peggotty and Mr. Micawber, which the actor-manager, with the modesty and discernment peculiar to his class, has appropriated for himself. Making due allowances for his difficulties, he has shown as much integrity in the solution of his problem as could reasonably be expected."

The huge success of Lionel Bart's modern era adaptation of Dickens' *Oliver Twist* to the musical stage as *Oliver!* (2,619 performances in London and 774 in New York) indicated the feasibility of other Dickens musicalizations. Consequently, *David Copperfield* emerged in 1981 in an unfortunate musical version called simply *Copperfield*, which opened on Broadway after twenty-six previews but survived just thirteen performances. "It is an enterprise that fails by a sustained mediocrity of intention and execution, and its failure is all the more painful because one perceives that there can never have been a moment from the very first runthroughs when any possibility of success lay within grasp," bemoaned *The New Yorker*'s Brendan Gill. In the *New York Post*, Clive Barnes felt, "What the musical lacks is a really strong score, and, in its book, a greater sense of compulsion...the book has not been dramatically shaped."

Frank Rich pinpointed the show's main problem in *The New York Times*: "After sitting through *Copperfield*... you may seriously question whether its creators have actually read their ostensible source material...You may even question whether they've read the *Classics Illustrated* version. But one thing you won't question. Al Kasha and Joel Hirschhorn, who wrote this show's book, music and lyrics, have definitely, but definitely, seen lots of his Broadway musicals." Comparing the Kasha-Hirschhorn score to that for the fondly remembered *Oliver!*, *Annie* and *Gypsy*, among others, critic Rich concluded that "the real problem is that [*Copperfield*'s] authors are not good mimics. From the music to the scenery to the cast, everything about this show looks tacky in comparison to its prototypes."

In the New York *Daily News*, critic Douglas Watt called *Copperfield* "a computerized cartoon...Under the busy and undistinguished staging of Rob Iscove, who is responsible for the commonplace dance routines, everything is done in broad strokes...and this, in turn, has obviously resulted from the puerile book and song reduction of David Copperfield by the team of Al Kasha and Joel Hirschhorn... *Copperfield* just barely qualifies as live theater. Push another button."

The earliest screen version of the famous tale was the three-part 1911 production by Thanhouser Pictures of *David Copperfield*, *Little Em'ly and David Copperfield*, and *The Loves of David Copperfield*, released in consecutive weeks in mid October. In the first, Flora Foster played David as a boy; in the second and third, Ed Genung was the grown-up David. A sixreel feature film of the Dickens classic was produced in Great Britain in 1913. "Readers of Dickens and particularly those who love the great author's favorite book...will be entertained and edified in seeing the pictured version of that story recently produced by the Hepworth Company," wrote *The Moving Picture World*. "American companies have given us, in a small way, some excellent motion pictures dealing with the Life of David Copperfield, but these have been brief character studies in the main, not attempting to cover the entire book... Much of the beauty of this picture lies in the scenes of Old England. Hepworth's gone to the actual places of which the story tells and given us views of Canterbury, the cliffs of Dover, and street scenes that have not materially changed in the past hundred years. The photography is excellent and the settings reveal great care in arrangement."

Denmark's 1922 screen adaptation of *David Copperfield* was well received in its American release in November 1923. *The New York Tribune* enthused: "The characters are Dickens to the life." *The New York Times* reported: "It is a film which brings this solace, this peace of mind, contentment and a wondering about the past...a picture that is different to others, and one that cannot be said to be perfect. Yet it holds the interest." The *Times* critic continued: "See the Nordisk Film Company's production of *David Copperfield* and for an hour and a half you will be in the Wonderful City of Dreams of the Past...This is a picture which Dickens lovers will enjoy in spite of its many deficiencies, as it is such a beatific change from the stories that are being bought, paid for and produced by film concerns."

The most memorable screen version of *David Copperfield* was produced by David O. Selznick in 1935. Overriding the objections of his father-in-law, Louis B. Mayer, Selznick succeeded in assigning noted British author Hugh Walpole to write the screenplay (Walpole also played the Vicar in the film) and George Cukor to direct the sumptuous all-star production. Selznick's hope was to shoot the picture on location in England but ended up making it on the MGM backlot. Disregarding Mayer's recommendation of his studio's resident juvenile, Jackie Cooper, to play young David, Selznick signed the ten-year-old British lad, Freddie Bartholomew, for the part. Oliver Hardy had been considered for the role of Micawber, but Selznick finally opted for Charles Laughton, at director George Cukor's suggestion. However, Laughton's continual agonizing over the definitive interpretation of Micawber forced a replacement in the person of W. C. Fields -- an inspired bit of casting in which Fields gave what many consider to be his finest performance. Although he unsuccessfully tried to persuade Selznick to let him perform his juggling routine, Fields was permitted to inject his comic routine that has him searching for his hat which is dangling above his head on a cane.

Director Cukor later recalled Fields' portrayal: "He was Micawber...he was marvelous, hard-working and would try anything...he realized he was working with something that was a classic and he behaved that way." The filming had started on September 27, 1934, and was completed two days before Thanksgiving. The following January, it premiered on Broadway at the Capitol Theatre. "It is my belief that this cinema edition of *David Copperfield* is the most profoundly satisfying screen manipulation of a great novel that the camera has ever given us," cheered *The New York Times*' Andre Sennwald. "Therein you will discover all the superb caricatures of blessed memory, led by a manly and heartbreaking David who is drawn to life in the person of Master Freddie Bartholomew...Being himself pretty generally a spiritual descendent of Mr. Micawber, W. C. Fields manages with the greatest of ease to become one with his illustrious predecessor...Although it is a film of enormous length, according to screen standards -- two hours and ten minutes -- Hugh Walpole's screenplay has been arranged with such uncanny correctness and each of the myriad episodes which go into the making of the varied canvas has been performed so perfectly that the photoplay slips by on an unwearying cavalcade."

David Copperfield was selected as one of the Ten Best pictures of 1935 and one of the twelve nominated as Best Picture of the Year by the Academy of Motion Picture Arts and Sciences. The Oscar, however, went to MGM's equally splendid version of *Mutiny on the Bounty*. The film also received Oscar nominations for Best Assistant Director (but not Best Director!) and for film editing.

The Dickens story was produced for television for the first time in 1954 as a two-parter on *Robert Montgomery Presents*. Directed by Norman Felton, the adaptation and teleplay by Doris Folliott was broadcast as *The Search*, on December 20, and *The Reward*, a week later. Philadelphia TV critic Bob William observed in *The Evening Bulletin*: "Doris Folliott's dramatization was a masterpiece of first-rate editing...there was never for a moment any doubt that this was Dickens or that the characters and story line were not those of a classic. The production also had the benefit of a fine performance by Rex Thompson as young David. Here is a child actor who always appears to have a clear concept of his assigned role and plays them with intelligence and polish."

Italy's RAI-TV in early 1966 serialized *David Copperfield* over an eight week period. The richly-produced telecasts were written and directed by Anton Guilio Majano and gave close attention to recreating Dickens' England. Each of the eight episodes, featuring Roberto Chevalier as young David and Giancarlo Giannini as the adult David, ran ninety minutes.

Four years later, a British filming of it for television, with a superlative allstar cast under the direction of Delbert Mann and featuring Jack Pulman's terrific adaptation of Dickens, premiered in America. Jack Gould, TV critic for *The New York Times*, felt however that "the power of the work is lost to movie theatrics" and "was so arranged by the director, Delbert Mann, that much of the cumulative power of the work was sacrificed to confusing cinema theatrics." Gould also aimed his criticism at the Hollywood mania for relating a story in flashback in which "a viewer had to settle for smidgens of Dickens rather than a cohesive whole...The film came alive as Sir Laurence Olivier invoked the brutality of the headmaster of Salem School...Not suprisingly, the best moment comes when Sir Ralph Richardson, playing Micawber with contagious relish, comes to grips with his conscience...Dame Edith Evans was grand as the compassionate Aunt Betsey...It must have broken Mr. Mann's creative heart that, with such a cast at his disposal, the tyranny of time on TV prevented him from developing many scenes."

Mann's film of *David Copperfield* was released theatrically abroad. Russell Campbell, reviewing it in Great Britain, wrote, "The best performance comes from Edith Evans, whose splendid portrayal of Aunt Betsey Trotwood is perhaps the only incarnation of the famous characters which will be remembered...Many of the cast are required to create caricatures more extreme than those of the novel...Perhaps it is wrong to judge a film by virtue of its adequacy in translating its source material into cinematic terms, but in the case of *David Copperfield* it is difficult to do otherwise... Mann's film has none of the style of the David Lean versions of Dickens nor the verve and visual exuberance of the equally sentimentalized *Oliver!*"

The British Broadcasting Corporation, in association with Time-Life Television, presented playwright Hugh Whitemore's ten-part dramatization of *David Copperfield* in the mid-1970s. It was telecast on PBS' *Once Upon a Classic* series in thirtyminute episodes beginning in early January 1977. Another BBC *David Copperfield* in the mid-1980s was seen in the U.S. on *Masterpiece Theatre* in the spring of 1988.

STAGE

Burton's Chambers Street Theatre, New York, opened November 30, 1850 82 performances

Produced and directed by William Evans Burton; A Play by Dr. Northall based on the novel by Charles Dickens

George Jordan (David Copperfield); Mrs. Hughes (Betsey Trotwood); T. B. Johnston (Uriah Heep); Jane Hill (Emily); William E. Burton (Mr. Micawber); Lizzie Weston (Martha); Miss Alderman (Agnes); J. W. Lester [Lester Wallack] (James Steerforth); William Rufus Blake (Daniel Peggotty); Mr. Henry (Mr. Wickfield); Mrs. Emma Skerrett (Mrs. Micawber); Josephine Russell (Rose Dartle); Humphrey Bland (Ham); Mr. Levers (Thomas Traddles); Mrs. George Homan (Mrs. Steerforth); Mrs. Henry (Mrs. Gummidge); Mr. Gourley (Waiter); Mr. Parsloe (Sheriff's Officer); Miss Cooke (Mary); Master Ralph, Master Wrag, Miss Wilson, Miss Dummie (Micawber's Children)

Bowery Theatre, New York, opened January 6, 1851 8 performances
A Play based on the novel by Charles Dickens

Susan Denin (David, as a child); Charles Pope (David, as a Young Man); Mrs. H. C. Jordan (Betsey Trotwood); Mr. Bowes (Uriah Heep); Mr. Martin (James Steerforth); A. W. Fenno (Mr. Micawber); Mrs. Charles M. Walcot (Mrs. Micawber); J. R. Scott (Daniel Peggotty); Catherine Wemyss (Emily); Caroline Hiffert (Agnes); John Winans (Mr. Dick); N. Johnson (Murdstone); E. L. Tilton (Ham); George Jordan (Thomas Traddles); Mr. Hamilton (Littimer); Mrs. Broadley (Mrs. Gummidge); Miss Barber (Janet); E. Forrester (Sailor)

Brougham's Lyceum Theatre, New York, opened January 6, 1851 24 performances
Produced and directed by John Brougham, adapted from the novel by Charles Dickens

Mr. Palmer (David Copperfield); Mrs. Vernon (Betsey Trotwood); J. E. Owens (Uriah Heep); John Brougham (Micawber); H. Lynne (Daniel Peggotty); John Dunn (James Steerforth); Stephen Leach (Mr. Dick); Mary Taylor (Agnes); Mrs. George Loder (Emily); Mr. Bristol (Littimer); Fred Lyster (Ham); H. Hunt (Barkis); H. B. Phillips (Mr. Wickfield); Mrs. W. R. Blake (Mrs. Micawber); Master Baker (Master Micawber); Miss Bishop (Miss Micawber); Kate Horn (Rosa Dartle); Mrs. John Brougham (Clara Peggotty); Mrs. James O. Dunn (Mrs. Gummidge); Mr. Fletcher (Bailiff)

Wallack's Lyceum Theatre, New York, opened August 19, 1856
Produced by William Stuart and J. W. Lester; Director, Dion Boucicault; A Play based on Charles Dickens' novel; Prompter, H. B. Phillips; Stage manager, J. W. Lester

Mr. Wentworth (David Copperfield); Mrs. H. P. Grattan (Betsey Trotwood); J. G. Bennett (Wilkins Micawber); T. B. Johnston (Uriah Heep); J. B. Howe (Peggotty); Miss Wilson (Agnes); Mr. Eytinge (James Steerforth); Mrs. Cooke (Mrs. Steerforth); Mr. Levere (Thomas Traddles); C. Peters (Ham); Mrs. T. B. Johnston (Emily); Mrs. Hough (Rose Dartle); C. Burnett, Jr. (Mr. Wickfield); Miss Deering (Mrs. Gummidge); Miss Payne (Mary); Miss Alleyne (Mrs. Micawber); Viola Grattan (Wilkins)

Walnut Street Theatre, Philadelphia, opened April 17, 1866
A Play by John Brougham, based on the novel by Charles Dickens

J. M. Barron (David Copperfield); Mary Carr (Betsey Trotwood); John Brougham (Wilkins Micawber); G. H. Griffiths (Uriah Heep); Annie Graham (Agnes Wickfield); Effie Germon (Mrs. Micawber); S. K. Chester (Peggotty); T. C. Green (Mr. Wickfield); Mrs. J. P. Brelsford (Clara Peggotty); F. Stull (Ham); C. V. Hess (Mr. Dick); R. Struthers (James Steerforth); Edward S. Marble (Barkis); Leonie Anderson (Emily); Mary Carr (Mrs. Gummidge); W. Osborn (Bailiff)

Olympic Theatre, New York, opened May 21, 1866
Produced by Mrs. John Wood; A Dramatization by George Fawcett Rowe of the novel by Charles Dickens

G. W. Garrison (David Copperfield); Mrs. G. H. Gilbert (Betsey Trotwood); George Fawcett Rowe (Wilkins Micawber); George C. Boniface (James Steerforth); Amelia Harris (Clara Peggotty); J. B. Studley (Daniel Peggotty); C. H. Morton (Ham); J. H. Stoddart (Uriah Heep); Henry L. Hinton (Traddles); Eliza Newton (Mrs. Micawber); T. J. Hind (Wickfield); Louisa Myers (Agnes Wickfield)

Walnut Street Theatre, Philadelphia, opened September 28, 1866*
A Play by John Brougham, based on the novel by Charles Dickens

J. M. Barron (David Copperfield); Mrs. W. A. Chapman (Betsey Trotwood); John Brougham (Wilkins Micawber); Charles Walcot, Jr. (Uriah Heep); Annie Graham (Agnes Wickfield); S. K. Chester (Daniel Peggotty); Mrs. J. P. Brelsford (Clara Peggotty); R. Struthers (James Steerforth); F. Stull (Ham); Leonie Arlington (Emily); Julia Porter (Mrs. Gummidge); Mrs. Charles Walcot, Jr. (Mrs. Micawber); J. B. Bradford (Bailiff)

* Restaged on January 24, 1867 with same cast except W. L. Stuart as Mr. Wickfield

LITTLE EM'LY, *Niblo's Garden Theatre*, New York, opened December 20, 1869
A Dramatization by George Fawcett Rowe of Charles Dickens' *David Copperfield*

Ione Burke (Little Em'ly); Frank Aiken (David Copperfield); George C. Boniface (Micawber); Mary Maddern (Mrs. Micawber); Mrs. Bardshaw (Betsey Trotwood); Mrs. Healey (Peggotty); L. R. Shewell (Dan'l Peggotty); F. C. Bangs (Ham Peggotty); F. A. Vincent (Uriah Heep); F. G. Maeder (James Steerforth); Kate Newton (Rose Dartle)

Niblo's Garden Theatre, New York, opened July 13, 1871
A Play by John Brougham, based on the novel by Charles Dickens

B. T. Ringgold (David Copperfield); John Brougham (Wilkins Micawber); C. H. Morton (Peggotty); Felix Rogers (Uriah Heep); Isabella Preston (Betsey Trotwood); E. B. Holmes (Mr. Wickfield); Pauline Markban (Agnes Wickfield); C. H. Rockwell (James Steerforth); Emma Cline (Mrs. Micwaber)

LITTLE EM'LY, *Olympic Theatre*, London, opened March 17, 1873
A Dramatization by Andrew Halliday of Charles Dickens' *David Copperfield*

Miss Dalton (Little Em'ly); Mr. Conway (David Copperfield); Sam Emery (Daniel Peggotty); Fanny Addison (Rosa Dartle); Joseph Eldred (Mr. Micawber); Mr. Peverill (James Steerforth); W. Rignold (Ham); A. Wood (Uriah Heep); Kate Rivers (Martha)

LOST EM'LY, *Surrey Theatre*, London, opened March 23, 1873
A Dramatization by Murray Wood of Charles Dickens' *David Copperfield*

Virginia Blackwood (Em'ly); Harold Jaye (David Copperfield); Murray Wood (Daniel Peggotty); Emilie Blackwood (Rosa Dartle); Clarke Nicholson (Ham); Maud Stafford (Agnes Wickfield); Miss Burnette (Mrs. Micawber); H. Cornwall (Uriah Heep)

MICAWBER, *Union Square Theatre*, New York, opened April 7, 1873
A Dramatization by George Fawcett Rowe of Charles Dickens' *David Copperfield*

Claude Burroughs (David Copperfield); George Fawcett Rowe (Wilkins Micawber); Emily Mestayer (Betsey Trotwood); Imogene Fowler (Agnes Wickfield); Welsh Edwards (Mr. Wickfield); F. F. Mackay (Uriah Heep); Josephine Laurens (Mrs. Micawber)

LITTLE EM'LY, *New Pavilion Theatre*, London, opened June 16, 1873
Produced by Morris Abrahams; A Play by Andrew Halliday, based on Charles Dickens' *David Copperfield*

J. Grainger (Little Em'ly); Mr. Reeves (David Copperfield); A. Rayner (Daniel

Peggotty); H. Clifton (Rosa Dartle); Mr. Bedford (Mr. Micawber); F. Thomas (Tommy Traddles); G. Yates (Uriah Heep)

LITTLE EM'LY, *Booth's Theatre*, New York, opened December 28, 1874 to January 30, 1875
A Dramatization by George Fawcett Rose of Charles Dickens' *David Copperfield*
Maude Granger (Little Em'ly); Claude Burroughs (David Copperfield); George Fawcett Rowe (Wilkins Micawber); Mary Wells (Betsey Trotwood); Charles Leclerq (Uriah Heep); Louise Henderson (Agnes Wickfield); C. H. Rockwell (James Steerforth); Frederick B. Warde (Daniel Peggotty); Emma Grattan (Mrs. Micawber); Helen Tracy (Rosa Dartle); Edwin Irving (Traddles); H. A. Weaver (Ham); Louisa Phillips (Martha); Augusta Raymond (Clara Peggotty); Estelle Mortimer (Mrs. Gummidge)

LITTLE EM'LY, *Touring Company*, season 1894-95
Produced and directed by George Holland; A Dramatization by Andrew Halliday of Charles Dickens' *David Copperfield*
Mabel Knowles (Little Em'ly); John F. McArdle (David Copperfield); Russ Whytal (Daniel Peggotty); Rose Barrington (Rosa Dartle); Eugene Jepson (Wilkins Micawber); Leigh McDowell (Uriah Heep); Carleton Macy (James Steerforth); Maggie Harold Davidge (Betsey Trotwood); Joseph Holland (Ham); Edwin Middleton (Traddles); James B. Everham (Mr. Wickfield); Mrs. Pennoyer (Mrs. Micawber); Miss Fisher (Mrs. Gummidge); Miss Lattimore (Peggotty Barkis); Alice Gale (Martha); Rodney Burton (The Bailiff)

LITTLE EM'LY, Castle Square Theatre, Boston, opened November 29, 1897
Produced by the Castle Square Theatre Dramatic Stock Company, J. H. Emery, manager; A Drama in four acts founded on Charles Dickens' *David Copperfield*; Director, James R. Pitman
Mary Sanders (Little Em'ly); N. H. Fowler (David Copperfield); Horace Lewis (Mr. Micawber); J. H. Gilmour (Daniel Peggoty); Lizzie Morgan (Betsey Trotwood); William Humphrey (Uriah Heep); Tony Cummings (James Steerforth); Florence Baker (Agnes Wickfield); J. L. Seeley (Mr. Wakefield); Teresa Ryan (Peggotty Barkis); William Charles Masson (Traddles); Rose Morison (Mrs. Micawber); Lillian Lawrence (Rosa Dartle); Charles Mackay (Ham); Lindsay Morison (Mrs. Gummidge); Master Charles Stovin (Wilkins Micawber, Jr.); Doris Bramson (Miss Micawber); Adelaide Cushman (Martha); Ada Rose, Master James Kelly (Twins); John J. Geary (Bill); John B. Walker (Jack); Roland Gillis (Smithers); James Wilson (Sternhold)

DAN'L PEGGOTTY, *King's Theatre*, London, opened March 10, 1907
A Play by H. Kellett Chambers, based on Charles Dickens' *David Copperfield*
Charles Cartwright (Dan'l Peggotty); Stanley Harrison (David Copperfield); Helen Vicary (Aunt Betsey Trotwood); Charles Collette (Mr. Micawber); A. B. Tapping (Uriah Heep); Gerald Lawrence (James Steerforth); Lionel Belmore (Ham); Ethel Ward (Little Em'ly); Miss Gordon Walker (Agnes Wickfield); J. D. Ross (Mr. Wickfield); Clarissa Selwynne (Rosa Dartle); Ethel Sarjient (Mrs. Steerforth); Nell Douglas (Mrs. Gummidge); Beatrice Grosvenor (Mrs. Barkis); Lillie Cavenagh (Martha); George de Lara (Littimer)

Touring Company, season 1909-10

Produced by Edward C. White; Directors, George Paxton and Mildred Holland; A Play adapted from Charles Dickens' novel; Company manager, Frank E. Morse; Stage managers, Del La Barre, Frank Backus

Franklin Pangborn (David Copperfield); Anna Barton (Betsey Trotwood); Dorothy Ryan (Agnes Wickfield); Wuld Scott (Uriah Heep); Harry W. Collins (Mr. Micawber); Del La Barre (Mr. Wickfield); Jane Dayton (Mrs. Micawber); Madeline Delmar (Little Em'ly); Andrew Guise (James Steerforth); Elizabeth Rathburn (Rose Dartle); Claude Gowand (Daniel Peggotty); Edwin A. Darby (Ham); Frank Backus (Traddles); Lucy Ryan (Martha); Sadie Lewis (Peggotty Barkis); John Glennon (Wilkins Micawber, Jr.); William Morse (Bailiff)

Crescent Theatre, New York, opened December 29, 1913
Produced by B.F. Keith; Adapted and directed by W.C. Masson, from the novel by Charles Dickens; Incidental music, George Purdy

M. J. Briggs (David Copperfield); Mabel Reed (Betsey Trotwood); George Alison (Daniel Peggotty); Charles Schofield (Mr. Micawber); Miss Isidore Martin (Little Em'ly); Wally Lestina (Agnes Wickfield); Harry Ireland (Mr. Wickfield); William H. Evarts (Uriah Heep); Ruth Byles (Peggotty Barkis); Frank Armstrong (Tommy Traddles); Edwin Maxwell (James Steerforth); Joseph Eggenton (Ham); Joseph Huntington (Jack); Ernest Wilkes (Smithers); Frank Harris (Sternhold); Bessie Lea Lestina (Mrs. Micawber); Gertrude Rivers (Rosa Dartle); Leah Winslow (Martha); Helen Scott (Mrs. Gummidge); Master Harry Coyne (Wilkins Micawber, Jr.)

THE HIGHWAY OF LIFE, *Wallack's Theatre*, New York, opened October 26, 1914
24 performances
Produced by the Liebler Company; A Play by Louis N. Parker, based on Charles Dickens' *David Copperfield*

J. V. Bryant (David Copperfield); Eva Vincent (Miss Betsey Trotwood); Prince Miller (Richard Babley, known as "Mr. Dick"); Edyth Latimer (Agnes Wickfield); Lennox Pawle (Wilkins Micawber); Vernon Steele (James Steerforth); Emmett Corrigan (Daniel Peggotty); Dorothy Parker (Little Em'ly); Maggie Fisher (Mrs. Micawber); O. P. Heggie (Uriah Heep); Philip Tonge (Tommy Traddles); Emma Chambers (Clara Peggotty); J. H. Greene (Ham); Louie Emery (Mrs. Gummidge); Anne Gaston (Martha Endell); Master Emmett Bradley (Wilkins Micawber, Jr.); Arline Dewey (Emma Micawber); Helen Westersby (Mrs. Heep); Mabel Stanton (Mrs. Crupp); Leslie Ryecroft (Littimer); Rhoda Beresford (Janet); Miss Rieser, Gladys Bradley (Micawber Twins); Master John Healy (A Donkey-Boy); Fred Nicholls (Golden Cross Waiter); Mr. Deane (A Cabman); Lionel Deane, Bouve Souther, Tracey Barrow (Old Fogies); A Young Gentleman (The Baby)

His Majesty's Theatre, London, opened December 24, 1914
Produced and directed by Herbert Beerbohm Tree; A Play by Louis N. Parker, based on Charles Dickens' novel; Scenery, Joseph Harker; Costumes, Percy Macquoid; Wigs by Clarkson; Music director, Adolf Schmid; Stage managers, Stanley Bell and Alfred Bellew

Owen Nares (David Copperfield); Sir Herbert Beerbohm-Tree (Wilkins Micawber/Dan'l Peggotty); Agnes Thomas (Betsey Trotwood); Basil Gill (James Steerforth); Charles Quartermaine (Uriah Heep); Evelyn Millard (Agnes Wickfield); Sydney Fairbrother (Mrs. Micawber); Nigel Playfair (Mr. Dick);

Frederick Ross (Ham); Jessie Winter (Little Em'ly); Mary Brough (Clara Peggotty); Ada King (Mrs. Gummidge); W. Gayer Mackay (Littimer); Deering Wells (Tommy Traddles); Rosamund Mayne-Young (Mrs. Heep); Mary Clare (Martha Endell; Stella St. Audrie (Mrs. Crupp); Maude Phillips (Janet); Sybil Sparkes (The Young Girl); Roy Byford (Waiter); W. J. Kemp (Sailor); J. William Mollison, Henry Byatt, Julian Cross (Old Fogies)

Lyceum Theatre, London, opened June 6, 1923 30 performances
Produced by Walter and Frederick Melville; A Play by Walter Frederick Evelyn, based on the novel by Charles Dickens; Director, Bransby Williams; Scenery, J. Leonard and E. Grimani; Lighting, John H. Walters; Music director, H. Sullivan Brooks; Acting manager, Cecil Schofield; Stage manager, Harcourt Brooke

Leslie Barrie (David Copperfield); Minnie Watersford (Betsey Trotwood); Charles Leighton (Mr. Wickfield); Fred E. Derrick (Uriah Heep); Ethel O'Shea (Agnes); Bransby Williams (Mr. Micawber/Dan'l Peggotty); Frederick Keen (James Steerforth); Nellie Hook (Mrs. Micawber); Eric B. Williams (Littimer); Douglas Ives (Thomas Traddles); William Lorimer (Ham); Grace Lester (Mrs. Gummidge); Katharine Carlton (Emily); Madeleine Temple (Mrs. Crupp); Betty Booth (Servant)

COPPERFIELD, *ANTA Theatre*, New York, opened April 16, 1981 13 performances
A Dome Production; Produced by Don Gregory and Mike Merrick; A Musical Play based on Charles Dickens' *David Copperfield*; Directed and choreographed by Rob Iscove; Book, music and lyrics by Al Kasha and Joel Hirschhorn; Scenery, Tony Stragis; Lighting, Ken Billington; Costumes, John David Ridge; Musical direction and vocal arrangements, Larry Blank; Orchestrations, Irwin Kostal; Dance arrangements and incidental music, Donald Johnston; Sound, John McClure; Hairstylists, Ray Iagnocco and Michael Heller; Company managers, Martin Cohen and Jill Cohen; Stage managers, Peter Lawrence, Jim Woolley, Edward Isser and Sarah Witham

Brian Matthews (David Copperfield); Evan Richards (Young David); Carmen Mathews (Aunt Betsey Trotwood); George S. Irving (Mr. Micawber); Barrie Ingham (Uriah Heep); Leslie Denniston (Agnes Wickfield); Lenny Wolpe (Mr. Dick); Linda Poser (Mrs. Micawber); Dana Moore (Vanessa); Mary Stout (Peggotty); Pamela McLernon (Clara Copperfield); Michael Connolly (Murdstone); Maris Clement (Jane Murdstone); Spence Ford (Victoria); Gary Munch (Mick Walter); Christian Slater (Billy Mowcher); Ralph Braun (Quinion); Darleigh Miller (Janet); Beulah Garrick (Mrs. Heep); Keith Perry (Mr. Wickfield); Mary Mastrantonio (Dora Spenlow); Richard Warren Pugh (Dr. Chillip/Baker); Katharine Buffaloe (Julia Mills/Nurse); David Horwitz (Bootmaker); Michael Danek (Constable); Brian Quinn (Mealy Potatoes); Michael Gorman (Ticket Taker); Bruce Sherman (Butcher); David Ray Bartee, Ralph Braunb, Katharine Buffaloe, Maris Clement, Michael Danek, Spence Ford, Michael Gorman, David Horwitz, Pamela McLernon, Darleigh Miller, Dana Moore, Gary Munch, Keith Perry, Linda Poser, Richard Warren Pugh, Brian Quinn, Lynne Savage, Bruce Sherman, Claude Tessier, Missy Whitechurch (Ensemble)

MUSICAL NUMBERS; "I Don't Want a Boy"; "Mama, Don't Get Married"; "Copperfield"; "Bottle Song"; "Something Will Turn Up"; "Anyone"; "Here's a Book"; "'Umble"; "The Circle Waltz"; "Up the Ladder"; "I Wish He Knew"; "The Lights of London"; "Villainy Is the Matter"; "With the One I Love"
Dropped from production during tryout: "Pay Us, Pay Us"; "Is There Anyone?"; "I Want to Share Them All"

SCREEN

Thanhouser Pictures, released in three parts in October 1911
Produced by Edward Thanhouser; Written and directed by Theodore Marston, based on the Charles Dickens novel

Anna Seer, Frank Crane, Alphone Ethier, Maude Fealy, Mignon Anderson, William Garwood, Harry Benham

Part 1: THE EARLY LIFE OF DAVID COPPERFIELD. Flora Foster as David as a boy

Part 2: LITTLE EM'LY AND DAVID COPPERFIELD. Ed Genung as David

Part 3: THE LOVES OF DAVID COPPERFIELD. Ed Genung as David

Hepworth/Walturdaw Pictures, Great Britain, released August 1913; in U.S. released by Albert Blinkhorn
Produced by Cecil M. Hepworth; Written and directed by Thomas Bentley, based on the Charles Dickens novel

Kenneth Ware (David Copperfield); Eric Desmond (Child David); Len Bethel (Youth David); Alma Taylor (Dora Spenlow); H. Collins (Wilkins Micawber); Jack Hulcup (Uriah Heep); Jamie Darling (Daniel Peggotty); Edna May (Little Em'ly as a child); Amy Verity (Little Em'ly); Cecil Mannering (James Steerforth); Ella Fineberg (Agnes Wickfield); Miss Harcourt (Aunt Betsey Trotwood); Johnny Butt (Murdstone); Miss West (Mrs. Micawber); Shiel Porter (Mr. Wickfield); Tom Arnold (Ham); Harry Royston (Mr. Creakle); Maria de Solla (Mrs. Gummidge)

Nordisk Films, Denmark, released 1922; in U.S., November 1923
Director, A.W. Sandberg; Screenplay, Laurids Skands, based on the Charles Dickens novel; Photography, Christen Jorgensen; Set decorator, Carlo Jacobsen; Musical score, Jacob Glade

Gorm Schmidt (David Copperfield); Martin Herberg (Young David); Marie Dinesen (Aunt Betsey Trotwood); Robert Schmidt (Murdstone); Karina Bell (Dora); Margaret Schlegel (Mrs. Copperfield); Ellen Rovsing (Miss Murdstone); Frederick Jensen (Mr. Micawber); Anna Marie Niehe (Mrs. Micawber); Poul Reumert (Mr. Wakefield); Else Nielsen (Young Agnes Wickfield); Karen Winther (Adult Agnes Wickfield); Rasmus Christiansen (Uriah Heep); Alfred Moeller (Barkis); Charles Wilken (Dr. Chillip); Karen Caspersen (Clara Peggotty); Peter Malberg (Mr. Dick)

Metro-Goldwyn-Mayer, released January 1935
Produced by David O. Selznick; Director, George Cukor; Screenplay, Howard Estabrook; Adapted by Hugh Walpole from Charles Dickens' novel; Photography, Oliver T. Marsh; Art directors, Cedric Gibbons and Merrill Pye; Set decorator, Edwin B. Willis; Costumes, Dolly Tree; Sound, Douglas Shearer; Editor, Robert J. Kern

W. C. Fields (replaced Charles Laughton) (Mr. Micawber); Lionel Barrymore (Daniel Peggotty); Maureen O'Sullivan (Dora Spenlow); Edna May Oliver (Aunt Betsey Trotwood); Lewis Stone (Mr. Wickfield); Frank Lawton (David Copperfield); Freddie Bartholomew (Young David); Elizabeth Allen (Mrs. Copperfield); Roland Young (Uriah Heep); Basil Rathbone (Mr. Murdstone); Elsa Lanchester (Clickett); Jean Cadell (Mrs. Micawber); Jessie Ralph (Nurse Peggotty); Lennox Pawle (Mr. Dick); Violet Kemble-Cooper (Jane Murdstone); Una O'Connor (Mrs. Gummidge); John Buckler (Ham); Hugh Williams (James

Steerforth); Ivan Simpson (Limmiter); Herbert Mundin (Barkis); Marilyn Knowlden (Young Agnes); Renee Gadd (Janet); Hugh Walpole (The Vicar); Harry Beresford (Dr. Chillip); Fay Chaldecott (Little Em'ly as a child); Florine McKinney (Little Em'ly); Mabel Colcord (Mary Ann); Arthur Treacher (The Donkey-Man)

TELEVISION

DAVID COPPERFIELD, *Robert Montgomery Presents*, televised December 20 and 27, 1954 NBC I hour each
Produced by Robert Montgomery; Director, Norman Felton; Teleplay, Doria Folliott, based on the novel by Charles Dickens

Rex Thompson (Young David); David Cole (Adult David); J. Pat O'Malley (Mr. Micawber); Isobel Elsom (Mrs. Micawber); Sarah Marshall (Agnes Wickfield); Betty Sinclair (Clara Peggotty); Ethel Owen (Aunt Betsey Trotwood); Frederic Warlock (Edward Murdstone); Cavada Humphrey (Jane Murdstone); Earl Montgomery (Uriah Heep); Carolyn Lee (Dora Spenlow); Lynn Bailey (Clara Copperfield); Ralph Bunker (Mr. Wickfield); Judson Rees (James Steerforth); Stafford Dickens (Mr. Dick); Anthony Kemple Cooper (Mr. Jorkins); Ronald Long (Mr. Creakle); Byron Russell (Dr. Chillip); Cecil Clovelly (Hodgins); Josephine Brown (Mrs. Crupp)

DAVID COPPERFIELD, televised December 26, 1965 through February 13, 1966 Italy 8 episodes 90 minutes each
Produced by RAI-TV; Adapted and directed by Anton Giulio Majano from the Charles Dickens novel; Production design, Emilio Voglino; Costumes, Maria Teresa Stella; Music, Riz Ortolani

Roberto Chevalier (Young David); Giancarlo Giannini (Adult David); Wanda Capodaglio (Aunt Betsey Trotwood); Fabrizio Moroni (James Steerforth); Stefano Sibaldi (Mr. Micawber); Elsa Vezzoler (Clara Peggotty); Anna Maria Guarnieri (Agnes Wickfield); Ileana Ghione (Clara Copperfield); Ubaldo Lay (Murdstone); Alberto Terrani (Uriah Heep); Enzo Cerusico (Tommy Traddles); Rina Franchetti (Dora Spenlow); Luigi Pavese (Barkis); Laura Ephrikian (Mrs. Micawber); Grazia Maria Spina (Emily); and Diana Torrieri, Mario Feliciani, Massimo Giuliani, Carla Del Poggio, Fosco Giachetti, Paolo Modugno, Pina Cei, Rolando Lupi, Nietta Zocchi, Rosella Spinelli, Elisa Cegani, Lida Ferro

DAVID COPPERFIELD, Omnibus Productions/20th Century-Fox, televised March 15, 1970 NBC 2 hours
A Sagittarius Production; Producer, Frederick H. Brogger; Associate producer, Hugh Attwool; Director, Delbert Mann; Teleplay, Jack Pulman, based on the Charles Dickens novel; Photography, Ken Godges; Art director, Alex Vetchinsky; Costumes, Anthony Mendelson; Music, Malcolm Arnold; Editor, Peter Boita

Robin Phillips (David Copperfield); Susan Hampshire (Agnes Wickfield); Ralph Richardson (Mr. Micawber); Edith Evans (Aunt Betsey Trotwood); Michael Redgrave (Dan'l Peggotty); Wendy Hiller (Mrs. Micawber); Ron Moody (Uriah Heep); James Donald (Mr. Murdstone); Emlyn Williams (Mr. Dick); Richard Attenborough (Mr. Tungay); Laurence Olivier (Mr. Creakle); Anna Massey (Jane Murdstone); Corin Redgrave (James Steerforth); Pamela Franklin (Dora Spenlow); Megs Jenkins (Clara Peggotty); Cyril Cusack (Barkis); Andrew McCulloch (Ham); Sinead Cusack (Emily); Isobel Black (Clara Copperfield);

Alistair MacKenzie (Child David); Nicholas Pennell (Tommy Traddles); Christopher Moran (Boy Steerforth); Helen Cotterill (Mary Ann); Liam Redmond (Mr. Quinion); Donald Layne-Smith (Mr. Wick-field); George Woodbridge (The Vicar); Ann Stallybass (Martha); Robert Lankesheer (Mr. Sharp); Kim Craik (Child Emily); Jeffrey Chandler (Boy Traddles); Phoebe Shaw (Prostitute); Gordon Rollings (Milkman); Brian Tipping (Boy); Alison Blair (Girl); James Hayter (Porter); William Lyon-Brown (Doctor); Christine Ozanne (Midwife)

DAVID COPPERFIELD, televised December 1, 1974 through January 5, 1975 BBC 6 parts 55 minutes each; in U.S. on PBS' *Once Upon a Classic*, televised January 8 through March 13, 1977 10 parts 30 minutes each
Produced by British Broadcasting Corporation in association with Time-Life Television; Executive producer, Jay Rayvid; Producer, John McRae; Coordinating producer, John Coney; Director, Joan Craft; Teleplay, Hugh Whitemore, based on the novel by Charles Dickens; Host, Bill Bixby

Jonathan Kahn (Young David); David Yellend (Adult David); Gail Harrison (Agnes Wickfield); Arthur Lowe (Mr. Micawber); Patience Collier (Aunt Betsey Trotwood); Marvin Jarvis (Uriah Heep); Anthony Andrews (James Steerforth); Pat Keen (Clara Peggotty); Ian Hogg (Dan'l Peggotty); Patricia Routledge (Mrs. Micawber); Melanie Hughes (Little Emily); Peter Bourke (Thomas Traddles); David Troughton (Ham); Beth Morris (Dora Spenlow); Colette O'Neil (Clara Copperfield); Gareth Thomas (Mr. Murdstone); Edward Sinclair (Barkis); Clifton Kershaw (Mr. Creakle); Godfrey Kenton (Mr. Wickfield); Timothy Bateson (Mr. Dick); Jacqueline Pearce (Rosa Dartle)

DAVID COPPERFIELD, animated version, televised in U.S. syndication 1983 75 minutes
Produced by Burbank Films Australia; Executive producers, Tom Stacey, George Stephenson; Producer, Eddy Graham; Director, Alex Nicholas; Adapted by Alex Buzo from the novel by Charles Dickens; Camera operators, Tom Epperson, Gary Page; Music, Richard Bowden and John Stuart; Animation supervisor, Cynthia Leach; Character design, Andrea Bresciani, Bob Fosbery; Background layouts, David Skinner; Editors, Peter Siegl and Chris Gardiner

Voices: Ross Higgins, Phillip Hinton, Robyn Moore, Judy Munn, Moya O'Sullivan, Robin Stuart, John Stone

DAVID COPPERFIELD, televised October 19 through November 21, 1986 BBC; in U.S. on *Masterpiece Theatre*, televised March 27 through April 24, 1988 PBS 5 parts 50 minutes each
A BBC-TV Production in association with WGBH Boston; Producer, Terrance Dicks; Director, Barry Letts; Adapted by James Andrew Hall from the novel by Charles Dickens; Script editor, Brian Wright; Designer, Gavin Davies; Visual effects, Dave Havard; Costume designer, Ann Arnold; Makeup designer, Maggie Thomas; Graphic designer, Marcus McGuinness; Lighting, Bob Chaplin; Sound, Alastair Askham; Production associate, Dave Edwards; Music, Stephen Deutch

Colin Hurley (Older David); Nolan Hemmings (Adult David); David Dexter (Young David); Natalie Ogle (Agnes Wickfield); Simon Callow (Mr. Micawber); Brenda Bruce (Aunt Betsey Trottwood); Paul Brightwell (Uriah Heep); Francesca Hall (Dora Spenlow); Thorley Walters (Mr. Dick); Oliver Cotton (Mr. Murdstone); Jeremy Brudenell (James Steerforth); Jenny McCracken (Clara Peggotty); Stephen Thorne (Dan'l Peggotty); Sandra Payne (Mrs. Micawber); Lee-Emma

Blakemore (Young Emily); Valerie Cogan (Emily); Neal Sweetenham (Thomas Traddles); Owen Teale (Ham); Ronald Herdman (Barkis); John Savident (Mr. Creakle); Artro Morris (Mr. Wickfield); Giles Older-shaw (Mr. Chillip); Hilary Mason (Mrs. Gummidge); Sarah Crowden (Jane Murdstone); Nyree Dawn Porter (Mrs. Steerforth); Ann Way (Mrs. Heep); Simon Sutton (Ostler); Reggie Oliver (Mr. Mull); Dylan Dolan (Young Traddles); Jonathan Lacey (George Dumple); Leon Eagles (Mr. Sharp); Terence Lodge (Mr. Spenlow); Alison Fiske (Rosa Dartle); Irene Richard (Julia Mills); Fanny Carby (Mrs. Crupp); John Baker (Tiffey); Mark Strickson (Markham); Philip Wright (Grainger); and Nicholas BondOwen, Chris Chandler, Alex Johnson, Margaret Clifton, Graham Cull, Gordon Salkilld

DAVY CROCKETT
A Play by Frank Murdock and Frank Mayo (1873)

Synopsis

Frontier scout Davy Crockett's childhood sweetheart, Eleanor Vaughan, then called Little Nell, returns from an extended stay abroad with her friend Neil Crampton and her guardian, Major Hector Royston. When Neil is injured, Davy suggests that the party stays in his rustic hut because of an oncoming blizzard. Isolated by the storm, they are attacked by wolves but Davy singlehandedly wards off the hungry and dangerous beasts. Eleanor, Neil and the major then leave for Oscar Crampton's estate where it is discovered that Neil's Uncle Oscar is blackmailing Major Royston with forged documents to force his consent to the marriage of Neil and Eleanor. Davy rescues Eleanor, destroys the forged papers, takes her back to this home in the wilderness and marries her.

Comment and Critique

Former actor Frank Hitchcock, who adopted his mother's name, Murdoch, for stage purposes, wrote his play, *Davy Crockett; or, Be Sure You're Right, Then Go Ahead,* especially for fellow thespian Frank Mayo. Murdoch died, however, seven months before the Broadway appearance of Mayo's *Davy Crockett*, largely rewritten by Mayo and the greatest success in the Bostonborn actor's career.

Stage historian George Odell wrote, "After having been seen at Wood's Museum and in Brooklyn, that very fine drama of the American frontier, Frank Murdoch's *Davy Crockett*, came to the attention of more fastidious playgoers on March 9th [1874], when Frank Mayo brought it to Niblo's and at once established his portrait of the brave pioneer as one of the gems of the American theater of that day. Unlike other border dramas, this was conceived in terms of simple art. The characterization was admirable and nothing was exaggerated." Odell continued, "A more thrilling scene than that in which the brave Crockett kept from the hut the besieging wolves by driving his arm as a bar through the iron sockets of the door we may not hope often to see. And his beloved Eleanor was in the hut, almost lifeless from the storm from which she had just sought shelter, so that chivalry was exalted as blood flowed downward from the arm of the doughty hero! And let us not forget the exhausted villain on the floor! The scene in which Davy played young Lochinvar charmed old and young alike...the charm of Mayo's acting, and the beauty of what the bills truly called Murdoch's 'charming backwoods idyl' carried Davy Crockett continuously to April 18th."

Mayo's Broadway debut in Murdoch's play at Wood's Theatre in June 1873 was judged by *The New York Times* as "a five-act drama portraying Western life as it was, rather than as it is. *Davy Crockett* is not exactly a sensational play...the scenery [is] quite new, and some of the situations are of a novel and striking character." Actor-writer Laurence Hutton later observed: "Mr. Frank Mayo's performance [is] a gem in its way. He is quiet and subdued, he looks and walks and talks like the trapper to live, never overacts and never forgets the character he represents...Mayo delineating Davy as a strong, brave young hunter of the Far West; bold but unassuming; gentle but with a strong will; skilled in woodcraft but wholly ignorant of the ways of the civilized world he had never seen...shy, sensitive, and proud; unable to read or to write... faithful, honest, truthful -- in short, a natural gentleman."

Folk songs were written in praise of Davy Crockett. Thomas D. Rice introduced his famous "Jump Jim Crow" at New York's American Theatre on November 12, 1832, and later added a verse about Crockett. George Washington Dixon praised Crockett in Congress in his 1834 song "Zip Coon," and by 1839, a 320-page *Crockett Free-and-Easy Song Book* was published in Philadelphia containing the day's popular ballads celebrating Crockett.

Several earlier plays also had been written about the legendary frontiersman. James Kirke Paulding's play, *The Lion of the West*, was produced in New York on April 25, 1831, starring James H. Hackett as Col. Nimrod Wildfire (Crockett). It subsequently was produced in London as *The Lion of the West; or, A Kentuckian's Trip to New York in 1815*. (England's R.R. Brown's song, "The Kentuckian," inspired by the play, became popular in Great Britain during the period.) In 1833, a play entitled *The Kentuckian* was written especially for Hackett, extending the adventures of Nimrod Wildfire.

Davy Crockett himself attended a performance of Paulding's play in New York, where the press enthused: "Colonel Crockett is making a great ado in the city of New York. On his entrance to the theater, he was received with as much applause as his brother, Mr. Hackett, the celebrated representative of Yankee characters. As the Colonel was sitting in a stage box, the eyes of Nimrod Wildfire met those of the former. Nimrod made a bow, and the Colonel, who kept a grave face the 'hull time,' made one also. The house was full, and the deafening applause which ensued fairly made the 'welkin ring.' Every city or town where the Colonel drives at, there is made as 'much ado' as if the General Lafayette was making another tour of the United States." (*Philadelphia Scrap Book*, June 15, 1833)

On December 13, 1833, a Washington newspaper reported, "Colonel Crockett made a prodigious figure last night at the theater. Hackett was to play Nimrod Wildfire...and Colonel Crockett attended by invitation. A whole box was assigned to the Colonel -- and the Colonel bowed and Nimrod Wildfire bowed -- both at each for a long time as if old acquaintances...while the theater rang with the cheers of the multitude assembled."

Davy Crockett was born on August 17, 1786, in Limestone, Tennessee. He served as a Tennessee congressman from 1827 to 1831 and from 1833 to 1835. In 1834, his *Narrative of the Life of David Crockett, of the State of Tennessee, Written by Himself* was published in Philadelphia by E.L. Carey and A. Hart. Crockett prefaced it with: "I leave this rule for others when I'm dead -- Be always sure you're right, THEN GO AHEAD!" (From it, Frank Murdoch derived the title of his 1873 play.) Colonel Davy Crockett died on March 6, 1836, defending the Alamo with his Tennessee Volunteers.

The Battle of Texas was staged at New York's Olympic Theatre in the waning days of 1846, with George Chapman as Crockett. Although other plays celebrated the frontiersman, it was Frank Mayo in the Murdoch play who became theatrically identified with Crockett in much the same way that Joseph Jefferson was forever remembered as Rip Van Winkle because of his many stage impersonations. Mayo was born in Boston on April 18, 1829, and began his career as a Shakespearean actor, but his enduring success in *Davy Crockett* consumed most of his nights on the stage. He played Crockett for two decades, and later his son Edwin F. Mayo assumed the role, not as successfully as his father. Frank Mayo died on June 12, 1896, while en route by train from Denver to Omaha touring in his adaptation of *Pudd'nhead Wilson*.

While Mayo was being acclaimed for his portrayal of Davy Crockett at Niblo's Garden in New York in March 1874, Bryant's Minstrels presented their burlesque version of the legendary hero at their Minstrel Hall beginning on April Fool's Day. Called *Davy Krocket*, the satire was played in conjunction with *Les Miserables; or, Old Times Rocks* and *The Calico Hop* and featured Dan Bryant, Nelse Seymour, Bob Hart and Dave Reed.

Under the title of *Ballet Ballads*, John Latouche wrote librettos for three works, *Susanna and the Elders*, *Willie the Weeper* and *The Eccentricities of Davey [sic] Crockett*, opening on Broadway in May 1948. "The idea here is the fusing of speech and song with dance, and it comes off interestingly in all three cases. The presentation is at once comparatively novel, witty and engrossing," reported critic George Jean Nathan. "The ballets, devoid of all artiness, present in *The Eccentricities of Davey Crockett*. choreography by Hanya Holm, the exploits of boyhood's hero in the fields of Indian fighting...The [Jerome] Moross music, particularly for *Willie the Weeper* and *Davey Crockett*, reveals its composer as one of uncommon range and ability, and the Latouche lyrics have humor, wit, delicacy and, when called for, dramatic force. All in all, a successful adventure in a synthesis of several of the theatrical arts." At the start of January 1961, *The Eccentricities of Davey Crockett* was revived Off Broadway at the East 74th St. Theatre, in conjunction with *Riding Hood Revisited* and *Willie the Weeper*.

A concert reading of *Davy Crockett; or, Be Sure You're Right, Then Go Ahead* was given by New York's Classic Theatre Company on December 2, 1982. The old Frank Murdoch play was one of six formerly popular on the American stage in the reading with Rob Neukrich as Davy Crockett.

For the screen, Bison Pictures produced *Davy Crockett in Hearts United* in 1909, a onereel picture featuring Charles K. French. Hobart Bosworth appeared in the lead in Selig's *Davy Crockett*, a 1910 one-reeler, and Superba Pictures issued a short film, *Davy Crockett Up-to-Date*, in 1915. D. W. Griffith's production, *Martyrs of the Alamo*, was released in October of that year, and in mid-July 1916, Paramount Pictures released the Pallas Company's production of *Davy Crockett* starring Dustin Farnum. Reviewing Farnum's film, the *New York Dramatic Mirror* found that "seldom have we seen more perfect photography...the settings throughout are worthy of much praise. The perfection of the photography and settings is almost nullified by a mediocre story...*Davy Crockett* may have been a fine play, but it is a conventional drama without suspense on the screen."

Several minor "B" productions featuring the Crockett character were produced during the 1920s and 1930s. Later Crockett westerns included *Davy Crockett, Indian Scout* (1980) starring George Montgomery as a namesake cousin of the original frontiersman. According to *The New York Times*, it contained "lots of fireworks and little logic." Republic Pictures' *The Last Command* (1955) featured Sterling Hayden as Jim Bowie and Arthur Hunnicutt as Crockett. *The Motion Picture Herald* described the film as "a well-built, actionful account of the battle of the Alamo simplifying but not entirely distorting the complicated events leading up to the legend of heroism. It moves rapidly if somewhat unevenly, focusing individually on each of the major heroes of Texas' War for Independence." Crockett was also a prominent figure in *The First Texan* (1956), in which Joel McCrea starred as Sam Houston. The film climaxed in the Battle of San Jacinto and touched on the prior historical highlights in Texas' history.

It was the "Frontierland" portion of Walt Disney's television series that ignited a Davy Crockett craze during the mid-1950s. Throughout America, Davy Crockett raccoonskin hats emerged on the heads of children everywhere and "The Ballad of Davy Crockett" hit the musical hit parade, in recordings by Bill Hayes and by Fess Parker (TV's Crockett personified). Three "Frontierland" episodes were consolidated into a feature film by Disney and released in June 1955 as *Davy Crockett, King of the Wild Frontier*. "The episodic form of this picture betrays its origins in a remarkably successful television series, but in the handsome presentation (set off by admirable Technicolor), this version has clearly been conceived for the cinema," wrote Britain's *Monthly Film Bulletin*. "Fess Parker is a pleasantly taciturn hero, the story of his adventure is vigorously told, and there are striking character studies by Buddy Ebsen and Basil Ruysdael."

With the unanticipated and flourishing popularity of Davy Crockett, Disney turned out two more one-hour episodes the following season, *Davy Crockett and the Keelboat Race* and *Davy Crockett and the River Pirates*. These two were combined and subsequently shown theatrically under the latter title in mid-1956.

For many years, John Wayne had envisioned a screen epic based on the historic battle at the Alamo with himself playing, of course, Colonel Davy Crockett. After having been refused financial backing by most of the Hollywood studios, he talked United Artists into risking $2.5 million, with Wayne himself raising a matching figure among well-heeled friends. Eventually, Clint Murchison and others contributed another $5 million, making Wayne's dream the most expensive production to that time. His company, Batjac, ultimately put its slice of Texas history on the screen, with John Wayne producing and directing (with a little uncredited help from his friend John Ford), for about $12 million.

Two years were consumed in constructing a detailed replica of San Antonio de Bexar and the former Franciscan mission built in 1744 and named for a grove of cottonwood trees (alamo) around which it was erected. John Wayne filmed his epic in Todd-AO and Technicolor on a ninety-one-day schedule beginning September 22, 1959, on the massive set covering hundreds of acres at Brackettville, Texas, 120 miles from San Antonio near the Mexican border. Filming ended on December 15.

The film ran three hours and twelve minutes initially when it premiered in New York on October 26, 1960 and in London the next day. Despite its special roadshow presentation, with reserved seating and increased admissions, *The Alamo* recouped only $8 million on its release. Running time was slashed but only the sale of television rights ultimately allowed for recovery of the initial investment.

Accolades for *The Alamo* came from directors George Stevens and John Ford. Stevens commented extravagantly that "When the roll call of the great ones is made, *The Alamo* will be among those few by which the films of the future will be measured. There are images in [it] that will haunt you for a lifetime: a glorious restoration in film of the historic Alamo epic...it is a modern classic." Ford enthused: "*The Alamo* is the greatest picture I've ever seen. It will last forever, run forever, for all peoples, all families everywhere."

Unfortunately, the critics were somewhat less enthusiastic than Wayne's colleagues. "*The Alamo* is the biggest western ever made. Wayne and Co. have not quite managed to make it the worst," reported *Time* Magazine. "The first three hours are as flat as Texas. Plenty happens...but it all seems to have happened before, in some other John Wayne western, and in any case, most of the action has nothing to do with the Alamo. When the film finally gets down to historical cases, it proves to be shamelessly inaccurate...Worse yet is the phony back-woodsiness of much of the dialogue -- and worst of all is the teary sentiment that blears every other frame of the film."

Bosley Crowther (*The New York Times*) found: "*The Alamo* for all its bigness -- and big and long it certainly is -- is but another beleagured blockhouse western...It cannot help but have certain moments and even long imagecrowded passages by which the audience is piercingly affected and visually overwhelmed...Mr. Wayne has unfortunately let his desire to make a 'big' picture burden him with dialogue. His action scenes are usually vivid, his talk scenes are long and usually dull." Crowther however did applaud the "dazzling graphic arrangements of panoramic views of the Mexican Army of General Santa Anna, gathering for the attack, arriving in companies and battalions like athletes at the opening of Olympic Games; bone-crushing sequences showing warm bodies hurling themselves against the walls; scenes of old-fashioned battle that fairly choke you with their clouds of smoke and dust."

In *Films and Filming*, John Cutts wrote that the film "isn't so much the epic entertainment that it claims to be as an endurance test of epic proportions...it isn't anywhere near the equal of *Davy Crockett* or *The Last Command*. The reasons why are too numerous to list fully -- but in the main, although Mr. Wayne's film has undeniable size, it is sadly lacking in sweep and vigor."

On November 14, 1960, ABC televised what amounted to as well-produced advertisement for the picture. Called *The Spirit of the Alamo*, the hourlong program featured the Wayne epic's principal players, together with guest commentators like former Vice President John Nance Garner, writer J. Frank Dobie and others. Wayne himself sauntered through as master of ceremonies, guiding viewers proudly through the massive Brackettville set (which still is being used). Dimitri Tiomkin's rousing title song and "Green Leaves of Summer" (written with Paul Francis Webster), were sung by a choir and, from the film, Ken Curtis, Ken Curtis sang "Lullaby," while Chill Wills and Frankie Avalon joined in a chorus of "Here's to the Ladies."

The Alamo might not have made too many Ten Best lists for 1960 but did receive Academy Award nominations as Best Picture (it lost to Billy Wilder's *The Apartment*), to Chill Wills for his supporting performance (losing to Peter Ustinov for *Spartacus*), to cinematographer William H. Clothier, to film editor Stuart Gilmore, and to Dimitri Tiomkin for his score and for his and Paul Francis Webster's "Green Leaves of Summer." Its sole Oscar was for sound. (The Harvard Lampoon acknowledged *The Alamo* with its special "Along the Mohawk Award" for "the film with the most drummed-up publicity campaign.")

The expansive, controversial, now-legendary campaign to capture the Academy Award for *The Alamo*, suggesting that not to vote for the film was unpatriotic, raised a number of industry eyebrows and some resentment. Additionally, Chill Wills' strenuous campaign to win votes as the year's Best Supporting Actor also was not wellreceived, causing what is thought to have been a "Forget the Alamo" backlash.

Lon Tinkle, an authority on the Alamo and a guest on Wayne's 1960 TV promotional, posthumously had his 1958 history, *Thirteen Days to Glory: The Siege of the Alamo*, adapted to television twenty-eight years later by Clyde Ware and Norman McLeod Morrill. Stockton Briggle, an extra in the Wayne film and a college buddy of Tinkle, obtained the television rights to Tinkle's book and produced it as *The Alamo: 13 Days to Glory*, with Brian Keith (at 65) as Davy Crockett and John Wayne's onetime protege, James Arness (at 63), as Jim Bowie. (Both actors were far more advanced in years than the characters they were portraying. Broadway star Raul Julia was signed to play Santa Anna (after Ricardo Montalban dropped out), and Lorne Greene, another veteran of the TV west, was cast as Sam Houston (a brief role and, unfortunately, Greene's last). Unable to obtain permission to film at the actual Alamo, producer Briggle and director Burt Kennedy took the company to Wayne's "Alamo" at Brackettville.

The Alamo: 13 Days to Glory was telecast in late January 1987 as a three-hour movie. In the view of *TV Guide*, "Unlike John Wayne's flagwaving 1960 production of The *Alamo,* this TV movie us a less romanticized and more balanced account of one of the most famous sieges in history." Atlanta-based television critic Frank Thompson found "The producer calls it 'the most truthful show ever done on the Alamo' and to a great extent it is. The issues are simplified, but there is little of the pure invention that marred Wayne's film." He also felt it "is very entertaining. The filmmakers have taken full advantage of the elements that the Alamo has always offered to the movies: tragedy, excitement, poignancy, colorful costumes and settings, interesting personalities, violence. The performances are uniformly good, the pacing is admirable and the action scenes are first rate." He concluded "The final section of the film is both its high and low points. The battle scene is filmed with energy and violence (sharp-eyed movie buffs will notice stock footage from *The Last Command* bolstering early moments of the fight; Mexicans from the Republic film fire cannon at the John Wayne set -- which gets more ironic the longer you think about it) and emerges as a truly thrilling -- and moving -- spectacle...While the script has gone to great pains to humanize the defenders, when it comes time for them to die, they are just as heroic and god-like as any grade-school pageant would have it. In the real battle, some men fled, others begged for their lives. Six men (including Crockett) surrendered and were executed after the fight. But in the movies, all defenders go down swinging -- and this one is no exception."

Two footnotes to this production: among the actors is Ethan Wayne, the Duke's youngest son who, as a young boy, also appeared with his dad in *The Alamo*; and an Emmy nomination for this exciting production went to cinematographer John Elsenbach.

Shelley Duvall's *Tall Tales & Legends* version of the Davy Crockett saga -- at least one incident in his colorful life -- was telecast on her ongoing Showtime cable series in 1987. Singer Mac Davis starred as Crockett and McLean Stevenson played Andrew Jackson. Somewhat over a year later, Walt Disney Productions felt the time was at hand to revive one of the company's most successful television characters in a new, five-episode series. Fess Parker was approached to repeat his original role, briefly, as an older Crockett recalling some of his younger adventures, when new star Tim Dunigan would step in. Parker declined and Johnny Cash took the role in the two-hour premiere (the subsequent shows were one hour each over a period of several months). Gary Grubbs played Georgie Russell, Davy's friend and sidekick, the part that Buddy Ebsen had done in the 1950s series.

STAGE

THE BATTLE OF TEXAS, *Olympic Theatre*, New York, opened December 29, 1846
George Chapman (David Crockett); Mr. Rodney (Santa Anna); H. Chapman (Lieutenant Dickinson); Mrs. George Chapman (Mrs. Dickinson)

THE KENTUCKIAN; OR, A TRIP TO NEW YORK IN 1815, Boston Theatre, Boston, opened February 17, 1848
Produced by Charles R. Thorne; A Play by James Kirke Paulding
James H. Hackett (Col. Nimrod Wildfire, a gay and eccentric young fellow from the Southwestern border of Kentucky); H. B. Phillips (Freeman); Harry Watkins (Percival); Moses R. Phillips (John Jenkins, a valet passing for Lord Granby); Mrs. H. Cramer (Mrs. Luminary); Mr. Byrnes (Caesar); Mr. Nelson (Tradesman); H. N. Sprague (Mary); Harriet Mace (Caroline); Mr. Miles (Servant); Mrs. Reid (Mrs. Freeman)

DAVY CROCKETT; OR, BE SURE YOU'RE RIGHT, THEN GO AHEAD, Wood's Museum, New York, opened June 2, 1873 12 performances
A Play by Frank Murdoch, revised by Frank Mayo
Frank Mayo (Davy Crockett); Rosa Rand (Eleanor Vaughan); T. W. Keene (Maj. Hector Royston); J. J. Wallace (Oscar Crampton); Mrs. Van Deren (Dame Crockett); Harry Stewart (Neil Crampton); Charles Sturges (Yonkers); C. M. Manley (Big Dan); R. J. Lewis (Briggs); L. R. Willard (Quickwitch); G. C. Charles (Watson); Welsh Edwards (Parson Ainsworth); Aggie Keene (Little Bob Crockett); Mary Page (Little Sally); Little Kittie (Little Kelly)

Niblo's Garden Theatre, New York, opened March 9, 1874 48 performances
A Play by Frank Murdoch, revised by Frank Mayo
Frank Mayo (Davy Crockett); Rosa Rand (Eleanor Vaughan); T. W. Keene (Maj. Hector Royston); W. B. Laurens (Oscar Crampton); Amy Crawford (Dame Crockett); Frank Percy (Neil Crampton); Orville Wallace (Yonkers); H. A. Weaver (Parson Ainsworth); Little Alice (Trot); W. Carpenter (Watson); H. Douglas (Big Dan); W. Williams (Briggs); W. Dalborn (Quickwitch); Master Buckingham (Little Bob Crockett); Katie Patterson (Little Sally)

Touring Company, season 1875-76
Produced and directed by Frank Mayo; A Play by Frank Murdoch, revised by Frank Mayo; Scenic effects, George Hielge; Machinery by M. A. Wright; Music arranged by Charles R. Dodworth; Stage manager, Charles M. Walcot
Frank Mayo (Davy Crockett); Josephine Laurens (Eleanor Vaughan); W. H. Bailey (Maj. Hector Royston); Frederic Bock (Oscar Crampton); Mrs. W. A. Chapman (Dame Crockett); W. A. Whitecar (Neil Crampton); W. H. Jones (Parson Ainsworth); Jule Reed (Little Bob Crockett); Walter Hubbell (Watson); B. W. Turner (Big Dan); Willis H. Page (Yonkers); H. Chase (Briggs); F. S. Julian (Quickwitch); Little Nellie (Little Sally)

Touring Company, season 1877-78
Produced and directed by Frank Mayo; A Play by Frank Murdoch, revised by Frank Mayo; Stage manager, Ralph Howard
Frank Mayo (Davy Crockett); Marie Burress (Eleanor Vaughan); George Robeling (Maj. Hector Royston); Edwin F. Mayo (Oscar Crampton); Florence Gerald (Dame Crockett); Harry Driscole (Neil Crampton); Paul Menifee (Parson Ainsworth); William Graham (Quickwitch); H. Carter (Watson); J. J. Murphy (Big Dan); Master Harry O'Lynn (Little Bob Crockett); R. C. Raymond (Yonkers); George Leonard (Briggs)

DAVY CROCKETT, Olympic Theatre, London, opened August 16, 1879
Written, produced and directed by Frank Mayo

Frank Mayo (Davy Crockett); Miss Ritta (Eleanor Vaughan); Master Phillips (Young Crockett); Maria Davis (Dame Crockett); Luigi La Blanche (Neil Crampton)

SAM HOUSTON, 3rd Avenue Theatre, New York, opened January 6, 1890

James H. Wallack (Sam Houston); Harold Leveson (Col. Davy Crockett); Will Muller (Col. Jim Bowie); Josie L. Fox (Victoria Legrand); Mrs. James H. Wallack (Senora Legrand)

THE BALLAD OF DAVY CROCKETT, American Historical Theatre, New York, season 1935-36 [presented at various theaters during the season]
Produced by The American Historical Theatre, Federal Theatre Works Progress Administration; A Play by Hofman R. Hays; Director, John Lyman; Settings, Wood MacLane, based on original designs by John Love; Costumes, Lillian Richter; Company manager, Charles Knapp; Stage manager, David Pardoll

Hiram Cooper (Davy Crockett); Henriette Brown (Ma Crockett); Edward Loeffler (Pa Crockett); Rei Terry (Sarah); Josephine Fox (Sarah's Ma); Wilbur Cos (Sarah's Pa); Robert Lawrence (Congressman Alexander); Lawrence Stanhope (Dare, Secretary to President Jackson); Edward West (President Andrew Jackson); Ellsworth Woods (Senator); Joan Arthur (Senator's Wife); Colfax Sanderson (Mr. Van Buren); Philip Clarke (Col. Barrett Travis); Joseph Rivera (Gen. Santa Anna); Cora Burlar (Fanny); Edward Loeffler (Capt. Morgan); Theodore Gros (Ballad Singer); Joseph Planck (Fiddler); Herbert Hunter (Uncle Josh); Bert Young (Schoolmaster); Hofmann R. Hays (Job Spindle); Samuel Wright (Carpenter); Harry Boden (Drunkard); Joseph McInerny (Capt. Edmonds); John Watkins, Joseph Gregory, George Matthews (Dying Men); Edgar Ballou (Lawyer Pitman); Allen Reeves (Saloonkeeper); Charles Craig (Watkins); Charles Downey (Rev. Wedgeford); Daniel Carew (Surveyor); George Matthews, Joseph Gregory (Soldiers); Colfax Sanderson (Granddaddy of the Snapping Turtles); Charles Downey (Granddaddy of the Bears); Kenneth Tittle (Granddaddy of the 'Coon'); Homer Lee, Thomas Doolan, Jack Saltzman, Solomon Goldstein (Backwoodsman); Myron Paulson, Harry Singer (Bystanders); Charles Craig (Watkins); Florence Hess (Mrs. Jones); Amelia Barleon (Elderly Lady); John Watkins (Flunkey); Edward Clare (Sentinel); Solomon Goldstein (Mexican Colonel); Marshall de Silva, Herbert Eisinger, George Sinclair (Mexican Soldiers); William Gallagher, Harlan Knight, George Sinclair, Wallance Banfield, Franklyn Merritt, Warren Pittinger, Eloise Ferrier, George Matthews, Leona Krauss, Nina Hibernian, Michael Defuso, Hattie Bainbridge, Wilfred Jessop, Herbert Eisinger (Backwoodsmen and Women)

THE ECCENTRICITIES OF DAVEY CROCKETT, Music Box Theatre, New York, opened May 18, 1948 62 performances
Produced by T. Edward Hambleton and Alfred R. Stern for the benefit of the American National Theatre and Academy; The Experimental Theatre's production of *Ballet Ballads*, three dance plays by John Latouche; Produced, Nat Karson; Director, Hugh Ross; Composer, Jerome Moross; Designed and lighted by Nat Karson; Choreographer, Hanya Holm; Musical director, Hugh Ross; Pianists, John Lesko, Jr. and Mordecai Sheinkman; General manager, Abe Cohen

Ted Lawrie (Davey Crockett); Barbara Ashley (Sally Ann); Lorin Barrett (Indian Chief); Carl Luman (Gen. Andrew Jackson); Betty Abbott (The Mermaid); Olga

Lunick (The Comet); William A. Meyers (Brown Brear); Robert Baird (Ghost Bear); John Costello (John Oldham [dancer]); William Ambler (John Oldham [singer]); Sharry Traver (Ann Hutchinson [dancer]); Gertrude Lockway (Ann Hutchinson [singer]); Barbara Downie (Grace Sherwood [dancer]); Arlouine Goodjohn (Grace Sherwood [singer]); Frank Seabolt (Nathaniel Bacon [dancer]); Eddie Varrato (Nathaniel Bacon [singer]); Harold Michener (President Andrew Jackson); Ellen R. Albertini, Margaret Cuddy, Barbara Downie, Sharry Traver, Beau Cunningham, John Costello, Frank Seabolt, Robert Trout, Spencer Teakle (Friends and Neighbors)

Presented in conjunction with *Susanna and the Elders* (choreographed by Katherine Litz) and *Willie the Weeper* (choreographed by Paul Godkin)

THE ECCENTRICITIES OF DAVEY CROCKETT, East 74th St. Theatre, New York, opened January 3, 1961 40 performances

Produced by Ethel Watt; Three dance plays, *Ballet Ballads*, written by John Latouche; Composed by Jerome Moross; Designed by Gary Smith; Lighting, Jules Fisher; Choreographer, Glen Tetley; Musical and choral director, Don Smith; Costumes, Hal George; General manager, James B. McKenzie; Stage managers, Don Lamb and Ted Bloecher; Presented in conjunction with *Riding Hood Revisited* and *Willie the Weeper*

Jack Mette (Davey Crockett); Sallie Bramlette (Sally Ann); Ed Zimmerman (Indian Chief/President Andrew Jackson); Alice Scott (The Mermaid); Carmen de Lavallade (The Comet); Steve Paxton (Brown Bear); Ted Lambrinos (Ghost Bear); Steve Paxton (John Oldham [dancer]); Ed Zimmerman (John Oldham [singer]); Ellen Graff (Ann Hutchinson [dancer]); Dianne Nichols (Ann Hutchinson [singer]); Betty de Jong (Grace Sherwood [dancer]); Lorraine Roberts (Grace Sherwood [singer]); Fred Herko (Nathaniel Bacon [dancer]); Ted Bloecher (Nathaniel Bacon [singer]); Fred Herko, Steve Paxton, Bob Powell, Jon Rager (Hunters/Indians/Congressmen); Ted Bloecher, Derek de Cambra, Ted Lambrinos, Gregg Nickerson (Soldiers); Betty de Jong, Pauline de Groot, Ellen Graff (Girls); Phyllis Lamhut, Douina Rathbone, Robert Helloway (Dancers); Sallie Bramlette, Lorraine Roberts, Alice Scott, Gregg Nickerson, Abbe Todd (Singers)

DAVY CROCKETT; OR, BE SURE YOU'RE RIGHT AND THEN GO AHEAD, Classic Theatre, New York, opened December 2, 1982 12 performances

Produced by The Classic Theatre Company in association with the East Lynne Company; A Play by Frank Murdoch; Director, Warren Kliewer. (Part of *A Festival of American Plays* consisting of six plays formerly popular on the American stage presented in concert readings.)

Rob Neukirch (Davy Crockett); Paula Gerhardt (Eleanor Vaughan); Richard Stack (Maj. Hector Royston); Jack Deisler (Oscar Crampton); Shirley Bodtke (Dame Crockett); David Higlen (Neil Crampton); Christian Deisler (Little Bob Crockett); Thomas L. Rindge (Narrator/Big Dan/Parson)

SCREEN

DAVY CROCKETT IN HEARTS UNITED, Bison Pictures, released May 1909

Director, Fred Balshofer; Screenplay by Charles K. French

Charles K. French (Davy Cockett); with Charles Inslee

DAVY CROCKETT, *Selig Pictures*, released April 1910
Director, Frank Boggs
Hobart Bosworth (Davy Crockett); with Betty Harte, Thomas Santachi

DAVY CROCKETT UP-TO-DATE, *Superba Pictures*, released May 1915
W. E. Browning, Rolinda Bainbridge

MARTYRS OF THE ALAMO, *Triangle Pictures*, released October 1915
Produced and supervised by D.W. Griffith; Written and directed by William Christie Cabane, based on a story by Theodosia Harris
Alfred Paget (James Bowie); A. D. Sears (David Crockett); Walter Long (Santa Anna); Ora Crew (Mrs. Dickinson); Fred Burns (Dickinson); John Dillon (Col. William Travis); Sam De Grasse (Silent Smith); Tom Wilson (Sam Houston); Augustus Carney (Revolutionary War Veteran); Juanita Hansen (Daughter of the Revolutionary War Veteran)

DAVY CROCKETT, *Paramount Pictures*, released July 1916
A Pallas Production; Director, William Desmond Taylor; Screenplay by Julia Crawford Ivers, from a story by Elliott J. Clawson; Photography, Homer Scott
Dustin Farnum (Davy Crockett); Winifred Kingston (Eleanor Vaughan); Herbert Standing (Maj. Hector Royston); Harry de Vere (James Vaughan); Howard Davies (Oscar Crampton); Page Peters (Neil Crampton); Lydia Yeamans Titus (Mrs. Crockett); Ogden Crane (Dan)

DAVY CROCKETT AT THE FALL OF THE ALAMO, *Sunset Productions*, released August 1926
Director, Robert North Bradbury; Screenplay, Ben Ali Newman; Photography, William Brown, Jr., and Elvert M. McManigal; Art directors, Wilson Silsby and Paul Cosgrove; Assistant directors, William Dagnell and Jack Pierce; Titles, Clover Roscoe; Editor, Della M. King
Cullen Landis (Davy Crockett); Joe Rickson (Col. William Travis); Bob Fleming (Col. James Bowie); Fletcher Norton (Gen. Santa Anna); Kathryn McGuire (Alice Blake); Steve Clemento (Mose); Anne Berryman (Kate Kennedy); Jay Morley (Zachary Kennedy); Frank Rice (Lige Beardsley); Betty Brown (Myra Winkler); Bob Bradbury, Jr. ("Pinky" Smith); Ralph McCullough (Col. Bonham); Thomas Lingham ("Dandy Dick" Heston)

THE PAINTED STALLION, *Republic Serial* (12 parts), released June 1937
Directors, William Witney, Alan James and Ray Taylor; Screenplay by Barry Shipman and Winston Miller, based on a story by Morgan Cox and Ronald Davidson; Photography, William Nobles and Edgar Lyons; Music, Raoul Kraushaar
Ray "Crash" Corrigan (Clark Stewart); Hoot Gibson (Walter Jamison); Jack Perrin (Davy Crockett); Hal Taliaferro (Jim Bowie); Duncan Renaldo (Zamoro); Sammy McKim (Kit Carson); Julia Thayer (The Rider); Leroy Mason (Dupre); Yakima Canutt (Tom); Maston Williams (Macklin); Duke Taylor (Joe); Laren Riebe (Pedro); Charles King (Bull Smith); Vinegar Roan (Oldham); Gordon de Main (Governor); George de Normand (Juan)

HEROES OF THE ALAMO, *Columbia Pictures*, April 1938
Director, Harry Fraser; Story and screenplay, Roby Wentz; Photography, Robert

Cline; Editor, Arthur A. Brooks

Lane Chandler (Davy Crockett); Rex Lease (Col. William Travis); Ruth Findley (Anne Dickinson); Edward Piel (Sam Houston); Bruce Warren (Almerian Dickinson); Julian Rivero (Gen. Santa Anna); Roger Williams (James); Earl Hodgins (Stephen Austin)

MAN OF CONQUEST, Republic Pictures, released April 1939
Associate producer, Sol C. Siegel; Director, George Nicholls, Jr.; Screenplay by E. E. Paramore, Jr., and Wells Root, based on a story by Harold Shumate, Wells Root; Photography, Joseph H. August; Art director, John Victor Mackay; Costumes, Adele Palmer; Music, Victor Young; Special effects, Howard Lydecker; Sound, Richard Tyler; Editor, Edward Mann

Richard Dix (Sam Houston); Gail Patrick (Margaret Lea); Edward Ellis (Andrew Jackson); Joan Fontaine (Eliza Allen); Victor Jory (William Travis); Robert Barrat (Davy Crockett); George Hayes (Lannie Upchurch); Ralph Morgan (Stephen Austin); Robert Armstrong (Jim Bowie); C. Henry Gordon (Santa Anna); Janet Beecher (Mrs. Lea); Pedro de Cordoba (Oolooteko); Max Terhune ("Deaf" Smith); Ferris Taylor (Jonas Lea); Kathleen Lockhart (Mrs. Allen); Leon Ames (John Hoskins); Charles Stevens (Zavola); Lane Chandler (Major Bonham); Sarah Padden (Mrs. Houston)

THE SON OF DAVY CROCKETT, Columbia Pictures, released July 1941
Produced by Leon Barsha; Written and directed by Lambert Hillyer; Photography, Benjamin Kline; Editor, Mel Thorsen

Bill Elliott (Davy Crockett); Iris Meredith (Doris Matthews); Dub Taylor (Cannonball); Kenneth MacDonald (King Canfield); Richard Fiske (Jesse Gordon); Eddy Wallar (Grandpa Matthews); Don Curtis (Jack Ridge); Paul Scardon (Zeke); Edmund Cobb (Lance); Harrison Greene (Pres. Ulysses S. Grant)

DAVY CROCKETT, INDIAN SCOUT, United Artists release, released March 1950
An Edward Small Production; Associate producers, Grant Whytock and Bernard Small; Director, Lew Landers; Screenplay, Richard Schayer, based on a story by Ford Beebe; Photography, George Diskant and John Mescall; Art directors, Rudolph Sternad and Martin Obzina; Music, Paul Sawtell; Editors, Stuart Frye and Kenneth Crane

George Montgomery (Davy Crockett); Ellen Drew (Frances); Philip Reed (Red Hawk); Noah Beery, Jr. (Tex); Addison Richards (Captain Weightman); Paul Guilfoyle (Ben); Robert Barrat (Lone Eagle); Erik Rolfe (Mr. Simms); William Wilkerson (High Tree); John Hamilton (Colonel Pollard); Vera Marshe (Mrs. Simms); Ray Teal (Captain McHale); Kenneth Duncan (Sergeant Gordon); Chief Thundercloud (Sleeping Fox); Jimmy Moss (Jimmy Simms)

DAVY CROCKETT, KING OF THE WILD FRONTIER, Buena Vista Pictures, released June 1955
A Walt Disney Production; Producer, Bill Walsh; Director, Norman Foster; Screenplay, Tom Blackburn; Adapted from the original "Disneyland" television productions; Photography, Charles P. Boyle; Art director, Marvin Aubrey Davis; Costumes, Norman Martien; Set decorators, Emile Kuri and Pat Delaney; Music, George Bruns; Song "The Ballad of Davy Crockett" by George Bruns, Tom Blackburn; Song "Farewell" by George Bruns (words by Davy Crockett);

Orchestrations, Edward H. Plumb; Makeup, Lon Philippi; Special processes, Ub Iwerks; Editor, Charles Schaeffer

Fess Parker (Davy Crockett); Buddy Ebsen (George Russel); Basil Ruysdael (Gen. Andrew Jackson); Kenneth Tobey (Col. Jim Bowie); Hans Conried (Thimblerig); Don Megowan (Col. William Travis); Helene Stanley (Polly Crockett); Mike Mazurki (Bigfoot Mason); William Bakewell (Tobias Norton); Nick Cravat (Bustedluck); Jeff Thompson (Charlie Two Shirts); Ray Whitetree (Johnny); Benjamin Hornbuckle (Henderson); Campbell Brown (Bruno); Eugene Brindle (Billy); Henry Joyner (Swaney); Pat Hogan (Chief Red Stick); Hal Youngblood (Opponent political speaker); Jim Maddox, Robert Booth (Congressmen)

THE LAST COMMAND, Republic Pictures, released August 1955

Produced by Herbert J. Yates; Associate producer and director, Frank Lloyd; Screenplay, Warren Duff, based on a story by Sy Bartlett; Photography, Jack Marta; Art director, Frank Arrigo; Music, Max Steiner; Song "Jim Bowie" by Sidney Clare and Max Steiner; Sound, Dick Tyler, Sr., and Howard Wilson; Editor, Tony Martinelli

Sterling Hayden (James Bowie); Anna Maria Alberghetti (Consuela); Richard Carlson (William Travis); Ernest Borgnine (Mike Radin); Arthur Hunnicutt (Davy Crockett); J. Carrol Naish (Santa Anna); John Russell (Lieut. Dickinson); Virginia Grey (Mrs. Dickinson); Ben Cooper (Jeb Lacey); Eduard Franz (Lorenzo de Quesada); Otto Kruger (Stephen Austin); Hugh Sanders (Sam Houston); Russell Simpson (The Parson); Roy Roberts (Dr. Sutherland); Slim Pickens (Abe)

THE FIRST TEXAN, Allied Artists release, released June 1956

Produced by Walter Mirisch; Associate producer, Richard Heermance; Director, Byron Haskin; Story and Screenplay, Daniel B. Ullman; Photography, Wilfrid Cline; Art director, David Milton; Music, Roy Webb; Conducted by Paul Sawtell; Title song, Roy Webb and McElbert Moore; Set decorator, John McConaghy; Editor, George White

Joel McCrea (Sam Houston); Felicia Farr (Katherine Delaney); Jeff Morrow (Col. Jim Bowie); James Griffith (Davy Crockett); Wallace Ford (Henry Delaney); Abraham Sofaer (Don Carlos); Jody McCrea (Baker); William Hopper (Col. William Travis); David Silva (Gen. Santa Anna); Dayton Lummis (Stephen Austin); Carl Benton Reid (President Andrew Jackson); Roy Roberts (Sherman); Frank Puglia (Pepe); Chubby Johnson ("Deaf" Smith); Rodolfo Hoyos (Colonel Cos); Lane Chandler (Colonel Fannin); Salvador Baguez (Veramendi); Nelson Leigh (Hockley)

DAVY CROCKETT AND THE RIVER PIRATES, Buena Vista Pictures, released July 1956

A Walt Disney Production; Producer, Bill Walsh; Director, Norman Foster; Screenplay, Tom Blackburn and Norman Foster; Adapted from the original "Disneyland" television productions; Photography, Bert Glennon; Art director, Field Grey; Costumes, Carl Walker; Set decorators, Emile Kuri and Bertram Granger; Music, George Bruns; Songs by George Bruns and Tom Blackburn; Orchestrations, Edward H. Plumb; Special processes, Ub Iwerks; Editor, Stanley Johnson

Fess Parker (Davy Crockett); Buddy Ebsen (George Russel); Jeff York (Mike Fink); Kenneth Tobey (Jocko); Irvin Ashkenazy (Moose); Paul Newlan (Big Harpe); Troy Melton (Hank); Dick Crockett (Ben); Clem Bevans (Cap'n Cobb); Mort Mills (Sam Mason); Frank Richards (Little Harpe); Hank Worden (The

Fiddler); Walter Catlett (Col. Plug); George Lewis (Black Eagle)

THE ALAMO, United Artists release, released October 1960
A Batjac Production; Produced and directed by John Wayne; Screenplay, James Edward Grant; Photography, William Clothier; Art director, Alfred Ybarra; Set decorator, Victor A. Gangelin; Costumes, Frank Beetson and Ann Peck; Music, Dimitri Tiomkin; Songs, Dimitri Tiomkin and Paul Francis Webster; Sound, Jack Solomon, Gordon Sawyer, Fred Haynes and Don Hall, Jr.; Special effects, Lee Zavitz; Technical supervisors, Frank Beetson and Jack Pennick; Editor, Stuart Gilmore

John Wayne (Davy Crockett); Richard Widmark (Col. Jim Bowie); Richard Boone (Gen. Sam Houston); Laurence Harvey (Col. William Travis); Frankie Avalon (Smitty); Linda Cristal (Flaca); Joseph Calleia (Juan Seguin); Patrick Wayne (Capt. James Bonham); Joan O'Brien (Mrs. Dickinson); Veda Ann Borg (Blind Nell); Chill Wills (Beekeeper); Ken Curtis (Captain Dickinson); Carlos Arruza (Lieutenant Reyes); Ruben Padilla (Gen. Santa Anna); Guinn "Big Boy" Williams (Lieutenant Finn); Denver Pyle (Gambler); John Dierkes (Jocko Robertson); Jester Hairston (Jethro); Bill Henry (Dr. Sutherland); Wesley Lau (Emil); Olive Carey (Mrs. Dennison); Hank Worden (Parson); Bill Daniel (Colonel Neill); Chuck Roberson (A Tennesseean); Alisa Wayne (Lisa Dickinson)

TELEVISION

DAVY CROCKETT, "Frontierland" segment of Walt Disney's Disneyland television series on ABC. Three hour-long programs devoted to the adventures of Davy Crockett:

DAVY CROCKETT, INDIAN FIGHTER, televised December 15, 1954
DAVY CROCKETT GOES TO CONGRESS, televised January 26, 1955
DAVY CROCKETT AT THE ALAMO, televised February 23, 1955

These programs were edited into the 1955 feature film, *DAVY CROCKETT, KING OF THE WILD FRONTIER*

THE LEGEND OF DAVY CROCKETT, "Frontierland" segment of Walt Disney's Disneyland series on ABC. Two hour-long sequels to the earlier Davy Crockett adventures:

DAVY CROCKETT AND THE KEELBOAT RACE, televised November 16, 1955
DAVY CROCKETT AND THE RIVER PIRATES, televised December 14, 1955

These programs were edited into the 1956 feature film, *DAVY CROCKETT AND THE RIVER PIRATES*

THE SPIRIT OF THE ALAMO, televised November 14, 1960 ABC 1 hour
Producer, Perry Cross; Coproducer and director, Seymour Robbie; Written by L. I. Salaman; Narrated by John Wayne

John Wayne (Davy Crockett), Richard Widmark, Laurence Harvey, Richard Boone, Frankie Avalon, Chill Wills, Linda Cristal, Joan O'Brien, Ken Curtis, Carlos Arruza. Special guests: John Nance Garner, J. Frank Dobie, Lon Tinkle

THE ALAMO, episode of *Time Tunnel* series, televised December 9, 1966 ABC 1 hour

Executive producer and creator, Irwin Allen; Director, Scobey Martin; Teleplay, Wanda and Bob Duncan; Photography, Winton Hoch; Music, Johnny Williams

Rhodes Reason (Col. William Travis), Jim Davis (Col. Jim Bowie); Edward Colmans (Davy Crockett); John Lupton (Captain Teynerson); Elizabeth Rogers (Mrs. Teynerson); Rodolfo Hoyos (Captain Rodriguez); and series regulars: James Darren (Dr. Tony Newman); Robert Colbert (Dr. Doug Phillips); Lee Meriweather (Ann); Whit Bissell (Gen. Heywood Kirk); John Zaremba (Dr. Raymond Swain)

YOU ARE THERE: THE SIEGE OF THE ALAMO, televised October 9, 1971 CBS 30 minutes

Executive producer, Burton Benjamin; Producer, Vern Diamond; Coproducer, Barbara Schultz; Director, Burt Brinckerhoff; Teleplay, Walter Bernstein; Commentators, Walter Cronkite, Dallas Townsend, Douglas Edwards and Bob Schieffer

Fred Gwynne (Davy Crockett); Philip Bosco (Gen. Sam Houston); Roger Davis (Col. William Travis); Bernard Kates (Col. Jim Bowie); Manuel Sebastian (Gen. Santa Anna); Hector Elias (Colonel Almonte); Arnie Freeman (Louise Rose); Tom Atkins (Almeron Dickinson); Melissa Murphy (Susannah Dickinson); James Hall (James Bonham); Gonzalo Madurga (Lorenzo de Zavala); Norman Bush (Ben); Donald Saunders (Hockley)

DAVY CROCKETT ON THE MISSISSIPPI, *Famous Classic Tales*, televised November 20, 1976 Animated cartoon CBS 1 hour

Hanna-Barbera Productions; Executive producers, William Hanna and Joseph Barbera; Producer, Iwao Takamoto; Director, Charles A. Nichols; Written by Sid Morse; Graphics, Iraj Paran; Animators, Carlos Alfonso, Oliver E. Callahan, Ken Muse, Juan Pina and Carlo Vinci; Music director, Hoyt Curtin; "Davy Crockett" theme, Gairden Cooke and Hoyt Curtin

Voices: Mike Bell, Ron Feinberg, Randy Gray, Kip Niven, Pat Parris, John Stephenson, Ned Wilson

THE ALAMO: 13 DAYS TO GLORY, televised January 26, 1987 NBC 3 hours

Finnegan/Pinchuk Productions; Executive producers, Stockton Briggle, Dennis D. Hennessy and Richard Carrothers; Producers, Bill and Pat Finnegan and Sheldon Pinchuk; Director, Burt Kennedy; Teleplay, Clyde Ware and Norman McLeod Morrill, based on the book *Thirteen Days to Glory: The Siege of the Alamo* by Lon Tinkle; Photography, John Elsenbach; Production designer, Ward Preston; Set decorator, Leonard Mazzola; Costume designer, Eileen Kennedy; Music, Peter Bernstein; Stunt coordinator/2nd unit director, David Cass; Editor, Michael N. Knue

James Arness (Jim Bowie); Brian Keith (Davy Crockett); Alec Baldwin (Col. William Travis); David Ogden Stiers (Colonel Black); Jim Metzler (James Bonham); Raul Julia (Gen. Santa Anna); Lorne Greene (Sam Houston); Tom Schanley (Danny); Fernando Allende (Almonte); Kathleen York (Susanna Dickinson); Isela Vega (Santa Anna's sister); Gene Evans (John McGregor); Michael Wren (Juan Seguin); Jon Lindstrom (Major Dickinson); Hinton Battle (Joe); David Sheiner (Luis); Noble Willingham (Dr. Pollard); Eloy Casados (Gregorio); Tony Becker (George Taylor); Thomas Callaway (Col. James Fannin); Buck Taylor (John Colorado Smith); Jerry Potter (Jacob Walker); Stan Ivar (Doc Sutherland); Ethan Wayne (Edward Taylor); Laura Martinez-Herring (Elena Musquiz); and Grainger Hines, Tom Everett, Jan Triska, Gary Karper,

John Furlong, Jay Baker, Dale Swann, Laura Fabian, Loyda Ramos, Del Sandre, Nicky Blair

DAVY CROCKETT, Shelley Duvall's "Tall Tales & Legends", televised September 20, 1987 Showtime 47 minutes
Platypus Productions in association with Gaylord Television Entertainment; Executive producer, Shelley Duvall; Producers, Bridget Terry and Frederic S. Fuchs; Director, David Grossman; Teleplay, Susan Denim, Jack Carrerow and Lisa A. Bannick; Production designer, Michael Erler; Costume designer, J. Allen Highfill; Music, Stephen Barber; Song performed by Mac Davis; Associate producers, Deveney Marking and Melissa Rhys Moore

Mac Davis (Davy Crockett); Adam Carl (Ben Parker); Mimi Kennedy (Mrs. Parker); McLean Stevenson (Andrew Jackson); Jane Alden (Congressman's wife); Daniel Davis (Congressman); Jennifer Joan Taylor (Polly); Gino DeMauro (Whitey); Michael McKean (Mr. Wallace)

DAVY CROCKETT: RAINBOW IN THE THUNDER, televised November 20, 1988 NBC 2 hours
Echo Cove Productions in association with Walt Disney Television; Executive producer, William Blinn; Supervising producer, Mark R. Ovitz; Producer, Frank Fischer; Director, David Hemmings; Developed and written by William Blinn; Photography, Isidore Mankofsky; Art director, Ian Thomas; Costume designer, Tom Bronson; Music, Joel McNeely; Editor, Andrew Cohen

Tim Dunigan (Davy Crockett); Johnny Cash (Col. Davy Crockett [older]); Gary Grubbs (Georgie Russel); Cheryl Arutt (Young Ory Palmer/Delia); Richard Tyson (Lute Newhouser); Samantha Eggar (Older Ory Palmer); Matt Salinger (Col. Andrew Jackson); David Hemmings (President Andrew Jackson); Jill Gamley (Mrs. Palmer); Brenda Crichlow (Mary); Jeff Irvine (Lieutenant North); Blu Mankuma (Butler); Freda Perry (Jess); Matt Walker (Woodrow Palmer)

DAVY CROCKETT: A NATURAL MAN, televised December 18, 1988 NBC 1 hour
Echo Cove Productions in association with Walt Disney Television; Executive producer, William Blinn; Supervising producer, Mark R. Ovitz; Producer, Frank Fischer; Director, Chuck Braverman; Developed by William Blinn; Teleplay, Steven Baum and Neil Alan Levy; Photography, Isidore Mankofsky; Art director, Ian Thomas; Costume designer, Tom Bronson; Music, Joel McNeely; Editor, Andrew Cohen

Tim Dunigan (Davy Crockett); Gary Grubbs (Georgie Russel); Barry Corbin (Jimmy Crockett); Molly Hagan (Mary Ann Gibbons); Jeff Irvine (Lieutenant North); Rodger Gibson (Eyes Like Sky); Stephen Dimopoulos (Hawkins)

DAVY CROCKETT: GUARDIAN SPIRIT, televised January 13, 1989 NBC 1 hour
Echo Cove Productions in association with Walt Disney Television; Executive producer, William Blinn; Supervising producer, Mark R. Ovitz; Producer, Frank Fischer; Director, Harry Falk; Developed by William Blinn; Teleplay, Robert Sonntag and Deborah Gilliland; Photography, Isidore Mankofsky; Art director, Ian Thomas; Costume designer, Tom Bronson; Music, Joel McNeely; Editor, Andrew Cohen

Tim Dunigan (Davy Crockett); Gary Grubbs (Georgie Russel); Garry Chalk (Major Benteen); Jeff Irvine (Lieutenant North); Evan Adams (Creek Boy); Henry Kingi (Creek Chief); Craig Brunanski (First Guard); Bill Croft (Second Guard)

DAVY CROCKETT: WARRIOR'S FAREWELL, televised June 18, 1989 NBC 1 hour

Echo Cove Productions in association with Walt Disney Television; Executive producer, William Blinn; Supervising producer, Mark R. Ovitz; Producer, Frank Fischer; Director, James J. Quinn; Developed and written by William Blinn; Photography, Isidore Mankofsky; Art director, Ian Thomas; Costume designer, Tom Bronson; Music, Joel McNeely; Editor, Andrew Cohen

Tim Dunigan (Davy Crockett); Gary Grubbs (Georgie Russel); Garry Chalk (Major Benteen); Jeff Irvine (Lieutenant North); Ken Swofford (Callahan); Sherri Stoner (Amy); Prudence Wright Holmes (Mrs. Pickering); Lloyd Berry (Willard); Clem Fox (Medicine Man); Maggie O'Hara (Teenage Girl); Sonny Surowiec (Young Settler)

THE DAYS OF WINE AND ROSES
A Television Play by JP Miller (1958)

Synopsis

Joe Clay is a San Francisco public relations man, required from time to time to line up party girls for clients, He stifles the acute distaste for this aspect of his job with whiskey. Meeting Kirsten Clay, a client's secretary, he is taken by her wholesome country-girl freshness, a sharp contrast to the girls he meets professionally. After a whirlwind courtship, they marry, although Kirsten, a teetotaler, is disturbed by Joe's hard drinking. They set up house-keeping and soon have a baby daughter. Under his job pressures, Joe's drinking becomes even heavier, and Kirsten is introduced to brandies alexanders. Soon she begins drinking more in self defense and both become confirmed alcoholics.

When Joe loses his job because of drunkenness, he realizes his and Kirsten's plight at the climax of a binge. He takes his family back to the country and they move in with Kirsten's father, who owns a nursery, and in a few weeks Joe and Kirsten are rehabilitated and happy, until Joe sneaks a few pints of whiskey into their bedroom and they go off on a bender. After a drunken rampage, Joe is taken to an alcoholic ward after a siege of d.t.'s. Coming out, he joins Alcoholics Anonymous, but Kirsten refuses to acknowledge her need for help, continuing to drink as her father attempts futilely to nurse her. Joe struggle for sobriety is thwarted by Kirsten and he is convinced to take his young daughter and moves away from her. A year later, he has a new job and Kirsten begs to be taken back, refusing however to admit to her alcoholism. Joe, though still desperately in love with her, finds he must refuse her and she leaves him and her daughter.

Comment and Critique

They are not long,
the days of wine and roses,
out of a misty dream
our path merges for a while,
then closes within a dream.

These gentle words of poet Ernest Dowson provided prolific television writer JP Miller with the title of his 1958 script which was produced to great acclaim on *Playhouse 90* at the start of that prestigious show's third season. *The Days of Wine and Roses* starred Cliff Robertson, Piper Laurie and Charles Bickford under the direction of John Frankenheimer. "A searching and frightening study of the tragedy of alcoholism...a brilliant and compelling work...a play of ascending power," is how *The New York Times'* Jack Gould described the drama on its premiere. "Mr. Miller's dialogue was especially fine, natural, vivid and understated. Miss Laurie's performance was enough to make the flesh crawl, yet it always elicited deep sympathy. Mr. Robertson achieved firstrate contrast between the sober man fighting to hold on and the hopeless drunk whose only courage came from the bottle...John Frankenheimer's direction was magnificent." All, however, were overlooked at Emmy Award time, although *Playhouse 90* was honored as Best Dramatic Series.

When Miller's play came to the screen four years later (minus the "The" in the title), industry eyebrows went up when all involved, save Charles Bickford, were bypassed for the film version (particularly since actors Robertson and Laurie and director Frankenheimer, who was especially disheartened), were known screen quantities equal at least to those chosen. Jack Lemmon's startling dramatic performance in the lead moved him to a new level as an actor previously known for his comedic talents. Lee Remick was equally astonishing as the alcoholic Kirsten. Both were nominated for Academy Awards. When the film opened at Radio City Music Hall at the start of 1963 (during a newspaper strike), *The New York Times'* Bosley Crowther found it "a grim, graphic, heartrending account of the agony of these two people in the clutch of booze...As a straight, ruthless visualization of an alcoholic's fate, with bouts of deterium tremens and 'dry-out' and all the rest, it is a commanding picture, and it is extremely well played by Mr. Lemmon and Miss Remick, who spare themselves none of the shameful, painful scenes." Crowther felt though that "for all their brilliant performing and the taut direction of Blake Edwards, they do not bring two pitiful characters to complete and overpowering life."

Director Blake Edwards and the film itself were overlooked at Oscar time, although nominations also went Joseph Wright and George James Hopkins for Art and Set Direction, and Don Feld for Costume Design. Powerful as the film was, it dated badly over the years. It's best remembered for Henry Mancini and Johnny Mercer's Academy Award-winning title song.

It would be three decades before Miller's play found its way to the stage and a production at the Cleveland Play House in spring 1992. "The newly written legit version has a plot similar to the screenplay Miller provided for Blake Edwards' widely seen 1962 film, except that the two characters now change from upright citizens into addicted incompetents without sufficient motivation or explanation," the *Variety* critic found. "Miller has added a potent sexuality to the new script...While it keeps things interesting, that change is insufficient reason to revive the chestnut, not least because the play treats the complex subject of alcoholism in such a simplistic fashion."

STAGE

DAYS OF WINE AND ROSES, *Cleveland Play House*, opened May 12 through June 7, 1992

Produced by the Cleveland Play House, Josephine R. Abady, artistic director; A Play in two acts by JP Miller; Director, Jack Hofsiss; Sets, David Jenkins; Lighting, Peter Kaczorowski; Costumes, Julie Weiss; Sound, Jefferson Montgomery; Production stage manager, Linda Cole

William Katt (Joe Clay); Mia Dillon (Kirsten Arnesen Clay); Christopher Wynkoop (Ellis Arnesen); Robert Hoffman (Fred Boyle)

SCREEN

DAYS OF WINE AND ROSES, *Warner Bros.*, released December 1962
Producer, Martin Manulis; Director, Blake Edwards; Screenplay, JP Miller; Photography, Philip Lathrop; Art director, Joseph Wright; Set director, George James Hopkins; Music, Henry Mancini; Title song, Henry Mancini and Johnny Mercer; Costume designer, Don Feld; Sound Jack Solomon; Editor, Patrick McCormick

Jack Lemmon (Joe Clay); Lee Remick (Kirsten Arnesen Clay); Charles Bickford (Ellis Arnesen); Jack Klugman (Jim Hungerford); Alan Hewitt (Leland); Tom Palmer (Ballefooy); Debbie Megowan (Debbie); Maxine Stewart (Dottie); Jack Albertson (Trayner); Ken Lynch (Proprietor)

TELEVISION

THE DAYS OF WINE AND ROSES, *Playhouse 90*, televised October 2, 1958 CBS 90 minutes
Producer, Fred Coe; Director, John Frankenheimer; Teleplay, JP Miller

Cliff Robertson (Joe Clay); Piper Laurie (Kirsten Arnesen Clay); Charles Bickford (Ellis Arnesen); Malcolm Atterbury (Jim Hungerford); Marc Lawrence (Scarface); Martha Wentworth (Mrs. Nolan)

DESTRY RIDES AGAIN

Various adaptations of the novel by Max Brand (Frederick Faust)(1930)

Synopsis

In lawless Bottleneck, a slick gambler named Kent, the town boss and owner of the Last Chance Saloon, uses his seductive entertainer, Frenchy, and her girls to lure ranchers into high stake poker games. After Sheriff Keogh is killed, Wash Dimsdale, the town drunk, is approached as his replacement. Wash sends for law-man Thomas Jefferson Destry, son of his a famous gunfighter and his old sidekick, to be his deputy and help bring law and order to Bottleneck. Tom Destry arrives by stagecoach with Janice Tyndall and Jack, her cattleman brother. Aware that the deceptively lackadaisical Destry carries no guns, and hearing that he's there to help clean up the town, Frenchy offers him a mop and a pail of water. When Lilybelle Callahan and Frenchy get into a knockdown fight over Lilybelle's husband Boris' pants, lost to Frenchy in a poker game, Destry dumps the pail of water over the battling females. He finally straps on his guns and wins the support of the townsfolk after Wash is killed by Kent's henchmen, and Frenchy joins him in enlisting the aid of the women of the town. Led by Destry and Frenchy, the townspeople march to the saloon. Kent shoots at Destry but Frenchy steps in front of him and is killed. Destry guns down Kent, brings peace and respectability to Bottleneck, and makes plans to marry Janice Tyndall.

Comment and Critique

Frederick Schiller Faust was a prolific writer of Western tales, most of them published by Street and Smith in *Western Story* magazine. Faust wrote under nineteen pseudonyms, the best known of which was Max Brand, author of *Destry Rides Again*. It originally was titled *Twelve Peers* and published in six installments in *Western Story* beginning February 1, 1930. The following August, Dodd, Mead published the book as *Destry Rides Again*. During World War II, Faust (Max Brand) was severely wounded by a German shell on May 11, 1944, and died the next day at age fifty-one.

The above synopsis of *Destry Rides Again* is the most familiar version of the Brand book, adapted for the popular 1939 Universal film by Felix Jackson, Gertrude Purcell and Henry Myers, although much truer to Brand's story was Tom Mix's 1932 screen version. Max Brand's original was set in the town of Wham, where Harrison Destry is framed and sent to prison for six years. After Destry's release, he returns to Wham and the First Chance Saloon to hunt down the twelve men of the jury which sentenced him. Betrayed by his best friend but still accomplishing his mission, Destry is reunited with his sweetheart, Charlotte "Charlie" Dangerfield. Brand ended his lively story with "...it meant the end of the old days and the beginning of a new regime in Wham, for Harrison Destry had put away his colt."

Two years after the publication of Brand's novel, Universal bought the story for Tom Mix, then fifty-three years old. Mix was the pride of Mix's Run, Pennsylvania, where he was born on January 6, 1879. He had first appeared in motion pictures for Selig in 1910, and after the retirement of William S. Hart, Mix became Hollywood's top Western star with his "Wonder Horse," Tony. After two decades of starring in wellproduced Westerns, mainly for Fox Studio, Mix made the transition to the talking screen. *Destry Rides Again* arguably was the best of Mix's talkies and was later reissued as *Justice Rides Again* after the famous Marlene Dietrich/James Stewart remake in 1939.

Marlene Dietrich made her American screen debut in 1930 in Paramount's *Morocco*, followed by a series of highly glamorized films directed by her mentor, Josef von Sternberg. It established her as an international film star, but her career began to sputter after her 1937 Ernst Lubitch-directed *Angel*. She accepted a relatively low salary to appear in Universal's remake of *Destry Rides Again*, replacing the originally advertised star, Paulette Goddard (who played the role on the Lux Radio Theatre in 1941), and found her career tremendously revived. The film also boosted the burgeoning screen career of second-billed James Stewart.

"Marlene Dietrich is the life of the part in *Destry Rides Again* and turns this fastmoving, old-time, hokum Western into a whopping comedy-melodrama, chock-full of fun, action, excitement and jamboree," *Cue* Magazine's Jesse Zunser enthused. "It's familiar stuff, true enough, but still good, as it is whammed across the screen." In *The New Yorker*, critic John Mosher wrote, "As a frontier siren of a Bloody Gulch saloon, Marlene Dietrich manages to be the heart and soul of a good old-fashioned Western which has everything in it except Indians, and Madame Dietrich makes up for that easy enough...Her scrap with Una Merkel, which is being so much talked about, isn't overestimated, and no one can see it and not believe the ladies weren't carried off the set in litters...*Destry Rides Again* holds its other surprises, one of them being the presentation of James Stewart..."

Frank S. Nugent (*The New York Times*) found the film "a jaunty and amusing chronicle with the novelty of finding a Dietrich and a Stewart in it playing it as wisely as though their names were Mr. and Mrs Hoot Gibson...Good fun, every minute of it." Howard Barnes added in the *New York Herald Tribune*: "The continuity is full of the usual Wild West hokum, but it has been handled with such exuberant good humor and with such telling melodramatic effect that the motion picture, instead of being a latter-day reprint of a successful formula, is one of the best examples of its genre."

Destry Rides Again was recycled by Universal in 1950 as *Frenchie* with Joel McCrea and Shelley Winters. A thinly-disguised adaptation as "story and screenplay by Oscar Brodney" (no mention of Max Brand), it had as its highlight a recreation of the famed Dietrich/Merkel brawl here performed by Shelley Winters and Marie Windsor. The studio's "official" remake came in 1954, with George Marshall once again directing (he had done the 1939 version). This Technicolor scene for scene remake using the same script merely changed the name of the town to Restful and the film's title to *Destry*. One critic noted: "It is now apparent that the wit and sophistication of the earlier film were due almost entirely to its stars, Marlene Dietrich and James Stewart. Audie Murphy offers his own kind of charm; Mari Blanchard, with her wild attempts to be hoydenish, has fewer attractions; but the impression is of a school revival of the original production."

Leonard Gershe adapted Max Brand's *Destry Rides Again* to the musical stage in 1959, with Harold Rome contributing the score. Starring Andy Griffith and Dolores Gray, with Scott Brady (replacing John Ireland) as the villainous Kent, the lively Western ran for 472 performances on Broadway. John Chapman (*Daily News*) called it "a ripsnorting musical...one word review of *Destry Rides Again*: Yippee!!!" Critical acclaim was showered on director/choreographer Michael Kidd's staging, and critic Chapman added, "Kidd's staging of *Destry* is electric, and he has found a remarkable company of singing dancers to do the work."

Robert Coleman, critic for the *Daily Mirror*, found the show "A musical whirlwind...It takes courage to transfer a film epic to the stage, for comparisons are inevitable. But Leonard Gershe has fashioned a taut book form the story by Max Brand, and Harold Rome has composed lyrics that make points and music that races the pulses...[it] is a riproaring rouser." In the *Journal-American*, John McClain thought *Destry Rides Again* to be the best musical of the season. "It has size and style, the most rousing ensemble numbers since *West Side Story*, and a surprisingly proficient book... *Destry* is not a milestone on the musical thruway by any means, but it will do until a better one comes down the pike."

In the thumbs-down corner was Brooks Atkinson, who reported in *The New York Times*: "By loyally working together, a regiment of dedicated show people have, indeed, made a Western out of *Destry Rides Again*...All this talent and labor have been squandered on a conventional Western story...There are times when it seems to be a cartoon on the Western stencil...Some fine talent has been wasted on unimaginative material." And Walter Kerr found in the *Herald Tribune*, "There is little genuine exuberance beneath the frenzies that have kept the front curtain whipping back and forth; there is simply skill. *Destry* does everything well except make you care. For some reason, fondness has been finessed right out of it."

Tony Award nominations for *Destry Rides Again* went to Andy Griffith and Dolores Gray as Best Actor and Actress in a Musical (they lost, respectively, to Jackie Gleason for *Take Me Along!* and Mary Martin for *The Sound of Music*) and to Michael Kidd as Best Director. Kidd won the Tony for his choreography. The musical itself went on to become a staple in summer stock in the early 1960s, but then disappeared from the circuit.

Universal Television's *Destry* series, starring John Gavin (later to be U.S. Ambassador to Mexico) in the title role, premiered in mid-February 1964. ABC advertised it as "one of the West's all-time reluctant heroes in a new Western with a sense of humor. Jack Gould, in *The New York Times*, detected "a nominal if not substantive relation to Max Brand's *Destry Rides Again* [which] turned into a pedestrian telling of an awkward adventure." The series made it through thirteen episodes before being cancelled.

STAGE

DESTRY RIDES AGAIN, *Imperial Theatre*, New York, opened April 23, 1959 472 performances

Produced by David Merrick in association with Max Brown; A Musical Comedy; Director and Choreographer, Michael Kidd; Book by Leonard Gershe, based on the story by Max Brand; Music and lyrics by Harold Rome; Production designer, Oliver Smith; Lighting, Jean Rosenthal; Costumes, Alvin Colt; Musical direction and vocal arrangements, Lehman Engel; Orchestrations, Philip J. Lang; Dance music arranged by Genevieve Pitot; Hairstylist, Ernest Adler; Directorial assistants, Deedee Wood and Marc Breaux; General manager, Jack Schlissel; Company manager, Joe Roth; Stage managers, Neil Hartley, Leonard Patrick and Ben Janney

Andy Griffith (Tom Destry); Dolores Gray (Frenchy); Scott Brady (Kent); Jack Prince (Wash); Libi Staiger (Chloe); Marc Breaux (Gyp Watson); Swen Swenson (Bugs Watson); George Reeder (Rockwell); Oran Osburn (Sheriff Keogh); Don McHenry (Mayor Slade); Elizabeth Watts (Rose Lovejoy); Nolan Van Way (Jack Tyndall); Reiko Sato (Ming Li); Ray Mason (Bartender); Don Crabtree (Claggert); Chad Block (Stage driver); May Muth (Mrs. Claggert); Rosetta Le Noire (Clara); Sharon Stone (Dimples); Ray Mason (Bailey); Don Crabtree, David London, Lanier Davis, Nolan Van Way (Prologue); Lynne Broadhurst, Joan Broderick, Shelah Hackett, Reiko Sato, Sharon Shore, Carol Stevens (Rose Lovejoy's girls); Shelly Chaplan, Lillian D'Honau, Maureen Hopkins, Betty Jenkins, Jillana, Andrina Miller, Shirley Nelson, Adriane Rogers, Carol Warner (Frenchy's girls); Jack Beaber, Chad Block, Mel Davidson, Al Lanti, Ken Malone, Frank Pietri, John Ray, Larry Roquemore, Merritt Thompson (Cowboys); Maria Graziano, Betty Kent, Sheila Mathews, May Muth, Don Crabtree, Lanier Davis, Ralph Farnworth, David London, Ray Mason, Oran Osburn, Nolan Van Way (Townsfolk)

MUSICAL NUMBERS: "Bottleneck"; "Ladies"; "Hoopde-Dingle"; "Tomorrow Morning"; "Ballad of the Gun"; "The Social"; "I Know Your Kind"; "I Hate Him"; "Rose Lovejoy of Paradise Alley"; "Anyone Would Love You"; "Once Knew a Fella"; "Every Once in a While"; "Fair Warning"; "Are You Ready, Gyp Watson?"; "Not Guilty"; "Only Time Will Tell"; "Respectability"; "That Ring on the Finger"; "Once Knew a Fella" (reprise); "I Say Hello"; "Ballad of the Gun" (finale)

Dropped from production during pre-Broadway tryout in Philadelphia and Boston: "A Handy Thing"; "The Smile Song"; "A Good, Good Thing"

Original cast recording: Decca Records

National Company, opened *Riviera Theatre*, Las Vegas, July 31, 1960; closed *O'Keefe Theatre*, Toronto, January 28, 1961

Produced by David Merrick in association with Max Brown; A Musical Comedy; Directed and choreographed by Michael Kidd; Book by Leonard Gershe, based on the story by Max Brand; Music and lyrics by Harold Rome; Production design, Oliver Smith; Lighting, Jean Rosenthal; Costumes, Alvin Colt; Dancing supervised by Shirley Nelson and Ben Vargas; Musical director, John Passaretti (succeeded by Shepherd Coleman, Louis Adrian); Orchestrations, Philip J. Lang); Dance music arranged by Genevieve Pitot; Production restaged and supervised by Leonard

Patrick; Production manager, George Eckert; Company manager, Tom Powers (succeeded by Manny Davis); Stage managers, Neil Hartley, George Wagner, Larry Pool and Jose Falcion

Gene Barry (succeeded by John Raitt, Stephen Douglass) (Tom Destry); Monique Van Vooren (succeeded by Anne Jeffreys, Gretchen Wyler) (Frenchy); Philip Reed (succeeded by Warde Donovan) (Kent); Tom Tully (succeeded by Edward Atienza) (Wash); Gene Kelton (Gyp Watson); James Weiss (Bugs Watson); Jose Falcion (Rockwell); Edmund Lyndeck (succeeded by Alan MacAteer) (Mayor Slade); Ethel Woodruff (Rose Lovejoy); Herb Mazzini (Jack Tyndall); Richard Holland (Bartender); Ian Bruce (succeeded by Hugh Brown) (Stagecoach driver); Misay (succeeded by Mei Ling Lee) (Ming Li); Robert Maxwell (Claggett); Eleanor Edie (Mrs. Claggett); Alyce Webb (Clara); Dugan Miller (Bailey); Lynn Broadhurst (succeeded by Sally Mortimer) (Dimples); Charles Dunn, John Roberson, Charles Scott, Herb Mazzini (Prologue); Lynn Broadhurst (succeeded by Martha Aguilar), Geralyn Donald, Alice Glenn (succeeded by Pat Colgate), Sally Mortimer, Toni Reither, Missy (succeeded by Mei Ling Lee) (Rose Lovejoy's girls); Renee Byrns, Shelly Chaplan, Marilyn Holland, Joan Hardy (succeeded by Rachelle Reyes), Betty Jenkins, Patti Kelton, Shirley Nelson, Carol Warner (Frenchy's girls); Ted August, Ian Bruce, Allen Byrns, Gene Cooper, Salador Juarez, Jerry Norman (succeeded by Clyde Laurents), John Rager, Andre St. John (Cowboys); Francesca Bell (succeeded by Marilyn Thomas), Eleanor Edie, Nancy Leighton, Phyllis Young, Hugh Brown, Charles Dunn, Dick Holland, Robert Maxwell, Herb Mazzini, Flynn McDonnell, Dugan Miller, John Roberson, Charles Scott (Townsfolk)

Touring Company, summer 1961

Produced by Lee Guber, Frank Ford and Shelly Gross; A Musical Comedy; Director, Jerome Eskew; Book by Leonard Gershe, based on the story by Max Brand; Music and lyrics by Harold Rome; Production design, Warwick Brown; Lighting, Lester Tapper; Costumes, Joseph Codori; Choreography, Bill Foster; Musical director, Phillip Ingalls

Jimmy Dean (Tom Destry); Monique Van Vooren (Frenchy); Earl Hammond (Kent); Bill Griffis (Wash); James Hutchinson (Gyp Watson); Ed Collins (Bugs Watson); Kip Andrews (Rockwell); Ned Wertimer (Mayor Slade); Richard Nieves (Sheriff Keogh); Lulu Bates (Rose Lovejoy); John Minto (Jack Tyndall); Rochelle Ross (Ming Li); Rosemary O'Shea (Chloe); Lila Herbert (Mrs. Claggett); Eulabelle Moore (Clara); Richard Nieves (Stagecoach driver); Larry Benson (Bartender); Geri Spinner (Dimples); Kay Brower, Roy Becker, Bob Becker, John Chiapuris, Larry Benson, Phyllis Ford, Wendel Gray, Lila Herbert, Violeta Landek, John Minto, Rosemary O'Shea, Richard Nieves, Gene Foote, June Eve Stony, Geri Spinner, Rochelle Ross, Vilma Vaccaro (Ensemble)

Touring Company, summer 1961

Produced by Melody Fair, Lewis T. Fisher, producer; A Musical Comedy; Director, Richard Casey; Book by Leonard Gershe, based on the story by Max Brand; Music and lyrics by Harold Rome; Settings, Robert Motley; Lighting, David Zierk; Costume coordinator, Richard Kalwicki; Choreography and musical staging, Peter Hamilton; Musical and choral direction, Harry Fuchs; Stage manager, James Boyd

Jack Irwin (Tom Destry); Libi Staiger (Frenchy); James Luisi (Kent); Keith Kaldenberg (Wash); Stefan Zema (Gyp Watson); Will Nagel (Bugs Watson); Glenn Gibson (Rockwell); Dan Merriman (Mayor Slade); Murray Olson (Sheriff

Keogh); Lawrence Hanratty (Claggett); Mirra Hinson (Mrs. Claggett); Herb Pordom (Jack Tyndall); Irene Byatt (Rose Lovejoy); Georgia Phillips (Chloe); Ben Reed (Bailey); Alyce Webb (Clara); Birgitta Kiviniemi (Ming Li); Kenneth Chapman (Stagecoach driver); Brian Crabb (Bartender); Nancy Robson (Dimples); Herb Pordam, Ben Reed, Murray Olson (Prologue); Herb Pordam, Brian Crabb, Ben Reed, Joseph Ilardo, Robert Ellinwood, Murray Olson, Penny Gasten, Mara Wirt, Joanne Myhal, Muriel James, Mirra Hanson, Sara Lynn Jansson, Dimitry Cheremeteff, William Martin-Viscount, Kenneth Chapman, Nancy Robson, Birgitta Kiviniemi, Elyse Zorgo, Gayle Lepine, Doug Weese (Ensemble)

St. Louis (Mo.) Municipal Opera Theatre, opened July 17, 1961
Produced by the Municipal Opera Theatre Association of St. Louis, John Kennedy, producer; A Musical Play; Director, James Vincent Russo; Book by Leonard Gershe, based on the story by Max Brand; Music and lyrics by Harolds Rome; Settings, Paul C. McGuire; Costumes, Bill Hargate; Choreography and ensembles by Dan M. Eckley; Musical director, Edwin McArthur; Musical numbers staged by Marc Breaux

Tom Poston (Tom Destry); Anne Jeffreys (Frenchy); Edmund Lyndeck (Kent); Edwin Steffe (Wash); Wayne McIntire (Sheriff Keogh); F.J. O'Neil (Mayor Slade); Marc Breaux (Gyp Watson); James Weiss (Bugs Watson); Alan Byrnes (Rockwell); Graham Green (Jack Tyndall); Walter Richardson (Claggett); Mary V. Cook (Mrs. Claggett); Rosetta Le Noire (Clara); Elizabeth Watts (Rose Lovejoy); Lila Gage (Chloe); Pablo Flores (Bartender); James Flynn (Stagecoach driver); Linda Shapiro (Ming Li); Robert Kelly (Bailey)

SCREEN

DESTRY RIDES AGAIN, Universal Pictures, released April 1932
A Carl Laemmle production; Producer, Stanley Bergerman; Directors, Ben Stoloff, Alan James; Screenplay, Isidore Bernstein, based on the novel by Max Brand; Dialogue, Robert Keith; Photography, Daniel N. Clark; Art director, Thomas F. O'Neil; Sound, C. Roy Hunter; Editors, Maurice Pivar and Arthur Hilton

Tom Mix (Tom Destry); Claudia Dell (Sally Dangerfield); Earle Foxe (Brent); Stanley Fields (Sheriff Wendell); ZaSu Pitts (Temperance worker); Andy Devine (Stagecoach passenger); Frederick Howard (Clifton); George Ernest (Willie); Francis Ford (Judd Ogden); Edward Piel, Sr. (Warren); John Ince (The Judge); Edward LeSaint (Mr. Dangerfield); Charles K. French (Jury foreman); Tony, the Wonder Horse (Himself)

DESTRY RIDES AGAIN, Universal Pictures, released November 1939
Produced by Joe Pasternak; Director, George Marshall; Screenplay, Felix Jackson, Gertrude Purcell and Henry Myers, based on the novel by Max Brand; Photography, Hal Mohr; Art director, Jack Otterson; Marlene Dietrich's costumes, Vera West; Music, Frank Skinner; Music director, Charles Previn; Songs by Frederick Hollander and Frank Loesser; Assistant director, Vernon Keays; Sound, Bernard B. Brown; Editor, Milton Carruth

Marlene Dietrich (Frenchy); James Stewart (Tom Destry); Brian Donlevy (Kent); Charles Winninger (Wash Dimsdale); Irene Hervey (Janice Tyndall); Una Merkel (Lilybelle Callahan); Mischa Auer (Boris Callahan); Allen Jenkins (Bugs Watson); Warren Hymer (Gyp Watson); Jack Carson (Jack Tyndall); Samuel S. Hinds (Judge Hiram J. Slade); Lillian Yarbo (Clara); Tom Fadden (Lem Claggett);

Virginia Brissac (Ma Claggett); Dickie Jones (Eli Whitney Claggett); Joe King (Sheriff Keogh); Ann Todd (Claggett's girl); Billy Gilbert (Loupgaru the Bartender); Edmund MacDonald (Rockwell); Harry Cording (Rowdy); Minerva Urecal (Mrs. DeWitt); and Carmen D'Antonio, Dick Alexander, Bob McKenzie, Billy Bletcher, Lloyd Ingraham, Bill Cody, Jr., Bill Steele Gettinger, Bud McClure, Harry Tenbrook, Alex Voloshin, Chief John Big Tree, Loren Brown, Harold DeCarro, Robert Keith, Dora Clement, Philo McCullough, Mary Shannon

SONGS: "Little Joe Wrangler"; "You've Got That Look"; "She What the Boys in the Back Room Will Have"; "I've Been in Love Before"

FRENCHIE, Universal-International Pictures, released December 1950
Producer, Michael Kraike; Director, Louis King; Story and screenplay by Oscar Brodney, based (uncredited) on *Destry Rides Again* by Max Brand; Photography, Maury Gertsman; Art directors, Bernard Herzbrun and Alexander Golitzen; Costumes, Yvonne Wood; Set decoration, Russell A. Gausman and Oliver Emert; Makeup, Bud Westmore; Music, Hans Salter; Editor, Ted J. Kent

Joel McCrea (Tom Banning); Shelley Winters (Frenchie Fontaine); Paul Kelly (Pete Lambert); Elsa Lanchester (Countess); Marie Windsor (Diane Gorman); John Russell (Lance Cole); John Emery (Clyde Gorman); George Cleveland (Jeff Harding); Regis Toomey (Carter); Paul E. Burns (Rednose); Frank Ferguson (Jim Dobbs); Vincent Renno (Tony); Larry Dobkin (Bartender); Lucille Barkley (Dealer)

DESTRY, Universal-International Pictures, released December 1954
Producer, Stanley Rubin; Director, George Marshall; Screenplay, Edmund H. North and D. D. Beauchamp, based on a story by Felix Jackson suggested by *Destry Rides Again* by Max Brand; Photography, George Robinson; Art directors, Alexander Golitzen and Alfred Sweeney; Costumes, Rosemary Odell; Choreographer, Kenny Williams; Music supervision, Joseph Gershenson; Songs "Empty Arms," "If You Can Can-Can" and "Bang! Bang!" by Arnold Hughes and Frederick Herbert; Sound, Leslie I. Carey; Editor, Ted J. Kent

Audie Murphy (Tom Destry); Mari Blanchard (Brandy); Thomas Mitchell (Rags Barnaby); Lyle Bettger (Decker); Lori Nelson (Martha Phillips); Edgar Buchanan (Mayor Hiram Sellers); Wallace Ford (Doc Curtis); Mary Wickes (Bessie Mae Curtis); Alan Hale, Jr. (Jack Larson); Lee Aaker (Eli Skinner); Trevor Bardette (Sheriff Joe Bailey); Walter Baldwin (Henry Skinner); George Wallace (Curley); Dick Reeves (Mac); Frank Richards (Dummy); Mitch Lawrence (Dealer); Ralph Peters (Bartender); John Doucette (Cowhand)

TELEVISION

DESTRY, televised February 14 to May 9, 1964 ABC Series 1 hour each
Produced by Universal Television; Producers, Howard Browne and Frank Telford; Directors, Donald Siegel and others; Teleplay, Robert Guy Burrows and others; Photography, Lionel Lindon; Art director, Raymond Beal; Music supervision, Stanley Wilson; Associate producer, Carter De Haven III; Editor, Richard M. Sprague

John Gavin (Tom Destry); plus assorted guest stars during the thirteen week series

DISRAELI
A Drama by Louis Napoleon Parker (1911)

Synopsis

England's Prime Minister Benjamin Disraeli is attempting to negotiate the purchase of Egypt's Suez Canal for the Queen, aware that it is "the Key to India." Mrs. Noel Travers, working for the opposing Russians, persuades Sir Michael Probert of the Bank of England to refuse the necessary financial backing for Disraeli's acquisition. Also standing in the way is his diplomatic struggle with his Liberal opponent, Sir William Gladstone, but Disraeli, called "the Sphinx of the Victorian Era," secures a loan from Jewish banker Hugh Meyers and sends his secretary Charles, Lord Deeford, to Cairo with Meyers' check, thereby securing controlling interest in the canal. Learning that Meyers is facing bankruptcy, Disraeli coerces Sir Michael into honoring Meyers' check at the Bank of England. Having assured her title of "Empress of India," Queen Victoria honors Disraeli at a reception at 10 Downing Street.

Comment and Critique

In 1910, actor George Arliss suggested a play on Benjamin Disraeli to producer George Tyler, who recommended playwright Louis Napoleon Parker to develop the material. Rehearsals for *Disraeli* began at the end of December, and the play starring Arliss opened at Montreal's Princess Theatre on the following January. After a successful Chicago engagement, *Disraeli* opened on Broadway at Wallack's Theatre in September. Arliss devised his own makeup for the role on the eminent British Prime Minister, and Elsie Leslie, Broadway's original *Little Lord Fauntleroy*, played Lady Clarissa. Arliss went on to play the starring role for the next five theatrical seasons.

In his work's preface, Louis N. Parker noted: "This is not a historical play, but only an attempt to show a picture of the days -- not so very long ago -- in which Disraeli lived, and some of the racial, social and political prejudices he fought against and conquered."

Of the play, the *New York Dramatic Mirror* reported, "Mr. Parker has evoked the character that he sought to portray, and with the help of painstaking work by the actors, he has created a play full of decided intellectual interest. Although he has not neglected dramatic effectiveness, it is subordinate to historical appeal as far as expediency permits. No other actor on our stage is so superlatively qualified for such a role as George Arliss. His makeup was a triumph, and his assumption of Disraeli's mannerisms was as complete as his own personality allowed."

Theatre magazine was less laudable: "Mr. Arliss received elsewhere a great deal of praise for his Prime Minister, but there are those who will insist, in spite of a masterly mask, that he has utterly missed the spirit of the proud and powerful few. and has submitted therefore the stage tricks and resources of a very capable character actor."

The New York Times critic described Arliss' Disraeli as "a highly finished portrait of an appealing and interesting character -- which will be chiefly responsible for the success of Mr. Parker's latest play...No one on our stage knows better than he how to make the blend of craft and charm, to convey the sense of latent power, which picturing a superficial softness of demeanor...Mr. Arliss' makeup is again a veritable triumph, and it would seem that, as far as anyone could do it, he conveys the pictorial suggestion needed to complete illusion."

Brilliant statesman and novelist Benjamin Disraeli (the family name originally was D'Israeli) was born of Jewish parents in London on December 21, 1804. He died at his home on Curzon Street in London on April 19, 1881, when George Arliss was thirteen years old. Augustus George Arliss-Andrews was born on Good Friday, April 10, 1868, on Duke Street in London's Bloomsbury section. On September 16, 1899, Arliss married his frequent leading lady on stage and screen, Florence Montgomery.

Arliss first came to America in January 1902 with Mrs. Patrick Campbell's Repertory Company. He later became Mrs. Minnie Maddern Fiske's leading man and starred on Broadway in Ferenc Molnar's 1908 comedy *The Devil*. He went on to receive acclaim in William Archer's 1921 drama *The Green Goddess* and in John Galsworthy's 1924 play *Old English*, among others. In 1928, after appearing on Broadway and touring as Shylock in *The Merchant of Venice*, Arliss retired from the stage.

Elswyth Thane (Mrs. William Beebe) wrote a play in 1934 depicting the early life of Benjamin Disraeli. Called *Young Mr. Disraeli*, it opened in London in November. *The London Times* found it unpromising, reporting, "It is true the play might have been about anyone else, for except that the effect of Disraeli's maiden speech is reported, there is no chance to imagine him at work, but his romance is related with discretion and without extravagance." (Alexander Korda in 1935 announced plans to film *Young Mr. Disraeli*, but the project was abandoned.)

Three years later, on November 10, 1937, *Young Mr. Disraeli* opened on Broadway at the Fulton Theatre. Derrick de Marney, who had the starring role in London, repeated it in New York. Brooks Atkinson wrote in *The New York Times*: "Faultless is the word for Elswyth Thane's *Young Mr. Disraeli*...But Disraeli, who loved subtlety and brilliance would be the first to declare that faultlessness and conscientiousness are not enough in public performance...A sober writer, Mrs. Beebe catches little of his brilliance or tempestuousness in the dialogue...Dizzy would be bored by this picture of himself."

Newsweek found the play "an exhibit which amounts to a succession of interminable speeches by its central character, describing the exciting things he has done in the immediate past and the exciting things he plans to do in the future. What movement there is, is confined solely to the profuse Hebraic gesticulations with which he accompanies his oratory. If ever there was an actor it was Disraeli, and if ever there was an actor double-plus, it is the Derrick de Marney who depicts him on this occasion. The combines impression [is] of a historic battle to the death between a barnstorming mongoose and a grease-paint snake."

George Arliss began his screen career in 1921 with *The Devil* and would later appear in film versions of his Broadway successes -- not once but twice. His *Disraeli* was brought to the screen in 1921 and remade as a talkie in 1929. *The Green Goddess*, filmed initially in 1923, was remade for the talking screen in 1930, the same year Arliss also starred for Warner Bros. in *Old English*. Arliss also starred in both the silent (1922) and sound (1932) versions of *The Man Who Played God*, adapted from Gouverneur Morris' short story *The Silent Voice* and Jules Eckert Goodman's play of the same name. Ironically, *Disraeli* first had been filmed in England in 1916 while George Arliss was still portraying the eminent statesman on America's stages.

Of Warners' 1929 *Disraeli*, critic Burns Mantle wrote: "The screen version of this drama and Mr. Arliss' performance therein probably had more to do with raising the standards of acting on the screen and more to do with cultivating an appreciation of the difference between true characterization and mugging in makeup before the camera, than any other drama that has figured in the growth of the talking picture. Disraeli and the Arliss performance were the first audible screen features that sold themselves on their merit than on the strength of circus advertising."

Harry Evans (*Life* Magazine) determined: "The talkies can perform no more important function than to preserve a permanent record of the stage personalities of great actors. In doing this they justify forgiveness for their manifold sins. It would have been a pity indeed if the Disraeli of George Arliss had been denied to posterity and to dramatic patrons of the present generation who have not been privileged to see Mr. Arliss give this remarkable piece of work on the stage...he plays the role with an impressive vigor and attention to detail that should live as a lesson in dramatics for ambitious young screen actors. The shading and color of Mr. Arliss' speeches and gestures differ from the average movie performance as a Rembrandt does from a magazine cover."

George Arliss won the Academy Award in 1929-30 for his portrayal of Disraeli (he also was nominated for *The Green Goddess* that year). Oscar nominations went to the film itself as Best Picture (it lost to *All Quiet on the Western Front*) and to Julian Josephson for his screenplay. There were only seven award categories in those days, and the ceremonies took less than fifteen minutes!

Based on a screenplay by Brock Williams and Michael Hogan, the British-made *The Prime Minister* (1941) starred John Gielgud as Disraeli. When it got to this country the following year, *The New York Times*' Bosley Crowther noted: "Considering the fact that Disraeli and George Arliss are synonymous in many minds, it seems almost effrontery that any other actor should attempt a full-length screen portrait of the great British statesman, yet that is what the young English actor, John Gielgud, has boldly essayed...To say that the young man has failed woefully to present a convincing or captivating character is simply to say that he is being repaid for his audacity. For on one can play Disraeli as George Arliss plays himself...It is not alone that Mr. Gielgud atrociously overacts, [the fault] is that *The Prime Minister* lacks dramatic structure utterly."

In his 1971 biography, *John Gielgud* (Random House), Ronald Hayman wrote, "The script was uninspired but John liked the part and accepted, though he knew it would be hard to rival George Arliss' famous characterization of Disraeli in the play and the film. As John afterwards discovered, the new scenarios had been written for Hollywood and been turned down by various film stars. It now had to be made on a very small budget...Often he has to play young scenes in the morning and old scenes in the afternoon...The blitz was just starting, so the extras were anxious to finish at Teddington early...Scenes were therefore set up and filmed very hastily and John did not get sufficient time to study his lines, many of them long excerpts from political speeches."

Other Disraelis on the screen included Arliss' stage rival Derrick de Marney, who played the part opposite Anna Neagle in both *Victoria the Great* (1937) and its sequel *Sixty Glorious Years* (1938), and Alec Guinness, Disraeli to Irene Dunne's Victoria in *The Mudlark* (1950). Of this production, which premiered in New York on Christmas Day 1950, Bosley Crowther wrote in *The New York Times*: "In the role of Disraeli, Alec Guinness gives a brilliant performance...endowing the famous British statesman with great shrewdness and eloquence. His rhythmic and clever histrionics in one long Parliamentary speech account for one of the most enjoyable passages in this show. Along side of his, the performance of Irene Dunne in the Victoria role is labored and superficial."

On television, Trevor Howard starred as the statesman in *The Invincible Mr. Disraeli* opposite Greer Garson on *Hallmark Hall of Fame* in the spring of 1963. In *Show* Magazine, critic Myra Magid felt that James Lee's teleplay "took some liberties with historic chronology to tell the complete story of Benjamin Disraeli" including "his identification with Jews despite an early conversion to Christianity." Magid cited Disraeli's retort to the taunting of a rival M.P. "Yes, I am a Jew, and when the ancestors of the Right Honourable gentleman were brutal savages in an unknown island, mine were priests in the Temple of Solomon." Summing up, she found the telecast "an outstanding original drama on an important subject."

Masterpiece Theatre presented BBC's superb four-part *Disraeli* in 1980 with talented British actor Ian McShane in the lead. John J. O'Connor said in *The New York Times*: "Much of this *Disraeli* is first rate. Mr. McShane brilliantly captures the character's ambitions and genius. Mary Peach is adorable as the ostensibly flighty Mary Anne. And, as is usual with BBC productions, the costumes and sets are splendid. But there are flaws. As Queen Victoria, Rosemary Leach has the misfortune to resemble Charlotte Rae preparing for a comedy routine...On balance, however, Disraeli is very much worth watching."

STAGE

DISRAELI, *Wallack's Theatre*, New York, opened September 18, 1911 280 performances

Produced by Lieber & Company; A Play written and directed by Louis Napoleon Parker; Associate director, Hugh Ford; Scenery, Gates and Morange; Costumes, Ramsey; Musical director, Harry Braham; Managing director, George C. Tyler; Stage manager, Dudley Digges

George Arliss (The Right Honourable Benjamin Disraeli, the Earl of Beaconsfield); Marguerite St. John (Lady Beaconsfield); Margaret Dale (Mrs. Noel Travers); Elsie Leslie (Lady Clarissa Pevensey); Ian MacLaren (Charles, Viscount Deeford); J.R. Torrens (Adolphus, Viscount Cudworth); Frances Reeve (Lady Cudworth); Guy Cunningham (Lord Brooke of Brooke-hill); Marie R. Quinn (Lady Brooke); Herbert Standing (Sir Michael Probert); Alexander Calvert (Mrs. Lumley Foljambe); J. L. Mackay (succeeded by Oscar Adye) (Mr. Hugh Meyers); Harry Chessman (Butler at Glastonbury Towers); George Reeves (Footman at Glastonbury Towers); Douglas Ross (Bascot, Disraeli's Butler); St. Clair Bayfield (Potter, Disraeli's Gardener); Rutherford Herman (Flooks); Dudley Digges (Clerk)

Touring Company, season 1912-13

Produced by Lieber & Company; A Play written and directed by Louis Napoleon Parker; Scenery, Gates and Morange; Costumes, Ramsey; Managing director, George C. Tyler; Stage managers, Frederick Stanhope and Dudley Digges

George Arliss (The Right Honourable Benjamin Disraeli); Florence Arliss (Lady Beaconsfield); Margaret Dale (Mrs. Noel Travers); Violet Heming (Lady Clarissa Pevensey); Arthur Eldred (Charles, Viscount Deeford); Henry Carvill (The Duke of Glastonbury); Leila Repton (The Duchess of Glastonbury); Harold Thomas (Adolphus, Viscount Cudworth); Lilla Campbell (Lady Cudworth); Noel Tearle (Lord Brooke of Brookehill); Marie R. Quinn (Lady Brooke); Charles Harbury (Sir Michael Probert); Dudley Digges (Mr. Lumley Foljambe); Oscar Adye (Mr. Hugh Meyers); Harry Chessman (Butler at Glastonbury Towers); Martin Greene (Footman at Glastonbury Towers); Douglass Moore (Bascot, Disraeli's butler); St. Clair Bayfield (Potter, Disraeli's gardener); Edmund Gorst (Flooks); Noel Arnold (A Clerk)

DISRAELI, *Metropolitan Theatre*, London, opened May 26, 1913

A Dramatic Sketch in two episodes by John Lawson and Samuel Gordon, based on the life of Benjamin Disraeli

John Lawson (Disraeli, Earl of Beaconsfield); W.A. James (Drummond); C.W. Somerset (Aguillar Montana); Lucille Sydney (Freda Montana); Henry Ludow (Sir Rupert Marsden); F. H. deQuincey (Mahmoud Bey); Charles Vane (Political Envoy); C. Stanford (De Costa); Frank Seddon (Royal Messenger); J. Camberyard (Political Envoy)

Royalty Theatre, London, opened April 4, 1916 128 performances
A Play written and directed by Louis Napoleon Parker

Dennis Eadie (Benjamin Disraeli); Mary Jerrold (Lady Beaconsfield); Mlle. Gabrielle Dorziat (Mrs. Noel Travers); Mary Glynne (Lady Clarissa Pevensey); Cyril Raymond (Charles, Viscount Deeford); C. Haviland Burke (The Duke of Glastonbury); Frances Ivor (The Duchess of Glastonbury); Ernest Cox (Adolphus, Viscount Cudworth); Gladys Young (Lady Cudworth); E. Pardoe Woodman (Lord Brooke of Brookehill); Adela Weekes (Lady Brooke); Hubert Harben (Sir Michael Probert); Campbell Gullan (Mr. Lumley Foljambe); Howard Sturge (Mr. Tearle); Vincent Sternroyd (Mr. Hugh Meyers); Morrice Seaton (Butler at Glastonbury Towers); Frank Denman (Footman at Glastonbury Towers); Harry Templeton (Bascot, Disraeli's Butler); Arthur Bowyer (Potter, Disraeli's gardener); J. Augustus Keogh (Flooks)

Knickerbocker Theatre, New York, opened April 9, 1917 48 performances
Produced by Klaw and Erlanger with George C. Tyler; A Play written and directed by Louis Napoleon Parker; Scenery, Gates and Morange; Costumes, Miss Spencer; Manager, H. C. Judge; Stage manager, Dudley Digges

George Arliss (The Right Honourable Benjamin Disraeli); Florence Arliss (Lady Beaconsfield); Margaret Dale (Mrs. Noel Travers); Jeanne Eagels (Lady Clarissa Pevensey); Arthur Eldred (Charles, Viscount Deeford); Langdon Bruce (The Duke of Glastonbury); Leila Repton (The Duchess of Glastonbury); Walter Grey (Adolphus, Viscount Cudworth); Lilla Campbell (Lady Cudworth); Noel Tearle (Lord Brooke of Brookehill); Helen Erskine (Lady Brooke); David Glassford (Sir Michael Probert); Dudley Digges (Mr. Lumley Foljambe); Edgar Kent (Mr. Hugh Meyers); Fred Nichols (Butler at Glastonbury Towers); C. M. Van Clief (Bascot, Disraeli's butler); Malcolm Morley (Potter, Disraeli's gardener); Martin Greene (Flooks)

QUEEN VICTORIA, *48th Street Theatre*, New York, opened November 15, 1923 44 performances
Produced by The Equity Players; A Play by David Carb and Walter Prichard Eaton; Director, Priestly Morrison

Beryl Mercer (Queen Victoria); Clarence Derwent (Benjamin Disraeli); Ulrich Haupt (Prince Albert); Arthur Maude (Edward, Prince of Wales); Anita Rothe (Baroness Lehzen); Winifred Hanley (Duchess of Kent); Donald Cameron (Viscount Melbourne); William Ingersoll (Lord Palmerston); Herbert Standing, Jr. (Lord Conyngham); Edward Fielding (Duke of Wellington); Albert Tavenier (Archbishop of Canterbury); Hubert Wilke (Baron Stockmar); Herbert Farjeon (Sir James Clark); Frances Goodrich (Lady Gay Hawthorne); George Farren (William Evert Gladstone); Borden Harriman (A Footman)

DIZZY, *Westminster Theatre*, London, opened October 5, 1932

A Domestic Comedy by Thomas Pellatt; Directed by Anmer Hall

Ernest Milton (Lord Beaconsfield); Gillian Scaife (Caroline, Lady Creech); Borisa Ranevsky (Count Schouvalov); Drelincourt Odlum (The Reverend Eustace Fayne); Alan Trotter (Montague Corry); Roger Maxwell (Baum); Nancy Russell (Lady Alice Lisle); Antony Eustrel (Baron Veurst); Archibald McLean (Hodnit); Andrew Churchman (Lord Wroxton); Geoffrey Toone (Lord Dailbraith); Vera Poliakoff (Renee de Montesson); Eugene Leahy (Mr. Gladstone); Peter Mather (Moses); Rollo Gamble (Peach); Carleton Hobbs (Lord Scarslake/John Wade); Ronald Waters (Foreign Service Messenger)

YOUNG MR. DISRAELI, *Kingsway Theatre*, London, opened November 12, 1934
A Comedy by Elswyth Thane (Mrs. William Beebe); Director, Maxwell Wray

Derrick de Marney (Benjamin Disraeli); Iris Ashley (Henrietta); Walter Fitzgerald (Edward Bulwer); Daphne Heard (Rosina Bulwer); Stanley Lathbury (Isaac Disraeli); Selma Van Dias (Sarah Disraeli); Elise Irving (Maria Disraeli); James Page (Tita); Sophie Stewart (Mrs. Wyndham Lewis); Annie Esmond (Rook); Douglas Burbridge (Wyndham Lewis); Barbara Dillon (Caroline Norton)

YOUNG MR. DISRAELI, *Fulton Theatre*, New York, opened November 10, 1937 6 performances
Produced by Alex Yokel; A Comedy by Elswyth Thane (Mrs. William Beebe); Director, Margaret Webster; Settings and costumes, David Ffolkes; Music directed by Henri Berchman

Derrick de Marney (Benjamin Disraeli); Selena Royle (Henrietta); Harry Redding (Edward Bulwer); Francis Amherst (Rosina Bulwer); Ben Webster (Isaac Disraeli); Lora Baxter (Sarah Disraeli); Molly Pearson (Maria Disraeli); Donald Arbury (Tita); Sophie Stewart (Mrs. Wyndham Lewis); Edgar Kent (Wyndham Lewis); Alice John (Rook); Lenore Sorsby (Caroline Norton)

BENJAMIN DISRAELI, *Workers' Theatre*, Tel Aviv, opened December 14, 1938
Produced by Ohel, The Workers' Theatre; A Play by Arthur Rundt; Hebrew translation by A. Shlonsky; Director, Frederick Lobe; Settings, J. Frankel

Z. Barban (Benjamin Disraeli); D. Kasteljanitz (Lady Dennam); M. Margalith (Lord Russell); D. Vogelson (Rothschild); S. Ponoch (Lady Bentinck); H. Sankovsky (Rahel); A. Nachtomi (Lord Dennam); S. Cechoval (Lord Derby); J. Einstein (Mortimer of March); J. Chalfi (Tita); B. Silberg (Traddles); J. Barkaith (Chambermaid); L. Senlonsky (Lady Wyndham)

PORTRAIT OF A QUEEN, *Vaudeville Theatre*, London, opened May 6, 1965
Produced by Donald Albery and H. Clay Blaney for Calabash Productions Ltd.; A Play by William Francis; Director, Val May; Production designer, Graham Barlow

Dorothy Tutin (Queen Victoria); Paul Eddington (Benjamin Disraeli); Peter Vaughan (William Gladstone); Derek Waring (Prince Albert); Norman Tyrell (Archbishop of Canterbury); Michael Barrington (Lord Melbourne and Other Ministers); Tim Minnikin (Bishop of Durham); Peter Whitbread (King Leopold of the Belgians); Heather Bell (Lady in Waiting); Boram Tyrell (*Times* Editor); Tim Minnikin, Edmund Coulter (Gentlemen of the Press); Tina Cousin (Lady in Waiting); Nicholas Smith (Ballad Singer); Rodney Archer, Martin Aubrey, John Challis, Edmund Coulter, Brian Haughton (Footmen); Heather Bell (Scottish Peasant Woman)

SCREEN

DISRAELI, NB Films, released November 1916
Produced by Arrigo Bocchi; Directors, Percy Nash and Charles Calvert; Screenplay, Louis Napoleon Parker, based on his play

Dennis Eadie (Benjamin Disraeli); Mary Jerrold (Lady Beaconsfield); Dorothy Bellew (Lady Clarissa Pevensey); Cyril Raymond (Lord Deeford); Daisy Cordell (Mrs. Noel Travers); Arthur Cullin (Sir Michael Probert); Cecil Morton York (Duke of Glastonbury); Evelyn Harding (Duchess of Glastonbury); Mrs. Lytton (Queen Victoria); Fred Morgan (Nigel Foljambe); A.B. Imeson (Hugh Meyers)

DISRAELI, United Artists release, released August 1921
Produced by Distinctive Productions; Director, Henry Kolker; Screenplay, Forrest Halsey, based on the play by Louis Napoleon Parker; Photography, Harry A. Fischbeck; Art director, Charles O. Seessel

George Arliss (Benjamin Disraeli); Florence Arliss (Lady Beaconsfield); Margaret Dale (Nrs. Noel Travers); Louise Huff (Lady Clarissa Pevensey); Reginald Denny (Lord Deeford); E.J. Ratcliffe (Sir Michael Probert); Henry Carvill (Duke of Glastonbury); Grace Griswold (Duchess of Glastonbury); Frank Losee (Hugh Meyers); Noel Tearle (Foljambe); Fred Nicholls (Butler)

DISRAELI, Warner Bros.-First National, released October 1929
Associate producer, Darryl F. Zanuck; Director, Alfred E. Green; Screenplay, Julian Josephson, based on the play by Louis Napoleon Parker; Photography, Lee Garmes; Titles, DeLeon Anthony; Music, Louis Silver; Editor, Owen Marks

George Arliss (Benjamin Disraeli); Florence Arliss (Lady Beaconsfield); Joan Bennett (Lady Clarissa Pevensey); Doris Lloyd (Mrs. Noel Travers); Anthony Bushell (Lord Deeford); David Torrence (Sir Michael Probert); Henry Carvill (Duke of Glastonbury); Gwendolen Logan (Duchess of Glastonbury); Ivan Simpson (Hugh Meyers); Michael Visaroff (Count Bosrinov); Margaret Mann (Queen Victoria); Norman Cannon (Foljambe); Cosmo Kyle Bellew (Mr. Tearle); Charles E. Evans (Potter, Disraeli's gardener); Jack Deery (Bascot, Disraeli's butler); Shayle Gardner (Dr. Williams); Powell York (Flooks)

THE PRIME MINISTER, Warner Bros.-First National, Great Britain, released March 1941; in U.S., February 1942)
Produced by Max Milder; Director, Thorold Dickinson; Screenplay, Brock Williams and Michael Hogan; Photography, Basil Emmott; Art director, Norman Arnold; Music, Jack Beaver; Editor, Leslie A. Norman

John Gielgud (Benjamin Disraeli); Diana Wynyard (Mary Anne WyndhamLewis); Will Fyffe (The Agitator); Owen Nares (Lord Derby); Fay Compton (Queen Victoria); Lyn Harding (Bismark); Stephen Murray (William Gladstone); Pamela Standish (Princess Victoria); Irene Browne (Lady Londonderry); Frederick Leister (Lord Melbourne); Nicholas Hannen (Sir Robert Peel); Barbara Everest (Baroness Lehzen); Kynaston Reeves (Lord Stanley); Anthony Ireland (Count D'Orsay); Gordon McLeod (John Brown); Glynis Johns (Miss A. Sheridan); Margaret Johnston (Miss G. Sheridan); Vera Bogetta (Lady Blessington)

THE MUDLARK, 20th Century-Fox, released December 1950
Produced by Nunnally Johnson; Director, Jean Negulesco; Screenplay, Nunnally Johnson, based on the novel by Theodore Bonnet; Photography, George Perinal; Art

director, C. P. Norman; Music, William Alwyn; Editor, Thelma Myers

Irene Dunne (Queen Victoria); Alec Guinness (Benjamin Disraeli); Finlay Currie (John Brown); Beatrice Campbell (Lady Emily Prior); Constance Smith (Kate Noonan); Andrew Ray (Wheeler); Anthony Steel (Lt. Charles McHatten); Marjorie Fielding (Lady Margaret Prior); Ronan O'Casey (Slattery); Raymond Lovell (Sgt. Footman Naseby); Wilfrid Hyde-White (Tucker); Ernest Clark (Hammond); Eric Messiter (Police Lieutenant Ash); Kynaston Reeves (General Sir Henry Ponsonby); Edward Rigby (Watchman); Robin Stevens (Herbert); William Strange (Sparrow); Ian Selby (Prince Christian); Pamela Arliss (Princess Christian); Howard Douglas (Broom); Alan Gordon (Disraeli's Valet); Richmond Nairne (Didbit); Maurice Warren (Christian); Michael Brooke (Prince Albert); Jane Short (Princess Victoria); Leonard Sharp (Ben Fox); Freddie Watts (Iron George); Bob Head (Dandy Fitch); Vi Stevens (Mrs. Dawkins); Leonard Morris (Hooker Morgan); George Dillon (Jailer); V. Kaley (Mrs. Feeney); Y. Yanai (Al Hook); Paul Gerrard (Petey); Marjorie Gresley (Meg Bownes); Grace Denbeigh Russell (Queen's maid)

TELEVISION

THE INVINCIBLE MR. DISRAELI, *Hallmark Hall of Fame*, televised April 4, 1963 NBC 90 minutes

A Compass Production; Produced and directed by George Schaefer; Teleplay, James Lee; Sets, Warren Clymer; Costumes, Noel Taylor; Makeup, Bob O'Bradowich

Trevor Howard (Benjamin Disraeli); Greer Garson (Mary Anne Wyndham-Lewis); Denholm Elliott (Corry); Hurd Hatfield (Rothschild); Geoffrey Keen (William Gladstone); Kate Reid (Queen Victoria); Eric Berry (Sir Robert Peel); Frederic Worlock (Derby); Joan White (Mrs. Gladstone)

DISRAELI: PORTRAIT OF A REBEL, televised September 5 through 26, 1978 ITV (London) 4 parts 1 hour each; in U.S. on PBS' *Masterpiece Theatre*, televised June 1 through 22, 1980

An ATV Network Production in association with BBC; Produced by Cecil Clarke; Director, Claude Whatham; Teleplay, David Butler; Set designer, Anthony Waller; Costumes, Shelagh Killeen and Ann Hollowood; Music, Wilfred Josephs

Ian McShane (Benjamin Disraeli); Mary Peach (Mary Ann Wyndham-Lewis); Rosemary Leach (Queen Victoria); Margaret Whiting (Lady Marguerite Blessington); John Carlisle (Dr. William Gladstone); Mark Dignam (Lord Lyndhurst); William Russell (Wyndham-Lewis); Aubrey Morris (Isaac D'Israeli); Madelena Nedeva (Henrietta Sykes); Leigh Lawson (Count Alfred D'Orsay); Brett Usher (Buliver); Anton Rodgers (Bentinck); Brewster Mason (Bismark); David DeKeyser (Rothschild); Rachel Bell (Clara Bolton); Patricia Hodge (Rosina); Sheila Ruskin (Caroline); Jenny Lipman (Sarah); Antony Brown (Sir Robert Peel)

EPISODES: I. "Dizzy" 2. "Mary Anne" 3. "The Great Game" 4. "The Chief"

EAST OF EDEN

Various adaptations of the novel by John Steinbeck (1952)

Synopsis

Austere Salinas Valley farmer Adam Trask has raised his twin sons Caleb and Aron alone after being deserted by his wife Kate, who has become the town madam. Partial to the studious Aron, Adam long ago alienated and embittered Caleb, whom he considers to be a ne'er-do-well. It is 1917, and the Trask lettuce farm is on the brink of failure. Caleb, trying to buy his father's love, goes to his mother after learning her whereabouts and of her profession. He borrows money from her to raise a crop of beans, which he is told will soar in price with the outbreak of war, and offers the substantial profit on the crop to his father as a birthday present. Adam, however, refuses the offer as he has rejected love for the son who reminds him of Kate. Angered, Caleb introduces his brother Aron to their mother. Appalled at Kate's existence and her profession, Aron gets drunk and enlists in the Army, while Caleb intense feeling of rejection leads him to Abra Bacon, Aron's fiancee. Adam, meanwhile, learning of Aron's enlistment and his sons' meeting with their mother, has a stroke. Abra goes to Adam and pleads that he forgive wayward Caleb and give his son some indication of his love. Relenting, Adam asks Caleb to stay and care for him, and Caleb ignores the urging of Sam Hamilton, Adam's longtime friend, that he (Caleb) leave, quoting from the Bible: "And Cain rose up against his brother Abel and slew him and Cain went away and dwelt in the land of Nod on the East of Eden."

Comment and Critique

John Steinbeck, author of sixteen novels and Nobel Prize recipient in 1962, was born at Salinas, California, on February 27, 1902, and died in New York City on December 20, 1968. During the writing of *East of Eden*, Steinbeck kept a diary which he later published as *Journal of a Novel: The East of Eden Letters*, in which he noted: "I am choosing to write this book to my sons...I will tell them [the] story of good and evil, of strength and weakness, of love and hate, of beauty and ugliness. I shall try to demonstrate to them how these doubles are inseparable...how neither can exist without the other and how out of their groupings creativeness is born."

East of Eden, remembered primarily for James Dean's performance as Caleb, was adapted to the screen by playwright Paul Osborn for Warner Bros.' 1955 production directed by Elia Kazan. (The Osborn adaptation comprised only the last ninety pages of the novel.) While Kazan's detailed direction extended to a beautiful mounted version, the film was criticized for the rather flamboyant, theatrically overburdened "style" and "excessive naturalism" displayed by the cast that also included Raymond Massey as Adam, Julie Harris as Abra and Richard Davalos as Aron. It was Jo Van Fleet, however, who won the Academy Award that year as Best Supporting Actress for her memorable characterization of Kate. Dean, Kazan and Osborn also were Oscar nominated.

The New York Times' Bosley Crowther questioned whether Osborn's compressed script "contains the best of the book." Reviewing *East of Eden*, which premiered at the Astor Theatre on Broadway in a benefit performance for the Actors Studio (as a bow to Kazan and Dean), Crowther appraised Dean's performance: "This young actor, who is here doing his first big screen stint, is a mass of histrionic gingerbread. He scuffs his feet, he whirls, he pouts, he stutters, he leans against walls, he rolls his eyes, he swallows his words, he ambles slack-kneed -- all like Marlon Brando used to do. Mr. Kazan should be spanked for permitting him to do such a sophomoric thing...To a lesser degree, Julie Harris exaggerates the role of the country coquette." The *Times* critic summed up: "In short, there is energy and intensity but little clarity and emotion in this film. It is like a great, green iceberg:

mammoth and imposing but very cold." He did, though, admire Kazan's use of color and CinemaScope, finding he captured the mood and expanse of the California settings described as "almost beyond compare."

Elia Kazan, in a later interview with Robin Bean of *Films and Filming*, recalled the making of *East of Eden* and working with James Dean, who was killed in an automobile accident on September 30, 1955 (prior to the release of his subsequent two films): "I was never very appreciative of Jimmy Dean becoming an idol; he's not an idol of mine, and I didn't particularly like what he was...I think I told the truth about him in *East of Eden*, or rather a character like that, but I didn't like the result...he *was* Cal Trask...He was vengeful; he had a sense of aloneness and of being persecuted. And he was suspicious. In addition, he was tremendously talented."

In 1968, *East of Eden* was adapted to the musical stage by Terrence McNally as *Here's Where I Belong*. During its road tryout, McNally was replaced by Alex Gordon. Legendary record executive Mitch Miller produced the show which featured a score by Robert Waldman (music) and Alfred Uhry (lyrics) that was considered by one critic as "too embarrassing for quotation." British actor Paul Rogers played Adam Trask with an impeccable American accent. *The New Yorker*, though, felt that "the star of the show was an electrifying young man named Walter McGinn who managed to make his silly part seem far better than it was" in what was described as Steinbeck's "sticky melodrama." (On March 31, 1977, in a bizarre coincidence, McGinn -- Caleb Trask in the musical -- was killed in a Los Angeles automobile accident at the age of forty. The role of Caleb again had taken its toll.)

Here's Where I Belong began previews at the Billy Rose Theatre on Broadway on February 8, 1968, and Mitch Miller had to sink an additional $100,000 (to the initial $450,000 provided by the Music Corporation of America) to sustain it through three weeks of repairs. It finally opened -- and closed -- on March 3.

A sampling of critical comments: Clive Barnes (*The New York Times*) called Alex Gordon's adaptation "clumsy and leaden-footed" while considering Steinbeck's story "unusually somber for a musical. The bland joint effort of Messrs. Gordon, Waldman and Uhry should probably have ended up not only East of Eden but West of Philadelphia...The director, Michael Kahn, had the unenviable task of attempting to direct a badly written and weakly plotted play continually being interrupted for a few songs or a little dancing, and he was unable to fuse these two disparate elements." Richard Watts, Jr. (*New York Post*) agreed that Steinbeck's *East of Eden* "would make unpromising material for a musical play...it provided a desperately dreary evening, despite the presence in a leading role of Paul Rogers, who is one of the most skillful actors on the English speaking stage...Everything appears to have gone wrong with *Here's Where I Belong*." And John Chapman (*Daily News*) concluded: "Somewhere along the line, producer Mitch Miller and his employees have lost the story of *Here's Where I Belong*."

In 1982, *East of Eden* came to television in a threepart, eight-hour ABC Novel for Television. Adapted by Richard Shapiro from Steinbeck's novel, and starring Jane Seymour and a stellar cast, it was given an elaborate production that encompassed several generations and virtually all of the book as written. *Time* magazine's summation of television's *East of Eden* was "Terribly tasteful and tastefully terrible." It received Emmy Award nominations as Outstanding Limited Series and for Frank Stanley's photography, and won Emmys for art direction and set decoration. At the Golden Globe Awards presentation, the production was chosen as Best Mini-Series and Jane Seymour was selected as Best Actress in a Mini-Series.

STAGE

HERE'S WHERE I BELONG, *Billy Rose Theatre*, New York, opened and closed March 3, 1968 1 performance
Produced by Mitch Miller in association with United Artists; A Musical play by Alex Gordon (succeeded Terrence McNally), based on John Steinbeck's *East of Eden*; Director, Michael Kahn; Music by Robert Waldman; Lyrics by Alfred Uhry; Settings, Ming Cho Lee; Lighting, Jules Fisher; Costumes, Ruth Morley; Musical direction and vocal arrangements, Theodore Saidenberg; Dance music, Arnold Goland (succeeded Genevieve Pitot); Dances and musical staging by Tony Mordente (succeeded Hanya Holm); Orchestrations, Glenn Osser, Norman Leyden, Jonathan Tunick; Company manager, Peter Neufield; Stage managers, William Dodd, D.W. Koehler and Gene Gavin

Paul Rogers (Adam Trask); Walter McGinn (Caleb Trask); Ken Kercheval (Aron Trask); James Coco (Lee); Heather MacRae (Abra Bacon); Nancy Wickwire (Kate); Casper Roos (Will Hamilton); Bette Henritze (Mrs. Bacon); Dena Dietrich (Mrs. Tripp); Patricia Kelly (Mrs. Heink); Aniko Morgan (Eva); Dorothy Lister (Della); Joetta Cherry (Juana); Taylor Reed (Newspaper man); Darrell Askey (British Purchasing Agent); Lee Wilson, Tod Miller (Schoolchildren); Darrell Askey, Joetta Cherry, Graciella Daniele, Elisa De Marko, Larry Devon, John Dickerson, Bud Fleming, John William Gardner, Gene Gavin, John Johann, Ray Kirchner, Jane Laughlin, Dorothy Lister, Andy Love, Richard Marr, David McCorkle, Joyce McDonald, Tod Miller, Aniko Morgan, Joan Nelson, Joseph Nelson, Donald Morris, Taylor Reed, Clifford Scott, Joy Serio, Michele Simmons, David Thomas, Barbara Webb, Lee Wilson (Townspeople, Field Workers, Denizens of Castroville Street)

[Characters and cast dropped from revised production prior to opening: David Thomas (Ernest Warren); Richard Marr (Sam Purcell); David McCorkle (Young Purcell); Donald Norris (Harry Grew); Andy Love (Humbert Heink); Larry Devon (Tyler Tripp); Joyce McDonald (Schoolteacher); Michele Simmons (Farmwoman); Gene Gavin (Bank teller); Bud Fleming (Baker); Clifford Scott (Dr. Edwards); William Gardner (Delivery boy); Joy Serio, John Dickerson, Ray Kirchner (Mexicans); Elisa De Marko (Salesgirl)]

MUSICAL NUMBERS: "We Are What We Are"; "Cal Gets By"; "Raising Cain"; "Soft Is the Sparrow"; "Where Have I Been?"; "No Time"; "Progress"; "Good Boy"; "Ballet"; "Act Like a Lady"; "The Send-Off"; "Top of the Train"; "Waking Up the Sun"; "Pulverize the Kaiser"; "You're Momma's"; "Here's Where I Belong"; "We're a Home"

Dropped from production in previews: "Sweeping Changes"; "Perfect"; "Tell Me About Your Eden"

Original cast recording: United Artists Records

SCREEN

EAST OF EDEN, *Warner Bros. Pictures*, released March 1955
Produced and directed by Elia Kazan; Screenplay, Paul Osborn, based on the novel by John Steinbeck; Photography, Ted McCord; Art directors, James Basevi and Malcolm Bert; Music, Leonard Rosenman; Editor, Owen Marks

Julie Harris (Abra Bacon); James Dean (Cal Trask); Raymond Massey (Adam

Trask); Burl Ives (Sam Hamilton); Richard Davalos (Aron Trask); Jo Van Fleet (Kate); Albert Dekker (Will Hamilton); Lois Smith (Ann); Harold Gordon (Mr. Albrecht); Richard Garrick (Dr. Edwards); Lonny Chapman (Roy); Timothy Carey (Joe); Nick Dennis (Rantini); Barbara Baxley (Nurse); Bette Treadville (Madame); Tex Mooney, Harry Cording (Bartenders); Mario Siletti (Piscora); Loretta Rush (Card Dealer); Bill Phillipd (Coalman); Jonathan Haze (Piscora's Son); and Jack Carr, Effie Laird, Wheaton Chambers, Ed Clark, Al Ferguson, Franklyn Farnum, Rose Plummer, John George, Earle Hodgins, C. Ramsey Hill, Edward McNally

TELEVISION

JOHN STEINBECK'S EAST OF EDEN, ABC Novel for Television, televised February 8, 9 and 11, 1981 ABC 8 hours
Executive producer, Mace Neufield for Warner Bros. Television; Producer, Barney Rosenzweig; Coproducer, Ken Wales; Director, Harvey Hart; Teleplay, Richard A. Shapiro, based on the novel by John Steinbeck; Photography, Frank Stanley; Art directors, Kim Swados and Ray Storey; Set decorator, Dennis Peeples; Costumes, Bob Magahay and Judy Truchan; Music, Lee Holdridge; Makeup, Tom Miller, Rodney Wilson; Hair styles, Cherie; Editors, Bill Brame and Michael Brown

Jane Seymour (Cathy Ames/Kate Trask); Timothy Bottoms (Adam Trask); Bruce Boxleitner (Charles Trask); Soon-Teck Oh (Lee); Karen Allen (Abra Bacon); Hart Bochner (Aron Trask); Sam Bottoms (Cal Trask); Warren Oates (Cyrus Trask); Howard Duff (Jules Edwards); Anne Baxter (Faye); Richard Masur (Will Hamilton); Nicholas Pryor (James Grew); Lloyd Bridges (Samuel Hamilton); Nellie Bellflower (Mrs. Trask); M. Emmet Walsh (Sheriff Horace Quinn); Vernon Weddle (Bill Ames); Grace Zabriskie (Mrs. Ames); Stymie Beard (Cotton Eye); Wendel Burton (Tom Hamilton); Timothy Agoglia Carey (Preacher); and Walter Brooke, Frederic Cook, Paul Harper, John Michael Johnson, Harry Lewis, Peter Maloney, Buck Taylor, Brett Williams, Brian Ann Zoccola

THE ELEPHANT MAN
A Drama by Bernard Pomerance (1977)

Synopsis

In 1884, Dr. Frederick Treves learns of a sideshow freak known as "The Elephant Man." Although the notorious show is closed by London police, Dr. Treves persuades Ross, the unscrupulous owner, to permit him to see his unique attraction. Treves, fascinated and repelled by, and agonizing over, the freak's appearance, pays Ross to bring "The Elephant Man" to Whitechapel Hospital for a secret examination. Discovering the vicious impresario has beaten the tragic creature, Treves secretly admits the freak as a patient, persuading the hospital's senior surgeon, Carr Gomm, that the man is indeed intelligent and in need of medical attention. Treves learns that "The Elephant Man" is an Englishman named John Merrick, and concentrates on his rehabilitation. Merrick's progress is heralded and publicized until he gains national recognition, and Treves rejects Ross' demand of the return of his "freak."

Noted English actress Madge Kendal visits Merrick in his hospital room and befriends him. Royal intervention secures Merrick's continued residence in the hospital, but he is disturbed by the ongoing fascination with his appearance and the fact that the hospital night porter has organized tours of his lowlife cronies to see "The Elephant Man" for a fee. Merrick escapes from the hospital and rejoins his former employer for a circus tour of the Continent. Ross cruelly locks Merrick in a cage with baboons, but the sympathetic circus freaks free him, and mortally ill, he returns to Treves. Back in the hospital, Merrick completes a cardboard model of a cathedral and is taken to see Madge Kendal perform. Never able to sleep other than in an upright position due to his hideously enlarged head, Merrick decides to emulate a normal human being one night and attempts to sleep on his back. He dies of suffocation.

Comment and Critique

In his *The Elephant Man and Other Reminiscences*, published in 1923, Dr. Frederick Treves, surgeon and professor of anatomy at London Hospital in Whitechapel, graphically described the amazing John Merrick: "The most striking feature about him was his enormous head. From the brow there projected a huge bony mass like a loaf, while from the back of the head hung a bag of spongy fungus-looking skin, the surface of which was comparable to brown cauliflower...From the upper jaw there projected another mass of bone. It protruded from the mouth like a pink stump, turning the upper lip inside out and making of the mouth a mere slobbering aperture...The back was horrible, because from it hung, as far down as the middle of the of the thigh, huge, sac-like masses of flesh covered by some loathsome cauliflower skin." (Treves later became surgeon to the Royal Family and received a knighthood.)

In 1973, anthropologist Ashley Montagu's *The Elephant Man: A Study in Human Dignity* was published, while Leslie Fiedler's 1978 *Freaks: Myths and Images* delineated an approach to "very special people" who provide "images of our secret selves." Michael Howell and Peter Ford's *The True History of the Elephant Man* appeared in 1980.

Author Bernard Pomerance, a New Yorker who relocated to London and learned the tale of "The Elephant Man," viewed the still preserved bones of John Merrick at London Hospital. Fascinated, he discovered that Merrick had been born in Leicester, England, in 1863, and based on *The Autobiography of Joseph Carey Merrick* (the name registered on his birth certificate), found that Merrick's affliction began in his mother's womb after she was knocked down by an elephant from a traveling circus. Pomerance went to work on a play relying on the intelligence of audiences to visualize Merrick's horrible appearance, and he later stated in an interview in *The New York Times*, "The most important element in theatre is the audience's imagination."

With his partner Roland Rees, Pomerance produced *The Elephant Man* on November 7, 1977 at London's Hampstead Theatre, with David Schofield as Merrick and David Allister as Treves. "Merrick's complex character is well drawn by the author; his loneliness, his gratitude for his salvation, his warm and gentle nature, the way he silently adores Mrs. Kendal, his thoughts," Ria Julian reported in *Plays and Players*. "His head is so big, he reflects, because it is full of dreams. It is a very moving observation that, despite 'the good life,' he still wants to hide in this patronizing society. He speaks about wanting to retire top a blind people's home, where no one would stare at him. David Schofield plays Merrick with great compassion and physical bravura."

The story of John Merrick, meanwhile, also interested two other playwrights. In

1978, Roy Faudree's play, also called *The Elephant Man*, was produced by the No Theatre of Northampton, Mass. And in March 1979, The Philadelphia Company produced a play of the same name by Tom Gibbons, with Lanie Robertson as Merrick.

San Francisco-born Philip Anglim, a twenty-six-year-old Yale graduate actor, arrived in London before the less-than-three-week run of Pomerance's *The Elephant Man* and purchased the American rights to the play. In mid January 1979, the first American production of the Pomerance drama opened Off Broadway at St. Peter's Church with Anglim as John Merrick. In *Time*, critic T. E. Kalem found: "Plays about historical figures rarely cast new light upon the figures or ourselves. Bernard Pomerance, an American living in London, has written a drama about a historical freak that movingly does both ...[The production] is done with impeccable taste and graced with skilled key performances that equal or surpass anything to be seen at present in the New York theater. Displaying no cosmetically applied malignancies, Philip Anglim's Merrick is like some sort of simple, twisted saint."

Richard Eder, in *The New York Times*, called *The Elephant Man* "a thoughtful and frequently moving play ...Philip Anglim plays Merrick with a questioning and affecting dignity. No makeup is used to make him grotesque; he presents deformity by twisting his body and speaking with a muffled effort that suggests a spirit struggling with impediments. It is a winning and impressive performance. Carole Shelley is at her finest as Mrs. Kendal...Kevin Conway's enthusiasm and doubt as Treves makes the third of three splendid performances...Jack Hofsiss' direction is an ideal blend of realism and stylization...It is an admirable production of a most worthwhile play."

The Elephant Man moved to Broadway's Booth Theatre the following April and amassed a run of 916 performances. "A true triumph" is how Douglas Watt described the play in the *Daily News*. "Pomerance's sensitive, never sentimental writing (he has revised the second half a bit, by the way, mostly to clarify a subsidiary situation in which Treves is swindled) is beautifully realized in all respects...The three principal characters -- Merrick, Treves and the actress Mrs. Kendal -- are impeccably performed by Philip Anglim, Kevin Conway and Carole Shelley...We can now add Anglim's name to the growing list of bravura performances by actors playing stricken people on Broadway...*The Elephant Man* is ravishing theater, and, because of the moral question it raises, profoundly disturbing."

The New York Drama Critics Circle Award as Best Play of the Year went to *The Elephant Man*. It also won the Tony as Best Play of the Season, while Jack Hofsiss received a Tony for his direction. Philip Anglim, nominated as Best Actor, lost to Tom Conti (for *Whose Life Is This Anyway?*), playing one of those "stricken people" critic Douglas Watt spoke of in his review. The Best Actress Tony Award was split between Carole Shelley for *The Elephant Man* and Constance Cummings for Arthur Kopit's *Wings*.

On December 2, 1980, with rock singer David Bowie (in his acting debut on Broadway) interpreting the role of Merrick, *The Elephant Man* was interpreted in sign language by Philip Giambaresi and Alan Champion.

For his Brooksfilms, director/comedian Mel Brooks announced plans in the spring of 1979 to film an adaptation of *The Elephant Man* using a screenplay by Christopher de Vore and Eric Bergren, based on the books by Sir Frederick Treves and Ashley Montagu. Suit was brought against Brooks by those involved with the Pomerance play to prevent him from filming, but since the Brooks version was based on documents in public domain and not on Pomerance's work, he was allowed to proceed. Filming in black and white was done at Elstree Studios in London with John

Hurt as Merrick, Anthony Hopkins as Treves and Anne Bancroft as Mrs. Kendal.

The New York Times' Vincent Canby found: "David Lynch's haunting new film that's not to be confused with the current Broadway play of the same time, though both are based on the life of the same unfortunate John Merrick... *The Elephant Man* uses some of the devices of the horror film, including ominous music, sudden cuts that shock and hint of dark things to come...Unlike the play, in which the actor playing John Merrick wears no makeup, his unadorned face representing the beauty of the interior man, the audience thus being forced to imagine his hideous appearance, the movie works the other way around. John Hurt, as John Merrick, is a monster with a bulbous forehead, a Quasimodo-like mouth, one almost-obscured eye, a useless arm and crooked torso. It's to the credit of Christopher Tucker's makeup and to Mr. Hurt's extraordinary performance deep inside it, that John Merrick doesn't look absurd...Mr. Hurt is truly remarkable."

A yes-and-no appraisal was given by critic Judith Crist. On the negative side, she felt that "Pomerance's theme is the sacrifice of inner grace and beauty entailed in accepting society's protection and by conforming to 'civilization.' Both Philip Anglim, who created the role, and [David] Bowie simply 'choreograph' the physical deformity and suggest the ugliness without horror makeup. It is the imprisoned spirit that interested Pomerance. The realism of the film allows no such symbolic interpretation." On the positive side, she said, "What we see initially is a triumph of the makeup man's art, and what we remain to watch is a remarkable performance by John Hurt... Anthony Hopkins' Frederick Treves [is] a masterpiece of understatement as the compassionate doctor."

The Elephant Man was Oscar-nominated in eight different categories: Best Picture, Best Actor, Best Director, Best Screenplay Adaptation, and for editing, original score, art direction and costume design. It won no awards.

At the start of 1982, ABC Television presented Bernard Pomerance's *The Elephant Man*, with Philip Anglim, Kevin Conway and Jack Hofsiss repeating their Broadway roles as stars and director. TV critic John J. O'Connor said in *The New York Times*: "What worked brilliantly on stage comes across as a bit of cheating in the almost rigidly naturalistic framework of a television drama...Once the story and social symbolism of Merrick have been established, the plot tends to meander...Still, *The Elephant Man* has a rewarding share of powerful dramatic moments in this outstanding production. Mr. Anglim is never less than compelling. Mr. Anglim is never less than compelling. Mr. Conway, despite some flabby enunciating in his British accent, scores sharply in his key scenes. And Penny Fuller [is] marvelously affecting as the actress...*The Elephant Man* represents, on balance, an exceptional television event."

Almost as bizarre as the life of John Merrick was rock star Michael Jackson's extraordinary mid-1980s pursuit to purchase the remains of "The Elephant Man" from the London Hospital Medical College. Jackson doubled his original $500,000 offer to $1-million in June 1987, with his manager, Frank DiLeo, explaining the star's fascination and necrological passion as an "absorbing interest, purely based on his awareness of the ethical, medical and historical significance of 'The Elephant Man.'"

Requiescat en pace Joseph Carey Merrick.

STAGE

THE ELEPHANT MAN, *Hampstead Theatre*, London, opened November 7, 1977
Produced by Bernard Pomerance and Roland Rees; A Drama by Bernard Pomerance; Director, Roland Rees; Production designer, Tanya McCallin; Lighting,

Alan O'Toole

David Schofield (John Merrick); David Allister (Dr. Frederick Treves); Jennie Stoller (Mrs. Madge Kendal); Arthur Blake (Ross); William Hoyland (Carr Gomm); Judy Bridgland (Pinhead); Ken Druary (Orderly); Pat Arrowsmith (Cellist)

St. Peter's Church, New York, opened January 14, 1979

Produced by the American National Theatre Academy; Producer, Raymond Crinkley; A Drama by Bernard Pomerance; Director, Jack Hofsiss; Setting, David Jenkins; Lighting, Beverly Emmons; Costumes, Julie Weiss; Stage manager, Pat DeRousie

Philip Anglim (John Merrick); Kevin Conway (Dr. Frederick Treves); Carole Shelley (Mrs. Madge Kendal); Richard Clarke (Carr Gomm/Belgian Policeman); I.M. Hobson (Ross/Conductor); Jarlagh Conroy (Pinhead manager); Jean DeBaer (Pinhead); Dennis Creagham (Orderly); David Heiss (Cellist)

Booth Theatre, New York, opened April 19, 1979 916 performances

Produced by The American National Theatre Academy; Producers, Raymond Crinkley, Elizabeth I. McCann and Nelle Nugent; A Drama by Bernard Pomerance; Director, Jack Hofsiss; Setting, David Jenkins; Lighting, Beverly Emmons; Costumes, Julie Weiss; Production supervisor, Brent Peck; Associate producers, Ray Larsen and Ted Snowden; Stage managers, William Dodds and William Chance

Philip Anglim (succeeded by Jack Wetherall, Bruce Davison, Jeff Hayenga, David Bowie, Benjamin Hendrickson, Mark Hamill) (John Merrick); Kevin Conway (succeeded by Donal Donnelly) (Dr. Frederick Treves/ Belgian Policeman); Carole Shelley (succeeded by Patricia Elliott, Carole Shelley) (Mrs. Madge Kendal/Pinhead); Richard Clarke (Carr Gomm/Conductor); I. M. Hobson (succeeded by Danny Sewell) (Ross/Bishop/Snork); Cordis Heard (succeeded by Concetta Tomei, Judith Barcroft) (Princess Alexandra/Countess/Miss Sandwich/Pinhead); John NevilleAndrews (succeeded by John C. Vennema, Jeffrey Jones) (Lord John/Earl/Will/Policeman/Pinhead manager); Dennis Creagham (succeeded by Munson Hicks, Dennis Creagham) (Orderly); David Heiss (succeeded by Michael Goldschlager, David Heiss) (Cellist)

Lyttelton Theatre, London, opened July 15, 1980

Produced by the National Theatre; A Drama by Bernard Pomerance; Director, Roland Rees; Setting, Tanya McCallin; Lighting, Gerry Jenkins; Costumes, Lindy Hemming

David Schofield (John Merrick); Peter McEnery (Dr. Frederick Treves); Jennie Stoller (Mrs. Madge Kendal); Arthur Blake (Ross/Bishop/Snork); Peter Howell (Carr Gomm); Peter Bourke (Lord John/Belgian Policeman); Anthony Falkingham (Conductor/Porter); Dallas Cavell (Pinhead manager/Policeman); Karina Knight, Heather Tobias (Pinheads); Audrey Noble (Duchess); Heather Tobias (Nurse/ Countess); Karina Knight (Princess Alexandra); Dan Meaden, Iain Rattray, Penny Ryder, Charles Spice, Charles Wegner (Citizens)

Touring Company, opened *Mechanic Theatre*, Baltimore, November 26, 1979; closed *Orpheum Theatre*, Minneapolis, March 8, 1981

Producers, Raymond Crinkley, Elizabeth I. McCann and Nelle Nugent; A Drama by Bernard Pomerance; Director, Jack Hofsiss; Setting, David Jenkins; Lighting, Beverly Emmons; Costumes, Julie Weiss; Musical arrangements, David Heiss; Associate producers, Ray Larsen and Ted Snowden; Stage managers, Robert Bruce Holley, Margaret Hatch and Mary Dierson

Philip Anglim (succeeded by David Bowie, Kensyn Crouch, Jeff Hayenga) (John Merrick); Ken Ruta (succeeded by Ralph Williams) (Dr. Frederick Treves/ Belgian Policeman); Penny Fuller (succeeded by Concetta Tomei) (Mrs. Madge Kendal/ Pinhead); Richard Neilson (succeeded by Dennis Lipscomb) (Carr Gomm); Danny Sewell (succeeded by Thomas Tomer) (Ross/ Bishop Walsham/ How/ Snork); Jeffrey Jones (succeeded by Dennis Lipscomb, Thomas Apple) (Pinhead manager/ London Policeman/ Will/ Lord John); Etain O'Malley (succeeded by Jeanette Landis) (Pinhead/ Miss Sandwich/ Princess Alexandra); Michael O. Smith (succeeded by Kensyn Crouch, Thomas Apple, Bruce Holley) (Orderly); Richard Sher (succeeded by David Heiss, Neal LoMonaco, Anthony Pirollo) (Cellist)

Touring Company, season 1980-81
A Drama by Bernard Pomerance; Director, Brent Peek; Setting, David Jenkins; Lighting, Beverly Emmons; Costumes, Julie Weiss; Musical arrangements, David Heiss; Production supervisor, Richard Martini; Stage managers, Leanna Lenhart and Gregory Nicholas

Courtney Burr (John Merrick); Kenneth Garner (Dr. Frederick Treves/Belgian Policeman); Joan Grant (Mrs. Madge Kendal/Pinhead); Larry Swanson (Carr Gomm/Conductor); K. Lupe O'Dell (Ross/Bishop/How/ Snork); Peter Bartlett (Will/Lord John/Pinhead Manager/Policeman); Judith Calder (Miss Sandwich/ Pinhead/Princess Alexandra); Michael Russell (Orderly); Larry J. Rowdon (Cellist)

SCREEN

THE ELEPHANT MAN, Paramount Pictures, released September 1980
An EMI Release of a Brooksfilm (Mel Brooks); Executive producer, Stuart Cornfeld; Producer, Jonathan Sanger; Director, David Lynch; Screenplay, Christopher de Vore, Eric Bergren and David Lynch, based on *The Elephant Man and Other Reminiscences* by Sir Frederick Treves and *The Elephant Man: A Study in Human Dignity* by Ashley Montagu; Photography, Freddie Francis; Production designer, Stuart Craig; Art director, Bob Cartwright; Set decorator, Hugh Scaife; Costumes, Patricia Norris; Special makeup, Christopher Tucker; Music, John Morris; Orchestrations, Jack Hayes; Performed by the National Philharmonic Orchestra; Editor, Anne V. Coates

John Hurt (John Merrick); Anthony Hopkins (Dr. Frederick Treves); Anne Bancroft (Mrs. Madge Kendal); John Gielgud (Carr Gomm); Wendy Hiller (Motherhead); Freddie Jones (Bytes); Hannah Gordon (Mrs. Treves); Helen Ryan (Princess Alexandra); John Standing (Fox); Lesley Dunlop (Nora); Phoebe Nicholls (Merrick's Mother); Michael Elphick (Night Porter); Pat Gorman (Fairground Bobby); Claire Davenport (Fat Lady); Orla Pederson (Skeleton Woman); Patsy Smart (Distraught Woman); Frederick Treves (Alderman); Richard Hunter (Hodges); James Cormack (Pierce); Robert Bush (Messenger); Roy Evans (Cabman); Joan Rhodes (Cook); Nula Conwell (Nurse Kathleen); Tony London (Young Porter); Alfrie Curtis (Milkman); Carole Harrison (Tart); Kenny Baker (Plumed Dwarf); Bernadette Milnes, Brenda Kempner (Fighting Women); Hugh Manning (Broadneck); Dennis Burgess (Committee Man); Fanny Carby (Mrs. Kendal's Dresser); Morgan Sheppard (Man in Pub); Gerlad Case (Lord Waddington); Deirdre Costello, Pauline Quirke (Whores); David Ryall (Man with Whores); Chris Greener (Giant); Marcus Powell, Gilda Cohen (Midgets);

Lisa Scoble, Teri Scoble (Siamese Twins); Eiji Kusuhara (Japanese Bleeder); Robert Day (Little Jim); Patricia Hodge (Screaming Mum); Tommy Wright, Peter Davidson (Bobbies); John Rapley (King in Panto); Hugh Spight (Puss in Panto); Teresa Codling (Princess in Panto); Marion Betzold (Principal Boy); Caroline Haigh, Florenzio Morgado (Tress); Victor Kravchenko (Lion/Coachman); Beryl Hicks (Fairy); Michele Arms, Lucie Alford, Penny Wright, Janie Kells (Horses); Lydia Lisle (Merrick's Mother); Kathleen Byron (Lady Waddington)

TELEVISION

THE ELEPHANT MAN, *ABC Theatre of the Month*, televised January 4, 1982 ABC 2 hours
A Marble Arch Production; Executive producer, Martin Starger; Producer, Raymond Crinkley; Director, Jack Hofsiss; Televison adaptation by Steve Lawson of the play by Bernard Pomerance

Philip Anglim (John Merrick); Kevin Conway (Dr. Frederick Treves); Penny Fuller (Mrs. Madge Kendal); Richard Clarke (Carr Gomm); Christopher Hewitt (Ross); Jarlath Conroy (Pinhead manager); Charlotte Moore (Nurse Sandwich); John NevilleAndrews (Lord John/Earl/Will/Policeman); and William Duff-Griffin, David Rounds, Josephine Nichole, Rex Everhart, Joe Grifasi, William Hutt, Myvanwy Jenn, Jean-Pierre Stewart

AN ENEMY OF THE PEOPLE
A Drama by Henrik Ibsen (1882)

Synopsis

In a small nineteenth century town on the south coast of Norway, Burgomaster Peter Stockmann has built a health resort. After an outbreak of typhoid fever, Peter's brother Dr. Thomas Stockmann proves that his father-in-law Morten Kiil's tannery is polluting the water system. Unable to persuade Peter to replace the system, Dr. Stockmann threatens to publish his findings in the local paper, supported by editors Hovstad and Billing but opposed by publisher Aslakeen. Peter warns at a public meeting that the cost of a new system will greatly increase taxes, and the townspeople brand Dr. Stockmann as a troublemaker. Hovstad and Billing withdraw their support and Dr. Stockmann is dismissed from his position as Officer of the Baths, his schoolteacher daughter Petra is fired and his family is terrorized in their home.

The manipulation and accumulation of the health resort's stock by Morten Kiil is misinterpreted as Dr. Stockmann's transaction, proving the safety of the town's water supply. The doctor, declining an offer to migrate to America by his loyal friend, Captain Horster, chooses to remain in his hometown and continue his fight for understanding and truth, despite being considered an enemy of the people.

Comment and Critique

In his book *A History of the Theatre* (written with John A. Reeves), historian George Freedley wrote: "*En Foldfiende (An Enemy of the People)*, despite its air of personal indignation, has proved one of [Ibsen's] most successful plays...It is in this play that the typical Ibsenism occurs, 'A minority may be right...a majority is always wrong.' It was chosen by the French as the play with which to honor him on his 70th birthday; Ermete Novelli triumphed in it in Italy; Sir Herbert Beerbohm-Tree played it for years in England and America; and Walter Hampden has revived it more than once in New York."

On April 8, 1895, Tree and his English company presented Ibsen's *An Enemy of the People* at Abbey's Theatre in New York for one performance as part of their repertory. *The New York Times* described the play as an "example of Ibsen's superior constructive skill and facility as a writer of stage dialogue...Mr. Tree, as the manager, treats it very skillfully but with an occasional lapse into farcical 'business' that is a little out of place...The whole performance, however, is sympathetic and natural. No actor is out of play...It is a pity that so many of Mr. Tree's actors persist in speaking their mother tongue so indistinctly. Miss Lily Hanbury can rarely be understood... Mr. Tree's performance as Dr. Stockmann is another striking example of the fineness and variety of his talent...the portrayal is wonderfully elaborate in details yet the effect is simple."

Together with Minnie Maddern, Alla Nazimova and Richard Mansfield, Walter Hampden was a staunch advocate of the plays of Henrik Ibsen, and he produced, directed and starred in *An Enemy of the People* at his New York theatre in October 1927. "Ibsen can scarcely be mangled by bad acting; Hampden can scarcely play a piece crudely. Many Ibsen plays have been give in Manhattan these past seasons; probably few better than this *Enemy of the People*," reported *Time* Magazine. Ten years later, Hampden revived the play, which was reviewed by a Boston critic as "a good production, and for much of it an exciting one. Hampden is a scholarly and clear actor, and his performance is a good reading, a good lecture platform reading of Ibsen...It is an artful production and it is a good play and Hampden and his company give it a good reading."

Arthur Miller adapted Ibsen's *An Enemy of the People* in 1950 with lessthansuccessful results. Fredric March and wife Florence Eldridge headed the cast. Robert Coleman (*Daily Mirror*) decided that Miller "has turned a stilted problem play into a rip-roaring muddle-mooded melodrama...interesting, if not always effective...We seem to recall that [the play] as presented by Walter Hampden in a conventional edition had stature and dignity; Miller's adaptation seldom has either of these qualities...The [Robert] Lewis staging missed fire, we thought, notably in the first act. This was not altogether his fault, for he had to project Miller's attempt to state a drama of protest in the jargon of a modern underworld thriller."

Howard Barnes, in the *New York Herald-Tribune*, felt that Miller "is far more successful in translating the work than in reconstructing its fierce defense of individual liberty in present day terms. Despite the staunch performing of Fredric March, Florence Eldridge, Morris Carnovsky and their colleagues, the production is very much like a 19th century canvas given a Picasso treatment...It is an interesting idea, but not particularly successful."

English critic Kenneth Tynan's explanation was that Arthur Miller had turned Ibsen's play "into a racy contemporary pamphlet. His temperament chimed with what he described as Ibsen's 'terrible wrath' and the dilemma of Stockmann, the betrayed crusader, duplicated Miller's own, that of a lifelong democrat who learns, from the example of his own country, that majority rule is not infallible...Anger is a great simplifier, and Miller is an angry writer."

In his preface to his published play, Arthur Miller wrote: "Throughout the play I have tried to peel away its trappings of the moment, its relatively accidental details which ring the dull green tones of Victorianism, and to show that beneath them there still lives the terrible wrath of Henrik Ibsen, who could make a play as men make watches, precisely, intelligently, and telling not merely the minute and the hour but the age."

Miller's adaptation of *An Enemy of the People* was revived by The Repertory Theatre of Lincoln Center in March 1971, and *Time* Magazine's T. E. Kalem observed, "When Arthur Miller adapted Ibsen's play in 1950, he was greatly concerned about the abuses of McCarthyism ...the play becomes a tirade against the venality of smalltown existence rather than a broad examination of when or whether the democratic principle of majority rule may legitimately be abrogated by a single individual...The present production at Lincoln Center begins slowly but develops cumulative power...Stephen Elliott is especially good as Stockmann."

Clive Barnes, in *The New York Times*, considered Miller's adaptation "one of the best plays [he] has ever written...More than Ibsen, Miller is dealing with issues rather than people. He has realized -- he make this much clear in a program note -- that he does not really intend the play as realistic drama...Miller is at his worst in conveying the atmosphere and essence of Ibsen's original, and at his fiery best when he is concentrating on the confrontation between the two brothers...The production is timely, although not for any modish ecological relevance hinted at in the program."

England's Chichester Festival Theatre revived *An Enemy of the People* in May 1975 in a version by John Patrick Vincent. "Ibsen's polemic, his response to the vitriol poured on *Ghosts*, is given a brisk, judiciously cut production," reported W. Stephen Gilbert in *Plays and Players*. "It's led by a performance from Donald Sinden which, though a perfectly legitimate reading, seems to me to diminish the play...As Katherine, Barbara Jefford gives selfless, true support in a blonde wig that does nothing for her. Donald Houston personifies extreme unction with unerring skill."

An all-black version of Ibsen's drama, with Arthur Miller's translation, played for as month in Chicago in 1980, with Paul Winfield heading the cast.

New York's Roundabout Theatre produced *An Enemy of the People* in April 1985, and Frank Rich (*The New York Times*) found that "The Roundabout production, as directed by Frank Hauser, is hardly first-rate but, thanks to the exemplary Stockman of Roy Dotrice, it usually holds the stage. Mr. Dotrice's performance even casts some fresh and appealing light on the play...As director, Mr. Hauser can be applauded for using an accurate rendering of the text rather than the skewered Arthur Miller adaptation."

Following the Young Vic's belated London premiere in 1988 of Arthur Miller's adaptation of the Ibsen play, *Variety* wrote: "As staged by David Thacker, Young Vic artistic director, the production seems stagey and a touch tentative at times, but it has a compensating all-stops-out performances by Tom Wilkinson as Dr. Stockmann...The greatness of this classic is the powerful tocsin it sounds for truth and the citizens' right to know as the cornerstone of democracy...It's a message that resonates in Miller's superior version with an emotional, spine-tingling force all too uncommon these days on the legitimate stage...If Wilkinson, by turns elated, astonished, despairing and finally fighting mad, is the clear standout, David Henry is also persuasive as a corrupt political leader and the show's chief heavy."

Steve McQueen, never noted for his classical acting abilities, raised a number of eyebrows when he announced he was planning a film of *An Enemy of the People* in 1976. He decided he did not want to continue wasting his time making "ordinary movies at this stage of my life. I chose Ibsen's *An Enemy of the People* because I thought he was wonderful and what he said was wonderful. [It] had real meaning for me. It reads like it was written yesterday. I've seen a change in our society over the years I've spent wheeling and dealing and staying alive." Produced by Solar

Productions for First Artists, the company formed by McQueen with Sidney Poitier, Barbra Streisand, Paul Newman and Dustin Hoffman, this ill-advised *An Enemy of the People* had McQueen, after several years off the screen, nearly unrecognizable in full beard and weighing in at more than 200 lbs. Warner Bros., which had agreed in February 1977 to distribute the film, withdrew its commitment after testing it in several cities in the spring of 1978, despite a smattering of favorable reviews. Noted film critic Arthur Knight has described the film as "a handsomely photographed, solid-looking movie, but it has no juice in it, no life to it at all. There's no way for that picture to make contact with a modern audience. McQueen has no understanding of the play, and it took me 20 minutes to recognize him under all those whiskers. It would make an ideal *Hallmark Hall of Fame* TV program." (Small wonder since it was directed by George Schaefer, long associated with *Hallmark Hall of Fame*.)

Gordon Gow (*Films and Filming*) felt that the film "did contain in its central portrait of Dr. Stockmann, whom McQueen portrays, some passing autobiographical references to the playwright himself... McQueen is dedicated in his representation of Stockmann, and he gets especially strong support from Charles Durning as his venal brother, the mayor...George Schaefer's direction of the film is careful rather than exciting, but maybe this is as well since Ibsen's anger, even when restrained a bit as it is here, remains palpable and potent enough." In Britain's *Monthly Film Bulletin*, Tom Milne found McQueen's adventure with Ibsen "straight-forward, sober, and acted with painstaking care...the one undeniably bright feature of the film is [Eugene] Lourie's production design, drained of color and making admirable use of stark wooden interiors and bleak lighting in the manner of Dreyer."

The film finally got a (brief) national release in 1979 before totally disappearing. The failure of *An Enemy of the People* was discouraging to McQueen, who was going through a variety of health problems. The onetime screen superstar was to make just one more movie before dying of cancer in November 1980 at the age of fifty.

Renowned Indian director Satyajit Ray's adaptation of the Ibsen play under the title *Ganashatru* premiered at the Cannes Film Festival in 1989. Spoken in Bengali and featuring Soumitra Chatterjee, one of the director's regular stars, it received only mediocre initial reviews in the western world. *Variety* called it "static and a bit dull" and that it "could have trouble attracting more than his faithful fans." And Britain's *Monthly Film Bulletin* felt that "The sad thing about Ray's adaptation of Ibsen's 107-year-old play, filmed under circumscribed conditions following his recuperation from heart trouble, is that there is little to recommend it" and that "the present version does it no favours by transposing it to a contemporary setting."

In March 1957, Silvio Narizzano directed a production of the Arthur Miller version of *An Enemy of the People* on British television for Granada's *Play of the Week*. The initial American television production of the Ibsen work was on *NET Playhouse* in December 1966. It again was Arthur Miller's adaptation, directed by Paul Bogart, and starred James Daly as Stockmann, Kate Reid as his wife, and Philip Bosco as his brother. Jack Gould said in *The New York Times*: "[It] may lack today the exceptional topicality that attended its presentation in 1951 as a protest against the ways of McCarthyism. But the Henrik Ibsen drama retains a timeless value as a reaffirmation of the value of dissent in a society where truth may be lost because it proves convenient to the majority." Gould found it "a thoroughly worthwhile production that extracted the lasting virtues of Ibsen's convictions from a script that is not totally free from contrivance and serious lapses in forcefulness...Paul Bogart's direction kept the program moving briskly over the many awkward spots...James Daly gives a lucid performance as the doctor, who is a mixture of incredible naivete and fierce determination. Kate Reid was altogether believable as his wife."

In 1990, *An Enemy of the People* again was staged for television, this time quite memorably on PBS' *American Playhouse*. "As a powerful depiction of social corruption and selfishness, the production provides a fascinating signpost to one major direction that theater and literature are likely to take in the 1990s: anger is back in fashion," wrote TV critic John J. O'Connor (*The New York Times*). Of the performers, he observed: "[John] Glover quite brilliantly and almost recklessly portrays Dr. Stockman as [Arthur] Miller envisions the character: a holy fool, fanatical, somewhat mad...Mr. Glover here emerges as a formidable leading man. His fire is perfectly balanced by the ice in [George] Grizzard's depiction of the calculating Mayor Stockman."

STAGE

AN ENEMY OF THE PEOPLE, Abbey's Theatre, New York, opened April 8, 1895 1 performance
Produced by Abbey, Schoeffel and Gray; A Drama, *En Foldfiende*, by Henrik Ibsen, English translation by William Archer; Director, Herbert Beerbohm-Tree; Performed in repertory with *Captain Swift*, *Hamlet*, *A Bunch of Violets*, *The Merry Wives of Windsor* and *Ballad Monger*

Herbert Beerbohm-Tree (Dr. Thomas Stockmann); Frances Ivor (Catherine Stockmann); Charles Allen (Peter Stockmann); Lionel Brough (Morten Kiil); Herbert Ross (Hovstad); E. Holman Clark (Billing); Lily Hanbury (Petra); Alfred Wigley (Aslaksen); Master J. Cookson (Eilif); Master S. Mead (Morten); C. M. Hallard (Captain Horster); Edward Maurice (A Drunken Man)

His Majesty's Theatre, London, opened May 5, 1909 2 matinee performances
Produced and directed by Herbert Beerbohm Tree; A Drama by Henrik Ibsen, English translation by William Archer; Music director, Adolf Schmid; General managers, Henry Dana and Frederick Whelan; Stage managers, Cecil King and Stanley Bell

Herbert Beerbohm-Tree (Dr. Thomas Stockmann); Mrs. Theodore White (Catherine Stockmann); Louis Calvert (Peter Stockmann); G.W. Hanson (Morten Kiil); Norman Page (Hovstad); E. Holman Clark (Billing); Beatrice Forbes-Robertson (Petra); E.M. Tobson (Aslaksen); Master Bobbie Andrews (Eilif); Master Sidney Sherwood (Morten); Sydney Hamilton (Captain Horster); Carleton Rex (Petersen)

Hampden's Theatre, New York, opened October 3, 1927 127 performances
Produced and directed by Walter Hampden; A Drama by Henrik Ibsen; Production designed and supervised by Claude Bragdon; Lighting, Frank Heins and Pierce Hodgins; Musical director, Elliott Schneck; Stage managers, Edwin Cushman and Albert West

Walter Hampden (Dr. Thomas Stockmann); Mabel Moore (Catherine Stockmann); C. Norman Hammond (Peter Stockmann); W. H. Sams (Morten Kiil); Dallas Anderson (Hovstad); Stanley Howlett (Billing); Marie Adels (Petra); Cecil Yapp (Aslaksen); Leroy Wade (Eilif); George Offerman, Jr. (Morten); Ernest Rowan (Captain Horster); Hart Jenks (Mr. Vik); P. J. Kelly (A Drunken Man); Edith Barrett, Caroline Meade, Hope Carey, Louis Polan, Franklin Salisbury, Howard Claney, Thomas Gomez, Gordon Hart, Albert West, Gage Bennett, Murray Darcy (Townsfolk)

Wyndham's Theatre, London, opened March 26, 1928 1 matinee perforance

A Drama by Henrik Ibsen (anonymous translation); Director, Rupert Harvey

Rupert Harvey (Dr. Thomas Stockmann); May Agate (Catherine Stockmann); Hubert Harden (Peter Stockmann); Hector Abbas (Morten Kiil); Keith Pyott (Hovstad); Geoffrey Dunlop (Billing); Ann Trevor (Petra); Philip Wade (Aslaksen); Barbara Smith (Eilif); Miriam Leighton (Morten); B. A. Pittar (Captain Horster)

Embassy Theatre, London, opened October 1, 1934
A Drama by Henrik Ibsen; Director, Eileen Thorndike

Ronald Adam (Dr. Thomas Stockmann); Elva Stuart (Catherine Stockmann); Vernon Sylvaine (Peter Stockmann); Mario Francelli (Morten Kiil); Alwyn Whatsley (Hovstad); John Angelo (Billing); Ann Titheradge (Petra); Victor Keefe (Eilif); John Jacques (Morten); Will Leighton (Captain Horster)

Old Vic Theatre, London, opened February 21, 1939
Produced and directed by Tyrone Guthrie; A Drama by Henrik Ibsen

Roger Livesey (Dr. Thomas Stockmann); Nora Nicholson (Catherine Stockmann); Edward Chapman (Peter Stockmann); Frederick Bennett (Morten Kiil); Colin Keith-Johnston (Hovstad); Jonathan Field (Billing); Ursula Jeans (Petra); Frank Napier (Aslaksen); Geoffrey Holiday (Eilif); David Baxter (Morten); Ballard Berkeley (Captain Horster)

Hudson Theatre, New York, opened February 15, 1937
Produced and directed by Walter Hampden; A Drama by Henrik Ibsen; Production designed by Claude Bragdon; Company manager, S.M. Weller; Stage managers, Edwin Cashman and Harvey Sayers

Walter Hampden (Dr. Thomas Stockmann); Mabel Moore (Catherine Stockmann); C. Norman Hammond (Peter Stockmann); Dodson Mitchell (Morten Kiil); Albert van Dekker (Hovstad); Allen Nourse (Billing); Marjorie Jarecki (Petra); Hannam Clark (Aslaksen); Walter Ward (Eilif); Dick Wallace (Morten); Albert Bergh (Captain Horster); Conrad Cantzen (Mr. Vik); Richard Freeman (A Drunken Man); Elizabeth Dean Farrar (A Maid); Mortimer Weldon, Arthur Gilmour, Paul Tripp, Murray D'Arcy, James C. Malaidy, Richard W. Bowler, Wyman Kane, Richard Ross, Boris Ulmar, Leslie Klein, Constance Pelissier, Harvey Sayers, John E. Wheeler, John C. Davis, Edward M. Grace, Walter James, G. B. Kingston, Sidney Palmer, Walter Kapp, John Rustad, Albert Allen, Richard Allen, Charles Brunswick, Haakon Ogle (Townsfolk)

Broadhurst Theatre, New York, opened December 28, 1950 36 performances
Produced by Lars Nordenson; A Drama by Henrik Ibsen, adapted by Arthur Miller; Director, Robert Lewis; Setting and costumes by Aline Bernstein; Lighting, Charles Elson; Stage managers, Robert F. Simon and James Awe

Fredric March (Dr. Thomas Stockmann); Florence Eldridge (Catherine Stockmann); Morris Carnovsky (Peter Stockmann); Art Smith (Morten Kiil); Martin Brooks (Hovstad); Michael Strong (Billing); Anna Minot (Petra); Fred Stewart (Aslaksen); Richard Traski (Eilif); Ralph Robertson (Morten); Ralph Dunn (Captain Horster); Lou Gilbert (A Drunken Man); Lulla Adler, Barbara Ames, Edith Case, Paul Fitzpatrick, James Karen, Michael Lewis, Salem Ludwig, Gene Lyons, John Marley, J. Berry Nathan, Charles Park, Richard Purcell, Arthur Row, Arnold Shulman, Robert F. Simon, Carl Specht, Rod Steiger (Townsfolk)

Provincetown Theatre, New York, opened February 25, 1958
Produced by Alexander Productions; A Drama by Henrik Ibsen; Adapted, directed and designed by Arthur Reel; Costumes, E. Blanche Barrett; Lighting, Henry Dencyger

David Moss (Dr. Thomas Stockmann); Pat Crawford (Catherine Stockmann); Sherman Lloyd (Peter Stockmann); James Colby (Morten Kiil); Iver Fischman (Hovstad); Jerry Weiss (Billing); Renay Granville (Petra); James Aipe (Aslaksen); Michael Aubrey (Eilif); Sam Flores (Morten); Lionel Habas (Captain Horster); Bill Corrie (Evensen); Carl Shelton (Anders); Cal Ander (Lumstad); Hugh Palmerston (Gunnar); Kay Hutchinson (Mrs. Helig); Christopher Tanner (Helig); Lisa Marshall (Drunk); Robert Bruce (Mr. Vik); Jean Harmel (Mrs. Lumstad); George Maisel (Nordsen); Richard Lienaweaver (Erik); Patti Killmurray (Erik's Wife); Edith Heller (Mrs. Evensen); Catherine Perkins (Mrs. Norden)

Actors Playhouse, New York, opened February 4, 1959
Produced by Gene Frankel, Al Sperduto and Richard Karp; A Drama by Henrik Ibsen, adapted by Arthur Miller; Director, Gene Frankel; Scenery, Richard Bianchi; Costumes, Oliver Olsen; Stage manager, Pamela Judson-Stiles

Ward Costello (Dr. Thomas Stockmann); Lois Holmes (Catherine Stockmann); Henderson Forsythe (Peter Stockmann); John Marley (Morten Kiil); Gerald Hiken (Hovstad); Ronald Nicholas (Billing); Joan De Marrais (Petra); Al Sperduto (Aslaksen); Spencer Duncan (Eilif); Howard Hilton (Morten); Joseph Warren (Captain Horster); Ted Tesser (Drunk); Gertrude Offstein (Hedvig); J. Thomas Degidon (Edvard); Al Viola (Nansem); Edward Chiaro (Henrik); Paul Ross (Gunnar); Bill Reilly (Knut); David Woodman (Finn); Stella Longo (Tora)

Arts Theatre, Cambridge, England, opened February 9, 1959
Produced by The Cambridge Arts Theatre Trust; A Drama by Henrik Ibsen, adapted by Arthur Miller; Director, John Hale; Production designer, Ken Bridgeman

George Coulouris (Dr. Thomas Stockmann); Elspeth MacNaughton (Catherine Stockmann); Brian Hawklsey (Peter Stockmann); Roger Milner (Morten Kiil); Tom Criddle (Hovstad); Henry Davies (Billing); Gillian Muir (Petra); William Wymar (Aslaksen); Robert Fyfe (Eilif); Richard Greenford (Morten); Arthur Skinner (Captain Horster); Paul Toseland (Drunk)

Actors Playhouse, New York, opened December 10, 1959
Produced by Gene Frankel, Al Sperduto and Richard Karp; A Drama by Henrik Ibsen, adapted by Arthur Miller; Director, Gene Frankel; Setting, Richard Bianchi; Costumes, Oliver Olsen

Joseph Warren (Dr. Thomas Stockmann); Lois Holmes (Catherine Stockmann); Nicholas Saunders (Peter Stockmann); Art Smith (Morten Kiil); William Sargent (Hovstad); Eric Tavares (Billing); Polly Campbell (Petra); Al Sperduto (Aslaksan); Spencer Duncan (Eilif); Dennis Duncan (Morten); Joseph L. Graham (Captain Horster); Ann Blackstone (Hedvig); Robert Bates (A Drunk); Richard Reeves (Edvard); Matt Rivera (Nansem); Ralph Faber (Gunnar); Alex Fox (Henrik); William Crossett (Finn); Ralph Lee (Gorg); Kathleen Scarlett (Tora)

Vivian Beaumont Theatre, New York, opened March 11, 1971 54 performances
Produced by The Repertory Theatre of Lincoln Center; A Play by Henrik Ibsen,

adapted by Arthur Miller; Director, Jules Irving; Settings, Douglas W. Schmidt; Lighting, John Gleason; Costumes, Carrie Fishbein Robbins; Hairstyles and makeup, Jim Sullivan; Stage managers, Barbara-Mae Phillips and Robert Benson

Stephen Elliott (Dr. Thomas Stockmann); Barbara Cason (Catherine Stockmann); Philip Bosco (Peter Stockmann); Sydney Walker (Morten Kiil); David Birney (Hovstad); James Blendick (Billing); Tandy Cronyn (Petra); Conrad Bain (Aslaksen); Barry Symonds or Michael Meyers (Eilif); Michael Meyers or Timmy Ousey (Morten); Don Plumley (Captain Horster); Macon McCalman (The Drunk); Esther Benson, Robert Benson, Joseph Boley, Richard Bowler, James Cook, Blaine Cordner, Ronald Frazier, Robert Levine, David Little, Michael Miller, Susan Sharkey, George Van Den Houten (Townsfolk)

Aldwych Theatre, London, opened April 18, 1975

Presented by the Royal Shakespeare Company; Produced by Compania di Prosotino Buazzelli of Italy in a Peter Daubeny World Theatre Season; A Drama by Henrik Ibsen; Director, Edmo Fenoglio, assisted by Nelly Cavallo; Production designer, Walter Pace; Lighting, Andrea Ori; Music, Lucia De Laurentiis

Tino Buazzelli (Dr. Thomas Stockmann); Nicoletta Languasco (Catherine Stockmann); Tino Bianchi (Peter Stockmann); Enrico Poggi (Morten Kiil); Massimo de Francovich (Hovstad); Gioacchino Maniscalco (Billing); Barbara Ney (Petra); Robertino Paoletti (Eilif); Massimo di Cecco (Morten); Claudio Dani (Captain Horster)

Chichester (Eng.) Theatre, opened May 27, 1975

Produced by the Chichester Festival Company; A Drama by Henrik Ibsen, translated by John Patrick Vincent; Director, Patrick Garland; Production designer, Stefanos Lazaridis; Lighting, Mick Hughes; Costumes, Michael Stennett

Donald Sinden (Dr. Thomas Stockmann); Barbara Jefford (Catherine Stockmann); Donald Houston (Peter Stockmann); Bill Fraser (Morten Kiil); Tony Robinson (Hovstad); David Henry (Billing); Sue Jones-David (Petra); Michael Coterill (Aslaksen); Julian Somers (Captain Horster); Sally Osborn (Randina); Rex Robinson (Rubeck); Jennifer Tudor (Mrs. Hinkle); Peggy Marshall (Mrs. Manders); Philip Anthony (Beckus); Michael Scholes (Evensen); Trevor Martin (A Drunk)

Seattle (Wash.) Repertory Theatre, season 1979-80

Produced by Peter Donnelly; A Drama by Henrik Ibsen, adapted by Arthur Miller; Director, Daniel Sullivan

Biff McGuire (Dr. Thomas Stockmann); Jeannie Carson (Catherine Stockmann); David White (Peter Stockmann); Barney O'Sullivan (Morten Kiil); Lawrence Ballard (Hovstad); John Procaccino (Billing); Marnie Mosiman (Petra); Clayton Corzatte (Aslaksen); Jeff Covell (Eilif); Christopher Briggs (Morten); John Aylward (Captain Horster); Michael Santo (A Drunk); Susan Ludlow, Cheryl Whitener, Richard E. Arnold, Daniel Noel, Jonathan Simmons, Dean Melang, Bill De Young, Randy Schaub, John Smiley, Tony Amendola, Charles Janasz, James Gordon, Mark Perry, William Crossett (Townsfolk)

Goodman Theatre, Chicago, opened January 24 to February 24, 1980

Produced by the Goodman Theatre of the Art Institute of Chicago, Janet Wade, managing director, Gregory Mosher, artistic director; A Drama by Henrik Ibsen, adapted by Arthur Miller; Director, Gregory Mosher; Scenery, Joseph Mieminski;

Lighting, Robert Christen; Costumes, Jessica Hahn; General manager, Roche Schulfer

Paul Winfield (Dr. Thomas Stockmann); Mary Cobb (Catherine Stockmann); William Marshall (Peter Stockmann); Mike Genovese (Morten Kiil); Gregory Williams (Hovstad); Terry Kinney (Billing); Jeanine Morick (Petra); Roy K. Stevens (Aslaksen); Ben Gundersheimer (Eilif); Carroll Valenzuela-Tyson (Morten); David Mink (Captain Horster); Robert Kahn (A Drunk); Arthur J. Burdett, Tim Campbell, Jim Egan, Marilyn Herrs, Paul Lapinski, Andrew Moore, Ernest Perry, Jr., William C. Renk, Mary Seibel (Townsfolk)

Roundabout Theatre, New York, opened March 27 through May 12, 1985
Produced by the Roundabout Theatre Company, Gene Feist, artistic director; A Drama by Henrik Ibsen; Director, Frank Hauser; Setting, Bob Mitchell; Lighting, Dennis Parichy; Costumes, A. Christina Giannini; Sound, Guy Sherman; Stage manager, K. Siobhan Phelan

Roy Dotrice (Dr. Thomas Stockmann); Ruby Holbrook (Catherine Stockmann); Paul Sparer (Peter Stock-mann); Jack Bittner (Morten Kiil); Mark Capri (Hovstad); Barrett Heins (Billing); Janet Zarish (Petra); Gordon Chater (Aslaksen); Sean H. M. Reynolds (Eilif); Bart Acocella (Morten); DeVeren Bookwater (Captain Horster); Robert Brownstein, Jared Roy, Alex Stul, Brian Tomlinson (Townsfolk)

Playhouse, London, opened November 30, 1988 through February 4, 1989
A Frank & Woji Gero presentation of a Young Vic production; A Play by Henrik Ibsen, adapted by Arthur Miller; Director, David Thacker; Setting, Fran Thompson; Lighting, Paul Denby

Tom Wilkinson (Dr. Thomas Stockmann); Margot Leicester (Catherine Stockmann); David Henry (Peter Stockmann); Clive Swift (Morten Kiil); Tom Mannion (Hovstad); Richard Graham (Billing); Suzan Sylvester (Petra); Richard Butler (Aslaksen); Stephen Evans (Eilif); Simon Mead (Morten); Harry Miller (Captain Horster); Susan Gott, Dominic Letts, Brian Southwood, Pancho Russell, Michael McElhatton

SCREEN

AN ENEMY OF THE PEOPLE, *Warner Bros.*, released March 1978
A Solar Production for First Artists; Executive producer, Steve McQueen; Produced and directed by George Schaefer; Associate producer, Philip Parslow; Screenplay, Alexander Jacobs, based on Arthur Miller's adaptation of the play by Henrik Ibsen; Photography, Paul Lohmann; Production designer, Eugene Lorie; Costumes, Noel Taylor; Set decoration, Anthony Mondello; Makeup, William and Tom Tuttle; Music, Leonard Rosenman; Special effects, William Doane; Editor, Sheldon Kahn

Steve McQueen (Dr. Thomas Strockmann); Bibi Andersson (Catherine Stockmann); Charles Durning (Peter Stockmann); Eric Christmas (Morten Kiil); Michael Cristofer (Hovstad); Michael Higgins (Billing); Pearson Rose (Petra); Richard A. Dysart (Askalsen); Ham Larsen (Eilif); John Levin (Morten); Richard Bradford (Captain Horster); Louise Hoven (Randine); Glen Ransom, Leon Charles, Harry Frazier, Jim Begg, Lilliam Adams, Steven Douglas Hartley, Jack Carol, Darel Glaser, Russ Marin, Thor Nielsen, Seamon Glass, Delos V. Smith, Jr., Kenneth White, Bart Williams, Michael Vandever, Kenneth W. Tanner, Stan Stratton, Joseph G. Medalis, Marc de Vries, Miriam Hendry, Gregory Bell,

Walter Stroud, Robert Clement, Zachary Lewis, Kay E. Kuter, Teddy Blue, John Volstad, Gene Ruymen, Michael Greene (Townsfolk)

GANASHATRU (AN ENEMY OF THE PEOPLE), India, released 1989
A National Film Development Corporation of India production; Executive producer, Ravi Malik; Producer; Anil Gupta: Adapted and directed by Satyajit Ray from the play by Henrik Ibsen; Photography, Barun Raha; Art director, Ashok Bose; Makeup, Ananta Das; Music, Satyajit Ray; Editor, Dulal Dutt

Soumitra Chatterjee (Dr. Ashok Gupta); Ruma Guharthakurta (Maya Gupta); Dhritiman Chatterjee (Nichit Gupta); Mamata Shankar (Ramu Gupta); Dipankar Dey (Haridas Bagchi); Subhendu Chatterjee (Biresh); Vischwa Gaharthakurta (Romen Holdar); Manoj Mitra (Adhir Mukherjee); Rajaram Yagnik (Bjhargava); Sarya Banerji (Manmatha)

TELEVISION

AN ENEMY OF THE PEOPLE, *Play of the Week*, televised March 20, 1957 Granada (London) 80 minutes
Produced and directed by Silvio Narizzano; Teleplay by Elspeth Cochrane from Arthur Miller's 1950 adaptation of the play by Henrik Ibsen

John Robinson (Dr. Thomas Stockmann); Jessica Spencer (Catherine Stockmann); Clive Morton (Peter Stockmann); Tony Sympson (Morten Kiil); Peter Wyngarde (Hovstad); Jill Dixon (Petra); John Salew (Aslaksen); Brian Franklin (Eilif); Anthony Wilson (Morten); Edward Forsyth (Captain Horster); Tom Criddle (Billing); and Reginald Marsh, Julia Chester, Malcolm Watson, Michael Ely, George Ricarde, Joanna Glass

NET Playhouse, televised December 2, 1966 PBS 2 hours
Produced by Jac Venza and Jack Landau; Director, Paul Bogart; Arthur Miller's 1950 adaptation of the play by Henrik Ibsen

James Daly (Dr. Thomas Stockmann); Kate Reid (Catherine Stockmann); Philip Bosco (Peter Stockmann); George Voskovec (Morten Kiil); James Olson (Hovstad); Barbara Dana (Petra); William Prince (Aslaksen); Earl Hedin (Eilif); Timothy Daly (Morten); Walter Klavin (Captain Horster)

American Playhouse, televised June 13, 1990 PBS 105 minutes
Produced by David Griffiths; Executive producer, Sam Paul; Director, Jack O'Brien; Arthur Miller's 1950 adaptation of the play by Henrik Ibsen; Production design, Ben Edwards; Lighting, Ken Dettling; Set decorator, Evette Siegel; Costume design, Lewis Brown; Musical director/composer, Bob James; Stage managers, Kelly D. Hommon and Richard Levin

John Glover (Dr. Thomas Stockmann); Valerie Mahaffey (Catherine Stockmann); George Grizzard (Peter Stockmann); Robert Symonds (Morten Kiil); Byron Jennings (Hovstad); Nina Siemaszko (Polly Stockman); Richard Easton (Anderson); William Anton (Billing); Dawn Didawick (Randine); James Morrison (Captain Horster); Robert Phalen (Drunk); Mitchell Edmonds, Anne Gee Byrd, James Whittle (Citizens)

FAME
Versions of the 1980 film written by Christopher Gore

Synopsis

The scene is the High School for the Performing Arts in midtown Manhattan. A disparate group of students have been selected by audition before music teacher Shorofsky, acting teacher Angelo and dance teacher Miss Berg. Among them are Doris Finsecker, a shy, mother-dominated aspiring actress; Raul Garcia (known to everyone as "Ralph Garcy"), a noisily overconfident Puerto Rican entertainer; Bruno Martelli, an obsessive electronic musician; Leroy Johnson, a brilliant black modern dancer with a chip on his shoulder; Lisa Monroe, a half-hearted ballet dancer; and Coco Hernandez, a singer with intense ambitions for herself. In the four years that follow, Doris manages to break the influence of her mother and befriends Montgomery, who eventually comes to terms with his sexuality; Leroy spars with Mrs. Sherwood, his English teacher, has an affair with WASPish Hilary Van Doren, and is accepted by the Alvin Ailey Dance Company; Ralph Garcy has a mutually liberating affair with Doris, acknowledges his deprived background and wins what turns out to be a temporarily prestigious gig as a nightclub comic; Coco has a brush with porno filmmaker Francois Lafete, develops a powerful voice, and sees Bruno's music finally accepted; Hilary appears to suffer a breakdown; and Lisa is expelled for lack of effort.

Comment and Critique

"Our film, I hope, will be a microcosm of New York. It's the glamour of the Great White Way of Broadway and the squalor of 42nd Street...the fine line between a Juilliard Scholarship and dancing topless at the Metropole [in Times Square]...A dozen races pitching in and having their own crack at the American Dream." So wrote British director Alan Parker in an open letter to the crew of *Fame*, which became one of the most invigorating contemporary musicals of its time and an overnight box office smash. Coming from the studio that was synonymous with the golden age of movie musicals, *Fame* brought the genre into a new generation. Written by Christopher Gore (brother of Lesley Gore, one of the top pop music stars of the 1960s), it boasted a vigorous score which he wrote with Dean Pitchford. The title song, in fact, won the Oscar and was to be theme of the subsequent TV series (with Debbie Allen, Albert Hague, Gene Anthony Ray and Lee Curreri repeating their film roles) and the later stage adaptation.

According to *Variety*, the film was shot not inside New York's venerable High School of the Performing Arts on 46th Street ("the educational institution would have none of the project") but in front of it, with an Episcopal church on the same block standing in for the school itself. Its critic said, "What director Alan Parker has come up with is exposure for some of the most talented youngsters seen on the screen in years...a rousing production bursting out of the screen with talent and exuberance..."

The New York Times' Janet Maslin called *Fame* "a jubilant, hugely entertaining movie by a man whose principal directing experience has been the making of commercials, and so it is happier, sexier and a little bit livelier than life...The cast is full of glowing newcomers, the score is emphatically upbeat, and the action moves swiftly from character to character, stringing together a lot of subplots in quick succession."

British critic John Pym, writing of *Fame* in *Monthly Film Bulletin*, felt: "The fragments of [the] youngsters' stories are cut together with a breathless immediacy that many will irresistible; and the punctuating sequences of non-stop 'entertainment'...communicate a genuine if limited sense of the world occupied by starry-eyed, over-energized *student* performers, as opposed to grittily or woefully determined old pros in the chorus lines of show business."

Fame emerged on television lasting for a year on NBC (1982-83) and then for four with original episodes produced for syndication. Debbie Allen not only starred (alphabetically) as the demanding dance teacher but also created three or four intricately-choreographed production numbers for each episode, and later she began directing a number of the episodes. Reviewing the premiere of the TV series in January 1982, *Variety* found: "Spinoff from 1980 feature film spills over with exuberance and juve pranks in a pitch to youthful audiences...Theme of a school for performers gives the new teleseries a shot at music numbers, something rare in commercial vid ventures...Debbie Allen has been recruited as the vivid dance instructor, and everyone seems on his toes for first assignment." John J. O'Connor (*The New York Times*) felt that "*Fame* gets off to a disarmingly sassy start, striking a reasonable balance between youthful realities and show business pizzazz. The rest will depend on good scripts and maintaining the momentum."

The show's fame, both in the U.S. and Great Britain, prompted the mounting of a Christmas 1982 British concert tour and an American television special in 1983 of *The Kids From Fame*, with a number of the TV series' talented performers (Debbie Allen, Valerie Landsburg, Erica Gimpel, Carlo Imperato, Lee Curreri, Lori Singer and Gene Anthony Ray).

In 1988, *Fame* was adapted to the stage and was given its premiere in Miami Beach. Conceived and developed by David De Silva, it combined the familiar *Fame* theme with a new score by Steven Margoshes and Jacques Levy. "The stage concept bumps into other models, notably *A Chorus Line*, in this outing and doesn't necessarily plow any new ground, but may prove good enough for another turn," *Variety* said of the world premiere of *Fame: The Musical*. "Author Jose Fernandez has taken a dramatic approach to his study of kids studying for the big time. His tale has rough edges and a hard center, on the far side of *Babes in Arms* with the movie version of *Fame* in the middle...Director David Saint maintains a smart pace and focus through it all, and gets a real boost from Jennifer Mueller's stylized, eyecatching choreography."

Following the show's spring 1989 staging at the Walnut Street Theatre in Philadelphia, *The Inquirer* critic William B. Collins enthused: "...perform is what the buoyant new musical, *Fame*, does, dance number after exhilarating number, song after sweet song, never losing sight of its mission to entertain...Composer Steven Margoshes and his lyricist, Jacques Levy, show a nice sensitivity to the condition of being young and hopeful and gifted...As in the film, the class is followed through its four years of schooling, but writer Jose Fernandez manages deftly to let us know that time is marching on without making us feel it is trampling on our consciousness."

Fame: The Musical has yet to make its way to Broadway.

STAGE

FAME: THE MUSICAL, *Coconut Grove Playhouse*, Miami, opened October 21 through December 3, 1988
Produced by the Coconut Grove Playhouse (Arnold Mittelman, producing artistic director) in association with David De Silva; A Musical in two acts, conceived and developed by David De Silva; Director, David Saint; Book by Jose Fernandez; Music by Steven Margoshes; Lyrics by Jacques Levy; "Fame" music and lyrics by Michael

Gore and Dean Pitchford; Choreography, Jennifer Muller; Sets, Alexander Okun; Lighting, Joshua Starbuck; Costumes, Randy Barcelo; Musical direction and incidental music, Kevin Stites; Orchestrations, Harold Wheeler and Steven Margoshes; Production stage manager, Rafael V. Blanco

Tom Acousti, Tener Brown, Christian Canciani, Monique Cintron, Juan Dinzey, Richard Frisch, Lyd-Lyd Gaston, Allen Hidalgo, Julia C. Hughes, Ebony JoAnn, Joyce P. King, Rosemary McNamara, Joel Malina, Gary Mendelson, Janet Metz, Stacy Morze, Guy Paul, Harold Perrineau, Jr., Marishka S. Phillips, Darnell D. Pritchard, Ken Seymour, Cherice Simmons

MUSICAL NUMBERS: "Pray I Make P.A."; "Hard Work"; "I Want to Make Magic"; "Can't Keep It Down"; "Tyrone's Rap"; "Let's Play a Love Scene"; "There She Goes/Fame"; "Bring on Tomorrow"; "The Teacher's Argument"; "Like Carmen, Not Me!"; "Shake the Foundation"; "I Want to Make Magic" (reprise); "Sugar Blues"; "Think of Meryl Streep"; "Dancin' on the Sidewalk"; "These Are My Children"; "Lemme Out!"; "In L.A."; "Let's Play a Love Scene" (reprise); "Bring on Tomorrow" (reprise)

FAME: THE MUSICAL, *Mechanic Theatre*, Baltimore, opened February 21 through March 19, 1989; *Walnut Street Theatre*, Philadelphia, opened March 25 through April 29, I989

Produced by the Walnut Street Theatre Company (Bernard Havard, artistic director) in association with the Baltimore Center for the Performing Arts; A Musical in two acts, conceived and developed by David De Silva; Director, David Saint; Book by Jose Fernandez; Music by Steven Margoshes; Lyrics by Jacques Levy; "Fame" music and lyrics by Michael Gore and Dean Pitchford; Choreography, Jennifer Muller; Sets, Alexander Okun; Lighting, Joshua Starbuck; Costumes, Randy Barcelo; Musical direction, Steven Margoshes; Incidental music, Kevin Stites; Orchestrations, Harold Wheeler and Steven Margoshes; Production stage manager, Jane Grey

Christian Canciani, Monique Cintron, Juan Dinzey, Dorothy R. Earle, Patricia Garvey, Lyd-Lyd Gaston, Allen Hidalgo, Ebony Jo-Ann, Omar Kabir, Joyce P. King, Rosemary McNamara, Joel Malina, Lisa Mayer, Louis Mazza, Gary Mendelson, Janet Metz, Stacy Morze, Michael O'Steen, Harold Perrineau, Jr., Marishka S. Phillips, Darnell D. Pritchard, David Rogers, Lee Shepherd, Cherice Simmons, Rondi Williams

MUSICAL NUMBERS: Same as previous production except "I Gotta Find a Way/Hard Work" and "The Pas-de-Deux" replaced "Shake the Foundation" and "Sugar Blues"

SCREEN

FAME, *Metro-Goldwyn-Mayer*, released 1980

Produced by David De Silva and Alan Marshall; Director, Alan Parker; Screenplay, Christopher Gore; Photography, Michael Seresin; Production designer, Geoffrey Kirkland, Set decorator, George DeTitta; Costumes, Kristi Zea; Music (see below); Choreography, Louis Falco; Editor, Gerry Hambling

Irene Cara (Coco Hernandez); Lee Curreri (Bruno Martelli); Laura Dean (Lisa Monroe); Antonia Franceschi (Hilary Van Doren); Paul McCrane (Montgomery MacNeil); Barry Miller (Raul Garcia, aka Ralph Garcy); Gene Anthony Ray (Leroy Johnson); Maureen Teefy (Doris Finsecker); Eddie Barth (Angelo); Boyd Gaines (Michael); Albert Hague (Shorofsky); Tresa Hughes (Naomi Finsecker); Steve Inwood (Francois Lafete); Anne Meara (Mrs. Sherwood); Joanna Merlin

(Miss Berg); Jim Moody (Farrell); Debbie Allen (Lydia); Richard Belzer (Richard, "Catch a Rising Star" MC); Frank Bongiorno (Truck Driver); Bill Britten (Mr. England); Eric Brockington (Plump Eric); Nicholas Bunin (Bunsky); Cindy Canuelas (Cindy); Nora Cotrone (Topless Student); Mbewe Escobar (Phenicia); Gennardy Filimonov (Violinist); Victor Fischbarg (Harvey Finsecker); Penny Frank (Dance Teacher); Willie Henry, Jr. (Bathroom Student); Steven Hollander, Ted Lambert, Loris Sallahian (Drama Students); Sang Kim (Oriental Violinist); Darrell Kirkman (Richard III); Judith L'Heureux (Nurse); Nancy Lee (Oriental Student); Sarah Malament (Dance Accompanist); James Manis (Bruno's Uncle); Carol Messenburg (Shirley, Leroy's Partner); Isaac Mizrahi (Touchstone); Raquel Mondin (Ralph's Sister); Alba Ohms (Ralph's Mother); Frank Oteri (Schlepstein); Traci Parnell (Hawaiian Dancer); Sal Piro (Himself, MC at "Rocky Horror" Screening); Leslie Quickley ("Towering Inferno" Student); Ray Ramirez (Father Morales); Ilse Sass (Mrs. Tossoff); Dawn Steinberg (Monitor on Stairs); Jonathan Strasser (Orchestra Conductor); Yvette Torres (Ralph's Little Sister); Frank X. Vitolo (Frankie); Stefanie Zimmerman (Dance Teacher; Tracy Burnett, Greg De Jean, Laura Delano, Michael DeLorenzo, Aaron Duigger, Neisha Folkes, Karen Ford, Robin Gray, Hazel Green, Eva Grubler, Patrick King, Cynthia Lochard, Julian Montenaire, Holly Reeve, Kate Snyder, Meg Tilly, Louis Venosta, Philip Wright, Ranko Yokoyana (Principal Dancers)

MUSICAL NUMBERS: "Fame" (Michael Gore, Dean Pritchford), performed by Irene Cara; "Out Here on My Own" (Michael Gore, Lesley Gore), performed by Irene Cara; "Hot Lunch Jam" (Michael Gore, Lesley Gore, Robert F. Colesberry, Irene Cara); "Dogs in the Yard" (Dominic Bugatti, arranged by Steven Margoshes), performed by Paul McCrane; "Red Light" (Michael Gore, Dean Pitchford), performed by Linda Clifford; "Is It Okay If I Call You Mine?" (Paul McCrane), performed on guitar by Paul McCrane; "Never Alone" (Anthony Evans), performed by the Contemporary Gospel Chorus, the High School of Music and Art; "I Sing the Body Electric" (Michael Gore, Dean Pitchford, arranged by Steven Margoshes), performed by Irene Cara, Paul McCrane, Traci Parnell, Eric Brockington

Original soundtrack recording: MGM Records

TELEVISION

FAME, televised January 7, 1982 through August 4, 1983 NBC 35 one-hour episodes; Syndication beginning October 1983 through May 1987 136 episodes total

An MGM-UA Television production; Executive producers, William Blinn and Gerald I. Isenberg; Producers, Stan Rogow, Mel Swope, David De Silva and Ken Ehrlich; Director, Bob Kelljan and others; Writers, Christopher Gore, William Blinn and others; Photography, Alan Metzger, Robert B. Hauser, William Spencer and Sherman Kunkel; Art directors, Ben Edwards and Ira Diamond; Music, Michael Gore, William Goldstein and Sue Sheridan; Theme, Michael Gore and Dean Pitchford; Performed by Erica Gimpel; Choreography, Debbie Allen and Otis Sallid; Editors, Eric Jenkins, Michael A. Hoey and Jim McElroy

Debbie Allen (Lydia Grant); Albert Hague (Prof. Benjamin Shorofsky); Carol Mayo Jenkins (Elizabeth Sherwood); Morgan Stevens (David Reardon); Ken Swofford (Quinton Murdoch); Ann Nelson (Gertrude Berg); Lori Singer (Julie Miller); Erica Gimpel (Coco Hernandez); Valerie Landsburg (Doris Schwartz); Lee Curreri (Bruno Martelli); Carlo Imperato (Danny Amatello); Gene Anthony Ray (Leroy Johnson); Cynthia Gibb (Holly Laird); Billy Hufsey (Christopher

Donlan); P. R. Paul (Montgomery MacNeil); Michael Thoma (Greg Crandall); Judy Farrell Mrs. Miller); Madlyn Rhue (Charlotte Schwartz); Carmine Caridi (Angie Martelli); Gerald S. O'Loughlin (Jack Schwartz); Alan Weeks (Leroy's Father); Royce Wallace (Leroy's Mother); Betty Karlen (Danny's Mother); Louis Gambalvo (Danny's Father); Janet Jackson (Cleo Hewitt); Nia Peeples (Nicole Chapman); Jesse Borrego (Jesse); *added cast for syndication*: Loretta Chandler (Dusty Tyler); Carrie Hamilton (Reggie Higgins); Page Hannah (Kate Reilly); Michael Cerveris (Ian Waire); Elisa Heinsohn (Jillian)

THE KIDS FROM FAME, televised March 7, 1983 NBC I hour
Produced by MGM/UA TV in association with NBC; Executive producers, William Blinn, Mel Swope, Charles Koppelman and Martin Bandler; Producer, Nicholas Clapp; Director, Terry Sanders; Teleplay, Draper Lewis; Photography, Erik Daarstad; Music conducted by Barry Fasman; Live concerts in London produced, staged and choreographed by Debbie Allen; Editors, Howard Block and William Cartwright; Host, George Burns

Debbie Allen, Lee Curreri, Erica Gimpel, Carlo Imperato, Valerie Landsburg, Gene Anthony Ray, Lori Singer

THE FIRST GENTLEMAN
A Play by Norman Ginsbury (1945)

Synopsis

The profligate, obese and extremely vain Prince Regent rules England due to the madness of his father, King George III. In June 1814 at Carlton House, the Prince, aptly described by his tutor as "either the most polished gentleman or the most accomplished blackguard in Europe -- possibly both," tries to force his strongwilled daughter Charlotte to marry Prince William of Orange. Charlotte, temperamental and as stubbornly determined as her tyrannical father, refuses Prince William and insists on marrying the man she loves, Prince Leopold of SaxeCoburg. The hedonistic Prince, beset with his embittered queen, Caroline, and his mistress, Lady Conynham, reluctantly consents to the marriage of Charlotte and Prince Leopold. After less than a year of marital bliss, Charlotte dies giving birth to a stillborn son. In June 1819, preening himself and insisting on being forcefully braced into a large, uncomfortable corset, the Prince Regent, England's future King George IV, dons his most magnificent royal robes to attend the christening of a niece who is to be named Victoria.

Comment and Critique

Norman Ginsbury, born in London on November 8, 1903, wrote a play called *Viceroy Sarah* in 1934 and made new translations of Ibsen's *Ghosts* and *An Enemy of the People* in 1937 and 1939. During the 1940s, he made English adaptations of Ibsen's *Peer Gynt* and *A Doll's House*, and in 1945 his successful play based on the life of England's future King George IV appeared. Six years later, the musical he wrote with Eric Maschwitz based on the life of Queen Victoria was banned for public performance in England by the Lord Chamberlain who reasoned the Queen did *not* sing!

The First Gentleman was described by *Theatre World* as a "clever historical play, which is finely acted by a brilliant cast and produced with a lavishness that does justice to the period...Robert Morley gives a masterly study of the Regent and Wendy Hiller brings youthful high spirits with some touches of real poignancy to the role of the illfated Charlotte." *The First Gentleman* ran for 654 performances in London, but despite an excellent production and excellent acting, the 1957 Broadway production faded after playing just twenty-eight times.

"Everything about *The First Gentleman* is done on a grand scale," wrote Brooks Atkinson (*The New York Times*). "Everything except the script, that is. For Mr. Ginsbury has written a conventional costume play... *The First Gentleman* is in that true-romance style, thrilled by the spectacle of royalty, titillated by the squalid follies of the great...But *The First Gentleman* is [Walter] Slezak's holiday...his bountiful portrait of a charming, subtly-mocking Prince with bland voice and witty eyes, with panache and drollery, is not the fruit of The Method. It is a personal creation that is lovable because it is genuine...*The First Gentleman* is no match for Mr. Slezak. The author does not have his freedom of spirit."

The *Daily Mirror*'s Robert Coleman conceded: "*First Gentleman* is interesting, but...runs the gamut from burlesque humor to tragedy...Walter Slezak is excellent as the plump peacock who preens his fine feathers, to the disgust of the populace." John Chapman (*Daily News*) called *The First Gentleman* "the most lavish dramatic production of the season...As a play it falls short of another historical romance, *Victoria Regina*, because it begins telling the real story too late in the evening."

Acknowledging that George Bernard Shaw could have made England's Prince Regent a more "fascinating and intellectually witty stage figure," Richard Watts, Jr. (*New York Post*) noted that playwright Norman Ginsbury "is at least more faithful to the facts of life, history and character, and his biographical drama about five years in the Hanoverian's career must pay the resulting penalty...*The First Gentleman* is remarkably without dramatic power...George was basically a cold, and he remains a cold, despite Mr. Slezak's ingenious acting, and the play cannot escape the results of that cloddishness. His picturesque peculiarities only partly conceal the fact that the Prince was also a bore."

Tom Donnelly (*New York World Telegram-Sun*) described the play as "a series of glimpses of a gilded cork bobbing about on a sea of satin...Tyrone Guthrie's direction is, by and large, expert, and I have nothing but praise for Ralph Alswang's prodigal settings and the sumptuous costumes by Motley." Walter Kerr (*Herald-Tribune*), reflecting on Slezak's encasement into a corset, commented, "If only author Ginsbury and director Tyrone Guthrie had been able to squeeze the random and rather double-faced play into an equally effective corset!"

John McClain (*Journal-American*) applauded the excellent cast, adding, "Historical accuracy has given way at times in the interest of dramatic impact, but it must be agreed that author Norman Ginsbury has achieved a suspenseful narrative which still retains the atmosphere of the era...*The First Gentleman* is large and luxurious, loaded with gusto and good humor."

Walter Slezak, born in Vienna on May 3, 1902, the son of famous opera tenor Leo Slezak, achieved success on the Broadway stage in several musicals (*Music in the Air*, *I Married an Angel*, *Fanny*) and in plays such as *My Three Angels* and *The Gazebo*. His long screen career included his memorable performance as the deceptively kindly but villainous German submarine captain in Alfred Hitchcock's *Lifeboat*. On April 21, 1983, after a long illness, a despondent Walter Slezak took his life in his home at Flower Hill, Long Island, New York.

The First Gentleman was filmed in England in 1948 and released in the United

States the following year under the title *Affairs of a Rogue*. A British critic wrote, "This film, in its essentials, keeps close to historic fact, and some of the dialogue is taken from words actually recorded in the memoirs of the time. The reconstruction of the period is, on the whole, brilliant. Cecil Parker, as the Prince Regent, is that princely buffoon to the life...Cavalcanti's direction makes of this film almost a window into the past."

The *Motion Picture Herald* reported, "Cavalcanti sacrificed dramatic punch for historical accuracy. The result is a slowpaced, often dull, film with little to recommend it for American audiences...The cast is competent but isn't given too much of a chance with the dialogue and situations..."

Southern Television of England produced *The First Gentleman*, which was televised in the United States on November 30, 1962. The principals in this version were Charles Gray, Susannah York and Michael Meachum.

STAGE

New Theatre, London, opened July 18, 1945 654 performances
Produced by Henry Sherek; A Play by Norman Ginsbury; Director, Norman Marshall; Setting by Laurence Irving; Costumes, Elizabeth Haffenden; Music, Herbert Griffiths, played by the Albert Cazabon Quintette; Sound effects, R. J. Jones; Stage managers, Martin Beckwith and Sebastian Minton

Robert Morley (Prince Regent of England); Wendy Hiller (Princess Charlotte); Philip Friend (Prince Leopold of Saxe-Coburg); Wilfred Walter (Edward, Duke of Kent); Madge Compton (Lady Conyngham); Brown Derby (Mr. Henry Brougham); Una Venning (Miss Cornelia Knight); Frances Waring (Charlotte, Queen of England); Sigrid Landstad (Lady Hertford); Amy Frank (Caroline, Princess of Wales); Ian Sadler (Dr. Stockmar); Christine Lindsay (Princess Elizabeth); Helen Stirling (Princess Augusta); Christina Horniman (Princess Mary); Martin Beckwith (Prince Regent's Dresser): Guy le Feuvre (Sir Richard Croft/ Bishop of Salisbury); Robert Beaumont (William, Hereditary Prince of Orange); Dorothy Gailbraith (Companion to Caroline); John Baker (Servant); Beryl Harrison (Mrs. Griffiths)

Belasco Theatre, New York, opened April 25, 1957 28 performances
Produced by Alexander H. Cohen and Ralph Alswang in association with Arthur C. Twitchell, Jr.; A Play by Norman Ginsbury; Director, Tyrone Guthrie; Settings and Lighting by Ralph Alswang; Costumes by Motley; Hairstylist, Ernest Adler; Stage managers, Rex Partington and Jon Wiley

Walter Slezak (Prince Regent of England); Inga Swenson (Princess Charlotte); Peter Donat (Prince Leopold of SaxeCoburg); Robert Goodier (Edward, Duke of Kent); Helen Burns (Lady Conyngham); Wesley Addy (Mr. Henry Brougham); Dorothy Sands (Miss Cornelia Knight); Maud Scherer (Charlotte, Queen of England); Isobel Elsom (replaced Maria Fein) (Caro-line, Princess of Wales); Frances Greet (Princess Elizabeth); Meg Wyllie (Princess Augusta); Joyce Ballou (Princess Mary); LeRoi Operti (Prince Regent's Dresser); Clarence Derwent (The Bishop of Salisbury); Guy Spaull (Sir Richard Croft); John Milligan (William, Hereditary Prince of Orange); Ludi Claire (Mrs. Griffiths); James Neylin (Caroline's Servant); Phena Darner (Claremont House Servant); MacGregor Gibb, Edward Dunne, Earl Simmons, Jon Wiley, Rosanna San Marco, Sally Kemp (Guests); Edmund Roney, Curt Lowens, Rex Partington, Dario Barri (Footmen)

SCREEN

THE FIRST GENTLEMAN, Columbia-British Pictures, released March 1948; in U.S. as *AFFAIRS OF A ROGUE*, released February 1949

Produced by Joseph Friedman; Director, Cavalcanti; Screenplay by Nicholas Phipps and Reginald Long, based on the play by Norman Ginsbury; Photography, Jack Hildyard; Art director, C. P. Norman; Music director, Sir Thomas Beecham; Editor, Margery Saunders

Cecil Parker (Prince Regent); Joan Hopkins (Princess Charlotte); Jean-Pierre Aumont (Prince Leopold); Margaretta Scott (Lady Hertford); Jack Livesey (Duke of Kent); Hugh Griffith (Bishop of Salisbury); Ronald Squire (Mr. Brougham); Athene Seyler (Miss Knight); Anthony Hawtrey (Sir Richard Croft); George Curzon (Duke of York); Frances Warning (Queen Charlotte); Amy Frank (Princess Caroline); Lydia Sherwood (Princess Augusta); Betty Huntley-Wright (Princess Elizabeth); Gerard Heinz (Mr. Stockmar); Tom Gill (Prince William)

TELEVISION

THE FIRST GENTLEMAN, NET Drama Festival, televised November 30, 1962 PBS 2 hours

Produced by Southern Television of England; The play by Norman Ginsbury

Charles Gray (Prince Regent); Susannah York (Charlotte); Michael Meachum (Prince Leopold); Margaret Courtenay (Lady Conyngham); John Wood (Duke of Kent); Marda Vann (Princess Charlotte)

FLAMINGO ROAD

A Melodrama by Robert and Sally Wilder (1946)

Synopsis

Sheriff Titus Semple, corrupt boss of Petersburg, Florida, orders carnival girl Lane Ballou to leave town. When she refuses, Semple has her jailed for prostitution. On her later release, Lane joins Lute-Mae Saunders' bordello and becomes the lover of Semple's political opponent, Dan Curtis. In anger, Semple sets out to destroy Curtis and continues to torment Lane who becomes enraged with his constant persecution and kills him.

Comment and Critique

"*Flamingo Road* shows why novelists can't write plays," reported Vernon Rice (*New York Post*) about Robert Wilder's stage adaptation of his novel in collaboration with his wife, Sally Wilder. "Giving a bit of play-going direction," advised Rice, "it would be wise not to cross *Flamingo Road*." Burton Rascoe (*New York World-Telegram*) described *Flamingo Road* as "one of those inbetween sort of plays which I must very reluctantly condemn with faint praise. Reluctantly, because it treats with high seriousness of a problem of deep concern to us all --that of the evil of political bossism."

*PM*s Kronenberger felt "The plot eats up the theme. Robert and Sally Wilder have let a good theme slip right through their fingers in *Flamingo Road*...A shapelier script and a sharper production would undoubtedly have helped; but *Flamingo Road* must even so have been wanting in solidity and impact. For it never sufficiently comes together to be indicted for falling apart." Robert Garland (*Journal-American*) felt the play "lacks the social significance to give it an excuse for being. Dramatically, it is just plain poppy-cock...With *Flamingo Road*, the scenery's the thing!"

Lewis Nichols (*The New York Times*) wrote "With all their gropings into the depths, it is a little too bad that Mr. and Mrs. Wilder did not find a play there." John Chapman (*Daily News*) applauded Francis J. ("Happy") Felton's portrayal of the fat, evil sheriff as "something like the late Huey Long, I suppose, in his political greed. Although I admire the author's conception of the character and the discovery of Mr. Felton to fit it, I found last evening that his hellish little schemes were failing to hold me."

Comedian Francis J. Felton was better known as "Happy" Felton, who, with Jay C. Flippen, had replaced Olsen and Johnson in their long-running 1938 vaudeville hit, *Hellzapoppin*. Felton had appeared for two performances on Broadway in 1927 in a flop called *The Seventh Heart* after working in burlesque, circus and vaudeville (with an act called *Adele Jason and the Boys*). He later headed his own orchestra advertised as "Music with a smile in the 'Happy' Felton style," and subsequently appeared in minor roles in several Hollywood films. He died in New York City on October 21, 1964, at age fifty-six. As the corrupt Sheriff Titus Semple, Felton at 278 pounds, proved, yet again, that comedians make the transition to drama with greater expertise than dramatic actors to comedy.

Despite the failure of *Flamingo Road* on Broadway, Warner Bros. filmed Robert and Sally Wilder's 1946 play three years later as a Joan Crawford vehicle. Howard Barnes (*New York Herald-Tribune*) reported, "[She] acquits herself ably in an utterly nonsensical and undefined part." *Photoplay* called *Flamingo Road* "a compelling drama...a spicy concoction of romance and politics." One British critic's appraisal of the film was "Joan Crawford as Lane gives one of the best performances of recent years, and Sydney Greenstreet's sinister and faintly salacious portrayal is brilliant. The character of the ruthless politician is well drawn, and though the story is not new, there is nothing tame or dull in this version. This is an adult film with good direction, clear photography and strong action."

Calling *Flamingo Road* "a murky thing...a jumbled melodrama," Bosley Crowther (*The New York Times*) felt: "Miss Crawford runs this gamut in 94 minutes flat, and we think it rather significant that she isn't even winded at the end...From one dramatic crisis to the next one, she moves like a sleek automaton. Her face, deeply plastered with makeup, is an ageless, emotionless mask. Here is a Spartan demonstration of bearing-up-under-it-all. And that appears all that this picture was really designed to achieve, a mechanized demonstration of Miss Crawford's fortitude..."

On May 12, 1980, NBC telecast a two hour TV-movie which served as a pilot film for a series based on Robert Wilder's novel. In *Flamingo Road*, produced by Lorimar Productions which is also responsible for *Dallas*, *Knots Landing* and *Falcon Crest*, network programmers obviously saw in Wilder's steamy story the ingredients for another long-running adult primetime soap opera. The teleplay by Rita Lakin had sufficient plots, counterplots and duplicitous characters to provide both daytime and nighttime sensations. The principal ones -- Howard Duff, the villainous Sheriff Titus Semple; Mark Harmon as Fielding; Morgan Fairchild as Constance; Barbara Rush as Eudora; Stella Stevens as Lute-Mae; and Kevin McCarthy as Claude Waldon -- were carried over to the NBC series with Cristina Raines continuing as the oppressed Lane Ballou. The *Flamingo Road* television series began January 6, 1981. It managed to hold the television public's interest for a season and a half.

STAGE

FLAMINGO ROAD, Belasco Theatre, New York, opened March 19, 1946 7 performances

Produced by Rowland Stebbins; A Melodrama by Robert and Sally Wilder, adapted from Robert Wilder's novel; Director, Jose Ruben; Settings, Watson Barratt; Lighting, Leo Kerz; Costumes, Emeline Roche; Production supervisor, Miriam Doyle; General manager, Charles Stewart; Stage manager, George W. Smith

Judith Parrish (Lane Ballou); Philip Bourneuf (Dan Curtis); Will Geer (replaced by Ralph Riggs) ("Doc" Watterson); Francis J. Felton (Titus Semple); Lauren Gilbert (Fielding Carlisle); Doris Rich (Lute-Mae Saunders); Tom Morrison (Burrell Lassen); Marcella Markham ("Red"); Olvester Polk (Boatright); Frank McNellis (Henry Veech); Paul Ford (Ulee Jackson); Bernard Randall (Tate Hadley); Martha Jensen (Goldie); Sally Carthage (Another "Lute-Mae" Girl); Hazele Burgess (Matron); Evelyn Davis (Virgie); Mahlon Naill (Grocery Boy)

SCREEN

FLAMINGO ROAD, Warner Bros. Pictures, released May 1949

Executive Producer, Michael Curtiz; Producer, Jerry Wald; Director, Michael Curtiz; Screenplay by Robert Wilder, based on the play by Robert and Sally Wilder; Photography, Ted McCord; Additional dialogue, Edmund H. North; Art director, Leo K. Kuter; Set decorator, Howard Winterbottom; Music, Max Steiner; Music director, Ray Heindorf; Costumes, Travilla; Sound, Robert B. Lee; Associate producer, George Amy; Assistant director, Robert Vreeland; Makeup, Percy Westmore, Eddie Allen; Second unit/Montage director, David Curtiz; Editor, Folmar Blangsted

Joan Crawford (Lane Bellamy); Zachary Scott (Fielding Carlisle); David Brian (Dan Reynolds); Sydney Greenstreet (Titus Semple); Gladys George (LuteMae Sanders); Fred Clark ("Doc" Waterson); Gertrude Michael (Millie); Alice White (Gracie); Sam McDaniel (Boatright); Virginia Huston (Annabelle Weldon); Tito Vuolo (Pete Ladas); Tristram Coffin (Ed Parker); Dale Robertson (Tunis Simms); Iris Adrian (Blanche); Pierre Watkin (Senator); Lester Kimmel (Lawyer); Dick Ryan, Pat Gleason (Barkers); Carol Brewster, Sunny Knight (Waitresses); Sam McKim (Bellboy); Frank Scannell (Man)

TELEVISION

FLAMINGO ROAD, televised May 12, 1980 NBC 2 hours

Produced by Lorimar Productions; Executive Producers, Lee Rich and, Michael Filerman; Producer, Edward S. Feldman; Director, Gus Trikonis; Teleplay by Rita Lakin, based on the play by Robert and Sally Wilder; Photography, Roland "Ozzie" Smith; Art director, Charles M. Zacha, Jr.; Music, Gerald Fried; Editors, Fred W. Berger and John Arthur Davis

Cristina Raines (Lane Ballou); Mark Harmon (Fielding Carlyle); Howard Duff (Titus Semple); Stella Stevens (Lute-Mae Sanders); Barbara Rush (Eudora Weldon); Melba Moore (Alma); John Beck (Sam Curtis); Woody Brown (Skipper Weldon); Morgan Fairchild (Constance Weldon); Kevin McCarthy (Claude Weldon); Mason Adams (Elmo Tyson); Norman Alden (Pete); Glenn Robards (Jasper, the Butler); Michael DeLano (Tom Coyne); Leonard Gaines (Horse

Auctioneer); Dianne Kay (Annabelle Troy); and Nick Angotti, Pat Colbert, John Furlong, Ted Lehman, Ed Kenney, Raymond Lynch, Bill McLaughlin, Tom Regan, Derek Thompson, Danil Torppe, Don Starr, Paul Sorensen, Lee Weaver, Karen Rushmore, Ben Young

NBC Series, televised January 6, 1981 through July 13, 1982 1 hour each episode
Produced by Lorimar Productions; Executive producers, Lee Rich and Michael Filerman; Supervising Producer, Rita Lakin; Producer-Director, Edward H. Feldman and others; Teleplay, Howard Lakin and others; Photography, Roland "Ozzie" Smith; Art director, James Bacon; Music, Gerald Fried and Elliot Kaplan

Howard Duff (Sheriff Titus Semple); Mark Harmon (Fielding Carlyle); Morgan Fairchild (Constance Weldon); Cristina Raines (Lane Ballou); Barbara Rush (Eudora Weldon); Stella Stevens (Lute-Mae); Kevin McCarthy (Claude Waldon); Woody Brown (Skipper Weldon); Alejandro Rey (Lorca); Peter Donat (Elmo Tyson); Judith Chapman (Terry); Joe Penny (Walker); Janis Paige (Jenny); John Beck (Sam Curtis); Joel Bailey (Tony); William Windom (Charles Banks); Peter Horton (Scott); Stacy Keach, Sr. (Senator Potter); Robert Rockwell (Timothy); David Selby (Michael Tyrone); Cynthia Sykes (Sande Swanson); Gina Gallego (Alicia Sancher); Andra Akers (Vanessa Curtis); Fernando Allende (Julie Sancher); Carmen Zapata (Lupe); Mike Kellin (Stern); Esther Rolle (Julia); Paul Lambert (Van Zandt); Bill Morey (Dr. Austin); Dana Elcar (Crane); Beverly Garland (Louise Stone)

FORTY-FIVE MINUTES FROM BROADWAY
A Musical play by George M. Cohan (1906)

Synopsis

Street-wise, glib young lightweight prizefighter Kid Burns is invited by his friend Tom Bennett, the recent heir of million dollars, to his New Rochelle mansion located forty-five minutes from Broadway. There Kid falls in love with the Bennett's housemaid, Mary Jane Jenkins. During a lavish reception for Tom's gold-digging fiancee, Flora Dora Dean, her mother conspires with a former accomplice and Mary's guardian, Daniel Cronin, to pilfer Bennett's safe. Mary and Kid catch Cronin and Mrs. Dean robbing the safe and have them arrested. Kid discovers Bennett's uncle's missing will leaving the entire estate to his faithful housemaid Mary and cutting off his playboy nephew Tom with one dollar. Impoverished Kid Burns gives the will to Mary and, feeling inferior to a sudden heiress, leaves for the New Rochelle railroad station. Declaring her love for Kid, Mary finds him at the station and tears up the will, and together they board the train which in forty-five minutes will take them to Manhattan.

Comment and Critique

George M. Cohan's *Forty-Five Minutes From Broadway* premiered in Columbus, Ohio, in late September 1905. Popular stage star Fay Templeton and Victor Moore, veteran vaudvillian here making his musical comedy debut, had the leads, with Cohan himself directing. Theodore T. Frankenbert (*Ohio State Journal*) considered Cohan's story "neither fish, flesh nor good red herring," but added, "the audience last night plainly liked the entertainment and it seems certain that audiences the country over (barring New Rochelle) will like it." George M. Cohan attended the Columbus opening of his latest musical play, then boarded an early morning train for Louisville, Kentucky, to rejoin his tour in his musical, *Little Johnny Jones*. Later, *Forty-Five Minutes From Broadway* arrived at Chicago's Colonial Theatre and remained there for a successful twelve-week run.

On New Year's Day 1906, Cohan's newest musical play opened on Broadway. "Mr. Cohan, who has a capital idea of the writing and staging of musical comedies, made the error of attempting something which, beginning in that vein, was interesting, and developing into melodrama of a very obvious sort, became most tiresome," *The New York Times* reported. "*Forty-Five Minutes From Broadway* is a case of oil and water. Its ingredients do not mix." *Theatre* magazine pooh-poohed the play and its author with "Mr. Cohan has little art. His pieces lack form and substance. He writes popular nonsense cleverly and voluminously. They have no permanent place in our drama and do not call for serious consideration."

Forty-Five Minutes From Broadway was performed ninety times at The New Amsterdam. In March 1912, the author returned to Broadway at the theater named after him to star in a revival of the show lasting thirtysix performances. Sallie Jenkins played Mary Jane Jenkins.

Charles Ray, whose motion picture career flourished as he portrayed shy country bumpkins in a long series of films including *Stringbean* in 1918, *Bill Henry* and *Hayfoot, Straw Foot* in 1919, and *The Clodhopper* in 1920, formed his own producing company to bring *Forty-Five Minutes From Broadway* to the screen. Critic Burns Mantle faulted Ray's ambitious effort to escape the perennial hayseed country boy, but supported the actor's decision with "Charles Ray's portrayal of Kid Burns is an epoch in his career, for he demonstrates that his screen talents are not limited to rural heroes," and found the picture was "a singularly successful conversion of the play."

The New York Times enthused, "George M. Cohan will have no regrets for having allowed his most popular stage production, *Forty-Five Minutes From Broadway*, to be adapted to the screen...Charles Ray adds another star to his film crown." The *New York Morning Telegraph* added, "Kid Burns is one of the best roles that Ray has played. *Forty-Five Minutes From Broadway* makes an excellent comedy-drama for the screen." The *New York Evening Sun* praised Ray's characterization of Kid Burns and noted, "The picture was well directed and is in every way a delightful entertainment."

Edward Weitzel (*The Moving Picture World*) wrote, "In the original play Kid Burns had to divide popularity with several of the other characters and a set of catchy musical numbers provided by the talented Mr. Cohan. In the screen version, Charles Ray has things pretty much to himself, and very few of his admirers will find any cause for a quarrel on this score...The plot of *Forty-Five Minutes From Broadway* is not startlingly original nor overburdened with incident, but it is clean, easy of comprehension and its humor is superior to its dramatic moments."

The 1942 screen biography of George M. Cohan, *Yankee Doodle Dandy*, starring James Cagney, featured an elaborate restaging of what was, purportedly, the finale of *Forty-Five Minutes From Broadway*, in which Irene Manning as Fay Templeton sang "Mary Is a Grand Old Name."

The *Omnibus* television production in 1959 of *FortyFive Minutes From Broadway* was viewed by Jack Gould (*The New York Times*) as "...the production as a whole so busy kidding itself that it often was only strained rather than amusing."

STAGE

FORTY-FIVE MINUTES TO BROADWAY, *New Amsterdam Theatre*, New York, opened January 1, 1906   90 performances
Produced by Klaw and Erlanger; A Musical play; Book, Music, Lyrics and Direction by George M. Cohan; Scenery and effects built by William Hoover; Exterior, Act I, painted by John Young; Interior, Act II, painted by Ernest Albert; Interior, Act III, painted by Frank Marsden; Costumes designed by F. Richard Anderson; Properties, John Brunton; Electrical effects, Harry Bissing; Musical director, Frederic Solomon; Company manager, Richard Dorney; Stage director, Walter Craven; Business director, Sam H. Harris

Fay Templeton (Mary Jane Jenkins); Victor Moore (Kid Burns); Donald Brian (Tom Bennett); Lois Ewell (Flora Dora Dean); Julia Ralph (Mrs. David Dean); James H. Manning (Daniel Cronin); Louis R. Grisel (Andy Gray); Marion Singer (Mrs. Purdy); Maurice Elliot (Station Master); Floyd E. Francis (Police Sergeant); Nat Royster (succeeded by Charles Friedland) (Messenger Boy); Mabel Ellis (succeeded by Miss Solomon) (Polly Poughkeepsie); Rhea G. Clemens (succeeded by Fern Minard, Miss Lawton) (Pauline Peekskill); Desiree Lazard (Tessy Tarrytown); Hazel Cox (Fannie Fordham); Madeline LeBoeuf (Rosie Rye); Marguerite Lane (Minnie Melrose); Nevada Maynard (Teresa Tuckahoe); Margaretta Masi (succeeded by Vivian Rushmore) (Winnie Wakefield); Eugene McGregor, Joe Simons, A. Claire Smith, Al DeBall (Reporters); J. S. Donnelly, Ned Achard, Frank Benor (Policemen)

MUSICAL NUMBERS: "Gentlemen of the Press"; "I Want to Be a Popular Millionaire"; "Mary Is a Grand Old Name"; "Forty-Five Minutes From Broadway"; "So Long Mary"

NOTE: This production premiered at the *Great Southern Theatre*, Columbus, Ohio, September 26, 1905, and then played the *Colonial Theatre*, Chicago, before coming to Broadway

George M. Cohan's Theatre, New York, opened March 14, 1912   36 performances
A Musical Play; Book, Music, Lyrics and Direction by George M. Cohan; Scenery, William Hoover; Costumes, F. Richard Anderson; Electrical effects, Harry Bissing; Musical director, Frederic Solomon; Business manager, Sam H. Harris

George M. Cohan (Kid Burns); Sallie Fisher (Mary Jane Jenkins); Lawrence Wheat (Tom Bennett); Louise Aichel (Flora Dora Dean); Ada Gilman (Mrs. Purdy); Lorena Atwood (Mrs. David Dean); Elmer Booth (James Blake); George Parsons (Daniel Krohman); Edgar Halsted (Andy Gray); John Klendon (Station Master); William Ford (Police Sergeant); James Denton (Messenger Boy); Hawley Brooks (Baggage Man); Elsie Artz (Fannie Fordham); Marion Donn (Pauline Peekskill); Rose Leslie (Tessie Tarrytown); Sydney Martineau (Polly Poughkeepsie); Lydia Scott (Rosie Rye); Paula Leslie (Minnie Melrose); Dorothy Lockhart (Theresa Tuckahoe); Elizabeth Young (Winnie Wakefield)

SCREEN

FORTY-FIVE MINUTES TO BROADWAY, *First National Pic-tures*, released August 1920
A Charles Ray Production. Produced by Arthur Kane; Director, Joseph De Grasse; Screenplay, Isabel Johnson and Bernard McConville, based on the musical play by George M. Cohan; Photography, Chester Lyons

Charles Ray (Kid Burns); Dorothy Devore (Mary Jane Jenkins); Donald McDonald (Tom Bennett); Hazel Howell (Flora Dora Dean); Eugenie Besserer (Mrs. David Dean); Harry Myers (Daniel Cronin); Mat Forster (Mrs. Purdy); William Courtwright (Andy Grey)

TELEVISION

FORTY-FIVE MINUTES TO BROADWAY, Omnibus, televised March 15, 1959 NBC
Director, Gower Champion; Music and Lyrics by George M. Cohan

Tammy Grimes (Mary Jane); Larry Blyden (replaced Robert Morse) (Kid Burns); Russell Nype (Tom Bennett); David Burns (Daniel Cronin); Howard St. John (Blake); Donna Millay (Flora Dora Dean)

FRANCES FARMER
Various adaptation based on the life of Frances Farmer

Synopsis

Ambitious, autocratic Lillian Farmer defends her daughter Frances' winning essay *God Dies* and her award of a trip to Russia against the outraged citizens of Seattle. On her twenty-first birthday, Frances signed a contract with Paramount Pictures but violently rebels against Hollywood and its tinsel glamour. After several films, Frances is signed for the leading female role in the leftist Group Theatre's Broadway production of *Golden Boy* by Clifford Odets with whom she has a steamy and traumatic affair. Rejected by Odets, Frances returns to Hollywood, alcohol and pills. National headlines report her arrest for drunk driving with pictures of her battling with police. Released from jail, she is shunned by Hollywood and the court assigns her to her mother's custody. Vindictive, slovenly Lillian Farmer, thirsting for the reflected glory of Frances' acting career, has her rebellious daughter institutionalized. Frances' actor husband Leif Erickson divorces her and she is reunited with a former lover, political activist Harry York, who obtains her release from the asylum. Lillian, however, has her recommitted. Before her final release from the asylum, Frances is given a transorbital lobotomy. Back in society, she finds her career finished, and flounders around during the next decade, ultimately finding work in local television in Indianapolis. Few of her former associates agree to participate when Frances appears on Ralph Edwards' television show *This Is Your Life*.

Comment and Critique

Frances Farmer made fourteen motion pictures and one uncompleted film with the prophetic title *There Is No Escape*. During her destructive affair with writer Clifford Odets, then married to Oscar-winning Viennese actress Luise Rainer, Frances was the wife of William Anderson, better known on the screen as Leif Erickson.

In 1972, G. P. Putnam's Sons published Frances Farmer's autobiography *Will There Really Be a Morning?*, the title taken from a poem by Emily Dickinson. The book was dedicated to Jeanvira Victoria Ratcliffe who became Frances' companion and mentor during her last years. After appearing on Ed Sullivan's television variety show, where she sang the folk song "Aura Lee" from her successful 1936 Samuel Goldwyn film, *Come and Get It* (the song later made famous by Elvis Presley as

"Love Me Tender"), Frances appeared to favorable notices with several stock companies in a variety of plays. She settled in Indianapolis, where she attained success as hostess on WFBM-TV of a television movie series that included interviewing show business figures. Frances Farmer died of cancer on August 1, 1970, at age fifty-six.

The production team and writers who brought Bernard Pomerance's drama *The Elephant Man* to the screen attempted to translate the harrowing and traumatic life of Frances Farmer to film in 1982 in *Frances*. Vincent Canby (*The New York Times*) called it "such a mixed up movie that is still seems to be unfinished, as if Graeme Clifford, the director, and the writers hadn't yet discovered the real point of the Frances Farmer story...Yet it also contains a magnificent performance by Jessica Lange in the title role...The excitement of watching her in *Frances* goes a long way toward transforming the film, which is a colossal downer, into an experience that is, if not exactly uplifting, genuinely memorable...In spite of the film's very real faults with structure and style, Miss Lange is consistently splendid."

In Britain's *Monthly Film Bulletin*, critic Paul Taylor wrote, "The Farmer biography, intersecting with so many current lines of both political concern and cinematic marketability, proves almost too rich for coherent encapsulation...while the film utilises conventional biopic ellipsis -- and a participant narrator -- to establish swiftly (if none to surely) Frances' intelligence, outspokenness, radicalism and talent, it soon settles for typing her as archetypal victim. Even if it can't decide of quite what or whom."

Noting that British film editor Graeme Clifford's transition to directing left a good deal to be desired, critic Desmond Ryan (*Films and Filming*) found, "*Frances* becomes a sensational document of the unspeakable way the mentally ill were and perhaps still are treated in this country. The fact that Jessica Lange is so sympathetic and frequently brilliant in the title role adds to the melodramatic effect of the film." Ryan also called *Frances* "a flawed film" that "offers little in the way of solace."

Prior to the release of *Frances*, a play called *The Frances Farmer Story* was produced Off-Broadway, featuring Elizabeth Hess in the lead. "The trouble with Sebastian Stuart's *The Frances Farmer Story*," reported Michael Feingold (*Village Voice*), "is that it doesn't give what its title promises, or rather, it does: a cursory, slicked up, Hollywood-style treatment of Farmer's life, slightly disconnected as if the editors and the censors had had their licks at it...The play [is] full of naivetes and awkwardness, including misguided waffling between sentimental dramatized history, and would-be experimental shorthand."

Clive Barnes (*The New York Times*) declared, "*Frances Farmer* is a disaster...[it] restores our faith in rottenness...*The Frances Farmer Story* is badly written badly conceived, badly constructed, badly characterized, badly directed, badly staged and -- with perhaps one exception -- badly acted. Have I left anything out?" Marilyn Stasio (*New York Post*) added, "Sebastian Stuart's play tries all the dirty details about its heroine's hair-raising life and career...the hopeless heroine winds up looking more foolish than anyone surely intended."

Less than a year later, a musical on Farmer's life came to the stage, with three different actress playing her at various ages. It had more than forty songs by Jack Eric Williams, who cowrote the book with director Tom O'Horgan and Joseph Stockdale. The production never made it to Broadway.

On February 22, 1983, CBS televised a production of Farmer's biography, *Will There Really Be a Morning?*, directed by Fielder Cook and featuring Susan Blakely as the self-destructive Frances and Lee Grant as her crazed mother.

"Obviously, the Frances Farmer story provides an actress with ample opportunities for demonstrating her acting range. At the same time, though, the story is so unrelentingly ghastly, so horrifyingly grim, that one cannot help wondering if there is much point in its being told at all," John J. O'Connor (*The New York Times*) felt. "*Will There Really Be a Morning?* sticks far closer to the facts of Miss Farmer's life than the film, *Frances*, which is something of a scripting mess ...[Susan] Blakely, like Miss Lange, provides a harrowing, in many ways memorable performance. Unlike Miss Lange, she is not as prettily attractive as Frances Farmer, but she fully captures the emotional turmoil of the woman. She and [Lee] Grant whip up scenes of almost frenzied power. In the end, though, it has to be remembered that the subject of all this energy is an actress who never was in the league of such contemporaries as Bette Davis or Katharine Hepburn. She was a modestly talented performer who never made an important picture. Somewhere along the line, there has developed a nagging imbalance in the perceptions of her."

Frances Farmer's films included:

Too Many Parents

Border Flight

Rhythm on the Range

Come and Get It

Ebb Tide

Toast of New York

Exclusive

Escape From Yesterday

South of Pago Pago

Flowing Gold

World Premiere

Among the Living

The Badlands of Dakota

There Is No Escape (Uncompleted)

Party Crashers

STAGE

THE FRANCES FARMER STORY, Chareeva Theatre, New York, opened October 29, 1982 11 performances

Produced by Ed Rubin and Didi Gough; A drama by Sebastian Stuart; Director, John Albano; Setting, Speed Hopkins; Lighting, Gerard Bourcier: Costumes, Gabriel Berry; Sound, Dave Schneider; Makeup/Hairstylist, Eugene Stiegler; General manager, Ed Rubin; Stage manager, Kate Mennone

Elizabeth Hess (Frances Farmer); John Jiler (Clifford Odets/ Dr. Freeman/ Justice/ Fraser/ Sheriff/ Stage manager); Penelope Rockwell (Lillian Farmer/ Betty/ Clara/ Lois/ Actress); J. P. Dougherty (Joe Halpern/ Judge/ Columnist/ Sid/ Cop/ Rooney/ Doctor Beatty/ Freddy/ Reporter); Chris Tanner (Lucky/ Jimmy/ Guard/ Cop/ Reporter/ Nurse); Mary Lou Wittmer (Sophie Rosenstein/ Belle McKenzie/ Actress/ Adelaide/ Delores/ Director/ Lady in Hart)

MRS. FARMER'S DAUGHTER, *Purchase's Center for the Arts*, Purchase, New York, opened July 20, 1983

Produced by PepsiCo Summerfare; A Musical play based on the life of Frances Farmer; Director, Tom O'Horgan; Book by Tom O'Horgan, Joseph Stockdale and Jack Eric Williams; Music and Lyrics by Jack Eric Williams; Setting, Bill Stabile; Lighting, John McLain; Choreography, Ted Rotante; Conductor and associate musical director, Marc Irwin; Costume coordinator, Randy Barcelo; Creative consultant, Barra Kahn; Sound, Monte Heath

Rhonda Coullet (Frances Farmer, mature years); Sharon Troyer Scruggs (Frances Farmer, middle years); Kristi Mordica (Frances Farmer, early years); Mary Dale (Lillian Farmer); Joseph Stockdale (Ernest Farmer); Larry J. Victor (Leif Erickson, early years); Don Chastain (Leif Erickson, mature years); Stephen Berger (Clifford Odets): Brian Hurley (Harold Clurman); Eve Martinez (Luise Rainer); William Kiehl (Adolph Zukor/Dr. Walter Freeman); Denise DeMirjian (Jean Ratcliffe); Raymond Patterson (Policeman/Guard)

MUSICAL NUMBERS: "God's Peculiar Care"; "Barnyard Blues"; "An Old Prayer"; "St. Agnes Eve"; "Frances Discovers Nietzsche"; "Jesus Sweetest Name I Know"; "Mother Love"; "She Showed Me"; "Jazztown Features"; "Manhattan"; "The Gospel According to Lillian"; "Nothing's Left But Hollywood"; "Hollywood Rag"; "The Bad Girl of West Seattle"; "Of When Stars Fall Down"; "Especially in the Dark"; "Inventory/In Flagrante Delicito"; "The Kingdom of Love"; "Christmas in Laurel Canyon"; "The Time of Your Life"; "The Thrill Is Gone"; "Too Bad"; "Board Meeting"; "Life as Rumor"; "The Garbo Bit"; "Knocking in Vain"; "Police Trouble"; "Vive Le Demimonde"; "That Feels Good"; "Slow Dancing"; "There Are B-Girls All Over Heaven"; "Mental Hugiene"; "Rib of Adam"; "Stub Me Out, I'm a Cigarette"; "A Boy Needs Love"; "The Lord's Prayer"; "Jacob's Ladder"; "The Full Moon"; "The Episodes"; "Maybe Now a Little House"; "Tomorrow: The Last Resort"; "Bird Americana"

SCREEN

FRANCES, *Universal Pictures*, released December 1982

A Brooksfilm Production for EMI; Produced by Jonathan Sanger; Coproducer, Marie Yates; Director, Graeme Clifford; Screenplay by Eric Bergren, Christopher DeVore and Nicholas Kazan; Photography, Laszlo Kovacs; 2nd Unit Photography, Laszlo Pal; Production designer, Richard Sylbert; Art director, Ida Random; Set decorator, George Gaines; Costume designer, Patricia Norris; Makeup, Dorothy Pearl; Medical advisor, Adrian J. Williams; Behavioral consultant, Melba Smith; Assistant directors, Ed Milkovich, William Scott and Michael Green; Screenplay consultants, Stewart O. Jacobson and Lois Kibbee; Music and Music director, John Barry; Orchestrations, Al Woodbury; Sound recording, David Ronne; Editor, John Wright

Jessica Lange (Frances Farmer); Kim Stanley (Lillian Farmer); Sam Shepard (Harry York); Bart Burns (Ernest Farmer); Christopher Pennock (Dick Steele); James Karen (Judge Hillier); Gerald S. O'Loughlin (Lobotomy Doctor); Sarah Cunningham (Alma Styles); Allan Rich (Mr. Bebe); Woodrow Parfrey (Dr. Doyle); Jack Riley (Bob Barnes); Darrell Larson (Louella's Spy); Jordan Charney (Harold Clurman); John Randolph (Kindly Judge); Keone Young (Chinese Doctor); Bonnie Barlett (Studio Stylist); Jeffrey DeMunn (Clifford Odets); Lane Smith (Dr. Symington); Jonathan Banks (Hitchhiker); James Brohead (Desk Sergeant); J. J. Chaback (Lady at Roosevelt Hotel); Daniel Chodos ("No Escape" Director); Rod Colbin (Sentencing Judge); Donald Craig (Ralph Edwards); Lee De Broux ("Flowing Gold" Director); Jack Fitzgerald (Clapper Man); Nancy Foy (Autograph Girl); Anne Haney (Hairdresser); Richard Hawkins (Bum on Street); Patricia

Larson (Mrs. Hillier); Albert Lord ("Flowing Gold" AD); Vincent Lucchesi (Arresting Sergeant); Jack Manning (Studio Photographer); Rod Pilloud (Martoni Kaminski); Larry Pines (Man on Phone, Bookie Joint); David V. Schroeder (Studio Lawyer); Helen Schustack (Wardrobe Mistress); Sandra Seacat (Drama Teacher); Charles Seaverns (Real Estate Man); Karin Strandjord (Connie); Vern Taylor (Studio Executive); Andrew Winner (Fire Chief); Bill Yeager (Motorcycle Cop); Alexander Zale (Man in Screening Room); Paul Fleming, M. C. Gainey, Roger Galloway, Matthew Goldsby, Paul Keith, F. William Parker, Charles Shull (Reporters, Publicists, Photographers); Teda Bracci, Jan Burrell, Flo diRe, Dodds Frank, Patricia Gaul, Robin Ginsburg, Pamela Gordon, Anjelica Huston, Jamie Johnston, Ola Kaufman, Donna LaMana, Sharmagne Leland-St. John, Jane Llig, Alexandra Melchi, Patricia Post, Zelda Rubenstein, Nina Schneider, Marlene Silvers, Vicki Williams, Susan Wolf (Mental Patients); Tom Amundsen, Anne Haslett, Barry Jamesby, Len Lookabaugh, Oceana Marr, Vahan Moosekian, Tom Pletts, Eileen T'Kaye, Lila Waters (Doctors, Nurses, Orderlies; Charles Prior, Carl Kraines (Soldiers)

TELEVISION

WILL THERE REALLY BE A MORNING?, televised February 22, 1983 CBS 3 hours An Orion TV Production in association with Jaffe-Blakely Films; Executive producers, Sandy Arcara and Stephen Jaffe; Producer, Everett Chambers; Supervising producer, Richard M. Rosenbloom; Director, Fielder Cook; Teleplay by Dalene Young, based on the autobiography of Frances Farmer; Photography, Michel Hugo; Production designer, Karen Bromley; Costume designer, Denita Del Signore; Music, Billy Goldenberg; Makeup, Ann Brodie and Ed Butterworth; Hairstyles, Paul LeBlanc, Carol Michaels and Lola Kemp; Associate producer, Steve Nicolaides; Editor, George Jay Nicholson

Susan Blakely (Frances Farmer); Lee Grant (Lillian Farmer); Royal Dano (Ernest Farmer); Joe Lambie (Bill Anderson); John Heard (Clifford Odets); Leonard Cimino (Adolph Zukor); Bruce Ornstein (John Garfield); Robert Hawkins (Franchot Tone); Michelle Leigh Stevens (Frances, age nine); Paul Perri (Luther Adler); James Eckhouse (Harold Clurman); Melanie Mayron (Sophie Rosenstein); Jack Greeley (Professor Williams); Jeanne Elias (Lottie); Ivor Francis (Drama Teacher); James Cahill (Howard Hawks); Joe Grifasi (William Wyler); Sydney Armus (Judge); Richard B. Shull (Publicist); Joseph Maher (First doctor); Neil Dainard (Justice of the Peace); Madeline Thornton-Sherwood (Second Doctor); Frederick Rold (Agent); George Touliatos (Makeup Man); Dalene Young (Hairdresser); Thomas Barbour (Director); Martha Gilson (Script Girl); Alan Scarfe (Third Doctor); John Kirby (Sailor); Roger Barton, Neil Affleck, Joe Pagano (Actors); Donnann Calvin (Actress); Ray Powers, Eric Stine (Photographers); Sean Moloney (Young Man); Meg Hogarth (Police Matron); Keith James, Paddy Carol, Jim Chad, Charles Prior, Bob Larkin, Clark Stevens, William Ward (Reporters); Joanne Strauss (Nurse); Angus McInnes (Policeman)

GEORGE M!

Musical comedy based on the life of George M. Cohan

Synopsis

Five-feet-six-inch, egotistical, cocky, multitalented George Michael Cohan was born at Corkie Hill, Providence, Rhode Island, on Wednesday, July 3, 1878 -- not his traditionally proclaimed "born on the Fourth of July" which earned him the sobriquet of the flagwaving "Yankee Doodle Dandy." George M.'s birth was registered at St. Joseph's Roman Catholic Church, Providence, on July 14, 1878, by his vaudevillian parents, Jeremiah John Cohan (an alteration by Jerry of his family name, Keohane) and Ellen (Helen Frances) Costigan Cohan.

George first appeared onstage with his parents in Jerry's sketch, "The Two Dans," and at the age of eight, he was playing violin in the orchestra of Peckmer Farsman's touring company of *Daniel Boone on the Trail*. Joined by George's younger sister, Josephine, the family became one of vaudeville's most successful acts as The Four Cohans. George, who wrote most of their material and songs -- and wore elevated heels to increase his small stature, acknowledged their increasing fame and prolonged applause with "My mother thanks you, my father thanks you, my sister thanks you, and I thank you."

In July 1889, George married Ethelia Fowler, known professionally as Ethel Levey, and they became the parents of a daughter, Georgette. On February 11, 1901, George's first musical comedy, *The Governor's Son* (an expansion of his vaudeville act), opened at Broadway's Savoy Theatre starring The Four Cohans with Ethel Levey. In 1904, George joined with Samuel Henry Harris to form the producing firm of Cohan & Harris, which was consolidated on a mere handshake. The partners' first production was Cohan's shamelessly flag-waving musical play, *Little Johnny Jones (The American Jockey)*, premiered on 42nd Street in Times Square at the Liberty Theatre on November 7, 1904. On New Year's Day 1906, Cohan's *Forty-Five Minutes From Broadway* opened at the New Amsterdam Theatre. It was followed six weerk later by his musical comedy *George Washington, Jr.* at the Herald Square Theatre, featuring his hit song "You're a Grand Old Rag," altered after a raging controversy to "You're a Grand Old Flag."

Ethel Levey divorced Cohan in February 1907, and in late June, George married Agnes Nolan, who had been in the chorus of *Little Johnny Jones*. His partner, Sam Harris, wed Agnes' sister, Alice. George and Agnes Cohan produced three children, George, Jr., Mary and Helen. George wrote another dozen or so musical comedies or rewrote plays by other authors until 1919. That year he unwisely organized the Actors Fidelity Association (in which he was joined by several important stars of the Broadway stage) to oppose the strike called by Actors Equity Association (founded December 22, 1912) arguing against deplorable working conditions imposed by theater producers, managers and owners. The Equity strike began on August 7, 1919 and successfully ended on September 6, after twenty-three productions had been closed on Broadway. For years, George M. was persona non grata at Actors Equity.

Cohan's greatest fame was based on a bugle call when he composed on April 6, 1917, the music and lyrics to what became the national theme song of World War I, "Over There." Published by Leo Feist, Inc., it sold over a million-and-a-half copies of sheet music and was professionally introduced by Broadway's celebrated singer, Nora Bayes.

Jerry and Ellen (called Nellie) Cohan's last stage appearance was in George's musical, *The Little Millionaire*, and on July 12, 1916, Josephine, who had married actor Fred Niblo (later to become a noted Hollywood director), died. George's beloved father, Jerry, passed on on August 1, 1917, and George, "The Prince of Broadway," kept his shows running. Not until October 2, 1933, did Cohan appear in a show that he himself did not write (or rewrite), when he returned to Broadway to portray Nat Miller in Eugene O'Neill's comedy, *Ah, Wilderness!*, remaining with it until February 1935.

In 1937, George M. Cohan agreed to appear in the first musical comedy he had not written: George S. Kaufman and Moss Hart's satirical *I'd Rather Be Right*, with music and lyrics by Rodgers and Hart, to whom Cohan maliciously referred as Gilbert and Sullivan. *I'd Rather Be Right* opened on Broadway on November 2, 1937, with George M. delighting audiences with his portrayal of President Franklin Delano Roosevelt, the first incumbent president to be portrayed on the stage. Cohan unloaded his full bag of tricks, tap-dancing, strutting his kangarooish walk and leaping up the proscenium arch in his remarkable characterizations of F.D.R., which was applauded by the President himself. Cohan completed his exhausting tour in *I'd Rather Be Right* in his hometown of Providence in February 1939 at age sixty-one.

George M. Cohan's last Broadway stage appearance was on May 17, 1940, at the National Theatre, for a disappointing seven performances, in *The Return of the Vagabond*. It was a retitled version of his successful 1920 play, *The Tavern*, which had a run of 252 performances. In May 1940, President Roosevelt presented George M. Cohan with the Congressional Medal of Honor in recognition of his contribution to America with his song "Over There" and of his long, impressive career in the theatre. On Thursday, November 5, 1942, George Michael Cohan, America's "Yankee Doodle Dandy," died in his New York City apartment at 993 Fifth Avenue at the age of sixty-four.

From the life of George M. Cohan, once known as "The Man Who Owns Broadway," Warner Bros. produced one of Hollywood's most beloved musical films, *Yankee Doodle Dandy*, in 1942. Although the movie lost out to MGM's *Mrs. Miniver* as Best Picture of the Year, the estimable James Cagney won not only a well-deserved Academy Award as Best Actor for his spirited portrayal of George M. Cohan but also the New York Film Critics Award for Best Actor. Walter Huston was Oscar-nominated as Best Supporting Actor for his delightful playing of Jerry Cohan but lost to Van Heflin for *Johnny Eager*. Nathan Levinson was awarded on Oscar for Sound Recording on *Yankee Doodle Dandy* and Ray Heindorf and Heinz Roemheld received Academy Awards for the Best Scoring of a Musical Picture.

Cohan had approval of the script, in which he insisted all references to his first wife, Ethel Levey, be deleted, and approval of the casting of James Cagney to portray him. Both wives were consolidated into one character, "Mary," played with ease and charm by young Joan Leslie. Cagney's own sister, Jeanne, played Josie Cohan and Rosemary De Camp was cast their mother. Cohan, paid $50,000 for the screen rights to his life story, was satisfied with the completed film and wired Cagney, "Dear Jim. How's my double? Thanks for a wonderful job. George M. Cohan."

Yankee Doodle Dandy has become a motion picture classic. Unlike some of his other recently "colorized" projects, TV mogul Ted Turner discovered that his new coloring process increased the impact of the musical numbers in *Yankee Doodle Dandy* in 1986, but only in the musical numbers. Otherwise, the crisp black-and-white photography was lost and the colorizing distracted from the film in scenes blurred or hazed. George Stevens, Jr., son of the famous director and former chairman of the American Film Institute, claims that color damages the integrity of black-and-white films, advising, "Psychologically, the films will cease to exist in black and white. It's a violation of the people who made the films, but also it shortchanges the audience."

Time magazine called *Yankee Doodle Dandy* "possibly the most genial screen biography ever made. Few films have bestowed such loving care on any hero as this one does on beaming, buoyant, wry-mouthed George M. (for Michael) Cohan. The result is a nostalgic, accurate recreation of a historic era of U.S. show business... [it] tries hard to squeeze the years of Cohan Americana into two hours and six minutes of celluloid. It succeeds best with the early years...the picture goes overboard with an elaborate presentation of *You're a Grand Old Flag*...The rest, down through scenes of Cohan's last stage appearances (in *I'd Rather Be Right*, 1937), is anticlimax." About Warners' $1.5 million production, *Time* added, "It is a remarkable performance, possibly Cagney's best, and it makes *Yankee Doodle* a dandy."

James Cagney, a gifted hoofer and song-and-dance man, was typecast by Hollywood, because of public demand, as a hoodlum, tough guy and far from the concept of a musical comedy star which he proved in *Yankee Doodle Dandy* he could be. The *New Yorker* noted, "He has had very little chance to dance in his career, as the public wanted something else, far from dancing, from him. Now he has his opportunity, and it is in his dancing, in the "numbers," the grand old Cohan numbers, that he is altogether at ease, altogether satisfactory. *Yankee Doodle Dandy* is a complete delight." The film began with President Roosevelt's awarding Cohan with the Congressional Medal of Honor and flashbacked to his great career, ending with a reprise of "Over There" (beautifully sung by Frances Langford) during World War II.

"*Yankee Doodle Dandy*, the story of the theatrical career of George M. Cohan, is the best film musical your correspondent ever saw -- and one of the finest pictures in any category," John Chapman wrote in *Redbook*. "Cagney's impersonation of Cohan is a miracle of good judgement for it is not too slavish in detail ...his dancing really *is* Cohan to perfection...It takes more than a star's performance to make a good picture, it takes excellence in all departments, and *Yankee Doodle Dandy* has it."

The New York Times' Bosley Crowther enthused, "...you will not find as warm and delightful a musical picture as has hit the screen in years, a corking good entertainment and as affectionate, if not accurate, a film biography as has ever -- yes, ever -- been made... The picture magnificently matches the theatrical brilliance of Mr. Cohan's career...And the performance of Mr. Cagney, as the one and original Song-and-Dance Man is an unbelievably faithful characterization, and a piece of playing that glows with energy."

James Cagney briefly reprised his George M. Cohan impersonation in *The Seven Little Foys*, Paramount's 1955 quasibiography of Eddie Foy. In his autobiography, *Cagney by Cagney* (1976), the author wrote, "Psychologically, I needed no preparation for *Yankee Doodle Dandy*, or professionally either. I didn't have to pretend to be a song-and-dance man, I was one." The film remained Cagney's favorite of the thirtyseven motion pictures he made for Warners from 1930 to 1942. To assure himself that his dancing would equate that of Cohan's, Cagney hired John Boyle, who had staged dances for George M.'s *The Cohan Revue of 1916*. Cagney was equally pleased that George M. saw the film "...and he gave it his blessing. I like to think that this only contact we had was professionally appropriate: one song-and-dance man saluting another, the greatest of our calling...So *Yankee Doodle Dandy* turned out to be something I could take real pride in. Its story abounds in all the elements necessary for a good piece of entertainment...*Yankee Doodle Dandy* has lots of reasons to be my favorite picture."

Michael Stewart and John and Fran Pascal created a musical play from the career of Cohan, appropriately called *George M!*, and which, with Cohan's music and lyrics, opened April 10, 1968 at Broadway's former vaudeville mecca, the Palace Theatre. In the title role was thirty-six-year-old Joel (Katz) Grey, who had lit up the stage two years earlier as the Master of Ceremonies in *Cabaret*. "Joel Grey is, of course, the star of *George M!*," reported John Chapman (*Daily News*), "for he gives a fabulous song-and-dance performance in the role of George M. Cohan. But he must share his stardom with at least two others -- Joe Layton, who directed and choreographed a show which has given the Broadway season a shot in the arm, and Jay Blackton, the musical director...Blackton's leading of the admirable orchestra was a performance all by itself..."

Unrestricted by Cohan's rearrangement of his life story for *Yankee Doodle Dandy*, the libretto for *George M!* included Ethel Levey as well as Cohan's loss of many friends after his bitter fight against Actors' Equity in 1919. Richard Watts (*New York Post*) advised, "*George M!* is fast-moving, dynamic and a little breathless, and it is happily filled to the brim with the great man's celebrated and delightful tunes, while it provides Joel Grey, late of *Cabaret*, with a large and vigorous role, and I think it is excellent fun...The story of Cohan is largely that of an arrogant and selfcentered man...The important matter is that he was a wonderful popular song writer and a gifted actor, and *George M!* plays a merited tribute to his high place in the American theatre."

Richard P. Cooke (*The Wall Street Journal*) reported, "*George M!* is an occasion for enjoyable nostalgia," and, although he found Joel Grey's dancing and assured stage presence admirable, added, "What he can't do, and it is probably asking too much, it to make us believe that it is, even for a fleeting moment, Cohan on stage rather than Grey...Mr. Grey is to be congratulated on his voice and dancing and his spirit, even though he couldn't quite reincarnate George M. himself."

Clive Barnes (*The New York Times*) appraised *George M!* as "a scrappy, ill-prepared, mediocrely written account of George M. Cohan, his life, career, loves and songs. It does one very smart thing to begin with -- it uses many of the old Cohan songs...Another smart thing was to cast Joel Grey as George M. Cohan...the story staggers along in fits and starts. When it is fitting rather than starting, you virtually forget about it altogether."

During the summer of 1970, Mickey Rooney (who previously had played Cohan on TV in 1957) replaced Bill Hayes in the title role of a touring *George M!*. Theatre critic Wayne Robinson reported, "Mickey Rooney makes a dandy Yankee Doodle Dandy as the George M. Cohan of *George M!*, the musical...the book is a cliche-ridden Broadway biography that makes a vaudeville turn of a legendary showman's life...Rooney had his lines and business letter perfect...His dancing right now is inclined to huff and puff...Singing is not a Rooney strong point, but Cohan was no Metropolitan Opera voice either...A young, attractive cast supports the star who, in the second act, manages somehow to look more like Ben Franklin of Paris days than George M. of Broadway..."

Joel Grey played *George M!* over a year (435 performances) on Broadway and headed an extensive national tour of the musical. In the summer of 1986, Joel Grey was back as *George M!* touring the summer theaters.

On September 12, 1970 John and Fran Pascal adapted *George M!* in a pared-down version for television with, again, Joel Grey as George Michael. Jack Cassidy, Nanette Fabray and Bernadette Peters portrayed the other three Cohans. *The New York Times* clarified the transfer to television as "What works well in the theater does not necessarily do so in television. The point unhappily was confirmed in the special derived from the Broadway musical *George M!* In the narrow confines of a home screen, the account of the career of George M. Cohan was a static affair. The qualities of illusion and nostalgia were decimated by the harsh reality of the camera closeups...Putting the musical in a closet was simply a mistake in judgement...Joel Grey [provided] the evening's central spark..." (Several years later, the original NBC ninety-minute special was rebroadcast on CBS in a sixty-minute version.)

Eleven years prior to the emergence of *George M!* on Broadway, the life of George M. Cohan was brought to television by Bella and Sam Spewack. Called *Mr. Broadway*, the 1957 special headlined Mickey Rooney as George M. *The New York Times*' Jack Gould found *Mr. Broadway* "...another example of television's skill in the use of confusion and ineptitude to produce rounded blah... Mickey Rooney and a large company, sought simultaneously to be drama, musical and documentary. It emerged as an exercise in superficiality without much entertainment or much insight into its principal figure...the playing version was so palpably truncated and in such a hurry to cover so much ground that it permitted only an episodic caricature of Mr. Cohan." Critic Gould felt that "the choice of Mr. Rooney to portray Mr. Cohan was ill-advised...Mr. Rooney's unrelieved emotional intensity can become somewhat oppressive, especially since he is not too adept at conveying the contrasting quality of mellowness...A major problem for live television, with its need for quick backstage changes, is the showing of the passing of the years in a biographical work. In depicting some 30 years in the life of Mr. Cohan, Mr. Rooney did not undergo any change in physical appearance, which meant that often he appeared either too old or too young."

STAGE

GEORGE M!, *Palace Theatre*, New York, opened April 10, 1968 435 performances
Produced by David Black, Konrad Matthaei and Lorin E. Prince; A Musical Comedy; Directed and Choreographed by Joe Layton; Music and Lyrics by George M. Cohan; Book by Michael Stewart and John and Fran Pascal; Musical and Lyric revisions by Mary Cohan; Scenery Tom John; Lighting, Martin Aronstein; Costumes, Freddie Wittop; Musical direction and vocal arrangements by Jay Blackton; Orchestrations, Philip J. Lang; Stage managers, Tony Manzi and Lee Welling

Joel Grey (George M. Cohan); Jerry Dodge (Jerry Cohan); Betty Ann Grove (Nellie Cohan); Bernadette Peters (succeeded by Patti Mariano) (Josie Cohan); Jill O'Hara (succeeded by Sheila Sullivan, Deborah Deeble) (Agnes Nolan); Jamie Donnelly (Ethel Levey); Jacqueline Alloway (Fay Templeton/ Draper's Assistant/ Wardrobe Lady); Harvey Evans (Sam Harris/ Violinist/ Bell Ringer); John Mineo (Archie/ Draper/ Dockhand/ Judge Anspacher/ First Policeman); Loni Ackerman (Dog Trainer/ Second Pianist/ Templeton's maid, Rose); Jonelle Allen (Living Statue/Cohan & Harris Secretary); Karin Baker (Living Statue/ Pushcart Girl); Susan Batson (First Little Girl/ Mrs. Red Deer/ Sharpshooter's Assistant); Janie Sell (Madame Grimaldi/ Mrs. Baker/ Flamethrower's Assistant); James Dybas (Stagehand/ Dog Trainer/ Louie/ Congressman Burkhardt/ Actor); Bill Brandon (Acrobat/ Boy in Pushcart); Roger Braun (Dr. Webb/ E.F. Albee/ Living Statue/ Ben/ Mayor); Gene Castle (Willie/ Sharpshooter/ Stage Manager Walt); Danny Carroll (Louis Behman/ Bell Ringer/ Vendor/ Fay Templeton's Manager); Patti Mariano (Second Little Girl/ Acrobat); Angela Martin (Ventriloquist/ Ma Templeton); Scotty Salmon (First Pianist/ Acrobat/ Bell Ringer/ Cohan Office Piano Player); Kathie Savage (Living Statue/ Pushcart Girl); Alan Weeks (Buck and Wing Dancer/ Designer's Assistant/ Frankie/ Sailor); Ronald Young (Saxophonist/ Flamethrower/ Bell Ringer/ Ship's Captain/ Alderman Hailey/ Accordionist/ Director)

MUSICAL NUMBERS: "Musical Moon"; "Oh, You Wonderful Boy"; "All Aboard for Broadway"; "Musical Comedy Man"; "I Was Born in Virginia"; "Twentieth Centruy Love"; "My Town"; "Billie"; "Push Me Along in My Pushcart"; "Ring to the Name of

Rose"; "Popularity"; "Give My Regards to Broadway"; "Forty-Five Minutes From Broadway"; "So Long, Mary"; "Down by the Erie"; "Mary"; "All Our Friends"; "Yankee Doodle Dandy"; "Harrigan"; "Nellie Kelly I Love You"; "Over There"; "You're a Grand Old Flag"; "The City"; "I'd Rather Be Right (Rodgers and Hart); "Dancing Our Worries Away"; "The Great Easter Sunday Parade"; "Hannah's A Hummer"; "Barnum and Bailey Rag"; "The Belle of the Barber's Ball"; "American Ragtime"; "All in the Wearing"; "I Want to Hear Yankee Doodle Tune"

Original cast recording: Columbia Records

Touring Company, opened *Curran Theatre*, San Francisco, May 8, 1969
Produced by James and Joseph Nederlander, George M. Steinbrenner III and Elizabeth Ireland McCann; A Musical Comedy; Directed and Choreographed by Joe Layton; Music and Lyrics by George M. Cohan; Book by Michael Stewart and John and Fran Pascal; Scenery, Tom John; Lighting, Martin Aronstein; Costumes, Freddy Wittop; Musical director, Jack Lee; Vocal arrangements, Jay Blackton; Orchestrations, Philip J. Lang; Production supervisor, Jose Vega; Lyrics and Musical revisions by Mary Cohan; Musical supervision, Laurence Rosenthal; Production stage manager, Joe Calvan; Stage managers, Robert Piper and Tony Manzi

Joel Grey (George M. Cohan); Jerry Dodge (Jerry Cohan); Betty Ann Grove (Nellie Cohan); Jennifer Williams (Josie Cohan); Pamela Peadon (Agnes Nolan); Judy Knaiz (Ethel Levey); Jacqueline Alloway (Fay Templeton/Draper's Assistant/Wardrobe Lady); Bill Gerber (Sam Harris/ Dr. Webb/ Violinist/ Bellringer); Roger Braun (E. F. Albee/Ben/Mayor/Mort/ Living Statue); Elaine Beener (Little Girl/Sharpshooter's assistant/Pushcart Girl); Gerard Brentte (Louis Behman/Bell Ringer); Tommy Breslin (Designer's assistant/ Sailor); Gene Castle (Willie/ Sharpshooter/Walt); Jennie Chandler (Living Statue); Kathy Conry (Rose/Pianist); Scott David (Acrobat/ Vendor); Cherry David (Mrs. Baker/Madame Grimaldi/Ma Templeton/Escape Artist's assistant); Ricky Doran (Escape Artist/Stagehand); Steve Holden (Acrobat); Tip Kelley (Ship's Captain/Alderman Hailey); Linda Larson (Ballerina); Susan McCollom (Little Girl/ Acrobat); Penny Pritchard (Living Statue/Pushcart Girl); Marion Ramsey (Living Statue/Secretary); Scotty Salmon (Pianist/ Bell Ringer/ Accordionist); Denny Shearer (Actor/ Congressman Burkhart/ Toe Tapper/ Bell Ringer); Sandra Brewer, Candace Cook (Siamese Twins); Ted Pritchard (Stage Doorman/ Frankie/Saxophonist); John Mineo (Archie the Drummer/ Judge Anspacker/ Draper/ Deckhand/ Policeman/ Man on Street)

Touring Company, summer 1970
Produced by Lee Guber and Shelly Gross; A Musical Comedy; Directed and Choreographed by Wakefield Poole; Music and Lyrics by George M. Cohan; Book by Michael Stewart and John and Fran Pascal; Scenery, David Chapman; Lighting, Barry A. Kearsley; Costumes, Sara Brook; Musical director, Milton Setzer; Lyrics and Musical Revisions by Mary Cohan; General manager, Bernard King; Production coordinator, Lester Topper

Mickey Rooney (replaced Bill Hayes) (George M. Cohan); William McDonald (Jerry Cohan); Mary Ann Niles (Nelie Cohan); Kathy Conry (Josie Cohan); Carol Fox (Agnes Nolan); Kathie Savage (Ethel Levey); Roger Braun (Sam Harris/Dr. Webb/Ben/ Dockworker); Marian Haraldson (Fay Templeton/Mrs. Baker/ Madame Grimaldi/Draper's Assistant); Don Douthit (Louie/Mayor/Draper); Neil Hartman (Alderman Hailey/ Sailor/Sharpshooter/Stagehand); Peter Morin

(Archie/ Piano Player/ Mad Violinist/ Sailor); Murray Moss (Louis Behman/ Man on the Street/ Director); Harriet All (Siamese Twin/ Secretary); Betty Chambers (Ma Templeton/ Piano Player/ Houdini's Assistant); Robin Kilgore (Judge Anspacher/ Walt); John Quinn (Houdini/ Ship's Captain/ Congressman Burkhardt/ Strike Actor); Steven Vincent (Freddy/ Dockworker/ Fast Tapper); Leonard Sanders (E. F. Albee/ Living Statue); Hermine Rochelle (Siamese Twin/ Little Girl); Myrna Charles (Mrs. Red Deer/ Little Girl/ Sharpshooter's Assistant); Fran Loeb (Living Statue); Kitty McDonald (Rose/ Little Girl/ Living Statue)

National Touring Company, September 1970 through March 1971
Produced by Tom Mallow; A Musical Comedy; Director, Billy Matthews; Music and Lyrics by George M. Cohan; Book by Michael Stewart and John and Fran Pascal; Lyrics and Musical Revision by Mary Cohan; Production designer, Leo B. Meyer; Lighting by Ralph Alswang; Costumes coordinated by Sanjora; Musical director, Milton Setzer; Dances and Musical numbers staged by Robert Pagent; Musical supervision and Additional Orchestrations, Julian Stein; Associate producer, Jane Friedlander; Production stage manager, Roger Franklin

Tony Tanner (George M. Cohan); Ray D'Amore (Jerry Cohan); Gloria Le Roy (Nellie Cohan); Maureen Maloney (Josie Cohan); Andrea Duda (Agnes Nolan); Sally Soldo (Ethel Levey); Donna Sanders (Fay Templeton); Ken Starrett (Sam Harris); Doug Newton (Archie); B. J. Harrod (E. F. Albee); Harriet Leider (Madame Grimaldi); Rita Abrams (Mrs. Laughin Water); Henry Victor (Mr. Behman); Bob La Croix (Louie); Arthur Whitfield (Freddie); Joe La Vigna (Actor on Strike); Richard Northcutt (Walt); Ritz Abrams, Betty Chambers, Charan Lee Cohen, Robbee Fian, Ellen Greene, B. J. Harrod, Lois Hathaway, Denis Hefner, Elizabeth Hines, Art Hutchinson, Bon LaCroix, Harriet Leider, Sandy Levitt, Pamela McLernon, Doug Newton, Richard Northcutt, Henry Victor, Joe La-Vigna, James E. Rogers, Arthur Whitfield (Singers and Dancers)

MUSICAL NUMBERS: "Always Leave Them Laughing"; "The Two of Us"; "The Four of Us"; "Musical Moon"; "Oh, You Wonderful Boy"; "Musical Comedy Man"; "All Aboard for Broadway"; "Virginia"; "Twentieth-Century Love"; "My Home Town"; "Billie"; "Push Me Along in My Pushcart"; "Ring to the Name of Rosie"; "Popularity"; "Give My Regards to Broadway"; "Forty-FiveMinutes From Broadway"; "Down by the Erie"; "Mary's a Grand Old Name"; "So Long, Mary"; "Auld Lang Syne"; "Yankee Doodle Dandy"; "Nellie Kelly"; "Harrigan"; "Johnny Get Your Gun"; "Over There"; "You're a Grand Old Flag"; "Musical Time Change"; "I'd Rather Be Right" (Rodgers and Hart)

GIVE MY REGARDS TO BROADWAY, *Marriott's Lincolnshire (Ill.) Theatre*, opened June 1, 1983
Produced by Kary M. Walker; A Musical Comedy; Director and Choreographer, David H. Bell; Music and Lyrics by George M. Cohan; Book and additional Lyrics by David H. Bell; Original music by David Siegel; Setting, Jeffrey Harris; Lighting, Terry Jenkins; Costumes, Doug Marmee; Sound, Todd Seisser; Musical direction and Musical arrangements, David Stites; Orchestrations, David Siegel

James W. Sudik (George M. Cohan); Mary Ernster (Josie Cohan); Mark Pence (Jerry Cohan); Peggy Roeder (Nellie Cohan); Scott Cervien (Tad); Kurt Johns (Stan); Carol Diley (Maisy); Barbara Robertson (Ethel Levey); Dana Kirk Sweeney (Pete); Rob Rahn (Al/Dance Captain); Ross Lehman (Sam Harris); Peter Anderson, Quin Aluni (Pages)

GIVE MY REGARDS TO BROADWAY, *North Shore Music Theatre*, Beverly, Mass. opened June 15, 1987
Executive Producer, Jon Kimbell, presented by arrangement with Artco Productions; A Musical Comedy; Directed and Choreographed by David H. Bell; Music and Lyrics by George M. Cohan; Music adaptation, Phil Hall; Book by David H. Bell; Setting, Michael Anania; Lighting, Bill Anderson; Costumes, Scaramouche; Additional music, Bradford Garside; Musical Direction and Orchestrations, Bradford Garside; Musical supervision and Vocal arrangements, Phil Hall; Production stage manager, Karl Lengel; Sound, Ed McDermid

P. J. Benjamin (George M. Cohan); J. T. Cromwell (Jerry Cohan); Carole Davis (Nellie Cohan); Carol Dilley (Josie Cohan); Louisa Flaningam (Ethel Levey); Paul Geraci (Thadeus); Tony Lillo (Stan); Tina Johnson (Maisy); Harrison McEldowney (Al); Larry Cahn (Sam Harris); Bradford Garside (Pete); Ed Tyler (Mr. Alpert); David Serko, Bruce Moore (Pages); Beth Blatt, Lisa Grant, Harrison McEldowney, Marina Mikelian, Bruce Moore, David Serko, Ed Tyler (Ensemble)

MUSICAL NUMBERS: "Broadway"*; "Second Balcony"*; "Steamer Trunk"*; "Harrigan"; "Mr. Keith"*; "You and I"; "All Aboard for Broadway"; "Running for the Station"*; "How You'd Like to Spoon With Me?" (Edward Laska, Jerome Kern); "American Ragtime"; "Maybe This Is It"*; "You Promised Me"*; "Yankee Doodle Dandy"; "Goodbye Johnny"; "Give My Regards to Broadway"; "Forty-Five Minutes From Broadway"; "Mary's a Grand Old Name"; "So Long, Mary"; "You're a Grand Old Flag"

*(written by David H. Bell, Bradford Garside)

SCREEN

YANKEE DOODLE DANDY, *Warner Bros. Pictures*, released May 1942
Executive Producer, Jack L. Warner; Producer, Hal B. Wallis; Associate producer, William Cagney; Director, Michael Curtiz; Screenplay by Edmund Joseph, Robert Buckner, Julius and Philip Epstein, based on a story by Robert Buckner; Photography, James Wong Howe; Art director, Carl Jules Weyl; Costumes, Milo Anderson; Choreographers, Leroy Prinz, Seymour Felix; Mr. Cagney's dances staged by Jack Boyle; Technical adviser, William Collier, Sr.; Montages, Don Siegel; Music director, Leo F. Forbstein; Music adaptation, Heinz Roemheld; Music and Lyrics, George M. Cohan; Orchestrations, Ray Heindorf; Dialogue director, Hugh MacMullan; Makeup, Perc Westmore; Sound, Everett A. Brown; Editor, George Amy

James Cagney (George M. Cohan); Walter Huston (Jerry Cohan); Rosemary De Camp (Nellie Cohan); Jeanne Cagney (Josie Cohan); Joan Leslie (Mary); Richard Whorf (Sam Harris); George Tobias (Dietz); Irene Manning (Fay Templeton); S. Z. Sakall (Schwab); George Barbier (Abe Erlanger); Walter Catlett (Manager); Frances Langford (Nora Bayes); Eddie Foy, Jr. (Eddie Foy); Odette Myrtil (Madame Bartholdi); Minor Watson (Edward Albee); Phyllis Kennedy (Fanny); Chester Clute (Harold Goff); Douglas Croft (George M. Cohan, age thirteen); Patsy Lee Parson (Josie Cohan, age twelve); Captain Jack Young (Franklin D. Roosevelt); Clinton Rosemond (White House Butler); Audrey Long (Receptionist); Spencer Charters (Providence Stage Manager); Dorothy Kelly, Marijo James (Sister Act); Thomas Jackson (Stage manager); Pat Flaherty (White House Guard); Leon Belasco (Magician); William B.

Davidson (New York Stage manager); Wallis Clark (Theodore Roosevelt); Georgia Carroll (Betsy Ross); Joan Winfield (Sally); Henry Blair (George M. Cohan, age seven); Jo Ann Marlow (Josie Cohan, age six); Syd Saylor (Boarder); Harry Hayden (Dr. Lewellyn); Francis Pierlot (Dr. Anderson); Dick Wessel, James Flavin (Union Army Veterans); Charles Smith, Joyce Reynolds, Dick Chandlee, Joyce Horne (Teenagers); Frank Faylen (Sergeant); Sailor Vincent (Schultz in *Peck's Bad Boy*); Fred Kelsey (Irish Cop in *Peck's Bad Boy*); Tom Dugan (Actor at Railway Station); Garry Owen (Army Clerk); Murray Alper (Wise Guy); Creighton Hale (Telegraph Operator); Ruth Robinson (Nurse); Eddie Acuff, Walter Brooke, Bill Edwards, William Hopper (Reporters); William Forrest, Ed Keane (Critics); Dolores Moran (Girl); Poppy Wilde, Leslie Brooks (Chorus Girls in *Little Johnny Jones*)

NOTE: Cagney reprised the role briefly in *The Seven Little Foys* (1955)

TELEVISION

MR. BROADWAY, NBC Color Special, televised May 11, 1957 90 minutes
Executive Producer, Paul Feigay; Producer/Director, Sidney Lumet; Teleplay by Sam and Bella Spewack; Music and Lyrics by George M. Cohan; Musical director, George Bassman; Choreography, Peter Gennaro; Narrator, Garry Moore

Mickey Rooney (George M. Cohan); James Dunn (Jerry Cohan); Gloria De Haven (Josie Cohan); Roberta Sherwood (Ellen Cohan); June Havoc (Trixie Friganza); Robert Ellenstein (Sam Harris); Bobby Mariano (George, as a child); Patricia Mariano (Josie, as a child); Henry Lascoe (Behman); Eddie Foy, Jr. (Joe Summerhalter); Amy Freeman (Jerry Armstrong); Dick Button (Newspaperman); with Paul Sparer, Bernard Lenrow, David Malen, Paul Mazursky, Bill Millikin, David De Haven, Charles Baxter, Tom Gorman, Dwight Marfield

MUSICAL NUMBERS: "Give My Regards to Broadway"; "Harrigan"; "The Shoes That Hurt"; "The Lively Bootblack"; "They're All My Friends"; "I'm Going to Telegraph My Baby"; "I'm Awfully Strong for You"; "Why Did Nellie Leave Her Home?"; "You're a Grand Old Flag"; "Yankee Doodle Dandy"; "Mary's a Grand Old Name"; "So Long, Mary"; "The ABC Song"; "Life Is Like a Musical Comedy"; "Over There"; "An Old Guy Like Me"; "You Remind Me of My Mother"; "Indians and Trees"

NOTE: Rooney reprised the role in the 1964 TV adaptation of the film *The Seven Little Foys* on the *Bob Hope Chrysler Theatre*

*GEORGE M!, NBC Special** televised September 12, 1970 NBC 90 minutes
Executive Producer, Joseph Cates; Producer, Martin Charnin; Directors, Walter C. Miller and Martin Charnin; Television adaptation by John and Fran Pascal of the 1968 musical comedy by Michael Stewart and John and Fran Pascal; Music and Lyrics by George M. Cohan; Musical Director, Elliot Lawrence, Choreographer, Alan Johnson; Art director, Peter Dohamos

Joel Grey (George M. Cohan); Jack Cassidy (Jerry Cohan); Nanette Fabray (Nellie Cohan); Blythe Danner (Agnes Nolan); Anita Gillette (Ethel Levey); Bernadette Peters (Josie Cohan); Red Buttons (Sam Harris); Jesse White (E. F. Albee); Lewis J. Stadlen (Stage Manager)

* Rebroadcast August 4, 1976 on CBS as a 1 hour special

THE GHOST AND MRS. MUIR
Various adaptations of the novel by R. A. Dick (1945)

Synopsis

At the turn of the century, widowed Lucy Muir escapes her wretched inlaws after a year of mourning for her dead husband, and rents a lovely English seaside cottage although warned the house is haunted. Unconcerned with ghosts, Mrs. Muir, her young daughter, Anna, and her maid, Martha, move into the charming Gull Cottage at White Cliffs. When the ghost of ruggedly handsome Captain Daniel Gregg, the former owner, appears, Mrs. Muir angrily upbraids him for unnecessary hollow laughter in the hallways and maliciously blowing out her candles. Captain Gregg's ghost is impressed with the courage and indomitable spirit of Mrs. Muir, and learning that her financial status has become desperate, he suggests that she write his biography. He dictates his fascinating, if salty, life story to Mrs. Muir and the book is a success. Aware that Mrs. Muir has become interested in Miles Fairley, a writer of children's books, Captain Gregg abandons the house, knowing he has fallen in love with Lucy Muir. Discovering Fairley is married with children and, again disillusioned with love, she returns to her home by the sea. Years pass and Anna has grown up and married, while Mrs. Muir remains at Gull Cottage with her maid, Martha. When aged Mrs. Muir dies in her sleep, Captain Gregg returns to take her with him to share an eternity of happiness.

Comment and Critique

R. A. Dick's (pseudonym for Josephine A. C. Leslie) 1945 novel *The Ghost and Mrs. Muir* was adapted to the screen by Philip Dunne. The 20th Century-Fox production began shooting on August 5, 1946, under the direction of Joseph L. Mankiewicz starring Rex Harrison and Gene Tierney in the title roles, George Sanders as Miles Fairley, and little Natalie Wood as young Anna.

"The romance between that disembodied old sea dog Captain Gregg and the earthly but ethereal widow Mrs. Muir, recounted with such captivating humor and tenderness in the R. A. Dick novel, has been made into a picture which notably recreates the haunting quality of the book," reported Thornton Delehanty (*Redbook* Magazine). "Though the acting burden is carried chiefly by Rex Harrison as the robustious ghost, and by Gene Tierney as his lady love, 20th Century-Fox has provided a supporting cast and a production background which are excellently in key with the story. To play a ghost and make him believable, to endow a spirit with flesh and blood and still keep him spiritual, is no slight achievement, and Mr. Harrison carries it off triumphantly. Miss Tierney, likewise, brings a fragile and sly humor as well as pathos to her role which, in this reviewer's opinion, makes it her most artful acting job to date."

The *Motion Picture Herald* proclaimed, "20th Century-Fox has come up with a beauty -- a delightful, imaginative film, well acted, skilfully directed and beautifully produced...as Gene Tierney, Rex Harrison and George Sanders act it, and as Joseph L. Mankiewicz has directed it, *The Ghost and Mrs. Muir* is a witty, believable and sophisticated offering, almost always avoiding an excess of sentiment and certainly always handling the fantasy with intelligence and sincerity... It's all done tastefully, with humor and with considerable skill."

Photoplay found "It's all done up cleverly with some bright comedy touches. You'll like Rex Harrison and wish he weren't just a spirit...you'll love Mr. Sanders and you'll find Gene Tierney, Edna Best, as the maid, and Vanessa Brown as the daughter thoroughly right in their roles..." The *New York Sun*, noting the absence of Rex Harrison's Ghost from the film during Mrs. Muir's romance with Fairley, reported, "[Harrison] makes a robust ghost, complete with beard and fiendish laugh. When he goes, audience interest goes with him."

Rex Harrison's summation of his ghostly Captain Gregg was "...in *The Ghost and Mrs. Muir*, I had to make passes at Gene Tierney without touching her. I'm going back to playing flesh-and-blood parts. Spiritual love-making is not exactly my cup of tea."

The Ghost and Mrs. Muir was adapted to television by Jean Holloway. The NBC series premiered in September 1968, and costarred Hope Lange and British actor Edward Mulhare. Jack Gould (*The New York Times*) called the television version "a salty manifestation. If *The Ghost and Mrs. Muir* doesn't succumb to an early attack of excessive cuteness, it just might turn into one of the season's hits. The half-hour comedy...is off to a head start in having two very strong leading characters played wittily by Edward Mulhare as the cantankerous ghost of a 19th-century sea captain and Hope Lange as the young widow with two children who buys his old seacoast home...What promises to make *The Ghost and Mrs. Muir* a little different are the characters of the two leads...Charles Nelson Reilly and Reta Shaw are amusing in the smaller roles..."

Prior to the successful 1968-70 television series, an hour-long film adaptation of *The Ghost and Mrs. Muir* was produced in 1956, During the mid-1950s, Otto Lang and Irving Asher produced for 20th Century-Fox several "pocket version" films for television, among them, *Cavalcade*, *Laura*, *The Ox-Bow Incident*, *The Late George Apley*, *The Late Christopher Bean*, *Miracle on 34th Street*, *Mr. Belvedere* and *Broken Arrow*, including a version of *The Ghost and Mrs. Muir* which was retitled *Stranger in the Night*. Joan Fontaine and Michael Wilding starred with Elsa Lanchester and Tom Conway (in the role similar to the one played originally by his real-life brother, George Sanders). The television version in no way erased the memory of the Gene Tierney-Rex Harrison film.

The production cycle of *The Ghost and Mrs. Muir* ran an unusual course from screen to television to, finally, the stage. On March 16, 1987, *The Ghost and Mrs. Muir* was produced by the PCPA Marian Theatre at Santa Monica, California, by Anita Phillips Berman. R. A. Dick's novel was adapted to the stage by Arthur Marx and Robert Fisher, with music and lyrics by Scott DeTurk and Bill Franceur. The musical version of *The Ghost and Mrs. Muir* featured Leanna Nelson as Mrs. Muir and Gale McNeeley as Captain Daniel Gregg. Reviewing its world premiere, *Variety* labeled it "a hit...a turn-of-the-century musical romance with 15 semioperatic tunes seamlessly and gracefully woven into the text, what was once merely light fare now has depth and resonance [which] transforms the cute-resident-ghost comic cliche into a bittersweet occult-tinged fantasy with the power and suspense of a *Brigadoon*."

STAGE

THE GHOST AND MRS. MUIR, *PCPA Marian Theatre*, Santa Monica, Calif., opened March 16, 1987

A PCPA Theatrefest Presentation; Produced by Anita Phillips Berman; A Musical Play by Arthur Marx and Robert Fisher, based on the novel by R. A. Dick; Director,

Jack Shouse; Music and Lyrics by Scott DeTurk and Bill Franceur; Settings, John Dexter; Lighting, Michael Peterson; Musical director, Brad Carroll; Sound, David R. White; Choreography, Carolyn Shouse; Costumes, Susan Snowden; Stage manager, Mary Emery

Leanna Nelson (Mrs. Muir); Gale McNeeley (Captain Daniel Gregg); Kathleen BradyGarvin (Martha Grant); Sheryl A. Joerger (Jessica Muir); and V. Craig Heidenreich, Pat Sibley, Carolyn J. Keith, Jeremy Mann, Phil Brotherton, James Wesley Mann, Michelle K. Mayorga, Maximillian Alexander Gough, David M. Huber, Job Martin, Andrew D. Oswald, Lee Shackelford, Douglas Harvey, Lisa Giorgi, Valerie Coulton, Nancy Dale Krebs, Deborah J. Norton, Heidi Hagopian

MUSICAL NUMBERS: "I've Always Loved You"; "A Reflection of Me"; "Shipshape and Bristol Fashion"; "Blood and Swash"; "Another Time Another Place"; and others

SCREEN

THE GHOST AND MRS. MUIR, 20th Century-Fox, released May 1947

Produced by Fred Kohlmar; Director, Joseph L. Mankiewicz; Screenplay by Philip Dunne, based on the novel by R. A. Dick; Photography, Charles Lang; Art directors, Richard Day and George Davis; Set decorators, Thomas Little, Stuart Reiss; Music, Bernard Herrmann; Special effects, Fred Sersen; Sound, Bernard Fredricks and Roger Heman; Editor, Dorothy Spencer

Gene Tierney (Lucy Muir); Rex Harrison (The Ghost of Captain Daniel Gregg); George Sanders (Miles Fairley); Edna Best (Martha); Anna Lee (Mrs. Miles Fairley); Vanessa Brown (Anna, grown); Natalie Wood (Anna, as a child); Isobel Elsom (Angelica); Robert Coote (Coombe); Victoria Horne (Eva); Whitford Kane (Sproule); Brad Slaven (Enquiries); Helen Freeman (Authoress); Willaim Stellin (Bill); David Thursby (Sproggins); Stuart Holmes (Man on Train); Heather Wilde (English Maid)

TELEVISION

STRANGER IN THE NIGHT, 20th Century-Fox Hour, televised October 17, 1956 CBS 60 minutes

Executive producer, Irving Asher; Producer, Peter Packer; Director, Lewis Allen; Teleplay, DeWitt Bodeen, based on the screenplay by Philip Dunne and the novel *The Ghost and Mrs. Muir* by R. A. Dick

Joan Fontaine (Lynne Abbott); Michael Wilding (Captain Robert Wilton); Elsa Lanchester (Ida Perkins); Tom Conway (Craig Eaton); Jack Raine (Royce); Philip Tonge (Smythe); Ashley Cowan (Mr. Enquiries); Mary Flynn (Mrs. Eaton); Queenie Leonard (Maid); Keith Hitchcock (Commuter)

THE GHOST AND MRS. MUIR, televised September 21, 1968 through September 6, 1969 NBC 30 minutes each; September 18, 1969 through September 9, 1970 ABC 30 minutes each (50 episodes total)

Producer, David Gerber; Director, Gene Reynolds and others; Teleplay, Jean Holloway and others (1968); Executive Producer, David Gerber; Producer, Howard Leeds; Director, Jay Sandrich and others; Teleplay, Dan Beaumont and Joel Kane and others (1969)

Hope Lange (Carolyn Muir); Edward Mulhare (Captain Daniel Gregg); Reta

Shaw (Martha Grant); Harlen Carraher (Jonathan Muir); Charles Nelson Reilly (Claymore Gregg); Guy Raymond (Ed Peevy); Dabbs Greer (Noorie Coolidge); Gil Lamb (Ed's buddy); Kellie Flanagan (Candy Muir); and weekly guests

GOODBYE, MR. CHIPS

Various adaptation of the novel by James Hilton (1933)

Synopsis

Ill with a severe cold on a frigid English November day, eighty-five-year-old Professor Chipping settles into his armchair by the fireplace and reflects on his long teaching career which began at the age of twenty-three in 1870 at Brookfield's School for Boys. On his first day, the headmaster warned him to maintain strict discipline over his classes, and when a student slammed his desk top, Chipping assigned him one hundred lines. The student's name was Colley, one of several generations of Colleys Professor Chipping would teach. On a walking tour in Austria, forty-eight-year-old Chipping met attractive much younger, Katherine Bridges. Falling in love with the Englishwoman, Chipping summoned sufficient courage after a nervous, uncertain courtship to ask her to marry him.

Kathy's enduring love brought him everlasting happiness, and through her, a greater understanding of his pupils to whom he became lovable, old Mr. Chips accepting his invitation to tea and friendship. After four years of marriage, Kathy died in childbirth on the very day several of the students, unaware of Chips' tragic loss, played April Fool's pranks on him. During World War I, Chips was appointed Brookfield's headmaster, placating a terrified Latin class during a German air raid with his unshakable calm and having them translate Caesar's description of warfare. In the school chapel at war's end, Chips, clad in his disreputable, worn gown, tearfully read the list of twenty-three former students lost in battle, clearly recalling their youthful faces.

Tended in his retirement by his housekeeper, Mrs. Wickett, Chips was frequently asked to welcome dignitaries visiting Brookfield, mainly former students now Parliament and Peerage members or public figures whose younger faces he remembered but whose names eluded him. The wise, bemused old man, aroused from his reverie by a freshman claiming he was told to report to Professor Chipping, recognized the old student prank and kindly agreed, offering the young lad tea and encouragement. The freshman was the last to see Mr. Chips, who died quietly in his sleep during the cold, harsh Winter night, but not before correcting his Doctor's comment, "He never had any children." Feisty Chip's last words were, "I had children, thousands of them, and all boys!"

Comment and Critique

James Hilton's sentimental story, *Goodbye, Mr. Chips*, in which he based the character of Chips on his own schoolmaster father John and a former Latin professor, was written for the Christmas 1933 supplement of *The British Weekly*. Later it ran serially in *The Atlantic Monthly*. Joseph Hennessey recommended the short novel to his employer, writer-critic-raconteur Alexander Woollcott, whose enthusiastic endorsement included going "quietly mad" over the tale. Woollcott persuaded Little, Brown & Co. to publish the book in June 1934 and its popularity grew into twenty-two English-language editions and twenty translations.

George S. Kaufman and Moss Hart, keenly aware of Woollcott's impact on the success of *Goodbye, Mr. Chips*, had the prematurely impressed Mrs. Ernest W. Stanley of Massilon, Ohio, hosting Sheridan Whiteside, their caricature of Woollcott, in their play *The Man Who Came to Dinner*, enthralled with the prospect that the invading Mr. Whiteside might even read *Goodbye, Mr. Chips* to the family.

In his biography, *Alexander Woollcott: The Man Who Came to Dinner*, Edwin P. Hoyt wrote, "James Hilton knew how this tremendous success had been achieved, by Aleck. He wrote on November 2 (1934), 'I want to tell you how well aware I am of the extent to which my present American reputation (let alone book sales) owes to your enormously influential advocacy, both in print and on the radio; and I count myself the most fortunate of writers to have had it so happen. Your review of *Goodbye, Mr. Chips* in *McCall's* magazine (to take but one instance) contained not only the best things I have ever had said about my work, but the most sympathetic understanding of Mr. Chips and all he signifies that I have read, either on your side of the Atlantic or mine.'"

MGM filmed *Goodbye, Mr. Chips* in England. The screen version was hugely successful, highlighted by a superb performance by English actor Robert Donat who, in 1939 (when most of the Academy Awards went to *Gone With the Wind*), captured the year's Best Actor Oscar for his beguiling portrayal of Mr. Chips. Greer Garson, making her first film playing the brief part of Chips' wife, Kathy, was Oscar-nominated as the year's Best Actress but lost to Vivien Leigh's Scarlett O'Hara.

"It has been rather tenderly done. Alexander Woollcott and the other authorities who have been quoted in the ads may be guilty of whooping up its merits overmuch, but basically they are right: it is a serene, heartwarming and generally satisfactory film edition of an edifyingly sentimental novelette," reported Frank S. Nugent (*The New York Times*). "Like the story, the film is nostalgic: if we never knew a Mr. Chips, we should have known him...The picture has no difficulty in using two hours to retell a story that was scarcely above short story length. Mr. Chips is worth its time. Particularly is he worth it with Mr. Donat's portrait of him. It is an incredibly fine characterization."

Howard Barnes (*New York Herald-Tribune*) found *Goodbye, Mr. Chips* "made into a beautiful and eloquently moving film. Keeping high faith with the spirit and letter of the original, Metro-Goldwyn-Mayer has translated it to the screen with remarkable vigor, understanding and feeling...Directed brilliantly by an American, Sam Wood, and performed consummately by Robert Donat and his British supporting company, it is a motion picture which you will want to see time and again and will remember long after the other offering of our day are forgotten."

John Mosher (*The New Yorker*) enthused, "Robert Donat's impersonation of the shy, unassuming Mr. Chips is a triumph." *Time* magazine found: "It is a lovingly faithful picturizing of the novelette," and Jesse Zunser (*Cue*) wrote, "It has been translated into a film as lovely, as memorable, and as perfectly satisfying in its celluloid medium, as it was in the original -- a rarely beautiful experience in the cinema...This is one of the best pictures of the year."

Prior to the release of the film version, James Hilton and Barbara Burnham dramatized the novel for the London stage. It opened at the Shaftesbury Theatre in late September 1938, and starred Leslie Banks as Chips with Constance Cummings as Katherine. London's *Bystander* praised the stage version: "Mr. Chips has thousands of friends, made through James Hilton's novel and through the broadcast play. But not one of them, however jealous of their imaginary picture, could grudge him to Leslie Banks. He *is* Mr. Chips, from his first class at Brookfield in 1870 to his last teaparty with a new boy in 1938. It is a faultless performance. Nothing could be added to it, nothing taken from it to make it more satisfying or more moving a portrait... Constance Cummings is enchanting..."

In summer 1982 Britain's Chichester Festival produced a musical version of *Goodbye, Mr. Chips*, with a book by Roland Starke and a score by Leslie Bricusse. Chichester's musicalized *Chips* starred seventy-two-year-old John Mills who had played the grown Colley in the 1939 film version. Thirteen years before Chichester's production, the Leslie Bricusse musical adaptation had been unsuccessfully brought to the screen and, as John Russell Taylor (*Plays and Players*) properly questioned, "Why it should be expected to work on stage if it could not work on film is a mystery. But perhaps the availability of Sir John Mills for the title role had something to do with it...[He] makes a remarkable attempt to look spry and youthful, and act that way, but inevitably there is a slowing of pace and a diminution of energy when it is all seen from nearly 40 years on. And pace and sharpness are just what a rather flaccid, undramatic piece like this needs to keep it ticking over at all...The show makes it hard to account for the perennial appeal of the story...Leslie Banks had a big hit with it on stage in 1938, and of course Robert Donat had his biggest screen success with it a year later. But since then the crisp side of the character has increasingly given place to the soppy. I must admit that as we neared the end at Chichester, there was scarcely a dry eye in the house."

In 1968, film producer Arthur P. Jacobs persuaded reluctant Metro-Goldwyn-Mayer that a musical remake of *Goodbye, Mr. Chips* was feasible without destroying Hilton's original concept. Jacobs assigned English playwright Terence Rattigan the task of updating the story from 1870-1914 to 1924-1968 and enlarging the role of Katherine. Peter O'Toole was cast as Chips and pop singer Petula Clark was signed for the expanded role of Katherine. (Rattigan reworked the part of Katherine as a disillusioned London music hall singer who is killed by a German buzzbomb during World War II.) Herbert Ross, a Broadway choreographer who had worked in that capacity on Jacobs' film production of *Doctor Dolittle* and the musical comedy sequences for Barbra Streisand's film version of *Funny Girl*, was given his first cinema directing assignment on *Goodbye, Mr. Chips*.

Films and Filming thought this about the reworked *Goodbye, Mr. Chips*: "Things are surprisingly jolly in this quaint reworking, to music, of James Hilton's old tribute to the dedicated breed of schoolmasters, whose like is still to be observed, here and there, in spite of everything. The present exercise, however, is chiefly successful because of its director's balletic eye. Herbert Ross has caused his camera to move, and has devised his every montage, in a style infinitely more musical than the actual tunes themselves..."

In Britain's *Monthly Film Bulletin*, critic Richard Combs wrote, "This luxuriant second spring for *Mr. Chips* arrives with the expressed intention of producer Arthur Jacobs and director Herbert Ross that it will also be a fresh starting-point for the film musical... But as a vehicle for such experimental thinking, *Mr. Chips* is a decidedly odd choice...For all Ross' (occasionally heavy-footed) grace, the astringent, realistic playing of Peter O'Toole and the earthy warmth and humor of Petula Clark, the film's origins in a very sentimental love story refuse to be buried" Combs also observed: "The musical embellishments do little to cover the yawning gaps in subject matter... the songs struggle to be more than banal -- they add nothing not already established elsewhere -- in this case by Rattigan's script, dryly accurate in detail while it is lacking overall, and Peter O'Toole's meticulous recreation of the aging schoolmaster and his lonely, incommunicable dedication. It is an excellent performance, sufficiently stark and bitter in tone in the early stages to deserve a more suitable framework than the film can provide. The same can be said for Herbert Ross, who could conceivably make his ideas work in something more promising that his patched-up, sadly dated vehicle."

Peter O'Toole won an Oscar nomination for his performance (losing ultimately to John Wayne for *True Grit*) and another nomination went to Leslie Bricusse for his score (music and lyrics) and John Williams for his musical adaptation.

"*Goodbye, Mr. Chips* is Welcome Once More," headlined John J. O'Connor's *New York Times* review of PBS' superlative *Masterpiece Theatre* production of Hilton's classic story, "Mr. Chipping, as he was baptized, is now being given a gently virtuosi turn by Roy Marsden ...Directed by Gareth Davies, this carefully measured and affecting BBC/MGM coproduction has the considerable benefits of superb performances with Mr. Marsden confidently leading the way, and wonderfully authentic locations (many of the school scenes were done at Repton in Derbyshire, the same one used in the Donat film). But the lion's share of credit still belongs to James Hilton. His little story seems to be a fail-safe classic."

Lee Winfrey (*TV Week*) wrote, "If you're weary of the sight of villainy on television, the sort of suspect behavior rampant on both nightly entertainment series and the evening newscasts, *Goodbye, Mr. Chips* will fill any need you feel for some genuine virtue...the role of Chips, the gentle English schoolteacher, is undertaken by Roy Marsden, hitherto best known on the television for playing a policeman. It is a complete change from the recurring *Mystery!* role of Adam Dalgliesch for Marsden, so skilled an actor that the last thing you would ever imagine he would do, as Chips, is to pick up a gun...A consistently artful piece of work, *Chips*, invariably lets viewers make up their own minds, settle on their own judgements, without pointing onlookers toward obvious conclusions as American prime-time entertainments conventionally do...Millions of readers and moviegoers have loved *Mr. Chips*...TV viewers can tune in and see for themselves the reasons for his enduring appeal."

STAGE

GOODBYE, MR. CHIPS, *Shaftesbury Theatre*, London, opened September 23, 1938
132 performances
Produced by O'Bryen, Linnit and Dunfee; Director, Murray MacDonald; A Play by James Hilton and Barbara Burnham, based on the novel by James Hilton

Leslie Banks (Mr. Chips); Constance Cummings (Katherine); Gillian Lind (Elaine); Nigel Stock (Colley/Redbrook); Michael Shepley (Sir Richard Colley/Mr. Blake); Charles Quartermaine (Mr. Weatherby/Dr. Redbrook); Hubert Harben (Mr. Stickleback); Godfrey Kenton (Mr. Upton/Mr. Ralston); Ronald Simpson (Mr. Temple); Ann Wilton (Annie); R. Meadows White (Tibbetts); Wilfrid Babbage (Mr. Rowden); Tony Halfpenny (Roberts); Lawrence Hardman (Mr. Chatteris); Robin Maule (Linford)

Chichester (Eng.) Festival Theatre, opened August 11, 1982
Produced by the Chichester Festival Company; A Musical based on the novel by James Hilton; Director, Patrick Garland and Christopher Selbie; Book by Roland Starke; Music and Lyrics by Leslie Bricusse; Production designer, Peter Rice; Lighting, Mick Hughes; Musical director, John Owen Edwards; Choreography, Lindsay Dolan

John Mills (Mr. Chips); Colette Gleeson (Kathie); Nigel Stock (Max); Paul Hardwick (Weatherby); Marcia Ashton (Mrs. Kirkby/Matron); Robert Meadmore (Bingham/ First Master/ Band Player/ Ellis/ Young Headmaster); Richard Freeman (Shane/Second Master/ Climber/ Passenger); Richard Evan (Porter/

Third Master/ Vickers/ Bank Player); Michael Sadler (Fourth Master/ Climber/ Passenger); Terence Conoley (Porter/ Landlord/ Passenger); Simon Butteriss (Colley/ Passenger/ Boy/ Maynard); Sue Withers (Flora/ Maid); June Bland (Nurse/ Passenger); Local Schoolboys (Edwards/ Cotter/ Morgan/ Martin/ Prefect/ Barton/ Passengers and Boys)

SCREEN

GOODBYE, MR. CHIPS, Metro-Goldwyn-Mayer, released May 1939

Produced by Victor Saville; Director, Sam Wood; Screenplay by R. C. Sherriff, Claudine West and Eric Maschwitz, based on the novel by James Hilton*; Photography, Freddie Young; Art director, Alfred Junge; Music, Richard Addinsell; Music director, Louis Levy; Sound, A. W. Watkins and C. C. Stevens; Editor, Charles Frend

Robert Donat (Mr. Chipping); Greer Garson (Katherine Chipping); Terry Kilburn (Peter Colley II/Peter Colley III/Peter Colley IV); John Mills (Peter Colley, as a Young Man); Paul Henreid (Staefel); Lyn Harding (Weatherby); Frederick Lister (Marsham); Judith Furse (Flora); Milton Rosmer (Charteris); Louise Hampton (Mrs. Wickett); David Tree (Jackson); Austin Trevor (Ralston); Jill Furse (Helen Colley); Edmond Breon (Colonel Morgan); Scott Sunderland (Sir John Colley)

* James Hilton's sequel, *Mr. Chips' Boys*, to be written for Alexander Korda's filming, never materialized.

Metro-Goldwyn-Mayer, released November 1969

Produced by Arthur P. Jacobs; Associate producer, Mort Abrahams; Director Herbert Ross; Screenplay by Terence Rattigan, based on the novel by James Hilton; Photography, Oswald Morris; 2nd Unit Photography, Brian West; Production Designer, Ken Adams; Art director, Maurice Fowler; Musical score and Songs by Leslie Bricusse; Music conductor and Supervisor, Johnny Williams; Associate Musical director, Ian Fraser; Associate choreographer, Nora Kaye; Costumes, Rita Davison; Costume Design, Julie Harris; Makeup supervisor, George Blackler; Mr. O'Toole's makeup created by Bill Lodge; Editor, Ralph Kemplen

Peter O'Toole (Arthur Chipping); Petula Clark (Katherine); Michael Redgrave (The Headmaster); Michael Bryant (Max Staefel); George Baker (Lord Sutterwick); Sian Phillips (Ursula Mossbank); Jack Hedley (William Baxter); Alison Leggatt (Headmaster's Wife); Clinton Greyn (Bill Calbury); Michael Culver (Johnny Longbridge); Barbara Couper (Mrs. Paunceforth); Elspeth March (Mrs. Summersthwaite); Clive Morton (General Paunceforth); Ronnie Stevens (Algy); Mario Maranzana (Pompeii Guide); John Gugolka (Sutterwick, Jr.); Michael Ridgeway (David); Tom Owen (Farley); Craig Marriott (New boy); Elspet Gray (Lady Sutterwick); Jeremy Lloyd (Johnson); Jack May (Price); Leo Britt (Elder Master); Royston Tickner (Policeman); Sheila Steafel (Tilly); Patricia Hayes (Miss Honeybun); The Boys of Sherborne School

MUSICAL NUMBERS: Overture; "Fill the World With Love"; "Where Did My Childhood Go?"; "London Is London"; "And the Sky Smiled"; "Apollo"; "When I Am Older"; "Walk Through the World"; "What Shall I Do With Today?" "What a Lot of Flowers"; "Schooldays"; "When I Was Younger"; "You and I"; "Fill the World With Love" (reprise); "You and I" (reprise)

Original soundtrack recording: MGM Records

TELEVISION

GOODBYE, MR. CHIPS, televised January 29 through March 4, 1984 BBC 6 parts (30 minutes each); in U.S. on PBS' *Masterpiece Theatre*, televised January 4, II, 18 1987 3 parts (1 hour each)
Produced by the British Broadcasting Corporation in conjunction with MGM/UA Entertainment; Producer, Barry Letts; Director, Gareth Davies; Teleplay by Alexander Baron, based on the novel by James Hilton; Music, Dudley Simpson; Editor, Terrance Dicks

Roy Marsden (Mr. Chips); Jill Meager (Katherine); Anne Kristen (Mrs. Wickett); Paul Hawkins (Colley); Peter Baldwin (Dr. Merivale); George Baker (Moldrum); Sarah Sherborne (Ethne); Davyd Harries (Mr. Farrell); Hilary Mason (Mrs. Fuller); Susan Dowdall (Aunt Elizabeth); Suzanne Halstead (Daisy); Mary MacLeod (Mrs. Farrell); Eryl Maynard (Amanda Farrell); John Harding (Mr. Kemp); Michael Cochrane (Ralston); Paul Williamson (Sir John); Christopher Reilly (Barrington); Elizabeth Milbank (Mrs. Tarrant); Stephen Jenn (Staefel); Daniel Flynn (Terriss); Richard Cordery (Chatteris); Michael Malnick (Ponsonby); Matthew Solon (Marlow)

THE GRAPES OF WRATH
A Novel by John Steinbeck (1939)

Synopsis

It is the depth of the Great Depression and sullen Tom Joad, returning home from prison after serving time for homicide, finds his family and others like them driven off their small tenant farms by large companies who can work vast tracts of land more economically. The Joads, with Casy, the preacher who has lost has calling, begin the difficult journey cross country to California only to find promises of work there empty. Going from one migrant camp to another, finding work occasionally only to be branded strikebreakers, Tom and his family and his fellow Okies press on with their seemingly hopeless search for the American dream, becoming increasingly embittered. Tom is forced to take direct action, ultimately, standing up for innocent folks by striking back and killing the labor camp contractor who gunned down the preacher, now a labor agitator, and then realizes he must leave his family once again -- a fugitive on the run.

Comment and Critique

Generally accepted to be the Great American Novel, *The Grapes of Wrath* brought John Steinbeck the Pulitzer Prize following its publication in 1939. An enduring testament to a historical and sociological phenomenon, the Dust Bowl, the book was to become an enormous bestseller -- more than 400,000 copies during its first year in print. Steinbeck was said to have finished the first draft in 1938, titling it then *L'Affaire Lettuceburg*, only to burn it unsatisfied and begin again, completing it in December. Not only did it take the literary world by storm but it caused Steinbeck himself to be denounced in Congress for writing such a radical, anti-American work.

In *The Grapes of Wrath: Trouble in the Promised Land*, author Louis Owens finds: "In his attempt to 'write history while it is happening' [Steinbeck's words from a letter to his agents in 1939], Steinbeck brilliantly documents the suffering of a people in flight, the tragic loss of homeland, and the discovery that in a land of plenty there isn't enough to go around." Owens concludes: "In American literature only one novel had previously brought together the political, sociological, and aesthetic power found in *The Grapes of Wrath*: Mark Twain's *Adventures of Huckleberry Finn*."

Darryl F. Zanuck purchased the rights to the book in 1940 for $100,000, giving Steinbeck no power over the screenplay. Zanuck then had Nunnally Johnson, his very best screenwriter, draft a script which Zanuck himself then edited. John Ford was given the job of directing Henry Fonda and a remarkable company of top-notch actors. (Ford and Fonda immediately before this had done *Young Mr. Lincoln* and *Drums Along the Mohawk* for Zanuck.)

"Actually the most important change Zanuck made on the picture, and the most controversial, was the new ending that he had wanted, and Zanuck made the change after Ford had finished the picture," Mel Gussow wrote in his biography of Zanuck, *Don't Say Yes Until I Finish Talking*. "Originally, in the end, Tom Joad leaves the family to become a labor organizer and activist, to do something not only for the Joads but all oppressed workers. Zanuck wanted something tidier, and he wrote a speech for Ma Joad. As she and the remainder of her family leave the government camp, which had provided the first stability they had known since Oklahoma, and headed once again for toward the promise of jobs, she said to her husband, 'For a while it looked like we was beat...we're the *people*. Can't nobody wipe us out...We'll go on forever 'cause we're the people.' This ended the movie on a note, many considered, of forced sentimentality, but Zanuck was -- and is -- proud of the speech..."

Even more memorable was Fonda's climactic speech ("...Wherever there's a fight so hungry people can eat, "I'll be there...") that made Tom Joad a legendary screen hero.

Following the film's premiere in late January 1940, *The New York Times*' Frank S. Nugent proclaimed: "In the vast library where the celluloid literature of the screen is stored there is one small, uncrowded shelf devoted top the cinema's masterworks, to those films which by dignity of theme and excellence of treatment seem to be of enduring artistry, seem destined to be recalled not merely at the end of their particular year but whenever great motion pictures are mentioned. To that shelf of screen classics, Twentieth Century-Fox yesterday added its version of John Steinbeck's *The Grapes of Wrath*, adapted by Nunnally Johnson, directed by John Ford, and performed by a cast of such uniform excellence and suitability that we should be doing its other members an injustice by saying it was 'headed' by Henry Fonda, Jane Darwell, John Carradine and Russell Simpson."

The Grapes of Wrath became one of the great classics of American filmmaking. The New York Film Critics named it Best Picture of 1940 and John Ford Best Director (for this and his other film of the year, *The Long Voyage Home*). Ford won the Oscar as Best Director and Jane Darwell (Ma Joad) received the Academy Award as Best Supporting Actress. Fonda was nominated (the first of only two Oscar nominations!) but lost to his friend James Stewart (for *The Philadelphia Story*). The film was among the ten nominated for Best Picture (losing to *Rebecca*), and other nominations went to Nunnally Johnson for his screenplay and editor Robert E. Simpson. Overlooked was cinematographer Gregg Toland (instead he was named for Ford's *The Long Voyage Home*).

It was to be forty-eight years before *The Grapes of Wrath* came to the stage in the magnificent production staged by Chicago's admirable Steppenwolf Theatre Company -- nearly two decades after Steinbeck's death. Adapted and directed by Frank Galati and underwritten by AT&T, the Steppenwolf production was faithful to the book to a fault. It boasted a huge cast, billed alphabetically, and drew generally positive reviews. *Variety*, for one, wrote that: "Gary Sinese's Tom Joad is a marvel of restrained rage, Lois Smith provides a strong dramatic center as Ma Joad, and Terry Kinney is superb as the strayed preacher, Jim Casy...It was obviously a labor of love for a book held in awe, particularly by Galati. The irony is that this company, a troupe that made its name via theatrical daring and panache, has been intimidated into conventionality by a writer, great though he may be." The size of the production and the budget it bore made future Steppenwolf stagings of *The Grapes of Wrath* problematical following its six week Chicago run in September-October 1988. It did play, however, in La Jolla, California, for four weeks in May-June 1989 before going to London, in repertory for twelve performances at the National Theatre beginning in June. Money eventually was found to bring it (slightly trimmed) to Broadway in spring 1990.

The Grapes of Wrath won the Tony as Best Play and Frank Galati was named Best Director. There were also six other nominations: Gary Sinise and Terry Kinney as Best Featured Actor, Lois Smith as Best Featured Actress, Kevin Rigdon for both Scenic Design and Lighting Design, Erin Quigley for Costumes. Despite its awards, the show and its downbeat theme could not attract enough of an audience to keep it going and it closed not long afterward -- but not before being preserved on videotape. It premiered on PBS' *American Playhouse* in 1991, one year to the day of its Broadway opening. John J. O'Connor (*The New York Times*) hailed the production as "superb...far more faithful to the 1939 John Steinbeck novel than was the classic 1940 film" and felt that "the performances tower over everything else...Beautifully realized, *The Grapes of Wrath* turns out to be very much a play of our time."

STAGE

Royal George Theatre, Chicago, opened September 17 through October 30, 1988
Produced by the Steppenwolf Theater Company, Randall Arney, artistic director, in association with AT&T; A Drama adapted and directed by Frank Galati from the novel by John Steinbeck; Scenery and lighting, Kevin Rigdon; Costumes, Kevin Rigdon and Erin Quigley; Original music, Michael Smith; Choreography, Peter Amster; Fight choreography, Michael Sokoloff; Sound, Rob Milburn; Production stage manager, Malcolm Ewen

Gary Sinise (Tom Joad); Lois Smith (Ma); Robert Breuler (Pa); Terry Kinney (Jim Casy); Lucina Paquet (Granma); Nathan Davis (Granpa); Tom Irwin (Noah); Cheryl Lynn Bruce (Elizabeth Sandy); and John D. Allison, Elizabeth K. Austin, Darryl D. Davis, Reliouse DeVar, Jim Donovan, Howard Elfman, Louise Freistadt, Jessica Grossman, Tim Hopper, Tonia Jackson, Nancy Lollar, Dana Lubotsky, Terrance MacNamara, Ramsay Midwood, James Noah, Rondi Reed, John C. Reilly, Christian Robinson, Paul G. Scherrer, Theodore Schultz, Eric Simonson, L. J. Slavin, Michael Smith, Rick Snyder, Miriam Sturm, Skipp Sudduth, Yvonne Suhor, Jim True, Elsa Wenzel, Alan Wilder

NOTE: This production was staged at the *La Jolla Playhouse* in California beginning May 14 through June 17, 1989 and then at the *Lyttleton Theatre* in London for 12 performances in a National Theatre summer repertory beginning June 22, 1989

Cort Theatre, New York, opened March 22, 1990 188 performances
Produced by the Shubert Organization, Steppenwolf Theater Company, Suntory International Corporation an Jujamcyn Theaters; A Drama adapted and directed by Frank Galati from the novel by John Steinbeck; Scenery and lighting, Kevin Rigdon; Costumes, Kevin Rigdon and Erin Quigley; Original music, Michael Smith; Choreography, Peter Amster; Fight choreography, Michael Sokoloff; Sound, Rob Milburn; Production stage manager, Malcolm Ewen

Gary Sinise (Tom Joad); Lois Smith (Ma); Robert Breuler (Pa); Terry Kinney (Jim Casy); Lucina Paquet (Granma); Nathan Davis (Granpa); Tom Irwin (Noah); Zoe Taleporos (Ruthie Joad); Cheryl Lynn Bruce (Elizabeth Sandy); Sally Murphy (Rose of Sharon); Francis Guinan (First narrator/ Car Salesman/ Man Going Back/ Weedpatch Camp Director/ Mr. Wainwright); Rick Snyder (Muley Graves/ Floyd Knowles); Ron Crawford (Willy/ Mayer of Hooverville); James Noah (Uncle John); Calvin Lennon Armitage (Winfield); Jim True (Al); Keith Byron-Kirk (Car Salesman); Terrance MacNamara (Camp Proprietor/ Car Salesman); Steve Ramsey (Gas Station Attendant); Michael Hartman (Gas Station Owner/ Contractor/ Third Narrator/ Hooper Ranch Guard); Theodore Schultz, P. J. Brown (Agricultural Officers); Skipp Sudduth (Deputy Sheriff/ Car Salesman/ Fourth Narrator); Nicola Sheara (Camp Nurse); Jessica Wilder (Al's Girl); Eric Simonson (Hooper Ranch Bookkeeper/ Car Salesman); Rondi Reed (Mrs. Wainwright); Kathryn Erbe (Aggie Wainwright); Lex Monson (Man in Barn); Jeremiah Birkett (His Son); Michael Smith, Miriam Sturm, L. J. Slavin, William Schwarz (Musicians)

SCREEN

THE GRAPES OF WRATH, 20th Century-Fox, released March 1940
Produced by Darryl F. Zanuck; Director, John Ford; Screenplay, Nunnally Johnson, based on the novel by John Steinbeck; Photography, Gregg Toland; Art directors, Richard Day and Mark Lee Kirk; Music, Alfred Newman; Editor, Robert Simpson

Henry Fonda (Tom Joad); Jane Darwell (Ma Joad); John Carradine (Casy); Charley Grapewin (Granpa); Dorris Bowdon (Rosasharn); Russell Simpson (Pa Joad); O. Z. Whitehead (Al); John Qualen (Muley); Eddie Quillan (Connie); Zeffie Tilbury (Granma); Frank Sulley (Noah); Frank Darian (Uncle John); Darryl Hickman (Winfield); Shirley Mills (Ruth Joad); Grant Mitchell (Guardian); Ward Bond (Policeman); Frank Faylen (Tim); Joe Sawyer (Accountant); Harry Tyler (Bert); Charles B. Middleton (Conductor); John Arledge (Davis); Hollis Jewell (Muley's Son); Paul Guilfoyle (Floyd); Charles D. Brown (Wilkie); Roger Imhof (Thomas); William Pawley (Bill); and Arthur Aylesworth, Charles Tannen, Selmar Jackson, Eddie C. Walker, David Hughes, Cliff Clark, Adrian Morris, Robert Homans, Irving Bacon, Kitty McHugh, Mae Marsh, Francis Ford, Jack Pennick, Peggy Ryan, Wally Albright

TELEVISION

American Playhouse, televised March 22, 1991 PBS 2 1/2 hours
Produced by Vanguard Films in association with FNM Films and 20th Century Fox Film Corporation; Executive producer, Lindsay Law; Producers, John Williams and Michael Bronson; The Steppenwolf Theatre Company production of the a play adapted and directed by Frank Galati from the novel by John Steinbeck; Television director, Kirk Browning; Scenery and lighting, Kevin Rigdon; Television lighting, Alan

Adelman; Costumes, Kevin Rigdon and Erin Quigley; Original music, Michael Smith; Choreography, Peter Amster; Fight choreography, Michael Sokoloff; Sound, Rob Milburn; Production stage manager, Malcolm Ewen; Oncamera introduction by Elaine Steinbeck

(for cast, see stage production at Cort Theatre in New York)

GREAT EXPECTATIONS

Various adaptations of the novel by Charles Dickens (1860-61)

Synopsis

Young orphan Pip, living with his sister and her blacksmith husband, Joe Gargery, wanders onto the neighboring marshes where he is grabbed by an escaped convict, Abel Magwitch, who demands that the boy bring him food and a file to remove the chains from his legs. Pip fearfully complies with Magwitch's demand and the convict promises the frightened boy he will someday be repaid him for his kindness. Later Pip is requested to visit the gloomy Havisham mansion where the day eccentric, reclusive Miss Havisham has lived since being deserted at the altar, the wedding breakfast molding on the dining room table. In her tawdry wedding dress, the old lady delights in encouraging her haughty ward Estella's dominance of all males.

Eventually Pip, having come of age, moves to London to become a gentleman through the generosity of an unknown benefactor arranged by London solicitor Jaggers. Sharing an apartment with Herbert Pocket, Pip quickly adapts to the upper classes but is embarrassed by a visit from rustic Joe Gargery carrying an invitation to visit Miss Havisham, whom Pip believes to be the provider of his great expectations. Using the name of Mr. Provis, Magwitch reappears on Pip's twenty-first birthday, acknowledging he is Pip's benefactor after having attained considerable wealth in the Colonies. He is under threat of death, however, for returning to England, especially from his old enemy, Arthur Compeyson, who, Herbert Pocket reveals to Pip, was the bridegroom who deserted Miss Havisham.

Revisiting the old lady, Pip learns Estella has married a disreputable London dandy, Bentley Drummle. Shortly thereafter, a fire accidentally ignites the Havisham mansion and, despite Pip's rescue attempt, the old lady perishes in her wedding dress. Pip soon discovers that Provis (Magwitch) is Estella's father and her mother is Mr. Jaggers' housekeeper. He also finds that Compeyson has traced Magwitch to London intent on turning him. Herbert and Pip attempt to smuggle elderly Magwitch to France. At the channel port, though, Compeyson attacks Magwitch but is killed by his old enemy. Magwitch is returned to prison but dies before his trial. Pip later falls ill, but the kindness of Joe Gargery who brings him back to his home to recuperate makes him realize the love the man has given to him since childhood. Eleven years after establishing a successful London business with Herbert Pocket, Pip returns to Miss Havisham's crumbling mansion to find Estella, now a widow, wandering among the ruins. The years have mellowed Estella, and she and Pip decide never again to part.

Comment and Critique

In 1860, Charles Dickens was editor of a popular British magazine, *All the Year Round*, and in December of that year, he began his fascinating novel *Great*

Expectations. He was published serially in the magazine throughout the following year, and in June 1861, Dickens completed the final chapter. The *London Times* reviewed the complete published novel the following October and found, "*Great Expectations* is not, indeed, his best work, but it is to be ranked among his happiest. There is that flowing humour in it which disarms criticism, and which is all the more enjoyable because it defies criticism. Faults there are in abundance, but who is going to find fault when the very essence of the fun is to commit faults?" The *Times* concept of *Great Expectations* a "fun" book is an arcane description. Dickens described it as "tragic-comic" but under any concept the novel is absorbing.

In 1861, George L. Aiken, who, in one week nine years before, had adapted the best and most enduring version of Harriet Beecher Stowe's *Uncle Tom's Cabin; or Life Among the Lowly* to the stage, adapted Charles Dickens' *Great Expectations*. Aiken's version of *Great Expectations* opened in October at Barnum's Museum in New York to play eight performances.

Nearly eighty years later, Alec Guinness adapted *Great Expectations* for the first production of the Actors Theatre Company which was produced at the Rudolf Steiner Hall on Baker Street in wartorn London on December 7, 1939. *Theatre World* reviewed Guinness' effort: "Aided by Motley's smooth and practical setting, and the device of a reader to link the scenes together, Mr. Guinness has achieved the nearmiracle of welding most of the unwieldy elements of a Dickens' novel into stage form without offending the zealots or confusing the uninitiated." Guinness played Herbert Pocket, the part he later had in David Lean's 1946 movie.

London's Mermaid Theatre Company produced Gerald Frow's adaptation of *Great Expectations* spring 1960 for a respectable run of 109 performances. "Dickens' novel, so difficult to adapt to the limitations of any stage, was given a lovable interpretation on the fine open acting area of the Mermaid Theatre," reported *Theatre World*, "and the play ran smoothly, gaining authenticity with each succeeding scene...tribute should be paid, particularly, to Gary Watson as Pip, the young man, and to John Hall as Pip, as a boy..."

At the beginning of January 1985, Peter Coe directed his ambitious version of *Great Expectations* at London's Old Vic. "Coe adapts and directs, restoring without actually bringing to theatrical life several important scenes omitted in the Manchester version, and must presumably be held responsible for a very long, very flat evening almost entirely lacking dramatic rhythm, resonance, tension and wit," reported Michael Ratcliffe (*Observer*). The *Daily Telegraph* found, "While in no way rivalling the Royal Shakespeare's imaginative handling of *Nicholas Nickleby*, the production plods manfully through a tortuous plot packed with everything you expect...But this is less a play than a panorama."

London's *Sunday Telegraph*, commenting on the three and onehalf hour performance, found that it contained "all that is least satisfactory in Dickens' teeming narrative -- its coincidences, melodrama, sentimentality -- become that much more blatant, without even the original prose to mesmerise one into an acceptance of it...Sadly, Ian McCurrach's plummy-voiced Pip [cannot] be described as more than acceptable...Roy Dotrice cleverly brings out the convict Magwitch's obsessional love for Pip, and that splendid actress Sheila Burrell gives a performance of rare pathos as Miss Havisham..."

Michael Billington (*The Guardian*) wrote, "Peter Coe's *Great Expectations* at the Old Vic reverts to the old Scenes-From-the-Novel approach and the result is a pedestrian strip cartoon curiously lacking in mood or emotion." Giles Gordon in *Punch* described the play as "Peter Coe's episodic script and uninterpretive direction recall his *Oliver!* or even RSC's *Nicholas Nickleby*. If you saw the point of the latter, you'll probably enjoy this less intense dramatization. But the British sport of putting novels on the stage is one I cannot understand unless the exercise results in an indigenous work of art being created."

There was a mid-1980s American version of the Dickens novel, adapted by Barbara Field and staged by the Guthrie Theatre of Minneapolis, as well as two musical versions. Financed by the Esther A. Simon Charitable Trust, the New York City Opera's thirteenth commissioned work was an opera based on Dickens' *Great Expectations*. Minneapolis composer Dominick Argento wrote an opera in 1979 in twoacts, fourteen scenes, with a prologue and epilogue based on an inquest into the death of Miss Havisham. John Olon-Scrymgeour, with a grant from the National Endowment for the Arts, did the libretto, titled *Miss Havisham's Fire*. Critic John David Richardson (*After Dark*) found the opera "flickered, sputtered, and at times flared brightly, but on the whole produced little heat..."

The spectacular Paper Mill Playhouse production in spring 1992 brought Dickens to another generation and wonderful notices from the critics. The New York *Daily News*' Howard Kissel, for one, found that Robert Johanson's adaptation of *Great Expectations* captures the theatricality of the novel quite grandly, compressing its many events into a comprehensible and compelling stage narrative" and called "this *Great Expectations* an enjoyable experience." *The New York Times* found that "As adapter and director, Mr. Johanson is true to Dickens, and by the second act, events proceed rippingly" and concluded that "the credibility of the Paper Mill production finally touches the heart, with its enobling panorama of incidental villainies and all-consuming humanity."

Daniel Frohman produced *Great Expectations* for the screen in 1917. The *New York Dramatic Mirror* called it "an artistic dramatization...Jack Pickford was Pip and a most wistful and lifelike Pip...Louise Huff, as Estella, gave the character all the quaint charm it deserves. If the acting were to be reviewed in detail, practically every member of the cast would deserve particular mention." A. W. Sandberg directed a Danish film version of *Great Expectations* in 1921, featuring Martin Herzberg and Harry Komdrup as young and elder Pip with Emile Helsengreen as Magwitch.

Universal Pictures in 1934 produced the only American sound version of *Great Expectations*. Featuring Phillips Holmes as Pip, the picture had compelling performances from recruits from the Broadway stage: Jane Wyatt, as Estella; Henry Hull, as Magwitch; Florence Reed as Miss Havisham, and a find, portly English actor Francis L. Sullivan as Mr. Jaggers. The picture was called "superb cinema entertainment" by *Time* magazine, "[that] should go a long way toward enlarging even further the prestige of Charles Dickens who has lately become the most fashionable author in Hollywood. Expertly condensed by Gladys Unger and directed by Stuart Walker, the task of preserving the vitality of *Great Expectations* rest principally on the cast."

For the filming of *Great Expectations*, Universal constructed fifty-four sets and installed a 175-foot tank filled with fan-blown water through two sound stages to create the River Thames. One huge set included a complete village of twelve thatched cottages plus a working blacksmith shop. The studio's expert makeup artist, Jack Pierce, who had created (and patented) the makeup for Universal's 1931 *Frankenstein* monster, devised four different makeups for Henry Hull's Magwitch and three graduating aging makeups for Florence Reed as Miss Havisham. Madame Hilda Grenier, former royal dresser to England's Queen Mary, acted as technical advisor for the picture's period costuming.

Photoplay magazine selected *Great Expectations* as one of its ten best pictures of the month, asking "Where has Dickens been all this time? Or possibly, where have the studios been? Here is superb movie material...The story unfolds with interest and mystery, and is clearly delineated on the screen. Florence Reed gives an outstanding performance, as does Henry Hull... a find and worthwhile production."

"While there is undeniable entertainment merit in this attraction, popularizing it to a degree that it will be profitably supported by both the classes and masses is not going to be an easy task," advised *The Motion Picture Herald*. "It is a Charles Dickens story, an asset justifying enthusiastic publicity. In the spirit of its story it is finely acted and intelligently directed. In Henry Hull and Jane Wyatt it brings two exceptionally talented principals to the screen. The other important principals as well the supporting cast provided many familiar names...It is expected that the lovers of Dickens literature will want to see this picture, likewise the more intelligent patrons..."

Twelve years after Universal's *Great Expectations* appeared, British director David Lean remade Dickens' story and created one of the screen's all-time masterpieces. *Great Expectations* was included in most of the year's ten best film lists and was recipient of the Academy Award for Guy Green's cinematography (for a Black and White film) and for John Bryan and Wilfred Shingleton's Art and Set decoration. The picture was also nominated for an Oscar as Best Picture of the Year but lost to Elia Kazan's *Gentleman's Agreement*.

Bosley Crowther (*The New York Times*) lauded *Great Expectations*: "Here, in a perfect motion picture, made in England (where it should have been made), the British have done for Dickens what they did for Shakespeare with *Henry V*; they have proved that his works have more life in them than in almost anything now written for the screen...But, somehow, the fullness of Dickens, of his stories and characters -- his humor, pathos and vitality and all his brilliant command of atmosphere -- has never been so illustrated as it is in this wonderful film, which can safely be recommended as screen story-telling at its best." Of the acting, Crowther found: "In the large cast of unsurpassed performers, John Mills, of course, stands out...He makes of this first-personal character such a full-bodied, gracious young man that Pip actually has more stature here than in the book. And little Anthony Wager, as the boy Pip, is so beautifully quiet and restrained...a deeply grateful salute to Bernard Miles for making of Joe Gargery, the blacksmith, a vivid memory...But we must say that all of them have managed to frame a Dickens portrait gallery to the life..."

James Agee (*The Nation*) wrote, "...the film is almost never less than graceful, tasteful, and intelligent, and some of it is better than that...It looks as if the director, David Lean, and his associates have understood Dickens' novel as a work of literature and as a literary but good moving picture...its first half unfolds as prettily as a Japanese paper flower on water." Writer-critic Paul Rotha considered *Great Expectations* one of two of the best films made by David Lean -- the other was *Brief Encounter*.

Gerald Pratley in his *The Cinema of David Lean* wrote about *Great Expectations*, "The result is a spellbinding picture rising to heights of poetry, imagination, sympathy, affection and love of mankind. Here is Lean the complete director at work, from the splendid control of the actors, all in the best Dickensian manner, the use of light and shade, sound and music, words and images. It is a constant procession of moving, charming, witty, lovely, despairing, sad and exciting events set against John Bryan's evocative creation of old London..."

Robert Montgomery produced a two-part TV *Great Expectations* in June 1954. "Television's propensity for biting off more than it can chew asserted itself once again in the earnest if ill-advised attempt of the Robert Montgomery program to condense Charles Dickens' work, *Great Expectations*," was the judgement of Jack Gould (*The New York Times*). "The novel was lost without the compensating reward of a good play...The telling of the story was so hurried that the people onstage never had an opportunity to be brought to life by the cast as flesh and blood humans of mid-19th-century England...were little more than cardboard caricatures done up in costume...Most successful was Rex Thompson as the boy Pip, who brought a measure of conviction to a difficult role. Estelle Winwood never had a chance to come to grips with Miss Havisham...All in all, *Great Expectations* could have been presented under a somewhat more accurate television title. *Pip Faces Life*, for example.."

A sumptuous Britishmade production of *Great Expectations* was televised over NBC in November 1974 as a Bell System Family Theatre presentation. Of the 124-minute film, British critic Sylvia Millar found: "Joseph Hardy and adapter Sherman Yellen have reduced one of Dickens' most subtle and complex novels to an insipid seasonal confection. Visually it contains no trace of authentic Dickensian atmosphere, so economically distilled in the 1946 Lean version...The intricate and sometimes rambling plot requires sensitive pruning and Yellen has hacked the story to pieces, altering motivations, dispensing with vital characters...transforming those that remain into types...this version denudes an untidy masterpiece of all terror, mystery, irony, humour and psychological depth...only Anthony Quayle as Jaggers manages to preserve something of the grim sidelong humour of the original."

Gordon Gow (*Films and Filming*) unfavorably compared the made-for-television *Great Expectations* with David Lean's highly praised film and concluded, "What we are offered is a generally perfunctory account in dramatised form of Pip's adventures...but in the prevailing gentleness, the melodrama, as much as social consciousness, is dissipated; and it was upon melodrama that Dickens thrived. All this makes matters difficult for the cast, but we can at least be grateful for a certain wryness in Margaret Leighton's etching of Miss Havisham, as well as for a cunning trace of cynicism in Anthony Quayle's study of the lawyer Jaggers, and for the bracing pleasure of Andrew Ray's performance as Herbert Pocket..."

In 1967, the BBC produced a ten-part *Great Expectations* with Christopher Guard and Francesca Annis as Pip and Estella, under Alan Bridges' direction, and in 1981, it turned out a twelve-part version, in conjunction with RCTV, Inc. and televised in six ninety-minute segments on the latter's ill-starred Entertainment Channel on American cable.

In summer 1989, a stunning new British-made *Great Expectations* premiered on American television in a three-part, six-hour version. Anthony Hopkins (as Magwitch) and Jean Simmons (this time playing Miss Havisham) headed an all-English cast which was directed by Kevin Connor. *The New York Times*' John J. O'Connor called it "splendid," feeling that "it is able to linger on the kind of finer points that the two-hour [Lean] films had to jettison. Many of the subsidiary characters, their eccentricities gloriously Dickensian, are given room to perform in this TV adaptation written by John Goldsmith...*Great Expectations* is a wonderful tale of greed and ambition, aspects of human nature that are not likely to become dated, no matter what styles of storytelling happen to be fashionable."

STAGE

GREAT EXPECTATIONS, Barnum's Museum, New York, opened October 7, 1861
8 performances

Produced by P. T. Barnum; A dramatization of the novel by Charles Dickens, adapted by George L. Aiken; Scenery by Hielge; Stage manager, E.A. Taylor

Addie Le Brun (Young Pip); Mrs. J. J. Prior (Older Pip); Mrs. R. France (Miss

Havisham); T. H. Hadaway (Joe Gargery); J. E. Nagle (Magwitch); C. Alford (Estella); E. Haviland (Jaggers); John Bridgman (Pumblechook); George Brookes (Wopsle); H. Cunningham (Compeyson); H. E. Chapman (Brownlow); George H. Clarke (Herbert Pocket); Addie Le Brun (Sarah Pocket); Jennie Walters (Mrs. Joe Gargery); Mr. Anderson (Mr. Camilla); W. L. Jamieson (Dolge Orlick); Mr. Ryley (Cousin Josh); Mr. Hughes (Herbert); Miss Thomas (Mrs. Hubble); Miss R. Moreland (Mrs. Camilla); Miss McCormick (Georgiana)

Rudolf Steiner Hall, London, opened December 7, 1939
Produced by The Actors Theatre Company; A Play by Alec Guinness, adapted from the novel by Charles Dickens; Director, George Devine; Settings and Costumes by Motley

Marius Goring (Storyteller in Act I/Pip); Roger Parker (Pip, as a boy); Yvonne Mitchell (Estella, as a Girl); Vera Lindsay (Estella); Roy Emerton (Magwitch); Wilfred Gaithness (Mrs. Jaggers); Martita Hunt (Miss Havisham); Alec Guinness (Herbert Pocket); Richard George (Joe Gargery); Beryl Measor (Mrs. Joe Gargery); Marne Maitland (Compeyson); Frank Tickle (Mr. Pumblechook); Mariott Longman (Clara Barley); James Donald (Policeman); Merula Salaman (Storyteller in Act II/Biddy); Alan Sykes (Mr. Wopsle); Herward Russell (Waiter); William Wightman (Sergeant)

Mermaid Theatre, London, opened April 13, 1960 109 performances
Produced by The Mermaid Theatre Company; A Drama by Gerald Frow, adapted from the novel by Charles Dickens; Director, Sally Miles; Production designer, Sean Kenny; Fights arranged by Patrick Crean

Gary Wilson (Pip); John Hall (Pip, as a Boy); Suzanne Fuller (Estella); Gillian Gale (Young Estella); Paul Curran (Magwitch); Josephine Wilson (Miss Havisham); Michael Logan (Mr. Jaggers); Richard Coe (Herbert Pocket); Brian Hewlett (Herbert Pocket, as a Boy/Client); Dan Meaden (Joe Gargery); Jocelyn Page (Mrs. Joe); Geoffrey Rose (Compeyson); Edgar K. Bruce (Uncle Pumblechook); Mairhi Russell (Biddy); Colin Ellis (Mr. Wemmick); Deirdre White (Amelia/Miss Stiggins); Michael Griffiths (Bentley Drummle); Raymond Farrell (William/The Colonel/ Soldier); John H. Garside (A Minister/Soldier/ Captain Tom); Terence Edmond (A Gentleman); Ronald Pember (Newgate Turnkey/Gatehouse Keeper); Blake Butler (The Aged P); Lewis Wilson (Sergeant/Custom House Officer/Drunken Clerk); Janet Pate, John Cole, John Gray, Nigel Keen, Andrew Thomas (Convicts, Soldiers, Brokers Men, Passersby)

MY GENTLEMAN PIP, *Opera House*, Harrogate, England, opened Decemebr 3, 1968
A Musical based on *Great Expectations* by Charles Dickens; Director, Brian Howard; Book and Music by Jack Sherman; Lyrics by Geoffrey Venis; Production designer, Alan Green; Lighting and Sound by Stephen Davey; Musical director, Derek Hardes; Movement by Molly Kenny

Tommy Risley (Pip, the boy); John Shorter (Magwitch); Jess Conrad (Pip, the man); Virginia Moore (Estella, the girl); Jill Howard (Estella, the woman); Jan Wilson (Miss Havisham); Keith Taylor (Joe Gargery); Nicholas Robinson (Herbet Pocket, as a boy); Paul Greenwood (Herbert Pocket, as a man); Robert Blacklock (Compeyson); Zara Jaber (Mrs. Joe); Andrew Manley (Pumblechook); Trish Tilley (Sarah Pocket); Simon Cuff (Jaggers); Alan Lyddiard (Hubble); Denis

Bond (Woppsie); Stephanie Daviel (Camilla); Zara Jaber (Georgina); Janet Lees Price (Biddy); Bill Anderson (Bentley Drummle); Martin Cochrane (Wemmick); Stephanie Daniel (Clara); Deborah Bateman (Mrs. Hubble)

MISS HAVISHAM'S FIRE, State Theatre, New York, opened March, 1979
Produced and commissioned by the New York City Opera Company; An Opera by Dominick Argento; Libretto by John Olon Scrymgeour, based on *Great Expectations* by Charles Dickens; Director, H. Wesley Balk; Scenery, John Conklin; Lighting, Gilbert V. Hemsley, Jr; Costumes, Charles Elsen; Choreography, Dorothy Frank Danner; Conductor, Julius Rudel

Rita Shane (Miss Aurelia Havisham); Alan Titus (Pip); Suzanne Morsee* (Estella); Lorna Wallach (Little Estella); John Lankston (Drummle); Paul Ikena (Magwitch)

*played and sung in later performances by Gianna Rolandi

J. I. Rodale Theatre, Allentown, Pa., opened December 3, 1980
Produced by the Pennsylvania Stage Company; A Musical play by Drew Kalter, based on *Great Expectations* by Charles Dickens; Director, Gregory S. Hurst; Music and Lyrics by Jeremiah Murray; Settings, Vittorio Capecce; Costumes, Elizabeth Palmer; Sound, Thomas Barrow; Lighting, Betsy Adams; Choreography, Diana Baffa-Brill; Orchestrations, Jeremiah Murray and Phil Hall; Musical director, Phil Hall

Gian-Carlo Vellutino (Young Pip); Richard White (Pip, grown); James Fleetwood (Magwitch); Whitney Webster (Young Estella); Catherine Gaines (Estella, grown); Victoria Boothby (Miss Havisham); Jack Davison (Joe Gargery); Sara Woods (Mrs. Joe Gargery); Ric Stoneback (Compeyson); J. R. Horne (Mr. Jaggers); Robert Hayman (Young Herbert Pocket); Dennis Warning (Herbert Pocket, grown); Scott Severance (Pumblechook/Butler/Wemmick); Barbara Marineau (Hannah); Michael Goldberg (Sergeant of the Guard/ Newgate Guard/ Policeman/ Anxious Man); Tricia O'Connell (Biddy); Ric Stoneback (Mr. Misfit); Trace Paterson (Mrs. Misfit); Stanton Cunningham (Sailor/ Bentley Drummle); Beth Leavel (Whore/Molly); Stephen Hope (Sharkie); Alice Morgan (Poll); Stanton Cunningham, Michael Goldberg, Stephen Hope, Beth Leavel, Patricia Ludd, Alice Morgan, Ric Stoneback (Ensemble)

MUSICAL NUMBERS: "The Holly and the Ivy"; "Please, Your Majesty"; "Tears of Joy"; "La Belle Dame Sans Meric"; "A Penny Dreadful"; "My Hero, My True Love"; "Great Expectations"; "You Can Depend on Me"; "Do I Dare Admit That I Love You?"; "Simply Super"; "Don't Come to Me"; "Entr'Acte"; "Where There's a Will"; "Letting Go"; "As the Fog Rolls In"; "Ghosts"; "A Better Dream"; "Now We Begin"

Royal Exchange Theatre, Manchester, England, opened October 30, 1984
Produced by The Royal Exchange Company; Adapted and Directed by Greg Hersov, James Maxwell and Braham Murray, from the novel by Charles Dickens; Production designer, Di Seymour; Lighting, Geoffrey Joyce; Music, Chris Monks; Sound, Julian Beech

Michael Mueller (Pip); Nick Stringer (Magwitch); Avril Elgar (Miss Havisham); Amanada Donohoe (Estella); Trevor Cooper (Joe Gargery); Wolfe Morris (Jaggers); Art Malik (Herbert Pocket); Janet McTeer (Mrs. Joe/Molly); Sean Arnold (Compeyson); Jenni George (Biddy); Amanda Jessiman (Sarah Pocket); Rory Edward (Orlick); John Southworth (Trabb); Cyril Nri (Trabb's Boy); Renny Krupinski (Wemmick); Kevin Doyle (Startop); Aden Gillett (Drummle); Charlotte Plowright (Figure)

Old Vic Theatre, London, opened January 2 through February 2, 1985
Produced by Nick Salmon for Hermes Production, Ltd.; The Churchill Theatre, Bromley and Birmingham Repertory Theatre Production; Adapted and directed by Peter Coe, from the novel by Charles Dickens; Production designer, Peter Rice; Lighting, Mark Henderson; Incidental Music, Grant Hossack, Charles Garland

Kent:
Ian McCurrach (Pip); Anthony Pearson (Young Pip); Leon Greene (Joe Gargery); Ken Wynne (Pumblechook); Angela Vale (Mrs. Gargery); Gabrielle Glaister (Biddy) Charles Lewsen (Mr. Trabb); Laura Brayne (Young Biddy); Lionel Hamilton (Mr. Wopsle); Nick Mercer (Trabb's Boy); Brendan Barry (Orlick); Robin Wentworth (A Stranger)

On the Marshes:
Roy Dotrice (Magwitch); Ronald Fernee (Compeyson); Brendan Barry (Sergeant)

At Satis House:
Sheila Burrell (Miss Havisham); Lynn Clayton (Estella); Yolande Palfrey (Young Estella); David Ellick (Young Herbert Pocket)

London:
Tony Jay (Jaggers); Owen John O'Mahoney (Mike); Michael Cogan, Nick Mercer (Petitioners)

Hammersmith:
Collin Johnson (Herbert Pocket); Patti Holloway (Mrs. Pocket); Angela Vale (Flopsom); Brendan Barry (Mr. Pocket); Yolande Palfrey (Jane); Nick Mercer (Startop); Ronald Fernee (Drummle); Gabrielle Glaister (Maid); Anthony Pearson, David Ellick, Laura Brayne, Giles Garnett (Children)

Wemmick Castle:
Charles Lewson (Wemmick); Ken Wynne (Aged Parent); Angela Vale (Miss Skiffins)

The Coach Station:
Michael Cogan (Sergeant); Robin Wentworth, Charles Garland (Convicts)

The Theatre:
Lionel Hamilton (The Cat); Leon Greene (The Ogre); Angela Vale (The Fairy); Gabrielle Glaister (The Marquis); Brendan Barry (The King); Yolande Palfrey (The Princess); Ken Wynne (The Dresser)

Other Personages:
Robin Wentworth (Narrator); Ray Browne (Barrister); Patti Holloway (Molly); Michael Wilcox (Pastry Cook); Michael Cogan (Customs Officer); Yolande Palfrey (Clara)

Musicians:
Michael Cogan, Charles Garland, Michael Wilcox

Touring Company, season 1985-86
The Guthrie Theatre Production; A Play by Barbara Field, adapted from the novel by Charles Dickens; Director, Stephen Kanee; Settings, Jack Barkla; Lighting, Marcus Dilliard; Costumes, Jack Edwards; Music composed and directed by Hiram Titus; Dialogue Coach, Elizabeth Smith; Dialogue assistant, Barbara Tirell; Action Coordinator, Bjorn Johnson; Dramaturg, Robert Cowgill; Sound designer, Tom Bolstad; Stage managers, Russell Johnson and Mary Manthis

Timothy Wahrer (Pip); Ann-Sara Matthews (Estella); Don R. Fallbeck (Magwitch); Darrie Lawrence (Miss Havisham/ Miss Skiffins); W. Alan Nebelthau (Joe Gargery/ Aged Parent); Jack McLaughlin-Gray (Jaggers/ Compeyson/ Clergyman); Matthew Kimbrough (Pumblechook/ Wemmick/ Bentley Drummle); Stephen D'Ambrose (Herbert Pocket/ Tailor); Barbara Kingsley (Clara Barley/ Biddy/ A Pocket/ Barmaid); Deirdre Peterson (Mrs. Joe Gargery/ Molly/ A Pocket); Gary Rayppy (Soldier/ Coachman/ Porter/ Stable Boy); Don R. Fallbeck (Undertaker/ A Pocket)

Paper Mill Playhouse, Millburn, N.J., opened February 12 through March 21, 1992
Produced by the Paper Mill Playhouse, Robert Johanson, artistic director; Adapted and directed by Robert Johanson from the novel by Charles Dickens; Scenic design, Michael Anania; Lighting, Timothy Hunter; Costume design, Gregg Barnes; Hair design, Paul Germano; Musaic, Albert Evans; Sound, David R. Paterson; Stage manager, Michael McEowen

On the Marshes: Michael James Reed (Pip); Daren Edward Higgins (Young Pip); John MacKay (Abel Magwitch); Michael O'Gorman (Joe Gargery); Suzanne Toren (Mrs. Joe); Joe Amrbose (Compeyson); Jim Hillgartner (Uncle Pumblechook); Kermit Brown (Mr. Hubble); Linda Poser (Mrs. Hubble); Jennifer Holmes (Estella as Young girl); Elizabeth Franz (Miss Havisham); Richard Woods (Mr. Jaggers); Michael Lewis (Miss Sarah Pocket); Jeff Woodman (Camilla); Timothy Wheeler (Raymond, Camilla's husband); Jeff Seelbach (Young Gentleman); Nancy Bell (Older Estella); Timothy Wheeler (Orlick); Marceline Hugot (Biddy); Robert Molnar (Trabb, the Tailor); Chris Rempfer (Trabb's Boy)

In London: Kermit Brown (Wemmick, Jaggers' Clerk); Carina Anderson, Andrew Segal (Jaggers' Clients); Michael Lewis (Herbert Pocket); Linda Poser (Mrs. Belinda Pocket, Herbert's Mother); Emily Blau, Dante Deianna, Daren Edward Higgins, Jennifer Holmes, Chris Rempfer, Jeff Seelbach (Pocket Children); Jim Hillgartner (Nursemaid Flopson); Timothy Wheeler (Nursemaid Millers); Robert Molnar (Mr. Matthew Pocket, Herber's Father/Wemmick's Father); Jeff Woodman (Bentley Drummle); Kyle Saunders (Startop/ Officer on the Thames); Nancy Bell (Molly, Jaggers' Housekeeper); Daren Edward Higgins (Little Pip)

SCREEN

GREAT EXPECTATIONS, *Paramount/Famous Players*, released January 1917
Produced by Daniel Frohman; Director, Robert G. Vignola; Screenplay, Paul West, based on the novel by Charles Dickens

Jack Pickford (Pip); Louise Huff (Estella); Frank Losee (Abel Magwitch, alias Provis); Marcia Harris (Miss Havisham); W. W. Black (Joe Gargery); Grace Barton (Mrs. Gargery); Herbert Prior (Mr. Jaggers)

STORE FORVENTNINGER (Great Expectations), Nordisk Films, Denmark, released 1921

Director, A. W. Sandberg; Screenplay, Laurids Skands, based on the novel by Charles Dickens; Photography, Louis Larsen and Einar Olsen; Settings, Carlo Jacobsen

Martin Herzberg (Young Pip); Harry Komdrup (Older Pip); Carlo Jacobsen (Joe Gargery); Emile Helsengreen (Magwitch); Marie Dinesen (Miss Havisham); Esther Kjaer Hansen (Estella); Ellen Rovsing (Mrs. Joe Gargery); Olga d'Org (Estella, as a child); Egill Rostrup (Mrs. Jaggers); Ellen Lillien (Biddy); Hialmar Bendtsen (Herbert Pocket); Alfred Meyer (Uncle Pumblechook); Peter Nielsen (Orlick)

Universal Pictures, released October 1934

Produced by Stanley Bergerman; Director, Stuart Walker; Screenplay by Gladys Unger, based on the novel by Charles Dickens; Photography, George Robinson; Art director, Albert D'Agostino; Sound, Gilbert Kurland; Technical director, Madame Hilda Grenier; Makeup, Jack Pierce; Editor, Edward Curtiss; Editorial supervision, Maurice Pivar

Phillips Holmes (Pip); Jane Wyatt (Estella); Henry Hull (Magwitch); Florence Reed (Miss Havisham); Francis L. Sullivan (Mr. Jaggers); George Breakston (Young Pip); Alan Hale (Joe Gargery); Rafaela Ottiano (Mrs. Joe Gargery); Forrester Harvey (Uncle Pumblechook); Eily Malyon (Sarah Pocket); Virginia Hammond (Molly); Jackie Searle (Young Herbert); Harry Cording (Orlick); Douglas Wood (Wopsle); Philip Dakin (Drummle); George Barraud (Compeyson); Ann Howard (Young Estella); Walter Armitage (Herbert Pocket); Valerie Hobson (Biddy [role deleted from final print])

General Film Distributors, England, released December 1946; in U.S., *Universal-International Pictures*, released April 1947

A Cine-Guild Production for the J. Arthur Rank Organisation; Executive producer, Anthony Havelock-Allan; Producer, Ronald Neame; Director, David Lean; Screenplay, David Lean and Ronald Neame with Kay Walsh and Carl McGivern, based on the novel by Charles Dickens; Photography, Guy Green; Production designed by John Bryan; Costumes, Sophia Harris (Motley) and Margaret Furse; Art director, Wilfred Shingleton; Choreography, Suria Magito; Music, Walter Goehr, Kenneth Pakeman and G. Linley; Walter Goehr conducting the National Symphony Orchestra; Sound, Stanley Lambourne, Desmond Dew and Gordon C. McCallum; Editor, Jack Harris

John Mills (Mr. Pip); Valerie Hobson (Estella); Anthony Wager (Pip, as a Boy); Jean Simmons (Estella, as a Girl); Finlay Currie (Magwitch); Martita Hunt (Miss Havisham); Alec Guinness (Herbert Pocket); John Forrest (Herbert, as a Boy); Francis L. Sullivan (Jaggers); Bernard Miles (Joe Gargery); Torin Thatcher (Bentley Drummil); Ivor Bernard (Wemmick); Freda Jackson (Mrs. Joe); Hay Petrie (Uncle Pumblechook); George Hayes (Compeyson); Everley Gregg (Sarah Pocket); Eileen Erskine (Biddy); Richard George (The Sergeant); John Burch (Mr. Wopsle); Grance Denbigh Russell (Mrs. Wopsle); O. B. Clarence (The Aged Parent); Anne Holland (A Relative); Frank Atkinson (Mike); Gordon Begg (Night Porter); Edie Martin (Mrs. Whimple); Walford Hyden (The Dancing Master); Roy Arthur (Galley Steersman)

TELEVISION

GREAT EXPECTATIONS, *Lucky Strike Theatre*, televised June 14 and 21, 1954
NBC 1 hour each
Produced by Robert Montgomery; Director, Norman Felton; Adapted by Doria Folliott from the novel by Charles Dickens; Settings, Syrjala
Part I: The Promise; Part II: The Reality

Rex Thompson (Young Pip); Jacques Aubuchon (Magwitch); Estelle Winwood (Miss Havisham); Mina Reader (Little Estella); Alistair Duncan (Pocket); Roddy McDowell (Pip); Joan Elam (Estella); Scott Forbes (Joe Gargery); Malcolm Lee Beggs (Mr. Jaggers); Lucie Lancaster (Mrs. Joe); Ronald Long (Uncle Pumblechook)

GREAT EXPECTATIONS, televised January 22 to March 26, 1967 BBC 10 parts (1 hour each)
A British Broadcasting Corporation production; Produced by Campbell Logan; Director, Alan Bridges; Adapted by Hugh Leonard from the novel by Charles Dickens; Designer, Stephen Bundy; Costumes, Joyce Hammond; Makeup, Pam Burns

Christopher Guard (Young Pip); Gary Bond (Older Pip); John Tate (Magwitch); Neil McCarthy (Joe Gargery); Shirley Cain (Mrs. Joe); Maxine Audley (Miss Havisham); Francesca Annis (Estella); Derek Lamden (later Richard O'Sullivan) (Herbert Pocket); Kevin Stoney (Compeyson); Peter Vaughan (Mr. Jaggers); Norman Scace (Uncle Pumblechook); Sidney Vivian (Mr. Hubble); Ursula Hirst (Mrs. Hubble); Elsie Wagstaff (Sarah Pocket); John Gill (Wopsle); Marjorie Wilde (Georgina); Joan Geary (Camilla); Christopher Steele (Raymond); Ronald Lacey (Orlick); Hannah Gordon (Biddy); Redmond Phillips (Trabb); Kenneth Nash (Trabb's Boy); Bernard Hepton (Wemmick); Jon Laurimore (Bentley Drummle); Hazel Bainbridge (Miss Skiffins); Mirabelle Thomas (Clara Barley); and Phillip Ross, Pamela Abbott, John Caesar, Frederick Piper, John Forrest, Hira Talfrey, John Roden, Henry Manning, Robert Sansom, Roger Ostime, Douglas Mann

LES GRANDES ESPERANCES, televised 1968 in France
Adapted from the novel by Charles Dickens

Jean-Claude Dauphin (Pip); Charles Vanel (Magwitch); Madeleine Renaud (Miss Havisham); Jean-Roger Caussimon (Mr. Jaggers)

GREAT EXPECTATIONS, Bell System Family Theatre, televised November 22, 1974
NBC 2 hours
Transcontinental Film Productions; Produced by Robert Fryer; Director, Joseph Hardy; Teleplay, Sherman Yellen, based on the novel by Charles Dickens; Photography, Freddie Young; Production designer, Terence Marsh; Art director, Alan Tomkins; Set decorator, Peter James; Assistant director, David Tringham; Associate producer, Johnny Goodman; Musical score and Music director, Maurice Jarre; Music performed by the New Philharmonia Orchestra of London; Costumes, Elizabeth Haffenden and Joan Bridge; Choreography, Eleanor Frazan; Sound recording, Claude Hitchcock; Editor, Bill Butler

Michael York (Pip); Sarah Miles (Estella); James Mason (Magwitch); Margaret Leighton (Miss Havisham); Anthony Quayle (Jaggers); Robert Morley (Uncle Pumblechook); Joss Ackland (Joe Gargery); Rachel Roberts (Mrs. Gargery); Simon Gipps-Kent (Young Pip); Andrew Ray (Herbert Pocket); Richard Beaumont (Young Pocket); Heather Sears (Biddy); James Faulkner (Bentley

Drummle); Peter Bull (Wemmick); John Clive (Mr. Wopsle); Patsy Samrt (Mrs. Wopsle); Celia Hewitt (Molly); Maria Charler (Sara Pocket); Elaine Garreau (Cousin Camilla); Sam Kydd (Scared Convict); Dudley Sutton (Criminal); Tow Owen (Trabb's Boy); Noel Trevarthen (Sergeant); Paul Ellison (Nephew Pip); Geoffrey Greenhill (Police Inspector); John Wireford (Police Officer); Michael Howarth, Ben Cross (Gentlemen at Ball); Eric Chitty (Old Man); Edward Brayshaw (Trabb)

GREAT EXPECTATIONS, televised October 4 to December 20, 1981 BBC 12 episodes (30 minutes each); in U.S. on The Entertainment Channel in six one-hour segments, June 13 to July 18, 1982
Produced by the British Broadcasting Corporation in association with RCTV, Inc.; Producer, Barry Letts; Director, Julian Amyes; A Dramtization by James Andrew Hall of the novel by Charles Dickens; Production Designer, Michael Edwards; Costumes, Ann Arnold; Senior Cameraman, Bob Hubbard; Vision Mixers, Mark Kershaw, Roger Sutton; Lighting, Peter Booth, Bob Chaplin; Sound, Ramon Bailey; Makeup, Gwen Arthy; Visual Effects Designer, John Horton; Graphic Designer, Lesley HopeStone; Film Editor, Oliver White; Music Composed and Conducted by Paul Reade; Production manager, Ann Aronsohn

Gerry Sundquist (Pip); Graham McGrath (Pip, age nine); Phillip Joseph (Joe Gargery); Joan Hickson (Miss Havisham); Paul Davies-Prowles (Pip, age twelve); Patsy Kensit (Estella); Sarah-Jane Varley (Estella, grown); Stratford Johns (Magwitch); Marjorie Yates (Mrs. Joe Gargery); John Stratton (Uncle Pumblechook); Peter Benson (Mr. Wopsle); Walter Sparrow (Mr. Hubble); Christine Ozanne (Mrs. Hubble); Peter Whitbread (Compeyson); Janet Henfrey (Camilla); Edmund Kente (Raymond); Christine Absolom (Biddy); Derek Francis (Mr. Jaggers); Linal Haft (Orlick); Jason Smart (Herbert Pocket); Mollie Maureen (Sarah Pocket); Tim Munro (Herbert Pocket, grown); Melanie Hughes (Clara Barley); Roger Bizley (Bill Barley); Colin Jeavons (Wemmick); James Belchamber (Mr. Trabb); Colin Mayes (Trabb's Boy); Richard Addison, Robert Demeger, Olwen Griffiths (Jaggers' Clients); Iain Ormsby-Knox (Bentley Drummle); Kevin Hart (Startop); Timothy Bateson (Mr. Pocket); Elizabeth Morgan (Mrs. Pocket); Judith Buckingham (Molly); Tony Sympson (Aged Parent); Annette Badlan (Flopson); Ray Faulkner, Howard Attfield (Jaggers' Clients); Charlotte West-Oram (Miss Skiffins); Alec Bregonzi (Wopsle's Dresser); Patrick Carter (Nightwatchman); Charles Bryer (Heckler); John Rutland (Patkins, the Waiter); Roger Bizley (Bill Barley); Edward Phillips (Landlord); Arthur Nightingale (Jack); Colin Fisher (Officer); Leonard Kavanagh (Governor); Ralph Nossek (Judge); Roy Kean (Waiter); Bernard Latham (Sheriff's Man); John Cannon, Harry Fielder, Billy Chimes, Peter Caton, Barney Lawrence, Ted Lane, Reg Turner (Soliders)

GREAT EXPECTATIONS, animated cartoon, syndicated 1988 1 hour
Burbank Films Australia; Executive producers, George Stephenson, Tom Stacey; Producer, Eddy Graham; Director of animation, Jean Tych; Adapted by Alex Buzo from the novel by Charles Dickens; Music, Richard Bowden; Conducted by Billy Burton; Animation supervisor, Warwick Gilbert; Animator, Maria Szemenyei, Gairden Cooke, Astrid Nordheim, Jacques Muller, Alain Costa, Kaye Watts, Janey Dunn, Pam Lofts, Lucie Quinn; Storyboard and Kevin Roper; Background Layouts, David Skinner; Character design, Jean Tych; Painting supervisor, Jenny Schowe; Editor, Peter Siegl; Camera operator, Tom Epperson; Production manager, Roz Phillips

Voices: Bill Kerr, Phillip Hinton, Simon Hinton, Barbara Frawley, Robin Stewart, Liz Horne, Marcus Hale, Moya O'Sullivan

GREAT EXPECTATIONS, televised July 9-II, 1989 The Disney Channel 3 parts (2 hours each)
Produced by PrimeTime Television, Ltd. and HTV, Ltd., in association with The Disney Channel; Producer, Greg Smith; Directed by Kevin Connor; Adapted by John Goldsmith from the novel by Charles Dickens; Photography, Doug Milsome; Production designer, Keith Wilson; Art director, Stephen Bream; Set decorator, Simon Wakefield; Costume designers. Joyce Stoneman, Tiny Nicholls; Music, Ken Thorne; Makeup Eddie Knight, Amanda Knight; Hair stylist, Eithne Fennell; Sound, Laurie Clarkson; Editor, Barry Peters

Anthony Hopkins (replaced Stacy Keach) (Magwitch); Jean Simmons (Miss Havisham); Anthony Calf (Pip); Martin Hervey (Young Pip); John RhysDavies (Joe Gargery); Ray McAnally (Mr. Jaggers); Kim Thomson (Estella); Adam Blackwood (Herbert Pocket); Sean Arnold (Compeyson); Niven Boyd (Orlick); Susan Franklyn (Biddy); Charles Lewson (Wemmick); Rosemary McHale (Mrs. Joe); Frank Middlemass (Uncle Pumblechook); John Quentin (Mr. Wopsle); Owen Teale (Mr. Drummble); Frank Thornton (Mr. Tabb); Henry Powers (Young Herbert); Preston Lockwood (Mr. Hubble); Eve Pierce (Mrs. Hubble); P. J. Davidson (Sergeant); Maria Charles (Sarah Pocket); Madeline Moffet (Georgina); Gerald Campion (Mr. Raymond); Hilary Mason (Mrs. Fragge); Shirley Stellfox (Mrs. Camilla); John Savage (Urchin); Martino Lazzari (Sneak); Simon Warwick (Startop); Charles Pemberton (Philbeam); Carolyn Jones (Molly); Angela Ellis (Mrs. Pocket); Jonathan Newth (Matthew Pocket); Paul Reynolds (The Avenger); Jonathan Stevens (Finch); Sarah Crowden (Miss Skiffins); Mark Williams (Trabb's Son); and Arthur Hewlett, Jeffrey Gardiner, Christine Moore, John Quarmby, Stephanie Schonfeld, Frank Moorey, John Sharp, Peter Corey, Peter Spraggon, Michael Kennedy, Ben Kennedy, Nicholas Taylor, Sara Hammond, Charlotte Payne

HELLZAPOPPIN
A Screamlined Revue by Olsen and Johnson (1938)

Synopsis, Comment and Critique

Describing *Hellzapoppin* is tantamount to comparing a musical version of *The Persecution and Assassination of Marat as Performed by the Inmates of the Asylum of Charenton Under the Direction of the Marquis de Sade* and the lunatic musical comedies of the Marx Brothers. Most Broadway critics were unimpressed with the zany vaudeville production and, like Anne Nichols' comedy, *Abie's Irish Rose* in 1922, which completed 2,327 performances despite critical cudgelling, *Hellzapoppin* became one the American stage's all-time hits. Before departing Broadway, *Hellzapoppin* accumulated 1,404 performances (a record for the time) and spawned road companies that toured successfully for several seasons.

The uninhibited revue created by Ole Olsen and Chic Johnson featured a plethora of wild acts including a man delivering a plant, which continued to grow in size throughout the evening and was last seen as a tree in the lobby; a woman roaming through the audience yelling for her husband, while vendors ballyhooed tickets for rival shows; carpenters with ladders passing through the audience en route to mythical construction; guns being fired incessantly; members of the audience being herded to the stage to participate in the lunacy while a woman screamed she had left her baby in the Automat and fled from the theater. Prologue to this madness was a newsreel in which Adolph Hitler (with a Jewish accent), Mussolini (spouting a Negro dialect), and Franklin D. Roosevelt (murdering the King's language) praised *Hellzapoppin*.

Time magazine described *Hellzapoppin* as "a cross between a fire in a lunatic asylum and the third day at Gettysburg. Billed as a 'screamlined revue,' it roars into action with bullets, bombs and sounds of heavy artillery backstage. Radios blare, sound films boom, gorillas growl, vendors hawk tickets for rival shows, people race across the stage, plunge down the aisles, dive among the audience, ride horseback in boxes." The critic concluded, though, "*Hellzapoppin* turns out to be a toothless bellowing babe...most of the acts are very bad."

Wolcott Gibbs (*The New Yorker*) wrote, "[Ole] Olsen and his associate, [Chic] Johnson, have rounded up every vaudeville act you ever heard of -- and I think they are all lowdown and wonderful...The newspaper reviews, you should know, were almost unanimous in denouncing it as an outrageous happening..."

In *The New York Times*, Brooks Atkinson admitted, "Folks, it is going to be a little difficult to describe this one...Anything goes in *Hellzapoppin* -- noise, vulgarity, practical joking -- and about every third number is foolish enough for guffawing...Very prominent in the proceeding are Olsen and Johnson, a pair of college cut-ups now well on toward middle life without much flowering of their culture...The taste of *Hellzapoppin* runs to second-rate vaudeville turns...But this is mainly a helter-skelter assembly of low-comedy gags to an ear-splitting sound accompaniment -- some of it ugly, all of it fast... but if you can imagine a demented vaudeville brawl without the Marx Brothers, *Hellzapoppin* is it, and a good part of it is loud, low and funny."

Walter Winchell unabashedly maintained his constant plugging of *Hellzapoppin* and propelled it into the smash hit it became. In his biography, *Winchell*, Bob Thomas truthfully noted, "He could make hit shows. When two old vaudeville hands, Olsen and Johnson, brought their *Hellzapoppin* to Broadway in 1938, drama critics sniffed at the unabashed corn. Winchell found it hilarious, and he told his readers so day after day."

George Jean Nathan, oddly enough, supported Winchell with, "*Hellzapoppin* is funnier than the Pulitzer Prize. I haven't laughed so much in a blue moon. It had me yelling my head off."

In its January 27, 1941 issue, *Time* magazine reported a few statistics on the madcap revue: "Last week the deranged festival called *Hellzapoppin* had passed its 1,009th performance. More than 2,000,000 people have seen *Hellzapoppin*, paid $3,450,000 for the privilege. During its lunatic history, 3,000 panes of glass have been shattered (the noise accompanies the waggling of a chorus girl doing the bumps), 150,000 pounds of ice have been dumped in the laps of the audience, 150,000 rounds of blank ammunition has been fired from 22 revolvers. *Hellzapoppin*'s Olsen & Johnson have changed costumes 60,000 times, a laugh-meter has recorded 510,000 gales of laughter..."

Billy House and Eddie Garr headed the 1940-41 national touring company of *Hellzapoppin*, while Jay C. Flippen and Happy Felton replaced Olsen and Johnson on Broadway and later toured in the comedy revue during the 1941-42 season when Olsen and Johnson were in Hollywood filming their mad theatrical adventure. Lew Parker and Jackie Gleason were featured in the 1942-43 national touring company of *Hellzapoppin*, and on April 10, 1948, Olsen and Johnson themselves unleashed a

London production at the Prince's Theatre. Despite their presence, *Hellzapoppin* had a meager West End run.

Life magazine pinpointed *Hellzapoppin*: "Vaudeville returns...but with a screw loose. During the World War, Londoners flocked to a great pseudo-Oriental hodgepodge called *Chu Chi Chow*. Perhaps it is the world crisis that now sends New Yorkers flocking to a hodgepodge called *Hellzapoppin*. Though practically every Broadway critic mauled it, within two weeks of is opening, *Hellzapoppin* was established as the first real smash of the Broadway season. Concocters of this crude, loud, funny and rowdy variety show are Ole Olsen and Chic Johnson who for 25 years have convulsed smalltown vaudeville and picture houses with antique gags and slapdash buffoonery. Supported by a score of other oldtime vaudevillians, they now make New York audiences laugh even louder..."

John Siguard "Ole" Olsen, born in Peru, Indiana, on November 6, 1892, teamed up in 1914 with Chicago-born Harold Ogden "Chic" Johnson (on March 5, 1891) for a rough and tumble, no-holds-barred comedy act. Early on, they appeared in a vaudeville sketch called "The Wager," a burlesque on Owen McGaveney's play *Oliver Twist*. The two zanies usually ended their routines with "May you live as long as you like" (Olsen) and "May you laugh as long as you live" (Johnson). The pair made their legitimate Broadway debut as replacements for Jack Haley and Sid Silvers in the musical comedy *Take A Chance* on June 5, 1933 at the Apollo Theatre. They also became coproducers of the show with Lawrence Schwab and Buddy De Sylva.

The genesis of *Hellzapoppin* was a wild, helter skelter vaudeville called *Atrocities of 1932*, which returned Olsen and Johnson to the stage after a lackluster career in Hollywood in such Warner films as *Oh! Sailor Behave!* (1930), *Fifty Million Frenchmen* and *Gold Dust Gertie* in 1931. Their *Atrocities of 1932* comprised the entire bill at Broadway's vaudeville mecca, The Palace, when it premiered August 21, 1932.

"Olsen and Johnson are turning the occasionally sedate Palace into a madhouse," reported *The New York Times*. "It is a nut comedy carried to extremes and it makes for lunatic and rowdy entertainment. Some of the revue is amusing, and all of it fast moving and remarkably noisy. Probably more firearms are being discharged on the stage of the Palace this week for no particular reason." The film *American Madness*, with Walter Huston, was shown between the scheduled madness of Olsen and Johnson's *Atrocities of 1932*, which, according to a publicist, had registered 1,529 laughs per performance.

Nils T. Granlund encouraged Lee Shubert to see Olsen and Johnson's manic show in Philadelphia at the Earle Theatre. Shubert agreed to back the comedians on a full-scaled revue on Broadway, investing little money and contributing sets and costumes from past Shubert shows such as *Hooray for What* and *The Show Is On*. The ever cagey Shuberts paid Olsen and Johnson 18 percent of the gross receipts which averaged about $34,000 a week against an operating cost of approximately $10,000.

Following the huge success of *Hellzapoppin*, Olsen and Johnson returned to Broadway in 1941 in their *Sons of Fun*, featuring Carmen Miranda and Ella Logan, for 742 performances. *Laffing Room Only* followed in 1944 with 233 performances, and, aided by sexy French Star Denise Darcel, the comedians starred in *Pardon Our French* in 1950 for 100 performances. In October 1954, Olsen and Johnson opened in Chicago with their latest madcap revue, *Pardon Our Antenna*, but were not pardoned and the show closed within two weeks. On June 24, 1959, Olsen and Johnson headlined George A. Hamid's production of *Hellzapoppin*, staged at Flushing Meadows Amphitheatre, which had been the site of Billy Rose's successful 1939

World's Fair Aquacade. In the vastness of the Amphitheatre, the comedians were lost.

Chic Johnson died in Las Vegas on February 25, 1962 at age seventy. Ole Olsen was seventy-one when he died the following January 26 in Albuquerque. The longtime partners probably did not live "as long as they liked" but certainly "laughed as long as they lived."

Alexander H. Cohen produced a version of *Hellzapoppin* for '67 Exposition in Montreal, starring Soupy Sales. In November 1976, another *Hellzapoppin*, produced by Cohen, opened in Baltimore, en route to Broadway, heavily ballyhooed as the Great White Way's debut of Jerry Lewis.

Unfortunately, most of 1976's *Hellzapoppin* occurred backstage. Director Abe Burrows, unsettled by Jerry Lewis' undisciplined theatrical behavior, resigned in favor of Jerry Adler. Additionally, Lewis refused "to do numbers with his costar, Lynn Redgrave" who was winning critical approval for her solo routines. *Hellzapoppin* stopped poppin offstage and on in Boston on Saturday, January 22, 1977. Although Alexander Cohen told the press the revue was being withdrawn because it was not ready for Broadway, he joined Jerome and Margaret Minskoff in bringing a law suit against Jerry Lewis for the $1.25 million *Hellzapoppin* disaster.

On Christmas Day 1941, Universal Pictures released the screen version of *Hellzapoppin* starring Olsen and Johnson with Martha Raye. "Of all the zany, nuttier-than-a-fruit-cake movies, this is it!" exclaimed *Photoplay*. "Olsen and Johnson, that indefatigable pair of clowns, have taken their show and transcribed it to the screen with all its wow and zest, fuss and feathers, madness and nitwitting." *Motion Picture Herald* announced, "Deliberately setting out to be the craziest film ever made, this picture uses every known camera and vaudeville trick to attain that end. The sheer novelty will bring laughs to every audience...the inspiration was the successful Broadway production by Olsen and Johnson, who give the picture what little unity it has."

Olsen and Johnson remained with Universal for three more comedies, *Crazy House* (1943), *Ghost Catchers* (1944) and *See My Lawyer* (1945). But Olsen and Johnson proved no threat to the studio's resident comedy team, Abbott and Costello.

Prior to the 1976 debacle of the proscenium *Hellzapoppin*, Alexander Cohen produced a television version of the show for ABC's Comedy Hour on March 1, 1972, featuring Lynn Redgrave, Jack Cassidy, the Jackson Five and Rex Reed. Rowan and Martin's *Laugh-In*, which made its television debut on January 22, 1968, owed a great deal to the madness and imagination of Olsen and Johnson's "screamlined revue." The *Laugh-In* pilot, televised on NBC on September 9, 1967, was viewed by many as a rip-off of *Hellzapoppin*. Cohen's 1976 television production of *Hellzapoppin* was filmed at Hollywood's Palace Theatre utilizing proscenium staging and, while entertaining and highly amusing, was ironically called a rip-off of *Laugh-in*.

STAGE

HELLZAPOPPIN, *46th Street Theatre*, New York; opened September 22, 1938; Transferred to *Winter Garden Theatre*, December 17, 1941 1,404 performances
Produced by Olsen and Johnson; A vaudeville revue assembled by Ole Olsen and Chic Johnson; Director, Edward Duryea Dowling; Music by Charles Tobias; Lyrics by Sammy Fain; Musical supervision, Harold Stern; Associate conductor, Edward A. Hunt; Additional dialogue and business by Tom McKnight; Vocal arrangemtns, Phil Ellis

Ole Olsen; Chic Johnson; Dewey Barto; George Mann; Hal Sherman; Shirley

Wayne; Bettymae Crane; Beverly Crane; Ray Kinney; Dorothy Thomas; Walter Nilsson; Bonnie Reed; Billy Adams; Mel Reed; Sidney Dean; Roberta and Ray; Radio Rogues; Berg and Moore; Theo Hardeen; James Hollywood; Sidney Gibson; Sidney Chatton; Cyrel Roodney; June Winters; Catherine Johnson; J. C. Olsen; Bob Barry; Mary Sutherland; Joe Wong; Henry Howe; John Callahan; The Charioteers; The Starlings; Phyllis McBride; Helen Felix; Claire Kaktin; Evelyn Deffon; Mary Barth; Dorothy Thomas; Helene Ecklund; Virginia Collins; Sally Bond; Evelyn Albright; Kay Wilson; Margaret Bacon; Dawn Greenwood; Blanche Poston; Elaine Caruso; Naomi Libby; Madeline O'Hara; Karl Lynn; Phyllis Lake; Evelyn Laurie; Jean Beryl; Regina Lewis; Marjorie Conrad; Renee Havel; Margie Young; Adolph Gudel; William Chandler; Phillip Johnson; Fuzzy Lentz; Frank Sheppard; Ned Coupland

MUSICAL NUMBERS: "Hellz-A-Poppin"; "Fuddle De Duddle"; "Strolling Thru the Park"; "It's Time to Say Aloha"; "When You Look in Your Looking Glass" (Music, Stephen Weiss; Lyrics, Paul Mann); "Abe Lincoln" (Music, Alfred Hayes; Lyrics, Earl Robinson); "Shaganola"

Touring Company, season 1940-41

Produced by Olsen and Johnson; A vaudeville revue assembled by Olsen and Johnson; Director, Edward Duryea Dowling; Book by Olsen and Johnson; Music and Lyrics by Sammy Fain and Charles Tobias; Costumes, Joan Personnette; Musical director, Jules Lenzberg; Dances arranged by Gae Foster; Dances staged by Alice Sullivan; Company manager, Gilman Haskell; Stage director, William Smythe; Stage managers, Dave Weinstein and Herman Kantor

Billy House; Eddie Garr; Grace and Nikko; Readinger Twins (succeeded by Sterner Sisters); Murtagh Sisters (succeeded by Read Sisters); The Four Pitchmen (succeeded by The Oxford Boys); Ben Dova; Paul Gordon; Frank Jerome (succeeded by Billy Potter); Bobby Jarvis; Eddie Nelson; Elizabeth Scott; Arleen Robinson; Harris Hines; T. Brauer; Stan Stanley (succeeded by Milton Ross); Annette Mills; Ben Wise; Tony Ross (succeeded by the Wynn Twins); Gail Andrews (succeeded by Billie Younger); Kay Clegg; Eleanor De Luca; Lorene Gray; Tracy Hunter (succeeded by Evelyn Shelby); Emily Jewell (succeeded by Mary Lee); Ronnie Kaye; Lee Laughlin; Ruth Maitland (succeeded by Ruth Morehouse); Frances Morris; Marilyn Robbins; Arleen Robinson (succeeded by Bette Learn); Helen Shepard (succeeded by Marjorie Behn); Doris Stuart (succeeded by Danita Kantor); Sonya Tonya; Violet Vincent; Helen Williams; Bob Cropsey; Dan Karry; Adrian Crosset; Jack Lyons; Bob Pitts; Irving Roppee

MUSICAL NUMBERS: "Hellz-a-Poppin"; "Perfect Day"; "I Tank I Go Home"; "Mosquito"; "Up High"; "Baloon"; "Boomps-A-Daisy"; "When McGregor Sings Off Key"; "Scarem Harem"; "Now You See It -- Now You Don't"; "Surprise Party"; "Now Comes the Time" (Sammy Fain and Charles Tobias); "Havana for a Night" (Gonzalo Curiel, Oscar Hammerstein, II)

Touring Company, season 1941-42 and *Winter Garden Theatre*, New York

Produced by Olsen and Johnson; A vaudeville revue arranged by Olsen and Johnson; Director, Edward Duryea Dowling; Book by Olsen and Johnson; Music and Lyrics by Sammy Fain and Charles Tobias; Dances, Gae Foster; Costumes, Joan Personette; Musical supervision, Harold Stern; Production consultant, Tom Greene; Company manager, L. S. Lawrence, Jr.; Stage director, Dennis Murray; Stage managers, Milton Stern and Fuzzy Lentz

Jay C. Flippen; Happy Felton; Barto and Mann; Charles Withers; The Radio Rogues; Walter Nilsson; The Charioteers; Lyda Sue; Theo Dardeen; Ben Beri (succeeded by Harry Reso); June Winters; Reed and Dean; Shirley Wayne; Ruth Faber; Stephen Olsen; Bergh and Moore; Dippy Diers; Billy Adams; Madelyn O'Hara; Phil Farley; Fuzzy Lentz; Bobby Barry; Adolf Gudel; John Callaghan; Billy Boyle; Jim Collins; Sidney Gibson; Bonnie Reed; Dolly Spence; Mary Sutherland; Peter Chan; Joey Ayrey; Milton Stern; Helen Felix; Claire Kaktin; Mary Barth; Dorothy Thomas; Mildred Clark; Margie Dale; Barbara Pond; Joan Bergere; Blanche Poston; Ila Marie Wilson; Phyllis Lake; Evelyn Laurie; Regina Lewis; Renee Havel; Dorothy Mathews; Anne Middleton; Louise Marsh; Pat O'Cleary; Ariel Ballard; Terry Lasky; Rit Karyl; Rita Horgan; Mary Boland; Eleanor Lamanna; Dick Langdon; Frank Sheppard; Eddie Murray; Ernest DiGennaro

Touring Company, season 1942-43
Produced by The Messrs. Shubert; A vaudeville revue arranged by Olsen and Johnson; Director, Edward Duryea Dowling; Directorial assistant, Milton Stern; Music and Lyrics, Sammy Fain and Charles Tobias; Scenery, Kolck-Meyer Company; Costumes, Fred Wittop; Dances, Dick Barstow

Lew Parker; Jackie Gleason; Barto and Mann; The Radio Rogues; Harry Reso; Charles Withers; Theodore Hardeen; The Biltmorettes; The Commandos; The Kim Loo Sisters; Stephen Olsen; Bergh and Moore; Mary McNamee; Dippy Diers; Joan Baker; Bobby Barry; Hickory Nuts; Billy Adams; Jack Pearson; J. C. Olsen; Edna Isenburg; Beverly Ferre; Jack Matis; Jack Reagen; Donna White; Patsy Newsome; Chubby Chuck; Dorothy Thomas; Stormy Bergh; George Holmes; Sidney Gibson; Mary Barth; Joan Bergere; Louise Marsh; June Ann; Mildred Clark; Pebby Baldwin; Helen Day; Lucille Carroll; Viola Ertoia; Renee Havel; Eleanor DaManna; Evelyn Laurie; Roma Leigh; Donna Misson; Phylliss McBride; Eunice Norris; Harriet Richter; Helen Vent; Florence Walsh; Muriel Ried; Ernest DiGennaro; Jack Purcell; Lucas Hovings; Arthur Walsh; Sidney Enkowe

Prince's Theatre, London, opened April 10, 1948
Produced by Olsen and Johnson; A vaudeville revue by Ole Olsen and Chic Johnson; Director, Edward Duryea Dowling; Music by Charles Tobias; Lyrics by Sammy Fain; Vocal arrangements, Phil Ellis

Ole Olsen; Chic Johnson; Gloria Gilbert; June Johnson; Zoe Gail; Three Pitchmen; J. C. Olsen; Michael Edwards; Clark Brothers; Shannon Dean; Frank Cook; Pat Basso; Dynamite Howes; Shorty Renna; Andy Ratouscheff; Billy Kay; Six Mighty Atoms; Six Rhythmaniacs; Twelve Olechics; Hallzapoppin Glee Club

HELLZAPOPPIN OF 1949, *Curran Theatre*, San Francisco, opened February 20, 1949
Produced by Olsen and Johnson; A vaudeville revue arranged by Olsen and Johnson; Director, Leon Leonidoff; Choreography, Dave Gould; Music/choreography, Pembroke Davenport; Conductor, Dave Schooler

Ole Olsen; Chic Johnson; Gloria Leroy; J. C. Olsen; June Johnson; Marty Kay; Harrison & Fisher; Nirska; Shirley, Sharon and Wanda; Jose Duval; Shannon Dean; Johnnie Howes; Maurice Millard; Billy Kay; Hank Whitehouse; Shorty Renna; Andrew Ratousheff; Six Mighty-Atoms; Frank Harty; Andy Wolandi; Helen Magna; Frank Cook

Golders Green Hippodrome, London, opened November 21, 1949
Produced by Bernard Delfont with Bertram Montague; A vaudeville revue based on Olsen and Johnson's production; Directors, Bertram Montague and Frank P. Adey; Scenery, Joseph Carl; Dances, Iris Kirkwhite

Dave and Joe O'Gorman; Hall, Norman and Ladd; The Three Monarchs; Slim Allan; Beryl Seton; Brian Kent; Helen Darmora; George Robertson; Dot Cunningham; Pat Stevenson; Betty Dayne; Sydney Bridge; The Four Yeomen; Iris Kirkwhite Dancers

MUSICAL NUMBERS: "The Fun Fair", "Mystery in the Madhouse"; "Civilization"; "The Dilemma"; "The Barn"; "Hotel Provence"; "Vice Versus Virtue, or Vice Versa"

Garden of Stars Theatre, La Ronde, Montreal, Canada's Expo '67
Produced by Alexander H. Cohen; A Musical Revue; Director, Jerry Adler; Music by Marian Grudeff; Lyrics by Raymond Jessel; Production designer, Raoul Pene Du Bois; Lighting, Jules Fisher; Musical direction and dance arrangements, John Berkman, Choreography, Buddy Schwab; Orchestrations, Don Walker; Company manager, Warren McClane

Soupy Sales; Betty Madigan; Luba Lisa; Claiborne Cary; Jackie Alloway; Brandon Maggart; Jack Fletcher; Ted Thurston; Suzan Clemm; Will B. Able; Graziella; Johnny Melfi (Principals); Barbara Brownell, Trudy Carson, Linda Grant, Sharon Hailey, Linda Jorgens, Marilyn Miles, Mabel Robinson, Lynn Winn, Mary Zahn, Dennis Edenfield, Bill Gerber, Tony Juliano, Rose Miles, Eddy Phillips, Scott Salmon, Fred Siretta, Michael Toles, Lester Wilson, Jeff Chambers (Ensemble)

PRODUCTION NUMBERS: "Hellzapoppin"; The Great Explodo; Songwriter; "Montreal"; "Love Revisited"; History Revisited; "The Umbrella"; Pyschiatrist Revisited; "Air Strip"

HELLZAPOPPIN, opened Baltimore, November 22, 1976; closed Boston, January 22, 1977
Produced by Alexander H. Cohen in association with Maggie and Jerome Minskoff; Coproducers, Hildy Parks and Roy A. Somlyo; A Musical Revue, based on a format by Olsen and Johnson; Director Jerry Adler (replaced Abe Burrows); Written by Abe Burrows, Bill Beyer, Hank Beebe and Joseph Stein; Music by Jule Styne, Hank Beebe and Cy Coleman; Lyrics by Carolyn Leigh and Bill Beyer; Settings and Lighting by Robert Randolph; Costumes, Alvin Colt; Choreography, Donald Saddler; Additional choreography, Tommy Tune; Musical supervision, Elliot Lawrence; Orchestrations, Ralph Burns; Musical conductor, John Lesko; Associate conductor, Louis Brown; Dance music, Gordon Lowry Harrell; Production assistants, Susan Guernsey and Juliet Wise

Jerry Lewis; Lynn Redgrave; Herb Edelman; Joey Faye; Brandon Maggart; Mace Barrett; Tom Batten; Marie Berry; Terry Calloway; Jill Choder; Susan Danielle; Mercedes Ellington; Robert Fitch; Trudie Green; Lisa Guignard; Lisa Haapaniemi; Bob Harvey; Peter Heuchling; Gwen Hillier; Justine Johnstone; Holly Jones; Leonardo; Michael Mann; P. J. Mann; Dana Jo Moore; Rick Pessagno; Rodney Reiner; Terry Rieser; Catherine Rice; Jeff Richards; Tudi Roach; Jane Robertson; Karen St. George; Fred Stretta; Robin Stone; The Villams; The Volantes; Bob Williams and Louie; Melanie Winter

MUSICAL NUMBERS: "Hellzapoppin"; "A Husband, a Love, a Wife"; "Bouncing Back for More"; "Dare to Do"; "Eighth Avenue"; "Once I've Got My Cane"; "Hello, Mom";

"Back to Him"; "A Miracle Happened"; "A Hymn to Her"; "One to a Customer"; "Let's Put a Man on the Sun"

SCREEN

HELLZAPOPPIN, Universal Pictures, released December 1941
A Mayfair Production; Producer, Jules Levy; Director, H. C. Potter; Screenplay by Nat Perrin and Warren Wilson, based on a story by Nat Perrin and the vaudeville revue by Olsen and Johnson; Photography, Woody Bredell; Special effects, John Fulton; Associate producers, Glenn Tyron and Alex Gottlieb; Editor, Milton Carruth

Ole Olsen (Ole); Chic Johnson (Chic); Robert Paige (Jeff Hunter); Martha Raye (Baby Betty Johnson); Jane Frazee (Kitty Rand); Lewis Howard (Woody Tyler); Nella Walker (Mrs. Rand); Clarence Kolb (Mr. Rand); Richard Lane (Director); Elisha Cook, Jr. (Assistant Director); Hugh Herbert (Detective Quimby); Shemp Howard (Louie); Jody Gilbert (Blonde); Andrew Tombes (Producer); George Davis (Butler); Hal K. Dawson, Frank Darien (Photographers); Billy Curtis (Taxi Driver); Harry Monti (Midget); Gus Schilling (Orchestra Leader); Sig Arno (Cellist); Don Brodie (Theatre Manager); Eddie Acuff (Drafted Devil); Gil Perkins (Butler in Pool); Dale Van Sickel (Man Who Falls into Pool); Bert Roach (Man in Audience); Mischa Auer (Prince Pepi); Katherine Johnson (Oscar's Wife); Dorothy Darrell (Girl); George Chandler (Man); Olive Hatch, Harlem Congaroo Dancers, The Six Hits, Slim and Sam (Specialties)

SONGS: "What Kind of Love Is This?"; "Watch the Birdie"; "You Were There"; "Heaven for Two"; "Hellzapoppin"; "Putting on the Dog"; "Congaroo"; "Congo Beso"; "Waiting for the Robert E. Lee"

TELEVISION

HELLZAPOPPIN, ABC Comedy Hour, televised March 1, 1972 ABC 60 minutes
Executive producer, Alexander H. Cohen; Producer, Carolyn Raskin; Director, Clark Jones; Writers, Sheldon Keller, Howard Albrecht, Gene Perret, John Rappaport, Kenny Solms, Gail Parent, Mark Richards, Dan Shapiro and Sol Weinstein; Music director, Nick Perito

Jack Cassidy, Ronnie Schell, Lynn Redgrave, Bob Williams and his dog Louie, June Wilkinson, Ruth Buzzi, Lyle Waggoner, Lou Wills, Will B. Able, The Volantes, The Jackson Five, Rex Reed, Richard M. Dixon, Jack Eagle

SONGS: "Why Must the Show Go On?"; "Nations United"; "Hellzapoppin"

HENRY VIII

A Play by William Shakespeare and various dramatizations of the life of King Henry VIII (also see A MAN FOR ALL SEASONS)

Synopsis

Seven weeks after becoming King of England, Henry VIII (born at Greenwich, England, on June 28, 1491) marries his late brother Arthur's widow, Katharine of Aragon, the daughter of King Ferdinand and Queen Isabella of Spain. Disappointed, though, in her subsequent deliverance of a daughter, Mary, and wary of her position as the aunt of King Charles V of Spain, head of the Roman Catholic Empire, Henry seeks a divorce through England's Cardinal Wolsey. Henry falls in love with Anne Boleyn but his divorce from Katherine is vigorously opposed by the Pope. Rebelling against the papal authority, the king disbands all the English Catholic monasteries, taking their enormous wealth into his treasury, and ruthlessly has his opposing friends, including Sir Thomas More, executed. After his marriage to Anne Boleyn, she bears him another daughter (the future Queen Elizabeth I) and a stillborn son. Henry, now enamored of Jane Seymour, has Anne beheaded on an unresolved charge of adultery with Mark Smeaton and others. Ten days later, the king marries Jane Seymour, who dies shortly after giving birth to the future Edward VI. Courting support for the throne from Germany, Henry then reluctantly weds independent and shrewd Anne of Cleves, who became known as "The Flanders Mare," but he later divorces her and has Thomas Cromwell beheaded for arranging the marriage in the first place. Henry takes for his fifth wife Catherine Howard, daughter of the Earl of Norfolk, and then has her beheaded after Archbishop Cranmer discovers her affair with Thomas Culpepper. Aging, feeble, ulcerated Henry next takes his sixth wife, Catherine Parr, a twice-wed divinity student. Catherine Parr survives (as did Anne of Cleves) to become Henry's widow when he dies on January 28, 1547, at age fifty-six to be buried in St. George's Chapel at Windsor Castle.

Comment and Critique

During a performance on June 29, 1613, by The Kings Players of William Shakespeare's *The Famous History of the Life of King Henry the Eight; or All Is True*, the original Globe Theatre in London was burned down. Sir Henry Wotton described the catastrophe, noting: "The Kings Players had a new Play called *All Is True*, representing some principal pieces of the Reign of Henry 8, which was set forth with many extraordinary Circumstances of Pomp and Majesty, even to the matting of the Stage; the Knights of the Order, with their Georges and Garter, the Guards with their embroidered Coats and the like...Now, King Henry making a Masque at Cardinal Wolseys House, and certain Cannons being shot off at his entry, some of the Paper, or other stuff wherewith one of them was stopped, did light on the Thatch, where [it] kindled inwardly and ran round a train, consuming within less than an hour the whole House to the very grounds...Only one man had his breeches set on fire, that would have perhaps broyled him, if he had not be the benefit of a provident wit put it out with a bottle of ale..."

King Henry VIII was initially printed in the First Folio edition of Shakespeare's plays in 1623 beginning a perpetual questioning of authorship. Editors John Hemminge and Henry Condell, however, assured that the plays as printed were "absolute in their number, as he [Shakespeare] conceived them." Historians, arguably, maintain that *Henry VIII* was written by Shakespeare in collaboration with playwright John Fletcher, with whom he had written *The Two Noble Kinsmen* in 1613 (published in 1634), both their names appearing on the title page as they were on a lost play, *Cardenio*, entered by the two playwrights in the *Stationer's Register* on September 9, 1653. Significantly, bolstering support for Fletcher's collaboration is usually condemnation of *Henry VIII* as a bad play "lacking unity."

Sir William Davenant adapted and produced *Henry VIII* at Lincoln's Inn Field on December 22, 1663, featuring Thomas Betterton as Henry. "The part of the King was so right and justly done by Mr. Betterton, he being instructed in it by Sir William Davenant who had it from old Mr. Lowen, that had his Instructions from Mr. Shakespeare himself, that I dare and will aver, none can, or will come near him in this Age, in the performance of that part," Downes wrote in his *Roscius Anglicanus*. "Mr.

Harris's performance of Cardinal Wolsey, was little Inferior to that, he doing it with such just State, Port and Mein, that I dare affirm, none hitherto has Eqall'd him...Every part by the great Care of Sir William, being all new Cloath'd and new Scenes; it continued Acting 15 Days together with general Applause."

Shakespeare's *King Henry VIII* was performed through the seventeenth and eighteenth centuries, but acting honors in the play were usually divided between the performer portraying Queen Katharine and the one the role of Cardinal Wolsey. Henry appeared to be in support.

Covent Garden's 1783 production of *King Henry VIII* was advertised as "Mainpiece: With the Procession From the Abbey at the Coronation of Anne Bullen. Afterpiece: :To End With a Representation of the Lord Mayor's Show on the Water. After which will be an Historical Procession of the Several Companies, with their respective Pageants, and the Chief Magistrates belonging to the City of London, from its Foundation, Books of the Songs, with an Explanation of the Procession to be had at the Theatre."

The legendary Sarah Siddons' portrayal of Queen Katharine at London's Drury Lane Theatre on November 25, 1788, was appraised by the *Public Advertiser* as "too laboured -- particularly in the Trial Scene, where the words came too slow and measured that they seemed to be distilled." John Palmer was Henry and Robert Bensley Cardinal Wolsey in this production.

American actress Charlotte Cushman, noted for several fine stage characterizations, had one of her most celebrated roles as Shakespeare's Katherine. For over a quarter century, she had sporadically played Katharine (she also took the role of Cardinal Wolsey on occasion), and on September 25, 1871, she returned to New York's Booth Theatre in the part. Noting her absence from the New York stage for several years, *The Herald* reported, "From the first moment of her coming on the stage it was evident that Time had laid his hand, though not urgently, on the great *tragedienne*. There was grace and cultivation in her every action, but somehow there was missing a force which we felt had been...At times it was painful to note how much the failure of the voice injured the conception of the actress. The facial action was accurate; finished delivery displayed Miss Cushman's genius...In the trail scene at Blackfriars, indeed, [she] seemed to call back her youthful vigor and rendered her conception with remarkable force...But it was in the dying scene [that] we liked her most. The nature of the scene required no violent exertions, and gave full scope for the display of the highest art..."

In March 1874, Mme. Francesca Janauschek, a formidable Czech actress, appeared at Booth's Theatre as Queen Katharine. *The New York Times*, noting the infrequency of productions of *King Henry VIII*, found the Janauschek presentation contained "such a distribution of characters as would hardly carry the general representation of the play beyond the description of mediocre," but that "Mme. Janauschek displayed those powers of intensely fervent acting which she undoubtedly possesses, coupled with womanly pride and queenly dignity. When the late Charles Kean used to perform in the role of Cardinal Wolsey, he was accustomed to dwarf all the other characters. Mme. Janauschek does not dwarf but she greatly surpasses even the Cardinal, who is intrinscially a more prominent and objective character than the Queen...The 'Bluff King Hal' of history had an efficient representative in Mr. Charles Walcot."

Two years before her death at age sixty, Charlotte Cushman returned Booth's Theatre (October 1874), for her farewell appearance in *Guy Mannering*, *Macbeth* and, as Queen Katharine in *King Henry VIII*. "*Henry VIII* is a great play, because it is Shakespeare's, but, for Shakespeare, it is not a great play. Indeed, it is notably lacking in dramatic plan and progress; being, in fact, less a tragedy, or even a simple drama, than a series of historical scenes grouped effectively together," wrote *The Herald*. "Miss Cushman's performance of Queen Katharine is too well known to need or bear special analysis. It is now what it has always been; for it showed no loss of force or spirit. Her reading is, as it always was, better than her action; and, indeed, in that respect, she is little short of perfection. The ease and naturalness of her enunciation...which almost conceals the fact that she is speaking in blank verse, while she never loses the fine rhythmical effect of verse..."

Madame Helena Modjeska, the Polish actress, successfully portrayed Queen Katharine to Otis Skinner's Henry on Broadway in 1892 andf again in 1893, while in 1892, Sir Henry Irving found one of his most colorful roles as Cardinal Wolsey in *Henry VIII* in the London production. (Over the years, Edmund Kean, John Philip Kemble amnd William Charles Macready had already put their stamp on Wolsey.) In December 1893, Henry Irving, William Terriss and Ellen Terry brought their production to Broadway. *The New York Times* hailed Irving's *King Henry VIII* as "a superb stage pageant," continuing: "Though this historical drama possesses some evidence of Shakespeare's genius, many students have attributed the work to Fletcher and Massinger...as a historical pageant it easily surpasses anything Mr. Irving has yet shown us...Properly speaking, or, rather, conventionally speaking, this is not a good acting play; It lacks certain elements that are looked for in a popular stage piece. But it has the merit of being truer to the facts of history, so far as they are known, than almost any other historical play...Mr. Irving's portrayal of Cardinal Wolsey is, of course, a dramatic performance of rare qualities, while the role of Queen Katharine brings into play artistic faculties which Miss Terry had not previously exhibited in New York."

The Times later described Irving's Cardinal Wolsey as "a sort of scarlet terror. His insolence and arrogance, his craft and cruelty...fairly make the spectator shiver...Mr. Irving does much for the illusion in the perfection of pictorial detail...There is nothing uglier or more malignant than the smile of his Wolsey ...Mr. Irving does nothing without a welldefined purpose, and by laying so much stress upon the craft and malevolence of the primate he increases the dramatic vitality..."

Henry VIII emerged as a character in William Brough's *The Field of the Cloth of Gold* (1831) and in Charles Major's novel *When Knighthood Was in Flower*, which was adapted to the stage in 1901. A musical version of Major's novel appeared on Broadway in 1904 under the title *A Madcap Princess*. In 1910, Sir Herbert Tree produced Shakespeare's *King Henry VIII* in London and played the part of Wolsey, and on March 14, 1916, he opened his Shakespeare Tercentenary Festival production of the play at Broadway's New Amsterdam Theatre, with Lyn Harding as Henry, Tree as Wolsey and Edith Wynne Matthison as Katharine.

"The performance of Henry VIII proved a splendid combination of acting and spectacle," reported *The New York Dramatic Mirror*, "Lynn Harding and Tree shared honors...The production is a fine example of London stage craft, as developed under Irving and Tree, to which the large deep stage of the New Amsterdam is peculiarly adapted...The reception accorded the distinguished guest amounted almost to an ovation...the English actor revealed powers which, while they are not as penetrating or as thrilling in their intensity of feeling as there is warrant for in the lines, enabled him to make a strong impression, and to score a substantial success...Harding's King Henry is remarkable for its broad humanity...Miss Matthison plays Katharine with engaging interest and in a musically monotonous voice."

The New York Times described Tree's import as "a brave, bouncing, brightly colored show...as written by Fletcher and Shakespeare, mercifully cut and revised by

Sir Herbert Tree, and gorgeously produced by him."

Sybil Thorndike produced and appeared as Queen Katharine in *Henry VIII* at London's Empire Theatre on December 23, 1925 for 127 performances. "Dramatically, poetically, and comically, it is inferior to all the other histories in the First Folio [and] was written as a pageant for the eye," London's *Sphere* noted. "Miss Thorndike [brings] a fine severity to bear on her interpretation of Katharine, speaking nobly and never ranting for a single syllable. Miss Angela Baddeley is a charming Anne Bullen...Mr. [Norman V.] Norman's Henry is great fun, but lacking in majesty...Mr. Lyall Swete's Wolsey is, however, the only real blot on the performance."

Tyrone Guthrie's production of *King Henry VIII* opened in London at the Sadler's Wells Theatre on November 7, 1933. "I wish I could have seen that fine actor, Charles Laughton, as Henry VIII in the Shakespearean play...before he had appeared as Henry VIII on the film," *Sphere*'s critic reflected. "He would not be human if he had remained uninfluenced by his share in that profitable buffooning. Not that Mr. Laughton does not have his moments of kingly dignity in the Sadler's Wells revival. In the trial scene no one could have been better. In the prayer scene very few people, I venture to think, could have been worse...In short, Mr. Laughton is not at his best as Henry, though he cannot fail to be interesting always. The part, in any serious presentation that is, suits him no more than Mr. Pickwick suited him." (Laughton starred on the London stage in *Mr. Pickwick* in 1928.)

In his autobiography, Tyrone Guthrie noted that Lillian Baylis, the austere director of the Old Vic, was not thrilled with the choice of Laughton as Henry. "[She] felt Charles could only be 'using' the Vic as a Stepping stone to his own career. She treated him with an icy, rather naive hauteur. To this, naturally, he reacted by imagining her to be a scheming, smallminded, mean-spirited old shrew."

In *Elsa Lanchester Herself*, Charles Laughton's widow wrote: "When the Old Vic chose to do Shakespeare's *Henry the Eighth*...they thought that they would cash in on the colossal success of the current film. Charles had Henry so in his bones that it was a foregone conclusion that he would give a great performance at the Old Vic. He did, but he suffered agonies in readjusting the celluloid character that he had already established. I think the result was disappointing to the public and the press."

The London Times critic believed there were moment when Laughton reverted to the character of Henry in Alexander Korda's 1933 film, yet in the trial scene thought the actor "spoke and stood -- not every inch King Henry, but every inch a King..." Although Laughton's performance in *The Private Life of Henry VIII* has arguably been considered his finest screen portrayal, some critics carped the characterization was "more Charles than Henry."

Henry VIII was produced at the Open Air Theatre in Regent's Park in London in June 1936 with a sterling cast that included Lyn Harding as Henry, Phyllis Neilson-Terry as Queen Katharine, Baliol Holloway as Wolsey, and Vivien Leigh as Anne Boleyn. London's *Bystander* reported, "Sydney Carroll's production of *Henry VIII* may lack the elaborate trappings and theatrical splendour we came to associate with Sir Beerbohm's [Tree] efforts, but there is something about Shakespeare's lines which seem to thrive on fresh air...In some circles -- but obviously not the Outer Circle in Regent's Park -- *Henry VIII* is held to be one of Shakespeare's dullest plays...Lyn Harding gives us a monarch whose mind is often as heavy as his figure, and not merely the bluff roysterer beloved of the film producers. Baliol Holloway's Wolsey makes that crafty cleric rather too much of the cold-blooded ascetic... Phyllis Neilson-Terry's Katharine is one of the highlights of the production, and this is undoubtedly the best thing she has ever done..."

Five years prior to the Regent's Park *Henry VIII*, Cornelia Otis Skinner had a successful theatrical experiment by portraying Henry's six wives in her monodrama, *The Wives of Henry VIII*. On November 6, 1946, actress Margaret Webster's newly established American Repertory Theatre produced *Henry VIII* at New York's International Theatre. "Out of an indifferent play the American Repertory Theatre has fashioned a memorable performance and a notable production. The play is *Henry VIII*, partly by Shakespeare, partly by Fletcher and the whole freely edited by Margaret Webster," Brooks Atkinson wrote in *The New York Times*. "As Katharine of Aragon, Miss [Eva] Le Gallienne is capping her career with one or two vividly acted scenes... Playing the sort of part that best becomes his talents, Mr. [Walter] Hampden is wearing imposing costumes again and speaking Elizabethan verse with mastery of tone. His Cardinal Wolsey is one of his best works. Victor Jory gives an altogether admirable portrait of a vigorous, strong-headed though friendly minded Henry VIII."

Maxwell Anderson's *Anne of the Thousand Days*, detailing the doomed love and marriage of Henry and Anne Boleyn became one of the big hits of Broadway's 1948-49 season. Although the year's Pulitzer Prize and the New York Critics Award went to Arthur Miller's *Death of a Salesman*), the *Herald-Tribune*'s Howard Barnes called *Anne* the "Best Play of the Season" and felt that "Maxwell Anderson, the foe of the critics, has confounded them brilliantly by writing a drama of lyric and dramatic consequence... The Motley costumes are enchanting. And Rex Harrison [Tony Award winner as Best Actor of the year] and Joyce Redman contribute superb performances to a consummate collaboration."

Newsweek noted, "For his 27th offering in a quarter century of playwrighting, Anderson goes back to the period that served him in *Mary of Scotland* and *Elizabeth the Queen*...Under H. C. Potter's expert direction, the play's costars are practically perfect. Harrison gives a masterful performance as the arrogant and lusty monarch...Miss Redman makes Anne Boleyn both a queen and a vivid, dangerous, fascinating woman."

Francis Hackett, author of *Henry VIII*, which became a bestseller with fourteen editions, had sued Sir Alexander Korda and United Artists in 1935 for using his biography as a basis for their *Private Life of Henry VIII*. In 1949, Mr. Hackett brought suit against Maxwell Anderson for basing *Anne of the Thousand Days* on his *Henry VIII* and his play *Anne Boleyn*. Korda settled the matter out-of-court for a substantial sum and acquired rights to Hackett's *Queen Anne Boleyn*. Anderson's comment on the situation was "Evidently Mr. Hackett feels somewhat possessive of Henry."

Henry VIII continued to be revived in London and other plays in which Henry was prominently featured were *The Boleyns* (1951); *Royal Gambit* (1959) *A Man for All Seasons* (1960), Robert Bolt's award-winning drama, based on the life of Sir Thomas More [see separate entry]. In 1966, Anita Loos adapted Jean Canooile's comedy-drama, *The King's Mare*, to the English speaking stage with Keith Michell as Henry and Glynis Johns as Anne of Cleves, and ten years later, Sheldon Harnick and Richard Rodgers set Sherman Yellen's book to words and music for Broadway's *Rex*.

"Richard Rodgers is a great man who has done the American musical theatre some service. But even Othello went wrong, and even Homer nodded. Mr. Rodgers' new musical *Rex* has almost everything not going for it," was Clive Barnes' appraisal in *The New York Times*. "One major difficulty of *Rex* is one of tone. Even if the book by Sherman Yellen had been modestly acceptable... [it] is not, being basically tedious and quite excessively vulgar on a number of planes or had the lyrics of Sheldon Harnick risen faintly and bravely above the submediocre there would still be the abiding problem of the music."

Douglas Watt (*Daily News*) felt: "*Rex* is hexed by history...handsome to look at but dull in the telling ...It has a potentially fascinating Henry in the brilliant Nicol Williamson...He even possesses a supple baritone...But although Williamson makes a pleasantly tempestuous Henry, Sherman Yellen's book doesn't allow his rich talents in this direction much scope."

Rex had a short life and, as noted by Gerald Bordman in his *The American Musical Theatre*, "Richard Rodgers suffered one of his most embarrassing failures when his *Rex* closed...Unfortunately, Sherman Yellen's book was unwieldy..."

Impressed with Sir Herbert Beerbohm-Tree's 1910 stage production of *King Henry VIII*, British producer Will L. Barker persuaded him to record it on film. Robert Hamilton Bell, in his definitive book *Shakespeare on Silent Film*, gives a detailed account of the filming of Tree's *Henry VIII* which began on February 9, 1911, at Barker's Ealing Studios:

"With Tree, he worked out an agreement which was entirely unprecedented and which marked the first English 'feature' picture and the first Shakespeare 'exclusive.' Tree was to paid the unprecedented sum of pound 1000. Only 20 prints were to be made, 10 for London, 10 for the provinces...Lest the film prove unsatisfactory, deteriorate, or interfere with the ticket sales of the theatre presentation, after six weeks the prints were to be called in and destroyed... at the end of the stipulated period the prints were called in, and on April 13th the press and various other visitors saw at Ealing an unusual ceremony which I wish had never taken place. After the prints had been counted and checked, they were unwound into a loose pile on an iron sheet. Barker himself applied a match to the films; as the flames shot up, everyone retired to a cooler distance and watched -- all except a cameraman for the company who shot a new film of the burning of Henry VIII."

The Kinematograph and Lantern Weekly praised Barker's film: "*Henry VIII* Successfully Filmed. Barker's Fine Picture of Sir Herbert Tree in His Greatest Production: Mr. Barker is to be all the more congratulated as the excellent photographic quality of the film secured on Thursday last is such as to more than compensate for the delay. That this film would be a great artistic triumph was a foregone conclusion."

British critic A. E. Taylor raved, "The great event in the Moving Picture World this week has been the production of *Henry VIII*...Words fail one to adequately describe this great triumph of the kinematographers' art. The picture is without doubt the greatest that has ever been attempted in this country, and I am almost tempted to say in any other...In it we have the best of dramatic talent, and consequently the acting surpasses anything ever seen in moving pictures before."

Henry was portrayed on the American screen by Tefft Johnson in Vitagraph's short film *Cardinal Wolsey*, written by Hal Reid, who played the title role. Thomas A. Edison produced *A Tudor Princess* with Robert Brower as Henry. Both short films were made in 1912. Laura Cowie, who had appeared as Anne Bullen in Sir Herbert Tree's 1910 London stage production of Shakespeare's play, portrayed the title role of *Anne Boleyn* in France's 1913 Gaumont film with Albert Decoeur as Henry VIII.

In 1920, Ernst Lubitsch directed *Anna Boleyn* in Germany starring Emil Jannings as Henry VIII and Henny Porten as Anna Boleyn. The Lubitsch film was released in the United States by Paramount Pictures in 1921 as *Deception*. "[It] is a feeble title of a masterly handled screen drama founded upon the unhappy romance between Anne Boleyn and the much-married and wholly disgraceful English monarch known to history as Henry VIII," reported Edward Weitzel (*Moving Picture World*). "History and fiction have been adroitly blended in a powerful drama...As a work of art, *Deception* ranks high in its color, form and onward march of actual drama...Ernest [sic] Lubitsch has cast and directed the picture with sound judgement and complete understanding of the material...Emil Jannings, an American[!], is Henry VIII...His bluff King Hal is a reasonable reproduction of the monarch...All the arrogance, individualism and kingly dignity that were in this detestable ruler are brought to play by the actor with consummate art."

Deception opened at New York's Rivoli Theatre on April 17, 1921, advertised in these words: "This version is based upon the only early copy known contained in manuscript 15117 in the British Museum...The authentic revelation of the world's strangest love story...7,000 persons in the cast...seven months in the making...sets, three months to construct."

The New York Times noted "*Anne Boleyn*, the second Ernst Lubitsch production to reach this country from Germany...has been renamed *Deception* as [his] *DuBarry* was renamed *Passion* for American consumption...The dramatic material of most of the American pictures, however, is puerile, and their treatment is mechanical, compared to the material and treatment of a photoplay like *Deception*...Here is a real story told so that intelligent people can enjoy it...Surely the Henry VIII of Emil Jannings [is] one of the finest pieces of character work ever done on the screen...The Anne Boleyn of Henny Porten is also convincing most of the time, though it is to be regretted that Miss Porten seems so heavy sometimes, and is not as personable as she seemed in Henry's eyes...The others in the cast, discreetly unnamed, are well enough suited to their parts, and persuasive in their acting...Rich, colorful, dramatic, *Deception* is a photoplay for those who want genuine realism..."

Burns Mantle (*Photoplay*) appraised the 10-million-mark production as "A big, solid, impressive picture, this German-made section of English history...It bulks large in crowds, actors, palaces and royal physiques, but it bulks large also, in art, and sets standards in the matter of the historical drama on the screen which native directors will have to consider if ever they become interested in pictures of this type."

The *Moving Picture News* added, "The spectator will forget time and environment -- to become an actual figure of Henry's period. Lubitsch has achieved this by presenting purely spectacular moments...What is presented is real, moving, dramatic and colorful. And the episodes are constructed in masterly fashion, all building to most effective climaxes, the final one being placed where it should be, at the conclusion, with no sop thrown at the sentimentalist..."

Alexander Korda had made only two marginally successful British films, *Service for Ladies* and *Wedding Rehearsal* when, in 1933, he produced and directed what would be called "one of the most important films in the development of the British cinema": *The Private Life of Henry VIII.* Korda later claimed the inspiration for making a motion picture based on the life of Henry came from hearing a London cab driver singing Harry Champion's music-hall song "I'm 'Enery the Eighth I Am," whereas he cleverly devised a vehicle for Charles Laughton and his wife, Elsa Lanchester.

The original script by Lajos Biro and Arthur Wimperis included only the boisterous marriage of Henry and Anne of Cleves. Seven scenarios later, the story had been expanded to include five of the King's wives, excluding Katharine of Aragon (a title frame reasoned her story was "uninteresting"). Production began at Herbert Wilcox's British and Dominion Studios in late spring 1933, and Korda wisely engaged famous French director Rene Clair's cinematographer, Georges Perinal, for his *Henry VIII* which was completed in five weeks. In August 1933, Douglas Fairbanks persuaded United Artists to release *The Private Life of Henry VIII* and to sign Korda and his London Films to a lucrative contract for future productions.

The Private Life of Henry VIII was given a "celebrity" premiere at London's

Leicester Square Theatre on August 17, 1933. The British press was not particularly enthusiastic. "Since Charles Laughton is doubly a king -- on stage and screen...it is probably high treason to say that his Henry VIII lacks the subtle, insinuating characterization of some of his previous performances. Physically, he may be every inch the Tudor monarch, but mentally he falls short of the heights and depths of that extraordinary personality. He is dominating without being regal, persuasive without omnipotence," was the judgment of *The Bystander*, "The background and costumes give the picture a pictorial richness, and Korda's direction is always polished; but it is episodic to the point of being fragmentary."

London's *Sphere*, however, considered *The Private Life of Henry VIII*, "a superb film -- a super-film in the best sense of the word. History has been twisted only a little in it...Mr. Charles Laughton's King Henry is occasionally Neronic; fine actor though he is, he finds it difficult to avoid the softly-sensual and the King was surely the hard sensualist, iron-like in his virility and determination. In the Katherine Howard episode, however, where he has to unbend, he unbent most touchingly..."

The Private Life of Henry VIII opened at Radio City Music Hall on Columbus Day 1933. Noting, and disregarding, the unenthusiastic reviews of the British press, Mordaunt Hall (*The New York Times*) reported, "Charles Laughton [is] at the top of his form in the title role...it is a really brilliant if suggestive comedy...Mr. Laughton not only reveals his genius as an actor, but also shows himself to be a past master in the art of make-up. In this offering he sometimes looks as if he had stepped from the frame of Holbein's painting of Henry...Mr. Laughton may be guilty of caricaturing the role, but occasionally truths shine in the midst of the hilarity..."

Time magazine praised the film, finding "Mr. Laughton's Henry is all that you might expect it to be after you have seen his Nero [the role he played in Cecil B. DeMille's *The Sign of the Cross* the previous year], his jealous husband in *Devil and the Deep*, his murderer in *Payment Deferred*...The picture shows up the regal old scamp as the tricky, gusty gentleman and sportsman that he was..."

Laughton received the Academy Award as Best Actor for his Henry although Korda's film itself lost the Oscar to Noel Coward's *Cavalcade*. Alexander Korda's plan to star Charles Laughton in a film version of William Brough's play, *The Field of the Cloth of Gold*, in which the actor would reprise his role of king Henry VIII, was abandoned in 1933; however, twenty years later, Laughton again played Henry VIII in *Young Bess*, described by a British critic as a "highly romanticised historical film which plays havoc with many facts."

Robert Shaw portrayed Henry VIII in the Oscar-winning 1966 screen version of Robert Bolt's play, *A Man For All Seasons*, opposite Paul Scofield's riveting Thomas More, recreating his stage role on the West End and later on Broadway.

In 1969, Richard Burton portrayed Henry in Hal Wallis' elegant production of Maxwell Anderson's *Anne of the Thousand Days*. Critic Brenda Davies wrote in Britain's *Monthly Film Bulletin* that "in spite of all its defects, the film retains a grip on one's attention simply through the impact of the playing. Burton's Henry profits from the actor's personal magnetism and authoritative voice, though it is a monotonous performance, written and played all on one note."

Keith Michell, who had played the role of Henry so brilliantly on the London stage in *The King's Mare* in 1966 and reprised the part in BBC's 1970-71 television series, *The Six Wives of Henry VIII*, portrayed the King again on the screen in *Henry VIII and His Six Wives* in 1972. British critic Colin Ford noted, "Michell's characterization, and the whole project, derives from a successful BBC television series. The film involves the same producer, Mark Shivas, and one of its script-writers, Ian Thorne, but its effect is as different from that of the television original as the title indicates...The film concentrates on Henry...His quest from wife to wife is more efficiently written and filmed than most of the products of EMI since it entered the film business, though it shares with them its apparent *raison d'etre*: after a successful television series and in the middle of a vogue for things Elizabethan and Tudor, it seems calculated to be a commercial success."

In director Trevor Nunn's lavish 1965 retelling of *Lady Jane Gray*, starring Helen Bonham Carter in the title role, the focus -- unlike the 1936 version with Nova Pilbeam (and Frank Cellier as Henry) -- was on the post-Henry VIII era and on his sickly son, Edward VI (played by Warren Saire). Henry, in fact, was out of the picture and off the screen, and therefore will not here be included.

In the debut of television's prestigious *Omnibus* series on November 9, 1952, a twenty-four-minute segment of the premiere program offered *The Trial of Anne Boleyn*, an original by Maxwell Anderson and starring Rex Harrison as Henry VIII and Lilli Palmer as Anne Boleyn. Jack Gould (*The New York Times*) found *The Trial of Anne Boleyn*, "Easily the most exciting and arresting segment -- written especially for the program by Maxwell Anderson. And as brought to life by Mr. Harrison and Miss Palmer, in superb portrayals of Henry VIII and Anne, it was a poignant and powerful delineation of human relations..."

The BBC's highly-acclaimed series, *The Six Wives of Henry VIII*, during the 1970-71 season starred Keith Michell as Henry with Annette Crosbie, Dorothy Tutin, Anne Stallybrass, Elvi Hale, Angela Pleasence and Rosalie Crutchley portraying his wives.

In the U.S., CBS televised the series during the summer of 1971 John J. O'Connor (*The New York Times*) joined other critics in praising the British series: "*The Six Wives of Henry VIII* scored among the highest ratings ever registered for British television. It's not difficult to see why...the series bubbles with fascinating history, personalities and complications. And, in the reliable British mode, the whole is magnificently acted, designed and costumed...As Henry, Keith Michell gives a dazzling performance. With a theatre background in musicals (*Irma La Douce*) and drama (*Abelard and Heloise*), Mr. Michell is given an opportunity for an acting tour de force, and he makes the superb most of it...The Wives do get the best of it in this series...On the whole, the series reflects the sophisticated attitude the British have toward their history. A more impressive collection of scoundrels and intriguers would be had to imagine. Americans would hardly appreciate a similar approach to their own history. If noting else, however, *The Six Wives of Henry VIII* reminds us that there were human being there."

Producer Mark Shivas' article *The Monarch Who Couldn't Stop Marrying*, published in *The New York Times*, compared the interpretation of Henry by Laughton, Burton and Robert Shaw wondering, "which is the true picture of Henry VIII, or are all the pictures true?...The BBC's series *The Six Wives of Henry VIII*, which I helped produced...began with the principle that while something was known of Henry himself, few people had any idea of what his wives were like, so six 90-minute plays were commissioned. Each was by a different author and each centered around one wife, with Henry seen through her eyes...Henry Tudor was shown by turns as eager scholar and sportsman, opportunist, tender lover, schemer, dupe and pathetic, diseased old man. He was a different character for each of his wives, and each view was right at one time or another..."

On April 25, 1979, the sixth and last production of PBS' first season of *The Shakespeare Plays* was *Henry VIII*. "The play is not a favorite in the Shakespeare repertory," reported John J. O'Connor (*The New York Times*). "One reason may be a question of authorship. Some scholars believe John Fletcher may have been a coauthor. Another reason is the blatantly uncritical portrait of Henry himself. No doubt politically understandable at a time when that was dominated by his daughter, Elizabeth I. *Henry VIII* is a pageant, a celebration of royal virtue." O'Connor went on, "The history is distorted and sometimes confusing but, this being Shakespeare, at least for the most part, there are numerous scenes of splendid power...The cast is generally impressive: John Stride as Henry, Claire Bloom as Katharine, Timothy West as Cardinal Wolsey, Ronald Pickup as Cranmer, Julian Glover as Buckingham and Barbara Kellerman as Anne Bullen. The production was filmed attractively in authentic castles. Unfortunately, the weather was obviously damp and cold, leading to a seeming epidemic of vocal nasality among many of the actors..."

Henry again came to television in the Charlton Heston production of *A Man for All Seasons* in 1988. Martin Chamberlain had the role, to Heston's Thomas More and John Gielgud's Wolsey.

STAGE

HENRY VIII, Lincoln's Inn Field, opened December 22, 1663
Produced, directed and adapted by Sir William Davenant, from the play by William Shakespeare

Thomas Betterton (King Henry VIII); Joseph Harris (Cardinal Wolsey); Mrs. Thomas Betterton (Queen Katherine); William Smith (Duke of Buckingham); Robert Nokes (Norfolk); Thomas Lilliston (Suffolk); Matthew Medburn (Cardinal Cranmer/Cardinal Campeius); John Young (Earl of Surrey); Cave Underhill (Bishop Gardiner); Joseph Price (Lord Sands)

Covent Garden, London, opened November 10, 1783
A Drama by William Shakespeare

Matthew Clarke (King Henry VIII); Elizabeth Younge (Queen Katherine); John Henderson (Cardinal Wolsey); Richard Wraughton (Duke of Buckingham); Charles Bonnor (Lord Chamberlain); Mrs. Gordon Inchbald (Anne Bullen); William Davies (Cromwell); James Chalmers (Sir Thomas Lovell); Mr. Fearon (Duke of Norfolk); Ann Pitt (A Lady); Mr. Jones (Lord Sands); John Whitfiled (Earl of Surrey); Thomas Hull (Cranmer); Joseph A. Booth (Duke of Suffolk); Richard Wilson (Gardiner)

Covent Garden, London, opened April 8, 1785
A Drama by William Shakespeare

Matthew Clarke (King Henry VIII); Elizabeth Younge (Queen Katherine); John Henderson (Cardinal Wolsey); Richard Wraughton (Duke of Buckingham); Charles Bonnor (Lord Chamberlain); Mrs. Gordon Inchbald (Anne Bullen); William Davies (Cromwell); Thomas Kennedy (Lord Sands); William Farren (Earl of Surrey); James Fearon (Duke of Norfolk); Ann Pitt (A Lady); James Chalmers (Sir Thomas Lovell); Thomas Hull (Cranmer); Joseph A. Booth (Duke of Suffolk); Ralph Wewitzer (Gardiner)

SONGS: "Tally ho!"; Mrs. Kennedy's Song, Act III; Production included Procession from the Abbey at the Coronation of Anne Bullen

Covent Garden, London, opened March 26, 1787
A Drama by William Shakespeare

Francis Aickin (King Henry VIII); Mrs. Alexander Pope (Queen Katherine); William Farren (Duke of Buckingham); William Davies (Cromwell); William Cubitt

(Lord Chamberlain); Mrs. Elizabeth Inchbald (Anne Bullen); Alexander Pope (Cardinal Wolsey); Thomas Hull (Cranmer); Joseph A. Booth (Lord Sands); William Macready (Earl of Surrey); James Fearon (Duke of Norfolk); William Gardner (Duke of Suffolk); John Edwin (Gardiner)

Drury Lane Theatre, London, opened November 25, 1788
A Drama by William Shakespeare

John Palmer (King Henry VIII); Sarah Siddons (Queen Katherine); Robert Bensley (Cardinal Wolsey); Richard Wraughton (Duke of Buckingham); Matthew Williams (Duke of Suffolk); Robert Palmer (Lord Chamberlain); John Hayman Packer (Cardinal Campeius); John Fawcett (Sir Thomas Lovell); Jane Farmer (Anne Bullen); Francis Aickin (Cranmer); William Barrymore (Lord Surrey); John Philip Kemble (Cromwell); Robert Baddeley (Lord Sands); Richard Suett (Winchester); Philip Lamash (Sir Henry Guildford); John Whitfield (Duke of Norfolk); Mrs. James Love (A Lady); Robert Benson (Surveyor); Francis Godolphin Waldron (Doctor Butts)

Drury Lane Theatre, London, opened March 26, 1792
A Drama by William Shakespeare

John Palmer (King Henry VIII); Sarah Siddons (Queen Katherine); Robert Bensley (Cardinal Wolsey); Richard Wraughton (Duke of Buckingham); John Philip Kemble (Cromwell); James Aickin (Cranmer); Mrs. Powell (Anne Bullen); John Fawcett (Sir Thomas Lovell); John Whitfield (Duke of Norfolk); William Barrymore (Earl of Surrey); Richard Suett (Gardiner); John Hayman Packer (Cardinal Campeius); Mrs. John Booth (Gentlewoman); Maria Theresa Bland (Patience); Francis Godolphin Waldron (Doctor Butts); Robert Benson (Surveyor); Miss Collins (Agatha); John Phillimore (Capucius); Robert Baddeley (Lord Sands); John Lyons (Sergeant); Mr. Jones (Doorkeeper); Thomas Banks (Brandon); Edward Alfred (Cryer)

Haymarket Theatre, London, opened March 9, 1793
A Drama by William Shakespeare

John Palmer (King Henry VIII); Sarah Siddons (Queen Katherine); Robert Bensley (Cardinal Wolsey); Richard Wroughton (Duke of Buckingham); Robert Palmer (Lord Chamberlain); Mrs. Powell (Anne Bullen); James Aickin (Cranmer); John Whitfield (Duke of Norfolk); Walter Maddocks (Lord Chancellor); Charles Kemble (Cromwell); John Hayman Packer (Cardinal Campeius); George Bland (Sir Henry Guilford); John Fawcett, Jr. (Sir Thomas Lovell); John Phillimore (Capucius); Thomas Caufield (Duke of Suffolk); William Barrymore (Earl of Surrey); Richard Suett (Gardiner); Robert Baddeley (Lord Sands); Francis Waldron (Doctor Butts); Robert Benson (Surveyor); Thomas Banks (Brandon); John Lyons (Servant); Mr. Jones (Doorkeeper); Edward Alfred (Cryer); Mrs. Booth (Gentlewoman); Mrs. Bland (Patience); Miss Collins (Agatha)

Covent Garden, London, opened May 24, 1793
A Drama by William Shakespeare (played in conjunction with *The Sailor's Festival* and *The Follies of a Day*)

John Holman (King Henry VIII); Mrs. Alexander Pope (Queen Katherine); Alexander Pope (Cardinal Wolsey); Mr. Farren (Duke of Buckingham); Thomas Hull (Cranmer); William Davies (Cromwell); William Cubitt (Lord Chamberlain); William C. Macready (Earl of Surrey); Miss Chapman (Anne Bullen); Thomas

Marshall (Duke of Suffolk); George Davies (Duke of Norfolk); John Quick (Bishop of Winchester)

New Theatre, New York, opened May 13, 1799 (American premiere)
Produced by John Hodginson and William Dunlap; A Drama by William Shakespeare; Scenery, Ciceri and Audin

Lewis Hallam (King Henry VIII); Mrs. George Barrett (Queen Katherine); George Barrett (Cardinal Wolsey); Mrs. Lewis Hallam (Anne Bullen); Ann Storer (Lady Denny); I. Cooper (Cromwell)

Covent Garden, London, opened May 15, 1799
A Drama by William Shakespeare

Joseph George Holman (King Henry VIII); Mrs. Alexander Pope (Queen Katherine); Alexander Pope (Cardinal Wolsey); M. G. Lewis (Cromwell); John Fawcett, Jr. (Lord Sands); Miss Charlotte Chapman (Anne Bullen); Henry Erskine Johnston (Duke of Buckingham); Charles Murray (Cranmer); Joseph Shepherd Munden (Bishop of Winchester); Thomas Knight (Earl of Surrey); John Emery (Doctor Butts); Eliza Atkins (Patience); John Whitfield (Duke of Norfolk); John Waddy (Duke of Suffolk); Charles Farley (Sir Thomas Lovell); James Whitmore (Chancellor); T. Abbott (Capucius); Max David Rees (Porter); William Wilde (Porter's Man); Mr. Curties (Lord Abergavenny); William Claremont (Brandon/Usher); John W. Clarke (Lord Chamberlain); Benjamin Thompson (Surveyor); James Street (Cryer); Henry Lee (Sergeant)

Park Theatre, New York, opened October 2, 1811
A Drama by William Shakespeare

George Frederick Cooke (King Henry VIII); Mrs. Stanley (Queen Katherine); Thomas Abthorpe Cooper (Cardinal Wolsey); Mr. Pritchard (Duke of Buckingham); Mrs. John Darley (Anne Bullen); William Wheatley (Campeius); Mr. Knox (Cranmer); Thomas Hilson (Lord Sands); Edmund Simpson (Cromwell); John Darley (Earl of Surrey); Mr. Carpenter (Suffolk); Mr. McFarland (Duke of Norfolk); Mr. Doyle (Bishop Gardiner); Lewis Hallam, Jr. (Capucius); Mr. Jones (Lord Chamberlain); Mr. Morrell (Sir Thomas Lovell); John Hogg (Sir Henry Guilford); Mrs. Claude (Patience); Mrs. William Wheatley (Cicely); Mrs. John Hogg (Lady Denny)

Park Theatre, New York, opened December 11, 1818
A Drama by William Shakespeare

George Bartley (King Henry VIII); Mrs. George Barley (Queen Katherine); Mr. Robertson (Cardinal Wolsey); Edmund Simpson (Cromwell); Mrs. Holman (Patience); James Pritchard (Duke of Buckingham)

SONG: "Angels Ever Fair and Bright"

Park Theatre, New York, opened May 26, 1826
A Drama by William Shakespeare

J. F. Foot (Henry VIII); Edmund Kean (Cardinal Wolsey); Mrs. John Barnes (Queen Katherine); Edmund Simpson (Cromwell); John H. Clarke (Cranmer); Mrs. Thomas Hilson (Anne Boleyn); Mr. Lee (Duke of Buckingham); Mr. Jervis (Sir Thomas Lovell); Mr. Stanley (Duke of Norfolk); Jacob Woodhill (Gardiner); J. Kent (Lord Sands); Henry Placide (Guilford)

Park Theatre, New York, opened December 11, 1826
A Drama by William Shakespeare
Charles Young (Henry VIII); William Conway (Cardinal Wolsey); Mrs. John Duff (Queen Katherine); George H. Barrett (Cromwell); Mrs. George H. Barrett (Anne Boleyn); John Duff (Duke of Buckingham); Mr. Williams (Lady Denny)

Park Theatre, New York, opened April 30, 1827
A Drama by William Shakespeare
J. F. Foot (Henry VIII); William C. Macready (Cardinal Wolsey); Mrs. B. Stickney (Queen Katherine); Edmund Simpson (Cromwell); Mr. Thomas Hilson (Anne Boleyn); Thomas Barry (Duke of Buckingham);

THE FIELD OF THE CLOTH OF GOLD, *Park Theatre*, New York, opened January 8, 1831
Produced by Stephen Price; A Play by William Brough
Thomas Barry (Henry VIII); Charles Robert Thorne (Lord Darnley); Miss Jessop (Katherine, Queen of England); Peter Richings (Francis I); Thomas Placide (Darby); Gilbert Nexsen (Cardinal Wolsey/William of Firstenberg); Joseph M. Field (Sir Caesar); Jacob Woodhill (Sir Payan Wileton); John Povey (Scrapeface); Mr. Bancker (Sir Henry Poynings); Mr. Collett (Sir Thomas Neville); Frederick Whestley (Richard Hartley); Mr. Hilson (Richard Hartley, Jr.); Henry Placide (Jekin Groby); Mr. Durie (Alesop/Lord of Arles); T. H. Blakeley (Wilson); Mr. Bissett (Penley); Mr. Hayden (Bertrand); Mr. Thornton (Schoenvelt); Mr. Charlton (Baron Wilsten); Mrs. Blake (Lady Constance de Grey); Mrs. Durie (Dame Hartley); Mrs. Spiller (Mrs. Alesop); Mrs. Wallack (Lady Catherine Bulmer); Mrs. Frederick Wheatley (Margaret); Miss Rogers (Queen of France); Mrs. Godey (Madelette Blaize)

HENRY VIII, *Park Theatre*, New York, opened May 2, 1834
A Drama by William Shakespeare
Mr. Harrison (King Henry VIII); Charles Kemble (Cardinal Wolsey); Fanny Kemble (Queen Katherine); John Kemble Mason (Cromwell); Henry Placide (Lord Sands); Mrs. Wheatley (Lady Denny); Julia Wheatley (Patience)

Wallack's Theatre, New York, opened April 9, 1838
A Drama by William Shakespeare
Henry Wallack (King Henry VIII); George Vandenhoff (Cardinal Wolsey); Emma Wheatley (Queen Katherine); Henry Horncastle (Duke of Suffolk); Mr. Matthews (Duke of Buckingham)

Touring Company, season 1843-44
A Drama by William Shakespeare, followed by the comedy *Simpson & Co.*
John Gilbert (King Henry VIII); Charlotte Cushman (Queen Katherine); J. B. Studley (Cardinal Wolsey); Mr. Carter (Duke of Buckingham); Viola Crocker (Anne Boleyn); L. Davenport (Cromwell); Mr. Rand (Duke of Norfolk); Mr. Fiske (Duke of Suffolk); Mr. Marston (Lord Sands); Mr. Kent (Earl of Surrey); Mr. Turner (Sir Thomas Lovell); Mr. Thompson (Cardinal Campeius); E Adah Grey (Patience); Mrs. Marshall (Lady Denny); Adele Hyde (Cecily); Mr. Eberle (Surveyor); Mrs. E. L. Davenport (Marchioness Dorset)
SONG: "Angels Ever Bright and Fair"

Park Theatre, New York, opened February 21, 1848
A Drama by William Shakespeare
Wyzeman Marshall (King Henry VIII); Thomas Barry (Cardinal Wolsey); Anne Shaw Hamblin (Queen Katherine); Mrs. H. Phillips (Anne Boleyn)

Bowery Theatre, New York, opened May 21, 1849
A Drama by William Shakespeare (played in conjunction with *Past Ten O'Clock)*
Redmond Ryder (King Henry VIII); John Gilbert (Cardinal Wolsey); Mrs. Shaw (Queen Katherine); H. E. Stevens (Duke of Buckingham); Mary Taylor (Anne Boleyn); John Winans (Lord Sands); Mr. McFarland (Cromwell); Mrs. John Gilbert (Lady Denny)

Broadway Theatre, New York, opened October 8, 1849
A Drama by William Shakespeare
W. R. Blake (King Henry VIII); Charlotte Cushman (Queen Katherine); Charles W. Couldock (Cardinal Wolsey); William Fredericks (Duke of Buckingham); Kate Horn (Anne Bullen); John Dyott (Cromwell); P. C. Byrne (Duke of Suffolk); George Jordan (Earl of Surrey); T. J. Hind (Sir Thomas Lovell); Mrs. Loder (Patience); Mrs. Hield (Lady Denny); Miss Carman (Agatha); C. Pope (Bishop); Mr. Chapman (Lord Sands); J. Lester (Gardiner)

Bowery Theatre, New York, opened November 14, 1853
A Drama by William Shakespeare
J. R. Scott (King Henry VIII); Mrs. Thomas Hamblin (Queen Katherine); Edward Eddy (Cardinal Wolsey); Amelia Parker (Anne Boleyn)

KATHARINE HOWARD, *Stadt Theatre*, New York, opened January 7, 1856
A German adaptation of the play by Alexandre Dumas
Frederick Schwan (King Henry VIII); Frau Otto Hoym (Queen Katharine); Frau Kress (Princess Margaret); Herr Wolff (Jack Fleming); Frau Worret (Herzogin of Oxford); Otto Hoym (Ethelwood); Frau Hubner (Herzogin of Rockeby); Herr Klein (Herzog von Sussex); Herr Czmock (Hamilton); Johann Wetzlau (Cranmer)

HENRY VIII, *Park Theatre*, New York, opened November 9, 1857
A Drama by William Shakespeare
Mark Smith (King Henry VIII); Charlotte Cushman (Queen Katherine); Charles Fisher (Cardinal Wolsey); W. H. Briggs (Cromwell); George C. Boniface (Duke of Buckingham); Ada Clifton (Anne Boleyn)
NOTE: On November 12 and 13, 1857, Charlotte Cushman played the role of Cardinal Wolsey

Niblo's Garden Theatre, New York, opened June 21, 1858
A Drama by William Shakespeare
John Gilbert (King Henry VIII); Charlotte Cushman (Queen Katherine); E. L. Davenport (Cardinal Wolsey); George C. Boniface (Duke of Buckingham); Ida Vernon (Anne Boleyn); L. R. Shewell (Cromwell); D. Whiting (Campeius); Joseph M. Dawson (Lord Sands); Josephine Orton (Patience); T. E. Morris (Duke of Norfolk); Mrs. Abbott (Lady Denny)

Broadway Theatre, New York, opened April 17, 1865
A Drama by William Shakespeare

George Jameson (King Henry VIII); Ellen Tree (Queen Katherine); Charles Kean (Cardinal Wolsey); G. Everett (Duke of Buckingham); J. F. Cathcart (Thomas Cromwell); Miss Chapman (Anne Bullen)

THE FIELD OF THE CLOTH OF GOLD, New York Theatre, New York, opened January 4, 1869
A Play by William Brough
C. Morton (Henry VIII); Agnes Wallace (Anne Boleyn); Mrs. Wright (Queen Katherine); George Lingard (Francis I); Jennie Worrell (Duke of Suffolk); Sophie Worrell (Lord Darnley); Mr. Rendle (Sir Guy); Jenny Gilmore (Rose de la Tour)

THE FIELD OF THE CLOTH OF GOLD, Wood's Museum and Metropolitan Theatre, New York, opened February 1, 1869
A Play by William Brough
Louis Mestayer (Henry VIII); Alice Logan (Anne Boleyn); M. C. Daly (Queen Katherine); W. J. Florence (Francis I); Rosa Cook (Duke of Suffolk); Rose Massey (Lord Darnley); Sol Smith, Jr. (Sir Guy); Fred G. Meader (Tete de Veau); Lillie Eldridge (Le Sieur de Boissy); Mrs. W. J. Florence (Lady Constance); H. Stuart (Von Schlascher); James Barnes (Von Mascher); Kate Logan (Rose La Foix); G. Mitchell (Citizen); Alice Mortimer (English Herald); Aggie Wood (French Herald); J. de Bonay (Von Scrascher)

THE FIELD OF THE CLOTH OF GOLD, Olympic Theatre, New York, opened June 20, 1870
A Burlesque by Henry J. Byron of the play by William Brough
John Dunn (King Henry VIII); Mr. H. T. Allen (Queen Katherine); Mrs. Oates (Lord Darnley); M. W. Fisher (Francis I); Professor O'Reardon (Tumbleronicon); Georgie Dickson (Lady Constance); Mr. Hernandez (Dancing Master)

THE FIELD OF THE CLOTH OF GOLD, Hooley's Opera House, Chicago, opened July 28, 1871
Produced by the Kate Putnam Troupe; A Burlesque of the play by William Brough
Mr. Jennings (King Henry VIII); Edwin Browne (Queen Katherine); Kate Putnam (Lord Darnley); John Dillon (Francis I); Belle Renick (Lady Constance); J. H. Rennie (Sir Guy); Lon Murphy (Tete De Vean)

HENRY VIII, Booth's Theatre, New York, opened September 25, 1871 24 performances
A Drama by William Shakespeare
D. W. Waller (King Henry VIII); Charlotte Cushman (Queen Katherine); William Creswick (Cardinal Wolsey); Theresa Selden (Anne Boleyn); Robert Pateman (Lord Sands); Mr. Wilson (Duke of Buckingham)

Booth's Theatre, New York, opened March 12, 1874
A Drama by William Shakespeare
Charles Walcot (King Henry VIII); Mme. Francesca Janauschek (Queen Katherine); Milnes Levick (Cardinal Wolsey); Gustavus Levick (Cromwell)

Booth's Theatre, New York, opened October 19, 1874
A Drama by William Shakespeare
John Jack (King Henry VIII); Charlotte Cushman (Queen Katherine); George

Vanderhoff (Cardinal Wolsey); Frederick B. Warde (Cromwell); Louise Henderson (Anne Boleyn); Charles Wheatleigh (Duke of Buckingham); Edwin Sheppard (Campeius); Edwin Irving (Lord Sands); Charles Leclercq (Capucius); C. H. Rockwell (Duke of Norfolk); Annie Kemp Bowler (Agatha); Mary Wells (Lady Denny)

Touring Company, season 1875-76
Produced and Directed by Edwin Booth; A Drama by William Shakespeare; Setting, George Heilge; Stage manager, Charles Walcot

Charles Walcot (King Henry VIII); Mrs. E. L. Davenport (Queen Katherine); Edwin Booth (Cardinal Wolsey); May Davenport (Anne Boleyn); W. H. Jones (Archbishop Cranmer); Frederick Bock (Duke of Buckingham); W. H. Bailey (Cardinal Campeius); Willis H. Page (Duke of Norfolk); A. Lawrence (Cromwell); B. W. Turner (Gardiner); W. A. Chapman (Capucius); W. A. Whitecar (Duke of Suffolk); C. E. Thomas (High Chancelor); H. E. Chase (Earl of Surrey); Roland Reed (Lord Sands); J. P. Deuell (Surveyor); F. H. Julian (Lord Thomas Lovell); W. Hubbell (Lord Chamberlain); J. K. Keane (Sir Thomas Guildford); C. Gibson (Sir William Brandon); Mrs. T. A. Creese (Patience); Julia Porter (Cicely); Louie Lawrence (Agatha); C. E. Fisher (Clerk of the Court); Miss Price (Marchioness of Dorset)

A CROWN OF THORNS; OR, ANNE BOLEYN, *Eagle Theatre*, New York, opened April 4, 1877
A Play be Anna Dickinson

Edward Arnott (Henry VIII); Anna Dickinson (Anne Boleyn); W. H. Leake (Cardinal Wolsey); J. A. Haworth (Cromwell); Henrietta Vaders (Jane Seymour); D. H. Chase (Duke of Norfolk); J. C. Padgett (Sir Thomas Boleyn); H. B. Bradley (Mark Smeaton); Stella Boniface (Madge Shelton); Louis Aldrich (Lord Henry Percy); C. A. Steadman (Lord Henry Norreys); Herbert Ayling (Lord George Boleyn)

HENRY VIII, *Booth's Theatre*, New York, opened September 23, 1878 32 performances
Produced by Jarrett and Palmer; A Drama by William Shakespeare; Scenery, W. B. Spong, W. Hann, Messender, T. Grieve & Son; Stage manager, Frank Little

James H. Taylor (King Henry VIII); Genevieve Ward (Queen Katherine); George Vandenhoff (Cardinal Wolsey); John Swinburne (Earl of Surrey); Frank Kilday (Sir Thomas Lovell); Eily Coghlan (Anne Boleyn); Milnes Levick (Duke of Buckingham); H. C. Kennedy (Duke of Norfolk); Frank Little (Cromwell); James L. Carhart (Lord High Chamberlain); Sam Carpenter (Duke of Suffolk); William V. Ranous (Lord Abdergavenny); C. H. Herbert (Campeius); H. A. Williams (Gardiner); Henry Rich (Lord Sands); Mr. Swinburne (Cranmer); George Jones (Capucius); Andrew Jacques (Surveyor); Charles McKean (succeeded by Mason Mitchell) (Sir Henry Guildford); Mrs. J. H. Rowe (Lady Denny); Julia Brunar (Patience); Miss A. Marion (Marchioness of Pembroke); Charles Fremont (Griffith)

This production reopened at the *Park Theatre*, Brooklyn, on October 28, 1878 with Mr. J. M. Hardie as Duke of Buckingham and Cora Tanner as Anne Boleyn.

Touring Company, season 1878-79
A Drama by William Shakespeare

Harry Edwards (King Henry VIII); Emily Gavin (Queen Katherine); John McCullough (Cardinal Wolsey); Mark M. Price (Duke of Buckingham); E. J. Buckley (Earl of Surrey); S. E. Springer (Duke of Norfolk); George Parks (Thomas Cromwell); A. Z. Chipman (Duke of Suffolk); J. W. Hague (Lord Chamberlain); Charlotte Blair (Patience); H. A. Cripps (Sir Henry Guildford); Horace Lewis (Capucius); E. Y. Backus (Brandon); H. E. Chase (Surveyor); Charles Addison (Gardiner); C. Leslie Allen (Campeius); James Taylor (Clerk of the Court); Gene Wiley (Sir Thomas Lovell)

Touring Company, season 1890-91
A Drama by William Shakespeare

B. W. Turner (King Henry VIII); Mrs. D. P. Bowers (Queen Katherine); Frederick Warde (Cardinal Wolsey); Catherine Coggswell (Lady Anne Boleyn); Harry Leighton (Cromwell); C. D. Herman (Duke of Buckingham/Earl of Surrey); H. C. Barton (Duke of Norfolk); Charles Clark (Duke of Suffolk); Robert Benedict (Lord Chamberlain); G. Marburg (Cardinal Campius); Lottie Sutton (Patience); Edwin Tanner (Gardiner) William Stuart (Sir Thomas Lovell); Percy Sage (Lord Sands); D. Talbot (Sir Henry Guildford); Robert Benedict (Cranmer); W. Purvis (Brandon); Thomas E. Lee (Surveyor); Annie Sutton (Lady Denny)

Garden Theatre, New York, opened October 17, 1892
Managing directors, Frank L. Perley and J. J. Buckley; Director, Beaumont Smith; A Drama by William Shakespeare; Scenery, Albert, Grover & Burridge; Music arranged by L. Tomaszewicz; Pastoral Gavotte by Prof. Mamert Bibeyran

Otis Skinner (King Henry VIII); Madame Helena Modjeska (Queen Katherine); John A. Lane (Cardinal Wolsey); Beaumont Smith (Duke of Buckingham); E. Peyton Carter (Duke of Norfolk); Rudolph De Cordova (Duke of Suffolk); Guy Lindsley (Earl of Surrey); Mrs. Beaumont Smith (Anne Bullen); Wadsworth Harris (Cromwell); George Hazelton (Lord Chamberlain); Ben G. Rogers (Griffith); Jules Cluzetti (Sir Henry Guildford); Alfred Carlisle (Sir Thomas Lovell); W. R. S. Morris (Capucius); Wadsworth Harris (Cardinal Campeius); Henry T. Vincent (Lord Sands); Frank Kemble (Surveyor); George Thomas (Brandon); Charles Kelley (Sergeant-at-Arms); M. J. Fenton (A Messenger); Henry G. Moore (Court Crier); Ellen Barnes (Patience); Maud Durbin (Prologue); Hannah E. Sargeant (An Old Lady); George Sargeant (Page); Lile Howard (A Scribe); Frederick Meadow, H. L. Sullivan (Gentlemen)

Lyceum Theatre, London, opened January 5, 1892 204 performances
Produced and directed by Henry Irving; A Drama by William Shakespeare; Scenery, Joseph Harker and Hawes Craven, William Telbin; Costumes, Seymour Lucas and Mrs. J. W. Comyns Carr; Chorus master, R. P. Tabb; Acting manager, Bram Stoker; Stage manager, H. J. Loveday

William Terriss (Henry VIII); Ellen Terry (succeeded by Amy Roselle) (Queen Katherine); Henry Irving (succeeded by Arthur Stirling) (Cardinal Wolsey); Gordon Craig (Thomas Cromwell); Violet Vanbrugh (Anne Bullen); Thomas E. Wenman (succeeded by William Haviland) (Duke of Norfolk); Henry Howe (Griffith); Frank Tyars (Duke of Suffolk); Allen Beaumont (Cardinal Campeius); William Haviland (succeeded by Acton Bond) (Duke of Buckingham's Surveyor); John Martin Harvey (Sir Henry Guildford); Arthur Stirling (succeeded by Mr. Vincent) (Cranmer); Clarence Hauge (Earl of Surrey); Gilbert Farquhar (succeeded by Mr. Johnson) (Lord Sands); R. P. Tabb (Capucius); Mr. Stewart

(Sir Thomas Lovell); Mr. Davis (Sir Anthony Denny); W. Lionel Belmore (Sir Nicholas Vaux); W. Belford (Garter King at Arms); Mr. Powell (Sergeant at Arms); W. J. Lorriss (Messenger); Mr. Seldon (Brandon); Johnston Forbes-Robertson (Duke of Buckingham); Alfred Bishop (Lord Chamberlain); Mr. Lacy (Gardiner); H. W. Cushing (succeeded by W. Marion) (Secretary); R. G. LeThiere (succeeded by Mrs. Edward Saker) (Old Lady); Mrs. Pauncefort (Patience); Mr. Johnson, W. J. Yeldham, John Archer (Gentlemen)

Garden Theatre, New York, opened October 10, 1893
A Drama by William Shakespeare

Otis Skinner (King Henry VIII); Madame Helena Modjeska (Queen Katherine); John A. Lane (Cardinal Wolsey); Rudolph de Cordova (Duke of Suffolk); Guy Lindsley (Earl of Surrey); Mrs. Beaumont Smith (Anne Bullen); William Harris (Cromwell); W. R. S. Morris (Capucius); Ben G. Rogers (Griffith); H. T. Vincent (Lord Sands); Helen Barnes (Patience); Beaumont Smith (Duke of Buckingham); Wadsworth Harris (Cardinal Campeius); Jules Cluzetti (Henry Guildford); Prologues and Epilogues spoken by Maud Durbin

Abbey's Theatre, New York, opened December 4, 1893
Produced and directed by Henry Irving; A Drama by William Shakespeare; Scenery, Hawes Craven, Joseph Harker, William Tolbin; Costumes, Mrs. J. W. Comyns Carr, Seymour Lucas; Acting manager, Bram Stoker

William Terriss (Henry VIII); Ellen Terry (Queen Katherine); Henry Irving (Cardinal Wolsey); Frank Cooper (Duke of Buckingham); Miss Coleridge (Anne Bullen); Henry T. Vincent (Archbishop Cranmer); William Haviland (Duke of Norfolk); Clarence Hague (Earl of Surrey); Mrs. Frank Tyars (Patience); R. P. Tabb (Capucius); Alfred Bishop (Lord Chamberlain); Mr. Archer (Gardiner); S. Johnson (Lord Sands); Frank Tyars (Duke of Suffolk); Lionel Belmore (Sir Thomas Lovell); Mr. Lacy (Cardinal Campeius); Mr. Davis (Sir Anthony Denny); H. N. Cushing (Sir Nicholas Vaux); John Martin Harvey (Cromwell); Henry Howe (Griffith); Mr. Buckley (Surveyor); Mr. Seldon (Brandon); Mr. Eldham (Sergeant-at-Arms); W. J. Lorriss (A Messenger); Mr. Reynolds (A Scribe); Maud Milton (An Old Lady); Mr. Marion (Secretary)

Touring Company, season 1894-95
A Drama by William Shakespeare

Eugene Jepson (King Henry VIII); Maggie Howard Davidge (Queen Katherine); Creston Clarke (Cardinal Wolsey); Rose Barrington (Anne Bullen); Edwin Middleton (Cromwell); Russ Whytal (Duke of Buckingham); Carleton Macy (Duke of Norfolk); Joseph B. Everham (Duke of Suffolk); Alice Gale (Lady Denny); John F. McArdle (Earl of Surrey); Arthur Raleigh (Cardinal Campeius); E. G. Moroney (Bishop Gardiner); Thomas J. Powers, Jr. (Sir Thomas Lovell); Rodney Burton (Henry Guildford); Arthur Raleigh (Brandon)

Touring Company, season 1901-02
Produced by Wagenhals and Kemper; A Drama by William Shakespeare; Director, Thomas Coffin Cooke; Scenery, Alexander B. Corbett; Company manager, John B. Reynolds

Norman Hackett (King Henry VIII); Madame Helena Modjeska (Queen Katherine); Louis James (Cardinal Wolsey); Aphie James (Anne Bullen); R. E. Jamison (Cromwell); Wadsworth Harris (Duke of Norfolk); Thomas Coffin Cooke

(Duke of Buckingham); Anthony Andre (Duke of Suffolk); Mrs. Evans-Welles (Patience); Jon Hons (Earl of Surrey); Jerome Harrington (Cardinal Campeius); Alexander Carleton (Lord Chamberlain); Girard Cameron (Sir Thomas Lovell); Charles Young (Capucius); Howard Woodruff (Surveyor); Louise Woelber (Lady Denny); James DuSang (Lord Sands); George Clinton (Griffith); Robert Carew (Scribe); Frank Dalton (Court Crier); George McCulla (Bishop Gardiner); W. H. Huffington (Henry Guildford); Louise Gale, Emma Jones, Alice B. Clarke, Louise Woelber, Emily Grey Bethel, Gertrude Patton, Georgia Frey, Clara Lane (Ladies of the Court)

WHEN KNIGHTHOOD WAS IN FLOWER, Criterion Theatre, New York, opened January 14, 1901 176 performances
Produced by Charles Frohman; A Play by Paul Kester based on the novel by Charles Major; Settings by Ernest Albert, Frank E. Gates, E. A. Morange; Costumes by Mrs. Charles Hone and Harper Pennington; Manager, C. B. Dillingham; Acting manager, L. J. Rodriguez; Stage Managers, Frank Reicher and Frank Colfax

Julia Marlowe (Mary Tudor); Charles Harbury (Henry VIII); David Torrence (Duke of Buckingham); Bruce McRae (Charles Brandon); Frank Reicher (Will Sommers); Norah Lamison (Lady Jane Bolingbroke); W. E. Morris (Duke De Longueville); Wilfrid North (Francis D'Angouleme); C. F. Gibney (Thomas Wolsey, Bishop of Lincoln); Donald MacLaren (Sir Edwin Caskoden); Frederic Burt (Master Cavendish); E. W. Morrison (Captain Bradhurst); Annie Clark (Queen Katherine); Claire Kulp (Anne Boleyn); Ellen Rowland (Jane Seymour); Frederick Leslie (Host of the Bow and String Tavern); William Charles (Tavern Servant); J. J. Elwyn (An Adventurer); Gwendolyn Valentine (Louise De Valois); Wilfrid North (Sir Adam Judson)

WHEN KNIGHTHOOD WAS IN FLOWER, Touring Company, season 1901-02
Produced by Charles Frohman; A Play by Paul Kester based on the novel by Charles Major; Settings by Ernest Albert, Frank E. Gates and E.A. Morange; Costumes, Mrs. Charles Hone and Harper Pennington; Manager, C.B. Dillingham; Acting manager, L.J. Rodriguez

Julia Marlowe (Mary Tudor); Charles Harbury (Henry VIII); Albert Bruning (succeeded by Sidney Toler) (Duke of Buckingham); Bruce McRae (Charles Brandon); Frank Reicher (Will Sommers); Charlotte Crane (succeeded by Norah Lamison) (Lady Jane Bolingbroke); A. Douzet (succeeded by John Lord) (Duke De Longueville); Wilfrid North (Francis D'Angouleme/Sir Adam Judson); C.F. Gibney (Thomas Wolsey); George S. Christie (Sir Edwin Caskoden); Frederic Burt (Master Cavendish); Algernon Tassin (Captain Bradhurst); Francis Ring (Anne Boleyn); Maud Lantry (Jane Seymour); Annie Clark (Queen Katherine); Frederic Leslie (Host of the Bow and String Tavern); William Charles (Tavern Servant); R. C. Beacroft (An Adventurer); Gwendolyn Valentine (Louise De Valois)

HENRY VIII, Shakespeare Memorial Theatre, Stratford-Upon-Avon, opened April 23, 1902
A Drama by William Shakespeare; Director, Frank R. Benson

Alfred Brydone (King Henry VIII); Ellen Terry (Queen Katherine); F. R. Benson (Cardinal Wolsey); Constance Benson (Anne Bullen); Arthur Whitby (Cranmer, Archbishop of Canterbury); Walter Hampden (Duke of Norfolk); Stuart Edgar (Sands); George Fitzgerald (Cardinal Campeius); Frank Rodney (Duke of

Buckingham); Charles Bibby (Gardiner); Percy D. Owen (Lord Chamberlain); H. O. Nicholson (Griffith); A. M. Lang (Duke of Suffolk); E. Harcourt Williams (Surrey)

A MADCAP PRINCESS, *Knickerbocker Theatre*, New York, opened September 5, 1904 48 performances

Produced by Charles B. Dillingham; A Comic-Opera founded on Charles Major's novel *When Knighthood Was in Flower*, Director, Edward Temple; Libretto by Harry B. Smith; Music by Ludwig Englander; Settings, Homer Emens and Edward G. Unitt

Lulu Glaser (Mary Tudor); William Pruette (Henry VIII); Bertram Wallis (Charles Brandon); Donald McLaren (Sir Edwin Caskoden); Frank Reicher (Will Sommers); H. Chambers (Sir Adam Judson); Arthur Barry (Duke of Buckingham); Maud Ream Stover (Queen Katherine); Ethel Wynne (Anne Boleyn); Olive Cox (Jane Seymour); Mary Conwell (Lady Jane Bolingbroke): Ralph Lewis (Cardinal Wolsey); Guy B. Hoffman (Duke de Longueville); Howard Chambers (Captain Bradhurst); Herbert Freer (Farmer Blake); Reginald Barlow (Landlord, The Bow and String Tavern); Elsie Thomas (Goody Blake); Maurice Sims (A Friar); Lillian Lipyeat (A Page); Estelle de Angelis, Helen Bancroft, Louise Wein, Rita Dean, Edith Hale, Miriam Norris, Virginia Courtney, Georgia Sage, Elise Thomas, Beatrice Anderson, Sadie Gerschoff, Vera Brewster, Estelle Peterson, Emma Spohr, Elizabeth Murray, Ella Reichter, Lucy Stone, Katherine La Tour, Anna Jarbeau, Luella Smith, Keannette Pawsey, George Hopper, J. D. Van Epps, A. Bellevue, Lacey Sampson, Joseph Frohoff, Louis Helle, Maurice Robinson, Adam Dockray, E. J. Kloville, E. F. Drew, Charles B. Baker, Joseph Miller, Peter Canova (Ladies and Gentlemen of the Court, Flower Girls, Attendants, Sailors, etc.)

A MADCAP PRINCESS, *Touring Company*, season 1905-06

Produced by Klaw and Erlanger; A ComicOpera founded on Charles Major's novel *When Knighthood Was in Flower*, Director, Edward Temple; Libretto by Harry B. Smith; Music by Ludwig Englander; Costumes, A. Koehler & Company, Klaw and Erlanger Costume Department; Musical director, Max Knauer; Production manager, Edwin O. Child; Stage managers, Bert Merket and Frederick McGee

Sophie Brandt (Mary Tudor); George O'Donnell (King Henry VIII); Frank Kelley (Charles Brandon); George Putnam (Sir Edwin Caskoden); Bert Merket (Will Sommers); F. L. Jordon (Sir Adam Judson); Adrian Bellvue (Duke of Buckingham); Emma Lewis (Queen Katherine); Ida May Lawrence (Anne Boleyn); Grace Nesmith (Lady Jane Bolingbroke); Frederick McGee (Cardinal Wolsey); Mary Shane (Goody Blake); Harry Bond (Duke de Longueville); Herman E. Stone (A Friar); F. L. Jordon (Captain Bradhurst); G. F. Northen (Landlord of the Bow and String Tavern); Elizabeth Murray (A Page); Frederick McGee (Farmer Blake); Nellie Shayne, Edna Roberts, Tilley Landman, Grace McUsher, Myrtle Jette, Alice Reed, May Holmes, Teddy Desmond, Daisy Leone, Georgie Spouner, Mary Shayne, Iren De Salo, Mary Theill, Mary Inverness, Pauline White, Florence Busby, Lottie Wade, Ethel Bridge, W. W. Roth, Frank Boyle, Authur Lee, M. E. Thomas, P. J. De Varney, William Readston, Carl Frederick, J. M. Windsor, W. F. Talbot, T. G. Cogney, Cliff Russell, Arthur G. Nash (Ladies and Gentlemen of the Court, Country Folk, Attendants, Sailors, etc.)

WHEN KNIGHTHOOD WAS IN FLOWER, *Touring Company*, season 1906-07

Produced and Directed by Ernest Shipman; A Play by Paul Kester, based on the novel by Charles Major; Scenery, Castle and Harvey; Directing manager, S. T. King; Company manager, B. B. Vernon; Stage managers, Edward Dillon and Joseph Hall Chase

Anna Day (Mary Tudor); Ogden Stevens (Henry VIII); Alfred Swenson (Charles Brandon); Frederic Siebke (Thomas Wolsey); John Alexander (Duke of Buckingham); Eloise Elliston (Lady Jane Bolingbroke); Joseph Hall Chase (Duke De Longueville); Thomas Irwin (Francis D'Angouleme); Edward Dillon (Sir Edwin Caskoden); John Sherman (Master Cavendish); Lorie Palmer (Anne Boleyn); Annie Ashley (Jane Seymour); Louise Derigney (Queen Katherine); Warren Evens (Sir Adam Judson); Harry Young (Captain Bradhurst); James Warren (Bow and String Tavern Host); Joseph Wood (Tavern Servant); Lewis Duncan, E. D. Wilson (Adventurers); Fred K. Wyatt (Will Sommers); Grace Fay, Francis Fay (Pages to Henry VIII)

WHEN KNIGHTHOOD WAS IN FLOWER, *Waldorf Theatre*, London, opened May 13, 1907 7 performances

Produced by the Waldorf Theatre Syndicate Ltd. and Estate of Sam S. Shubert; A Play by Paul Kester, based on the novel by Charles Major; Managers, E. E. Eldridge, A. T. Worm and John Major; Stage managers, Francis Powell, Frank Colfax and Frederick Kaufman

Julia Marlowe (Mary Tudor); Mr. Mawson (Henry VIII); Henry Vibart (Duke of Buckingham); E. H. Sothern (Charles Brandon); Miss Lamison (Lady Jane Bolingbroke); Frank Reicher (Francis D'Angouleme/Will Sommers); Frederick G. Lewis (Sir Edwin Caskoden); Rowland Buckstone (Captain Bradhurst); Mr. Cromptom (Thomas Wolsey); Mr. Crawley (Duke de Longueville); Mr. Anderson (Master Cavendish/Adventurer); Fred Eric (Sir Adam Judson); Alma Kruger (Queen Katherine); Miss Baird (Anne Boleyn); Miss Clement (Jane Seymour); Mr. Aspland (Host); Mr. Robertson (Officer); Mr. Howson (An Adventurer); Miss Alexander (Louise De Valois); Mr. Kelly (Tavern Servant); Mr. Taylor (Officer of Ship); Mr. Howson, Mr. Walsh, Mr. Harris (Adventurers); Mr. Wilson (Page)

HENRY VIII, *His Majesty's Theatre*, London, opened September 1, 1910 252 performances

Produced and Directed by Sir Herbert Beerbohn-Tree; A Drama by William Shakespeare; Assistant director, Louis N. Parker; Settings and Costumes by Percy Macquoid; Scenery, Joseph Harker; Original Music, Edward German; Musical director, Adolf Schmid; Dances arranged by Margaret Morris; "Morris Dance" and "Pastime and Good Company" written and composed by King Henry VIII; General manager, Henry Dana; Stage managers, Cecil King and Stanley Bell

Arthur Bourchier (King Henry VIII); Violet Vanbrugh (Queen Katherine); Sir Herbert Tree (Cardinal Wolsey); Laura Cowie (Anne Bullen); Reginald Owen (Thomas Cromwell); Henry Ainsley (Duke of Buckingham); Edward O'Neill (Duke of Suffolk); S. A. Cookson (Cardinal Campeius); Lila Barclay (Patience); Charles Fuller (Cranmer); Gerald Lawrence (Earl of Surrey); Edward Sass (Lord Chamberlain); William Burchill (Gardiner); Clarence Derwent (Lord Abergavenny); Henry C. Hewitt (Sir Thomas Lovell); Charles James (Sir Nicholas Vaux); W. R. Creighton (Lord Sands); Clifford Heatherley (Garter King); Henry Morrell (Griffith); Acton Bond (Surveyor); Edmund Goulding (A Crier); Ross Shore (Jester); Mrs. Charles Calvert (An Old Lady); Edmund Gurney (Sir Henry Guildford); Arthur Gaskill (Sergeant-at-Arms); W. B. Abington (Servant);

Francis Chamier (A Scribe); A. E. George (Duke of Norfolk); Cyril Sworder, Charles Howard (Gentlemen)

His Majesty's Theatre, London, opened April 17, 1911
Produced and Directed by Sir Herbert Beerbohm-Tree; A Drama by William Shakespeare; Assistant Director, Louis N. Parker; Settings and Costumes by Percy Macquoid; Scenery, Joseph Harker; Original music by Edward German; Musical director, Adolf Schmid; Dances arranged by Margaret Morris; "Morris Dance" and "Pastime and Good Company" written and composed by King Henry VIII; General manager; Henry Dana; Stage managers, Cecil King and Stanley Bell

Arthur Bourchier (King Henry VIII); Violet Vanbrugh (Queen Katherine); Sir Herbert Tree (Cardinal Wolsey); Laura Cowie (Anne Bullen); Cyril Sworder (Thomas Cromwell); Basil Gill (Duke of Buckingham); A. E. George (Duke of Norfolk); Gerald Lawrence (Earl of Surrey); S. A. Cookson (Cardinal Campeius); Lila Barclay (Patience); Edward Sass (Lord Chamberlain); Francis Chamier (Capucius); Clarence Derwent (Lord Abergavenny); Walter R. Creighton (Lord Sands); Edmund Gurney (Sir Henry Guildford); Henry C. Hewitt (Sir Thomas Lovell); Clifford Heatherley (Sir Nicholas Vaux); Acton Bond (Surveyor); Arthur Gaskill (Sergeant-at-Arms); Edmund Goulding (Court Crier); James Smythson (A Scribe); Ross Shore (Jester); Mrs. Charles Calvert (An Old Lady); E. Ion Swinley, Charles Howard (Gentlemen); Henry Morrell (Griffith); W. B. Abingdon (Servant)

WHEN KNIGHTHOOD WAS IN FLOWER, *Chestnut Street Theatre*, Philadelphia, opened April 8, 1912
Produced by The Orpheum Players; A Play by Paul Kester, based on Charles Major's novel; Director, Percy Winter

Carolyn Gates (Mary Tudor); Edward M. Kimball (King Henry VIII); William Ingersoll (Charles Brandon); Walter Lewis (Will Sommers); Virginia Howell (Lady Jane Bolingbroke); Wilmer L. Walter (Duke of Buckingham); Frank Peters (Adam Judson); Fraunie Fraunholz (Sir Edwin Caskoden); Charles Ashley (Duc De Longueville); John J. Geary (Thomas Wolsey); Ralph Kline (Master Cavendish); Marion Tiffany (Anne Boleyn); Lilian Corbin (Jane Seymour); Florence Roberts (Katherine of Aragon); Charles M. Stuart (Host of the Bow and String Tavern); George Peddle (Servant); Pierre Francis (Captain Bradhurst); William Macauley (Francis D'Angouleme); Annette Paulson (Countess d'Hauteville); John Mitchell (Lord Chamberlain); C. G. Kilby, Charles Hudson, John Mitchell, Ralph Hingerford, Henry McLaughlin (Adventurers)

BLUFF KING HAL, *Garrick Theatre*, London, opened October 10, 1914 43 performances
A Play written and directed by Louis N. Parker

Arthur Bouchier (King Henry VIII); Violet Vanbrugh (Katharine Parr); Baliol Holloway (Sir Thomas Seymour); Cecil Humphreys (Sir Thomas Wroithsley); Roland Pertwee (Eustace Chappuys); Odette Goimbault (Lady Jane Grey); Master Donald Buckley (Prince of Wales); Herbert Bunston (Stephen Gardiner); Cyril Sworder (Dr. Butts); Ray Raymond (William Morice); Clifford Heatherley (Signor Vendramin); Mina Leonesi (Princess Mary); Lathleen Jones (Princess Elizabeth); Enid Rose (Lady Herbert); W. S. Hartford (An Officer); Christopher Steels (Duke of Najera); John Liege (Fitton); Mary Dibley (Lady Tyrwhit); Alice Lonnen (Anne Askew); Betty Linley (Mistress Barbara); I. Solney (Earl of

Surrey); Robin Cuff (Lord Oxford); M. Summers (William Parr); R. J. Tippett (Sir William Herbert); Eric Fowler (Sir Robert Tyrwhit); John C. Rice (Sir Nicholas Throckmorton); B. D. Wood (Sir George Blagge); W. S. Beard, Cyril Raymond (Spanish Gentlemen); Wilfred Herbert (Chaplain); Howard Douglas, Matthew Lawrence (Secretaries); Osmond Wilson (A Page); Madeline Bellew (The Countess of Rutland); Alice Stuart (Lady Strickland); Sarah Brindly (Lady Suffolk); Mary Fowler (Lady Margaret Douglas); Margaret Ost (Lady Katharine Willoughby); Isolde le Roy (Lady Margaret Neville); E. BinghamHall (Mistress Aghonby); K. Bingham-Hall (Mistress Ashley); Gladys Preatoa, Monica Mellor (Venetian Dancers); Rene Waler, (Lord Dudley); Patricia Manners (Shade of Katharine of Aragon); Belle Lind (Shade of Anne Boleyn); Louie Barnes (Shade of Jane Seymour); Olive Temple (Wraith of Anne of Cleaves); Winifred Bateman (Shade of Katharine Howard)

HENRY VIII, *His Majesty's Theatre*, London, opened July 5, 1915
Produced by Sir Herbert Beerbohm-Tree; A Drama by William Shakespeare; Director, Louis N. Parker

Arthur Bourchier (King Henry VIII); Violet Vanbrugh (Queen Katherine); Sir Herbert Tree (Cardinal Wolsey); Laura Cowie (Anne Boleyn); Henry B. Irving (Cardinal Campeius); Lewis Waller (Duke of Buckingham); Henry Ainley (Earl of Surrey); Sydney Valentine (Cranmer); Alma Murray (Dowager Duchess of Norfolk); A. E. George (Duke of Norfolk); Hubert Carter (Duke of Suffolk); Edward Sass (Lord Chamberlain); J. Fisher White (Capucius); Leon Quartermaine (Lord Abergavenny); Gerald du Maurier (Lord Sands); Godfrey Tearle (Sir Henry Guildford); Basil Gill (Sir Thomas Lovell); Ben Webster (Sir Nicholas Vaux); Owen Nares (Thomas Cromwell); Herbert Waring, Murray Carrington (Gentlemen); E. Holman Clark (Griffith); Eille Norwood (Garter King-at-Arms); Acton Bond (Surveyor to Buckingham); J. H. Barnes (Sergeant-at-Arms); Dion Boucicault (Scribe); Donald Calthrop (Messenger); O. B. Clarence (A Servant); George Grossmith (Jester); Lady Tree (An Old Lady); Constance Collier (Patience); Frederick Ross (A Crier); Ada Crossley, Clara Evelyn, Winifred Barnes (Singing Ladies); and: Clifton Alderson, Isabel Alison, J. G. Anderson F. J. Arlton, Robert Atkins, Dora Barton, Phyllis Bedells, Kryle Bellew, Richard Rodney, John Booth, Lilian Braithwaite, Henry Byatt, Leonard Calvert, G. Campion, Laurence Cecil, Joan Chaloner, Arthur Cleave, P. Clive, Amy Coleridge, Margaret Cooper, Vernon Crabtree, Elise Craven, F. Cremlin, Julian Cross, Winifred Dalby, Louise Dale, Reginald Dance, Grace Darby, Irene Delisse, Clarence Derwent, Kenneth Douglas, Jennie Earle, F. S. Edgar, Claud Edmonds, Grace Egbert, R. Fairfax, Madeline Fitzgerald, Archibald Forbes, Henry Fowler, Florence Glossop-Harris, A. Houghton Goddard, Aithna Glover, Alfred Corney Grain, A. C. Hardle, Clifford Heatherley, Gilbert Heron, Henry Hewitt, Maxine Hinton, Julia James, Douglas Jeffries, P. Jones, M. Keen, Percy Keitley, W. Kershaw, George Laundy, Gerald Lawrence, Mina Leonesi, Victor M. Lewisohn, A. Lubimoff, Dorothy McBain, James McLeod, Georgina Milne, Dawson Milward, J. W. Mollison, Phyllis Monkman, Fred Morgan, Arthur Morris, Alan Nichols, Herbert Norris, T. O'Brien, Reginald Owen, Maude Phillips, J. G. Preston, George Raymond, Louise Regnis, S. Rendall, F. Forbes Robertson, Roy Royston, Stella St. Audrie, Leonard Shepherd, Sybil Sparkes, Edith Stock, Christopher Steele, D. Sullivan, Madge Titheradge, Chris Walker, C. Dernier Warren, Victor Wiltshire, Herbert Woodward, Leonard Yorke

New Amsterdam Theatre, New York, opened March 14, 1916
Produced and Directed by Sir Herbert Beerbohm-Tree; A Play by William Shakespeare; Scenery, Joseph Harker; Furnishings and Costumes, Percy Macquoid, Perruquier and William Clarkson; Incidental Music, Edward German by arrangement with the executors of the late Sir Henry Irving; Musical director, Anton Heindl; Dances arranged by Elizabeth Rothe; "Morris Dance" and "Pastime and Good Company" written and composed by King Henry VIII; Pageantry, Louis N. Parker; General manager, Percy Burton; Stage managers, Eric Snowdon, George G. Carr
(Sir Herbert Beerbohm Tree's Shakespeare Tercentenary Festival Production)

Lyn Harding (King Henry VIII); Edith Wynne Matthison (Queen Katharine); Herbert Beerbohm-Tree (Cardinal Wolsey); Willette Kershaw (Anne Bullen); Charles Fuller (Archbishop Cranmer); Fred Eric (Duke of Norfolk); Charles Dalton (Duke of Buckingham); Reginald Carrington (Duke of Suffolk); Claude Beerbohm (Cardinal Champeius); Earl Maxon (Earl of Surrey); Lionel Braham (Lord Chamberlain); Edward S. Forbes (Lord Abergavenny); Arthur Bow (Lord Sands); A. D. Mavity (Sir Henry Guildford); Craig Ward (Sir Thomas Lovell); Douglas Ross (Thomas Cromwell); Henry Herbert (Usher); Alfred Shirley (Sir Nicholas Vaux); H. R. Irving (Garter King at Arms); Gerald Hamer (Surveyor); Arthur Gaskill (Sergeant-at-Arms); Cecil Nixon (A Crier); Frank Arnold (A Scribe); Maud Milton (An Old Lady); Katherine Sayre (Patience); Henry Herbert (Jester); George C. Carr, Charles Howard (Gentlemen); Walter Plinge (Servant)

A KING OF NOWHERE, Maxine Eliott's Theatre, New York, opened March 20, 1916; moved to *39th Street Theatre*, March 27, 1916 58 performances
Produced by the Garrick Company; A Romantic Comedy by J. and L. du Rocher Macpherson; Director, Jessie Bonstelle

Sydney Greenstreet (King Henry VIII); Lou Tellegen (Godred); Olive Tell (The Lady Margaret Silchester); Corliss Giles (Lord Harry Fitzwalter); Wilda Mari Moore (Queen Catherine Parr); Robert Adams (Sir Dick Denny); Cameron Mathews (Sir Anthony Fairfax); Charles Rogers (John Skinner); Roselle Cooley (Mistress Lettice Plantagenet); Galwey Herbert (Fenwolf); Irene Bell (Mistress Eleanor Courtenay); Eileen Wilson (Mistress Phyllis Arundel); Armsby Ayers (A Doctor); Harry Chessman (A Chaplain); Robert Vivian (A Jester); Charles Derickson (A Page); Dana Parker (Attendant); Martin Snell, Norman Rolfe (Guards)

HENRY VIII, Touring Company, season 1916-17
Produced and Directed by Sir Herbert Beerbohm-Tree; A Play by William Shakespeare; Scenery, Joseph Harker; Furnishings and Costumes, Percy Macquoid; Dances arranged by Elizabeth Rothe; Incidental Music, Edward German; "Morris Dance" and "Pastime and Company" written and composed by King Henry VIII; Pageantry, Louis N. Parker; General manager, Percy Burton; Stage managers, Eric Snowdon and George G. Carr

Lyn Harding (King Henry VIII); Edith Wynne Matthison (Queen Katherine); Herbert Beerbohm-Tree (Cardinal Wolsey); Elise Mackay (Anne Bullen); Charles Fuller (Archbishop Cranmer); George Hayes (Duke of Norfolk); Henry Herbert (Duke of Buckingham); St. Clair Bayfield (Duke of Suffolk); Charles Coleman (Lord Chamberlain); Edward Forbes (Thomas Cromwell); Warburton Gamble (Earl of Surrey); Katherine Sayre (Patience); Gerald Hamer (Cardinal

Campeius); Walter Plinge (Lord Abergavenny); Arthur Jackson (Lord Sands); Bernard Savage (Sir Henry Guildford); Craig Ward (Sir Thomas Lovell); Alfred Shirley (Sir Nicholas Vaux); G. W. Anson (Griffith); Julian Justine (Surveyor); H. R. Irving (Garter King at Arms); Arthur Gaskill (Sergeant-at-Arms); Alice Augarde Butler (An Old Lady); Cecil Nixon (A Crier); Frank Arnold (A Scribe); G. W. Anson (Jester); George G. Carr, Charles Howard (Gentlemen); George Curtis (Servant)

Shakespeare Memorial Theatre, Stratford-Upon-Avon, England, opened August 16, 1916
A Drama by William Shakespeare; Director, Ben Greet
Norman V. Norman (King Henry VIII); Lillian Braithwaite (Queen Katherine); R. Rawson Buckley (Cardinal Wolsey); Florence Saunders (Anne Bullen); E. Ion Swinley (Duke of Buckingham); Austin Revor (Duke of Suffolk); Robert Atkins (Duke of Norfolk); Orlando Barnet (Lord Chamberlain); A. Corney Grain (Thomas Cranmer, Archbishop of Canterbury); Russell Thorndike (Bishop Gardiner); Madge Whiteman (Patience); Royston Wood (Sir Thomas Lovell); Jerrold Robertshaw (Cardinal Campeius); Claire Pauncefort (Old Lady)

Royal Victoria Hall, London, season 1917-18
Produced by Lillian Baylis; A Drama by William Shakespeare; Director, Ben Greet; Costumes and Wigs by Messrs. Rayne; Dances and Vision of Angels arranged by Jean Anderton; Musical director, Charles Corri; Vocal Trio by Edward German; Stage managers, Wilfred Lyndon, Madge Whiteman
Norman V. Norman (King Henry VIII); Sybil Thorndike (alternate Beatrice Wilson) (Queen Katherine); Russell Thorndike (Cardinal Wolsey); Mary Sumner (Anne Bullen); Cowley Wright (Duke of Buckingham); John Leslie (Duke of Norfolk); Gordon Douglas (Thomas Cromwell); Martyn Reynolds (Duke of Suffolk); Florence Saunders (Sir Thomas Lovell); Philip Barry (Lord Chamberlain); Wilfred Lyndon (Sir Henry Guildford); Ernest Meads (Surveyor to the Duke of Buckingham); Viola Lyel (Lord Abergavenny); Roger Williams (Lord Sands); Winifred Oughton (An Old Lady); Ben Greet (Cardinal Campeius); Joseph Peters (Griffith); Mark Stanley (Earl of Surrey); Madge Whiteman (Capucius); Ernest Meads (Thomas Cranmer, Archbishop of Canterbury); Betty Potter, Viola Lyel (Gentlemen); Roger Williams (Bishop Gardiner); Noel Mackern (Patience)
NOTE: "Owing to the order to shorten performances, five of the text scenes must be omitted from this representation. Arrangements have been made that warning a threatened air raid will be communicated by the Military Authorities to this Theatre. On receipt of any such warning the audience will be informed with a view to enable persons who may wish to proceed home to do so."

Empire Theatre, London, opened December 23, 1925 127 performances
Produced by Sybil Thorndike, A Drama by William Shakespeare; Director, Bronson Albery; Scenery, J. Crosbie-Frazer, Alick Johnstone and Arthur Le Maistre; Production designer, Charles Ricketts; Costumes, Bruce Winston, J. H. Edgcombe, H.& M. Rayne and Thomas Wallis; Music and Music director, John H. Foulds; Choreography, Penelope Spencer; Stage manager, Thomas Warner; Assistant stage managers, Matthew Forsyth and Laurence Olivier
Norman V. Norman (King Henry VIII); Sybil Thorndike (Queen Katherine); E. Lyall Swete (Cardinal Wolsey); Angela Baddeley (succeeded by Primrose

Morgan) (Anne Bullen); Lewis T. Casson (Griffith); Arthur Wontner (Duke of Buckingham); Eugene Leahy (Duke of Norfolk); Harold Scott (Cromwell); H. Reyner Barton (Duke of Suffolk); Hubert Carter (Lord Chamberlain); William Fazan (Surveyor to the Duke of Buckingham); Cyril Hardingham (Gardiner/Capucius); H. R. Hignett (Cardinal Campeius); Lawrence Anderson (Earl of Surrey); John H. Moore (Garter King-at-Arms); Chris Walker (Sergeant-at-Arms); O. B. Clarence (Lord Sands/Cranmer, Archbishop of Canterbury); William J. Miller (Sir Thomas Lovell); Matthew Forsyth (Sir Nicholas Vaux); Stockwell Hawkins (Porter); Laurence Olivier (First Serving Man); Philip Clowes (succeeded by George Blackwood) (Second Serving Man); Osborne Adair, Stockwell Hawkins, Bruce Winston (succeeded by J. Henry Twyford) (Gentlemen); Mrs. Arthur Whitby (Duchess of Norfolk); Beatrice Smith (Patience); Ada King (Old Lady); Doris Kealy (Singer); Lawrence Anderson (succeeded by R. Caton Woodville) (Brandon); Desmond Deane (Scribe); Charles Bond (Wolsey's Servant); Iris Baker, Zillah Carter, Brenda Cleather, Gwen Harker, Agnes Lauchlan, Vere Shepstone, Peggy (Margaret) Webster, Eileen Archer, Mudah Findlay, Betty Gwynne, Joan Halls, Dorothy Holliday, Margaret Neeson, Dorothy Rickinson, Rosalind Snow, Ronald Bayne, Holland Bennett, Charles Bond, John Clifford, Philip Clowes, Ernest Fosbrooke, H. Hesslegrave, Alfred Hilliard, Ronald Kerr, Michael Logan, Wilfred Lyndon, Frank Macrae, H. Melrose, David Olive, Laurence Olivier, James Parish, Sam Pickles, Cecil Rayne, Terence Ranson, Carol Reed, B. Russell, Richard Turner, J. Henry Twyford, Guy Vivian (Members of the Court, Ladies, Gentlemen)

THE WOOING OF KATHERINE PARR, *Borough Theatre*, Stratford, England, opened February 28, 1927
Produced and Directed by Fred Terry; A romantic play by William Devereux

Fred Terry (Henry VIII); Julia Neilson (Katherine Parr); John Cabot (Duke of Norfolk); David G. Noble (Thomas Cranmer); Donald Fergusson (Sir Thomas Seymour); Frank Milray (Wriothesley); Maris Morden-Wright (Prince Edward); Frank Royde (Stephen Gardiner); Denis Banyard (Sir Nicholas Throckmorton); Hugh F. S. Casson (Dr. William Buttes); Alfred Hearne (Hans Holbein); E. Waddy (Sir Andrew Crosswell); Richard Seaton (Sir Miles Partridge); Tom Roydan (Bishop Jackson); W. H. Garbois (Marbeck); Harold Melvill (Clem o' the Dales); Esther McPherson (Cecile Bellingham); Edmund Grogan (Sir Francis Bryan)

HENRY VIII, *Old Vic Theatre*, London, opened April 8, 1929
Produced by Andrew Leigh; A Drama by William Shakespeare; Costumes and Settings by Owen P. Smyth; Principal costumes designed by Charles Ricketts by arrangement with Lewis Casson; Dances arranged by Ninette De Valois; Music director, Charles Corri; Stage managers Michael Watts and Eric Spear

Percy Walsh (King Henry VIII); Esme Church (Queen Katherine); Reyner Barton (Cardinal Wolsey); Adele Dixon (Anne Bullen); John Laurie (Duke of Buckingham); Peter Taylor-Smith (Duke of Norfolk); Eric Phillips (Lord Abergavenny); Godfrey Kenton (Cromwell); Wilfred Babbage (Earl of Surrey/Surveyor); Torin Thatcher (Duke of Suffolk); Eric Adeney (Lord Chamberlain); Horace Sequeira (Lord Sands/Cranmer/ Cardinal Campeius); Rafe Thompson (Sergeant-at-Arms); Eric Spear (Sir Thomas Lovell); Phillip Fothergill (Gardiner); Iris Baker (Patience); Michael Watts (Capucius); Charles Smyrk (Servant); Rafe Thompson (Sir Harry Guildford); Leslie Young (Wolsey's

Servant); Rita Daniel (An Old Lady); H. Stanley Beers (A Crier); Mary Hull (Singer); Eric Phillips (A Gentleman); Owen P. Smyth (Griffith); Rosamond Brune, Monica Brett, Beryl Ede, Mary Hull, Mary Lamb, Peggy Hunter (Guests, Attendants, etc.)

THE WIVES OF HENRY VIII, *Avon Theatre*, opened November 15, 1931 69 performances
Produced by James B. Pond; Written and directed by Cornelia Otis Skinner; A Series of Character Studies including *Eve of Departure*; *In a Gondola*; *Homework*; *Monte Carlo*; *A Lady Explorer*; Incidental music selected by Miss Skinner, arranged by Lowell Patton and orchestrated by Adolf Schmid; Music director, Chris Arth; Costumes, Helen Pons Studio

Cornelia Otis Skinner as Catharine of Aragon, Anne Boleyn, Jane Seymour, Anne of Cleaves, Kathryn Howard, Katherine Parr

HENRY VII, Sadler's Wells Theatre, London, opened November 7, 1933
Produced and directed by Tyrone Guthrie; A Drama by William Shakespeare

Charles Laughton (King Henry VIII); Flora Robson (Queen Katherine); Robert Farquharson (Cardinal Wolsey); Ursula Jeans (Anne Bullen); Nicholas Hannen (Duke of Buckingham); James Mason (Cromwell); Dennis Arundell (Duke of Norfolk); Ernest Hare (Lord Abergavenny); Frank Napier (Earl of Surrey); Roger Livesey (Lord Chamberlain); Bertram Grimley (Sir Henry Guildford); Richard Goolden (Lord Sands/Thomas Cranmer); Philip Thornley (Surveyor to Duke of Buckingham); Christopher Hassall (Sir Thomas Lovell); Marius Goring (Cardinal Campeius/Garter King at Arms); Athene Seyler (An Old Lady); Elsa Lanchester (A Singer); Oxford St. John (Sir Nicholas Vaux); Evelyn Allen (Patience); Peter Copley (Capucius); Morland Graham (Griffith); Cecil Scott-Paton (Gardiner); Ernest Hare (Duke of Suffolk); Thorley Walters (A Messenger)

THE ROSE WITHOUT A THORN, *Duke of York's Theatre*, London, opened November 6, 1933
A Drama by Clifford Bax; Director, Nancy Price

Frank Vosper (King Henry VIII); Lawrence Hanray (Thomas Cranmer); Joan Maude (Kathryn Howard); Mabel Constanduros (Anne of Cleves); Alistair Sim (Sir Thomas Audley); Tristan Rawson (Earl of Hertford); William Fox (Thomas Culpeper); Grizelda Hervey (Margery Morton); Mary Alston (Mary Lassells); Robert Speaight (John Lassells); Douglas Allen (Tom Tiler); Arthur Pusey (Francis Derham); Alison Leggatt (Katherine Tilney); David Lewis (Strife); Ivan Craig (Paris); Maureen King (Juno); Daphne Newton (Minerva); Margery Vosper (Venus); John Gardner, Dan Callaghan (Soldiers); Ursula Marx (Page); Geoffrey Wilkinson (Tom Taylor)

HENRY VIII, *Open Air Theatre*, Regent's Park, London opened June 22, 1936
Produced by Sydney Carroll; A Drama by William Shakespeare; Director, Robert Atkins

Lyn Harding (King Henry VIII); Phyllis Neilson-Terry (Queen Katherine); Baliol Holloway (Cardinal Wolsey); Vivien Leigh (Anne Bullen); Christopher Casson (Cromwell); Gyles Isham (Duke of Buckingham); John Abbott (Sir Thomas Lovell); Jack Carlton (Duke of Suffolk); W. E. Holloway (Duke of Norfolk); Lawrence Baskcomb (Lord Chamberlain); Valentine Rooke (Lord Sands); Gordon Edwards (Sir Henry Guildford); C. W. Anson (Campeius); George Hagan

(Lord Abergavenny/ Scribe/Capucius); Hugh Thurston (Sir Nicholas Vaux/Sergeant); Clement Hamelin (Crier/Surveyor); M. Acton-Bond (Wolsey's Servant); Ion Swinley (Earl of Surrey); Franklyn Kelsey (Griffith); Hilda Trevelyan (Old Lady); Lindisfarne Hamilton (Patience); Kenneth Evans, John Lonquet (Gentlemen)

Shakespeare Memorial Theatre, Stratford-Upon-Avon, England, opened April 23, 1938

A Drama by William Shakespeare; Director, B. Iden Payne; Production designer, Herbert Norris

Gyles Isham (King Henry VIII); Phyllis Neilson-Terry (Queen Katherine); James Dale (Cardinal Wolsey); Valerie Tudor (Anne Bullen); Guy Belmore (Duke of Suffolk); G. Sheldon Bishop (Duke of Norfolk); Stanley Howlett (Lord Sands/Archbishop Cranmer); Francis James (Duke of Buckingham); Andrew Leigh (Lord Chamberlain); Gerald Kau Souper (Cardinal Campeius); Kenneth Wicksteed (Griffith); Anne Dalston (Patience); Michael Goodliffe (Surrey); Ethel Griffies (Old Lady); George Hagan (Capucius/Guildford)

Shakespeare Memorial Theatre, Stratford-Upon-Avon, England, opened May 17, 1945

A Drama by William Shakespeare; Director, Robert Atkins; Production Designer, Guy Sheppard

Antony Eustrel (King Henry VIII); Viola Lyel (Queen Katherine); George Skillian (Cardinal Wolsey); Moira Lister (Anne Bullen); C. Rivers Gadsby (Cromwell); H. Worrall-Thompson (Duke of Suffolk); Tristan Rawson (Duke of Norfolk); Thomas Dance (Bishop of Lincoln Brandon); David Read (Lord Chamberlain); Peter Bell (Lovell); Andrew Faulds (Vaux/Crier/ Surrey/Lord Abergavenny); Clement Hamelin (Cardinal Campeius); David Peel (Guildford); Horace Sequeira (Lord Sands/Griffith)

International Theatre, New York, opened November 6, 1946 39 performances

Produced by the American Repertory Theatre; A Drama by William Shakespeare; edited by Margaret Webster; Director, Margaret Webster; Scenery and Costumes by David Ffolkes; Dances arranged by Felicia Sorel; Music by Lehman Engel; Managing director, Cheryl Crawford; Played in repertory with James M. Barrie's *What Every Woman Knows* and Henrik Ibsen's *John Gabriel Borkman*

Victor Jory (Henry VIII); Eva Le Gallienne (Katherine of Aragon); Walter Hampden (Cardinal Wolsey); June Duprez (Anne Bullen); Philip Bourneuf (The Prologue); Eli Wallach (Cromwell); Richard Warning (Duke of Buckingham); Raymond Greenleaf (Duke of Norfolk); Ernest Truex (Lord Chamberlain); William Windom (Earl of Surrey/Sergeant of the Guard); Robert Rawlings (Lord Abergavenny/A Messenger); Emery Battis (Sir Thomas Lovell); Efrem Zimbalist, Jr. (Duke of Suffolk); Angus Cairns (Surveyor); Arthur Keegan (Sir Harry Guildford); John Becher (Lord Sands); Donald Keyes (Sir Nicholas Vaux); John Straub (Cardinal Campeius); Margaret Webster (An Old Lady); Theodore Tenley (Archbishop of Canterbury); Marion Evenson (Patience); Eugene Stuckmann (Capucius); Mary Alice Moore (Duchess of Norfolk); Philip Bourneuf, Eugene Stuckmann (Chroniclers); Donald Keyes (Griffith); Ruth Neal (Lady-in-Waiting to Katherine); Angus Cairns (Garter King of Arms); Cavada Hamphrey, Anne Jackson, Mary Alice Moore, Ruth Neal (Ladies of the Court); Don Allen, John Behney, Michael Corhan, Tom Grace, Bart Henderson, Frederic Hunter, Robert

Leser, Mark McCardle, Gerald McCormack, Walter Neal, James Rafferty, Theodore Tenley, Ed Woodhead (Lords, Bishops, Monks, Guards, Servants, Heralds, Pages)

HENRY VIII AND HIS WIVES, *Metropolitan Opera House*, New York, opened October 17, 1947
A Ballet by Rosella Hightower; Music by Rossini; Adapted and arranged by Robert Zeller; Director, James Starbuck; Costumes, Russell Hartley and Rose Schogel

Performed by: Anton Dolin, Natalie Conlon, Alicia Markova, Rozsika Sabo, Bettina Rosay, Kirsten Valbor, Royes Fernandez, George Resch, Wallace Seibert and Oleg Tupine

ANNE OF THE THOUSAND DAYS, *Shubert Theatre*, New York, opened December 8, 1948 288 performances
Produced by The Playwrights' Company and Leland Hayward; A Drama by Maxwell Anderson; Director, H. C. Potter (replaced Bretaigne Windust); Setting and Lighting by Jo Mielziner; Costumes by Motley; Music by Lehman Engel; Company manager, Walter Fried; Stage managers, Walter Wagner, Scott Jackson, Maury Tuckerman, Cecil Clovelly and Terence Anderson

Rex Harrison (Henry); Joyce Redman (Anne Boleyn); Percy Waram (succeeded by Charles Francis, Frederic Worlock) (Cardinal Wolsey); John Merivale (Mark Smeaton); John Williams (Duke of Norfolk); Robert Duke (Percy, Earl of Northumberland); Viola Keats (Elizabeth Boleyn); Charles Francis (Thomas Boleyn); Allan Stevenson (succeeded by Francis Bethencourt) (Henry Norris); Louise Platt (succeeded by Janet Ward) (Mary Boleyn); Margaret Garland (succeeded by Avril Keiller); (Madge Shelton); Monica Lang (succeeded by Valerie Cardew) (Jane Seymour); Russell Gaige (succeeded by Claude Horton) (Sir Thomas More); Harry Irvine (Bishop Fisher); George Collier (succeeded by Cecil Clovelly, Charles Ellis) (Prior Houghton); Ludlow Maury (Servant); Cecil Clovelly (succeeded by Walter Matthau) (Servant); Harry Selby (A Messenger); Terence Anderson (Clerk); Kathleen Bolton (Serving Woman); Fred Ayres Cotton (succeeded by Walter Reimer) (Bailiff); Harold McGee (succeeded by William MacDougal (Bailiff); Wendell K. Phillips (Thomas Cromwell)

HENRY VIII, *Shakespeare Memorial Theatre*, Stratford-Upon-Avon, England, opened July 23, 1949
Produced by the Shakespeare Memorial Theatre; A Drama by William Shakespeare; Director, Tyrone Guthrie; Production designer, Tanya Moiseiwitsch; Incidental Music by Cedric Thorpe-Davis; Masque arranged by Paulien Grant; Music advisor, Leslie Bridgewater; Manager, Patrick Donnell; Production manager, H. Nancy Burman; Resident stage manager, Desmond Hall; Stage managers, Julia Wootten and Christopher West

Anthony Quayle (King Henry VIII); Diana Wynyard (Queen Katherine); Harry Andrews (Cardinal Wolsey); Kathleen Michael (Anne Bullen); Leon Quartermaine (Duke of Buckingham); Philip Guard (Cromwell); Edmund Purdom (Lord Abergavenny); Robert Shaw (Duke of Suffolk); Michael Gwynn (Duke of Norfolk); Paul Hardwick (Gardiner); Julian Amyes (Archbishop Cranmer); Paul Hansard (Sir Thomas Lovell); Richard Dare (Cardinal Campeius); William Squire (Lord Chamberlain); Norman Mitchell (Sergeant-at-Arms); Harold Kasket (Surveyor); Michael Bates (Lord Sands); George Rose (A Gentleman/Porter); Wynne Clarke (Prologue/An Old Lady); Robert Hardy (Griffith); Timothy Bateson

(Bishop of Lincoln); Eric Lander (Earl of Surrey); Lorna Whitehouse (Patience); David Lytton (A Messenger); John Money (Capucius); Bertram Shuttleworth (Porter's Man); Geoffrey Curtis (Sir Henry Guildford); Jill Bennett, Margaret Courtenay, Jean Fox, Penelope Munday, Pat Sandys, Robin Dowell, John Dunbar, John Gay, Alexander Graham, Leslie Heritage, Keith Herrington, Peter Norris, John Stewart, David Wroe (Ladies, Men-at-Arms, Clerics, Choristers); Alexander Lowe, John Roland, Clifford Asher, Leslie Black, Roy Goodwin, Richard Hodgkins, Lionel Jarman, Kenneth McNulty, Frederick Neale, John Pollard, Norman Smith, Bernard Tebbutt, Philip Wilson, Robert Woodburn (Soldiers)

Shakespeare Memorial Theatre, Stratford-Upon-Avon, England, opened March 28, 1950
Produced by the Shakespeare Memorial Theatre; A Drama by William Shakespeare; Director, Tyrone Guthrie; Production designer, Tanya Moiseiwitsch; Incidental Music, Cedric Thorpe-Davis; Masque arranged by Pauline Grant; Music advisor, Leslie Bridgewater; Stage director, Patrick Donnell; Assistant stage director, Desmond Hall; Stage managers, Julia Wootten and Tony Riddell

Anthony Quayle (King Henry VIII); Gwen Ffrangcon-Davies (Queen Katherine); Andrew Cruickshank (Cardinal Wolsey); Barbara Jefford (Anne Bullen); Leon Quartermaine (Duke of Buckingham); Brian Brockman (Cromwell); Peter Norris (Lord Abergavenny); Robert Shaw (Duke of Suffolk); Richard Dare (Cardinal Campeius); Michael Gwynn (Duke of Norfolk); Paul Hardwick (Gardiner); Alan Badel (Lord Chamberlain); Harold Kasket (Surveyor); John Hayes (Sergeant-at-Arms); Harold Siddons (Sir Henry Guildford); Nigel Green (Sir Thomas Lovell); Geoffrey Bayldon (Cranmer); Michael Bates (Lord Sands/Porter's Man); Robert Hardy (Griffith); Timothy Bateson (Bishop of Lincoln); Eric Lander (Earl of Surrey); Rosalind Atkinson (Prologue/An Old Lady); George Rose (A Gentleman/Porter); Maxine Audley (Patience); David Lytton (A Messenger); John Money (Capucius); Mairhi Russell, Romany Evens, Hazel Penwarden, Felicity Barrington, Marjorie Steel, John Gay, John Dunbar, Cyril Conway, Ronald Hines, Peter Halliday, Harold Siddons, Michael Ney, Michael Atkinson, Ward Williams, Peter Jackson, David Woodman, Charles Lepper, Godfrey Bond, John York, Edward Atienza, Michael Ferrey, Peter Hechie, Basil Hoskins, Oliver Cox, Michael Kelly, Bernard Collingwood, Percy Herbert, Anthony Service, Reginald Marsh, Brendon Barry, John Wright (Ladies, Men-at-Arms, Clerics, Choristers)

THE BOLEYNS, *Watergate Theatre*, London, opened January 18, 1951
A Chronicle Play by Laura Wildig; Director, Chloe Gibson

Gillian Maude (Anne Boleyn); Antony Kearey (King Henry VIII); Peter Smallwood (George Boleyn); Sylvia Shaw (Lady Boleyn); Barbara New (Alice Boleyn); Joss Ackland (Sir Henry Norris); Noel Davis (Sir Francis Weston); Geoffrey Hibbert (Will Somers); Joyce Appleton (Mary Carey); James Thomason (Duke of Suffolk); Harold Young (Sir Thomas Boleyn); Elizabeth Thorndike (Jane Seymour); Michael Jackson (Mark Smeaton)

ANNE OF THE THOUSAND DAYS, *Flatbush Theatre*, Brooklyn, New York, opened June 6, 1950
Produced by George Brandt; A Drama by Maxwell Anderson; Director, Maury Tuckerman; Costumes by Motley; Music by Lehman Engel; Company manager,

Maurice Turet

John Loder (Henry VIII); Sylvia Sidney (Anne Boleyn); Walter Matthau (Cardinal Wolsey); Earl Oxford (Mark Smeaton); Bernice Marsh (Jane Seymour); Haskell Coffin (Thomas Cromwell); Henry Craig Neslo (Thomas Boleyn); Rosemary Murphy (Mary Boleyn); Margaret Garland (Madge Shelton); Bernard Pollock (Henry Norris); Erik Rhodes (Duke of Norfolk); Shirley Dale (Elizabeth Boleyn); Frank Rowan (Sir Thomas More); Bruce Hall (Percy, Earl of Northumberland); William MacDougall (Bishop Fisher); Walter Riemer (Prior Houghton); Walter Sands (Servant); Terence Anderson (Servant)

HENRY VIII, Old Vic Theatre, London, opened May 6, 1953
Produced by The Old Vic Company; A Drama by William Shakespeare; Director, Tyrone Guthrie; Sets and Costumes, Tanya Moiseiwitsch; Music composed by Cedric Thorpe-Davis; Manager, J. A. Titcombe; Stage manager, Elizabeth Butterfield; Dances, Tom Brown

Paul Rogers (King Henry VIII); Gwen Ffrangcon-Davies (Queen Katherine); Alexander Knox (Cardinal Wolsey); Jeanette Sterke (Anne Bullen); Leo Genn (Duke of Buckingham); Timothy Bateson (Cromwell); Eric Thompson (Lord Abergavenny); John Phillips (Duke of Norfolk); Laurence Hardy (Gardiner); David Waller (Brandon); James Ottaway (Lord Sands); Alan Dobie (Sir Thomas Lovell); Bernard Kilby (Sir Henry Guildford): Bruce Sharman (Bishop of Lincoln); Denis Raymond (Capucius); William Squire (Cranmer); Norman Fraser (Messenger); Margaret Courtenay (Patience); Daniel Thorndike (Earl of Surrey); Newton Blick (Porter/Gentleman); John Warner (Porter's Man/ Cardinal Campeius); Terry Wale (Page); Wynne Clark (Prologue/Old Lady); Garth Adams (Sergeant); Wolfe Morris (Surveyor/Griffiths); Robert Hardy (Lord Chamberlain); Patrick Wymark (Duke of Suffolk); David Benson, Malcolm Black, Fred Braun, Don Burgess, Howell Davies, Denzil Ellis, Norman Fraser, Philip Gale, Rupert Harvey, Pat Horgan, William Job, Fletcher Lightfoot, Gerald Limbrick, Johan Malherbe, Leslie Pitt, Desmond Rayner, Elsa Bach, Sonia Graham, Barbara Grimes, Phyllida Law, Barbara St. Ledger (Nobles, Bishops, Clerks, Masquers, Men at Arms, Ladies); Albert Barker, Lucas Bassett, Desmond Campbell, Felix Dabrowa, Robert Davies, J. R. Evans, Roland Lucantonio, Michael O'Farrell, Brian Matthews, David Saron, David Sharpe, Jeremy Wilkin (Choir)

NOTE: Produced at the Old Vic Theatre in the Presence of H. M. The Queen at a Gala Performance on Wednesday, May 6, 1953, in honour of the coronation

Old Vic Theatre, London, opened May 13, 1958
Produced by the Old Vic Company; A Drama by William Shakespeare; Director, Michael Benthall; Production designer, Loudon Sainthill; Music by Gordon Jacob

Harry Andrews (King Henry VIII); Edith Evans (Queen Katherine); John Gielgud (Cardinal Wolsey); Jill Dixon (Anne Bullen); Jack Gwillim (Duke of Buckingham); Richard Wordsworth (Duke of Norfolk); Barry Ingham (Lord Abergavenny); Dennis Chinnery (Cromwell); David Dodimead (Sir Nicholas Vaux); Paul Daneman (Lord Chamberlain); Daniel Thorndike (Duke of Suffolk); Rosalind Atkinson (An Old Lady); Margaret Courtenay (Patience); Roy Patrick (Sergeant-at-Arms); Ronald Fraser (Surveyor to the Duke of Buckingham); Oliver Neville (Sir Thomas Lovell); John Humphry (Sir Henry Guildford); Derek Godfrey (Cardinal Campeius); David Dodimead (Cranmer); Charles West (Lord Sands); David Waller (Gardiner); Harold Innocent (A Crier); Juliet Cooke (A Singer); Keith Taylor (A Messenger); Crispian Woodgate (A Boy); John Humphry (Earl of

Surrey); Brian Badcoe (Capucius); James Culliford, Edward Hardwicke (Gentlemen); Derek Francis (Griffith)

ROYAL GAMBIT, *Sullivan Street Playhouse*, New York, opened March 4, 1959 87 performances

Produced by David Ellis; A Play by Hermann Gressieker, translated and adapted by George White; Director, Philip Lawrence; Setting by Glenn Hill; Lighting by Nicola Cernovich; Costumes by Michael De Marco; Production manager, Matthew Tobin

Russell Gold (Henry VIII); M'el Dowd (succeeded by Tani Seitz, Eileen Letchworth) (Katherina of Aragon); Tani Seitz (succeeded by Susan Brown) (Anne Boleyn); Dolores Rashid (Jane Seymour); Alice Drummond (Anna of Cleaves); Elizabeth Perry (Kathryn Howard); Grace Chapman (Kate Parr)

A MAN FOR ALL SEASONS, *Globe Theatre*, London, opened July 1, 1960 315 performances

(see separate entry)

HENRY VIII, *Stratford Shakespearean Theatre*, Stratford, Ontario, Canada, opened June 21, 1961

Produced by the Stratford Shakespearean Festival of Canada; Michael Langham, artistic director; A Drama by William Shakespeare; Director, George McCowan; Production designer, Brian Jackson; Music, Louis Applebaum; Dances, Alan and Blanche Lund; Company manager, Bruce Swerdfager; Stage managers, Jack Hutt, Graham Spicer, Thomas Bohdanetzky and Peter Mannering

Douglas Campbell (King Henry VIII); Kate Reid (Queen Katherine); Douglas Rain (Cardinal Wolsey); Pat Galloway (Anne Boleyn); Jack Creley (Duke of Buckingham); Eric Christmas (Lord Chamberlain); John Vernon (Duke of Suffolk); Peter Donat (Earl of Surrey); Leo Ciceri (Duke of Norfolk); Edward Holmes (Lord Abergavenny); James Peddie (Cromwell); Max Helpmann (Gardiner); Peter Needham (Sir Thomas Lovell); Fred Euringer (Sergeant-at-Arms); Robin Gammell (Dr. Butts/Surveyor to Buckingham/ Porter's Man); Robert Goodier (Lord Sands); Bernard Behrens (Sir Henry Guildford); William Needles (Cardinal Campeius); Mervyn Blake (Griffith); Maureen Fitzgerald (Old Lady); Christine Bennett (Patience); Barbara Collier (Singer); Bruno Gerussi (Cranmer); Garrick Hagon (Messenger); Louis Negin (Capucius); Douglas Chamberlain (Porter); Dinah Christie (Marchioness of Dorset); Christine Bennett (Marchioness of Norfolk); Louis Negin, Garrick Hagon (Attendants to Wolsey); Louis Turenne (Lord Chancellor); Mary Anderson, Claude Bede, Guy Belanger, Ingi Bergman, Dinah Christie, Marcia Clare, Michael Davidson, Miranda Davies, Lewis Gordon, Adrienne Harris, Al Koslik, Gary Krawford, Barry Lord, John McKay, Hedley Mattingly, Nelson Phillips, Anthony Robinow, Joseph Rutten (Lords, Ladies, Soldiers, etc.)

ROYAL GAMBIT, *Vanguard Playhouse*, Detroit, opened November 17, 1961

Produced by the Vanguard Playhouse Company; A Drama by Hermann Gressieker, translated and adapted by George White; Director, William A. Gregory; Settings and Lighting by Tom A. Aston; Costumes, Helen King

Robert Rounsville (King Henry VIII); Jan Kosta (Katharina of Aragon); Elaine Hyman (Anne Boleyn); Alice Rolph (Jane Seymour); Shirley Davidson (Anna of Cleves); Bev Pemberthy (Kathryn Howard); Mady Correll (Kate Parr)

ROYAL GAMBIT, Ashcroft Theatre, Croydon, England, opened November 5, 1962
Produced by Hubert Woodward and Clement Scott Gilbert for New Pembroke Theatre Ltd.; A play by Hermann Gressieker; Director, Clement Scott Gilbert; Production designer, Michael Young

Michael Denison (King Henry VIII); Dulcie Gray (Katherina of Aragon); Pamela Ann Davy (Anne Boleyn); Jean Robinson (Jane Seymour); Carole Boyer (Anna of Cleves); Polly Adams (Kathryn Howard); Gillian Reine (Kate Parr)

A MAN FOR ALL SEASONS, ANTA Theatre, New York, opened November 22, 1961
637 performances

(see separate entry)

A MAN FOR ALL SEASONS, Paper Mill Playhouse, Milburn, N.J., opened February 16, 1965

(see separate entry)

A MAN FOR ALL SEASONS, Coconut Grove Playhouse, Los Angeles, opened April 12, 1966 8 performances

(see separate entry)

THE KING'S MARE, Garrick Theatre, London, opened July 20 1966
Produced by Stanley Gordon and Jerry Wayne; A Comedy-Drama by Jean Canooile; Adapted from the French by Anita Loos; Director, Peter Coe; Production designer, Ralph Koltai; Lighting, Robert Ormbe

Keith Michell (Henry VIII); Glynis Johns (Anne of Cleves); Jane Morrow (Kathryn Howard); Brian Murphy (Thomas Cranmer); Michael Logan (Duke of Norfolk); Sydney Tafier (Thomas Cromwell); Michael Gwynn (Wriothsley); Roger Ostime (Holbein); Shelia Bernette (Frau Schwartzenbroch); Mollie Maureen (Frau Willick); Blake Butler (Chancellor in Cleves); Valerie Dunico, Vilma Stuttle (Court Ladies); Dennis Tynsley, Stanley Dawson, Reg Templar, Michel Julian (Guards)

HENRY VIII, Shakespearean Festival Theatre, Lithia Park, Ashland, Oregon, opened July 23, 1968
Produced by the Oregon Shakespearean Festival, Augus L. Bowmer, Producing Director; A Drama by William Shakespeare; Director, Richard Risso; Settings, Clayton Karkosh; Costumes, Jack A. Byers; Lighting, Steven A. Maze

Patrick Hines (King Henry VIII); Ann Kinsolving (Queen Katherine); Danny Davis (Cardinal Wolsey); Amanda McBroom (Anne Bullen); Vincent Landro (Duke of Buckingham); Milt Tarver (Duke of Norfolk); P. A. Rudolph (Cardinal Campeius); Dennis Smith (Duke of Suffolk); Rick Hamilton (Earl of Surrey); Cindy Veazey (Duchess of Norfolk); Patrick McNamara (Lord Chamberlain); Derek Evans (Archbishop of Canterbury); Philip Davidson (Cranmer); Scott Van Fossen (Prologue/Epilogue); Arnold Hummasti (Cromwell); William Tate (Lord Chancellor/Secretary); Bill McClaren (Gardiner/Crier); Timothy Casey (Bishop of Lincoln); Larry Alan Haynes (Lord Abergavenny); Dennis Higgins (Lord Sands); Thomas O. Martin (Sir Henry Guildford/Griffith); Ron Gural (Sir Thomas Lovell); Scott Porter (Brandon, Sir Nicholas Vaux); Les Barnum (Garter King-at-Arms); Timothy Cassey (Surveyor); Charles Edelman (Doorkeeper); John M. Gavigan (Porter); Tom Oleniacz (Porter's Man); Randy Bowser (Page); Karen Sue Boettcher (Patience); Linda Johnson (Singer); Cathy Wright (An Old Lady); John Shephard (First Gentleman); Frank Kelly, Robert Singleton, Karl Weakley

(Maskers); Betsy Hamilton, Barbara Acker, Jo Guthrie, Emily Carpenter, Cathy Christie, Carol Clark (Visions); Joyce Dever, Mollie Byers, Carol Clark (Ladies-in-Waiting); Charles Coldwell, Russell Elliott, Lawrence E. Hirtzel, Jon Holland, John S. Koehler, Jane Sanborn, Scott Wagoner (Musicians); Larry Alan Haynes, David Kent Nale, Stephen Stearns, Cragi Mann, Scott Van Fossen, Tom Oleniacz, Jon Harrison, Dwight Dunn, Les Barnum, Randy Bowser, Timothy Casey, Charles Edelman, Randall Stothers, Dan Hays, Robert Ground (Lords, etc.)

Royal Shakespeare Theatre, Stratford-Upon-Avon, opened October 9, 1970; moved to *Aldwych Theatre*, London, December 17, 1970
Produced by the Royal Shakespeare Company; A Play by William Shakespeare; Director, Trevor Nunn, assisted by Buzz Goodbody and David Benedictus; Production designer, John Bury; Costumes, Ann Curtis; Lighting, John Bradley; Music composed by Guy Woolfenden; Deputy Music Director, Gordon Kember; Music includes arrangements of two tunes written and composed by King Henry VIII

Donald Sinden (King Henry VIII); Peggy Ashcroft (Queen Katherine); Brewster Mason (Cardinal Wolsey); Lisa Harrow (Anne Bullen); Richard Pasco (Duke of Buckingham); Jeffrey Dench (Duke of Norfolk); Anne Dyson (Duchess of Norfolk/ An Old Lady); Denis Holmes (Duke of Suffolk); Emrys James (Archbishop Cranmer); Janet Whiteside (Marchioness of Dorset/ Patience); Basil Clarke (Lord Chancellor/Lord Sands); Nicholas Selby (Lord Chamberlain); Richard Mayes (Sir Thomas Lovell); Miles Anderson (Sir Henry Guildford); David Dundas (Sir Nicholas Vaux/Masquer); Anthony Pedley (Campeius/ Guard/ Commoner); Michael Gambon (Earl of Surrey/ Secretary/ Sergeant/ Scribe); John Berwyn (Capucius/ Brandon/ Reveller); Michael Shannon (Surveyor/Dr. Butts/ Bishop of London/ Commoner); David Sinclair (Lord Abergavenny/ Executioner/ Scribe); Sydney Bromley (Griffith/ Reveller); Peter Messaline (Doorkeeper/ Masquer/ Secretary); Boyd Mackenzie (Sergeant - at - Arms/A Crier/ Masquer/ Porter's Man); Don Henderson (Porter/ Commoner); George Collis (Gardiner's Page); Geoffrey Hutchings (Cromwell); Pip Donaghy (Guard/ Scribe); Peter Geddis (Scribe/ Gentleman); David Ballie (Gentleman/ Reveller/ Guard); Christopher Biggins (Wolsey's Servant/ Guard/ Scribe); Gordon Reid (Gentleman/ Scribe); Maev Alexander, Madeleine Cannon, Basil Clarke, Michael Gambon, Don Henderson, Peter Messaline, Juliet Aykroyd, Madeleine Cannon, Carol Hall, Stephen Brown, George Collis, David Harrison, Richard Heywood, Joseph Jones, Martin Samuels, Adrian Wistreich (Lord, Bishops, Ladies, Spirits, Pages, Choristers, Common Children)

CATHERINE HOWARD, *Theatre Royal*, York, England, opened May 23, 1972; (Premiered at *Bournemouth Playhouse*, May 9, 1972)
A Play by Beverley Cross, adapted from his television script for *The Six Wives of Henry VIII*, Director, Richard Digby Day; Scenery, Hugh Durant; Costumes, Kit Surrey

John Humphry (King Henry VIII); Elizabeth Bennett (Catherine Howard); Martin Potter (Thomas Culpepper); Michael Cadman (Duke of Norfolk)

REX, *Lunt-Fontanne Theatre*, New York, opened April 25, 1976 48 performances
Produced by Richard Adler, in association with Roger Berlind and Edward R. Downe, Jr.; A Musical Drama by Sherman Yellen; Director, Edwin Sherin; Music by Richard

Rodgers; Lyrics by Sheldon Harnick; Scenery and Costumes, John Conklin; Lighting, Jennifer Tipton; Choreography, Dania Krupska; Orchestrations, Irwin Kostal; Dance arrangements, David Baker; Musical director, Jay Blackton; Hairstylists, Bert Anthony, Werner Sherer; Technical director, Mitch Miller; Company manager, Leo K. Cohen; Wrestling advisor, John Andoska; Stage managers, Jack Timmers, Bob Bernard and Elise Warner

Nicol Williamson (Henry VIII, King of England); Penny Fuller (Anne Boleyn/Princess Elizabeth); William Griffis (Cardinal Wolsey); Barbara Andres (Queen Catherine of Engalnd); April Shawhan (Lady Jane Seymour); Martha Danielle (Queen Katherine Parr of England/Queen Claude of France/Lady Margaret); Tom Aldredge (Will Somers); Ed Evanko (Mark Smeaton); Glenn Close (Princess Mary); Stephen D. Newman (Francis, King of France); Keith Koppmeier (Dauphin); Merwin Goldsmith (Comus); Charles Rule (Norfolk); Michael John (Prince Edward); Danny Ruvolo ("Te Deum" Herald); Jeff Phillips (replaced Buddy Teijelo) (French Herald); Lillian Shelby (replaced Melanie Vaughan) (Nursemaid); Melanie Vaughan (Lady-in-Waiting); Sparky Shapiro (Young Princess Elizabeth); Gerald R. Teijelo (Thomas Cromwell); Valerie Mahaffey (Catherine Howard); Ken Henley, Dennis Daniels (Guards); Dennis Daniels, Harry Fawcett, Paul Forrest, Pat Gideon, Ken Henley, Dawn Herbert, Robin Hoff, Don Johanson, Jim Litten, Craig Lucas, Carol Jo Lugenbeal, Valerie Mahaffey, G. Eugene Moose, Jeff Phillips, Charles Rule, Danny Ruvolo, Lillian Shelby, Jo Speros, Gerald R. Teijelo, Jr., Candace Towar, John Ulrickson, Melanie Vaughan (Ladies and Gentlemen of the Court); Dennis Daniels, Ken Henley, Don Johanson, Jim Litten, Jeff Phillips, Danny Ruvola (Sword and Morris Dancers)

MUSICAL NUMBERS: "Te Deum"; "No Song More Pleasing"; "At the Fields of Cloth of Gold"; "The Chase"; "Where Is My Son?"; "As Once I Love You"; "Away From You"; "Elizabeth"; "Christmas at Hampton Court"; "The Wee Golden Warrior"; "From Afar"; "In Time"; "Basse Dance"; "What Now"; "The Masque"

Dropped from Production: "Tell Me"; "Dear Jane"; "So Much You Loved Me"; "I Brought You a Gift"; "The Pears of Anjou"; "Long Live the King"

Original cast recording: RCA Records

KING HENRY THE EIGHTH, *Royal Shakespeare Theatre*, Stratford-Upon-Avon, England, opened June 9, 1983

Produced by the Royal Shakespeare Company; A Drama by William Shakespeare; Directors, Howard Davies and David Elgar; Production Designer, Hayden Griffin; Lighting, David Hersey; Costumes, Deidre Clancy; Music, Ilona Sekacz; Choreography, Stuart Hopps

Richard Griffiths (King Henry VIII); Gemma Jones (Katherine of Aragon); John Thaw (Cardinal Wolsey); David Schofield (Duke of Buckingham); Bruce Alexander (Duke of Norfolk); John Dicks (Duke of Suffolk); Nigel Cooke (Earl of Surrey); Sarah Berger (Anne Bullen); John Nolan (Lord Abergavenny/ Capucius/Archbishop of Canterbury); Geoffrey Beevers (Lord Chamberlain); Henry Goodman (Sir Thomas Lovell); Eileen Page (Patience); Paul Greenwood (Thomas Cromwell); Christopher Neame (Sir Walter Sands); Stanley Page (Doctor Butts/Bishop of Lincoln); Richard O'Gallaghan (Thomas Cranmer); Roger Hume (Cardinal Campeius/Porter); Caroline Harris (Anne's Lady); Sheridan Ball, Lesley Duff, Emma Watson (Ladies-in-Waiting); Clyde Pollitt (Griffith/Buckingham's Surveyor); Oliver Ford Davies (Gardiner); Martin Milman,

Charles Lawson, Cyril Nri (Gentlemen); Campbell Morrison (Sergeant-at-Arms); Charles Lawson, Paul Mooney (Soldiers); Richard Garnett (Brandon); Paul Mooney (Porter's Man); Sheridan Ball, Nigel Cooke, Lesley Duff, Richard Garnett, Caroline Harris, Roger Hume, Paul Mooney, John Nolan, Cyril Nri, Richard O'Callaghan, Eileen Page, Emma Watson (Courtiers and Dancers)

Barbican Theatre, London, opened September 6, 1984
Produced by the Royal Shakespeare Company; A Drama by William Shakespeare; Director, Howard Davies; Production designer, Hayden Griffin; Lighting, David Hersey; Costumes, Deidre Clancy; Music, Ilona Sekacz; Assistant director, David Edgar

Richard Griffiths (Henry VIII); Gemma Jones (Katherine of Aragon); Stephen Moore (Cardinal Wolsey); Lesley Duff (Anne Bullen); David Schofield (Duke of Buckingham); Bruce Alexander (Duke of Norfolk); Martin Milman (Duke of Suffolk); Nigel Cooke (Earl of Surrey); John Nolan (Lord Abergavenny/ Lord Mayor/ Capucius/ Archbishop of Canterbury); Geoffrey Beevers (Lord Chamberlain); Richard Garnett (Sir Thomas Lovell); Alexander Wilson (Sir Walter Bands); Henry Goodman (Thomas Cranmer); Eileen Page (Patience); Graham Sinclair (Sergeant-at-Arms); Caroline Harris (Anne's Lady); Campbell Morrison (Cardinal Campeius); Roger Hyams (Bishop of Lincoln/ Messenger): Paul Greenwood (Cromwell); Clyde Pollitt (Griffith/ Buckingham's Surveyor); Oliver Ford Davies (Gardiner); Jill Connick, Tina Jones, Tilda Swinton (Ladies-in-Waiting); David Haig, Stanley Page (Gentlemen)

A MAN FOR ALL SEASONS, *Savoy Theatre*, London, opened October 19, 1987
(see separate entry)

A MAN FOR ALL SEASONS, *Roundabout Theatre Company* (Christian C. Yegen Theater), opened January 4, 1987
(see separate entry)

SCREEN

KING HENRY VIII, *Barker Motion Photography Ltd.*, released February 1911 (Great Britain's first 2-reel film)
Produced, Directed and Photographed by Will L. Barker; A Drama by William Shakespeare as produced by Sir Herbert Beerbohm-Tree at His Majesty's Theatre on September 1, 1910

Arthur Bourchier (King Henry VIII); Sir Herbert Tree (Cardinal Wolsey); Violet Vanbrugh (Queen Katherine); Laura Cowie* (Anne Bullen); Reginald Owen (Thomas Cromwell); Basil Gill (Duke of Buckingham); A. E. George (Duke of Norfolk); Edward O'Neill (Duke of Suffolk); Gerald Lawrence (Duke of Surrey); Edward Sass (Lord Chamberlain); Walter R. Creighton (Lord Sands); Charles James (Sir Nicholas Vaux); Clarence Derwent (Lord Abergavenny); S. A. Cookson (Cardinal Campeius); Charles Fuller (Cranmer); Henry Morrell (Griffith); Acton Bond (Surveyor); Arthur Gaskill (Sergeant-at-Arms); Lila Barclay (Patience); Mrs. Charles Calvert (An Old Lady); Ross Shore (Jester); Clifford Heatherly (Garter King-at-Arms); Cyril Sworder, Charles Howard (Gentlemen); W. B. Abington (Servant); Edmund Goulding (A Crier); James Smythson (A Scribe)

* Laura Cowie appeared in the title role of *Anne Boleyn*, produced in France by

Gaumont in 1913 with Albert Decoeur as Henry VIII

CARDINAL WOLSEY, *Vitagraph*, released March 1912
Produced by J. Stuart Blackton; Director, Lawrence Trimble; Screenplay by Hal Reid
Tefft Johnson (Henry VIII); Julia Swayne Gordon (Queen Katherine); Hal Reid (Cardinal Wolsey); Clara Kimball Young (Anne Boleyn); Logan Paul (Archbishop of Canterbury); George Ober (Bishop of Essex); Robert Gaillard (King's Scretary, Cromwell)

A TUDOR PRINCESS, *Edison*, released December 1912 2 reels
Produced by Thomas A. Edison; Director, Walter Edwin
Robert Brower (King Henry VIII); Mrs. Wallace Erskine (Queen Katherine); Charles Ogle (Cardinal Wolsey); Mary Fuller (Princess Mary) Benjamin F. Wilson (Charles Brandon); Barry O'Moore (King Louis XII); Elizabeth Miller (Lady Jane Bolingbroke); Rex Hitchcock (Francis, the Dauphin); Harry Grady (Duke de Lougueville); Allan Crelius (Will Somers); George Anderson (Jean Freisot)

ANNA BOLEYN, *UFA* (Germany), released December 1920; in U.S. as *DECEPTION*, released by *Famous Players-Lasky*, April 1921
A Union-UFA Production; Meester-Film GmbH, Berlin and Projektions-AG-Union; Director, Ernst Lubitsch; Screenplay, Hans Kraly and Fred Orbing; Photography, Theodor Sparkuhl; Settings, Kurt Richter; Costumes, Ali Hubert
Emil Jannings (King Henry VIII); Henny Porten (Anna Boleyn); Aud Egede Nissen (Jane Seymour); Paul Hartmann (Sir Henry Norris); Ludwig Hartau (Duke of Norfolk); Hedwig Pauly (Queen Catherine); Hilde Muller (Princess Marie); Ferdinand von Alten (Mark Smeaton); Maria Reisenhofer (Lady Rochford); Adolf Klein (Cardinal Wolsey); Karl Platen (Physician); Erling Hanson (Court Percy); Paul Biensfeldt (Jester); Wilhelm Diegelmann (Cardinal Cambeggio); Sophie Pagay (Nurse); Josef Klein (Sir William Kingston); Friedrich Kuhne (Archbishop Cranmer)

WHEN KNIGHTHOOD WAS IN FLOWER, *Paramount Pictures*, released December 1922
A Cosmopolitan Production; Producer, William Randolph Hearst; Director, Robert G. Vignola; Screenplay by Luther Reed, based on the novel by Charles Major; Photography, Ira Morgan and Harold Wenstrom; Settings designed by Joseph Urban; Costumes, Gretl Urban; Fencing supervisor, James Murray; Assistant director, Philip Carle; Armor advisor, Bashford Dean; Musical Score by William Frederick Peters; "Marion Davies March" by Victor Herbert
Lyn Harding (King Henry VIII); Marion Davies (Mary Tudor); Forrest Stanley (Charles Brandon); Pedro De-Cordoba (Duke of Buckingham); Arthur Forrest (Cardinal Wolsey); Arthur Donaldson (Sir Henry Brandon); Theresa Maxwell Conover (Queen Katherine); Ruth Shepley (Lady Jane Bolingbroke); Ernest Glendenning (Sir Edwin Caskoden); Johnny Dooley (Will Somers); Charles Gerrard (Sir Adam Judson); Downing Clarke (Lord Chamberlain); William H. Powell (Francis I); George Nash (Captain Bradhurst); William Norris (Louis XII); Macey Harlam (Duc de Longueville); Gustav von Seyffertitz (Grammont); Paul Panzer (Captain of the Guard); William Kent (King's Tailor); Guy Coombes (Buckingham's follower); Flora Finch (French Countess); Mortimer Snow, Charles Ogle (Men)

THE PRIVATE LIFE OF HENRY VIII, United Artists, Great Britain premiere, August 17, 1933; in U.S. released October 1933

A London Film Production, Produced and directed by Alexander Korda; Screenplay by Arthur Wimperis, based on a story by Lajos Biro and Arthur Wimperis; Photography, Georges Perinal; Production designer, Vincent Korda; Music director, Kurt Schroeder; Costumes, John Armstrong; Sound, A. W. Watkins; Production manager, David Cunynghame; Historical Consultant, Philip Lindsay; Supervising Editor, Harold Young; Editor, Stephen Harrison

Charles Laughton (Henry VIII); Merle Oberon (Anne Bullen); Robert Donat (Thomas Culpeper); Binnie Barnes (Catherine Howard); Elsa Lanchester (Anne of Cleves); Wendy Barrie (Jane Seymour); Everley Gregg (Katherine Parr); Franklyn Dyall (Cromwell); Miles Mander (Wriothesly); Lady Tree (Henry's Old Nurse); John Loder (Thomas Peynell); Lawrence Hanray (Cranmer); William Austin (Duke of Cleaves); Frederick Culley (Duke of Norfolk); John Turmbull (Holbein); Sam Livesey (English Executioner); Judy Kelly (Lady Rochford); Gibb McLaughlin (French Executioner); Claude Allister (Cornell)

SONG: "What Shall I Do For Love?" by King Henry VIII, sung by Binnie Barnes

TUDOR ROSE (aka *Lady Jane Grey*), *Gaumont-British*, released April 1936; in U.S. as *Nine Days a Queen* released October 1936

A Gainsborough Production; Producer, Michael Balcon; Directed and adapted by Robert Stevenson; Photography, Mutz Greenbaum; Art director, Alex Vetchinsky; Costumes, J. Strassner; Wardrobe, Marianne; Music, Louis Levy; Sound, W. Salter; Editor, Terence Fisher

Nova Pilbeam (Lady Jane Grey); Cedric Hardwicke (Earl of Warwick); Frank Cellier (Henry VIII); John Mills (Lord Guilford Dudley); Felix Aylmer (Edward Seymour); Gwen Ffrangcon-Davies (Mary Tudor); Desmond Tester (Edward VI); Leslie Perrine (Thomas Seymour); Sybil Thorndike (Ellen); Martita Hunt (Frances Grey); Miles Malleson (Henry Grey)

THE SWORD AND THE ROSE, Walt Disney/RKO Radio Pictures, released June 1953

Produced by Walt Disney; Producer, Perce Pearce; Director, Ken Annakin; Screenplay, Lawrence Edward Watkin, based on the novel *When Knightwood Was in Flower* by Charles Major; Photography, Geoffrey Unsworth; Art director, Carmen Dillon; Costumes, F. Arlington Valles; Makeup, Geoff Rodway; Hairstyling, B. Chrystal; Music, Clifton Parker; Muir Matheson directing the Royal Philharmonic Orchestra; Assistant director, Peter Bolton; Editor, Gerald Thomas

Richard Todd (Charles Brandon); Glynis Johns (Princess Mary Tudor); James Robertson Justice (King Henry VIII); Michael Gough (Duke of Buckingham); Rosalie Crutchley (Queen Katherine); D. A. Clarke-Smith (Cardinal Wolsey); Jane Barrett (Lady Margaret); Peter Copley (Sir Edwin Caskoden); Ernest Jay (Lord Chamberlain); Bryan Coleman (Earl of Surrey); Jean Mercure (King Louis XII); Gerard Oury (The Dauphin of France); Fernand Fabre (French Ambassador); Gaston Richer (Grand Chancellor); Philip Glasier (Royal Falconer); Philip Lennard (Chaplain); John Vere (Lawyer Clerk); Robert Le Beal (Royal Physician); Helen Goss (Princess Claude); Caven Watson (Captain Bradhurst); Richard Molinas (Father Pierre); Hal Osmond (Costermonger); Norman Pierce (Innkeeper); Patrick Cargill, Anthony Sharpe (French Diplomats); Douglas Bradley-Smith (Squire); Ewen Solon (Guardsman); John Serrett

(French Squire); Bob Simmons (French Champion); Thomas Heathcoate (Wrestling Second); Arthur Brander (First Mate); Russell Waters (Sailor); Paddy Ryan, Rupert Evans (Bargemen)

YOUNG BESS, *Metro-Goldwyn-Mayer*, released May 1953
Produced by Sidney Franklin; Director, George Sidney; Screenplay by Jan Lustig and Arthur Wimperis, based on the novel by Margaret Irwin; Photography, Charles Rosher; Art directors, Cedric Gibbons and Urie McCleary; Costumes, Walter Plunkett; Music, Miklos Rozsa; Editor, Ralph E. Winters

Jean Simmons (Young Bess); Stewart Granger (Thomas Seymour); Deborah Kerr (Catherine Parr); Charles Laughton (Henry VIII); Kathleen Byron (Anne Seymour); Rex Thompson (Edward); Guy Rolfe (Ned Seymour); Kay Walsh (Mrs. Ashley); Cecil Kellaway (Mr. Parry); Leo G. Carroll (Mr. Mums); Robert Arthur (Barnaby); Norma Varden (Lady Tyrwhitt); Alan Napier (Robert Tyrwhitt); Ivan Triesault (Danish Envoy); Noreen Corcoran (Young Bess, age six); Elaine Stewart (Anne Boleyn); Lumsden Hare (Archbishop Cranmer); Lester Matthews (Sir William Paget); Dawn Addams (Kate Howard); Reginald Sheffield (Court Recorder); Anny Tyrrell (Mary); Doris Lloyd (Mother Jack); Fay Wall (Woman); Frank Eldridge, John Sheffield (English Officers); Carl Saxe (Executioner); Patrick Whyte (Officer); Ian Wolfe (Stranger); John Trueman (Yeoman); Major Sam Harris, Raymond Lawrence, David Cavendish (Council Men); Clive Morgan, Charles Keane (Halbadiers)

A MAN FOR ALL SEASONS, *Columbia Pictures*, released April 1966
(see separate entry)

ANNE OF THE THOUSAND DAYS, *Universal Pictures*, released December 1969
Produced by Hal Wallis; Director, Charles Jarrott; Screenplay by John Hale and Bridget Boland, based on Maxwell Anderson's play; Adaptation by Richard Sokolove; Photography, Arthur Ibbetson; Production designer, Maurice Carter; Art director, Lionel Couch; Set decorators, Peter Hewitt and Patrick McLoughlin; Costume designer, Margaret Furse; Choreography, Mary Skeaping; Music, Georges Delerue; Makeup, Tom Smith; Production supervisor, James Ware; Technical and historical advisor, Patrick McLoughlin; Associate producer, Richard McWhorter; Editor, Richard Marden

Richard Burton (King Henry VIII); Genevieve Bujold (Anne Boleyn); Irene Papas (Catherine of Aragon); Anthony Quayle (Cardinal Wolsey); John Colicos (Thomas Cromwell); Michael Hordern (Thomas Boleyn); Katharine Blake (Elizabeth Boleyn); Valerie Gearon (Mary Boleyn); Michael Johnson (George Boleyn); William Squire (Thomas More); Esmond Knight (Kingston); Peter Jeffrey (Norfolk); Joseph O'Connor (Fisher); Nora Swinburne (Lady Kingston); Lesley Paterson (Jane Seymour); Nicola Pagett (Princess Mary); Terence Wilton (Harry Percy); Vernon Dobtcheff (Mendoza); T. P. McKenna (Norris); Denis Quilley (Weston); June Ellis (Bess); Kynaston Reeves (Willoughby); Brook Williams (Bereton); Gary Bond (Smeaton); Marne Maitland (Campeggio); Cyril Luckham (Prior Houghton); Lilian Hutchins, Ann Tirard (Catherine's Spanish Ladies-in-Waiting); Amanda Walker, Charlotte Selwyn, Elizabeth Counsell (Anne's Ladies-in-Waiting); Juliet Kempson, Fiona Hartford (Catherine's English Ladies-in-Waiting); Kate Burton (Serving Maid); Elizabeth Taylor (Courtesan); Liza Todd Burton (Beggar Maid)

HENRY VIII AND HIS SIX WIVES, *Anglo-EMI Productions*, released September 1972

Executive producer, Mark Shivas; Producer, Roy Baird; Director, Waris Hussein; Screenplay by Ian Thorne, based on the television series *The Six Wives of Henry VIII*; Photography, Peter Suschitzky; Production designer, Roy Stannard; Set decorator, Ian Whittaker; Costumes, John Bloomfield; Production supervisor, John Comfort; Music and music director, David Munro; Music performed by The Early Music Consort of London; Choreography, Terry Gilbert; Keith Michell's makeup, Pam Meager; Sound recording, Brian Simmons; Editor, John Bloom

Keith Michell (Henry VIII); Frances Cuka (Catherine of Aragon); Charlotte Rampling (Anne Boleyn); Jane Asher (Jane Seymour); Jenny Bos (Anne of Cleves); Lynne Frederick (Catherine Howard); Barbara LeighHunt (Catherine Parr); Donald Pleasence (Thomas Cromwell); Brian Blessed (Suffolk); Michael Gough (Norfolk); Bernard Hepton (Cranmer); John Bryans (Cardinal Wolsey); Michael Byrne (Edward Seymour); Damien Thomas (Mark Smeaton); Michael Goodliffe (Thomas More); Robin Sachs (Thomas Culpepper); Garfield Morgan (Gardiner); David Ballie (Norris); Clive Merrison (Weston); Peter Clay (Thomas Seymour); Mark York (Brereton); Nicholas Amer (Chapuys); Sarah Long (Mary); Peter Madden (Fisher); Basil Clarke (Abbot); Simon Henderson (Prince Edward); John Bennett (Wriothesley); Richard Warner (Warham); Michael Godfrey (Sir Ralph Ellerker); Alan Rowe (French Ambassador); Margaret Ward (Lady Rochford); Colin Rix (Bowes); Imogene Claire (Maria de Salinas)

TELEVISION

THE TRIAL OF ANNE BOLEYN, *Omnibus*, televised November 9, 1952 CBS 24 minutes

Produced by the CBS and the TV-Radio Workshop of the Ford Foundation; Producer, Alan Anderson; Director, Alex Segal; Teleplay by Maxwell Anderson; Host, Alistair Cooke. Premiere of the *Omnibus* series

Rex Harrison (Henry VIII); Lilli Palmer (Anne Boleyn); with Richard Kiley, Edwin Jerome, Jonathan Harris, Susanne Bloch, Robert Pastene

Premiere of Omnibus; Executive Producer, Robert Saudek; Producer, William Spier

Included: Excerpts from Gilbert & Sullivan's *The Mikado* with Martyn Green, Ella Halman; conducted by Lehman Engel

The Bad Men; a 22-minute teleplay by William Saroyan with Russell Collins, Joshua Shelley, Sidney Poitier, Mary Stuart, James Westerfield, Harry Bellaver, Malcolm Broderick, Sharon Porter

Film: *The Witch Doctor* with dancers Jean Leon Destine, Jeanne Damon, Alphonse Comber

THE SIX WIVES OF HENRY VIII, televised January 1 to February 5, 1970 BBC 6 episodes (90 minutes each); in U.S., televised August 1 to September 5, 1971 CBS

A British Broadcasting Corporation production; Producer, Mark Shivas; and Ronald Travers; Directors, John Glenister and Naomi Capon; Series based on an idea by Maurice Cowan; Production designer, Peter Seddon; Lighting, Robert Wright; Costumes, John Bloomfield; Makeup, Pam Burns; Music arranged by David Munrow; Narrator, Anthony Quayle; Teleplays, as noted:

CATHERINE OF ARAGON, televised January 1, 1970; Teleplay by Rosemary Anne Sisson; Director, John Glenister
Keith Michell (Henry VIII); Annette Crosbie (Catherine of Aragon); Dorothy Tutin (Anne Boleyn); John Baskcomb (Cardinal Wolsey); Patrick Troughton (Duke of Norfolk); Raymond Adamson (Duke of Suffolk); Charles Workman (Archbishop Warham); Geoffrey Lewis (Bishop Fisher); John Woodnutt (Henry VII); Martin Ratcliffe (Prince Arthur); Ken Wynne (Dr. De Puebla); Sally Travers (Dona Elvira Manuel); Joyce Mandre (Francesca De Carceres); Peter Stephens (Don Guiterre Gomez de Fuensalida); Robert Hartley (Bishop Fox); Will Leighton (Tutor); Ina de la Haye (Inez De Venegas); Ronald Adam (Cardinal Campeggio); Richard Burnett (Usher); Donald Bisset (Earl of Surrey); Margaret Ford (Marie De Salinas); Valentine Palmer (Lord Willoughby); Verina Greenlaw (Princess Mary); Edward Atienza (Eustache Chapuys); Peter Bennett (Nobleman)

ANNE BOLEYN, televised January 8, 1970; Teleplay by Nick McCarty; Director, Naomi Capon
Keith Michell (Henry VIII); Dorothy Tutin (Anne Boleyn); Michael Osborne (Mark Smeaton); Wolfe Morris (Thomas Cromwell); Patrick Troughton (Duke of Norfolk); Christopher Hancock (Sir Henry Norreys); Christopher Beeching (Earl of Surrey); Sheila Burrell (Lady Rochford); Hilary Mason (Lady Boleyn); Jonathan Newth (George Viscount Rochford); Bernard Hepton (Archibishop Cranmer); Anne Stallybrass (Jane Seymour); Arnold Peters (Armourer); Robert Cawdron (Sir William Kingston); Patricia Heneghan (Lady Kingston); Peter Cellier (Sir Christopher Hales)

JANE SEYMOUR, televised January 15, 1970; Teleplay by Ian Thorne; Director, John Glenister
Keith Michell (Henry VIII); Anne Stallybrass (Jane Seymour); Daniel Moynihan (Edward Seymour); Gillian Bailey (Dorothy Seymour); Dorothy Black (Lady Margaret Seymour); Howard Lang (Sir John Seymour); William Abney (Sir Francis Bryan); Alison Frazer (Princess Mary); Marion Methie (Lady Exeter); Louis Haslar (Sir Nicholas Carew); Jo Kendall (Anne Stanhope); Bernard Hepton (Thomas Cranmer); Sheila Burrell (Lady Rochford); Patrick Troughton (Duke of Norfolk); Basil Dignam (Bishop Gardiner); Wolfe Morris (Thomas Cromwell); John Ronane (Thomas Seymour)

NOTE: Thorne's teleplay won Italy's Prix d'Iatlia Award for 1970.

ANNE OF CLEVES, televised January 22, 1970; Teleplay by Jean Morris; Director, John Glenister
Keith Michell (Henry VIII); Elvi Hale (Anne of Cleves); Bernard Hepton (Thomas Cranmer); Jody Schaller (Princess Elizabeth); Angela Pleasence (Catherine Howard); Peter Reeves (Philip of Hesse); Patrick Godfrey (Sir Thomas Wriothesley); Wolfe Morris (Thomas Cromwell); Basil Dignam (Bishop Gardiner); James Mellor (Hans Holbein); William Maxwell (Wilhelm of Cleves); David Butler (Sir Christopher Mont); Norman Tyrrell (Chancellor of Cleves); Mollie Sugden (Lotte); Robert Jamee (Robert Barnes); Stephanie Lacey (Lady Frances); Melanie Ackland (Lady Margaret);

Michael Cullen (Servant); Freddy Wilson (Page); Norman Atkyns (Henry's Gentleman); Carol Macready (Amalie); Patrick Troughton (Duke of Norfolk)

CATHERINE HOWARD, televised January 29, 1970; Teleplay by Beverley Cross; Director, Naomi Capon
Keith Michell (Henry VIII); Angela Pleasence (Catherine Howard); Catherine Lacey (Dowager Duchess of Norfolk); Patrick Troughton (Duke of Norfolk); Ralph Bates (Thomas Culpepper); Simon Prebble (Francis Dereham); Bill Riley (Stanton); Sheila Burrell (Lady Rochford); Howard Goorney (Will Somers); Julia Cornelius (Anne Carey); Alberto Colzi (Ambassador of the Order of St. John of Jerusalem); John Richmond, William Curran (Surgeons); Sue Bishop, Unity Grimwood (Ladies-in-Waiting); Ruth and Paula Mills (Children); Frederick Clemson, Alistair Meldrum, Michael Pattern, Bill Jenner (Knights and Soldiers)

CATHERINE PARR, televised February 5, 1970; Teleplay by John Prebble; Director, Naomi Capon
Keith Michell (Henry VIII); Rosalie Crutchley (Catherine Parr); Howard Goorney (Will Somers); John Ronane (Sir Thomas Seymour); Daniel Moynihan (Lord Hertford); Basil Dignam (Stephen Gardiner); Patrick Godfrey (Sir Thomas Wriothesley); Karen Ford (Lady Lane); Jim Kennedy (Anthony Knevet); Elizabeth Bell (Anne Askew); Edward Atienza (Chapuys); Bernard Hepton (Thomas Cranmer); Alison Frazer (Princess Mary)

HENRY VIII, The Shakespeare Plays, televised February 25, 1979 BBC 3 hours; in U.S. on PBS, April 25, 1979
A Production of BBC and Time-Life; Producer and script editor, Cedric Messina; Director, Kevin Billington; Series Producer, Ann Blumenthal;
John Stride (King Henry VIII); Claire Bloom (Queen Katherine); Barbara Kellerman (Anne Bullen); Timothy West (Cardinal Wolsey); Michael Poole (Cardinal Campeius); Ronald Pickup (Archbishop Cranmer); Jeremy Kemp (Duke of Norfolk); Julian Glover (Duke of Buckingham); Peter Vaughan (Bishop of Winchester); David Rintoul (Lord Abergavenny); John Rowe (Thomas Cromwell); David Troughton (Surveyor)

A MAN FOR ALL SEASONS, televised December 7, 1988 TNT 3 hours
(see separate entry)

HOBSON'S CHOICE
A Comedy by Harold Brighouse (1915)

Synopsis

Blustering, hard-drinking Henry Horatio Hobson despairs of ever finding a son-in-law who could tolerate his domineering, abusive, self-sufficient oldest daughter, Maggie, who manages his Lancashire bootshop. Maggie, meanwhile, has noticed meek, bashful cobbler Willy Mossop, whose talents as a bootmaker have been admired by the village grand dame who will have her shoes made only by him.

Maggie decides that, despite his engagement to Ada Figgins, Mossop will be her husband. She gets her sisters married and forces her penurious, overbearing father into providing ample dowries for them. Then she establishes Willy in their own shoemaking shop and through her constant but deceptively tender dominance instills authority and assertiveness in her timid uneducated new husband. When Horatio's drinking increases and his business declines, Maggie returns home and coerces her nearly apoplectic father into signing an agreement for the establishment of one shop to be called Mossop and Hobson.

Comment and Critique

Harold Brighouse's title for his delightful comedy inspired by seventeenth century British deliveryman Thomas Hobson, who required every customer arriving at his stable to take the horse in the stall nearest the door; or, as Webster defines Hobson's choice, "apparently free choice with no real alternative."

Although a typically British play about an Englishman in the North Country, Brighouse's comedy curiously had its world premiere on Broadway at the Princess Theatre in November 1915. *The New York Dramatic Mirror* reported, "Mr. Brighouse is one of the Stanley Houghton group of playwrights brought into prominence through the activities of Miss Horniman and her Manchester Repertory Theatre...[He] retains his gift for the whimsical but has enveloped his whimsicality, his love for the quaint and picturesquely provincial, with such freshness of observation... accuracy of caricature, and humanness of dialogue that he has provided one of the most delightful plays of recent years."

Munsey magazine found that *Hobson's Choice* "does for Lancashire what *Bunty Pulls the Strings* did for Scotland, and the Shuberts were fortunate enough to secure Molly Pearson, the famous *Bunty*, for the string-puller in *Hobson*...As Willy Mossop, Whitford Kane gives a really wonderful performance...Old man Hobson falls to A. G. Andrews, who, though he is an American, born in Buffalo in 1857, has done much of his work on the other side of the Atlantic, where he played for several seasons with Henry Irving's company."

The play opened the following year in London, had a successful 246 performance run and went on to become a hardy perennial on the British stage.

Nearly a half century after *Hobson's Choice* first appeared on the stage, Britain's National Theatre revived the comedy at London's Old Vic in January 1964. "The National Theatre people were wise to bring *Hobson's Choice* into their repertoire. It is the best of its kind; it is robust, richly comic and at times -- although, one suspects, in spite of oneself -- moving. It is also a classic...No audience could fail to enjoy it hugely," Hugh Leonard (*Plays and Players*) reported. "Michael Redgrave's Hobson has been criticised -- unjustly I think -- for being a Lancastrian King Lear... Joan Plowright as Maggie was quite magnificent...As Willy, Frank Finlay went at it the hard way. He gave us a very human person, instead of the usual Formbyish clown...This was the Willy of whom Brighouse wrote: 'He is not stupid, but stunted mentally by a brutalised childhood.'" Critic Leonard concluded, "John Dexter's production had a lively pace to begin with, and later settled down comfortably."

London's *Sphere* added, "This play gained a huge success in America, and a smaller success in London. In the new production, it at last finds its right place as a classic of British comedy. This is the sort of revival which the National Theatre should undertake and which it has brought off with scrupulous care."

The following season, The National Theatre recast *Hobson's Choice*, proving the play be virtually actor-proof. Peter Roberts (*Plays and Players*) admired both Billie

Whitelaw's portrayal of Maggie and Colin Blakely's "lightweight Falstaff...a rather pathetic creature under all the blustering. As a performance it lacks the sinister undertones that Charles Laughton brought to the famous film performance of the part, [but] Mr. Blakely's reading dovetails beautifully with Frank Finlay's very human Willy Mossop."

New Haven's Long Wharf Theatre revived the Brighouse comedy in 1977. "*Hobson's Choice*, the 62-year-old play about a comic but effective revolution in a shoe shop, is more than a chestnut but less than a classic. Harold Brighouse's play...is like an old well-made sofa. Its frame is solid and it has details of craftsmanship that are quite out of the ordinary, and a long, slow sag in the middle," Richard Eder wrote in *The New York Times*. "The main strength of the Long Wharf production is the acting of Joyce Ebert as Maggie ...Frank Converse is a fine counterpoint as the rabbity Massop...William Swetland gives a sharp, well-timed performance as Hobson."

Hobson's Choice was revived at London's Haymarket Theatre in 1982. Richard Findlater (*Plays and Players*) complimented Triumph Productions' "shrewd and successful choice in picking Harold Brighouse's 1915 comedy about 1880 Salford for the opener of its Hay-market repertory season...*Hobson's Choice* is the hardiest perennial of the so-called Manchester school -- virtually its only survivor on the stage in the last twenty years..." Trevor Peacock's portrayal of Willy Mossop was described as "an infectiously gleeful performance stuffed with clownish subtleties...a joy to watch, a pleasure to remember." Anthony Quayle's Hobson "seems, from the start, crumbling and bemused; a heavy drinker approaching a crisis of alcoholism, a failed family tyrant on the brink of defeat." Penelope Keith, one of England's excellent comediennes, cast as the domineering Maggie was found to be "enjoyable" with "a skillful performance" in which "she makes the comic machinery work all the better because of her impassive refusal to prettify the part."

Roger O. Hirson and Ketti Frings adapted *Hobson's Choice* to the Broadway musical stage in 1966 as *Walking Happy*, starring England's Norman Wisdom, along with Louise Troy and George Rose. "*Walking Happy* Is a Glad Show Packed With Songs and Dances," reported John Chapman (*Daily News*). "This is a completely professional work in the musical theatre, and it rejoices in good taste as well as high spirits...The libretto by Roger O. Hirson and Ketti Frings is thoroughly expert ...And the songs -- lyrics by Sammy Cahn, music by Jimmy van Heusen -- shimmer with good spirits."

"The big asset *Walking Happy* has to offer is Norman Wisdom," wrote Richard Watts, Jr. (*New York Post*). "The popular English comedian is making his overdue American debut...and his endearing portrayal of a plaintive, woebegone little underdog is the brightest and most appealing feature of the evening that is cheerful, friendly and goodhearted but has the misfortune to be otherwise disappointingly lacking in exhilaration." Norman Nadel (*Herald Journal Tribune*) added, "*Hobson's Choice* is a lovely play, though you'd scarcely suspect it from *Walking Happy*...The one joy of *Walking Happy* is the American debut of England's favorite entertainer, Norman Wisdom...[He] is a superb comedian, and so fine an actor that his comedy seems ingrained in the man he portrays, rather than merely superimposed."

Walter Kerr (*The New York Times*) found *Walking Happy* "an easygoing, unpretentious, minor-league musical that is neatly put together.: Wisdom was described as looking "rather like Fred Astaire crossed with Stan Laurel...Perhaps with a few shreds of Jimmy Savo thrown in...but he is, it must be said, his own man, a zany original with ruffled hair, rueful eyes, and an altogether irresistible appeal...He is Harlequin come to life among the British lower classes and it was nice getting to know him..."

Harold Brighouse's play had been brought to the screen in England twice, in 1920 and 1931, both versions long-forgotten, before the definitive 1954 *Hobson's Choice* was released. "David Lean has produced and directed a delightful and rewarding British film," reported Bosley Crowther (*The New York Times*). "Those who have wished for some time that Charles Laughton might have a role worthy of his skill and his perception in transmitting character will be pleased to discover that he has it in this particularly characterful film...and [John] Mills is hilariously revealing of an humble slavey who is made to grow." (John Mills had replaced ill Robert Donat as Willy Mossop.) David Lean later commented on the making of *Hobson's Choice*, his last black and white film: "Most of the time, directing actors is a matter of gentle suppression and gentle encouragement. This was certainly true of Laughton, a remarkable artist...My job is to make the best use of their talents, and there are various ways of doing it with different actors."

Gerald Pratley (*The Cinema of David Lean*) wrote, "The film is attractively made, a comedy-drama from Lancashire life and manners, close to the characters and their time, larger than life perhaps, as in Dickens, but still recognisable as natural and determined people. Lean again turned a play into a fine piece of cinema with perfect settings."

English critic Penelope Houston was less enthused about Lean's classic writing, "*Hobson's Choice* is unmistakingly the work of a craftsman; but an over-elaborate pursuit of effects, alien to the tone of the play, cannot but overweight the material...In this version, Charles Laughton's playing, for all its technical finesse, fails to bring Hobson convincingly to life, and John Mills is none too happily cast as Mossop. Brenda de Banzie, though, plays the hard-headed, bullying Maggie with warmth and real human feeling; her performance is the best thing in the film." She concluded by observing that David Lean "displays his customary technical proficiency, and his customary coldness in the handling of human relationships."

The BBC mounted two television productions of *Hobson's Choice*: an hour-long version in 1950 with Edgar K. Bruce, Belle Chrystall and Wilfred Pickles in the leads, and a three-part one in 1967 with Peter Woodthrope, Mary Miller and Kenneth Colley.

In December 1983, the first American television *Hobson's Choice* premiered, with the setting switched from 19th century Lancashire to New Orleans, circa 1914. The made-for-TV film adapted by Burt Prelutsky and directed by Gilbert Cates was, according to John J. O'Connor (*The New York Times*), "Never quite as sharp, or even convincing, as it should be." Ever-reliable Jack Warden was seen as being "...not terribly persuasive as a New Orleans gentleman, albeit a drunken one. Sharon Gless is more successful with Maggie, giving the character an admirably unyielding integrity." Richard Thomas' Mossop was to critic O'Connor, "a somewhat unsympathetic wimp." Only one performance was a stand-out -- that of Lillian Gish as the crisp matron Miss Molly Winkle whom O'Connor properly appraised as "a twinkling delight."

STAGE

Princess Theatre, New York, opened November 2, 1915; moved to *Comedy Theatre*, November 8, 1915 135 performances
Produced by F. Ray Comstock; A Comedy by Harold Brighouse; Director B. Iden Payne

A. G. Andrews (Henry Horatio Hobson); Molly Pearson (Maggie Hobson); Whitford Kane (Willy Mossop); Viola Roach (Alice Hobson); Olive Wilmet Davis (succeeded by Alice Seymour) (Vickey Hobson); Barrett Parker (Fred Beenstock); Marie Hudspeth (Mrs. Hepworth); Harry J. Ashford (Timothy "Tubby" Wadlow); Agnes Dorntee (Ada Figgins); Harold de Becker (Albert Prosser); Walter Fredericks (Jim Heeler)

Apollo Theatre, London, opened June 22, 1916; moved to *Prince of Wales's Theatre*, November 20, 1916 246 performances
Produced and Directed by Albert De Courville; A Comedy by Harold Brighouse

Norman McKinnel (Henry Horatio Hobson); Edyth Goodall (Maggie Hobson); Joe Nightingale (Willy Mossop); Lydia Billbrooke (Alice Hobson); Hilda Davies (Vickey Hobson); Jefferson Gore (Fred Beenstock); Dora Gregory (Mrs. Hepworth); Sydney Paxton (Timothy "Tubby" Wadlow); Mary Byron (Ada Figgins); Reginald Fry (Albert Prosser); J. Cooke Beresford (Jim Heeler); J. Fisher White (Dr. Macfarlane)

Arts Theatre, London, opened June 4, 1952
A Comedy by Harold Brighouse; Director, Roy Rich

David Bird (Henry Horatio Hobson); Pauline Jameson (Maggie Hobson); Donald Pleasance (Willy Mossop); Julia Braddock (Alice Hobson); Marcia Ashton (Vickey Hobson); Barbara Cavan (Mrs. Hepworth); Denis Holmes (Fred Beenstock); Beryl Bainbridge (Ada Figgins); Hal Osmond (Jim Heeler); Jack Howarth (Timothy Wadlow); Willoughby Gray (Dr. MacFarlane); Patrick McGoohan (Albert Prosser)

Old Vic Theatre, London, opened January 7, 1964
Produced by The National Theatre Company; A Comedy by Harold Brighouse; Director, John Dexter; Assistant director, Piers Haggard; Production designed by Motley; Lighting, Ronald Cox

Michael Redgrave (Henry Horatio Hobson); Joan Plowright (Maggie Hobson); Frank Finlay (Willy Mossop); Mary Miller (Alice Hobson); Jeanne Hepple (Vickey Hobson); Harry Lomax (Jim Heeler); Reginald Green (Tubby Wadlow); Enid Lorimer (Mrs. Hepworth); Raymond Clarke (Fred Beenstock); Terence Kanpp (Albert Prosser); Jean Rogers (Ada Figgins); Anthony Nichols (Dr. MacFarlane); Elizabeth Burger, Alan Ridgway (Customers); Christopher Chittell, Alan Ridgeway (Children)

Old Vic Theatre, London, opened March 9, 1965
Produced by The National Theatre Company; A Comedy by Harold Brighouse; Directed by John Dexter and Piers Haggard; Production designed by Motley; Lighting, Ronald Cox

Colin Blakely (Henry Horatio Hobson); Billie Whitelaw (Maggie Hobson); Frank Finlay (Willy Mossop); Jeanne Hepple (Alice Hobson); Sheila Reid (Vickey Hobson); Harry Lomax (Jim Heeler); Reginald Green (Tubby Wadlow); Enid Lorimer (Mrs. Hepworth); George Innes (Fred Beenstock); Terence Knapp (Albert Prosser); Petronella Barker (Ada Figgins); Frank Wylie (Dr. MacFarlane)

WALKING HAPPY, *Lunt-Fontanne Theatre*, New York, opened November 26, 1966 161 performances
Produced by Feuer and Martin; A Musical comedy based on the play *Hobson's Choice* by Harold Brighouse; Director, Cy Feuer; Book by Roger O. Hirson and Ketti Frings; Music by James Van Heusen; Lyrics by Sammy Cahn; Settings and Lighting,

Robert Randolph; Costumes, Robert Fletcher; Musical Direction and Vocal Arrangements, Herbert Grossman; Dances and Musical Numbers staged by Danny Daniels; Orchestrations by Larry Wilcox; Dance music arranged by Ed Scott; Company manager, Milton M. Pollack; Stage managers, Phil Friedman and Merritt Thompson

Norman Wisdom (Will Mossop); Louise Troy (succeeded by Anne Rogers) (Maggie Hobson); George Rose (Henry Horatio Hobson); Lucille Benson (Mrs. Figgins); Gordon Dilworth (Tubby Wadlow); Ed Bakey (succeeded by Leonard Drum) (George Beenstock); Thomas Boyd (Minns); Casper Roos (Denton); Carl Nicholas (Tudsbury); Sharon Dierking (Alice Hobson); Gretchen Van Aken (Vickie Hobson); Michael Berkson (Freddie Beenstock); Emma Trekman (Mrs. Hepworth); Jane Lughlin (Ada Figgins); Ian Garry, Al Lanti (Figgins Brothers); Richard Sederholm (Handbill Boy); Steven Jacobs (Footman); Eleanor Bergquist (Customer); Burt Bier (Thief); Chad Block (Policeman); Richard Korthaze (Beggar); James B. Spann (Albert Beenstock); Michael Quinn (Heeler); Burt Bier, Chard Block, Thomas Boyd, Ian Garry, Gene Gavin, Steven Jacobs, Richard Korthaze, Al Lanti, Carl Nicholas, Don Percassi, Michael Quinn, Casper Roos, Richard Sderhom, Dan Siretta (Townsmen); Eleanor Berquist, Diane L. Blair, Sandra Brewer, Ellen Graff, Marian Haraldson, Jane Laughlin, Marie Patrice O'Neill, Nada Rowand, Anne Wallace (Townswomen)

MUSICAL NUMBERS: "Think of Something Else"; "Where Was I?"; "How D'Ya Talk to a Girl?"; "Clog and Grog"; "If I Be Your Best Chance"; "A Joyful Thing"; "What Makes It Happen"; "Use Your Noggin"; "You're Right, You're Right"; "I'll Make a Man of the Man"; "Walking Happy"; "I Don't Think I'm in Love"; "Such a Sociable Sort"; "It Might as Well Be Her"; "People Who Are Nice"

Original cast recording: Capitol Records

WALKING HAPPY, *Curran Theatre*, San Francisco, opened April 25, 1967
Produced by Feuer and Martin, by arrangement with Lester Linsk; Presented by the San Francisco Civic Light Opera Association; A Musical comedy based on the play *Hobson's Choice* by Harold Brighouse; Director, Cy Feuer; Book by Roger O. Hirson and Ketti Frings; Music by James Van Heusen; Lyrics by Sammy Cahn; Scenery and Lighting, Robert Randolph; Costumes, Robert Fletcher; Dance and Musical numbers staged by Danny Daniels; Music director, Julian Stein; Orchestrations, Larry Wilcox; Dance music arranged by Ed Scott

Norman Wisdom (Willy Mossop); Anne Rogers (Maggie Hobson); George Rose (Henry Horatio Hobson); Sharon Dierking (Alice Hobson); Lucille Benson (Mrs. Figgins); Hallie Walker (Vickie Hobson); Leonard Drum (George Beenstock); Thomas Boyd (Minns); Burt Bier (Denton); Gordon Dilworth (Tubby Wadlow); Emma Trekman (Mrs. Hepworth); Michael Berkson (Freddie Beenstock); Ellen Graff (Ada Figgins); Ian Garry, Dan Siretta (Figgins Brothers); Carl Nicholas (Tudsbury); Michael Quinn (Heeler); James B. Spann (Albert Beenstock); Richard Korthaze (Footman); Al Lanti (The Clog Man); Eleanor Bergquist (Customer); Sam Schuman (Handbill Boy); Burt Bier, Gene Cooper, Larry Devon, Dom Salinara, Thomas Boyd, Ian Garry, Gene Gavin, Richard Korthaze, Al Lanti, Stan Mazin, Carl Nicholas, Michael Quinn, Sam Schuman, Dan Diretta (Townsmen); Eleanor Bergquist, Diane L. Blair, Annette Cummings, Joyce Driscoll, Ellen Graff, Marian Haraldson, Karen Kristin, Marie Patrice O'Neill, Nada Rowand (Townswomen)

WALKING HAPPY, *Kenley (Ohio) Theatre*, opened July 27, 1969
Produced by John Kenley; A Musical Comedy based on Harold Brighouse's play *Hobson's Choice*; Director, Jack Leigh; Book by Roger O. Hirson and Ketti Frings; Music by James Van Heusen; Lyrics by Sammy Cahn; Choreography, Mario Melodia; Setting, Patrick Belew; Scenic artist, Phil Rozen; Technical director, Wayne Muller; Musical director, John De Main; Stage manager, Paul Stetz

Noel Harrison (Willy Mossop); Linda Lavin (Maggie Hobson); Dean Dittmann (Henry Horatio Hobson); Betty Kovacs (Alice Hobson); Dana Snyder (Vickey Hobson); Carol Trigg (Mrs. Hepworth); Leonard Drum (George Beenstock); Michael Arle (Albert Beenstock); Don Amendolia (Freddie Beenstock); Jack De Leon (Tubby Wadlow); Roxanne Ebner (Ada Figgins); Leo Muller (Minns); Renato Vellutino (Denton); Philip Lucas (Tudsbury); Frank Echols (Heeler); Carol Trigg (Mrs. Figgins); Marti Deats (Customer); Rick Runyeon (Handbill Boy); Georgia Neu, Carol Trigg, Roxanne Ebner, Chris Carlson, Melissa Bassford, Betty Kovacs, Penny Smyser, Diane Mauthe, Marti Deats, Judy Simon, Dana Snyder, John Daenen, Don Amendolia, Bill Smith, Philip Lucas, Renato Vellutino, Leonard Liberman, Sammy Williams, Steve Mesaros, Leo Muller, Rick Runyeon (Singers and Dancers)

HOBSON'S CHOICE, *Young Vic Theatre*, London, opened January 29, 1973
Produced by the Young Vic Company; A Comedy by Harold Brighouse; Director, Bernard Goss; Decor, Alan Barlow; Lighting, David Watson

Peter Bayliss (Henry Horatio Hobson); Anne Stallybrass (Maggie Hobson); Andrew Robertson (Willy Mossop); Lois Daine (Alice Hobson); Mel Martin (Vickey Hobson); Ian Charleston (Fred Beenstock); Julia McCarthy (Mrs. Hepworth); Ian Taylor (Jim Heeler); Alun Lewis (Albert Prosser); Alan Foss (Tubby Wadlow); Michael Byrne (Dr. MacFarlane); Ursula Mohan (Ada Figgins)

Long Wharf Theatre, New Haven, opened October 23, 1977
Produced by the Long Wharf Theatre, Arvin Brown, artistic director; Edgar Rosenblum, executive director; A Comedy by Harold Brighouse; Director, Arvin Brown; Settings by David Jenkins; Lighting by Jamie Gallagher; Costumes by Bill Walker; Music written and arranged by Terrence Sherman; Production stage manager, Anne Keefe

William Swetland (Henry Horatio Hobson); Joyce Ebert (Maggie Hobson); Frank Converse (Willy Mossop); Laurie Kennedy (Alice Hobson); Susan Sharkey (Vickey Hobson); Mary Fogarty (Mrs. Hepworth); Richard Backus (Albert Prosser); Philip Polito (Tubby Wadlow); Harry Groener (Fred Beenstock); Ellin Roskin (Ada Figgins); Emery Battis (Dr. MacFarlane); Richard Mathews (Jim Heeler)

Lyric Hammersmith, London, opened February 2 through March 8, 1981
A Comedy by Harold Brighouse; Director, David Giles; Settings, Kenneth Mellor; Lighting, Mark Dawson; Costumes, Mark Negin

Arthur Lowe (Henry Horatio Hobson); Julia McKenzie (Maggie Hobson); Ronald Pickup (Willy Mossop); Lesley Manville (Alice Hobson); Veronica Sowerby (Vickey Hobson); Joan Cooper (Mrs. Hepworth); Jenny Howe (Ada Figgins); Stephen Reynolds (Fred Beenstock); Clifford Parrish (Dr. MacFarlane); Adam Bareham (Albert Prosser)

Theatre Royal Haymarket, London, opened February 11, 1982

Produced by Duncan C. Weldon for Triumph Theatre Productions Ltd; A Comedy by Harold Brighouse; Director, Ronald Eyre; Settings, Kenneth Mellor; Lighting, Mark Pritchard; Costumes, Michael Stennett

Anthony Quayle (Henry Horatio Hobson); Penelope Keith (Maggie Hobson); Trevor Peacock (Willy Mossop); Anita Carey (Alice Hobson); Belinda Lang (Vickey Hobson); Carmen Silvera (Mrs. Hepworth); Michael Bilton (Timothy "Tubby" Wadlow); Gordon Kaye (Jim Heeler); Annette Badland (Ada Figgins); Mark Drewry (Fred Beenstock); John Grieve (Dr. MacFarlane); Jonathan Coy (Albert Prosser)

SCREEN

HOBSON'S CHOICE, Master Films (BEF), released March 1920
Director, Percy Nash; Screenplay by W. C. Rowden, based on the play by Harold Brighouse

Arthur Pitt (Henry Horatio Hobson); Joe Nightingale (Will Mossup); Joan Ritz (Maggie Hobson); George Wynn (Albert Prosser); Joan Cockram (Vickey Hobson); Charles Heslop (Fred Beenstock); Mary Byron (Ada Figgins); Louis Rihill (Jim Heeler); Ada King (Mrs. Hepworth); Phyllis Birkett (Alice Hobson); Charles Stone (Tubby Wadlow); Judd Green (Landlord)

Wardour Film (BIP), released October 1931
Director, Thomas Bentley; Screenplay by Frank Launder, based on the play by Harold Brighouse

James Harcourt (Henry Horatio Hobson); Frank Pettingell (Will Mossup); Viola Lyel (Maggie Hobson); Reginald Bach (Albert Prosser); Belle Chrystal (Vickey Hobson); Basil Moss (Freddy Beenstock); Kathleen Harrison (Ada Figgins); Herbert Lomas (Jim Heeler); Amy Veness (Mrs. Hepworth); Joan Maude (Alice Hobson); Jay Laurier (Tibby Wadlow)

British Lion Films, released February 1954
Produced by London Films; A David Lean Production; Associate producer, Norman Spencer; Director, David Lean; Screenplay, David Lean, Norman Spencer and Wynward Browne, based on the play by Harold Brighouse; Photography, Jack Hildyard; Art director, Wilfrid Shingleton; Costumes, John Armstrong; Music, Malcolm Arnold; Sound, John Cox; Assistant director, Adrian Pryce-Jones; Editor, Peter Taylor

Charles Laughton (Henry Horatio Hobson); John Mills (Willy Mossop); Brenda de Banzie (Maggie Hobson); Richard Wattis (Albert Prosser); Prunella Scales (Vickey Hobson); Derek Bolmfield (Freddy Beenstock); Dorothy Gordon (Ada Figgins); Joseph Tomelty (Jim Heeler); Helen Haye (Mrs. Hepworth); Julian Mitchell (Sam Minns); Gibb McLaughlin (Tudsbury); Philip Stainton (Denton); Daphne Anderson (Alice Hobson); Madge Brindley (Mrs. Figgins); John Laurie (Dr. MacFarlane); Raymond Huntley (Pat Beenstock); Jack Howarth (Tubby Wadlow); Herbert C. Wanton (Printer)

TELEVISION

HOBSON'S CHOICE, televised April 2, 1950 BBC I hour
A British Broadcasting Corporation production; Director, Eric Fawcett; A Comedy by Harold Brighouse; Production designer, James Bould

Edgar K. Bruce (Henry Horatio Hobson); Belle Chrystall (Maggie Hobson); Wilfred Pickles (Willy Mossop); Sonia Williams (Alice Hobson); Sylvia Clarke (Vickey Hobson); Alan Bromly (Albert Prosser); Beatrice Varley (Mrs. Hepworth); Jack Howarth (Timothy "Tubby" Wadlow); Frank Atkinson (Jim Heeler); Sibell Gill (Ada Figins); Dennis Fraser (Fred Beenstock); Alistair Hunter (Dr. Macfarlane)

HOBSON'S CHOICE, televised September 19 to October 10, 1967 BBC 3 episodes 30 minutes each
A British Broadcasting Corporation production; Director, Michael Simpson; A Comedy by Harold Brighouse, adapted for television by Michael Simpson; Production designer, Don Brewer; Costumes, Maureen Muggeridge; Makeup, Jackie Jeffries; Sound, Brian Forgham; Cameras, Dennis Channon, Tommy Claydon

Peter Woodthorpe (Henry Horatio Hobson); Mary Miller (Maggie Hobson); Kenneth Colley (Willy Mossop); Shirley Stelfox (Alice Hobson); Sian Davies (Vickey Hobson); Patrick Godfrey (Albert Prosser/Dr. Macfarlane); Ann Mitchell (Ada Figgins); Daphne Heard (Mrs. Hepworth); Joby Blanshard (Jim Heeler); John Gill (Tubby Wadlow); Struan Rodger (Fred Beenstock)

HOBSON'S CHOICE, televised December 21, 1983 CBS 2 hours
A Blue-Green Production in association with CBS Entertainment; Produced by Blue Andre and Vanessa Greene; Associate producer, Alice Pardo; Director, Gilbert Cates; Teleplay by Burt Prelutsky, based on the play by Harold Brighouse; Photography, Isidore Mankofsky; Art director, Richard Berger; Set decorator, Joe D. Mitchell; Costumes, Patricia Nantz; Music, Robert Drasnin; Editor, Peter E. Berger

Richard Thomas (Willy Mossop); Sharon Gless (Maggie Hobson); Jack Warden (Henry Hobson); Lillian Gish (Miss Molly Winkle); Robert Englund (Freddy Beenstock); Wynn Irwin (A. D. Hallem); Lenora May (Vickey Hobson); Jennifer Holmes (Alice Hobson); Henry G. Sanders (Tubby); Frank Dent (Albert Prosser); Duncan Ross (Dr. MacFarlane); Jack Hollahan (Father Lawrence); Michael Morrison (Joey); Ron Gural (Red); Becki Davis (Mabel Higgins); Lenore Banks (Mrs. Higgins); Stocker Pontelieu (Jason Monroe); Barbara Chaney (Miss Amy); Bert Remsen (Homer Ralston); Robert Earle (Ross Ferber); Bill Holliday (Bob McCaulley); Lyla May Owen (Waitress); Matt Sorel (Taxi Driver); Donna Thompson (Bank teller); John Schluter (Chauffeur); Nimard File (Bank teller); Charles Szasley (Trumpeterfather); Kenyatto Szasley (Trumpeterson); Joe Catalanotto (Weight guesser)

HOLIDAY

A Comedy by Philip Barry (1929)

Synopsis

Socialite Julia Seton introduces her prospective husband, young lawyer Johnny Case, who has struck it rich in the stock market, to her very wealthy Manhattan family. Edward Seton, Julia's stuffy, imperious father, strongly opposes Johnny's plan for an extended holiday on the French Riviera after the marriage with his free-spirited friends, Nick and Susan Potter. Julia's non-conformist sister, Linda, however, approves of Johnny's philosophical holidaying while young and working when older.

Brother Ned Seton is blissfully happy on his extensive alcoholic holiday to oblivion. Julia and Johnny separate but Linda and Johnny find they are kindred souls and leave for their honeymoon and that disputed holiday.

Comment and Critique

Few American playwrights wrote more trenchant and witty dialogue depicting his generation than Philip Jerome Quinn Barry. *Holiday* followed Barry's 1927 hit comedy *Paris Bound* and was called "a holiday in playmaking" by Brooks Atkinson of *The New York Times*. "With his marvelous gift for spinning, spiraling humors, Philip Barry keeps life gay through most of his new spindrift comedy *Holiday*...[he] is effortless with dialogue and characters. But pressing a story around them still keeps him uneasy. *Holiday* does not flow as graciously as *Paris Bound* and does not curl around ideas so amiably. But it has savor, fresh color and sunny merriment."

Robert Benchley (*The New Yorker*) advised, "The greatest cause for thanksgiving which the week devoted to that occupation gave Broadway is Philip Barry's new play, *Holiday*...[with] dialogue, which is half nonsense, half wisdom, and together different from the dialogue anyone else writes." *Time* magazine noted, "Author Philip Barry suddenly twists the mood of *Holiday* from one of gaiety to one of longing. [He] wrote *Paris Bound*, a light cocktail of adultery and wit; like that fine play, *Holiday* begins frivolously ...the people are almost real and the ones who should be are completely charming. So are the actors who make them real."

Robert Garland (*New York World-Telegram*) reported, "In the sparking new piece at the Plymouth -- *Holiday* by Philip Barry -- there is a great moral lesson. In three wise and worldly acts and a couple of likely looking scenes, the playwright does what he can to prove that all shirk and no pay make Johnny Case a bright boy...*Holiday* may not be another *Paris Bound*, but, nevertheless, it is a smart and topsy-turvy comedy."

Holiday returned to Broadway forty-five years later in 1973. Clive Barnes (*The New York Times*), conceding that Philip Barry remained known mainly as the playwright of *The Philadelphia Story*, felt *Holiday* has "too long been shamefully neglected" and that Barry's plays "survive better than those of his weightier contemporaries...language and character are the two keys to a playwright. With Mr. Barry, the language can be really dazzingly...*Holiday* has come up very bright and interestingly." *Time* magazine, however, felt, "Barry was not quite up to the company he tried to keep. He lacked [Noel] Coward's dry crystal tone, [Cole] Porter's slyly sexy urban ennui. [F. Scott] Fitzgerald's tender romantic imagination and [George Bernard] Shaw's intellect..."

Barry, one of American's finest playwrights of sophisticated comedy, died on December 3, 1949, at age fifty-three, long before seeing *Holiday*, or for that matter even *The Philadelphia Story*, musicalized -- both with Cole Porter scores.

In 1979, Burt Shevelove devised *Happy New Year*, a musical version of Philip Barry's *Holiday* paced with obscure Cole Porter songs. The combination of Barry and Porter, again, would have appeared to be a winning, if posthumous, collaboration but, despite Barry's witty dialogue and Porter's equally sophisticated lyrics and music, the spark was not there.

Happy New Year had first been tested at the Stratford, Ontario, Canada Festival in the summer of 1979, and on April 27, 1980, Shevelove's musicalized *Holiday* opened on Broadway. Douglas Watt (*Daily News*) called it "a pale imitation of the genuine article... The result is a limp period show doing justice to neither Barry nor Porter...Shevelove hasn't had sufficient faith in the story, which Barry's buoyant dialogue carried off, to leave it alone, or simply trim it to musical needs...And I kept wishing for something else, for Barry and Porter locked up right now in a New Haven or Boston hotel room, dashing off new scenes and new songs and, of course, a whole new show."

Clive Barnes (*New York Post*) felt, "Making a musical from a Barry play and throwing in Porter music ought to be a unalloyed delight...the result was distinctly alloyed." Shevelove's tinkering with Barry's script was viewed by Barnes as creating "awesome mayhem on Barry's original play *Holiday*. He has turned a stylish comedy of manners into a commonplace book musical...The scenery by Michael Eagan looks rather like chunks of monumental masonry reduced to jumblesale trivia, but the costumes by Pierre Balmain, and supervised by John Falabella, are gems."

In *The New York Times*, Mel Gussow applauded *Happy New Year* as "a musical bouquet of gentle charm and piquancy. Porter and Barry are partners in urbanity and wit...Mr. Shevelove has matched Barry's happy-go-lucky book with a fountain of effervescent Porter tunes. In the Stratford tryout, songs were largely lesser known and of middling quality. At the Morosco most of them are first-class and include many Porter favorites..."

Holiday was revived at London's Old Vic in January 1987, stage by Lindsay Anderson. In Kenneth Hurren's *Plays and Players* review, he felt, "Of course, there was no disguising the fact that it is an *Old* play...and its two expensive sets, not to mention four or five more characters than a contemporary playwright would think essential...Whether it should have turned up on a London stage, when we have plenty of second-rate old plays of our own, is something else...Why Lindsay Anderson and his stars (Malcolm McDowell and Mary Steenburgen, husband and wife, themselves fugitive from the motion pictures) were attracted to it is almost as mysterious as why Barry wrote it. Barry was a writer who always seemed guilt-ridden because he had money and, in his comedies, cultivated a detached, mildly ironic attitude towards the gilded milieu in which his characters moved...The curious results, in *Holiday*, was that he came down in favour of the rich so long as they were idle rich..."

Mary Harron (London *Observer*) added, "Lindsay Anderson has never been noted for his feather-light touch, and he is hampered here by an unfamiliar American idiom and by the gross miscasting of Malcolm McDowell -- now a distinguished older man with silvering hair -- as the thrusting young American from the streets. Perhaps it seemed a cute idea to partner McDowell with his real-life wife Mary Steenburgen as Linda. In the event she saves the evening, for there would be no reason to recommend *Holiday* were it not for her radiant performance."

Holiday first came to the screen in 1930 with Ann Harding and Mary Astor as Linda and Julia Seton and Robert Ames as Johnny Case. "Two years ago Philip Barry's *Holiday* was one of the most popular plays on Broadway," reported *Liberty* magazine. "It has been expanded a little for the screen, but otherwise it is still Philip Barry's play and good entertainment...It is an amusing picture and sparkles with bright dialogue." *Time* magazine found Ann Harding "less mannered and more attractive than was Hope Williams on the stage" and that "the witty, rich and velvet sophistication out of which Philip Barry fashioned the best comedy of the 1928-1929 theatrical season has not, in translation to the screen, been exchanged for the crude, stuffy plushes of Hollywood naivete." *The New Yorker* added, "The acting in the picture is excellent, without that note of the gifted amateur which characterized the stage performance. The picture is long, a wordy affair as such an argumentative piece must be, but the sound mechanism carries it off with definite success."

Life magazine congratulated Pathe "for the excellent job they have done in transferring Philip Barry's play to the screen...We nominate Miss Harding's performance as one of the finest things of the year." Ann Harding was Oscar-nominated as Best Actress of the Year for her performance in *Holiday*, but the award went to Marie Dressler for her memorable work in *Min and Bill*.

Columbia Pictures several years later purchased several properties from RKO Radio (Pathe) Pictures for $80,000 including *Holiday*. Katharine Hepburn, who had understudied Hope Williams on Broadway as Linda Seton, was assigned the leading role in 1938 Columbia remake of the comedy, and her sparkling performance in it under George Cukor's direction refuted a recent poll of exhibitors labeling her "box-office poison." Donald Ogden Stewart (the Nick Potter of Broadway's 1928 production), a personal friend of Philip Barry, adapted *Holiday* to the screen. Edward Everett Horton again played the role of Nick Potter as he had in the 1930 film and, portraying the carefree Johnny Case to perfection, was Cary Grant, in the second of his four movies with Hepburn.

The star was labeled by Columbia "The New Hepburn," and *The New Yorker* acknowledged, "That Katharine Hepburn manages to make her role of Linda Seton in *Holiday* as appealing as she does is a triumph for her appearance and her talent. And doubtless Mr. Cukor's able handling had something to do with it. The distinction of the film and all its vitality rest upon the beautiful Hepburn moments..."

"Usually a second making of a picture suffers when it is compared with the original", reported *Motion Picture Herald*. "The condition is particularly true when the original was an outstanding audience and showman picture. When Philip Barry's *Holiday* was produced by E. B. Derr for Pathe in 1930, it was regarded as a model of picture making craftsmanship...As smart and dignified, while down-to-earth interment in which there is a wealth of showmanship material, the 1938 version stands shoulder to shoulder with its ancestor." The magazine's critic also felt that "Katharine Hepburn returns to that standard which marked her first screen appearances. Cary Grant continues in the stride of his last several pictures. Lew Ayres comes up with the kind of performance that makes one wonder what was the matter with those who had been handling him for several years."

Howard Barnes, in the *New York Herald-Tribune*, applauded "Cukor's expert direction and a vibrant, moving performance by Katharine Hepburn," and observed: "Even though the comic edge of the original has been considerably blunted in translation, humor and romance have been skillfully blended to make a beguiling show."

Holiday was celebrated on live television on *Studio One* in 1949. Directed by Worthington Miner, Barry's play benefited from excellent performances from Valerie Bettis and John Forsythe as the iconoclastic lovers.

STAGE

HOLIDAY, *Plymouth Theatre*, New York, opened November 26, 1928 229 performances

Produced and directed by Arthur Hopkins; A Comedy by Philip Barry; Settings by Robert Edmond Jones; Gowns by Charles Kondazian, Hattie Carnegie

Hope Williams (Linda Seton); Ben Smith (Johnny Case); Monroe Owsley (Ned Seton); Dorothy Tree (Julia Seton); Walter Walker (Edward Seton); Barbara White (Susan Potter); Donald Ogden Stewart (Nick Potter); Rosalie Norman (Laura Cram); Thaddeus Clancy (Seton Cram); Cameron Clemens (Charles); Beatrice Ames (Delia); J. Ascher Smith (Henry)

Road Company, 1930

Produced by George Sharp; A Comedy by Philip Barry; Director, Addison Pitt; Settings by B. W. Nichols

Dorothy Gish (Linda Seton); George Blackwood (Johnny Case); Charlotte Wynters (Julia Seton); Arthur Stuart Hill (Edward Seton); William Carey (Ned Seton); Doris Rankin (Susan Potter); Don Beddoe (Nick Potter); Nancy Allan (Laura Cram); Albert Loew (Seton Cram); William Hitch (Charles); Addison Pitt (Henry)

Road Company, 1930
Produced by George Sharp; A Comedy by Philip Barry; Director, Harry Manners; Settings by B. W. Nichols; Technical director, Joseph Lawrence

Edith King (Linda Seton); Emmett Vogan (Johnny Case); Henry Wadsworth (Ned Seton); Mabel Kroman (Julia Seton); Walter F. Jones (Edward Seton); Lucette Parker (Susan Potter); Hugh Banks (Nick Potter); Alice Ann Baker (Laura Cram); Robert Fiske (Seton Cram); Allen Gracey (Charles); Joseph Lawrence (Henry)

Road Company, 1930
Produced by Henry Duffy; A Comedy by Philip Barry; Director, Ferdinand Munier

Dale Winter (Linda Seton); Alexander Clark, Jr. (Johnny Case); Philip Tead (Ned Seton); Mia Marvin (Julia Seton); Clarence Geldart (Edward Seton); Ann Little (Susan Potter); Robert Keith (Nick Potter); Dorothy La Mar (Laura Cram); Harry Adams (Seton Cram); Russell Parker (Charles); Cecil Drummond (Henry); Hilda Onkalo (Delia)

Ethel Barrymore Theatre, New York, opened December 27, 1973 18 performances
Produced by the New Phoenix Repertory Company, T. Edward Hambleton and Michael Montel, managing directors; Harold Prince and Stephen Porter, artistic directors; A Comedy by Philip Barry; Director, Michael Montel; Settings, Edward Burbridge; Lighting, Ken Billington; Costumes, Carolyn Parker, Nancy Potts and Donald Brooks; Musical consultant, Paul Gemignani; General manager, Marilyn S. Miller; Stage managers, Murray Gitlin, Louis Pulvino and Valentine Mayer

Constance Moore (Linda Seton); John Glover (Johnny Case); George Ede (Edward Seton); Robin Pearson Rose (Julia Seton); Thomas A. Stewart (Ned Seton); David Dukes (Nick Potter); Bonnie Gallup (Susan Potter); Curt Karibalis (Seton Cram); Ellen Tovatt (Laura Cram); Bill Moor (Henry); Nicholas Hormann (Charles)

HAPPY NEW YEAR, *Avon Theatre*, Stratford, Ontario, opened June 9, 1979
Produced by the Stratford, Ontario, Canada Festival; A Musical play; Written and directed by Burt Shevelove, adapted from Philip Barry's comedy *Holiday*; Music and Lyrics by Cole Porter; Choreography, Donald Saddler; Setting, Michael Eagan; Lighting, Michael J. Whitfield; Costumes, Robin Fraser Paye; Musical director, Buster Davis; Orchestrations, Daniel Troob

Victoria Snow (Linda Seton); Edward Evanko (Johnny Case); Leigh Beery (Julia Seton); Eric Donkin (Edward Seton); David Dunbar (Ned Seton); Ted Follows (Narrator); William Copeland, Carol Forte, Wally Michaels, Marylu Moyer, Maida Rogerson, Hank Stinson, Heather Summerhayes, Barry Van Elen, Barrie Wood (Linda's Friends, Servants)

MUSICAL NUMBERS: "After You, Who?"; "When Your Troubles Have Started"; "Ours"; "Find Me a Primitive Man"; "To Hell With Everyone But Us"; "Boy, Oh Boy!";

"Let's Make It a Night"; "Bless the Bride"; "I'm in Love at Last"; "Once Upon a Time"; "See for Yourself"; "Nervous"; "Goodbye, Little Dream, Goodbye"; "My Lover Loves Me!"

HAPPY NEW YEAR, *Morosco Theatre*, New York, opened April 27, 1980 25 performances

Produced by Leonard Soloway, Allan Francis and Hale Matthews, in association with Marble Arch Productions; A Musical Play; Written and directed by Burt Shevelove, based on Philip Barry's comedy *Holiday*; Music and lyrics by Cole Porter, edited by Buster Davis; Setting, Michael Eagan; Lighting, Ken Billington; Costumes, Pierre Balmain; Choreography, Donald Saddler; Musical direction and vocal arrangements, Buster Davis; Orchestration, Daniel Troob; Dance music arrangements, Charles Coleman; Assistant choreographer, Mercedes Ellington; Associate producer, Dorothy Cherry; Production stage manager, Nina Seely

John McMartin (Narrator); Leslie Denniston (Linda Seton); Michael Scott (Johnny Case); William Roerick (Edward Seton); Kimberly Farr (Julia Seton); Richard Bekins (Edward Seton, Jr.); Roger Hamilton (Frazer); Morgan Ensminger (Charles/Anderson); J. Thomas Smith (Patrick); Tim Flavin (George/Thompson); Richard Christopher (Steven/Harrison); Lara Teeter (Victor/ Dixon); Lauren Goler (Rose/Nancy); Mary Sue Finnerty (Maude/ Mary/ Miss Madden); Bobbie Nord (Annie/ Gloria); Michelle Marshall (Bridget/Joan)

MUSICAL NUMBERS: "You Do Something to Me" (*Fifty Million Frenchmen* [1929]); "Night and Day"; "After You, Who?" (*Gay Divorce* [1932]); "Ridin' High"; "Red, Hot and Blue"; "Ours" (*Red, Hot and Blue* [1936]); "Easy to Love" (*Born to Dance* [1936 film]); "At Long Last Love" (*You Never Know* [1938]); "Let's Be Buddies" (*Panama Hattie* [1940]); "I Am Loved" (*Out of This World* [1950]); "When Your Troubles Have Started" (unused--*Red, Hot and Blue*); "Let's Make It a Night" (unused--*Silk Stockings*); "Once Upon a Time" (title song for unproduced 1933 show); "Boy, Oh Boy" (unused)

Incidental Music: "Let's Do It" (*Paris* [1928]); "What Is This Thing Called Love?" (*Wake Up and Dream* [1929]); "You've Got That Thing" (*Fifty Million Frenchmen* [1929]); "Let's Fly Away"; "Where Have You Been?"; "Take Me Back to Manhattan" (*The New Yorkers* [1930]); "Just One of Those Things" (*Jubilee* [1935]); "It's DeLovely" (*Red, Hot and Blue* [1936]); "Make It Another Old Fashioned, Please" (*Panama Hattie* [1940]); "Girls" (*Mexican Hayride* [1944]); "Ev'ry Time We Say Goodbye" (*Seven Lively Arts* [1944]); "They Couldn't Compare to You" (*Out of This World* [1950])

HOLIDAY, *Goodman Theatre*, Chicago, opened April 12, 1979

Produced by the Goodman Theatre Company; A Comedy by Philip Barry; Director, Tony Tanner; Scenery, Joseph Nieminski; Lighting, Robert Christen; Costumes, Clifford Capone; Production stage manager, John Drummond; Stage manager, Marsha Gitkind

Lindsay Crouse (Linda Seton); Norman Snow (Johnny Case); Nancy Snyder (Julia Seton); Tony Mockus (Edward Seton); W. H. Macy (Ned Seton); Jodean Culbert (Laura Cram); James Deuter (Seton Cram); Colin Stinton (Nick Potter); Kathleen Melvin (Susan Potter); James R. Keith (Henry); Fred Tumas (Charles); Jeanine Morick (Delia)

Ahmanson Theatre, Los Angeles, opened October 3, 1980 51 performances

Produced by Robert Fryer; A Comedy by Philip Barry; Director, Robert Allan Ackerman; Setting, John Lee Beatty; Lighting, Arden Fingerhut; Costumes, Robert Wojewodski; Production associate, Robert Linden; Stage managers, Bill Holland and Patrick Watkins

Sally Kellerman (Linda Seton); Kevin Kline (Johnny Case); Marisa Berenson (Julia Seton); Carole Kean (Laura Cram); Nicholas Hormann (Nick Potter); Marya Small (Susan Potter); Maurice Evans (Edward Seton); Colby Chester (Charles); Ivor Barry (Henry)

Long Wharf Theater, New Haven, opened November 26, 1982 47 performances
Produced by the Long Wharf Theater, Arvin Brown, artistic director; A Comedy by Philip Barry; Director, John Pasquin; Scenery, Marjory Bradley Kellogg; Lighting, Ronald Wallace; Costumes, Bill Walker

Jill Eikenberry (Linda Seton); Richard Jenkins (Johnny Case); Joanne Camp (Julia Seton); David Pierce (Ned Seton); Peggy Cosgrave (Laura Cram); Jonathan Hadary (Nick Potter); Sofia Landam (Susan Potter); William Swetland (Edward Seton); Clayton Berry (Seton Cram); Robert Koon (Charles); William Barry (Henry); Dana Cashman (Delia)

Williamstown (Mass.) Theatre Festival, opened June 30 through July 16, 1983
Produced by the Williamstown Theatre Festival, Nikos Psacharopoulos, artistic director; A Comedy by Philip Barry; Director, Nikos Psacharopoulos; Setting, Hugh Landwehr; Lighting, Roger Meeker; Costumes, Jess Goldstein; Stage manager, Liza C. Stein

Blythe Danner (Linda Seton); Ken Howard (Johnny Case); Marisa Berenson (Julia Seton); Christopher Reeve (Ned Seton); Chris Weatherhead (Laura Cram); Edmond Genest (Nick Potter); Jennifer Harmon (Susan Potter); Jerome Dempsey (Edward Seton); Christian Clemenson (Seton Cram); James Horgan (Charles); Peter Herrick (Henry); Mary Tharp (Delia)

Old Vic Theatre, London, opened January 14 through February 28, 1987
Produced by the Old Vic Company; A Comedy by Philip Barry; Director, Lindsay Anderson; Production designer, Michael Pavelka; Lighting, Mick Hughes; Costumes, Tom Rand

Mary Steenburgen (Linda Seton); Malcolm McDowell (Johnny Case); Cherie Lunghi (Julia Seton); Geoffrey Burridge (Nick Potter); Clare Clifford (Susan Potter); Frank Grimes (Ned Seton); Don Fellows (Edward Seton); Daniel Benzali (Seton Cram); Susan Denaker (Laura Cram); Peter Schofield (Henry); Peter Merrill (Charles); Marie Collett (Delia)

SCREEN

HOLIDAY, Pathe Pictures, released July 1930
Produced by E. B. Derr; Director, Edward H. Griffith; Screenplay, Horace Jackson; Photography, Norbert Brodine; Art director, Carroll Clark; Costumes, Gwen Wakeling; Music, Josiah Zuro; Assistant director, Paul Jones; Editor, Daniel Mandell

Ann Harding (Linda Seton); Robert Ames (Johnny Case); Monroe Owsley (Ned Seton); Hedda Hopper (Susan Potter); Edward Everett Horton (Nick Potter); Mary Astor (Julia Seton); William Holden (Edward Seton); Creighton Hale (Pete Hedges); Hallam Cooley (Seton Cram); Elizabeth Forrester (Laura Cram); Mabel Forrest (Mary Jessup); Mary Forbes (Mrs. Pritchard Ames)

Columbia Pictures, released May 1938
Associate producer, Everett Riskin; Director, George Cukor; Screenplay, Donald Ogden Stewart; Photography, Franz Planer; Art directors, Stephen Goosson and Lionel Banks; Set decorator, Babs Johnstone; Music, Sidney Cutner; Music director, Morris Stoloff; Costumes, Kalloch; Assistant on screenplay, Sidney Buchanan; Editors, Otto Meyer and Al Clark

Katharine Hepburn (Linda Seton); Cary Grant (Johnny Case); Lew Ayres (Ned Seton); Jean Dixon (Susan Potter); Edward Everett Horton (Nick Potter); Doris Nolan (Julia Seton); Henry Kolker (Edward Seton); Binnie Barnes (Laura Cram); Henry Daniell (Seton Cram); Mitchell Harris (Jennings); Charles Richman (Thayer); Marion Ballou (Grandmother); Matt McHugh (Taxi Driver); Luke Cosgrove (Grandfather); Bess Flowers (Countess); Maude Hume (Maid); Charles Trowbridge (Banker); George Pauncefort (Henry); Neil Fitzgerald (Edgar); Esther Peck (Mrs. Jennings); Lillian West (Mrs. Thayer); George Hickman (Telegraph Boy); Maurice Brierre (Steward); Frank Shannon (Farmer); Margaret McWade (Farmer's Wife); Hilda Plowright, Howard Hickman (Church Members); Harry Allen, Edward Cooper (Scotsmen); Aileen Carlyle (Farm Girl)

TELEVISION

HOLIDAY, Kraft Television Theatre, televised December 17, 1947 NBC I hour
Produced and directed by Stanley Quinn; Adapted from the play by Philip Barry

Margaret Phillips (Linda Seton); Walter Brooke (Johnny Case); Don Keefer (Ned Seton); Patricia Jenkins (Julia Seton)

Studio One, televised February 20, 1949 CBS I hour
Produced and directed by Worthington Miner; Adapted from the play by Philip Barry

Valerie Bettis (Linda Seton); John Forsythe (Johnny Case); Oliver Thorndike (Ned Seton); Staats Cotsworth (Nick Potter); Virginia Dwyer (Susan Potter); Patricia White (Julia Seton); James Van Dyk (Edward Seton)

HOME IS THE HERO
A Drama by Walter Macken (1953)

Synopsis

Ignorant Irish bully Paddo O'Reilly returns home after five years in prison for killing a neighbor in a drunken rage. During his absence, his crippled son, Willie, has established a successful shoe-repairing business. Paddo's wife, Daylia, has taken in lodgers to provide the family with additional support. Blusteringly attempting to reestablish his former dictatorial position in the family, Paddo is vigorously opposed by his daughter, Josie. Willie's decision to marry Lily, the daughter of Paddo's victim, further enrages the bitter Paddo who nearly kills Daylia's lodger, Dovetail. Alone with his gnawing inner guilt and aware that he inflicts nothing but unhappiness on his family, Paddo decides to leave Daylia, Willie and Josie.

Comment and Critique

Actor/author Walter Macken made his Broadway debut as Bartley Dowd in Michael J. Molloy's 1951 play *The King of Friday's Men*, which lasted four performances in February of that year. Macken had written four plays in Gaelic and two in English, in addition to four novels, when Dublin's Abbey Theatre first produced his drama, *Home Is the Hero*, in 1952. Brian O'Higgins was the original Paddo O'Reilly, but the author himself took the part when his play first came to America.

Brooks Atkinson (*The New York Times*) appraised *Home Is the Hero* when it opened on Broadway two years later, calling it "three acts of conscientious writing and acting," while finding that "the writing is pedestrian...In the final analysis, it is a dull play about a disagreeable fellow." Robert Coleman (*New York Daily Mirror*) also felt that the Macken play failed to please. "Its leading character is a heel, a bully and something of a bore...*Home Is the Hero* has its merits, but it is an unpleasant and repetitious play."

In the *New York Post*, Richard Watts, Jr., said: "The prestige of the contemporary Irish theater is hardly likely to be enhanced in America by *Home Is the Hero*... Mr. Macken was endeavoring to provide a kind of free tragic paraphrase of that masterpiece of comedy, *The Playboy of the Western World* -- I hasten to add that the similarity is merely in theme, and not in skill, effectiveness or sardonic power...Despite Mr. Macken's ability to write occasional effective scenes...his semi-tragedy rises to the bitterly ironical climax or achieves the quality of sardonic, brooding pity that he seems to have intended...Whatever his defects are as a playwright, Mr. Macken is an excellent actor."

Home Is the Hero was filmed in Ireland in 1959, again starring Walter Macken, along with the Abbey Players and fine, underrated American actor Arthur Kennedy. *Films and Filming*'s Max Neufeld called it "an indifferent play by Walter Macken, set in Ireland...the whole thing is sentimental, unconvincing and too Irish by half, despite the fact that the cast is drawn from the Abbey Theatre." Bosley Crowther wrote in *The New York Times* that it was "played with conspicuous devotion by Arthur Kennedy and a clearly Irish cast... But Mr. Macken has failed in his play and Henry Keating has failed in his screenplay to clarify it and give it a point. There is no sense of benighted background, of the cruel grip of poverty or any other peculiar circumstances that have affected these people's fates." Crowther added about the characters, "they are simply other stupid people dancing attendance to a dunce."

Between the original play and the film version of it came its staging on the *Kraft Television Theatre* in January 1956. Veteran actor Brian Donlevy was the brutish Paddo and up-and-coming Anthony Perkins was his son Willie. The play, it was felt, was given good performances but remained depressing television fare.

STAGE

HOME IS THE HERO, Queen's Theatre, Dublin, Ireland, opened August 4, 1952
Produced by the Abbey Theatre; A Drama by Walter Macken; Director, Ria Mooney; Settings, Vere Dudgeon

Brian O'Higgins (Paddo O'Reilly); Michael Hennessy (Willie O'Reilly); Eileen Crowe (Daylia O'Reilly); Ita Mathews (Josie O'Reilly); Harry Brogan (Dovetail); Maire Kane (Bid); Joan Eager (Lily Green); Brid Lynch (Mrs. Green); Liam Foley (Manchester Monaghan); Eddie Golden (Trapper O'Flynn)

Booth Theatre, New York, opened September 22, 1954 29 performances
Produced by The Theatre Guild and Worthington Miner; A Drama by Walter Macken; Director, Worthington Miner; Production designer, Marvin Reiss; Stage managers,

Elliott Martin and Mike Thoma

Walter Macken (Paddo O'Reilly); Donald Harron (Willie O'Reilly); Glenda Farrell (Daylia O'Reilly); Peggy Ann Garner (Josie O'Reilly); J. Pat O'Malley (Dovetail); Ann Thomas (Bid); Loretta Leversee (Lily Green); Frances Fuller (Mrs. Green); Christopher Plummer (Manchester Monaghan); Art Smith (Trapper O'Flynn)

Richmond Theatre, London, opened August 29, 1955

Produced by the Abbey Theatre; A Drama by Walter Macken; Director, Toni Wyatt

Brian O'Higgins (Paddo O'Reilly); Jack MacGowren (Willie O'Reilly); Bea Duffell (Daylia O'Reilly); Rita Foran (Josie O'Reilly); Kenin Stoney (Dovetail); Sally Travers (Bid); Cepta Fennell (Lily Green); Aithna Gover (Mrs. Green); Michael Seaver (Manchester Monaghan); Gordon Daisley (Trapper O'Flynn)

Billy Munk Theatre, New York, opened March 17, 1975 16 performances

Produced by Barry Moss; Artistic directors, Barbara Loden and Mary Tierney; A Drama by Walter Macken; Director, Barbara Loden; Setting, Robertson Carricart; Lighting, Brett Landow Lewis; Costumes, Susan Harris; Stage managers, Ellen Casey and Estelle Fenbnell

Pat McNamara (Paddo O'Reilly); John Burke (Willie O'Reilly); Janet Ward (Daylia O'Reilly); Mary Tierney (Josie O'Reilly); Diarmuid McNamara (Dovetail); Audrey Bell (Bid); Allison Corbett-Smith (Lily Green); Maggie Burke (Mrs. Green); James Handy (Manchester Monaghan); Walt Gorney (Trapper O'Flynn)

SCREEN

HOME IS THE HERO, British-Lion/Britannia Films, released 1959; in U.S., released by *Show Corporation of America*, January 1961

Produced in Ireland by Emmet Dalton Productions; Producers, Robert S. Baker and Monty Berman; Director, Fielder Cook; Screenplay, Henry Keating, based on Walter Macken's play; Photography, Stanley Pavey; Art director, Allan Harris; Music, Bruce Montgomery; Musical director, Philip Martell; Editor, John Ferris

Walter Macken (Paddo O'Reilly); Arthur Kennedy (Willie O'Reilly); Eileen Crowe (Daylia O'Reilly); Joan O'Hara (Josie O'Reilly); Harry Brogan (Dovetail); Maire Kean (Bid); Maire O'Donnell (Maura Green); Patrick Layde (Mr. Green); Michael Hennessey (Manchester Monaghan); Philip O'Flynn (Trapper O'Flynn); Eddie Golden (Shannon); John Hoey (Finegan)

TELEVISION

HOME IS THE HERO, Kraft Television Theatre, televised January 25, 1956 NBC I hour

Produced and directed by Robert Herridge; Adapted from the play by Walter Macken

Brian Donlevy (Paddo O'Reilly); Anthony Perkins (Willie O'Reilly); Loretta Leversee (Josie O'Reilly); J. Pat O'Malley (Dovetail); Ann Thomas (Bid)

HUCKLEBERRY FINN

Various adaptations of *The Adventures of Huckleberry Finn* by Mark Twain (1884)

Synopsis

Huckleberry Finn, a brash young scamp from a small Mississippi town, despairs of the discipline, cleanliness and mothering of the Widow Douglas and her pious old maid sister, Miss Watson. Knowing of the money Huck and his pal Tom Sawyer found and gave to Judge Thatcher for investment, Huck's brutal father kidnaps his son. Huck, however, escapes from his drunken father's isolated, dirt floor hut, leaving the place with the appearance of robbery and murder. Soon he meets Jim, Miss Watson's slave, who is aware of his mistress' intent to sell him down the river and has run off. Huck and Jim construct a large raft and drift down the Mississippi. After several close calls and invigorating adventures, the two take aboard a couple of drifters who call themselves the King of France and the Duke of Bridgewater. The imposters have Huck and Jim attend them as befits royalty while they bilk a rural camp meeting, and in other towns, attempt scenes from Shakespearean plays.

Despite a reward of $200, The King turns Jim in for $40, but Huck manages to locate his traveling companion on the farm of Silas Phelps. There Huck is greeted by Aunt Sally Phelps who mistakes him for his sister Aunt Polly's young nephew Tom Sawyer, en route for a visit. Ever a masterful liar, Huck pretends to be Tom until the real Tom arrives and claims to be his half-brother, Sid Sawyer. Tom's active imagination creates fictions to set Jim free and produces havoc in the Phelps household. After the arrival of Aunt Polly, true identifications are restored and Tom confesses his various adventures in which he supposedly received a bullet wound attempting to free Jim. Miss Watson, he says, had died and freed Jim in her will. Huck's fear of returning home to face his father are quelled when Jim tells him that the body they found in as floating house during a flood was the old man. But Huck, aware that Aunt Sally plans to adopt and civilize him, decides to "light out for the territory."

Comment and Critique

Samuel Langhorne Clemens, better known as Mark Twain, wrote his book *Adventures of Mark Twain (Tom Sawyer's Comrade)* in the first person singular and it was introduced:

> "You don't know about me without you have read a book by the names of *The Adventures of Tom Sawyer*, but that ain't no matter. That book was made by Mr. Mark Twain, and he told the truth, mainly. There was things which he stretched, but mainly he told the truth."

It later would fall to Ernest Hemingway to write astutely, "All modern American literature comes from one book by Mark Twain called *Huckleberry Finn*. Twain's book was started in the summer of 1876 as a sequel to his successful *Tom Sawyer*. Episodes of Huck's adventures appeared in the *Century* magazine and, in February 1885, Charles L. Webster and Company published the novel with 175 illustrations by Sacramento artists Edward Windsor Kemble. The book was attacked, however, by most reviewers. *The New York World* described it as "cheap and pernicious stuff -- what can be said of a man of Mr. Clemens' wit, ability and position deliberately imposing upon the unoffending public a piece of careless hack-work in which a few good things are dropped amid a mass of rubbish."

The Boston Transcript reported: "The Concord [Mass.] Public Library has to exclude Mark Twain's latest book from the library. One member of the committee says that, while he does not wish to call it immoral, he think it contains little humor and that of a very coarse type. He regards it as the veriest trash." Through the years, *Huckleberry Finn* has been banned by self-styled moralists. In 1902, Denver and Omaha banned the book and the Brooklyn Public Library removed it from its shelves in 1905. In his *The Day They Came to Arrest the Book* (adapted to television in 1987), Nat Hentoff noted that the nineteenth chapter of the Book of Judges in the Bible as inflicting more harm on the juvenile mind than Twain's book. As one TV critic wrote of the adaptation of Hentoff's book about the "arresting" of *Huckleberry Finn*: "Unfortunately for contemporary readers, one of the words that ordinary people used a lot along the banks of the Mississippi River a century ago was 'nigger'. The frequency with which the word pops up in *Huckleberry Finn* has made the novel a frequent target of school-censorship drives during the last few years."

In November 1902, Klaw and Erlanger premiered *Huckleberry Finn*, a musical version of Twain's book, at Parson's Theatre in Hartford, and it then moved to the Chestnut Street Theatre in Philadelphia. The show's book was credited to Mark Twain and Southern playwright Lee Arthur with music by Frederick Solomon. "Mark Twain as a dramatist has studiously ignored the well-beaten paths that have marked the course of the better known play writers and has gone off on a by-road of his own," judged the theater critic of *The Philadelphia Inquirer*. "There are none of the subdivisions of plays under which this effusion can be placed. It is in reality, to be perfectly plain, no play at all. It is an entertainment and as such it is spectacular, it is musical and it is tedious."

The Evening Bulletin in Philadelphia felt: "It is useless to attempt to classify the production...The program announces that the work of dramatizing this story was performed by Mark Twain in conjunction with Lee Arthur, and the audience doubtless expected to see a more or less coherent summary of the chief episodes of the book. What they did see was something altogether different. The events and characters of both the Twain stories, *Tom Sawyer* and *Huckleberry Finn*, had been drawn upon as material, but these were so jumbled by a succession of songs, dances, and various other specialties that the result was a musical extravaganza, diversified at times by a few melodramatic situations and devoid of anything like a consecutive portrayal or narration..."

Klaw and Erlanger's handsomely mounted musical comedy did not attempt Broadway and closed on the road.

Francis Fergusson's adaptation of Twain's Huck Finn story, called *The King and the Duke*, was produced Off Broadway at Circle in the Square in June 1955, with Jose Quintero directing. In *The New York Times*, critic Lewis Funke wrote: "Just what Mr. Fergusson intended in this work is not entirely clear...The material he has used is the interlude in which Huck and his slave friend Jim fall in with those two rapscallions The King and The Duke...There is a blatant insistence on atmosphere in the telling of the tale. There also is a heavy interlarding of music, choral and solo, provided by G. Wood, some of it rather pleasant and rhythmic. But there is little than can be called theatre...But what sort of brew all this is supposed to make is difficult to say...Ralph Williams is an authentic Huck, John Armstrong a corpulent, loud-wailing, wicked scoundrel of a King, and James Greene, a sleek, dapper, smooth-talking Duke..."

Huckleberry Finn finally landed on Broadway in April 1957 in the musical play *Livin' the Life*, based on an adaptation of *The Adventures of Tom Sawyer* by Dale Wasserman and Bruce Geller. The world premiere of *Big River: The Adventures of Huckleberry Finn* was presented by the American Repertory Theater of Cambridge, Massachusetts, during the 1983-84 season and then the show was polished at the La Jolla Playhouse on the West Coast. It opened on Broadway on April 25, 1985, and was an immediate smash, garnering seven Tony Awards including Best Musical and playing for two-and-one-half years, accumulating 1,005 performances.

"*Big River: The Adventures of Huckleberry Finn* is the last Broadway musical of the season -- but, more important, it is the first that audiences can attend without fear of suffering either profound embarrassment or terminal boredom," Frank Rich reported in *The New York Times*. "This show has a lot going for it: a tuneful score by the country-music songsmith Roger Miller, exuberant performers and a gifted young director, Des McAnuff, who is full of clever ideas about how to bring Mark Twain's masterpiece to the stage... The music and lyrics, often riding on giddy banjo-and-fiddle-flecked hoedown arrangements at first rise well above the text. Mr. Miller write in indigenous Southern and Western American idioms that are ideally expressive of Twain's characters and their salty vernacular." Of Daniel H. Jenkins, who played Huck, Rich felt: "...he's always charming company, and in that sense, he's the perfect Huck Finn for an ingratiating musical that can't quite bring itself to raise hell."

In the *New York Post*, Clive Barnes wrote: "*Big River* is much more a musical play than your ordinary common or prairie Broadway musical. Its story line is American-epic, and its staging is as important in itself as anything it stages...The book of the musical, by William Hauptman, is pretty fair to American literature's first anti-hero or non-conformist scamp...The scenic focus is the raft, and the river -- beautifully lit by Richard Riddell...[Des] McAnuff, [Roger] Miller, Hauptman and Twain are lucky in the luminously innocent Huck of Daniel H. Jenkins and the warily honest Jim of Ron Richardson -- although I am more than prepared to accept that luck had anything to do with it. Anyway, they are both perfect..."

Not as enthusiastic was Douglas Watt in the *Daily News*, who called *Big River* "amiable, tuneful, rambling and almost totally uninvolving. The great American novel is a work whose breadths and incident seem to defy the conventions of the musical stage. Of its several movie treatments, only one has dare set it to music, and that was a failure. Possibly the closest it would have come to realization was the Maxwell Anderson-Kurt Weill *Raft on the River* [in 1950], cut short by Weill's untimely death after the completion of just five songs...William Hauptman's book is a decent enough condensation of the novel, though a great deal of [it's] flavor is lost and some of the alterations are questionable...So what we're left with is a respectable, and reasonably honest, version of Twain's classic that commits the unpardonable sin of being dull."

In any event, *Big River* won Tony Awards not only as Best Musical but also for Book, Score, Direction, Scenic Design, Lighting Design, and Featured Actor (Ron Richardson). It also won Drama Desk Awards for Richardson (Outstanding Actor), Rene Auberjonois (Outstanding Featured Actor), Score and Lyrics, Orchestrations, Scenery and Lighting.

In 1988, Richardson recreated his role of Jim in a Japanese version of the production that also starred Hiroyuski Sanada as Huck. He spoke his lines in Japanese and did his singing in English.

Bernard Sabath had written three plays based on the life of Mark Twain and, in 1981, his offbeat drama (having nothing to do with Twain) entitled *The Boys in Autumn* opened in San Francisco for a sold-out month-long engagement. The reason for the sell-out was its casting of sixty-four-year-old Kirk Douglas and sixty-seven-year-old Burt Lancaster in the roles of middle-aged Tom Sawyer and Huckleberry Finn respectively.

"When Kirk Douglas and Burt Lancaster step out on the stage together, instant electricity is generated. The two charismatic superstars opened last night in *The Boys in Autumn*...the event had to be one of the most exciting theatrical happening in memory," critic Jeanne Miller gushed in the *San Francisco Examiner*. "The two gifted actors offer virtuoso performances that make the evening a towering success despite the insubstantial quality of Bernard Sabath's two-character play about the twilight years of Mark Twain's Tom Sawyer and Huckleberry Finn...Douglas' performance is sheer delight as he juggles, plays the banjo and does a soft-shoe tap routine to explain his way of life to his old friend. Lancaster is a taciturn, embittered man whose life has turned sour after the death of his wife. The actor brings strength, dignity and marvelous authority to the role...The two actors' dynamic performances serve the playwright's purpose with great distinction. One suspects that the play's fragility in terms of strength, substance and vigor would be more apparent in less accomplished hands."

In the *San Francisco Chronicle*, Bernard Weiner called it "a great idea for a play. Would that I could report that *The Boys in Autumn* matches its potential. Sadly, it's pretty thin stuff, a talky non-drama that relies far too much on offstage description and on the movie-star reputations of its two stars...with some major rewriting, [it] could prove to be a popular vehicle for Douglas and Lancaster. The basic idea is so rich, using Mark Twain's universally understood rapscallions in elaborating a tale of undying friendship, that it's difficult to see how, with proper refashioning, the play couldn't do well, especially given it two familiar stars in their role."

Other commitments prevented Douglas and Lancaster from touring with the show and perhaps bringing it to Broadway. It was remounted, however, five years later and came to New York with John Cullum and George C. Scott as Tom and Huck. Reunited after fifty years since their youthful Missouri adventures, Huck, now a retired hardware merchant, has condoned the mercy killing of his obese redheaded wife, a former nurse. Tom, with his wife Tillie Green, became a vaudevillian touring as Gray and Green when he was not being arrested for molesting young girls, all of whom reminded Tom of Becky Thatcher.

The New York Times' Frank Rich slammed the play, calling it "a terminally innocuous speculation about Huckleberry Finn and Tom Sawyer in middle age...It's hard to know what attracted either star to *The Boys in Autumn*. They'd find more challenge playing the Duke and the King in a bus-and-truck tour of *Big River*." Douglas Watt agreed in the *Daily News*: "You might expect at least a bit of enchantment to accrue from the reunion of Huckleberry Finn and Tom Sawyer atop a Mississippi bluff fifty years after their early adventures. But you'd be dead wrong. The idea never occurred to Mark Twain, and Bernard Sabath... should have cast it from his mind immediately." *The Boys in Autumn* faded away after thirty-eight performances.

Between the San Francisco and New York productions of *The Boys in Autumn*, two ambitious works dealing with Huckleberry Finn premiered in 1983 within two weeks of one another. A musical entitled *Huck and Jim on the Mississippi*, directed by Joshua Logan with book and lyrics by Logan and music by Bruce Pomahac, premiered at Florida Atlantic University Theatre in Boca Raton. *Variety* wrote: "Mark Twain's Huckleberry Finn had been a problem child on both stage and screen throughout this century. Logan himself admits in the current project's program notes to both enthusiasm and frustration in dealing with the material 'for many years' with Maxwell Anderson, Kurt Weill, Alan Jay Lerner and Burton Lane. *Huck and Jim on the Mississippi*...appears as good a stab as any after a week of rewrites, reshuffling and recasting during the university run. Much more is needed for the show to have commercial potential, and Logan's performance changes indicated a drive to achieve as much of that as possible during the limited, sellout engagement. Many of the problems inherent in dramatizing such a sprawling tale are reflected in Huck and Jim, though Logan has chosen his focal points carefully."

At the other end of the country, the Seattle Repertory Theater mounted a drama by James Hammerstein and Christopher Harbon called *The Adventures of Huckleberry Finn*, staged by Hammerstein. It premiered to middling reviews. "It's a good, ambitious effort, but this adaptation of the classic American novel doesn't make it. James Hammerstein and Christopher Harbon's adaptation comes out in bits and pieces, only a few of which have dramatic impact," *Variety* found. "Only briefly does Robert MacNaughton as Huck Finn capture the common sense, mischievousness and disregard of current conventions that made the novel's character great. David Toney, as Jim, runaway slave and Huck's friend, is good, steadfast and loyal, and eloquently dramatizes the plight of black slaves circa 1836. The large cat, mostly playing multiple roles, created confusion, with few having time to delineate a memorable character that has impact on the drama or the audience."

Mark Twain's Huckleberry Finn and Tom Sawyer became favorite characters for the screen dating back to the earliest days. In 1917, William Desmond Taylor directed Jesse L. Lasky's production of *Huck and Tom* featuring Robert Gordon and Jack Pickford in those roles. "The realistic scenes laid in Hannibal, Missouri, where the story was written -- so much of the atmosphere of the original work has been transferred to the screen that Mr. Taylor deserves the highest praise for his masterly direction," *The New York Dramatic Mirror* reported. "Jack Pickford has duplicated his good work in the *New Adventures of Tom Sawyer*...As Huck, Robert Gordon gives the same delightful performance that won him praise in the first picture in which he essayed the part...It is a wholly delightful story of adventure..."

Taylor had directed Pickford and Gordon in 1917's *Tom Sawyer*, and *Huck and Tom*, its sequel, was equally successful. Edward Weitzel (*Moving Picture World*) found: "Jack Pickford hardly looks a fourteen-year-old boy, but plays the part so naturally and makes Tom so like the character as Mark Twain drew him that everything else is forgotten. Robert Gordon fits the part of Huck admirably...The incidents in the picture are among the most interesting in the story, and the author's wonderful sympathy with everything connected with boys of all ages and his knowledge of the habits and customs in a Missouri River town before the Civil War are brought out in complete detail in the Jesse L. Lasky production."

When Taylor's next version of the work, *Huckleberry Finn*, opened in New York in February 1920, *The Times* found that he "did not seek to use Mark Twain's book as material for a conventional movie of his own, and so escaped being shot. He did seek, with care and intelligence, to translate as much as possible of the book into moving pictures, and so has won the gratitude of the public. His translation, as far as it goes and can go, is remarkably, and most enjoyably, good. Of course, only a part of what Mark Twain wrote can be said in the language of moving pictures...Lewis Sargent, a fifteen-year-old boy practically unknown on the stage and screen, but with an apparent aptitude for the part, is Huck, and will undoubtedly convince nearly every one that he is the original brought to life." *The Times* critic continued: "The settings of *Huckleberry Finn* appear to verify the report that Mr. Taylor and his company went to the Mississippi River to make their picture. Some of the scenes might have been under Mark Twain's own direction...no matter what its shortcomings may be it should be a joy to every one..."

Paramount again followed its silent pictures trend into the talkies by filming *Huckleberry Finn* as a sequel to its 1930 *Tom Sawyer*, with most of the same cast. *Photoplay* called the l931 Huck "another of Paramount's delightful series of kid pictures. Not as great as *Skippy*, not quite as good as *Tom Sawyer*, but withal a splendid successor to both...Junior Durkin as Huck Finn turns in the finest performance of his career; he doesn't just act Huck, he just is Huck. Jackie Coogan makes good again as Tom Sawyer..."

Mordaunt Hall (*The New York Times*) found that "It is an offering which will be heartily welcomed, in spite of changes due to the demands of the screen, by all admirers of the great American humorist. As in the production *Tom Sawyer*, Junior Durkin impersonates Huckleberry Finn, Jackie Coogan acts Tom Sawyer, Jackie Searl impersonates Sid Sawyer, and Mitzi Green, now a blonde, undertakes the role of the flirtatious little Becky Thatcher...Master Coogan does quite well with his role. Young Durkin is capital, and he actually looks like the illustrations of Huck..."

MGM's 1939 *The Adventures of Huckleberry Finn* starred Mickey Rooney, and remains the most famous of the screen's Hucks. In the *New York Herald Tribune*, Robert W. Dana said: "Anyone would admit that Mark Twain's rambling, almost fabulous story of Huck Finn and his river travels, with their unending bypaths and flavorsome adventures, could not be put between the first and last feet of film with any degree of completeness. The new film with the popular and talented Mickey Rooney, is no exception...It is a tight, well-acted and generally amusing screen drama. Yet, however bright and deserving has been the attempt, the film is an uneasy reminder of a comprehensive and utterly delightful story."

John Mosher wrote in *The New Yorker*. "Mickey Rooney naturally had to check off Huck Finn before he got any older. Now he's done his duty, and I don't feel either he or those others involved in this production did more. It's a perfunctory, commonplace job, pretty creaky and in the manner of those revival pieces some think quaint...Aside from being a step for Mr. Rooney, this picture accomplished nothing."

The New York Times' B. R. Crisler considered the film "an average, workmanlike piece of cinematic hokum -- Master Rooney's latest vehicle affords little, if any, insight into the realistic boyhood of which old Mark wrote with such imperishable humor. How could the story be Mark Twain when the river isn't the Mississippi (it's the Sacramento, if you can stand it) and when the Finn part of the proceedings is more Mickey than Huckleberry?"

In the mid-1940s, Metro-Goldwyn-Mayer producer Arthur Freed planned a Technicolor production of *Huckleberry Finn* featuring up-and-coming young actor Claude Jarman, Jr., star of the company's *The Yearling*. Sally Benson was to do the screenplay and a musical score was to be provided by Hugh Martin and Ralph Blane (Benson, Martin and Blane instead got sidetracked to *Meet Me in St. Louis*). In August 1951, the studio began rehearsals of yet another musical attempt at *Huckleberry Finn* -- this time with a screenplay by Alan Jay Lerner, who also wrote the lyrics to music by Burton Lane. Vincente Minnelli was to direct Dean Stockwell as Huck, Gene Kelly as the Duke (he was also to choreograph the film), Danny Kaye as the Dauphin, Margaret O'Brien as Mary Jane Wilks, and William Warfield as the runaway slave, Jim. Irene Sharaff designed the costumes, and Minnelli recalled in his autobiography, *I Remember It Well*, "Marvelous bits of business were being concocted for Danny and Gene in their roles as itinerant con men...This was probably the best score ever written for films..." For one reason or another, the film never got made.

Some of the Lerner-Lane Huck Finn score did get used, however, in MGM's 1960 Technicolor version of *The Adventures of Huckleberry Finn*, produced by Samuel Goldwyn, Jr., and starring Eddie Hodges, the freckle-face young actor from Broadway's *The Music Man* and the screen's *A Hole in the Head*. Jim was played by boxer Archie Moore, but the picture was stolen by Tony Randall as The King and Mickey Shaughnessy as The Duke. Among the cast of veteran actors in support were Judy Canova, Andy Devine, John Carradine, Sterling Holloway, even Buster Keaton. "It is sumptuously photographed in sometimes too vivid color, and much of it was shot out of doors, in the broad, flat Sacramento River Valley, which reasonably resembles the Mississippi's, *Bosley Crowther* observed in *The New York Times*. "But the film takes its basic characteristic from the quality of Eddie Hodges as Huck -- and that, we must tell you quite frankly, is not on the order of Marks' deathless boy...As a consequence, this pretty film version might likewise be classified as 'cute' -- cheerful, chummy, sentimental, and, eventually, monotonous and dull. But don't take your youngster to see it in the expectation of introducing him to Huck Finn. Explain that this is but entertainment -- a plush one. Then give him a copy of the book."

In the early 1970s, *Reader's Digest* got into movie-making with a production of *Tom Sawyer* and followed it naturally with a musicalized *Huckleberry Finn*, with a score by Robert B. and Richard M. Sherman, the brother songwriting team responsible for *Mary Poppins*. In *The Hollywood Musical*, Clive Hirschhorn judged: "The results were disastrous. It bore no relation in mood and atmosphere to Twain's original, and the Sherman Brothers' screenplay (they also wrote instantly forgettable tunes) was cloying, and the film deadly dull. It was directed by J. Lee Thompson, who deserved a special Oscar for his underachievement in turning a hitherto foolproof property into a dud, and starred Jeff East -- whose performance was nowhere as effective as it had been in *Tom Sawyer* -- as Huck..."

Lawrence Van Gelder decided in *The New York Times*: "After an hour, just when *Huckleberry Finn* is about to drown in its own treacle, up bob Harvey Korman as the King and David Wayne as the Duke, and for half an hour or so, life on the Mississippi seems well worth living. But all too soon, Messrs. Korman and Wayne disappear behind the bars of the Jackson's Landing jail. And *Huckleberry Finn*, all sunsets, leafiness and thin riparian righteousness, drags its way to the finish ...The setting is Disneyland South; Jeff East as Huck gives one of those performances that afflict child actors with a bad name [and] J. Lee Thompson directs as though excitement hadn't been invented yet...Paul Winfield merits praise for a strong, dignified performance as Jim..."

An unexpected *Huckleberry Finn* arrived on the screen in 1972 -- from Russia, with the Dnieper River substituting for the Mississippi. Georgi N. Daneliya directed eleven-year-old Moscow schoolboy, Roma Madyanov, and Nigerian geology student from Patrice Lumumba University, Felix Imokuede, as Huck and Jim. The wide-screen, color production from the USSR was found by *The Christian Science Monitor*'s Leo Grukow to be in "the Russian tradition of broad character acting [and] lends itself to the nineteen-century place and gives the picture a curiously Dickensian flavor."

On television, CBS' *Climax!* series presented a production of *The Adventures of Huckleberry Finn* in September 1955 with Charles Taylor as Huck, John Carradine as The Duke, and Thomas Mitchell as Pap Finn. Two years later, on the *United States Steel Hour*, Jimmy Boyd starred in the title role of a musical *Huck Finn*, along with Jack Carson and Basil Rathbone as the King and the Duke, Earle Hyman as Jim, and Florence Henderson as Mary Jane Wilks. Then in October 1960, on the *Shirley Temple Theatre*, Mickey Rooney's young son Teddy reprised his dad's old role as Huck Finn to Alan Ladd's son David's Tom Sawyer in the production *Tom and Huck*, also starring Janet Blair, Dan Duryea and a long-ago Tom Sawyer, now-grown Jackie Coogan.

A 1975 made-for-television movie, adapted from the Twain story by Jean Holloway (she also had adapted a Tom Sawyer TV-movie two years earler), starred Ron Howard and Donny Most -- both from TV's *Happy Days* -- as Huck and Tom, with Antonio Fargas as Jim, Jack Elam as the King and country star Merle Haggard as the Duke. Six years later, a *Classics Illustrated* adaptation of *The Adventures of Huckleberry Finn* premiered (it was shot in 1978) with unknowns Kurt Ida and Dan

Monahan as, in *Variety*'s opinion, "well-scrubbed Huck Finn and Tom Sawyer [who] go through the paces in a marshmallow-soft version of Mark Twain's novel." The 1982 TV-movie *Rascals and Robbers--The Secret Adventures of Tom Sawyer and Huck Finn* was, in the view of *Variety*, a "valiant attempt to extend Mark Twain's characters into a loose collection of anecdotes" that "doesn't give Twain much credit and doesn't catch much of his spirit, either. As Twain said to his wife when, trying to cure him of cussing, she tried quoting him, 'You've got the lyrics fine, Livy, but you ain't got the tune.'"

In 1985, a superlative four-part *Adventures of Huckleberry Finn* was presented on PBS' *American Play-house*, marking Mark Twain's 150th birthday and the Huck Finn centennial. English novelist and critic Jonathan Raban, in a lengthy piece at the time in *TV Guide*, began his article by noting "*Huckleberry Finn* is *the* American classic...the only novel in American literature that has the permanent, enchanting and mysterious power of an ancient myth" and concluded: "I can't even copy out the words (of Huck's speeches) on the type-writer without wanting to be the. That is what *Huckleberry Finn* does: it makes you want to live intensely inside it. It is incomparable." A large cast headed by relative unknowns Patrick Day (Huck), Eugene Oakes (Tom) and Samm-Art Williams (Jim) had in support the likes of Geraldine Page (Aunt Sally), Sada Thompson (Widow Douglas), Jim Dale and Barnard Hughes as the Duke and the Dauphin), and Richard Kiley, Lillian Gish, Frederic Forrest, Butterfly McQueen and others.

"Filmed strikingly like a parade of Thomas Hart Benton paintings by Walter Lassally, [it] dares point out that *Adventures of Huckleberry Finn* is not a youngsters' story," *Variety* felt, "but a story of the human condition. [Director Peter H.] Hunt unfolds grief, joy and vitality in a drama whose final moments are startlingly poignant. Exec producer William Perry, whose *Life on the Mississippi* [previously on PBS] was an elegy for an age, turns *Finn* into an amber idyll; he and his company may not convey all the appropriate laughter, but they have found the heart of darkness."

The Nat Hentoff novel *The Day They Came to Arrest the Book*, a fictional tale of the banning of *Huckleberry Finn* in a number of school systems around the country, came to television as an award-winning *CBS Schoolbreak Special*, airing late in the afternoon. Melvin Van Peebles wrote the adaptation and Gilbert Moses directed a cast of young pros, plus veteran actress/comedienne Anne Meara as the put-upon and defiant school librarian who fought the ban.

In fall 1990, a new Huck Finn/Tom Sawyer movie adventure came to television in the form of *Back to Hannibal*, produced for The Disney Channel, with Huck, now a newspaperman, and Tom, a successful big city lawyer, reuniting in Hannibal to defend Jim, the former slave, against charges of killing Becky Thatcher's husband. Mitchell Anderson played Huck; Raphael Sbarge was Tom.

STAGE

HUCKLBERRY FINN, *Parson's Theatre*, Hartford, opened November 11, 1902; moved to *Chestnut Street Theatre*, Philadelphia, November 20, 1902*
Produced by Klaw and Erlanger; A Musical Play based on the novel by Mark Twain; Director, Ben Teal; Book and lyrics by Mark Twain and Lee Arthur; Music by Frederick Solomon; Scenery, Ernest Gros; Lighting effects, Harry Bissing; Mechanical effects, P. J. McDonald; Costumes, F. Richard Anderson; Musical director, John Harding; Company manager, Frank W. Martineau; Stage managers, Robert Harold and Julian Myers

Arthur Dana (Huckleberry Finn); John C. Slavin (Tom Sawyer); Jack Ryan (Joe

Harper); James Devlin (Ben Goers); Archie Anderson (Billy Fisher); Charles K. French (Jim, a Negro Slave); Leonie Darmon (Becky Thatcher); Marie Bingham (Aunt Polly); Flora Parker (Amy Lawrence); Robert Harold (Mr. Lawrence); Mabelle de Rhana (Mrs. Lawrence); Mrs. Weston (Widow Douglas); Webb Raum (Sid Sawyer); Charles W. Stokes (Judge Thatcher); Charles Stanley (The Duke); William Sampson (The Dauphin); W. C. Kelly (Mr. Doughton); Samuel Reed (Mr. Walters); A. T. Ernest (Silas Finn); Edward J. Connolly (Hannibal Johnson); Hughey Flaherty (Pete, a Negro); Julie A. Herne (Mary Ann); Virginia Ross (Palmyra); Lizette Le Baron (Agatha); Jane Dara (Cresy); Beatrice Walsh, Lillian Rice, Edna McClure, Nellie Harris, Lucille de Mendez, Angie Wiemers, Louise Elton, Lola Merrill, Babe Adams, Sallie Bergere, Evelyn Carrette, Jean Ryson, Geraldine Royal, Saide Haynes, Edith Williams, Mabel Mordaunt (Chorus)

MUSICAL NUMBERS: "Pierrot Dance"; "I Want to Be a Drummer in the Band" (Music, Silvio Heine; Lyrics, Matthew C. Woodward); "Good Night, Lucindy" (McHerson and Brown); "The Temperance Union Band"; "Courting"; "Madrigal"; "The Sunflower and the Violet"; "Oh, Isn't It Fine to Be Robbers"; "My Own Sweetheart"; "Tarantella"; "A Tender Spot for Father"; "Animal's Convention" (Cole and Johnson); "Country Dance"; "We Are Glad We Are Alive"

* This production continued to play on the road but never reached Broadway

THE KING AND THE DUKE, *Circle in the Square*, New York, opened June 1, 1955
Produced by the Circle in the Square Cabaret Theatre; A Melodramatic Farce by Francis Fergusson, adapted from Mark Twain's *Huckleberry Finn*; Director, Jose Quintero; Settings, Keith Cuerden; Lighting, Jan Marascek; Music, G. Wood; Dances, William Hooks

Ralph Williams (Huckleberry Finn); John Armstrong (The King); James Greene (The Duke); Stanley Greene (Jim); Patsy Bruder (Mary Jane); Robin Oliver (Susanna); Patricia Brooks (Joanna); G. Wood (Deacon Lot Hovey); Bruce Kirby (Ben Rucker); Ron Soble (Dr. Robinson); James Ray (Lafe Buckner); John Gregory (Hank Buckner); Jean Stephens (Widow Bartley); Doree Simmons (Mrs. Hovey); Betty James (Mrs. Rucker); Alfonso Gonzales (Abner); Robert Marchand (Luke/ William Wilks); Philip Minor (Ames/ Rev. Harry Wilks); Danny Rivituso (Zeke)

DOWN RIVER, *St. Clements Church*, New York, opened December 19, 1975
Produced by the American Repertory Company; A Musical Play by Jeff Tambornino, based on Mark Twain's *Huckleberry Finn*; Director, Brian Murphy; Music and lyrics by John Braden; Setting, David Mitchell

David Patrick Kelly (Huckleberry Finn); Samuel E. Wright (Nigger Jim); James Greene (The King); John Bottoms (The Duke)

HUCK AND JIM ON THE MISSISSIPPI, *Florida Atlantic University Theater*, Boca Raton, opened November 11, 1983
Produced by Joshua Logan and the Florida Atlantic University Foundation; Producer, Joe Conway; A Musical based on Mark Twain's *Huckleberry Finn*; Direction, Book and lyrics by Joshua Logan; Music by Bruce Ponahac; Sets, Rex Fluty; Lighting, Edward Maddern; Costumes, Beverly Jane Thomas; Choreography, Robert Simpson; Musical director, Vicki Carter; Musical conductor, William Prince; Stage manager, Priscilla Pearl Farley

Jonathan Ward (Huckleberry Finn); Ray Forchion (Jim); Howard Da Silva (The King); Don Sparks (The Duke); and Melissa Hart, Ann Turner, Alan S. Reynolds, Caroline Viglione, Ken Thiboult, Karen Holroyd, Jack Brenner, Bob Mello, Roger Paul DuBois, Paul A. Yager, Arnold Dolan, Lori Galante, Juliann Pugh, Julie Prosser, Michael J. A. Cappola

MUSICAL NUMBERS: "Stretchers"; "The Widow's Song"; "The Widow Douglas' House"; "An Almost Nearly Friend"; "Jackson Island"; "Good Mornin' Mornin'; "The Escape"; "Goin' Where the River Goes"; "Grangerford Prayer"; "Critters"; "A Love Like Mine"; "My Kind of Bastid"; "Vignettes"; "The Touch of a Woman"; "Song of Mourning"; "England"; "I'm Old Enough to Know"; "The Gates of Hell"; Finale

THE ADVENTURES OF HUCKLEBERRY FINN, *Bagley Wright Theatre*, Seattle, opened November 20, 1983 37 performances

Produced by the Seattle Repertory Theatre; A Play by James Hammerstein and Christopher Harbon, based on the novel by Mark Twain; Director, James Hammerstein; Settings, Robert Dahlstrom; Lighting, Arden Fingerhut; Costumes, Liz Covey; Original music, Ralph Affoumado; Musical direction, Daniel Birnbaum; Musical staging, Nancy Cranbourne; Sound, Michael Holten

Robert Macnaughton (Huckleberry Finn); William O'Leary (Tom Sawyer/Emmeline); David Toney (Jim); Brian Faker (Ben/Buck Grangerford/Boy in Traveling Clothes/Boy In Canoe); Ted D'Arms (The King/Judge Thatcher/Riverman); John Procaccino (Bob Grangerford/The Duke); Susan Ludlow (Miss Watson/Widow Bartley); Glenn Mazen (Pap Finn/Col. Grangerford/ Silas Phelps); Kathryn Mesney (Aunt Polly/Judith Loftus/Mrs. Grangerford/Mary Jane Wilkes); Sharon Ullrick (Hank/Sophia Grangerford/Joanna Wilkes/ Aunt Sally); Michael Santo (Dancing Riverman/ Ferryboat Captain/ Parker/ Judge/ Harvey Wilkes/ Luke); Karen Kay Cody (Jo/Charlotte Grangerford/Mrs. Shackleford); Frank Corrado (Man with Gun/Tom Grangerford/ Hines/Earl); Marjorie Nelson (Widow Douglas/Miss Rucker); Corky Dexter (Violinist/William Wilkes/ Farmer); Tamu Gray (Lula/Betsy/ Lize); Mark Jenkins (Singing Canoeist/Rev. Shackleford/Doctor); Michael Greer, Keith Nicholai (Rivermen); Carl August Sander (Banjo Player/ Harnery Sheperdson/ Auctioneer/ Jed); Steve Sneed (Slave/Shadrach)

THE ADVENTURES OF HUCKLEBERRY FINN, *Goodman Theatre*, Chicago, opened February 4, 1985

Produced by the Organic Theatre Company; A Play written and directed by Stuart Gordon, based on the novel by Mark Twain; Settings, John Paoletti; Lighting, Geoffrey Bushor; Costumes, Mary Griswold; Musical director, Jonathan Pearthree

James Cameron Mitchell (Huckleberry Finn); Meshach Taylor (Jim); J. Pat Miller (The King); Richard Henzel (The Duke/Ben Rogers/Bob Grangerford); Carolyn Purdy-Gordon (Aunt Polly/Mary Jane Wilks/Sophia Grangerford/Miss Watson/Mrs. Loftus); Eric Berg (Tom Sawyer); Tom Towles (Pap Finn/Col. Grangerford); Roberta Custer (Aunt Sally/Widow Douglas/Mrs. Grangerford/Joanna Wilks)

BIG RIVER: THE ADVENTURES OF HUCKLEBERRY FINN, *Eugene O'Neill Theatre*, New York, opened April 25, 1985 1,005 performances

Produced by Rocco Landesman, Heidi Landesman, Rick Steiner, M. Anthony Fisher and Dodge Productions; Associates producers, Arthur Katz, Emily Landau, Fred Mayerson and TM Productions; A Musical Play based on the novel by Mark Twain;

Director, Des McAnuff; Book by William Hauptman; Music and lyrics by Roger Miller; Scenery, Heidi Landesman; Lighting, Richard Riddell; Costumes, Patricia McCourty; Choreography, Janet Watson; Musical director and vocal arrangments, Linda Twine; Musical supervision, Danny Troob; Orchestrations, Steven Margoshes and Danny Troob; Dance and incidental music, John Richard Lewis; Stage movement and fights, B. H. Barry; Sound, Otto Munderloh; Stage managers, Frank Hartenstein, Steven Adler and Marianne Cane

Daniel H. Jenkins (succeeded by Martin Moran, Brian L. Green, Jon Ehrlich) (Huckleberry Finn); Ron Richardson (succeeded by Larry Riley, George Merritt) (Jim); John Short (succeeded by Clint Allen, Roger Bart) (Tom Sawyer); Gordon Connell (Mark Twain); Susan Browning (Widow Douglas/Sally Phelps); Bob Gunton (succeeded by Michael McCarty) (The King); Rene Auberjonois (succeeded by Russell Lieb, Brent Spiner, Ken Jenkins, Stephen Mellor) (The Duke); Evalyn Baron (Miss Watson/Harmonica Player); John Goodman (succeeded by Leo Burmester, Roger Miller, Graham Pollock) (Pap Finn/Sheriff Bell); Ralph Byers (Judge Thatcher/Harvey Wilks/Silas Phelps); William Youmans (Ben Rogers/Young Fool); Andi Henig (Jo Harper/Joanna Wilks); Aramis Estevez (Simon); Patti Cohenour (succeeded by Karla DeVito, Patti Cohenour, Marin Mazzie) (Mary Jane Wilks); Peggy Harmon (Susan Wilks); Michael Brian (Dick/Andy/Hired Hand/Man in Crowd); Reathel Bean (Lafe/Counselor Robinson/Hired Hand); Carol Denis (Alice, a Slave); Jennifer Leigh Warren (Alice's Daughter); Franz Jones (Bill)

MUSICAL NUMBERS: "Do You Want to Go to Heaven?"; "The Boys"; "Waiting for the Light to Shine"; "Guv'ment"; "Hand for the Hog"; "I Huckleberry Me"; "Muddy Water"; "Crossing Over"; "River in the Rain"; "When the Sun Goes Down in the South"; "The Royal Nonesuch"; "Worlds Apart"; "Arkansas"; "How Blest We Are"; "You Ought to Bed Here With Me"; "Leaving's Not the Only Way to Go"; "Free at Last"

Original cast recording: MCA Records

Touring Company, opened *State Theatre*, Cleveland, July 11, 1987; closed *Opera House*, Lexington, Ken., May 15, 1988

Presented by Tom Mallow, Arthur M. Katz, William H. Kessler, Jr., by arrangement with Rocco Landesman, Heidi Landesman, Rick Steiner, M. Anthony Fisher and Dodge Productions; A Musical Play based on the novel by Mark Twain; Director, Michael Grieg; Book by William Hauptman; Music and lyrics by Roger Miller; Scenery, Heidi Landesman; Lighting, Richard Riddell; Costumes, Patricia McCourty; Choreography, Janet Watson; Musical director and vocal arrangments, Linda Twine; Musical supervision, Danny Troob; Orchestrations, Steven Margoshes and Danny Troob; Dance and incidental music, John Richard Lewis; Stage movement and fights, B. H. Barry; Sound, Otto Munderloh; Stage manager, Charles Collins

Romain Fruge (Huckleberry Finn); Michael Edward-Stevens (Jim); Kevin Cooney (succeeded by Jordan Bowers) (Mark Twain/Counselor Robinson/Doctor); Barry Lee (Tom Sawyer); Frances Ford (Widow Douglas/ Sally Phelps); Walker Joyce (The King); Michael Calkins (The Duke); Lucina Hitchcock Cone (Miss Watson/Woman in Shanty/Harmonica Player); Dale Radunz (Pap Finn/Sheriff Bell/Hired Hand); Bruce Vernon Bradley (Judge Thatcher/Harvey Wilks/Silas Phelps); Robert Lambert (Ben Rogers/Hank/Hired Hand); Beth Musiker (Jo Harper/Joanna Wilks); Thom Cagle (Simon/Dick Young Fool); Carol Carmello (succeeded by Jessie Janet Richards) (Mary Jane Wilks); Heidi Karol Johnson

(Susan Wilks); Fred Sanders (Lafe/Counselor Robinson/Man in Crowd/Hired Hand); Ivan Thomas (succeeded by Brian Evart Chandler) (Bill, a Servant); Gwendolyn L. Stewart (Alice, a Slave); Angela Hall (Alice's Daughter); Steven Riddle (Man of Skiff); Lawrence Patrick (St. Pete Boy)

THE BOYS IN AUTUMN, Marines Memorial Theatre, San Francisco, opened September 3, 1981 32 performances
Produced by the Kennedy Center and James B. McKenzie, in association with Peter Owens and Theatre Now, Inc.; Associate producer, Harry Berensen; A Play by Bernard Sabath; Director, Tom Moore; Setting, Douglas W. Schmidt; Lighting, Martin Aronstein; Costumes, Robert Blackmand; Sound, Susan Harvey

Kirk Douglas (Thomas Gray); Burt Lancaster (Henry Finnigan)

THE BOYS IN AUTUMN, Circle in the Square, New York, opened April 30, 1986 38 performances
Produced by the Circle in the Square, Theodore Mann, artistic director; A Play by Bernard Sabath; Director, Theodore Mann; Setting, Michael Miller; Lighting, Richard Nelson; Costumes, Jennifer Von Mayrhauser; Stage managers, Michael F. Ritchie and Carol Klein

John Cullum (Thomas Gray); George C. Scott (Henry Finnigan)

SCREEN

HUCK AND TOM, Famous Players Lasky-Paramount Pictures, released March 1918
A Jesse L. Lasky production; Director, William Desmond Taylor; Screenplay, Julia Crawford Ivers, based on the novel by Mark Twain; Photography, Homer Scott

Robert Gordon (Huck Finn); Jack Pickford (Tom Sawyer); George Hackthorne (Sid Sawyer); Edythe Chapman (Aunt Polly); Clara Horton (Becky Thatcher); Anitra Short (Joe Harper); Frank Lanning (Injun Joe); Tom Bates (Muff Potter); Alice Marvin (Mary); Jack Keckley (Mrs. Thatcher); John Burton (Judge Thatcher)

HUCKLEBERRY FINN, Famous Players Lasky-Paramount Pictures, released February 1920
A Jesse L. Lasky production; Director, William Desmond Taylor; Screenplay, Julia Crawford Ivers, based on the novel by Mark Twain; Photography, Homer Scott

Lewis D. Sargent (Huck Finn); Gordon Griffith (Tom Sawyer); Edythe Chapman (Aunt Polly); Thelma Salter (Becky Thatcher); Esther Ralston (Mary Jane Wilks); Orral Humphrey (The Duke); Tom D. Bates (The King); George Reed (Jim); Martha Mattox (Miss Watson); L. M. Wells (Judge Thatcher); Frank Lanning (Pap Finn); Katherine Griffith (Widow Douglas); Fay Lampert (Johanna); Harry Rattenburg (Uncle Harvey); Eunice Van Moore (Mrs. Sally Phelps); Charles Elder (School Teacher)

HUCKLEBERRY FINN, Paramount Pictures, released August 1931
Director, Norman Taurog; Screenplay, Grover Jones and William Slavens McNutt, based on the novel by Mark Twain; Photography, David Abel

Junior Durkin (Huck Finn); Jackie Coogan (Tom Sawyer); Mitzi Green (Becky Thatcher); Jackie Searl (Sid Sawyer); Clarence Muse (Jim); Clara Blandick (Aunt Polly); Jane Darwell (Widow Douglas); Guy Oliver (Judge Thatcher); Cecil Weston (Mrs. Thatcher); Eugene Pallette (Junior); Oscar Apfel (Senior); Warner

Richmond (Pap Finn); Charlotte V. Henry (Mary Jane Wilks); Doris Short (Ella); Lillian Harner (Abigail Prentice); Frank McGlynn (School Teacher)

THE ADVENTURES OF HUCKLEBERRY FINN, *Metro-Goldwyn-Mayer*, released February 1939

Producer, Joseph L. Mankiewicz; Director, Richard Thorpe; Screenplay, Hugo Butler, based on the novel by Mark Twain; Photography, John Seitz; Art directors, Cedric Gibbons and Randall Duell; Music, Franz Waxman; Editor, Frank E. Hull

Mickey Rooney (Huckleberry Finn); Walter Connolly (The Dauphin); William Frawley (The Duke); Rex Ingram (Jim); Lynne Carver (Mary Jane Wilks); Elizabeth Risdon (Widow Douglas); Jo Ann Sayers (Susan Wilks); Minor Watson (Captain Brandy); Victor Kilian (Pap Finn); Clara Blandick (Miss Watson); Anne O'Neal (Miss Batlett); Harlan Briggs (Mr. Rucker); Sarah Edwards (Mrs. Rucker); Janice Chambers (Mary Adams); Harry Watson (Ben Donaldson); Billy Watson (Eliot); Johnny Walsh (Sam); Delmar Watson (Joe); E. Allyn Warren (Mr. Skackleford); Nora Cecil (Mrs. Shackleford); and Sarah Padden, Roger Gray, Wade Boteler, Irving Bacon, Robert Emmett Keane, Roger Imhof, Arthur Aylesworth, George Guhl, Erville Anderson, Jessie Graves, John Ince, Edwin J. Brady, Joe Bernard, Mickey Rentschler, Leni Lynn, Frank Darien, Alonzo Price, Harry Cording, Lew Kelly

THE ADVENTURES OF HUCKLEBERRY FINN, *Metro-Goldwyn-Mayer*, released May 1960

Producer by Samuel Goldwyn, Jr.; Director, Michael Curtiz; Screenplay, James Lee, based on the novel by Mark Twain; Photography, Ted McCord; Art directors, George W. Davis and McClure Capp; Musical director, Jerome Moross; Songs, Burton Lane and Alan Jay Lerner; Editor, Frederic Steinkamp

Eddie Hodges (Huckleberry Finn); Tony Randall (The King); Mickey Shaughnessy (The Duke); Archie Moore (Jim); Patty McCormack (Joanna); Neville Brand (Pap Finn); Judy Canova (Sheriff's Wife); Andy Devine (Mr. Carmody); Sherry Jackson (Mary Jane Wilks); Finlay Currie (Captain Sellers); Josephine Hutchinson (Widow Douglas); Royal Dano (Sheriff); Buster Keaton (Lion Tamer); Parley Baer (Grangerford Man); John Carradine (Slave Catcher); Dolores Hawkins (River Boat Singer); Sterling Holloway (Barber); Dean Stanton (Slave Catcher); Minerva Urecal (Miss Watson); Roy Glenn (Drayman); Rickey Murray (Cabin Boy); Sam McDaniel (Servant); Fred Coby (Sheriff); Eddie Fetherston (Townsman); Fred Kohler, Jr. (Mate); Virginia Rose (Woman at Circus); Henry Corden (Mate); Haldane Zajic (Percy); Patric Whyte (Uncle Harvey)

MUSICAL NUMBERS: "I Ain't Never Felt So Good Before"; "The World Is Full of Suckers"; "Pittsburgh Blue"; "Huckleberry Finn"

THE ADVENTURES OF HUCKLEBERRY FINN, *Mosfilm* (USSR), released 1972-73

Director, Georgi N. Daneliya; Screenplay, Viktoriya Tokareva and Georgi N. Daneliya, based on the novel by Mark Twain; Photography, Vadim I. Yusov; Music, Andrei Petrov

Roma Madyanov (Huck Finn); Felix Imokuede (Jim); Vakhtang Kikabidze (The Duke); Yevgeny Leonov (The King); Vladimir P. Bassov (Pap Finn); Irina Skobstyeva (Widow Douglas)

THE ADVENTURES OF HUCKLEBERRY FINN, *United Artists*, released May 1974

An APJAC-Reader's Digest production; Producer, Arthur J. Jacobs; Associate producer, Robert Greenhut; Director, J. Lee Thompson; Screenplay, Richard M. and Robert B. Sherman, based on the novel by Mark Twain; Photography, Laszlo Kovacs; Production designer, Philip Jefferies; Costumes, Donfeld; Choreography, Marc Breaux; Musical director, Fred Werner; Music and lyrics, Richard M. and Robert B. Sherman; Editor, Michael F. Anderson

Jeff East (Huckleberry Finn); Paul Winfield (Jim); Harvey Korman (The King); David Wayne (The Duke); Gary Merrill (Pap Finn); Arthur O'Connell (Colonel Grangerford); Lucille Benson (Widder Douglas); Natalie Trundy (Mrs. Loftus); Kim O'Brien (Mary Jane Wilks); Jean Fay (Susan Wilks); Ruby Leftwich (Miss Watson); Odessa Cleveland (Jim's Wife); Joe Boris (Jason); Danny Lantrip (Kyle); Van Bennett (Wayne); Linda Watkins (Mrs. Grangerford); Jean Combs (Miss Emmeline); Frances Fawcett (Miss Charlotte); Suzanne Prystup (Miss Maryanne); H. L. Rowley (Horatio); Doris Woebs (Marybelle); Frank Mills (Buck); Sherree Sinquefield (Miss Sophia); Morris Denton (Boat Captain); Hoskins Deterlly (Lot Hovey); Elliott Trimble (Uncle Harvey); Forrest Colebank (Abner); Charles C. Burns (Sheriff); Orville Meyer (Tomkins); R. Norwood Smith, Jack Millstein (Hunters); Larry Ferney, Albert Schilling, Clayton Sterling (Men at Theater); Rex Commack (Bartender); George Prescott (Man at Jackson's Landing); Mrs. James Torrey, Rose Pansanol, John Schwartzman (Auction Members); Gray Montgomery, Pat O'Connor, Sam Blackmon (Guards); Louis Wentworth III, Andrew Knight (Roughmen); Ken Wannberg (Piano Player)

MUSICAL NUMBERS: "Freedom"; "Huckleberry Finn"; "Someday Honey Darlin'"; "Cairo, Illinois"; "A Rose in a Bible"; "Royalty"; "What's Right, What's Wrong"; "Rotten Luck"; "Royal Nonesuch"; "Into His Hands"

TELEVISION

THE ADVENTURES OF HUCKLEBERRY FINN, *Climax!*, televised September 1, 1955 CBS 1 hour

Producer, Martin Manulis; Director, Herbert Swope, Jr.; Adapted from the novel by Mark Twain

Charles Taylor (Huck Finn); John Carradine (The Duke); Walter Catlett (The Dauphin); Thomas Mitchell (Pap Finn); Minor Watson (Judge Thatcher); Elizabeth Patterson (Widow Douglas); Catherine Warren (Mary Jane Wilks)

HUCK FINN, *United States Steel Hour*, televised November 20, 1957 CBS 1 hour

Producer, David Alexander; Director, Elliot Silverstein; Teleplay, Leo Pockriss, Anne Croswell and Frank Luther, adapted from the novel by Mark Twain; Songs, Frank Luther

Jimmy Boyd (Huck Finn); Earle Hyman (Jim); Jack Carson (The King); Basil Rathbone (The Duke); Florence Henderson (Mary Jane Wilks); Karin Wolfe (Johanna Wilks)

MUSICAL NUMBERS: "Loafin' on the Water"; "My Friend Huckleberry Finn"; "The Boasting Song"; "The Time Has Come to Say Goodbye"; "We All Shout Together in the Morning"; "Storm A-Risin' in the Night"; "Funny But Likeable"; "Too Wonderful for Me"; "You Are One to Wonder"

TOM AND HUCK, *Shirley Temple Theatre*, televised October 9, 1960 NBC 1 hour

Producer, Alvin Cooperman; Director, Paul Nickell; Adapted by Bruce Geller from Mark Twain's Tom Sawyer and Huckleberry Finn stories; Narrator, Shirley Temple

Teddy Rooney (Huck Finn); David Ladd (Tom Sawyer); Janet Blair (Aunt Polly); Dan Duryea (Muff Potter); Paul Stevens (Injun Joe); Ruthie Robinson (Becky Thatcher); Ray Teal (Judge Thatcher); Jackie Coogan (Marshal Rogers); Lee Richardson (Doc Robinson)

THE NEW ADVENTURES OF HUCKLEBERRY FINN, televised September 15, 1968 through March 21, 1969 NBC 20 episodes 30 minutes each
Executive producers, William Hanna and Joseph Barbera; Producer, Edward Rosen; Directors (live action), Bruce Bilson, Byron Haskin, Walter Burr and Hollingsworth Morse; Director (animation), Charles A. Nichols; Written by Frank Crew, Les Rifkin; Music, Hoyt Curtin and Ted Nichols

Michael Shea (Huckleberry Finn); Kevin Schultz (Tom Sawyer); Lu Ann Haslam (Becky Thatcher); Ted Cassidy (Injun Joe); Anne Bellamy (Aunt Polly); Dorothy Tennant (Mrs. Thatcher); and the voices of Dennis Day, Daws Butler, Hal Smith, Ted DeCorsia, Peggy Webber, Jack Kruschen, Bernard Fox, Jay Novello, Keye Luke, Janet Waldo, Charles Lane, Vic Perrin, Julie Bennett, Paul Frees, Marvin Miller, Paul Stewart, John Myhers, Abraham Sofaer

HUCKLEBERRY FINN, televised March 25, 1975 ABC 90 minutes
Produced by ABC Circle Films; Producer, Steven North; Director, Robert Totten; Teleplay, Jean Holloway, based on the novel by Mark Twain; Photography, Andrew Jackson; Art director, Peter M. Wooley; Music, Earl Robinson; Song "Mississippi (Said the River, I'm Your Friend)" by Earl Robinson and Steven North; Sung by Roy Clark; Editors, Diane Adler and Marsh Hendry

Ron Howard (Huckleberry Finn); Donny Most (Tom Sawyer); Jack Elam (The King); Merle Haggard (The Duke); Royal Dano (Mark Twain); Antonio Fargas (Jim); Dee Carroll (Aunt Sally Phelps); Rance Howard (Pap Finn); Patty Weaver (Mary Jane Wilks); Jean Howard (Widow Douglas); Clint Howard (Arch); Shug Fisher (Old Doc); Sarah Selby (Aunt Polly); Bill Erwin (Harvey Wilks); Frederic Downs (Ben Bucker); James Almanzar (Uncle Silas Phelps); Woodrow Chambliss (Auctioneer)

THE ADVENTURES OF HUCKLEBERRY FINN, televised July 9, 1981 NBC 2 hours
Schick Sunn Classics/Taft International Pictures; Executive producer, Charles E. Sellier, Jr.; Producer, Bill Cornford; Director, Jack B. Hively; Teleplay, Tom Chapman, based on the novel by Mark Twain; Photography, Paul Hipp; Art director, Charles Bennett; Music, Bob Summers; Editor, Michael Spence

Kurt Ida (Huck Finn); Dan Monahan (Tom Sawyer); Brock Peters (Jim); Forrest Tucker (The Duke); Larry Storch (The Dauphin); Lurene Tuttle (Miss Watson); Jack Kruschen (Judge Thatcher); Helen Kleeb (Widow Douglas); Cliff Osmond (Pap Finn); Prentiss Rowe (Constable Burns); Michele Marsh (Mrs. Loftus); Elvia Allman (Aunt Sally Phelps); James Griffith (Uncle Silas Phelps); Mike Mazurki (Logan); and John Sterling Arnold, John G. Bishop, Jeff Craggs, Richard Blomgren, Loren Ewing, Robert J. Gallagher, Don Haggerty, Richard Hansen, Henry Max Kendrick, H.E.D. Redford, Michael Ruud, Theophis Ross, Tim Winters, Bill Zuckert, William F. West

RASCALS AND ROBBERS -- THE SECRET ADVENTURES OF TOM SAWYER AND HUCK FINN, televised February 27, 1982 CBS 2 hours
A CBS Entertainment production; Executive producer, Hunt Lowry; Produced and

written by Carlos Davis and David Taylor, based on characters created by Mark Twain; Director, Dick Lowry; Photography, James Pergola; Art director, Albert Heschong; Costumes, Rosanna Norton; Music, James Horner; Editor, Byron "Buzz" Brandt

Anthony Michael Hall (Huck Finn); Patrick Creadon (Tom Sawyer); Anthony James (Scree); Allyn Ann McLerie (Aunt Polly); Anthony Zerbe (Arco the Magnificent); Ed Begley, Jr. (Jeb); Cynthia Nixon (Alice); John Harkins (Mr. Clinch); Hansford Rowe (Colonel Beeton); William Le Messena (Judge Thatcher); J.D. Hall (George); Gretchen West (Callie); Eugenia Wright (Reba); and Robert Adams, Ed Bakey, Dave Cass, Lydy Henley Caldwell, Hoskins Deierl, Chris Ellis, Blake Brocksmith, Ron Gural, Boyce Holliman, Jerry Leggio, Robert Lussier, John Quern, Al Scott, Edward Seamon, Sam Serrill, Neil Summers, Laddy Sartin, Patti Tierce

THE ADVENTURES OF HUCKLEBERRY FINN, *CBS Family Classics*, televised November 26, 1982 CBS 1 hour

Produced by John Erichsen in association with Triple Seven Concepts; Executive producer, Walter J. Hucker; Director, Paul McAdam; An animated version by John Palmer of the novel by Mark Twain; Music, Richard Bowden; Editors, John Mandelberg, Nancy Davenport

Voices: Simon Hinton, Alistair Duncan, Scott Higgins, Philip Hinton, Jane Harder

ADVENTURES OF CON SAWYER AND HUCKLEMARY FINN, *ABC Weekend Special*, televised September 7 and 14, 1985 30 minutes each part

An ABC Production; Executive producer, Diane Silver; Producers, Doro Bacharach and Marcus Viscivi; Director, Joan Darling; Teleplay, Ann Elder and Cynthia Chenault; Photography, Curtis Clark; Art director, Richard James; Music, Paul Chihara; Editor, Katherine Wenning

Drew Barrymore (Con Sawyer); Randy Ward (Hucklemary Finn); Patricia Richardson (Pamela Sawyer); James Rebhorn (Charlie Riley); Alan North (Skeezer); James Naughton (Mr. Sawyer); Terri Hanauer (Sarah); Melissa Hart (Cindy); M. Emmet Walsh (Rocco); Raymond Serra (Stubby); Ken Olfson (Reverend); Kimber Shoop III (Bobby Thatcher); and Dennis Haskins, Hopi Morton, Liz Porazzo, Ray Spruell, David Wilson

ADVENTURES OF HUCKLEBERRY FINN, *American Playhouse*, televised February 10 through March 2, 1986 PBS 4 episodes 1 hour each

Produced by The Great Amwell Co., in association with WGBH Boston; Executive producer, William Perry; Producer, Jane Iredale; Director, Peter H. Hunt; Teleplay, Guy Gallo, based on the novel by Mark Twain; Photography, Walter Lassally; Production designer, Bill Groom; Costumes, Jennifer Von Mayrhauser; Music, William Perry; Editor, Jerrold L. Ludwig

Patrick Day (Huckleberry Finn); Eugene Oakes (Tom Sawyer); Samm-Art Williams (Jim); Geraldine Page (Aunt Sally Phelps); Jim Dale (The Duke); Barnard Hughes (The King); Frederic Forrest (Papp Finn); Sada Thompson (Widow Douglas); Butterfly McQueen (Blind Woman); Richard Kiley (Colonel Grangerford); Lillian Gish (Mrs. Loftus); Anne Shropshire (Miss Watson); Jack Reidelberger (Buck Grangerford); Bill Chamness (Judge Thatcher); Robert Stocker (Minister); Jason Hankins (Billy); Richard Niehaus (Sheriff); David Watters (Reverend Sprague), Harriet Cartmell (Mrs. Sprague), Amy Shouse (Agnes); Omer W. Johnson (Pete); Robert Bowen (Clerk); Lewis Hankins

(Deputy); Fay Washington (Servant); Shag Adamson (Mr. Bradish); Fay Thomas (Cook); Allan Schmitt (Heber); Hula Duke (Aunt Polly); Barry Moser (Hank); Jeff Seibert (Slade); Mark Perraut (Ned); Ralph Pace (Bob); Royce Clark (Arkansas); Ivan Green (Davy); David Gray (Scotty); Ronnie French (John); Kelley Kalb (Bob Grangerford); Shirley Toncray (Rachel Grangerford); Michael Jones (Tom Grangerford); Kimberley Skeens (Sophia Grangerford); James McDaniel (Jack); Michael Kalman (Minister); Andy Duke (Stover); Phil Weber (Buck Harkness); Mark Vaughan (Horace); Roberta Wooden (Hannah); Conrad McLaren (Silas Phelps)

THE DAY THEY CAME TO ARREST THE BOOK, CBS Schoolbreak Special, televised January 27, 1987 CBS 1 hour
Produced by Ruby-Spears Enterprises in association with Sunrise Films Ltd. and Zorah Productions, Inc.; Executive producers, Joe Ruby and Ken Spears; Supervising producer, Edward Ledding; Producer, Eda Godel Hallinan; Coproducer, Paul Saltzman; Line producer, Rob Iveson; Director, Gilbert Moses; Teleplay, Melvin Peebles, based on the novel by Nat Hentoff; Photography, Doug Kiefer; Production designer, Perri Gorrara; Music, Udi Harpaz; Editor, Richard Uber

Anne Meara (Mrs. Saltars); Jonathan Crombie (Barney); Real Andrews (Gordon); Jeremy Ratchford (Luke); Jessica Steen (Kate); Michelle St. John (Maggie); Maureen McRae (Mrs. Baines); Tony Rosato (Mr. Lopez); David Ferry (Mr. Phelps); Barry Flatman (Mr. Moore); Ardon Bess (Mr. McLean); and Lynn Cormack, Matsu Anderson, Lorna Wilson, Gloria Reuben, Glairey Richardson, David B. Nichols, Martin Louis

BACK TO HANNIBAL: THE RETURN OF TOM SAWYER AND HUCKLEBERRY FINN, televised October 21, 1990 The Disney Channel 95 minutes
Produced by Gay-Jay Productions in association with The Disney Channel and WonderWorks; Producer, Hugh Benson; Coproducer, Thomas Lane; Director, Paul Krasny; Teleplay, Roy Johansen, based on characters created by Mark Twain; Photography, James W. Roberson; Production designer, Robert J. Bacon; Costumes, Donna Roberts; Music, Lee Holdridge; Editor, Richard E. Rabjohn

Raphael Sbarge (Tom Sawyer); Mitchell Anderson (Huck Finn); Megan Follows (Becky Thatcher Newman); William Windom (Judge Thatcher); Ned Beatty (The Duke of Bridgewater); Paul Winfield (Jim Watson); Graham Jarvis (Pruitt); George O. Petrie (Judge Cochran); Shea Farrell (Lyle Newman); Joseph Bova (The King of France); Hank Woessner (Willie Dawes); Zachary Bennett (Marcus); Mark Dakota Robinson (Henry); Kenny Davis (Allie Karcher); Val Saffron (Aunt Lucille); T. Max Graham (Steve Carswell); Burt Marshall (Wesley Cramer); Robert Crowley (Fowler); Grady Smith (Kevin Blevins); Eric Cole (Nevil Wainwright); Ralph Seeley (Ringland); Terry Sneyd (Samuel Biggs); and Addison Myers, Brad Holiday, Harry Gibbs, Elias Eliadis, James Anthony, Larry McKeever, Holmes Osborne, Whit Reichert, Sweeney LaBarge, Tim Snay, Read James, Hollis Huston, Cynthia Harness, Dorothy Farmer Davis, Len Pighini, Tina Chappel

THE HUMAN COMEDY

Various adaptations of the novel by William Saroyan (1943)

Synopsis

When Marcus Macauley marches off to war after Pearl Harbor, he leaves his fourteen-year-old brother Homer as head of the household back in Ithaca, California. Besides looking after his widowed mother, sister Bess and four-year-old Ulysses, Homer works after school and at night in the telegraph office managed by kindly Thomas Spangler. Spangler's telegrapher, old Willie Grogan, manages to get drunk every night despite his weak heart, but also nurtures the eager teenager whose kid brother daily is discovering the world around him. Marcus' frequent letters praise his new Army buddy, Tobey George, who has adopted the Macauley family as his own and is being encouraged by Marcus eventually to marry Bess and really become a family member. One night, Willie Grogan suffers a heart attack and dies before Homer returns from the drug store with his medicine. The old man's final effort was to type out a telegram from the War Department to Katie Macauley advising her of Marcus' death, and it has fallen to Homer to deliver it. The same night, Tobey George arrives in Ithaca and persuades Homer to destroy the telegram, assuring him Marcus is not dead when there are so many who love him. Because of a premonition, Mrs. Macaualey is aware that Marcus has been killed and embraces her two remaining sons. Ulysses takes Tobey's hand and leads him into the house when Mrs. Macauley welcomes her "new son" into the family.

Comment and Critique

My Heart's in the Highlands was the first produced play (in 1939) by William Saroyan, who was born in Fresno, California, on August 31, 1908. It was followed later the same year by *The Time of Your Life*, the first American play to win both the Pulitzer Prize and the New York Drama Critics Circle Award. The iconoclastic novelist created a furor when he refused the Pulitzer, claiming "wealth had no right to patronize art." Instead, he went to work for Louis B. Mayer at $300 a week. Aware of Mayer's dedication to family oriented fare, Saroyan submitted an outline of a screenplay called *The Human Comedy*, rhapsodizing the American way of life during the early days of Word War II. Mayer enthusiastically accepted it, and then Saroyan's agent Stanley Ross stunned MGM's boss by asking $300,000 for the screen rights. The negotiation was finally resolved by payment of $50,000 to Saroyan and the agent's 10% fee to be paid by the studio. Mayer, however, drew the line at Saroyan's demand to direct the movie and assigned the task to Clarence Brown. He then had writer Howard Estabrook complete the screenplay. Saroyan, meanwhile, rewrote *The Human Comedy* as an overnight best-selling novel, published in 1943 by Harcourt, Brace just before the film's release.

Time magazine's critic found that "at its best, *The Human Comedy* is immensely moving. Even its preaching sometimes achieves an eloquence that gives the picture a psychological fifth dimension. The Saroyan touch leaves nothing ordinary; the film is electric with the joy of life."

Thornton Delehanty, writing in *Redbook* magazine, reported: "*The Human Comedy* is William Saroyan's first feature-length story, and it lives up to its title. In its wealth of material, its accurate portraiture and its warm understanding, it is inescapably human, and Saroyan's light-hearted approach to the trials and tribulations of his characters causes it to glow with hidden laughter even when it is unashamedly sad...It is a simple account of simple people, told without affection or idiosyncrasy."

The critic for *The New Yorker*, while regretting the "diabetic quantities" of sentimentality in *The Human Comedy*, found: "What makes the picture worth seeing, which it is, oddly enough, is a fine lack of pretension, combined with a sort of mobility, a certain effect of outdoor freedom that you don't get from the smart interiors that the players are confined in most movies. Also, there's quite a lot of intentionally funny dialogue mixed in with the hallelujahs."

And following the film's New York opening, *The Times*' Bosley Crowther said that "here, cheek by jowl and overlapping, are set some most charming bits of fine motion picture expression and some most maudlin gobs of cinematic goo...here, in a picture which endeavors to speak such truths about Americana as should be spoken, pop up such artificialities as make one squirm with rank embarrassment...The whole simple idea of the story is that people are essentially good and that sorrow is a grim, inevitable burden and that faith and love will elevate men's hearts." Crowther concluded, "*The Human Comedy* is sentimental showmanship."

Mickey Rooney and Frank Morgan headed the cast, playing young Homer Macauley and old Willie Grogan, which brought a roster of future stars to the fore: Van Johnson, Marsha Hunt, James Craig, Donna Reed, young Bob Mitchum (he was still Bob at the time), Don DeFore and Barry Nelson. There also were veterans like Fay Bainter and Henry O'Neill, and a youngster being introduced by the name of Jackie "Butch" Jenkins -- the six-year-old son of actress Doris Dudley and Captain Jack Jenkins -- who well-nigh stole the movie from Mickey Rooney. Jenkins was to make only nine more movies (his final one, *Summer Holiday*, also had him playing Rooney's kid brother) before approaching adolescence and retiring from the screen.

The Human Comedy earned an Oscar nomination as Best Picture (losing to *Casablanca*). Mickey Rooney received his second Best Actor nomination, but lost the Oscar to Paul Lukas (for *Watch on the Rhine*). There was also a nomination for Harry Stradling's cinematography. An Academy Award did go, however, to William Saroyan (his only one) for Best Original Story.

Forty years after the film of *The Human Comedy*, William Dumaresq adapted the Saroyan story to the stage for which a musical score was written by Galt MacDermot (of *Hair* fame). Produced by Joseph Papp initially in late December 1983 for the New York Shakespeare Festival, *The Human Comedy* moved briefly to Broadway the following April.

Frank Rich lauded the musicalized *The Human Comedy*, feeling, "Both Saroyan and Mr. MacDermot share a rhapsodic Whitmanesque vision of this country; both men set that vision to warming idiomatic music... Virtually the entire show is sung...The result is a *Human Comedy* with the feel of *Our Town* -- and that sentiment is upheld by the ensemble fabric of the company and the all-American heterogeneity of the music...Perhaps that ideal American community never really existed as Saroyan and Mr. MacDermot have imagined it...But in *The Human Comedy*, you can go home again -- at least for a while -- and rediscover what a happy place it was meant to be."

Michael Walsh wrote in *Time* magazine: "The line between art and entertainment is often indistinct, and never more so than in musical theatre...The latest composer to blur that line is Galt MacDermot... The hero is not an individual but the imaginary, indomitable town of Ithaca. This poses a problem that MacDermot and his librettist, William Dumaresq, never quite overcome...The composer needs to be more careful about prosody; misplaced accents make some lines sound as if they were translated from Czech..."

In the *New York Post*, Clive Barnes, not overly impressed with Saroyan set to music, felt: "For me by far the best part of the show remains MacDermot's music -- his most considerable score since those far off days when he gave us *Hair*...Many people will find this show lovable, homespun, whimsical and altogether adorable.

Even moving, I myself find it -- apart from MacDermot's vibrantly alive score, mawkish and, like all of Saroyan for me, fundamentally insincere and therefore phony."

And *Newsweek*'s Jack Kroll observed: "Its chief virtue is hardly theatrical excitement but rather the tenderness, sweetness and compassion that pulsate through MacDermot's music...a kind of pop cantata... It's Norman Rockwell set to music in its portrait of hope and heartbreak."

In March 1959, David Susskind brought *The Human Comedy* to television, with Burgess Meredith narrating. The *DuPont Show of the Month* production was described by Richard F. Shepard (*The New York Times*) as "beautifully produced...There was no story to tell, yet it was a touching fable...S. Lee Pogostin adapted the novel magnificently, bringing dignity and love to the television version. Robert Mulligan's direction caught the comedy, the pathos, the loneliness, the unabashed sentimentality of the work. The acting was brilliant, particularly that of Michael J. Pollard, as the 14-year-old, and of seven-year-old David Francis, as his younger brother." CBS aired a pilot for a weekly series of *The Human Comedy* in 1964 with Timmy Rooney in the part his dad Mickey had in the film version two decades earlier.

STAGE

Public/Anspacher Theatre, New York, opened December 20, 1983 79 performances; moved to *Royale Theatre*, April 5, 1984 13 performances

Produced by the New York Shakespeare Festival and the Shubert Organization; Producer, Joseph Papp; Associate producer, Jason Steven Cohen; A Musical Comedy based on the novel by William Saroyan; Director, Wilford Leach; Libretto by William Dumaresq; Music by Galt MacDermot; Scenery, Bob Shaw; Lighting, James F. Ingalls; Costumes, Rita Ryack; Sound, Tom Morse; Music director and orchestrations, Galt MacDermot; Conductor, Tania Leon; Makeup and hairstyles, Marlies Vallant; Stage managers, Alan Fox and K. Siobhan Phelan

> Josh Blake (Ulysses Macauley); Stephen Geoffreys (Homer Macauley); Bonnie Koloc (Katie Macauley); Rex Smith (succeeded by Walter Hudson (Tom Spangler); Mary Elizabeth Mastrantonio (Bess Macauley); Anne Marie Bobby (Helen); Laurie Franks (Miss Hicks); Gordon Connell (Mr. Grogan); Daniel Noel (Felix); Christopher Edmonds (Thief); Delores Hall (succeeded by Debra Boyd) (Beautiful Music); Caroline Peyton (Mary Arena); Joseph Kolinski (Tobey George); Leata Galloway (Diana Steed); Walter Hudson (Minister); David Lawrence Johnson (Trainman); Olga Merediz (Mexican woman); Don Kehr (succeeded by Grady Mulligan) (Voice of Matthew Macauley); Kathleen Rowe McAllen (A Neighbor); Kenneth Bryan, Louis Padilla, Michael Wilson (Soldiers); Marc Stephen DelGatto, Lisa Kurchner, Vernon Spencer, Dan Tramon (Townspeople)

MUSICAL NUMBERS: "In a Little Town in California"; Hi Ya Kid"; "We're a Little Family"; "The Assyrians"; "Noses"; "You're a Little Young for the Job"; "I Can Carry a Tune"; "Happy Birthday, Happy Anniversary"; "I Think the Kid Will Do"; "Beautiful Music"; "Coconut Cream Pie"; "When I Am Lost"; "I Said Oh No, Daddy Will Not Come Walking Through the Door"; "The Birds in the Sky"; "Remember Always to Give"; "Long Past Sunset"; "Don't Tell Me"; "The Fourth Telegram"; "Give Me All the Money"; "Everything Is Changed"; "The World Is Full of Loneliness"

SCREEN

THE HUMAN COMEDY, Metro-Goldwyn-Mayer, released March 1943
Produced and directed by Clarence Brown; Screenplay, Howard Estabrook, based on the novel by William Saroyan; Photography, Harry Stradling; Art directors, Cedric Gibbons and Paul Groesse; Set decorators, Edwin B. Willis and Hugh Unt; Music, Herbert Stothart; Sound, W. R. Sparks; Editor, Conrad A. Nervig

Mickey Rooney (Homer Macauley); James Craig (Tom Spangler); Frank Morgan (Willie Grogan); Fay Bainter (Katie Macauley); Marsha Hunt (Diana Steed); Van Johnson (Marcus Macauley); Donna Reed (Bess Macauley); John Craven (Tobey George); Dorothy Morris (Mary Arena); Jackie "Butch" Jenkins (Ulysses Macauley); Mary Nash (Miss Hicks); Katherine Alexander (Mrs. Steed); Ray Collins (Matthew Macauley); Henry O'Neill (Charles Steed); Darryl Hickman (Lionel); S. Z. Sakall (Mr. Ara); Alan Baxter (Brad Stickman); Barry Nelson (Fats); Don DeFore (Texas); Bob Mitchum (Horse); Ann Ayars (Mrs. Sandoval); Ernest Whitman (Negro); Mark Daniels (First Soldier); William Roberts (Second Soldier); Rita Quigley (Helen Elliott); David Holt (Hubert Ackley); Byron Foulger (Blenton); Wallis Clark (Principal); Wally Cassell (Flirt); Mary Servoss (Mrs. Beaufrere); Morris Ankrum (Mr. Beaufrere); Lynn Carver (Daughter); Carl "Alfalfa" Switzer (Augie); Clem Bevans (Henderson); Adeline de Walt Reynolds (Librarian); Hobart Cavanaugh (Drunk at Bar); Emory Parnell (Policeman); Connie Gilchrist (Dolly); Frank Jenks (Larry); Howard Freeman (Reverend Holly); Jay Ward (Felix); Robert Emmet O'Connor (Bartender)

TELEVISION

THE HUMAN COMEDY, DuPont Show of the Month, televised March 28, 1959 CBS 90 minutes
Produced by David Susskind; Director, Robert Mulligan; Teleplay, S. Lee Pogostin, based on William Saroyan's novel and the motion picture

Burgess Meredith (Narrator); Ray McHugh (Homer Macauley); David Francis (Ulysses Macauley); Jo Van Fleet (Katie Macauley); Robert Geringer (Tom Spangler); Thomas Chalmers (Willie Grogan); Russell Collins (Mr. Covington); Anne Helm (Bess Macauley); Molly McCarthy (Mary Arena); John F. Hamilton (Charlie); R. G. Armstrong (Chris); Leo Penn (John)

THE HUMAN COMEDY, televised September 19, 1964 CBS Pilot 30 minutes
Produced by Metro-Goldwyn-Mayer Television; Producer, Rudy E. Abel; Director, Robert Ellis Miller; Based on characters created by William Saroyan

Timmy Rooney (Homer Macauley); Phyllis Avery (Alice Macauley); Jimmy Homer (Ulysses Macauley); Arthur O'Connell (Willie Grogan); Minerva Urecal (Mrs. Windler)

NOTE: Timmy Rooney has the part his father played in the 1943 movie

I, CLAUDIUS

Various adaptations of the novel by Robert Graves (1934)

Synopsis

To remain alive, scholarly Claudius, crippled Roman historian, plays the fool alive while his early marriage to Urganalia develops into mutual hatred. Claudius is fascinated with his grandmother, Empress Livia, who casually poisons anyone interfering with his thirst for power. Having divorced her husband and married Emperor Augustus, she arranges for the return to Rome of her son, Tiberius. Although victorious in war against the barbarians, Tiberius remains unpopular in the capital, and after Augustus' death, which Claudius suspects Livia has arranged, Tiberius kills his own brother, Postumus. Claudius' brother, Germanicus, is poisoned, assuring Tiberius of the throne. Livia slowly starves Tiberius' wife, Julia, to death, but aging Tiberius refuses to return to Rome from Capri when his mother Livia dies at eighty-six. After having Tiberius killed, mad Caligula ascends to the throne and then forces a marriage between his cousin, Messalina, and Claudius after banishing Calpurnia, Claudius' only true friend in Rome. The infamous Caligula's declaration of his transformation into a god and his orgiastic excesses and depravities at the expense of increased levies against the citizens foments revolt and he is assassinated. Claudius, born Tiberius Claudius Druses Nero Germanicus, at last becomes Emperor of Rome.

Comment and Critique

John Mortimer's play *I, Claudius* opened in London in 1972 to so-so notices and had a meager run of seventy-one performances. In *Plays and Players*, John Crosby wrote: "[Mortimer] went on to try to compress both of Robert Graves' delicious books *I, Claudius* and *Claudius the God* into one evening of theatre...[and] foolishly enough to try to grapple with not only Claudius but also the reigns of Augustus, Tiberius and Caligula. For a minute or so, I thought he was going to try to encompass all of *Decline and Fall*, all six of Gibbons' volumes!...In fact, *I, Claudius* is hardly a play at all, more a recital, a narration, a comic monologue... David Warner, a many-faceted actor, uses his stammer, his lisp, his flowing hands and large eyes with great skill to rivet our wandering wits on the complexities of Roman high life. Some of the others, I fear, ought to be arrested for impersonating actors. Tony Richardson's direction was fairly hysterical but I'm not sure that the script didn't demand it."

Robert Bryden, reporting to *The New York Times* from London, found: "Mortimer's script [is] well below the usual level of his stage writing, reducing the lives of the Caesars to a *Lion in Winter* mixture of palace-stair gossip and facetious anachronism. Richardson's direction seems to have limited itself to a few splashy crowd effects and bared breasts. Of its many promises, the only one the production keeps is the Claudius of David Warner."

The screen rights to Graves' best-selling *I, Claudius*, published in 1934, were purchased by Alexander Korda and its sequel, *Claudius the God*, three years later . Korda accepted a screen treatment from Graves but then turned the project over to Lajos Biros and Arthur Wimperis, who rewrote the screenplay. Screenwriter Carl Zuckamayer, who had written the dialogue for the screenplay of Korda's 1936 *Rembrandt*, was engaged with Lester Cohen to further collaborate on the script, and Graves' original scenario disappeared by committee.

I, Claudius was to star Charles Laughton and advance the career of actress Merle Oberon, whom Korda was intent on making not only an international film star but also his wife (on June 3, 1939). Reputedly having had enough of Laughton's agonizing, dedicated "character immersion" during his direction of *Rembrandt*, Korda sought another director to guide the rather undisciplined actor through *I, Claudius*. Marlene Dietrich agreed to release Korda from his final $100,000 payment on her $350,000 contract for starring in his 1937 *Knight Without Armour* if he would use the services of her mentor, Josef von Sternberg, then shunned in Hollywood and ill in a London hospital. Sternberg accepted Korda's offer to direct *I, Claudius*, but Laughton had agreed to star under the direction of his friend, William Cameron Menzies, and was furious about Korda's selection of Sternberg.

Alexander Korda's brother Vincent designed stunning sets for the projected epic, which began production at Denham Studios on February 15, 1937, budgeted at 120,000 pounds. Laughton's maddening insistence on "immersing" himself in the role of Claudius became a nerve-racking exercise in his search for a definitive interpretation. (His similar difficulties in 1934 attempting to "find" Micawber in MGM's memorable version of *David Copperfield* caused the studio to replace him with W. C. Fields.) In 1932, Laughton had successfully played Nero in Cecil B. DeMille's *The Sign of the Cross*, but the Emperor Claudius eluded him. His frenetic search for Claudius' speaking voice included constantly playing a recording of Edward VIII's abdication speech until his stuttering as Claudius became such a perfect imitation that Korda, unwilling to offend the Royal Family, refused to permit it. Additionally, Laughton received almost no direction from the autocratic Sternberg (clad in riding breeches and laced up boots and wearing a turban), who treated the actor with unmasked disdain.

In his autobiography *Fun in a Chinese Laundry* (which one wag felt should be subtitled *Film History Reshaped by Josef von Sternberg*), the director viewed his *I, Claudius* as bringing "to life an old empire and to depict the arrogance and decay of its civilization but to hold it up as a mirror to our tottering values and to investigate the diseased roots of excessive ambitions." He felt that the plot of the film-to-be was "highly dramatic and was to relate how a stuttering cripple became Emperor Claudius by allowing his enemies to consider him an idiot." Sternberg went on: "In selecting the actors and actresses who were to become my fellow sufferers, I was faced with the refusal of at least two of them to participate in the honor of acting in what was meant to be the film of the century; in particular, Raymond Massey, who told me that nothing on earth could persuade him to work with Laughton...but a part had been made to order for Laughton...he was Claudius. As the countdown approached, my star performer suddenly his majestic behavior and seemed to be in the throes of an agony, which at first I thought to be stage fright or an attack of constipation."

Disregarding the production schedule, Laughton wandered from set to set out of camera range, never dragging the same foot twice, trying to discover "better vibrations." He appalled Sternberg and Korda by further insisting that he could not play certain scenes on established sets but required moving to another setting where, as he told them, "the aura was move favorable to emanations." An impossible clash of egos was at work, and on March 1, Laughton informed the press that his contract with London Films would expire on April 21, and on that date he would be leaving the production. On March 16, Merle Oberon was involved in a serious auto accident, and Korda, distraught by his protege's injuries, at Sternberg's profligate direction, and at Laughton's tantrums, shut down his troubled set. He received 80,000 pounds from his insurance company to cover current production costs.

Sternberg later claimed: "Actors had truncated my film...When Merle Oberon had a bad concussion in an auto accident, which meant so much delay that all our preparations and contracts were invalidated, it was decided to halt the film. It might have been my most successful work." He added, however, "It was not a nightmare. It was a daymare."

In his 1974 book, *The Great British Picture Show*, George Perry wrote about the filming: "It was an unhappy experience. Laughton suffered desperate agonies in his quest for the interpretation of his part. Von Sternberg was difficult, temperamental and disliked, and after Merle Oberon was injured in a car accident, the film was abandoned, a third of it shot and thousands of pounds spent on massive and spectacular sets. What remains depicts what might have been one of Laughton's greatest performances."

On Christmas Eve 1965, the BBC first televised *The Epic That Never Was*, Bill Duncalf's remarkable chronicle of the making of *I, Claudius*. Negatives of the uncompleted and abandoned production were discovered in the Denham Studios of London Films, including five reels of rough-cut sequences, outtake and scrapped footage, which required two hours to screen. The film was edited and included in the BBC documentary, narrated by Dirk Bogarde. In the seventy-minute telecast were interviews with Josef von Sternberg, Merle Oberon, Flora Robson and Emlyn Williams. Author Robert Graves felt Claudius defied interpretation but, at least, Korda's purchase of the property paid off the mortgage on Graves' Majorca home. Merle Oberon insisted the film was abandoned because of her accident, but Emlyn Williams, who had given a superb performance as Caligula, realistically claimed that the actress easily could have been replaced and it was hostility between Laughton and his director that ended the production.

BBC's much-acclaimed, thirteen-part 1976 adaptation of *I, Claudius*, which earned Derek Jacobi the British equivalent of the Emmy Award as Best Actor, was televised in the U.S. on PBS' *Masterpiece Theatre* beginning on November 6, 1977, and a decade later was again broadcast in all its brilliance. John J. O'Connor (*The New York Times*) hailed it as "a fiendishly sophisticated concoction of Roman history, political intrigues, murderous ambitions and consuming passions. In the BBC/London Film Productions venture, they add up to fascinating spectacle and perhaps, with fitting perversity, great fun." Jack Pulman's scripts "are extremely successful in capturing the peculiar flavor of Mr. Graves' books" and Sian Phillips' portrayal of Livia was "played with absolutely gorgeous malevolence." Derek Jacobi's unforgettable playing of Claudius refuted Graves' concept that the stuttering scholar pretending to be an idiot defied impersonation.

STAGE

I, CLAUDIUS, Queen's Theatre, London, opened July 11, 1972 71 performances
Produced by Michael White in association with Woodfall Ltd.; A Play by John Mortimer, based on *I, Claudius* and *Claudius the God* by Robert Graves; Director, Tony Richardson; Decor, William Dudley; Costumes, Sue Palmer; Movement by Eleanor Fazan; Music by John Addison

David Warner (Claudius); Freda Jackson (Livia); Charles Lloyd Pack (Augustus); Warren Clarke (Caligula); David Foxxe (Tiberius); Rosalind Ayres (Calpurnia); Linda Liles (Sybil); John Gregg (General Drusus); John Turner (Cassius); Sean Roantree (Germanicus); Yvette Vanson (Camilla); Joolia Cappleman (Urganalia); Desmond Gill (Narcissus); Sara Kestleman (Messalina); Trevor T. Smith (Gemellus); Peter Dennis (Minester); Ben Aris (Vincius); Geoffrey Bateman (Silius); John Meredith (The Sergeant); Gerard Murphy (Interpreter); Stuart Mungall (The Doctor); Henry Szeps (Senator); Meg Clancy, Michael Hamilton, Fiona Victory (Citizens)

SCREEN

I, CLAUDIUS, London Films (unfinished 1937 film)
Produced by Alexander Korda; Director, Josef von Sternberg; Screenplay by Josef

von Sternberg, Lajos Biros, Arthur Wimperis, Carl Zuckmayer, Lester Cohen and Robert Graves, based on the Graves novels *I, Claudius* and *Claudius the God*; Photography, Georges Perinal; Production designer, Vincent Korda; Costumes, John Armstrong; Choreography, Agnes de Mille; Assistant director, Geoffrey Boothby; Technical advisor, Professor Ashmole.

Charles Laughton (Tiberius Claudius Drusus); Merle Oberon (Messalina); Flora Robson (Livia); Emlyn Williams (Caligula); Robert Newton (Cassius); John Clements (Valenz); F. Forbes Robertson (Tiberius)

TELEVISION

THE EPIC THAT NEVER WAS, televised December 24, 1965 BBC 70 minutes
Produced by the British Broadcasting Corporation; Producer/director, Bill Dincalf; Narrator, Dirk Bogarde

Josef von Sternberg, Merle Oberon, Flora Robson, Emlyn Williams, Robert Graves

I, CLAUDIUS, televised September 28 through November 30, 1976 BBC 13 episodes (60 minutes each); in U.S. on PBS' *Masterpiece Theatre*, televised November 6, 1977 through January 29, 1978
Produced by the British Broadcasting Corporation and and London Films Ltd.; Producer, Martin Lisemore; Directed by Herbert Wise; Teleplay by Jack Pulman, based on the novels by Robert Graves; Production designer, Tim Harvey; Title music, Wilfred Josephs; Incidental music, David Wulstan, performed by the Clerkes of Oxonford; Production advisor, Robert Erskine; Story editor, Betty Willingale

Derek Jacobi (Claudius); Sian Phillips (Livia); Brian Blessed (Augustus); Margaret Tyzack (Antonia); John Hurt (Caligula); George Baker (Tiberius); Patrick Stewart (Sejanus); Stratford Johns (Piso); Sheila White (Messalina); Ian Ogilvy (Drusus); Frances White (Julia); David Robb (Germanicus); Patricia Quinn (Livilla); John Castle (Postumus); James Faulkner (Herod); John Paul (Agrippa); Christopher Guard (Marcellus); Angela Morant (Octavia); Irene Hamilton (Plancina); Fiona Walker (Agrippina); Kate Lansbury (Apicata); Liane Aukin (Aelia); Beth Morris (Druscilla); John Rhys-Davies (Macro); Douglas Melbourne (Gemellus); Lockwood West (Senator); Jon Laurimore (Lentulus); Jo Rowbottom (Calpurnia); Freda Dowie (Caesonia); Sam Dastor (Cassius); Norman Eshley (Marcus); Anne Dyson (Briseis); Bruce Purchase (Sabinus); Moira Redmond (Domitia); Bernard Hill (Gratus); Geoffrey Hinsliff (Rufrius); John Cater (Narcissus); Lyndon Brook (Silanus); Bernard Hepton (Pallas); Nicholas Amer (Minester); Stuart Wilson (Silius); Charlotte Howard (Scylla); Norman Shelley (Horace); Kevin McNally (Castor); Donald Eccles (Pollio); Denis Carey (Livy); Alan Thompson (Praxis); Guy Slater (Courier); John Truscott (Librarian); Vivian Clifford (Postumus' wife); Jennifer Croxton (Urganalia); Charles Kay (Gallas); Karen Foley (Helen); Richard Hunter (Drisos); Alan Tucker (Slave); Robert Bateman (Singer); William Bond (Usher)

EPISODES: A Touch of Murder; Family Affairs; Waiting in the Wings; What Shall We Do About Claudius?; Poison Is Queen; The Crowd Calls for Death (Some Justice); A Partner to His Labors (Queen of Heaven); Reign of Terror; Zeus, By Jove; Hail, Who?; Fool's Luck; A God in Colchester; Old King Log

I NEVER SANG FOR MY FATHER
A Play by Robert Anderson (1968)

Synopsis

Gene Garrison is a recent a widower who finds a desperate need to reconcile his relationship with his aging, tyrannical father who has always been indifferent and cold toward him. The father is obsessed with himself, having lost his own mother when he was young and his own father to drink and abandonment of family. The elder Garrison had become a cold, unlovable martinet who had driven his daughter Alice from his house when she married a Jew, and never sang to him, never understood him. The failure of communication gives way to an emotional confrontation during Gene's visit when his mother suddenly dies and Alice, returning for the funeral, attempts to help her brother come to a more reasonable understanding of his relationship with their father.

Comment and Critique

Playwright Robert Anderson was born in New York City on April 28, 1917, and educated at Harvard, and began acting in summer stock at the South Shore Playhouse in Cohasset, Mass. He went on to create a playwriting course at New York's American Theatre Wing and taught at the Actors Studio. He wrote his first play, a musical called *Hour Town*, while a Harvard undergraduate, and first was featured as a playwright on Broadway with *Come Marching Home* in 1946. His *Tea and Sympathy* became one of the dramatic hits of the 1953-54 season and remains his best known work. He also wrote the 1956 screen version of it and stayed in films to do the screenplay to *The Nun's Story*, for which he received an Oscar nomination, and to *The Sand Pebbles*. His next Broadway hit was the comedy *You Know I Can't Hear You When the Water's Running* (1967) and then *I Never Sang for My Father* that had a mediocre run following its January 1968 opening. His wife, Teresa Wright, played the "exiled" sister in a family that never was able to communicate, and Hal Holbrook was the son who "never sang for my father."

In *The New York Times*, critic Clive Barnes felt it "often has the poignancy of a personal document. But the poignancy of the situation, real enough and believable in all conscience, is constantly betrayed by the over-obviousness and sentimentality of the writing, and by a lack of genuine dramatic focus...The saddest aspect of the play is that while its sincerity is as transparent as glass, the writing, the simulation of agony, even the actual story [has] the hearts-and-flowers, tear-jerking anguish of a woman's TV serial." Barnes liked Holbrook's "finely conveyed" despair and Lillian Gish's "delicately fluttery mother...[a] performance worthy of a more productive cause." He carped at Teresa Wright's "monotonous" acting in her role, but enthused over Alan Webb's picture of the father, which despite his playing the part with a British accent, "was perhaps a small price for a performance of telling sensibility."

Robert Anderson then adapted his play to the screen and for it won his second Oscar nomination. (He won the Writers Guild award for his screenplay.) The 1970 film version, starring Melvyn Douglas, in probably his greatest screen role, and Gene Hackman as the son, earned both actors Academy Award nominations, in starring and supporting roles, respectively. (Anderson lost to Ring Lardner, Jr., for *M*A*S*H*; Douglas to George C. Scott for *Patton*; Hackman to John Mills for *Ryan's Daughter*.) However, it was not overly popular with audiences or critics, although it made a number of Ten Best lists. Vincent Canby of *The New York Times* found: "Characters fret and argue, but the attitudes have been learned not from life but from archaic television. When eyes brim with tears, you are simply reminded of air pollution, and although people never stop speaking, they never really talk ...[Gilbert] Cates' direction is full of solemn, romantic movie affection that at time give this purported slice-of-life a touch of pure commercial fantasy." Canby summed up: "Melvyn Douglas and Dorothy Stickney, as the old couple, perform with the kind of professional sufficiency one expects of them, but Gene Hackman and Estelle Parsons, as their children, left me cheerless, which is the nature of the entire enterprise. *I Never Sang for My Father* is, by definition, a wretched motion picture."

Tom Milne wrote in Britain's *Monthly Film Bulletin*: "One is reminded, inevitably, of *Long Day's Journey Into Night*. Although Robert Anderson never presumes to match the tearing cannibalistics of O'Neill's family reunion, something of the same sense of a despairing *huis clos* emerges." Milne continued: "Melvyn Douglas gives the performances of his life [as] the tough, vulnerable old man, and is beautifully supported by Gene Hackman and Estelle Parsons in particular. The only pity is that Gilbert Cates evidently felt obliged to introduce some 'cinema.'"

Between the film version in 1970 and the revival of the play in 1987, Anderson wrote *Solitaire/Double Solitaire* and *Free and Clear* for Broadway, several novels, and the 1981 television movie, *The Patricia Neal Story*. The new mounting of *I Never Sang for My Father* in the summer of 1987 began with its opening at the Berkshire Festival on what was hoped to be the road to Broadway once again, but the production ended in Los Angeles after a cross-country tour. *Variety*, reviewing opening night at Washington's Eisenhower Theater, said: "A timeless theme about relationships and understanding is explored in this insightful dramatic study of a son's private battle with his conscience...Under Josephine Abady's sensitive direction, each member of the trio is a classic study in desperation. [Daniel] Travanti is just right as the sensible son who tries vainly to uphold traditional values before pent up rage engulfs him...[Harold] Gould gives new meaning to the word irascible as the selfish and bombastic father... Dorothy McGuire is moving as the faithful and long-suffering wife who offers constant excuses for her husband, as well as displaying the virtues he lacks...The production is not flawless [but] it is off to a promising start. It will give audiences a worthwhile second look at Anderson's fine play."

This production was later taped and broadcast on PBS' *American Playhouse* in mid-June 1988. "Realism as staged by Jack O'Brien almost does the drama in...[he] unleashes Harold Gould's querulous old man to a fare-thee-well; Gould builds the self-centered rambling father with sustained control, even in the more flamboyant portions," *Daily Variety* wrote of the TV production. "The play, which suggests an autobiographical unloading, boasts texture if not dramatic balance. It also wears away at the son's failure to make his father proud or even caring, a point that borders on the unstable. Travanti plays him with a restraint implying emptiness rather than regret... Problem with *I Never Sang for My Father* seems to be that in all its versions it comes off as more catharsis than objective dramaturgy."

John J. O'Connor, in *The New York Times*, felt: "As the United States grows older, demographically speaking, the play is more touching and pertinent than ever." He found, of the acting: "Giving another of his subdued, sometimes recklessly understated performances, Mr. Travanti at times turns Gene into a wimp. His goodness and compassion threaten to become exasperating. Tackling the father, Mr. Gould goes to the other extreme, doing an aggressive turn that captures the man's New York roots but little of the shrewd corporate executive who wound up as something of a suburban lord...[but] in the final confrontation scene, Mr. Travanti and Mr. Gould end up demonstrating just how powerfully affecting this play remains. Miss

McGuire... is as charming and gently elegant as ever, and [Margo] Skinner manages to be both biting and sympathetic as the hardened Alice. In the end, there are no comforting solutions for either parents or their children."

STAGE

I NEVER SANG FOR MY FATHER, Longacre Theater, New York, opened January 25, 1968 125 performances

Presented by Gilbert Cates in association with Doris Vidor; A Play by Robert Anderson; Director, Alan Schneider; Setting and Lighting by Jo Mielziner; Costumes, Theoni V. Aldredge; Production stage manager, Paul A. Foley

Hal Holbrook (Gene Garrison); Teresa Wright (Alice); Alan Webb (Tom Garrison); Lillian Gish (Margaret Garrison); Sloane Shelton (Mary); Laurinda Barrett (Nurse); Matt Crowley (Marvin Scott); Daniel Keyes (Dr. Mayberry); Allan Frank (Reverend Pell); James A. Spearman (Waiter); Earl Sydnor (Porter)

Revival tour, opened *Eisenhower Theater*, Washington, September 2, 1987, closed *Ahmanson Theater*, Los Angeles, January 31, 1988

A Jay H. Fuchs, Kennedy Center/ANTA, and PACE Theatrical Group presentation with Sports Entertainment Group, Inc.; A Play by Robert Anderson; Director, Josephine R. Abady; Scenery, David Potts; Lighting, Jeff Davis; Costumes, Linda Fisher; Sound, Scott Lehrer

Daniel J. Travanti (Gene Garrison); Caroline Aaron (Alice); Harold Gould (Tom Garrison); Dorothy McGuire (Margaret Garrison); Sonja Lanzener (Mary); Jeni Royer (Nurse); Edward Penn (Marvin Scott); William Cain (Dr. Mayberry); John Wylie (Reverend Pell); Scott Kanoff (Porter/Waiter)

(This production was taped in Los Angeles for television presentation, with Margo Skinner in the role played by Caroline Aaron, who had inherited it as a last minute replacement for Mary Kay Place.)

SCREEN

I NEVER SANG FOR MY FATHER, Columbia Pictures, released October 1970

Produced and directed by Gilbert Cates; Screenplay by Robert Anderson, based on his play; Photography, Morris Hartzband and George Stoetzel; Art director, Hank Aldrich; Costumes, Theoni V. Aldredge; Music, Barry Mann and Al Gorgoni; Song "The Strangers" by Barry Mann and Cynthia Weill; Sung by Roy Clark; Sound, Charles Federmack; Editor, Angelo Ross

Melvyn Douglas (Tom Garrison); Gene Hackman (Gene Garrison); Dorothy Stickney (Margaret Garrison); Estelle Parsons (Alice); Elizabeth Hubbard (Peggy); Lovelady Powell (Norma); Daniel Keyes (Dr. Mayberry); Conrad Bain (Reverend Pell); Jon Richards (Marvin Scott); Nikki Counselman (Waitress); Carol Peterson, Sloane Shelton (Nurses); James Karen (Old Age Home Director); Gene Williams (State Hospital Director)

TELEVISION

American Playhouse, televised June 15, 1988 PBS 2 hours

A Coproduction of Brandeman Productions, Ltd., Duet Productions, Ltd., and KCET/Los Angeles, in association with Columbia Pictures Television; Executive producers, Michael Brandeman, Jay H. Fuchs, Ricki Franklin and Phyllis Geller;

Producer, Iris Merlis; Director, Jack O'Brien; The play by Robert Anderson; Production designer, Roy Christopher; Art director, Greg Richman; Costume designer, Noel Taylor; Makeup, Jo Ann Kozloff; Music, Conrad Susa

Daniel J. Travanti (Gene Garrison); Margo Skinner (Alice); Harold Gould (Tom Garrison); Dorothy McGuire (Margaret Garrison); Sonja Lanzener (Mary); Jennifer Royer (Nurse); Edward Penn (Marvin Scott); William Cain (Dr. Mayberry); Richard Thomson (Reverend Pell)

AN IDEAL HUSBAND
A Play by Oscar Wilde (1895)

Synopsis

At the invitation of her friend Lady Markby, Mrs. Cheveley attends a reception at the Grovesnor Square home of Sir Robert Chiltern, a prominent Member of Parliament. Lady Chiltern, considering him to be "the ideal husband, incapable of doing a foolish thing, as he is of doing a wrong thing," is unaware that years before, while Under Secretary of Foreign Affairs to cabinet minister Lord Radley, he had tipped stock speculators to the government's plan to purchase the Suez Canal and in turn was paid a small fortune. Chiltern's original letter advising the stock purchase is now in the possession of Mrs. Cheveley, a woman of questionable reputation, and she plans to use it to blackmail him into supporting a proposed fraudulent South American canal project in which she has heavily invested.

Recognizing her though as a former schoolmate expelled for cheating, and noting her attraction to Sir Robert, Lady Chiltern orders her to leave. The scheming Mrs. Cheveley denounces Lady Chiltern's "ideal husband" as a fraud who sold cabinet secrets for a fortune, and calls on Lord Goring who, she is convinced, is having an affair with Lady Chiltern, "finds" a letter exchanged between the two. She offers Sir Robert's incriminating letter to him if he agrees to marry her. He declines but catches her with some stolen jewelry. In turn, she offers the letter in exchange for Goring's silence about her thievery, but keeps the one from Lady Chiltern to Goring. Hoping to destroy an "ideal" marriage, Mrs. Cheveley sends Lady Chiltern's letter to Sir Robert, but since it stated only "I want you, I trust you. I am coming to you," Sir Robert mistakenly believes his wife sent it to him in forgiveness. The Chilterns are happily reunited and Sir Robert is appointed to the cabinet after his brilliant House of Commons denouncement of the South American canal project. Wicked Mrs. Cheveley's various schemes, meanwhile, all collapse and Lady Chiltern lives happily ever after with her forgiven, not-so-ideal husband.

Comment and Critique

Oscar Wilde completed *An Ideal Husband* in his rooms at Nos. 10 and 11 St. James's Place in London, and first sent the script to John Hare, actor-manager of the Garrick Theatre. Hare rejected it and the play was finally produced by Lewis Waller and H. H. Morell at the Haymarket just after the New Year 1895. Not too long after its opening, Wilde was exposed as a good deal less than an ideal husband, capped with revelation of his homosexual affair with Lord Alfred Douglas. (All of this made for two juicy, competing 1960 films, *Oscar Wilde* and *The Trials of Oscar Wilde*, with Robert Morley and Peter Finch, respectively, as Wilde.)

Fellow writer George Bernard Shaw, then drama critic for the London's *Saturday Review*, wrote: "Mr. Oscar Wilde's new play at the Haymarket is a dangerous subject, because he has the property of making his critics dull. They laugh angrily at his epigrams, like a child who is coaxed into being amusing in the very act of setting up a yell of rage and agony. They protest that the trick is obvious, and that such epigrams can be turned out by anyone like-minded enough to condescend to such frivolity. As far as I can ascertain, I am the only person in London who cannot sit down an write an Oscar Wilde play at will. The fact that his plays, though apparently lucrative, remain unique under these circumstances, says much for the self-denial of our scribes."

Reviewing the play's debut, London's *Morning Advertiser* reported: "Anyone happening to look in at the Haymarket Theatre on the fall of the curtain last night would have come to the conclusion that Mr. Oscar Wilde had written a brilliant play, and no doubt many of those who cheered so lustily were quite of that opinion. But viewed dispassionately, *An Ideal Husband* was a thing of shreds and patches, a stringing together of a number of inconsequent incidents whose only dramatic value was that they have been in use for years past, and are therefore to be borne with as we bear the ancient jokes of an elderly, highly respectable, and, above all, wealthy member of one's family. There is nothing in it which gives Mr. Wilde the right to class himself as a playwright either of promise or experience."

The Morning Post in London considered "*An Ideal Husband*, as a dramatic work, is as inferior to *A Woman of No Importance* as *A Woman of No Importance* was inferior to *Lady Windermere's Fan*. Mr. Wilde is not progressing in the dramatist's art. There is no mere 'story' in *An Ideal Husband* than there was in its two predecessors, but that story is no so well worked out...[It] was not a first-night success by reason of the absorbing interest of its story or the masterly fashion in which that story was handled. It was a success in spite of its framework. It was a success, perhaps, in the first place, because evidently the audience was sympathetically disposed towards Mr. Wilde and the new sublessees of the theatre, Mr. Waller and Mr. Morell, in the second place, because much of the characterization and a good deal of the dialogue is admirable either in its truth to life or in his literary cleverness. Mr. Wilde knows the fashionable world, and supplies of it a graphic and effective picture."

Three months after the London premiere of Wilde's play, it opened on Broadway at the Lyceum Theatre, produced "in a sumptuous manner by Mr. Daniel Frohman." *The New York Times* reviewer was delighted with the playwright's latest effort, noting, "It is only a few months old, but he has written another since. It is, however, the best piece we have yet seen from his whimsical and impudent pen. Until the third of its four acts is reached, it is reasonably logical, which is rare for Oscar, and even then it is diverting...A deus ex machina is needed to straighten things...otherwise the play is expert and effective. The richness of the setting has not been surpassed even at the Lyceum, and the ladies' dresses are marvels...[Herbert] Kelcey leads all the others with a portrayal as consistent with human nature as Mr. Wilde's text would permit ...[Rhoda] Cameron is showy and effective in the easy and grateful role of the adventuress."

An Ideal Husband was revived for several seasons, and in November 1943, Robert Donat's production opened in London. "The early Wilde play is verbally as witty as *The Importance of Being Earnest* and in some ways less forced, though it cannot compare with the later comedy as a complete work of art," British critic Ashley Dukes observed. "The plot is quite astoundingly false and it drags along two hopeless prigs as leading man and woman; the secondary characters abound either in charm, like Lord Goring, or vitality, like Mrs. Cheveley. I think these two are beautifully played by Roland Culver and Martita Hunt...the whole play of three hours is first-class entertainment...I foresee a Wilde boom in which Lady Windermere will bring out her fan and some other nonentity will be of no importance."

Theatre World praised the Donat production, noting that "this play is a noteworthy instance both for the technical skill of Wilde in dramatic construction and in the polished wit and neat epigrams by which his writings are distinguished. His insight into human natures, and firm grasp of character are nowhere more clearly expressed than in the theme portrayed here... Rosemary Scott gives a sympathetic interpretation of the conventional Lady Chiltern, while Manning Whiley's portrayal of Sir Robert Chiltern is in every way convincing...Martita Hunt is suavely sinister as the unscrupulous Mrs. Cheveley...Roland Culver is altogether excellent as the witty and urbane Viscount Goring."

Peter Bridge revived Wilde's play in London in mid-December 1965. The comedy was directed by James Roose-Evans and became one of the season's biggest hits. Following a long run on the West End, it made two provincial tours and returned to London a year later. Michael Billington (*Plays and Players*) found, "The great paradox of this revival is that it succeeds where Wilde is at his melodramatic worst and stumbles where he is at his epigrammatic best...Margaret Lockwood is still a tower of strength as the villainous Mrs. Cheveley -- it is a performance of real voluptuous splendor...Unfortunately, the casting of Richard Todd as Lord Goring helps to sink a good many of Wilde's most pregnant epigrams and damages one of the play's chief points: namely that underneath a flippant, debonair exterior, one often finds a man of shrewdness and principle. Mr. Todd is about as debonair as a gumboot."

The 1970s saw several revivals of *An Ideal Husband*, and in mid-May 1987, Wilde's play was again staged successfully at the Chichester Festival in England. "At the time Oscar Wilde wrote *An Ideal Husband*, his private life was becoming ominously public." observed Kenneth Hurren in *Plays and Players*. "The playwright must have been a touch aware that the breakers of scandal were rolling towards him. There is a hint in the play that the possibility of exposure was preoccupying him when the worried Sir Robert Chiltern, under threat of blackmail by Mrs. Cheveley, discusses the situation with his friend, Lord Goring, confessing to having done 'a thing that I suppose most men would call shameful and dishonorable...men who, every one of them, have worse secrets in their own lives...And, after all, whom did I wrong by what I did? No one...'"

The Times' Benedict Nightingale wrote of the 1992 London revival "a Victorian fin-de-siecle comedy whose message reaims equally pertinent at the end of our own century."

In 1947, Alexander Korda produced and directed a screen version of Wilde's play with Paulette Goddard, as Mrs. Cheveley, heading an all-British cast. Filmed at Shepperton Studios in England, it was beautifully costumed by Cecil Beaton. "The star system," sniffed London's *Sphere*, "is presumably the excuse for giving the leading part in so essentially English a comedy of manners to an American actress, but Diana Wynyard has been cast in the role of Lady Chiltern." *Photoplay* also carped, "Despite stunning sets and costumes in dazzling Technicolor, Oscar Wilde's satire on London society of 1895 is a disappointing affair...A brittle comedy of manners, the emphasis is more on manners than comedy...Paulette Goddard spiritedly portrays the calculating Mrs. Cheveley, long on looks but short on character."

Bosley Crowther wrote in *The New York Times*: "For some reason Sir Alexander

Korda has chosen to film the ancient Wilde play, *An Ideal Husband*, as though its people were the most consequential of folks and its ridiculously old-fashioned problem as vital as atomic power...Yet with all the solemnity and pomposity that even Oscar found supremely dull, he has turned out a handsome film in color with a conspicuously antiquated plot...with Paulette Goddard playing the siren among a lot of stuffy English swells as though she were the gal living next to the firehouse." And James Agee, in *The Nation*, felt, "Vincent Korda's sets are good. Cecil Beaton's costumes are mouth-watering, and most of the players were visually right. The composing and cutting of this fine raw material is seldom above medium grade. Wilde's lines are unevenly and in general too slowly and patiently delivered, and the whole production is too slow and realistic."

In her biography, *Alexander Korda: The Man Who Could Work Miracles*, Karol Kulik noted: "Alex Korda intended *An Ideal Husband* to be his last directorial effort, and many wondered why he had chosen Oscar Wilde's play for his 'swan song.' Korda had long believed in the selling advantages of films taken from popular literary sources and had produced a number of these...Sadly, Korda permitted his fondness for the subject matter and dialogue to be subjugated to the color visualization of the 'period' and the need for a box-office Hollywood 'star' ...In a time of widespread austerity, *An Ideal Husband* had been a shallow testament to the glories of bygone days: the 1890s of the play and the mid-1930s of Korda's own career..."

In *Charmed Lives*, the biography of his illustrious family, publishing executive Michael Korda saw his famed uncle's *An Ideal Husband* this way: "Alex's love of irony and paradox...The cost of Cecil Beaton's costumes alone would have been enough to finance a small movie, and the sets were planned with reckless extravagance...he was reputed to have had an affair with Paulette Goddard (this may have been the reason for the otherwise inexplicable decision to cast her as Mrs. Cheveley)..."

The second, and to date last, filming of Wilde's play was done in 1981 by Russia's Mosfilm! "This quaint and sometimes agreeable Russian rendering of Oscar Wilde's *An Ideal Husband*," British critic John Pym found, "keeps anachronisms and solecisms to a minimum ...with the Soviet view of capitalist skullduggery, there is little need for editorializing: the titled classes look after their own, and indulge in a typically English cover-up, with never a twinge of conscience."

BBC's ninety-minute television production in May 1969 of *An Ideal Husband*, shown on the *NET Playhouse* on PBS in mid-January 1971, was blessed with delightful performances by Margaret Leighton and Keith Michell as Mrs. Cheveley and Sir Robert Chiltern. (A 1952 *Theatre Guild on the Air* radio version starred Rex Harrison as Lord Goring and then-wife Lilli Palmer as Mrs. Cheveley.) Reviewing the BBC *Play of the Month* production, the critic for the *London Times* noted: "The serious plays of Oscar Wilde are melodramatically determined statements of Victorian ethics which tend to the sonorously hollow. They are redeemed into humanity by the author's own inescapable representative, not only epigrammatic in himself, but a cause that other people are epigrammatic too. Wilde could not, thank goodness, resign himself entirely to solemnity. Rudolph Cartier and a notable cast kept this firmly in mind for [the BBC] production." Of the central quintet, the *Times* found: "Keith Michell's threatened Foreign Secretary and Dinah Sheridan's Lady Chiltern were as little stiff as the author allowed them to be. Jeremy Brett's Wildean Lord Goring's occasional offhandedness was the price we paid for a performance which refused to regard wit as public statement. Susan Hampshire was a deliciously gay Mabel. Mrs. Cheveley, the *femme fatale*, was beautifully done by Margaret Leighton. Miss Leighton shone, was witty, glamourous, poised and, in defeat, quite human."

STAGE

AN IDEAL HUSBAND, Haymarket Theatre, London, opened January 3, 1895; moved to *Criterion Theatre*, April 13, 1895 124 performances
Produced by Lewis Waller and H.H. Morell; A Comedy by Oscar Wilde; Settings, Walter Hann and William Harford; Lighting, E. Wingfield Bowles; Music director, Carl Armbruster

Lewis Waller (Sir Robert Chiltern); Florence West (Mrs. Cheveley); Charles H. Hawtrey (Lord Goring); Julia Neilson (Lady Chiltern); Maude Millett (succeeded by Sydney Fairbrother) (Mabel Chiltern); Fanny Brough (succeeded by Vane Featherston) (Lady Markby); Alfred Bishop (succeeded by Charles Good-hart) (Earl of Caversham); Vane Featherston (succeeded by Enid Spencer) (Lady Basildon); Helen Forsyth (Mrs. Marchmont); Cosmo Stuart (Vicomte de Nanjac); H. Deane (Mason); Charles Meyrick (Footman); Henry Stanford (Mr. Montford); Charles H. E. Brookfield (Phipps)

Lyceum Theatre, New York, opened March 12, 1895 40 performances
Produced by Daniel Frohman; A Comedy by Oscar Wilde; Settings, Wilfred Buckland; Art director, William Hawley; Lighting, Milnor Wells; Stage manager, Fred Williams

Hebert Kelcey (Lord Goring); Rhoda Cameron (Mrs. Cheveley); Stephen Grattan (Sir Robert Chiltern); Isabel Irving (Lady Chiltern); Katherine Florence (Mabel Chiltern); Mrs. Charles Walcot (Lady Markby); W. J. LeMoyne (Earl of Caversham); Bessie Tyree (Lady Basildon); Mrs. Thomas Whiffen (Mrs. Marchmont); David Elmer (Vicomte de Nanjac); Charles A. Goettler (Mason); Frank Short (Mr. Montford); Ernest Tarleton (Phipps); Misses Stannard, Peixotto, Okie, Converse, Cruger, Chester, Perry, Cochrane, La Balle, and Messrs. Meyer, Steppling, Rudd, Bostwick, Hards, Flood, Olmstead, Crawford, Harris (Guests)

St. James's Theatre, London, opened May 14, 1914 77 performances
Produced by George Alexander; A Comedy by Oscar Wilde; Production supervisor and director, George Alexander; Settings, Walter Hann and G. Sackmann

Arthur Wontner (Sir Robert Chiltern); Hilda Moore (Mrs. Cheveley); Sir George Alexander (succeeded by Reginald Owen) (Viscount Goring); Phyllis Neilson-Terry (succeeded by Elizabeth Chesney) (Lady Chiltern); Amy Brandon-Thomas (Mabel Chiltern); Henrietta Watson (Lady Markby); Alfred Bishop (Earl of Caversham); Elizabeth Chesney (succeeded by Cecil Otway) (Countess of Basildon); Muriel Barnby (Mrs. Marchmont); J. S. Russell (Vicomte de Nanjac); Guy Dawson (James); Walter C. Randolph Rose (Brook); W. Coats Bush (Harold); George Bishop (succeeded by John Ridley) (Mr. Montford); A. Glascodine (succeeded by Frank Hughbert Dane) (Mason); E. Vivian Reynolds (Phipps)

Irving Place Theatre, New York,opened October 28, 1915
A Comedy by Oscar Wilde; Director, Arnold Koroff

Richard Feist (Sir Robert Chiltern); Jennie Valliere (Mrs. Cheveley); Arnold Koroff (Lord Goring); Annie Rub-Foerster (Lady Chiltern); Iffi Engel (Mabel Chiltern); Marie Kierschner (Lady Markby); Heinrich Matthaes (Earl of Caversham); Flora Arndt (Countess Basildon); Bertha Schoenfeld (Mrs.

Marchmont); Paul Schuetz (Vicomte de Nanjac); Henrich Falk (Mason); Willy Frey (Phipps); Curt Manthey (James); Eugen Kellar (Harold)

Comedy Theatre, New York, opened September 16, 1918 80 performances
Produced and directed by John D. Williams; A Comedy by Oscar Wilde; Stage managers, Henry Crocker and Milton C. Herman

Norman Trevor (succeeded by Wilton Lackaye) (Sir Robert Chiltern); Constance Collier (succeeded by Julia Arthur, Merle Maddern) (Mrs. Cheveley); Julian L'Estrange (succeeded by Norman Trevor) (Lord Goring); Beatrice Buckley (Lady Chiltern); Gretchen Yates (Mabel Chiltern); Alice Augarde Butler (Lady Markby); Cyril Harcourt (Earl of Caversham); Merle Maddern (succeeded by Grace Nolan) (Lady Basildon); Elizabeth Feimel (Mrs. Marchmont); George Hayes (Vicomte de Nanjac); Alfred Helton (Mason); S. V. Phillips (Mr. Montford); Henry Crocker (Phipps); Vincent Sartori (Count Strelic); Dorothy Clay (Lady Jane Barford); Kate Davenport, Caroline Darling, Rose Wood, Allen Lanner, Millicent McLaughlin Herman, Georgiana Such, Margaret Scobie, Milton C. Herman, David Hayward (Guests)

Loew's 7th Avenue Theatre, New York, opened January 30, 1919
Produced and directed by John D. Williams; A Comedy by Oscar Wilde; Costumes by Lucille, Farquharson and Wheelock; Stage manager, Alfred Helton

Lumsden Hare (Sir Robert Chiltern); Selene Johnson (Mrs. Cheveley); Fred Tiden (Lord Goring); Geraldine Beckwith (Lady Chiltern); Rose Wood (Mabel Chiltern); William Eville (Lord Cavashaw); Alice Augarde Butler (Lady Markby); Cyril Harcourt (Earl of Caversham); Grace Van Dusen (Mrs. Marchmont); Georgiana Such (Lady Basildon); Milton C. Herman (Vicomte de Nanjac); S. V. Phillips (Mr. Montford); Alfred Helton (Mason); Charles Hanna (Phipps)

Hudson Theatre, New York, opened May 4, 1924
A Comedy by Oscar Wilde

George Alison (Sir Robert Chiltern); Merle Maddern (Mrs. Cheveley); Norman Trevor (Lord Goring); Elizabeth Valentine (Lady Chiltern); Berenice Vert (Mabel Chiltern); Elizabeth Patterson (Lady Markby); Albert Bannister (Count Streleck); Lalive Brownell (Lady Basildon); Myrtle Bauer (Mrs. Marchmont); Francis M. Verdi (Vicomte de Nanjac); John Seymour (Mr. Montford); William Seymour (Phipps)

Westminster Theatre, London, opened November 16, 1943 268 performances
Produced by Robert Donat; A Comedy by Oscar Wilde; Director, Jack Minster; Settings and costumes, Rex Whistler; Incidental music, Edward Sackville-West

Manning Whiley (Sir Robert Chiltern); Martita Hunt (Mrs. Cheveley); Roland Culver (Viscount Goring); Rosemary Scott (Lady Chiltern); Peggy Bryan (Mabel Chiltern); Irene Vanburgh (Lady Markby); Rosamund Greenwood (Mrs. Marchmont); Nan Hopkins (Countess of Basildon); Ian Lubbock (Vicomte de Nanjac); Charles Deane (Mr. Montford); Esme Percy (Earl of Caversham); John Vere (Mason); Townsend Whitling (Phipps); John Baker (James); Ian Morris (Harold); Mary Pemberton, Ian Morris, John Baker, Ursula Bradley, Joan Hart (Guests)

Oxford (Eng.) Playhouse Theatre, opening February 11, 1946
Produced by Oxford Repertory Players; A Comedy by Oscar Wilde; Director,

Christopher Fry; Setting, Hutchinson Scott; Company manager, Celia Chaundry; Stage manager, Anne Winkeworth

Clement Ashby (Sir Robert Chiltern); Barbara Cavan (Mrs. Cheveley); Gordon Whiting (Viscount Goring); Judith Glick (Lady Chiltern); Margaret Still (Mabel Chiltern); Nell Carter (Lady Markby); Joanna Moorer (Countess of Basildon); Terence Duggan (Vicomte de Nanjac); T. Hannam-Clark (Earl of Caversham); Kenlisa Taylour (Mrs. Marchmont); Brian Cornwell (Mr. Montford/Harold); Martin Bretherton (Mason); Michael Hitchman (Phipps)

Pitlochry (Eng.) Festival Theatre, opened 25, 1959

Produced by Pitlochry Festival Theatre; A Comedy by Oscar Wilde; Director, Peter Steuli; Settings, Stephen Doncaster

Peter Whitbread (Sir Robert Chiltern); Elizabeth Hart (Mrs. Cheveley); Gordon Fairclough (Viscount Goring); Una McLean (Lady Chiltern); Petronella Byrnes (Mabel Chiltern); Anthea Holloway (Lady Markby); Hamish Roughead (Earl of Caversham); Moira Lamb (Countess of Basildon); Elizabeth Richman (Mrs. Marchmont); Simon Carter (Vicomte de Nanjac); Gary Hope (Mr. Montford); Victor Carin (Mason); Roy Boutcher (Phipps); Jon Croft (Harold); Terence Lane (James); Edwina Ireland, Pamela McGrath, Terence Lance, Jon Croft (Guests)

Birmingham (Eng.) Repertory Theatre, summer 1965

Produced by Birmingham Repertory Theatre; A Comedy by Oscar Wilde; Director, John Harrison

Donald Douglas (Sir Robert Chiltern); Lillias Walker (Mrs. Cheveley); John Turner (Lord Goring); Barbara Barnett (Lady Chiltern); Linda Gardner (Mabel Chiltern)

Strand Theatre, London, opened December 16, 1965; moved to *Piccadilly Theatre*, August 13, 1966 339 performances

Produced by Peter Bridge in association with Howard & Wyndham, Ltd.; A Comedy by Oscar Wilde; Director, James Roose-Evans; Production designer, Anthony Holland; Costumes, L. & H. Nathan, Ltd; Production manager, John H. de Lannoy; Company manager, Brian Tyler; Stage managers, Martin Fowler, Lesley Lee and Keith Bowles

Michael Denison (Sir Robert Chiltern); Margaret Lockwood (Mrs. Cheveley); Richard Todd (Lord Goring); Dulcie Gray (Lady Chiltern); Perlita Neilson (Mabel Chiltern); Ursula Jeans (Lady Markby); Roger Livesey (Earl of Caversham); Anne Cameron (Lady Basildon); Gillian Raine (Mrs. Marchmont); Richard Dennis (Vicomte de Nanjac); Keith Bowles (Mr. Montford/James); John Atkinson (Mason); Cyril Wheeler (Phipps); Martin Fowler (Harold); Lesley Lee (Maid)

Garrick Theatre, London, opened December 13, 1966

Produced by Peter Bridge; A Comedy by Oscar Wilde; Director, James Roose-Evans; Production designer, Anthony Holland; Production manager, John H. de Lannoy

Michael Goodliffe (Sir Robert Chiltern); Margaret Lockwood (Mrs. Cheveley); Richard Todd (Lord Goring); Rachel Gurney (Lady Chiltern); Perlita Neilson (Mabel Chiltern); Joyce Cary (Lady Markby); Raymond Huntley (Earl of Caversham); Anne Cameron (Lady Basildon); Yvette Rees (Mrs. Marchmont); Richard Dennis (Vicomte de Nanjac); Keith Bowles (Mr. Montford/James); Leader Hawkins (Mason); Cyril Wheeler (Phipps); Martin Fowler (Harold); Lesley

Lee (Maid)

National Arts Center, Ottawa, Canada, opened February 22, 1977 6 performances
Produced by the National Arts Center Company; Producer, Paul Elliott; A Comedy by Oscar Wilde; Director, Val May; Setting, Terry Parsons; Lighting, Andrew A. Garnder; Costumes, Jane Robinson

Edward Hardwicke (Sir Robert Chiltern); Sylvia Sims (Mrs. Cheveley); Simon Williams (Lord Goring); Rachel Gurney (Lady Chiltern); Judy Geeson (Mabel Chiltern); Margaretta Scott (Lady Markby); Wilfrid Hyde-White (Earl of Caversham); Bernice Stegers (Lady Basildon); Graham Callan (Vicomte de Nanjac); Julie Neubert (Mrs. Marchmont); Simon Clarke (Mr. Montford); Robert Tunstall (Phipps); Barry Wilmore (Mason/Guest); Ethel Drew (Maid/Guest); John Benjamin (Footman)

Greenwich Theatre, London, opened February 2, 1978 34 performances
A Comedy by Oscar Wilde; Director, Robert Kidd; Production designer, Bernard Culshaw; Lighting, Nick Chelton

Robert Swann (Sir Robert Chiltern); Anna Carteret (Mrs. Cheveley); Frank Barrie (Viscount Goring); Lucinda Gane (Lady Chiltern); Michelle Newell (Mabel Chiltern); Barbara Atkinson (Lady Markby); Arthur Howard (Earl of Caversham); Susan Porrett (Countess of Basildon); Michael Tudor Barnes (Vicomte de Nanjac/Harold); Beverley Walding (Mrs. Marchmont); Robin Meredith (Phipps/Mr. Montford); Ewan Hooper (Mason)

Wimbledon Theatre, London, opened August 6, 1979 9 performances
Produced by the Horseshoe Theatre Company by arrangement with Paul Elliott; Associate producer, Brian Hewitt-Jones; A Comedy by Oscar Wilde; Director, Guy Slater; Stage managers, Marc Ashley and Jane Myerson

Richard Coleman (Sir Robert Chiltern); Hildegarde Neil (Mrs. Cheveley); John Fraser (Lord Goring); Bridget deCourcy (Lady Chiltern); Haren Dotrice (Mabel Chiltern); Betty Marsden (Lady Markby); Raymond Francis (Earl of Caversham); Mary Mitchell (Lady Basildon); Mark Dowse (Vicomte de Nanjac); Sheila Felvin (Mrs. Marchmont); Marc Ashley (Mr. Montford); Michael Sharvell Martin (Mason); Jonathan Cecil (Phipps); Jane Myerson (Maid); Nicholas Bell (Guest)

Citizens Theatre, Glasgow, Scotland, opened August 29, 1986
Produced by the Citizens Theatre Company; A Comedy by Oscar Wilde; Director and designer, Philip Prowse; Lighting, Gerry Jenkinson

Mark Lewis (Sir Robert Chiltern); Roberta Taylor (Mrs. Cheveley); Harry Gibson (Lord Goring); Anne Lashton (Lady Chiltern); Claire Hirsch (Mabel Chiltern); Jill Spuerier (Lady Markby); Robert David Macdonald (Earl of Caversham); Imogen Claire (Lady Basildon); Laurence Rudic (Vicomte de Nanjac); Yvonne Drengo (Mrs. Marchmont); Colin Wells (Mr. Montford); Derwent Watson (Mason); Patrick Hannaway (Phipps); David Monteath (Tommy Trafford); Laurence Brady, Mandy Bryan, Neil Dougan, Christopher Gee, Piero Jamieson, Elaine Kidd, Calum Macaninch (Guests)

Chichester (Eng.) Festival Theatre, opened May 13, 1987
Produced by the Chichester Festival; A Comedy by Oscar Wilde; Director, Tony Britton; Production designer, Peter Rice; Lighting, Bill Bray

David Gwillim (Sir Robert Chiltern); Joanna Lumley (Mrs. Cheveley); Clive

Francis (Viscount Goring); Lucy Fleming (Lady Chiltern); Amanda Waring (Mabel Chiltern); June Whitfield (Lady Markby); William Fox (Earl of Caversham); Rebecca Roper-Caldbeck (Countess of Basildon); Lynn Clayton (Mrs. Marchmont); Malcolm Browning (Mr. Montford); Collin Johnson (Vicomte de Nanjac); Caroline Linott (Lady Jane Barford); Valerie Minifie (Duchess of Marlborough); Mary Harris, David Head, Anna Kohler, Christopher Phillips, Rosemary Phillips, Ralph Shuter, Mary Webb, Rowland White (Guests)

Westminster Theatre, London, opened April 26, 1989* 292 performances
Presented by Ian Liston and Westminster Productions; A Comedy by Oscar Wilde; Director, Patrick Sandford; Production designer, Juliet Shillingford; Lighting: Vincent Herbert

Jeremy Child (Sir Robert Chiltern); Delia Lindsay (Mrs. Chevely); Jeremy Sinden (Lord Goring); Liz Bagley (Lady Chiltern); Emma Watson (Miss Mabel Chiltern); Moira Redmond (Lady Markby); Richard Murdoch (Earl of Caversham); Rachel Preece (Lady Basildon); Shauna Baird (Mrs. Marchmont); Sean Aita (Vicomte de Nanjac); Deborah Blake (Mason); Roy Boutcher (Phipps)

* This production initially opened at the *Grand Theatre*, Leeds, January 24, 1989

Globe Theatre, London, opened November 13, 1992
A Comedy by Oscar Wilde; Director, Peter Hall; Designer, Carl Tom

David Yelland (Sir Robert Chiltern); Anna Carteret (Mrs. Cheveley); Martin Shaw (Lord Goring); Hannah Gordon (Lady Chiltern); Victoria Hasted (Miss Mabel Chiltern); Dulcie Gray (Lady Markby); Michael Denison (Earl of Caversham); Deborah Makepeace (Lady Basildon); Kate Isitt (Mrs. Marchmont); Dominic Hawksley (Vicomte de Nanjac); Roderick Nelson (James); Peter Gordon (Phipps); Diana van Proosdy (Duchess of Marlborough); Teresa Forsyth (Lady Jane Barford)

SCREEN

AN IDEAL WOMAN, *British Lion Films*, released in Great Britain November 1947; in U.S. by *20th Century-Fox*, January 1948
A London Films production; Produced and directed by Alexander Korda; Screenplay by Lajos Biro, based on the Oscar Wilde play; Photography, Georges Perinal; Production designer, Vincent Korda; Costumes, Cecil Beaton; Production manager, Jack Clayton; Music, Arthur Benjamin; Musical director, Dr. Hubert Clifford; Make-up, U. P. Hutchinson and Dorrie Hamilton; Hairstylist, Gladys Weston; Associate producers, Phil Brandon and Hugh Stewart; Editor, Oswald Hafenrichter

Paulette Goddard (Mrs. Cheveley); Michael Wilding (Viscount Goring); Diana Wynyard (Lady Chiltern); Hugh Williams (Sir Robert Chiltern); Glynis Johns (Mabel Chiltern); Sir C. Aubrey Smith (Earl of Caversham); Constance Collier (Lady Markby); Harriette Johns (Countess of Basildon); Christine Norden (Mrs. Marchmont); Michael Anthony (Vicomte de Nanjac); Peter Hobbes (Mr. Montford); Michael Medwin (Duke of Nonsuch); Fred Groves (Phipps); Johns Clifford (Mason); Michael Ward (Trafford)

IDEALNY MUZH (AN IDEAL HUSBAND), *Mosfilm*, Russia, released 1981
Produced by Mosfilm; Executive producer, Boris Gostinsky; Adapted and directed by Viktor Georglyev, based on the Oscar Wilde play; Photography, Fyodor Dobronravov; Special photography, A. Renkov and Z. Moryakova; Production manager, M.

Konchakivsky; Settings, Konstantin Forostenko; Costumes, Ganna Genyevkaya; Makeup, M. Ermakova; Music, E. Denisov; Music director, S. Skripka; Editor, K. Aleyeva

Yuri Yakovlyev (Sir Robert Chiltern); Ludmila Gurchenko (Mrs. Chevely); Eduard Martsevich (Viscount Goring); Anna Tvelenyova (Lady Chiltern); Elena Korenyeva (Mabel Chiltern); E. Khanayeva (Lady Markby); Pavel Kadochnikov (Earl of Caversham); E. Kivi (Lady Basildon); I. Dmitriev (Vicomte de Nanjac); A. Budnitskaya (Mrs. Marchmont); K. Karelskikh (Phipps); A. Filozov (Mr. Trafford); L. Voronov (Mason); B. Khimchev (James)

TELEVISION

AN IDEAL HUSBAND, *Play of the Month*, televised May 11, 1969 BBC 90 minutes; in U.S. on *NET Playhouse*, televised January 14, 1971 PBS
Produced by British Broadcasting Corporation; Producer, Cedric Massina; Directed by Rudolph Cartier; A Comedy by Oscar Wilde, adapted by Rosemary Hill; Production designer, Roger Andrews

Keith Michell (Sir Robert Chiltern); Margaret Leighton (Mrs. Cheveley); Jeremy Brett (Viscount Goring); Dinah Sheridan (Lady Chiltern); Susan Hampshire (Mabel Chiltern); Zena Dare (Lady Markby); Charles Carson (Earl of Caversham); Raymond Graham (Mason); Michael Faure (Vicomte de Nanjac); Erik Chitty (Phipps); Magda Miller (Basildon); Penelope Lee (Mrs. Marchmont)

IDIOT'S DELIGHT
A Drama by Robert E. Sherwood (1936)

Synopsis

Second-rate song-and-dance man Harry Van and his tired troupe of six chorus girls arrive in the Italian Alps at the Hotel Monte Gabrielle after a tour of the Balkans. There Harry meets Russian Countess Irene, mistress of wealthy, amoral munitions manufacturer, Achille Weber. Despite her elegant facade and thick, bogus accent, Harry recognizes Irene as a former vaudevillian with whom he had a steamy love affair ten years before in Room 974 of the Governor Bryan Hotel back in Omaha. The disparate guests, trapped by the closing of borders and the threat of war, are advised to leave. Irene's League of Nations passport, however, is unacceptable to Italian authorities and Weber deserts her to leave with the other hotel guests for the safety of Switzerland at the outbreak of idiot's delight: War. Harry remains in the emptyhotel with Irene, and during a massive air raid, they watch bombs destroying the world around them as they share a bottle of champagne.

Comment and Critique

Following a revival of Shakespeare's *The Taming of the Shrew* in 1935, Alfred Lunt asked Robert Sherwood to write a play for him an Lynn Fontanne involving a vaudeville performer and a fake heiress. Sherwood had been toying with a similar idea since 1933 and had been in Budapest not long before where he saw a troupe of dreary, bedraggled American chorus girls doing an act at the Club Arizona which, he later recalled, "formulated the connecting line on which the whole play could be strung."

Just before Christmas 1935, Sherwood submitted his anti-Fascist, antiwar play to the Lunts after reading it to his friend, paralyzed playwright Edward Sheldon, and accepting Sheldon's perceptions and comments. The Lunts made further suggestions for tightening or expanding certain scenes. Rehearsals began for *Idiot's Delight* three weeks later after two hundred chorus girls were auditioned for Harry Van's chorines by Sherwood, Lunt, producer Vinton Freedley and playwright Russel Crouse, then press agent for the Theatre Guild. Lunt asked Milton Berle to tutor him in the timing of a nightclub performer, and to coach him in belting songs, he sought out Sophie Tucker. To tap dance, he turned to Jacqueline "Jackie" Paige, a dancer from *Anything Goes* who would play the part of the chorine, Shirley, in *Idiot's Delight*. Lynn Fontanne meanwhile immersed herself in the flashy role of Irene by virtually duplicating the thick Russian accent of noted costume designer Valentina.

The final dress rehearsal for *Idiot's Delight* in Washington, D.C. continued through the night until eight the next morning. The show opened twelve hours later to great acclaim. During the play's Washington tryout, Hitler's army invaded the Rhineland and Sherwood's seemingly prophetic play was gaining unpleasant focus. The second testing of the play was in Pittsburgh beginning in mid-March when the spring thaw created a flood, and several cast members had to wade through water in the basement of the Nixon Theatre to get on-stage. The following day, all transportation in and out of Pittsburgh was halted, telephone service was dead and the city water was considered unsafe to drink. Despite the failure of electricity, the dedicated cast played *Idiot's Delight* to improvised auxiliary power and many in the audience arrived by rowboat.

The Broadway opening of *Idiot's Delight* on March 24, 1936, was greeted with nineteen curtain calls, and two months later, Sherwood won the Pulitzer Prize for his play. (He dedicated the published play to the Lunts for whom he had written *Reunion in Vienna* in 1931, and later would write a second Pulitzer Prize drama, *There Shall Be No Night*.)

Brooks Atkinson (*The New York Times*) reported Sherwood's play to be one of his "most likeable entertainments...[although] the discussion of war is inconclusive...the mood of the play is somewhat too trivial for such a macabre subject." Atkinson continued: "Mr. Sherwood's play is a robust theatre charade, not quite so heroic and ebullient as *The Petrified Forest* but well inside the same tradition...[he] has spoken passionately about a grave subject and settled down to write a gutsy show." In *The New Yorker*, Robert Benchley wrote: "*Idiot's Delight* is a fine combination of rage, despair and good humor...it is Mr. Lunt at his best. It is also Mr. Sherwood at his best...a fine play, slightly diffused, perhaps, in its twin allegiance to good entertainment and its lesson...It is one of the few plays which everyone should see..."

John Mason Brown's opinion in the *New York Post* was: "In *Idiot's Delight*, Mr. Sherwood shows once again his uncommon ability to combine entertainment of a fleet and satisfying sort with an allegory which reaches for a larger meaning...Haphazard as the dramaturgy may be by which Mr. Sherwood achieves his results, the production which Bretaigne Windust has directed for the Theatre Guild is precision and surety itself." And in the *Journal-American*, critic Robert Garland found: "With bitterness in his heart, with mockery in his pen, Mr. Sherwood has turned out as bizarre a theatre-piece as you have seen...If this sound mad and moody, mad and moody is what the Theatre Guild's new production is."

Following its Broadway run, *Idiot's Delight* made a cross-country tour, although in San Antonio, the Legion of Decency wanted to cut several lines in the play and change the title which the Legion claimed implied God was an idiot. When the production reached Omaha, the mayor denounced its opening, citing the romantic liaison between Harry and Irene in the city's fictitious Hotel Governor Bryan, and condemned the play as immoral, demanding sixteen script deletions. Dorothy Parker even suggested changing the play's title to *Idiot's Delete*, without a justifiable subtitle for hizzoner the Mayor of Omaha-ha-ha -- as the city was pronounced in the play by Lynn Fontanne. In the end, it opened uncut, intact and sold out in Omaha.

Prior to the play's March 1938 London opening, the Lord Chamberlain took a different approach to censorship, recommending removal of all references to fascists and dictatorship "to ward off any complaint from the Continent (which then was being overrun by Hitler)." Sherwood's play premiered at London's Apollo Theatre eleven days after Germany's invasion of Austria. In *The Bystander*, Herbert Farjeon reviewed *Idiot's Delight* as "an intensely moving play...I warm to [it] because, while, it is rather the cry of pain of a wounded world than a sermonistic expression of opinion, it seems ultimately to bear out this view...It is, on the whole, a remarkable entertainment...for though you may complain that it's bad enough reading the newspapers every dreaded morning, an entertainment *Idiot's Delight* unquestionably succeeds in being...And, above all, there are Mr. Raymond Massey and his terribly funny blondes."

London's *Sphere* added, "No one nowadays needs to be told that war is a fool's business, a thing that can delight only idiots. Mr. Robert Sherwood...has been congratulated widely on having arrived at this not very novel conclusion and on having achieved an effective piece of antiwar propaganda...*Idiot's Delight* is a live play, and if it is not a perfect one it is in every sense of the word a thundering good entertainment."

Mel Gussow (*The New York Times*) reviewed a 1970 revival of *Idiot's Delight* starring Jack Lemmon and Rosemary Harris at Los Angeles' Ahmanson Theatre, appraising director Garson Kanin's program note ("time has caught up with Sherwood's Passionate Prophecy and given it added dimension and deeper purpose") with "Time may not have damaged the playwright's intentions, but it certainly has put a severe dent in his dramaturgy." Gussow also suggested, "This is one play that might benefit from musical expansion." Alan Jay Lerner toyed with a musical adaptation of it for the next twelve years. His "toying" resulted in a misadventure called *Dance a Little Closer*.

Before the opening of the musical, Lerner told the press: "What I've tried to do is preserve the fundamental structure of the play and to replace some characters who would not be relevant today with characters I think are. I wanted to write an antinuclear play. Even though it does have a rather serious background, it is still a love story and a romantic comedy in a strange way." Lerner's "strange way" was to alter Sherwood's munitions mogul, Achille Weber, to Dr. Josef Winkler, a European-born American diplomat patterned on Henry Kissinger. Irene was reincarnated as a phony English aristocrat, former nightclub singer Cindy Brooks (played by sixty-three-year-old Lerner's eighth wife, Liz Robertson, a twenty-four-year-old British actress making her Broadway debut). The precious newlyweds, Mr. and Mrs. Cherry, became a gay Pan Am twosome seeking contemporary wedlock.

Dance a Little Closer, set "in the avoidable future," opened and closed at the Minskoff Theatre on May 11, 1983, following twenty-seven previews and an investment of $2.5 million. In the *New York Post*, Clive Barnes described the fiasco: "It looks like a good idea half-baked...the whole show has gone subtly but awfully wrong. Everything about it could work -- but nothing does." *The New York Times*' Frank Rich called it "a huge, extravagant mishmash -- one of those musicals that seems to have taken on a rampaging, self-destructive life of its own; an initially shaky premise is steadily dismantled by errors of judgment on all front." And Douglas Watt, in the *Daily News*, considered Charles Strouse's music one of his better scores but was less inclined toward Lerner's book and direction: "Simply put, it is a chilly, charmless and foolhardy musical...Lerner's book -- which he has also, and probably unwisely, directed himself -- is a generally disagreeable patchwork, and his lyrics show sign of strain."

Metro-Goldwyn-Mayer had purchased the screen rights to Robert Sherwood's drama for $135,000 and hired him to adapt the screenplay, insisting on the deletion of all references to fascists, dictators and identification of the country of origin of raiding aircraft. Military uniforms were to be designed to establish no specific country. *Newsweek* magazine reported that "Clark Gable's hard-boiled hoofer is a fine characterization. Norma Shearer plays a difficult and purposely exaggerated role to the hilt and perhaps a little farther. With an extra credit for its worthy intention, *Idiot's Delight* is refreshingly intelligent entertainment."

Graham Greene (*The Spectator*) was less impressed with the film version, adding, "Mr. Clark Gable does his best, but Miss Norma Shearer adds to the heavy saturated ennui the weight of a far too powerful personality. Overacting could hardly go further." *The Commonweal*, in February 1939, noted: "It is seldom that a play makes such an intelligent movie as does *Idiot's Delight*. Norma Shearer and Clark Gable come through in grand style in the role made famous by the Lunts. This is a strong and bitter condemnation of a civilization tottering on the verge of war."

Loosely based on *Idiot's Delight* was the delightful 1957 MGM Gene Kelly musical, *Les Girls*, with a sprightly Cole Porter score. George Cukor directed and Kay Kendall, Mitzi Gaynor and Taina Elg played the dancers. John Patrick's screenplay was based on a story by Vera Caspary (best known for *Laura*), with no mention at all going to Robert Sherwood.

In September 1963, NBC televised the premiere of its comedy series *Harry's Girls*. The thirty-minute sitcom featuring Larry Blyden as Harry had a short television run. *Harry's Girls* began life based on *Idiot's Delight* but became more of an extension of *Les Girls*. Disguised as an extension of either property, *Harry's Girls* was no special delight.

STAGE

IDIOT'S DELIGHT, Sam S. Shubert Theatre, New York, opened March 24, 1936
300 performances

Produced by the Theatre Guild; A Play by Robert E. Sherwood; Director, Bretaigne Windust; Production conceived by Alfred Lunt and Lynn Fontanne; Setting by Lee Simonson; Miss Fontanne's costumes designed and executed by Valentina; Chorus costumes by Irene Sharaff; Dances staged by Morgan Lewis; Company manager, Lawrence Farrell; Stage manager, George Greenberg

Alfred Lunt (Harry Van); Lynn Fontanne (Irene); Francis Compton (Achille Weber); Richard Whorf (Quillery); Sydney Greenstreet (Dr. Waldersee); Edward Raquello (Captain Locicero); George Meader (Dumptsy); Edgar Barrier (Auguste); S. Thomas Gomez (Pittaluga); Bretaigne Windust (Mr. Cherry); Jean McIntyre (Mrs. Cherry); Barry Thomson (Donald Navadel); Jacqueline Paige (Shirley Laughlin); Connie Crowell (Beulah Tremoyne); Frances Foley (Edna Creesh); Etna Ross (Francine Merle); Marjorie Baglin (Elaine Messiger); Ruth Timmons (Bebe Gould); Stephan Sandes (Signor Paloto); Le Roi Operti (Signor Rossi); Ernestine De Becker (Signora Rossi); Giorgio Monteverde (succeeded by Gordon Nelson) (Major); Alan Hewitt (succeeded by Charles Ansley) (First Officer); Winston Ross (Second Officer); Gilmore Rush (Third Officer); Tomasso Tittoni (succeeded by David Selva) (Fourth Officer); Una Val (Anna); Gerald Kunz, Max Rich, Joseph Knopf (Musicians)

Program Note: The Theatre Guild wishes to thank Irving Berlin for the use of some of his songs and for the special lyric for "Swanee River," sung by Mr. Lunt, and for invaluable suggestions in the staging of the musical numbers in Act II.

Apollo Theatre, London, opened March 22, 1938; transferred to *His Majesty's Theatre*, October 24, 1938 230 performances

Produced by Raymond Massey and Henry Sherek, by arrangement with the Theatre Guild and Alec L. Rea; A Drama by Robert E. Sherwood; Director, Raymond Massey; Setting by Lee Simonson; Mechanical effects, Alexander Black; Costumes by Motley, Karinska, and Max Weldy; Company manager, Stanley Brightman; Stage managers, Peter Gyll and Ambrose Day

Raymond Massey (succeeded by Lee Tracy) (Harry Van); Tamara Geva (succeeded by Tatiana Lieven) (Irene); Hugh Miller (Achille Weber); Carl Jaffe (Quillery); Franklin Dyall (Dr. Waldersee); Terence Neill (Captain Kirvlin); Ralph Roberts (Dumptsy); Cecil G. Calvert (Auguste); Charles Paul (Pittatek); Valentine Dyall (Mr. Cherry); Janet Johnson (Mrs. Cherry); Richard Rudi (Donald Navadel); Pat Denny (Shirley); Peggy Hamilton (Beulah); Joan Clarkson (succeeded by Elaine Murray) (Edna); Audrey Boyes (Francine); Eileen McCarthy (Elaine); Carol Dexter (Bebe); Benjamin Wright (Mr. Preva); Kara Shera (Mrs. Preva); Reginald Atkinson (Major); Elizabeth Adair (Maid); Peter Gyll (First Officer); Edward Stuart (Second Officer); Robert Beatty (Third Officer); Patrick Jenkins (succeeded by Ambrose Day) (Fourth Officer); Jack Jacobs (Orchestra Leader); Tony Hatley, Bert Jacobs, Len Johnson (Musicians)

Cape Playhouse, Dennis, Mass., opened July 25 through 30, 1938

Produced by Raymond Moore in association with Richard Aldrich; A Drama by Robert E. Sherwood; Director, Arthur Sircom; Setting, Eugene Fitsch; Dances arranged and directed by Una Val Castle

Phil Baker (Harry Van); Muriel Hutchison (Irene); Otto Hulett (Achille Weber); Jose Ruben (Quillery); Forrest Orr (Dr. Waldersee); Louis Veda Quince (Captain Locicero); Albert Bergh (Dumptsy); Fred Sears (Auguste); Charles Paul (Pittaluga); Guy Kingsford (Mr. Cherry); Mary Brian (Mrs. Cherry); Philip Huston (Donald Navadel); Frances Hammond (Shirley); Una Val Castle (Beulah); Elizabeth Hechscher (Edna); Marion O'Brien (Francine); Barbara Harris (Elaine); Mary Ellen Tindall (Bebe); Giovanni Martini (Signor Palota); Charles Baker (Signor Rossi); Monica Muller (Signora Rossi); Michael Robinson (Major); Marcis Ward (Anna); Philip Carr (First Officer); Walter Hill (Second Officer); Bernard Malek (Third Officer); Robert Mazur (Fourth Officer)

City Center Theatre, New York, opened May 23, 1951 16 performances

Produced by the New York City Theatre Company; A Drama by Robert E. Sherwood; Director, George Schaefer; Settings and Lighting, Eldon Elder; Costumes, Emeline Roche; Choreography, Ted Cappy; Company manager, Edward A. Haas; Stage managers, Thelma Carpenter and Tom Hughes Sand; Artistic supervisor, Maurice Evans

Lee Tracy (Harry Van); Ruth Chatterton (Irene); Emmett Rogers (Quillery); John C. Becher (Dumptsy); Stiano Braggioti (Achille Weber); Stefan Schnabel (Dr.

Waldersee); Chester Stratton (Donald Navadel); Rock Rogers (Pittaluga); Theodore Tenley (Auguste); Louis Borell (Captain Locicero); Winston Ross (Mr. Cherry); Sybil Baker (Mrs. Cherry); Irene Dailey (Shirley); Gretchen Houser (Beulah); Lillian Udvary (Bebe); Rita Barry (Francine); Joanne Woodlock (Elaine); Nancy Pearson (Edna); Dan Rubinate (First Officer); Scott Fielding (Second Officer); Felice Orlandi (Third Officer); Bruce Jewell (Fourth Officer); John Weaver (Signor Rossi); Martine Bartlett (Signora Rossi); Sarah Marshall (Anna); Alan Furlan (Major); Max Merlin, Michael DuChesne, Sidney Rich, Phil Salomon (Musicians)

Ahmanson Theatre, Los Angeles, opened March 17, 1970 47 performances
Produced by the Center Theatre Group and Elliot Martin; A Drama by Robert E. Sherwood; Director, Garson Kanin; Production designer, Harry Horner; Lighting, H. R. Poindexter; Costume designer, Lewis Brown; Choreographer and assistant director, Wally Strauss; Production supervisor, David Pardoll; Interpolated music, John Ulmer Lemmon III; Musical arranger, John Guanieri; Sound, Glenn Hayes; Company manager, Charles Mooney; Stage manager, Dom Salinaro

Jack Lemmon (Harry Van); Rosemary Harris (Irene); Sam Jaffe (Dr. Waldersee); Pierre Olaf (Quillery); Sandor Szabo (Achille Weber); Leon Askin (Dumtsy); John Myhers (Donald Navadel); Anthony Caruso (Captain Locicero); Terence Scammell (Mr. Cherry); Flora Plumb (Mrs. Cherry); Marti Ralph (Shriley); Trayce Johnson (Beulah); Linda Gandell (Edna); Lisa Pharren (Bebe); Corinne Carroll (Elaine); Trish Mahoney (Francine); Sam Scar (Major); Remo Pisani (Pittaluga); John Guarnieri (Paleta); Reuben Singer (Auguste); Jennifer Moore (Anna); Beppy De Vries (Signora Rossi); Peter Brocco (Signor Rossi); Susan Ohman (Flower girl); Dom Salinaro, Colin Higgins, Leo Morrell, Michael Sevareid (Italian officers); Georgie Auld (Saxophonist); Dick Berk (Drummer); Shirley Cornell (Violinist)

DANCE A LITTLE CLOSER, *Minskoff Theatre*, New York, opened/closed May 11, 1983
Produced by Frederick Brisson, Jerome Minskoff, James Nederlander and John F. Kennedy Center Center for the Performing Arts (Roger L. Stevens, chairman); A Musical play based on Robert E. Sherwood's *Idiot's Delight*; Director, Alan Jay Lerner; Book and lyrics by Alan Jay Lerner; Music by Charles Stouse; Musical staging and choreography, Billy Wilson; Scenery, David Mitchell; Lighting, Thomas Skelton; Costumes, Donald Brooks; Dance music, Glen Kelly; Orchestrations, Jonathan Tunick; Musical director, Peter Howard; Production supervisor, Stone Widney; Sound design, John McClure; Skating staged by Blair Hammond; Hairstylist, Joe Tubens; Associate producer, Paul N. Temple; Company manager, Mitzi Harder; Stage managers, Alan Hall, Steven Adler and Diane Trulock

Len Cariou (Harry Aikens); Liz Robertson (Cynthia Brookfield-Bailey); George Rose (Dr. Josef Winkler); Don Chastain (Roger Butterfield); David Sabin (Johannes Hartog); Elizabeth Hubbard (Countess Carlo Pirianno); Noel Craig (Captain Mueller); Brent Barrett (Charles Castleton); Jeff Keller (Edward Dunlop); I. M. Hobson (Rev. Oliver Boyle); Joyce Worsley (Hester Boyle); Joseph Kolinski (Heinrich Walter); Diane Pennington, Cheryl Howard, Alyson Reed (The Delights--Shirley, Bebe, Elaine); Philip Mollet (Harry/Bellboy); Brian Sutherland (Waiter/ Harry's double/Harry); James Fatta (Rink attendant/ Violinist/Harry); Colleen Ashton (Ice Skater); Robin Stephens (Cynthia's double); Colleen Ashton, Candy Cook, Brian Sutherland, Peter Wendel (Hotel guests)

MUSICAL NUMBERS: "It Never Would've Worked"; "Happy, Happy New Year"; "No Man Is Worth It"; "What Are You Going to Do About It?"; "A Woman Who Thinks I'm Wonderful"; "Pas de Deux"; "There's Never Been Anything Like Us"; "Another Life"; "He Always Comes Home to Me"; "Why Can't the World Go and Leave Us Alone?"; "I Got a New Girl"; "Dance a Little Closer"; "There's Always One You Can't Forget"; "Homesick"; "Mad"; "I Don't Know"; "Auf Wiedersehen"; "I Never Want to See You Again"; "On Top of the World"

Eisenhower Theatre, Washington, opened February 17, 1986 24 performances
Produced by the John F. Kennedy Center for the Performing Arts, Roger L. Stevens, chairman; Artistic director, Marta Istomin for the American National Theatre; A Play by Robert E. Sherwood; Director, Peter Sellars; Setting, George Tsypin; Lighting, James F. Ingalls; Costumes, Kurt Wilhelm; Sound, Bruce Orland; Choreography, Baayork Lee; Dance and vocal arrangements, Randolph Mauldin; Stage manager, Lani Bell

Stacy Keach (Harry Van); JoBeth Williams (Irene); Werner Klemperer (Achille Weber); Tim Choate (Quillery); Richard Woods (Dr. Waldersee); Marc Epstein (Donald Navadel); Paul Stolarsky (Dumptsy); Barbara Sharma (Shirley); Jacklyn Ross (Beulah); Helen Schneider (Bebe); Sam Robards (Mr. Cherry); Anne Beresford Clarke (Mrs. Cherry); Merwin Goldsmith (Pittaluga); Jan Triska (Captain Locicero); Nick Mathwick (Signor Rossi); Brian McCue (Auguste/ Signora Rossi/Anna)

SCREEN

IDIOT'S DELIGHT, *Metro-Goldwyn-Mayer*, released January 1939
Produced by Hunt Stomberg; Director, Clarence Brown; Screenplay, Robert E. Sherwood, based on his play; Photography, William Daniels; Art directors, Cedric Gibbons and Wade B. Rubottom; Set decorator, Edwin B. Willis; Montage, Slavo Vorkapich; Gowns, Adrian; Music director, Herbert Stothart; Choreography, George King; Song "How Strange" by Gus Kahn and Herbert Stothart; Editor, Robert J. Kern

Clark Gable (Harry Van); Norma Shearer (Irene Fellara); Edward Arnold (Achille Weber); Charles Coburn (Dr. Walderace); Burgess Meredith (Quillery); Joseph Schildkraut (Captain Kirvline); Laura Hope Crews (Madame Zuleika); Skeets Gallagher (Donald Navadel); Peter Willes (Mr. Cherry); Pat Paterson (Mrs. Cherry); Virginia Grey (Shirley Laughlin); Lorraine Kreuger (Bebe Gould); Paula Stone (Beulah Tremeyne); Joan Marsh (Elaine Messiger); Bernadene Hayes (Edna Creesh); Virginia Dale (Francine); William Edmunds (Dumptsy); Fritz Feld (Pittatek); Edward Raquello (Chiari); Frank Orth (Benny Zinssar); Bernard Suss (Auguste); William Irving (Sandro); George Sorel (Major); Hobart Cavanaugh (Frueheim); Harry Strang (Sergeant); Bud Geary (Ambulance driver); Emory Parnell (Policeman); Mitchell Lewis (Indian); Jim Conlin (Stagehand); Rudolph Myzet (Czech announcer); Joe Yule (Comedian); Gertrude Bennett, Bonita Weber (Women)

LES GIRLS, *Metro-Goldwyn-Mayer*, released October 1957
Produced by Sol C. Siegel; Director, George Cukor; Screenplay, John Patrick, based on a story by Vera Caspary; Photography, Robert Surtees; Art directors, William A. Horning and Gene Allen; Set decorator, Edwin B. Willis; Costumes, Orry-Kelly; Choreography, Jack Cole; Songs by Cole Porter; Music adapted and conducted by Adolph Deutsch; Orchestrations, Alexander Courage and Skip Martin; Sound, Wesley

C. Miller; Associate producer, Saul Chaplin; Editor, Ferris Webster

Gene Kelly (Barry Nichols); Kay Kendall (Lady Wren); Mitzi Gaynor (Joy Henderson); Taina Elg (Angele Ducros); Jacques Bergerac (Pierre Ducros); Leslie Phillips (Sir Gerald Wren); Henry Daniell (Judge); Stephen Vercoe (Mr. Outward); Patrick Macnee (Sir Percy); Philip Tonge (Associate Judge); Owen McGiveney (Court usher); Francis Ravel (French stage manager); Maurice Marsac (French house manager); Adrienne d'Ambricourt (Wardrobe mistress); Cyril Delevanti (Fanatic); Nestor Paiva (Spanish peasant); George Navarro (Waiter); Maya Van Horn (French woman); Louisa Triana (Flamenco dancer); Genevieve Pasques (Shopkeeper); Lilyan Chauvin (Dancer); Dick Alexander (Stagehand)

TELEVISION

HARRY'S GIRLS, NBC comedy series, televised September 13, 1963 through January 3, 1964 NBC 30 minutes each

Produced by MGM Television; Executive producers, Joe Stein and Bruce Cohn; Producer, Billy Friedberg; Director, Richard Kinon; Written by Joe Stein; Music, Van Alexander, Jerry Fielding

Larry Blyden (Harry Burns); Diahn Williams (Terry); Dawn Nickerson (Lois); Susan Silo (Rusty)

THE INVISIBLE MAN

Various adaptations of the novel by Herbert George Wells (1897)

Synopsis

For three years, scientist Jack Griffin experiments with refractions of light, believing that body cells will become transparent and the human body invisible. With the success of his experimentations, Griffin becomes invisible and robs his father, who commits suicide. After setting fire to his room and destroying all evidence of his research, Griffin begins terrorizing London and then, wearing dark glasses, whiskers and heavy bandages to cover his face, he escapes to Iping. Badgered for payment of his overdue rent bill by Herbert Hall, landlord of the Coach and Horses Inn, Griffin perversely removes his bandages to the horror of both the constable and Hall, who watch him physically vanish. Pursued by police and villagers alike, the invisible Griffin is shot but finds refuge in the home of his former university friend, Dr. Kemp, who is convinced that Griffin is insane -- especially after a series of robberies and grisly murders. Griffin warns Kemp that he has embarked on a reign of terror and that the latter is his next victim. Outside the Inn, invisible Griffin attacks Kemp, but gauging the position of the unseen assailant, a villager swings a sharp spade. Kemp is suddenly released as a crowd gathers to watch Griffin's nude body materialize before their eyes.

Comment and Critique

The pseudo-scientific novels written by H. G. Wells began in 1895 with the publication of *The Time Machine*, and two years later, Harper & Brothers published his fascinating tale of *The Invisible Man*. Early stage adaptations of the novel were failures, and even a "work in progress" musical adaptation of the Wells story in the late 1980s never got far out of Portland, Oregon, but in 1933, Universal Pictures released a film version that was to become an early horror classic and would spawn several sequels.

Universal originally assigned Robert Florey to direct its production of *The Invisible Man* with Boris Karloff as star. Florey was replaced by Cyril Gardner, who was succeeded by E. A. DuPont. Karloff, meanwhile, during a financial disagreement with the studio, refused to play the part of Griffin and was replaced by fellow English actor Claude Rains (in his American screen debut). James Whale, who had made the studio's landmark 1931 film, *Frankenstein*, signed on as director number four.

In their informative *Science Fiction: Studies in Film*, authors Frederik Pohl and Frederik Pohl IV wrote: "The H. G. Wells novel was a natural for filming, and R. C. Sheriff's script followed the book with under-standing...Making the film only awaited a time when the technical problems could be solved, and by 1933, Universal's John P. Fulton had done so with wires, double-printing and an army of retouchers who painted out the hardware that was not meant to be seen on the negatives...*The Invisible Man* did not spark its audiences to terror. Wells' gently Fabian style seldom displayed violence...[It] is about as close to perfection -- that is, to the successful realization of its creator's aims -- as a film ever gets."

The New York Times' Mordaunt Hall found that "No actor has ever made his first appearance on the screen under quite as peculiar circumstances as Claude Rains does...[his] countenance is beheld for a mere half minute at the close of the proceedings. The rest of the time his head is either completely covered with bandages of he is invisible, but his voice is heard... This eerie tale evidently afforded a Roman holiday for the camera aces. Photographic magic abounds in the production, the work being even more startling than was that of Douglas Fairbanks' old picture *The Thief of Bagdad*. The story makes such superb cinematic material that one wonders that Hollywood did not film it sooner. Now that it has been done, it is a remarkable achievement."

Universal's persistence in turning out sequels to profit-makers was reflected in the follow-ups to *Frankenstein*, *The Wolf Man* and other popular properties and continued with *The Invisible Man*, which a half dozen years later begat *The Invisible Man Returns* -- with Vincent Price making his entry into the realm of the horror/scifi genre. Although the 1940 sequel was sprightly directed by Joe May and contained flashy performances mainly from Cedric Hardwicke and Cecil Kellaway, the *New York Herald Tribune* caustically appraised the Price performance: "I think he is better in the disembodied section than in the final sequence [where he appears]."

Critic Frank Nugent (*The New York Times*) felt that "*The Invisible Man Returns* is a mite on the ghostly side, too, although neither so horrendous nor so humorous as the first one was. Blame that on time and Topper, which have given us several other peeks at the unseen...The camera hocus-pocus still has its fascination, of course, for fantasy has been fascinating since Melies made his *Trip to the Moon*, but the script is annoyingly unoriginal."

The following year came Universal's *The Invisible Woman*, about which *Photoplay* astutely noted: "Hollywood never lets go of a good thing. It hands on and on until the good thing becomes a dull thing...*The Invisible Woman* is far from good." John Barrymore, on the downward spiral of his once illustrious career, took second billing to Virginia Bruce (in the title role). Observed the *Motion Picture Herald*: "The film also marks in all probability the first appearance -- or non-appearance -- of 'invisible nudity' on the screen, the fair subject of the experiment having to take off her clothes behind a screen to make the machine effective. For much of the picture, she parades about 'invisibly nude.'"

Invisible Agent starring Jon Hall came the next year. "Universal has had lots of fun with its series of Invisible Men pictures (sometimes more than audiences have) but now it produces one that everyone will enjoy," felt *Photoplay*, and of the studio's follow-up two years later, *The Invisible Man's Revenge*, again with Hall, the magazine noted: "Jon Hall delivers a punchy and credible performance as the invisible man... It isn't a bad little show at all providing one accepts in advance the fact that the proceedings are entirely out of this world."

In its endless search for vehicles for the studio's resident comedy team, Universal in 1951 had *Abbott and Costello Meet the Invisible Man*, which most A&C buffs feel is right up there with the boys' best -- and arguably their last good one. In his *Movie Comedy Teams*, Leonard Maltin calls it "one of team's funniest outings, and the special effects are just about the best ever devised for this kind of film. Scenes like the one where [Arthur] Franz unwraps his bandages, revealing nothing but air, are eye-popping."

Loosely based on the original H. G. Wells tale was the 1960 Mexican-produced *El Hombre que Legre ser Invisible* (aka *The Invisible Man in Mexico*) starring Arturo de Cordova. The previous year, Mexico's Jaime Salvador had directed *Los Invisibles*, another variation on the Wells story.

The first time *The Invisible Man* was "seen" on television was in an hour-long adaptation on NBC's *Matinee Theatre* in the summer of 1957, with Chester Stratton in the lead. A syndicated British series of twenty-six half-hour episodes began airing the following year. In 1975, Universal dusted off its very successful property of several decades earlier and offered a ninety-minute television adaptation with David McCallum. Of it, John J. O'Connor (*The New York Times*) noted that despite the liberties it took with the Wells tale, "the visual tricks are clever, using TV technology to good advantage. The invisibility is ingeniously made visible. The plotting however is noticeably tired. The characters, like most TV characters, seem to exist in a vacuum [and] inhabit a world having little contact with logic, no contact with reality."

It was followed by a relatively unsuccessful weekly hour-long series which faded away like its star (again David McCallum) after just eleven episodes. Next incarnation, and a silly one it was, was *The Invisible Woman* (1983) from the producers of "Gilligan's Island," Lloyd J. and Sherwood Schwartz, a two-hour comedy pilot as a vehicle for their venerable Gilligan, Bob Denver, and for newcomer Alexa Hamilton in the title role.

BBC's six-part *The Invisible Man* was telecast in Great Britain in the fall of 1984 and turned up in the U.S. on the A&E channel in the spring of 1987. The adaptation for television by James Andrew Hall remained close to Wells' concept and the excellent production made the special effects noteworthy. Pip Donaghy, little known on these shores, starred as Griffin in this lavishly produced series.

STAGE

THE INVISIBLE MAN, *Coliseum Theatre*, London, opened No-vember 3, 1913
A Farce by Cyril Twyford and Leslie Lambert, based on the story by H. G. Wells

G. Trevor Roller (Denis Stuart); Miss Tommy Clancy (Evelyn Cooper); Cecil Bevan (Harry Hamber); Herbert Russell (P. C. Harris); Frank Snell (Police Inspector)

Storefront Theater, Portland, Oregon, opened June 29, 1987
Director, Lesley Conger; A Musical by Lesley Conger and Ted Deane, based on the novel by H. G. Wells; Music by Steve Schaubel, Jamie Eoff and Fred Chalenor;

Scenery, Charles Tyndall; Lighting, Polly Suttles and Tom Newson; Costumes, Shaune Wunder; Special effects, Jane Herrold; Sound, Bill Reinhardt

Joseph Cronin (The Invisible Man); Kathy Philpott (Nellie Carmichael); Edie Baker (Mrs. Janny Hall); David Beetham-Gomes (Roger Kemp); Cherie Price (Lydia Oliver); Kris Bluett (Katie); Randy Knee (Dr. Archibald Cuss); R. Dee (Vicar); Dan DePrez (Sandy Wadgers); Alan King (Bill Fearenside); Ken Colburn (Constable Jeffers); Alice Lane (Mrs. Madeline Fearenside); Cathryn Cushing (Mrs. Agnes Cuss); Barbara Low (Mrs. Betsy Jeffers; Thorn Cosgriff (Narrator)

SCREEN

THE INVISIBLE MAN, Universal Pictures, released November 1933

Produced by Carl Laemmle, Jr.; Director, James Whale; Screenplay, R. C. Sherriff and Philip Wylie, based on the novel by H. G. Wells; Photography, Arthur Edeson and John Mescall; Art director, Charles B. Hall; Special effects, John P. Fulton; Makeup, Jack Pierce; Editors, Maurice Pivar and Ted Kent

Claude Rains (Jack Griffin); Gloria Stuart (Flora Cranley); Henry Travers (Dr. Cranley); William Harrigan (Dr. Kemp); Una O'Connor (Jenny Hall); Forrester Harvey (Herbert Hall); Holmes Herbert (Chief of Police); E. E. Clive (Jaffers); Dudley Digges (Chief of Detectives); Dwight Frye (Reporter); Harry Stubbs (Inspector Bird); Donald Stuart (Inspector Lane); Merle Tottenham (Milly); Walter Brennan (Man with bike); Jameson Thomas (Doctor); John Carradine (Informer); John Merivale (Young Man)

THE INVISIBLE MAN RETURNS, Universal Pictures, released January 1940

Produced by Ken Goldsmith; Director, Joe May; Screenplay, Lester Cole, Cedric Belfrage, Curt Siodmak, based on a story by Joe May and Curt Siodmak and characters created by H. G. Wells; Photography, Milton Krasner; Art directors, Jack Otterson and Martin Obzina; Gowns, Vera West; Special effects, John P. Fulton; Music, H. J. Salter and Frank Skinner; Music director, Charles Previn; Editor, Frank Gross

Vincent Price (Geoffrey Radcliffe); Sir Cedric Hardwicke (Richard Cobb); Nan Grey (Helen Manson); John Sutton (Dr. Frank Griffin); Cecil Kellaway (Inspector Sampson); Alan Napier (Willis Spears); Forrester Harvey (Ben Jenkins); Frances Robinson (Nurse); Ivan Simpson (Cotton); Harry Stubbs (Constable Dukesbury); Edward Fielding (Governor); and Harry Cording, Mary Gordon, Bruce Lester, Leyland Hodgson, Dave Thursby, Jimmy Aubrey, Frank Hagney, Frank O'Connor, Matthew Bolton, Frank Hill, Dennis Tankard, George Kirby, George Hyde, George Lloyd, Ellis Irving, Louise Brien, Ernie Adams, Mary Field, Edmund MacDonald, Paul Englund, Eric Wilton

THE INVISIBLE WOMAN, Universal Pictures, released January 1941

Associate producer, Burt Kelly; Director, A. Edward Sutherland; Screenplay, Robert Lees, Frederic I. Rinaldo and Gertrude Purcell, based on a story by Joe May and Curt Siodmak; Photography, Ellwood Bredell; Art director, Jack Otterson; Gowns, Vera West; Special effects, John P. Fulton; Music, Charles Previn; Editor, Frank Gross

Virginia Bruce (Kitty Carroll); John Barrymore (Pro-fessor Gibbs); Charles Ruggles (George); John Howard (Dick Russell); Oscar Homolka (Blackie Cole); Margaret Hamilton (Mrs. Jackson); Thurston Hall (John Hudson); Mary Gordon (Mrs. Bates); Charles Lane (Mr. Crowley); Kathryn Adams (Peggy); Anne Nagel

(Jean); Maria Montez (Marie); Ed Brophy (Bill); Shemp Howard (Hammerhead/Frankie); Donald McBride (Foghorn); Kay Leslie (Model); Eddie Conrad (Hernandez); Kitty O'Neil (Mrs. Patton); Kernan Cripps (Postman); Harry C. Bradley (Want-Ad man); Kay Linaker, Sarah Edwards (Buyers at Fashion Show)

INVISIBLE AGENT, Universal Pictures, released July 1942
Producer, Frank Lloyd; Associate producer, George Waggner; Director, Edwin L. Marin; Screenplay, Curt Siodmak, suggested by H. G. Wells' *The Invisible Man*; Photography, Lester White; Art director, Jack Otterson; Gowns, Vera West; Special effects, John P. Fulton; Music, Charles Previn; Assistant director, Vernon Keays; Editor, Edward Curtiss

Jon Hall (Frank Raymond/Griffin); Ilona Massey (Maria Sorenson/Goodrich); Peter Lorre (Baron Ikito); Sir Cedric Hardwicke (Conrad Stauffer); J. Edward Bromberg (Karl Heiser); Albert Basserman (Arnold Schmidt); John Litel (John Gardiner); Holmes Herbert (Sir Alfred Spencer); Keye Luke (Surgeon); Lee Tung-Foo (General Chin Lee); Henry Zynder (General Kelenski); Philip Van Zandt (Nazi SS man); Matt Willis (Nazi assassin); John Holland (Spencer's secretary); Wolfgang Zilzer (Von Porten); Michael Visaroff (Verichen); Lee Shumway (Brigadier General); and Sven Hugo-Borg, Mabel Colcord, Marty Faust, Alberto Morin, Henry Guttman, Ferdinand Munier, Eddie Dunn, Hans Schumm, John Burton, Milburn Stone, Walter Tetley, Pat West, Leslie Denison, William Ruhl, Otto Reichow, Wally Scott, Bobby Hale, James Craven, Charles Regan, Victor Zimmerman, Bill Pagan, Ferdinand Schumann-Heink, Mabel Conrad, Charles Flynn, Phil Warren, Paul Byar, John Merton, Pat McVey, Lane Chandler, Duke York, Donald Curtis

THE INVISIBLE MAN'S REVENGE, Universal Pictures, released June 1944
Producer and director, Ford Beebe; Screenplay, Bertram Milhauser, based on the character created by H. G. Wells; Photography, Milton Krasner; Art director, John B. Goodman; Costumes, Vera West; Special effects, John P. Fulton; Music, H. J. Salter; Editor, Saul A. Goodkind

Jon Hall (Robert Griffin); Evelyn Ankers (Julie Herrick); Alan Curtis (Mark Foster); Leon Errol (Herbert Higgins); John Carradine (Dr. Peter Drury); Gale Sondergaard (Lady Irene Herrick); Lester Matthews (Sir Jasper Herrick); Halliwell Hobbes (Cleghorn); Doris Lloyd (Maude); Billy Bevan (Sgt. Fredric Travers); Ian Wolfe (Jim Feeny); Skelton Knaggs (Al Perry)

ABBOTT AND COSTELLO MEET THE INVISIBLE MAN, Universal-International, released March 1951
Produced by Howard Christie; Director, Charles Lamont; Screenplay, Robert Lees, Frederic I. Rinaldo and John Grant, from a story by Hugh Wedlock, Jr., and Howard Snyder, based on the character created by H. G. Wells; Photography, George Robinson; Art directors, Bernard Herzbrun and Richard H. Riedel; Music, Joseph Gershenson; Song "Good Old D.D.T." by Frederick Herbert, Milton Rosen and Joseph Gershenson; Editor, Virgil W. Vogel

Bud Abbott (Bud Alexander); Lou Costello (Lou Francis); Nancy Guild (Helen Gray); Arthur Franz (Tommy Nelson); Adele Jergens (Boots Marden); Sheldon Leonard (Morgan); William Frawley (Detective Roberts); Gavin Muir (Dr. Philip Gray); John Day (Rocky Hanlon); Paul Maxey (Dr. James C. Turner); George J. Lewis (Torpedo); Sid Saylor (Waiter); Bobby Barber (Sneaky); Billy Wayne

(Rooney); Sam Balter (Radio announcer); Frankie Van (Referee); Carl Sklover (Lou's handler); Charles Perry (Rocky's handler); Ed Gargan (Milt); Herbert Vigran (Stillwell); Ralph Dunn (Motorcycle Cop); Harold Goodwin (Bartender); Richard Bartell (Bald-headed man); Pete Launders (Cop); Edith Sheets (Nurse); Milt Bronson (Ring announcer)

LOS INVISIBLES (The Invisible Man), Mexican, released 1959
Director, Jaime Salvador; Based on the novel by H. G. Wells

Firuta; Capulina; Martha Elena; Cervantes; Eduardo Fajardo; Jose Jasso; Rosa Maria Gallardo; Chucho Salinas

EL HOMBRE QUE LEGRE SER INVISIBLE (The Invisible Man in Mexico), *Cinematografica Calderon SA*, released 1960
Produced by Guillermo Calderon; Director, Alfredo B. Cravenna; Screenplay, Alfredo Salazar, based on the novel by H. G. Wells; Photography, Raul Martinez Solares

Arturo de Cordova (Carlos Hill); Ana Luisa Peluffo (Beatriz); Augusto Benedico (Luis Hill); Raul Meraz (Conandante Flores); Jorge Mondragon (Don Ramon); Nestor de Borbosa (Enrique Salas); Roberto G. Ribera (First agent); Jose Munoz (Capataz); Roy Fletcher (Second agent); Jose Chavez (First policeman); Enrique Diaz Indiano (Juez)

TELEVISION

THE INVISIBLE MAN, *Matinee Theatre*, televised August 8, 1957 NBC 60 minutes
Producer, Albert McCleary; Director, Larry Schwab; Adapted by Robert Esson from the novel by H. G. Wells

Geoffrey Toone (Dr. Howard Kemp); Chester Stratton (Griffin); Angela Thornton (Addy); Molly Roden (Mrs. Bunting); Terrence de Marney (Teddy); Bob Kerr (Double); Suzie Davison (Millie); Gene Lawton (Farmer); Dean Howard (Postman)

THE INVISIBLE MAN, syndicated British series, televised in U.S. beginning November 4, 1958 CBS 26 episodes (30 minutes each)
Producer, Ralph Smart; Directors, Ralph Smart, C. Pennington Richards, Peter Maxwell and Quentin Lawrence; Writers, Ralph Smart, Michael Connor, Michael Carmey, Ian Stuart Black and others, based on the character created by H. G. Wells; Music, Sydney John Kay

Tim Turner (Dr. Peter Brady/The Invisible Man); Lisa Daniely (Diane Wilson); Deborah Watling (Sally Wilson); Ernest Clark (succeeded by Ewan McDuff) (Sir Charles); Lloyd Lamble (Dr. Hanning); and guest stars including Adrianne Corri, Martin Benson, Peter Sallis, Dennis Price, Griffith Jones, Betta St. John, Lee Montague, Derek Bond, Walter Fitzgerald, Andre Morrell, Vivian Matalon, Gary Raymond, Barbara Shelley, Dermot Walsh, Ralph Michael, Ronald Fraser, Mai Zetterling, Anton Diffring, Geoffrey Keen, Esmond Knight, Zena Marshall, Rupert Davies, Lana Morris, Charles Gray, Greta Gynt, Edward Judd, Redmond Phillips, Philip Friend, Honor Blackman, Jack Watling, Louise Allbritton, Bruce Seton

EPISODES: Secret Experiment; Crisis in the Desert; Behind the Mask; Strange Partners; Point of Destruction; Play to Kill; The Decoy; The Rocket; Shadow Bomb; Man in Disguise; Bank Raid; Picnic With Death; Odds Agains Death; Man in Power; The Big Plot; Jail-break; The Prize; Flight Into Darkness; The Locked Room; The

White Rabbit; The Mink Coat; Death Cell; The Vanishing Evidence; Shadow on the Screen; Blind Justice; The Gun Runners

THE INVISIBLE MAN, televised May 6, 1975 NBC 90 minutes
Produced by Silverton Productions in association with Universal Television; Executive producer, Harve Bennett; Producer, Steven Bochco; Director, Robert Michael Lewis; Teleplay, Steven Bochco, based on a story by Bochco and Harve Bennett, adapted from the novel by H. G. Wells; Photography, Enzo A. Martinelli; Art director, Frank T. Smith; Music, Richard Clements; Editor, Robert F. Shugrue

David McCallum (Dr. Daniel Weston/The Invisible Man); Melinda Fee (Kate Weston); Jackie Cooper (Walter Carlson); Henry Darrow (Dr. Nick Maggio); Alex Henteloff (Rick Senter); Arch Johnson (General Turner); John McLiam (Blind Man); Ted Gehring (Gate Guard); Paul Kent (Security Chief); and Milt Kogan, Jon Cedar, Lew Palter

THE INVISIBLE MAN, televised September 8, 1975 to January 9, 1976 NBC 11 episodes (60 minutes each)
Produced by Silverton Productions in association with Universal Television; Executive producer, Harve Bennett; Producers, Steven Bochco, Leslie Stevens, Robert F. O'Neill; Directors, Robert Michael Lewis, Alan J. Levi, Leslie Stevens and Sigmund Neufeld, Jr.; Music Henry Mancini, Pete Rugolo and Richard Clements; Music supervisor, Hal Mooney

David McCallum (Dr. Daniel Weston/The Invisible Man); Melinda Fee (Kate Weston); Craig Stevens (Walter Carlson); Henry Darrow (Dr. Nick Maggio); and guest stars including Nehemiah Persoff, Robert Alda, Barry Sullivan, Conrad Janis, Pat Harrington, Ross Martin, Michael Pataki, John Vernon, Jack Colvin, Robert Douglas, Shirley O'Hara, Barbara Anderson, Bobby Van, William Prince, John Kerr, Thayer David, Paul Shenar, James McEachin, Roger C. Carmel, Scott Brady, Frank Aletter, Nancy Kovack Mehta, Peter Donat, David Opatoshu, Richard X. Slattery, Cliff Osmond

THE INVISIBLE WOMAN, televised February 13, 1983 NBC 2 hours
Produced by Redwood Productions in association with Universal Television; Executive producers, Lloyd J. Schwartz and Sherwood Schwartz; Producer and director, Alan J. Levi; Teleplay, Lloyd J. Schwartz and Sherwood Schwartz, suggested by the *The Invisible Man* by H. G. Wells; Photography, Dean Cundey; Art director, Richard B. Lewis; Music, David Frank; Song "She Must Be Around Here Someplace" by Lloyd J. Schwartz, Sherwood Schwartz and David Frank; Special effects, Alan Hall; Editor, Houseley Stevenson

Bob Denver (Dr. Dudley Plunkett); Alexa Hamilton (Sandy Martinson/The Invisible Woman); Jonathan Banks (Darren); David Doyle (Neil Gilmore); George Gobel (Dr. Farrington); Anne Haney (Mrs. Van Dam); Harvey Korman (Carlisle Edwards); Art La Fleur (Phil); Garrett Morris (Lt. Greg Larkin); Ron Palillo (Spike Mitchell); Richard Sanders (Orville the Janitor); Mel Stewart (Security Guard); Jack Bruno Tate (Lt. Dan Williams); Scott Nemas (Rodney Sherman); Jack Steinfeld (Attendant); Ken Sansom (Lionel Gilbert); Teri Beckerman (Receptionist); Ronald E. Morgan (Cop #1); Joseph Phelan (Cop #2); Dan Woren (Gallery Guard); Marsha Warner (Sales-lady); Clinton Chase (Officer); David Whitfield (Marvin Carter); Valerie Hall (Miss Tomkins)

THE INVISIBLE MAN, televised September 4 through October 9, 1984 BBC 6

episodes (60 minutes each); in U.S. on Arts and Entertainment Channel April 30 through June 4, 1987

Produced by British Broadcasting Corporation; Producer, Barry Letts; Director, Brian Lighthill; Teleplay, James Andrew Hall, based on the novel by H. G. Wells; Production designer, Don Giles; Lighting, John Wiggins; Costumes, Anna Stubley; Makeup, Cheryl Wright; Visual effects, John Brace; Music, Stephen Deutsch

Pip Donaghy (Griffin); Lila Kaye (Mrs. Hall); Ron Pember (Mr. Hall); Michael Sheard (Reverend Bunting); Gerald James (Dr. Cuss); David Gwillim (Samuel Kemp); Donald Bissett (Professor Hobbema); Merelina Kendall (Lucy); Frank Middlemass (Thomas Marvel); Frederick Treves (Colonel Adye); Alan Mason (Wickstead); John Quarmby (Constable Jeffers); Jiggy Bhore (Barmaid); Ivor Salter (Barman); Roy Holder (Sandy Wadgers); Jonathan Adams (Teddy Henfrey); Deddie Davies (Mrs. Bunting); David Trevena (Postman); Anna Wing (Mrs. Roberts); Nigel Gregory (Youth); Rachel Heaton-Armstrong (Girl); Anthony Brown (Mariner); Esmond Knight (Blind Man); Cyril Shaps (Landlord); Bernard Stone (Shop Owner); Ruby Buchanan (Miss Hood); Janos Kurucz (Bearded Man); Helen Gold (Cook); John Patrick (Prison Officer); Keith Ashton (Navvy)

EPISODES: The Strange Man's Arrival; The Unveiling of the Stranger; Mr. Marvel's Visit to Iping; Dr. Kemp's Visitor; Certain First Principles; The Hunting of the Invisible Man

IT'S A WONDERFUL LIFE

Adaptations of the story *The Greatest Gift* by Philip Van Doren Stern and the 1947 movie by Frances Goodrich, Albert Hackett and Frank Capra

Synopsis

It is Christmas Eve in the small town of Bedford Falls. George Bailey, a happily married banker who grew up there, wed his high school sweetheart Mary Hatch, and stayed behind to manage his father's building and loan company when his kid brother went off to war, now fears his ability to keep the company afloat. When his bumbling uncle Billy loses a $3,000 deposit, George faces charges of embezzlement -- his generous nature his undoing. In desperation he turns to banker Henry Potter, but Potter will do nothing to help him -- he wants the building and loan company for himself. Distraught, George, thinking the world would be better off if he never existed, stands on a snow-covered bridge, and jumps into the icy river below. To his rescue comes on old fellow named Clarence Oddbody, a novice angel eager to earn his wings. Introducing himself as George's guardian angel, he suggests that before George commits suicide he should look at Bedford Falls and what it would be like if he had never lived. It would be a much different place. Henry Potter would own the town; Mary Hatch would be a lonely spinster; George's brother would have died because nobody would have saved him from a near drowning; the town pharmacist would have been ruined had not delivery boy George Bailey noticed a bungled prescription; his many friends would be leading dismal lives. "Strange, isn't it?" Clarence asks. "Each man's life touches so many other lives, and when he isn't around he leaves an awful hole, doesn't he? You see, George, you really had a wonderful life."

George decides that he really wants to live and returns home to his family. There he finds that his friends have rallied to his support and collected enough money to keep his business out of Henry Potter's hands. He and his neighbors joyfully ring in Christmas and George realizes that life is indeed wonderful. A tinkling bell atop the family Christmas tree announces that even Clarence has a present -- he's gotten his wings.

Comment and Critique

It's a Wonderful Life has emerged as an American film classic. When it was released initially -- the comeback movie for both James Stewart and Frank Capra after the war and made for a newly emerging company -- it was hardly the smash hit that all had envisioned. Following the war, Capra joined fellow directors George Stevens and William Wyler and producer Samuel Briskin to form Liberty Films. Capra had come across a delightful short story that evoked all of the American values of the time. "We had both been out of the service for several months," James Stewart later recalled, "and I had had no offers to play in pictures of any kind, but Frank called me [they had done *Mr. Smith Goes to Washington* and *You Can't Take It With You* together in the late 1930s] and said he had an idea for a picture, and I went over to his house. He started a rather rambling story about a guardian angel and a man about to commit suicide and wishing he had never been born. It was all rather confusing. However, I frankly didn't ask many questions and simply said that I would like, with all my heart, to play the part of George Bailey."

It was RKO's Christmas film of the year in 1946, and following its opening in New York, Bosley Crowther called it in *The Times* "a quaint and engaging modern parable on virtue being its own reward...Mr. Capra, back from the war, has resumed with a will his previously manifest penchant for portraying folks of simple, homely warmth...In composing this moralistic fable, [he] and his writers have tossed in a great abundance of colloquial incidents and emotional tangles of a mistful, humorous sort...As the hero, Mr. Stewart does a warmly appealing job, indicating that he has grown in spiritual stature as well as in talent during the years he was in the war. And Donna Reed is remarkably poised and gracious as his adoring sweetheart and wife." Crowther, however, wasn't completely taken by *It's a Wonderful Life*, and he failed to include it in his Ten Best list, noting that it "would have got into the charmed circle if its philosophy had been less candified."

Although it received Oscar nominations as Best Picture and for James Stewart, director Frank Capra, editor William Hornbeck, and John Aalberg (for sound recording), *It's a Wonderful Life* practically disappeared. Liberty Films made one other movie, Capra's subsequent *State of the Union*, before disbanding, and its maiden film's copyright subsequently lapsed. It fell to television to rediscover *It's a Wonderful Life* nearly three decades later and turn it into one of the most beloved movies of them all and a Christmas perennial. Since it is in public domain, virtually every TV station in the country seems to have a print (it's free to them) and its running time various quite drastically from one print to another. It is now shown in its original black and white and in newly colorized versions, almost, as some have groused, to the point of overkill. (In the New York area during the 1989 Christmas season, for instance, it was shown more than two dozen times on various commercial and public television stations!)

In 1977, actress Marlo Thomas dusted off the Capra classic, had the parts recast for a change-of-gender look at the story, and remade it as *It Happened One Christmas*, playing the Jimmy Stewart role. Wayne Rogers had the Donna Reed part, Cloris Leachman was the Guardian Angel, and Orson Welles chewed the scenery as the sinister banker. "Lovingly photographed by Conrad Hall (with additional lensing by Charles Correll) and handsomely produced by [Marlo] Thomas and Carole Hart, telefilm still smacks of the artificial," wrote *Variety*'s critic. "Main problem is Mary Bailey, character assayed by Thomas. [She] ricochets between Lady Bountiful and Joan of Arc in her endeavors to straighten out the little people of Bedford Falls...and defeat nasty banker Potter." *Variety* concluded: "Director Donald Wrye has failed to keep out the treacle as Mary runs about dispensing her sunshine."

In late 1990, the *It's a Wonderful Life* angel, Clarence Oddbody, was resurrected (as a younger man) in a syndicated television movie called *Clarence*. Starring Robert Carradine, it was produced in Canada as a venture by Television New Zealand for The Family Channel in America.

During the 1980s, composer Joe Raposo and lyricist Sheldon Harnick joined to create a musical of the famed movie, calling simply *A Wonderful Life*. It was first performed as a work in progress at the University of Michigan in April 1986 with cast comprised solely of drama students. Not much was heard about the musical subsequently until 1989, following the death of Raposo. Interest in further stagings of *A Wonderful Life* was revived and it received what seems to have been its first professional production (billed a "West Coast Premiere") in December 1989 at the Laguna Playhouse in California, with Harnick personally assisting in the staging. The Arena Stage in Washington, D.C., mounted another production of the musical in late 1991, but *Variety*'s theater critic, Jeremy Gerard, had few good words for it: "...a tedious musical comedy version from Sheldon Harnick and the late Joe Raposo that is neither musical nor intentionally comical ...Prospects for this lavish but unyieldingly cool production are limited, not to say undetectable. Missing from *A Wonderful Life* is any sense of the big themes and thwarted dreams that give the film its emotional resonance and durability."

STAGE

A WONDERFUL LIFE, *Power Center for the Performing Arts*, University of Michigan, Ann Arbor, opened April 17 through 20, 1986

Produced by the Musical Theatre Program, University of Michigan School of Music; A Musical in two acts, based on the Frank Capra film; Director, Brent Wagner; Book and lyrics by Sheldon Harnick; Music by Joe Raposo; Set designer, David Leugs; Lighting, Ken Yunker; Musical director and orchestrator, Jerry DePuit; Conductor, Bradley Bloom; Choreographer, Tim Millett; Stage manager, Brett Finley

An all-student cast including: Andrew A. Lippa (Frank Bailey); Paul Winberg (Jimmy Bailey); Stephen Bryant (Herb Miller); Doug LaBrecque (Sam Korman); Christopher Taylor (Joseph); Mark E. Doerr (Clarence); Paul Martinez (Mr. Hepner/Bank Examiner Carter); Ty Hreben (Ernie Bishop); Karen Seguin (Mrs. Bishop); Edward J. Smit (Tom Bailey/Martini Nephew); Connie Sa Loutos (Mrs. Bailey); Jeff Schneiter (Uncle Billy); Fred Vipond (M.C./Minister/Martini Nephew); Sue Kenny (Band Vocalist); Robin Robinson (Mary Lou); Beth Spencer (Kathy Wainwright); John Casey Ganun (Matt the Cop); Matt Chellis (Mr. Martini); Gabrielle Gustav (Mrs. Martini); Gilles Chiasson (Martini Nephew); Elizabeth A. Staton (Mrs. Wainwright); Hilary James (Dorothy Korman); Thomas Pasley (Priest); Brett Stockdill (Miller's Accountant); Sharen MacEnulty (Harriet the Bank Teller); Robert Coelius (Tommy Bailey); Amy Cohen (Margie Bailey); Paola Bollester (Beth Bailey); Judge Luckey, Brett Stockdill, Paul Martinez, Gilles Chiasson (Board of Directors)

MUSICAL NUMBERS: "Opening: Prayer"; "Show Me a Suitcase"; "One of the Lucky Ones"/"Can You Find Me a House?"; "In a State"; "A Wonderful Life"; "If I Had a

Wish"; "Can You Find Me a House?" (reprise); "A Mystery"/"Wings"; "Ruth"/"On to Pittsburgh"; "Good Night"; "Not What I Expected"; "Panic at the Building and Loan"; "A Wonderful Life" (reprise); "Prayer" (reprise); "Can You Find Me a House?" (reprise); "Linguine"; "First Class All the Way"; "I Couldn't Be With Anyone But You"; "Welcome a Hero"; "Christmas Gifts"; "Precious Little"; "Unborn (Sequence)"; "A Wonderful Life" (reprise); "Welcome a Hero" (reprise); "Christmas Gifts" (reprise)

A WONDERFUL LIFE, *Laguna Playhouse*, Laguna Beach, Cal., opened December 5 through 17, 1989
A Laguna Playhouse production, Douglas Rowe, artistic director; Associate producer, Mary Jo Slater; Directed by Douglas Rowe; A Musical based on the film by Frank Capra; Book and lyrics by Sheldon Harnick; Music by Joe Raposo; Set design, Proscenery; Lighting design, Jeff Calderon; Costumes, Karen Weller; Musical director, Mark Turnbull; Choreography, Steve Josephson; Stage manager, Blanche Mickelson

> Ralph Burneau (Frank Bailey); Jeff Parker (Jimmy Bailey); Nils Anderson (Herb Miller); Jeffrey B. Schlichter (Sam Korman); John Weston (Joseph); Harper Robinson (Clarence); Eric Hansen (Mr. Hepner/ Dominick Martini); Don Clinebell (Ernie Bishop); Rita Butler (Mrs. Bishop); Lloyd Castleton (Tom Bailey); Genie Ranney (Mrs. Bailey); Michael C. Miller (Uncle Billy); Laura Wells (M.C./Band Vocalist); Dierdre West (Mary Lou Howerton); Valerie Perri (Kathy Wainwright); Bill Littleton (Matt the Cop); Joe Wilson (Morgan); David A. Nelson (Minister/Priest); Norman Weingarten (Mr. Martini); Greta D. Henson (Mrs. Martini); Camilla Ming (Ruth); Angela Bauer (Mrs. Wainwright); Tisha Bellantuoni (Sarah); Flynn Lundh (Harriet); Steve Glaudini (Anthony Martini); Hilary James (Dorothy Korman); Terry Christopher (Miller's Accountant); Brad Charlton (Bank Examiner); Randall Dodge (Teller); Nathan Wood (Tommy Bailey); Claire Gaboury (Margie Bailey); Katy Killackey (Beth Bailey); Eric Hansen, Terry Christopher, David A. Nelson, Joe Wilson (Board of Directors); Jeff Parker, Dierdre West, Karen Angela, Steve Glaudini, David A, Nelson, Donna L. Getzinger, Randall Dodge, Cameron Ahia, Terry Christopher, Promise La Marco (Charleston Dancers); Eric Hansen, Steve Glaudini, Brad Charlton (Toughs); Camilla Ming, April Morgan, Karen Angela, Donna L. Getzinger, Dierdre West (Dames)

MUSICAL NUMBERS: Same as previous production, except "Can You Find Me a House?" dropped; "Blessing of the House" and "Frank's Prayer" added

A WONDERFUL LIFE, *Arena Stage*, Washington, opened November 21, 1991 through January 5, 1992
An AT&T OnStage presentation of an Arena Stage production; Directed by Douglas C. Wager; A Musical based on the film by Frank Capra; Book and lyrics by Sheldon Harnick; Music by Joe Raposo; Sets, Thomas Lynch; Lighting, Allen Lee Hughes; Costumes, Jess Goldstein; Musical director, Jeffrey Saver; Orchestrations, Michael Straobin; Choreography, Joey McNeely; Stage manager, Martha Knight

> Casey Biggs (George Bailey); Brigid Brady (Mary Hatch); Scott Wise (Harry Bailey); James Hindeman (Sam Wainwright); Richard Bauer (Mr. Potter); Jeffrey V. Thompson (Clarence); Ralph Cosham (Joseph); Terrence Currier (Mr. Martini/Tom Bailey); Michael W. Howell (Ernie Bishop); Halo Wines (Milly Bailey); Henry Strozier (Uncle Billy); Deanna Wells (Violet Bick); Kiki Moritsugu (Ruth Reynolds); and Hannahlee Casler, Heather Casler, Tyron Jon Chasez, Gabrielle Dummyer, Joel Eskowitz, Tracy Flint, Michael Forrest, Harriet D. Foy,

Kari Lynn Ginsburg, M. E. Hart, Tana Hicken, David Marks, John McInnis, Embrey Minor, Pamela Nyberg, Benjamin H. Salinas, David Trusnikoff, Wendall Wright

MUSICAL NUMBERS: "George's Prayer"; "This Year, Europe"; "One of the Lucky Ones"/"Can You Find Me a House?"; "In a State"; "A Wonderful Life"; "If I Had a Wish"; "Can You Find Me a House?" (reprise); "Wings"; "Ruth"/"On to Pittsburgh"; "Good Night"; "Not What I Expected"; "Panic at the Building and Loan"; "A Wonderful Life" (reprise); "George's Prayer" (reprise); "Can You Find Me a House?" (reprise); "Linguine"; "First Class All the Way"; "I Coulrdn't Be With Anyone But You"; "Welcome a Hero"; "Christmas Gifts"; "Precious Little"; "George's Prayer" (reprise); "Unborn (Sequence)"; "A Wonderful Life" (reprise); "Welcome a Hero" (reprise); "Christmas Gifts" (reprise)

SCREEN

IT'S A WONDERFUL LIFE, RKO Pictures, released January 1947

A Liberty Films Production; Produced and directed by Frank Capra; Screenplay, Frances Goodrich, Albert Hackett, Frank Capra and (uncredited) Michael Wilson and Clifford Odets; Additional scenes by Jo Swerling; Based on the short story *The Greatest Gift* by Philip Van Doren Stern; Photographers, Joseph Walker and Joseph Biroc; Art director, Jack Okey; Set decoration, Emile Kuri; Costumes, Edward Stevenson; Music, Dimitri Tiomkin; Editor, William Hornbeck

James Stewart (George Bailey); Donna Reed (Mary Hatch); Lionel Barrymore (Mr. Potter); Thomas Mitchell (Uncle Billy); Henry Travers (Clarence); Beulah Bondi (Mrs. Bailey); Ward Bond (Bert); Frank Faylen (Ernie); Gloria Grahame (Violet Bick); H. B. Warner (Mr. Gower); Todd Karns (Harry Bailey); Frank Albertson (Sam Wainwright); Samuel S. Hinds (Pa Bailey); Mary Treen (Cousin Millie); Virginia Patton (Ruth Dakin); Charles Williams (Cousin Eustace); Sara Edwards (Mrs. Hatch); Bill Edmunds (Mr. Martini); Lillian Randolph (Annie); Argentina Brunetti (Mrs. Martini); Bobby Anderson (Little George); Ronnie Ralph (Little Sam); Jean Gale (Little Mary); Jeanine Anne Roose (Little Violet); Danny Mummert (Little Marty Hatch); Georgie Noaks (Little Harry Bailey); Sheldon Leonard (Nick); Frank Hagney (Potter's Bodyguard); Ray Walker (Joe, at luggage shop); Charles Lane (Real Estate Salesman); Carol Coombs (Janie Bailey); Karolyn Grimes (Zuzu Bailey); Larry Simms (Pete Bailey); Jimmy Hawkins (Tommy Bailey); Carl "Alfalfa" Switzer (Freddie); Hal Landon (Marty Hatch); Harry Holman (High School Principal); Charles Halton (Bank Examiner Carter); Ed Featherstone (Bank Teller); Stanley Andrews (Mr. Welch); J. Farrell MacDonald (House Owner); Marion Carr (Mrs. Wainwright); Max Wagner (Bartender); Gary Owen (Bill Poster); Harry Cheshire (Dr. Campbell); Bobby Scott (Mickey); Ellen Corby (Mrs. Davis); Alan Bridge (Deputy with Summons); Tom Fadden (Watchman); and Almeira Sessions, Lee Frederick, Bert Moorhouse, Harry Rosenthal, Frank Fenton, Dick Elliott, Ernie Adams, Sam Flint

TELEVISION

IT HAPPENED ONE CHRISTMAS, televised December 11, 1977 ABC 2 1/2 hours

Daisy Productions in association with Universal Television; Produced by Marlo Thomas and Carole Hart; Director, Donald Wrye; Teleplay, Lionel Chetwynd, based on the Frank Capra film *It's a Wonderful Life* and the story *The Greatest Gift* by Philip Van Doren Stern; Photography, Conrad Hall; Additional photography, Charles Correll;

Production designer, John J. Lloyd; Set decorator, Hal Gausman; Music, Stephen Lawrence; Editors, Robbe Roberts and Bill Martin

Marlo Thomas (Mary Bailey Hatch); Orson Welles (Henry F. Potter); Wayne Rogers (George Hatch); Cloris Leachman (Clara); Barney Martin (Uncle Willie); Karen Carlson (Violet); Dick O'Neill (Mr. Gower); Doris Roberts (Mrs. Bailey); Cliff Norton (Mr. Martin); Richard Dysart (Peter Bailey); Christopher Guest (Harry Bailey); Morgan Upton (Bert Andrews); Lynn Woodlock (Mary, age 12); Archie Hahn (Ernie Baker); Ceil Cabot (Cousin Tillie); Jim Lovelett (Sam Wainwright); Robert Emhardt (Judge); Gino Conforti (Sassini); Bryan O'Byrne (Doctor); Med Flory (Nick the Bartender); Rita George (Helen Bailey); Dan Barrows (Toll Keeper); James E. Brodhead (Bank Examiner)

CLARENCE, televised November 22, 1990 The Family Channel 2 hours
Clarence Productions Inc.; Produced by Atlantis Films Ltd./South Pacific Pictures Ltd. and Television New Zealand in association with The Family Channel; Executive producers, Michael MacMillan, S. Harry Young, Terry A. Botwick and Don Reynolds; Producer, Mary Karlin; Supervising producer, Seaton MacLean; Director, Eric Till; Teleplay, Lorne Cameron and David Hoselton; Photography, Glen MacPherson; Art director, Ed Hanna; Music, Louis Natale; Editor, Bruce Lange

Robert Carradine (Clarence Oddbody); Kate Trotter (Rachel Logan); Louis Del Grande (Harold Brimble); Richard Fitzpatrick (Jeremy); Barbara Hamilton (Mrs. Duckworth); Jamie Rainey (Casey Logan); Nicolas Van Burek (Brent Logan); Jason McSkimming (Joseph); and Larry Albrey, Rachel Blanchard, Chris Campbell, Claire Celluci, Conrad Coates, Alvin Crawford, Murray Crutchley, Kevin Frank, Marvin Karon, Deborah Kirshenbaum, Shawn Lawrence, Bruce McFee, Jeff McGibbon, B. J. McQueen, Jack Newman, James Oregan, Paul Ranville, Julian Rewed, Alan Richards, Robbie Rick, Todd Schroeder, Harvey Sokoloff, Philip Williams

IVANHOE

Various adaptations of the novel by Sir Walter Scott (1819)

Synopsis

During the Holy Land Crusade of King Richard I, his brother Prince John, aided by traitorous Normans, attempts to usurp the British throne. After imprisonment in Austria, Richard makes his way back to England and, with Wilfred of Ivanhoe, defeats John's men. Wounded during the battle, Ivanhoe is nursed back to health by Rebecca, the Jewess who loves him. Rebecca is, in turn, desired by treacherous Sir Brian de Bois-Guilbert, the Templar, who captures Ivanhoe, his father Cedric, Lady Rowena, Rebecca and her father Isaac, and takes them to Norman Torquilstone Castle. Richard and his Saxons, aided by Robin of Lockley (Robin Hood) and his Sherwood Forest men, take the castle and release the prisoners except for Rebecca, who has been spirited away by Sir Brian. To the delight of Prince John, Rebecca is accused of witchcraft and is to be burned at the stake as a sorceress. Ivanhoe defends Rebecca in a trial by combat, defeating Sir Brian, as King Richard and his Saxon army arrive to oppose Prince John. Rebecca is freed but, aware that Ivanhoe is in love with Lady Rowena, leaves England with her father.

Comment and Critique

Sir Walter Scott was born in Edinburgh, Scotland, on August 15, 1771. After translating several German ballads and dramas, he began writing his own ballads and poems in 1799. His *Lady of the Lake* appeared in 1810. In 1814, Scott turned to prose, anonymously publishing his *Waverly Novels* (consisting of *Guy Mannering*, *The Antiquary*, *The Black Dwarf*, *Old Morality*, *Rob Roy* and *The Heart of Midlothian*). Also included was his most popular novel, *Ivanhoe*. Following were *Kenilworth*, *The Bride of Lammermoor*, *Quentin Durward*, *Redgauntlet*, *The Talisman* and others. In 1820, Scott became Sir Walter when honored with the title of baronet. Not until 1827 was it known that the popular author of the *Waverly Novels* was Sir Walter Scott.

He never recovered from a paralytic stroke in 1830 and, prior to his death at age sixty-one at his estate, Abbotsford, in Scotland on September 21, 1832, he had completed his eight-volume biography of Napoleon. His literary legacy was voluminous, but *Ivanhoe* remained his most popular work. One year after its publication, is was adapted to the stage as *Ivanhoe; or, The Jew and His Daughter*. Other anonymous adaptations followed, and in 1823, it appeared at New York's Park Theatre as *The Hebrew*. From a libretto by Rophino Lacy, Gioacchino Antonio Rossini composed an opera based on *Ivanhoe* called *The Maid of Judah*, which was performed at the Park Theatre in New York early in 1832. (The following year, Rossini used Scott's *The Lady of the Lake* as the basis for his *La Donna del Lago*.)

During the 1840s, dramatizations of Scott's novel appeared on the New York stage simply as *Ivanhoe*. Julian Sturgis' adaptation of it was set to music by Sir Arthur Seymour Sullivan and was successfully produced for 160 performances by Richard d'Oyly Carte at London's Royal English Opera House in January 1891. Thomas Dibdin's earlier dramatization, *Ivanhoe; or, Rebecca the Jewess*, had a meager run in London five years later. Lauderdale Maitland, who was favorably received for his portrayal of Ivanhoe at London's Lyceum Theatre in May 1913, repeated his characterization that same year in a screen version of *Ivanhoe*. But the British Zenith Film production with Maitland was completely overshadowed by the arrival in England of America's Herbert Brenon to film his version of Scott's saga for Universal's Imp Pictures.

Brenon started shooting *Ivanhoe* -- and playing the role of Isaac of York -- at Chepstow, England, utilizing the picturesque Chepstow Castle situated on the River Wye in Mommouthshire. Fellow American actors King Baggot and Leah Baird played Ivanhoe and Rebecca. The British press coverage of the first day of filming on June 23, 1913, continued throughout the production. Multitudes of townspeople were enlisted for scenes at the castle and reporter from London's *Daily Express* signed on as an extra to obtain firsthand coverage of the siege of the thirteenth century Chepstow Castle by Universal Studios. "We have carried Chepstow Castle at the sword's point, just as I foretold last Wednesday," the scribe reported, "and as I write, half of Ivanhoe's green-coated foresters are drinking pints at the Tuns Tavern to celebrate the victory. The other half are getting their wounds dressed at a local surgery...We gripped our weapons as grimly as Ivanhoe stood up in his stirrups and pointed the way with his sword. There was no holding us, but when Mr. Brenon stood beside the camera and bellowed through a megaphone, 'Fight, like blazes, boys, and there's sandwiches and beer when you get inside' -- well, that was just about the point when we began to see red. Both Ivanhoe's ranks and the Normans were recruited at five shillings a day from the local iron-works, which closed down for the battle, and some of these blacksmiths and riveters got a great swing on sword or battle-ax when they were in the thick of the scrimmage..."

Brenon's *Ivanhoe* received excellent notices. *The Cinematograph* review enthused, "What a wonderfully perfect actor is Mr. King Baggott, and what an enormous amount of energy he puts into his work. He seems to inspire the rest of the company whenever he is in the picture, with the result that they put much more force into their work than they would otherwise deem necessary." W. Stephen Bush (*Moving Picture World*) extolled "the splendid acting of the principal characters [and] the magnificence of the settings."

Having accumulated over the years large profits in England which were frozen by the British Government unless spent in Great Britain, Metro-Goldwyn-Mayer opened a studio consisting of 120 acres at Borehamwood near London. The prestigious Hollywood studio inaugurated its expansive new British facilities filming a screen version in 1949 of Robert Morley and Noel Langley's play, *Edward, My Son*. The following year, MGM constructed a replica of the enormous Torquilstone Castle on the studio's Borehamwood acreage with a moat twenty feet wide and ten feet deep, preliminary to the studio's proposed production of Scott's *Ivanhoe*. (Walter Wanger's publicized proposal for the filming of *Ivanhoe* in 1935 for Paramount, with Gary Cooper, Sylvia Sidney and Madeleine Carroll, never materialized.) Initially Ava Gardner, then Deborah Kerr were announced for the role of Rebecca and Margaret Leighton as Rowena. Rebecca ultimately was played by Elizabeth Taylor, and Joan Fontaine was signed to portray Rowena. Robert Taylor always was the choice to play the lead. George Sanders was signed for the evil Sir Brian and the remaining cast was well chosen from the seemingly endless array of top English actors.

Produced by Pandro S. Berman and directed by Richard Thorpe, MGM's *Ivanhoe* premiered at Radio City Music Hall in the summer of 1952 and made most of the year's Best Film lists. It was nominated for an Oscar as Best Picture of the Year, but lost to Cecil B. DeMille's *The Greatest Show on Earth*. In his *The Great Adventure Films*, Tony Thomas wrote: "The action sequences of *Ivanhoe* called for from 500 to 1,000 extras each day and the training required was nothing less than military. Dozens of men were drilled in the use of lances, spears and maces for the jousting scenes, and squads of men were given instruction in the use of the longbow and crossbow..."

Bosley Crowther wrote in *The New York Times*, "Out of Sir Walter Scott's glorious panoramic novel, *Ivanhoe*, which also contains an ample measure of twelfth-century social overtones, [producer] Berman and Metro-Goldwyn-Mayer have fetched a motion picture that does them, Scott and English history proud...we are much obliged to Metro, which has herein brought to the screen almost as fine a panorama of medievalism as Laurence Olivier gave us in *Henry V*...Production of this picture in England endowed it with a rich, distinctive air. It is a grand picture, told in what Sir Walter himself called his 'big bow-wow style.'"

During the 1957-58 season, Sydney Box Productions filmed in England a thirty-eight-episode television series which was syndicated in the United States through 1959. The Wales-based production of *Ivanhoe* starred Roger Moore and was dubbed into six different languages. A decade later, a ten-episode British series had Eric Flynn in the title role. In 1981, Norman Rosemont produced a lavish *Ivanhoe* in England featuring a somewhat miscast Anthony Andrews in the lead. Janet Maslin (*The New York Times*) found "This *Ivanhoe* is still lavish and bright. It doesn't run deep, and watching it is certainly no substitute for reading the novel it abridges, or even the feature film that starred Robert Taylor, Elizabeth Taylor and Joan Fontaine...there is plenty of jousting and frolicking...If the inventiveness of the effort can't entirely be applauded, its energy and ambition can..."

STAGE

IVANHOE; OR, THE JEW AND HIS DAUGHTER, *The Theatre*, New York, opened June 19, 1820
A Play based on the novel by Sir Walter Scott
Edmund Simpson (Ivanhoe); Mrs. John Barnes (Rebecca); Robert Campbell Maywood (Isaac of York); Jacob Woodhull (Sir Brian de Bois-Guilbert); Miss Johnson (Lady Rowena); John Barnes (Wamba); Mr. Spiller (Gurth); Harry George Moreland (Sir Reginald Front de Boeuf); Thomas Kilner (Cedric of Rotherwood); Mrs. Joseph Baldwin (Ulrica)

THE HEBREW, *Park Theatre*, New York, opened December 15, 1823
A Play based on the novel *Ivanhoe* by Sir Walter Scott
Edmund Simpson (Ivanhoe); Miss Johnson (Rebecca); Thomas Hilson (Isaac of York); Jacob Woodhull (Robin of Locksley); John H. Clarke (Sir Brian de Bois-Guilbert); Peter Richings (Maurice de Bracey); J. F. Foot (Cedric of Rotherwood); Frederick Wheatley (Prior Aymer); Mr. Kent (Friar Tuck); D. Reed (Grant Master)

THE MAID OF JUDAH, *Park Theatre*, New York, opened February 27, 1832 12 performances
An Opera by Gioacchino Antonio Rossini; Libretto by Rophino Lacy, based on the novel *Ivanhoe* by Sir Walter Scott
John Jones (Ivanhoe); Elizabeth Hughes (Rebecca); Jacob Woodhull (Isaac of York); Thomas Barry (Sir Brian de Bois-Guilbert); Edmund Simpson (Robin Hood); Thomas Placide (Gurth); John Barnes (Wamba); James Thorne (Malvoisin)

IVANHOE, *Bowery Theatre*, New York, opened April 19, 1841 8 performances
Produced and directed by Thomas S. Hamblin; A Play based on the novel by Sir Walter Scott (performed in conjunction with a circus and a play *Raphael's Dream*)
T. McCutcheon (Ivanhoe); Mrs. Anderson (Rebecca); Thomas Barry (Isaac of York); Mrs. Herring (Lady Rowena); Mr. Harrison (Sir Brian de Bois-Guilbert); Mr. Addis (Cecil of Rotherwood); Mr. Jackson (Maurice de Bracey); Mrs. Lansing (Elgiva); Mrs. Stickney (Ulrica); Mr. McClusky (Athelstane); Mr. Foster (Black Knight); W. F. Gates (Wamba); Mr. Jervis (Prior Aymer); N. H. Needham (Gurth)

IVANHOE, *Bowery Theatre*, New York, opened February 8, 1846
Produced by A. W. Jackson; A Play based on the novel by Sir Walter Scott, with Rockwell & Stone's Equestrian Troupe
Edward L. Davenport (Ivanhoe); Mrs. George Jones (Rebecca); John R. Scott (Isaac of York); Corson W. Clarke (Sir Brian de Bois-Guilbert); Mrs. Phillips (Rowena); Mr. Proctor (Robin of Locksley); Mrs. Sargent (Elgiva); Francis Chanfrau (Cedric of Rotherwood); Mr. Blanchard (Black Knight); Barkham Cony (Gurth); Thomas Hadaway (Wamba)

REBECCA, *Drury Lane Theatre*, London, opened February 21, 1875
An adaptation by Andrew Halliday, based on Sir Walter Scott's *Ivanhoe*
Genevieve Ward (Rebecca); William Terriss (Wilfrid of Ivanhoe); Samuel Phelps (succeeded by Mr. Fernandez) (Isaac of York); Miss Gainsborough (Lady Rowena); A. C. Lilly (Robin of Locksley); James Johnstone (Friar Tuck); Miss

Page (Ulrica); A. Mattheson (Richard Coeur de Lion)

IVANHOE, Royal English Opera House, London, opened January 31, 1891 160 performances
Produced and directed by Richard d'Oyly Carte; A Light Opera based on the novel by Sir Walter Scott; Music by Arthur Sullivan; Book by Julian Sturgis; Musical director, Francois Cellier; Conductor, Ernest Ford; Scenery, Hawes Craven, T. E. Ryan, Joseph Harker and William Telbin; Costumes designed by Percy Anderson; Stage manager, Hugh Moss; Mechanical effects, W. P. Dando

Ben Davies (succeeded by Joseph O'Mara) (Wilfrid of Ivanhoe); Margaret MacIntyre (succeeded by Miss Thuddicum, Lucille Hill) (Rebecca); Norman Salmond (succeeded by Franklin Clive) (Richard Coeur de Lion); Richard Green (succeeded by Wallace Brownlow) (Prince John); Esther Palliser (succeeded by Lucille Hill) (Lady Rowena); Eugene Oudin (succeeded by Francois Noije) (Sir Brian de Bois-Guilbert); Marie Groeble (Ulrica); Charles Kenningham (Maurice de Bracey); Adams Owen (Lucas de Beaumont); Ffrrangcon Davies (succeeded by W. H. Burgon) (Cedric the Saxon); Avon Saxon (Friar Tuck); Charles Copland (Isaac of York); W. H. Stephens (Robin of Locksley); David Cowis (Wamba); Frederick Bovill (The Squire)

Royal English Opera House, London, opened November 6, 1891 6 performances
Produced and directed by Richard d'Oyly Carte; A Light Opera, based on the novel by Sir Walter Scott; Music by Arthur Sullivan; Book by Julian Sturgis; Musical conductor, Ernest Ford; Scenery, Hawes Craven, T. E. Ryan, Joseph Harker and William Telbin; Costumes by Percy Anderson

Barton McGukin (Wilfrid of Ivanhoe); I. Thuddicum (Rebecca); Norman Salmond (Richard Coeur de Lion); John Wallace Brownlow (Prince John); Medora Henson (Lady Rowena); Eugene Oudin (Sir Brian de Bois-Guilbert); Marie Groeble (Ulrica); Charles Kenningham (Maurice de Bracey); Adams Owen (Lucas de Beaumont); Ffrangcon Davies (Cedric the Saxon); Avon Saxon (Friar Tuck); Charles Copland (Isaac of York); W. H. Stephens (Robin of Locksley); David Cowis (Wamba)

Irving Place Theatre, New York, opened May 8, 1893
Produced by Columbia College Dramatic Club; An All-Male Burlesque by Benjamin Aymar and John Reginald Blake (Columbia Law School, 1892) of the novel by Sir Walter Scott

The Columbia College "Strollers": William F. Wall (Ivanhoe); Melvin Henry Dalberg (Rebecca); Giles Augustus Taintor (Isaac of York); Edward Rush Duer (Lady Rowena); Richard Stockton Emmet, Jr. (King Richard); Albert La Montague (Sir Brian); Arthur Middleton Balke (Prince John); George Newell Hamlin (Cedric); John Reginald Blake (Oswald); Joseph G. Lamb (Wamba); John B. Brazier (De Bracey); J. R. de la Torre Bueno (Athelstane); Louis Fitzgerald, Jr. (Premiere Danseuse); Bertram de Lancey Drake (Second Danseuse)

On December 18, 1894, the "Strollers" returned to the *Broadway Theatre* with *IVANHOE UP TO DATE* featuring the above cast with the following exceptions: Mortimer Kennedy Flagg (King Richard); J. R. de la Torre Bueno (Prince John); James A. Donaghey (Athelstane/De Bracey)

IVANHOE; OR, REBECCA THE JEWESS, Novelty Theatre, London, opened

September 21, 1896 6 performances
A Historical Drama by Thomas Dibdin, based on the novel by Sir Walter Scott; Manager, Walter Tyrell

Bernard Copping (Ivanhoe); V. St. Lawrence (Rebecca); Newman Maurice (Isaac of York); Cybel Wynne (Lady Rowena); Robert Smith (King Richard); Percy Murray (Sr Brian de Bois-Guilbert); Henry Bertram (Cedric of Rotherwood); Harold Child (Wamba); Margaret Marshall (Elgiva); Thea Lesbrooke (Ulrica); Frank Ashton (Friar Tuck); Harry Danby (Maurice de Bracey); Cecil Hill (Sir Reginald Font de Boeuf); Charles Hilding (Lucas de Beaumont); Jack Haddon (Gurth)

IVANHOE, Lyceum Theatre, London, opened May 22, 1913 52 performances
A Play by Walter and Frederick Melville, based on the novel by Sir Walter Scott

Lauderdale Maitland (Ivanhoe); Miss Tittell-Bruns (Rebecca); Hubert Carter (Isaac of York); Ethel Bracewell (Lady Rowena); Fred Morgan (Prince John); Henry Lonsdale (Sir Brian de Bois-Guilbert); W. E. Hall (Maurice de Bracey); Austen Milroy (Reginald Font de Boeuf); E. A. Warburton (King Richard); Allan Wilkie (Cedric the Saxon); Allen Ellis (Philip Malvoisin); Norman Leyland (Athelstane); Raymond Wood (Lucas de Beaumont); Frank Harvey (Will Locksley); Jerrold Manville (Prior Aylmer); Fred Ingram (Wamba); J. T. MacMillan (Gurth); Richard Bode (Allan-A-Dale); Nancy Bevington (Elgiva); Marjorie Battis (Sarah); F. Willing (Francis); Charles Wingate (Stamford); George Milton (Much the Miller); Percy Baverstock (Oswald); K. McBean (Fitz Urse); Grace Lester (Ulrica); F. Elsworthy (Conrad); Mr. Gustave (Ahmed); H. Sullivan (Abdul)

SCREEN

IVANHOE, Zenith Films, England, released July 1913; in U.S. released as *REBECCA THE JEWESS*
Written and directed by Leedham Bantock; Based on a play by Walter and Frederick Melville, adapted from the novel by Sir Walter Scott

Lauderdale Maitland (Ivanhoe); Edith Bracewell (Rebecca); Hubert Carter (Isaac of York); Nancy Bevington (Lady Rowena); Henry Lonsdale (Sir Brian de Bois-Guilbert); Austen Milroy (Reginald Font de Boeuf); Raymond Wood (Lucas de Beaumont); Fred Morgan (Prince John); W. E. Hall (Maurice de Bracey); Fred Ingram (Wamba)

Universal-Imp Pictures, released September 1913
Produced and directed by Herbert Brenon; Based on the novel by Sir Walter Scott

King Baggott (Ivanhoe); Leah Baird (Rebecca); Herbert Brenon (Isaac of York); Evelyn Hope (Lady Rowena); Wallace Widdecombe (Sir Brian de Bois-Guilbert); George Courtney (Prince John); Arthur Scott Craven (King Richard); Jack Bates (Sir Reginald Font de Boeuf); Wallace Boscoe (Cedric the Saxon); W. Thomas (Robin Hood); H. Holles (Friar Tuck); A. J. Charlwood (Athelstane); W. Calvert (Gurth); Mr. Norman (Wamba)

Metro-Goldwyn-Mayer, released July 1952
Produced by Pandro S. Berman; Director, Richard Thorpe; Screenplay, Noel Langley, based on the adaptation by Aeneas MacKenzie of the novel by Sir Walter Scott; Photography, F. A. Young; Art director, Alfred Junge; Costumes, Robert Furse;

Makeup, Charles Parker; Music, Miklos Rozsa; Special effects, Tom Howard; Sound, A. W. Watkins; Editor, Frank Clarke

Robert Taylor (Ivanhoe); Elizabeth Taylor (Rebecca); Joan Fontaine (Lady Rowena); George Sanders (Sir Brian de Bois-Guilbert); Robert Douglas (Sir Hugh de Bracey); Emlyn Williams (Wamba); Felix Aylmer (Isaac of York); Guy Rolfe (Prince John); Finlay Currie (Cedric the Saxon); Norman Wooland (King Richard); Basil Sydney (Waldemar Fitz Urse); Francis DeWolff (Reginald Font de Boeuf); Harold Warrender (Locksley); Patrick Lovell (Philip Malvoisin); Roderick Lovell (Ralph de Vipont); Sebastian Cabot (Copmanhurst clerk); Megs Jenkins (Isaac's servant); Valentine Dysell (Norman guard); John Ruddock (Hundebert); Michael Brennan (Baldwin); Lionel Harris (Roger of Bermondsley); Earl Jaffe (Austrian Monk)

TELEVISION

IVANHOE, Harlech Television, syndicated 1957-59 38 episodes (30 minutes each)
Sydney Box Productions for Harlech Television, Cardiff, Wales; Executive producer, Peter Rogers; Producers, Bernard Coote, Herbert Smith and Seymour Friedman; Directors, David MacDonald, Tim Mitchell, Anthony Moreton, Lance Comfort, Don Sharpe and others; Teleplay, Benedict Berenberg, Richard Fielder, Geoffrey Orme and others; based on the novel by Sir Walter Scott; Music, Edwin Astley and Albert Elms

Roger Moore (Ivanhoe); Bruce Seton (King Richard); Robert Brown (The Monk); Paul Whitsum (Sir Maverick); John Pike (Bart); Brian Thomas (Will of Underhill); Jack Watson (Garrick); Richard Green (Sir Robert of Locksley); Alfie Bass (The Thief)

EPISODES: Freeing the Serfs; Ragan's Forge; Slave Traders; German Knight; Rinaldo; Whipping Boy; The Witness; The Ransom; Wedding Cake; Lyman the Pieman; Face to Face; Black Boar; Freelance; Masked Bandit; The Weavers; The Masons; Arms and the Woman; The Circus; The Escape; Murder at the Inn; Prisoner in the Tower; The Cattle Killers; By Hook or By Crook; The Treasures of Cathay; Brothers in Arms; The Double-Edged Sword; The Kidnapping; The Widow of Woodcote; The Princess; Gentle Jester; Counterfeit; Search for Gold; The Devil's Dragon; Three Days to Worchester; The Night Raiders; The Raven; The Fledgling; The Swindler

IVANHOE, syndicated 1971 BBC 10 episodes (30 minutes each)
Produced by British Broadcasting Corporation. Producer, John McRae

Eric Flynn (Ivanhoe); Vivian Brooks (Rebecca); John Franklyn Robbins (Isaac of York); Clare Jenkins (Lady Rowena); Anthony Bate (Sir Brian de Bois-Guilbert); Tim Preece (Prince John); Bernard Horsfell (King Richard); Eric Woolfe (Receptor)

IVANHOE, televised February 23, 1982 CBS 3 hours
A Norman Rosemont Production in association with Columbia Pictures Television; Producer, Norman Rosemont; Associate producer, William Hill; Director, Douglas Camfield; Teleplay, John Gay, based on the novel by Sir Walter Scott; Photography, John Coquillon; Production designer, John Blezard; Art director, Ken Court; Costume designer, Olga Lehmann; Music, Allyn Ferguson; Second-unit director, David Tringham; Makeup, Robin Grantham, Edie Knight and Jane Royle; Editor, Bill Blunden

Anthony Andrews (Wilfrid of Ivanhoe); James Mason (Isaac of York); Olivia Hussey (Rebecca); Lysette Anthony (Lady Rowena); Sam Neill (Sir Brian de Bois-Guilbert); Julian Glover (King Richard); John Rhys-Davies (Reginald Font de Boeuf); Ronald Pickup (Prince John); Michael Hordern (Cedric the Saxon); George Innes (Wamba); Stuart Wilson (Maurice de Bracey); Michael Gothard (Athelstane); David Robb (Robin Hood); Anthony Haygarth (Friar Tuck); Timothy Morand (Prince John's attendant); Dean Harris (Phillippe); Philip Locke (Grant Master); Geofrey Veevers (Beaslin); Stewart Bevan (Edward); Debbie Farrington (Alicia); Robert Russell (Leader); Chloe Franks (Attendant); John Forgeham (Font's Lieutenant); John Allam (Herald); Kenneth Gilbert (Marshal)

IVANHOE, syndicated 1983 (animated) 65 minutes
An API Television production; Producer, Walter J. Hucker; Director, Leif Gram; Teleplay, Michael Robinson, based on the novel by Sir Walter Scott; Music, John Sangster; Editor, Eddy Graham

Voices: Ron Haddrick, John Kingley, John Llewellyn, Bruce Montague

IVANHOE, syndicated 1984 (animated) 72 minutes
Burbank Films Australia; Executive producer, Tom Stacey; Producer, Tim Brooke-Hunt; Animation director, Warwick Gilbert; Teleplay, Alex Nicholas, Kit Ontcon, based on the novel by Sir Walter Scott; Music, Mark Isaacs

Voices: Lewis Fitzgerald (Ivanhoe); Liz Alexander (Lady Rowena); Robert Coleby (Robin Hood); Nick Tate (Sir Cedric); and Phillip Hinton, Ron Haddrick, Robin Stuart, Sean Hinton, Bill Conn, Ross Higgins, Barbara Frawley

JACK AND THE BEANSTALK

Various adaptations of the British fairy tale

Synopsis

To make ends meet, Jack's impoverished mother reluctantly decides to sell their cow whose milk, sold daily in the village market, has been their only source of income. On the way to market, Jack meets a strange old man who persuades him to trade the cow for a handful of magical beans. Infuriated, Jack's mother thrashes her son when he comes home, tosses the beans out of the window, and sends the impulsive boy to bed without dinner. Awakening the next morning, Jack is astonished to see that a giant beanstalk has grown overnight, reaching to the sky. He scurries up the beanstalk to the clouds where he finds himself on a long road leading to a great house. A large woman tentatively greets him at the door and disagreeably offers him breakfast, warning him that her husband is an ogre -- literally -- who'd eat little boys broiled on toast. With a terrible rumble, her giant spouse ambles into the kitchen but his wife has hidden Jack in the oven. "Fee-fi-fo-fum, I smell the blood of an Englishman. Be he alive or be he dead, I'll grind his bones to make my bread," grumbles the giant. Jack escapes from the oven after the giant drifts off to sleep, but passing the snoozing ogre, the youngster notices several bags of gold. Grabbing one, he races back to the beanstalk and retreats down it.

Jack and his mother live well on the gold but when it is exhausted, he makes another trip skyward to the house of the giant where, again, he is admitted by the ogre's wife. It's back to the oven for Jack when the giant appears and demands his hen "that lays the golden eggs." When nap time comes for the giant, Jack grabs the hen and flees down the beanstalk proudly displaying his latest fortune to his mother. Each time Jack commands "Lay!" the hen produces a golden egg. Another return to the great house in the sky gives Jack the chance to gaze on the giant's golden harp which plays and sings on command. He attempts to steal the harp when the giant begins snoozing, but it screams for its master, awakening the ogre, who lumbers after Jack and chases him down the beanstalk. The boy reaches his home safely, however, gets an axe and chops the beanstalk until it breaks, hurling the giant to the ground, killing him. Jack continues to sell his golden eggs and grows to be a very rich man, wedding a beautiful princess and living happily ever after.

Comment and Critique

The British fairy tale *Jack and the Beanstalk* has had various stage incarnations over the past 150 years. One of the earliest: at New York's Bowery Theatre early in January 1863. George Washington Lafayette Fox, described in his day as "the greatest American exponent of classical pantomime," prior to his success in the title role of his 1868 play *Humpty Dumpty*, produced *Jack and the Beanstalk* while manager of the Bowery. He was then America's highest paid entertainer. (Fox died in 1877 at the age of fifty-two.)

In his *Annals of the New York Stage*, George Odell wrote: "Fox mounted high to success in a pantomime, *Jack and the Beanstalk*...This had a really splendid run, in company, of course, with established dramas... Jack was still climbing the beanstalk. By February 16th, however, he ceased to do so..." Throughout the late 1880s, *Jack and the Beanstalk* was a popular, often elaborate, pantomime in London.

In November 1896, Klaw and Erlanger produced *The Strange Adventures of Jack and the Beanstalk* at New York's Casino Theatre. *The New York Times* considered the production "an amusing piece of nonsense and very likely to succeed...[It] is distinctly amusing in its frivolous, foolish way, and anybody who wants to rest his thinking apparatus for a couple of hours can hardly do it more innocently and effectively than by watching for that space of time this latest of Mr. R. A. Barnet's achievements. He has taken half a dozen Mother Goose stories, mixed them up with one from the Arabian Nights and several from the Newgate Calendar, and then set the ludicrously incongruous characters thus obtained to singing a lot of songs more or less original with Mr. A. B. Sloane [and] others. The result is incomprehensible, inconsequential, and neither comic opera nor farcical comedy, but it is lively and ingenious, occasionally humorous, almost constantly admirable, as a spectacle..."

Edward A. Dithmar later added in *The Times*: "The nursery play at the Casino is a remarkably pretty show in the manner of the English Christmas pantomimes...One cannot help admiring the unclassified skill of Mr. R. A. Barnet, who puts this sort of stuff together as ingeniously...Mr. Sloane's music is often very tuneful, and in never tiresome, though there is a full measure of it."

Pantomimes became annual Christmas stage traditions in England with productions of *Cinderella*, *Aladdin*, *Puss 'n' Boots*, and other tales for children, including *Jack and the Beanstalk*. The art of pantomime is as old as the theater. In his 1941 *A History of the Theatre*, George Freedley observed, "Despite the fact that the mime undoubtedly descended directly from the Doric mime, it was not until the time of the Roman Empire that it won its highest esteem...All authorities unite in referring to it as being a play of low life... The last important form of Roman drama was the *pantomimus* or pantomime." In England, noted Freedley, "Colley Cibber records what must have been the first pantomime, a mimic story about Mars and

Venus in dance and gesture..."

In 1929, the scribe for London's *Sphere* recalled: "I return again to my playbook of *Jack and the Beanstalk* 35 years ago at Drury Lane. I glance at the list of actors. I see such well-loved names as Dan Leno, Harriet Vernon, Harry Nicholls, George Conquest, Jun., Charles Lauri, the Griffiths Brothers and Herbert Campbell -- but I never liked Herbert Campbell; I can never laugh at large men dressed up as little girls with fair ringlets and socks. But that was certainly a notable cast and it is quite surprising, if you glance through the Christmas programmes at Drury Lane for 50 years, to see what a number of pantomime celebrities there have been."

Beginning December 21, 1931, the opera by Louis Gruenberg and John Erskine of *Jack and the Beanstalk* gave sixteen performances at the 44th Street Theatre in New York to generally good reviews. Erskine, author of *The Private Life of Helen of Troy* and other novels, explained his contribution to the opera that was commissioned by the Juilliard School of Music: "A libretto should be entertaining, and it should be a comedy...should be based on a plot already familiar to the audience. The pleasure of recognition belongs to art...if you don't know the story before the curtain rises, the singers are not likely to let you into the secret."

Jack and the Beanstalk continued to delight audiences in London as a Yuletide pantomime, and on Christmas Eve 1935, Marriott Edgar's production opened at London's Drury Lane Theatre starring Binnie Hale as Jack. *The London Times* found: "Though firm in the tradition, this is one of the liveliest and best-looking pantomimes of recent years. It is always within range of the story it has to tell and, whenever some diversion threatens to become tedious, promptly returns to it for support...In brief, the entertainment is more various and better balanced than such entertainments commonly are...The giant, too big for even the stage of Drury Lane to hold all of him at once, appears first amid thunder as a pair of vast boots, then as a ravishing hand, then by implication when, in a transformation scene, his beanstalk grows before our eyes, and finally, as a head when the beanstalk is cut and his downfall accomplished. Meanwhile, Miss Binnie Hale, in or out of shining armour, performs prodigies of romantic attack...a brisk and decorative evening..."

For the next half century, a pantomime of *Jack and the Beanstalk* continued as an English Christmas event. Of a contemporary London version, in 1991, there was this view from *The Times'* Jeremy Kingston: "This glittering mega-panto starts off with a flash of lightning and a giant's roar loud enough to knock the plugs out of your ears. The curtain lifts and the forces of good and evil; begin throwing couplets at each other that will not end till three hours later." Kingston found onetime rock star Cilla Black as Jack "irrepressible and captivating...I should have liked to see Cilla climb a few leaves further up the beanstalk, but these are minor carpings against an evening of great joy."

In the mid-1980s, Stephen Sondheim and James Lapine put together an elaborate musical combining many of the great fairy tale legends in revisionist looks at Cinderella, Jack the Giant Killer, Little Red Riding Hood, and Rapunzel, with Sleeping Beauty and Snow White included briefly. Their show, *Into the Woods*, came to Broadway in 1987, received fifteen thumbs up out of twenty-three reviews from the New York critics and played for twenty-two months. Ben Wright was Jack originally, Barbara Byrne Jack's mother, and Merle Louise the Giant. One of the striking sights for those in the vicinity of the Martin Beck Theater on West 45th Street was that of the massive leg of the Giant stepping over the side of the building above the marquee. *Into the Woods* received ten Tony Award nominations including Best Musical (it lost to *The Phantom of the Opera*). Awards went to Joanna Gleason (The Baker's Wife) as Best Actress in a Musical and to Sondheim and Lapine for their score and book.

Into the Woods subsequently toured the United States for thirteen months with Cleo Laine initially starring as The Witch. In late September 1990, it had its London premiere with Julia McKenzie in the lead. It played for six months and went on to be chosen Best Musical by the *Evening Standard*. It also was nominated for the Olivier Award as Best Musical, but lost to Sondheim's *Sunday in the Park With George*.

The earliest screen adaptations of the popular fairy tale were produced by Thomas Edison in 1902 and Sigmund Lubin the following year. In 1912, Edison's Kinetoscope Films released another short screen version of it. He advertised his motion picture as "A fairy tale, as familiar in the homes as a household word, unfolding the adventures of Jack, his triumphant return from the mystic height of the beanstalk with the giant's ill-gotten treasures. The photographic work, in showing the size of the giant and his wife, is little short of wonderful."

Five years later, William Fox's first "Fox Kiddie Features" was *Jack and the Beanstalk*. The ten-reel feature film premiered at New York's Globe Theatre on a two-a-day schedule beginning July 30, 1917. The reserved-seat policy was scaled at admissions of twenty-five to fifty cents for matinees and up to $1.00 for evening performances. It was released nationally in late August.

Edward Weitzel (*The Moving Picture World*) reported: "In preparing *Jack and the Beanstalk*, the ten-part film deluxe of the juvenile classic, for screen representation, the producers have evidently gone to a great deal of expense. More than this, the money has been spent intelligently and most of the picture displays excellent taste. Reduced to eight reels by judicious cutting it would form an entertainment that would prove equally pleasing to youngsters and the grownups...The adventures of the greatest hero in juvenile fiction are carried out in a wonderfully impressive manner, not the least effective feature being the acting of the little stars, Francis Carpenter and Virginia Lee Corbin, and the other members of the youthful cast...Young Master Carpenter, in the title role, measures up to his work amazingly. He has the force, stride, personality and method of a well-seasoned actor, and makes all his points with the ease of a veteran...Heroic cutting will save the day, and the good work of the producers, C. M. and S. A. Franklin, will receive its full value..."

The New York Times noted: "*Jack and the Beanstalk* in the Fox Films' most spectacular movie, made in California, furnished the young season's youngest first night on old Broadway in some years at the Globe...The fairy tale, as a piece of workmanship, was admirably clear and varied, with the constant shift of scenes quick as thought, and a well-sustained climax of interest in the little hero."

Bud Abbott and Lou Costello's 1952 color screen version of the story was founded on Jack (Costello) falling asleep while reading the fairy tale to a child and dreaming he is the story's Jack who, with his partner Dinkelpuss (Abbott), climbs the magic beanstalk, saves a prince and a princess and destroys the evil giant (played by wrestler Buddy Baer). "Frequently funny in a highly visual sort of way and there is plenty of action...As Jack the Giant Killer, Costello cuts a very funny figure indeed," wrote the critic for the *New York Herald Tribune*.

"There is always room for improvement," *The New York Times* found, "and *Jack and the Beanstalk* -- the Lou Costello-Bud Abbott version of the Teutonic fairy tale -- proves accuracy of the maxim...the spotlight is on the pratfalls and mayhem that [they] concoct. They have not refined their particular brand of slapstick to any great degree, and the marked improvement can be traced mainly to their choice of a story. While the pair have turned out a film that falls far short of distinguished slapstick comedy, they deserve plaudits for leaving behind the dreary routine of inane stories and meaningless antics."

Jack and the Beanstalk, produced by the comedy pair's own company at approximately $450,000, was Abbott and Costello's first color film (SuperCinecolor) but did little to bolster their then waning box office popularity. One British critic dismissed the boys' version as "fair pantomime, with wide opportunities for the talents of Messrs. Abbott and Costello. But the level is uneven and the music disappointing."

A variation on the fairy tale was filmed in 1961. Called *Jack the Giant Killer*, the Edward Small production featured Kerwin Mathews in the title role. It was not well received. *The New York Times*' Howard Thompson dismissed it by saying: "The whole thing hops the make-believe track in short order...The acting is terrible, the dialogue is even worse, and some extremely jarring touches of the macabre -- yowling skeletons, and witches, splashed around in rather messy special effects -- simply aren't for the small fry. And some of the combats involving the giants (there are two), various monsters (rubber), and the slender Mr. Mathews are a gory eyeful."

Tom Cruise had one of his earlier starring roles playing Jack in Ridley Scott's elaborate but less-than-successful *Legend* in 1985. "It is a fairy-tale produced on a grand scale, a classic tale of the stuggle between darkness and light, good and evil, set in some timeless world peopled with fairies, elves and goblins, plus a spectacularly satisfying Satan," wrote the critic for *Variety*. "At the same time, the basic premise is alarmingly thin, a compendium of ancient fairy-tales including *Jack and the Beanstalk* and *The Sleeping Beauty*, with borrowings from dramatic works such as *A Midsummer Night's Dream* and *Peter Pan*." In Britain's *Monthly Film Bulletin*, critic Kim Newman felt that "*Legend* does its best to live up to its blunt title and seem archetypal. However, like [director Scott's] *Blade Runner* before it, the film suffers so much from an overemphasis on details at the expense of the actual story that it becomes a plodding bore. The force of Nature is represented by Tom Cruise with long hair and a vacant expression."

On television, the prestigious *Producers' Showcase* in 1956 offered a "live and in color" musical version of *Jack and the Beanstalk* with Joel Grey as Jack and a cast that included Cyril Ritchard, Peggy King, Billy Gilbert and (as narrator) Dennis King.

"Jack went up a Hollywood beanstalk last night," wrote Jack Gould in *The New York Times*. "The musical version of the fairy tale [had] sets and stars galore. Someone merely forgot to send out for the spirit of make-believe. It was to be expected that Helen Deutsch, who prepared the book and lyrics, and Jerry Livingston, who contributed the score, would necessarily take considerable liberties with the original of *Jack and the Beanstalk*. But it was hardly to be anticipated that they would sacrifice the story's precious qualities of childlike revelation and discovery...Joel Grey was cast as Jack and, frankly, was much too old for the part. He surmounted the obstacles barring his way to the giant, but never with a deep sense of relish or anticipation. And as a singer, Mr. Grey is not yet a Mel Torme. But it was not entirely Mr. Grey's fault. Miss Deutsch's book had Jack go out of focus." Critic Gould continued: "*Jack and the Beanstalk* too often wavered between *Captain Video* in a vegetable patch and soap opera... The production was extremely lavish and quite overwhelming. The trick camera shots and the literal stage settings were very cumbersome and intrusive...No amount of electronics can ever substitute for the enchantment of that everlastingly exciting phrase, 'Once upon a time...'"

The engaging Hanna and Barbera 1967 TV musical of *Jack and the Beanstalk* starred Gene Kelly (as the man with the magic beans) and nine-year-old Bobby Riha (as Jack) and a score by Sammy Cahn and James Van Heusen. Kelly had danced with cartoon characters in MGM's *Anchors Aweigh* in 1945 and in his later *Invitation to the Dance*. In NBC's *Jack and the Beanstalk*, which he also produced and directed, he again performed with animated figures. Ben Gross (New York *Daily News*) called the TV musical "a charming show...[it] may well become a television classic." Less enthusiastic were some of his colleagues. Harry Harris (*The Philadelphia Inquirer*) found it "pleasant, but not especially imaginative...Michael Morris/Larry Marks' script seemed aimed at children of all ages -- under eight...Kelly, who also served as producer and director, was amiable and agile [and] Bobby Riha impressed as actor, singer and hoofer."

Jack Gould wrote in *The New York Times*: "Any shotgun marriage of the fantasy of cartoon animation and the actuality of life-size people is something to be avoided, most of all in a children's classic...A viewer was merely conscious of the ability of Hollywood technology to match the film and soundtrack of a drawing and a living performer... The oppressive automation of show business took its toll of the gifted composers, along with Mr. Kelly and everyone else."

Another *Jack and the Beanstalk* materialized on television in 1983 when Shelley Duvall assembled a cast that included Dennis Christopher (as Jack), Elliott Gould (as The Evil Giant) and Jean Stapleton (as The Kindly Giantess), among others, for her acclaimed *Faerie Tale Theatre* version of the oft-told tale for Showtime. In the spring of 1991, the production of *Into the Woods*, taped during the end of its run at the Martin Beck Theater in New York with most of the original cast, was presented on PBS' *American Playhouse*.

STAGE

JACK AND THE BEANSTALK, Bowery Theatre, New York, opened January 5, 1863
48 performances
A Pantomime produced and directed by George Lafayette; Played in conjunction with *The Wept of Wishton-Wish*; *Mary Price, or The Adventures of a Servant Girl*; *El Hyder*, and *The Co-Lean Born*

George L. Fox (Happy-Go-Lucky the Clown); George Davenport (Harlequin Jack); Giant Bihin (Swallow-allup the Giant); Charles K. Fox (Uppercrust/ Pantaloon); Louisa Browne (Rosine/ Columbine); Jackson Haines (Rollerskater)

Astley's Theatre, London, opened January 14, 1869
Produced by E. T. Smith and H. T. Friend; A Pantomime by Harry Lemon; Scenery, William Brew and J. Rutland Potts; Costumes, Mr. S. May and Miss Bennett

Caroline Parks (alternate Tilly Wright) (Jack of the Beanstalk); E. Robertha Erskine (Jill); George Yarnold (Demon Indigestion); Louise Fosbrooke (Burlesque); Georgie Clare (Pantomime); Mrs. Levettez (Scarlet Runner); Edmund Coles (Squire Chevy); Frank Lacey (Harlequin); E. St. Albyn (Grimgrief); Master Percy Roselle (Number Nip); Minnie Ashton (Rigmarole); Rose Clare (Fun); Constance Brabant (Dame Gossip); Master Davidson (Broad Bean); Harry Pritchard (Lawyer Mumps); Henry Dudler (Gaffer Kroner); Mr. Parchmont (Sheepskins); Mr. Hopple (Pippin)

Astley's Theatre, London, opened January 8, 1870
Producer, E. T. Smith; A Pantomime by Harry Lemon; Scenery, William Brew

Caroline Parks (Jack of the Beanstalk); E. Robertha Erskine (Jill); George Yarnold (Demon Indigestion); Louise Fosbrooke (Burlesque); Frank Lacey (Harlequin); Mlle. Wright (Columbine); Master Percy Roselle (Number Nip); Minnie Ashton (Rigmarole); Rose Clare (Fun); Mr. Stoinette (Clown); J. Buckingham (Pantaloon)

THE BEANSTALK: OR, HARLEQUIN JACK THE GIANT KILLER AND THE SEVEN CHAMPIONS, Standard Theatre, London, opened January 17, 1870
Produced and directed by John Douglas

C. Roby (Harlequin Jack); Miss Russell (Princess Fairplay); Ida Hertz (Ariadne); J. W. Wallace (Baron Slion); Marie Leslie (Champion of Scotland); Fanny Lang (Champion of Wales); J. F. Brian (Champion of Ireland); Alice Herbert (Champion of France); Lizzie Dashwood (Champion of Italy); Bella Stanley (Champion of Spain); Alice St. Maine (Saint George of England); Albert Thomas (His Squire); E. Roby (Columbine); Gordine Boleno (Clown); Mr. Stewart (Pantaloon); Brothers Roberts (Sprites)

JACK THE GIANT KILLER, Adelphi Theatre, London, opened December 25, 1872
A Pantomime Burlesque by C. Millward

Caroline Parks (Jack the Giant Killer); Charlotte Saunders (Jack's Mother); B. Egan (The Giant); Harwood Cooper (Policeman A-1); A. C. Lilly (King Ti-lol-lol the Last); Miss Hudspeth (Queen Bountiful); Fanny Montague (Prince Broadbean); Maud Howard (Princess Rosatinta); Robert Romer (Ye Butcher)

JACK AND THE BEANSTALK, Covent Garden, London, opened December 26, 1873
Produced by Mr. Chatterton; A Pantomime by Frank W. Green; Scenery, Julian Hicks; Ballets, Mr. Beverley

Fanny Leslie (Jack); Clara Jenks (Princess Pomsie); Lizzie Coote (Quicksilver); George Vokes (Lord Chamberlain); G. H Macdermott (Thomas); Master Laurie (Poodle); Herbert Campbell (Widow Simpson); W. George (King Pippin); Harry Payne (Harlequin); Miss Lewes, Miss Grainger, Mme. Paradise, Mme. Archer, Mme. Carthew, Mme. Clifton, Messrs. Miller, Spencer, Davis (Ballet); Mlles. Limido and Sidonis (Premiere Danseuse)

JACK THE GIANT KILLER, Marylebone Theatre, London, opened December 26, 1873
Produced by Albert West; A Pantomime by Frank Hall

Laura Sedwick (Jack); Jessie Garratt (Count Palo-myne); Laura Marsden (Mary); George Skinner (Mrs. Jack); Charles Fox (Twitters); Henry Evans (King Arthur); Charles Beverley (Coromoranto the Giant); Agnes Warden (Robin); Adah Garratt (Fairy Fairstar)

JACK THE GIANT KILLER, Gaiety Theatre, London, opened December 26, 1877
Produced by John Hollingshead; A Pantomime by H. J. Byron

Jenny Hill (Jack); Miss Wadman (Sybil); Miss Hazel (Fairy); Mr. Clifford (Gorgibuster); W. Elton (Tremoloso); Misses Gilchrist and Wilson (Columbines); Mlle. Aenea and W. Warde (Dancers)

JACK THE GIANT KILLER, Imperial Theatre, London, opened December 26, 1882
A Pantomime by Frank Green and Hugh J. Didcott; Music, Mr. Frewin

Marie Longmore (Jack); Bertie Stokes (Jill); Jessie Mayland (The Good Fairy); W. H. Wallace (King Arthur); Sam Wilkinson (Jack's Mother); Mr. Frome (Cormoran the Giant); Mr. Nye (Blunderbore the Giant); George Vokes (Clown); Lily Lee (Premiere Danseuse); Rose Fox (Dancer)

JACK AND THE BEANSTALK, *Drury Lane Theatre*, London, opened January 29, 1885

Produced and directed by Augustus Harris; A Pantomime by Horace Lennard; Scenery, William Beverley, W. Talbin, Henry Emden, T. W. Grieve and F. Fenton; Costumes, Auguste et Cie; Ballet, John D'Auban; Music, Oscar Barrett

Emily Duncan (Jack); William Morgan (Mrs. Simpson, Jack's Mother); John D'Auban (Silly Billy); Russell Crauford (King of Hearts); Jenny Lee (Queen of Hearts); E. S. Vincent (Lord Chamberlain); Charles Ross (Old Smock); Annie Poole (Princess Heartsease); Emma D'Auban (Spirit of Pantomime); Bertie Vann (Spirit of Culture); Mr. Rowella (Old Father Time); Alfred West (Julius Caesar, the Dog); Messrs. Gerard and Leslie (Daisy the Cow); Mlle. Luna (Principal Dancer); Mr. Lawless (Bird Charmer); *The Harlequinade*: The Great Little Rowella (Clown); Arthur Bolton (Pantaloon); George Canning (Harlequin); Marie Knight (Columbine); Charles Ross (Policeman)

JACK THE GIANT KILLER, *Pavilion Theatre*, London, opened December 26, 1885

Produced by Morris Abrahams; A Pantomime by Oswald Allen; Director, Isaac Cohen

Katie Barry (Jack); George English (King Domino); Arthur Alexander (Chamberlain Dismallo); Annie Dunbar (Prince Charming); Amy Graham (Prince Courtly); Ada Graham (Prince Rooster); with C. Reeves, C. Danby, Brothers Le Fre, Julia Kent, Ada Reeves, Ida Heath, C. Kent, Baby Langtry, F. Harrington

JACK AND THE BEANSTALK, *Surrey Theatre*, London, opened December 26, 1886

A Pantomime by George Conquest and Henry Spry; Scenery, J. Soames; Limelights and pyrotechnic effects by Mordey; Gas effects, W. Dimes; Mechanical effects, F. Gayden; Special scenery, Richard Douglass; Music by Mr. Phillips

Maude Stafford (Jack); Dan Leno (Dame Durden); Lillie Ernest (Mary); George Conquest (Baron Grim'um/Giant); Lydia Reynolds (Mercury); Tom Costello (Irish Mephistopheles); The Sisters Watson (Jupiter and Mars); E. S. Vincent, John Danvers, Mlle. Phillipini (Dancers); and Frank Sims, Maude Humm, Claire Danvers, George Conquest Jr., Florrie West, Ada Clarissa

JACK THE GIANT KILLER AND THE BUTTERFLY QUEEN; OR, HARLEQUIN KNIGHTS OF THE ROUND TABLE, *Elephant and Castle Theatre*, London, opened December 24, 1887

Produced by W. Burton Green; A Pantomime by Oswald Allen; Director, George Skinner; Libretto by H. G. French; Scenery, Grimani; Acting manager, T. Crauford

Maud Stafford (Jack); G. B. Priot (Jack's Mother); Clara St. Leger (Prince Penniless); Lizzie Russell (Realjam); Kitty Tyrrell (Fairy Silverwing); Carrie Braham (The Baroness); Pete Dwight (Punchap); Mr. Fitzgerald (The Demon); Mr. Kellino, J. G. Johnson, Mr. Maddison, Lilly Beatrice, Jessie Noit, W. Lacy, T. Matthews, Monsieur Eli (Company)

FE FI FO FUM; OR, HARLEQUIN JACK THE GIANT KILLER, *National Standard Theatre*, Bishopsgate, London, opened December 24, 1887

Produced by John Douglass; A Pantomime with scenery by John Douglass; Music, W. Corri; Songs "Two Lovely Black Eyes," "God Blee Ye, Merrie Gentlemen"

Jennie Lee (Jack); Richard Purdon (Jack's Mother); Alice Burville (Polly Primrose); Eric Thorne (Billy the Blockhead); John Barnum (Squire's Page); Mr. Lonadel, Lizzie Dashwood, Madame Ada Doree, Florence Lavender, Kate Leslie, Ida Millais, The Grovani Troupe (Dancers)

JACK AND THE BEANSTALK AND THE SEVEN CHAMPIONS, *Royal Covent Garden*, London, December 26, 1887

Produced by Freeman Thomas and W. T. Purkiss; A Pantomime by Henry Hersee and Horace Lennard; Director, J. A. Cave; Scenery by Messrs. Bruce Smith, A. Callcott, L. Hart and E. Banks; Magnificent armour by Messrs. Kennedy of Birmingham; Ballets arranged by Mons. Bertrand; Music by Messrs. A. Gwyllym Crowe and H. M. Higgs; Chorus master, Mr. Stedman; Wigs by Clarkson; Limelight effects by Wells & Company; Costumes and dresses by Mons. and Mme. Alias, Miss Fisher, Mr. Isidore Nathan and Company; Feathers and flowers by Rean; Horses by Ginnett and Hales; Musical director and conductor, A. Gwyllym Crowe; Acting manager, T. S. Carlton

Fanny Leslie (Jack Simpson); Frank M. Wood (The Widow Simpson); George Conquest, Jr. (Fee-Fo-Fum, the Giant); Sam Wilkinson (Fee-Fo-Fa, his Wife); Tom Squire (Billy Loblolly); W. H. Harvey (Abel Armstrong); Frank Hall (Old King Cole); Mrs. Bennett (The Queen); Hallen Mostyn (Baron Rampajus); Mr. J. W. Braithwaite (The Baroness); Minnie Mario (Prince Amaroso); Jessie Mayland (Princess Rosabelle); Ilma Norina (Little Bo-Peep); Little Sandy (The Giant's Chief Cook); Messrs. Griffin and Ardell (Two Black Cooks); Mr. Athol (Tommy Truant); Mr. Rowe (The Grof); Signor Carlo Huberti (The Giant's Hen); H. Hearne (Daisy Dimple the Cow); The Famous Jee Family (The Musical Smith); J. F. Brian (Herald); Florence Audrey (Amethyst); Rosie Nott (Beryl); Miss Wolff (Cornelian); Nelly Moon (Diamond); Miss Verral (Trip); Miss Fairlie (Skip); T. F. Nye (The Gnome King); Mr. Borani (Fly-by-Night); Susetta Fenn (The Fairy of the Beanstalk); Mabel Love (Sunbeam); Ida Heath (Moonbeam); *The Seven Champions*: Kate Paradise (St. George of England); Flo Edgcumbe (St. David of Wales); Julia Hamilton (St. Andrew of Scotland); Annie Temple (St. Patrick of Ireland); Kate Terry (St. Denis of France); Josephine O'Mara (St. James of Spain); Florence Lancaster (St. Anthony of Italy)

LITTLE JACK AND THE BIG BEANSTALK, *Prince of Wales Theatre*, Greenwich, England, opened January 16, 1888

Produced and directed by William Morton; A Pantomime by Arthur Lloyd; Scenery, W. R. Martin

Katty King (Jack); Horace Wheatley (Jack's Mother); Arthur Lloyd (King Mooney); Gracie Mainstone (Prince Dazzle); Cissie Judge (Princess Moonlight); A. Fenwick (The Giant); Bob Bradford (Buttons); Master Panlo (The Oodle, Towzer); Kate Gower (Premiere Danseuse)

JACK AND THE BEANSTALK; OR, HARLEQUIN AND THE MIDWINTER NIGHT'S DREAM, *Drury Lane Theatre*, London, opened December 26, 1889

Produced and directed by Augustus Harris; A Pantomime by Harry Nicholls and Augustus Harris; Regisseur, Arthur P. Collins; Scenery by Messrs. Dayes, Caney, Kautsky and Perkins; Decorations, J. M. Boekbinder; Costumes by Wilhelm; Dresses by Auguste et Cie, Rouy & Osborne, Mrs. S. May, Messrs. H. L. Nathan, J. A. Harrison, J. Simmons & Sons, M. Landolff, Miss Palmer, Mrs. Chapion and Mrs. Atkins; Armour and jewelry, Gutpere of Paris, Kennedy and Phillips; Limelight effects by Mr. Pearce; Music composed and arranged by Walter Slaughter

Harriett Vernon (Jack Simpson); Dan Leno (Mrs. Simpson); Harry Nicholls (King Henry, the Bounder); Herbert Campbell (Queen Fanny, the Flirt); George Conquest, Jr. (The Giant Gorgibuster); Charles Lauri (Puck); Frederick Griffiths

(The Cow); Joseph Griffiths (The Cow Keeper); The Brothers Leopold (Giant's Attendants); Tom Pleon (Cabman); Maggie Duncan (Princess Diamond Duckz); Agnes Hewitt (Oberon); Marie Faudelle (Titania); W. H. Partridge (Flunkey); Frank Harrison (Schoolmaster); Madame AEanea (Scarlet Runner/Zephyr/Ariel); Sybil Gray (Housemaid); Miss Cole (Princess Olivia/Mars/House-maid); Miss Hodges (Lysander/One of the Graces/ Housemaid); Lillie Comyns (Dairy Maid); Lydia Rachel (Schoolmistress); Rose Darling (Johnnie Deahboi); Lizzie Wilson (Johnnie Oldflah); Mabel Coates (Johnnie Hullothih/Isabella/Cerces); Ida Francis (Fairy Moth/Portia/ Flora); Marguerite Etoile (Fairy Cobweb/Claudio); May Palfrey (Fairy Peach Blossom/ Juliet); Miss Malvern (Fairy Mustard Seed/Arabella); Miss Nicholls (Jupiter/Anthony); Minnie Sannon (Juno/Lorna); Maud Pinder (Helie/Anne/Page); Miss Hammack (Apollo/Ferdinand); Miss Wilson (Iris/ Neptune); Lily Brooking (Bessano); Flo Lummerton (Amphritrite/Katherine); Alice Frazer (Pluto/Lady Macbeth); Cissy St. George (Prosperpine/Rosalind); Clarice Clayton (Minerva/Hamlet); Lilian Vincent (Vanios/Princess Katherine); Bride Jennings (Aurora/ Mirando); Florence Talbot (Bacchus/Tybalt); Miss Ingreville (Mercury/Constance); Miss Verner (Master Slander); Mr. Garraud (Mr. Page); Miss Heddington (Mrs. Ford); Miss Williams (Mrs. Page); Mr. Real (Duke Orsini); Miss H. Powell (Viola); Miss Lowe (Sebastian); Miss Hastings (Maria); Mr. Francis (Sir Foly); Mr. Beawane (Sir Andrew); Mr. French (Malvolio); Mr. Bassanarde (Duke); Mr. Mortimer (Angelo); Mr. Denvil (Benedict); Miss Fisher (Beatrice); Miss Bradshaw (Hero); Mr. Artelli (Antonio); Mr. B. Robins (Shylock); Miss E. Ward (Gelia); Mr. Harrison (Touchstone); Miss Strathmore (Orlando); Mr. N. Strathmore (Jacques); Miss J. Woolcott (Helena); Mr. Cree (Petruchio); Miss Montague (Romeo); Miss Carew (Mercutio); C. Rouse (Friar Lawrence); Mrs. Brandon Ellis (Nurse); Miss Tivoli (Queen); Miss Wolff (Horatio); Mr. Seaton (Ghost); Miss E. Stanley (Cassio); Miss Delorine (Desdemona); Agnes Cameron (Demetrius); Miss G. Powell (Hermia); Miss M. Stuart (Helena); Miss Stratton (Arthur); Mr. Uridge (Richard III); Miss A. Powell (Queen); Misses M. and G. Fisher (Two Princes); Miss B. Harcourt (Lady Anne); W. Murray (Camillo); Miss Routsky (Perdita); Miss A. Marsden (Paulina); Miss M. Johnstone (Hermione); Mr. Weston (Macbeth); Miss Popham (Malcolm); Master Lorraine (Donaldbain); Miss Werendel (Anne Boleyn); Miss E. Brandon (Egos); Miss McKee (Cleopatra); Miss Hawthorne (Iris); Miss Slingo (Charman); Mr. Lorraine (King Lear); Miss A. Lurman (Regan); Miss Kingsley (Goneril); Miss Lyons (Fool); Miss D. Johnstone (Cordelia); Mr. Mayes (Albany); Mr. Ashworth (Cornwall); *Harlequinade*: Harry Payne (Clown); Fred Artelli (Harlequin); Tully Lewis (Pantaloon); Annie Evans (Columbine); W. H. Patridge (Policeman); The Leopold Troupe

THE STRANGE ADVENTURES OF JACK AND THE BEANSTALK, *Casino Theatre*, New York, opened November 2, 1896 65 performances*
Produced by Klaw and Erlanger; A Musical Extravaganza; Director, Ben Teal; Book by R. A. Barnet; Music by A. B. Sloane; Ballets by Carl Marwig; Scenery, Ernest Albert; Costumes, F. Richard Anderson; Musical director, Paul Schindler); Electrical effects, H. Harndin; Mechanical effects, Claude Hagen; Tricks by Robert Cutler; Company manager, Edwin H. Price; Stage manager, Will Carleton

Madge Lessing (Jack Hubbard); Henry V. Donnelly (succeeded by Alexander Clark) (Old King Cole); Eddie Girard (succeeded by Harry Kelley) (Sinbad); Hubert Wilke (Sir Harry Haitewurk); Hilda Hollins (Marquis de Carabas); Basil Tetson (Neverwash); J. Craig (Evertyrd); Justine Batlo (Rowland); Kitty Perry

(Oliver); A. C. Butler (succeeded by H. L. Traub); (Sir Guy Coffin); Maude Hollins (Princess Mary "Quite Contrary"); Merri Osborne (Little Miss Muffett); Rose Snow (Sonanum Tuberoseum); H. M. Morse (Giant Ruse); Harry Kelley (succeeded by Daniel Baker) (Mrs. Ruse); Donna Dean (succeeded by Miss Hearn) (Asparagus Blossom); Carrie Perkins (Old Mother Hubbard); Marie Godoy (Puss in Boots); Nellie Lynch (Cyclometrix); Misses Mills, Ashton, Leslie Sanford, Warren (succeeded by Hening), David, Howe, Browne (succeeded by Riseva) (Eight Pretty Maids); Archie Gillis (Jack Sheppard); Fred Lewis (Joe Blueskin); Carl Kehn (Jonathan Wild); John James (Dick Turpin); Charles Wilson (Robin Hood); George Pyke (Robert Mecaire); William Dorfman (Jacques Strop); William Morgan (Claude Duval); William Pullman (Lafitte); Misses Hearn, Borani, Caldwell, Payne, Schwartz, Knight, Siegel, Warren, Mayer, Schwarz (Ten Good Fairies)

MUSICAL NUMBERS: "A Lock of Hair" (Gustav Kerker); "Dangerous Girls" (Paul Schindler); "Drinking Song" (Gustav Kerker); "Comprendez Vous?" (W. A. Jennings, John A. Golden)

* This production toured during the 1896-97 season and then returned to the *Harlem Opera House* on April 5, 1897 for eight performances

JACK AND THE BEANSTALK, *Drury Lane Theatre*, London, opened December 12, 1899 141 performances

Produced and directed by Arthur P. Collins; A Pantomime by Arthur Sturgess and Arthur P. Collins; Scenery, Bruce Smith, William Perkins, R. C. McCleery, Robert Caney, Henry Emden, W. Cross and William Harford; Costumes designed by Comelli; Choreography, John d'Auban and Carlo Coppi; Music director, J. M. Glover; Stage managers, Frank Damer and Michael Ring

Nellie Stewart (Jack); Mabel Nelson (Princess Pretty); Dan Leon (Dame Trot); Le Brun (Cow Queen); Johnny Danvers (King Rattatat); William Morgan (Demon Worm); T. Hendon (Giant Blunderbore); Rita Presano (Prince Racket); Mollie Lowell (Marjorie); Birdie Sutherland (Fairy Queen Ant); Herbert Campbell (Bobbie); Charles Trevor (Pitapat); H. A. Lonsdell (Bessie); George Lake Grange (Thomas); Grigolati (Spirit of Spring); Horace Pollock (The Mayor); Phil Sturgess (The Doctor); Mr. Freeman (Tradesman); Alfred Balfour (The Auctioneer); Ernest d'Auban (Bronson the Cat); Rita Barrington (Fifi the Cat); Mrs. Webb (Chief Cook); Florence Hooten, Edith Russell, Lizzie Wilson, Evie Grand (Huntsmen); Rita Barrington, Nellie Pounds, Bob Robina, Violet Neville, Maude Jennings, Florence Hooten, Edith Russell, M. Marsden, Lizzie Wilson, Evie Grand, Ernest d'Auban, Alfred Balbour, Phil Sturgess, Horace Pollock, Ainslie, Burton, Webb, Freeman (Ensemble)

Drury Lane Theatre, London, opened December 26, 1910

Produced and directed by Arthur P. Collins; A Children's Pantomime; Book by J. Hickory Wood, Frank Dix and Arthur P. Collins; Music composed, selected and arranged by J. M. Glover; Lighting, H. Mather; Costumes designed by Comelli; Ballets by Jean Pratesi; Incidental dances by Jon d'Auban

Dolly Castles (Jack Halleybut); George Graves (Mrs. Halleybut); Harry Randall (Prince Spinach); Julia James (Princess Dorothy); George Barrett (Rupert Halleybut); Barry Lupino (Alexis the Page); Johnny Danvers (King Rattatat); Arthur Conquest (Priscilla the Cow); William Downes (Professor Hypno); Ernest Langford (dr. Lanky); Bennett and Martell (Nim and Rod); Maudie Thornton (Marjorie); Anita Edis (Puck); Hilda Playfair (Titania); Kitty Emson (Moth); Beta

Emson (Mustard Seed); Miss Lovell (Cobweb); Miss L. Graham (Peas-Blossom); Miss Jimmie Jones (The Lord Chamberlain); Austin Melford (Uncle Tom Cobbley); Will and Joe Pender (Horace and Percy); Mr. Clarke (The Giant); E. Morgan (Scoutmaster); Will Compo (An Old Woman); The Penders (Storks); Mmes. Lewis, Pragnell, C. Murray. R. Murray, Barrington, Grimaldi, Messrs. Kemp, Brian, Delfosse, Freeman, Reynolds, Baldwin (Ensemble)

Hippodrome Theatre, London, opened December 23, 1921 137 performances
Produced by Moss Empires Ltd., R. H. Gillespie, Managing Director; A Pantomime; Director, Julian Wylie; Staged by Gus Sohlke; Book and lyrics by J. James Hewson, Clifford Harris and Valentine; Music by James W. Tate; Scenery, Conrad Tritschler, Philip Howden and Marc Henri; Lighting, W. P. Chester; Costumes, Dolly Tree and V. de St. Martin; Music director, Julian Jones; Stage managers, Claud Vernon, W. Armstrong

Clarice Mayne (succeeded by Dorothy Ward (Jack); George Robey (Dame Trot); Madge Saunders (Princess Sylvia); Jay Laurier (Miffins); Tom Walls (King Gerald XXX); Winifred Roma (Fairy Hyacinth); Walter Hubert (Fee-Fo-Fum); Phil Lester (Bill); Harry Terry (Sam); Kiddy Kennedy (Sarah Jane); Bob Pender (Clown); The Pender Troupe of Giants (Jessie); Nora Roylance (Dancer)

Lyceum Theatre, London, opened December 26, 1923 116 performances
Produced and directed by Walter and Frederick Melville; A Pantomime; Book and lyrics by Leedham Bantock; Music by Guy Jones; Scenery, J. Leonard and E. Grimani; Lighting, John H. Waters; Costumes, Willie Clarkson; Choreography, Euphan MacLaren; Music director, Guy Jones; Stage managers, Cecil de Lee and H. G. Wright

Sybil Arundale (Jack); Bertie Wright (Dame Dimple); Robert Woollard (Demon Mischief); Dick Henderson (King Klondike); Sybil Coulthurst (Princess Alice); Fred Sayers (Mr. Hops); Percy Mead (Pickles); Connie Wilde (Spirit of the Moon); May Carpenter (Fairy Sunstar); Iris Field (Sir Randolph); John Brown (Bobby Feeler); Harry Farmer (Sir Archibald); Jack Hurst (Felix); Charles Wilton (Old Moore); Fred Stone (succeeded by Frank Attree) (Horatio); Stern and Austin (Clara the Cow); Bertram Dench (Willie Watkyn Welks); George Jackley (Bill); Frank Attree ('Erb); Jack Kellaway (Mercury); Eileen Dagmar (Mrs. Pussyfoot); Lydia Crane (Venus); Winifred Yorke (Percy Vere); Master Kiddy King (Giant's Juggler); William Stern (Pantaloon); Betty Ray (succeeded by Eileen Dagmar); Poor Flo); Raymond Wood (Giant Blunderbore); Frank Lampton (succeeded by D. Urquhart) (Mars); Boganny Troupe (Giant's Cooks); Charles Sparrow (succeeded by Betty Ray (Officer); Freddy Austin (Clown); Baby Love (Cupid); John Brown, Connie Wilde (Specialty Dancers); The Lottie Stone Troupe

THE STRANGE ADVENTURES OF JACK AND THE BEANSTALK, *Repertory Theatre of Boston*, opened December 26, 1927
Produced by the Repertory Theatre of Boston, Frances Jewett, executive director; A Fairy Extravaganza by R. A. Barnet and A. B. Sloane; Director, William Mason; Scenery, Jonel Jorgulesco; Lighting, Per Lee Sibila; Costumes, Grace Ripley; Music director, David Kuntz; Ballets, Thayer Roberts; Production supervisor, Henry Jewett; Stage managers, Josef Lazarovici and Robert Cass

Cecile Benson (alternate Katherine Warren) (Jack); Milton Owen (Old Mother Hubbard); William Faversham, Jr. (The Giant Ruse); Leo Cass (The Cow,

Mooing End); Robert Cass (The Cow, Kicking End); Arthur Sircom (Evertyred); Harlan Grant (Never-wash); Thayer Roberts (Madame Rose Geranium); Thomas Shearer (Old King Cole); Margaret Conklin (Princess Mary); Arthur Bowyer (Sir Guy Coffin); William Mason (Sinbad the Sailor); Dennis Cleugh (Bluebeard); Irving Marston Jackson (Sir Harry Haitework/Marquis de Carabas); Olga Birkbeck (Fairy Asparagus Blossom); Adelaide George (Fairy Caterpillar); Dana Sieveling (Little Miss Muffet); Robert Cass (Rowland); Cecelia Radcliffe (Old Woman Who Lived in a Shoe); Charles S. Flato (Giant's Private Secretary); Cecile Benson (Little Bo-Peep); Doris Peel (Little Boy Blue); Lucille Paulus (Alice in Wonderland); Gorden Bullett (Mad Hatter); Joan Damon (Jack); Mina Baylarian (Jill); Willa Rickard (Little Red Riding Hood); Ruth Butler, Patricia Teague, Mina Baylarian, Margaret Morgan, Jean Damon, Lucille Paulus (Six Pretty Maids); Eugenia Frothingham, Dorothea Symington, Olive Cousens, Margaret Ross, Mary Pedrazzi, Maxine Blake, Nancy Bremer, Gertrude Hunt, Katherine Allen, Helen Samonski, Margaret Hall (The Good Fairies); Mary Stuart, Willa Richard, Doris Peel, June Smith, Dorothy Streets, Lois Harrington, Dorothy Schweikhart (Bluebeard's Wives); Harlan Grant, Gordon Bullett, Vahan Tashjian (Fiddlers Three); Fred Assad, Laverne Finch, Ian Fraser, Robert Hall, Burlin Maine, Reginald Macelhiney, Walter Hale, Robert Peel, John Tennant, F. C. Williams, Charles Assad, Roderick Dwyer, Charles Joseph, Edward Roberson (Some of the Forty Thieves)

MUSICAL NUMBERS: "A Captain Bold"; "King Cole"; "Georgie"; "Sinbad the Sailor"; "Come Along With Me"; "I've Sold My Cow"; "Duette"; "'Tis With Love"; "Whispering of Flowers"; "Entrance of the Giant"; "Sing a Song of Sixpence"; "Sabre Bout"; "On the Road to Mandalay"; "Clementine"; "Dance of the Golden Siamese"; "The Vamp"; "When Daisies Pied"; "Nymphs and Shepherds"; "Slumber Song"; "Bluebeard's Wives"; "Once There Lived a Pretty Maid Mary"; "When Dull Care"; "Wedding Ceremony"

JACK AND THE BEANSTALK, *Children's Theatre*, London, opened December 23, 1930

Produced by The Children's Theatre; A Pantomime written and directed by Margaret Carter

Geoffrey Wincott (Jack); Maud Jolliffe (Mother Grubble); Norman Shelley (Prince Donzil); Elfrida Burgiss (Princess Chrystabel); Mary Cobb (Lady Flavia); Patrick Glover (The King); Nan Jacobs (Dame Gallibantus); Eric Anderson (Gallibantus); Beatrice Elburn (Cherry Girl); Joan Luxton (Azelle); Brember Wills (Peterkins); Arthur Goullet (Rufus); Doris Little, Elfrida Burgiss (Cuckoo)

44th Street Theatre, New York, opened December 21, 1931 16 performances

Produced by George Bye; A Fair Play by John Erskine; Music by Louis Gruenberg; Settings, Margaret Linley; Opera Orchestra of the Juilliard School of Music; Musical director, Albert Stoessel; Associate conductors, Gregory Ashman and Charles Lichter

Mary Katherine Akins or Alma Milstead (Jack); Beatrice Hegt or Marion Selee (Mother); Pearl Besuner or Ruby Mercer (Princess); Raymond Middleton or Julius Huehn (The Giant); Roderic Cross and George Newton (Cow); Willard Young (Locksmith); John Barr (Tanner); Roland Partridge (Barker); Roy Nichols or Mordecai Bauman (Butcher); Apolyna Stoskus, John Barr, Janice Kraushaar (Magic Harp Soli); Misses Antoine, Chapelle, Couchman, Dorff, Gilman, Huddle, Kraushaar, Lapidus, Leshure, Lockwood, Malolie, Marshall, O'Connell, Olson, Schwan, Stoskus, Strickler, Waltenberg, Wisecup, Wooten, and Messrs.

Bauman, Haywood, Hill, Marsh, Partridge, Pratt, Worthington, Young (Ensemble)

Embassy Theatre, London, opened December 24, 1932
Produced by The Children's Theatre; A Pantomime by Margaret Carter; Director, Geoffrey Wincott

Geoffrey Wincott (Jack); Maud Jolliffe (Mother Grubble); Patrick Glover (The King); Rupert Bruce (Prince Donzil); Elfrida Burgiss (Princess Chrystabel); Ann Casson (Lady Flavia); Margaret Carter (Dame Gallibantus); J. Forbes Williams (Gallibantus); Sylvia Shaw (Cherry Girl); Joan Luxton (Azelle); Brember Wills (Peterkins); Mackenzie Ward (Rufus); Mary Ramey, Elfrida Burgiss (Cuckoo); Paul Kirkland (Oldest Inhabitant); Margaret Carter, Nan Jacobs, Mary Ramey (Weavers); J. Forbes Williams, Jean Manson, Ronald Hickman, Nan Jacobs (Reapers)

Wimbledon Theatre, London, opened December 26, 1934
Director, Henry Wright; A Pantomime by Reginald Cooper; Music by David Cochrane and Laurie Jackson

Betty Huntley Wright (Jack Durden); Barry Lupino (Dame Durden); Charles Rolfe (The Demon); Reginald Newson (King Hunky Dorum); George Gulliver (Giant Blunderbore); Mary Saunders (Ralph); Myrtle Peter (Helen); Gwen Kay (Princess); Ernie Leno (Simple Sammy); Oliver and Proctor (Jessie the Cow); Roy Lane (King's Steward); Con Kenna (Bill); J. H. Graham (Walter); Pegi Rhys (The Fairy)

King's Theatre, Hammersmith, London, opened December 26, 1935
Director, Ivan Campbell; A Pantomime by Reginald Cooper; Music by David Cochrane and Charles Lawrie

Betty French (Jack Durden); Barry Lupino (Dame Durden); Charles Rolfe (The Demon); Guy North (King Hunky Dorum); George Gulliver (Giant Blunderbore); Eda Peel (Ralph); Tonie Lupino (Helen); Rita Cooper (Princess); Fred Miller (Simple Sammy); Oliver and Proctor (Jessie the Cow); The Three Stoogers and Al Oakes (The King's Brokers); John Bucklin (The King's Bailiff); Millie Deane (The Bailiff's Daughter); Cherie (The Fairy)

Drury Lane Theatre, London, opened December 24, 1935
Produced by Prince and Blance Littler; A Pantomime by Marriott Edgar; Director, Ralph Reader; Music by Charles Prentick, Gordon Stewart and Eric Coates; Scenery, Alick Johnstone; Costumes, Gladys E. Calthrop; Company manager, F. C. Marshall

Binnie Hale (Jack); Gavin Gordon (The Rag Man); Clifford Heatherley (The King); Charles Heslop (Muggles); Marjorie Browne (Princess Annabel); Jack Glyn (Giles); Bert Brownbill (Clown); Douglas Wakefield (Pinch); Billy Nelson (Scrape); Shaun Glenville (Mrs. Hubbard); Brothers Griffiths (The Cow); Baby Terry (Fairy Thistle Down); The Hartman Troupe (The Giant's Family); Irene Busby, Alethea Jermaine (Principal Dancers); Walter Dare Wahl, Emmett Oldfield (Entertainers); Irene Lister (Anne); Eugene's Super Flying Ballet

MUSICAL NUMBERS: "Barnsley Fair" (Arthur Wood); "Common People" (Harry Perritt); "Love's Everywhere" (Harry Parr Davies); "Everybody's Got to Wear a Smile" (Bert Elden); "Dairy Maids" (Gordon Stewart); "Moo Maa" (Sam Mayo); "March While the Bugles Blow" (Charles Prentice); "You Can't Do That There 'Ere" (Raymond Wallace); "As Long As Our Hearts Are Young" (Ronald Hill); "Cinderella" (Eric

Coates); "Coal 'Ole" (Charles Prentice); "Slaves of the Giant" (Gordon Stewart); "Congratulate Me" (Lou Handman); "March of the Giants" (Herman Finck); "Dainty Doll" (Bernard Barnes); "Where Did You Get That Name?" (Bob Miller)

Brixton Theatre, London, opened December 26, 1935
A Pantomime written, produced and directed by Frederick Melville; Music by Charles J. Moore and Frank Brockett

June Melville (Jack); Fred Moule (Demon Mischief); Norman Greene (Gobblywobbly); Chester Barclay (The King); Joan Collier (Princess Rosamund); Jessica Roland (Fairy Starlight); John E. Conan (Dame Dimple); Fred Wolgast (Simple Simon); Roberta Petley (Margery); Dave May (Juggins/Huggins); Cleve Cothan (Their Assistant); Ivy and Eva Linde (King's Attendants); Sybil Lane (Lord Chamberlain)

Streatham Hill Theatre, London, opened December 27, 1937
Produced and directed by Prince Littler; A Pantomime by Marriott Edgar; Music by Charles Prentice, Gordon Stewart and Eric Coates

Marie Burke (Jack); Eric Fort (The Rag Man); Bert Brownbill (The King); Ted Ray (Muggles); Eve Lister (Princess Annabel); Charles Wingrove (Giles); John Warwick (Clown); Leonie Pounds (Spirit of the Beanstalk); Phyllis Cardew (Anne); The Brothers Griffiths (The Cow); Three Loose Screws (The Broker's Men); Joy Keech (Premier Danseuse)

Golder's Green Hippodrome, London, opened December 24, 1938
Produced and directed by Prince Littler; A Pantomime by Marriott Edgar; Music by Charles Prentice, Gordon Stewart and Eric Coates

Ivy Tresmand (Jack); Hilton Porter (The Rag Man); Bert Weston (The King); Leslie Hatton (Muggles); Nancy Burne (Princess Annabel); Charles Wingrove (Giles); Bertie Hare (Clown); Harry Moreny (Pinch); Jack Farr (Scrape); Charmain Innes (Spirit of the Beanstalk); Joan Seaton (Anne); The Brothers Griffiths (The Cow); Henry Latimer (Giant); Harold Childs (Nuisance); Jane Cain (Fairy Thistledown); Marjorie Field (Premier Danseuse)

Coliseum Theatre, London, opened December 26, 1941
A Pantomime adapted and directed by Francis Laidler; Based on the book by J. Hickory Wood

Jean Collin (Jack); Norman Evans (Dame Durden); Lorely Dyer (Princess Twinkle); Joe P. Kennedy (Giant Blunderbore); Jimmy Plant (Squire of Widdicombe); Betty Jumel (Polly); Joe Crastonian (Simon); Dimitri Vetter (Demon Grimm); Kathleen Livingston (Fairy Gleam); Shanks Brothers (Constance the Cow)

Grand Theatre, Croydeon, London, opened December 26, 1946
Produced and directed by Barry Lupino; A Pantomime by Barry Lupino and Arty Ash

Marjorie Sandford (Jack); Barry Lupino (Dame Durden); Sybil Summers (Princess Beauty); Reg Kinman (Archie); Theo Hook (The King); Bert Thompson (Giant Blunderbore); Leopold Brothers (Jessie the Cow); Marton Clifford (Mother Shipton); Angela Kinman (Marion); Armour Boys (Bob and Bill); Frances Hughes (Fairy Lamar)

Golder's Green Hippodrome, London, opened December 24, 1947

Prince Littler presents The Drury Lane Pantomime by Marriott Edgar; Director, Leonard Dainton; Music by Charles Prentice, Gordon Stewart and Eric Coates; Dances and ensembles, Anita Foster; Scenery, Bert Reynolds; Costumes, Mae Rogers; Company manager, Martin Adeson; Stage manager, Betty Smith

Greta Fayne (Jack Hubbard); Eddie Childs (Mother Hubbard); Richard Littledale (The King); Patricia Lang (Fairy Thistledown); Tom Lucas (The Giant); Marian Pola (Spirit of the Beanstalk); Beverly Wright (Princess Annabel); Anita Foster (Anne); Leon and Partner (Irene the Cow); Tom Singer (Clown); Max Wall (Muggles); Lenox Dalton (The Ragman); Lupe (Pinch); Valez (Scrape); Lupe & Valez, Vic & Joe Crastonian, Eleanor Beams' Twelve Babes, Twelve J. W. Jackson Girls (Specialties); Julie Bond, Valerie Carton, Audrey Cooper, Pamela Corderoy, Doreen Dale, Margaret Fairhurst, June Garland, Peggy Garland, Jackie Joyner, Phyllis King, Maudie Mayne, Joan Walker, Althea Walton, June White, Pamela Williams, Jose Williamson (Ladies of the Chorus); Mary Barr, Olivia Bioletto, Eileen Cecil, Mavis Clapp, Celia Coleman, Moya McCormack, Violet Stoneham, Dora Thomas, Georgia Winter, Gloria Wyse, Sylvia Wyse, Pamela Young (The J. W. Jackson Girls); Van Dam and His Orchestra

MUSICAL NUMBERS: "Clown"; "Jack and the Beanstalk"; "Barnsley Fair"; "Happy-Go-Lucky"; "Pat Away a Ray of Sunshine"; "Chorus of Welcome"; "You've Got to Know How to Dance"; "I Can't Believe"; "We'll Have to Sell the Cow"; "Train Number"; "When I'm Not Near the Girl I Love"; "I Believe"; "March While the Bugles Blow"; "We're the Slaves"; "Beetle Dance"; "Pomp and Circumstance"; "My Desire"; "Butterflies"; "Where Is My Sunday Potato?"; "Down the Mall"

Wimbledon Theatre, London, opened December 24, 1948

A Pantomime directed by Frank P. Adey

Marion Gordon (Jack Durden); Bunny Doyle (Dame Durden); Marjorie Russell (Princess Crystal); Alec Duck (Giant Blunderbore); Frankie Howerd (Simple Simon); Gordon Jenson (Squire of Widdecombe); Shanks and Gay (Constance the Cow); Eva Kane (Fairy Gleam); John Essex (Grimm); Eddie Falcon (Snap); Jack Falcon (Snorum)

Chiswick (Eng.) Theatre, opened December 24, 1949

Produced by Prince Littler; A Pantomime by Marriott Edgar; Director, Leonard Dainton; Music by Charles Prentice, Gordon Stewart and Eric Coates; Scenery, Bert Reynolds; Costumes, Mae Rogers; Choreography, Doreen Austin; Music director, Dermot MacDermott; Stage managers, Douglas Fraser and Leonard Morris

Dorothy Ward (Jack); Judy Kemp (Princess Annabel); Henry Caine (The King); Tom Lucas (Giant Blunderbore); Patricia Lang (Fairy Thistledown); Zola and Mattie (Jessie the Cow); Shaun Glenville (Mrs. Hubbard); Clive Dunn (Muggles); Lennox Dalton (The Ragman/Clown); Patricia Webb (Anne); Doug and Eddie Wilcoxz (Pinch and Scrape); The Lyemun Juveniles (Specialties); Cilla's Football Dogs

Chelsea Palace Theatre, London, opened December 26, 1950

A Pantomime written, produced and directed by Dan Leno, Jr.

Jessie Jewel (Jack); Dan Leno, Jr. (Dame Dimple); Patricia Penfold (Princess Sylvia); Jan Kemp (Giant); Jan Harding (Sammy); Jack Walters (The King); Three Oxfords (Giant's Henchmen); George Barnes (Demon); Joan Lovatt (Fairy); Delysia Duo (Daisy the Cow)

London Palladium, London, opened December 17, 1968
Produced by Leslie A. Macdonnell and Leslie Grade in association with Bernard Delfont; Devised and directed by Albert J. Knight; Original book, music and lyrics by Ronnie Cass and Peter Myers; Decor, Tod Kingman; Costumes, Cynthia Tingey; Choreography, Pamela Davis

Jimmy Tarbuck (Jack Durden); Arthur Askey (Dame Durden); Ivor Emmanuel (The King); Audrey Jeans (The Queen); Jean Bayliss (The Princess); David Davenport (Giant Blunderbore); Bill Tasker (Town Crier); Mary Laine (The Witch); Rosemarie Cockayne (Fairy); Desmond & Marks (Daisy the Cow); Jane Dowling (Old Woman Who Lives in a Shoe); Bertie Hare and Jack Francois (Giant's Henchmen); Mary Laine (Old Crone); Bertie Hare (Royal Chamberlain); Charlie Cairoli with Paul, Little Henry, Dik and Dok (Strolling Clowns); The Veterans (Themselves); The Pamela Davis Dancers; The Bel Canto Singer; The Peggy O'Farrell Children

Wimbledon Theatre, London, opened December 23, 1972
Produced by Bernard Delfont and Richard M. Mills for Tom Arnold and Bernard Delfont Enterprises Ltd.; A Pantomime by Phil Park; Directed and choreographed by Malcolm Goddard; Decor, Tod Kingman; Music director, Bob Probst; Assistant choreographer, Arvil Gaynor; Company manager, Derek Ensor; Stage managers, John Cleaver and Nick Emery

Jimmy Tarbuck (Jack Trot); Ken Wilson (Dame Trot); Gerald Martin (Giant Blunderbore); Wendy Walsh (The Princess); Audrey James (The Queen); Gillian Price (The Fairy); Virginia Drinkwater (The Witch); Helen Garton (Queen of the Gypsies); Trevor Griffiths (Royal Chamberlain); Gerald Martin (The Sheriff); Keefe and Annette (Daisy the Cow); Clive Kennard, Peter Kenyon, Tina Townley, The Derek Tavener Singers, The Peggy O'Farrell Children (Specialties)

London Palladium, London, opened December 18, 1973
Produced by Bernard Delfont; A Pantomime devised and directed by Albert J. Knight; Book by Phil Park; Additional material by Dick Hills; Decor, Tod Kingman; Costumes, Cynthia Tingey; Choreography, Pamela Davis

Mark Wynter (Jack Durden); Dora Bryan (Dame Durden); Elizabeth Larner (The Queen); Alfie Bass (The King); Michael Kilgarriff (Giant Blunderbore/The Story Teller); Mary Laine (The Witch); Frankie Howerd (Simple Simon); Bertie Hare (Court Chamberlain); Calli (The Princess); Leon Greene (The Giant's Henchman); Lynton and Dickman (Daisy the Cow); Karin Gaeng, David Wright (Principal Dancers); The Pamela Davis Dancers, The Bel Canto Singers, The Peggy O'Farrell Children (Townspeople)

Wimbledon Theatre, London, opened July 8, 1975
Produced by the Actors Company; A Pantomime written and directed by Edward Petherbridge; Decor, Gordon Aldred; Lighting, Brian Harris; Costumes, Chris Kinman; Presented in conjunction with *The Bacchae* by Euripides

Sharon Duce (Jack); Keith Drinkel (Jack's Mother); Gary Raymond (The Giant); Ralph Michael (Pierrot); Sheila Burrell (Fairy Godmother); John Horwood and Jonathan Adams (Bailiff's Men); Juan Moreno (Fairground Men); Sheila Reid (Shadowplay Puppeteer); Helen Cotterill and Sheila Reid (The Cow); Edward Petherbridge (Ringmaster)

Theatre Royal, Bristol, England, opened December 26, 1979

Produced by Bristol Old Vic Company; A Play by John Moffatt; Director, Adrian Noble; Production designer, John McMurray; Lighting, John A. Williams; Musical numbers staged by Rae Landor; Musical director, Neil Rhoden; Sound, Craig Nell; Stage managers, Moira Hunter, Hazel Chrisup, Sara Byers, Russell Harvey and Robert Cavendish

Belinda Lang (Jack Trot); John Moffatt (Dame Trot); Rosamund Shelley (Margery Daw); Andrew Hilton (Giant Blunderbore); John Boswall (The Baron); Michael Derrington (Snatchit); Michael Tudor Barnes (Grabbit); John Telfer (Simple Simon); Peter Ackerman (Robin); Amanda Redman (Phoebe); Elizabeth Ashley (Fairy Queen); David Foxxe (Demon King); Nicholas Cook and Steve Armley (Miranda the Cow); Andrew Fotheringham, Nicholas Cook, Steve Armley, Paula Dane, Kay Jones, Kim McCarthy, Peter Ackerman, Amanda Redman (Villagers and Servants)

MUSICAL NUMBERS: "Derrydownderry"; "The Motor Car"; "Where There's a Boy There's a Girl"; "I'm Going to Keep Off the Grass No More"; "Complaints"; "When the Sun Says 'Good Morning' to You"; "When Daisies Pied"; "Look at Her"; "Kidnap Me"; "Trust in Me"; "What Is the Use of Loving a Girl?"; "Four Terrible Men"; "On the Road to Anywhere"; "Til We Meet Again"; "You Can't Buy a Thousand Rays of Sunshine"; "The Rest of the Day's Your Own"; "Strike Up the Band"; "One Hour of Love With You"

Piccadilly Theatre, London, opened December 13, 1991 through January 19, 1992

Presented by Paul Elliot by arrangement with Bobby Willis and John Ashby; A Pantomime directed and staged by Tudor Davies; Designer, Alan Miller-Bunford; Lighting, Benny Ball; Choreography, Christopher Robinson; Musical director, Gary Hind

Cilla Black (Jack Trot); Tudor Davies (Dame Trot); Patrick Mower (Demon Blackspider); Sophie-Louise Dann (Princess Apricot); Jean Boht (The Cauliflower Fairy); Bob Carolgees (Simple Simon); Mike Edmunds (King Drumble the First); Jerelle Hydes (Fairy Queen); Paul Scott and James Skegs (Gertie the Cow); The Mosaics (The Beanstalk Transformation); Richard Chandler (The Magic Hen); Sandra Bossy (Little Bo-Peep); Maria Bossy (Little Miss Muffet); Jacqueline Dunnley (Mary-Mary); Claire Becket (Old Woman Who Lives in a Shoe); Jason Maher (Little Boy Blue); Jonathon Blazer (Bobby Shafroe); Kelvin Warren (Little Jack Horner); Steve Houghton (Tom the Piper's Son); Babette Langford's Young Set (Children and Fairies); and Spit the Dog

INTO THE WOODS, *Old Globe Theatre*, San Diego, opened December 4, 1986 through January 11, 1987

Produced by the Old Globe Theatre Company, Donald and Darlene Shirley, executive producers; A Musical Play in two acts; Book and direction by James Lapine; Music and Lyrics by Stephen Sondheim; Settings, Tony Straiges; Lighting, Richard Nelson; Costumes, Ann Hould-Ward; Orchestrations, Jonathan Tunick; Musical director, Paul Gemignani; Musical staging, Lar Lubovitch; Magic consultant, Charles Reynolds; Sound, Michael Holten; Stage manager, Douglas Pagliotti

Ellen Foley (The Witch); Chip Zien (Baker); Joanna Gleason (Baker's Wife); George Coe (Cinderella's Father/Mysterious Man); John Cunningham (Narrator/Wolf/Steward); Ben Wright (Jack the Giant Killer); Barbara Bryne (Jack's Mother); Merle Louise (Giant); Kim Crosby (Cinderella); Joy Franz (Cinderella's Stepmother/Wolf); Lauren Mitchell (Lucinda); Lu Anne Ponce (Little Red Riding

Hood); Kenneth Marshall (Cinderella's Prince); Merle Louise (Cinderella's Mother/Grandmother/Wolf/Giant); Kay McClelland (Rapunzel/Florinda); Chuck Wagner (Rapunzel's Prince); Pamela Tomasetti (Snow White); Terri Cannicott (Sleeping Beauty)

INTO THE WOODS, Martin Beck Theater, New York, opened November 5, 1987 750 performances

A Heidi Landesman, Rocco Landesman, Rick Steiner, M. Anthony Fisher, Frederic H. Mayerson and Jujamcyn Theaters presentation, Michael David, executive producer; A Musical Play in two acts; Book and direction by James Lapine; Music and Lyrics by Stephen Sondheim; Settings, Tony Straiges; Lighting, Richard Nelson; Costumes, Ann Hould-Ward; Orchestrations, Jonathan Tunick; Musical director, Paul Gemignani; Musical staging, Lar Lubovitch; Magic consultant, Charles Reynolds; Sound, Alan Stieb and James Brousseau; Associate producers, Greg C. Mosher, Paula Fisher, David B. Brode and Mutual Benefit Companies/Fifth Avenue Productions; Stage manager, Frank Hartenstein

Bernadette Peters (succeeded by Phylicia Rhashad, Betsy Joslyn, Nancy Dussault, Bernadette Peters, Nancy Dussault) (The Witch); Chip Zien (Baker); Joanna Gleason (succeeded by Lauren Mitchell, Kay McClelland, Mary Gordon Murray, Cynthia Sikes, Joanna Gleason, Kay McClelland) (Baker's Wife); Tom Aldredge (succeeded by Dick Cavett, Tom Aldredge) (Narrator); Tom Aldredge (succeeded by Edmund Lyndeck, Tom Aldredge) (Mysterious Man); Ben Wright (Jack the Giant Killer); Barbara Bryne (Jack's Mother); Merle Louise (Giant); Kim Crosby (Cinderella); Joy Franz (Cinderella's Stepmother); Lauren Mitchell (Lucinda); Danielle Ferland (succeeded by Lu Anne Ponce) (Little Red Riding Hood); Robert Westenberg (Wolf/Cinderella's Prince); Edmund Lyndeck (Cinderella's Father); Merle Louise (Cinderella's Mother/Grandmother); Pamela Winslow (succeeded by Marin Mazzie) (Rapunzel); Chuck Wagner (succeeded by Dean Butler) (Rapunzel's Prince); Philip Hoffman (Steward); Jean Kelly (Snow White); Maureen Davis (Sleeping Beauty)

MUSICAL NUMBERS; "Into the Woods"; "Hello, Little Girl"; "I Guess This Is Goodbye"; "Maybe They're Magic"; "I Know Things Now"; "A Very Nice Prince"; "Giants in the Sky"; "Agony"; "It Takes Two"; "Stay With Me"; "On the Steps of the Palace"; "Ever After"; "So Happy"; "Agony" (reprise); "Lament"; "Any Moment"; "Moments in the Woods"; "Your Fault"; "Last Midnight"; "No More"; "No One Is Alone"; "Children Will Listen"; "Into the Woods" (reprise)

Original cast recording: RCA Records

INTO THE WOODS, National tour, opened *Parker Playhouse*, Fort Lauderdale, November 22, 1988; closed *Naples/Marco Philharmonic*, Naples, Florida, December 17, 1989 (including *Ahmanson Theatre*, Los Angeles, January 3 through March 5, 1989)

Produced by Pace Theatrical Group, Ahmanson Theatre (Los Angeles) and Jujamcyn Theaters; Producers, Heidi Landesman, Rocco Landesman, Rick Steiner, M. Anthony Fisher and Frederic H. Mayerson; A Musical Play in two acts; Book and direction by James Lapine; Music and Lyrics by Stephen Sondheim; Settings, Tony Straiges; Lighting, Richard Nelson; Costumes, Ann HouldWard; Orchestrations, Jonathan Tunick; Musical director, Randy Booth; Musical staging, Lar Lubovitch; Magic consultant, Charles Reynolds; Sound, Alan Stieb and James Brousseau; Associate producer, Rod Kaats; Stage manager, Dan W. Langhofer

Cleo Laine (succeeded by Betsy Joslyn) (The Witch); Mary Gordon Murray (Baker's Wife); Rex Gill (Baker); Rex Robbins (Narrator/Mysterious Man); Robert Duncan McNeill (Jack); Charlotte Rae (succeeded by Nora Mae Lyng) (Grandmother/Giant/Jack's Mother); Kathleen Row McAllen (succeeded by Jill Geddes) (Cinderella); Chuck Wagner (The Wolf/Cinderella's Prince); Susan Gordon-Clark (Florinda); Danette Cuming (Lucinda); Don Crosby (Cinderella's Father); Anne Rickenbacker (Cinderella's Mother); Tracy Katz (Red Riding Hood); Marguerite Lowell (Rapunzel); Douglas Sills (Rapunzel's Prince); Marcus Oldon (Steward); Jody Walker-Lichtig (Snow White)

INTO THE WOODS, *Phoenix Theatre*, London, opened September 25, 1990 186 performances
An Ed Mirvish presentation; A Musical Play in two acts; Director, Richard Jones; Book by James Lapine; Music and Lyrics by Stephen Sondheim; Scenery, Richard Hudson; Lighting, Pat Collins; Costumes, Sue Blane; Choreography, Anthony Van Laast; Orchestrations, Jonathan Tunick; Musical director, Peter Stanger; Sound, Andrew Bruce

Julia McKenzie (The Witch); Ian Bartholomew (Baker); Imelda Staunton (Baker's Wife); Nicholas Parsons (Narrator); Richard Dempsey (Jack the Giant Killer); Patsy Rowlands (Jack's Mother); Jacqueline Dankworth (Cinderella); Ann Howard (Cinderella's Stepmother); John Rogan (Cinderella's Father/Mysterious Man); Liza Sadovy (Lucinda); Elizabeth Price (Florinda); Tessa Burbridge (Little Red Riding Hood); Clive Carter (Wolf/Cinderella's Prince); Eunice Grayson (Cinderella's Mother/Grandmother); Mary Lincoln (Rapunzel); Mark Tinler (Rapunzel's Prince); Peter Ledbury (Steward); Megan Kelly (Snow White); Kate Arnell (Sleeping Beauty)

NOTE: The song "Our Little World" was added to this production.

Original London cast recording: RCA Records

SCREEN

JACK AND THE BEANSTALK, *Edison Pictures*, released January 1912
Produced by Thomas A. Edison Kinetoscope Company

Gladys Hulette (Jack); Miriam Nesbitt (Jack's Mother); Harry Eytinge (The Giant); Gertrude Clarke (The Giant's Wife); Gertrude McCoy (The Fairy)

Fox Pictures, released August 1917
Written and directed by C. M. and S. A. Franklin; Photography, Frank Good

Francis Carpenter (Francis/Jack); Virginia Lee Corbin (Virginia/Princess Regina); Violet Radcliffe (Princess Rudolphe); Carmen Fay (DeRue, King of Cornwall); J. G. Tarver (Blunderbore the Giant); Vera Lewis (The Giantress); Eleanor Washington (Francis' Mother); Ralph Lewis (Francis' Father); Ione Glennen (Virginia's Mother)

Warner Bros., released April 1952
An Exclusive Production; Producer, Alex Gottlieb; Director, Jean Yarbrough; Screenplay, Nat Curtis, based on a story by Pat Costello adapted from the Fairy Tale; Additional comedy material, Felix Adler; Photography, George Robinson; Art director, McClure Capps; Music, Heinz Roemheld; Music supervisor, Raoul Kraushaar; Songs "He Never Looked Better in His Life" and "I Fear Nothing" by Bob Russell and Lester

Lee; Choreography, Johnny Conrad; Editor, Otho Lovering

Bud Abbott (Dink Dinklepuss); Lou Costello (Jack); Buddy Baer (Sergeant Riley/The Giant); Dorothy Ford (Polly, the Giant's Housekeeper); Shaye Cogan (Eloise Larkin/The Princess); James Alexander (Arthur Royal/The Prince); Barbara Brown (Mother); William Farnum (The King); David Stollery (Donald); Joe Kirk (Villager); Johnny Conrad and Dancers

Primrose Productions (Great Britain) released 1955 12 minutes
A Silouette Film produced by Vivian Milroy and Louis Hagen; Design and animation by Lotte Reinger; Assistant animator, Carl Koch; Music, Freddie Phillips; Narrator, Deryck Guyler

Tigon Picture for *United Artists* release, released Great Britain 1961; in U.S., June 1962
A Zenith Films production; Producer, Edward Small; Associate producer, Robert E. Kent; Director, Nathan Juran; Screenplay, Nathan Juran and Orville Hampton, based on the Fairy Tale and an original story by Hampton; Photography, David S. Horsley; Special effects in Fantascope by Howard A. Anderson; Art directors, Fernando Carrere and Frank McCoy; Costumes, David Berman; Set decorator, Edward G. Boyle; Makeup, Charles Gemora; Music, Paul Sawtell and Bert Shefter; Sound, John Kean; Editor, Grant Whytock

Kerwin Mathews (Jack); Judi Meredith (Princess Elaine); Torin Thatcher (Pendragon); Walter Burke (Garna); Roger Mobley (Peter); Barry Kelly (Sigurd); Don Beddoe (Imp in Bottle); Dayton Lummis (King Mark); Anna Lee (Constance); Helen Wallace (Jack's Mother); Tudor Owen, Robert Gist, Ken Mayer (Men)

Cinetron Corp., released December 1970
An R & S Film Enterprises production; Executive producer, C. T. Robertson; Producer/Director/Writer, Barry Mahon; Photography and lighting, Bill Tobin; Scenic design, Thelma Raniero; Costumes, Peggy Praigg; Music and Lyrics, George Linsenmann and Ralph Falco; Arrangements, Eugene Ventresca; Makeup; Tom Brumberger; Sound, Jon Williams; Editor, Steve Cuiffo

Mitchell Poulos (Jack); Dorothy Stokes (Mother), Chris Brooks, John Loomis, Renato Boracherro, Sami Sims, George Wadsworth

Nippon Herald Films, Japan, Feature-length animated cartoon, released 1974
A Production of Group TAC; Executive producer, Mikio Nakada; Producer, Katsumi Furukawa; Assistant producer, Makoto Kato; Director, Gisaburo Sugil; Screenplay, Shuji Hirami; Photography, VAC; Art directors, Takoa Kodama, Yoshiyuki Uchida, Koji Abe and Shiro Fujimoto; Music, Takashi Miki, Tadoa Inoue and Shunichi Tokura; Musical director, Morihisa Shibuya; Music coordinator, Yuh Aku; Editor, Masashi Furukawa

LEGEND, *Universal Pictures* (U.S.), *20th Century-Fox* (Great Britain), released August 1985
A Legend Production; Producer, Arnon Milchan; Co-producer, Tim Hampton; Director, Ridley Scott; Screen-play, William Hjortsberg, based on *Jack and the Beanstalk*, *Sleeping Beauty*, *Peter Pan* and *A Midsummer Night's Dream*; Photography, Alex Thomson; Production designer, Asheton Gorton; Art directors, Norman Dorme and Les Dilley; Costumes, Charles Knode; Special effects, Nick

Allder; Music, Jerry Goldsmith; Set decorator, Ann Mollo; Choreography, Arlene Phillips; Special makeup, Rob Bottin; Editor, Terry Rawlings

Tom Cruise (Jack of the Beanstalk); Mia Sara (Princess Lili); Tim Curry (Darkness); David Bennent (Gump); Alice Playten (Blix); Billy Barty (Screwball); Cork Hubbert (Brown Tom); Peter O'Farrell (Pox); Kiran Shah (Blunder); Annabelle Lanyon (Oona); Robert Picardo (Meg Mucklebones); Tina Martin (Nell); Ian Longmuir and Mike Crane (Demon Cooks); Liz Gilbert (Dancing Black Dress); Eddie Powell (Mummified Guard)

TELEVISION

JACK AND THE BEANSTALK, *Producer's Showcase*, televised December 12, 1956 NBC 90 minutes

Produced by Alvin Cooperman; Director, Clark Jones; A Musical Fantasy with book and lyrics by Helen Deutsch and music by Jerry Livingston; Narrated by Dennis King

Joel Grey (Jack); Peggy King (Tillie); Leora Dana (Jack's Mother); Cyril Ritchard (The Peddler); Celeste Holm (Mad Maggie); Billy Gilbert (Poopledoop/The Giant); Arnold Stang (The Little Giant); Ray Charles Singers

MUSICAL NUMBERS: "Ballad of Jack and the Beanstalk"; "This Is the One"; "He Never Looks My Way"; "Where Are the White Birds Flying?"; "People Should Listen to Me"; "Sweet World"; "The March of the Ill-Assorted Guards"; "Twelve Feet Tall"; "Looka Me"; "I'll Go Along With You"

JACK AND THE BEANSTALK, NBC Special, televised February 26, 1967 NBC 60 minutes

A Hanna-Barbera Production; Executive producers, William Hanna and Joseph Barbera; Producer-Director, Gene Kelly; Written by Michael Morris and Larry Marks; Music and Lyrics, Sammy Cahn and James Van Heusen; Music arranged and conducted by Lennie Hayton; Animation by Hanna-Barbera Studios

Gene Kelly (Jeremy Keen); Bobby Riha (Jack); Marion McKnight (Jack's Mother); Voices: Ted Cassidy (Giant); Janet Waldo (Princess Serena [speaking]); Marni Nixon (Princess Serena [singing]); Dick Beals (The Cat); Cliff Norton, Leo DeLyon (Woggle Birds); Chris Allen (Arnold the Mouse)

MUSICAL NUMBERS: "Half-Past April and a Quarter to May"; "A Tiny Bit of Faith"; "One Starry Moment"; "I Sure Hate Love"; "It's Been Nice"; "Stiffen Up That Upper Lip"; "The Woggle-Bird Song"

Original soundtrack recording: Hanna-Barbera Records

JACK AND THE BEANSTALK, Shelley Duvall's *Faerie Tale Theatre*, televised September 8, 1983 Showtime 47 minutes

Platypus Productions and Gaylord Television Entertainment in association with Lion's Gate Films; Executive producer, Shelley Duvall; Producer, Jonathan Taplin; Director, Lamont Johnson; Teleplay, Ron Ash and Mark Curtiss

Dennis Christopher (Jack); Elliott Gould (The Evil Giant); Jean Stapleton (The Kindly Giantess); Katherine Helmond (Jack's Mother); Jerry Hall (Lady in the Harp); Lamont Johnson (Voice of Spot the Cow); Mark Blankfield (Narrator/Little Man/Fairy)

INTO THE WOODS, *American Playhouse*, televised March 20, 1991 PBS 2 1/2 hours (see 1987 Broadway production at the Martin Beck Theater)

JESSE JAMES

Various adaptations of the life of Jesse James, including *Missouri Legend*, a comedy by Elizabeth B. Ginty (1938)

Synopsis

Notorious bank robber Jesse James, who had been the scourge of the Old West, has retired with his faithful wife, Zee, and his outlaw brother, Frank, to St. Joseph, Missouri, under the guise of Thomas Howard, a respectable, law-abiding, scripture-quoting Baptist. Jesse, who neither smokes nor drinks, permits no swearing in his home from visiting gang members but reluctantly goes out to rob a bank to save impoverished Widow Weeks, a neighbor, from eviction, and then relieves the bank of the mortgage payment. "Mrs. Howard" is embarrassed at having to line her bustle with a newspaper announcing a $10,000 reward for the capture of her husband dead or alive. To uphold his outlaw reputation and honor, Jesse and his gang stage a new train robbery. Home again as the respectable Mr. Howard, Jesse is able to let down his guard. Young Robert Ford, alias Bob Johnson, a gang member paying a visit, shoots Jesse in the back for the reward money, and ultimately becomes known in ballads written about Jesse as "that dirty little coward that shot Mr. Howard has laid poor Jesse in his grave."

Comment and Critique

Long called in this country's folklore "the greatest criminal in America," the infamous Jesse James was born on September 5, 1847, in Clay Country, Missouri, to Baptist minister Robert James and his wife, Zerelda. By the time Jesse died thirty-five years later, he had become a true folk hero of the Old West for his bank robbing exploits and his train holdups with his gang that included his brother, Frank. During the Civil War, at seventeen, Jesse had joined William Clarke Quantrill's marauders of which his brother, Alexander Frank James, and his cousins Cole, Jim, Bob and John Younger were members. Ten years later, on April 23, 1874, he married his first cousin, Zerelda (Zee) Mimms, and apparently planned on settling down, but equally as apparently, outlawry was in his blood. On April 3, 1882, he was killed by a member of his gang and was buried in Kearney, Missouri. A tombstone was erected over his grave with this inscription:

> "Jesse James
> Died April 3, 1882
> Murdered by a traitor and a coward
> Whose name is not worthy to
> Appear here."

The *New York Daily Graphic* on April 11, 1882, reserved its front page for a tribute to Jesse James. It read: "The most renowned murderer and robber of his age. He quickly rose to eminence in his gallant and dangerous profession and his exploits were the wonder and admiration and excited the emulation of the small boys of the period. He was cut off in the prime of his strength and beauty, not by the hands of a hangman but by the shot of a base assassin of whom the Governor of the State of

Missouri was the accomplice. He was followed to his grave by mourning relatives, hosts of friends, officers of the law and the *reverend clergy*, who united in paying extraordinary honors to his memory. Go thou and do likewise."

On October 4, 1882, Frank James surrendered to Governor Francis T. Crittendon, whose reward offer inspired Bob Ford to shoot Jesse down. Taking off his guns, Frank was reported to have said, "Governor Crittendon, I want to hand over to you that which no living man except myself has been permitted to touch since 1861, and to say that I am your prisoner." Nationwide empathy for Jesse largely influenced the acquittal of his brother Frank, who was released from custody in February 1885 and died of natural causes on February 18, 1915. On June 24, 1892, Ed. O'Kelly entered the saloon in Creedo, Colorado, being run by Bob Ford and shot to death "the dirty little coward who murdered Mr. Howard."

Nineteenth-century dime novelists exploited and glamorized Jesse James' career of crime while magazines published stories of his bravery and gallantry as an American Robin Hood. Street and Smith's dime novels about the James Brothers sold an estimated six million copies with their first adventure, *Jesse James, the Outlaw*. Some 277 titles appeared in Frank Tousey's *James Boys Weekly*.

A year after Jesse's death, James J. McCloskey wrote a six-act melodrama entitled *Jesse James, The Bandit King*. Produced by James H. Wallick, the "dramatic triumph" opened in Chicago in October 1883, featuring Wallick himself as Jesse and R. M. Olson as Frank. The play was lavishly advertised as a "complete unparalleled success" and theater manager James H. Meade was stating: "The business of the Jesse James Company surpasses anything ever experienced at the Olympic Theatre under my management." The *Chicago Tribune* noted: "Manager Meade of the Olympic has been obliged to ask for police protection at his theater this week, as the huge crowds who are hungry to witness the exploits of the noted bandit in the play *Jesse James* threaten to break down the doors."

One of the play's greater excitements was the use of Jesse's horses, authenticated by an item published in a St. Joseph, Missouri, newspaper on April 10, 1882, a week after Jesse's murder, stating that E. F. Mitchell had purchased the Roan Charger and Bay Raider horses found in Jesse's stable the day he was killed. "The Bay is the horse he made his famous ride from the Winston Train Robbery to Kansas City, and sold Saturday, April 1, to C. A. Alderman." The two horses were resold to the managers of McCloskey's Jesse James Company, S. H. Barrett & Company of Hoboken, New Jersey, the following July. The Ford Brothers, Charles and Robert, later signed an affidavit before James J. McCloskey certifying the horses were indeed the property of Jesse James.

On October 3, 1883, Chicago's *Interocean* newspaper reported, "Mr. Wallick gives a creditable piece of acting in the title role and infuses it with a vigor akin to realism. Incidental to the play are introduced 'Roan Charger' and 'Bay Raider,' authenticated as the property of the late Jesse James by affidavits." The *Chicago News* added, "Nothing like horse-drama and Kansas banditti to draw. *Jesse James* is the greatest draw the Olympic has had under its present management."

In its review of *Jesse James, The Bandit King*, the *Chicago Herald* said, "Jesse James, though dead, will long live in the annals of crime and the dime novels of the future. In mimic shape, he walked the boards of the Olympic Theatre last night, and a crowded house witnessed his sensational deeds without a shudder...the performance last night was full of exciting emanations, pistol-shots and ludicrous situations."

The tale of Jesse James was turned into a comedy called *Missouri Legend* in 1938 by Elizabeth B. Ginty, who had spent several years as secretary to flamboyant producer and playwright David Belasco. Max Gordon and Guthrie McClintic mounted a production of it on Broadway with a cast that included Dean Jagger, Dorothy Gish, Karl Malden, Jose Ferrer, Dan Duryea and Mildred Natwick, among others. It ran only forty-eight performances. *The New York Times*' Brooks Atkinson called it "romantically humorous, written with a salty tongue in cheek...Miss Ginty's dry and laconic sense of humor [is] a generous thing in our callous theater." Richard Watts in the *Herald Tribune* found it "filled with humor and excitement, and it gives the theater a much needed touch of popular amusement. *Missouri Legend* is good fun."

Walter Winchell (*New York Mirror*) reported: "*Missouri Legend*, a spellbinding saga about Jesse James came last night to the Empire Theatre...It is from the robust pencil of an historian named E. B. Ginty, plus the exciting direction of Guthrie McClintic, and is played by a talented cast. John Mason Brown (*Evening Post*) considered the comedy well acted but found it lacking structure, "true creativeness and point of view ...It is in her constant contrast between the moral and amoral Jesse James that Miss Ginty is at her most amusing in her dramatization of the James saga. Her play is not by any means a skillful one...one leaves *Missouri Legend* wishing its writing were more consistently worthy of its acting...In the redoubtable Jesse James, Miss Ginty has a fascinating subject of which for the most part she makes passably entertaining, if undistinguished, use in her saga of his last eight days.

Classifying the play as "half a clowning comic strip, half a romantic daguerreotype," *Time* magazine felt that "Playwright Ginty's triumph of make believe is that she has created out of one part pious bluenose and one part murderous bandit, a lively, attractive, fun-loving Tom Rover."

Jesse James, Jr., was seven years old when his father was shot down. In 1921, Jesse Jr. appeared in two films based on his dad's legend, *Jesse James Under the Black Flag* and *Jesse James the Outlaw*. (An early film about Jesse, a 1908 one-reeler produced by Essanay Films called *The James Boys in Missouri*, was banned in Chicago.)

Western actor Fred Thomson had the title role in Paramount's *Jesse James* in 1927. Mordaunt Hall (*The New York Times*) found this film "as a whole disappointing as a character study of the famous outlaw [in which] Fred Thomson fills the part of Jesse James. He is a performer of no mean ability -- in this picture he is a superman and the others characters are often quite dense." *Photoplay* considered *Jesse James* one of the year's best films, although qualifying it, noting, "Fred Thomson's exciting film version may seem to whitewash the famous bandit of Clay County. Still, there were many Americans of the '70s who believed that James had a real grievance and that he was a persecuted man. Thomson's film version presents him in this light."

Darryl F. Zanuck filmed his studio's adventuresome Technicolor version of the James legend with Tyrone Power and Henry Fonda as Jesse and Frank at Pineville, Missouri, on the Elk River at the cost of some $2 million. William R. Weaver observed in *Motion Picture Herald*, "It contained just about everything melodramatic the cinematograph has discovered since *The Great Train Robbery*...It may well turn out to be an American classic. Certainly it is a Zanuck triumph." *Liberty* magazine called the 1939 epic "a picturesque fabrication of the Missouri border bandits. You probably will like Tyrone Power as the lad who rode hard and recklessly..." Most, however, felt the incredibly handsome romantic leading man generally miscast in his first Western.

Of 20th Century-Fox's *Jesse James*, directed by Henry King (the fourth of eleven teamings with Power), *The New York Times'* B. R. Crisler thought it to be "handsomely produced...stirringly directed...beautifully acted" and noted that Power "makes an excellent melodramatic case against himself as Jesse, although, as far as we are concerned, the verdict is still 'Not guilty.'" The critic for *Time* magazine decided that "purified in the person of Tyrone Power, *Jesse James* emerges brilliantly in Technicolor as an amiable brigand, genuinely devoted to his aged mother, and generally more sinned against than sinning...[He] excels modern cinema gangsters in horseback riding, marksmanship and chivalry [and] treats his gun moll with devotion."

The scenario for *Jesse James* was based on data assembled by Rosalind Schaeffer and Miss Jo Frances James of Los Angeles, a descendent of Jesse's. Jo Frances James later capsulated the film as "about the only connection it had with fact was that there was a man named James and he did ride a horse."

A year after the release of Jesse James came Fox's sequel, *The Return of Frank James*, with Henry Fonda reprising his role. It was a far more tightly constructed tale of the Missouri legend, giving an account, if fictionalized, of Frank's dedicated revenge of his brother's murder. *The Return of Frank James* opened with the closing scenes from *Jesse James*, and for many years in reissue was shown on a double bill with it -- often in black and white during the war years and in Technicolor later.

Motion Picture Herald, reviewing the sequel, noted: "Henry Fonda, who played Frank in the first picture, and was credited by the critics with stealing the picture from Tyrone Power up to the point where the writers dropped him out of the script, is presented here as determined to lead a life of rectitude but forced to take the trail in pursuit of his brother's killers when they are granted a pardon for the killing ...Directed by Fritz Lang, the picture is in Technicolor, as was *Jesse James*, and contains exteriors, chases over open country and river bed, canyon and peak, which do for the eye and pulse all that was done for them in the first production." *The New York Herald Tribune* admired the film for "its emphasis on small things like gestures and shadows and sounds of nature revealing the Western in a new and interesting light."

Over the next decade, Jesse James was a portrayed in such films as *Bad Men of Missouri* (about the Young Brothers), *Badman's Territory*, *I Shot Jesse James*, *Gunfire*, *The Return of Jesse James*, *Kansas Raiders* and *Best of the Badmen*, among others.

Nunnally Johnson's 1939 screenplay for *Jesse James* was revised by 20th Century-Fox in 1957 for *The True Story of Jesse James* (released in Great Britain as *The James Brothers*) featuring Robert Wagner as Jesse and Jeffrey Hunter as Frank. Two years later, in *Alias Jesse James*, Wendell Corey is a mean-looking Jesse to whom Bob Hope, as an inept insurance salesman mistakenly sells a life insurance policy. Universal's 1972 *The Great Northfield Minnesota Raid* (Robert Duvall as Jesse) came closest to being a factual reconstruction of the last outlawing days of Jesse and Frank James, but was, in the view of critic Judith Crist, "just another killers-and-psychos-at-play exercise in incredibility." In 1980 the James brothers Jesse and Frank again rode on the big screen in *The Long Riders* in the guise of the Keach brothers James and Stacy.

Missouri Legend was adapted to television in 1956 by Ernest Kinoy and starred Robert Preston as Jesse James. *The New York Times* reported, about Ginty's play on television and Preston's performance, "He's a fine actor whose abilities should be put to better use. There was nothing in this threadbare story about the last days of Jesse James to add to Mr. Preston's reputation or to entertain a viewer."

In September 1965, ABC premiered its series *The Legend of Jesse James*. It featured Christopher Jones as Jesse and Allan Case as Frank, and lasted thirty-four episodes. Jack Gould (*The New York Times*) viewed the first one, "Three Men from Now," and felt, "This series avers Jesse in part may have been the victim of the permissiveness of frontier society but the viewer may be puzzled how a legend could grow around such a bore on the draw!"

Fourteen years later, producer-director Dan Curtis brought one of those "best of the badmen" Westerns, once so dear to Hollywood, to television in the form of *The Last Ride of the Dalton Gang*, in which the Daltons and Jesse James (here played by Harris Yulin) team up for the legendary raid on the bank in Coffeyville, Kansas. (In TV's 1975 *The Last Day*, the Coffeyville raid also was staged but only the Daltons were involved in this version -- Jesse James was not portrayed.)

Another seven years would pass before Jesse rode again on TV, in William A. Graham's *The Last Days of Frank and Jesse James*, featuring a number of country music stars such as Kris Kristofferson (as Jesse), Johnny Cash (as Frank), and Willie Nelson (who stole the picture in a brief role as Confederate General Jo Shelby). Filming was done near Nashville, so the stars could be close to their recording studios. Interesting is the fact that Johnny Cash's wife June Carter Cash (of the famed Carter Family, pioneers in the field of country music) played his and Kris Kristofferson's mother! *TV Guide*'s Judith Crist gave this assessment of the film: "Beginning in 1877, when, after 15 years of outlawry, the brothers attempt to settle down to farming with their families, the story provides a study of contrasts between Kristofferson's womanizing, money-hungry, prideful Jesse and Cash's Shakespeare-quoting, book-loving, family-oriented Frank. Vengeance, greed and betrayal lead to Jesse's death and loyalty leads to Frank's survival. It's a rich and illuminating story complete with an effective cameo appearance by Willie Nelson."

STAGE

THE OUTLAW BROTHERS, *National Theatre*, New York, opened February 19, 1883
Henry Belmer (Jesse James); F. K. Wallace (Frank James); Mamie Wallace (Zee James); James McCauley (Bob Ford); D. Franks (Charley Ford)

THE OUTLAW BROTHERS, *Volks Theatre*, New York, opened March 24, 1883
Henry Belmer (Jesse James); W. D. Chalfin (Frank James); William C. Cameron (Mussey); Fanny Davenport (Mrs. Samuels); Mai Estelle (Fanny Ralston/ Zerelda James); with Horses, "Wildfire" and "Ginger"

THE OUTLAW BROTHERS, *Park Theatre*, New York, opened November 17, 1884
Henry Belmer (Jesse James); William Lee (Frank James); John H. McVickers (Mussey); Billy Williams (Peter Corndodger)

THE BANDIT KING, *Niblo's Garden Theatre*, New York, opened March 23, 1885
Produced by James H. Wallick; A Drama by James J. McCloskey*
James H. Wallick (Jesse James); R. H. Olson (Frank James); Elmer E. Grandin (Kansas Jake); Fred Lyons (Colored Man); with Horses, "Bay Charger" and "Roan Charger"

* The McCloskey play was originally staged in Chicago on October 2, 1883 as *Jesse James, The Bandit King*, with James H. Wallick as Jesse James and R. H. Olson as Frank James

THE JAMES BOYS; OR, THE MISSOURI OUTLAWS, *National Theatre*, New York, opened March 15, 1886

Produced by the Sid C. France Grand Double Specialty & Comedy Company

Frank Keenan (Jesse James); Thomas Brantford (Frank James); Sid C. France (Buckskin); Robert Allen (Bob Ford); Maud Hillman (Jenny Somers); Bertie Brantford (Mrs. Grayson); Ada West (Eliza Jane Green)

JESSE JAMES, *Standard Museum*, New York, opened December 5, 1887

Harry Belmer (Jesse James); Tex Bender (Frank James)

MISSOURI LEGEND, *Empire Theatre*, New York, opened September 19, 1938 48 performances

Produced by Guthrie McClintic, in association with Max Gordon; A Comedy by E. B. Ginty; Director, Guthrie McClintic; Production design, John Koenig; Costumes, Pons Studio and Eaves Costume Company; Music director, Albert Pearl; General manager, Stanley Gilkey; Company manager, William G. Tisdale; Stage managers, John Cornell and Vincent Copeland

Dean Jagger (Thomas Howard); Dorothy Gish (Mrs. Howard); Karl Malden (Charlie Johnson); Dan Duryea (Bob Johnson); Mildred Natwick (The Widow Weeks); Russell Collins (Jim Cummins); Jose Ferrer (Billy Gashade); Richard Bishop (Frank Howard); Clare Woodbury (Aunt Belle); Joseph Sweeney (Hosea [Pop] Hickey); John Woodworth (Sam); Vincent Copeland (George); James Craig (succeeded by Hudson Shotwell) (Asa); John Philliber (Old Timer); Ben Roberts (Police Commissioner Gregg); Cliff Heckringer (succeeded by John Winthrop) (The Reverend)

MISSOURI LEGEND, *Temple University Theatre*, Philadelphia, opened March 1951

Produced by Temple University; A Musical version of the play by E. B. Ginty; Director, Paul E. Randall; Music by John Shuman; Lyrics by Peg Randall; Adaptation, Olga Larkin; Musical arrangements, Robert Drumm; Costumes, Patricia Gleason; Choreography, Sherry Betchen; Lighting, Mort Mossman; Technical director, Clemen M. Peck; Production manager, M. Harris Schaeffer

Gilbert Thompson (Thomas Howard); Florence King (Mrs. Howard); Elwood Maschmeyer (Charlie Johnson); Paul Stockbine (Bob Johnson); Charlene Becker (The Widow Weeks); William E. Fischelis, Jr. (Jim Cummins); Louis Lippa (Billy Gashade); Herbert Dufine (Frank Howard); Norman Feld (Hosea [Pop] Hickey); Arthur Zigouras (Sam/The Reverend); Zeke Berlin (George); John Levy (Asa); Marvin Levin (Old Timer); Norman Garfield (Police Commissioner Gregg)

Mule-Power Merry-Go-Round Ballet: Danny Spizzirri (Jesse); Ruth Leon (Zee); Willa Broome (Flower Girl); and Zelma Weisfeld, Fran Gilligan, Ruthe Fischer, Bobby Weinsweig, Betty Jane Leuchtener, Hancy Honneger, Sarah Berlin, Bill Bonsall, Ronald Barbeck, Joe Tyrell, Bill Christianson, Fred Russo, Mike Marston, Len Rittenberg

Train Robbery Ballet: Danny Spizziri (Jesse); Fred Russo (Billy Gashade); Len Rittenberg (Salesman); Mike Marston (Politician); Bill Christianson (Groom); Joe Tyrell (Frank); Ronald Barbeck (Jim); Ruth Leon (Bride); Ruthe Fischer (Daughter); Willa Broome (Indian); Bobby Weinsweig (Prostitute)

MUSICAL NUMBERS: "Ballad of Jesse James"; "I Gave Him a Gun"; "'Twas a Summer Night"; "Some Day You Won't Come Back"; "What's a Gal Ter Do?"; "I'll Buy You a Bustle"; "I Hadda Move Along"; "What's Right What's Wrong"; "Maisie"; "I Can Tell a Book by Its Cover"; "Yours Till and Through Death"

INDIANS, *Aldwych Theatre*, London, opened July 4, 1968 (World Premiere)
Produced by the Royal Shakespeare Company; A Play by Arthur Kopit; Director, Jack Gelber; Production designer, John Bury; Costumes in collaboration with Ann Curtis; Music, Guy Woolfenden; Company director, Terry Hands

Barrie Ingham (Buffalo Bill); Daniel Moynihan (Jesse James); Peter Geddis (Billy the Kid); Gay Brown (Belle Starr); Jeffrey Dench (Ned Buntline); Michael Jayston (General Custer); Morgan Sheppard (Wild Bill Hickok); Phillip Hinton (Bob Dalton); William McGuirk (Emmett Dalton); Geoffrey Hutchings (Geronimo); Peter Geddis (General Sheridan); Don Henderson (Spotted Tail); Roger Rees (Caddo); Emrys James (Sitting Bull); Vanessa Miles (Annie Oakley); Sydney Jayston (Lord Throgmorton); Daniel Moynihan (Grand Duke Alexis); Philip Taylor (His Interpretor); David Healy (Chief Joseph); Richard Mayes (Gunter Hookman); Don Henderson (Doc Holliday); Susan Sheers (Flora); Sydney Bromley (Ol' Klondike); Boyd Mackenzie (Joe the Bartender); Jeffrey Dench (Senator Dawes); Richard Mayes (Senator Morgan); Ron Daniels (John Grass); John Noland (A Lieutenant); Morgan Sheppard (Colonel Forsyth); Geoffrey Hutchings (Apache Pete); Phillip Hinton (Finley, a Soldier); Derek Smith (Ol' Time President); Rudy Head (First Lady); Gaye Brown (Paula Monduli); David Rowland (Sam the Piano Player); Michael Jayston (Senator Logan); Peter Geddis, Phillip Hinton (Reporters); Vanessa Miles, Christina Greatrex (Saloon Hostesses); Ron Daniels, Brian Forster, Oscar James, Alton Kumalo, Tony McEwan, Peter Messaline, Gregg Palmer, Roger Rees, John Rogan, Keith Washington (Indians); Stephan Chase, Boyd Mackenzie, John Noland, Philip Taylor (Cowboys, Soldiers, Phony Indians); Philip Box, Peter Hastings, Edward Hobart, Aneurin James, Edward Joory, David Munden (Musicians)

INDIANS, *Brooks Atkinson Theatre*, New York, opened October 13, 1969 96 performances
Produced by Lyn Austin, Oliver Smith, Joel Schenker and Roger L. Stevens; A Play by Arthur Kopit; Director, Gene Frankel; Setting, Oliver Smith; Lighting, Thomas Skelton; Costumes, Marjorie Slaiman; Choreography, Julie Arenal; Music, Richard Peaslee; Company manager, James Walsh; Stage managers, Kathleen A. Sullivan, Fritz Holt and Moose Peting

Stacy Keach (Buffalo Bill); Ronny Cox (Jesse James); Ed Rombola (Billy the Kid); Raul Julia (Uncas/Grand Duke Alexis); Sam Waterston (John Grace); Pamela Gray (Annie Oakley); Manu Tupou (Sitting Bull); Charles Durning (Ned Buntline); Barton Hayman (Wild Bill Hickok); Tom Aldredge (Senator Logan); Richard McKenzie (Senator Dawes); Jon Richards (Senator Morgan); James J. Sloyan (Spotted Tail); Andy Torres (Red Cloud); Kevin Conway (Black Hawk); Gary Weber (Kicking Bear); Ted Goodridge (Howling Wolf); Tom Fletcher (White Antelope); Philip Arsenault (Low Dog); Juan Antonio (Naiche); Peter MacLean (Colonel Forsyth); Yusef Bulos (Interpreter); George Mitchell (Chief Joseph); Brian Donahue (Bartender); Dino Laucinia (Crazy Horse); Robert MacLean (He-Who-Hears-Thunder); Jay Fletcher (Little Hawk); Princeton Dean (Kiokuk); Ed Henkel (Satanta); Michael Ebbin (Old Taza); Peter MacLean (Ol' Time President); Dortha Duckworth (First Lady); Darryl Croxton (Master Valet); Dimitra Arliss (Teskan-javila); Bob Hamilton, Richard Nieves (Trial Soldiers); Richard Novello (Lieutenant); Ronny Cox, Brian Donahue, Darryl Croxton (Reporters); Pasqual Vaquer (Tecumseh); Leon Oxman, Allan Silverman (Indian Drummers); Tony Posk, Peter Rosenfelt (White House Orchestra); Joseph Ragno, Richard Novello, Brian Donahue (Valets); Richard Nieves, Richard

Miller, Clint Allmon, Bob Hamilton (Cowboys); Wesley Fata (Yellow Cloud); Peter DeMaio (Touch-the-Clouds)

DIAMOND STUDS (THE LIFE OF JESSE JAMES), Westside Theatre, New York, opened January 15, 1975 232 performances
Produced by The Chelsea Theater Center of Brooklyn; A Saloon Musical; Director, John L. Haber; Book by Jim Wann; Music and Lyrics by Bland Simpson and Jim Wann; Musical numbers staged by Patricia Birch; Musical consultant, Mel Marvin; Design advsior, Larry King; Sound, Laddy Savetin; Company manager, Catherine Boyer; Stage manager, Brenda Mezz

The Southern States Fidelity Choir: Jim Wann (Jesse James/Guitar); John Foley (Bob Ford/12-string Guitar); Mike Sheehan (Allen Pinkerton/Percussion); Bland Simpson (Governor Thomas Crittendon/Piano); Jan Davidson (Major Edwards/Bass)

The Red Clay Ramblers: Tommy Thompson (Zerelda Samuels/Cole Younger/Banjo); Jim Watson (Jim Younger/Mandolin); Mike Craver (Dr. Reuben "Pappy" Samuels/Piano); Bill Hicks (Bob Younger/ Fiddle)

And Friends: Scott Bradley (William Clark Quantrill); Joyce Cohen (Zee James); Rick Simpson (Frank James); Madelyn Smoak (Belle Starr); Francis Tamburro (Tourist)

MUSICAL NUMBERS: "Jesse James Robbed This Train"; "These Southern States That I Love"; "The Year of Jubilo"; "The Unreconstructed Rebel"; "Mama Fantastic"; "Saloon Piano"; "I Don't Need a Man to Know I'm Good"; "Northfield, Minnesota"; "King Cole"; "New Prisoner's Song"; "K. C. Line"; "Cakewalk Into Kansas City"; "When I Was a Cowboy"; "Pancho Villa"; Put It Where the Moon Don't Shine"; "Sleepy Time Down South"; "Bright Morning Star"; "When I Get the Call"

JESSE AND THE BANDIT QUEEN, Other Stage Public Theatre, New York, opened November 2, 1975 155 performances
Produced by the New York Shakespeare Festival Public Theatre, Joseph Papp, producer; A Play by David Freeman; Director, Gordon Stewart; Setting, Richard J. Graziano; Lighting, Arden Fingerhut; Costumes, Hilary M. Rosenfeld; Stage managers, Penny Gebhard and Miklos Horvath

Kevin O'Connor (succeeded by Barry Primus) (Jesse James); Pamela Peyton-Wright (succeeded by Dixie Carter) (Belle Starr)

MISSOURI LEGEND, Equity Library Theatre, New York, opened February 12, 1976 14 performances
Produced by the Equity Library Theatre; A Play by E. B. Ginty; Director, Thom Molyneaux; Scenery, Maria Schweppe; Lighting, Timothy Garvin; Costumes, Paula Davis; Musical director, Earl Wentz; Additional music and lyrics by Earl Wentz and Thom Molyneaux; Stage managers, Ed Oster, Amy F. Leveen and Tom Nagle

Bill Tatum (Thomas Howard); Sofia Landon (Mrs. Howard); Michael Cutt (Charlie Johnson); Michael Oakes (Bob Johnson); Susanne Marley (The Widow Weeks); Peter Looney (Jim Cummins); Earl Wentz (Billy Gashade); Todd Drexel (Frank Howard); Jeanne Schlegel (Aunt Belle); Bill Wiley (Hosea [Pop] Hickey); James Galvin (Sam); Ray Rantapaa (George); Michael Zeke Zaccaro (Asa); Jody Hingle (Martha); Annie O'Neill (Jenny); Georgia Southcotte (Trapper's Wife); Harry Carlson (Police Commissioner Gregg); Ray Rantapaa (The Reverend)

THE DEATH AND LIFE OF JESSE JAMES, Westside Airlines Terminal, New York, opened May 11, 1978 22 performances

A Lion Theatre Company Productions; Produced and directed by Gene Nye; A Drama by Len Jenkin; Scenery, Henry Millman; Lighting, Frances Aronson; Costumes, Bob Wojewodski; Music, John McKinney; Choreography, Kathy Kramer; Company director, Garland Wright; Managing director, Ellie Meglio; Stage managers, Steve Shlansky and Kathy Arlt

Allan Carlsen (Jesse James); William Brenner (Frank James); James McLure (Bob Ford); Maria Cellario (Zee James); John Ingle (Cole Younger); Peter Noel-Duhamel (Huey Dalton); Jerry Lazarus (Louie Dalton); M. Patrick Hughes (Dewey Dalton); Tamara Daniel (Mom); Rebecca Malka (Rosita); Janice Fuller (Conchita); Collette Connor (Pepita); Deirdre Keogh (Child); Don Auspitz (Captain Sheeta/Speedy Gonzalez); John Genke (Reverend/President/Sheriff); Russell Duffy (Immigrant); Rob Anderson (Commissioner/Interviewer)

THE MAN WHO SHOT THE MAN WHO SHOT JESSE JAMES, *Manhattan Punch Line Theatre*, New York, opened April 24, 1980 16 performances

Produced by Faith Catlin; A Play by Thornebrake Theatre; Director, Christopher Coddington; Setting, Tony Castrigno; Lighting, Gregory Chabay; Costumes, Karen Hummel; Choreographer, Janet Watson; Stage manager, John Kingsbury

Brad Bellamy (Bob Ford); Evelyn Seubert (Dottie Evans Ford); Tom Shelton (Charley Ford/J. Benjamin Tuthill); Andy Lerner (Dell/LeSinge/Tom Drayson); Jane Unger (Ma/Mormon Queen); Doug Baldwin (Soappy Siddons/Bill Saul Tutland); Marcia Hepps (Virginia Marlotte/Stranger/Dog/Lola Montez); Maggie Low (Lulu Slain/Emma Evans); Lucy Lee (Mary/Darla Deulappe)

JESSE AND THE BANDIT QUEEN, *Kingston Playhouse*, San Diego, Cal., opened June 4 through 30, 1990

Produced by the Bowery Theater; A Play by David Freeman; Director, Ollie Nash; Set, John Blunt and Ralph Elias; Lighting, Kris Sabel; Sound, Lawrence Czoka

Tim Reilly (Jesse James); Mickey Mullany (Belle Starr)

SCREEN

JESSE JAMES UNDER THE BLACK FLAG, *Mesco Pictures*, released April 1921

Director, Franklin B. Coates; Setting, Edgar Kellar

Jesse James, Jr. (Himself/Jesse James); Diana Reed (Lucille); Marguerite Hungerford (Zee); Franklin B. Coates (Himself)

JESSE JAMES AS THE OUTLAW, *Mesco Pictures*, released April 1921

Director, Franklin B. Coates; Setting, Edgar Kellar

Jesse James, Jr. (Himself/Jesse James); Diana Reed (Lucille); Marguerite Hungerford (Zee); Franklin B. Coates (Himself)

JESSE JAMES, *Paramount Famous Players/Lasky*, released October 1927

Produced by Adolph Zukor and Jesse L. Lasky; Director, Lloyd Ingraham; Production supervisor, Alfred L. Werker; Story and screenplay, Frank M. Clifton; Photography, Allen Siegler; Technical advisor, Jesse James, Jr.

Frank Thomson (Jesse James); Nora Lane (Zerelda Mimms); Montagu Love (Frederick Mimms); Mary Carr (Mrs. Samuels); James Pierce (Frank James); Harry Woods (Bob Ford); William Courtright (Parson Bill); Silver (King of the Wild Horses)

JESSE JAMES, 20th Century-Fox, released January 1939
Produced by Darryl F. Zanuck; Associate Producer, Nunnally Johnson; Director, Henry King; Screenplay, Nunnally Johnson, based on historical data assembled by Rosaline Schaeffer and Jo Frances James; Photography, George Barnes; Technicolor director, Natalie Kalmus; Art directors, William Darling and George Dudley; Set decorator, Thomas Little; Music director, Louis Silvers; Sound, Roger Heman and Arthur von Kirbolt; Editor, Barbara McLean

Tyrone Power (Jesse James); Henry Fonda (Frank James); Nancy Kelly (Zerelda [Zee] Cobb James); Randolph Scott (Will Wright); Henry Hull (Major Rufus Cobb); Brian Donlevy (Barshee); John Carradine (Bob Ford); Jane Darwell (Mrs. Samuels); John Russell (Jesse James, Jr.); Spencer Charters (Preacher); J. Edward Bromberg (Pinkerton Agent George Runyon); Donald Meek (McCoy); Willard Robertson (Clark); Paul Sutton (Lynch); Slim Summerville (Jailer); Charles Tannen (Charles Ford); Claire Du Brey (Mrs. Ford); Paul Burns (Hank); Arthur Ayles-worth (Tom); Charles Halton (Banker Heywood); George Chandler (Roy the Printer); Erville Anderson (Old Marshal); Harry Tyler (Farmer); George Breakston (Farmer's Boy); Virginia Brissac (Boy's Mother); Charles Middleton (Doctor); Eddy Waller (Deputy); Lon Chaney, Jr. (Member of Jesse's Gang); and Don Douglas, Leonard Kibrick, Tom London, John Elliott, Edward LeSaint, George O'Hara, James Flavin, Wylie Grant, Ethan Laidlaw, Harold Goodwin, Ernest Whitman

DAYS OF JESSE JAMES, Republic Pictures, released December 1939
Associate producer/director, Joseph Kane; Screenplay, Earle Snell, based on an original story by Jack Natteford; Photography, Reggie Lannings; Music director, Cy Feuer; Editor, Tony Martinelli

Roy Rogers (Roy); George "Gabby" Hayes (Gabby); Donald Barry (Jesse James); Pauline Moore (Mary); Harry Woods (Captain Worthington); Arthur Loft (Sam Wyatt); Wade Boteler (Dr. Samuels); Ethel Wales (Mrs. Samuels); Monte Blue (Fields); Olin Howland (Under Sheriff); Glenn Strange (Cole Younger); Fred Burns (Sheriff); Michael Worth (Frank James); Scotty Beckett (Buster Samuels); Jack Rockwell (McDaniels)

THE RETURN OF FRANK JAMES, 20th Century-Fox, released August 1940
Produced by Darryl F. Zanuck; Associate producer, Kenneth Macgowan; Director, Fritz Lang; Screenplay, Sam Hellman; Photography, George Barnes, William V. Skall; Art directors, Richard Day and Wiard B. Ihnen; Technicolor consultant, Natalie Kalmus; Set decorator, Thomas Little; Costumes, Travis Benton; Music, David Buttolph; Sound, Roger Heman and W. D. Flick; Editor, Walter Thompson

Henry Fonda (Frank James); Gene Tierney (Eleanor Stone); John Carradine (Bob Ford); Henry Hull (Major Rufus Cobb); Jackie Cooper (Tom Grayson); J. Edward Bromberg (George Runyon); Donald Meek (McCoy); Ernest Whitman (Pinky Washington); Charles Tannen (Charles Ford); Lloyd Corrigan (Randolph Stone); Edward McWade (Colonel Fentridge Jackson); Barbara Pepper (Nellie Blane); George Barbier (Judge Ferris); Victor Kilian (Preacher); Russell Hicks (Prosecutor); Bud Fine (Deputy); Frank Shannon (Sheriff Daniels); Stymie Beard (Bellboy Mose); Eddie Collins (Eldora Station Agent); George Chandler (Roy); Louis Mason (Watchman Wilson); William Pawley ("Jesse James" Actor); Bob Battier ("Frank James" Actor); Frank Sully (Old Actor--"Pappy"); Davison Clark (Officer); Edmund Elton (Jury Foreman); Sherry Hall (Court Clerk); A. S. Byron

(Engineer); Lee Phelps (Bartender); Hattie Noel (Chambermaid); Almeda Fowler (Mrs. Edna Stone); Adrian Morris (Detective); Irving Bacon (Man at Wagon Sale); and Lillian Yarbo, James Morton, Bob McKenzie, Kernan Cripps, Lew Meehan, Russ Powell, Nelson McDowell, Milton Kibbee, Dale Van Sickel, Frank Melton, Lester Dorr, Kermit Maynard

BAD MEN OF MISSOURI, *Warner Bros. Pictures*, released July 1941
Produced by Harlan Thompson; Director, Ray Enright; Screenplay, Charles Grayson, based on a story by Robert E. Kent; Photography, Arthur Todd; Dialogue director, Robert Foulk; Editor, Clarence Kolster

Dennis Morgan (Cole Younger); Wayne Morris (Bob Younger); Arthur Kennedy (Jim Younger); Jane Wyman (Mary Hathaway); Victor Jory (William Merrick); Alan Baxter (Jesse James); Russell Simpson (Hank Younger); Walter Catlett (Mr. Pettibone); Howard da Silva (Greg Bilson); Faye Emerson (Martha Adams); Virginia Brissac (Mrs. Hathaway); Erville Alderson (Mr. Adams); Hugh Sothern (Fred Robinson); Sam McDaniel (Wash); Dorothy Vaughan (Mrs. Dalton); Dix Davis (Bob Dalton); Sonny Bupp (Grat Dalton); Henry Blair (Tod Dalton); William Gould (Sheriff Brennon); Tom Tyler (Deputy Sheriff); Robert Winkler (Willie Younger); Ann Todd (Amy Younger); Roscoe Ates (Lafe); Frank Wilcox (Minister); Spencer Charters (Clem); Creighton Hale (Bank Representative); and Duncan Renaldo, Frank Mayo, Jack Mower, Leah Baird, John Beck, Ed Stanley, Charles Middleton, Milton Kibbee, Vera Lewis

JESSE JAMES AT BAY, *Republic Pictures*, released October 1941
Associate producer/director, Joseph Kane; Screenplay, James R. Webb, based on an original story by Harrison Jacobs; Photography, William Nobles; Music Director, Cy Feuer; Song "Just for You" by Sol Meyer and Jule Styne; Sung by Roy Rogers; Editor, Tony Martinelli

Roy Rogers (Jesse James/Clint Burns); George "Gabby" Hayes (Sheriff "Gabby" Whittaker); Sally Payne (Polly Morgan); Gale Storm (Jane Fillmore); Pierre Watkin (Krager); Ivan Miller (Judge Rutherford); Hal Taliaferro (Sloane); Roy Barcroft (Vern Stone); Jack Kirk (Rufe Balder)

THE REMARKABLE ANDREW, *Paramount Pictures*, released January 1942
Produced by Richard Blumenthal; Director, Stuart Heisler; Screenplay, Dalton Trumbo, based on his novel *The Remarkable Andrew: Being the Chronicle of a Literal Man*; Photography, Theodor Sparkuhl; Editor, Archie Marshek

William Holden (Andrew Long); Ellen Drew (Peggy Tobin); Brian Donlevy (General Andrew Jackson); Rod Cameron (Jesse James); Richard Webb (Randall Stevens); Porter Hall (Art Slocumb); Frances Gifford (Halsey); Nydia Westman (Miss Van Buren); Montagu Love (George Washington); George Watts (Benjamin Franklin); Brandon Hurst (Justice Marshall); Gilbert Emery (Thomas Jefferson); Jimmy Conlin (Henry Smith); Spencer Charters (Dr. Upjohn); Wallis Clark (R. R. McCall); Tom Fadden (Jake Pearl); Minor Watson (Orville Beamish); Thomas W. Ross (Judge Krebbs); Clyde Filmore (Mayor Ollie Lancaster); Martha O'Driscoll (Secretary); Ben Taggart (Bailiff); Harlan Briggs (Clem Watkins); Milton Parsons (Sam Savage); Helene Phillips (Mrs. Grundes); Emory Parnell, Monte Blue (Policemen); James Millican (Onlooker)

BADMAN'S TERRITORY, *RKO Pictures*, released April 1946
Produced by Nat Holt; Director, Tim Whelan; Screenplay, Jack Nattleford and Luci

Ward; Additional sequences, Clarence Upton Young and Bess Taffel; Photography, Robert de Grasse; Art directors, Albert S. Agostino and Walter E. Keller; Set decorators, Darrell Silvera and James Altwies; Music, Roy Webb; Music director, C. Bakaleinikoff; Montage, Harold Palmer; Sound, Jean L. Speak and Terry Kellum; Editor, Philip Martin

Randolph Scott (Mark Rowley); Ann Richards (Henryette Alcott); George "Gabby" Hayes (Coyote Kid); Lawrence Tierney (Jesse James); Tom Tyler (Frank James); Isabel Jewell (Belle Starr); Steve Brodie (Bob Dalton); Phil Warren (Grat Dalton); William Moss (Bill Dalton); Nestor Paiva (Sam Bass); Ray Collins (Colonel Farewell); Virginia Sale (Meg); James Warren (John Rowley); Morgan Conway (Bill Hampton); John Halloran (Hank McGee); Andrew Tombes (Doc Grant); Chief Thundercloud (Chief Tahlequah); Richard Hale (Ben Wade); Harry Holman (Hodge)

JESSE JAMES RIDES AGAIN, *Republic Pictures*, released June 1947 13 episode serial

Associate producer, Mike Frankovitch; Directors, Fred C. Brannon and Thomas Carr; Screenplay, Franklin Adreon, Basil Dickey, Jesse Duffy and Sol Shor; Photography, John MacBurnie; Music, Mort Glickman; Editors, Cliff Bell and Sam Starr

Clayton Moore (Jesse James); Linda Stirling (Ann); John Compton (Steve); Roy Barcroft (Lawton); Tristram Coffin (Clark); Tom London (Bolton); Holly Bane (Tim); Edmund Cobb (Wilkie); Gene Stutenroth (The Sheriff); Fred Graham (Hawks); LeRoy Mason (Finlay); Edward Cassidy (Captain Flint); Tom Steele (Goff); Dale Van Sickel (Brock)

EPISODES: The Black Raiders; Signal for Action; The Stacked Deck; Concealed Evidence; The Corpse of Jesse James; The Traitor; Talk or Die; Boomerang; The Captured Raider; The Revealing Truth; The Spy; Black Gold; Deadline at Midnight

ADVENTURES OF FRANK AND JESSE JAMES, *Republic Pictures*, released July 1948 13 episode serial

Associate producer, Franklin Adreon; Directors, Fred C. Brannon and Yakima Canutt; Screenplay, Franklin Adreon, Basil Dickey and Sol Shor; Photography, John MacBurnie; Music, Morton Scott; Editors, Cliff Bell and Sam Starr

Clayton Moore (Jesse James); Steve Darrell (Frank James); Noel Neill (Judy Powell); George J. Lewis (Rafe Henley); Stanley Andrews (Powell); John Crawford (Amos Ramsey); Sam Flint (Thatcher); House Peters, Jr. (Sheriff Towey); Dale Van Sickel (Dale); Tom Steele (Steele); James Dale (Nichols); I. Stanford Jolley (Ward); Gene Stutenroth (Marshal); Lane Bradford (Bill); George Chesebro (Station Agent); Jack Kirk (Stage Driver)

EPISODES: Agent of Treachery; The Hidden Witness; The Lost Tunnel; Blades of Death; Roaring Wheels; Passage to Danger; The Secret Code; Doomed Cargo; The Eyes of the Law; The Stolen Body; Suspicion, Talk or Die; Unmasked

I SHOT JESSE JAMES, *Lippert Pictures*, released February 1949

Executive producer, Robert L. Lippert; Produced by Carl K. Hittleman; Written and directed by Samuel Fuller, based on an article by Homer Croy; Photography, Ernest W. Miller and Archie Dalzell; Art director, Frank Hotaling; Set decorators, John McCarthy and James Redd; Music, Albert Glasser; Editor, Paul Landres

Reed Hadley (Jesse James); John Ireland (Bob Ford); Preston Foster (John Kelley); Barbara Britton (Cynthy Waters); Barbara Woodell (Zee James); Tom Tyler (Frank James); Tom Noonan (Charles Ford); J. Edward Bromberg (Harry

Lane); Victor Killian (Soapy); Byron Foulger (Room Clerk); Eddie Dunn (Bartender); Margia Dean (Barroom Singer); Gene Collins (Gunslinger); Jeni Le Gon (Maid); Phil Pine (Man in Saloon); Robin Short (Troubadour); Chuck Robertson (Jesse James' Double)

THE JAMES BROTHERS OF MISSOURI, *Republic Pictures*, released October 1949
12 episode serial
Associate producer, Franklin Adreon; Director, Fred C. Brannon; Screenplay, Royal Cole, William Lively and Sol Shor: Photography, Ellis W. Carter; Art director, Fred A. Ritter; Set decorators, John McCarthy, Jr., and James Redd; Music, Stanley Wilson; Special effects, Howard and Theodore Lydecker; Editors, Cliff Bell and Sam Starr

Keith Richards (Jesse James); Robert Bice (Frank James); Noel Neill (Peggy Sawyer); Roy Barcroft (Ace); Patricia Knox (Belle); Lane Bradford (Monk); Eugene Roth (Marshal Rand); John Hamilton (Lon); Edmund Cobb (Sheriff); Hank Patterson (Dufy); Dale Van Sickel (Martin); Tom Steele (Slim); Lee Roberts (Knox); Frank O'Connor (Citizen); Marshall Reed (Dutch); Wade Ray (Deputy Sheriff); Nolan Leary (Pop Keever)

EPISODES: Frontier Renegades; Racing Peril; Danger Road; Murder at Midnight; Road to Oblivion; Missouri Manhunt; Hangman's Noose; Coffin on Wheels; Dean Man's Return; Galloping Gunslingers; The Haunting Past; Fugitive Code

GUNFIRE, *Lippert Pictures*, released July 1950
Executive producer, Robert L. Lippert; Produced and directed by William Berke; Screenplay, Victor West and William Berke; Photography, Ernest W. Miller; Music Director, Albert Glasser; Editor, Carl Pierson

Don Barry (Frank James); Robert Lowery (Kelly); Pamela Blake (Cynthy); Wally Vernon (Clem); Paul Jordan (James' Son); Roger Anderson (Bob Ford); Barbara Wendell (Mrs. James); Gaylord Pendleton (Charlie Ford); Steve Conti (Riley); Claude Stroud (Mundy); Leonard Penn (Simons); Tommy Farrell (Lerner); Kathleen Magrinetti (James' Daughter); Gil Folliman (Bank President); Dean Reisner (Cashier); Bill Bailey (Officer); Jane Adrian (Flo)

THE RETURN OF JESSE JAMES, *Lippert Pictures*, released August 1950
Executive producer, Robert L. Lippert; Produced by Carl K. Hittleman; Director, Arthur David Hilton; Screenplay, Jack Nattleford, based on a story by Carl K. Hittleman; Photography, Karl Struss; Art director, F. Paul Sylos; Music Director, Albert Glasser; Editor, Harry Croswick

John Ireland (Johnny); Ann Dvorak (Sue Younger); Reed Hadley (Frank James); Hugh O'Brian (Lem); Henry Hull (Hank Younger); Clifton Young (Bob Ford); Margia Dean (Margie); Victor Killian (Rigby); Byron Foulger (Bakin); Tom Noonan (Charlie Ford)

FRANK JAMES RIDES AGAIN, *Lippert Pictures*, released September 1950
Executive producer, Robert L. Lippert; Produced and directed by William Berke; Screenplay, Victor West and William Berke; Photography, Ernest W. Miller; Art director, Fred W. Preble; Music Director, Albert Glasser; Editor, Carl Pierson

Don Barry (Fenton/Frank James); Robert Lowery (Kelly); Pamela Blake (Cynthy); Wally Vernon (Clem); Claude Stroud (Mundy); Leonard Penn (Simonds)

THE GREAT MISSOURI RAID, *Paramount Pictures*, released December 1950

Produced by Nat Holt; Director, Gordon Douglas; Screenplay, Frank Gruber; Photography, Ray Rennahan; Art director, John Goodman; Music, Paul Sawtell; Editor, Philip Martin

Macdonald Carey (Jesse James); Wendell Corey (Frank James); Ellen Drew (Bee Moore); Anne Revere (Mrs. Samuels); Ward Bond (Major Trowbridge); Bruce Bennett (Cole Younger); Bill Williams (Jim Younger); Edgar Buchanan (Dr. Samuels); Louis Jean Heydt (Charlie Ford); Whit Bissell (Bob Ford); Lois Chartrand (Mary Bauer); Barry Kelley (Mr. Bauer); James Millican (Sgt. Trowbridge); Paul Lees (Bob Younger); Guy Wilkerson (Clell Miller); Ethan Laidlaw (Jim Cummings); Tom Tyler (Allen Parmer); Steve Pendleton (Arch Clements)

KANSAS RAIDERS, *Universal-International*, released December 1950
Produced by Ted Richmond; Director, Ray Enright; Screenplay, Robert L. Richards; Photography, Irving Glassberg; Art directors, Bernard Herzbrun and Emrich Nicholson; Music, Joseph Gershenson; Editor, Milton Carruth

Audie Murphy (Jesse James); Richard Long (Frank James); Brian Donlevy (Quantrill); Scott Brady (Bill Anderson); Marguerite Chapman (Kate Clarke); Anthony [Tony] Curtis (Kit Dalton); James Best (Cole Younger); Dewey Martin (Jim Younger); Richard Arlen (Union Captain); George Chandler (Willie); John Kellogg (Red Leg Leader); Charles Delaney (Pell); David Wolfe (Tate); Richard Egan (First Lieutenant); Sam Flint (Bank President); Mira McKinney (Woman); Buddy Roosevelt (Another Red Leg); Larry McGrath (Man in Crowd); Ed Peil, Sr. (Bank Teller)

BEST OF THE BADMEN, *RKO Pictures*, released June 1951
Produced Herman Sclom; Director, William D. Russell; Screenplay, John Twist and Robert Hardy Andrews, based on a story by Andrews; Photography, Edward Cronjager; Art directors, Albert S. D'Agostino and Carroll Clark; Music, Paul Sawtell; Music director, C. Bakaleinikoff; Editor, Desmond Marquette

Robert Ryan (Jeff Clanton); Claire Trevor (Lily Fowler); Robert Preston (Matthew Fowler); Jack Buetel (Bob Younger); Lawrence Tierney (Jesse James); Tom Tyler (Frank James); Walter Brennan ("Doc" Butcher); Bruce Cabot (Cole Younger); John Archer (John Younger); Barton MacLane (Joad); Bob Wilke (Jim Younger); John Cliff (John Younger); Lee MacGregor (Lieutenant); Carleton Young (Wilson); Byron Foulger (Judge); Emmett Lynn (Oscar); Larry Johns (Jury Foreman); William Tannen (Adjutant); Harry Woods (Trading Post Proprietor); Everett Glass (Doctor); David McMahon (Perk); Ed Max (Hawkins)

THE GREAT JESSE JAMES RAID, *Lippert Pictures*, July 1953
Produced by Robert L. Lippert, Jr.; Director, Reginald Le Borg; Screenplay, Richard Mandau; Photography, Gilbert Warrenton; Art director, George Van Marter; Music, Bert Shefter; Editor, Carl Pierson

Willard Parker (Jesse James); Barbara Payton (Kate); Tom Neal (Arch Clements); Wallace Ford (Elias Hobbs); Jim Bannon (Bob Ford); Richard Cutting (Sam Wells); James Anderson (Jorette); Barbara Woodall (Zee James); Mary Treen (Mrs. Angus); Earl Hodgins (Soapy Smith); Tom Walker (Jesse James, as a youth); Rory Mallinson (Cavalry Officer); Ed Russell (Sheriff); Joann Arnold (Brunette); Helene Hayden (Redhead); Steve Pendleton (Todd); Bob Griffin (Morgan); Robin Morse (Anderson)

THE WOMAN THEY ALMOST LYNCHED, Republic Pictures, released March 1953
Associate producer/director, Allan Dwan; Screenplay, Steve Fisher, based on a *Saturday Evening Post* story by Michael Fessier; Photography, Reggie Lanning; Art director, James Sullivan; Set decorators, John McCarthy, Jr., and George Milo; Costumes, Adele Palmer; Music, Stanley Wilson; Songs, "How Strange" by Victor Young and Peggy Lee, "All My Life" by Sidney Mitchell and Sam Stept; Special effects, Howard and Theodore Lydecker; Editor, Fred Allen

John Lund (Lance Horton); Audrey Totter (Kate McCoy Quantrill); Brian Donlevy (Charles Quantrill); Joan Leslie (Sally Maris); Reed Hadley (Bitterroot Bill Maris); Ben Cooper (Jesse James); James Brown (Frank James); Jim Davis (Cole Younger); Ann Savage (Glenda); Minerva Urecal (Mrs. Stuart); Virginia Christine (Jenny); Nina Varela (Delilah Courtney); Marilyn Lindsey (Rose); Nacho Galiade (John Pablo); Richard Simmons (Captain); Gordon James (Sergeant); Frank Ferguson (Bartender); Post Park (Driver); Tom McDonough (Quantrill's Henchman); and Ted Ryan, Richard Crane, Carl Pitti, Joe Yrigoyen, Jimmie Hawkins, James Kirkwood, Paul Livermore, Hal Baylor, Ellen Corby, Fern Hall

JESSE JAMES VS. THE DALTONS, Columbia Pictures, released February 1954
Produced by Sam Katzman; Director, William Castle; Screenplay, Robert E. Kent, based on a story by Edwin Westrate, adapted by Samuel Neuman; Photography, Lester H. White; Art director, Paul Palmentola; Music director, Mischa Bakaleinikoff; Editor, Viola Lawrence

Brett King (Joe Branch); Barbara Lawrence (Kate Manning); James Griffith (Bob Dalton); Bill Phipps (Bill Dalton); John Cliff (Grat Dalton); William Tannen (Emmett Dalton); Rory Mallinson (Bob Ford); Richard Garland (Gilkie); Nelson Leigh (Father Kerrigan); Raymond Largary (Corey Sayles)

JESSE JAMES' WOMEN, United Artists, released September 1954
A Panorma Picture; Produced by Lloyd Royal and T. V. Garraway; Director Donald Barry; Screenplay, D. D. Beauchamp; Photography, Ken Peach; Music, Walter Greene; Songs "Careless Lover" by George Antheil, "In the Shadows of My Heart" by Stan Jones; Editor, Burton E. Hayes

Don Barry (Jesse James); Jack Buetel (Frank James); Peggie Castle (Waco Gans); Lita Baron (Delta); Joyce Rhed (Caprice Clark); Betty Brueck (Cattle Kate Kennedy); Laura Lee (Angel Botts); Sam Keller (Cole Younger)

OUTLAW TREASURE, New Realm Pictures, released 1955 (filmed in 1952)
A Favorite Film production, presented by Evelyn L. Wheeler; Written and produced by John Carpenter; Director, Oliver Drake; Photography, Clark Ramsey; Music, Darrell Calker; Editor, J. Ogilvie

John Forbes [John Carpenter](Dan Parker); Adele Jergens (Rita); Glenn Langan (Lieutenant); Michael Whalen (Major); Frank "Red" Carpenter (Jesse James); Hal Baylor (Frank James)

THE TRUE STORY OF JESSE JAMES, 20th Century-Fox, released February 1957
Produced by Herbert B. Swope, Jr.; Director, Nicholas Ray; Screenplay, Walter Newman; based on a 1939 screenplay by Nunnally Johnson and historical data assembled by Rosalline Schaeffer and Jo Frances James; Photography, Joe MacDonald; Costumes, Mary Wills; Music, Leigh Harline; Music director, Lionel Newman; Special effects, Ray Kellogg; Editor, Robert Simpson

Robert Wagner (Jesse James); Jeffrey Hunter (Frank James); Hope Lange (Zee

James); Agnes Moorehead (Mrs. Samuels); John Carradine (Reverend Jethro Bailey); Alan Hale, Jr. (Cole Younger); Biff Elliot (Jim Younger); Anthony Ray (Bob Younger); Alan Baxter (Remington); Barney Phillips (Mr. Samuels); Rachel Stephens (Anne); Frank Overton (Major Cobb); Marian Seldes (Rowena Cobb); Frank Gorshin (Charley Ford); Carl Thayler (Robby); Barry Atwater (Attorney Walker); Chubby Johnson (Askew); John Doucette (Hillstrom); Robert Adler (Sheriff Trump); Clancy Cooper (Sheriff Yee); Sumner Williams (Bill Stiles); Tom Greenway (Deputy Leo); Aaron Saxon (Wiley); Mike Steen (Deputy Ed); Jason Wingreen (Peter); Clegg Hoyt (Tucker Bassham); Tom Pittman (Houghie); Louis Zito (Clell Miller); Mark Hickman (Sam Wells); Adam Marshal (Dick Liddell); Joseph Di Reda (Bill Ryan); Frederik Albeck (Jorgenson); Kellogg Junge, Jr. (Archie, age four)

ALIAS JESSE JAMES, *United Artists*, released March 1959
A Hope Enterprises Production; Executive producer, Bob Hope; Producer, Jack Hope; Director, Norman Z. McLeod; Screenplay, William Bowers and D. D. Beauchamp, based on a story by Robert St. Aubrey and Jack Lawrence; Photography, Lionel Linden; Art directors, Hal Pereira and Roland Anderson; Set decorators, Sam Comer and Bertram Granger; Costumes, Edith Head; Music arranged and conducted by Joseph J. Lilley; Songs, "Ain't A-Hankerin'" and "Protection" by Arthur Altman (music) and Bud Burtson (lyrics), Title theme by Marilyn and Joe Hooven (music) and Dunham (lyrics); Special effects, John P. Fulton; Editors, Marvin Coil and Jack Bachom

Bob Hope (Milford Farnsworth); Rhonda Fleming (The Duchess); Wendell Corey (Jesse James); Jim Davis (Frank James); Will Wright (Titus Queasley); Mary Young (Ma James); Gloria Talbot (Indian Maiden); Sid Melton (Fight Fan); James Burke (Bartender Charlie); George E. Stone (Gibson Girl Fan); Joe Vitale (Sam Hiawatha); Lyle Latell (Conductor); Mike Ross (Killer); Emory Parnell (Sheriff); Stan Jolley (Conductor); Dick Alexander (Jeremiah Cole); Oliver Blake (Undertaker); Jack Lambert (Snake Brice); J. Anthony Hughes (Dirty Dog Saloon Keeper); Iron Eyes Cody (Indian); Harry Tyler (Stationmaster Elmo); Mike Mazurki, Mickey Finn (Toughs); Nestor Paiva (Bixby); Ethan Laidlow, Glenn Strange (Henchmen); *Special Guest Appearances*: Bing Crosby, Gene Autry, Roy Rogers, Gary Cooper (Themselves); Hugh O'Brian (Wyatt Earp); James Arness (Matt Dillon); Fess Parker (Davy Crockett); Gail Davis (Annie Oakley); James Garner (Bret Maverick); Ward Bond (Majors Seth Adams); Jay Silverheels (Tonto)

YOUNG JESSE JAMES, *20th Century-Fox*, released August 1960
An Associated Producers Production; Producer, Jack Leewood; Director, William Claxton; Screenplay, Orville H. Hampton and Jerry Sackheim; Photography, Carl Berger; Art directors, Lyle R. Wheeler and John Mansbridge; Music, Irving Gertz; Title song by Irving Gertz and Hal Levy; Sung by Johnny O'Neill; Editor, Richard C. Meyer

Ray Sticklyn (Jesse James); Willard Parker (Cole Younger); Merry Anders (Belle Starr); Robert Dix (Frank James); Emile Meyer (Quantrill); Jacklyn O'Donnell (Zerelda); Bob Palmer (Bob Younger); Johnny O'Neill (Jim Younger); Sheila Bromley (Mrs. Samuels); Rayford Barnes (Pitts); Rex Holman (Zack); Leslie Bradley (Major Turnbull); Norman Leavitt (Folsom); Lee Kendall (Jennison); Tyler McVey (Banker); Britt Lomond (Federal Lieutenant)

JESSE JAMES MEETS FRANKENSTEIN'S DAUGHTER, *Embassy Pictures*, released 1965

Produced by Circle Productions; Producer, Carroll Case; Director, William Beaudine; Story and screenplay, Carl H. Hittleman; Photography, Lothrop Worth; Art director, Paul Sylos; Set decorator, Harry Reiff; Music, Raoul Kraushaar; Makeup, Ted Coodley; Editors, William Austin and Roy Livingston

John Lupton (Jesse James); Cal Bolder (Hank Tracy); Estelita (Juanita); Narda Onyx (Maria Frankenstein); Steven Geray (Rudolph Frankenstein); Raymond Barnes (Lonny); Jim Davis (Marshal McFee); Rosa Turich (Nina); William Faucett (Pharmacist Jensen); Felipe Turich (Manuel); Page Slattery, Nestor Paiva, Dan White, Roger Creed, Fred Stromsoe, Mark Norton (Men)

A TIME FOR DYING, *Etoile Distribution Release*, released September 1971 (filmed in 1964)

A Fipco (Audie Murphy) Production; Written and directed by Budd Boetticher; Photography, Lucien Ballard; Art director, Les Thomas; Music: Harry Betts; Editor, Harry Knapp

Richard Lapp (Cash); Anne Randall (Nellie); Audie Murphy (Jesse James); Victor Jory (Judge Roy Bean); Beatrice Kay (Mamie); Bob Random (Billy); Peter Brocco (Ed); Burt Mustin (Seth)

THE GREAT NORTHFIELD, MINNESOTA RAID, *Universal Pictures*, released April 1972

Produced by Jennings Lang and Robertson and Associates; Associate producer, Bruce Graham; Written and directed by Philip Kaufman; Photography, Bruce Surtees; Art directors, Alexander Golitzen and George Webb; Set decorator, Hal Gausman; Costumes, Helen Colvig; Music, Dave Grusin; Production manager, Harker Wade; Editor, Douglas Stewart

Robert Duvall (Jesse James); Cliff Robertson (Cole Younger); Luke Askew (Jim Younger); Matt Clark (Bob Younger); John Pearce (Frank James); R. G. Armstrong (Clell Miller); Elisha Cook, Jr. (Bunker); Dana Elcar (Allen); Donald Moffat (Manning); Royal Dano (Gustavson); Mary-Robin Redd (Kate); Wayne Sutherlin (Charley Pitts); Robert H. Harris (Wilcox); Jack Manning (Heywood); Arthur Peterson (Jefferson Jones); Liam Dunn (Drummer); Erik Holland (Sheriff); Marjorie Durant (Maybelle); Madeleine Taylor Holmes (Granny); Herbert Nelson (Chief Detective); Anne Barton (Clell's Wife); Valda J. Hansen (Nude Girl); Inger Stratton (Singing Whore); Bill Callaway (Calliopist); Craig Curtis (Chadwell); Barry Brown (Henry Wheeler); Nellie Burt (Doll Woman); Robert Gravange (Farmer); William Challee (Old Timer)

BUFFALO BILL AND THE INDIANS; OR, SITTING BULL'S HISTORY LESSON,* *United Artists*, released July 1976

A Dino De Laurentiis Production in association with Lion's Gate Films, Talent Associates, and Norton Simon; Executive producer, David Susskind; Produced and directed by Robert Altman; Screenplay, Alan Rudolph and Robert Altman, suggested by the play *Indians* by Arthur Kopit; Photography, Paul Lohmann; Production designer, Tony Masters; Set decorators, Dennis J. Parrish, Graham Sumner; Costumes, Anthony Powell; Makeup, Monty Westmore; Music, Richard Baskin; Editors, Peter Appleton and Dennis Hill

Paul Newman (Buffalo Bill Cody); Burt Lancaster (Ned Buntline); Geraldine Chaplin (Annie Oakley); Joel Grey (Nate Salsbury); Kevin McCarthy (Major John

Burke); Harvey Keitel (Ed Goodman); John Considine (Frank Butler); Allan Nichols (Prentiss Ingraham); Frank Kaquits (Sitting Bull); Will Sampson (William Halsey); Robert DoQui (Osborne Dart); Denver Pyle (McLaughlin); Bert Remsen (Crutch); Pat McCormick (President Grover Cleveland); Shelley Duvall (Frances Folsom); Mike Kaplan (Jules Keen); Bonnie Leaders (Margaret); Noelle Rogers (Lucille Du Charmes); Evelyn Lear (Nina Cavalini); Ken Krossa (Johnny Baker); Fred N. Larsen (Buck Taylor); Humphrey Gratz (Old Soldier)

* This screen adaptation of the Kopit play bears little resemblance to the stage production. The character of Jesse James has been eliminated, as have others, and it is chronicled here only for the record.

THE LONG RIDERS, *United Artists*, released August 1980

Produced by Huka Films; Executive producers, James Keach and Stacy Keach; Producer, Tim Zinnemann; Director, Walter Hill; Screenplay, Bill Bryden, Steven Phillip Smith, Stacy Keach and James Keach; Photography, Ric Waite; Production designer, Jack Collis; Set decorator, Richard Goddard; Costumes, Bobbie Mannix, Tom Bronson, Marie Brown and Dan Moore; Makeup, Michael Germain; Music, Ry Cooder; Choreography, Katina Savvidis; Editors, David Holden and Freeman Davies

James Keach (Jesse James); Stacy Keach (Frank James); David Carradine (Cole Younger); Keith Carradine (Jim Younger); Robert Carradine Bob Younger); Dennis Quaid (Ed Miller); Randy Quaid (Clell Miller); Christopher Guest (Charlie Ford); Nicholas Guest (Bob Ford); Harry Carey, Jr. (George Arthur); Pamela Reed (Belle Starr); James Remar (Sam Starr); Fran Ryan (Mrs. Samuels); Savannah Smith (Zee James); Shelby Levington (Annie Ralston); Kevin Brophy (John Younger); Felice Orlandi (Mr. Reddick); James Whitmore, Jr. (Mr. Rixley); Amy Stryker (Beth Mimms); John Bottoms (Mortician); West Buchanan (McCorkindale); Edward Bunker (Chadwell); Martina Deignan (Shirley Biggs); Allan Graf (Bank Customer); Chris Mulkey (Veron Biggs); Thomas R. Myers (Gallatin Bank Cashier); Marlise Pieratt (Wilhelmina); Glenn Robards (Doctor); Tim Rossovich (Pitts); Lin Shaye (Kate); Gary Wilkins (Bank Teller Heywood); Peter Jason, Steve Chambers, Duke Storud, William Traylor (The Pinkertons); Prentiss Rowe (Sheriff Rowe); Stuart Mossman (Engineer); Michael Lackey (Gustavson); Mitch Greenhill (Guitarist); Bill Bryson (Banjo Player); Tom Stauber (Fiddle Player); Hugh McGraw (Singer); J. Don Ferguson (Preacher); Jimmy Medearis (Farmer); Edgar McLeod (Photographer); Luis Contreras (Man at Bar); Kalen Keach (Little Jesse); R. B. Thrift (Archie)

TELEVISION

YOU ARE THERE: THE CAPTURE OF JESSE JAMES, televised February 8, 1953 CBS 30 minutes

Producer, Charles W. Russell; Director, Sidney Lumet; Host, Walter Cronkite

James Dean (Jesse James)

FRANK AND JESSE JAMES, episode of *Stories of the Century*, syndicated 1954

Producer, Rudy Ralston

Jim Davis (Matt Clark); Mary Castle (Frankie Adams); Lee Van Cleef (Jesse James)

THE LEGEND OF JESSE JAMES, televised September 13, 1965 to September 5, 1966 ABC 34 episodes (30 minutes each)

Produced by 20th Century-Fox Television; Producer, Don Siegel; Director, James Clark; Teleplay, Anthony Spinner, others; Music: Joseph Hooven

Christopher Jones (Jesse James); Allen Case (Frank James); Ann Doran (Ma James); Robert J. Wilke (Marshal Sam Corbett); John Milford (Cole Younger); Tim McIntire (Bob Younger); David Richards (Jim Younger); with guest stars including George Kennedy, Jack Elam, Victor Jory, Mariette Hartley, Kevin McCarthy, Ann Sothern, Tom Tully, Marie Windsor, Mickey Shaughnessy, Nehemiah Persoff, John Carradine, Gary Lockwood, Charles Bronson, Strother Martin, Joseph Wiseman, Susan Strasberg, Dennis Hopper, John Cassavetes, Michael Anderson, Jr., John Mitchum, Lyle Talbot, John Marley, Harry Carey, Jr., Gene Evans, Lloyd Bochner, Mike Mazurki, Slim Pickens

EPISODES: Three Men From Now; The Dead Man's Hand; Put Me in Touch With Jesus; The Pursuers; The Raiders; Vendetta; The Quest; The Judas Root; Jail Break; One Too Many Mornings; Manhunt; The Celebrity; The Man Who Was; The Widow Fay; The Man Who Killed Jesse; The Empty Town; The Reunion; The Colt; A Real Tough Town; Return to Lawrence; The Cave; South Wind; The Lonely Place; James' Raid; The Chase; Things Just Don't Happen; As Far As the Seas; 1863; The Last Stand of Captain Hummel; The Hunted and the Hunters; Dark Side of the Moon; A Field of Wild Flowers; Wanted: Dead or Alive; A Burying for Rosey

THE LAST RIDE OF THE DALTON GANG, televised November 20, 1979 NBC 3 hours*

Dan Curtis Productions; Executive producer/directror, Dan Curtis; Producer, Joseph Stern; Teleplay, Earl W. Wallace; Photography, Frank Stanley; Art director, Ned Parsons; Music, Bob Cobert; Editor, Dennis Virkler

Cliff Potts (Bob Dalton); Randy Quaid (Grat Dalton); Larry Wilcox (Emmet Dalton); Royal Dano (Pa Dalton); Mills Watson (Bill Dalton); Harris Yulin (Jesse James); Jack Palance (Will Smith); Sharon Farrell (Flo Quick); Dale Robertson (Judge Isaac Parker); Julie Hill (Julie Williams); Matt Clark (Bitter Creek/George Newcombe); John Karlen (Charlie Powers); Elliott Street (Potts); Bo Hopkins (Bill Doolin); Don Collier (Frank Dalton); James Crittendon (Hugh McElhennie); Terry Kiser (Nafius); John Fitzpatrick (Texas Jack Broadwell); Dennis Fimple (Blackface/Charlie Bright); Eric Lawson (Willie Powers); R. G. Armstrong (Leland Stanford); Kathleen Freeman (Ma Dalton); Harry Townes (Reverend Johnson); Jorge Moreno (Archulleta); Larry Block (Leroy Keenan); Buff Brady (Buffalo Bill); Allen Williams (Preacher); Scott Brady, H. M. Wynant, Jack Collins, Robert Karnes, Sid Conrad (Card Players); Orin Cannon (Bartender); Dean Smith (Deputy); Tony Palmer (Stationmaster); Mitch Carter (Gunfighter); John Calvin (Cop)

* Originally made as *Raid on Coffeyville*, a four-hour film edited before its premiere showing to three hours.

BELLE STARR, televised April 2, 1980 CBS 2 hours

Produced by Hanna-Barbera Productions/Entheos Unlimited Productions; Executive Producers, Barry Krost and Joseph Barbera; Producer, Doug Chapin; Directed and photographed by John A. Alonzo; Teleplay, James Lee Barrett; Art director, Robert Kinoshita; Music, Dana Kaproff; Editor, David Garfield

Elizabeth Montgomery (Belle Starr); Cliff Potts (Cole Younger); Michael Cavanaugh (Jesse James); Jesse Vint (Bob Dalton); Alan Vint (Grat Dalton); Gary Combs (Frank James); Fred Ward (Ned Christie); Geoffrey Lewis (Reverend Weeks); Michelle Stacy (Pearl Younger); Peter Hobbs (Jenkins);

Sandy McPeak (Pratt); David Knell (Ed Reed); Geno Silva (Blue Duck); Morgan Paull (Latham); Sarah Cunningham (Mrs. Chandler); Burt Edwards (Bank Manager); Stony Bower (Summerville); James Burke (Fuller); Dee Cooper (Morris); Gilbert Combs (Baggage Clerk); Kate Williams (Woman); John Edwards (Stockyard Clerk)

THE LAST DAYS OF FRANK AND JESSE JAMES, televised February 16, 1986 NBC 2 hours
A Joseph Cates Company Production; Executive producer, Joseph Cates; Producer, Philip Cates; Director, William A. Graham; Teleplay, William Stratton; Photography, Tony Imi; Production designer, David Gropman; Costume designer, Faye Sloane; Music, Paul Chihara; Song "The Legend of Jesse James" sung by Johnny Cash; Editor, Patrick McMahon

Kris Kristofferson (Jesse James); Johnny Cash (Frank James); Willie Nelson (General Jo Shelby); June Carter Cash (Mother James); Ed Bruce (Major Edwards); Darrel Wilks (Bob Ford); Gail Youngs (Anna James); Margaret Gibson (Zee James); David Allan Coe (Whiskeyhead Ryan); Marcia Cross (Sarah Hite); Andrew Stahl (Dick Liddel); James Sinclair (Charlie Ford); Cherie Elledge Grapes (Martha Bolton); Peter Bradshaw (Wood Hite); Jack Barlow (Uncle George Hite); Mac Bennett (Clarence Hite); John Ramsey (Jake Iglehart); William Newman (Sheriff Timberlake); Buck Ford (William Pinkerton); Ed Evans (Governor Tom Crittendon); Jim McDaniels (Jimmy Little); Earle Poole Bell (Squire Farnum); John Brown (Gentleman); Dan Butler (New York Reporter); Glen Clark (Angry Man); David Cobb (Dr. Samuel); Bruce Darnaham (Sedalia Reporter); Marshall Falwell (Jim Ward); Donnie Fritts (Jury Foreman); Lecille Harris (Bartender); Mary Jane Harrill (Actress); Dan Hoffman (Conductor Westfall); John Jay Hecker, Jr. (John Phillip); G. W. Jones (Colonel Sariston); Irv Kane (John Eulich); Joe Kurtzo (French Joe Duval); Jack Lawrence (Galatin Sheriff); and Slick Lawson, Kal Roberts, Jack Wesley Routh, John Jackson Routh, Rick Schulman, Dennis Tucker, Byron Warner, Charlie Williams

JOURNEY'S END
A Drama by R. C. Sherriff (1928)

Synopsis

After three years on the Western Front during World War I, British Captain Dennis Stanhope turns to the bottle to alleviate the constant death, dirt and destruction in a dugout before St. Quentin. Further increasing his trauma is the arrival of Second Lieutenant James Raleigh, a former schoolmate and brother of his fiancee. Raleigh idolizes Stanhope as a war hero. Stanhope's close friend, former schoolmaster Lieutenant Osborne, reassures Raleigh of Stanhope's abilities and courage, but to cowardly Second Lieutenant Hibbert, adept at avoiding battle by faking illness, Stanhope confesses his own mounting dread. When chosen to lead a raiding party, Osborne calms Raleigh's fear with reminiscences of home and quotations of the Walrus in *Alice in Wonderland*. Osborne is killed, and later, Raleigh is mortally wounded and dies in the dugout. Now alone, Stanhope tries to control his grief and loneliness with liquor as he departs at dawn to face yet another German attack. An enemy shell lands next to the dugout, the timber door props cave in and sandbags block the entrance, and in the flickering candlelight, the first rays of dawn are seen through the rubble.

Comment and Critique

Prior to *Journey's End*, "the most credible of all war plays" had been Maxwell Anderson and Laurence Stalling's 1924 *What Price Glory?* R. C. Sherriff, a thirty-two-year-old insurance broker, was asked to write something for the amateur players of his Kingston Rowing Club. Recalling his World War I experiences during four years in the trenches with the East Surrey Regiment, during which time he rose to Second Lieutenant, Sherriff turned out *Journey's End*. (Robert Cedric Sherriff, born on June 6, 1896, at Kingston-on-Thames, subsequently became a prolific screenwriter of such classics as *The Invisible Man*, *Goodbye, Mr. Chips*, *The Four Feathers*, *Lady Hamilton*, *This Above All* and *Odd Man Out*, among others. He was seventy-nine when he died on November 13, 1975.)

The Incorporated Stage Society and the Three Hundred Club presented Sherriff's play for two performances in December 1928 at London's Apollo Theatre. While considering the play relatively unimportant, a young Laurence Olivier played Stanhope in the tryout of *Journey's End*, looking on the role merely as an audition for the more coveted part in the lead of the forthcoming London production of *Beau Geste* -- a failure when it opened the following month at His Majesty's Theatre and ran a paltry thirty-nine performances.

Journey's End, on the other hand, reopened at the Savoy Theatre on the West End the same week, now with Colin Clive as Stanhope, to become one of London's greatest stage successes. Produced by Maurice Browne and directed by James Whale, it ran 593 performances. Several road companies toured the provinces in Sherriff's war drama, which subsequently was translated into more than two dozen languages. In March 1929, Maurice Browne and Gilbert Miller staged another production of it at the Arts Theatre in London, transporting it to Broadway later that month. It played in New York for 485 performances.

Reviewing the Savoy Theatre production in London, James Challoner wrote in *The Bystander*, "Were there such a decoration as the theatrical V. C. it should have been pinned to the breast of R. C. Sherriff, the author, [and] Maurice Browne, the actor-manager; the one for writing and the other for staging this play... Our young dramatist merely gives us a series of incidents which go to make up a picture of life in the trenches and the effect of that life on various individuals. Yet so vivid, and so instinct with truth, is the picture, that throughout the evening, one's attention is gripped as in a vice....A picture of war, beautifully composed and beautifully painted by a sincere and brilliant artist. That is *Journey's End* by R. C. Sherriff."

Arthur Hornblow (*Theatre* Magazine) raved about the New York production: "*Journey's End* has come to be one of the genuine sensations of the current dramatic season, and logically so, for it is not alone the best drama that has sprung out of the World War, but one of the sincerest efforts in playwriting given to the stage in decades...The emotional power of the piece is tremendous...Mr. Sherriff shows his consummate artistry, his sense of proportion, the nice balance of what seems to be an occasional and very natural outburst of humor with the sense of impending disaster." Hornblow also compared the "decency of its dialogue" with the "deluge of profanity and obscenity" heard in *What Price Glory?*

Time magazine extolled the virtues of *Journey's End*: "It deals with elemental emotions, this play, with a simplicity that is devastating. It is as fine a series of psychological studies as one will find outside a casebook. And it has the added benefit of perfect interpretation. *The New Yorker* reported: "*Journey's End* is not only about war but is a singularly beautiful play. The war it reveals is a gentleman's war in contradistinction to the profane scrap of *What Price Glory?*"

When *Journey's End* was revived for a limited Broadway run in 1939 on the brink of another war, critic John Mason Brown wrote in *The Evening Post*: "The play remains one of the most poignant of our theatrical experience...[It] was for us almost unbearable in its heartbreak." But the poorly directed revival went generally unpraised except for the return of Colin Keith-Johnston in his original role of Stanhope. *Time* magazine found it "much less remarkable than when first produced here ten years ago...[but] on its picture of people afraid of being afraid, *Journey's End* has at times a bat-like psychological terror more harrowing than the physical horror of an *All Quiet on the Western Front*."

The New York Times' Brooks Atkinson found: "*Jour-ney's End* is an honest play about a real subject, but, like nearly everything else that is written and said today, it is inadequate in the face of the current emergency." He added "No one can remain wholly indifferent to a sincere and ably written play about men risking their lives under orders."

New York's Roundabout Theatre remounted *Journey's End* almost thirty years later. Jerry Talmer (*New York Post*) reported: "I thank director Gene Feist for this revival, and for the great daring of attempting it with a young cast of American actors...Sterling Jensen is by far the most sure as Lieutenant Osborne." In *The New York Times*, Dan Sullivan viewed this Roundabout revival this way: "Unfortunately, the all-male cast, as directed by Gene Feist, contribute a good deal less... all the energy of its members goes toward convincing us (which it doesn't) that they are British. What gets lost is how it felt to be a soldier 50 years ago...But the expressionist method simply does not fit Mr. Sherriff's tender-tough realism."

London's Mermaid Theatre production of Sherriff's play in 1972 featured Peter Egan as Captain Stanhope. John Russell Taylor (*Plays and Players*) considered that the revival succeeded in overcoming that "thin but very definite line to be drawn between the period and the dated...To that extent, the play is clearly period rather than dated. With whatever minor reservations, it still enforces a serious hearing for itself."

London critic Bernard Weinraub wrote: "The evening of January 21, 1929, remains a landmark in British theatrical history. *Journey's End*, a World War I drama by an unknown 32-year-old insurance clerk, R. C. Sherriff, opened at the old Savoy Theatre to 19 curtain calls...The play became a success in New York, a Hollywood film, and was translated into 27 languages. Now, quite suddenly and quietly, Journey's End has returned to London at the Mermaid Theatre. If there were any misgivings before the recent opening about the play's relevance, its stiff-upper-lip values, its class ethos, its period uniforms and 'jolly decents,' all were swiftly dispelled." *The London Times* termed it "a magnificent revival." And the *Guardian* said, "Sherriff's play is a fascinating document of war, and this production does it justice."

Of the spring 1988 revival at London's Whitehall Theatre, Irving Wardle (*The London Times*) said: "R. C. Sherriff's masterpiece of the 1918 trenches belongs among a small group of plays that are revisited rather than revived. An endless soap opera could be developed from the lives of Captain Stanhope and his brother officers in the St. Quentin dug-out, except that Sherriff packed it all into two and a half hours. In retrospect, *Journey's End* falls into place as a theatrical equivalent of Sassoon's poems; simultaneously an anthem for doomed youth and an unforgiving epitaph for the top brass. But whenever it returns to the stage it opens up a wealth of living detail that cannot be boiled down to any single argument." The Stanhope of this production was Jason Connery, Sean's actor son.

Gainsborough-Tiffany Pictures filmed *Journey's End* and imported Colin Clive to reprise his role of Stanhope. Clive, who in the following year would create the role of Dr. Frankenstein for Universal, was given a six week leave of absence from the London stage production. James Whale, who had directed each British stage production as well as the American ones (and later would direct the film *Frankenstein*), was engaged to oversee the filming of Sherriff's acclaimed play. Clive completed his Hollywood work in *Journey's End* in ten days and return to the London stage production. (Clive died an alcoholic in Hollywood on June 25, 1937, at age thirtyseven.)

"The film version of *Journey's End*," reported *Life* magazine, "is a meticulously faithful reproduction of the successful stage play, for which Heaven and director James Whale (who directed the stage production) be praised...It is one of the finest talkies to date." Frederick James Smith, critic for *Liberty* magazine, wrote, "Tiffany presents one of the finest pictures ever made in *Journey's End*...It is a great picture." *The New Yorker*, on the other hand, preferred the stage version "for the simple reason that, other things being equal, the spectacle of living human beings is more compelling than any picture of them can be."

In 1976, *Journey's End* was remade as a British/ French coproduction with a stellar cast. Now called *Aces High*, and reset from the trenches to an air squadron, it failed to attract much attention. "The most depressing thing about *Aces High* is not so much the wanton butchery performed on *Journey's End* as the crudity with which anti-Establishment and antiwar graffiti borrowed from fashionable models like *If...* and *Oh! What a Lovely War* (film version) have been grafted onto it," wrote British critic Tom Milne in *Monthly Film Bulletin*. "Sherriff's delicate little masterpiece survives only in the relationship between Croft and the aging Sinclair, very well played by Peter Firth and Christopher Plummer. Otherwise, apart from a nice performance by David Wood, the acting ranges from the disastrously overwrought (Malcolm McDowall) to the equally disastrously underwrought (most of the 'guest stars')."

For television, the BBC produced a splendid adaptation of Sherriff's play in 1960 featuring Richard Johnson as Stanhope, reaffirming the author's powerful, well-paced, brilliant character study of men in war. An American production of *Journey's End* was taped for TV in the early 1980s for the *Broadway on Showtime* cable series of dramas, comedies and musicals. Heading the cast were Maxwell Caulfield and Andrew Stevens.

STAGE

JOURNEY'S END, *Apollo Theatre*, London, opened December 9, 1928 2 performances

Presented by the Incorporated Stage Society and the Three Hundred Club; Produced by Maurice Browne; A Drama by R. C. Sherriff; Direction and setting by James Whale; Scenery, Francis Bull; Costumes, Hyman; Special effects, H. H. Martin, Ltd.; Music director, Philip Braham; Stage managers, John Fernald and Madge Whiteman

Laurence Olivier (Captain Dennis Stanhope); Maurice Evans (2nd Lieutenant Raleigh); Melville Cooper (2nd Lieutenant Trotter); Robert Speaight (2nd Lieutenant Hibbert); Percy Walsh (Company Sergeant-Major); H. G. Stoker (Colonel); Alexander Field (Private Mason); David Horne (Captain Hardy); George Zucco (Lieutenant Osborne); Geoffrey Wincott (German Soldier); Richard Caldicott (Lance Corporal Broughton); John Fernald, Leslie Mitchell, J.M.W.E. Curtis, Owen Griffith (Private Soldiers)

Savoy Theatre, London, opened January 21, 1929; transferred to *Prince of Wales's Theatre*, June 3, 1929 593 performances
Produced by Maurice Browne; A Drama by R. C. Sherriff; Direction and setting by James Whale; Scenery, Francis Bull; Costumes, Hyman; Special effects, H. H. Martin, Ltd.; Music, Philip Braham; General manager, Clifford Hamilton; Stage managers, Thomas Warer and Walter Lindsay

Colin Clive (Captain Stanhope); Maurice Evans (2nd Lieutenant Raleigh); Melville Cooper (2nd Lieutenant Trotter); Robert Speaight (2nd Lieutenant Hibbert); Tristan Rawson (Company Sergeant-Major); H. G. Stocker (Colonel); Alexander Field (Private Mason); Reginald Smith (Captain Hardy); George Zucco (Lieutenant Osborne); Geoffrey Wincott (German Soldier); Richard Caldicott (Lance Corporal Broughton); John Curtis, Geoffrey Clarke, Frank Prebble, John Fernald (Private Soldiers)

Arts Theatre, London, opened March 7, 1929 6 performances
Produced by Maurice Browne and Gilbert Miller; A Drama by R. C. Sherriff; Direction and setting by James Whale; Scenery, Francis Bull; Costumes, Hyman; Special effects, H. H. Martin, Ltd.; General manager, Stanley Bell; Stage manager, Herbert Lugg

Colin Keith-Johnson (Captain Stanhope); Derek Williams (2nd Lieutenant Raleigh); Henry Wenman (2nd Lieutenant Trotter); Jack Hawkins (2nd Lieutenant Hibbert); Sidney Seaward (Company Sergeant Major); Geoffrey Clarke (succeeded by Eric Stanley) (Colonel); S. Victor Stanley (Private Mason); Evelyn Roberts (Captain Hardy); Leon Quartermaine (Lieutenant Osborne); Terence de Marney (German Soldier); Kenneth Ware (Lance Corporal Broughton); Fordham Ellis, Victor Hilton, David Pearson (Private Soldiers)

Henry Miller's Theatre, New York, opened March 22, 1929 485 performances
Produced by Gilbert Miller, by arrangement with Maurice Browne; A Drama by R. C. Sherriff; Direction and setting by James Whale; Scenery, Francis Bull; Uniforms, John Hyman of London; Firearms, Bapty & Co. of London; Production manager, Clifford Hamilton; General manager, Lodewick Vroom

Colin Keith-Johnson (Captain Stanhope); Derek Williams (2nd Lieutenant Raleigh); Henry Wenman (2nd Lieutenant Trotter); Jack Hawkins (succeeded by Walter Hudd) (2nd Lieutenant Hibbert); Sidney Seaward (succeeded by Arthur Gilbert) (Company Sergeant Major); Eric Stanley (Colonel); S. Victor Stanley (Private Mason); Evelyn Roberts (succeeded by Colin Hunter) (Captain Hardy); Leon Quartermaine (Lieutenant Osborne); Salo Douday (German Soldier); Kenneth Ware (Lance Corporal Broughton)

National Road Company, season 1929-30
Produced by Gilbert Miller, by arrangement with Maurice Browne; A Drama by R. C. Sherriff; Director, Stanley Bell; Setting, James Whale; Uniforms, Morris Angel of London; Company manager, Samuel L. Tuck; Stage manager, Arthur Stenning

Richard Bird (Captain Stanhope); Frederick Catling (2nd Lieutenant Raleigh); Norman Pierce (2nd Lieutenant Trotter); G. P. Huntley, Jr. (2nd Lieutenant Hibbert); John Parrish (Company Sergeant-Major); George Thorpe (Colonel); Dan Blocker (Private Mason); Robert Noble (Captain Hardy); Henry Stephenson (Lieutenant Osborne); Ben Kranz (German Soldier); Vernon Dowling (Lance Corporal Broughton); Arthur Stenning (Private)

West Coast Company, season 1929-30
Produced by Gilbert Miller, by arrangement with Maurice Browne; A Drama by R. C. Sherriff; Direction and setting by James Whale; Scenery, John F. Gallagher; Uniforms, John Hyman of London; Firearms, Bapty & Co. of London; General manager, Clifford Hamilton; Company manager, Frank Perley; Stage manager, Herbert Lugg

Hugh Williams (Captain Stanhope); Wallace Douglas (2nd Lieutenant Raleigh); Forrester Harvey (2nd Lieutenant Trotter); Walter Hudd (2nd Lieutenant Hibbert); Desmond Roberts (Company Sergeant-Major); Edwin Ellis (Private Mason); Tom Macauley (Captain Hardy); Wellington Briggs (Colonel); Basil Gill (Lieutenant Osborne); Gerrit Kraber (German Soldier); Frank Arundel (Lance Corporal Broughton)

Henry Miller's Theatre, New York, opened August 4, 1930
Produced by Gilbert Miller, by arrangement with Maurice Browne; A Drama by R. C. Sherriff; Direction and setting by James Whale; Scenery, Francis Bull; Uniforms, John Hyman of London; Firearms, Bapty & Co. of London; General manager, Lodewick Vroom

Richard Bird (Captain Stanhope); Maury Tuckerman (2nd Lieutenant Raleigh); Harry Ratcliffe (2nd Lieutenant Trotter); G. P. Huntley, Jr. (2nd Lieutenant Hibbert); John Parrish (Company Sergeant-Major); Fred Monti (Private Mason); Wilfrid Seagram (Captain Hardy); Wilfred Jessop (Colonel); William Sauter (Lieutenant Osborne); Salo Douday (German Solider); Arthur Stenning (Lance Corporal Broughton); Willian Hitch, James Grainger (Soldiers)

Criterion Theatre, London, opened November 27, 1934
A Drama written and directed by R. C. Sherriff

Reginald Tate (Captain Stanhope); Lewis Shaw (2nd Lieutenant Raleigh); Norman Pierce (2nd Lieutenant Trotter); Alexander Archdale (2nd Lieutenant Hibbert); Reginald Smith (Company Sergeant-Major); S. Victor Stanley (Private Mason); David Horne (Captain Hardy); H. G. Stoker (Colonel); Basil Gill (Lieutenant Osborne); Geoffrey Wincott (German Soldier); Owen Griffith (Lance Corporal Broughton)

Empire Theatre, New York, opened September 18, 1939 16 performances
Produced and directed by Leonard Sillman; A Drama by R. C. Sherriff; Setting, Lemuel Ayres; Scenery, Karle O. Amend; Uniforms, Brooks Costume Company; Production manager, Blanche Lederer; Stage manager, Wylie Adams

Colin Keith-Johnson (Captain Stanhope); Jack Merivale (2nd Lieutenant Raleigh); A. P. Kaye (2nd Lieutenant Trotter); Glenn Hunter (2nd Lieutenant Hibbert); Ralph Sumpter (Company Sergeant-Major); Hugh Rennie (Captain Hardy); Victor Beecroft (Private Mason); Richard Temple (Colonel); Reginald Mason (Lieutenant Osborne); Everett Ripley (German Soldier); Philip Huston (Lance Corporal Broughton); Houseley Stevens, Jr. (Bert)

Westminster Theatre, London, opened October 5, 1950
Director, John Gordon Ash; A Drama by R. C. Sherriff

Peter Randall (Captain Stanhope); David Oake (2nd Lieutenant Raleigh); Neil Wilson (2nd Lieutenant Trotter); Gerald Dawtrey (2nd Lieutenant Hibbert); Maxwell Jackson (Company Sergeant-Major); John Gordon Ash (Captain

Hardy); Arthur Lovegrove (Private Mason); Harold Young (Colonel); Kevin Stoney (Lieutenant Osborne); Carl Duering (German Soldier); Edward Hall (Lance Corporal Broughton)

Roundabout Theatre, opened October 4, 1958 32 performances
Produced and directed by Gene Feist; A Drama by R. C. Sherriff; Scenery, Valle Blake; Lighting, Dev Kerman and Dan Stowens; Technical director, Lindsay Romanow; Sound, Michael Czajowski

Gene Galusha (Captain Stanhope); Jon Carlson (2nd Lieutenant Raleigh); David Bates (2nd Lieutenant Trotter); Julian Sulmonetti (2nd Lieutenant Hibbert); Robert Barger (Company Sergeant-Major); Lyle J. Lorenz (Captain Hardy); Gil Pacheco (Private Mason); Sterling Jensen (Lieutenant Osborne); Jerry Norvell (German Soldier); Anthony Reilly (Lance Corporal Broughton); Ray Ascencio (Private)

Mermaid Theatre, London, opened May 18, 1972; transferred to *Cambridge Theatre*, July 20, 1972
Produced by Eddie Kulukundis and Richard Pilbrow; A Drama by R. C. Sherriff; Director, Eric Thompson; Setting, Alan Pickford; Scenery, Watts and Corry; Lighting, Michael O'Flaherty; Costumes, Berman and Nathan; Sound, Ian Gibson; Production managers, John Wallbank and Thomas Elliott; Company and stage manager, Michael Cass Jones

Peter Egan (Captain Stanhope); Christopher Good (2nd Lieutenant Raleigh); Colin Prockter (2nd Lieutenant Trotter); Christopher Timothy (2nd Lieutenant Hibbert); Harry Walker (Company Sergeant-Major); Ivor Danvers (Colonel); Harry Landis (Private Mason); Christopher Hancock (Captain Hardy); James Maxwell (Lieutenant Osborne); Steven Barnes (German Soldier); Jeremy Sinden (Lance Corporal Broughton); John Green (Private)

Long Wharf Theatre, New Haven, opened October 19 through November 19, 1978
Produced by the Long Wharf Theatre, Arvin Brown, artistic director; A Drama by R. C. Sherriff; Director, Kenneth Frankel; Sets, John Conklin; Costumes, Carol Oditz; Lighting, Ronald Wallace

Edward Herrmann (Captain Stanhope); Harry Groener (2nd Lieutenant Raleigh); Douglas Sadler (2nd Lieutenant Trotter); Joel Stedman (2nd Lieutenant Hibbert); Stephen Mendillo (Company Segeant-Major); Emery Battis (Colonel); Nicholas Woodeson (Private Mason); Roger Newman (Captain Hardy); John McMartin (Lieutenant Osborne); William Sadler (German Soldier); Jim Abrams (Lance Corporal Broughton); William Groth (Private)

Whitehall Theatre, London, opened April 19, 1988* 103 performances
Produced and directed by Justin Greene; A Drama by R. C. Sherriff; Designed by Sarah Jane-McClelland; Lighting, Jenny Crane; Sound, Matt McKenzie

Jason Connery (Captain Stanhope); Andrew Castell (2nd Lieutenant Raleigh); Timothy Kightley (2nd Lieutenant Trotter); Alan Barker (2nd Lieutenant Hibbert); Barry Ewart (Company Sergeant-Major); Michael McStay (Colonel); Andrew Latham (Private Mason); Alan Gill (Captain Hardy); Nicky Henson (Lieutenant Osborne); Edward Pinner (German Soldier); Michael Sheldon (Lance Corporal Broughton)

* This production premiered at *Nuffield Theatre*, Southampton, February 23, 1988

SCREEN

JOURNEY'S END, Tiffany Pictures, released April 1930

A Gainsborough Production, George Pierson, supervisor; Director, James Whale; Screenplay, Joseph Moncure March, based on the play by R. C. Sherriff; Photography, Benjamin Kline; Art director, Hervey Libbert; Sound, Buddy Myers; Editor, Claude Berkeley

Colin Clive (Captain Stanhope); David Manners (2nd Lieutenant Raleigh); Billy Bevan (2nd Lieutenant Trotter); Anthony Bushell (2nd Lieutenant Hibbert); Thomas Whitely (Company Seregeant-Major); Jack Mitcairn (Colonel); Charles Gerrard (Private Mason); Robert A'Dair (Captain Hardy); Ian MacLaren (Lieutenant Osborne); Warner Klinger (German Boy); Leslie Sketchley (Corporal Ross)

ACES HIGH, EMI Distributors, released May 1976

Produced by S. Benjamin Fisz Productions (London) and Productions Jacques Roitfeld (Paris); Producer, S. Benjamin Fisz; Director, Jack Gold; Screenplay, Howard Baker, based on *Journey's End* by R. C. Sherriff; Additonal material from *Sagittarius Rising* by Cecil Lewis; Photography, Gerry Fisher; Aerial photography, Peter Allwork; Production designer, Syd Cain; Costumes, Philippe Pickford; Music, Richard Hartley; Music advisor, Charles Chilton; Sound, Ivan Sharrock; Associate producer, Basil Keys; Editor, Anne V. Coates

Malcolm McDowell (Major John Grehsam); Christopher Plummer (Sinclair); Simon Ward (Crawford); Peter Firth (Stephen Croft); Sir John Gielgud (Headmaster); Trevor Howard (Lt. Colonel Silkin); Richard Johnson (Colonel Lyle); Ray Milland (Brigadier Whale); David Wood (Thompson); Barry Jackson (Joyce); David Daker (Bennett); Ron Pember (Eliot); Elliott Cooper (Wade); Tim Piggott-Smith (Stoppard); Jane Anthony (Katherine); Christopher Blake (Roberts); James Walsh (Grehsam's Batman); Pascale Christophe (Croft's French Girlfriend); Jacques Maury (Ponnelle); Gilles Behat (Beckenauer); and Evelyn Cordeau, Judy Buxton, Penny Irving, Tricia Newby, Jeanne Patou, John Serret, Gerard Paquis, Paul Henley, Paul Rosebury, David Arnold, Jean Driant, James Cormack, Ronald Viner, Steven Pacey, Kim Lotis, Colin Rix

TELEVISION

JOURNEY'S END, televised March 6, 1960 BBC 90 minutes

Produced by the British Broadcasting Corporation; Director, John Jacobs; The Play by R. C. Sherriff; Photography, Frank Cresswell; Production designer, Richard Henry; Lighting, Keith Edelsten; Costumes, Sheila Glassford; Makeup, Christine Hillcoat

Richard Johnson (Captain Stanhope); Derrick Sherwin (2nd Lieutenant Raleigh; Harry Locke (2nd Lieutenant Trotter); John Warner (2nd Lieutenant Hibbert); Campbell Singer (Company SergeantMajor); Cyril Raymond (Colonel); Victor Maddern (Private Mason); Peter Sallis (Captain Hardy); Joseph O'Connor (Lieutenant Osborne); Andrew Lieven (German Soldier); Dudley Foster (Lance Corporal Broughton); Robert Vahey (Signaller); Allan Casley, John Dawson, Ray Grover, Frank Mills, John Scott-Martin, Frank Seton, Tony Starr, Peter Stockbridge (Soldiers)

JOURNEY'S END, Broadway on Showtime, televised January 20, 1983 Showtime 2 hours

A production of Roger Berlind and Catalina Production Group Ltd., in association with MGM/UA Entertainment; Produced by Roger Berlind, Franklin R. Levy and Gregory Harrison; Coproducer, Matthew Rushton; Director, Kent Gibson; The Play by R. C. Sherriff; Taped at Cast-at-the-Circle, Hollywood

Maxwell Caulfield (Captain Stanhope); Andrew Stevens (2nd Lieutenant Raleigh); Ian Abercrombie (2nd Lieutenant Trotter); and Wayne Alexander, Robert Anton, Robert Englund, Grant Gottschall, Bert Hinchman, Ken Letner, Lawrence Poindexter, Dale Reynolds, George Wendt

KEAN

Various dramatizations based on the life of Edmund Kean

Synopsis

Vain, hedonistic, hard-drinking early nineteenth century English actor Edmund Kean is sponsored by the Prince of Wales and closely protected by his devoted valet, Solomon. Kean's acting genius is equaled by his insatiable passion for women from whore to royalty. A trap door has been conveniently installed in his Drury Lane Theatre dressing room to accommodate discreet entrances and exits of impassioned ladies including Elena, Countess de Koefeld, wife of the Danish Ambassador. Elena barely discovers exposure when her husband arrives at Kean's door and the trap door refuses to open until she and the egocentric actor dislodge it by dancing a frantic jig. Drunkenly carousing in seedy London taverns, frequently engaging in brawls and bawds, Kean rescues lovely young Anna Danby from an unwanted affair with an elderly lord. Anna falls madly in love with Kean and becomes his mistress. Stage-struck Anna is entrusted with the role of Desdemona opposite Kean's acclaimed Othello, except that she forgets not only her handkerchief but also her lines. During the play's onstage debacle, the Prince of Wales, sitting in his box with Elena, can be heard offering caustic comments on the performance, and an enraged Kean vociferously insults his loyal, royal sponsor. Forced to publicly apologize to the Prince from the stage, Kean selects various lines from Shakespeare to mask his insincere words of regret, then seeking a less critical climate, he and Anna leave for America.

Comment and Critique

Illegitimately-born (1787) Edmund Kean was a child prodigy who went on to become the most famous if not tempestuous English actor of his time, greatly praised for his *Othello* and *Richard III*. American audiences hailed him (in New York and Boston) in tours in 1820 and 1825. On March 25, 1833, Kean collapsed on the stage of London's Covent Garden Theatre while playing Othello and died six weeks later at his Richmond home. He was forty-five.

Three years after Kean's death, Emanuel Theaulon's play based on the actor's life, created specifically for France's foremost star, Frederick Lemaitre, was rewritten by Alexandre Dumas. Dumas' *Kean, ou Desordre et Genie* starring Lemaitre premiered at the Varietes Theatre in Paris in the summer of 1836. Noted French writer and critic, Theophile Gautier, wrote: "Kean himself could not have played his own part any better. Never has a better role been written for Lemaitre. At this moment, Frederick is undoubtedly the greatest actor in the world; no one has ever had a wider range."

Lemaitre and Kean were kindred souls in many ways. During an early performance of *Kean*, Lemaitre arrived at the theater so intoxicated he could barely stand, but, after keeping the audience waiting for nearly an hour, he insisted that the curtain rise and proceeded to give a compelling performance. German writer Heinrich Heine stated: "The whole production is true to life...I really though I was watching the late Edmund Kean again."

In his *Paris Sketch Book*, William Makepeace Thackery wrote: "M. Dumas' piece of *Kean* was brought out by the author as a satire upon the French critics who, to their credit be it spoken, had generally attacked him, and was intended by him, and received by the public, as a faithful portraiture of English manners."

Robart Baldick, in his comprehensive biography, *The Life and Times of Frederick Lemaitre*, clarified Thackery's observations: "It is clear that Dumas' intention in writing or rewriting the play was not so much to satirize the Press -- though both he and his interpreter settled some old scores in Kean's diatribe against venal critics -- or to present a realistic picture of English life, as to provide Frederick with a vehicle designed to show off every aspect of his many-sided genius. If he made Kean get drunk and go mad, play Romeo and Falstaff, make polite conversation and ardent protestations of love, fight with a pugilist and shout abuse at the Prince of Wales, it was because Frederick was equally at home as a drunkard, madman, brawler, lover, wit, tragic actor or brokenhearted, clown."

Sarah Bernhardt's first success on the Paris stage was as Kean's fictitious mistress, Anna Danby, opposite Pierre Berton's less effective Kean in a revival of Dumas' play in spring 1868. In October 1891, noted French actor Lucien Guitry appeared as the passionate tragedian in Dumas' comedy about Kean at Paris' Odeon Theatre. Guitry was praised for playing the role with superb diction; criticized for playing it without magnetism.

Various plays fictitiously based on Kean's life and career appeared in the late nineteenth century. George M. Caprico starred in P. A. Fitzgerald's frivolous melodrama, *Edmund Kean; or, Life Among the Gypsies*, at Wood's Museum in New York in mid-January 1875. In Great Britain, Haddington Templin's play, *Edmund Kean*, opened on November 20, 1893, and J. Edgar Pemberton's English translation of Dumas' comedy, retitled *Edmund Kean, Tragedian*, was produced on October 23, 1896.

New York's German-speaking theater companies presented several productions of Dumas' play as *Genie und Leidenschaft*, using a translation by Schneider. Kean was played by Adolph Sonnenthal (March 14, 1885); Frederick Mietterwurger (November 30, 1885); Ludwig Barnay (March 15, 1888); Maurice Morrison (October 20, 1890), and others. Italian actor Ernesto Rossi included *Kean* in his repertory on Broadway in 1875.

Charles Francis Coghlan, the noted English actor imported to America in 1876 by Augustin Daly, adapted Dumas' *Kean; ou Desordre et Genie* as *The Royal Box*, which opened at the Fifth Avenue Theatre just before Christmas 1897. *The New York Times* found, "Coghlan's adaptation of that eccentric romantic drama by the elder Dumas called *Kean*, is free from some of the worst extravagance of the original, and while it is not likely to be taken very seriously, it is all thoroughly entertaining...To be sure, the hero is still far from impeccable, and represents genius in disorder with a vengeance...*The Royal Box* still seems a little passe as a play...Coghlan's adroit, richly varied and absorbingly interesting acting would make a poorer piece than this worthwhile." Coghlan toured America with his play during the 1898-99 season, and

Ermente Novelli included *The Royal Box* in his Broadway repertory in 1907. In 1928, Walker Whiteside revived the Coghlan play on Broadway for thirty-nine performances and an extensive tour.

In the early 1950s, Jean-Paul Sartre rewrote Dumas' comedy for French actor Pierre Brasseur. Sartre's *Kean* was a success following its opening at the Theatre Sarah Bernhardt in Paris in late 1953 with Pierre Brasseur, but seventeen years later, Frank Hauser's English translation of Sartre's play was even more successful in Great Britain. The synopsis of Kean given here is the Sartre version which wisely substituted Kean's greatest role of Othello for his unpraised acting in Dumas' inclusion of *Romeo and Juliet*. Originally produced in September 1970 at the Oxford Playhouse by the resident company under Hauser's direction with Alan Badel in the title role, *Kean* moved to London's Globe Theatre in January 1971.

Noting that Kean's life was "Depicted in a Comedy of Style" and "given a virtuoso performance by Alan Badel," Clive Barnes (*The New York Times*) called Sartre-Hauser's *Kean* "an amusing, entertaining and civilized evening in the theater. It also embraces one of the London stage's current best performances -- Alan Badel, playing the actor as to the life...Mr. Hauser has not only directed the play but also translated it into English and in both capacities he shows style and resource...this *Kean* becomes a most diverting evening."

Peter Stone, who would later write the libretto for Broadway's *1776*, adapted Sartre's *Kean* to the musical stage in 1961 with music and lyrics by Robert Wright and George Forrest of *Song of Norway* (to Greig's music) and *Kismet* (to Borodin's) fame. The musical version of *Kean* opened in New York at the beginning of November, but despite a bravura turn by Alfred Drake, it lasted only ninety-two performances.

"This lavishly mounted, richly costumed wide-stage dramarama is the most elaborate fiasco of the new theater season," reported *Time* magazine. "To see Alfred Drake, in his one lamentable lapse of the evening, as Othello is to read Shakespeare by the flash of a lightning bug." John Chapman, critic for the New York *Daily News*, added: "It strikes me that *Kean*...has been unable to make up its mind about being a music drama, a musical comedy or a biography with songs added. Being thus unsettled to its ambitions, it is not particularly convincing even though it does have Alfred Drake."

The *Herald Tribune*'s Walter Kerr found: "Mr. Drake is so effective, beneath his lowering brows, that one constantly wishes all this nonsense about a musical could be dismissed forthwith and the whole Edmund Kean repertory played straight...but a musical it must be, no matter how the hours stretch on, and the commitment is stubbornly honored." Howard Taubman (*The New York Times*) felt "Peter Stone, the librettist of the American *Kean*, has been reasonably faithful to the contemporary Frenchman's work, and in their songs, Robert Wright and George Forrest have not strayed too far from Sartre or the quality of the magnetic actor and lover who was Kean...and in Alfred Drake, nonpareil of musical performers, here is Kean to the life."

In 1981, *Kean* was revived in an acclaimed production at the John W. Huntington Theatre in Hartford directed with panache by Mark Lemos and acted with great gusto by Keith Baxter. *The New York Times*' Mel Gussow found this *Kean* "a marvelous charade overflowing with the life of the theater...As delineated by Mr. Baxter, Kean's force of personality is irresistible... So much of the play deals with the actor as a second-class citizen, a clown, subject to the whim of the aristocracy. Mr. Baxter takes a Kean-like pleasure in the play's flashes of melodrama and never overlooks the element of self-mockery, repeatedly piercing the armor of pretension."

Raymond FitzSimons' two-hour, one-act play, *Edmund Kean*, based on his own

1976 biography, *Edmund Kean: Fire From Heaven*, became a successful vehicle for Krishna Bhanji, a British actor of Indian descent better known as Ben Kingsley. The Kingsley portrayal of Kean opened at England's Harrowgate Theatre in August 1981, and in 1983, he repeated it at the Hay-market Theatre. Christopher Edwards reported in *Plays and Players*: "The adoring reception given to Oscar-winner [for *Gandhi*] Ben Kingsley at the opening of this one-man show is precisely the sort of experience Kean would have reveled in...The script is a modern prose narrative -- tart, lively, informative...FitzSimons' success is to have dovetailed the biography into the extracts from Shakespeare -- the parts which constitute the *raison d'etre* of the piece. Kingsley's success is in being convincing, at times moving, in an alien rhetorical idiom, although not all the parts are equally effective..."

In September 1983, Kingsley open in *Edmund Kean* on Broadway. Frank Rich found in *The New York Times*: "As a portrait of Kean, or as a satisfying theater piece of any kind, Raymond FitzSimons' script is perilously weak. But Mr. Kingsley turns nearly every worthwhile moment into a passionate image haunted by a character larger than the one in the text...As resourcefully directed by Alison Sutcliffe, *Edmund Kean* unfolds in a musty, heavily draped dressing room that John Watt's inventive lighting can instantly turn into a footlit Regency stage...Yet Mr. FitzSimons is less interested in integrating Kean's neuroses into a coherent characterization than in yanking Mr. Kingsley from one Shakespearean interpolation to the next. Some of the transitions are absurdly literal-minded..."

Critic Douglas Watt (*Daily News*) wrote: "Kingsley, whose name is joint to Kean's in bold type on the program's title page as if they were one and the same, is an accomplished actor. But while he is rarely less than entertaining in his one-man show...he does not command the role, the stage or the audience with the bravura called for...All this is missing is Kean."

French actor Robert Hossein directed a revival of Jean-Paul Sartre's *Kean* which opened at Paris' Theatre Marigny in March 1987. with Jean-Paul Belmondo, returning to the stage after a successful screen career. Playing the title role with great abandon and all the dash of a D'Artagnan, Belmondo was a smash. Commenting on his twenty-seven-year hiatus from the stage and his return, Belmondo said: "I could have died by my legend. But I wanted to take a risk, prove myself, hear my own fears, have doubts, conquer them and tell myself I'm nuts to do this stunt." His "stunt" proved to be one of the great successes of the modern Paris theatre.

Derek Jacobi's much-heralded *Kean* opened at the Old Vic in London in summer 1990, and Benedict Nightingale, in his review in *The London Times*, wrote that "the turbulence that Jacobi continually expresses is still primarily fun. His performance is packed with flamboyant energy and bravura mischief. He lolls, fidgets uncontrollably, leaps up, thumps the woodwork or his chest, and launches his arms into some new melodramatic gesture, his face into an imitation of his gentry, his voice into yet another hoot of glee. If it is not the Kean of the history books, it is one whose restlessness we can certainly appreciate and possibly share." Jacobi subsequently brought his *Kean* to Toronto at the beginning of 1991.

The motion picture was a natural showcase for the turbulent career and tempestuous live of Edmund Kean. In 1909 from Denmark came *Kean, or Disorder et Genie* with Einar Zangenberg, and the following year came the release of the Royal Theatre of Copenhagen's screen version of the actor's life, *Kean, or The Prince and the Actor*, starring Martinus Nielsen. Charles Coghlan's play, *The Royal Box*, was filmed by Selig in 1914, with Coghlan's daughter, Gertrude, in the female lead opposite Thomas J. Carrigan's Clarence (Kean). In 1916, Italy's film about Kean starred Ciro Galvani, and two years after that, Friedrich Zelnick directed himself as Kean in Germany's *Leichtsinn und Genie*. It was filmed again in Germany in 1921 with the screen adaptation of the Dumas play being directed by Rudolph Biebach and starring Heinrich George as Kean.

Fox Films in 1922 produced Dumas' play, *Kean, ou Desordre et Genie*, as *A Stage Romance* starring William Farnum as Kean. France's 1923 screen treatment of the Dumas play, *Kean, The Madness of Genius*, starring Ivan Mosjoukine, was released in the United States in 1927 as *Edmund Kean, Prince Among Lovers*. Mosjoukine's performances was described by one critic, paraphrasing Othello, as "acting too much and not so well." In 1929, Germany filmed Dumas' play once again, as *Der Mann, der nicht liebt*.

Warner Bros.' first German language film in 1929, *Die Koenigslodge*, was based on Charles Coghlan's play about Kean and released in the U.S. as *The Royal Box*. Alexander Moissi had the lead. Noting that *The Royal Box* was Hollywood's first German-speaking motion picture, *Photoplay* found Camilla Horn (as Anna) "appealing and her voice records well" and reported Moissi's acting "distinguished but his vociferous style is cumbersome." Allowing for those who did not understand the German dialogue, the magazine advised: "The action is too slight to follow the story. *Die Koenigslodge* was directed by Bryan Foy, one of the original Seven Little Foys.

Vittorio Gassman adapted the Dumas-Sartre play to the Italian stage with co-playwright Luciano Lucignani as *Genie e Sregelatezza* and starred as Kean at Rome's Teatro d'Arte during the 1954-55 season. Then he starred in the 1957 screen version and won Italy's Silver Riband Award.

A three-hour BBC television production of Sartre's play, *Kean*, translated by Frank Hauser, was taped in 1978 after two weeks of rehearsal and one day of camera rehearsal. Lauded by the British critics, especially for Anthony Hopkins' performance in the lead, it also got raves when shown on PBS' *Masterpiece Theatre* in two parts the following year. About the hectic television schedule, Hopkins said: "The first five days were like a traffic jam. Every section I was involved in, I staged myself. Robert Stephens [who plays the Prince of Wales] and I worked together on our scenes. You have to practice positive selfishness." Comparing his own drive for perfection with Kean's similar passion, Hopkins admitted that "I'm a perfectionist. I think it's a vice. I'm very demanding. Kean was like that." About Kean, he said: "He was a very modern actor, with a great eye for detail. But he was very exasperating for the people around him. He wanted to rehearse all the time, like Olivier."

In 1984, Ben Kingsley repeated his Kean on TV. *Ben Kingsley as Edmund Kean* was reduced from the two-hour stage presentation to a one-hour television program. It benefited by close-ups of Kingsley but greatly diminished his portrayal of Kean in a swiftly paced although too accelerated television adaptation.

STAGE

KEAN, OU DESORDRE ET GENIE, *Theatre des Varietes*, Paris, opened August 31, 1836

A Play by Emmanuel Theaulon, adapted by Alexandre Dumas

Frederick Lemaitre (Edmund Kean); Mme. A. Beauchene (Anna Danby); M. Bressant (Prince of Wales); Mlle. Mazurier (Juliette); Mlle. Pauline (Countess Koefeld); Mlle. Georgina (Ketty); M. Dussert (Lord Melville); M. Prosper (Solomon); M. Adrien (Pistol); M. Rebard (A Constable); M. Dumoulin (Peter Patt); Mlle. Jolivet (Countess of Gosswill); M. Dandel (Count Koefeld); M. Cazot (Stage Manager); Mlle. Alberti (Lady in Waiting); M. Lamarre (John); M. Sainville

(Tom); M. Edouard (David); Mlle. Louisa (Wet Nurse); Aimee (Maid Servant); M. Hyacinthe (Darius); M. Renaud (Bardolph); M. Emmanuel (Steward); M. Louis (Wine Waiter); M. Mayer (First Valet); M. Adolphe (Second Valet)

KEAN, OU DESORDRE ET GENIE, *Theatre de l'Odeon*, Paris, opened March 1868
Director, A. Grevin; A Play by Emmanuel Theaulon, adapted by Alexandre Dumas
Pierre Berton (Edmund Kean); Sarah Bernhardt (Anna Danby); M. Reynald (Prince of Wales); Mlle. L'Enfant (Juliette/Gidsa/La Nourrice); Mlle. Ferraris (Countess Koefeld); Mlle. Bode (Ketty); M. Richard (Lord Melville); M. Saint-Leon (A Constable); M. Parfait (Peter Patt); Mlle. Guerin (Countess of Gosswill); M. Laute (Count Koefeld); M. Coquelin-Cadet (Darius)

EDMUND KEAN; OR, LIFE AMONG THE GYPSIES, *Wood's Museum*, New York, opened January 11, 1875
A Melodrama by P. A. Fitzgerald
George M. Caprico (Edmund Kean)

EDMUND KEAN, *Academy of Music*, New York, opened January 18, 1882 3 performances
A Comedy based on Alexandre Dumas' *Kean, ou Desordre et Genie*
Ernesto Rossi (Edmund Kean); Carrie Turner (Anna Danby); Leslie Gossin (H.R.H. Prince of Wales); Louis Muldener (Helen); Constance Hamblin (Amy); Harry Weaver, Jr. (Lord Neville); E. A. Eberle (Solomon); W. J. Shea (Pistol); Charles Kent (A Constable); T. F. Kelly (Peter Patt); Mrs. H. A. Weaver Gidsa); Harry A. Weaver (Count Koefeld); William V. Ranous (Drury Lane Theatre Manager); S. Jackson (A Servant)

GENIE UND LEIDENSCHAFT, New York, opened March 15, 1885
A Play based on Alexandre Dumas' *Kean, ou Desordre et Genie*
Adolf Sonnenthal (Edmund Kean)

GENIE UND LEIDENSCHAFT, New York, opened November 30, 1885
A Play based on Alexandre Dumas' *Kean, ou Desordre et Genie*
Frederick Mietterwurger (Edmund Kean)

GENIE UND LEIDENSCHAFT, New York, opened March 15, 1888
A Play based on Alexandre Dumas' *Kean, ou Desordre et Genie*
Ludwig Barnay (Edmund Kean); Lucie Werner (Amy)

KEAN, *Thalia Theatre*, New York, opened April 9, 1888
A Play based on Alexandre Dumas' *Kean, ou Desordre et Genie*; Produced by the German Theatre
Ludwig Barnay (Edmund Kean); Lucie Werner (Amy); Jacques Kruger (Prinz von Wales); Elisabeth Hagedorn (Grafin Elena); Emanuel Lederer (Regisseur of Covent Garden Theatre); Ernst Possart (Solomon)

GENIE UND LEIDENSCHAFT, New York, opened October 20, 1890
A Play based on Alexandre Dumas' *Kean, ou Desordre et Genie*
Maurice Morrison (Edmund Kean)

EDMUND KEAN, London, opened November 20, 1893

A Play by Haddington Templin

EDMUND KEAN, TRAGEDIAN, London, opened October 23, 1896
A Play based on Alexandre Dumas' *Kean, ou Desordre et Genie*, translated by Edgar Pemberton

THE ROYAL BOX, *Fifth Avenue Theatre*, New York, opened December 21, 1897, moved to *Garden Theatre*, January 10, 1898   63 performances
Produced by The Liebler Company; A Romantic Play written and directed by Charles Coghlan, based on Alexandre Dumas' *Kean, ou Desordre et Genie*; Settings, Louis Young; Costumes by Eaves; Stage manager, Claude Brooke

Charles Coghlan (Clarence, an actor); E. J. Ratcliffe (succeeded by Harold Russell) (Prince of Wales); Gertrude Coghlan (Juliet); Albert Bruning (Count Felsen); Mrs. Thorndyke-Boucicault (succeeded by Elizabeth Garth) (Countess Helen Felsen); Grace Filkins (Celia Pryse); Lulu Klein (Lady Robert); Walter Craven (succeeded by Mervyn Dallas) (Lord Bassett); Charles Stanley (Tipps); Claude Brooke (Winch/Drury Lane Theatre Stage Manager); Edwin Hoff (succeeded by C. W. King) (Marmaduke/ Mercutio); Frank Sheridan (succeeded by Harry Hanlon) (Benvolio); Guy Nichols (Montmorency); Addie Plunkett (Ebba); Taylor Granville (Widgets); Harry Hanlon (Swedish Servant); William Morton, Jr. (Rickards)

THE ROYAL BOX, *Touring Company*, season 1898-99
Produced by The Liebler Company; A Romantic Play written and directed by Charles Coghlan, based on Alexandre Dumas' *Kean, ou Desordre et Genie*; Settings, P. J. McDonald; Costumes by Eaves; Company managers, George C. Tyler and J. A. Reed; Stage manager, Claude Brooke

Charles Coghlan (Clarence, an actor); Andrew Robson (Prince of Wales); Nora O'Brien (Juliet); Alexander Kearney (Count Felsen); Lotta Linthicum (Countess Helen Felsen); Gertrude Coghlan (Celia Pryse); Mabel Bart (Lady Robert); Palmer Collins (Lord Bassett); Charles Stanley (Tipps); Claude Brooke (Winch/ Drury Lane Theatre Stage Manager); Harry Hanlon (Marmaduke/ Benvolio); James W. Bankson (Montmorency/ Mercutio); Josephine Adams (Ebba); Edgar George (A Servant)

EDMUND KEAN, *Vaudeville Theatre*, London, opened January 10, 1903   4 matinee performances
Produced by A. & S. Gatti and Charles Frohman; A Play by Gladys Unger; Director, Seymour Hicks; Scenery, William Harford; Costumes, Percy Anderson

Seymour Hicks (Edmund Kean); Henrietta Watson (Jennifer); Vincent Sternroyd (Lord Trecome); Norman McKinnel (Benet); Charles Daly (Peter); Irene Rooke (Gregory)

EDMUND KEAN, *Prince's Theatre*, Manchester, England, opened June 24, 1922
A Play by Arthur Shirley, based on the life of Edmund Kean

Act I (August 1812): H. A. Saintsbury (The Barnstormer); Louise Regnis (The Barnstormer's Wife); Violet Adcock, Renie Davis (The Barnstormer's Children); H. Halladay Hope (The Squire); William Farren (Gentleman from London); W. R. Staveley (The Constable); W. H. Vernon (The Tramp); Georgette Thiery (The Hostess)

Act II (November 23, 1813): H. A. Saintsbury (Edmund Kean); Louise Regnis

(Mary Kean); Miss Violet Adcock (Howard Kean); W. H. Vernon (Bob Clifford); Edward Cooper (The Captain); J. Henry Twyford (Squire Willett); Frank Goodyear (A Doctor)

Act III (November 30, 1813): Royce Milton (Earl of Essex); William Farren (Doctor Drury); H. Halladay Hope (Landlord); Kathleen Deville (Phoebe); W. R. Staveley (Reuben); Price and Randall (Roger and William); Wallace Rayland (Simon Andrew); Ruth Rozella (Susan); Frank Goodyear (A Postillion); Angus Adams (Sheriff's Officer)

Act IV: Edward Cooper (Lord Byron); W. R. Staveley (Mr. Raymond); J. Henry Twyford (Mr. Rae); H. Halladay Hope (Dowton); Angus Adams (Phillips); Kathleen Deville (Miss Smith); Ruth Rozella (Mrs. Bland); Renie Davis (Call Boy); Claire Pauncefort (Mrs. David Garrick); Georgette Thiery (Miss Williams); Queenie Cox (Charles Kean)

NED KEAN OF OLD DRURY, *Drury Lane Theatre*, London, opened May 9, 1923 61 performances

Director, Arthur Collins; A Play by Arthur Shirley, originally produced as Edmund Kean

H. A. Saintsbury (Edmund Kean); Louise Regnis (Mary Kean); Miss Gabrielle Casartolli (Howard Kean); Miss Violet Aubert (Charles Kean); Thomas Paucefort (Bob Clifford); William Farren (Doctor Drury); Henry Hallett (Earl of Essex); Edward Cooper (Lord Byron); Haldee Wright (Mrs. David Garrick); Frank E. Petley (Captain); J. Henry Twyford (Squire Willett/Mr. Rae); H. Halladay Hope (The Landlord/The Squire/ Dowton); Fred J. Little (Mr. Jennifer); Rothbury Evans (Barnaby/Raymond); Constance Robertson (Mrs. Pengelly/Miss Smith); Kathlyn Clifford (Jane/Annie); Esme Shirley (Phyllis/Charlotte/Jane); Gwen Yvonne (Polly/Ann); Teddie Barrie (Soldier/Simon/Andrew); Horace Corbyn (Sailor/Roger/Powell); G. Aubyn Bourne (The Fiddler/A Postillion/The Call Boy); Fred Grove (A Country Doctor/Watkins); Violet Vivian (Landlady); Edwin Austin (Joe/Anthony); Jack Stephens (William); Aida Kaye (Caroline/Anne); Hilda Sims (Susan Quech/Mrs. Bland); Augustus Bowerman (Sheriff's Officer/A Linkman); Margaret Yarde (Miss Williams); Leonard Ashdowne (Phillips)

THE ROYAL BOX, *Belmont Theatre*, New York, opened November 30, 1928 39 performances

Produced and directed by Walker Whiteside; A Comedy Romance by Charles Coghlan, adapted from Alexandre Dumas' *Kean, ou Desordre et Genie*

Walker Whiteside (James Clarence); Lulu Mae Hubbard (Countess Felsen); Catherine Proctor (Lady Robert); Manart Kippen (Count Felsen); Hugh Huntley (H.R.H. Prince of Wales); Daisy Belmore (Mrs. Barker); Frank Henderson (Tommy Widgets); Charles Penman (Lord Bassett; Franc Hale (Celia Pryse); Elwyn Eaton (Bailiff Tipps); William Dunne (Rickards); Don Currie (Ebba); Alexander F. Frank (Davis); Richard Ranier (Stage Manager); Carl Vose (Call Boy); A. Syms (Footman)

KEAN, *Theatre Sarah Bernhardt*, Paris, opened December 14, 1953

Produced by A. M. Julien; A Play by Jean-Paul Sartre, adapted from Alexandre Dumas' *Kean, ou Desordre et Genie*; Director, Pierre Brasseur; Settings and costumes, Alexandre Trauner; Music, J. A. Petit

Pierre Brasseur (Edmund Kean); Marie Olivier (Anna Danby); Roger Pigaut (Prince of Wales); Claude Gensac (Elena); Henri Nassiet (Count de Koefeld);

Camille Fournier (Amy)

KEAN, *Broadway Theatre*, New York, opened November 2, 1961 92 performances
Produced by Robert Lantz; A Musical Play based on the comedy by Jean-Paul Sartre; Staged and choreographed by Jack Cole; Book by Peter Stone; Music and lyrics by Robert Wright and George Forrest; Production design, Ed Wittstein; Lighting, John Harvey; Ballet and incidental music, Elie Siegmeister; Musical direction and vocal arrangements by Pembroke Davenport; Orchestrations, Philip J. Lang; Stage managers, Peter Bronte, Walter Neal and Malcolm Marmorstein

Alfred Drake (Edmund Kean); Lee Venora (Anna Danby); Joan Weldon (Countess Elena de Koeberg); Patricia Cutts (Lady Amy Gosswell); Christopher Hewett (Barnaby); Oliver Gray (Prince of Wales); Arthur Rubin (Francis); Robert Penn (Ben); Roderick Cook (Lord Neville); Alfred DeSio (Christie); Truman Smith (Solomon); Patrick Waddington (Lord de Koeberg); John Lankston (Lord Delmore); Larry Shadur (Maxwell); George Harwell (Pott); Margaret Gathright (Sparrow); Rene Jarmon (St. Albands); Gloria Warner (Bolt); Randy Doney (Tim); John Jordan (David); Paul Jordan (Pip); Charles Dunn (Patrick); Martin Ambrose (Major Domo); Alfred Toigo (Stage Manager); Eddie Ericksen (Prop Boy); Joseph McGrath (Secretary); Martin Ambrose (Henchman); Larry Shadur, John Wheeler (Guards); John Aristides, Barbara Beck, Johanna Carothers, Louis Castle, Charles Corbett, Kenneth Creek, Randy Donbey, Judy Dunford, Larry Fuller, Mickey Gunnersen, Pamela Hayford, Jim Hutchinson, Lisa James, Rene Jarmon, Richard Lyle, George Martin, Roger Puckett, Susanne Shirley (Dancers); Martin Ambrose, Charise Amidon, Charles Dunn, Eddie Ericksen, Nancy Foster, Margaret Gathright, Maggie Goz, George Harwell, John Lankston, Joseph McGrath, Lispet Nelson, Mary Nettum, Larry Shadur, Susan Terry, Alfred Toigo, Gloria Warner, John Wheeler (Singers)

MUSICAL NUMBERS: "Penny Plain"; "Twopence Colored"; "Man and Shadow"; "Mayfair Affair"; "Sweet Danger"; "Queue at Drury Lane"; "King of London"; "To Look Upon My Love"; "Let's Improvise"; "Elena"; "Social Whirl"; "The Fog and the Grog"; "Civilized People"; "Service for Service"; "Willow, Willow"; "Fracas at Old Drury"; "Chime In"; "Swept Away"; "Domesticity"; "Clown of London"; "Apology"

Original cast recording: Columbia Records

KEAN, *Globe Theatre*, London, opened January 28, 1971 300 performances
Produced by Bernard Delfont, by arrangement with The Oxford Playhouse Company; A Play by Jean-Paul Sartre, based on Alexandre Dumas' *Kean, ou Desordre et Genie*, translated by Frank Hauser; Director, Frank Hauser; Production design, Peter Farmer; Lighting, Robert Bryan; Costumes by Nathan's and Barbara Higgins; Stage manager, Byron Chandler

Alan Badel (Edmund Kean); Felicity Kendal (Anna Danby); Philip Voss (Prince of Wales); Lisa Daniely (Elena, Countess de Koefeld); Frank Gatliff (Count de Koefeld); Maggie Jones (Amy, Countess of Gosswill); Ken Wynne (Solomon); Peter Yapp (Lord Neville); William Ridoutt (Peter Potts); Pamela Danton (Sadie); Eve Karpf (Gidsa); Roderick Horn (Darius); Denis De Marne (Stage Manager); Peter Yapp (Major Domo); Keith Varnier (Footman); Thomas Chesleigh (Constable); Denis De Marne (First Tumbler); Thomas Chesleigh, Johnny Clayton, Pamela Denton, Patrick Gibson, Peter Gregory, Eve Karpf, Anne Lieven, Keith Vernier (Tumblers, Servants, etc.)

NOTE: This production premiered at the *Oxford Playhouse* on September 8, 1970

KEAN, *Arena Theatre*, Washington, opened March 26, 1981 33 performances
Produced by the Arena Stage Company, Zelda Fichandler, producting director; Associate producer, Nancy Quinn; A Comedy by Jean-Paul Sartre, adapted from Alexandre Dumas' *Kean, ou Desordre et Genie*; Director, Martin Fried; Settings, Marjorie Kellogg; Lighting, Hugh Lester, Costumes, Nan Cibula

Stanley Anderson (Edmund Kean); Annalee Jefferies (Anna Danby); Richard Bauer (Prince of Wales); Halo Wines (Elena, Countess de Koefeld); Joe Palmieri (Count de Koefeld); Gerry Lasarda (Amy, Countess of Gosswill); Mark Hammer (Solomon); Robert W. Westenberg (Lord Neville); Charles K. Bortell (Philips); John Neville-Andrews (Major Domo/Peter Potts/Inn-keeper/Stage Manager); Kim Merrill (Gidsa/Tumbler/ Audience); David Toney (Audience/Constable/ Footman); John Elko (Darius/ Assassin/Footman/Audience); Michael Hartford, John Prosky, Robert Shampain (Footmen, Tumblers, Assassins, Audience); Cam Magee (Sadie/Audience)

KEAN, *John W. Huntington Theatre*, Hartford, Conn., opened November 13, 1981 44 performances
Produced by the Hartford Stage Company, Mark Lamos, artistic director; A Comedy by Jean-Paul Sartre, based on Alexandre Dumas' *Kean, ou Desordre et Genie*, translated by Frank Hauser; Director, Mark Lamos; Production design, John Conkin; Lighting, Pat Collins; Wigs, Paul Huntley

Keith Baxter (Edmund Kean); Mary Layne (Anna Danby); David Schramm (Prince of Wales); Jean Smart (Elena, Countess de Koefeld); Nafe Katter (Count de Koefeld); Patricia Connolly (Amy, Countess of Gosswill); Timothy Meyers (Solomon); Ian Stuart (Lord Neville); Stephen Rust (Stage Manager/Consatble); Chris Ceraso (Darius); Deborah Stenard (Sadie/ Gidsa); William Verderber (Major Domo/Peter Potts); Craig Pinder (Butler); Chris Ceraso, Talbott Dowst, David H. Lawrence, Ted McAdams, Mark Wayne Nelson, Criag Pinder, Deborah Stenard, David Watson (Tumblers, Assassins, Audience Members)

BEN KINGSLEY AS EDMUND KEAN, *Lyric Theatre Hammersmith*, London, opened April 14 through May 7, 1983; reopened at *Theatre Royal Haymarket*, London, June 13 through July 23, 1983*
Produced by Duncan C. Weldon, Paul Gregg, Lionel Becker; A Solodrama by Raymond FitzSimons, adapted from his biography, *Edmund Kean: Fire From Heaven*; Director, Alison Sutcliffe; Production design, Martin Tilley; Lighting, John Watt; Choreography, Cleone Rive

Ben Kingsley as Edmund Kean

*This solodrama was originally staged at the *Harrogate Theatre* in Yorkshire August 1981.

BEN KINGSLEY AS EDMUND KEAN, *Brooks Atkinson Theatre*, New York, opened September 27, 1983 29 performances
Produced by Alexander H. Cohen and Hildy Parks, in association with Duncan C. Weldon, Paul Gregg, Lionel Becker; A Solodrama by Raymond FitzSimons, adapted from his biography, *Edmund Kean: Fire From Heaven*; Director, Alison Sutcliffe; Production design, Martin Tilley; Lighting, John Watt; Choreography, Cleone Rive; Coordinating producer, Roy Somlyo; Stage managers, Alan Hall, Josh Moss and Ruth E. Ranklin

Ben Kingsley as Edmund Kean

KEAN, *Theatre Marigny*, Paris, opened March 5, 1987
Produced by Theatre Marigny, ALAP, Spectacles Lumbroso, Hachette One Premiere et Cie, UGC and SPPS; A Comedy by Jean-Paul Sartre; Director, Robert Hossein; Production design, Pierre Simonini; Costumes, Sylvie Poulet; Pantomimes, Gilles Segal; Stunt director, Claude Carliez

Jean-Paul Belmondo (Edmund Kean); Sabine Haudepin (Anna Danby); Pierre Vernier (Prince of Wales); Beatrice Agenin (Elena); Gabriel Cattand (Count de Koefeld); Danielle Volle (Amy); Michel Beaune (Solomon); Jacques Mignot (Peter Potts); Bernard Dumaine (Major Domo); Olivier Belmont (Young Philips); Bertrand Gohaud (Footman); Estelle Kingold (A Maid); Pierre Hossein (Clown); Marcel Cuegan, Gilles Dimicelli, Jean-Lionel Breuil, Patrick John-Hathan, Danielle Benhamou, Claude Lancelot, Michel Bros, Marc Dubreuil, Marie Casterez, Odile Le Nissonais, Catherine Lesnoff, Estelle Kingold, Candice Berner, Beatrice Hailmi, Natalie Aussant, Virginie Patou, Bernard Dumaine, Hubert Noel, Serge Berry, Max Fournel, Stephen James Back, Yvan Ormand (Guests, Friends, Actors)

KEAN, OR DISORDER AND GENIUS, *Old Vic Theatre*, London, opened August 2, 1990 144 performances
Produced by Duncan C. Weldon and Jerome Minskoff for Triumph Proscenium Productions Ltd.; A Play by Jean-Paul Sartre, based on Alexandre Dumas' *Kean, ou Desordre et Genie*, translated by Frank Hauser; Director, Sam Mendes; Production design, Simon Higlett; Lighting, Mick Hughes; Music, Jeremy Sams; Sound, John A. Leonard; Movement, Lindsay Dolan

Derek Jacobi (Edmund Kean); Sarah Woodward (Anna Danby); Nicholas Farrell (Prince of Wales); Eleanor David (Elena, Countess de Koefeld); Michael Godley (Count de Koefeld); Kate Duchene (Amy, Countess of Gosswill); Ian McNeice (Solomon); Malcolm Mudie (Lord Neville/Major Domo); Stanley Page (Peter Potts); Tricia Morrish (Sadie/Gidsa); Christopher Luscombe (Darius); Tom Dunne (Stage Manager); Tim Wallers (Constable); Andrea Duncan, Mark Southworth, Terry Whan (Old Bob's Tumblers)

NOTE: This production moved to the *Royal Alexandra Theatre*, Toronto, January 4 through February 16, 1991, with Kate Duchene playing Elena, Abigail McKern as Amy, Charlotte Harvey as Sadie/Gidsa, Tom Hallander as Darius, and Paul Daintry as Stage Manager

SCREEN

KEAN, OU DESORDRE ET GENIE, *Nordisk Films* (Denmark), released 1909
Director, Viggo Larsen, adapted from Alexandre Dumas' play

Einar Zanenberg (Kean); Oda Alstrupp (Anna); Lauritz Olsen (Prince of Wales)

KEAN, OR THE PRINCE AND THE ACTOR, *Nordisk Films* (Denmark), released April 1910
Produced by The Royal Theatre of Copenhagen; Director, Holger Rasmussen, adapted from Alexandre Dumas' play

Martinius Nielsen (Kean); Agnete Nyrop Christensen (Anna); August Blom (Prince of Wales); and Einar Zanenberg, Alfi Zanenberg, Charlotte Sannom, Poul Welander, Edward Jacobsen, Thilda Fonss, Oscar Stribolt, Edvard Schroder, O. Lagoni, Axel Boesen, Schioler-Linck, L. Olsen

THE ROYAL BOX, *Selig Pictures*, released May 1914
Director, Oscar Eagle, based on the play by Charles Coghlan, adapted from Alexandre Dumas' *Kean, ou Desordre et Genie*
Thomas J. Carrigan (James Clarence); Gertrude Coghlan (Celia Pryce); Clifford Bruce (Prince of Wales); Palmer Bowman (Count Felson); Adrienne Kroell (Lady Felson)

KEAN, OU DESORDRE ET GENIE, Italy, released 1916
Director, Armando Brunero, adapted from Alexandre Dumas' play
Ciro Galvani (Kean); Delia Bicchi (Anna)

KEAN, LEICHTSINN UND GENIE, Germany, released 1918
Written and directed by Friedrich Zelnick, based on Alexandre Dumas' play
Friedrich Zelnick (Kean); Hanni Weiss (Anna); Maria Zelenka (Countess de Koefeld)

KEAN, LEICHTSINN UND GENIE, Germany, released 1921
Director, Rudolf Biebach, based on Alexandre Dumas' play
Heinrich George (Kean); Carola Toelle (Anna); Fritz Junkermann (Prince of Wales); Olga Limburg (Countess de Koefeld); Curt Vespermann (Count de Koefeld)

A STAGE ROMANCE, *Fox Films*, released March 1922
Produced by William Fox; Director, Herbert Brennon; Screenplay, Paul H. Sloane, based on Alexandre Dumas' *Kean, ou Desordre et Genie*; Photography, Tom Malley
William Farnum (Edmund Kean); Peggy Shaw (Anna Danby); Holmes Herbert (Prince of Wales); Myrtle Bonillas (Countess Elena de Koefeld); Paul McAllister (Count de Koefeld); Etienne Girardot (Solomon); Mario Carillo (Lord Neville); Paula Shay (Countess Amy Gosswill); Viva Verone (Gidsa); Bernard Siegel (Mr. Sleeker); Jack Collins (Bardolph); America Chedister (Lady Anne Boyle); Hal DeForrest (Old Bob); Edward Kipling (Darius); Harry Grippe (Prizefighter John); Austus Balfour (Stage Manager); Cuyler Supplee (Tom); Edward Boring (Needles); Florence Ashbrook (Mrs. Bob); Ruth D. Goodwin (Little Emily)

KEAN, OU DESORDRE ET GENIE, *Compagnie Vitagraph de France*, released 1923; in the U.S. in May 1927 as *EDMUND KEAN, PRINCE AMONG LOVERS*
A Films Albatross production; Producer, Alexandre Kamenka; Director, Alexandre Volkoff; Screenplay, Kenelm Foss, Alexandre Volkoff and Ivan Mosjoukine, based on Alexandre Dumas' play; Photography by Jean-Louis Mundviller, Fedor Bourgassoff and Ivan Mosjoukine; Production designer, Ivan Locknoff
Ivan Mosjoukine (Edmund Kean); Mary Odette (Anna Danby); Otto Detlefsen (Prince of Wales); Nathalie Lissenko (Elena); Georges Deneubourg (Count de Koefeld); Constant Mic (Amy); Nikolai Koline (Solomon); Kenelm Foss (Lord Neville); Pauline Po (Ophelia/ Juliet); Albert Bras (Constable); Morlas (Gidsa)

DER MANN, DER NICHT LIEBT (L'ETERNELLE IDOLE), Germany, released 1929
Director, Guido Brignone; Screenplay, Hans H. Zerlett and Lother Knud Frederik, based on Alexandre Dumas' *Kean, ou Desordre et Genie*; Photography, Willy Winterstein; Art director, Heinrich Richter
Gustav Diesel (Merone); Daisy D'Ora (Lucile Destang); Agnes Estherhazy

(Elena); Suzanne Bianchetti (The Duchess); Suzanne Delmas (Ginette); and Harry Hardt, Colette Darfeuil, Alexander Murski, Max Gulstorff, Pino Bradamante, Valery Boothby, Alexander Bondireff, Nico Turoff, Carla Bartheel

DIE KOENIGSLOGE (THE ROYAL BOX), Warner Bros. Pictures (filmed in German), released December 1929
Director, Bryan Foy; Screenplay, Murray Roth, based on Charles Coghlan's play, adapted from Alexander Dumas' *Kean, ou Desordre et Genie*; Adaptation and dialogue, Edmund Joseph, Arthur Hurley; German translation, Arthur Rundt; Photography, E. B. Du Par and Ray Foster; Art directors, Frank Namczy and Tom Darby

Alexandre Moissi (Edmund Kean); Camilla Horn (Alice Doren); Elsa Ersi (Countess Toeroek); William F. Schoeller (Prince of Wales); Egon Brecher (Count Toeroek); Lew Hern (Solomon); Leni Stengel (Lady Robert); Carlos Zizold (Lord Neville); Greta Mayer (Mrs. Barker); Siegfried Rumann (Bailiff); William Gade (Tom Widgets)

KEAN, Scalera Productions (Italy), released 1940
Director, Guido Brignone; Screenplay, Guido Brignone and Tomaso Smith, based on Alexandre Dumas' play; Photography, Otello Martelli; Art directors, Gino Franzi and Giuseppe Vaccaro; Music, Edgardo Carducci; Sound, Adolfo Alessandrini; Editor, Giuseppe Fatigati

Rossano Brazzi (Edmund Kean); Mariella Lotti (Anna); Filippo Scelzo (Prince of Wales); Germana Paolieri (Elena); Dino Di Luca (Comte de Koefeld); Sandro Salvini (Amy); and Dina Sassoli, Giuseppe Porelli, Tao Ferrari, Oreste Fares, Nicola Maldacea, Edoardo Borelli

KEAN, GENIO E SREGOLATEZZA, Lux-Vides Films (Italy), released 1956
Produced by Franco Cristaldi; Director, Vittorio Gassman; Screenplay, Suso Cecchi D'Amico, Francesco Rosi and Vittorio Gassman, based on Jean-Paul Sartre's adaptation of Alexandre Dumas' *Kean, ou Desordre et Genie*; Photography, Gianni di Venanzo; Art director, Gianni Polidori; Costumes, Giulio Coltelacci and Marilu Carteny; Music, Roman Vlad; Editor, Enzo Alfonzi

Vittorio Gassman (Edmund Kean); Anna Maria Ferraro (Anna Danby); Eleanora Rossi-Drago (Elena, Contessa de Koefeld); Gerard Landry (Prince of Wales); Nerio Bernardi (Comte de Koefeld); Dina Sassoli (Amy); Cesco Baseggio (Solomon); Helmut Dantine (Lord Neville); Mario Carotenuto (Peter Patt); Maria Fabbri (Prima Attrice); and Amedeo Girard, Carlo Mazzarella, Bruno Smith, Pietro Tordi, Alberto Carloni, Ferrucio Stagni, Mario Passante, Masssimo Burrelli, Renato Terra, Roberta Benedetti, Jean Molier, Winni Riva, Nada Cortese, Angelo Zanolli, Armando Annuale, Maria Luisa Rolando, Hedda Linton, Claudio Perone

TELEVISION

KEAN: UN ROI DE THEATRE, ORTF-Television (France), televised December 21, 1968
Adapted and directed by Marcel Moussy from Alexandre Dumas' *Kean, ou Desordre et Genie*

Robert Hirsch (Edmund Kean); Nicole Jamet (Anne Danby), Jean-Francois Remy (Prince of Wales); Marie Laforet (Elena, Countess de Koefeld); Jean

Leuvrais (Count de Koefeld); Monique Nevers (Amy, Countess of Gosswill); Van Doude (Lord Neville); Francois Beaulieu (Charles Young); Jacqueline Monsigny (Mrs. Clarke); Georges Spanelly (Mrs. Clarke's servant); Catherine Brevent (Miss Carey); Jean Obe (John); Robert Favart (Elliston); Annick Alane (Lisbeth); Raymond Danjou (de Koefeld's servant); Patrick Pezin (Constable); Edmond Beauchamp (Richardson); Serge Gamby (Young Kean); and Jean Rupert, Pierre Negre, Francoise Gingal, Renee Villers, Marius Laurey, Raoul Curet, Michel Charrel, Jean-Pierre Janio, Andre Gagnard, Aristide Demonico, Gaetan Noel, Marc Blanchard, Michel Ferrand, Jacques Francial, Jacques Le Glou, Gaetene Lore

KEAN, televised November 26, 1978 BBC 2 hours; in U.S. on PBS' *Masterpiece Theatre* in two parts September 9 and 16, 1979
A British Broadcasting Corporation Production; Produced by David Jones; Director, James Cellan Jones; Based on Frank Hauser's translation of the play by Jean-Paul Sartre; Script editor, Stuart Griffiths; Designer, Geoff Powell; Lighting, Sam Barclay; Costumes, Betty Aldiss

Anthony Hopkins (Edmund Kean); Cherie Lunghi (Anna Danby); Robert Stephens (Prince of Wales); Sarah Kestelman (Elena, Countess de Koefeld); Barrie Ingham (Count de Koefeld); Frank Middlemass (Solomon); Adrienne Corri (Amy, Countess of Goss-will); Julian Fellowes (Lord Neville); George Tovey (Peter Potts); Jennifer Granville (Sadie); Helena Breck (Gidsa); Hugh Walters (Darius); Roger Elliott (Constable); Mike Savage (Stage Manager)

BEN KINGSLEY AS EDMUND KEAN, televised February 27, 1983 Yorkshire Television; in U.S. on PBS May 21, 1984 1 hour
Produced by Yorkshire Television; Director, Michael Ferguson; Written by Raymond Fitzsimons, based on his biography *Edmund Kean: Fire From Heaven.*

Ben Kingsley as Edmund Kean

KIND SIR
A Comedy by Norman Krasna (1953)

Synopsis

A worldly actress, Jane Kimball, is introduced at a party to Philip Clair, a suave banker who works for the State Department, and is swept off her feet. He's charmed by her but doesn't want to get trapped, so he lies to her about being married and unable to get a divorce. She, however, continues to arrange that they keep running into one another, and then stumbles onto his little romantic subterfuge. Annoyed that he'd been playing on her heartstrings, she decides that she'll chase him in earnest until he catches her.

Comment and Critique

Stage and movie producer/writer Norman Krasna, born in Corona, Long Island on November 7, 1909, is best known for his romantic comedies that range from *Dear Ruth* and *John Loves Mary* to *Who Was That Lady I Saw You With?* and *Sunday in New York*. Before writing hit plays, he had been a New York drama critic and a publicity executive in Hollywood, and eventually, in the 1950s, formed a film producing partnership with Jerry Wald, turning out both comedies and dramas. Among the movies he wrote were *Fury*, *Bachelor Mother*, *It Started With Eve*, *The Devil and Miss Jones*, *Princess O'Rourke*, for which he won the 1943 Academy Award for Best Original Screenplay, and *White Christmas*.

Late in 1953, with Mary Martin and Charles Boyer in the leads, his sprightly comedy, *Kind Sir*, opened on Broadway. Mary Martin was "between musicals" -- *South Pacific* preceded it, *Peter Pan* followed it -- and Boyer had recently been praised for his *Don Juan in Hell* on Broadway and during a lengthy cross-country tour. Both the stars and the top-notch supporting cast that included Dorothy Stickney, Frank Conroy and Margalo Gillmore led the critics to have high hopes going in.

"In a way, I suppose *Kind Sir* symbolizes the current plight of the American theater," wrote the *New York Post*'s Richard Watts Jr. "A talented and distinguished cast has been assembled for it. There is a handsome setting, and some lavish costumes for its leading actress. One of the ablest of contemporary directors [Joshua Logan] has staged it affectionately. A particularly fancy audience of celebrities was even willing to stop acting in the lobby long enough to watch it. Everything that theatrical skill and popular interest could provide was present, and then there was no play forthcoming to go with it...a feeble antic worth no one's effort, including Mr. Krasna's...The dialogue, if it has few other virtues, is strewn with song cues, and Mary Martin is present to go on from there with the songs but there's aren't any. And it is quite possible that *Kind Sir* might have been a nice intimate musical play."

Brooks Atkinson agreed in *The New York Times*: "Since everyone is devoted to Mary Martin and Charles Boyer, it would be a pleasure to report that their play is equal to their quality...Superbly cast and directed by Joshua Logan, with opulent settings, including a gold-plated piano, by Jo Mielziner, it is fashionable and trivial theatre that is spasmodically entertaining ...Every detail is carefully attended to. But what a waste of talent. Mr. Krasna's routine script is not worth the work and is not worth of the people."

Walter Kerr sneered, as well, in the *Herald Tribune*: "The stage at the Alvin is littered with talent [and] I suppose it would take a bandwagon of a play to carry this resplendent company to glory. Author Norman Krasna has provided a kiddie-car....The actors seem perfectly aware of the void they are working in: Nearly every sentence is bravely uttered; but it is immediately followed by a strained and apprehensive silence, as though the show were being played on the brink of the Grand Canyon and the players had to wait for the echoes to stop before conversation could be resumed."

The cast alone kept the play running for 165 performances. Krasna, several years later, wrote a screen-play from *Kind Sir*, and called it *Indiscreet*. "Krasna's [1958] screen adaptation of his 1953 Broadway hit [is] a vast improvement over the original," *Newsweek*'s critic found. "For one thing, the comedy of manners is now set against a posh and technicolored backdrop of London at its loveliest. For another, director [Stanley] Donen's stars are Cary Grant and Ingrid Bergman. Together for the first time since 1946 and *Notorious*, the actors volley Krasna's ebullient dialogue with masterful adroitness and manage romance with a subtlety that detracts not for a moment from its ardor." In *Time* there was this: "*Indiscreet* is a conventional comedy of what Hollywood supposes to be upper-class manners, but it is flicked off in the high old style of hilarity that U.S. movie-makers seem to have forgotten in recent years. Director Donen deserves a cash-register-ringing cheer. Actress Bergman, always lovely to look at, is thoroughly competent in the first comedy role that she has played for Hollywood. And Cary Grant is in a class by himself when it comes to giving a girl a yacht."

A. H. Weiler wrote in *The New York Times*, "Call it a tiny miracle or a testament to perseverance, but *Kind Sir*, Norman Krasna's comedy that did not capture the heart of every critic and Broadway playgoer in 1953, has been retitled *Indiscreet* and transformed into a thin but impishly gay and enchanting film that was unveiled at the Musical Hall. Mr. Krasna, who adapted his still weightless play, has not given it any added body. But with the assistance of Ingrid Bergman and Cary Grant [and] producer-director Stanley Donen...they have concocted a frivolous and diverting antic."

Norman Krasna died at seventy-four in Los Angeles on November 1, 1984, but his movie screenplay was later adapted (in 1988) to a lavish made-for-television remake of *Indiscreet*, to which most critics gave a firm thumbs down. Said *Daily Variety*: "Someone wasn't thinking very clearly to begin with when they decided to remake *Indiscreet*, a rather slight story carried entirely by the charisma of Cary Grant and Ingrid Bergman. Casting Robert Wagner and Lesley-Anne Down demonstrates that they weren't thinking any better later on, resulting in about as lifeless and wooden a vidpic as one is likely to ever see -- or better yet, miss...It ends up playing like a 96-minute perfume commercial, though the smell is decidedly unflattering."

STAGE

KIND SIR, *Alvin Theatre*, New York, opened November 4, 1953 165 performances
Produced and directed by Joshua Logan; A Comedy by Norman Krasna; Associate producer and director, Marshall Jamison; Setting and lighting, Jo Mielziner; Costumes, Main Bocher

Mary Martin (Jane Kimball); Charles Boyer (Philip Clair); Dorothy Stickney (Margaret Munson); Margalo Gillmore (Anna Miller); Frank Conroy (Alfred Munson); Robert Ross (Carl Miller)

Cape Playhouse, Dennis, Mass., opened July 13 through 18, 1963
Produced by Charles Mooney; A Comedy by Norman Krasna; Director, Gus Schirmer, Jr.; Gowns, Burton Miller; Setting, Herbert Senn

John Forsythe (Philip Clair); Patricia Barry (Jane Kimball); Mary Cooper (Margaret Munson); Hildegarde Halliday (Annie Miller); Frank Milan (Alfred Munson); Don Doherty (Carl Miller)

SCREEN

INDISCREET, *Warner Bros. Pictures*, released June 1958
A Grandon Production; Produced and directed by Stanley Donen; Screenplay, Norman Krasna, from his play *Kind Sir*; Photography, Frederick A. Young; Art director, Don Ashton; Costumes, Quintino; Music, Richard Rodney Bennett and Ken Jones; Musical conductor, Muir Mathieson; Title song, Sammy Cahn and James Van Heusen; Editor, Jack Harris

Cary Grant (Philip Adams); Ingrid Bergman (Anna Kaufman); Cecil Parker (Alfred Munson); Phyllis Calvert (Margaret Munson); David Kossoff (Carl Banks); Megs Jenkins (Doris Banks); Oliver Johnston (Finleigh); Middleton Woods (Finleigh's Clerk)

TELEVISION

INDISCREET, televised October 24, 1988 CBS 2 hours

A Republic Pictures Production in association with HTV Ltd.; Executive producer, Karen Mack; Executive producers for HTV, Patrick Dromgoole and Johnny Goodman; Producer, John Davis; Supervising producer, Jane Petteway; Director, Richard Michaels; Teleplay, Walter Lockwood and Sally Robinson, based on Norman Krasna's play *Kind Sir* and his 1958 screenplay; Photography, Bob Edwards; Production designer, Ken Sharp; Costume designer, Graham Williams; Music, Arthur B. Rubinstein; Editor, Terry Maisey

Robert Wagner (Philip Adams); Lesley-Anne Down (Anne Kingston); Maggie Henderson (Margaret Munson); Robert McBain (Alfred Munson); Jeni Barnett (Erica James); Fanny Carby (Smitty); Derek Royle (Harry Lawford); Timothy Davies (Peterson); Geoffrey Chater (Herbert Finley); Barry Wolger (Andrew Aukwell); Michael Howarth (Alan Seacove); David Ashford (Charles); Remy Beard (William); Stanley Davies (Taxi Driver); Pavel Douglas (Makeup Man); Barry Andrew (Director); Jerry Harte (Senator Blake); Robert Swales (Actor); Kevin Francis (Runner)

LADY WINDERMERE'S FAN

A Comedy by Oscar Wilde (1892)

Synopsis

Lady Margaret Windermere, a naive young woman, learns from the snobbish Duchess of Berwick that her husband has been having an affair with the notorious, divorced Mrs. Erlynne, hoping to reestablish her in London society. Overwrought with jealousy, she discovers ckecks in her husband's desk written to Mrs. Erlynne. Lord Windermere's insistence that flirty Mrs. Erlynne be invited to the forthcoming ball Margaret further reinforces her belief in his infidelity. However, Mrs. Erlynne charms one and all at the Windermere's ball, especially Lord Augustus Lorton, who proposes marriage. Upset by her guests' fascination and acceptance of Mrs. Erlynne, and of her husband's continuing attention to the attractive woman, Margaret decides to begin an affair of her own -- with Lord Darlington, and leaves a note for her husband. Mrs. Erlynne discovers the note and rushes to the Darlington manor to plead with Lady Windermere to reconsider and return home.

When Lord Darlington and his friends, including Lord Windermere, unexpectedly return from their club for a nightcap. the two women hide in an adjoining room. Gossipy Cecil Graham finds a fan left behind in the drawing room and confronts Darlington about his secret affair. Lord Windermere recognizes the fan and demands an explanation from his host, as Lady Windermere slips out and Mrs. Erlynne appears in the drawing room to claim the fan, returning it the next day to the Windermere's home. Out of gratitude, Margaret becomes devoted to Mrs. Erlynne, but later, when Lady Windermere is out, her husband upbraids Mrs. Erlynne for her disgraceful behavior at Darlington's. Mrs. Erlynne then confesses that she merely was saving her daughter for a similar experience she herself had gone through, and then asks Margaret on her return for permission to keep the fan since they both share the same name. Lord Augustus then arrives to announce he and Mrs. Erlynne plan to wed; the Windermeres are reunited, and Margaret's puritanical views of moralistic Victorian discrimination have mellowed.

Comment and Critique

Oscar Fingall O'Flahertie Wills Wilde was born in Dublin on October 16, 1854. Despite the failure of his first two works, *Vera* and *The Duchess of Padua*, he was paid one hundred pounds by George Alexander to write a play for him. In the summer of 1891, Wilde secluded himself in England's Lake District near Lake Windermere and there wrote his first theatrical success, *Lady Windermere's Fan*. Four years later, there followed his "Trivial Comedy for Serious People," *The Importance of Being Earnest*, which garnered even greater acclaim.

Wilde's original title for the play for Alexander was *A Good Woman*, until his mother reminded him that no one was really interested in "a good woman" -- even in the Victorian era. His brilliant dialogue, sparkling, cynical wit, and deft characterizations of London society delighted audiences on both continents. Ellen Terry's sister, Marion, scored a great personal success as the notorious Mrs. Erlynne in George Alexander's 1892 London production, and *Lady Windermere's Fan* became one of Margaret Anglin's hits on Broadway and later on the road.

Of his fellow playwright, George Bernard Shaw wrote: "He has the property of making his critics dull. They laugh angrily at his epigrams, like a child who is coaxed into being amused in the very act of setting up a yell of rage and agony. They protest that the trick is obvious and that such epigrams can be turned out by the score by anyone lightminded enough to condescend to such frivolity. As far as I can ascertain, I am the only person in London who can sit down and write an Oscar Wilde play at will. The fact that his plays, though apparently lucrative, remain unique under the circumstances says much for the self-denial of our scribes."

The Shaw-Wilde relationship confirmed Dr. Johnson's oft-quoted observation on the Irish as being "fair-minded people": "They never speak well of each other." Wilde's comment on Shaw: "He had no enemies, but all of his friends dislike him."

The first American production of *Lady Windermere's Fan* was seen in New York at Palmer's Theatre in February 1893. "The first American cast...had played the much discussed Wilde piece in Boston, before they presented it in New York," theater historian George Odell wrote. "The chief honors of the performance went to Mrs. Bowers and Maurice Barrymore, to whom, indeed, fell the most showy parts in the play, and who delivered the precious lines with an unction truly remarkable. Mrs. Bowers came to the younger playgoers as a revelation of what the older school could do in the way of crisp, trenchant diction; nothing like her delivery of Wilde's brilliant lines had for years been heard in New York...The talk of the party of men, in Darlington's rooms, and Mrs. Erlynne's self-sacrifice in saving Lady Windermere from social error made an ineradicable impression on all beholders; it was very good theatre..."

The New York Times predicted, about the opening at Palmer's Theatre: "It will have a long run here, and deserves it, too, for it is clever and interesting, if neither profound nor particularly wise...Mr. Wilde is generally whimsical and often absurd...But in *Lady Windermere's Fan*, he shows that he has, after many misadventures in the field of dramatic authorship, learned at last how to write a play that pleases the fancy of the large public and does not make the most painfully judicious grieve very seriously." On October 4, 1893, *The Times* reported the Harlem Opera House production of Wilde's comedy to be "smooth and enjoyable in every respect, and the setting is handsome." The performance by Virginia Harned was described as "graceful and buoyant, yet infused with a sort of fascinating languor."

Charles H. E. Brookfield's travesty on Wilde's *Lady Windermere's Fan*, called

The Poet and the Puppet, played in London for forty performances. Henry Miller's company of comedians (including May Robson, Alice Johnson and Maurice Barrymore) appeared in it in the spring of 1893 at New York's Garden Theatre. "The house echoed with laughter from the moment May Irwin appeared in the prologue as a plump blonde fairy to the end of the performance, two hours later," said *The New York Times*. "Many of the actors succeed in making themselves counterparts of the Palmer company, both in looks and speech, and among these there is but little trace of burlesque...They turn Mr. Wilde's epigrams inside out and end for end...Nobody need be offended, even Mr. Wilde."

Margaret Anglin produced and starred in the 1914 production of Wilde's comedy that opened on Broadway at the Hudson Theatre. "The revival of *Lady Windermere's Fan* is in the nature of a triumph," *The New York Times* reported. "Worn and threadbare as was the material of the story when the play was produced, it still catches and holds the attention here and now. And for all the score and more of years since first it was written, and for all the innumerable imitations of it that have been attempted since, the brilliance of the dialogue seems still undimmed...One reason is because from the first to last, the comedy in this revival is very well acted."

The *New York Dramatic Mirror* wrote that "[it] is one of the most artistic plays ever written, with an intrigue delicately handled, characters wholly unconventional, and situations whose dramatic interest never falters...And very prettily performed by Miss Anglin's company of Shakespearean players...For the part of a polished woman of English society commend us to Miss Anglin. Her whole manner shows breeding and class. And Mrs. Erlynne is a part after her own heart."

On July 3, 1930, *Lady Windermere's Fan* was revived in London, and the critic for the British stage journal *Curtain* wrote: "[It] is still a brilliant play, as is proven in the present revival. The wit of Oscar Wilde lives in the lines, even if his sentiment is somewhat moribund...Wilde told it in the theatrical fashion of his time and redeemed it for future audiences by the supreme quality of the dialogue extraneous to the story."

Fifteen years later, John Gielgud directed a postwar version of the comedy which opened at Theatre Royal Haymarket in a beautiful production designed by Cecil Beaton. "London has rarely seen such elegance as in this John Gielgud production which," *Theatre World* found, "with its Cecil Beaton decor, is a feast of the exquisite and spacious. Against such a background, Wilde's polished wit is doubly satisfying...A talented cast takes full advantage of the stylised wit of Oscar Wilde...Isabel Jeans is the ideal Mrs. Erlynne...This is indeed a production with the theatergoer of discrimination cannot afford to miss."

The following year, Cecil Beaton's stunning production opened on Broadway with Cornelia Otis Skinner as Mrs. Erlynne. (Beaton received the year's Donaldson Award for settings and costumes.) "The revival of Oscar Wilde's *Lady Windermere's Fan*...is such a gorgeous thing, optically, that it should have been done in glorious Technicolor," John Chapman judged in the *Daily News*. "As a comedy, [it] is something of a piece of bric-a-brac, too -- something one might take off the back corner of a whatnot and, after blowing the dust off it, remark affectionately, 'This was quite a piece in its time'...*Lady Windermere's Fan* is the handsomest curio to be mounted on the New York stage in many seasons. The settings are endlessly and fascinatingly fussy, and within them is presented a fashion parade of great beauty. Certainly the stage could offer no lovelier a sight than Penelope Ward as Lady Windermere..."

In the *New York World-Telegram*, William Hawkins called the revival "a spectacularly beautiful production...The 55 years since Wilde wrote the play have not dimmed the wit of his lines, except in so far as they have been quoted and paraphrased...Estelle Winwood gave a knowing and superb picture of the tattletale Duchess...Cornelia Otis Skinner, who is starred as Mrs. Erlynne, is an imposing, handsome figure...John Buckmaster is elegant and sincere as the Lord Darlington... Mr. Beaton himself appears as an effete crony of the principal blades, and garners several lusty laughs..."

Brooks Atkinson (*The New York Times*) felt that: "At the age of 54, Oscar Wilde's *Lady Windermere's Fan* is, to tell the truth, growing a trifle seedy. It is too old to be smart, but not old enough to be a classic like *The School for Scandal*...The scene and costume designer, who is Cecil Beaton, and the actors [come] close as anyone can to persuading you that there is a dance of two in the old girl yet. In fact, Mr. Beaton has contributed as much to the production as Oscar Wilde."

Richard Watts, Jr. (*New York Post*) recalled seeing the Gielgud London production and found it to be "one of the most completely satisfying things I have ever seen in the theatre. The current version [is] by no means that fine, but, for that matter, the play is not as good, either, as *The Importance of Being Earnest*, being among the classic comedies of the English-speaking stage, while, by comparison, *Lady Windermere's Fan* is virtually commonplace." Watts concluded, however, "In our chaotic day, an Oscar Wilde comedy, with its charming artificiality, is particularly welcome, and *Lady Windermere's Fan* should be a comfort to us all."

Noel Coward, in 1954, adapted Wilde's comedy to the musical stage as *After the Ball*. The Coward operetta ran nearly six months at London's Globe Theatre. "Embellished with Mr. Coward's witty lyrics and pleasant music, *After the Ball* is finely mounted, and a first rate company has been assembled to put over effectively both the new songs and the Wilde dialogue, much of which has been left intact," reported *Theatre World*'s Frances Stephens. "Robert Helpmann has produced with an eye to visual effect, and Doris Zinkeisen's scenery and costumes are elegantly in period. The thing to do is forget Wilde, and bask in the Coward wit and music and in the lovely production by Helpmann... This is a musical of style and wit which cannot but please."

Eric Keown (*Punch*) wrote: "One of Noel Coward's difficulties in turning *Lady Windermere's Fan* into a musical comedy is that, not unnaturally, he finds the Victorian period funny, so that, although he uses some of Wilde's epigrams in addition to his own, he cannot escape a spoiling note of burlesque...In other words, the tincture of Wilde is a very uncertain asset, but if one can forget it there is still a good deal in *After the Ball* to be enjoyed simply as musical comedy."

St. John Terrell produced Coward's *After the Ball* in the United States in the summer of 1955 at his Lambertville (N.J.) theatre-in-the-round. Wayne Robinson noted in the *Philadelphia Evening Bulletin*: "Since Oscar Wilde has been called the Noel Coward of his day, it is only apt that Mr. Coward should take Mr. Wilde's *Lady Windermere's Fan* and turn, it some 70 years after it was written, into an operetta...The 'new' book keeps pretty closely to Wilde's original...By its very nature, *After the Ball* is no thermonuclear blockbuster of a musical. 'People,' says Lord Darlington, 'are either tedious or charming.' This musical is both... The Victorian era was a leisurely one, and so it the Wilde-Coward *Ball*...pleasant entertainment with its roots in old-fashioned theatre which takes it own good time (three hours by our watch last night) to tell a story."

In his book *Noel*, Charles Castle wrote of *After the Ball*: "Although it was expertly directed by Robert Helpmann, and had enchanting music and lyrics, it flopped." Castle cited Sir Robert's explanation: "You would have thought that a play of Wilde's with music by Coward would be marvelous but I suddenly realised at the first rehearsal it was like having two funny people at a dinner party. Everything that Noel sent up Wilde was sentimental about, and everything that Wilde sent up Noel was sentimental about. It was two different points of view and it didn't work. It could never have worked."

A second musical, *A Delightful Season*, adapted by Don Allan Clayton from Wilde's play, opened in New York at the Gramercy Arts Theatre in late September 1960. It lasted just seven performances.

Three quarters of a century after the first production of Wilde's comedy, it once again was revived in London, under Anthony Quayle's direction at the Phoenix Theatre. "Once again, Cecil Beaton has designed the settings -- no, not designed, *mounted*! This time, the interior decorator in him has run amok. With the exception of the ballroom scene, which is conventionally pretty, the sets are hideous," thought Frank Marcus of the 1966 staging in *Plays and Players*. "The acting is equally ill-assorted...the two main elements in Wilde's play are melodrama and comedy of manners. The comedy is efficient, with patches of brilliance, but the melodrama is contrived, so wooden and so dull -- and in *Lady Windermere's Fan* so predominant -- that the whole experience becomes an ordeal rather than an entertainment."

Lady Windermere's Fan first was brought to the screen in 1916 by Britain's Ideal Pictures, and in 1925, for Warner Bros., Ernst Lubitsch gave Wilde's play his soon-to-be-legendary "Lubitsch Touch." Ted Shane (*The New Yorker*) said of the Warner version, "Oscar Wilde will have no cause to turn over in his grave. Der Herr Lubitsch has done magnificently, if somewhat Germanically, by the Gifted Magpie of the perfumed sayings, He has attempted and succeeded in transforming a Wilde without use of a single tinseled Wilde epigram from the play, rather trusting to his own great sense of cinematic wit and the dramatic. The result is a Wilde of wondrous characterization and situation...well interspersed with pictorial wit, acted by the usual splendid hand-held Lubitschean actors." Shane summed up: "It comes closer to perfection than any production of the year, with the inevitable exception of *The Last Laugh*."

Life magazine labeled *Lady Windermere's Fan* by Wilde, out of Lubitsch, "One of the best pictures of the year -- a brilliant production; an amazingly skillful and intelligent adaptation...in which Lubitsch again demonstrates the cerebral superiority that has placed him in a class by himself among movie directors." And *Time* magazine, allowing for the difficulties in transferring drawing-room comedy to the screen, added: "Mr. Lubitsch has done it about as well as one could wish."

The New York Times, on the other hand, decided: "While the screen translation of Oscar Wilde's *Lady Windermere's Fan* is a worthy production, rivaling most of the sophisticated subjects of its type, it shrinks in importance beside the original effort."

Twenty-four years later, Wilde's *Lady Windermere's Fan* again got the Hollywood treatment -- as *The Fan*. Director Otto Preminger later admitted: "It was a mistake on my part to have remade this play. Whatever I did to the film was wrong. It is one of the few pictures I disliked while I was working on it." Preminger's *The Fan*, with Jeanne Crain in the lead, was a decided flop. *Time* magazine viewed it as featuring "a group of talented actors pretending to be characters in a play by Oscar Wilde...At its 20th Century ersatz movie worst, it emerges as a sentimental woman's drama -- a sort of *Stella Dallas* in turn-of-the-century stays."

Bosley Crowther (*The New York Times*) wrote: "Most of the brittle wit and satire of Mr. Wilde's conversation piece has been lost in the making of this picture, except for a few scattered scenes, an occasional epigrammatic sally and the shadow of one character. The Duchess of Berwick, that old windbag of Victorian pomp and snobbery, is brilliantly indicated by Martita Hunt in a couple of brief scenes...but the rest of this nicely costumed picture which Otto Preminger has directed and produced for 20th Century-Fox is a strangely uninspired nostalgic romance."

On television, *Lady Windermere's Fan* was produced several times in Great Britain. It was a "Play of the Week" in 1967, "crisply directed by Joan Kempson," according to the critic for *The London Times*, who also felt that "Stanley Miller's adaptation ironed out most of the verbal problems." *The Times* also found that "Barbara Jefford [as Mrs. Erlynne] was admirable in this role, suggesting a woman who combined a mind like a cash register with a heart as big as, say, South Kensington Station." Wilde's comedy later was a lavish BBC production that premiered in London in 1985 and came to the States on cable TV the following year. The crisply directed teleplay featured Stephanie Turner as Mrs. Erlynne, Kenneth Cranham as Lord Darlington, Helene Little as Lady Windermere, and Tim Woodward as Lord Windermere.

STAGE

LADY WINDERMERE'S FAN, *St. James's Theatre*, London, opened February 20, 1892

Produced and directed by George Alexander; A Comedy by Oscar Wilde; Decor, Frank Giles and Company; Costumes, Mme. Savage and Mme. Purdue; Wig, C. H. Fox; Incidental music, Walter Slaughter; Company manager, Alwyn Lewis; Stage manager, Robert V. Shone

Marion Terry (Mrs. Erlynne); Lily Hanbury (succeeded by Winifred Emery) (Lady Windermere); George Alexander (Lord Windermere); Nutcombe Gould (Lord Darlington); H. H. Vincent (Lord Augustus Lorton); Fanny Coleman (Duchess of Berwick); Laura Graves (succeeded by Edith Chester) (Lady Agatha Carlisle); Ben Webster (Mr. Cecil Graham); A. Vane Tempest (Charles Dumby); Alfred Holles (Mr. Hopper); Miss A. DeWinton (Mrs. Cowper-Cowper); Miss B. Page (Lady Jedburgh); Miss M. Girdlestone (Lady Stutfield); Mr. V. Sansbury (Parker); Miss W. Dolan (Rosalie); Miss Granville (Lady Plymdale)

THE POET AND THE PUPPETS, *Comedy Theatre*, London, opened May 19, 1892
40 performances

Produced by Charles H. Hawtrey; A Travesty by Charles H. E. Brookfield, based on Oscar Wilde's *Lady Windermere's Fan*; Director, Frederick Glover; Music director, James M. Glover; Acting manager, E. F. Bradley; Stage manager, Charles Milton

Charles H. Hawtrey (A Poet); Cynthia Brook (Lady Winterstock); Lottie Venne (Mrs. Earlybird/ Ophelia/ Fairy); Charles H. E. Brookfield (Lord Pentonville/ Hamlet/ A Moralist/ Spirit of Fair Arbitration); Eric Lewis (Lord Winterstock/ An Author); James Nelson (Lord Gonbustus Often); Lizzie Ruggles ("The Duchess"); E. Gross (Mrs. Nicey-Nicey); E. Gordon (Mrs. Lummy-Lummy); Ernest Cosham (A Realist/ First Young Man); William Wyes (Parker); Violet Austin (Mrs. Willoughby Mydear); Florence Wilson (Mrs. Welly Nearly); William Philip (A Bard/ Second Young Man); John Phipps (An Optimist); Harley Granville-Barker (Third Young Man); Charles Milton (Fourth Young Man); Lizzie Wilson (Mrs. McNaughtie-Naughtie)

LADY WINDERMERE'S FAN, *Palmer's Theatre*, New York, opened February 6, 1893
69 performances

Produced by A. M. Palmer Stock Company; A Comedy by Oscar Wilde; Presented by special arrangement with Mr. Charles Frohman; Director, A. M. Palmer; Settings by Marston

May Brooklyn (Mrs. Erlynne); Julia Arthur (Lady Windermere); Edward Bell (Lord Windermere); Maurice Barrymore (Lord Darlington); E. M. Holland (Lord Augustus Lorton); Mrs. D. P. Bowers (Duchess of Berwick); Ann Urhart (Lady Agatha Carlisle); Walden Ramsay (Mr. Cecil Graham); J. G. Saville (Charles Dumby); Edward S. Abeles (Mr. Hopper); Rose Barrington (Mrs. Cowper Cowper); Emily Seward (Lady Jedburgh); Marie Henderson (Lady Stutfield); Guido Marburg (Parker); Zenaide Vislaire (Rosalie); Fanny Jackson (Lady Plymdale)

*Replaced during a performance by Walden Ramsay during the second week of the run. Edward S. Abeles took over the role of Cecil Graham

THE POET AND THE PUPPETS, *Garden Theatre*, New York, opened April 3, 1893
A Travesty by Charles H. E. Brookfield, based on Oscar Wilde's *Lady Windermere's Fan*; Preceded by a one-act farce, *His Wedding Day*

Henry Miller (The Poet, Oscar O'Flaherty Wilde); Elaine Ellison (Lady Winterstock); Alice Johnson (Mrs. Earlybird); May Irwin (A Fairy/Ophelia); Max Finegan (Hamlet); May Robson (Miss Yesmama); H. Lillford (Lord Pentonville); H. A. Roberts (Lord Winterstock); Harry Mills (Spirit of Arbitration); Harry Brown (Lord Gonbustus Often); Hawtry Webb (Sir Charles Stillwater); Harry Woodruff (Gwynne Bennett/ A Realist); Fred Strong (Parker)

NOTE: On opening night, Maurice Barrymore played the Man in Darlington's Chamber scene

MUSICAL NUMBERS; "Daddy Won't Buy Me a Bow-Wow" performed by May Irwin; "Three-Legged Dance" performed by May Robson

LADY WINDERMERE'S FAN, *Harlem Opera House*, New York, opened October 3, 1893
A Comedy by Oscar Wilde

Virginia Harned (Mrs. Erlynne); Evelyn Campbell (Lady Windermere); Frank Gillmore (Lord Windermere); Howard Hansel (Lord Darlington); J. C. Saville (Lord Augustus Lorton); Mrs. E. J. Phillips (Duchess of Berwick); Beulah Staff (Lady Agatha Carlisle); Edward S. Abeles (Mr. Cecil Graham); Herbert Ayeling (Charles Dumby); Guido Harburg (Mr. Hopper); Etta Morris (Mrs. Cowper-Cowper); Marie Henderson (Lady Jedburg); Anne Standard (Lady Stutfield); Fanny Jackson (Lady Plymdale)

St. James's Theatre, London, opened November 19, 1904 93 performances
Produced and directed by George Alexander; A Comedy by Oscar Wilde; Decor, Walter Hann; Lighting, W. Barbour; Costumes, Mme. Frederic, Mme. Hayward, Mme. Brown, Marshall and Snelgrove, Mrs. Evans, Mme. Elsie; Music director, William Robins; General manager, C. T. H. Helmsley; Stage managers, E. Vivian Reynolds and H. R. Kimpton

Marion Terry (Mrs. Erlynne); Lilian Braithwaite (Lady Windermere); Ben Webster (Lord Windermere); C. Aubrey Smith (Lord Darlington); Sydney Brough (succeeded by Eric Lewis) (Lord Augustus Lorton); Fanny Coleman (Duchess of Berwick); Corisande Hamilton (succeeded by Barbara Hannay)(Lady Agatha Carlisle); Selwyn Seymour (Mr. Cecil Graham); A. Vane-Tempest (succeeded by Robert Horton) (Charles Dumby); Eileen Lewis (Mrs. Cowper-Cowper); Elinor Aickin (Lady Jedburgh); Maud Harcourt (Rosalie); Pauline French (Lady Plymdale)

Touring Company, season 1907-08
A Comedy by Oscar Wilde

Leah Winslow (Mrs. Erlynne); Josephine Lovett (Lady Windermere); William Ingersoll (Lord Windermere); Robert Cummings (Lord Darlington); Frederick Summer (Lord Augustus Lorton); Helen Reimer (Duchess of Berwick); Evelyn Francis (Lady Agatha Carlisle); Harmon MacGregor (Mr. Cecil Graham); John Stellping (Charles Dumby); Edith Walls (Mrs. Cowper-Cowper); J. Hammond Dailey (Mr. Hopper); Mayme Zorb (Lady Stutfield); May Callahan (Lady Jedburgh); Kitty Raye (Rosalie); Myra Jackson (Lady Plymdale); Mark Price (Parker); Vera Berrie (Miss Graham); Kenneth Bisbee (Sir James Royston); John Flemmings (Mr. Rufford)

Hudson Theatre, New York, opened March 30, 1914; moved to *Liberty Theatre*, April 13, 1914 72 performances
Produced by Margaret Anglin; A Comedy by Oscar Wilde; Director, George Foster Platt; General manager, James Shesgreen; Acting manager, Lodewick Vroom; Stage manager, Howard Lindsay

Margaret Anglin (Mrs. Erlynne); Margery Maude (Lady Windermere); Pedro De Cordoba (Lord Windermere); Arthur Byron (Lord Darlington); Sarah Cowell LeMoyne (Duchess of Berwick); Sidney Greenstreet (Lord Augustus Lorton); Margery Card (Lady Agatha Carlisle); Norman Tharp (Mr. Cecil Graham); Wallace Widdecombe (Charles Dumby); Donald Cameron (Mr. Hopper); Sally Williams (Mrs. Cowper-Cowper); Lillian Thurgate (Lady Jedburgh); Florence Wollerson (Lady Stutfield/Rosalie); Ruth Holt Boucicault (Lady Plymdale); Harry Barfoot (Parker); Helen Joseffy (Miss Graham); Louise Gilmore, Ethel Lawrence, Silvia Zan, Jane Page, William Lod, Frank Durand, Shirley Braithwaite (Guests)

Touring Company, season 1914-15
Produced by Margaret Anglin; A Comedy by Oscar Wilde; Director, George Foster Platt; General manager, James Shesgreen; Acting manager, Lodewick Vroom; Stage manager, Howard Lindsay

Margaret Anglin (succeeded by Margery Maude) (Mrs. Erlynne); Florence Carpenter (Lady Windermere); Leonard Willey (Lord Windermere); Stanley Dark (Lord Darlington); Ruth Holt Bouciçault (Duchess of Berwick); Sidney Greenstreet (Lord Augustus Lorton); Carolyn Darling (Lady Agatha Carlisle); Harry Redding (Mr. Cecil Graham); Wallace Widdecombe (Charles Dumby); Donald Cameron (Mr. Hopper); Catherine Ainsley (Mrs. Cowper-Cowper); Virginia Palmer (Lady Jedburgh); Jane Houston (Lady Stutfield); Louise Van Wageman (Rosalie/Lady Paisley); Helene Sinnott (Lady Plymdale); Harry Barfoot (Parker); Helen Joseffy (Miss Graham); Roy Porter (Footman)

Everyman Theatre, London, opened July 3, 1930
A Comedy by Oscar Wilde; Director, Stephen Thomas

Kate Cutler (Mrs. Erlynne); Kathleen O'Regen (Lady Windermere); Cecil Parker (Lord Windermere); Eric Maturin (Lord Darlington); Margaret Yarde (Duchess of Berwick); George Merritt (Lord Augustus Lorton); Pamela Carme (Lady Agatha Carlisle); Michael Shepley (Mr. Cecil Graham); Ernest Thesiger (Charles Dumby); Eric Lugg (Mr. Hopper); Lumena Edwardes (Mrs. Cowper-Cowper); Nona Hoffe (Lady Jedburgh); Madge Snell (Rosalie); John V. Trevor (Parker); Mary Hinton (Lady Plymdale)

Recital Theatre (Daly's 63rd Street Theatre), New York, opened January 26, 1932 4 performances
Produced by the Afternoon Theatre; A Comedy by Oscar Wilde; Director, Arthur William Row

Theresa Maxwell (Mrs. Erlynne); Ellis Baker (Lady Windermere); Richard Stevenson (Lord Windermere); Sherling Oliver (Lord Darlington); Essex Dane (Duchess of Berwick); Herbert Standing (Lord Augustus Lorton); Florence Williams (Lady Agatha Carlisle); Carl Emory (Mr. Hopper)

Theatre Royal Haymarket, London, August 21, 1945 602 performances
Produced by Tennent Plays Ltd. in association with C.E.M.A. by arrangement with Frederick Harrison Trust Ltd.; A Comedy by Oscar Wilde; Director, John Gielgud; Decor, Cecil Beaton; Lighting, William Conway

Isabel Jeans (Mrs. Erlynne); Dorothy Hyson (Lady Windermere); Geoffrey Toone (Lord Windermere); Griffith Jones (Lord Darlington); Athene Seyler (Duchess of Berwick); Michael Shepley (Lord Augustus Lorton); Patricia Dickson (Lady Agatha Carlisle); Denys Blakelock (Mr. Cecil Graham); Deering Wells (Charles Dumby); Hugh Stewart (Mr. Hopper); Phyllis Thomas (Mrs. Cowper-Cowper); Phyllis Relph (Lady Jedburgh); Diana Marshall (Lady Stutfield); Stuart Bull (Parker); Hilda Bruce-Potter (Rosalie/Lady Paisley); Thomas Hutcheson (Lord Paisley); Gladys Wykeham Edwards (Lady Plymdale); Gillian Raine (Miss Graham); Anthony Massie, Victor Albany (Footmen)

Cort Theatre, New York, opened October 14, 1946 227 performances
Produced by Homer Curran in association with Russell Lewis and Howard Young*; A Comedy by Oscar Wilde; Director, Jack Minster; Scenery, lighting and costumes, Cecil Beaton; Company manager, Emmett R. Callahan; Stage manager, Robert Linden

Cornelia Otis Skinner (Mrs. Erlynne); Penelope Ward (Lady Windermere); Henry Daniell (succeeded by David Manners) (Lord Windermere); John Buckmaster (Lord Darlington); Estelle Winwood (Duchess of Berwick); Rex Evans (Lord Augustus Lorton); Sally Cooper (Lady Agatha Carlisle); Cecil Beaton (succeeded by Rex O'Malley) (Mr. Cecil Graham); Evan Thomas (Charles Dumby); Stanley Bell (Mr. Hopper); Leonore Elliott (succeeded by Jeri Sauvinet) (Mrs. Cowper-Cowper); Elizabeth Valentine (Lady Jedburgh); Anne Curson (Lady Stutfield); Jack Merivale (Sir James Royston); Marguerite Gleason (Lady Paisley); Thomas Louden (Parker); Marjorie Wood (succeeded by Pamela Wright) (Rosalie); Jeri Sauvinet (succeeded by Dorothy Kelley) (Miss Rufford); Paul Russell (succeeded by Richard Burns) (Mr. Rufford); Nan Hopkins (succeeded by Louise Prussing) (Lady Plymdale); Pamela Wright (Miss Graham); Tanagra Thayer (Hon. Paulette Sonning); Peter Keyes (The Bishop); Guy Blacke, Richard Burns (Footmen)

*This production opened at the *Curran Theatre*, San Francisco, on August 26, 1946 with this cast, except Jack Merivale (Mr. Cecil Graham); George Pembroke (Charles Dumby); Guy Blake (Sir James Royston)

Touring Company, season 1947-48
Produced by Homer Curran in association with Russell Lewis and Howard Young; A Comedy by Oscar Wilde; Director, Jack Minster; Scenery, costumes and lighting, Cecil Beaton; Company manager, Emmett R. Callahan; Stage managers, Peter

Keyes and Arthur Stenning

Cornelia Otis Skinner (Mrs. Erlynne); Judith Fellows (Lady Windermere); David Manners (Lord Windermere); Bramwell Fletcher (Lord Darlington); Estelle Winwood (Duchess of Berwick); Rex Evans (Lord Augustus Lorton); Suzette Meredith (Lady Agatha Carlisle); George Thirlwell (Mr. Cecil Graham); Evan Thomas (Charles Dumby); Michael Sadler (Mr. Hopper); Joyce Harris (Mrs. CowperCowper); Peter Keyes (Sir James Royston); Matilde Baring (Lady Jedburgh); Chaucy Horsley (Lady Stutfield); Madge Preston (Miss Rufford); Richard Harrison (Mr. Rufford); Mary Brady (Miss Graham); Mary MacLeod (Rosalie); Henry Vincent (Parker); Louise Prussing (Lady Plymdale); Nola Haines (Hon. Paulette Sonning); Arthur Stenning (The Bishop); Richard St. John (Footman)

AFTER THE BALL, *Globe Theatre*, London, opened June 10, 1954

Produced by Tennent Productions Ltd.; A Musical Comedy, based on Oscar Wilde's *Lady Windermere's Fan*; Director, Robert Helpmann; Music and lyrics by Noel Coward; Scenery and costumes, Doris Zinkelman; Costumes for Miss Browne and Miss Cree by Jacqmar; Music director, Philip Martell; Orchestrations, Philip Green; General manager, Bernard Gordon; Production manager, Ian Dow; Stage managers, Jane Shirley and Andrew Sachs

Mary Ellis (Mrs. Erlynne); Vanessa Lee (Lady Windermere); Peter Graves (Lord Windermere); Shamus Locke (Lord Darlington); Irene Browne (Duchess of Berwick); Donald Scott (Lord Augustus Lorton); Tom Gill (Mr. Cecil Graham); Dennis Bowen (Charles Dumby); Graham Payn (Mr. Hopper); Aileen Gamley (Mrs. Cowper-Cowper); Pam Marmont (Lady Stutfield); John Morley (Lord Paisley); Betty Felstead (Lady Jedburgh); Anna Halinka (Lady Paisley); Bill Horsley (Mr. Rufford/Darlington's Footman); Margaret Gibson (Mrs. Arthur Bowden); Leslie Pearson (Parker); Maureen Quinney (Miss Graham); Lois Green (Lady Plymdale); Silvia Beamish (Lady Ruckinge); Marion Grimaldi (Mrs. Hurst-Green); Raymond Savigar (Guy Berkeley)

MUSICAL NUMBERS: "Oh, What a Century It's Been"; "I Knew That You Would Be My Love"; "Mr. Hopper's Chanty"; "Sweet Day"; "Stay on the Side of the Angels"; "Quartette"; "Creme de la Creme"; "Light Is the Heart"; "May I Have the Pleasure?"; "I Offer You My Heart"; "Why Is It the Woman Who Pays?"; "Aria"; "Go, I Beg You Go"; "London at Night"; "Clear Bright Morning"; "All My Life Ago"; "Something on a Tray"; "Farewell Song"; "Faraway Land"

Dropped during tryout: "Oh, What a Season This Has Been"

Original cast recording: Phillips Records

AFTER THE BALL, *Music Circus*, Lambertville, N.J., opened August 2, 1955 8 performances

Produced by St. John Terrell; A Musical Comedy, based on Oscar Wilde's *Lady Windermere's Fan*; Director, Bertram Yarborough; Music and lyrics by Noel Coward; Setting, Donn Fischer; Costumes, Charles Macri; Musical director, Oscar Kosarin; Assistant conductor and choral director, Donald Pippin; Choreography, Duncan Noble; General manager, Arthur Gerold; Production manager, Bruce Laffey; Stage managers, St. John Terrell and John Conboy

Eleanor Lutton (Mrs. Erlynne); Gloria Hamilton (Lady Windermere); Dick Smart (Lord Windermere); Eric Brotherson (Lord Darlington); Cynthia Latham (Duchess of Berwick); Fred Harper (Lord Augustus Lorton); Kirsten Valbor (Lady Agatha

Carlisle); Jerome Reed (Mr. Cecil Graham); David Gard (Charles Dumby); Doug Rogers (Mr. Hopper); Barbara George (Mrs. Cowper-Cowper); Marilyn Hodges (Lady Jedburgh); Joyce Barker (Lady Stutfield); Dorring Seymour (Lord Paisley); John Conboy (Parker); Robert Reim (Mr. Rufford); Susan Shaute (Lady Plymdale); Randy Simmons (Lady Ruckinge); Harold Jagel (Guy Berkeley); Elaine Nochumson (Mrs. Hurst-Green); Baird Searles (Darlington's Footman)

A DELIGHTFUL SEASON, *Gramercy Arts Theatre*, New York, opened September 28, 1960 7 performances
Produced by New Enterprises, Allan Stern and Gerada Burke, producers, in association with Nicholas Pavlik and Jerri Kenneally; A Musical Comedy, based on Oscar Wilde's *Lady Windermere's Fan*; Director, Bill Butler; Book, music and lyrics by Don Allan Clayton; Scenery and lighting, Robin Wagner; Costumes, Domingo A. Rodriguez; Musical direction and orchestrations, Jay Brewer

Joan Copeland (Mrs. Erlynne); Karen Thorsell (Lady Windermere); Donald Symington (Lord Windermere); Nick Todd (Lord Darlington); Jane Lambert (Duchess of Berwick); Charles French (Lord Augustus Lorton); Kay Brewer (Lady Agatha Carlisle); Brian Desmond (Mr. Cecil Graham); Jonathan Taylor (Charles Dumby); Fred Mueller (Mr. Hopper); Frances Parker (Mrs. Cowper-Cowper); Estelle Ritchie (Lady Stutfield); Ruth Livingston (Lady Jedburgh); James Baker (Sir James Royston); William Eddy (Mr. Rufford); Edward Zimmerman (Parker); Barbara Newborn (Lady Plymdale)

MUSICAL NUMBERS: "A Delightful Season"; "Gentle and Kind"; "I Don't Like to Talk"; "Once to Every Woman"; "Someone That I Love"; "A Good Husband"; "Love Song"; "Yes, Mamma"; "Would All Were Well"; "Living Up to the Past"; "Windermere Waltz"; "Who's the Girl?"; "If I Were Not the Butler"; "I Discovered My Heart" (Bill Butler and Jay Brewer, based on a theme by D. A. Clayton)

LADY WINDERMERE'S FAN, *Phoenix Theatre*, London, opened October 13, 1966 146 performances
Produced by H. M. Tennent Ltd.; A Comedy by Oscar Wilde; Director, Anthony Quayle; Production designer, Cecil Beaton

Coral Browne (Mrs. Erlynn); Juliet Mills (Lady Windermere); John Humphry (Lord Windermere); Ronald Lewis (Lord Darlington); Isabel Jeans (Duchess of Berwick); Wilfrid Hyde-White (Lord Augustus Lorton); Carolyn Montagu (Lady Agatha Carlisle); Corin Redgrave (Mr. Cecil Graham); Anthony Royle (Charles Dumby); Terence Bayler (Mr. Hopper); Anne Sherwin (Mrs. Cowper-Cowper); Molly Veness (Lady Jedburgh); Billie Hill (Lady Stutfield); Peter Jackson (Sir James Royston); Martin Aubrey (Guy Berkeley); Maria Warburgh (Miss Graham); Geoffrey King (Parker); Celestine Randall (Rosalie); George Desmond (The Bishop); Jacqueline Lacey (Lady Plymdale); Roy Boyd (Darlington's Footman)

Toronto Truck Theatre, New York, opened April 7, 1977
Produced by Toronto Truck Theatre Company; A Comedy by Oscar Wilde; Director, Peter Peroff; Stage management and Set design, Antoine Martine; Lighting, Tim Fort; Costumes, Ken Nye

Irene Hanson (Mrs. Erlynne); Virginia Reh (Lady Windermere); James Bartley (Lord Windermere); Alan Fawcett (Lord Darlington); Jo Haviland (Duchess of Berwick); Daniel Hyatt (Lord Augustus Lorton); Adrienne Eisnor (Lady Agatha Carlisle); Allan Habberfield (Mr. Cecil Graham); Tim Fort (Charles Dumby);

Raymond Storey (Mr. Hopper); Garnet Truax (Parker); Pat Boothman (Lady Plymdale)

SCREEN

LADY WINDERMERE'S FAN, *Ideal Pictures* (Great Britain), released July 1916; in U.S. released January 1917
Director, Fred Paul; Screenplay, Benedict James, based on the play by Oscar Wilde

Irene Rooke (Mrs. Erlynne); Netta Westcott (Lady Windermere); Milton Rosmer (Lord Windermere); Arthur Wontner (Lord Darlington); Alice de Winton (Duchess of Berwick); Joyce Kerr (Lady Agatha Carlisle); Nigel Playfair (Lord Augustus Lorton); Evan Thomas (Mr. Cecil Graham); Vivian Reynolds (Mr. Dumby); Sidney Vautier (Mr. Hopper)

Warner Bros. Pictures, released December 1925
Director, Ernst Lubitsch; Adaptation and screenplay, Julien Josephson, based on the play by Oscar Wilde; Photography, Charles J. Van Enger; Assistant cameraman, Willard Van Enger; Decor, Harold Grieve; Assistant director, George Hippard

Irene Rich (Mrs. Erlynne); May McAvoy (Lady Windermere); Bert Lytell (Lord Windermere); Ronald Colman (Lord Darlington); Edward Martindel (Lord Augustus Lorton); Billie Bennett (Gossipy Duchess); Carrie Daumery (Duchess of Berwick); Wilson Benge (Parker); Larry Steers (Cecil Graham)

HISTORIA DE UNA MALA MUJER, *Argentine Sono Films*, released 1948
Director, Luis Saslavsky; Screenplay, Pedro Miguel Obligado, based on Oscar Wilde's *Lady Windermere's Fan*; Photography, Alberto Erchebechere; Settings, Gori Munoz; Music, Victor Slister; Editor, Jorge Garate

Dolores Del Rio (Mrs. Erlynne); Maria Duval (Lady Windermere); Francisco de Paula (Lord Windermere); Alberto Closas (Lord Darlington); Fernando Lamas (Lord Augustus Lorton); Amalia Sanchez Arino (Duchess of Berwick)

THE FAN, *20th Century-Fox*, released April 1949
Produced and directed by Otto Preminger; Screenplay, Dorothy Parker, Walter Reisch and Rose Evans, based on Oscar Wilde's *Lady Windermere's Fan*; Photography, Joseph LaShelle; Art directors, Lyle R. Wheeler and Leland Fuller; Set decorators, Thomas Little and Paul S. Fox; Costumes, Charles Le Maire and Rene Hubert; Special visual effects, Fred Sersen; Music, Daniele Amfitheatrof; Music director, Alfred Newman; Orchestrations, Edward Powell and Maurice de Packh; Editor, Louis R. Loeffler

Madeleine Carroll (Mrs. Erlynne); Jeanne Crain (Lady Windermere); Richard Greene (Lord Windermere); George Sanders (Lord Darlington); Martita Hunt (Duchess of Berwick); Virginia McDowall (Lady Agatha Carlisle); Hugh Dempster (Lord Augustus Lorton); Richard Ney (Mr. Hopper); John Sutton (Cecil Graham); Hugh Murray (Dawson); Frank Elliott (The Jeweler); John Burton (Hoskins); Trevor Ward (The Auctioneer); Winifred Harris (The Maid); Alphone Martell (Philippe); Colin Campbell (The Tailor); Terry Kilburn (Messenger); Felippa Rock (Rosalie); Tempe Pifott (Mrs. Rudge); Patricia Walker (An American); Eric Noonan (Underwood)

TELEVISION

LADY WINDERMERE'S FAN, televised September 25, 1967 Yorkshire Television 1 hour
Executive producer, Peter Willes; Director, Joan Kemp-Welch; A Play by Oscar Wilde; Designer, John Clements

Barbara Jefford (Mrs. Erlynne); Jennie Linden (Lady Windermere); Ian Ogilvy (Lord Windermere); James Villiers (Lord Darlington); Richard Vernon (Lord Augustus Lorton); Joan Benham (Duchess of Berwick); Mia Martin (Lady Agatha Carlisle); John Steiner (Mr. Dumby); Elliott Cairnes (Mr. Hopper); Jennifer Wright (Lady Plymdale); Barbara Bolton (Lady Jed-burgh); John Lee (Parker)

LADY WINDERMERE'S FAN, televised September 15, 1985 BBC 2 hours; in U.S. on Arts and Entertainment Channel, televised September 9, 1986
Produced by British Broadcasting Corporation; Producer, Louis Marks; Director, Tony Smith; A Play by Oscar Wilde; Script editor, David Snodin; Production designer, Don Taylor; Costumes, Phoebe De Gaye; Makeup, Marion Richards; Lighting, Alan Horne; Production associate, Chris Cherry; Choreography, Geraldine Stephenson; Graphic designer, Graham Kern; Sound supervisor, Richard Chubb

Stephanie Turner (Mrs. Erlynne); Helena Little (Lady Windermere); Tim Woodward (Lord Windermere); Kenneth Cranham (Lord Darlington); Robert Lang (Lord Augustus Lorton); Sara Kestelman (Duchess of Berwick); Amanda Royle (Lady Agatha Carlisle); John Clive (Mr. Dumby); Geoff Morrell (Mr. Hopper); Veronica Lang (Lady Plymdale); Gloria Connell (Mrs. Cowper-Cowper); Vivien Lloyd (Lady Stutfield); Diana Fairfax (Lady Jedburgh); Mary Kurowski (Rosalie); Ian Burford (Parker); Sally Sinclair (Nanny); Danielle Colairo (Baby); Giles Oldershaw (Footman); Gary Dean (Sir James Royston); Peter Gates Fleming (Guy Berkeley); Kay Springle (Miss Graham; Leslie Adams (Lord Paisley); Sheila Rennie (Lady Paisley); Russell Brook (Mr. Rufford); George Ballantine (Arthur Bowden); Margaret McKechnie (Mrs. Arthur Bowden); Johnny Mack (Duke of Berwick); Brychen Powell, Derek Suthern, Tony Snell, Pat Butler, Elaine Hopkins (Servants); Paul Sadler, Gaynor Seago, Paul Ellison, Lesley Burt, Nigel Descombes, Carol Freeman, Oscar Peck, Cindy Blow, Mike Mungarven, Jane Bough, Kenneth Sedd, Ray Knight, Jacqueline Noble, Juliette James, Geoff Whitestone, Liz Adams, Nicholas Segrue, Ellison Kemp, Kevin O'Brien, Susan Eddy, Hilary Michelle, Bert Crome, Wendy Danvers, Reg Thomason, Elaine Williams, Maureen Stevens, Douglas Auchterlonie, David Cleeve, Fred Reford, Rosalyn Cole, Iben Hutzelsider, Jinty Coventry, Kay Zimmermann, Ina Claire, Joan Chorlton, Su Bishop, Christopher Beeching, Rodney James, Peter Jessup, Sean Bartley, Ken Laurie, Barry Grantham, Michael Sherwin (Guests)

THE LADY WITH THE LAMP
A Play by Reginald Berkeley (1929)

Synopsis

Born in Florence, Italy, of English parents on May 12, 1820, she was named for the city of her birth. Florence Nightingale was appointed Superintendent of Nursing at London's Hospital for Invalid Gentlewomen. A royal commission of inquiry's investigation into the inadequate care of casualties in the Crimean War's wretchedly equipped field hospitals causes Nurse Nightingale to offer her services to her longtime friend, Sidney Herbert, Secretary of War. She is sent to the Crimea in complete charge of hospitals and head of the nursing corps, and arrives with thirty-eight nurses at Scutari where the hordes of wounded were coming back from Balaklava and Inkerman. The dedication and determination of Nurse Nightingale gradually results in sanitizing the deplorable barrack hospitals and improving nursing conditions. At night she makes the hospital rounds with her lamp, offering comfort and encouragement. She soon is placed in charge of all Bosphorus hospitals housing over ten thousand wounded while bureaucratic military resistance, red tape and regulations threaten her accomplishments.

By June 1855, Nurse Nightingale's stern supervision has reduced the high hospital death rate to two percent. Despite her failing health, she refuses to leave the Crimea, and in July 1856, she shuns a British warship sent to return her to England. She finally arrives in London aboard a French vessel, thereby avoiding a tumultuous reception arranged for her. Queen Victoria has granted her request for vital reforms on all military hospitals. Florence Nightingale, who has helped found the Nightingale Home for training nurses at St. Thomas Hospital, in 1907 receives the Order of Merit of the British Empire. She dies in London on August 13, 1910, at age ninety and is buried at East Wellow, Hampshire, England.

Comment and Critique

Based on Lytton Strachey's biography, *Eminent Victorians*, Reginald Berkeley's 1929 play, appropriately called *The Lady With a Lamp*, opened in London at the Arts Theatre with Edith Evans as Florence Nightingale. London's *Bystander* described the drama: "[It] is Reginald Berkeley's series of tableaux, well told and well acted. Not-so-long-dead people figure in this play. Fair Florence is shown as a young girl; with pentup passions, finding expression at last in ruthless campaigning, driving strong men to despair, and herself to senile old age...Miss Edith Evans gives an astonishing performance of the great lady both in youth and age."

The critic for London's *The Curtain* called it: "A chronicle of Florence Nightingale from girlhood to old age. The heroism of the woman is depicted with a reality rarely found in stage writing...Edith Evans, less mannered than usual, sails splendidly through the part...Reginald Berkeley has given us an impressive work, albeit an amalgam of history and histrionics. Edith Evans, as Florence, from youth to old age, contributes a performance which must rank as one of the greatest of the year 1929..."

In mid November 1931, Edith Evans' *The Lady With a Lamp* arrived on Broadway for a disappointing twelve performances. *Time* magazine found, "Between the play and the Strachey piece, however, there are noticeable differences in characterization and fact. The play-wright Berkeley, Nurse Nightingale, revertly and somewhat palely acted by Edith Evans, is a sort of Maid of Orleans...to Mr. Strachey, however, Florence Nightingale was more like the kind of person Carrie Nation might have turned out to be has she been interested in caring for the sick instead of breaking up bars with umbrella and hatchet."

Brooks Atkinson (*The New York Times*) reported that this legend of Florence Nightingale was presented "in the form of undramatic recitatives, successive episodes in her career. Especially with Edith Evans to play the chief part with a kind of exalting radiance, it is a noble story; it is profoundly moving in various scenes ...Save for the quietly exalting final scene of the investiture, the last part of *The Lady With a Lamp* lets its heroine down badly...As a feeble old lady in a wheelchair, blind, faltering and limp, she (Edith Evans) represents grandeur without having to describe it. The nobility of Mr. Berkeley's Florence Nightingale is the true property of Miss Evans' acting."

Robert Garland wrote in the *New York World-Tele-gram*: "A magnificent performance illuminates an indifferent play...The magnificent performance is that of Miss Edith Evans, the celebrated English actress, who is making her American debut. The indifferent play is *The Lady With a Lamp*, Mr. Reginald Berkeley's dialogic biography of the Florence Nightingale Mr. Lytton Strachey knows...The trouble with *The Lady With a Lamp* -- and of trouble there is plenty -- is that it casts the rules of playmaking aside and offers nothing that can be looked upon as a substitute...Having used 'magnificent' in connection with Miss Evans' Florence Nightingale, I can do no more than use magnificent again. From eight-thirty until eleven, the visitor from London acts circles around the author's stilted and unnatural lines."

In April 1968, London's Royal Court Theatre premiered a production of *Early Morning*, a bizarre fantasy written by Edward Bond. It was promoted as "A Private Performance for Critics and Friends" -- who must have been staggered. Bond's play had Prince Albert and Disraeli planning assassination of Queen Victoria, who wants one of her Siamese twins (!), Prince George, to marry Florence Nightingale, then preoccupied with a lesbian affair with the Queen. All is resolved when Prince Albert and one half of the world's population engage in a tug of war with the other half led by Queen Victoria atop a precipice. Victoria's cry for "Peace" releases the rope on her side and Albert and his world crumble. Albert goes to heaven where Victoria has replaced God, and he falls in love with Florence Nightingale who managed to hop aboard the last hearse. Albert becomes a saint, at last, and ascends to a more heavenly heaven.

Early Morning had a Royal Court revival the following year. Alluding to playwright Edward Bond's program notes, "The events of this play are true," critic Martin Esslin (*Plays and Players*) reported: "There is nothing that is historically true in the play ...But the events of the play are also true, perhaps even more so, in the way in which they portray the process by which out of this half-understood, and therefore already mythical, fairy-tale material, a child would build up its private mythology using the strange mythical beings it has been told about to express its subconscious fears and desires...the title pointing to the fact that this is a picture of the world as it might appear in childhood life's early morning."

When Bond's offbeat play opened Off-Off-Broadway at New York's La Mama Theatre in November 1970, Clive Barnes (*The New York Times*) ameliorated its shock by writing: "What an absolutely extraordinary playwright the Englishman Edward Bond is! His first play, *The Pope's Wedding*, betoken a certain eccentricity of subject matter." Barnes went on to assess *Early Morning*: "It is the kind of play that first blows the mind and then tramples on it...The play starts mad and gets progressively madder...But black farce is a form even more difficult than black comedy...A strange play -- with its last half scarcely knowing what its first half is doing...but I found myself enjoying the fun of the acting and the crazy, demon spirit of the play."

In December 1990, Elizabeth Diggs' *Nightingale* opened Off Broadway after having premiered earlier as *St. Florence* at the Capital Repertory Theatre in Albany. Florence Nightingale, in this version, is portrayed as a pioneer for women's rights. "The production is especially fortunate in its casting of the title role with Kathryn Pogson," Mel Gussow wrote in *The New York Times*. "In her striking performance, she merges aspects of Lewis Carroll's Alice and Bernard Shaw's St. Joan. Her passion to be a nurse (a profession previously dominated by prostitutes) leads her into a black, comic wonderland, where practically everyone seems anxious to undermine her...In its style and spirit, *Nightingale* is not unrelated to *The Elephant Man*, dealing as it does with the inhumanity of English traditions."

The British-made four-reel 1915 film, *Florence Nightingale, Founder of the Red Cross*, starred Elizabeth Risdon who portrayed the noted nurse from early childhood through the Crimea War to her death. "Obvious care has been exercised in making the production historically accurate," said *Motion Picture World*. "Subtitles are sufficiently explicit and Miss Risdon displays a knowledge of makeup in changing from a radiant girl to a venerable woman. Some of the settings will appear rather artificial to audiences accustomed to American methods of production; but technical shortcomings are overbalanced by the educational value of the subject."

Warner Bros.-First National's 1936 *The White Angel* was based on Lytton Strachey's biography, directed by William Dieterle and starring Kay Francis. Filmed during the Warner era of ersatz movie biographies of the great and not-so-great, it presented a hopelessly miscast Florence Nightingale. The attractive and sophisticated Kay Francis with her unmistakable lisp, costumed in nurse's uniform, obviously had not even a nodding acquaintanceship with the subject. Her performance was called "antiseptic," together with less complimentary descriptions. Dieterle later admitted "That was a beautiful story, but it was, shall I say, written by the wrong people -- they wanted to be so correct with the English...The film itself could have been a lot better."

Anna Neagle in 1938 had portrayed Queen Victoria in her husband Herbert Wilcox's *Sixty Glorious Years*, in which Joyce Bland had the part of Florence Nightingale. In 1951, Wilcox got around the filming Reginald Berkeley's play, *The Lady With a Lamp*, starring Neagle as Nightingale. Much of it was shot at Lea Hurst in Derbyshire, the home of Florence Nightingale purchased by J. P. Mitchelhill from the Nightingale family as a convalescent home for nurses. The Wilcox's London home was also opposite 60 South Street where Nurse Nightingale had lived. Anna Neagle did extensive research on Nightingale's life, discovering at the Imperial War Museum the well-publicized Grecian urn lantern she had carried through the Crimea at night to be a much brighter Chinese lantern. Filming was also done at Embley Park in Hampshire, a residence of the Nightingales. It is in the small churchyard near Embley Park that Florence Nightingale is buried, her tombstone merely bearing the initials F.N. Other scenes were filmed at Broadlands, home of Lord and Lady Mountbatten, where Florence had spent a good deal of time.

As a benefit for the Royal College of Nursing, headed by Lady Edwina Mountbatten, Herbert Wilcox arranged charity performances of *The Lady With a Lamp* throughout the Commonwealth. The film was advertised as a "Royal Premiere" at Leicester Square's Warner Theatre. Due to the illness of the King, Princess Elizabeth, attended by the Mountbattens, substituted for her parents, and Lady Mountbatten presented the director and the star with a silver cigarette box engraved: "To Herbert Wilcox and Anna Neagle, with gratitude from nurses in all parts of the world and from all those devoted to the cause of nursing."

The Lady With a Lamp, unfortunately, did not receive the same accolades from the press. British critic Penelope Houston wrote: "What the handling and the performance conspicuously and disastrously lack is the quality of toughness -- physical, mental and moral -- which was the basis of Florence Nightingale characters...Anna Neagle's performance, although marked by obvious sincerity of intention, has softened the redoubtable Florence Nightingale into a figure of dull and conventional nobility...Michael Wilding is in every respect unsuited to the demands of Sidney Herbert..." (The film received little or no distribution in the United States, and if it opened in New York, *The Times* failed to review it.)

On television, Sarah Churchill starred in *The Story of Florence Nightingale*, a half-hour *Hallmark Hall of Fame* production in 1952. This ill-conceived misstep for the consistently prestigious program that has spanned nearly the entire history of TV was corrected in its ninety-minute drama about Florence Nightingale thirteen years later with Julie Harris. Called *The Holy Terror*, James Lee's original teleplay brought out the expected raves. Jack Gould (*The New York Times*) praised the Harris performance as "adding another superb achievement to her list of achievements on the home screen" and then found that "Mr. Lee's work often took the form of a vivid and searing documentary on the suffering, filth and jungle environment in the barracks for the wounded and dying at Scutari. In color TV, at times the sight was not pleasant...But it was Miss Harris' evening. As the genteel young girl hearing the angels call to do God's duty...she projected a diversification that had absorbing power and sensitivity."

The Philadelphia Bulletin's Harry Harris felt: "Although this was an 'original' work and infinitely superior to most TV drama, in mood, content and period trappings, it was virtually indistinguishable from the historic biographies that have become the 'Hall of Fame's' prime staple." Critic Rex Polier had a negative view: "Author James Lee did not do right by either Florence Nightingale or actress Julie Harris...His Nightingale did not develop into a real and believable woman until the final half hour of this heavily upholstered period piece...The George Schaefer production just didn't have the verve and impact it should have."

Jaclyn Smith starred as "the lady with the lamp" in the three-hour 1985 motion picture for television, *Florence Nightingale*. "Florence Nightingale deserves better," reported John J. O'Connor in *The New York Times*. "Brought to television in a script by Ivan Moffat and Rose Leiman Goldemberg, Florence Nightingale becomes a rather genteel creature whose presumably fierce determination too often comes out looking like little more than tasteful pertness. She is played by Jaclyn Smith, an American actress whose British accent, when turned on, manages to be just studied enough to be pretentiously arch. Miss Smith, who has come a respectable distance from her days as one of *Charlie's Angels* is a strikingly beautiful woman whose more recent television efforts, including the title role in *Jacqueline Bouvier Kennedy*, have done well in the ratings...Although surrounded by a supporting cast of very accomplished British actors, Miss Smith is clearly the centerpiece, dominating the screen with a tenacity that only certain types of stars can command." O'Connor concluded: "*Florence Nightingale* drifts by us easily enough on the television screen. There is nothing that is truly dreadful about the fairly elaborate production, which was directed by Daryl Duke...but neither is there anything particularly memorable."

STAGE

THE LADY WITH A LAMP, *Arts Theatre*, London, opened January 5, 1929; moved to *Garrick Theatre*, January 24, 1929

Produced and directed by Leslie Banks and Edith Evans; A Play by Reginald Berkeley, based on Lytton Strachey's biography *Eminent Victorians*

Edith Evans (Florence Nightingale); Eille Norwood (Lord Palmerston); Gwen Ffrangeon-Davies (Elizabeth Herbert); Leslie Banks (Henry Tremayne); Richard Goolden (William Nightingale/Corporal Jones/Pursivant); Clare Harris (Selina Bracebridge); Dona Barton (Lady Christabel Deane); Neil Porter (Sydney Herbert/Secretary of State); Muriel Asked (Mrs. Nightingale); Olga Slade (Lady Heritage); Muriel Dole (Mrs. Calden); Leslie Braham (A Nurse); Edith Martyn

(Miss Pelt/Mrs. Williams/A Mother); Frederick Burtwell (Dr. Smith/Mr. Macdonald/A Pressman/Lord Mayor of London); Basil Beale (A Surgeon); Henry Oscar (Dr. Sutherland); Reginald Purdell (Mr. Bramford); Albert A. Raynor (Dr. Cumming); Dolys Stevens (Nurse Bates); Graham Stuart (Court Chamberlain); Horace Lyons (Little Boy); Stringer Davis (*Times* Representative); Basil Beale (Tankerton); Leslie Mitchell (German Diplomat)

Maxine Elliott Theatre, New York, opened November 12, 1931 12 performances
Produced by Kenneth Macgowan and Joseph Verner Reed; A Play by Reginald Berkeley, based on Lytton Strachey's biography *Eminent Victorians*; Director, Leslie Banks

Edith Evans (Florence Nightingale); J. W. Austin (Lord Palmerston); Patricia Collinge (Elizabeth Herbert); Stuart Casey (Henry Tremayne); Edgar Kent (William Nightingale/Dr. Cumming/Pursivant); Leslie Barrie (Sidney Herbert/Corporal Jones/Court Chamberlain); Anne Revere (Miss Pelt/Nurse); Nellie Malcom (Mrs. Nightingale); Philip Tonge (Surgeon/Tankerton); Jane Savile (Selina Bracebridge); St. Clair Bayfield (Dr. Southerland); H. Langston Bruce (Dr. Smith/Lord Mayor of London/Mr. Macdonald); Virginia Tracey (Mrs. Williams); Joaquin Souther (Mr. Bamford/American Red Cross President); Hilda Plowright (Lady Heritage); Barbara Allen (Mrs. Calder/First Lady); Frank Carew (German Diplomat); Barbara Bruce (Lady Christabel Deane/A Mother); Frances Simon (Nurse/Little Girl); Ann Lynwood (Nurse/Second Lady); Betty Upthegrove (Nurse Bates/Maid); David Hughes (Orderly); Harry Sothern (Pressman); James Barrow (*Times* Representative); Arthur Metcalf (Secretary of State); Harry E. Allen, Peter Martin (Stretcher Bearers); Alix Holland, Elizabeth Farrar, Mary Kemble, Helene Willard (Nurse); Joseph Kennedy, James Milaidy, Frank Munnell, David Hughes, Harry E. Allen, Wilbur Young (Veterans)

DIE LADY MIT DER LAMPE (THE LADY WITH A LAMP), *Schauspielhaus*, Zurich, Switzerland, opened June 26, 1958
Produced by the Schauspielhaus; A Play by Elsie Attenhofer; Director, Karlheinz Streiberg; Settings, Ted Otto; Lighting, Walter Gross; Costumes, Elisabeth Schmid; Technical direction, Ferdinand Lange

Rosemarie Gertsenberg (Florence Nightingale); Peter Schuette (Sidney Herbert); Herman Wisch (William Nightingale); Traute Carlsen (Fanny Nightingale); Alfred Schlageter (Lord Penmure); Richard Muench (Dr. John Hall); Hans Krassnitzer (Dr. Sutherland); Wolfgang Stendar (Richard Ashley); Otto Maschtlinger (Michael Morton); Claus A. Landsittel (Robert Watson); Anneliese Betschart (Mabel Watson); Maria Magdalena Thiezing (Elizabeth a Court); Margrit Winter (Miss Galton); Edith Golay (Julia Woolton); Valerie Steinmann (Rose); Elisabeth Wenger (Terry); EvaMaria Bing (Kate); Anneliese Eggar (Emma); Armin Schweizer (Warden); Hans Jeditschka, Kurt Brunner (Soldiers); Albert Gemperio, Max Wuetbrich (Voices)

EARLY MORNING, *Royal Court Theatre*, London, opened April 7, 1968
Produced by the Royal Court Theatre Company; A Play by Edwin Bond; Director, William Gaskill; Production designer, Deirdre Clancy

Marianne Faithfull (Florence Nightingale); Nigel Hawthorne (Prince Albert); Moira Redmond (Queen Victoria); Malcolm Tierney (Benjamin Disraeli); Tom Chadbon (Prince George); Prince Eyre (Prince Arthur); Roger Booth (Lord Chamberlain); Norman Eshley (Lord Mennings); Dennis Waterman (Len); Jane Howell (Joyce);

Gavin Reed (Doctor); Jack Shepherd (Gladstone); Bruce Robinson (Ned); Hugh Armstrong, Harry Meacher (Soldiers)

EARLY MORNING, Royal Court Theatre, London, opened March 13, 1969
Produced by the Royal Court Theatre Company; A Play by Edwin Bond; Director, William Gaskill; Production designer, Deirdre Clancy

Shirley Ann Field (Florence Nightingale); Nigel Hawthorne (Prince Albert); Moira Redmond (Queen Victoria); Henry Woolf (Benjamin Disraeli); Tom Chadbon (Prince George); Jack Shepherd (Prince Arthur); Peter Needham (Lord Chamberlain); Peter Blythe (Lord Mennings); Kenneth Cranham (Len); Queenie Warris (Joyce); James Hazeldine (Doctor); John Barrett (Gladstone); Don Hawkins (Ned); Peter Spromie (Officer); Brian Croucher (Corporal Jones); Billy Hamon (Private Griss)

EARLY MORNING, La Mama Theatre, New York, opened November 25, 1970
Produced by La Mama E.T.C.; A Play by Edwin Bond; Director, Melvin Bernhardt; Setting, Michael Mossee; Lighting, David Adams; Costumes, Nancy Potts; Music, James Reichert; Stage manager, Larry Ziegler

Alix Elias (Florence Nightingale); Tresa Hughes (Queen Victoria); Joe Daly (Prince Albert); Edward Zang (Benjamin Disraeli); William Macadam (Prince George); Lenny Baker (Prince Arthur); Ray Stewart (Lord Chamberlain); Patrick Cook (Lord Mennings); A. Rockefeller Grant (Len); Jeanne Hepple (Joyce); John Harkins (Gladstone); Christopher Leahy (Corporal Jones); Gordon Clapp (Private Griss); Peggy Cohen, Harvey Noel (Mob)

NIGHTINGALE, Vineyard Theatre, New York, opened December 2, 1990
Present by the Vineyard Theatre, Douglas Aibel, artistic director; A Play by Elizabeth Diggs; Director, John Rubinstein; Scenic design, William Barclay; Lighting, Phil Monat; Costumes, James Scott; Music, Robert Waldman; Musical staging, Jane Lanier; Production stage manager, Kate Broderick

Kathryn Pogson (Florence Nightingale); James A. Stephens (William Edward Nightingale/Dr. Hall); Pippa Pearthree (Parethenope Nightingale); Sloane Shelton (Fanny Nightingale); John Curless (Sidney Herbert); and Robertson Carricart, Jane Lanier, Edmund Lewis, Elizabeth Logun, Jodie Lynne McClintock, Emily Arnold McCully, Patrick O'Connell, Gregg Porretta, Diana Van Fossen

* Originally staged as *St. Florence* at the *Capital Repertory Theatre*, Albany, New York

SCREEN

FLORENCE NIGHTINGALE, FOUNDER OF THE RED CROSS, Ideal Film Service, released November 1915
Director, Maurice Elvey; Screenplay, Eliot Stannard, based on *The Life of Florence Nightingale* by Edward Cook

Elizabeth Risdon (Florence Nightingale); A. V. Bramble (Sidney Herbert); Fred Groves (Doctor)

THE WHITE ANGEL, Warner Bros.-First National, released June 1936
Produced by Henry Blanke; Director, William Dieterle; Screenplay, Michael Jacoby and Mordaunt Sharp, based on Lytton Strachey's biography *Eminent Victorians*;

Photography, Tony Gaudio; Dialogue director, Stanley Logan; Music director, Leo F. Forbstein; Editor, Warren Low

Kay Francis (Florence Nightingale); Ian Hunter (Fuller); Nigel Bruce (Dr. West); Donald Crisp (Dr. Hunt); Henry O'Neill (Dr. Scott); George Curzon (Sir Henry Herbert); Donald Woods (Charles Cooper); Phoebe Foster (Elisabeth Herbert); Georgia Caine (Mrs. Nightingale); Lillian Kemble-Cooper (Parthe Nightingale); Charles Croker-King (Mr. Nightingale); Billy Mauch (Tommy); Montagu Love (Mr. Bullock); Halliwell Hobbes (Lord Raglan); Frank Conroy (Mr. LeFroy); Ara Gerald (Mrs. Elda Stevens); Eily Malyon (Sister Columbo); Egon Brecher (Fieldner); Gaby Fay (Queen Victoria); Barbara Leonard (Minna); Ferdinand Munier (Soyer); Tempe Pigott (Mrs. Waters); Lawrence Grant (Colonel); Nelson McDowell (Hospital Superintendent); Eric Wilton (Servant); Robert Bolder, James May, Arthur Turner Foster (Doctors); Daisy Belmore, Alma Lloyd, May Beatty, Kathrine Clare Ward (Nurses)

THE LADY WITH A LAMP, *British Lion Films*, released 1951

A Wilcox-Neagle Production/Imperadio; Producer and director, Herbert Wilcox; Screenplay, Warren Chetham-Strode, based on the play by Reginald Berkeley; Photography, Max Green; Art director, William C. Andrews; Music, Anthony Collins; Editor, Bill Lewthwaite

Anna Neagle (Florence Nightingale); Michael Wilding (Sidney Herbert); Felix Aylmer (Lord Palmerston); Rosalie Crutchley (Mrs. Sidney Herbert); Barbara Couper (Fanny Nightingale); Helen Shingler (Parthenope Nightingale); Edwin Styles (William Nightingale); Henry Edwards (Howard Edward Russell); Monckton Hoffe (Lord Stratfor); Gladys Young (Mrs. Bracebridge); Julian D'Albie (Mr. Bracebridge); Arthur Young (Gladstone); Cecil Trouncer (Sir Douglas Dawson); Maray Mackenzie (Nurse Johnson); Maureen Pryor (Sister Wheeler); Andrew Osborn (Dr. Sutherland); Helena Pickard (Queen Victoria); Peter Graves (H.R.H. Prince Albert); Dame Sybil Thorndike (Miss Bosanquet); Clement McCallin (Richard M. Milnes)

TELEVISION

THE STORY OF FLORENCE NIGHTINGALE, *Hallmark Hall of Fame*, televised February 3, 1952 NBC 30 minutes

Produced and directed by William Corrigan; Teleplay, Jean Holloway

Sarah Churchill (Florence Nightinagel); Isobel Elsom (Fanny Nightingale); Robin Craven (William Nightingale); John Moore (Dr. Sutherland); Alexander Clark (Dr. Poole); John O'Hara (Richard Milnes); and A. J. Herbert, Dick Fraser, Mary Barclay

THE HOLY TERROR, *Hallmark Hall of Fame*, televised April 7, 1965 NBC 90 minutes

Produced and directed by George Schaefer; Teleplay, James Lee; Settings, Warren Clymer; Makeup, Bob O'Bradovich; Music, Bernard Green

Julie Harris (Florence Nightingale); Denholm Elliot (Sidney Herbert); Brian Bedford (Billy Sims); Leueen McGrath (Fanny Nightingale); Torin Thatcher (Dr. Poole); Kate Reid (Aunt Mai); Alan Webb (William Nightingale)

FLORENCE NIGHTINGALE, televised April 7, 1985 NBC 3 hours

A Cyprus Point Productions; Executive producer, Gerald W. Abrams; Producers,

Tony Richmond and Ron Carr; Director, Daryl Duke; Teleplay, Ivan Moffat and Rose Leiman Goldemberg; Photography, Jack Hildyard; Production designer, Harry Pottle; Music, Stanley Myers; Editor, Bill Lenny

Jaclyn Smith (Florence Nightingale); Timothy Dalton (Richard Milnes); Claire Bloom (Fanny Nightingale); Jeremy Brett (William Nightingale); Timothy West (Russell); Ann Thornton (Parthe Nightingale); Peter McEnery (Sidney Herbert); Stephan Chase (Dr. Sutherland); Jeremy Child (Dr. Hall); Michael Elwyn (Dr. Menzies); Carol Gilles (Nurse Davis); Brian Cox (Dr. McGrigor); Marjorie Yates (Trude); Emma Watson (Elizabeth Marshall); Lorna Heilbron (Selina); Julian Fellowes (Charles); Patrick Drury (Henry Nicholson); Denis Lill (Dr. Howe); Wolf Kahler (Gunther)

THE LAST DAYS OF POMPEII

Various Adaptation of the novel by Edward George Bulwer-Lytton (1834)

Synopsis

Glaucus, a young Athenian, is loved by Nydia, a blind Thessalonian slave girl own by a cruel innkeeper in Pompeii. He buys Nydia and gives her as a handmaiden to his beloved Ione, who in turn is passionately desired by Arbaces, an evil Egyptian priest of Isis. Julia, daughter of wealthy Diomed, also in love with Glaucus, plots with Arbaces to drug Glaucus into submission. Arbaces kills Ione's Christian brother, Apaecides, and blames the murder on Glaucus, who is sentenced to fight wild beasts in the arena. Declaring her belief in Glaucus' innocence, Ione is seized by Arbaces and made a prisoner in his palace. Nydia, aware of Arbaces' guilt, persuades a slave to carry a message to Glaucus' friend, Sallust. The gladiator games begin in the arena but Glaucus is saved by the timely arrival of Sallust demanding the arrest of Arbaces. The bloodthirsty spectators are insisting that Arbaces be thrown to the lions in place of Glaucus when the volcano Vesuvius erupts, raining death and destruction upon Pompeii. Thousands of the inhabitants are killed, including Arbaces. Nydia and Glaucus rescue Ione and sail out to sea in a small boat as Vesuvius continues wreaking havoc on the city. The following morning, Glaucus and Ione discover that Nydia, resigned to the hopelessness of her love for Glaucus, has drowned herself, and they see their once beautiful, hedonistic Pompeii in ruins.

Comment and Critique

Edward George Bulwer-Lytton, first Lord Lytton born in London on May 25, 1803, was a prolific author encouraged by actor William Charles Macready to turn to playwriting. Bulwer-Lytton's best known plays included *The Lady of Lyons* (1838), *Richelieu, or The Conspiracy* (1839), *Not as Bad as We Seem* (1851) and *Walpole, or Every Man Has His Price* (1869). He was made Baron Lytton of Knebworth in 1866 and died at age sixty-nine in Devonshire on January 18, 1873. Lord Lytton lived in Italy for nearly all of 1833, examining the excavations of the ruins of Pompeii and vividly describing in detail the construction, customs, costumes and mores of the fascinating but doomed city in his most lasting work, *The Last Days of Pompeii*, published in 1834.

A year after its publication, Louisa H. Medina adapted the novel to the stage.

The play was produced by her husband Thomas S. Hamblin at his Bowery Theatre in New York in February 1835, featuring Charles Robert Thorne as Glaucus. It had a run of twenty-nine performances. Louisa Medina Hamblin died three years later, but sporadic revivals of her dramatization of Bulwer-Lytton's fictionalized Pompeii were staged through the mid-1800s. James H. Wallack, Jr. starred as Glaucus in the 1839 Hamblin production, hailed by critics as "a spectacular production." After the Bowery Theatre was destroyed by fire that year, Hamblin rebuilt it and again produced his late wife's play there in 1843 and 1849.

The Last Days of Pompeii, adapted by *London Times* critic John Oxenford, opened at London's Queen's Theatre in January 1872. "Let us say at once that the piece failed to realize the anticipations that had been formed of it. It was, to come to the point quickly, a virtual failure," reported London's *Entre'act*. "To invite the public to witness a play in such an unprepared state was an insult...Mr. Oxenford has not done his work well...No interest is aroused; the characters, if not colourless, are repulsive; the plot seems involved and purposeless, and the curtain falls on situations that neither excite nor please." Despite the critical lambasting, the play ran for two months. Clifford Rean's version of the Bulwer-Lytton novel reappeared on the stage of the Queen's Theatre in the spring of 1914. Few of the stage adaptations of *The Last Days of Pompeii*, however, could be classified as successful.

The earliest known film adaptation of the novel by Edward Bulwer-Lytton was an Italian one directed by Luigi Maggi in 1898; the first British one three years later, directed by Walter Booth.

In 1913, Italy produced two screen version of *The Last Days of Pompeii*. The Pasquali eight-reeler was imported and released in the United States by H. J. Streyckmans. He advertised the Italian film as "Genuine dramatization of Lord Bulwer-Lytton's masterpiece in *nine* reels, staged at Pompeii and Turin, Italy. This production is without question the most sensational and spectacular artistic film ever conceived, costing hundreds of thousands of dollars...The conflagration was staged during one of the most violent eruptions of Mt. Vesuvius, and the burning of the City of Pompeii in connection with the flaming volcano presents an awe-inspiring spectacle." The film claimed a cast of 3,000 people, 50 gladiators and 100 lions and tigers.

Reviewing the Pasquali production in *The Moving Picture World*, Louis Reeves Harrison claimed: "The story is suited to photodramatic purposes -- a grand spectacle of destruction of a city at its eminence of voluptuous luxury, of debauchery and decadence...but it would have been more realistic if actual views of the volcano had been added at certain moments instead of a studio eruption. There is not attempt to give this feature an added educational value by indicating the relation of Pompeii and Vesuvius and by actual photographs of interesting remains...It would have helped to give us a genuine picture of Vesuvius still breathing forth smoke...Aside from its lack of realism, the Pasquali feature has a disadvantage from my point of view of being too long..."

Two weeks after Pasquali's film went into release, George Kleine premiered Ambrosio Films' version of *The Last Days of Pompeii* in the United States. Ambrosio has produced a short film version of the Bulwer-Lytton novel in 1908, directed by Luigi Maggi, which an Italian critic described in these words: "The theme of this drama is splendidly rendered in the arena scene when the historical episodes of the eruption of Vesuvius begins, with the terror of the fleeing spectators suffocated by the terrible effects of molten lava." Ambrosio's 1913 celluloid spectacle with a cast of thousands was shown in the U.S. with an astounding $1.00 admission charge.

Reviewing the six-reeler, *The Moving Picture World* felt that "the fact that the

Ambrosio company has not followed very faithfully the story of *The Last Days of Pompeii* as written by Bulwer-Lytton, [but] it is a very interesting and entertaining picture that has been made by that great Italian producer...Exceptionally beautiful are the settings of the various interior scenes and some magnificent effects have been produced in the exteriors. Rare photography characterizes the whole... By the use of an ancient Roman arena and the employment of sufficient people to fill the seats within the field of the camera, a most realistic view of what might have happened on the occasion when Glaucus was compelled to fight the lions is given. The scene of the eruption of Vesuvius and the efforts of the populace to escape the doomed city is startling in its conception and awful in its rendition..."

In 1926, Italy again produced a screen version of *The Last Days of Pompeii.* Arthur Knight described it in his book *The Liveliest Art* as "only demonstrating again how out of date their techniques and values had become." Directed by Amleto Palermi but completed by Carmine Gallone, it featured Maria Corda (then Mrs. Alexander Korda) as Cicca, Victor Varconi as Glaucus and Bernhard Gietzke as Arbaces. In his 1972 book *The Italian Cinema*, translated from the French by Roger Greaves and Oliver Stallybass, Pierre Leprohon noted the period of decline of Italian films and cited *Gli Ultimi Giorni di Pompei* as a sterling example, classifying the 1926 movie as "the final episode in the fall of the Italian cinema."

Leprohon cited actor Emilio Ghione's recall of the filming: "Amleto Palermi got all the papers to announce that he was shortly to direct a monumental historical film called *Gli Ultimi Giorni di Pompei*...He hired, at enormous expense, the largest studio at Cines where no film had been made for years...filled the sports stadium with 5,000 extras dressed as ancient Romans, and in this improvised arena shot some remarkable scenes with gladiators, lions, etc." Palmeri, in exchange for needed capital, agreed to replace his stars, Diomira Jacobini and Lido Menetti, with more bankable international players Maria Corda and Vincent Varconi. With the film only half completed, Palermi had spent three million lire and persuaded directed Carmine Gallone to finish it while he went about unearthing sufficient funds. The final production cost seven million lire. "This was the last important film to be shot in Italy," claims Ghione. "Instead of *The Last Days of Pompeii*, it could have been called *The Last Days of the Italian Cinema*."

In 1935, Merian C. Cooper and Ernest B. Schoedesack, the men who created *Grass* (1925), *Chang* (1927), *Four Feathers* (1929) and *King Kong* (1933), produced an epic version of *The Last Days of Pompeii* for RKO. It was based on an original story by James Ashmore Creelman and Melville Baker, with little remaining of Bulwer-Lytton except the title.

"Spectacular in story quality and production value -- a massive feature, reflecting in every phase the care, thought and diligence put into it by the producers, director and players," was the judgement of the critic for *The Motion Picture Herald*. "In every way this is a big picture, rich in all the necessities required...The strength or weakness of cast names -- and the personalities presented are worthy of anyone's best efforts -- is of little comparative significance."

Film Daily praised the film as "One of the Ten Best of this or any season...Audiences broke into applause in the middle of it...It makes all other spectacular productions fade in comparison...And for the climactic smash, the eruption of Vesuvius followed by earthquakes with thousands of people feeling the arena has never been equaled for sheer magnitude...Everything about the production is superb -- musical score, photography, directing, acting..."

In *The New York Times*, Andre Sennwald reported: "The historical fable...borrows its title from Bulwer-Lytton, together with such items of large-scale disaster as might contribute to the spectacle of Pompeii's flaming end. Otherwise it tells an entertaining fiction of its own...*The Last Days of Pompeii* is a shade too long for complete comfort. Although it is persuasively staged and excitingly narrated, the work is rather more absorbing in its straightforward melodrama than in the later phases when the defiant gladiator is getting religion...This is, in fact, an ably managed historical work up to the time when it begins to bludgeon the moral and to drag in a foolish little romance between the exgladiator's adopted son and one of the slaves whom he is bent on rescuing from the arena. Mr. [Preston] Foster dominates the photoplay as the self-made man and performs his role with thoroughness and skill. But the hero of the occasion is Basil Rathbone, whose Pilate is a fascinating aristocrat, scornful in his hauteur and sly in his reasoning."

The French version of Bulwer-Lytton's novel was filmed in 1948 by Marcel L'Herbier under the title *Les Derniers Jours de Pompei*. Starring Micheline Presle and Georges Marchal, it was never shown in the United States. In 1959, another Italian-made version of *Gli Ultimi Giorni di Pompei* starred muscleman Steve Reeves, an American who had gained screen fame a few years before as *Hercules*.

Films and Filming reviewed the Reeves version, released in Great Britain and the United States in 1960: "[He] is probably making more money acting with his muscles than, for instance, Olivier is making acting with his intellect. But we should not underestimate Mr. Reeves because cinemagoers enjoy watching him change costumes in every reel (in this picture, a series of flounce-skirted togas with a hem line way above that currently recommended by Dior)...Of course, we cannot take this genre of film seriously...It is not surprising that these Hollywood-inspired epics should be filmed in Italy. It was the Italians who were making big spectacle films of ancient Rome in the silent days...The acting is poor, the dialogue turgid (there is no relation here, or intended, to Lord Lytton's book), and the dubbing of the American voices very carelessly engineered; but what magnificent sets, what wonderfully reconstructed costumes...But the story -- surely the clapperboy could have devised a better story about Pompeii than this!"

Writing in the *New York Herald Tribune*, Joe Morgenstern felt: "What a shame that Mt. Vesuvius couldn't have erupted a few days sooner. That would have spared Steve Reeves the trouble of doing away with a band of scoundrels who were terrorizing Pompeii. As it happens, [he] has his hands full of marauders and his mouth full of dubbed dialogue. It's quite a strain, but he manages things nicely..." *The New York Times*' Howard Thompson found: "The color is splashy...under Mario Bonnard's square-cut direction, the picture soon drops into a typical, old fashioned rut."

Britain's 1971 spoof *Up Pompeii* was derived from a BBC television comedy by Talbot Rothwell and headlined Frankie Howerd. The film was judged to be nearly indistinguishable from the television entry -- in the mold of the popular series of "Carry On" comedies -- including a clumsily staged Vesuvius eruption but contained an amusingly slapdash performance by Howerd and a delightful one by Patrick Cargill as a very bored Nero.

The elaborate three-part 1984 television miniseries of *The Last Days of Pompeii* was described by Lee Winfrey (*The Philadelphia Inquirer*) as "Spectacle pure and sinful...Fully accoutered with seductive dancing girls, muscular gladiators, suffering Christians, hungry lions, dissipated nobles, and even a dwarf painter...In depth of characterization, *Pompeii* seldom arises above the pedestrian. But it does have a good violent volcano eruption, and that's really all you need in a show about how Pompeii was buried under the ash from Mt. Vesuvius...As the high priest of Isis, [Franco] Nero employs only one expression: a glower. As a wealthy, social-climbing merchant, the usually excellent [Ned] Beatty mugs through perhaps the hammiest performance he has every given. [Lesley-Anne] Down has the ripest role: a variation on the old whore-with-a-heart-of-gold..."

Critic Winfrey noted that the script for the seven-hour, $19 million TV epic was written by Carmen Culver, author of the previous season's highly-praised *The Thorn Birds*, but added: "Star billing here, though, belongs not to Culver's pot-boiling script but to Jack Cardiff's luminous photography and, even more, to production designer Michael Stringer and special effects supervisor Peter Hutchinson... Sometime it seems a long wait for the eruption, since many of the players look as if they graduated from the Victor Mature School of Acting. [Duncan] Regehr, in particular, is as stiff as an arthritic elbow. The acting of Laurence Olivier and Anthony Quayle...is pure and smooth in comparison and often it looks as if they must have wandered into *Pompeii* from the set of another show."

The critic for *Variety* had this assessment: "More like a Roman circus than a respectful adaptation of Edward Bulwer-Lytton's 1834 warhorse, *The Last Days of Pompeii* gives kitsch a bad name. Filmed in Italy and London (with miniatures looking like they were filmed in someone's garage, [it] gallops along with acting styles ranging from Laurence Olivier's fragile nobleman to Ned Beatty's low-comedy used car dealer-type. Title was used in 1935 when Preston Foster and Dorothy Wilson took on the lions, but that opus sings compared to what's been doing here...Mount Vesuvius looms over all -- though its base looks like the meadow of a toy-train layout. By way of warning, the volcano belches puffs of smoke before blowing its top. The earthquakes look like camera jiggling, and the ashes sometimes filter past the camera lens without touching the people. The lions look bored."

STAGE

THE LAST DAYS OF POMPEII, *Bowery Theatre*, New York, opened February 9, 1835 29 performances
Produced and directed by Thomas S. Hamblin; A Play by Louisa H. Medina adapted from the novel by Edward Bulwer-Lytton

Charles R. Thomas (Glaucus); A. Pickering (Calenus); Mrs. Thorne (Ione); Thomas S. Hamblin (Arbaces); Mr. Stevenson (Apaecides); Mrs. Lenox (Clodius); Mrs. Flynn (Nydia); Mr. Maconachy (Medon); Mr. Brittingham (Lepidus); Mrs. McClure (Saga); Mr. Gates (Burbo); Mr. Ingersoll (Lydon); Mr. McClure (Tetraides); Mr. Lewis (Niger); Mr. Addis (Sporus); Mrs. Stickney (Stratonice)

Park Theatre, New York, opened January 7, 1839
Produced and directed by Thomas S. Hamblin; A Play by Louisa H. Medina adapted from the novel by Edward Bulwer-Lytton

James W. Wallack, Jr. (Glaucus); Mrs. Rogers (Ione); Thomas S. Hamblin (Arbaces); Miss Monier (Nydia); E. S. Conner (Lydon); Mrs. Sefton (Saga)

Bowery Theatre, New York, opened October 9, 1843
Produced and directed by Thomas S. Hamblin; A Play by Louisa H. Medina adapted from the novel by Edward Bulwer-Lytton

Corson Walton Clarke (Glaucus); Mrs. Sutherland (Ione); John R. Scott (Arbaces); Mrs. Webster (Nydia)

Chatham Theatre, New York, opened May 19, 1845

Produced and directed by Thomas S. Hamblin; A Play by Louisa H. Medina adapted from the novel by Edward Bulwer-Lytton

Mr. Morton (Glaucus); Matilda Phillips (Ione); James W. Wallack, Jr. (Lydon); Mrs. James W. Wallack, Jr. (Nydia); P. F. Williams (Medon); Harry A. Perry (Clodius)

Bowery Theatre, New York, opened February 20, 1849
Produced and directed by Thomas S. Hamblin; A Play by Louisa H. Medina adapted from the novel by Edward Bulwer-Lytton

J. H. Hall (Glaucus); John Gilbert (Arbaces); Mrs. Sutherland (Ione); J. M. Scott (Medon); Catherine Wemyss (Nydia)

American Theatre, Cincinnati, opened October 24, 1849
Produced by Henry Lewis; A Play based on the novel by Edward Bulwer-Lytton

William M. Fleming (Lydon); Mrs. Wilkinson (Nydia); Joseph P. Breisford (Arbaces); Mrs. Kent (Ione); Thomas G. Booth (Burbo)

Queen's Theatre, London, opened January 15, 1872 80 performances
Produced by E. Clifton; A Drama by John Oxenford, dramatized by special permission from Lord Lytton, based on his novel; Director, Mr. Ryder; Scenery, George Gordon and W. Harford; Mechanical effects, Mr. Cawdrey; Costumes, Hope and Gell, arranged by Henrietta Hodson, executed by Madame Reid; Properties, Mr. Boulanger; Music composed and arranged by Mr. Schoening

George Rignold (Glaucus); Henrietta Hodson (Nydia); Miss Hibbert (Ione); Mr. Ryder (Arbaces); H. Dalton (Sallust); Keet Webb (Pansa); W. Howard (Diomed); J. Gardiner (Lepidus); Mr. Vollaire (Calenus); H. C. Sidney (Apaecides); Alice Phillips (Julia); Miss Graham (Syra); B. Egan (Niger); R. Dolman (Sporus); H. Reeves (Tetraides); W. D. Graham (Burbo); Mr. Dempsey (Roman Centurion); Miss Corgon (Slave); H. Everhard (Stratonice); W. Ryder (Lydon); The Sexillian Troupe (Eumolpus, Nepimus, Berbix, Nobilior); Messrs. Brand, Martin, Butler, Thorpe (Citizens); Messrs. Evans, Haisman, Anderson, Edwards (Officers)

THE VERY LAST DAYS OF POMPEII, *Vaudeville Theatre*, London, opened February 13, 1872
A Burlesque by written and directed by Richard Reece, based on the Edward Bulwer-Lytton novel *The Last Days of Pompeii*; Music director, Mr. Nicholson

Nelly Power (Glaucus); Mr. Ryder (Arbaces); Maria Rhodes (Nydia); Lizzie Russell (Ione); Mr. Thorne (Apaecides); David James (Sallust)

THE LAST DAYS OF POMPEII, *Queen's Theatre*, London, opened April 13, 1914
A Play by written and directed by Clifford Rean, based on the novel by Edward Bulwer-Lytton

William Melvyn (Glaucus); Edith Loraine (Ione); T. B. Woulfe (Arbaces); Gertrude Glanmor (Nydia); Annie Boyd (Apaecides); Fred Blake (Diomed); Hy Parr (Gallus); Frank Pettingell (Calenus); Mary Irene Wright (Saga); William Young (Modon); Arthur Gordon (Lydon); Charles West (Sporus); Terry Davies (Burbo); Ruby Lee (Julia); Marie Thorne (Strathonice)

SCREEN

GLI ULTIMI GIORNI DI POMPEI, *Ambrosio Films*, Italy, released 1898

Director, Luigi Maggi; Based on the novel by Edward Bulwer-Lytton
Lydia de Roberti (Nydia), Mirra Principi

THE LAST DAYS OF POMPEII, England, released 1901
Producer, Robert William Paul; Director, Walter Booth; Based on the novel by Edward Bulwer-Lytton

GLI ULTIMI GIORNI DI POMPEI, Italy, released 1913 (released in the U.S. by H. J. Streyckmans)
Director, Enrico Vidali; Based on the novel by Edward Bulwer-Lytton
Suzanne De Labroy, Ines Melidoni

GLI ULTIMI GIORNI DI POMPEI, Ambrosio Films, Italy, released 1913
Director, Mario Caserini; Screenplay, Arrigo Frusta, based on the novel by Edward Bulwer-Lytton; Photography, Giovanni Vitrotti; Musical score, Walter C. Graziani
Antonio Grisante (Arbaces); Eugenia Tettoni (Ione); Cesare Gani Canini (Apaecides); Fernanda Negri-Pouget (Nydia); Ubaldo Stefano (Glaucus); Mario Bonnard (Clodius)

GLI ULTIMI GIORNI DI POMPEI, Italy, released February 1926
Directed by Carmine Gallone (replaced Amleto Palermi); Based on the novel by Edward Bulwer-Lytton; Photography, Donelliad Armenise
Victor Varconi (replaced Lido Menetti) (Glaucus); Maria Corda (replaced Diomira Jacobini) (Nydia); Bernhard Goetzke (Arbaces); Emilio Ghione (Apaecides); Rina de Liguoro (Ione)

THE LAST DAYS OF POMPEII, RKO Radio Pictures, released October 1935
Produced by Merian C. Cooper; Director, Ernest B. Schoedsack; Screenplay, Ruth Rose, based on an original story by James Ashmore Creelman and Melville Baker; Adaptation collaborator, Boris Ingster; Photography, J. Roy Hunt; Photographic technician, Eddie Linden; Photographic effects, Vernon Walker; Special effects, Harry Redmond; Sound effects, Walter Elliott; Art director, Van Nest Polglase; Set decorator, Thomas Little; Costumes, Aline Bernstein; Music, Roy Webb; Chief technician, Willis O'Brien; Associate art director, Al Herman; Editor, Archie F. Marshek
Preston Foster (Marcus); Basil Rathbone (Pontius Pilate); Alan Hale (Burbix); Dorothy Wilson (Claudia); Louis Calhern (Prefect); Wyrley Birch (Leaster); Frank Conroy (Gaius); David Holt (Flavius, as a Boy); John Wood (Flavius, as a Man); Gloria Shea (Julia); William V. Mong (Cleon); Edward Van Sloan (Clavius); Zeffie Tilbury (The Wise Woman); Henry Kolker (Warder); Murray Kinnell (Judean Peasant); John Davidson (Slave); Ward Bond (Gladiator)

GLI ULTIMI GIORNI DI POMPEI, Italy, released 1937
Director, Mario Mattoli; Based on the novel by Edward Bulwer-Lytton

LES DERNIERS JOURS DE POMPEI, Pathe-Consortium Arts (France), released April 1950 (filmed in 1948) (unreleased in the U.S.)
Produced by Franco London Films (Paris) and Universalia (Rome); Director, Marcel L'Herbier; Screenplay, Marcel L'Herbier, Jean Laviron and Pierre Brive, adapted from the novel by Edward Bulwer-Lytton; Photography, Roger Hubert; Decor and costumes, Colassanti; Music, Roman Vlad; Editor, Gisa Levi

Jaque Catelain (Clodius); Georges Marchal (Lycias); Micheline Presle (Helene); Marcel Herrand (Arbaces); Laura Alex (Julia); Adriana Benetti (Nydia); Roldano Lupi (Glaucus); Mariella Lotti (Ione); and Alain Quercy, Camillo Pilotto, Peter Trent, A. Pierifiderci, Marcella Rovena

GLI ULTIMI GIORNI DI POMPEI, Cineproduzioni (Italy), release 1959; in U.S. released as *THE LAST DAYS OF POMPEII* by *United Artists*, June 1960
A Production of Cineproduzioni (Rome), Procusa (Madrid) and Transocean (Monaco); Produced by Paolo Moffa; Director, Mario Bonnard; Screenplay, Ennio De Concini, Luigi Emmanuele, Sergio Leone, Duccio Tessari and Sergio Corbucci, based on the novel by Edward Bulwer-Lytton; Photography, Antonio Lopez Ballesteros; Art directors, Augusto Lega, Francisco R. Asenzio and Ramiro Gomez; Costumes, Vittorio Rossi; Special effects, Magasoli Erasmo Bacci; Music, Angelo Francesco Lavagnino; Sound, Mario Amari and Giovanni Percelli; Editors, Eraldo Da Roma and Julio Pena

Steve Reeves (Glaucus); Christine Kaufmann (Ione); Annemarie Baumann (Julia); Fernando Rey (Arbaces); Barbara Carroll (Nydia); Angel Aranda (Antonius); Guillermo Marin (Ascanius); Carlo Tamberlani (Leader of the Christians); Mimmo Palmara (Galenus); Mino Doro (Consul); Mario Berriatua, Mario Morales, Angel Ortiz (Praetorian Guards); and Lola Torres, Ignazio Dolce, Antonio Casas, Tony Richards

UP POMPEII, Anglo-EMI Associated/London Films, released March 1971
Executive producer, Beryl Vertue; Producer, Ned Sherrin; Associate producer, Terry Glinwood; Director, Bob Kellett; Screenplay, Sid Colin, based on an idea by Talbot Rothwell and the BBC television series; Photography, Ian Wilson; Art director, Seamus Flaherty; Costumes, Penny Lowe; Music, Carl Davis; Title song, Ken Howard and Alan Blaikley; Sung by Frankie Howerd; Editor, Al Gell

Frankie Howerd (Lurcio); Patrick Cargill (Nero); Michael Hordern (Ludicrus); Barbara Murray (Ammonia); Lance Percival (Bilius); Bill Fraser (Prosperus); Adrienne Posta (Scrubba); Julie Ege (Voluptua); Bernard Bresslaw (Gorgo); Royce Mills (Nausius); Rita Wedd (Cassandra); Madeline Smith (Erotica); Ian Trigger (Odius); Audrey Woods (Villanus); Hugh Paddick (Priest); Laraine Humphreys (Flavia); Roy Hudd (M.C.); George Woodbridge (Fat Bather); Andrea Lloyd (Dolly Bird); Derek Griffiths (Steam Salve); Carol-Anne Hawkins (Palanquin Girl); Barrie Gosney (Major Domo); Dave Prowse (Muscular Man); Veronica Clifford (Boobia); Russell Hunter (Jailer); Kenneth Cranham, Andy Foray (Hippies); Maya Zell (Pretty Girl); Irlin Hall (Fat Lady); Nicola Austine (Naked Lady); Anna Bret (Slave Girl); Robert Tayman (Noxius); Kenneth Rodway (Rumpus); Reuben Martin (Masseur); Ken Wynne (Wine Seller); Lally Bowers (Procuria); Billy Walker (Prodigous); and Ritchie Stewart, Gaye Brown, Warwick Sims, Jonathan Dennis, Mischa de la Motte, Robert Grange, William Cordery, Candice Glendenning, Valerie Stanton, Patsy Snell, Sally Douglas, Ann Collins, Corinne Skinner, Laura Marshall, Janet Pearce, Mark York, Ian Sheridan

TELEVISION

THE LAST DAYS OF POMPEII, televised May 6-8, 1984 ABC 7 hours
David Gerber Productions in association with Columbia Pictures Television; Executive producer, David Gerber; Produced by Richard Irving and William Hill; Director, Peter Hunt; Teleplay, Carmen Culver, based on the novel by Edward

Bulwer-Lytton; Photography, Jack Cardiff; Production designer, Michael Stringer; Art directors, Fred Carter and John Roberts; Costumes, Anthony Mendelson; Special effects, Peter Hutchinson; Music, Trevor Jones; Performed by London Symphony Orchestra, Marcus Dods conducting; Editors, Richard Marden and Michael Ellis

Nicholas Clay (Glaucus); Olivia Hussey (Ione); Franco Nero (Arbaces); Linda Purl (Nydia); Duncan Regehr (Lydon); Ernest Borgnine (Marcus); Ned Beatty (Diomed); Lesley-Anne Down (Chloe); Anthony Quayle (Quintus); Laurence Olivier (Gaius); Siobhan McKenna (Fortunata); Brian Blessed (Olinthus); David Robb (Sallust); Tony Anholt (Lepidus); Benedict Taylor (Antonius); Gerry Sundquist (Clodius); Stephen Greif (Sporus); Peter Cellier (Calenus); Barry Stokes (Gar); Howard Lang (Medon); Joyce Blair (Lucretia); Marilu Tolo (Xenia); Brian Coburn (Burbo); Michael Quill (Catus); Malcolm Jamieson (Petrus); Catriona MacColl (Julia)

THE LAST OF THE MOHICANS

Various dramatizations of the novel by James Fenimore Cooper (1826)

Synopsis

In the summer of 1757, Major Duncan Heyward and David Gamut are escorting Alice and Cora Munro to Fort William Henry where the girls' father, Colonel Munro, is commandant, but along the way, they are captured by Magua, a ruthless Huron Indian. Coming to the rescue is Nathaniel "Natty" Bumpo, a famous frontier scout for the English known as "Hawkeye." With his close friend, Mohican chief Chingachgook, also called Sagamore, and the latter's son Uncas, Hawkeye tries to persuade Magua to allow the party to go to Fort Henry, but Magua insists that Cora stay behind to be his squaw -- although her refusal enrages him. Hawkeye and Chingachgook force the issue and, after Magua escapes, the weary travelers get to the Fort only to find it under siege by the French led by Major General Montcalm. The treacherous Magua and his renegade Hurons join forces with the French in a massacre at the Fort, and then he kidnaps Cora and holds Alice and David prisoners. Uncas finally locates the captives in Magua's camp, which is infiltrated by Hawkeye and Heyward in disguise. They free Alice and Uncas, while Cora is spirited off into the hills by Magua. Uncas manages to pick up the trail but is ambushed and stabbed to death by Magua who is then shot and killed by Hawkeye. Cora dies at the hands of a Huron and is buried in the forest next to Uncas. Major Heyward, Colonel Munro and Alice safely reach English territory, and Hawkeye promises his friend Chingachgook, the last of the Mohicans in deep mourning for his son Uncas, to stay with him forever and they return to live in the forest.

Comment and Critique

James Kent Cooper, born on September 15, 1789, at Burlington, New Jersey, attained lasting literary fame for his five novels published in 1850 under the general heading of *The Leatherstocking Tales*. The first, *The Pioneers*, was written in 1823 and was followed by *The Last of the Mohicans* three years later when the author changed his middle name from Kent to Fenimore and left the United States for Europe where he lived for the next seven years. His first two adventure novels were followed by *The Prairie* (1827), *The Pathfinder* (1840) and *The Deerslayer* (1841). The most popular of the series remains the second.

Cooper was severely criticized by his contemporaries and later authors for *The Leatherstocking Tales*. Mark Twain's essay, "Fenimore Cooper's Literary Offenses," took Cooper to task for Hawkeye's dialogue, claiming he "talks like an illustrated, gilt-edged, tree-calf, hand-tooled, seven-dollar Friendship's Offering in the beginning of a paragraph...and like a Negro minstrel in the end of it." Stephen Crane ridiculed Cooper's "noble savages," and Henry Nash Smith found in his 1950 *The American West as Symbol and Myth*: "[Cooper's] conflict of allegiances was truly ironic, and if he had been able -- as he was not -- to explore to the end the contradictions in his ideas and emotions, the *Leatherstocking* series might have become a work of art."

In a preface to his 1850 edition of the complete *Tales*, Cooper wrote, "If anything from the pen of the writer of these romances is at all to outlive himself, it is, unquestionably, the series of *The Leather Stocking Tales*." Cooper arranged the *Tales* according to chronological events in Natty "Hawkeye" Bumpo's life whereas the original books haphazardly covered it in his early to mid-thirties, in *Mohicans*, his death in *The Prairie*, his younger days in *The Pathfinder* and his early youth in *The Deerslayer*.

The Last of the Mohicans remains a thrilling adventure story but, as Henderson Kincheloe has written in an evaluation of Cooper's work, "It is easy to complain of Cooper's faulty style, his verbosity, his heavy-handed humor (with David Gamut), his improbable actions, the insufficient motivation of his characters, the inconsistency and inaccuracy of his dialogue, yet many readers willingly suspend their disbelief or modify their critical objections in order to enjoy the rush of action which makes up so much of [it]."

Five years after its publication, Captain Glover adapted Cooper's novel to the stage. It was first produced by Richard Russell at New York's Richmond Hill House and Gardens Theatre just after Christmas 1831. Ambitious playwright and actor George Fawcett Rowe presented his stage adaptation of *The Last of the Mohicans* at Niblo's Garden in February 1874. *The New York Times* reported: "As Mr. Rowe [has] honestly tried to frame out of Cooper's *The Last of the Mohicans* a substantial and impressive American drama, we should be glad to record the success of *Leatherstocking*, done last evening for the first time at Niblo's. Unhappily, the author's performance did not prove equal to his intentions...The acting was of diverse qualities...Mr. Rowe himself donned the garb of Hawkeye, but reminded us more of Salem Scudder (in *The Octoroon*) and of Rip Van Winkle than of Cooper's hero. Mr. Rowe is skilled in all of the arts of the comedian, but we cannot recall a less felicitous attempt to embody a well-defined character than his latest endeavor."

The New York Clipper appraised Rowe's stage adaptation in these words: "The language is good, bordering at times almost upon the poetical, and the situation and effects have been well arranged. It is a difficult task to present a satisfactory version of any novel upon the dramatic stage, but particularly so is it the case with any of Cooper's romances...[It] received a beautiful mounting, the closing scene of each act being a marvel of the painter's art..."

The motion picture was a medium more adaptable to Cooper's outdoor adventures, of course, and it was D. W. Griffith who first brought his works to the screen. Griffith made a one-reel film called *Leatherstocking* for Biograph in 1909, and in 1911, both Powers and Thanhouser issued short films of *The Last of the Mohicans*. Vitagraph then produced *The Deerslayer* featuring Harry T. Morey as Hawkeye and Wallace Reid as Chingachgook. In late 1920, Associate Producers released Maurice Tourneur's *The Last of the Mohicans*, filmed at Big Bear Lake with directorial assistance from Clarence Brown.

In *The Moving Picture World*, critic Edward Weitzel headed his review: "Cooper's

The Last of the Mohicans Finely Filmed by Maurice Tourneur," and maintained: "The public owes Maurice Tourneur a vote of thanks for putting [it] on the screen. As the most representative of James Fenimore Cooper's *Leatherstocking Tales*, it should take its place among the standard film productions that serve to hand on the fame of a master of American literature...There are scenes of carnage in this picture that are truthful illustrations of the price paid by the hardy beings who made out present civilization possible. Sensitive souls who refuse to face the facts of life may find the massacre at the fort too realistic...Courage, fidelity and noble aspirations are at the root of every scene of violence in *The Last of the Mohicans*." Weitzel continued: "Looked at merely as a directorial exploit, the picture has many merits. The locations are often of great beauty, the cast has been admirably chosen, in most cases, and the accessories of all kinds fulfill every requirement. There are movements of troops and the management of Indian bands and of groups of settlers that reveal the signal ability of Maurice Tourneur in this branch of his profession...There are no stars in the cast...First honors should go to Wallace Beery for a forceful interpretation of the savage villain Magua...Honorable mention is due Philip R. Du Bois and Charles E. Van Enger for the excellence of the camera work."

Photoplay enthused: "If we had a National Cinematographic library, as we should have, into the archives of which each year were placed the best pictures and finest examples of the cinematographic art...I certainly should include *The Last of the Mohicans* in my list of eligible exhibits. There is, to me, an impressive effort made in this fine picture of Maurice Tourneur's to treat a big subject with dignity and a certain reverence to which its traditions entitle it, and yet to do so without losing sight for an instant of its picture possibilities ...Tourneur differs from most of the directors in his class in that he can achieve great beauty of background without sacrifice of story value...there is more good melodrama in *The Last of the Mohicans* than in a half dozen crook plays; more fine, hair-raising fights, and one supreme climax in the leap from the cliff that has not been equalled for several season..."

In 1932, Harry Carey and Edwina Booth (who had costarred in *Trader Horn*) battled their way through a twelve-episode Mascot serial of *The Last of the Mohicans*. Hobart Bosworth, then sixty-five and an actor in films since 1908, played Chingachgook, here called Sagamore.

Edward Small's 1936 production of the Cooper classic was an especially fine version blessed with an admirable cast headed by Randolph Scott as Hawkeye. "Thrill action melodrama, heart-touching romance, courageous adventure, savage passion, stark tragedy and pulse-tingling danger are the elements of which this picture is woven," wrote the critic for *Motion Picture Herald*. "Elaborately produced, panoramic vistas of natural scenic beauty constituting the principal backgrounds, the show completely translates James Fenimore Cooper's semi-historical literary classic to screen entertainment. Preserving and embellishing the full essences of the original, quality acting endows the film with an impressive and believable appeal to both class and mass patronage."

Not quite so enthusiastic but still positive was *The New York Times* review: "It may seem captious, perhaps to quibble over details in the telescoping of so ponderous an item as *The Last of the Mohicans* into a mere hour or so of screen entertainment...[The writers] have, of course, done a grand job of bringing the high spots of the story to the screen, even if it did require technical aid from the Boy Scouts to teach the modern Redskins how to whoop and holler in the accepted James Fenimore Cooper manner. Bruce Cabot's Magua is as evil a Huron as ever you pictured him...The massacre of Fort William Henry is by far the bloodiest, scalpingest morsel of cinematic imagery ever produced ...Randolph Scott, we must admit, is our Hawkeye to the life, despite his newfound falling for a pretty face, something you must admit about Binnie Barnes."

Eleven years later, Columbia Pictures remade the tale under the title *Last of the Redmen*, with Jon Hall (as Major Heyward) given top billing. Michael O'Shea was a mediocre Hawkeye in the so-so film that was somewhat salvaged by Buster Crabbe's villainous Magua.

Germany, Canada, even the BBC have done productions of the instinctively American adventure tale. Germany's Luna-Film Company had produced a 1920 version of *Leatherstocking Tales* under the title *Lederstrumpf*, consisting of two parts: *Der Wiltoter (The Deerslayer)* and *Der Letzte der Mohikaner (The Last of the Mohicans).* Directed by Arthur Wellin, the two-parter was edited from twelve reels to five and released in the United States as *The Deerslayer* the following year. Bela Lugosi gave a convincing performances as Uncas. In 1965, Germany remade *Der Letzte Mohikaner*, of which one British critic felt: "No one can ever complain of a dearth of incident in this European Western, even if it leaves the impression that the script was built up scene by scene rather than worked out as a whole...The story owes more to Karl May than to Fenimore Cooper, but its scrappiness is more than compensated for by a pace that never lets up."

The spectacular 1992 remake of the 1936 *Last of the Mohicans* starred Oscar-winning British actor Daniel Day-Lewis, of whom Janet Maslin (*The New York Times*) wrote: "Dominating every scene, and greatly missed whenever he happens to be off-camera, is Mr. Day-Lewis, who understands Hawkeye as a living, breathing American artifact and plays him with all the brooding energy that requires." She also felt, "The film seems meant to be watched as closely for its background detail -- beadwork, tattoos, uniforms, weapons, canoes, particularly Irish-sounding music -- as for its central theme. It can also be watched for its enlightened and uncommonly interesting treatment of the story's Indian characters, who are played by American Indian actors." David Ansen (*Newsweek*) felt that "[director Michael Mann's] gorgeous *The Last of the Mohicans* gets off to a bumpy start, gathers feeling and momentum, and comes roaring into the homestretch at full gallop. When this historical adventure kicks in, it's thrilling in the way old-fashioned epics used to be, but its romanticism has a fierce, violent physicality that gives it a distinctively modern stamp.

Canada's Normandie Productions turned out the 1957 television series (syndicated in the U.S.) called *Hawkeye and the Last of the Mohicans*. John Hart and Lon Chaney, Jr., played Hawkeye and Chingachgook through thirty-nine half-hour episodes. In 1962, four feature films for television were edited from the series: *Along the Mohawk Trail*, *The Redmen and the Renegades*, *The Long Rifle and the Tomahawk* and *The Pathfinder and the Mohican*.

It remained for the BBC in 1971 to recreate definitively (if uncharacteristically) Cooper's all-American classic. Following the U.S. premiere on PBS' *Masterpiece Theatre* of the eight-part series, *The New York Times*' John J. O'Connor queried: "So what if Uncas has a British accent?...In *The Last of the Mohicans*, little emphasis is put on Cooper's ambiguous attitudes toward the role of France and England in the Colonial wars of North America...Instead, it hews, not always closely, to the obvious line of romantic adventure. Filmed in Scotland near Loch Ness, the setting is excellent, perfectly recreating Cooper's description of dense forests and lakes in upper New York...*The Last of the Mohicans* is tightly woven...There are faults. Some of the British accents are incongruous...The eight episodes, running about 40 minutes each before the addition here of Alistair Cooke's commentaries, are not true to the exact letter of Cooper's novel. They do, however, capture much of the spirit, and the result in 'quality' television that is also remarkably entertaining."

As *Variety* reviewed it: "The BBC-Masterpiece Theatre voyage across the Atlantic into James Fenimore Cooperland is, to put it succinctly, quaint...No matter how much host Alistair Cooke explains away the pervasive British accents, it sounds funny to hear frontiersman Hawkeye say 'I'll get my own head into the nosebag, too' as though he were going out for a crumpet, or Mohicans do everything but ask for tea." Hailed, on the other hand, were "David Maloney's meticulous direction" and John McRae's "lively and lovely" production.

Stephen Lord's "Classics Illustrated" TV adaptation of Cooper's novel premiered in November 1977 starring Steve Forrest as Hawkeye and Ned Romero as Chingachgook. Forrest and Romero reprised those roles the following year in a TV version of *The Deerslayer*.

STAGE

THE LAST OF THE MOHICANS, Richmond Hill House and Gardens Theatre, New York, opened December 27, 1831
Produced by Richard Russell; A Play by Captain Glover, based on the novel by James Fenimore Cooper; Director, J. H. Clarke

Richard Russell (Hawkeye); J. H. Clarke (Chingachgook); Charles R. Thorne (Magua); Mrs. Richard Russell (Cora Munro); Mrs. C. R. Thorne (Alice Munro); Emanuel Judah (Uncas); Joseph Field (Major Duncan Heyward); Mr. Wray (Tamenund); Mr. Lindsley (General Montcalm); Mr. Phillips (David Gamut)

Niblo's Garden Theatre, New York, opened February 16, 1874 24 performances
Written and directed by George Fawcett Rowe, based on the novel by James Fenimore Cooper

George Fawcett Rowe (Hawkeye); W. L. Street (Chingachgook); Fanny Cathcart (Cora Munro); Louise Henderson (Alice Munro); J. B. Studley (Magua); Fanny Herring (Uncas); H. Dalton (Major Duncan Heyward); F. F. Mackay (General Montcalm); J. J. Prior (Tamenund); M. W. Leffingwell (David Gamut); W. B. Cahill (Patrick Rooney)

SCREEN

LEATHERSTOCKING, Biograph Pictures, released September 1909
Produced and directed by D. W. Griffith; Based on the novel by James Fenimore Cooper; Photography, Billy Bitzer and Arthur Marine; Filmed at Cuddebackville, New York

James Kirkwood (Hawkeye); and Linda Arvidson, Mack Sennett, Billy Quirk, Marion Leonard, Vernber Clarges, Owen Moore, Adele de Garde

THE LAST OF THE MOHICANS, Powers Pictures, released August 1911
Based on the novel by James Fenimore Cooper

THE LAST OF THE MOHICANS, Thanhouser, released November 1911
Written and directed by Theodore Marston; Based on the novel by James Fenimore Cooper; Filmed at Lake George, New York

Frank Crane (Hawkeye); William Russell (Chingach-gook); Alphonse Ethier (Uncas)

THE DEERSLAYER, *Vitagraph*, released February 1912
Directed and written by Lawrence Trimble, based on the novel by James Fenimore Cooper

Harry T. Morey (Hawkeye); William Wallace Reid (Chingachgook); Hal Reid (Hurry Harry March); Ethel Dunn (Hist); Florence Turner (Betty Hutter); Evelyn Dominicus (Judith Hutter); William F. Cooper (Chief Rivenoak); Edward Thomas (Thomas Hutter)

LEDERSTRUMPF (LEATHERSTOCKING), *Luna-Film GmbH* (Germany), released December 1920; in U.S. released as *THE DEERSLAYER*, 1921
Director, Arthur Wellin; Screenplay, Robert Heymann, based on novels by James Fenimore Cooper

1) *DER WILDTOTER (The Deerslayer)*: Bela Lugosi as Chingachgook
2) *DER LETZTE DER MOHIKANER (The Last of the Mohicans)*: Bela Lugosi as Uncas, with Margot Sokolowska, Emil Mamelok, Gottfried Krause, Herta Heden, Eduard Eyseneck

THE LAST OF THE MOHICANS, *Associated Producers*, released November 1920
Directors, Maurice Tourneur and Clarence Brown; Screenplay, Robert A. Dillon, based on the novel by James Fenimore Cooper; Photography, Philip R. Du Bois and Charles E. Van Enger; Art director, Floyd Mueller

Wallace Beery (Magua); Harry Lorraine (Hawkeye); Theodore Lorch (Chingachgook); Barbara Bedford (Cora Munro); Lillian Hall (Alice Munro); Albert Roscoe (Uncas); Henry Woodward (Major Duncan Heyward); James Gordon (Colonel Munro); George Hackathorne (Captain Randolph); Jack MacDonald (Tamenund); Sidney Deane (General Webb); Nelson McDowell (David Gamut); Boris Karloff (Indian Chief)

LEATHERSTOCKING, *Pathe*, released 1924, a 10-part serial
Director, George B. Seitz; Based on James Fenimore Cooper's *Leatherstocking Tales*

Edna Murphy, Harold Miller, Frank Lackteen

EPISODES: The Warpath; The Scarlet Trail; The Hawk's Eyes; The Paleface Law; Ransom; The Betrayal; Rivenoak's Revenge; Out of the Storm; The Panther; Mungo's Torture

THE LAST OF THE MOHICANS, *Mascot Pictures*, released May 1932, a 12-part serial
Directors, B. Reeves Eason and Ford Beebe; Screenplay, Colbert Clark, John Francis Natteford, Ford Beebe and Wydham Gittens, based on the novel by James Fenimore Cooper

Harry Carey (Hawkeye); Edwina Booth (Alice Munro); Junior Coghlan (Uncas); Hobart Bosworth (Sagamore); Lucille Browne (Cora Munro); Robert Kortman (Magua); Walter Miller (Major Duncan Heyward); Nelson McDowell (David Gamut); Mischa Auer (General Montcalm); Edward Hearn (General Munro); Yakima Canutt (Black Fox); Joan Gale (Red Wing); John Big Tree (Indian)

EPISODES: Wild Waters; Flaming Arrows; Rifle or Tomahawk; Riding With Death; Red Shadows; Lure of Gold; Crimson Trail; Tide of Battle; Redskin's Honor; The Enemy's Stronghold; Paleface Magic; End of the Trail

THE LAST OF THE MOHICANS, *Reliance Pictures*, released September 1936

Presented by Harry M. Goetz; Producer, Edward Small; Director, George B. Seitz; Screenplay, Philip Dunne, adapted by John L. Balderson, Paul Perez and Daniel Moore from the novel by James Fenimore Cooper; Photography, Robert Planck; Art director, John Ducasse Schulze; Associate director, Wallace Fox; Research director, Edward P. Lambert; Music, Roy Webb; Sound, John L. Case; Editor, Jack Dennis

Randolph Scott (Hawkeye); Phillip Reed (Uncas); Bruce Cabot (Magua); Binnie Barnes (Alice Munro); Robert Barrat (Chingachgook); Henry Wilcoxon (Major Duncan Heyward); Heather Angel (Cora Munro); Hugh Buckler (Colonel Munro); Willard Robertson (Captain Winthrop); William Stack (General Montcalm); Lumsden Hare (General Abercrombie); Frank McGlynn, Sr. (David Gamut); Will Stanton (Jenkins); William V. Mong (Sachem); Ian MacLaren (William Pitt); Reginald Barlow (Duke of Newcastle); Olaf Hytton (King George II); Lionel Belmore (Patroon); Claude King (Duke of Marlborough); Art Di Puis (deLevis)

DEERSLAYER, *Republic Pictures*, released November 1943
Produced by P. S. "Pete" Harrison and M. B. Derr; Director, Lew Landers; Screenplay, P. S. Harrison and M. D. Derr, based on John W. Krafft's adaptation of the novel by James Fenimore Cooper; Photography, Arthur Martinelli; Music, Mort Glickman; Editor, George McGuire

Bruce Kellogg (Deerslayer); Jean Parker (Judith Hutter); Larry Parks (Jingo-Good); Warren Ashe (Hurry Harry March); Wanda McKay (Hetty Hutter); Yvonne de Carlo (Wah-Tah); Addison Richards (Mr. Hutter); Johnny Michaels (Bobby Hutter); Phil Van Zandt (Briarthorne); Trevor Bardette (Chief Rivenook); Robert Warwick (Chief Uncas); Many Treaties (Chief Brave Eagle); Clancy Cooper (Mr. Barlow); Princess Whynemiah ("Duenna"); William Edmund (Huron Sub-Chief)

LAST OF THE REDMEN, *Columbia Pictures*, released August 1947
Produced by Sam Katzman; Director, George Sherman; Screenplay, Herbert Dalmas, George H. Plympton, based on James Fenimore Cooper's *The Last of the Mohicans*; Photography, Ray Fernstrom, Ira H. Morgan; Art director, Paul Palmentola; Music director, Mischa Bakaleinikoff; Editor, James Sweeney

Michael O'Shea (Hawkeye); Jon Hall (Major Heyward); Evelyn Ankers (Alice Munro); Julie Bishop (Cora Munro); Buster Crabbe (Magua); Rick Vallin (Uncas); Guy Hedlund (General Munro); Buzz Henry (David Gamut); Frederick Warlock (General Webb); Emmett Vogan (Bob Wheelwright)

THE IROQUOIS TRAIL, *United Artists*, released June 1950
An Edward Small Production; Producer, Bernard Small; Director, Phil Karlson; Screenplay, Richard Schayer, based on James Fenimore Cooper's *Leatherstocking Tales*; Photography, Henry Freulich; Art director, Edward Ilou; Editor, Kenneth Crane

George Montgomery (Hawkeye); Brenda Marshall (Marion Thorne); Glenn Langan (Captain West); Reginald Denny (Captain Brownell); Monte Blue (Sagamore); Sheldon Leonard (Ogane); Paul Cavanaugh (Colonel Thorne); Holmes Herbert (General Johnson); Dan O'Herlihy (Lieutenant Blakeley); Don Gerner (Tom Cutler); Marcel Gourmet (General Montcalm); Arthur Little, Jr. (Adjutant Dickson); Esther Somers (Ma Cutler); John Doucette (Sam Girty)

THE PATHFINDER, *Columbia Pictures*, released January 1953
Produced by Sam Katzman; Director, Sidney Salkow; Screenplay, Robrert E. Kent, based on the novel by James Fenimore Cooper; Photography, Henry Freulich; Art director, Paul Palmentola; Music director, Mischa Bakaleinikoff; Editor, Jerome

Thoms

George Montgomery (Pathfinder); Helena Carter (Welcome Alison); Jay Silverheels (Chingachgook); Walter Kingsford (Colonel Duncanson); Rodd Redwing (Chief Arrowhead); Stephen Bekassy (Colonel Brasseau); Elena Verdugo (Lokawa); Bruce Lester (Captain Bradford); Chief Yowlachie (Eagle Feather); Ed Coch, Jr. (Uncas); Russ Conklin (Togamak); Vi Ingraham (La-Letan); Adele St. Maur (Matron)

THE DEERSLAYER, 20th Century-Fox, released September 1957

Produced and directed by Kurt Neumann; Screenplay, Kurt Neumann and Carroll Young, based on the novel by James Fenimore Cooper; Photography, Karl Struss; Music, Paul Sawtell and Bert Shefter; Editor, Jodie Coplan

Lex Barker (Deerslayer); Rita Moreno (Hetty Hutter); Forrest Tucker (Hurry Harry Marsh); Cathy O'Donnell (Judith Hutter); Jay C. Flippen (Old Tom Hutter); Carlos Rivas (Chingachgook); John Halloran (Old Warrior); Joseph Vitale (Huron Chief)

DER LETZTE MOHIKANER, German/Italian/Spanish, released 1965

A Coproduction of International Germania Film (Cologne)/Cineproduzioni Associates ((Rome)/P. C. Balcazar (Barcelona); Executive producer, Alfons Carcasona; Produced by Frank Thierry; Director, Harald Reinl; Screenplay, Joachim Bartsch, based on James Fenimore Cooper's *The Last of the Mohicans*; Photography, Ernst Kalinke and Francisco Marin; Art director, Jurgen Kiebach; Costumes, Irma Pauli; Music, Martin Bottcher; Editor, Hermann Haller

Joachim Fuchsberger (Captain Heyward); Anthony Steffens [Antonio De Teffe] (Strongheart); Karin Dor (Cora Munro); Marie France (Alice Munro); Ricardo Rodriguez (Magua); Carl Lange (Colonel Munro); Dan Martin (Uga); Stelio Gandelli (Roger)

THE LAST OF THE MOHICANS, 20th Century-Fox, released August 1992

Executive producer, James G. Robinson; Producers, Michael Mann and Hunt Lowry; Supervising producer, Ned Dowd; Director, Michael Mann; Screenplay, Michael Mann and Christopher Crowe, based on the novel by James Fenimore Cooper and the 1936 screenplay by Philip Dunne, adapted by John L. Balderston, Paul Perez and Daniel Moore; Photography, Dante Spinotti and Doug Milsome; Production designer, Wolf Kroeger; Music, Trevor Jones; Editors, Doug Hoenig and Arthur Schmidt

Daniel Day-Lewis (Hawkeye); Madeleine Stowe (Cora); Russell Means (Chingachgook); Eric Schweig (Uncas); Jodhi May (Alice); Steven Waddington (Heyward); Wes Studi (Magua); Maurice Roeves (Colonel Munro); Patrice Chereau (General Montcalm); Terry Kinney (John Cameron); Tracy Ellis (Alexandra Cameron); Justin Rice (James Cameron)

TELEVISION

HAWKEYE AND THE LAST OF THE MOHICANS, syndicated 1957-58 39 episodes (30 minutes each)

Produced by Canadian Normandie Productions; Producer, Sigmund Neufeld; Directors, Sam Newfield, Sigmund Neufeld; Teleplays, Andre Boehm, Louis Vittes, others, adapted from James Fenimore Cooper's *The Last of the Mohicans*

John Hart (Natty Bumpo, aka Hawkeye); Lon Chaney, Jr. (Chingachgook); Michael Ansara (Magua)

EPISODES: Hawkeye's Homecoming; The Threat; Franklin Story; The Wild One; Delaware Hoax; The Coward; The Ethan Allan Story; The Witch; The Medicine Man; The Servant; The Search; Snake Tattoo; False Witness; Powder Keg; Scapegoat; Way Station; The Brute; Stubborn Pioneer; Promised Valley; The Girl; The Soldier; Huron Tomahawk; The Tolliver Gang; The Colonel and His Lady; The Washington Story; Winter Passage; The Reckoning; LaSalle's Treasure; The Prisoner; False Fracas; The Morristown Story; Revenge; The Contest; The Truant; The Royal Grant; The Long Rifles; The Printer; The Indian Doll; Circle of Hate

THE LAST OF THE MOHICANS, televised January 1 to February 20, 1971 BBC 8 episodes (60 minutes each); in U.S. on PBS' *Masterpiece Theatre*, televised March 26 to May 14, 1972
Produced by British Broadcasting Corporation; Producer, John McRae; Director, David Maloney; Teleplay, Harry Green, based on the novel by James Fenimore Cooper; Production designer, David Spode; Makeup, Sandra Hurll; Fight arranger, Peter Diamond

Kenneth Ives (Hawkeye); Patricia Maynard (Cora Munro); Joanna David (Alice Munro); John Abineri (Chingachgook); Philip Madoc (Magua); Richard Warwick (Uncas); Tim Goodman (Major Duncan Heyward); David Leland (David Gamut); George Pravda (General Montcalm); Andrew Crawford (Colonel Munro); Noel Coleman (General Webb); David King (Huron Sagamore); Terence Brook (Huron Chief); Prentis Hancock (Lieutenant Grant); Michael Cullen (Lieutenant Otley); John Wentworth (Tamenund); Vernon Joyner (Surgeon); James Snell (Delaware Scout); Michael Lynch (Delaware Chief)

THE LAST OF THE MOHICANS, Schick Sunn Classics, televised November 23, 1977 NBC 2 hours
Executive producer, Charles E. Sellier, Jr.; Producer, Robert Stambler; Director, James L. Conway; Teleplay, Stephen Lord, based on the novel by James Fenimore Cooper; Photography, Henning Schellerup; Art director, Charles Bennett; Music, Bob Summers; Editors, Jim Webb and Steve Michael

Steve Forrest (Hawkeye); Ned Romero (Chingachgook); Jane Actman (Alice Morgan); Michele Marsh (Cora Morgan); Andrew Prine (Major Duncan Heyward); Don Shanks (Uncas); Robert Tessier (Magua); Robert Easton (David Gamut); John G. Bishop (Colonel Munro); Dehl Berti (Tamenund); and Beverly Rowland, Coleman Creel, Rosalyn Mike, Reid Sorenson

THE DEERSLAYER, Schick Sunn Classics, televised December 18, 1978 NBC 90 minutes
Executive producers, Charles E. Sellier, Jr., James L. Conway; Producer, Bill Conford; Director, Dick Friedenberg; Teleplay, S. S. Schweitzer, based on the novel by James Fenimore Cooper; Photography, Paul Hipp; Art director, Scott Lindquist; Music, Bob Summers and Andrew Belling; Stunt coordinator, Alan Gibbs; Editor, Carl Kress

Steve Forrest (Hawkeye); Ned Romero (Chingachgook); John Anderson (Hutter); Victor Mohica (Rivenook); Joan Prather (Judith Hutter); Charles Dierkop (Hurry Harry March); Brian Davies (Lieutenant Plowden); Ted Hamilton (Sieur de Beaujeur); Madeline Stowe (Hetty Hutter); Ruben Moreno (Tamenund); Betty Ann Carr (Wa-Wa-Ta); and Alma Beltran, Rosa Maria Hudson, Andrew William Lewis, Stephen Craig Taylor

THE LAST OF THE MOHICANS, syndicated 1987 Animated 70 minutes
Produced by Burbank Films Australia; Executive producer, Tom Stacey; Producers, Roz Phillips and Tim Brookehunt; Animation director, Warwick Grant; Director, Geoff Collins; Teleplay, Leonard Lee, based on the novel by James Fenimore Cooper; Storyboard, Bob Fosbery; Layout supervisor, Glen Lovett; Music, Simon Walker; Editors, Peter Jennings and Caroline Neave

Voices: John Waters (Hawkeye), Andrew Clarke, Bill Conn, Wallas Eaton, Russ Higgins, Scott Higgins, Phillip Hinton, Juliet Jordan, Judy Morris

THE LAST TYCOON
Various adaptation of the novel by F. Scott Fitzgerald (1941)

Synopsis

Monroe Stahr, the charismatic head of a major Hollywood studio, is literally worshipped by compnay president Pat Brady's daughter Cecelia. A minor Los Angeles earthquake that shakes up the backlot puts Stahr together with starlet Kathleen Moore, who disturbingly reminds him of his deceased actress-wife Minna Davis Stahr. His persistent pursuit however finally seduces Kathleen into his bed at his un-completed Malibu home, much to the dismay of Cecelia, who runs to daddy with the distressing news. Stahr, meanwhile, is beset with the traumatic problems of Rodriguez, the studio's top star and playboy around town who is obsessed with the possibility of impotency; the ineffectual contract director Red Ridingwood, and the temperamental tantrum's of Rodriguez' frequent co-star, Didi. Then comes unexpected word of Kathleen's impending marriage to someone else. Stahr, a tee-totaler, feels himself near the edge and braces himself with too many cocktails prior to a meeting with Brimmer, the powerful union organizer, and it ends in a drunken brawl. Brady, increasingly eager to rid himself of his high-profiled, publicity-wise production genius, seizes the opportunity to suggest to Stahr that the time has come for the latter to leave the studio for a well-earned rest.

Comment and Critique

F. Scott Fitzgerald has had more books written about him than he himself wrote in his lifetime. *The Last Tycoon* was Fitzgerald's uncompleted last novel. He died of a heart attack on December 21, 1940, after finishing Chapter Six. He was only thirty-four. Edmund Wilson, who edited the manuscript for publication in 1941 for Scribner's, called *The Last Tycoon* "Fitzgerald's most mature piece of work."

Hollywood columnist Sheilah Graham, with whom Scott spent his final years and in whose home he died (their story was told from her viewpoint in *Beloved Infidel*), forwarded to Wilson a copy of her letter detailing Fitzgerald's plans for the ending of his novel. (It was published by *The New York Times* in 1976 prior to the release of the film version of *The Last Tycoon*.) "This is how it was going to end. Brady was to ruin Stahr in the same way that at one time, and perhaps all the time, L. B. Mayer was out to wrest control of Metro from and/or to ruin Irving Thalberg. Stahr was almost kicked out and decided to remove Brady. He resorted to Brady's own gangster methods -- he was going to have him murdered. On a plane back to Hollywood, Stahr decides not to go through with the murder which has already been planned and which other people are doing for him; if he did, he would be as bad as the Brady crowd. So at the next airplane stop, he plans a cancellation of orders. I imagine the murder was to take place within a few hours. Before the next stop, however, the plane crashes and Stahr is killed. Which left the murder to go through..."

Graham also thought that the final scene would be Stahr's funeral and that Fitzgerald would have used the strange mix-up in usher invitations. Bob Thomas also indicated in his biography *Thalberg: Life and Legend* that "F. Scott Fitzgerald was intrigued that Harry Carey has been invited to usher, his invitation having been meant for [director] Carey Wilson. Fitzgerald's notes indicated he intended to use the incident in *The Last Tycoon.* A faded cowboy star, Johnny Swanson, was to have been a pallbearer for Monroe Stahr, along with Hollywood's most powerful figures -- 'Johnny goes through the ceremony rather dazed, and then finds out, to his astonishment, that his fortunes have been gloriously restored. From this time on, he is deluged with offers of jobs.' The Carey incident, alas, was merely legend."

In his biography *Scott Fitzgerald*, Andrew Turnbull noted that Fitzgerald "had studied Thalberg, the young Napoleon of films, who would be the model for the hero of *The Last Tycoon*." Turnbull also wrote that "Thalberg had dazzled Fitzgerald with 'his peculiar charm, his extraordinary good looks, his bountiful success, the tragic end of his great adventure.' Fitzgerald conceded that it was Thalberg who 'inspired the best part of Monroe Stahr -- though I have put in some things drawn from other men and inevitably much of myself ...Fitzgerald saw the struggle at MGM between Thalberg and Louis B. Mayer (the struggle between Stahr and Brady in *The Last Tycoon*)."

Stephen Vincent Benet (*Saturday Review of Literature*) appraised *The Last Tycoon* as showing "what a really first-class writer can do with material...It is character that dominates the book, the complex yet consistent character of Monroe Stahr, the producer, hitched to the wheels of his own preposterous chariot ...Had Fitzgerald been permitted to finish the book, I think there is not a doubt that it would have added a major character and a major novel to American fiction."

Hy Kraft's stage adaptation of *The Last Tycoon* was tested at the Woodstock (New York) Playhouse on August 31, 1954. The Kraft script entailed the final twenty-four hours of Monroe Stahr. David Stewart was cast as Stahr and Felicia Montealegre portrayed Kathleen Moore. Although plans were made for *The Last Tycoon* to come to Broadway in the 1954-55 season, Kraft's adaptation folded in Woodstock.

Prior to the aborted stage version of *The Last Tycoon*, Robert Montgomery in 1951 produced and starred in a television adaptation by Thomas W. Phipps, directed by Norman Felton. June Duprez was Kathleen Moore in this production. A second TV version was directed by John Frankenheimer on *Playhouse 90* six years later. In the all-star cast were Jack Palance as Stahr, Lee Remick as Cecilia and Viveca Lindfors as Kathleen Moore. Jack Gould wrote in *The New York Times* of the March 1957 production adapted by Don M. Mankiewicz: "Palance...contributed a searching and gripping study of the lonely, ruthless and tragic Hollywood film genius...[He] may have been just a shade too young in facial appearance for the part of the tycoon. But as he developed his characterization, he made the part of Monroe Stahr seem a man of dimension and determination ...To Mr. Mankiewicz and the director, John Frankenheimer, must go generous praise. Thanks to their efforts, *The Last Tycoon* did not lose its dark mood."

A British TV staging of *The Last Tycoon* with John Ireland and Constance Cummings in 1959 led *The London Times* to comment: "There were some unusually exciting, oblique glimpses of work in film studios, but the presentation of the play with little vivid action, an offbeat love affair that leads nowhere and an atmosphere of frustrating inevitability was an act of considerable courage...Mr. Ireland's performance had the hard, sensitive integrity of the novel's hero...The dramatization had the effect of increasing our admiration for Scott Fitzgerald's unfinished book."

Aware that film rights to *The Last Tycoon* had reverted to Fitzgerald's daughter, Mrs. Frances Fitzgerald Smith, after being owned for years by MGM and by Lester Cowan who had Irwin Shaw draft a screenplay that was never filmed, Sam Spiegel in the 1970s purchased the property. Mike Nichols was to direct the Harold Pinter screenplay and Al Pacino, Dustin Hoffman and Robert De Niro each was approached to play Stahr. De Niro got the part but apparently had a falling out with Nichols who withdrew from the project in favor of Elia Kazan (his last movie to date).

In *The New York Times*, Vincent Canby wrote of Kazan's movie of *The Last Tycoon*: "[It] echoes '30s Hollywood...De Niro, whose lean, dark good looks seem an idealization of Thalberg's becomes a casualty of the 'new' Hollywood of Wall Street investors, bankers and union organizers that Fitzgerald could see in the future...In one of his final notes for *The Last Tycoon*, Fitzgerald wrote in capital letters: 'Action Is Character.' It is one of the achievements of Messrs. Kazan, Pinter and De Niro that so much of Monroe Stahr in the novel succeeds in coming though in the film...None of the changes seems to me to damage the style or mood of the book. More than any other screen adaptation of a Fitzgerald work...*The Last Tycoon* preserves the original feeling and intelligence."

Equally generous with his praise was Andrew Sarris, who in *The Village Voice* found "*The Last Tycoon* eminently worth supporting if we are to preserve a literate cinema in the English language...Edmund Wilson's introduction to the novel entirely misses the point of Fitzgerald's involvement with the film industry and with the characters in the novel [and] treats *The Last Tycoon* as if it were an Upton Sinclair tract on the abuse of meat packers." Sarris continued: DeNiro's Stahr dominates every scene in *The Last Tycoon*. Even Jack Nicholson's showy cameo as a Communist organizer of Hollywood writers merely illuminates Stahr's suicidal despair after his Kathleen has vanished into the mists of otherness...It's all De Niro's show, and Kazan's and Pinter's, as they transform [it] into a sustained Hollywood hallucination... *The Last Tycoon* is an accomplished film."

Other critics were somewhat less enthusiastic about *The Last Tycoon*, and the Academy of Motion Picture Arts and Sciences overlooked De Niro (for this film; he was nominated for *Taxi Driver* that year), Kazan, Pinter, and others down the line, as well as the film itself. Its lone nomination was for Art Direction/Set Decoration.

STAGE

THE LAST TYCOON, Woodstock (N.Y.) Playhouse, opened August 31, 1954
Produced by the Woodstock Playhouse by arrangement with Albert Selden and Morton Gottlieb; A Drama by Hy Kraft, based on the novel by F. Scott Fitzgerald; Director, Michael Howard; Setting, Robert Jillson

David Stewart (Monroe Stahr); Felicia Montealegre (Kathleen Moore); Norman Rose (Dr. Baer); Edward Cullen (Mr. Boxley); Mary James (Miss Doolan); Michael Lewin (Pat Brady); Betty Bendyk (Cecilia Brady); Howard Wierum (Charles Buckley); Robert Thornell (Red Ridingwood); Bernard Kates (Tommy)

SCREEN

THE LAST TYCOON, Paramount Pictures, released November 1976
Produced by Sam Spiegel; Director, Elia Kazan; Screenplay, Harold Pinter, based on

the novel by F. Scott Fitzgerald; Photography, Victor Kemper; Production designer, Gene F. Callahan; Art director, Jack Collis; Set decorator, Jerry Wunderlich; Costumes, Anna Hill Johnstone; Additional costumes, Anthea Sylbert; Music, Maurice Jarre; Special effects, Henry Millar; Editor, Richard Marks

Robert De Niro (Monroe Stahr); Robert Mitchum (Pat Brady); Ingrid Boulting (Kathleen Moore); Tony Curtis (Rodriguez); Jeanne Moreau (Didi); Jack Nicholson (Brimmer); Ray Milland (Fleishacker); Dana Andrews (Red Ridingwood); Donald Pleasence (Boxley); Peter Strauss (Wylie White); Theresa Russell (Cecilia Brady); Tige Andrews (Popolos); Morgan Farley (Marcus); John Carradine (Guide); Jeff Corey (Doctor); Diane Shalet (Stahr's Secretary); Angelica Huston (Edna); Leslie Curtis (Mrs. Rodriguez); Seymour Cassell (Seal Trainer); Eric Christmas (Norman); Lloyd Kino (Butler); Bonnie Bartlett, Sharon Masters (Brady's Secretaries); Brendan Burns (Assistant Editor); Peggy Feury (Hairdresser); Betsy Jones-Moreland (Lady Writer); Carrie Miller (Lady in Restaurant); Patricia Singer (Girl on Beach)

TELEVISION

THE LAST TYCOON, Lucky Strike Theatre, televised February 26, 1951 NBC 1 hour

Produced by Robert Montgomery; Director, Norman Felton; Teleplay, Thomas W. Phipps, based on the novel by F. Scott Fitzgerald; Settings, Syrjala; Music, Raymond Scott; Narrator, Hedda Hopper

Robert Montgomery (Monroe Stahr); June Duprez (Kathleen Moore); Louis Hector (Pat Brady); Judy Parrish (Cecelia Brady); Robert Harris (George Boxley)

Playhouse 90, televised March 14, 1957 CBS 90 minutes

Produced by Martin Manulis; Director, John Frankenheimer; Teleplay, Don M. Mankiewicz, based on the novel by F. Scott Fitzgerald; Settings, Walter Herndon

Jack Palance (Monroe Stahr); Viveca Lindfors (Kathleen Moore); Keenan Wynn (Lou Myrick); Lee Remick (Cecilia Brady); Robert F. Simon (Pat Brady); John Hudson (Wylie White); Peter Lorre (Pete Zavras)

Armchair Theatre (Great Britain), televised December 27, 1959 Granada 90 minutes

Produced by Independent Television; Producer, Sydney Newman; Director, William Kotcheff; Adapted by Don M. Mankiewicz from the novel by F. Scott Fitzgerald; Designer, Timothy O'Brien

John Ireland (Monroe Stahr); Constance Cummings (Kathleen Moore); Peter Dyneley (Lou Myrick); Betta St. Johns (Cecilia Brady); Bud Knapp (Pat Brady); Sean Sullivan (Wylie White); Karel Stepanek (Pete Zavras); Olga Lowe (Birdy); William Peacock (Mark Gilligan); Bernard Archard (George Boxley); Vic Wise (Mike van Dyke); Paul Whitsun-Jones (Charles Kellogg)

THE LEGEND OF SLEEPY HOLLOW

Various adaptations of the story by Washington Irving (1819)

Synopsis

In the small Revolutionary Era village of Sleepy Hollow, near Tarrytown, New

York, on the Hudson River, long, lanky and rather gawky Ichabod Crane is the sole teacher in the local one-room schoolhouse. He occupies his spare time fascinating the locals with witchcraft yarns and is himself intrigued by their ghost stories. He is even more intrigued with young Katrina Van Tassel, daughter of a wealthy landowner but finds himself constantly vying for her favors with roistering, swaggering Abraham Van Brunt, known to all as Brom Bones. Following a party at the Van Tassels, Ichabod goes out into the night on his scrawny plough horse, Gunpowder, borrowed for the occasion from Hans Van Ripper, and in the darkness is pursued by one of the curses of local legend, the Headless Horseman. Gunpowder refuses to gallop faster, and, looking back, a now terrified Ichabod sees the mysterious caped figure behind him rise up in the stirrups of his black stallion and hurl what appears to be a severed head at him. The next morning, a search is made for the school-master, but nothing is found except Ichabod's hat lying on the ground next to a smashed jack-o'-lantern. As time passes, memories of the odd-looking teacher fade in Sleepy Hollow, Brom Bones marries Katrina, and the locals puzzle over Brom's laughter whenever the tale of Ichabod Crane and his disappearance is related.

Comment and Critique

Washington Irving's *The Sketch Book of Geoffrey Crayon*, published in England in 1819, contained two of his classic tales, *Rip Van Winkle* and *The Legend of Sleepy Hollow*. Composer Max Maretzek set the latter one to music in 1848 with a libretto titled *Sleepy Hollow* by Charles Gaylor. *Rip Van Winkle* was memorialized on stage by legendary American actor Joseph Jefferson, and *The Legend of Sleepy Hollow* initially by George Fawcett Rowe, whose 1879 adaptation of it as *Wolfert's Roost* opened in New York at Wallack's Theatre.

Written with popular actor John T. Raymond in mind, it was reviewed by *The New York Times*: "We fail to see that [he] has risen beyond its scenes and incidents; his individuality, as embodied in Ichabod Crane, is scarcely of a kind to make more than a respectable impression upon the mind...*Wolfert's Roost* is another illustration of a poetic subject treated theatrically, and lowered by his treatment from the place of imagination to that of conventionality. Irving's legend of Sleepy Hollow is perfect in its way as a combination of humor and fantasy, the delicate play of good-natured satire over vague shadows and strange visions. To put such a story upon the stage is practically impossible ...[Rowe's] play is not altogether a bad one, although it spoils a lovely conception and verges at times on the ridiculous...The scenery was exceedingly elaborate and beautiful..."

Actress Miriam Battista and her husband, Russell Maloney, a writer for *The New Yorker*, did the book and lyrics for *Sleepy Hollow*, a musical comedy adaptation of Irving's tale. George Lessner, a Viennese composer whose light opera *The Queen's Maid* was produced in Austria when he was sixteen, set the Battista/Maloney book to music, and the show opened on Broadway in June 1948. Unfortunately, it disappeared quicker than did the headless horseman after a mere dozen performances.

Sleepy Hollow the *Time* magazine critic found to be "passably tuneful and monumentally tedious...Washington Irving's famous yarn [would] seem likely material for a musical...But *Sleepy Hollow* has lost the flavor of Irving's old tale...The show is incredibly pokey and protracted; it just won't keep movin' along...As Ichabod, angular Gil Lamb is likeable and pleasant, but by no means a tide-turner..."

Reported *Billboard*: "...what has come out of the notion via a book by Russell Maloney and Miriam Battista suggests that Ichabod Crane and his Dutch pals might better have been left in Mr. Irving's *Sketch Book*...Not even some ear-appealing ballads by George Lessner, splendidly delivered by Betty Jane Watson and Hayes Gordon, nor occasional winning clowning by Gil Lamb, nor some expert stepping by James Starbuck and Dorothy Bird, can make *Sleepy Hollow* seem other than a cumbersome, drowsy operetta [which] gets progressively wearier as the evening wears on."

Eighteen years later, in October 1966, another musical version was attempted of Irving's *The Legend of Sleepy Hollow*. Called *Autumn's Here*, with book, music and lyrics by Norman Dean and staging and choreography by dancer Hal Le Roy, it opened on Broadway at the Bert Wheeler Theatre and lasted for eighty performances. It inaugurated the one-time Plantation Room of the Dixie Hotel on West 43rd Street, and the former vaudevillian and film headliner for whom the theatre was named was present for the opening. He was seventy-one at the time.

Dan Sullivan (*The New York Times*) criticized Norman Dean for taking "most of the atmosphere our of Irving's masterly tale, and made it into a vigorous but rather clumsy animated cartoon...What hurts is the lack of sensitivity to the lazy, hazy, harvest-home aura of the tale [and] the author's strange decision to make his characters talk like Broadway touts...The show does have a certain dash to it, thanks to Hal Le Roy's direction and several fine performers. Bob Riehl couldn't have been better as Ichabod..."

Alice Hale's adaptation of Irving's classic opened at the Theatre of the Open Eye in New York in November 1985. This version was geared for children, but Walter Goodman, writing in *The New York Times*, felt the confused production might divert youngsters "by the commotion on the stage and in the aisles of the Open Eye's new quarters" and those "who have not grown blase over horror movies may get some shivers from the climactic appearance of the Headless Horseman." Goodman thought, however, that "they may also enjoy the few songs and dances of the period and place..."

Despite these assorted stage version of Irving's *The Legend of Sleepy Hollow* over the years, the tale appeared to be more adaptable to the motion picture screen, and was first filmed by Kalem in 1908 in a fourteen-minute reel and by Eclair in 1912. Hodkinson produced a screen version in 1922 as *The Headless Horseman* with Will Rogers as Ichabod Crane.

The Moving Picture World's Charles S. Sewell described *The Headless Horseman* as having been "conscientiously produced -- with Will Rogers in the famous character of Ichabod Crane...the visualization seems as near perfect...the whole production shows great care, an unusual faithfulness in the characters and settings that bespeaks fine direction...Will Rogers has achieved the unusual in picturing the loveless Ichabod...He is funny in a natural, consistent way, as one can imagine the author intended. The ride of the headless horseman is the dramatic highlight of the picture...comic and weird by turns. These scenes have been vivified by skillful lighting and shading, and some spectacular shots of the sky at night..."

In 1949, Walt Disney combined Irving's *The Legend of Sleepy Hollow* in an animated version with Kenneth Grahame's tale of Mr. Toad in *The Wind in the Willows*, calling the feature *Ichabod and Mr. Toad*. Bing Crosby narrated the Washington Irving yarn and sang a couple of songs. Disney-phile Leonard Maltin found in his *The Disney Films* that "*Ichabod and Mr. Toad* is one of Disney's most beguiling animated features; *The Wind in the Willow* in particular has some of the finest work the studio ever did." Maltin said of the Sleepy Hollow portion: "The gags come fast and funny throughout... with dozens of throwaways, in depicting Ichabod's lack of dedication to the teaching profession [and] more broadly in his competition with Brom Bones for Katrina's attention. Naturally the showiest part of the film is Ichabod's ride home at night, which is masterly done...It really is a frightening vision, and gives impetus to the frantic chase scene that follows."

The New York Times' A. H. Weiler applauded Disney's return to all-animation, but felt that "This is not to report that Disney has reached perfection in 'Ichabod.' He is still short of the mark...Although Mr. Crosby states that the 'colonies' also produced a few notable characters in his introduction to 'Old Icky,' the tale of Ichabod Crane lacks the subtlety and satirical bite of its predecessor. Following the 'facts' as relayed by Diedrich Knickerbocker to Washington Irving, the saga of the lanky, pin-headed, 'posturing pedagogue' is related almost literally and in broad splashy sequences...That famous scene where the gullible and terrified Yankee schoolmaster, astride his bony nag, is chased through the Hollow by the Headless Horseman may be as terrifying to youngsters as any previous Disney hairraiser. The amiable Mr. Crosby's narration...is smooth and professional. The same may also be said of 'The Legend of Sleepy Hollow.' It, too, is smooth and professional but it lacks the inventiveness and genuine whimsy of 'Mr. Toad.'"

Britain's *Monthly Film Bulletin* rated the Mr. Toad part of the Disney movie superior to the Sleepy Hollow segment, noting: "In view of the success of Mr. Toad, it is a great pity that [it] cannot be separated and shown apart from Ichabod [which] is inferior in artistry and conception."

On television, costumed as Washington Irving, Boris Karloff acted as narrator for the 1958 *Shirley Temple Storybook* telecast of *The Legend of Sleepy Hollow*, opening the proceedings by announcing, "I am not Shirley Temple!" The entertaining production, part-live and part-film, starred Shirley Temple as Katrina and Jules Munshin as Ichabod.

Finding the production "rather uneven," *The New York Times*' Jack Gould wrote: "In part it was engagingly spooky and faithful to the spirit of make-believe; in part it suggested a Western staged on the Pennsylvania Turnpike...Miss Temple, playing her first dramatic role since her return to the entertainment world, was both fetching and believable...Boris Karloff, dressed as Washington Irving, was superb. His offscreen narration enormously heightened the mood...In the filmed ride sequences, Mr. Munshin seemed more frightened of his own horse than anybody else's...John Ericson played Brom Bones with vigor and virility..."

A segment of *CBS Library's "Once Upon a Midnight Dreary"* hosted by Vincent Price during Halloween week of 1979 offered an abbreviated version of *The Legend of Sleepy Hollow* with Rene Auberjonois as Ichabod Crane. The following year, on Halloween Night, a two-hour "Classics Illustrated" version, bowdlerized by Jack Jacobs, Marvin Wald and Tom Chapman, starred Jeff Goldblum. The cast did what it could with a script that resorted to low comedy and outright slapstick turned the Irving tale into silly time on television, complete with a happy sitcom ending -- with Ichabod remaining in town, winning Katrina from bullying Brom Bones and announcing "All's well that ends well!" The committee of writers seemed to have figured Shakespeare had a better ending than Irving.

Truer to Washington Irving was the 1986 adaptation on *Shelley Duvall's Tall Tales and Legends* on Showtime, with Ed Begley, Jr., as Ichabod, Beverly D'Angelo as Katrina, Tim Thomerson as Brom Bones, and Charles Durning as the Narrator. "Shelley Duvall, exec producer and host for this latest edition...earns high praise for the charming, assured adaptation (by Lan O'Kun) of Washington Irving's 1819 story," reviewed *Variety*. "Ed Begley, Jr., falling heir to the Ichabod Crane role, does a fine job of interpreting the 1800s schoolmaster...Performances belong in the knowing-wink school of acting and adapt well to the proceedings." This was followed two years later by a beautifully designed half-hour animated version of the classic narrated by Glenn Close.

In October 1974, the United States Postal Service, as one of a series of American Revolution Bicentennial issues, produced a commemorative tencent *Legend of Sleepy Hollow* stamp, depicting the Headless Horseman chasing Ichabod Crane, silhouetted against a full moon.

STAGE

WOLFERT'S ROOST; OR, A LEGEND OF SLEEPY HOLLOW, Wallack's Theatre, New York, opened August 18, 1879 48 performances

Written and directed by George Fawcett Rowe, based on the story by Washington Irving; Scenery, George Heister and J. Clare

John T. Raymond (Ichabod Crane); Kate Forsythe (Katrina Van Tassel); F. Hardenberg (Brom Van Brunt); J. W. Shannon (Baltus Van Tassel); E. M. Holland (Coroner John Tappan); Henry Lee (Dolf Haverstraw); Mme. Ponisi (Dame Haverstraw); Courtney Barnes (Emma Haverstraw); P. A. Anderson (The Ghost of Wolfert); C. E Edwin (Jake, a Negro); Connie Thompson (Phoebe, a Mulatto Girl); Josie Myers (Widow Perkins); H. Pearson (Ploos); F. Lull (Anstel); Allie Dorrington (Katie Van Schaick)

SLEEPY HOLLOW, Academy of Music, New York, opened September 25, 1879 11 performances

An Opera by Max Maretzek, based on the story by Washington Irving; Libretto by Charles Gaylor

W. C. Gardion (Ichabod Crane); Annis Montague (Katrina Van Tassell); Charles Turner (Brom Bones); Charles Collins (Herr Van Tassell); H. Gardier (Rip Van Ripper); J. Fink (Van Ness); Ada Whitman (Frau Van Tassel); Florence Rice Knox (Frau Van Spuyten)

SLEEPY HOLLOW, St. James Theatre, New York, opened June 3, 1948 12 performances

Produced by Lorraine Lester; A Musical Comedy based on the story by Washington Irving; Director, John O'Shaughnessy; Book and lyrics by Russell Maloney and Miriam Battista; Music by George Lessner; Settings and lighting, Jo Mielziner; Costumes, David Ffolkes; Musical numbers and dances staged by Anna Sokalow; Musical director, Irving Actman; Orchestrations, Hans Spialek, Ted Royal and George Lessner; Choral arrangements, Elie Siegmeister; Additional lyrics, Ruth Hughes Aarons; Company manager, Joe Moss; Stage manager, Ed Brinkmann

Gil Lamb (Ichabod Crane); Mary McCarty (Eva); Betty Jane Watson (Katrina Van Tassel); Ruth McDevitt (Mrs. Van Tassel); Tom Hoier (Mr. Van Tassel); Laura Pierpont (Mrs. Van Brunt); Bert Wilcox (Mr. Van Brunt); Bobby White (Jacob Van Tassel); Hayes Gordon (Brom "Bones" Van Brunt); Ward Gardner (Hendrick); Ellen Repp (Wilhelmina); Walter Butterworth (Willie Van Twiller); Alan Shay (Hans Van Ripper); Jean Handzlik (Mrs. Van Ripper); Morley Evans (Mr. Van Ripper); Russell George (Luther); James Starbuck (Walt); Jo Sullivan (Margaret); Margery Oldroyd (Annie); William Ferguson (Ike); Larry Robbins (Roelf); Lewis Scholle (Stuyveling Van Doorn); Kaja Sundsten (Elizabeth); Shaun O'Brien (Piet); Ray Drakeley (Balt); John Ward (Chris); Margaret Ritter (Bertha); Ann Dunbar (Jenny); Peggy Ferris (Lena); Franklin Wagner (Nick); Ken Foley (Mr. Van Hooten); John Russel (Joost); Ty Kearney (Conscience);

Kenneth Remo (Indian); William Mende (Cotton Mather); Dorothy Bird (The Lady from New Haven); Sylvia Lane (Greta); Robin Sloan (Hilda); Doreen Lane (Tina); Richard Rhoades (Martin Van Horsen); Aza Bard, Clara Courdery, Ann Dunbar, Kate Friedlich, Saida Gerrard, Carmella Guiterrez, Margaret McCallion, Kaja Sundsten, Alex Dunseff, Dan Farnworth, Jay Lloyd, Remi Martel, Joseph Milan, Shaun O'Brien, Franklin Wager, John Ward (Dancers); Ilona Albok, Joan Barrett, Peggy Ferris, Deda La Petina, Margery Oldroyd, Margaret Ritter, Janice Sprei, Jo Sullivan, Ray Drakeley, William Ferguson, Ken Foley, Russell George, Vincent Lubrano, William Mende, Larry Robbins, John Russel (Singers); Walter Butterworth, Doreen Lane, Sylvia Lane, Richard Rhoades, Lewis Francis Scholle, Alan Shay, Robin Sloan (Children)

MUSICAL NUMBERS: "Time Stands Still"; "I Still Have Plenty to Learn"; "Ask Me Again"; "Never Let Her Go"; "There's History to Be Made"; "Here and Now"; "Why Was I Born on a Farm?"; "If"; "My Lucky Lover"; "A Musical Lesson"; "You've Got That Kind of Force"; "I'm Lost"; "Goodnight"; "The Englishman's Head"; "Pedro"; "Ichabod"; "Poor Man"; "The Things That Lovers Say"; "Bouree"; "Headless Horseman Ballet"; "The Gray Goose"

Dropped during tryout: "Hereabouts"; "Alma"; "In the Hay"

AUTUMN'S HERE, *Bert Wheeler Theatre*, New York, opened October 25, 1966 80 performances

Produced by Bob Hadley; A Musical adaptation of *The Legend of Sleepy Hollow* by Washington Irving; Directed and choreographed by Hal Le Roy; Book, music and lyrics by Norman Dean; Settings, Robert Conley; Lighting, Arthur Terieson; Costumes, Eve Hendriksen; Musical director, Gordon Munford; Stage manager, Ross Hertz

Bob Riehl (Ichabod Crane); Karin Wolfe (Katrina Van Tassel); Fred Gockel (Brom Bones); James L. O'Neill (Diedrich Knickerbocker); Allan Lokos (Mr. Van Tassel); Joyce Lynn (Mrs. Van Tassel); Joyce Devlin (Jo); Les Freed (Ben); John Johann (Douglas); Zona Kennedy (Etta); Dan Leach (Will); Regina Lynn (Dora); Pamela Privette (Della); Gordon Ramsey (Lew)

MUSICAL NUMBERS: "Sleepy Hollow"; "Boy, Do I Hate Horse Races"; "Me and My Horse"; "Autumn's Here"; "Song of the 13 Colonies"; "Patience"; "For the Harvest Safely Gathered"; "Who Walks Like a Scarecrow"; "This Is the Girl for Me"; "Do You Think I'm Pretty"; "Fine Words and Fancy Phrases"; "Private Hunting Ground"; "It's a Long Road Home"; "Brom and Katrina"; "Dark New England Night"; "Dutch Country Table"; "You Never Miss the Water"; "Any Day Now"; "You May Be the Someone"; "Beware As You Ride Through the Hollow"; "The Chase"

THE LEGEND OF SLEEPY HOLLOW, *Theatre of the Open Eye*, New York, opened November 5, 1985

Produced by The Theatre of the Open Eye; A Play by Alice Hale, based on the story by Washington Irving; Director, Amie Brockway; Settings and lighting, Adrienne J. Brockway; Costumes, David Kay Mickelson; Assistant director, James H. Sweeney; Stage manager, Thomas Spence

Hugh Hodgin (Ichabod Crane); Ebba James (Katrina Van Tassel); William Ellis (Diedrich Knickerbocker); Elizabeth Gee (Mistress Van Tassel); Bruce Anthony (Balt Van Tassel); John Moser (Brom Bones); Chris Gifford (Joseph/Daredevil); Harry Bennett (Gunpowder/Farmer York); Mark Peters (Fiddler/Farmer Van Wart); Elizabeth Geraghty (Mistress Van Wart/Jacob); Frank Deal (John/Farmer

Van Ripper); Katherine Barry (Mistress York/Johanna)

SCREEN

THE HEADLESS HORSEMAN, W. W. Hodkinson Corp., released November 1922
Produced by the Sleepy Hollow Corporation; Director, Edward Venturini; Screenplay, Carl Stearns Clancy, based on *The Legend of Sleepy Hollow* by Washington Irving; Photography, Ned Van Buren; Settings, Tec-Art Studios

Will Rogers (Ichabod Crane); Lois Meredith (Katrina Van Tassel); Ben Hendricks, Jr. (Abraham Van Brunt); Mary Foy (Dame Martling); Charles Graham (Hans Van Ripper); Nicholas Burnham (Doffue Martling)

ICHABOD AND MR. TOAD, Walt Disney/RKO Pictures, released October 1949
Produced by Walt Disney; An Animated Cartoon; Directors, James Algar, Clyde Geronimi and Jack Kinney; Production supervisor, Ben Sharpsteen; Directing animators, Franklin Thomas, Oliver Johnson, Jr., Wolfgang Reitherman, Milt Kahl, John Lounsbery and Ward Kimball; Story, Erdman Penner, Winston Hibler, Joe Rinaldi, Ted Sears, Homer Brightman and Harry Reeves; Character animators, Fred Moore, John Sibley, Marc Davis, Hal Ambro, Harvey Toombs, Hal King, Hugh Fraser and Don Lusk; Music director, Oliver Wallace; Vocal arrangements, Ken Darby; Orchestrations, Joseph Dubin; Editor, John O. Young; Special process, Ub Iwerks; Songs for *Ichabod*: "Katrina," "Ichabod" and "The Headless Horseman" by Don Raye and Gene DePaul; Song for *Mr Todd*: "Merrily on Our Way" by Frank Churchill and Charles Wolcott, Larry Morey and Ray Gilbert

Bing Crosby as narrator of the story of Ichabod Crane; Basil Rathbone as narrator of the story of Mr. Toad; Voices of Eric Blore (Mr. Toad); Pat O'Malley (Cyril); Claud Allister (Water Rat); John Ployardt (Prosecutor); Collin Campbell (Mole); Campbell Grant (Angus MacBadger); Ollie Wallace (Winky)

TELEVISION

THE LEGEND OF SLEEPY HOLLOW, Shirley Temple Storybook, televised March 5, 1958 NBC 1 hour
Produced by Alvin Cooperman; Director, Paul Bogart; Teleplay, Norman Lessing, based on the story by Washington Irving

Jules Munshin (Ichabod Crane); Shirley Temple (Katrina Van Tassel); John Ericson (Brom Bones); Boris Karloff (Narator); Russell Collins (Alpheus Dankendorf); Fred Essler (Baltus Van Tassel); Barbara Morrison (Dame Van Tassel); and John Mylong, Jimmy Carter, Tiger Farfarh, Jim Bridges

THE LEGEND OF SLEEPY HOLLOW, CBS Library: Once Upon a Midnight Dreary, televised October 21, 1979 CBS I hour
Asselin Productions, Inc.; Produced by Diane and Paul Asselin; Director, Nell Cox; Written by Kimmer Ringwald; Photography, David Sanderson; Editor, Steve Muscarella; Presented in conjunction with *The Ghost Belongs to Me* by Richard Peck and *The House With a Clock in the Walls* by John Bellair; Narrator/Host, Vincent Price

Rene Auberjonois (Ichabod Crane); Pamela Brown (Katrina Van Tassel); Guy Boyd (Brom Bones); Robert Forster (The Headless Horseman)

THE LEGEND OF SLEEPY HOLLOW, Schick Sunn Classics, televised October 31,

1980 NBC 2 hours
Executive producer, Charles E. Sellier, Jr.; Producer, James L. Conway; Director, Henning Schellerup; Teleplay, Jack Jacobs, Marvin Wald and Tom Chapman, based on the story by Washington Irving; Photography, Paul Hipp; Production designer, Paul Staheli; Music, Bob Summers; Editor, Michael Spence

Jeff Goldblum (Ichabod Crane); Meg Foster (Katrina Van Tassel); Dick Butkus (Brom Bones); Paul Sand (Frederic Dutcher); Michael Witt (Ted Vanderhoof); James Griffith (Squire Van Tassel); Laura Campbell (Thelma Vanderhoof Dumke); John Sylvester White (Fritz Vanderhoof); Michael Ruud (Winthrop Palmer); Karin Issacson (Jenny); H.E.D. Redford (Karl); Tiger Thompson (Jan Van Tassel)

THE LEGEND OF SLEEPY HOLLOW, Shelley Duvall's Tall Tales and Legends, televised October 6, 1986 Showtime 50 minutes
A Platypus Production in asociation with Gaylord Productions; Executive producer, Shelley Duvall; Producers, Bridget Terry, Frederic S. Fuchs; Director, Edd Griles; Teleplay, Lan O'Kun, based on the story by Washington Irving; Production designer, Michael Erler; Costume designer, J. Allen Highfill; Music, Robert Folk; Makeup, Sheryl Leigh and Ron Figuly

Ed Begley, Jr. (Ichabod Crane); Beverly D'Angelo (Katrina Van Tassel); Charles Durning (Uncle Doffue/ Narrator); Tim Thomerson (Brom Bones); Barret Oliver (Hendrick); Dean Dittman (Mr. Van Tassel); Diana Bellamy (Mrs. Van Tassel); Walter Olkewicz (Van Epps); David McCharen (Van Der Meer); Harry Frazier (Van Ripper); Michael Dalae (Van Der Kar)

THE LEGEND OF SLEEPY HOLLOW, Children's Storybook Classics, televised October 10, 1988 Showtime 30 minutes
Rabbit Ears Productions; Executive producer, Mark Sottnick; Associate producer, Doris Wilkowsky; Adapted by Robert Van Nutt from the Washington Irving story; Paintings, Robert Van Nutt; Title art, Julia Van Nutt; Titles designed by Henrietta Condak; Production designer, C. W. Rogers; Music composed, arranged and conducted by Tim Story

Glenn Close (Narrator)

LEGS DIAMOND

Various productions inspired by the life of Jack "Legs" Diamond

Synopsis (the musical)

Jack Diamond, having done time in a Pennsylvania prison for Arnold Rothstein, then a small-time hood, arrives in New York and looks up his former on- and offstage dance partner, Flo, at her nightspot, the Hotsy Totsy Club and Grill. He interrupts her floor-show with one of his own that displays his dance technique. Backstage, he asks her for a spot in her show, but quickly learns that the place isn't hers -- it belongs to Rothstein, who's now in the bigtime. Diamond figures that Rothstein owes him and goes to him for a job, but Bones and Moran, henchmen of A. R., as he likes to be known, let Jack know that Rothstein considers his debt paid by not having him killed. A. R.'s moll, Kiki Roberts, however, takes to Jack and escapes the watchful eye of her constant bodyguard Little Augie to invite him to her show at A. R.'s Club

Tropicabana. The two strike a spark, but his main interest is getting into the show. A. R. drops by one night, doesn't recognize Jack but admires his technique as a dancer and nicknames him "Legs."

Eventually Jack eases his way into A. R.'s operation and the big-time gangster decides to eliminate him. Jack survives the hit -- two of them, in fact -- and then, while saving Kiki's life, accidentally kills A. R. Jack and Kiki marry so that she can't testify against him when he's picked up as the prime suspect, and the cops have to release him. As Jack is on the verge of taking over A. R.'s crime empire, the feds step in with needed evidence to send him up the river, but after reluctantly sending Kiki out of his life, he arranges with one of A. R.'s boys to fake another hit on him. Now that the authorities think he's dead, he's free to take off -- with the older woman in his life, Flo. And they're Cuba bound.

Comment and Critique

He was born John T. Noland in Philadelphia in 1896 and was shot down in a rooming house in Albany in 1931. During that time, he gained a modicum of infamy in the annals of crime as Legs Diamond. In *The Encyclopedia of American Crime* by Carl Sitakis (Facts on File, 1982), in which Jack "Legs" Diamond is identified simply as "Racketeer and Murderer," there is this: "Two things often said about Jack 'Legs' Diamond, one of the most notorious gangsters of the 1920s -- 'the only woman who ever loved him was his mother and she died when he was a kid' and 'the bullet hasn't been made that can kill Legs Diamond' -- both were inaccurate...[His] main problem in life was that almost everyone in the under-world hated him."

Diamond, legend has it, clawed his way from small-time bootlegging in the 1920s to top of big-time gangsterdom, and eventually became a sport in Manhattan with his own joint, the Hotsy Totsy Club, a second-floor bistro on Broadway in the Fifties. A small-time dancer himself (hence the nickname), Legs was always nattily dressed, usually in pin-stripes and spats. Ultimately he got into turf trouble with Dutch Schultz and they became mortal enemies. Over the years, he took a number of bullets but always survived and became convinced he couldn't be killed. When gangster kingpin Arnold Rothstein was gunned down in 1931, and his empire divided, Legs wanted a bigger share of the New York nightclub rackets than he got and further embittered himself to the other crime lords. Unknown hit man, sent allegedly by Dutch Schultz, finally did Legs in a week before Christmas 1931.

Ironically it was the day after Christmas 1988 that a lavish Broadway musical based on his life opened just around the corner from his long-gone Hotsy Totsy Club. Like Legs himself, the show had a troubled history, going on to become one of the legendary bombs of the musical stage. With a score by Peter Allen, Australian song-and-dance man and recording star (and one time husband of Liza Minnelli), and starring Allen in the title role, *Legs Diamond* (the show) made initial stage history with no pre-Broadway tryout but nine weeks of previews with customers paying full price. The book by playwrights Harvey Fierstein and Charles Suppon was based on the 1960 movie *The Rise and Fall of Legs Diamond* -- an unlikely source for a Broadway musical. And this Broadway musical was met with venom by the critics. "[It] wistfully bills itself as a 'big new Broadway musical.' That it's not, since it isn't particularly big or new or musical," wrote *The New York Times*' Frank Rich. "But was it too much to hope for the next big thing -- a big new Broadway bomb along the demented lines of *Kelly* or *Dude* or *Carrie*?...The creators of *Legs Diamond* could not even come up with the riotous larger-than-life fiasco of which theatrical legends are made...One must charitably assume that the lyrics, with their tiresome imitations of brighter tomorrows and ships coming in and roads not taken, are put-ons."

Clive Barnes said in the *New York Post*: "When the best moments of a show are provided by the curtain calls, it is a safe bet at least to suspect that the show itself is in trouble. And Peter Allen's *Legs Diamond*...is in the kind of trouble that might here be characterized as fractured paste. At least the backers can see where their money went. It's lavish. But lavish is as lavish does -- and it doesn't do much here...Mind you, there is nothing wrong with it that a completely new book, new lyrics, new score and new concept could not fix overnight."

In the *Daily News*, Howard Kissel complained: "*Legs* isn't even bad enough to laugh it. It's just dull. It needed an imagination as wild and elegant as its subject's, not as tame as its star's."

Legs Diamond didn't even manage to receive a Tony Award nomination as Best Musical in a season was so bereft of musicals that the roster of nominees was pared down to three. Veteran musical comedy star Julie Wilson was nominated, however, as Best Featured Actress in a Musical, and nominations also went to choreographer Alan Johnson, and costume designer Willa Kim.

Ray Danton (later a TV director) starred as Legs in Warner Bros.' 1960 gangster epic *The Rise and Fall of Legs Diamond*, directed by Budd Boetticher, and reprised the role the following year in *Portrait of a Mobster* (about Dutch Schultz) for the same studio. (That was the year Danton also starred in the title role of *The George Raft Story*, a-swarm with Legs Diamond-era gangsters.) An entertaining gangster melodrama that played fast and loose with the facts in the grand Warner style, *The Rise and Fall of Legs Diamond* "takes a breezy approach to his rise, and audiences may see him as the hero as often as they do the villain," *Variety*'s critic found. Howard Thompson (*The New York Times*) reported that "the unhealthy keynote of Warners' flashy screen portrait of the notorious Jack Diamond is that his 'rise' is quite entertaining to watch... Although Diamond is frankly labeled an ice-cold opportunist, both Mr. Danton and the picture also project him as a natty, glittering personality, bland, limber and not without humor. Mr. Danton smiles engagingly even as he mows 'em down."

Steven Hill was the Legs Diamond tracked down Robert Stack's Eliot Ness on TV's *The Untouchables* in October 1960 (although this not only never happened but Ness never was involved with Legs). It made, though, for an enjoyable hour in the rat-a-tat-tat format of the famed television series.

STAGE

LEGS DIAMOND, Mark Hellinger Theater, New York, opened December 26, 1988
72 previews and 64 performances
Produced by James M. and James L. Nederlander, Arthur Rubin, The Entertainment Group and George Steinbrunner 3d, in association with Jonathan Farkas and Marvin A. Krauss; A Musical comedy based on the film *The Rise and Fall of Legs Diamond*; Director, Robert Allan Ackerman; Book by Harvey Fierstein and Charles Suppon; Music and lyrics by Peter Allen; Settings, David Mitchell; Lighting, Jules Fisher; Costumes, Willa Kim; Choreo-graphy, Alan Johnson; Musical direction and vocal arrangements, Eric Stern; Orchestrations, Michael Starobin; Dance music arrangements, Mark Hummel; Production stage manager, Peter B. Mumford

Peter Allen (Jack Arnold); Julie Wilson (Flo); Randall Edwards (Kiki Roberts); Joe Silver (Arnold Rothstein); Christian Kauffmann (Bones); Raymond Serra (Augie); Pat McNamara (Devane); Brenda Baxton (Madge); Deanna Dys (Cigarette Girl); Mike O'Carroll (Hotsy Totsy Announcer); Jim Fyfe (Moran);

James Brandt (Tropicabana Announcer); Adrian Bailey, Quin Baird, Frank Cava, Norman Wendall Kauahi, Bobby Moya, Paul Nunes, Keith Tyrone, Stephen Bourneuf, Rick Manning, Carol Ann Baxter, Colleen Dunn, Deanna Dys, Gwendolyn Miller, Wendy Waring, Jonathan Cerullo, K. Craig Innes, Kevin Weldon, Ruth Gottschall (Ensemble)

MUSICAL NUMBERS: Prelude/"When I Get My Name in Lights"; "Speakeasy"; "Applause"; "Knockers"; "I Was Made for Champagne"; "Tropicabana Rhumba"; "Sure Thing Baby"; "Speakeasy Christmas"; "Charge It to A.R."; "Only an Older Woman"; "Taxi Dancers' Tango"; "Only Steal From Thieves"; "When I Get My Name in Lights" (reprise); "Cut of the Cards"; "Gangland Chase"; "Now You See Me, Now You Don't"; "The Man Nobody Could Love"; "The Music Went Out of My Life"; "Say It Isn't So"; "All I Wanted Was the Dream"; Finale

Original cast recording: RCA Records

SCREEN

THE RISE AND FALL OF LEGS DIAMOND, *Warner Bros.*, released January 1960

Producer, Milton Sperling; Associate producer, Leon Chooluck; Director, Budd Boetticher; Screenplay, Joseph Landon; Photography, Lucien Ballard; Art director, Jack Poplin; Costumes, Howard Shoup; Music, Leonard Rosenman; Sound, Samuel F. Goode; Editor, Folmar Blandsted

Ray Danton (Jack "Legs" Diamond); Karen Steele (Alice Shiffer); Elaine Stewart (Monica Drake); Jesse White (Leo Bremer); Simon Oakland (Lieutenant Moody); Robert Lowery (Arnold Rothstein); Judson Pratt (Fats Walsh); Warren Oates (Eddie Diamond); Frank de Kova (Chairman); Gordon Jones (Sergeant Cassidy); Joseph Ruskin (Matt Moren); Diane [Dyan] Cannon (Dixie); Richard Gardner (Vince "Mad Dog" Coll); Sid Melton (Little Augie); Nesdon Booth (Fence); Buzz Henry, Dyke Johnson, Roy Jenson (Body-guards); Joe Marr, Jim Drum (Officers); Dorothy Neumann, Frances Mercer (Women); Judd Holdren (Haberdashery Clerk); George Taylor (Switchboard Operator); Robert Herron, Carey Loftin (Thugs); Norman Dupont (Maitre d')

PORTRAIT OF A MOBSTER, *Warner Bros.*, released April 1961

Director, Joseph Pevney; Screenplay, Howard Browne, based on the book by Harry Grey; Photography, Eugene Polito; Art director, Jack Poplin; Costumes, Howard Shoup; Music, Max Steiner; Sound, M. A. Merrick; Editor, Leo H. Shreve

Vic Morrow (Dutch Schultz); Leslie Parrish (Iris Murphy); Ray Danton (Jack "Legs" Diamond); Peter Breck (Frank Brennan); Norman Alden (Bo Wetzel); Robert McQueeney (Michael Ferris); Ken Lynch (Lieutenant Corbin); Frank de Kova (Anthony Parazzo); Stephen Roberts (James Guthrie); Evan McCord (Vincent "Mad Dog" Coll); Arthur Tenen (Steve Matryck); Frances Morris (Louise Murphy); Larry Blake (John Murphy); Joseph Turkel (Joe Noe); Eddie Hanley (Matty Krause); John Kowal (Lou Rhodes); Harry Holcombe, Jr. (Captain Bayridge); Anthony Eisley (Legal Adviser); Poncie Ponce (Master of Ceremonies); Gil Perkins (Joe Murdoch); Roy Renard (Bartender)

TELEVISION

THE JACK "LEGS" DIAMOND STORY, episode of *THE UNTOUCHABLES*, televised October 20, 1960 ABC 1 hour

A Quinn Martin production; Executive producer, Jerry Thorpe; Producer, Joseph Shaffer; Associate producer, Lloyd Richards; Director, John Peyser; Teleplay, Charles O'Neil, based on a story by Harry Essex; Photography, Charles Straumer; Music, Nelson Riddle; Narrator, Walter Winchell

Robert Stack (Eliot Ness); Steven Hill (Legs Diamond); Lawrence Dobkin (Dutch Schultz); Suzanne Storrs (Dixie); Peter Whitney (Nick); Norma Crane (Kate); Abel Fernandez (Agent William Youngfellow); Nick Georgiades (Agent Enrico Rossi); Paul Picerni (Agent Lee Hobson); Steve London (Agent Rossman)

LI'L ABNER

A Musical Comedy by Norman Panama and Melvin Frank (1956)

Synopsis

Called "the most useless place in America," the tiny backwoods community of Dogpatch has been selected as the testing ground for an atomic bomb. Amiable, handsome, slightly dense Li'l Abner Yokum, that hundred percent red-blooded American boy, leaves his devoted girlfriend, beautiful Daisy Mae, whose sole purpose in life is the get Abner to marry her, and hurries to Washington to have his maw's Mammy Yokum's Yokumberry Tonic tested and approved to establish the importance of Dogpatch. Mammy's tonic has made Li'l Abner a magnificent physical specimen without increasing his mental abilities or libido -- a revolutionary formula seen by unscrupulous General Bullmoose as an ideal antidote for Washington. Eager to steal the formula, Bullmoose enlists voluptuous Appassionata von Climax to use her charms on innocent Abner, but he resists her allure and returns home in time for Sadie Hawkins Day, the annual event when local spinsters may claim any bachelor they can catch. Abner, however, is put into a trance by Appassionata, who has followed him, and he is whisked back to Washington. Crestfallen, Daisy Mae agrees to marry slovenly Earthquake McGoon if he will save her true love, Abner. The citizens of Dogpatch march on Washington, make a shambles of Bullmoose's lavish ball, and rescue Abner. But time is running out and the government is moving in. When attempting to move the town's imposing statue of Dogpatch's equestrian hero, General Jubilation T. Cornpone, however, the citizens discover a plaque commemorating the place as a national shrine by Abraham Lincoln. McGoon, seeing how much Daisy Mae has been pining for Abner Yokum, releases her from her promise of marriage -- rather than share a home with her repulsive relatives, he tells her. An extra strong potion prepared by Mammy Yokum from her Yokumberry Tonic awakens Abner's dormant libido and he and Daisy Mae prepare for Marryin' Sam's blessing and the matrimonial stomp toward a happy future.

Comment and Critique

Cartoonist Al Capp was an American original. Pundit, satirist, media celebrity, he created one of the most enduring comic strips of his time, from its introduction on August 12, 1935, into the 1970s, and its celebration such juicy individuals as Mammy and Pappy Yokum, Stupefyin' Jones, Evil Eye Fleagle, Moon-beam McSwine, the Scragg Family, and even the Schmoo. In 1940, his Li'l Abner came to the screen in a live-action low-budget movie. "Faithful to Al Capp's United Features comic strip, *Li'l Abner*, first production of Vogue Pictures Ltd., is what is known in the trade as an exploitation special," *Motion Picture Herald* reported. "The film itself is a translation of the cartoon to the screen in terms of a cartoon, not of the motion picture...Its chief characters are portrayed, for the most part, by unknown players acting as the residents of Dogpatch and Skunk Hollow, not as players giving their interpretation of what Capp had in mind."

In the early 1950s, first with composer Burton Lane and later with Arthur Schwartz, Alan Jay Lerner attempted to create a musical comedy based on Al Capp's comic strip characters. After Lerner abandoned the project, rights were acquired by Norman Panama and Melvin Frank, the successful Hollywood producing-directing-screenwriting team, who developed the property into a Broadway smash, with Michael Kidd directing and choreographing, and an engaging Johnny Mercer-Gene DePaul score. Robert Coleman, critic for the New York *Daily Mirror*, home of Capp's daily syndicated cartoon strip, wrote, "Nothing so cyclonic has struck the Main Stem since Olsen and Johnson's *Hellazapoppin*!...Edith Adams look so much like Daisy Mae and Peter Palmer, like Li'l Abner, that they might have stepped right out of the *Daily Mirror* page...Kidd has staged *Li'l Abner* with supersonic speed. His choreography breaks the sound barrier. It's furiously fast and funny."

John McClain (*Journal-American*) considered the show "often guilty of questionable taste" but he admitted: "It has as sprightly and decorative chorus as we've seen in recent semesters and the dancers are beautifully schooled by Michael Kidd...*Li'l Abner* is bountiful, lively and tuneful. We won't all agree with its taste or its tenets, but it is a cinch to be with us for many a Dogpatch moon." And John Chapman of the *Daily News* called it "wonderful -- simply wonderful... Al Capp, inventor of this comic strip, may have created many delightful characters [but] the people who created last night's musical were a great team of lovable lunatics...The plot is a satisfying mixture of hillbilly nonsense and sharp, critical humor...*Li'l Abner* is a top-flight American musical."

And from *The New York Times*' Brooks Atkinson, praise for Michael Kidd's brilliant direction and choreography which "captures, the distinguishing characteristics of Al Capp's comic strip style...It is amusing to see Dogpatch come to life in [William and Jean] Eckart's good-natured scenery and to see the comic strip characters appear in Alvin Colt's raffish costumes... Since Dogpatch is populated by affable and vigorous people, *Li'l Abner* has a pleasant spirit. But like its local citizens, it is happiest when it is content to stay at home. When it moves to Washington and into our industrial complex, it is out of its element. The innate decency of Dogpatch is sound enough to satirize the rest of the world."

Norman Panama and Melvin Frank moved their Broadway smash to the screen in 1959 in a garish movie musical with most of the cast from the stage version intact. (Two critical exceptions: Edie Adams and Tina Louise. Plus the addition of "surprise guest" Jerry Lewis.) It was Paramount Pictures' Christmas hit that year. In his review of the movie, Bosley Crowther (*The New York Times*) commented on the successful two-year run of Dogpatch on Broadway, noting that "it pretty well stood to reason that [Panama and Frank] wouldn't change it much in putting it on the screen. They haven't...To be sure, Edie Adams is no longer the well-put-together Daisy Mae. That role falls to Leslie Parrish, who fills it out generously. Nor is Appassionata von Climax played by Tina Louise. That sly dish is played by Stella Stevens, who is almost as svelte...They're here in the same proportions, state of minds and outrageous costumes as they were on the stage, and they are doing almost precisely the same things...Not since *Seven Brides for Seven Brothers* has there been such splendid roughhouse dancing on the screen -- and the dances in that one, you'll remember, were also created by Mr. Kidd." (The score also was by Johnny Mercer and Gene DePaul.)

One British view of this uniquely American musical was that of Tony Keniston, writing in *Films and Filming*. "For once it seems 40 million Americans cannot be wrong Panama and Frank's musical production, *Li'l Abner*, is a sheer delight. The rich, earthy humour and satire of Al Capp's remarkable cartoon strip has been brought to the screen as vividly as it was played for two years on the Broadway stage ...A stage musical has been transferred to the screen without the whole character of the production being lost in wide open spaces ...With few exceptions, the entire Broadway cast, led by Peter Palmer in the title role, was reassembled for the film...There is not doubt about it, *Li'l Abner* is a big success on the screen."

In 1967, NBC televised a pilot for a prospective *Li'l Abner* series, with Sammy Jackson (star of the single-season *No Time for Sergeants* series a few years earlier) in the title role. Poor ratings and dismal reviews with the consensus being that the players lacked the enthusiasm for their roles, possibly in recognition of the unfunny script, made NBC drop series plans. ABC Television offered a hokey one-hour musical special, *Li'l Abner*, in the spring of 1971. Al Capp should have sued. The amateur night playing of the principals in a preposterous story made the original *Li'l Abner* look like a classic.

NBC brought the Dogpatch gang back to television in an updated entry in November 1978 as *Li'l Abner in Dogpatch Today*. Of this special, geared as a pitch by women-libbers to chase careers, not men, despite the annual Sadie Hawkins Day festivities, Tom Buckley wrote in *The New York Times*: "With its already old-hat references to the women's liberation movement, its unbelievably lame jokes, inert performances, unimaginative sets, costumes and choreography, and six new songs that are hard to remember even as they are being performed, it is a creaking, cobwebbed and mildewed antique."

STAGE

LI'L ABNER, *St. James Theatre*, New York, opened November 15, 1956 693 performances

Produced by Norman Panama, Melvin Frank and Michael Kidd; A Musical Comedy based on characters created by Al Capp; Director and choreographer, Michael Kidd; Book by Norman Panama and Melvin Frank; Music by Gene de Paul; Lyrics by Johnny Mercer; Scenery and lighting, William and Jean Eckart; Costumes, Alvin Colt; Musical director, John Passaretti; Orchestrations, Philip J. Lang; Ballet music arranged by Genevieve Pitot; General manager, Joseph Harris; Company manager, Ira Bernstein; Stage managers, Terence Little, Lawrence N. Kasha and Lanier Davis

Peter Palmer (Li'l Abner); Edith Adams (succeeded by Wynne Miller) (Daisy Mae); Charlotte Rae (succeeded by Billie Hayes) (Mammy Yokum); Joe E. Marks (Pappy Yokum); Stubby Kaye (Marryin' Sam); Howard St. John (General Bullmoose); Julie Newmar (Stupefyin' Jones); William Lanteau (Available Jones); Ted Thurston (Senator Jack S. Phogbound); Tina Louise (succeeded by DeeDee Wood) (Appassionata von Climax); Al Nesor (Evil Eye Fleagle); George Reeder (succeeded by Chad Block) (Dr. Smithborn); Ralph Linn (succeeded by Anthony Saverino) (Dr. Krogmeyer); Marc Breaux (Dr. Schleifitz/Romeo Scragg); James Hurst (succeeded by John Craig) (Clem Scragg); Chad Block (Hairless Joe); Anthony Mordente (succeeded by Robert Karl) (Lonesome Polecat); Anthony Saverino (Alf Scragg); Stanley Simmonds (Dr. Rasmussen T. Finsdale); Carmen Alvarez (succeeded by Maureen Hopkins) (Moonbeam McSwine); Bern Hoffman (Earthquake McGoon); Oran Osburn (Mayor

Dawgmeat); Richard Maitland (succeeded by Joe Calvan) (Government Man); Lanier Davis (State Department Man); George Reeder (succeeded by Lanier Davis) (Colonel); Robert McClure, Jack Matthew, James Hurst (succeeded by John Craig) (Radio Commentators); Carmen Alvarez (succeeded by Maureen Hopkins), Pat Creighton (succeeded by Christie Reeder); Lillian D'Honeau, Bonnie Evans, Hope Holiday, DeeDee Wood (succeeded by Sharon Shore) (Wives); Marc Breaux, Ralph Linn (succeeded by Chad Block), Jack Matthew, Robert McClure, George Reeder (succeeded by Merritt Thompson) (Cronies); Lanier Davis (President); Lanier Davis, Robert McClure, Jack Matthew, George Reeder (succeeded by Merritt Thompson) (Secretaries); James J. Jeffries (succeeded by Robert McClure (Butler); Margaret Baxter, Joan Cherof, Hope Holiday, Katherine Williams, John Craig, Lanier Davis, Bob Gorman, Jack Matthew, Oran Osburn, Robert McClure, Anthony Saverino (Singers); Lillian D'Honeau, Bonnie Evans, Valerie Harper, Maureen Hopkins, Barbara Klopfer, Joan Lindsay, Shirley Nelson, Patti Nester, Christy Reeder, Carol Stevens, Sharon Shore, Chad Block, Marc Breaux, Joe Calvan, Mel Davidson, Robert Karl, John Kessler, John Ray, Larry Roguemore, Merritt Thompson, George Zina (Dancers)

MUSICAL NUMBERS: "A Typical Day"; "If I Had My Druthers"; "Jubilation T. Cornpone"; "Rag Offen the Bush"; "Namely You"; "Unnecessary Town"; "What's Good for General Bullmoose"; "The Country's in the Very Best of Hands"; "Sadie Hawkins Day"; "Oh Happy Day"; "I'm Past My Prime"; "Love in a Home"; "Progress Is the Root of All Evil"; "Put 'Em Back"; "The Matrimonial Stomp"

* Following the show's Broadway run, the above company toured (with noted cast replacements), opening at the *Riviera Theatre*, Las Vegas, on September 1, 1958, and closing at the *Royal Alexandra Theatre* in Toronto on January 3, 1959

Original cast recording: Columbia Records

Touring Company, season 1958-59

Produced by Lee Guber, Frank Ford and Shelly Gross, in association with Norman Panama, Melvin Frank and Michael Kidd; A Musical Comedy based on characters created by Al Capp; Director, Lawrence Kasha, based on the original direction and choreography by Michael Kidd; Book by Norman Panama and Melvin Frank; Music, Gene de Paul; Lyrics, Johnny Mercer; Choreography, George and Christy Reeder; Settings and lighting, William and Jean Eckart; Costumes, Alvin Colt; Orchestrations, Philip J. Lang; Ballet, Genevieve Pitot; Musical director, Phil Ingalls; Musical supervision, Salvatore Dell'Isola; General manager, Marvin V. Krauss; Stage managers, Sherwood Goozee and Jay Gerber

Robert Kaye (Li'l Abner); Patricia Northrop (Daisy Mae); Charlotte Nolan (Mammy Yokum); Don Potter (Pappy Yokum); Dean Dittman (Marryin' Sam); Henry Norell (General Bullmoose); Ginny Gan (Stupefyin' Jones); Herb Giron (Available Jones); Sammy Smith (Senator Jack S. Phogbound); Norma Kessler (Appassionata von Climax); Duane Bodin (Evil Eye Fleagle/ Government Man); Allen Charlet (Dr. Schleifitz/Alf Scragg); Mark Ross (Romeo Scragg); Chuck Arnett (Dr. Krogmeyer/Clem Scragg); Leslie Guinn (Hairless Joe/State Department Man); Bob Becker (Lonesome Polecat); Jay Gerber (Mayor Dawgmeat/Dr. Rasmussen T. Finsdale/President); Margo DeBarr (Moonbeam McSwine); Peter Costanza (Earthquake McGoon); Dick Keller (Colonel); Mark Ross, Chuck Arnett, Allen Charlet, Dick Keller (Cronies); Ellen Fluhr, Jean Ann

Einwick, Margo DeBarr, Dolores Bagley (Wives); Dick Keller, Mark Ross, Leslie Guinn (Secretaries); Andrew Massa, Konstantin Moskalenko, Nick Siggelakis, Vern Weaver (Muscle Men); Dolores Bagley, Jean Bledsoe, Joan Coddington, Barbara Creed, Margo DeBarr, Jean Ann Einwick, Ellen Fluhr, Ginny Gan, Priscilla Morrow, Jayne Mylorie, Dellas Rennie, Chuck Arnett, Bob Becker, Duane Bodin, Allan Charlet, Charles Floyd, Jay Gerber, Herb Giron, Leslie Guinn, Thomas Hester, Dick Keller, Mark Ross (Ensemble)

Touring Company, summer 1959

Produced by Musicarnival, John L. Price, Jr., producer and general manager; A Musical Comedy based on characters created by Al Capp; Director, Jerome Eskow; Book by Norman Panama and Melvin Frank; Music by Gene de Paul; Lyrics by Johnny Mercer; Choreography and musical staging, Birgieta Kiviniemi and Gordon Marsh; Settings, Paul Rodgers; Lighting, Sam Kleinman; Musical and choral director, Boris Kogan; Orchestra conductor and concertmaster, Ben Silverberg; Costume supervision, Sheila Pearl; Stage managers, Lawrence Vincent and Richard Alan Woody

John Craig (Li'l Abner); Barbara Lee Smith (Daisy Mae); Maggie Dillon (Mammy Yokum); Jerry Rice (Pappy Yokum); Tom Batten (Marryin' Sam); T. J. Halligan (General Bullmoose); Diane Torgler (Stupefyin' Jones); Brownie Bradley (Available Jones/Romeo Scragg); Frank Shaw Stevens (Senator Jack S. Phogbound); Lynne Osborne (Appassionata von Climax); Joel Craig (Evil Eye Fleagle); Ray Wilde (Clem Scragg); Art Kalin (Alf Scragg); Stan Rich (Hairless Joe); Paul Lubera (Lonesome Polecat); Suzanne Werner or Marilyn Tschda (Moonbeam McSwine); Larry Ward (Earthquake McGoon); Malcolm Morton (Mayor Dawgmeat); Alan Greenwald (Colonel); William Skelton (Dr. Rasmussen T. Finsdale); Mark Rose (Speedy McRabbit); Edith Johnson (Scarlett); Bob McHaffey (Creighton); Gary Batinte, Joseph Berch, Richard Podboiy, Norman Zenisek (Converted Dogpatchers); Lloyd Lawrence, Malcolm Morton, Art Kalin, Ray Wilde (Secretaries); Brownie Bradley, Patricia Brooker, Joel Craig, Carol Davidson, Lonnie Davis, Sandra Dietrich, Bobby Franklin, Louis Gasparinetti, Ilona Hirschl, Art Kalin, John Kole, Lloyd Lawrence, James Malcolm, Malcolm Morton, Maurice Nystrom, Judith Panzer, Lynne Osborne, Stan Rich, Mark Rose, Marilyn Stark, Connee Teaman, Marilyn Tschida, Ray Wilde (Company)

Touring Company, summer 1959

Produced by Melody Fair, Lewis T. Fisher, producer; A Musical Comedy based on characters created by Al Capp; Director, Richard Casey; Book by Norman Panama and Melvin Frank; Music by Gene de Paul; Lyrics by Johnny Mercer; Settings, Sonia Lowenstein, Lighting, David Zierk; Choreography and musical numbers staged by Zachary Solov; Musical director, William Janson; Production manager, Kenneth Gill; Stage manager, Gene Lasko

Peter Lombard (Li'l Abner); Patricia Northrup (Daisy Mae); Renie Riano (Mammy Yokum); Andy Thomas (Pappy Yokum); Dean Dittman (Marryin' Sam); Herbert Beattie (General Bullmoose); Danica d'Hondt (Stupefyin' Jones); Toby Nicholson (Available Jones); Sam Kressen (Senator Jack S. Phogbound); Doreen Kent (Appassionata von Climax); Anthony Paella (Evil Eye Fleagle); Joe Frazier (Dr. Smithborn); Reid McRae (Dr. Krogmeyer); Peter Johl (Dr. Schleifitz); Herbert Pordum (Hairless Joe); Tom Larson (Mayor Dawgmeat); Nino Golenti (Lonesome Polecat); Catherine Gerry Gale (Moonbeam McSwine); Don Merriman (Dr. Rasmussen T. Finsdale); Michael Contos (Government Man);

Dan Olejniczak (Colonel); Carl Seltzer (State Department Man); Robert Rancour (Butler); Joy Alexander, Ian Bruce, Joe Frazier, Catherine Gerry Gale, Nino Galenti, Garold Gardner, Helen Guile, Kent Hatcher, Danny Kasinski, Peter Johl, Bill Kisling, Tom Larson, Jean McPhail, Reid McRae, Carole Anne Noble, Linda North, Joan Osborne, Nira Paez, Nancy Robson, Nada Rowand, Mara Wirt (Dogpatchers)

Touring Company, summer 1959

Produced by Lee Guber, Frank Ford and Shelly Gross in association with Norman Panama, Melvin Frank and Michael Kidd; A Musical Comedy based on characters created by Al Capp; Director, Lawrence Kasha, based on original direction and choreography by Michael Kidd; Settings, Warwick Brown; Lighting, Lester Tapper; Costumes, Ann Roth;, Muscial director, Peter Laurini

Stuart Damon (Li'l Abner); Barbara Lee Smith (Daisy Mae); Diana Banks (Mammy Yokum); Lou Fryman (Pappy Yokum); Al Medinets (Marryin' Sam); T. J. Halligan (General Bullmoose); Beverly Sanders (Stupefyin' Jones); Mark Ross (Available Jones/Dr. Smithborn); Jack Hollander (Senator Jack S. Phogbound); Gloria Hudson (Appassionata von Climax); Edward Greene (Evil Eye Fleagle); John Blanchard (Dr. Krogmeyer); Gene Foote (Dr. Schleifitz); Daniel P. Hannafin (Romeo Scragg/State Department Man); Robert Hocknell (Clem Scragg/Colonel); Lee Howard (Mayor Dawgmeat/ Dr. Rasmussen T. Finsdale/President); Margo DeBarr (Moonbeam McSwine); Steve Vincent (Earthquake McGoon); Don Byars (Lonesome Polecat); Oscar Torres (Hairless Joe); Bob Gorman (Government Man/Butler); Daniel P. Hannafin, Robert Hocknell (Secretaries); Mark Ross, Bob Gorman, Gene Foote, John Blanchard, Oscar Torres (Cronies); Margo DeBarr, Ellie Zalon, Amelia Haas (Wives)

SCREEN

LI'L ABNER, RKO Radio Pictures, released November 1940

Produced by Vogue Pictures, Ltd.; Producer, Lou Ostrow; Associate producer, Herman Schlom; Director, Albert S. Rogell; Screenplay, Charles Kerr and Tyler Johnson, based on an original story by Al Capp; Photography, Harry Jackson; Art director, Ralph Berger; Editors, Otto Ludwig and Donn Hayes

Granville Owen (Li'l Abner); Martha O'Driscoll (Daisy Mae); Mona Ray (Mammy Yokum); Johnnie Morris (Pappy Yokum); Buster Keaton (Lonesome Polecat); Maude Eburne (Granny Scraggs); Kay Sutton (Wendy Wildcat); Billie Seward (Cousin Delightful); Johnny Arthur (Montague); Walter Catlett (Barber); Edgar Kennedy (Cornelius Cornpone); Lucien Littlefield (The Sheriff/Mister Oldtimer); Charles A. Post (Earthquake McGoon); Bud Jamison (Hairless Joe); Frank Wilder (Abijah Gooch); Chester Conklin (Mayor Gurgle); Dick Elliott (Marryin' Sam); Mickey Daniels (Cicero Gruntz); Doodles Weaver (Hannibal Hoops); Marie Blake (Miss Lulubelle); Al St. John, Eddie Gribbon, Heinie Conklin, Hank Mann (Men)

Paramount Pictures, released December 1959

Produced by Norman Panama; Director, Melvin Frank; Screenplay, Norman Panama and Melvin Frank, based on their musical comedy and characters created by Al Capp; Photography, Daniel L. Fapp; Music by Gene de Paul; Lyrics by Johnny Mercer; Art directors, Hal Pereira and J. MacMillan Johnson; Costumes, Alvin Colt; Choreography, DeeDee Wood, based on the original choreography by Michael Kidd;

Music scored and conducted by Nelson Riddle and Joseph L. Lilley; Special photographic effects, John P. Fulton; Editor, Arthur P. Schmidt

Peter Palmer (Li'l Abner); Leslie Parrish (Daisy Mae); Stubby Kaye (Marryin' Sam); Howard St. John (General Bullmoose); Julie Newmar (Stupefyin' Jones); Stella Stevens (Appassionata von Climax); Billie Hayes (Mammy Yokum); Joe E. Marks (Pappy Yokum); William Lanteau (Available Jones/Hairless Joe); Ted Thurston (Senator Jack S. Phogbound); Al Nessor (Evil Eye Fleagle); Bern Hoffman (Earthquake McGoon); Robert Strauss (Romeo Scragg); Carmen Alvarez (Moonbeam McSwine); Alan Carney (Mayor Dawgmeat); Stanley Simmonds (Dr. Rasmussen T. Finsdale); Diki Lerner (Lonesome Polecat); and Jerry Lewis

MUSICAL NUMBERS: "A Typical Day"; "If I Had My Druthers"; "Jubilation T. Cornpone"; "Don't That Take the Rag Offen the Bush"; "Room Enuf for Us"; "Namely You"; "The Country's in the Very Best of Hands"; "Unnecessary Town"; "I'm Past My Prime"; "Otherwise"; "Put 'Em Back as They Wuz"; "The Matrimonial Stomp"

Original soundtrack recording: Columbia Records

TELEVISION

LI'L ABNER, televised September 5, 1967 NBC 30 minutes

UA Television in association with NBC Entertainment; Executive producer, Al Capp; Producer, Howard Leeds; Director, Coby Ruskin; Teleplay, Al Capp

Sammy Jackson (Li'l Abner); Jeannine Riley (Daisy May); Judy Canova (Mammy Yokum); Jerry Lester (Pappy Yokum); Robert Reed (Senator Henry Cabbage Cod); Larry Mann (Marryin' Sam)

LI'L ABNER, televised April 26, 1971 ABC l hour

Producers, Allan Blye and Chris Bearde; Director, Gordon Wiles; Written by Coslough Johnson, Ted Zeigler, Chris Bearde and Allan Blye; Art director, Gene McAvoy; Costume designer, Ret Turner; Music and lyrics by Earl Brown and Jimmy Dale; Choreography, Claude Thompson

Ray Young (Li'l Abner); Nancee Parkinson (Daisy Mae); Billie Hayes (Mammy Yokum); Billy Bletcher (Pappy Yokum); Dale Malone (Marryin' Sam); Tom Solari (Lonesome Polecat); H. B. Haggarty (Hairless Joe); Ted Zeigler (Jack Lemming); Bobo Lewis (Nightmare Alice); Jackie Kahane (Captain Rickety-back); Jennifer Narin-Smith (Snow Blight); Inga Neilson (Beautify America); and Eddie Albert, Ken Berry, Carol Burnett, Monte Hall, Donald O'Connor

SONGS: "Your World"; "Infamous Revival Stomp"; "All Over the World"; "Super Gettin' Method Power"

LI'L ABNER IN DOGPATCH TODAY, televised November 8, 1978 NBC 1 hour

George Schlatter Productions in association with NBC Entertainment; Producer, George Schlatter; Director, Jack Regas; A Musical written by Norman Panama with songs by Billy Barnes, based on characters created by Al Capp; Additional material, Digby Wolfe

Stephan Burns (Li'l Abner); Debra Feuer (Daisy Mae); Don Potter (Pappy Yokum); Susan Tolsky (Mammy Yokum); Polly Bergen (Phyllis Shoefly); Kaye Ballard (Bella Asgood); Deborah Zon (Moonbeam McSwine); Cisse Cameron (Mitzi Galore); Rhonda Bates (Appassionata); Louis Nye (General Bullmoose); Diki Lerner (Lonesome Polecat); Charlene Ryan (Stupefyin' Jones); Ben

Davidson (Hairless Joe); Leonard Feiner (Marryin' Sam); Jim Staal (Pythagoras Scragg); Tino Insana (Virgil Scragg); Jim Fisher (Romeo Scragg); Jason Roberts (Worthless); Mindy Sterling (Tooth-less); Prudence W. Holmes (Sexless); Darcel Wynne (Strokin' Yokum); Candy McCoy (Smokin' Yokum)

LITTLE LORD FAUNTLEROY

Various dramatizations of the novel by Frances Hodgson Bennett (1886)

Synopsis

Young Cedric Errol, who makes his way on the streets of New York to help his impoverished widowed mother, has become friends with both streetwise bootblack Dick Tipton and Mr. Hobbs, the local grocer. The gruff, aged Earl of Dorincourt, owner of one of Great Britain's great estates, who had disinherited his son after the latter's marriage to an American commoner, sends for Cedric as the sole Dorincourt heir. Mrs. Errol, whose husband was killed in the war and is "Dearest" to young Cedric, agrees to the Earl's invitation to the boy, providing no mention is made to Cedric of the Earl's dislike of her. In England, "Dearest" is consigned to a cottage on the Dorincourt estate while Cedric lives in the castle with his grandfather. The boy's conviction that his grandfather is loving, caring and benevolent slowly alters the autocratic, irritable old man into Cedric's vision. The youngster enchants everybody and he even persuades his grandfather to improve the estate's out cottage long in disrepair. Delighted with his grandson, the Earl is appalled to learn that a coarse American actress named Minna has filed a claim in favor of her son, sired by the old man's late ne'er-do-well elder son Bevis, as the legal heir to Dorincourt.

Cedric writes to his friends back on Hester Street in New York, enclosing a newspaper photograph of Minna. Dick Tipton recognizes her as the wife who deserted his older brother and left for England with their baby boy. Havisham, the Dorincourt retainer, arranges for Dick, his brother and Mr. Hobbs to come to England where they succeed in exposing Minna's deception. Cedric is then acknowledged as the Earl's rightful heir, and in gratitude and love for the boy, the irascible grandfather invites "Dearest" to live with them in the castle.

Comment and Critique

Frances Hodgson Burnett's classic story of *Little Lord Fauntleroy* was first serialized by London's *St. Nicholas* magazine in November 1885 and later published as a novel by Frederick Warne and Company. The novel, and eventual play, ignited a mania for "Little Lord Fauntleroy" black velvet suits with lace collars for young boys who were also required -- usually unhappily -- to wear their hair in long curls as did Cedric of the story. They understandably resented emulating Cedric and, worse, being labeled a "sissy" by their peers. But doting mothers persisted as in a later day they attempted to mold their young daughters to the "Shirley Temple look."

Little Lord Fauntleroy also became a cause celebre in the British courts. On February 23, 1888, E. V. Seebohm's unauthorized adaptation of the Burnett story opened in London at the Prince of Wales's Theatre. Mrs. Burnett sued, not impressed with a letter from Seebohm that stated, "I sincerely trust that I have written nothing that could cast a slur on one of the most beautiful stories it has ever been my pleasure to read." Mrs. Burnett wrote a friend, "A thief has quietly dramatized

Fauntleroy...The brigand, whose name is Seebohm, knew he was doing a miserable, dishonest thing, and knew I thought myself protected by the 'All Rights Reserved' of the title-page. He kept his plan most discreetly secret until he was ready and it was too late for me to hurry *my* play and secure myself." The case was heard in the Chancery Division of the High Court of Justice on March 24, 1888, not entirely supported by the British press.

London's *Era* reported: "If Mrs. Burnett thought that *Little Lord Fauntleroy* was worth preserving for the adaptor, why did she not secure it in the legal way? A copyright performance can be easily done for 30 pounds, a mere trifle to a successful lady novelist... Why do the novelists not all 'pull together,' agitate fiercely and get the law altered?" Under the antiquated British Copyright Act of 1842, "Seebohm," as suggested by Ann Thwaite, Mrs. Burnett's biographer, in *Waiting for the Party (The Life of Frances Hodgson Burnett)*, "might have the right, under the law as it stood, to represent the novel on the stage; but he had no right to make copies of any part of the book." Much of the dialogue in Seebohm's play indeed was lifted verbatim from the novel. Because of Frances Hodgson Burnett's law suit and battle for the stage rights to *Fauntleroy*, the creaky Copyright Act of 1842 was altered to protect authors from unauthorized dramatizations.

Mrs. Burnett's own dramatization of her novel, called *The Real Little Lord Fauntleroy* and produced by Madge Kendal, opened at Terry's Theatre in London in May 1888. Nine-year-old Vera Beringer portrayed the little lord and kindly Mr. Havisham was acted by Brandon Thomas, better known as author of *Charley's Aunt*.

William Archer (*London World*) praised the authentic adaptation: "Mrs. Burnett shows herself a true poet though her Pegasus may be a rocking-horse...Novelists need no longer fear to see their brainchildren kidnapped, distorted and sent forth to pick up pence for the kidnapper in the theatrical highways and byways." *The London Times* applauded the play, feeling "*The Real Little Lord Fauntleroy* proved to be in all respects superior to the pirated version which Mr. Seebohm has been restrained from performing. It reflects in a great measure the fresh, delicate, exquisitely pretty sentiment of the book...the piece is exceptionally well-acted."

The Real Little Lord Fauntleroy first came to America in September 1888, premiering at the Boston Museum Theatre. The *Boston Transcript* called it "a play for moist eyes, even in its comic parts...A susceptible person will hardly get the tears down out of his throat through the whole piece." The *Spirit of the Times* in New York later reported: "Last week when the news of the immense success of the author's version of *Little Lord Fauntleroy* at the Boston Museum reached New York, a young Englishman committed suicide at the Hoffman House. He had been known as Lawrence Herbert, had talked much about the chances of English dramatists in this country, and had expended all his money. On the London tailor's tab in the pocket of his overcoat was written the name of E. V. Seebohm. It will be remembered that Mr. Seebohm dramatized *Little Lord Fauntleroy* in London and was stopped by an injunction."

An extraordinary child-actress, Elsie Leslie (nee Lyde), played the title role in the first American production. Theater historian George Odell later wrote, "Elsie Leslie, in long curls and most aesthetic, unboyish costumes, copied from Reginald Birch's pictures for the book, established a fashion that doting mothers tried in vain to make their recalcitrant little sons follow; the Russell boy did not -- perhaps because he was a boy -- quite 'click' in the part, certainly not to the same extent...In the week of December 10th-15th, we were informed that the victorious Elsie Leslie would play the lord in all performances except Wednesday matinees and Saturday evenings, when Tommy Russell [brother of noted stage actress Annie Russell] would show what he could do with the part..."

Vera Beringer, who initiated the role of Cedric in Mrs. Burnett's first London production of the play, recalled before her death in 1971 at age ninety-two to author Thwaite, "I played the part between six and seven hundred times -- and with a wonderful cast...I remember so vividly the first performances of all, at Terry's Theatre, when Mrs. Burnett sat in a stage box, and in her enthusiasm flung me an immense bouquet of pink roses, saying, 'Bless the child, and she did not forget a single word.'"

Frances Eliza Hodgson was born at Cheetham Hill outside of Manchester, England, on November 24, 1849. In 1865, the Hodgson family migrated to Knoxville, Tennessee, and eight years later, Frances Eliza married Dr. Swan Burnett. Two sons, Lionel and Vivian, were born within the following two years. Mrs. Burnett's sons called her "Dearest," the term she later used for Mrs. Errol in *Little Lord Fauntleroy*. (She also turned out another children's classic, *The Secret Garden*.) A few weeks before her seventy-fifth birthday, Frances Hodgson Burnett died (October 29, 1924) and was buried at God's Acre in Roslyn, Long Island.

The Burnett novel (and play) was turned into a musical called *Fauntleroy* in 1981 by composer Mavor Moore. Hollywood songwriter Johnny Burke provided the music and lyrics for the show that opened "out of town" -- in Prince Edward Island, Canada. The score included not only new material but several songs Burke had written with either Arthur Johnston or James V. Monaco for Bing Crosby movies during the 1930s. *Fauntleroy* never made it to Broadway.

Great Britain's Kineto Productions produced the first screen version of *Little Lord Fauntleroy* in 1914. It was in a revolutionary color process called Kinemacolor and featured young Gerald Royston as Cedric. *The New York Dramatic Mirror* found, "A pleasant enough picture, offering suitable entertainment for children, is this film interpretation of Frances Hodgson Burnett's classic. It was made in England by an English company, and in point of photography, at least, deserves high commendation. The settings, too, are pleasing, as is the acting of the somewhat precocious boy in the part of Little Lord Fauntleroy. His elders are not always so successful in their histrionic efforts...Moreover, the titles, in addition to their extensive number, frequently are unnecessarily wordy and difficult to read and comprehend in the short time they remain on the screen...Many of the exterior locations give glimpses of the charming English scenery, whereas the interiors have depth and clearness ...As mentioned previously, the photography is unfailingly good. None of the acting suggests particular comment."

Mary Pickford produced *Little Lord Fauntleroy* for United Artists in 1921 and played both Cedric and "Dearest." *The New York Times* reported, "Mary Pickford as Little Lord Fauntleroy -- and also 'Dearest,' his mother. Can't you imagine it?...Miss Pickford, and the story, and those who think it's laid on somewhat too thick could not be satisfied with *Little Lord Fauntleroy*...unless they are capable of enjoying some of the best photography seen on the screen for a long time and some truly excellent acting by several members of the cast, notably Claude Gillingwater as the old Earl of Dorincourt. And also by Miss Pickford, especially as Lord Fauntleroy's mother...The staging and photography of the picture is, in fact, one of its chief claims to distinction." The *Times* critic continued: "It is not probable that many persons will be disappointed by Miss Pickford...She is herself, distinctively feminine and often obviously too old for the part. Here is the greatest weakness of the film...Miss Pickford does not maintain the illusion that she is a sturdy little boy, despite her attractive antics, her genuinely boyish walk and all of the tricks she employs to make her role appealing. She succeeds in making it appealing but not convincing...But as the mother, Miss Pickford is entirely satisfactory."

In her autobiography, *Sunshine and Shadow*, Mary Pickford wrote: "I was 27 years old when I played one of my most successful children -- Little Lord Fauntleroy. In this film, I also portrayed Little Lord Fauntleroy's mother. Nowadays, trick photography, trick sets, and parallel takes are commonplace, but in those days every new device was an adventure, every new camera angle a discovery...The scene in which 'Dearest' kisses her son took 15 hours to accomplish. It lasted exactly three seconds on the screen."

The Mary Pickford Company, in 1973, released a series of her most famous silent pictures as "Motion Picture Classics" with added musical score played by Gaylord Carter on the Wurlitzer organ. *Little Lord Fauntleroy* was among them.

In the late 1970s, David Robbins reviewed the 1921 *Little Lord Fauntleroy* as a retrospective for Britain's *Monthly Film Bulletin*, noting: "Even if the settings are over-upholstered by modern tastes, and Dorincourt Castle is a rather extravagant notion of English baronial style, the visual aspect of the film of Stephen Goosson's design and Charles Rosher's photography remains sumptuous. Rosher is the true star of the picture; the trick photography by which he enabled Pickford to play the dual roles of Cedric and his mother is still unsurpassed...Mary Pickford [is] charming, acts well and conscientiously in the slightly emphatic style of the earlier silent screen. The dual role was evidently calculated both to show off her range and to give her an opportunity to escape to a degree from the child roles which, at 27, were still obligatory to her career. As 'Dearest' she has enormous grace; as Cedric Lord Fauntleroy, she never for a moment looks like a real boy or a real infant (despite the use of extremely tall supporting players to emphasize her slight stature), and yet she compels belief by her own integrity and conviction..."

Ironically, the last public appearance of Frances Hodgson Burnett was at the opening at New York's Apollo Theatre of Pickford's *Little Lord Fauntleroy*. Miss Pickford, pressed by the audience of a speech, expressed regret that the famous author of the story could not be present, unaware that Mrs. Burnett was quietly sitting in a box in the theater.

In 1935, David O. Selznick selected *Little Lord Fauntleroy* as the maiden production for his newlyformed Selznick International Pictures. To adapt the book and write the screenplay. Selznick engaged British author Hugh Walpole, who, as a youngster, had himself been forced into a velvet Fauntleroy suit and heavily starched, stiff collar, thanks to the story's Cedric Errol. Freddie Bartholomew, who has charmed audiences in Selznick's MGM production of *David Copperfield*, was perfectly cast as Cedric, and to portray "Dearest," Selznick coaxed beautiful Dolores Costello Barrymore out of retirement. For his 1935 remake, Selznick hired cameraman Charles Rosher whose innovative photography was the highlight of the 1921 Pickford version.

"A gentle, tear-misted affair," is how *Liberty* magazine described the Selznick *Fauntleroy*. "[It] retains the pristine flavor of the story and yet manages to become never actually maudlin. Master Freddie Bartholomew -- minus the traditional curls, sash and velvet knickers -- gives a perfect interpretation of the Victorian idea of a perfect little gentleman, handling a variety of scenes with his childish charm and mature technique. And since Hugh Walpole's adaptation of Frances Hodgson Burnett's story fully recaptures the essence of a bygone day, the film does exactly what it sets out to do: supplies a pleasantly lachrymose evening...As for the players, they are universally fine ...lovely Dolores Costello is still the screen's best exponent of noble suffering, and her handling of dialogue is superb."

Frank S. Nugent (*The New York Times*) considered: "Although Frances Hodgson

Burnett's *Little Lord Fauntleroy* scarcely merits association with *David Copperfield* and *Anna Karenina*, Mr. Selznick has transferred it to the screen with equal consideration and understanding. It may not be a classic in the literary sense, but it approaches that stature in the warm, sentimental and gently humorous film edition which Selznick International Pictures has spread upon the screen of the Radio City Music Hall." *The New Yorker*, on the other hand, was "bored to extinction by *Little Lord Fauntleroy*...Too great a burden has been put, I think, on the Bartholomew shoulders. His precise quaintness, so really good in *David Copperfield*, is a bit overworked here...Even Dolores Costello Barrymore, the 'Dearest' of the sketch, might have been more assertive."

In 1977, BBC's six-episode television production of *Little Lord Fauntleroy* aired in the United States on PBS. Glenn Anderson was featured as Cedric, Jennie Linden as "Dearest" and Paul Rogers as the crotchety Earl of Dorincourt. Three years later came the sumptuous Norman Rosemont production as a two-hour made-for-television movie teaming Ricky Schroder as Cedric with Sir Alec Guinness as the Earl. Of this version, Judith Crist enthused in *TV Guide*: "The kind of heart-warming period piece it's said isn't made anymore." Kay Gardella wrote in the New York *Daily News*, "It's the kind of film that made movies a delight years ago." And *The Phildelphia Inquirer*'s critic, Lee Winfrey, hailed it as "a joy to watch. It has charm, grace, beauty, wit, class and style...The reason I am beguiled by *Fauntleroy* is Alec Guinness. Most people know that Guinness is a stupendous actor. What most people won't know until *Fauntleroy* begins [is] that this sentimental novel, now almost a century old, serves as a vehicle for one of his finest performances." The lavish Rosemont production earned an Emmy Award for Arthur Ibbetson's lush photography.

Rosemont's television film was shown theatrically in Great Britain and reviewed by critic Geoff Brown in *Monthly Film Bulletin*, who called it "a computerised confection" and said, disparagingly, "Ricky Schroder fails to tug at the heartstrings with the cloying insistence of Freddie Bartholomew, and Alec Guinness, in a cast sprinkled with friendly British faces, gives one of his more routine performances. He isn't helped by Jack Gold's irritating tendency to cut away to reaction shots of servants smiling knowingly or shaking their heads despairingly at the Earl's irascibility. Otherwise, the film is shot with bland anonymity."

Encouraged by otherwise critical acclaim, generally, Rosemont and CBS decided to attempt a *Little Lord Fauntleroy* series, but the pilot which was televised in the summer of 1982 -- with Jerry Suprian in the title role and Sir John Mills as the Earl -- was not well received and the prospective series was abandoned.

STAGE

LITTLE LORD FAUNTLEROY, *Prince of Wales's Theatre*, London, opened February 23, 1888 I matinee performance (repeated March 23, 1888)
Produced by Horace Sedger; A Play by E. V. Seebohm, based on the novel by Frances Hodgson Burnett; Director, William Sidney

Annie Hughes (Cedric Errol); C. W. Somerset (Earl of Dorincourt); Mary Rorke (Mrs. Errol); Royce Carleton (John Havisham); Arthur Williams (Silas Hobbs); Cicely Richard (Mary O'Brien); Windham Guise (Simpkins); Stephen Caffrey (Dawson); W. Cheesman (Reverend Jacob Mordaunt)

THE REAL LITTLE LORD FAUNTLEROY, *Terry's Theatre*, London, opened May 14, 1888 5 performances

Produced and directed by Madge Kendal; A Play by Frances Hodgson Burnett, based on her novel; Musical director, J. Bayliss; Stage manager, C. Valentine

Vera Beringer (Cedric Errol); Alfred Bishop (Earl of Dorincourt); Winifred Emery (Mrs. Errol); Brandon Thomas (Mr. Havisham); Albert Chevalier (Silas Hobbs); Esme Beringer (Dick Tipton); Helen Leigh (Minna); Fanny Brough (Mary); Mr. Hendrie (Wilkins); Mr. Branscombe (Higgins); Maurice Vaughan (Thomas)

LITTLE LORD FAUNTLEROY, *Broadway Theatre*, New York, opened December 3, 1888 185 performances

Produced by T. H. French; A Play written and directed by Frances Hodgson Burnett, based on her novel; Scenery, Messrs. Goatcher and Young; Liveries by W. Dazian & Company; Original music, Ernest Neyer; Mechanical effects, A. C. Fillot and Assistants; Gas and electric effects, James Stewart; Stage manager, Frank E. Loeb

Elsie Leslie (alternate Tommy Russell) (Cedric Errol); J. H. Gilmour (Earl of Dorincourt); Kathryn Kidder (Mrs. Errol); F. F. Mackay (Mr. Havisham); George Parkhurt (Silas Hobbs); Frank E. Lamb (Dick, a Bootblack); Effie Gerson (Mary); Alice Fischer (Minna); Carrie Vinton (Jane); John Swinburne (Higgins, a Farmer); Alfred Klein (Wilkins, a Groom); John Sutherland (Thomas, a Footman); T. J. Plunkett (Servant)

THE REAL LITTLE LORD FAUNTLEROY, *Opera Comique Theatre*, London, 1889

Produced by Mrs. Oscar Beringer; A Play by Frances Hodgson Burnett; Director, Mrs. Madge Kendal; Music director, Ernest Bucalussi; Stage manager, E. Hendrie

Vera Beringer (Cedric Errol); C. W. Somerset (Earl of Dorincourt); Marion Terry (Mrs. Errol); George Canninge (Mr. Havisham); Etienne Girardot (Silas Hobbs); Fred Baxter (Dick Tipton); E. Hendrie (Wilkins); Helen Leigh (Minna); Fanny Brough (Mary); Mr. Branscombe (Higgins)

LITTLE LORD FAUNTLEROY, *Madison Square Theatre*, New York, opened November 12, 1899 (Matinees only)

Produced by Palmer and Providence; A Play by Frances Hodgson Burnett

Wallace "Wallie" Eddinger (alternate Ray Maskell) (Cedric Errol); J. H. Gilmour (Earl of Dorincourt); Isabelle Evesson (Mrs. Errol); F. F. Mackay (Mr. Havisham); Emily Lytton (Minna)

Touring Company, season 1889-90

Produced and directed by T. H. French; A Play by Frances Hodson Burnett, based on her novel

Ray Maskell (alternate Tommy Russell) (Cedric Errol); Frank E. Aiken (Earl of Dorincourt); Helen Lowell (Mrs. Errol); M. B. Snyder (Mr. Havisham); George Parkhust (Silas Hobbs); Graham Henderson (Dick Tipton); Alfred Klein (Higgins); Emily Lytton (Minna); Rose Snyder (Mary); Irving Williams (James); Pearson Adams (Wilkins); A. G. Smith (Thomas)

Park Theatre, New York, opened April 28, 1890

Produced by I. Fleishman; A Play by Frances Hodgson Burnett, based on her novel; Director, T. H. French; Company manager, Charles E. Power; Stage manager, Carl A. Haswin

Tommy Russell (alternate Gertie Homan) (Cedric Errol); Carl A. Haswin (Earl of Dorincourt); Isabelle Evesson (Mrs. Errol); Adolph Bernard (Mr. Havisham); C. J. Williams (Silas Hobbs); Charles Klein (Dick Tipton); Dorothy Rossmore (Minna);

Emma Marble (Mary); I. W. Browning (James); George Marston (Wilkins); Charles R. Gilbert (Thomas)

Windsor Theatre, New York, opened May 11, 1891
A Play by Frances Hodgson Burnett, based on her novel
Ray Maskell (Cedric Errol); Carl A. Hoswin (Earl of Dorincourt); Frances Wheatcroft (Mrs. Errol); Frank Opperman (Mr. Havisham); George Conway (Silas Hobbs); J. Commeyer (Dick Tipton); Florence Foster (Minna); Hugh Ford (Thomas)

Castle Square Theatre, Boston, opened August 9, 1897
Produced by Castle Square Theatre Dramatic Stock Company, J. H. Emery, manager; A Play by Frances Hodgson Burnett, based on her novel; Director, James R. Pitman
Johnnie McKeever (Cedric Errol); J. H. Gilmour (Earl of Dorincourt); Grace Atwell (Mrs. Errol); William Humphrey (Mr. Havisham); William Charles Masson (Silas Hobbs); Tony Cummings (Dick Tipton); Lillian Lawrence (Minna); Agnes Findlay (Mary); Lindsay Morison (Wilkins); M. H. Fowler (Thomas); Howard Hall (Higgins)

Wyndham's Theatre, London, opened December 26, 1901 32 performances
Produced by Charles Wyndham; A Play by Frances Hodgson Burnett, based on her novel; Director, Ernest Hendrie; Costumes, Don Company and Mme. Oliver Hoomes; Musical director, Alick MacLean; Stage manager, Christmas Grose
Master Vyvian Thomas (Cedric Errol); Will Dennis (Earl of Dorincourt); Marion Terry (Mrs. Errol); George Canninge (Mr. Havisham); Arthur Williams (Silas Hobbs); Christmas Grose (Dick Tipton); Alice Esden (Minna); Kate Phillips (Mary); Ernest Hendrie (succeeded by Welton Dale) (Higgins); Welton Dale (succeeded by T. P. Haynes) (Wilkins); Charles Carey (Thomas)

Court Theatre, London, opened December 26, 1908 40 performances
Produced by Gertrude Mouillot; A Play by Frances Hodgson Burnett, based on her novel; Director, Frederick Stanhope; Costumes, Marie Luzette and Roberteau; Musical director, Albert Cazabon; General manager, James Anning; Stage manager, Christmas Grose
Master Lenton Murray (Cedric Errol); Will Dennis (Earl of Dorincourt); Eva Moore (succeeded by Ada Ferrer) (Mrs. Errol); George Canninge (Mr. Havisham); William Lockhart (Silas Hobbs); Christmas Grose (Dick Tipton); Gertrude Netterville (Minna); Mary Brough (Mary); T. Norman (Higgins); Norman Clifton (Wilkins); J. Poole Kirkwood (Thomas)

Gate Theatre, London, opened January 7, 1931
An abbreviated version of the play by Frances Hodson Burnett, based on her novel; Director, Peter Godfrey
Elsa Lanchester (Cedric Errol); Alan Napier (Earl of Dorincourt); Prudence Vanburgh (Mrs. Errol); Walter Fitzgerald (Mr. Havisham); Arthur Chesney (Silas Hobbs); Peter Ridgeway (Dick Tipton); Hermione Gingold (Minna); Elsie French (Mary); Harold Young (Thomas)

FAUNTLEROY, Charlottestown Festival Theatre, Prince Edward Island, Canada, opened July 2, 1981

Produced by Charlottestown Festival Company; Producers, Robert E. Dubberley and David L. March; A Musical Play by Mavor Moore, based on *Little Lord Fauntleroy* by Frances Hodgson Burnett; Director and choreographer, Alan Lund; Music and lyrics by Johnny Burke; Additional lyrics by Mavor Moore; Additional lyrics by Arthur Johnston and James Monaco; Settings and costumes, Brian Jackson; Lighting, Ronald Montgomery; Orchestrations, John Fenwick and Doug Randle; Music director, Fen Watkin

Duane Woods (Fauntleroy); Douglas Chamberlain (Earl of Dorincourt); Maida Rogerson (Mrs. Errol); James Hobson (Mr. Havisham); Terry Doyle (Mr. Hobbs); Larry Herbert (Dick Tipton); Joy Thompson (Jane); Darlene Hirst (Mary); Janelle Hutchinson (Lady Fauntleroy); Hank Stinson (Reverend Mordaunt); Michael Rainbird (Lord Harry); William Hosic (Newick); Elizabeth Mawson (Lady Loridale)

MUSICAL NUMBERS: "I've Got a Pocketful of Dreams" (Burke and Monaco, from the film *Sing You Sinners*); "He Made Me Feel Lovely"; "4th of July Parade"; "Pennies From Heaven" (Burke and Johnston, from the film *Pennies From Heaven*); "I'm Myself"; "God Bless You All the Day"; "Dee-lightful"; "I Hate Little Boys"; "If the Girl Has Charm"; "It's the Company"; "Refer Them to Me"; "Worry Not a Whit, Not I"; "I Wish You Needed Me"; "I Have Only My Own Way of Loving Him"

SCREEN

LITTLE LORD FAUNTLEROY, Kineto Productions Ltd. (Great Britain), released July 1914

Produced by the Natural Colour Kinematograph Company; Director, F. Martin Thornton; Based on the novel by Frances Hodgson Burnett; Filmed in Kinemacolor

Gerald Royston (Cedric, Little Lord Fauntleroy); Jane Wells ("Dearest"); H. Agar Lyons (Earl of Dorincourt); Bernard Vaughan (Mr. Haversham); Fred Eustace (Bevis); Edward Viner (Captain Cedric Earl); F. Tomkins (Silas Hobbs); V. Osmond (Minna Tipton); Frank Strather (Ben Tipton); Harry Edwards (Dick Tipton); D. Callan (Tommy Tipton); John M. East (Thomas); Stella St. Audrie (Bridget); B. Murray (Maurice)

United Artists, released November 1921

Produced by Mary Pickford; Directors, Alfred E. Green and Jack Pickford; Screenplay, Bernard McConville, based on the novel by Frances Hodgson Burnett; Photography, Charles Rosher; Art Director, Stephen Goosson; Lighting effects, William S. Johnson; Music, Louis F. Gottschalk

Mary Pickford (Cedric, Little Lord Fauntleroy/ "Dearest," his mother); Claude Gillingwater (Earl of Dorincourt); Joseph Dowling (Mr. Havisham); James Marcus (Silas Hobbs); Fred Malatesta (Dick Tipton); Kate Price (Mrs. McGinty, the Apple Woman); Rose Dione (Minna); Frances Marion (Minna's Son); Arthur Thalasso (Minna's Husband); Colin Kenny (Bevis); Emmett King (Reverend Mordaunt); Madame de Bodamere (Mrs. Higgins)

Selznick International/United Artists, released March 1936

Produced by David O. Selznick; Director, John Cromwell; Screenplay, Hugh Walpole, adapted from the novel by Frances Hodgson Burnett; Photography, Charles Rosher; Art director, Sturges Carne; Set decorator, Casey Roberts; Wardrobe, Sophie Wachner; Special effects, Jack Cosgrove and Virgil Miller; Musical score, Max Steiner; Editor, Hal C. Kern

Freddie Bartholomew (Cedric); Dolores Costello ("Dearest"); C. Aubrey Smith

(Earl of Dorincourt); Henry Stephenson (Mr. Havisham); Guy Kibbee (Silas Hobbs); Mickey Rooney (Dick, the Bootblack); Constance Collier (Lady Lorridaile); E. E. Clive (Lord Lorridaile); Jackie Searle (Tom, the Claimant); Helen Flint (Minna); Una O'Connor (Mary); Jessie Ralph (The Apple Woman); Ivan Simpson (Reverend Mordaunt); Eric Alden (Ben); May Beatty (Mrs. Mellon); Virginia Field (Miss Herbert); Reginald Barlow (Newick); Lionel Belmore (Higgins); Tempe Pigott (Mrs. Dibble); Gilbert Emery (Purvis); Lawrence Grant (Lord Chief Justice); Walter Kingford (Snade); Eily Malyon (Landlady); Fred Walton (Landlord); Robert Emmett O'Connor (Policeman); Elsa Buchanan (Susan); Mary McLaren (Woman); Prince the Dog ("Dougal")

TELEVISION

LITTLE LORD FAUNTLEROY, televised November 21 through December 26, 1976 BBC 6 episodes (30 minutes each); in U.S. on PBS' *Once Upon a Classic*, April 2 through May 7, 1977
Produced by the British Broadcasting Corporation and Time-Life Television; Executive producer, Jay Rayvid; Producer, Barry Letts; Coordinating producer, John Coney; Director, Paul Arnett; A dramatization of the novel by Frances Hodgson Burnett; Story editor, Alistair Bell; Music, Kenny Clayton

Glenn Anderson (Cedric Errol); Paul Rogers (Earl of Dorincourt); Jennie Linden ("Dearest"); Preston Lockwood (Mr. Havisham); Betty McDowall (Mary); Ray Smith (Silas Hobbs); Paul D'Amato (Dick Tipton); Valerie Lush (Mrs. Mellon); Ian Thompson (Higgins); Elizabeth Chambers (Mrs. Higgins); Ray Armstrong (Newick); Mischa de la Motte (Hooper); Ellis Dale (Wilkins); Cherry Morris (Dawson); Max Faulkner (Mather); Michael Keet (Young Higgins); Ralph Nossek (Reverend Mordaunt); Dorothy Reynolds (Lady Lorridaile); Ruby Head (Mrs. Dibble); Marianne Stone (Woman in Street); Eileen Beldon (Ragged Woman); Frederick Bennett (Sedgewick); Nicholas McArdle (Innkeeper); Tom Beckley (Braxton); Carole Hayman (Minna); Peter Hale (Tom); Dan Meaden (Police Sergeant); John Barrett (Maggs); Christopher Jenkinson (First Man); Tony Scannell (Second Man); Hal Galli (Sailor)

LITTLE LORD FAUNTLEROY, televised November 25, 1980 CBS 2 hours
Produced by Rosemont Productions; Producer, Norman Rosemont; Associate producer, William Hill; Director, Jack Gold; Teleplay, Blanche Hanalis, based on the novel by Frances Hodgson Burnett; Photography, Arthur Ibbetson; Production designer, Herbert Westbrook; Art director, Martin Atkinson; Set decorator, Tessa Davies; Costumes, Olga Lehmann; Makeup, Roy Ashton; Music, Allyn Ferguson; Editor, Keith Palmer

Ricky Schroder (Cedric Errol); Alec Guinness (Earl of Dorincourt); Connie Booth ("Dearest"); Eric Porter (Mr. Havisham); Rachel Kempson (Lady Lorridaile); Colin Blakely (Silas Hobbs); Carmel McSharry (Mary); Rolf Saxon (Dick Tipton); Kate Harper (Minna); Edward Wylie (Ben Tipton); Antonia Pemberton (Dawson); John Cater (Thomas); Peter Copley (Reverend Muldaur); Patsy Rowlands (Mrs. Dibble); Ann Way (Mrs. Smiff); Patrick Stewart (Wilkins); Gerry Cowper (Mellon); Barry Jackson (Hustings); Tony Melody (Kimsey); Rohan McCullough (Lady Grace); Dicon Murray (Georgie); Ballard Berkeley (Sir Harry); John Southworth (Higgins); Norman Pitt (Lord Ashby-Delefant)

THE ADVENTURES OF LITTLE LORD FAUNTLEROY, televised August 14, 1982

CBS 1 hour

Produced by Rosemont Productions; Producer, Norman Rosemont; Associate producer, William Hill; Director, Desmond Davis; Teleplay, Blanche Hanalis, based on the novel by Frances Hodgson Burnett; Photography, Alan Hume; Production designer, John Stell; Costume designer, Olga Lehmann; Music, Allyn Ferguson; Editor, Keith Palmer

Jerry Superian (Cedric Errol); Sir John Mills (Earl of Dorincourt); Caroline Smith ("Dearest"); Godfrey James (McGregor); Dennis Savage (Billy); Pat Keen (Dawson); Avis Bunnage (Mrs. Lemmy); Gerry Cowper (Mellon); David Cook (Hustings); Carmel McSharry (Mary); Kenneth Midwood (The Groom); Jim Norton (Tom Muller); Kate Binchy (Mrs. Mulley); Jeremy Hawk (Doctor)

A LITTLE NIGHT MUSIC

A Musical by Hugh Wheeler (1973) based on the film *Smiles of a Summer Night* by Ingmar Bergman (1955)

Synopsis

It is turn-of-the-century Europe and to the provincial Swedish town where Fredrik Egerman, a prosperous middle-aged lawyer, now lives with his young, inexperienced second wife Anne, comes Desiree Armfeldt, a famous actress. Teenaged Anne soon learns that Desiree, a famous actress, is there to resume an old liaison with Fredrik, who, while discussing his and Anne's unconsummated marriage with Desiree, is interrupted by her present lover, Count Malcolm. Deciding that she still needs Fredrik, Desiree plans an elaborate intrigue to regain his favor. She arranges an elegant house party at the mansion of her mother, a sly, aged courtesan, and invites Fredrik and Anne, along with Henrik (Fredrik's moody son from a former marriage with a crush on his lovely stepmother), and Count Malcolm and his wife Charlotte, a proud woman who resents her husband's romantic indiscretions.

The traditional, "symbolic" Swedish summer night affects their destinies in strange and unexpected ways. Anne and Henrik finally realize their love for one another and run off together. Malcolm interrupts a romantic rendezvous between Fredrik and Charlotte, taunts the lawyer in a game of Russian roulette, and after satisfying his honor, returns to his wife. And Desiree successfully ensnares the deserted Fredrik. Out in the fields, meanwhile, Anne's maid, Petra, finds her own happiness with the Armfeldt's groom, Frid.

Comment and Critique

Ingmar Bergman, fast making a name for himself internationally as Sweden's premiere moviemaker, in 1955 created one of his few comedies, *Sommarnatens Leende (Smiles of a Summer Night)*, which Britain's *Monthly Film Bulletin* felt "evoked the spirits of Schnitzler, Wilde and Strindberg in this decidedly Nordic morality play." Bergman's spicy period comedy of manners, with many members of his stock company of players, scored a big hit on both sides of the Atlantic. It won top honors at the 1956 Cannes Film Festival and on its New York premiere on Christmas Eve 1957, Bosley Crowther wrote in *The Times*: ""Who would have thought that august Sweden would be sending us a film comedy as witty and cheerfully candid about the complexities of love as any recent French essay on l'amour. Yet this is what Ingmar

Bergman's *Smiles of a Summer Night* is -- a delightfully droll contemplation of amorous ardors."

It was to influence such disparate talents as Woody Allen, who was to pay homage to the Bergman film with his later *A Midsummer Night's Sex Comedy*, and playwright Hugh Wheeler, composer Stephen Sondheim, and director Harold Prince, who remolded the Bergman story into what would become one of the treasures of the musical stage as *A Little Night Music*.

The inventive Sondheim score, made up entirely of waltzes, the urbane and witty Wheeler book, and the cast headed by Glynis Johns, Len Cariou and Hermione Gingold (who also was to repeat her grande dame role on the London stage and in the later film version), all were embraced by the critics on the show's Broadway premiere in February 1973. Clive Barnes (*The New York Times*) called it "heady, civilized, sophisticated and enchanting. It is Dom Perignon. It is supper at Laserre. It is a mixture of Cole Porter, Gustav Mahler, Antony Tudor and just a little of Ingmar Bergman. And it is more fun than any tango in a Parisian suburb...*A Little Night Music* is soft on the ears, easy on the eyes and pleasant on the mind. It is less than brash but more than brassy, and it should give a lot of pleasure. It is the remembrance of a few things past, and all to the sound of a waltz and the understanding smile of as memory. Good God! -- an adult musical!"

Douglas Watt (*Daily News*) was a bit more tempered: "Exquisiteness is so much the concern of *A Little Night Music*, a beautifully designed and staged operetta of intimate proportions...that there is little room for the breath of life...Between them, director Harold Prince and [choreographer Patricia] Birch have given the movement sweep and flourish. Everywhere, in fact, *A Little Night Music* reveals the work of superior theatrical craftsmanship. But stunning as it is to gaze upon and as clever as the score is, with its use of trio and ensemble singing, it remains too literary and precious a work to stir the emotions."

A Little Night Music went on to win the Tony and the New York Drama Critics Award as Best Musical. Glynis Johns and Patricia Elliott won Tonys as Best Actress and Best Featured Actress in a Musical, Stephen Sondheim for his score, Hugh Wheeler for his book, and Florence Klotz for her costume design. Harold Prince was nominated for his direction but lost to Bob Fosse for *Pippin*. Len Cariou received as nomination as Best Actor in a Musical, Laurence Guittard as Best Featured Actor, and Hermione Gingold as Best Featured Actress, with nominations also going to Boris Aronson (set design) and Tharon Musser (lighting). And from the score of the show came one of Stephen Sondheim's most endearing and accessible songs, *Send in the Clowns*, which has remained a pop classic.

One year after *A Little Night Music*'s Broadway premiere, the national company began its tour with Jean Simmons in the lead making her musical stage debut. The tour ran for nearly a year and then she went to London for the show's West End debut, first with Angela Baddeley and then with Hermione Gingold from the original Broadway company. Harold Prince restaged it at the Adelphi Theatre where it played for a year beginning in April 1975. "*A Little Night Music* remains a charming as well as distinguished show in this West End production," wrote the critic for *Variety*. "The production as a whole is a fine example of ensemble playing, a strong directorial hand being noted throughout. It is visually stunning..." Irving Wardle (*The London Times*) found that it could "amount to an evening of schmaltz. It is saved by the most rigorous stylistic self-discipline I have seen in a Broadway musical." He felt that Jean Simmons "manages to get through a wardrobe of steadily mounting magnificence and to plan the downfall of her old friend's marriage, while retaining a manner of buoyantly sympathetic charm. As she does it without the least betrayal of character, it ranks as an achievement almost matching Miss Gingold's." Wardle concluded: "Altogether it is a show that effects a reunion between Broadway and the artistic conscience."

In 1985, *A Little Night Music* had its first major New York revival in a staging at the Equity Library Theater. "...a scintillating production" is how *The New York Times*' Walter Goodman described it. "The virtuoso display of wit in waltz began its memorable Broadway run in 1973, and among the incidental pleasures of seeing it now are the hints of the musical and literary themes that have engaged Mr. Sondheim's talents in the years since." The Opera Ensemble of New York staged a version of *A Little Night Music* in March 1988, an "ambitious, fully orchestrated revival [showing] the skill with which the production evoked a mood of idealized Old World elegance, using a minimum of resources," as *The Times'* Stephen Holden observed. Mary Beth Peil starred as Desiree. The New York City Opera produced an acclaimed version of the musical in September 1990, with musical comedy star Sally Ann Howes making her debut with the company, along with George Lee Andrews (who was Frid in the original Broadway production and Fredrik in the national tour) and Regina Resnick, the opera diva returning "home" to the New York City Opera where she first sang in 1944. This production was performed in repertory once a week and then was televised on PBS' *Live From Lincoln Center* in early November 1990.

Harold Prince, whose only other film was *Something for Everyone* (1970) with Angela Lansbury, brought *A Little Night Music* to the screen in 1977 in association with Sascha-Wien Films of Austria. He engaged Elizabeth Taylor to star as Desiree and Diana Rigg as Charlotte, and recruited Len Cariou, Hermione Gingold and Laurence Guittard from the original cast to repeat their roles as, respectively, Fredrik, Madame Armfeldt and the Count. Lesley Anne-Down and Christopher Guard played the younger couple. The film encountered a myriad of production and monetary problems and finally got a release (quite spotty in the United States, where Roger Corman's New World Pictures distributed it). It was not well received, despite the cast and the popularity of the musical itself. "Having elected to transform the Sondheim show into a film, Mr. Prince appears to have made every decision that could sabotage the music and the lyrics," Vincent Canby wrote in *The New York Times*. He has cast the film with people who don't sing very well and then staged almost every number in such a way that we can't respond to the lyrics. It is, of course, possible to hear the songs, but in this movie it seems like work. 'Send in the Clowns' will survive Miss Taylor's game way with a lyric, but *A Little Night Music* shouldn't be a matter of survival. It should be ebullient and fun. It isn't. It often seems mean-tempered."

In the *New York Post*, criitic Judith Crist observed: "The casting of Elizabeth Taylor as the edging-over-the-hill Desiree -- obviously the box-office draw for this $7.5 million extravaganza -- is surface viable, even though the camera is only intermittently kind to her particular plump maturity. One can even accept her recitative-like singing, given the plum of 'Send in the Clowns.' But Taylor is unfortunately surrounded by stylish performers and is left to her own prosaic talents, with an overwhelming opulence of bosom too often a total distraction."

STAGE

A LITTLE NIGHT MUSIC, Shubert Theatre, New York, opened February 25, 1973
600 performances
Produced by Harold Prince in association with Ruth Mitchell; A Musical by Hugh Wheeler, suggested by Ingmar Bergman's *Smiles of a Summer Night*; Director,

Harold Prince; Music and lyrics by Stephen Sondheim; Scenery, Boris Aronson; Lighting, Tharon Muser; Costumes, Florence Klotz; Choreography, Patricia Birch; Musical director, Harold Hastings; Orchestrations, Jonathan Tunick; Sound, Jack Mann; Hairstylist, Charles LaFrance; Production supervisor, Ruth Mitchell; Stage managers, George Martin, John Grigas and David Wolf

Glynis Johns (Desiree Armfeldt); Len Cariou (succeeded by William Daniels) (Fredrik Egerman); Hermione Gingold (Madame Armfeldt); Judy Kahan (succeeded by Sheila K. Adams) (Fredrika Armfeldt); Laurence Guittard (Count Carl-Magnus Malcolm); Patricia Elliott (Countess Charlotte Malcolm); Despo (Malla, Desiree's Maid); Benjamin Rayson (Mr. Lindquist); Teri Ralston (succeeded by Joy Franz) (Mrs. Nordstrom); Barbara Lang (succeeded by Sherry Mathis) (Mrs. Anderssen); Gene Varrone (Mr. Erlanson); Beth Fowler (Mrs. Segstrom); George Lee Andrews (succeeded by Dick Sabol) (Frid, Madame Armfeldt's Butler); Mark Lambert (Henrik Egerman); Victoria Mallory (Anne Egerman); D. Jamin-Bartlett (Petra); Will Sharpe Marshall (Bertrand, a Page); Sherry Mathis (Osa)

MUSICAL NUMBERS: Overture; "Night Waltz"; "Now"; "Later"; "Soon"; "The Glamorous Life"; "Remember?"; "You Must Be My Wife"; "Liaisons"; "In Praise of Women"; "Every Day a Little Death"; "A Weekend in the Country"; "The Sun Won't Set"; "It Would Have Been Wonderful"; "Perpetual Anticipation"; "Send in the Clowns"; "The Miller's Son"; Finale

Original cast recording: Columbia Records

National Tour, opened *Forrest Theatre*, Philadelphia, February 26, 1974; closed *Shubert Theatre*, Boston, February 15, 1975

Produced by Harold Prince in association with Ruth Mitchell; A Musical by Hugh Wheeler, suggested by Ingmar Bergman's *Smiles of a Summer Night*; Director, Harold Prince; Music and lyrics by Stephen Sondheim; Scenery, Boris Aronson; Lighting, Tharon Muser; Costumes, Florence Klotz; Choreography, Patricia Birch; Musical director, Richard Parrinello; Orchestrations, Jonathan Tunick; Sound, Jack Mann; Hairstylist, Richard Allen; Production supervisor, Ruth Mitchell; Stage managers, Ben Strobach, Patricia Drylie and Arlene Caruso

Jean Simmons (Desiree Armfeldt); George Lee Andrews (Fredrik Egerman); Margaret Hamilton (Madame Armfeldt); Marti Morris (Fredrika Armfeldt); Ed Evanko (Count Carl-Magnus Malcolm); Andra Akers (Countess Charlotte Malcolm); Elliott Savage (Mr. Lindquist); Kris Karlowski (Mrs. Nordstrom); Marina MacNeal (Mrs. Anderssen); Joe McGrath (Mr. Erlanson); Karen Zenker (Mrs. Segstrom); Jonathan Banks (Frid, Madame Armfeldt's Butler); Stephen Lehew (Henrik Egerman); Virginia Pulos (Anne Egerman); Mary Ann Chinn (Petra); James Ferrier (Bertrand, a Page); Verna Pierce (Osa)

Adelphi Theatre, London, opened April 15, 1975 406 performances

Ruth Mitchell, Frank Milton, Eddie Kulukundis and Richard Pilbrow, in association with Bernard Delfont, presentation of a Harold Prince production; A Musical by Hugh Wheeler, suggested by Ingmar Bergman's *Smiles of a Summer Night*; Director, Harold Prince; Music and lyrics by Stephen Sondheim; Scenery, Boris Aronson; Lighting, Tharon Muser; Costumes, Florence Klotz; Choreography, Patricia Birch; Musical director, Ray Cook; Orchestrations, Jonathan Tunick; Sound, David Collinson; Production supervisor, George Martin

Jean Simmons (Desiree Armfeldt); Joss Ackland (Fredrik Egerman); Angela

Baddeley (succeeded by Hermione Gingold) (Madame Armfeldt); Christine McKenna (Fredrika Armfeldt); David Kernan (Count Carl-Magnus Malcolm); Maria Aitken (Countess Charlotte Malcolm); John J. Moore (Mr. Lindquist); Chris Melville (Mrs. Nordstrom); Liz Robertson (Mrs. Anderssen); David Bexon (Mr. Erlanson); Jacquey Chappell (Mrs. Segstrom); Michael Harbour (Frid, Madame Armfeldt's Butler); Terry Mitchell (Henrik Egerman); Veronica Page (Anne Egerman); Diane Langton (Petra); Christopher Beeching (Bertrand, a Page); Penelope Potter (Osa)

Original cast recording: RCA Red Seal

NOTE: Jean Simmons and Hermione Gingold were joined by Paul Vicena in a summer 1977 U.S. tour of the musical

Studio Arena Theatre, Buffalo, New York, opened March 26, 1976 35 performances
Produced by the Studio Arena Theatre, Neal DuBrock, executive producer; A Musical by Hugh Wheeler, suggested by Ingmar Bergman's *Smiles of a Summer Night*; Director and choreographer, Tony Tanner; Music and lyrics by Stephen Sondheim; Scenery, Robert D. Soule; Lighting, Robby Monk; Costumes, Clifford Capone; Musical director, Dorothy Opalach; Orchestrations, Jonathan Tunick; Sound, Richard Menke

Rosemary Prinz (Desiree Armfeldt); William Chapman (Fredrik Egerman); and Paula Laurence, David Holliday, Alan Brasington, Karen Good, Gail Johnston, Jay Lowman, Leila Martin, Sarah Rice, Howard Shalwitz

Church of the Heavenly Rest, New York, opened March 20, 1981 21 performances
Produced by the York Players Company; A Musical by Hugh Wheeler, suggested by Ingmar Bergman's *Smiles of a Summer Night*; Director, Fran Soeder; Music and lyrics by Stephen Sondheim; Scenery, James Morgan; Lighting, David Gotwald; Costumes, Sydney Brooks; Choreography, Helen Butleroff; Musical director, Eric Stern; Orchestrations, Jonathan Tunick; Sound, Joseph D. Sukaskas; Stage manager, Molly Grose

Lynn Metternich (Desiree Armfeldt); Jay Stuart (Fredrik Egerman); Helen Lloyd Breed (Madame Armfeldt); Jane Krakowski (Fredrika Armfeldt); Kenneth Kantor (Count Carl-Magnus Malcolm); Barbara Broughton (Countess Charlotte Malcolm); Don Woodman (Mr. Lindquist); M. Lynne Wieneke (Mrs. Nordstrom); Gail Titunik (Mrs. Anderssen); Gordon Stanley (Mr. Erlanson); Terry Baughan (Mrs. Segstrom); Robert Sanders (Frid, Madame Armfeldt's Butler); Keith Rice (Henrik Egerman); Kathryn Morath (Anne Egerman); Diane Pennington (Petra); Melissa Ann Green (Osa)

Opera Ensemble of New York, opened March 9, 1988 9 performances
Produced by the Opera Ensemble of New York; A Musical by Hugh Wheeler, suggested by Ingmar Bergman's *Smiles of a Summer Night*; Director, John J. D. Sheehan; Music and lyrics by Stephen Sondheim; Scenery, Dain Marcus; Lighting, Clifton Taylor; Costumes, Hope Hanafin; Choreography, William Whitener; Musical director, Richard Parrinello; Orchestrations, Jonathan Tunick; Production stage manager, Stan Schwartz

Mary Beth Piel (Desiree Armfeldt); Ron Raines (Fredrik Egerman); Lucille Patton (Madame Armfeldt); Cady McClain (Fredrika Armfeldt); David Trombley (Count Carl-Magnus Malcolm); Rebecca Mercer-White (Countess Charlotte Malcolm); Gregg Lauterbach (Mr. Lindquist); Kelly Hogan (Mrs. Nordstrom); Jacqueline

Marx (Mrs. Anderssen); Craig Collins (Mr. Erlanson); Julia Davidson (Mrs. Segstrom); Matthew McClanahan (Frid, Madame Armfeldt's Butler); Franc D'Ambrosio (Henrik Egerman); Colby Thomas (Anne Egerman); Kate Egan (Petra)

Piccadilly Theatre, London, opened October 10, 1989 152 performances
An H. M. Tenant presentation; Executive producer, John Gale; A Musical by Hugh Wheeler, suggested by Ingmar Bergman's *Smiles of a Summer Night*; Director, Ian Judge; Music and lyrics by Stephen Sondheim; Scenery, Mark Thompson; Lighting, Nick Chelton; Choreography, Anthony Van Laast; Musical director, Roger Ward; Orchestrations, Jonathan Tunick; Sound, Matthew Gale

Dorothy Tutin (Desiree Armfeldt); Peter McEnery (Fredrik Egerman); Lila Kedrova (Madame Armfeldt); Debra Beaumont (Fredrika Armfeldt); Eric Flynn (Count Carl-Magnus Malcolm); Susan Hampshire (Countess Charlotte Malcolm); David Hitchen (Frid, Madame Armfeldt's Butler); Alexander Hanson (Henrik Egerman); Deborah Poplett (Anne Egerman); Sara Weymouth (Petra); Mandi Martin (Malla); Susan Paule (Osa)

New York State Theater, opened August 3, 1990 (I performance per week through November)
Presented by the New York City Opera; A Musical by Hugh Wheeler, suggested by Ingmar Bergman's *Smiles of a Summer Night*; Director, Scott Ellis; Music and lyrics by Stephen Sondheim; Scenery, Michael Anania; Lighting, Dawn Chiang; Costumes, Lindsay W. Davis; Choreography, Susan Stroman; Musical director, Paul Gemingani; Orchestrations, Jonathan Tunick; Sound, Abe Jacob

Sally Ann Howes (Desiree Armfeldt); George Lee Andrews (Fredrik Egerman); Regina Resnick (Madame Armfeldt); Danielle Ferland (Fredrika Armfeldt); Michael Maguire (Count Carl-Magnus Malcolm); Maureen Moore (Countess Charlotte Malcolm); Ron Baker (Mr. Lindquist); Lisa Saffer (Mrs. Nordstrom); Barbara Shirvis (Mrs. Anderssen); Michael Rees Davis (Mr. Erlanson/Bertrand, a Page); Susanne Marsee (Mrs. Segstrom); David Comstock (Frid, Madame Armfeldt's Butler); Kevin Anderson (Henrik Egerman); Beverly Lambert (Anne Egerman); Raven Wilkinson (Malla, Desiree's Maid); Susan Terry (Petra); Michael Cornell, Ernest Foederer, Kent A. Hancock, Ronald Kelley, Brian Michels, Brian Quirk, Christopher Shepherd, John Henry Thomas (Serving Gentlemen)

NOTE: This production was televised on PBS' *Live From Lincoln Center* on November 7, 1990. A restaging with the same cast, except Elaine Bonazzi as Madame Armfeldt, opened at the *State Theater*, July 9, 1991, for seven performances over six weeks

James A. Doolittle Theatre, Los Angeles, opened April 18 through June 30, 1991
A Center Theatre Group/Ahmanson revival; A Musical by Hugh Wheeler, suggested by Ingmar Bergman's *Smiles of a Summer Night*; Director, Gordon Davidson; Music and lyrics by Stephen Sondheim; Scenery, Robert Israel; Lighting, Paulie Jenkins; Costumes, Noel Taylor; Choreography, Onna White; Musical director, Arthur B. Rubinstein; Orchestrations, Jonathan Tunick; Vocal staging, David Craig; Sound, Jon Gottlieb; Production stage manager, Mark Wright

Lois Nettleton (Desiree Armfeldt); John McMartin (Fredrik Egerman); Glynis Johns (Madame Armfeldt); Polly Heard (Fredrika Armfeldt); Jeff McCarthy (Count Carl-Magnus Malcolm); Marcia Mitzman (Countess Charlotte Malcolm);

Joe H. Crest (Frid, Madame Armfeldt's Butler); Franc d'Ambrosio (Henrik Egerman); Michelle Nicastro (Anne Egerman); Patricia Fraser (Malla, Desiree's Maid); Kathleen Rowe McAllen (Petra); Kelli Rabke (Osa); Robert E. Lauder, Jr., Marnie Moslman, Ray Benson, Rita Baretta, Sarah Tattersall (Ensemble)

SCREEN

SOMMARNATTENS LEENDE (SMILES OF A SUMMER NIGHT), Svensk Filmindustri, released 1955; in U.S. released by *Rank Films*, December 1957
Written and directed by Ingmar Bergman; Photography, Gunnar Fischer; Art director, P. A. Lundgren; Costumes, Mago; Music, Erik Nordgren; Sound, P. O. Pettersson; Editor, Oscar Rosander

Eva Dahlbeck (Desiree Armfeldt); Gunnar Bjornstrand (Fredrik Egerman); Ulla Jacobsson (Anne Egerman); Harriet Andersson (Petra); Jarl Kulle (Count Malcolm); Margit Carlquist (Charlotte Malcolm); Bjorn Bjelvenstam (Henrik Egerman); Naima Wifstrand (Madame Armfeldt); Ake Fridell (Frid); Julian Kindahl (The Cook); Gull Natorp (Malla, Desiree's Maid)

A LITTLE NIGHT MUSIC, New World Pictures, released 1977
A Sascha-Wien Film in association with Elliott Kastner; A Roger Corman presentation; Executive producer, Heinz Lazek; Producer, Elliott Kastner; Director, Harold Prince; Screenplay, Hugh Wheeler, based on his musical play suggested by Ingmar Bergman's *Smiles of a Summer Night;* Music and lyrics by Stephen Sondheim; Photography, Arthur Ibbetson; Production designer, Laci von Ronay; Art directors, Herta Pischinger and Thomas Riccabona; Costumes, Florence Klotz; Choreography, Patricia Birch; Music scored and supervised by Jonathan Tunick; Editor, John Jympson

Elizabeth Taylor (Desiree Armfeldt); Len Cariou (Fredrik Egerman); Hermione Gingold (Madame Armfeldt); Chloe Franks (Fredrika Armfeldt); Laurence Guittard (Count Carl-Magnus Mittelheim); Diana Rigg (Countess Charlotte Mittelheim); Lesley-Anne Down (Anne Egerman); Christopher Guard (Erich Egerman); Heinz Maracek (Kurt); Lesley Dunlop (Petra); Jonathan Tunick (Conductor); Hubert Tscheppe (Franz); Rudolph Schrympf (Band Conductor); Franz Schussler (Mayor); Johanna Schussler (Mayoress)

Original soundtrack recording: Columbia Records

TELEVISION

A LITTLE NIGHT MUSIC, Live From Lincoln Center, televised November 7, 1990
PBS 3 hours

(see New York City Opera production under Stage; television production directed by Kirk Browning)

THE LIVES OF A BENGAL LANCER

Adaptations of the book by Francis Yeats-Brown (1930)

Synopsis

On India's Northwest frontier, coldly detached but regally proper British Colonel

Stone is in command of a regiment of Bengal Lancers, most of them well-bred, Sandhurst-educated Englishmen, his own son, a lieutenant, among them. The corps of Lancers vigorously has defended its position against marauding Afridis guerrillas. Virile Lieutenant MacGregor, a Scotsman, and flippant Lieutenant Fortesque are captured by the Afghans and savagely tortured but steadfastly refuse to disclose to Mohammed Khan the route of a reinforcing munitions train. Lieutenant Stone, betrayed by Tania, a seductive Russian spy, is also taken by the rebels and tortured, but rebelling against his father's stern discipline, he breaks under the torture and reveals Lancer secrets. Ultimately, the three disparate officers escape and manage to bring honor to themselves and their regiment when their fortress comes under a savage Afghan attack. MacGregor is killed when the Lancers blow up the ammunition depot sought by Mohammed Khan, and is posthumously awarded the Victoria Cross.

Comment and Critique

This synopsis is of the screenplay by John L. Balderston, Achmed Abdullah and Waldemar Young for Paramount Pictures' zesty, action-packed 1935 filming of the book by Major Francis Yeats-Brown. Engrossing, exciting, well-made, *The Lives of a Bengal Lancer* became one of the year's Ten Best movies and was nominated for several Academy Awards, including Best Picture. Other than the title, however, *The Lives of a Bengal Lancer* had little in common with the Yeats-Brown book beyond the background of a regiment of Lancers serving in India.

Francis Yeats-Brown's adventure autobiography (not a novel) was published by Viking Press and became a bestseller in 1930, and was purchased by Paramount for Gary Cooper, loosely adapted to the screen and directed by Henry Hathaway against authentic, previously filmed India backgrounds. Its screen success doubtless surprised the author, whose book related his long experience in the Seventeenth Cavalry of the Bengal Lancers to which he has been commissioned as a nineteen-year-old.

The Bengal Lancers regiment at Bantu on the Northwest Frontier was commanded by British officers but consisted primarily of Indian natives of varying and frequently opposing religions. Through the years with the Lancers, Yeats-Brown related experiences in hunting wild boars with a lance and becoming expert at polo. Much of his autobiography deals with his fascination with and study of Yoga, meeting with various gurus, and striving to understand India's complexities.

During World War I, Francis Yeats-Brown was assigned to duty as an airborne observer of Turkish troop movements until his capture and imprisonment in Baghdad. He eventually escaped and returned to England. As a Major, he went back to India in command of his own squadron and continued his search for spiritual fulfillment, chronicling it for his book.

Following the release of Paramount's movie using that book's title and appending to it a scenario more in line with a Kipling tale, Andre Sennwald (*The New York Times*) wrote, "*The Lives of a Bengal Lancer* is as joyous in its gunplay as it is splendid and picturesque in its manufacture, and it proves to be consistently lively despite its great length...Henry Hathaway, the director, executes a skillful and convincing blend of the studio scenes and the authentic, atmospheric films made in India several years ago by a Paramount expedition headed by Ernest Schoedsack...[It] is a superb adventure story and easily the liveliest film in town."

The *New York World-Telegram* reported: "The acting is of a superior quality. Gary Cooper has seldom had a more sympathetic or effective part than MacGregor, and he performs the task imposed upon him expertly and effectively...The direction is of a high quality and the photography is splendid. The *London Daily Telegraph* extolled the film as "Terrific...the best army picture ever made. There is no love story. The theme is the conflict between duty and sentiment [and] Gary Cooper and Franchot Tone are magnificent as the two subalterns. Henry Hathaway has directed brilliantly."

Photoplay also was enthused: "No phrase, no matter how majestic, could quite describe the dramatic majesty of the picture...Brittle, pointed dialogue, swift direction, pictorial grandeur, and an intelligent production make this picture definitely important to see."

In 1985, William Ayot adapted Francis Yeats-Brown's autobiographical chronicle to the stage as a one-man play, *Bengal Lancer*, starring Tim Piggott-Smith and directed by Michael Joyce at London's Lyric Theatre Hammersmith. Clare Colvin wrote in *Plays and Players*: "[His] one-man show is the most elaborately staged I have seen for some time. The set by Bob Crowley is draped with vast swathes of mosquito netting and tailors' dummies stand surrealistically among the heaps of sand...The actor makes full use of the props. He is in and out of several changes of costume during the evening, from Lancers' dress uniform to a saddu's dhoti, unconcernedly changing down to his underpants or retreating behind a flimsy piece of mosquito netting when shedding underpants as well. It is a debatable point whether all this business adds much to William Ayot's play." The critic proceeded to point out: "The trouble with the with the Yeats-Brown book is that the man suffered from the sort of emotional paralysis that was the lot of so many subjected to the public school system. The quality of India is filtered through a mind trained not to acknowledge the overwhelming." Of Tim Piggott-Smith: "[He] skillfully impersonates crusty colonels, effete officers and headwagging Indian officials, but the central character, the outsider hidden behind an English mask, remains a slightly sad enigma." Like, from most reports, Francis Yeats-Brown.

In the *London Standard*, Christopher Grier found: "Fifty years ago, Hollywood's British acting community was recruited into a lovely, toshy film remotely connected with Francis Yeats-Brown's autobiographical *The Lives of a Bengal Lancer*...Nothing like that about Tim Pigott-Smith's one-man show -- closely derived from the same source with an economical script by William Ayot. This version called simply *Bengal Lancer* sticks to the original...Professionally it counts as a tour-de-force by a clever character actor, but there is more to it than that. His act represents a labour of conviction as well as love. It rings true!"

Michael Billington, critic for *The Guardian*, felt: "The strength of the evening lies partly in what it tells one about the sub-continent, but even more in the actor's palpable identification with the hero who goes to India for vocational reasons and ends up being seduced by the world of Yogis, gurus and the tantalizing deceptiveness of Indian religion...Not the least of the show's fascinations is Pigott-Smith's physical recreation of the fetishistic business of donning uniforms...Pigott-Smith switches with wonderful agility from the wide-eyed hero to tough Scots major... headwagging bureaucrats and brolly-brandishing gurus. He gives a real performance...not a recital."

In late October 1956, the Lancers came to television in the NBC series, *Tales of the 77th Bengal Lancers*, produced by Herbert B. Leonard (creator of *Route 66*). It featured Phil Carey in the old Gary Cooper role (under a different character name) and Warren Stevens in the part that Franchot Tone had played. Cast as the regimental commander was British actor Patrick Whyte, himself a onetime Lancer and technical adviser for the singleseason series. All told, *Tales of the 77th Bengal*

Lancers, described as Kiplingesque and rather preposterous *fin de siecle*, swashbuckled through twenty-five episodes. Reporting on the premiere show, *Billboard* noted: "The debut program was far from adequate. Mistakes were made in conception, production and scripting. It was the story of the manner in which the two costars covered up the cowardice of the glory boy of the regiment..."

STAGE

BENGAL LANCER, Lyric Theatre Hammersmith, London, opened July 5, 1985
A Monodrama by William Ayot, based on *The Lives of a Bengal Lancer* by Francis Yeats-Brown; Director, Michael Joyce; Production designer, Bob Crowley, Lighting, John A. Williams; Assistant designer, Rod Langsford; Music, George Fenton

Tim Pigott-Smith (Francis Yeats-Brown and numerous others)

SCREEN

THE LIVES OF A BENGAL LANCER, Paramount Pictures, released January 1935
Produced by Louis D. Lighton; Director, Henry Hathaway; Screenplay, Waldemar Young and John L. Balderston, based on the adaptation bu William Slavens McNutt, Grover Jones and Achmed Abdullah of the novel my Major Francis Yeats-Brown; Photography, Charles Lang; Art directors, Roland Anderson and Hans Dreier; Choreography, LeRoy Prinz; Music, Milan Roder; Sound, Harold C. Lewis; Editor, Ellsworth Hoagland

Gary Cooper (Lieutenant MacGregor); Franchot Tone (Lieutenant Fortesque); Richard Cromwell (Lieutenant Stone); Sir Guy Standing (Colonel Stone); C. Aubrey Smith (Major Hamilton); Kathleen Burke (Tania Volkanskaya); Colin Tapley (Lieutenant Barrett); Douglass Dumbrille (Mohammed Khan); Monte Blue (Hanzulia Khan); Noble Johnson (Ram Singh); Akim Tamiroff (Emir); Jameson Thomas (Hendrickson); Lumsden Hare (Major General Woodley); J. Carrol Naish (Grand Vizier); Boswhan Singh (Nuim Shah); Mischa Auer (Afridi); George Rigas (Kushal Khan); Rollo Lloyd (The Ghazi); Charles Stevens (MacGregor's Servant); Leonid Kinsky (Snake Charmer); Eddie Das (Servant); Clive Morgan (Lieutenant Norton); James Warwick (Lieutenant Gilhooley); Reginald Sheffield (Novice); Myra Kinch (Solo Dancer); Abdul Hassan (Ali Hamdi); Hussain Hasri (Muezzin); Major Sam Harris, Carli Taylor (British Officers); James Bell, F. A. Armenta, General Ikonnikoff, Jamiel Hasson, Ram Singh (Indian Officers); Claude King (Clerk); Ray Cooper (Grand Vizier's Assistant); Lya Lys (Girl on Train)

I TRE SERGENTI DEL BENGALA (ADVENTURES OF THE BENGAL LANCERS), Filmes/Fono (Rome); *Olympic Pictures* (Madrid), released 1965
Produced by Solly V. Bianco; Director, Humphrey Humbert (Umberto Lenzi); Screenplay, Victor A Catena and Fulvio Gicca; Photography, Angelo Lotti; Art director and costumes, Arrigo Equini; Music, John Wellman (Italian version, Giovanni Fusco); Sound, Mario Del Pezzo; Editor, Jolanda Benvenuti

Richard Harrison (Frankie Ross); Hugo Arden (Burt Wallace); Nick Anderwon (John Foster); Wandisa Guida (Mary Stark); Aldo Sambrell (Sikidama); Andrea Bosic (Colonel Lee); Luz Marquez (Helen)

TELEVISION

TALES OF THE 77TH BENGAL LANCERS, televised October 21, 1956 through May 17, 1957 NBC 25 episodes (30 minutes each)
Created and produced by Herbert B. Leonard; Director, Douglas Hayes and others; Written by Patrick Whyte, Douglas Hayes and others; Technical adviser, Patrick Whyte

Phil Carey (Lt. Michael Rhodes); Warren Stevens (Lt. William Storm); Patrick Whyte (Colonel Standish): also guests including Brett Halsey, Patric Knowles, Eva Gabor, Jean Byron, Abraham Sofaer, Rex Evans, Patricia Medina, Douglass Dumbrille, Ted De Corsia, Walkter Kingsford, Michael Ansara, John Hubbard, Kathleen Crowley, Peter Coe, June Vincent, Sean McClory, Reginald Denny, Rex Reason, Leon Askin, Abel Fernandez, Damian O'Flynn, Queenie Leonard, Lee Aaker, Terence de Marney, Reginald Sheffield, John Sutton, Edgar Barrier, Frances Robinson, Jay Novello

EPISODES: The Regiment; The Pawn; Hostage; Steel Bracelet; The Traitor; Stepping Stones; Golden Ring; The Weakling; The Handmaiden; Shadow of the Idol; The Maharani; The Gentle Vise; Silent Trumpet; Cecil of Kabul; The Barbarian; Imposter; Test of a Titan; The Enemy; Relentess Man; The Courtship of Colonel Standish; Pit of Fire; The Glass Necklace; Ten Thousand Rupees; Akbar the Great; Challenge of the Chundra Sing

LOOK BACK IN ANGER
A Drama by John Osborne (1956)

Synopsis

Jimmy Porter, a working-class Englishman, rebels angrily against brave causes lost or discredited and the lack of new ones to support. He spews venom on what he considers a hypocritical, self-deceiving society and rails against middle-class morality represented by his wife, Alison, and her family. In the Porters' squalid, Midlands attic flat, their friend, Cliff, who works with Jimmy in the latter's street market candy stall, tries to quell the ambivalence between the couple. Alison, learning that she is pregnant, leaves Jimmy and returns to her family. Jimmy, meanwhile, turns to their mutual friend, young actress Helena Charles. Cliff finds the adulterous situation untenable and moves out, not long before Alison, having lost her child, comes back to the dismal flat. Unable to understand the love-hate relationship between Jimmy and Alison, Helena leaves them to their uneasy reconciliation.

Comment and Critique

London-born John Osborne (December 12, 1929) began his career in the theater as an actor, making his stage debut in Sheffield in *No Room at the Inn*. Osborne joined The English Stage Company Ltd. founded in 1956 by, among others, Dame Peggy Ashcroft, at the Royal Court Theatre. He appeared as Antonio in *Don Juan* with the company and not long afterward had his first play, *Look Back in Anger*, produced there. With *Look Back in Anger*, Osborne found himself in the front ranks of Britain's new group of "Angry Young Playwrights."

Despite the tremendous success of *Look Back in Anger* in London as well as in most of the European capitals, plus Moscow, where The English Stage Company produced it for the World Youth Festival in 1959, Osborne's drama was not initially well received in the London press. In *Plays and Players*, Anthony Merryn wrote: "John Osborne in *Look Back in Anger* has certainly succeeded, if he has done little else, in putting on the stage one of the most irritatingly boorish, verbose and bitter young men that ever exasperated an audience ...This is a stagy, conventional, unauthentic conception of the reality of working people...Even so, there is an undeniable quality in the writing, a creative, poetic, witty use of words that might serve better for a non-naturalistic theme. What it lacks is character-drawing, economy and subtlety. The story itself does not amount to much...Kenneth Haigh showed a remarkable fluency and stamina in the leading role, and the urge to get up on the stage and strangle him at least showed that there was some kind of compelling life in his performance."

In spite of the lukewarm reviews for his play, John Osborne received the Evening Standard Drama Award in 1956 as "the most promising British playwright." The Bristol Old Vic then staged a production of Osborne's drama in spring 1957, notable for the casting in the lead role of a young Peter O'Toole, then a member of the Bristol company.

Look Back in Anger came to Broadway in October 1957 with the principals of the London company, including Mary Ure, Osborne's wife. The play was lauded by the New York Critics Circle who gave it their "Best Foreign Play" award over Osborne's previous play *The Entertainer*, Peter Ustinov's *Romanoff and Juliet*, and Jean Anouilh's *Time Remembered*.

"*Look Back in Anger* hit England with a bang last year and it is clear enough why, reported *Time* magazine. "On the one hand, it clangingly echoed a new generation's call to disorder in English life. And it had something more than the *Zeitgeist* or England's general theatrical anemia to recommend it; it had a man who could really write...Not for a good many years has anyone come out of England with playwright Osborne's verbal talent for throwing stones..."

Brooks Atkinson announced in *The New York Times*: "John Osborne has written the most vivid British play of the decade...[He] is a fiery writer with a sharp point of view and a sense of theater...If Mr. Osborne is disgusted with England today, he is also disgusted with the pallor of British drama." Walter Kerr (*Herald-Tribune*) added: "Under Tony Richardson's now fiery now quickly sensitive direction, the performance as a whole is beautifully articulated...The play isn't pleasant. It solves nothing at all. But Mr. Osborne is, first of all, a writer -- a real one. He has, in addition, opened up an environment, an atmosphere, a jungle of contemporary experience that is fresh to the theater, and freshly observed..."

John Chapman (*Daily News*) claimed: "John Osborne's *Look Back in Anger* [is] the most virile and exciting play to come out of London in a long, long time -- something to set the wits tingling...Playwright Osborne is a showman as well as a cynic, and there are several neat twists of the plot. Best of all, he writes with economy and punch. *Look Back in Anger* has put the drama season on its toes."

In 1959, Tony Richardson directed the screen version of Osborne's play, with Richard Burton starring. Reviewing it for *Films and Filming*, Roger Manvell wrote, "I was impressed, like others, by the vituperative power of its dialogue rather than by any particular manners (in the theatrical sense) that John Osborne might seem to be projecting in his play... Osborne has the ability to write dialogue which, apart from muscularity of phrasing, lives and breathes at its best with the sustenance of a meaning beyond its immediate statement...Burton's coruscating performance as Jimmy Porter -- the best I have ever seen him give -- reveals through Tony Richardson's emphatic close-ups the agony of this man...*Look Back in Anger* is Tony Richardson's debut as a feature film director, just as *Room at the Top* was Jack

Clayton's. In them we have gained overnight (as it were) two men capable of putting mature work on the screen with undeniable strength."

British critic Penelope Houston found Mary Ure (repeating her stage role) "the least distinctive" member of the film's cast but that "Tony Richardson, directing his first feature, has given it a tough, vital style, which represents something new in British cinema...All in all, from 'the best young play of its generation' has invigoratingly come the best young (British) film of our generation."

In *The New York Times*, Bosley Crowther said: "The fury and hate that John Osborne was able to pack into a flow of violent words in his stage play, *Look Back in Anger*, are not only matched but also documented in the film that the original director, Tony Richardson, has made from that vicious play...Richardson uses his camera in a hard, crisp documentary style that recalls the way Carol Reed used one in his memorable *The Stars Look Down*." Crowther went on, "In getting performances from his actors, Mr. Richardson repeats the quality of the play. Richard Burton is frenzied to the point of mania as the husband who hates the agony of life...Mary Ure makes a touching slavey as his nerve-jangled, fear-cluttered wife...And Claire Bloom is delightful, sharp and catty as the neighborhood friend who won't take the blowhard's guff."

Twenty-four years after the London premiere of *Look Back in Anger*, Osborne's drama was revived at the Roundabout Theatre in New York with Malcolm McDowell as Jimmy Porter. Walter Kerr (*The New York Times*) considered McDowell's performance as being on a steady course of controlled rage which tended to equate emotions and neutralize them ..."There's a sober evenness about him here, a lack of real velocity, that keeps this early, urgent dropout from fully igniting...the absence is in part due, I think, to the fact that director [Ted] Craig has allowed or encouraged his people to perform all at the same pitch." The Roundabout Theatre production subsequently was taped and televised on cable in February 1981 on the *Broadway on Showtime* series. Noted British director Lindsay Anderson, making his American television debut, was brought in to oversee this version. An earlier TV version was produced by the BBC in 1976, with James Hazeldine and Ciaran Madden starring and John Glenister directing.

STAGE

LOOK BACK IN ANGER, Royal Court Theatre, London, opened May 8, 1956
Produced by The English Stage Company Ltd., George Devine, artistic director; A Drama by John Osborne; Director, Tony Richardson; Setting, Alan Tagg; Lighting consultant, Peter Theobald; Music, Thomas Eastwood; Production manager, John Harrison; Artistic director assistant, John Dexter; Stage managers, Diana Watson and Neville Pearson

Kenneth Haigh (succeeded by Richard Pasdco) (Jimmy Porter); Mary Ure (succeeded by Wendy Williams) (Alison Porter); Alan Bates (Cliff Lewis); Helena Hughes (succeeded by Vivienne Drummond) (Helena Charles); John Welsh (succeeded by Deering Wells) (Colonel Redfern)

Theatre Royal, Bristol, England, opened April 22 through May 5, 1957
Produced by The Bristol Old Vic Company; A Drama by John Osborne; Director, John Moody; Setting, Patrick Robertson; Production manager, Nat Brenner; Stage manager, Ann Spiers

Peter O'Toole (Jimmy Porter); Wendy Williams (Alison Porter); Barry Wilsher (Cliff Lewis); Phyllida Law (Helena Charles); Joseph O'Connor (Colonel Redfern)

Lyceum Theatre, New York, opened October 1, 1957; moved to *Golden Theatre*, March 17, 1958 408 performances
Produced by David Merrick; A Drama by John Osborne; Director, Tony Richardson; Setting, Alan Tagg; Lighting and costumes supervised by Howard Bay; Costumes, Motley; Music, Thomas Eastwood; General manager, Jack Schlissel; Stage manager, Howard Stone

Kenneth Haigh (succeeded by Donald Madden) (Jimmy Porter); Mary Ure (succeeded by Susan Oliver) (Alison Porter); Alan Bates (succeeded by Dino Narizzano) (Cliff Lewis); Vivienne Drummond (succeeded by Patricia Devon) (Helena Charles); Jack Livesey (Colonel Redfern)

41st Street Theatre, New York, opened November 11, 1958 116 performances
Produced by Chelsea Productions; A Drama by John Osborne; Director, George Mully; Setting, Tom Jewett; Music, Thomas Eastwood; General manager, Charles Harrow; Stage managers, Elizabeth Caldwell and Robert Zolnick

William Daniels (succeeded by William Shust) (Jimmy Porter); Audree Rae (Alison Porter); Gene Rupert (Cliff Lewis); Diana Herbert (Helena Charles); Michael Lewis (Colonel Redfern)

Touring Company, opened *Ford's Theatre*, Baltimore, September 22, 1958; closed *Geary Theatre*, San Francisco, May 9, 1959
Produced by David Merrick; A Drama by John Osborne; Director, Tony Richardson; Setting, Alan Tagg; Lighting and costumes supervised by Howard Bay; Costumes, Motley; Music, Thomas Eastwood; Company manager, Tom Powers; General manager, Jack Schlissel; Stage managers, David Pardoll and Edward Shelton

Kenneth Haigh (succeeded by Donald Madden, Donald Harron) (Jimmy Porter); Diana Hyland (succeeded by Pippa Scott) (Alison Porter); Al Muscari (succeeded by John Milligan) (Cliff Lewis); Elizabeth Hubbard (Helena Charles); Jack Livesey (Colonel Redfern)

Arena Stage, Washington, D.C., opened April 11, 1967 40 performances
Produced by the Arena Stage; A Drama by John Osborne; Director, Hy Kalus; Setting and costumes, Judith Haugan; Lighting, William Eggleston

Douglas Rain (Jimmy Porter); Martha Henry (Alison Porter); Robert Foxworth (Cliff Lewis); Jane Alexander (Helena Charles); James Kenny (Colonel Redfern)

Royal Court Theatre, London, opened November 5, 1968
Produced by The English Stage Company Ltd.; A Drama by John Osborne; Director, Anthony Page; Setting, Tony Abbott; Lighting, Andy Phillips; Costumes, Anne Gainford

Victor Henry (Jimmy Porter); Jane Asher (Alison Porter); Martin Shaw (Cliff Lewis); Caroline Mortimer (Helena Charles); Edward Jewkesbury (Colonel Redfern)

Young Vic Theatre, London, opened December 12, 1972
Produced by the Young Vic Theatre Company; A Drama by John Osborne; Director, Bernard Goss; Setting, Patrick Robinson; Lighting, David Watson; Costumes, Rosemary Vercoe

Nicky Henson (Jimmy Porter); Mel Martin (Alison Porter); Alun Lewis (Cliff Lewis); Lois Daine (Helena Charles); Ian Taylor (Colonel Redfern)

Young Vic Theatre, London, opened February 1, 1979
Produced by the Young Vic Theatre Company; A Drama by John Osborne; Director, Mel Smith; Production designer, Marty Flood

John Labanowski (Jimmy Porter); Susan Woolridge (Alison Porter); Christopher Ashley (Cliff Lewis); Laura Cox (Helena Charles); Ian Taylor (Colonel Redfern)

Roundabout Theatre, Stage One, New York, opened October 26, 1980 148 performances
Produced by Gene Feist and Michael Fried; A Drama by John Osborne; Director, Ted Craig; Setting, Roger Mooney; Lighting, Dennis Parichy; Costumes, A. Christina Giannini; Musical supervision, Philip Campanella; Stage manager, Martha R. Jacobs

Malcolm McDowell (Jimmy Porter); Lisa Baines (Alison Porter); Raymond Hardie (Cliff Lewis); Fran Brill (Helena Charles); Robert Burr (Colonel Redfern)

SCREEN

LOOK BACK IN ANGER, Associated British-Pathe Films (in U.S., released by *Warner Bros.*), released September 1959
Produced by Woodfall Films; Executive producer, Harry Saltzman; Produced, Gordon L. T. Scott; Director, Tony Richardson; Screenplay, Nigel Kneale, based on the play by John Osborne; Additional dialogue, John Osborne; Photography, Oswald Morris; Art director, Peter Glazier; Music by Chris Barber and His Band; Music supervisor, John Addison; Music Hall song by Thomas Eastwood; Editor, Richard Best

Richard Burton (Jimmy Porter); Claire Bloom (Helena Charles); Mary Ure (Alison Porter); Dame Edith Evans (Mrs. Tanner); Gary Raymond (Cliff Lewis); Glen Bryan Shaw (Colonel Redfern); Phyllis Neilson-Terry (Mrs. Redfern); Donald Pleasence (Hurst); Jordan Lawrence (Producer); George Devine (Doctor); Bernice Swanson (Sally)

TELEVISION

LOOK BACK IN ANGER, televised November 21, 1976 BBC 90 minutes
Produced by the British Broadcasting Corporation; Producer, Cedric Messina; Director, John Glenister; A Play by John Osborne

James Hazeldine (Jimmy Porter); Ciaran Madden (Alison Porter); Chrissy Iddon (Helena Charles); Neil Daglish (Cliff Lewis); Thorley Walters (Colonel Redfern)

Broadway on Showtime, televised February 3, 1981 Showtime 90 minutes
The Roundabout Theatre Production/Crossover Programming Company; Producers, Chuck Braverman and Donald Boyd; Director, Lindsay Anderson; The Play by John Osborne; Scenic designer, Roger Mooney; Costumes, A. Christina Giannini; Musical supervision, Philip Campanella; Associate producers, Peggy Sloan and Julian Goldberg

Malcolm McDowell (Jimmy Porter); Lisa Banes (Alison Porter); Fran Brill (Helena Charles); Raymond Hardie (Cliff Lewis); Robert Burr (Colonel Redfern)

LOVERS AND OTHER STRANGERS
A Comedy by Renee Taylor and Joseph Bologna (1968)

Synopsis

Episode 1: Jerry, a passionate if rather inept bachelor, picks up demure, ladylike Brenda, brings her to his apartment, and discovers her to be a great deal more eager for seduction than he is prepared to accommodate.

Episode 2: Wilma, a sexually neglected housewife, decides to spice things up by greeting Johnny, her advertising salesman husband, at the door in a revealing negligee and an overdose of exotic perfume, getting him to forgo his traditional after dinner nap before the TV.

Episode 3: Mike Vecchio, getting last minute wedding jitters, turns up at the apartment of his fiancee, Susan Henderson, to call off their forthcoming nuptials, but, patiently listening to his tirade against the shackles of marriage, she eases him back to rationality by turning the topic to the arrangements he still has to make for his ushers. Meekly, he accepts his once-fancied entrapment and agrees to marital plans.

Episode 4: Blustery Frank Vecchio and his wife, Bea, after thirty tumultuous years of marriage, arrive at the home of their son, Richie, to dissuade him and his wife, Joan, from breaking up. Frank confesses that life with Bea hasn't always been bliss but their marriage has been a necessary institution in which he has survived -- something which ends up convincing the bickering younger couple to remain firm in their decision to separate.

(The revamped film version was set against the wedding of Frank and Bea Vecchio's son Mike to Susan Henderson, who've been secretly living together for more than a year, and at the ceremony, the elder Vecchios learn that their older son, Richie, has decided to break up with his wife, Joan.)

Comment and Critique

Actor-writers Renee Taylor and Joseph Bologna met in 1964 and married the following year. Each a relatively successful actor and writer separately, they first collaborated on a short film called *"2"* which was shown at the 1966 New York Film Festival. On September 18, 1968, their episodic comedy *Lovers and Other Strangers* opened on Broadway. (Renee Taylor had the role of Wilma in the second episode.) Richard P. Cooke, critic for *The Wall Street Journal*, suggested: "It could be that if George Bernard Shaw were alive, he would have approved of *Lovers and Other Strangers*, a parcel of four small comedies...There isn't an intellectual or political line in them, but there are reports on the endless war between the sexes and it is the women who prove the stronger..."

John Chapman (*Daily News*) wrote about the "four little one-act comedies" that "all four are by Renee Taylor and her husband, Joseph Bologna, who are newcomers to stage writing. The first two playlets are simply awful. As they hammer away at one topic, the sexual act, they are witless enough to make sex unpopular. Then, after an intermission for fresh air, there are two simply delightful comedies about marriage, and marriage involves more than Act One. Here, the humor is warmer and deeper -- and somehow the actors seem better..."

In the *New York Post*, Richard Watts, Jr., added: "The first three are mildly pleasant little exercises, but the fourth is a fresh, wise and wryly delightful contemplation of disturbed domesticity, beautifully played by Richard Castellano, and it is good enough to lift the entire evening into something of interest...At their best, the two authors of *Lovers and Other Strangers* can write with realistic and observant humor and posses a gift for sketching a character with a few strokes. They are by no means sentimental writers, and they know how to be caustic, but they can bring in a shyly warmhearted moment that Mr. Castellano handles to perfection."

Clive Barnes wrote in *The New York Times*: "This four-in-hand view of wilder shores of love, sex and New York apartments has been provided by Renee Taylor and Joseph Bologna. There are compassion, insight and irony here, and a lot of fun. I would rank it a little lower that Neil Simon's *Plaza Suite* and a little higher that *You Know I Can't Hear You When the Water's Running*. It was a happy, lighthearted opening of the new Broadway season...Each sketch has the effect of a perfectly judged cartoon. What the authors are showing is nothing like all the truth, but enough like part of the truth for us to grin with shame-faced recognition."

Lovers and Other Strangers earned beefy actor Richard Castellano a Tony Award nomination as Outstanding Feature Actor in a Drama for his performance as Frank Vecchio, the morose, henpecked father of the groom. (He lost the award to Al Pacino that year for *Does a Tiger Wear a Necktie?*) Subsequently, Castellano received an Oscar nomination as Best Supporting Actor for reprising the role in David Susskind's screen version of the Taylor/Bologna comedy, becoming a rather unlikely film star whose often repeated line "So, what's the story?" became one of the catchphrases of the day. (The Oscar ultimately went to John Mills for *Ryan's Daughter*.) Castellano's promising film career, which next included the role of Clemenza, one of Don Corleone's loyal soldiers, in *The Godfather*, fell apart after he held up producer/director Francis Ford Coppola for too much money to recreate the part in *The Godfather, Part 2* and he was written out -- and virtually written off by Hollywood, never again to have a major movie role. He died on December 10, 1988, at age fifty-five.

The 1969 movie *Lovers and Other Strangers* was, in effect, a melding of the last two (of four) sketches from the Broadway play, rewritten by Renee Taylor and Joseph Bologna. Joining veteran actors Anne Jackson, Gig Young and Harry Guardino were then-relatively-new-to-filmgoers Diane Keaton, Beatrice Arthur, Bonnie Bedelia, Anne Meara and Richard Castellano. In his review in *Films and Filming*, critic Richard Davis felt: "...this is very much a photographed stage piece, and the wit springs from the dialogue...[It] is a commentary on the different kinds of sexual love. It is ritualistically patterned...Love, separated from hypocrisy, is what *Lovers and Other Strangers* is all about, and the messages are conveyed without a nude in sight. A word about the acting. It is uniformly excellent, and Beatrice Arthur, as the prospective groom's mother, is a joy to watch..."

Roger Greenspun reported in *The New York Times* that although the film "never adequately balances its various strands, and ultimately remains so open-minded as to seem almost bitterly fatalistic, it is pleasant in most of its parts and sometimes very funny individual scenes...Cy Howard's direction is straight-forward and efficient. But the film has been miserably edited -- in the rather elementary sense that shots that should fit together don't, and you repeatedly find yourself jarred by merely mechanical discontinuities in sequences that are clearly meant to flow smoothly. The real attraction of *Lovers and Other Strangers* is its cast, which is large and excellent, and with a few exceptions (Anne Jackson and the wonderful Gig Young) not very well known..."

In the *New York Post*, Archer Winsten wrote: "This kind of movie a reviewer should pay to see...The funniest movie I've seen this year. It's about marriage, love, sex, passion, lack of passion, seduction divorce, religion, freedom and happiness, not necessarily in that order...Just go, run, to see it." And *Newsday* hailed it as "One of the best American films of the year."

For an opposing opinion, drama critic Ernest Schier (*Philadelphia Evening Bulletin*) found that "an excellent cast tackles a miserable scenario -- and loses...The would-be comedy is a tasteless treatment of the middle class, this time Irish and Italian instead of Jews, that revolves around a wedding much like the wedding in *Goodbye, Columbus* ...The movie, produced by David Susskind and clumsily directed by Cy Howard, wastes some fine talents..."

For their screenplay to *Lovers and Other Strangers*, Taylor and Bologna were Oscar-nominated, losing to Ring Lardner, Jr., for *M*A*S*H.* The film however did introduce "For All We Know," which not only won the Academy Award as Best Song but also became a wedding anthem of sorts for an entire generation of young marrieds.

David Susskind, who had produced the screen version, was the executive producer for the Renee Taylor-Joseph Bologna 1983 television adaptation of their Broadway comedy. Starring Harry Guardino (who also was in the film version but in a different role) and directed by Burt Brinckerhoff, it was a pilot for a proposed television series but suffered from TV sitcom-itis and serious overplaying by most of the cast. Despite a dominating performance by Guardino as Frank Vecchio attempting to salvage his son's marriage, the adaptation failed and the series never materialized.

STAGE

LOVERS AND OTHER STRANGERS, *Brooks Atkinson Theatre*, New York, opened September 18, 1970 70 performances

Produced by Stephanie Sills in association with Gordon Crowe; A Play by Renee Taylor and Joseph Bolgna; Director, Charles Grodin; Settings, Robin Wagner; Lighting, John Gleason; Costumes, Domingo A. Rodriguez; Hair styles, David Crespin; Production associate, Lee Bletzer; Associate producer, Maury Kanbar; General manager, Richard Seader; Stage managers, Joe Calvan, Hal Halvorsen and William Lazarus

Renee Taylor (Wilma); Gerald S. O'Loughlin (Johnny); Zohra Lampert (Brenda); Ron Carey (Jerry); Mariclare Costello (Susan); Marvin Lichterman (Mike); Richard Castellano (Frank); Helen Verbit (Bea); Bobby Alto (Richie); Candy Azzara (Joan)

Touring Company, summer 1972

Produced and directed by Charles Forsythe; A Play by Renee Taylor and Joseph Bologna; Settings, Darrell Kiester

Tom Poston (Jerry/ Johnny/ Hal/ Frank Vecchio); Abby Dalton (Brenda/ Wilma/ Cathy/ Bea); Margaret Linn (Joan/ Susan); Marvin Lichterman (Mike Vecchio/ Richie)

Touring Company, summer 1973

Produced and directed by Charles Forsythe; A Play by Renee Taylor and Joseph Bologna; Settings, Darrell Kiester

Tom Poston (Jerry/ Johnny/ Hal/ Frank Vecchio); Marian Mercer (Brenda/ Wilma/ Cathy/ Bea); Brenda Broome (Joan/ Susan); Roy London (Mike Vecchio/ Richie)

SCREEN

LOVERS AND OTHER STRANGERS, ABC Pictures for Cinerama Releasing Co., released August 1970

Producer, David Susskind; Associate producer, Anthony Loeb; Director, Cy Howard; Screenplay, Renee Taylor and Joseph Bologna with David Zelag Goodman, based on the play by Taylor and Bologna; Photography, Andy Laszlo; Production designer, Ben Edwards; Set decorator, John Alan Hicks; Costume designer, Albert Wolsky; Music, Fred Karlin; Songs "For All We Know," "Comin' Thru to Me" and "Keepin' Free" by Fred Karlin, Robb Wilson and Arthur James; "For All We Know" sung by Larry Meredith; Editors, David Bretherton and Sidney Katz

Beatrice Arthur (Bea Vecchio); Bonnie Bedelia (Susan Henderson); Michael Brandon (Mike Vecchio); Richard Castellano (Frank Vecchio); Bob Dishy (Jerry); Harry Guardino (Johnny); Marian Hailey (Brenda); Joseph Hindy (Richie Vecchio); Anthony Holland (Donaldson); Anne Jackson (Cathy); Diana Keaton (Joan Vecchio); Cloris Leachman (Bernice Henderson); Mort Marshall (Father Gregory); Anne Meara (Wilma); Gig Young (Hal Henderson)

TELEVISION

LOVERS AND OTHER STRANGERS, ABC Comedy Special, televised July 22, 1983
ABC 30 minutes

Executive producer, David Susskind; Producers and writers, Renee Taylor and Joseph Bologna, based on their play; Director, Burt Brinckerhoff; Art director, Ken Johnson; Music, Fred Karlin

Harry Guardino (Frank Vecchio); Brian Benben (Mike Vecchio); Carol Teitel (Bea Vecchio); Randi Oakes (Susan Henderson Vecchio); Helen Verbit (Pauline); Bruce Kirby (Father Gregory); Clkaudia Wells (Mary Claire Vecchio); R. J. Williams (Bruno Vecchio); Keri Houlihan (Marie Vecchio); Alan Hayes (Jerry Vecchio); Joanne Baron (Brenda)

LUTHER
A Drama by John Osborne (1961)

Synopsis

Martin Luther, a Catholic priest of the Augustinian Order of Eremites in Erfurt, Germany, in 1506, teaches theology at the University of Wittenberg while physically ill and consumed with spiritual doubts. The church's practice of selling indulgences and forgiving sins in exchange for money infuriates Luther who defiantly nails his historic ninety-five protests against papal dogma onto the door of the Wittenberg Church on October 31, 1517. Pope Leo X and the church demand that Luther recant but he persists, denying the holy supremacy of the pleasure-loving Medici Pope and the mercenary practices of the priests and the church itself. Excommunicated, Luther continues his protests and is safely secured from the retaliation of Charles V and Pope Leo by the Elector of Saxony, soon establishing his own church, giving Germany an identity, and marrying Katherine, a former nun, who bears him a son.

Comment and Critique

John Osborne, who has established a reputation in the late 1950s as Britain's "angry" young playwright after his brilliant *Look Back in Anger* (1957) and his follow-up plays *The Entertainer* and *Epitaph for George Dillon* (with Anthony Creighton), in 1961 chronicled the life of Martin Luther, which brought Osborne another wave of acclaim. (Martin Luther was born at Eisleben, Germany on November 10, 1483, and died there on February 18, 1546, to be buried at Wittenberg's Castle Church.

London's *Theatre World* reported of Osborne's *Luther*: "The strong feeling of our most provocative playwright found the ideal outlet in the character of the sin-obsessed and body-conscious Martin Luther of his play, and Albert Finney was accorded the Best Actor prize at the 1961 Paris Festival for his remarkable performance in the title role. [Finney also was named Best Actor by the London Theatre Critics for 1961-62, but lost the Tony to Alec Guinness (for *Dylan*) when recreating the role on Broadway several years later.] *Luther* was also seen at the 1961 Edinburgh Festival and on 5th September began a successful run at the Phoenix. The direction by Tony Richardson and Jocelyn Herbert's decor received high praise."

In *Plays and Players*, Caryl Brahms, reviewing the opening of *Luther* at the Royal Court Theatre, noted: "Man bites dogma...to reduce the struggle towards God of any human being to scenes of a stage play is even more impossible than to catch a part of history under the neat little headings of the programme note to a chronicle piece...Mr. Osborne set out to write a play and not an autobiography and the play he has written [is] a play of strength and, going by the text, of clarity...Led by Albert Finney in a performance that should sweep off all awards and assuredly will, the actors were beautifully cast and superbly directed by Tony Richardson...Finney, at all times a compulsive actor, is more than compelling as Luther. He *is* Luther...This was the most convincing performance that I can remember ever to have seen."

London's *Sphere* continued the accolades for *Luther*: "It was given its world premiere at the Theatre des Nations in Paris, where it caused a deal of commotion and enabled its leading actor, Albert Finney, to win the annual award for best actor of the season. Without doubt, *Luther* has solidified John Osborne's reputation ...[His] play captures much of the powerful atmosphere of grim piety and earthly fanaticism of Luther and his era."

When *Luther* moved to the Phoenix Theatre, *Plays and Players* re-reviewed it, finding that "John Osborne's play, the most ambitious and impressive he has yet given up, presents a compelling portrait of Martin Luther -- racked by spiritual doubt, emotionally unbalances, physically sick, yet dominating the whole age in which he lived."

In September 1963, *Luther* arrived on Broadway, and Howard Taubman wrote in *The New York Times*: "Led by Albert Finney, in a superb performance as Martin Luther, the play arrived...in a production that honors an achievement on the stage in a parlous time when such achievements are rare. Whatever your allegiance of faith may be, you owe it to yourself to rediscover the excitement that a vital play can generate...It is about matters worth talking and thinking about. It makes the theatre ten feet tall."

Theatre Arts magazine felt that Osborne was not one to write a play about Martin Luther: "His virtue us that he can clothe protest in eloquence. Like a Welsh politician -- Lloyd George, say, or Aneurin Bevan -- he covers familiar sentiments with his gift of gab. He is not particularly good at telling a story; he has no original thoughts to display; he depends on the flash of bright instinctive theatre. And so what he has made of *Luther* is the subject of a brilliant historical pageant rather than a play...This unfolding pageant is kept together by the Luther of Albert Finney in an incandescent performance or rare authority. Finney is a young man of extraordinary range..."

Luther won the Tony Award as Best Play, and John Osborne won as Best Playwright. (Finney, as mentioned above, was nominated as Best Actor, but lost to Alec Guinness.)

The life of Martin Luther first had been brought to the screen in 1913 as *Martin Luther, the Nightingale of Wittenberg*, written by Erwin Baron and directed by Louis Gero. Eleven years later, the Lutheran Film Division released their controversial *Martin Luther, His Life and Times*. Adapted by the Reverend M.G.G. Scherer and Ernest Maas from the book by P. Kurz, it featured middle-aged Eugen Kloepfer as Luther. It did not receive a theatrical release in the United States until June 1929, and was found to be overly repetitive with endless religious processions, ceremonies and dogma, appealing largely to members of the Lutheran Church.

In 1953, for Lutheran Church Productions, Louis de Rochemont Associates produced *Martin Luther*, starring Niall MacGinnis in the title role. "This well made film about a historically important man is irrefutable proof that motion pictures on religions and religious history need not be dull," Henry Hart wrote in *Theatre World*. "Financed by the Lutheran Church, produced on location in Western Germany by Lothar Wolff (for Louis de Rochemont), and directed by Irving Pichel. *Martin Luther* is more dramatic than most fiction films, and makes the beginning of the Protestant Reformation visually interesting and intellectually exciting...The performance of Niall MacGinnis as Luther is inspired."

Bosley Crowther wrote in *The New York Times*: "A tough and unusual subject has been squarely and intelligently embraced in the film called *Martin Luther*...In any responsible handling of a subject such as this, there must be a great deal of discourse, which is perilous to the playing of a film. And discourse there is, beyond question, in this fully responsible job... Thanks to a splendid performance by Mr. MacGinnis under the direction of Irving Pichel, a man of strong will and ardent nature is portrayed in the title role. This Martin Luther is a titan, full of courage and integrity...The settings and production, too, are excellent...As an impress of personal drama, it applies powerful pressure to the mind."

Twenty years later in 1973, Ely A. Landau produced Edward Anhalt's screen adaptation of John Osborne's play, featuring Stacy Keach as Luther. Tom Milne, in Britian's *Monthly Film Bulletin*, felt: "*Luther*, frankly is a mess. It never was one of John Osborne's better plays, chiefly because in modeling it on Brecht's *Galileo*, he failed to achieve the correct dialectical balance between the personal drives and public caveats that beset a man of destiny. Stacy Keach, although be-deviled by the fact that his American Luther is given an Irish father and an English social context, does very well with the tormented soul of the beginning who is desperately trying to grapple with his own doubts and sense of inadequacy. That his performance never builds, as Albert Finney's stage original did, into a vitriolic Jimmy Porter [of Osborne's *Look Back in Anger*] diatribe against a world (including himself) content to settle for life without good brave causes...is less Keach's fault than the film's."

In 1966, the BBC's television production of Osborne's play, adapted and directed by Alan Cooke, premiered to enthusiastic reviews. Alec McCowan's portrayal of Luther was favorably compared to Albert Finney's stage original. Two years later, Robert Shaw starred in ABC Television's American production of Osborne's *Luther*. In the *Philadelphia Evening Bulletin*, it was called "a brilliant 90-minute adaptation ...Robert Shaw *was* Luther [and] with the magnificent closeups TV can provide, was stronger and more powerful [than] Albert Finney's tremendous portrayal of Luther on Broadway...the cast was equally brilliant, and settings and costumes were in keeping."

And in *The New York Times*, Jack Gould praised it: "Robert Shaw gives an intense portrayal of Luther -- [He] was the embodiment of overwhelming intensity in his portrayal. A condensed version of John Osborne's play *Luther*...had many moments of forceful eloquence ...as done on television, [it] was three-quarters play and one-quarter hurried narrative of highlights of the man's life. But even where events had to be skeletonized and abruptly covered, it was a competent and often inspired effort. The subject matter simply warranted the greater latitude enjoyed by stage or film."

STAGE

LUTHER, Royal Court Theatre, London, opened July 27, 1961; moved to *Phoenix Theatre*, September 5, 1961* 266 performances
Produced by The English Stage Company and Oscar Lewenstein; A Drama by John Osborne; Director, Tony Richardson; Settings and costumes, Jocelyn Herbert; Music composed and arranged by John Addison; Chorus master, John McCarthy

Albert Finney (Martin Luther); Bill Owen (Hans); James Cairncross (Prior/Eck); Dan Meaden (Weinand); Robert Robinson (Miltitz); Peter Duguid (Lucas); Peter Bull (Tetzel); George Devine (Staupitz); John Moffatt (Cajetan); Charles Kay (Pope Leo); Meryl Gourley (Katherine); Julian Glover (Knight); Stacey Davies, Murray Evans, Derek Fuke, Malcolm Taylor (Monks, Peasants, Lords); Ian Partridge, Frank Davies, Andrew Pearmain, David Read (Singers); Roger Harbird, Paul Large (Children)

*This production had its world premiere at the *Theatre Sarah Bernhardt* in Paris, July 6, 1961, and subsequently was performed at the 1961 Edinburgh Festival in Scotland

St. James Theatre, New York, opened September 25, 1963 212 performances
Produced by David Merrick by arrangement with The English Stage Company and Oscar Lewenstein; A Drama by John Osborne; Director, Tony Richardson; Settings and costumes, Jocelyn Herbert; Supervised by Thea Neu; Music composed and arranged by John Addision; Choral director, Max Walmer; General manager, Jack Schlissel; Company manager, Eugene Wolsk; Stage managers, Mitchell Erickson and B. Lester

Albert Finney (suceeded by John Heffernan) (Martin); Kenneth J. Warren (succeeded by George Mathews) (Hans); Ted Thurston (Prior); John Heffernan (succeeded by Harry Carlson) (Weinand); Robert Burr (Miltitz); Luis Van Rooten (Lucas); Alfred Sandor (Reader); Peter Bull (succeeded by Lionel Stander) (Tetzel); Frank Shelley (Staupitz); John Moffatt (succeeded by Hugh Franklin) (Cajetan); Michael Egan (Pope Leo); Martin Rudy (Eck); Lorna Lewis (Katherine); Glyn Owen (Knight); Thor Arngrim, Harry Carlson, Stan Dworkin, Roger Hamilton, Konrad Matthaei, Alfred Sandor (Monks, Peasants, Lords); Perry Golkin, Joseph Lamberta (Children); Paul Flores, Dan Goggin, Robert L. Hultman (Singers); Marvin Solley (Soloist)

Touring Company, season 1963-64
Produced by David Merrick by arrangements with The English Stage Company and Oscar Lewenstein; A Drama by John Osborne; Director, Tony Richardson; Settings and costumes, Jocelyn Herbert; Music composed and arranged by John Addison; Choral director, Max Walmer; General manager, Jack Schlissel; Stage managers, Mitchell Erickson and B. Lester

John Heffernan (Martin); George Mathews (Hans); Alfred Sandor (Prior/Eck); Harry Carlson (Weinand); Ed Zimmermann (Miltitz); Donald Mayre (Lucas); Stan Dworkin (Reader); Lionel Stander (succeeded by Michael Egan) (Tetzel); Frank Shelley (Staupitz); Hugh Franklin (Catejan); Michael Egan (succeeded by Stan Dworkin) (Pope Leo); Lorna Lewis (Katherine); Alan Bergmann (Knight); Gunnar Dahlberg, James Rado (Monks, Peasants, Lords); Murray Goldkind, Dan Goggin, Robert L. Hultman, Peter Johl (Singers); Marvin Solley (Soloist)

Touring Company, opened Norfolk, Virginia, October 2, 1964; closed Toronto, February 27, 1965
Produced by Joel Spector, Julina Olney and B. B. Randolph; A Drama by John Osborne; Director, Mitchell Erickson; Scenery and costumes, Jocelyn Herbert; Music composed and arranged by John Addison; Choral director, Marvin Stolley; General manager, Monty Shaff; Stage managers, Irving Sudrow and William Countryman

Alan Bergmann (Martin); Herman Rudin (Hans); Alfred Sandor (Prior/Catejan); Donald Mayre (Weinand); Jay Gregory (Miltitz); John Eames (Lucas/Eck); William Countryman (Reader); Sam Kreesen (Tetzel); George Cotton (Staupitz); Jack Hollander (Pope Leo); Anne Countryman (Katherine); Barry Snider (Knight); Thomas Boyd, Gunnar Dahlberg, Dan Goggin, Jay Gregory, Gilbert Williams (Monks, Peasants, Lord, Singers); Marvin Stolley (Soloist)

SCREEN

MARTIN LUTHER, THE NIGHTINGALE OF WITTENBERG, released 1913
Director, Louis Gero; Screenplay, Erwin Baron

MARTIN LUTHER, HIS LIFE AND TIMES, *Reformation Films* (Germany), released 1924; in U.S. released as *LUTHER*, June 1929
Produced by Cob-Film, Lutheran Film Division; Director, Hans Kyser; Screenplay, Reverend M.G.G. Scherer and Ernest Maas, adapted from the book by P. Kurz; Photography, M. Paetz

Eugen Kloepfer (Martin Luther); Elsa Wagner (Katherine); with Jakob Tiedtke, H.K. Mueller, Bruno Kastner, Carl Elzer

MARTIN LUTHER, *British Lion Films*, released August 1953
Produced by Louis de Rochemont Associates for the Lutheran Church and Lutheran Film-Gesellschaft MbH.; Producer, Lother Wolff; Director, Irving Pichel; Research and screen preparation by Allan Sloane and Lothar Wolff with Dr. Jaroslav Pelikan and Dr. Theodore G. Tappert; Photography, Joseph C. Brun; Art directors, Fritz Maurischat and Paul Markwitz; Music, Mark Lothar

Niall MacGinnis (Martin Luther); John Ruddock (Vicar von Staupitz); Pierre Lefevre (Spalatin); Guy Verney (Malenchthon); Alastair Hunter (Carlstadt); David Horne (Duke Frederick, Elector of Saxony); Fred Johnson (Prior); Philip Leaver (Pope Leo X); Dr. Egon Strohm (Cardinal Aleander); Alexander Gauge (Tetzel); Irving Pichel (Brueck); Annette Carell (Katherine von Bora); Leonard White (Emissary); Hans Lefebre (Charles V, Emperor of the Holy Roman Empire)

LUTHER, *Ely Landau Productions*, released November 1973
Ely Landau Organization in association with American Express Films (New York) and Canada Cinevision Ltd.; Executive producer, Mort Abrahams; Producer, Ely A.

Landau; Associate producer, Henry T. Weinstein; Director, Guy Green; Screenplay, Edward Anhalt, based on the play by John Osborne; Photography, Freddie Young; Production designer, Peter Mullins; Costumes, Elizabeth Haffenden and Joan Bridge; Music, John Addison; Assistant director, Kip Gowans; Editor, Malcolm Cooke

Stacy Keach (Martin Luther); Patrick Magee (Hans); Hugh Griffith (Tetzel); Robert Stephens (Von Eck); Alan Badel (Cajetan); Julian Glover (Kinght); Leonard Rossiter (Weinand); Thomas Heathcoate (Lucas); Peter Cellier (Prior); Judi Dench (Katherine); Maurice Denham (Johann von Staupitz); Malcolm Stoddard (Charles V); Bruce Carstairs (Duke of Saxony); Matthew Guinness (Reading Monk)

LUTHER IST TOT (LUTHER IS DEAD), Pan-Film (Germany), released 1984

Producer, Hans der Kirche; Writer/director, Frank Burckner; Photography, Hartmut Jahn, Armin Faust and Tom Preiss; Production designer, Maya Dubois; Music, Reiner Bohm, Reinhard Hoffmann and Dagmar Jaenicke; Editor, Goetz Meyer

Hermann Treusch (Luther as a Monk); Ulrich Kuhlmann (Luther as a Rebel); Wolfgang Bathke (Luther as Junker Jorg); Gerhard Friedrich (Luther as Opponent of the Peasants); Eberhard Wechselberg (Luther as Prophet); Ingeborg Drewitz (Speaker); and Walter Alich, Andreas Bissmeyer, Jockel Baumann, Johns Dengler, Erika Fuhrmann, Frank Glaubrecht, Alexander Herzog, Ulrich Hass, Klaus Jepson, Helmut Kraus, Rainer Johannes Kolble, Krikor Melikyan, Manfred Petersen, Rainer Pigulla, Erich Scwarz, Peter Schlesinger, Britta Toegel, Eric Vaessen, Manuel Vaessen, Wolfgang Unterzaucher, Horst-Deiter Wildner

TELEVISION

LUTHER, televised October 19, 1965   BBC   90 minutes

Produced by British Broadcasting Corporation; Producer, Cedric Messina; Adapted and directed by Alan Cooke, from the play by John Osborne; Story editor, James Barbazon; Production designer, Barry Learoyd; Costumes, Rupert Jarvis; Makeup, Lillian Munro; Vision mixer, Dave Hanks; Music, Herbert Chappell; Sound supervisor, Chick Anthony

Alec McCowen (Martin Luther); Jerold Wells (Hans); Patrick Magee (Tetzel); Gerry Duggan (Lucas); Philip Stone (Weinand); James Cairncross (Prior); Charles Carson (Staupitz); Geoffrey Bayldon (Cajetan); William Ingram (Miltitz); Tom Criddle (Pope Leo); Fulton Mackay (Eck); Etain O'Dell (Katherine); Ray Barrett (Knight); Douglas Ditta, Peter Purves, Darroll Richards, Rex Robinson (Monks, Lords, Peasants)

LUTHER, televised January 29, 1968   ABC   90 minutes

Executive producer, Bill Murphy; Producers, Michael Style and Trevor Wallace; Director, Stuart Burge; Adaptation by Robert Furnival of the play by John Osborne

Robert Shaw (Martin Luther); Kenneth J. Warren (Hans); Robert Morley (Pope Leo); Ronald Fraser (Tetzel); Frank Middlemass (Staupitz); Reginald Barratt (Lucas); Bernard Kay (Weinand)